LIFE IN MEXICO

The Letters of Fanny Calderón de la Barca

LIFE IN MEXICO

The Letters of
Fanny Calderón de la Barca

WITH NEW MATERIAL FROM
THE AUTHOR'S PRIVATE JOURNALS

Edited and annotated by
Howard T. Fisher and Marion Hall Fisher

DOUBLEDAY & COMPANY, INC., GARDEN CITY, NEW YORK, 1966

Contents

BALLS AND MASSES

"REVOLUTION IN MEXICO!"

FAMILIAR SIGHTS AND FRIENDLY FACES

A JOURNEY THROUGH THE SUGAR COUNTRY

THE END OF CALDERON'S MISSION

REVOLUTION AGAIN: SANTA ANNA RETURNS

FIVE WEEKS ON HORSEBACK IN MICHOACAN

FAREWELL TO MEXICO

Illustrations

During the years embracing Fanny Calderón de la Barca's sojourn in Mexico a number of outstanding illustrators were at work there. To their compositions, and to the innumerable copies which they inspired, we are greatly indebted today for our knowledge of the look of Mexico in the mid-nineteenth century.

Mexico, then as now, seems to have had a special fascination for foreigners, and the majority of those whose work is best known today bear foreign names: Claudio Linati, an Italian who worked in Mexico in the late 1820's; Carl Nebel, from the vicinity of Hamburg, who began working in Mexico in 1828 and whom the Calderóns seem to have met there in 1840; Pedro Gualdi, whose *Monumentos de Méjico* appeared at the very time of the Calderóns' stay; and Johann Moritz Rugendas, who painted in many parts of Latin America and whose Mexican sketches served as the basis for engravings published in the 1850's. To these may be added a visiting amateur of unusual competence: Mrs. H. G. Ward, illustrator of her husband's well-known book *Mexico in 1827*.

While all of those mentioned are represented in this volume (either directly or by old linear copies of their work), our greatest debt of gratitude is to Casimiro Castro, who in the 1850's was working with the Mexican lithographic establishment of José Decaen. The jacket, endpapers and approximately twenty of our plates are from lithographs which he drew, either alone or with others.

The work of those so far mentioned has all been reproduced from published books. In contrast, we have also been able to present, with kind permission, a number of original works from museums and private ownership. These include the productions of several anonymous or all-but-forgotten Mexican artists of distinction, together with the anonymous portraits of the author and her husband.

In the selection of old illustrations suitable for use as linecuts, we have of necessity been largely dependent upon material available in the form of book illustrations—frequently, in treatment as well as in technique, better suited for our purpose than the more formal originals from which they may have been derived. Mostly anonymous, such illustrations oc-

casionally bear names—though in a large percentage of cases the names
serve only to identify the author of the particular copy. Some pictures,
with or without modifications, proved especially popular and recur repeatedly in a wide variety of publications produced in Mexico and elsewhere. While in many instances the original source may be assumed
with confidence (as we have done in some cases), to have tried to
determine true authorship for the purpose of giving unconditional credit
would have required both time and competence we did not possess. In
our use of such material, all now in the public domain, we thus continue an old tradition—with apologies to any we may have unjustly
slighted.

As will be obvious, for many of our illustrations we have employed
less than the entire composition available—at times preferring to select
mere fragments to illustrate particular points. In addition, our captions
do not necessarily bear any relationship to those that may have been
previously assigned to the same subjects.

ABBREVIATIONS

AGC   Antonio García Cubas, *Atlas Pintoresco e Histórico de los
           Estados Unidos Mexicanos.*
AM   *Album Mejicano; Tributo de Gratitud al Civismo Nacional.*
ARC   Alfred R. Conkling, *Appleton's Guide to Mexico.*
ASE   Albert S. Evans, *Our Sister Republic.*
BM-M   Brantz Mayer, *Mexico as It Was and as It Is.* (While a state-
           ment on the title page of this book refers to "numerous
           illustrations on wood, engraved by Butler from drawings
           by the author," there has appeared to be no reliable basis
           for establishing credit—as the illustrations clearly must
           have been drawn from a wide variety of sources.)
BM-MASR   Brantz Mayer, *Mexico, Aztec, Spanish and Republican.*
BN   Biblioteca Nacional, Mexico, one of a collection of single
           pictures pasted into a copy of Pedro Gualdi's *Monumentos
           de Méjico.*
CL   Charles Lempriere, *Notes in Mexico in 1861 and 1862.*
CN   Carl Nebel, *Voyage pittoresque et archéologique dans la partie
           la plus intéressante du Mexique* (or other edition).
CO   *Calendario de Ontiveros.*
CSM   *Calendario de las Señoritas Megicanas.*
FAO   Frederick A. Ober, *Travels in Mexico.*
FCB-J   Fanny Calderón de la Barca, manuscript journal.
FCB-LM   Fanny Calderón de la Barca, *Life in Mexico* (first American
           edition; music from second English edition).

FJC   Francisco Javier Clavijero, *Historia Antigua de Mégico* (or
           earlier editions).
GH   Gilbert Haven, *Our Next-Door Neighbor: A Winter in Mexico.*
HGW   H. G. Ward, *Mexico in 1827.*
HTF   Photograph by Howard T. Fisher.
IM   *La Ilustración Mexicana.*
JF   John Frost, *The History of Mexico and Its Wars.*
JL   Jules Leclercq, *Voyage au Mexique de New-York à Vera-
           Cruz.*
MB   Mark Beaufoy, *Mexican Illustrations.*
MNHC   Museo Nacional de Historia, Chapultepec.
MRC   Manuel Rivera Cambas, *Los Gobernadores de México.*
MoM   *Mosaico Mexicano.*
MuM   *Museo Mexicano.*
MSA   *México y Sus Alrededores.*
NZ   Niceto de Zamacois, *Historia de Méjico.*
PB   P. Blanchard and A. Dauzats, *San Juan de Ulúa.*
PC   Private collection.
RAW   Robert A. Wilson, *Mexico: Its Peasants and Its Priests.*
SH   Samuel Hazard, *Cuba with Pen and Pencil.*
VRP   Vicente Riva Palacio, editor, *México a Través de los Siglos.*

Text Illustrations

MAPS

(By Raleigh Spinks)

PLATES

Following page 258

ENDPAPERS

Introduction

This book as first published bore the date of 1843. Fanny Calderón de la Barca, its author, was a Scotswoman married to a Spanish diplomat who served as his country's first minister to Mexico. She was a sophisticated and zestful woman, with an eye and an ear for delectable detail and with the ability to share her experiences in generous measure. Mexico and she seem to have been made for each other, and the result was a book which age has only enhanced.

Life in Mexico, which appeared first in Boston and very shortly afterwards in London, was greeted with pleasure in the English-speaking world. Most American and British comment was strongly favorable (though one British reviewer doubted that the author had ever set foot in the country she described). In Mexico, where serialization in Spanish was begun shortly after a few copies of the book arrived on the local scene, the effect was a violent front-page newspaper storm of protest. Over the years *Life in Mexico* has become a quiet persistent classic, admired alike by serious students and those reading for pleasure—a book that is read and read again, and passed appreciatively from hand to hand. Its basic good will, admittedly somewhat astringent at times, and its fundamental honesty may be judged by the fact that nowhere today is it more highly regarded than in Mexico itself.

Work on the present version of *Life in Mexico* was initiated more than twenty-five years ago when, with great good fortune, access was obtained to significant new material, coupled with the most generous co-operation on the part of its possessor. The task was begun with confidence and in something of a holiday spirit. But, as any professional historian would have known at the outset, each fresh vista inevitably opened to others. Histories of the times beckoned to what lay behind them. One newspaper file suggested comparison with others. Diplomatic correspondence and the memoirs and accounts of other travelers demanded to be read. Yet a time finally comes when a halt must be called, even though there remains much more to be learned.

In planning this edition of *Life in Mexico,* here, in sum, is what we have tried to do: To fill in for the reader the background of some of the events chronicled and things described, and to round out from many sources the portraits of people whom the author met and knew. To assemble illustrations broadly contemporary with her time. To clarify her sometimes approximate dates. To provide a comprehensive index to the storehouse of information on Mexico which the book contains. And also, for our own pleasure as much as for use in this volume, to tie the past to the present—by retracing the author's Mexican journeys, by identifying the places she mentioned, and by recording in photographs some of the scenes through which she passed. We feel that she would have been more than sympathetic with the inclusion of such illustrations in her book, for she and her husband also had a camera in Mexico, undoubtedly among the first to reach its shores. (Alas, the awesome apparatus was far less simple to operate than its modern counterparts, and no tangible results of its use seem to have survived.)

But by far the most important contributor to this new edition is Fanny Calderón de la Barca herself. According to the original preface written by William Hickling Prescott, who later made appreciative use in his *Conquest of Mexico* of her descriptions of the country he himself never saw, her book was developed from letters written to her relatives. This was no doubt the case; but what Prescott did not say was that the core of her material consisted of intermittent journals to which she frequently confided her Mexican experiences. Parts of this Journal (as we will call it)—unfortunately only two volumes of what were probably three—have been preserved as a valued possession by a family descended from her older sister. A spirited document, written at times under the greatest pressure and largely unparagraphed and unpunctuated except by dashes, it recognizably parallels those parts of the book which were developed from it.

In drawing on this material the author reorganized, smoothed, and revised, sometimes substituting for her first succinct and lively phrases others more consciously literary. In the process she also censored. Many of the revisions incorporated in her printed text were obviously made for the sake of discretion, and to conceal the identities of living people. Others were made, evidently, because of a realization that her feelings on many subjects had changed with time and experience—a fact that she acknowledged on more than one occasion in her published book.

Material from the Journal not originally made use of is presented in this volume. Carefully correlated with the previously printed text, it has been interpolated in such a way as to preserve so far as possible the full flavor and vitality of the original within the context of the whole. Slightly differentiated type has been employed to indicate thus all material, hitherto unpublished, taken from the Journal. We hope that readers will find of interest these old yet new contributions by Fanny Calderón de la Barca which now for the first time are imparted to her public. We have also used the same typographic device to indicate names previously censored, in whole or in part, but here provided from a marked first-edition copy of *Life in Mexico* made available to us by the kindness of a descendant of the author's younger sister. (A more detailed explanation of the precise procedure employed in the preparation of this edition, as well as our grateful acknowledgments of help, appears following the main text of this volume.)

The Journal of the Spanish minister's Scottish wife has yielded much that is of historic as well as human interest. It helps to illuminate a small segment of the nineteenth-century past as first seen by a sometimes critical but highly intelligent observer who found many things in an alien place to like and some to dislike; who obviously liked more the longer she stayed; and who departed with the greatest regret.

The author of *Life in Mexico* was born Frances Erskine Inglis in Edinburgh on December 23, 1804. When her father William Inglis (pronounced Ingalls) welcomed his new daughter—named for her great-grandmother Lady Frances Erskine—he was already the head of a family of four children under seven years of age. A member of that specialized branch of the legal profession known as Writers to the Signet, he was a strong Whig, a leading Mason, the subject of a portrait by Raeburn, and the owner of a house on pleasant Queen Street in Edinburgh and of Middleton Hall in the nearby countryside. He was also the husband of Jane Stein, beautiful daughter of James Stein of Kilbogie, whose family business was that sure source of income, a thriving distillery.

One cannot help but speculate on the possibility that if he had been less well born, with fewer important family connections, he might have been more cautious. He was descended on his father's side from a line of Lowland landholders that went straight back to the Sir William Inglis who felled a marauding English knight in single combat and was rewarded with a barony in 1396. His mother's mother, of the noble Erskine family, had provided him with an extraordinary international array of forebears, with descent from the royal Stuarts, the Plantagenets, and various princely houses of France, Spain, and northern Italy. His living Erskine cousins included the eleventh Earl of Buchan, two of the ablest lawyers of the day (one of whom was briefly Lord High Chancellor), and a minister plenipotentiary.

The Inglis family continued to grow. By 1816, the eleven-year-old Fanny—for so Frances was always called—was one of five daughters and four sons. With the belated arrival of another daughter, Lydia, the family of ten handsome children was complete.

William Inglis undoubtedly earned well through the years, and it is a matter of record that he was able to make large investments in land. At the same time, the problem of maintaining his household in what seemed appropriate style, bringing up so ample a family, and launching its sons must have been formidable. It is evident that little expense was spared in educating the children, and it is known that some of them, including Fanny, enjoyed periods of travel in Italy.

The second oldest daughter, Richmond, was the first to marry. At seventeen she became the wife of Alexander Norman Macleod, laird of the island of Harris. She will play an important role in what is to follow. The oldest daughter, Catherine, married a few years later, died young, and left a widower—Captain E. W. H. Schenley, who will reappear later with calamitous results.

More sorrow and a major disaster struck them all when Fanny was twenty-three. In the spring of 1828 news arrived that the eldest son, a young army officer, had died of fever in Madras. And in the early summer William Inglis, by this time in his late sixties, was forced into bankruptcy for a hopelessly large sum. He was totally and irretrievably ruined. Broken in health, he took refuge in Normandy, where his womenfolk loyally bore him company. He lived only two years longer, and died in a farmhouse near Le Havre in June 1830.

It is possible only to guess at the reasons behind the final decision that some members of the large family should emigrate to the United States and establish a school in Boston. A compelling one was, surely, the determination not to burden their kinsmen or the two Inglis sons who were to remain in Scotland. There may also have been the urgent wish to put past problems behind them, including difficulties that had developed in regard to Richmond's marriage. Time has obscured the circumstances that led to her separation from her husband, but it is clear that her relatives stood firmly with her and that she and they assumed responsibility for the upbringing of her four little girls. Her husband, who lost his island patrimony of Harris, emigrated to Jamaica, where he kept with him, at least at this time, their only son. The youth bore his father's name of Alexander Norman Macleod and, with his younger sister Kate, he will appear in this book.

The Inglis contingent that came to Boston, apparently in the autumn of 1831, was entirely feminine. The roster numbered at least nine, four of whom could be counted upon as breadwinners: the widowed Mrs. Inglis, in active middle age; Richmond, a little over thirty, with her Macleod daughters (Jane, Emmeline, Agrippina, and Kate, ranging from eleven to five); Fanny, the author of this book, nearing twenty-seven; Harriet, in her early twenties; and Lydia, last of her generation and near in age to her older Macleod nieces. Alexander Duff Inglis, man of the transplanted family at fifteen, joined them about a year later.

By educational standards of the day, the Inglis women were undoubtedly well prepared for their new role as schoolmistresses. Their establishment on Mount Vernon Street enjoyed distinguished patronage and their affairs seem to have gone well, but trouble was soon to follow—and Fanny was at the center of it. In May 1833 it was bruited about that an anonymous pamphlet caricaturing a number of prominent Bostonians

who had staged an elaborate bazaar for charity—and perhaps, in so doing, had exhibited uncharitable foibles—was written by Fanny Inglis and
a young man known to admire her. Victims who had daughters in the
school showed their ire by withdrawing them. The young man in the case
insisted valiantly that he was the sole author and apologized in print, but
the truth of his confession was seriously doubted. (His gallantry did his
courtship no good as Fanny evidently refused him, for he put himself on
record as still despairing even after her marriage years later.)

The school continued in Boston for about two years more. Perhaps
because of the old embroilment over the pamphlet, or possibly because
of increasing competition, the Inglis ladies sought a fresh field. Their
choice fell upon Staten Island. Dotted with handsome Greek Revival
villas as well as farms, it was also noted for two or three excellent
summer hotels patronized by southern families of means and by foreign
diplomats seeking relief from the damp heat of Washington. Beyond
any reasonable doubt, their move—to Belmont House in the village of
New Brighton—brought Fanny Inglis her husband.

Angel Calderón de la Barca was born in 1790 in Buenos Aires, then
a part of Spain's vast colonial domain. One of eight children of a
Spanish-born official, he was sent at an early age to England for his
schooling. He later enlisted for the defense of Spain during the
Napoleonic struggle, and fell a prisoner to the French. After the re-
establishment of peace, he entered government service in the mother
country and over the following years served on diplomatic assignments
in Germany and Russia. In 1835 he was sent to the United States as
Spanish minister.

Calderón, as he was called, emerges from his letters and from fragmentary descriptions by others as a man of varied interests and studious bent;
conservative, cautious, and upright; solid rather than brilliant; and endowed with flawless, easy manners. To William Hickling Prescott, he
was "a frank, manly caballero"—for thus the historian described him after
their first meeting in New York in the spring of 1838, a meeting to discuss ways in which Calderón might further Prescott's efforts to obtain
source materials from Spain. Calderón was likewise attracted to the
scholarly open-hearted New Englander (whom Fanny had known earlier
in Boston), and a staunch, lasting friendship ensued.

There is meager but unmistakable evidence that Angel Calderón de la
Barca and Fanny Inglis knew each other well for at least a year and a
half before their marriage. During much of this period, Calderón was at
odds with the current government in Spain and out of its diplomatic
service, but a few months after returning to duty, on September 24, 1838,
he and Fanny Inglis were married in New York by the Cuban-born
priest of the Church of the Transfiguration. The bridegroom gave his
age for the record as forty-eight. The age of the tall, blooming young

woman who had been born in Scotland thirty-three years before was
entered as twenty-eight.

Following their marriage Fanny and Calderón saw a winter of Washington life under the Van Buren administration. The following summer,
however, found them living with their Staten Island relatives, preparing
for Calderón's important new assignment as the first envoy sent by Spain
to independent Mexico. On October 27, 1839—the opening date of *Life
in Mexico*—they left New York for Havana.

Two and a half years later, while lingering in Havana on their return
from Mexico, Fanny and Calderón learned of a disaster that had struck
her school-keeping relatives on Staten Island. The ladies had shortly
before welcomed as a visitor Captain Schenley, widower of Fanny's oldest
sister Catherine Inglis. The well-tailored captain (who had been remarried and re-widowed and who was now fiftyish and the wearer, according to one report, of corsets as an aid to trimness) repaid them by
eloping with one of their pupils, a motherless fifteen-year-old who was
sole heiress to a notable fortune. The reverberations of the affair, dwelt
upon with relish in the public prints, effectively wrecked the school.

The luckless Inglises felt obliged to move once more. Encouraged, apparently, by various impeccable sponsors, they turned again to Boston,
and the resilient "Mrs. Inglis's Establishment for Young Ladies" soon
opened its doors at No. 5 Chestnut Street. It was there, in the hard-
working household which the Calderóns shared for the major part of a
year, that *Life in Mexico* was put together and readied for the publishers.

What followed, for Fanny and for Calderón, is a story which can
only be touched upon here.

They passed the next year abroad, accompanied by Fanny's niece,
Kate Macleod. Following an initial round of visits in Scotland they
settled in Madrid. After a rather uncertain winter in a chilly apartment,
waiting for a suitable new assignment, Calderón was again appointed
Spanish minister to the United States.

The next nine years were spent in Washington, with Calderón involved in a variety of challenging diplomatic encounters, and with Fanny
interested, as always, in people and events, and warmly concerned in the
developing lives of her young Macleod nieces. The girls and their mother
maintained independence by continuing the family school in Boston
and later in Baltimore. They were often guests of the Calderóns, however, and almost certainly it was in the home of their diplomatic aunt
that three of the four accomplished Macleod girls met their future
husbands, each of a different nationality. Emmeline married a prominent
Washington lawyer; Agrippina, a Spanish diplomat of noble family; and
Kate, a Frenchman who was later named his country's minister to China.

In 1847 Fanny took a step for which she had been consciously preparing for at least two years and toward which, perhaps, she may have

been tending ever since her sojourn in Mexico. On May 10 of that year she was received into the Catholic faith at Georgetown's Holy Trinity Church. That she was a whole-hearted and deeply committed convert there cannot be the slightest doubt.

The year 1853 brought diplomatic advancement and upheaval when Calderón was named Spain's minister of foreign affairs. He and Fanny left the United States in August, and with them went Fanny's youngest sister Lydia, about thirty and still unmarried. Two days after their arrival in Madrid, the ministry that had promoted Calderón resigned. The new leaders—men evidently less to his liking—offered him the same post. He refused; but subsequently, after a plea from the Queen herself, he reluctantly accepted office.

During subsequent months Spain seethed with rumors, factions, plots, and repression. After a bad harvest and increasing tension, revolt broke out in various parts of the country. The government of which Calderón was a part fell on July 17, 1854. Mobs surged through the streets of Madrid and there was an outcry for the arrest of the fallen ministers. Calderón, after concealment in one foreign legation and then another, and with the aid of dyed hair and a false passport, escaped over the Pyrenees disguised as a French wine merchant. In due time Fanny, also traveling under an assumed identity, followed. She was accompanied by two adolescent nieces whom, with characteristic enthusiasm, she had borrowed for a season from her sister Harriet Addison, their mother.

The exiles, who were joined by Fanny's sister Lydia, spent two philosophical years living outside Paris in a little house in Neuilly. There Fanny went back to her old resource, her pen. Following the publication in New York of a two-volume translation from the Italian of Father Daniel Bartoli's book on the life of St. Ignatius Loyola, there appeared, also in New York, in 1856 a lively account covering the recent turbulent events which the Calderóns had experienced in Spain. For this book Fanny sought effective anonymity: *The Attaché in Madrid* was presented as an English translation of the work of an unnamed young German diplomat. Unlike *Life in Mexico*, which had appeared as by "Madame C_____ de la B_____," it kept the secret of its authorship for many years.

By the time they were able to return to Spain in 1856, Calderón was in his mid-sixties. As a life member of the senate he had occupation and standing, but he never again took a prominent public role, and they were no longer a part of the circle that lived and breathed politics and court affairs. Parts of each year were spent in the picturesque little fishing village of Zarauz on Spain's north coast, near San Sebastián. They had just finished building there a modest holiday villa when Calderón, past seventy, died in 1861.

The widowed Fanny, while making a conventual retreat following Calderón's death, received a message from the Queen, asking her to undertake the education of the Infanta Isabel, who would soon be ten years of age. Fanny is said to have declined the royal summons at first, but a second request brought acceptance. Thus, at the age of fifty-seven, she returned to the profession she had left upon her marriage some twenty-three years before, but now her classroom and her home were in the Royal Palace.

This new part of her life lasted nearly as long as her marriage. During the next few years, as she observed the royal children of whom her Infanta was the oldest—with only one male heir of less than robust health—Fanny, and others also, must have recognized the possibility that she was training the girl who might one day be Queen of Spain.

Her charge was married at sixteen to a young cousin with little to distinguish him other than a good army record. He was Don Cayetano de Borbón, Conde de Girgenti, a prince of the deposed royal house of the Kingdom of the Two Sicilies. The wedding was in May 1868 and during the following months Fanny, perhaps again facing a time of decision, made a visit to the United States. As a consequence she missed the outbreak of what would have been her fourth and most sweeping revolution. Time had run out for the good-natured, mismanaging, generous, amoral Queen Isabel II, and the entire royal family was obliged to seek refuge in France.

Tragedy brought Fanny back to her former pupil. The Infanta's husband Don Cayetano developed severe epileptic seizures about a year after their marriage and Fanny's aid as the Infanta's companion was sought and obtained. Following one unsuccessful attempt on his own life, Don Cayetano shot himself fatally at Lucerne in November 1871. His widow was only nineteen.

Meanwhile, the exiled Queen's only son Alfonso was growing up. His mother abdicated her rights in his favor, and at the end of 1874 his supporters succeeded in making him King of Spain at the age of seventeen. In due course his older sister the Infanta Isabel returned to Spain as Princess of Asturias, next in line to the throne until her brother should marry and father an heir. Fanny, with an appointment as lady of honor to her ex-pupil and friend, likewise returned to the enormous palace in Madrid which once more became her home. On September 18, 1876, in recognition of her husband's services as well as her own, she was accorded the title of Marquesa de Calderón de la Barca by her young sovereign, to whom she is said to have given his first childhood lessons in English.

She lived for five years more under the reign of Alfonso XII: through his marriage, for love, to his first cousin Mercedes; through the eighteen-year-old Queen's death a few months later; and through the King's dutiful remarriage to the capable, reserved Austrian archduchess who became the mother of his children.

These palace years were not without the warmth of family ties.

Fanny's niece Agrippina, wife of a Spanish *marqués,* was happily rooted in Madrid with a family of children. Harriet Addison, Fanny's next younger sister, now a widow, with one of her daughters married to a Spanish diplomat and another to an Italian nobleman, seems to have spent long periods in Europe. And near at hand was her youngest sister Lydia who, subsequent to the death of the Spanish diplomat whom she had married in 1859, followed in Fanny's footsteps by becoming governess to the King's younger sisters.

Fanny is said to have kept her splendid health and her supple intellect until the end of her life. One evening in the winter of 1882, when dressed according to custom in brave décolletage for a dinner, she took cold. Worsening rapidly, she died in her apartments on February 6. She was seventy-seven.

A charming photograph taken in her last years survives. Her costume, topped with a decorous white cap perched upon her pompadour, was conservative but modish. She looked exactly what she was: an elderly Scotswoman of firm character who, by a curious chain of circumstances, was being photographed in Madrid, with a Spanish decoration pinned to her shoulder. It was the insignia of the Banda de las Damas Nobles de María Luisa, an order she had mentioned in *Life in Mexico* some forty years before.

NEW YORK TO
THE CITY OF MEXICO

1

To Havana on a Merchant Packet

Sunday: October 27th, 1839
On board the Packet Ship *Norma*

This morning at ten o'clock we left New York and stepped on board the steamboat *Hercules,* destined to convey us to our packet with its musical name. The day was foggy and gloomy, as if refusing to be comforted, even by an occasional smile from the sun. All prognosticated that the *Norma* would not sail today, but all were mistaken—"where there's a will, there's a way."

Several of our friends had come to see us off and accompanied us to the wharf: Bodisco, the Russian minister, who is about taking a part in *El Sí de las Niñas;*[1] Mr. Krehmer, who tried hard to look sentimental, and even brought tears into his eyes by some curious process he must have learned in St. Petersburg—"The tear forgot as soon as shed";[2] Judge Patterson; Mariquita Harmony; Suárez, who looked like a stale lemon; Trueman, who appeared on the scene to increase the effect at the last moment; also General Alvear, the minister of Buenos Aires; &c., &c.

Richmond, A. Norman, Jane, and Mary Jones, from whom we were truly sorry to part, accompanied us as far as the ship.[3]

The *Norma* was anchored in one of the most beautiful points of the bay—and, luggage hoisted in, the steamboat towed us five miles, until we had passed the Narrows. The wind was contrary, but the day began to clear up, and the sun to scatter the watery clouds. Stoughton came in a boat, and made the amiable. His motto is, "Welcome the coming, speed the parting guest."[4]

Still, there is nothing so sad as a retreating view. It is as if time were visibly in motion; and as here we had to part from [my family] we could only distinguish, as through a misty veil, the beauties of the bay; the shores covered to the water's edge with trees rich in their autumnal colouring; the white houses on Staten Island—the whole gradually growing fainter till, like a dream, they faded away.

The pilot has left us, breaking our last link with the land. We still see the mountains of Navesink, and the lighthouse of Sandy Hook.[5] The sun is setting, and in a few minutes we must take our leave, probably for years, of places long familiar to us. We have said adieu to Richmond, and Jane, and A. Norman, and Mary Jones—and Spanish-Yankee Stoughton—and Zaldo, who makes fair promises. And now we are alone, Calderón and I and Mme Martin, my French *femme de chambre*, with her air of offended dowager duchess, and moreover sea-sick.

Our fellow passengers do not appear very remarkable. There is Madame Albini—returning from being prima donna in Mexico, in a packet called after the opera in which she was there a favourite—with an awful looking man, her husband, Señor Vellani, with moustaches like a bird's nest, and a baby and nurse;[6] a Mme de Roy, a pretty widow in deep affliction, at least in deep mourning, of whom more anon; an old maiden lady, Miss Fay, going out as a governess, under our protection they say; a family whose names I do not know; and every variety of ugly Spaniard, from Bird's-Nest Vellani to an old Habanero consul, going out to replace the disgraced Trist.[7]

Monday evening: October 28th, 1839

When I said I liked a sea life, I did not mean to be understood as liking a nasty dirty merchant ship, full of vulgar Spaniards who smoke and spit worse than the most be-Trolloped Americans.[8] I did not mean that I liked a cabin without air, and with every variety of bad smell—and no chance of a good one. As the Albini, with the air of an afflicted porpoise and with more truth than elegance expresses it: *"Tout devient puant, même l'eau de cologne!"*[9]

The wind is still contrary and the *Norma*, beating up and down, makes but little way. The captain says we have not gone more than seventy-four miles, and of these *advanced* but forty. He, Captain Barton, has now made fifty-four voyages to and fro Havana.

Nothing very remarkable has occurred today. Most people sick—passively or actively—and the deck is nearly deserted. The most interesting object I have yet discovered on board is a pretty little deaf and dumb girl, very lively and with an intelligent face, who has been trying to teach me to speak on my fingers. There is a large iron sugar machine on board, which looks enough to weigh down the vessel. Spent the day on deck, to avoid the purgatory of bad odours which pervades the cabin. Mme de Roy made her first appearance on deck—and gave a mortal blow to the interest with which her history had inspired me by her performance in public. It is said that her husband being at New York, and dying of consumption, she rejected every entreaty and advice that was given her to advise him to have his will made, saying that his last moments should not be disturbed—by which means, he dying without a will, she has been left destitute.

The only commendable part of the ship is the food, which is very decent indeed—but ah! the difference between this and a Liverpool or Havre packet! Charles Napoleon, the infant heir of the houses of Albini and Vellani, has shown his good taste by passing the day in screaming. Bird's-Nest Vellani, pale, dirty, and much resembling a brigand out of employ, has traversed the deck with uneasy footsteps, and a cigar appearing from out his moustaches, like a light in a tangled forest, or a jack-o'-lantern in a marshy thicket. A horrid fat Spaniard has been discoursing on the glories of garlic and *olla podrida*.[10] *Au reste*, we are slowly pursuing our way and if we go on at this rate might reach Cuba in three months.

And the stars are shining, quiet and silvery. All without is soft and beautiful, and no doubt the *Norma* herself with her white sails spread looks all in unison with the scene, balancing herself like a lazy swan, white and graciously. So it is without, and *within* there is miserable seasickness, bilge water, bad smells, fat Spaniards, and Bird's-Nest Vellani!—and all the unavoidable disagreeables of a small packet.

Tuesday: October 29th, 1839

Pitching and tossing—pitching and tossing—creak-creak-creak. All the passengers sick or sickish. Wind so-so.

Wednesday: October 30th, 1839

Fair wind. Mme de R's romance is ended. It appears she *knew* her husband had made a will in her favour—and is left very rich. Her affliction now appears to me affectation. *"Entre callar y trompeta,"* &c.[11]

It appears that this extraordinary rolling of the ship is caused in great part by a huge sugar machine, hollow in the middle. Impossible to write —and not much to say. Imagine seasickness in all its varieties—a *valse infernale* with variations.

Thursday: October 31st, 1839

Three days have passed without anything worthy of notice having occurred, except that we already feel the difference of temperature. The passengers are still enduring seasickness in all its phases.

This morning opened with an interesting angry dispute between two of the gentlemen (Spaniards) on the subject of Cuban lotteries, and they ended by calling each other liars.[12] But by dinner time they were amicably engaged in concocting together an enormous tureen of *gazpacho*, a sort of salad, composed of bread, oil, vinegar, sliced onion and garlic— and the fattest one declares that in warm weather a dish of *gazpacho* with plenty of garlic in it makes him feel as fresh as a rose. He must indeed be a perfect bouquet.

A little less rolling—fair wind. The opening of morning is dramatic in our narrow cabin. About twenty voices in Spanish, German, Italian, and broken English strike up by degrees. From nextdoor Nid d'Oiseau[13] puts forth his head.

"Stooar! A toomlar! Here is no vater!"

"Comin, sir, comin."

"Caramba! Stooard!"

"Comin, sir, comin!"

"Stuart? *Vasser und* toel!"

"Here, sir!"

"Amigo! How is the wind?" (This is the waking up of El Señor Ministro, putting his head half suffocated out of his berth.)

"Oh steward! Steward!"

"Yes, miss."

"Come here, and look at *this!*"

"I'll fix it, miss."

&c., &c., &c.

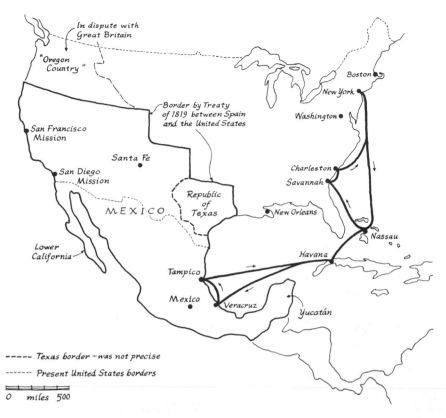

In dispute with
Great Britain

"Oregon
Country"

Border by Treaty
of 1819 between Spain
and the United States

Boston
New York
Washington

San Francisco
Mission

Santa Fe

San Diego
Mission

Charleston
Savannah

Republic
of
Texas

MEXICO

New Orleans

Lower
California

Nassau

Havana

Tampico

Mexico   Veracruz

Yucatán

----- Texas border ~ was not precise

------ Present United States borders

0   miles 500

Friday: November 1st, 1839

A fair wind after a stifling night, and strong hopes of seeing the
Bahama Banks on Sunday. Beautiful day. During all this time our
Dowager Duchess has been sick and below.[14]

Most people are now gradually ascending from the lower regions,
dragging themselves on deck with pale, miserable and dejected countenances, and sitting down to dinner with looks of disgust. The widow
with two or three men round her lies down on a bench. I do not
believe her inconsolable. Madame A[lbini] and Bird's-Nest are so very
well conducted, so quiet and *comme il faut*, that there is nothing to be
said. She is rather agreeable with such a sweet-toned voice in speaking,
especially in her accents of her *bella Italia*, that it is refreshing to
listen to her.

There is a boy who appears half imbecile on board and who is very
curious in straw hats—letting one overboard every now and then. Also
a *Havana Catlin*.[15]

Saturday: November 2nd, 1839

Beautiful weather—wind pretty fair. Passed as usual all day lounging on deck, with intervals of eating—and reading, after a desultory fashion, *Les Enfants d'Edouard* by Casimir Delavigne, Washington Irving, D'Israeli's *Curiosities of Literature*, &c.[16] It is rather singular that while there is a very tolerable supply of English and French books here I see but one or two odd volumes in Spanish, although these packets are constantly filled with people of that nation, going and coming. Is it that they do not care for reading, or that less attention is paid to them than to the French or American passengers? One would think Cervantes, Lope de Vega, Calderón or Moratín better worth buying than many commonplace novels which I find here.

The Dowager Duchess appeared on deck. In fact, there is now a pretty general muster. The A[lbini] put on a white wrapper, in which she looks à la Zamora. The heat becomes tolerably great. The wind is not very favourable this evening. What is of it is soft and balmy, making one feel lazy and dreamy. So now for our hen coop.

Sunday: November 3rd, 1839

Wind contrary. Yesterday the wind blew soft as on a summer morning. A land bird flew into the ship. Today the wind has veered round, but the weather continues charming. Read prayers and then novels, and sat on deck all day. Nothing remarkable but the sea is covered with multitudes of small flying fish. An infantile waterspout appeared, and died

in its birth, not a *ship* birth. Mr. Smith, the consul, has been giving me an account of the agreeable society in the Sandwich Islands!!! *Caramba!*—and the agreeable fêtes at Tooloombooroolooboo, or some such name!

A magnificent sunset, the sight of which compensates for all the inconveniences of the voyage. The sky was covered with black clouds lined with silver, and surrounded by every variety of colour: deep blue, fleecy-rose, violet, and orange. The heavens are now thickly studded with stars, numbers shooting across the blue expanse like messengers of light, glancing and disappearing as if extinguished.

It is well to read the *History of Columbus* at sea, but especially in these waters where he wandered in suspense, high-wrought expectation, and firm faith; and to watch the signs which the noble mariner observed in these latitudes: the soft serenity of the breezes, the clear blue of the heavens, the brilliancy and number of the stars, the seaweeds of the gulf which always drift in the direction of the wind, the little land birds that come like harbingers of good tidings, the frequency of the shooting stars, and the multitude of flying fish.

As the shades of evening close around, and the tropical sky glitters with the light of innumerable stars, imagination transports us back to that century which stands out in bold relief amidst other ages rolling by comparatively undistinguished, and we see as in a vision the Discoverer of a World, standing on the deck of his caravel as it bounded over the unknown and mysterious waste of waters, his vigilant eyes fixed on the west, like a Persian intently watching the rising of his god —though his star was to arise from whence the day-god sets. We see him bending his gaze on the first dark line that separated the watery sea from the blue of the heavens, striving to penetrate the gloom of night, yet waiting with patient faith until the dawn of day should bring the long-wished-for shores in sight.

Monday: November 4th, 1839

Wind contrary. Long faces like merchants' before a crash—not *after*. Notwithstanding, I have passed a not disagreeable day, sitting on deck in a large chair, and reading a French novel! The wind is soft and dreamy. I feel rather an unchristian distaste to our fellow passengers— at least the Habaneros.

Tuesday: November 5th, 1839

Wind dead ahead! C'est désespérant. Faces lengthen, and patience decreases. We shall certainly not have a very short passage—which will shorten our stay at Havana. I came down to write my Journal, when a Spaniard—the Havana Catlin, who has the air of a *perruquier*—very quietly took off his coat, drew in a chair opposite, set down a looking glass, comb, brush, &c.—and proceeded to dress his hair, clean his nails, lather his face with soap, shave—until, not foreseeing where he might go, I thought it wise to make a retreat. Now, methinks, no Yankee, however vulgar, would have so coolly taken the opportunity of coming to dress and clean himself before a lady. If an Englishman had done the same, it would of course have been an insult—but this man, with an air of ineffable conceit, sat examining his nose and chin in the glass, evidently thinking he was making a most agreeable display of his personal charms and graces.

Wednesday: November 6th, 1839

For three days, three very long and uncomfortable days, the wind, with surprising constancy, has continued to blow dead ahead. In ancient days, what altars might have smoked to Æolus! Now, except in the increased puffing of consolatory cigar smoke, no propitiatory offerings are made to unseen powers. There are indeed many mourning signs amongst the Spanish or Habanero passengers. Everyone has tied up his head in an angry-looking silken bandana, drawn over his red nose with a dogged air. Beards are unshaven, a black stubble covering the lemon-coloured countenance, which occasionally bears a look of sulky defiance, as if its owner were, like Juliet, "past hope, past cure, past help" and as if each said, "Here grief and I together sit—not to be parted."[17]

Thursday: November 7th, 1839

On Wednesday morning the monotony of fine weather was relieved by a hearty squall, accompanied by torrents of rain, much thunder and frequent forked lightning. The ship reeled to and fro like a drunken man, and the passengers, as usual in such cases, performed various involuntary evolutions, cutting right angles, sliding, spinning round, and rolling over, almost as if Oberon's magic horn were playing an occasional blast amidst the roaring winds. The only firm of footstep and of purpose were the stewards. Like Horace's good man, they walked serene amidst the wreck of crockery and the fall of plates.[18] Driven from our stronghold on the deck, we were forced to take refuge indiscriminately crammed in below like figs in a drum or Dutch herrings in a barrel. "Weltering," as Carlyle has it, "like an Egyptian pitcher of tamed vipers," we submitted tant bien que mal to our hard fate. The cabin windows all shut in, we tried to take it coolly, in spite of the suffocating heat. It is strange that the ancient Greeks, so alive to all that touched their senses, had no Goddess of Perfume!—one who presided over sweet smelling odours. Certain it is, no trace of such a deity was to be seen or smelt that day.

There is a child on board, brother of the little dumb girl, who is certainly possessed, not by a witty, malicious demon, a *diable boiteux*, but by a teasing, stupid, wicked imp, which inspires him with the desire of universally tormenting everything human that comes within his reach. Should he escape being thrown overboard, it will show a wonderful degree of forbearance on the part of the passengers.

Friday: November 8th, 1839

On Thursday we had again fine weather—thank heaven!—after a night even more disagreeable than the day. The passengers, with their heads tied up, look more gloomy than ever. Some sit dejected in corners, and some take to quarrelling with their neighbours, thus finding a safety valve by which their overflowing wrath may escape.

This day the weather is perfect—cool and pleasant—but the wind is inexorable. Nevertheless, the passengers have all brightened up, taken off their red and black headkerchiefs and shaved, as if ashamed of their six days' impatience, and making up their minds to a sea life.

This morning we saw land: a long, low ridge of hills on the island of Eleuthera, belonging to the English—where they make salt and where

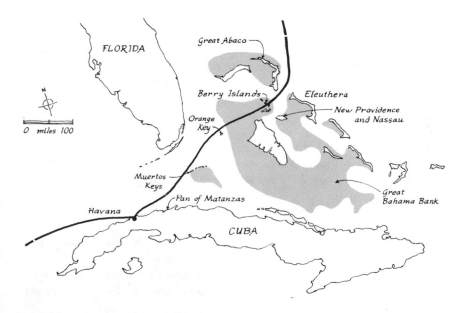

there are many Negroes. But neither salt nor Negroes were visible to the naked eye; nothing but the gray outline of the hills melting into the sea and sky. Still, to see land is something. One might almost consent to be numbered among the things that have been to have stood on the deck of Columbus' vessel when the first shout of *Land!* was heard. However, it was not remarkably pleasant when, after having tacked about all day, we found ourselves in the evening precisely at the same distance from and opposite to the island of salt and Negroes. We did not feel either like discoverers, or wayfaring men in sight of home. When we may reach Havana, we cannot even conjecture. There are Job's comforters on board who assure us that they have been thirty-six days between New York and *"la joya más preciosa de la corona de España."*[19]

For my part I do not feel very impatient, having rather a dislike to changing my position even when it is a disagreeable one, and the air is so fresh and laden with balm that it seems to blow over some paradise of sweets, some land of fragrant spices. The sea also is a mirror, and I have been reading Captain Marryat's *Pirate* for the first time, which is energetic and well told. The sea is his element—and there he should remain, both in imagination and reality.[20]

Thus then we stand, on this eighth day of November—at eight o'clock p.m.—wind ahead, and little of it, performing a zigzag march between Eleuthera and Abaco.

On deck, the pretty widow lies in her easy chair, surrounded by her countrymen, who are disputing as usual about sugar, molasses, chocolate, and other local topics—anything, everything that turns up—together with the relative merits of Cuba as compared with the rest of the known world. Madame Albini is trying to study her part of Elisabetta in the opera of *Roberto Devereux,* which she is to bring out in Havana, but the continued creaking of the *Norma* is sadly at variance with divine harmony.[21] El Señor Ministro is translating the *History of Photogenic Drawing* into pure Castilian.[22] A pale German creature, in dressing gown and slippers, is studying Schiller—and an ingenuous youth whose name I know not, but shall take the liberty of supposing to be Mollycoddle, is carefully conning a well-thumbed note, which looks like a milliner's girl's last billet doux. The little *possédé* is burning brown paper within an inch of the curtains of a stateroom, while the steward is dragging it from him. Others are gradually dropping into their berths, like ripe nuts from a tree. Thus are we all pursuing our vocations.

Saturday: November 9th, 1839

Wind dead ahead! This gets to be no joke. I console myself with *Cinq-Mars* and *Jacob Faithful.*[23] But the weather is lovely. A young moon in her first quarter, like a queen in her minority, glitters like a crescent on the brow of night.

Towards evening the long-wished-for lighthouse of Abaco (built by the English) showed her charitable and revolving radiance. But our ship, Penelope-like, undoes by night what she has performed by day, and her course is backward and crabbish. A delicious smell of roses and violets is blowing from the land.

Sunday morning: November 10th, 1839

A fair wind! The good tidings communicated by the Albini, *toute rayonnante de joie.* A fair wind and a bright blue sea, cool and refreshing breezes, the waves sparkling, and the ship going gallantly over the waters. The captain thinks we shall reach Havana by Wednesday. So far, our voyage may have been tedious, but the most determined landsman must allow that the weather has been charming.

Sunday at sea. Here we are where no bells toll, and no hymns are chanted, nor mass is sung—nor where are any temples made with hands, but none are needed here. The blue sky above and the blue ocean beneath us form one vast temple, pure and unprofaned, where, since the foundations of the earth and sea were laid, "Day unto day uttereth speech, and night unto night sheweth knowledge."[24]

This morning we neared the Berry Islands, unproductive and rocky, as the geography books would say. One of these islands belongs to a coloured man, who bought it for fifty dollars—a cheaply-purchased sovereignty. He, his wife and children, with their several Negro slaves —slaves to a coloured man!—live there. They have a house with outhouses—and cultivate vegetables, &c. to sell at the New York market—or to the different ships that pass that way. Had the wind been favourable, they would probably have sent us out a boat with fresh vegetables, fish, and fruit, which would have been rather agreeable. If the mulatto wished to escape from the contempt of the white man he has done wisely.

We saw, not far from the shore, the wreck of a two-masted vessel—sad sight to those who pass over the same water to see

A brave vessel,
Who had, no doubt, some noble creatures in her,
Dashed all to pieces!

Who had, at least, some of God's creatures in her. Anything but that! I am like Gonzalo, and "would fain die a dry death."[25]

We are now on the Bahama Banks, the water very clear and blue, with a creamy froth, looking as if it flowed over pearls and turquoises. An English schooner man-of-war (or rather *boy*-of-war in size) made all sail towards us, doubtless hoping we were a slaver; but, on putting us to the test of his spyglass, the captain, we presume, perceived that the general tinge of countenance was lemon or olive rather than Negro, and so abandoned his pursuit.[26]

This evening on the Banks. It would be difficult to imagine a more placid and lovely scene. Everything perfectly calm, all sail set, and the heavens becoming gradually sprinkled with thousands of silver stars. The sky blue, and without a cloud, except where the sun has just set, the last crimson point sinking in the waves and leaving a long retinue of rainbow-coloured clouds, deep crimson tinged with bright silver, and melting away into gray, pale vapour.

On goes the vessel, stately and swanlike; the water of the same bright turquoise blue, covered with a light milky froth, and so clear that we can see the large black sponges at the bottom. Every minute they heave the lead.

"By the mark three."

"By the mark three, less a quarter."

"By the mark twain and a half." Fifteen feet, the vessel drawing thirteen—two feet between us and the bottom. The sailor sings it out like the first line of a hymn in short metre, doled out by the parish clerk. I wish Madame A[lbini] were singing it instead of he.

"By the mark three, less a quarter."

To this tune, the only sound breaking the stillness of the night, I dropped to sleep. The captain passed the night anxiously, now on the topmast looking out for lights on the Banks, now at the helm, or himself sounding the lead:

> For some must watch whilst others sleep;
> Thus wags the world away.[27]

Monday: November 11th, 1839

Beautiful morning, and fair wind. About eight we left the Banks. Just then we observed that the sailor who sounded, having sung out five, then six, then in a few minutes seven, suddenly found no bottom— as if we had fallen off all at once from the brink of the Bank into an abyss. We passed the Orange Keys at four o'clock. We shall probably reach Havana tomorrow. This is the fifteenth day of our passage. With fair wind, a voyage to Havana must be a mere trip. I have written letters to New Brighton—perhaps we may hear from them before leaving Havana. Captain Brown, a fellow captain and passenger of our Captain Barton's, told me this morning that he spoke the ship which carried out

Governor and Mrs. Maclean to Cape Coast Castle—the unfortunate L. E. L. He says report said they were already on bad terms. Her death was by prussic acid—and it is supposed that she took it herself—and was in the habit of taking it—but whether she increased the quantity intentionally or not is unknown, except to those perhaps who were with her at the time. Poor L. E. L.! To die poisoned at Cape Coast Castle! What a romance she would have written about her own death if she had lived! With which bull I give way to a black steward with a dirtyish tablecloth.[28]

We have been accompanied all the morning by a magnificent large ship, going full sail, the *Orleans*, Captain Sears, bound for New Orleans.

A long semicircular line of black rocks in sight; some of a round form, one of which is called the Death's Head; another of the shape of a turtle, and some two or three miles long. At the extremity of one of these the English are building a lighthouse.

Tuesday: November 12th, 1839

We are opposite the Pan of Matanzas—why so called I have not been informed—about sixty miles from Havana.[29] Impatience becomes general, but the breeze rocks us gently up and down, and we gain but little. This day, like all last days on board, has been remarkably tedious, though the country as we approach nearer gradually becomes more interesting. A still more interesting spectacle was the universal *cleaning up* of the passengers; some shaving, some with their heads plunged into tubs of cold water—so that the ship resembled Noah's ark when the dove did not return, and all the passengers prepared for *terra firma*, after a forty days' voyage. Our Mount Ararat was the Morro Castle which, black and

frowning, presented itself to our much wearied eyes about six o'clock p.m. An interchange of unintelligible noises having taken place between the captain and the commander, we continued on our way.

Nothing can be more striking than the first appearance of this fortress, starting up from the solid rock, with its towers and battlements of dark gray stone.[30] Here for the first time to remind us of our latitude, we see a few feathery cocoas growing amidst the thick herbage that covers the banks near the castle. By its side, covering a considerable extent of ground, is the fortress called Cabaña, painted rose colour, with the angles of its bastions white.

But there is too much to look at now. I must finish my letter in Havana.

[Tuesday evening: November 12th, 1839
Havana]

As we entered the beautiful bay, everything struck us as strange and picturesque. The soldiers of the garrison, the prison built by General Tacón, the irregular houses with their fronts painted red or pale blue, and with the cool but uninhabited look produced by the absence of glass windows; the palace of the Captain-General, large but not very remarkable; that of the *Intendente*. In the bay, the merchant ships and large men-of-war; vessels from every port in the commercial world, the little boats gliding amongst them with their snow-white sails; the Negroes on the wharf—nothing European. The heat was great, that of a July day in England and without the same freshness in the air.

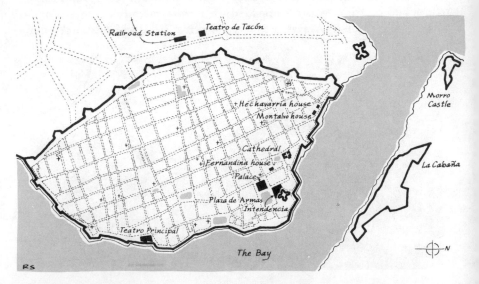

As we approached the wharf the noise and bustle increased. The passengers all crowded upon deck, and we had scarcely anchored when numerous little boats were seen making for the *Norma*. First boat brought a little pale officer with the salutations of the Captain-General to His Excellency Don Angel, with every polite offer of service, putting himself at his feet—and his property at his disposition. Second boat brought the *administrador* of the *Intendente* (the Count de Villanueva), with the same civilities—ditto, ditto; the third, the master of the house where we now are, and whence I indite these facts;[31] the fourth, the Italian opera, which rushed simultaneously into the arms of the Albini; the fifth, prosaic customhouse officers; the sixth, a Havana count and marquis— the Count de S. (which may stand for *Somebody*, his name I forget) and a small shrivelled marquis; the seventh, the family of General Montalvo— five boys like little old gentlemen with large heads (ditto hats) and one older little gentlemen with spectacles—the elder and younger brethren of Don Ramón[32]—much resembling the family of the chicken merchant.

Finally we—that is, El Señor Ministro, I, the Dowager Duchess, the *gouvernante* of the Count de la Reunión, the Count de S.—were hoisted over the ship's side in a chair, into the government boat, and rowed over to the shore. Much have I complained in the course of my voyagings by land and by sea that there was nothing new under the sun. I revoke my opinion, for I have seen nothing like Havana—the houses—people— modes and customs—in short the whole—whether en *masse* or en *détail*.

As it was rather dusk when we arrived, and we were driven to our destination—the Casa Hechavarría—in a *volante*, we did not see much of the city. We could but observe that the streets were narrow, the houses irregular, most people black, and the *volante* an amusing-looking vehicle —about the ugliest sort of carriage I ever saw. Behind it looks like a black

insect with high shoulders, and with a little black postilion on a horse or mule, stuffed into an enormous pair of jack boots and with a dirty fancy uniform.

The house in which, by the hospitality of the Hechavarría family,[33] we are installed has from its windows, which front the bay, the most varied and interesting view imaginable. As it is the first house, Spanish fashion, which I have entered, I must describe it to you before I sleep. The house forms a great square, and you enter the court, round which are the offices, the rooms for the Negroes, coal-house, bath room, &c., and in the middle of which stand the *volantes*. Looking up you see a large gallery which runs all round the house. Mount the staircase, arrive at the gallery, and pass into the *sala*—a large cool apartment with marble floor and handsome marble tables, and chaise longues with elastic cushions, chairs, and cane-bottomed armchairs. A drapery of white muslin and blue silk divides this from a second and smaller drawing room, now serving as my dressing room, and beautifully fitted up with Gothic toilet table, inlaid mahogany bureau, marble centre and side tables, handsome mirrors, cane sofas and chairs, green and gold paper. A drapery of white muslin and rose-coloured silk divides this from a bedroom, also fitted up with all manner of elegances for the toilette. A handsome French bed—blue silk drapery with blue silk coverlids and clear mosquito curtains, fringed sheets, fine lace and embroidered pillowcases, &c. A *drapery* divides this on one side from the gallery, on the other from the chamber of the host and hostess. This room [thus] opens into others which run all around the house.

The floors are marble or stucco—the roof's beams of pale blue-coloured wood placed transversely. Spit boxes adorn the floor. The whole has an air of agreeable coolness. Everything is handsome without being gaudy, and admirably adapted for the climate. Much luxury—with numerous inconsistencies—but commend me to one's own house—be it a cottage with a mud floor. The publicity of all things is primitive and amusing to see—but not agreeable to take a part in. To sleep in public—dress in public—&c. &c. &c.—one must have early habits to that effect. The sleeping apartments have no windows, and are dark and cool, while the drawing rooms have large windows down to the floor, with green shutters, kept closed till the evening.

Calderón having gone to pay his respects to the Captain-General and *Intendente*, I was left with the ladies of the house, the wife and the sister of H[echavarría]. To describe the former would require the pencil of a Hogarth. *Figurez-vous*, a little wild-looking mulatto—all hunched up in white muslin and dirty blonde[34]—without stays—biting her fingers and tearing her handkerchief with her teeth. Never have I been more astonished—seeing that her husband is good-looking and fond of show—a true Habanero, [who] dresses *en petit maître*—while she with her bare brown arms, uncombed hair, gown open behind, and rolling along generally cleaning her teeth with a toothpick is something "*more* than won-derful." The sister is large, good-looking, rather clever and awfully con-ceited—in comparison with the other, a perfect princess—but vulgar—*horrid* voice—spitting all over the floor—and eternally picking her teeth. Two or three ladies came to look at me—also the major-domo of the *Intendente* who told me that Scotland was a province belonging to England. One remarkable fact is that the women cannot understand that there is any difference between the U.S. and England—*el Norte* is for them all the same. Sweetmeats and *tea* ordered out of compliment to us.

The mosquitoes have now commenced their evening song, a signal that it is time to put out the lights. The moon is shining on the bay, and a faint sound of military music is heard in the distance, while the sea moans with a sad but not unpleasing monotony. To all these sounds I now retire to bed in view of the whole house if they choose to look.

2

A Glimpse of Spanish Colonial Life[1]

Wednesday: November 13th, 1839
Havana

No, never do I recollect having passed such a night. To avoid being seen by the whole house, we were foolish enough to shut the doors—and for this love of solitude we have paid dearly. The heat was suffocating. The mosquitoes, those winged demons of the night, kept up their perpetual and horrible *buzz.* [We were] like Catholic monarchs lying in state in beds with canopies and coverlids of blue silk—I for my part upon an elastic mattress which kept me dancing all night in time to the mosquitoes' singing. To sleep was impossible, but morning came at last, bringing at least light and air to the prisoners.

Breakfast at nine o'clock. A long table placed in the gallery with about twenty dishes—soup of garlic, oil, bread, &c.—*delicious,* to those who like it. *Beef-tek!*—small pieces of beef fried in oil and garlic. Hashes of meat and banana—eggs, fish, buffalo's tongue, *café au lait,* wine, &c. Everything in handsome French porcelain, white and gold. Little dirty Negro boys like juvenile apes, with their arms folded, standing behind the chairs.

About ten o'clock commence the visits. We have held a levee to all that is most distinguished in Havana. Counts, marquises, generals—all with orders, lace frills, diamond pins, ruby stars, fingers covered with rings, &c., &c.—have poured in and poured out ever since our arrival.[2]

At three o'clock, dinner—consisting of at least one hundred dishes, all with a delicious odour of garlic, and a dessert of sweetmeats, ripe oranges, preserved lemons and tropical fruits which I have not yet learnt to like, even though they are certainly wonderful and delicious productions of nature. But to eat eggs and custards and lumps of butter off the trees seems unnatural. I cannot pretend to say that I like Spanish cookery—the *fond* of oil and garlic formeth a groundwork which does not suit my notions. They had an *olla podrida* which I did not taste. It is a national dish, and like all national dishes unfashionable, but in reality much liked by the natives—like sheep's head and hodge-podge in Scotland (oh! that I had some of the latter!), or roast beef and plum pudding in England. After dinner toothpicks handed round to the guests, ladies and gentlemen; coffee, &c.

Received this morning the prettiest thing I have yet seen in Cuba—a large bouquet of roses and verbinum from the Countess de Villanueva, lady of the *Intendente,* with a message that she will come this evening. Received a visit from Mme de Montalvo and her daughter. It is the custom here for the ladies to accompany their female guests to the top of the staircase. [Then] at the bottom of the first landing takes place another salutation from the lady at the top. The description of a Spanish grandee, written I think by Poinsett and which I thought ridiculously *brodée,* is *exact.*[3]

About seven o'clock arrived the *Intendenta,* [the Countess de Villanueva]. ✕—mark her name with a cross—for at last I have seen a Spanish *lady.* Amongst the ladies who have called on me I find none more charming. Her manners cordial and easy, voice agreeable, dress quiet and rich, expression beautiful from goodness, her features good without being regular, with animated black eyes and fine teeth—altogether a charming person. She is universally beloved here. I receive from her nearly every morning a bouquet of the loveliest flowers from her *quinta*—roses, carnations, heliotrope, &c.[4] She spoke of poor Mrs. S. with tears in her eyes, and of her death as peculiarly melancholy from the mistaken method pursued with her in which the English doctor seems universally blamed. However, she died young and innocent, was buried at home, and mourned by her mother—there are worse fates.

> Death, which doth sin and sorrow thus prevent,
> Is the next blessing to a life well spent.[5]

At nine o'clock we got into the *volante* to go to the theatre and arrived at the last act of the first piece. The streets dark and crowded with *volantes* jostling each other. Soldiers at the door of the theatre. The sudden change from Yankee Land to this military, monkish, Spanish Negroland is *dreamy.*

After the first piece, a pantomime well represented, Calderón went to the box of the Countess de Fernandina—the great politician of the island. She is surnamed "*La Cacica.*" A handsome woman for her age which may be forty-five or so, wearing her hair dressed like a crop—à la Ninon—with fine shoulders and arms, very rich dress, and big diamonds here and there. Rather a fashionable-looking dame, with an intelligent but supercilious expression. The count a little thin gentlemanly man, lemon-coloured, and an invalid—but quiet and noble in his manners.[6]

The pantomime was an affair of brigands—stealing into a house on a dark night to murder the lady of the establishment. Heaven only knows what extraordinary hallucination came over me—a feeling unknown to

me—but whether it was that the whole appears so like a fiction that the representation seemed as real as the rest I cannot tell. So it was that over me crept a horror—a kind of stealing fear—to such an extent that I could scarcely forbear from screaming out loud. I never felt it before, and hope I shall not again. It lasted the whole evening—so that if on leaving the theatre anyone had touched me I should certainly have *shrieked*.[7]

I was introduced to La Fernandina, in the midst of a long file of soldiers—and came home very tired and frightened.

Thursday: November 14th, 1839

As no lady ever puts her foot on the streets of Havana, I cannot go out. Besides which, we are holding a perfect levee—very *flattering*, but extremely tedious. The *General de la Marina—anglisé*: Admiral of the Station—has been here to inform us that there is a brigantine of war prepared to take us to Veracruz, so they are treating us with *proper* consideration.[8] Visits the whole morning, from ten till three.

In the evening we found time to go to the opera—*Lucia di Lammermoor* by Donizetti. The prima donna, La Rossi, has a voice of much sweetness, sings correctly and with taste, is graceful in movement, but sadly wanting in strength. Still, for the character represented, she suits well and comes up exactly to my idea of poor Lucy, devoted and brokenhearted, weak physically and morally. But the story is altered, and the interest weakened. The music is lovely, graceful and full of melody—now and then a little like Bellini. The orchestra is excellent—and, strange to say, is composed of blacks and whites, mingled in harmonious confusion like the notes of a piano. They applaud, but never seem to encore.

The theatre is remarkably pretty and airy, and the pit is remarkable for its cleanness and respectability. All the seats are red leather armchairs, and all occupied by well-dressed people.

At the end of the first act we went round to the box of the Countess de Fernandina to return a visit she had made me in the morning. We found her very agreeable and full of intelligence, also with a very decided air of fashion. She was dressed in fawn-coloured satin, with large pearls. She and the count seem devoted to music. At the end of the second act, Lucia was taken ill—her last air missed out—and her monument driven on the stage without further ceremony. Montresor, the Ravenswood of the piece, came in, sung, and stabbed himself with immense enthusiasm and *bonne volonté*—but unfortunately with very little voice.[9] It is a pity that his voice is deserting him, for he has taste and feeling. The theatre is pretty and altogether French looking. The boxes are private—i.e., taken by individuals—but not shut in which, in this climate, would be suffocating. We passed out through a long file of soldiers.

Friday: November 15th, 1839

A continuation of our levee—which lasted till near dinner time. Some navy officers who called advised us to go off soon on account of the north winds. The whole day large birds like turkeys are flying slowly up and down before the windows, which front the bay and command a beautiful view of the Morro and the ships that enter or go out. Negroes with bare

legs, in fact with *next* to nothing on, are walking on the wall, carrying parcels, &c. *Volantes* pass by, with their black-eyed occupants in full dress: ladies dressed in white, with short sleeves, flowers in their hair, and black or white mantillas. Well-dressed, martial-looking Spanish soldiers marching by, and making tolerably free remarks upon the ladies in the *volantes*.

A great dinner given today to us by the master of the house. Just as I had gone to dress arrived the *Intendente*, [the Count de Villanueva]. The heat today is suffocating; [but] Calderón, thinking it necessary I should see him, hurried me in the most uncharitable manner. I found the *Intendente* a gentlemanly man, with manners of the old school—a little formal and very kind—[with] a very agreeable, benevolent expression. He paid *me* a great many compliments upon Calderón.[10]

The dinner at Hechavarría's today was a perfect *feast*. I sat between the Count de Fernandina and the Count de Santovenia, who is a millionaire. There were the Count de Peñalver and his brother, the latter a gentlemanly and intelligent man with a great taste for music, very pleasant and well informed, and whose daughter is a first-rate singer and a charming person, Domingo Herrera, &c., &c., &c.[11]

After dinner we rose, according to custom, and went into the next room while they set the dessert, consisting of every imaginable and unimaginable sort of sweetmeat, ice, fruits, &c. Everything was served in French white and gold porcelain, which looks particularly cool and pretty in this climate, with quantities of French ornaments (rather *gimcrack*). The whole cookery was *à l'espagnol*, garlic predominating. They do not seem to me very curious in their wines here—claret, champagne, and sherry. For one thing, much wine would be *killing* in such a climate.

The heat today is horrible, with a suffocating south wind blowing, and were the houses not built as they are, would be unbearable. The dinner is served in the gallery, which is spacious and cool.

After dinner the brother of H, Señor Don Prudencio Hechavarría, *qui fait le bel esprit*—a noisy, talkative democrat, but with some eloquence and a good deal of superficial talent—rose and, addressing Calderón, pronounced a poetical impromptu *tal cual* in verse on the late victory of Espartero and congratulating Calderón on his mission to the Mexican republic—which, being much applauded, I insert as a souvenir of this festival, he having sent it this morning.[12]

Improvisation

of Don Prudencio Hechavarría at the feast given by his brother Don Bernardo on November 15, 1839 for Señor Don Angel Calderón de la Barca, Minister Plenipotentiary of Her Catholic Majesty to the Mexican Republic. (The part more particularly addressed to Calderón will serve as a specimen of the style of the whole.)

> Listen, now, Minister of Isabela
> To Tenochtitlan, once the
> Treasure chest of her Monarchy:[13]
> Thou knowest, Calderón, the bitter school
> Of liberty, of crime, of passions
> Which today sets the world in convulsion
> And reveals a terrible truth to us.
> Peoples and nations have awakened!!
> Diplomacy, in which your genius shines
> With your majestic vision, &c., &c., &c., &c., &c.

Cela suffit. After dinner it became cooler and on the balcony was delicious. The air was delightful, a cool evening breeze having suddenly sprung up. A large ship, full sail, passed the Morro, and numerous barks. The bay was covered with little boats.

Many visitors came in, amongst others the Chief Justice with his wife and daughter from Madrid, the latter of whom is remarkably pretty, ladylike and quiet—more so than any unmarried lady I have yet seen.[14]

We then proceeded in *volantes* to pay a visit to the Countess de Villanueva at her pretty *quinta,* about three miles from town. As it was late, she was alone at her *prières du soir* in an inner room with the door open. The *Intendente* received us, and shortly after she came in with the little count—the only son and heir—rather a pretty, graceful child, but brought up like a little creole prince. Already he is attached as one of the Lords of the Bedchamber or chamberlains to Queen Cristina, who has sent him a diamond key in token of her approbation of his father's services.[15]

The countess has a good picture—an engraving—of Queen Victoria with the Duchess of Sutherland and Lady Normanby.[16] Apropos to queens, she told us an anecdote of the little Queen Isabel and the Infanta of Spain. They were playing together, and the Queen beat her sister. The Queen Regent insisted upon Her Majesty's going on her knees, kissing the Infanta's hand, and asking pardon. The Infanta, still crying, said to her mother: "When the Queen beat me first, I knelt down and, kissing her hand, called out, 'Viva Isabel Segunda! Viva Isabel Segunda!'—but the more I called out 'Viva Isabel Segunda' and kissed her hand, the harder she knocked!"

We visited and walked in the garden by moonlight, amongst flowers and fountains. These country retreats are delightful after the narrow streets and impure air of the city. Went to the Countess Fernandina's and home. The Captain-General had called and left his card, finding we were at dinner.

Saturday: November 16th, 1839

Visits—visits—visits. Having a headache, I did not get up. Calderón being out, an officer came from the Captain-General with dispatches, and as he wished to give them into the hands either of Calderón or me he was nearly introduced à l'espagnol, when I was in bed. However, I excused myself, got up, and received the Conde de la Reunión, a millionaire and formerly a merchant—so large that he looks as if he kept all his money within himself for safety—very civil and good-natured.[17]

This is the day of the patron saint San Cristóbal, and the saint is to be carried in [a] great procession this evening. Accordingly, we went about seven o'clock to the balconies of the Intendencia. It is a fine spacious building and, together with the Captain-General's palace,[18] stands in

the Plaza de Armas, a square with trees—the only place where the Habaneras find rest for the sole of their foot, exercise being totally unknown, and a lady on foot in the streets an impossibility. The square and all the streets were crowded with Negroes. The Negresses [were] all dressed in white with white muslin and blonde mantillas which showed off and framed their black faces to peculiar advantage.

Two regiments, with excellent bands of music, conducted the procession. Monks and priests composed it. San Cristóbal, a large figure remarkably fat with thick gold legs and gold angels with gold wings surrounding him, was carried on the shoulders of the priests to the music of "Suoni la tromba" from the Puritani to which were adapted the words of a hymn in praise of Liberty!—the whole being very consistent —the golden saint—Italian opera—military music—and freedom—to which add the slaves, and you have a whole composed of odd parts. The scene was curious and worth seeing.[19]

Paid a visit to La Fernandina, who has a fine house. Went to the Theatre of Tacón, which is superb, and saw the *Lucia*.

Sunday: November 17th, 1839

On Sunday morning rose at seven, took a cup of chocolate, put on a black silk gown and a white lace mantilla, and with a fan and a *livre d'heures* went to mass at the church of San Felipe![20] I hope that is being Spanish enough for once. *Ahime!* I would that were all. Preceded according to custom by a little Negro footman in livery carrying carpets, we entered the middle aisle of the church, where groups of women with black gowns and mantillas were kneeling on carpets—with little liveried Negroes standing behind them. There were not a great number

in the church, but the grouping was picturesque. The black faces of the Negresses with their white mantillas and white satin shoes; the black silk dresses and black lace mantillas of the Havana ladies, with their white faces and black eyes; the officers, the music, the long-bearded priests—all was very effective. As for the *devotion,* there was a good deal of crossing, much ringing of bells, and much low muttering in Latin on the part of the priest. Then the fair penitents, much fatigued with the unusual exertion of kneeling for ten minutes, sat down on their carpets, talked a little, crossed themselves, got up—and, followed by their Negroes and carpets, entered their respective *volantes* and drove off. We then proceeded to make a short tour in the *volante,* the morning being delicious though warm, and returned to breakfast.

Found, on my return, a very fine Erard harp, sent me by the Marchioness of Arcos, a pretty woman and female Crœsus. At four o'clock, having dressed ourselves, we repaired to the house of General Montalvo.

A splendid entertainment was given us today by General Montalvo. His house very large and cool. We were introduced to four daughters, five sons, several grandchildren, and two nieces.[21] Of these, the daughters look for the most part pale, awkward, and languishing; the sons very fat or very thin; the grandchildren good-looking and old-fashioned; the nieces extremely handsome but very *gauche*—which seems odd for Spanish women. Shortly after entered: Mme de Peñalver and her daughter—the latter very nice-looking, *rather* handsome, [with] good manners but a little too *prononcées;* the Marchioness of Arcos, rather good-looking, very good-natured and unaffected, like a little black-eyed indolent creole; her daughter, dark and with a pretty face; Mme Cárdenas, pretty and coquettish; Count de Fernandina; Marquis of Arcos; Domingo Herrera; &c., &c., &c., &c.

Although in all there were ninety-seven guests and as many Negroes in waiting, the heat was not oppressive. As they were amazingly long of assembling, I had to *play the piano!*—besides walking all through the rooms, which are almost completely unfurnished. Everywhere the same thing—floors of stucco or marble, a few handsome tables, cane chairs, and mirrors, a large gallery going all round the house and looking down on the court where the *volantes* stand.

In the gallery as usual was the dinner. It certainly has the advantage of coolness—dining in so large a barn, where the wind blows in from all quarters. The dinner was in fact an immense, luxurious, ill-regulated feast—composed by several cooks, amongst whom is one Frenchman who was cook to Queen Hortense and who for three ounces per month consents to roast and be roasted, or rather to stew and be stewed.[22] But notwithstanding this, garlic and oil were the groundwork of all. As England is said to smell of coal, and Russia of leather, so does Havana boast a universal fragrance of oil and garlic. Everything you come near—the gentlemen you waltz with, the opera, the theatre, the streets—all remind you that you are in a Spanish colony. Add to this a dash of tobacco—and a very strong flavour of Negro—and you have before you the *smell of Havana*—the fragrance emitted by *la joya más preciosa de la corona de España.*[23]

For my own part I do not think I exaggerate when I calculate that I was offered 350 different *plats*—and, as the pressing is excessive, one runs some danger of being suffocated. It is the custom after dinner for everyone to ask you *how you have dined*—and, if you have eat little, you are not only overwhelmed with friendly reproaches, but the circumstance and the probable causes of it are the topic of conversation the next day.

There was a wonderful display of jewels. The jewels of the ladies were superb, especially the diamonds of the Montalvo family: sprays, necklaces, earrings—really beautiful. The handsome cousins, with ill-made dark silk gowns, wore on their heads superb sprays of diamonds with diamond chains going round their heads, earrings, immense brooches, &c. The Marquesa de Arcos was smothered in a set of emeralds the size of pigeons' eggs. She had with her a pretty, graceful-looking daughter, the *marquesita,* with beautiful eyes, immense diamond earrings, and her hair dressed very high—probably to make her look older and taller.[24] The *marquesa,* who appears very amiable, is a desperate gambler. Even the men were well sprinkled with diamonds and rubies; and the jewels of the gentlemen fully equal those of the ladies. They have sets of superb rubies, buttons, stars, shoebuckles—occasionally sporting a set of diamonds or emeralds according to the occasion. Add to this a black velvet waistcoat embossed in gold and sparkling with stones, ruffles of point lace at the wrists and, on the breast of his shirt, as many orders as he can lay claim to, three or four chains of different styles of gold, a coloured and embroidered cravat, hair or wig curled and perfumed—and you have before you a Habanero count or marquis. You must add to this a profusion of bows and compliments, reiterated assurances that he and all he has—his house and furniture, wife and daughters, jewels and orders—and, what is perhaps of least value, himself into the bargain, are at your disposition. Nor are these entirely empty compliments, for if in an evil hour you admire anything belonging to him it is sent to you the next day. Whether this love of giving proceeds from custom or vaingloriousness or good nature or a mixture of all three, it is not easy nor perhaps necessary to determine.

After dinner a toast was proposed: "To the health of *El Señor Ministro y su Señora.*" Then rose our Havana Mirabeau—and gave out that he was inspired with an impromptu, which poetical address, from its absurdity, merits to be recorded:[25]

To Calderón's Lady in the Name of Montalvo's

To thee, blonde nymph of Caledonia,
Admiring friend of the great Walter Scott,
A toast is dedicated by the sincere Antonia,
Wife of Montalvo, respected in Havana.
May thy lucky Angel,[26] with lasso of flowers,
Produce in thee, sweet Fanny, a little one—
And like Juan and Antonia, with six glories of love,
May you have grandchildren to cradle!!!!!![27]

To Señor de Calderón

May a fair wind bear you to Anáhuac,
Minister of Isabel, angel of good will.
Your graciousness and knowledge lend confidence
That loving peace may reunite
The peoples of Iberia and Mexico
In the mutual esteem of brothers.

No more the memory of three centuries:
The happy eagle on its nopal
Toasts the lion and its noble children
With brotherly affection in place of insults.
Exalted is your mission, dear Angel;
Montezuma and Cortés applaud it.

Take note of Cuba, haven of security
For a thousand prows that plough the sea,
Center of rich enterprise, and of practical wisdom;
And of Spain in whose debt we stand.
The Hispanic scepter we will keep secure,
All of us loyal—and Montalvo, a leader.

After this effusion we rose and adjourned to the other apartments which by this time were lighted up, and in about half an hour we returned to a dessert which, from variety and immensity, was a real curiosity. I regret infinitely that I have not a *carte* of the *whole* feast. Immense alabaster vases of flowers and candelabra of alabaster were placed at different distances on the table. Hundreds of porcelain dishes were filled with *dulces* and fruits—*dulces* of every description unheard of and fruits with unknown or at least with Spanish names untranslatable —from little meringues called *bocado de la reina,* "mouthful for a queen," to the blancmanger made of *suprême de volaille* and milk strained, *confitures* of eggs, &c., &c., &c.

And now the noise which had always been great became greater, and now the Negroes tumbled more and more over each other, and now the *hissing* increased—not that malignant hissing which proceeds from the mouth of angry critic pouring vinegar on the wounds of enraged author nor yet that hissing which, issuing from the throats of *flocks* of geese, impatient of intrusion, betokens indignation—but that continuous hiss with which the languishing Habanera calls upon her ebony attendants, so that the uninitiated might imagine himself suddenly transported amidst a company of serpents. But all things have an end. The remark seems trite, but at a Havana dinner the reflection is consolatory.

In the same order in which we entered we made our *exeunt omnes,* and found coffee, cakes, &c., &c., spread out on a large table. Moreover the harp of Mme de Arcos had arrived for me to play upon! Moreover Pepe Peñalver was putting himself *en train* to perform the *Norma* with me, accompanying me on the piano. Moreover I was particularly requested to take my place in a Spanish country dance with Domingo Herrera! *Vogue la galère—ce n'est que le premier pas qui coûte.*[28] I had already played; the ice was broken. Dancing was but another step forwards or backwards, as the case may be found to be one of these days. Accordingly I stood up and joined in a Spanish dance—but which I imagine is rather *Habanera.* The music very good and lively, performed by Pepe Peñalver. Any number of couple stand up as in the old English country-dance. The two first go down the middle and back again—the four first right and left twice; the four first then perform a sort of *balancé* and then waltz with a very slow lazy movement—and so on till you reach the bottom, and then go back again if you choose. It is a really Havana dance for laziness—not ugly, but very monotonous. There is generally an inelegant scramble as to who shall get the highest places. The girls dance badly—nearly as ill as in Boston and not unlike, which may be accounted for by their being taught by the same person, Mme Papanti, who, having left her husband in Boston, has come out to Havana and *married* one of the orchestra.[29]

The dance over, the harp was tuned by me, and Peñalver and I performed *Norma*—tolerably well—after which Miss Peñalver sung from *Lucia* an aria—uncommonly well—her father being her sole preceptor. Having then sat and talked in low continuous murmur for about an hour, it seemed to me that we might cry, "Hold—enough!"[30] As to conversation, the women apparently have very little, with a few exceptions such as La Fernandina and La Villanueva, both of whom, particularly the former, can talk—and talk well. Having then shaken hands with every lady in the room, which seems to be a universal practice, we took our leave—much pleased with the host and hostess who appear to have more genuine hospitality than I have yet seen—much astonished at the sumptuosity and size of the feast—and much wondering that I, *la fille de mon père*, should have spent such a Sunday!

Monday: November 18th, 1839

Sweetmeats sent me by Mme Montalvo—meringues and cakes.

The hostess has fortunately fallen into, or rather acceded to, my request of leaving me alone all the morning—and goes to play with or scold her Negroes. Her grandmother was a woolly-headed Negress—and it is said that there are not more than three or four families *de sang pur* in the Island—among whom are reckoned the Fernandinas, the Marquesa de Arcos, and the *Intendenta*—he is of the proscribed race. It is not, however, as in the U.S., any disgrace.[31]

One or two persons dined with us, and as usual our morning was devoted to receiving visitors. This evening was set apart for returning visits. In the first, to_____, we encountered a musical prodigy—a little boy of ten years old, a very beautiful child with a pale face and dark hair, and that melancholy expression almost invariably seen in the eyes of children whom nature had endowed with premature genius, such as in "the Infant Lyra"—a sort of half-angel look, as if they knew that they were doomed to pass away early, and were merely visiting earth for a brief springtime before going home. On the earth but not of it. After having listened with admiration to this child's singing and playing we continued our course of visits to various other houses—the *Regente's*,[32] Montalvos', &c.

One thing is remarkable in regard to these visits. First, in no place did I see a *gentleman*. Only the ladies in two straight rows of chairs, fronting each other, and forming the true definition of parallel lines— lines at equal distances which may extend *ad infinitum,* but never meet. Second, never did I see a lady *occupied*. Never did I see work, or books, or anything. A fan gently moving—a chiaroscuro light—and an occasional monosyllable prove that the vital spark, as the coroner says, is not extinct. If with this indolence there were ease, as there probably is among the Turkish beauties—*á la bonne heure*—but no; they are all stiff—embarrassed—and have evidently put on their stays—and stockings —and clean gowns—and abandoned their cigars and slaves for a short and sad evening.

Tuesday: November 19th, 1839
Queen of Spain's birthday—
Viva Isabel Segunda![33]

A brighter sun rises on the Spanish horizon. Don Carlos has fought a good fight, and may now repose upon remembered laurels. The young Queen may unbend her brows—and the [Queen] Regent may once more show her dimples. But though the capital doubtless sends forth a cry of jubilee, Spain's most precious jewel gives no violent demonstrations of joy. The ships hang out their streamers; and the Morro keeps up a continued cannonading; and the *Intendente* has chosen this day to give us a dinner at the Intendencia—which, says our would-be Mirabeau in his bad French, is *"une grande coup de politique"*—and much does he regret that he is prevented from going there this day, and giving us a touch of his inflated oratory. Not, he takes care to inform us, that the impediment arises from his wife's being on her deathbed, gradually extinguishing, he says himself, "like a spent lamp," but because "he has *mal au ventre*"—which the count's good dinner might increase! Disgusting brute!

Meanwhile the Captain-General Ezpeleta *gives nothing*—nor dinner, nor levee, nor any other token that he takes part in the peace of Spain. Perhaps he thinks that the best way of celebrating peace is to keep at peace; perhaps he is a Carlist *au fond,* or perhaps, as he is old and about to depart from Havana, he prefers pleasing himself to pleasing them.[34] He is not so far wrong, but the *Habaneros* cannot forgive such an opportunity being lost for displaying their rings—and diamonds

—and buckles—and buttons—and crosses and orders—and lace—and waistcoats—and stockings—and cravats—&c., &c., &c. It is said that a *besamanos* at Havana is as good as a comedy. Cruel Ezpeleta—thus to balk the loyalty and vanity of the tropical Spaniards.

But the hour arrives for the *Intendente's* dinner. Emilie having performed a very elaborate and magnificent coiffure upon my head, and Calderón having been persuaded to put on one order in honour of the Queen—he not being, as he says, *"un homme à plaques"*—we set out for the Intendencia, an immensely large building of no particular architecture, unless it be the Habanero order. [We] passed through some soldiers on guard, and were met by the *Intendente* who, giving me his hand (not his *arm*), led me up several flights of stairs to a very large room at the upper end of which sat the Countesses de Villanueva and Fernandina—and, having passed through groups of bowing *caballeros*, landed me on a seat at the right of the *Intendenta*. How often in the course of five minutes I had to say, *"Para servir a usted, Señor,"* I cannot pretend to say. The only other ladies were the mother and sister of Mme *la Intendenta;* the men, innumerable. Yet, notwithstanding the numbers, the dinner appeared more like a *diner de famille* than a *diner d'etiquette*. I sat between the *Intendente* and the Conde de Fernandina. On the left side of the *Intendente* was the Countess Fernandina. Opposite us was the *Intendenta,* with Calderón on one side and the little count on the other.[35]

The dinner was very elegant, not only extremely handsome, but for the most part excessively well-dressed and French. To say that oil and garlic were forgotten would be to start a most unnatural fallacy—but it was *kept under,* like a scarlet tone by a skillful painter, and in many dishes amounted to nothing more than a *soupçon*. The variety—quantity —and *showoffosity* of a Habanera dinner must be seen to be appreciated. And as generally, according to Spanish custom, *les grands seigneurs ici se tutoient*[36] and give each other their Christian names—indeed, they are almost all connected by intermarriages—and as the well-bred, low-toned monotony of a London dinner has not yet found its way to the Cuban capital, the conversation (if it may be so called) is amusing.

"Antonio! *Hombre!* Some turkey with calf's head and brains! You eat nothing."

"Pepe! Some *pescado* with olives—very delicate."

"Teresa! A glass of Cyprus wine—you have eat nothing at all. *Cómo? Nada más!* What does *nada más* mean? Is the dinner bad?"

"Juan! *Hombre!* A small piece of partridge—*chiquitito*."

"Hiss! Psss—— My compliments to the Señor Don Angel. I send him a plate of piquéd veal—"

"Try it, Señora, only try it. You have no appetite. You find the dinner bad? A glass of Málaga—*muy dulce*—a paté—a little Xeres—"

"Eat some of that dish, Pepe, *hombre!*"

"The health of *el Señor Calderón y su Señora*—a good voyage!"

You may guess at an inferior in rank only by their increased respect towards him.

Her Majesty's health was proposed by Don Bernardo Hechavarría, and so well timed that all the guns of the forts fired a salute, it

being sunset, just as the toast was concluded, which was drank standing with real enthusiasm and hearty good will.

Once more [we were] led into another apartment through eight or ten others. The house for size is a palace, and the apartments innumerable. We then were led to the dessert, arranged in another room, which for profusion and variety was as usual a real curiosity. Having tasted several hundred different dishes, we finished at length, and were taken to a large suite of rooms, with a long balcony fronting the *place d'armes*.

It is difficult to imagine a more beautiful scene. The night was cloudless, the temperature, though rather warm, delicious from the softness of the evening breeze. The moon rose so bright that she seemed like the sun shining through a silvery veil, and night seemed a softened image of day. Groups of Habaneros—gentlemen and ladies, the latter in white with mantillas—were sauntering about in the square, under the trees. To complete the beauty of the whole, two bands, having ranged themselves with lamps and music, played alternately the music of Mozart and Bellini. We regretted much leaving so delightful a scene for the theatre, where we arrived in time to hear La Pantanelli sing an aria, dressed in helmet and tunic. Her voice is powerful, and her science and correctness great. She sings with much expression, but it seems to me that she is a little wanting in feeling and softness. After this there was a stupid play, and then the *jota aragonesa,* a peasant national dance—very spirited, and danced by two handsome Spanish girls in very good style.

Wednesday: November 20th, 1839

Went out in a *volante,* devoting one morning to shopping. Not a lady to be seen on the streets. The narrowness, mud, and crowd of *volantes* make it impossible.[37] And they are so lazy that when they do go in a *volante* to buy anything, which is very rarely, the shopkeepers bring their goods out to them, it not being the fashion for ladies to enter the shops—though I took the privilege of a foreigner to infringe this rule occasionally. They will not even go to a dentist's—the dentist comes to them.

I found the dearness of everything *enormous.* The French modistes seem to be improving their time by charging respectable prices for their work. Mme Retant, a Frenchwoman, very wisely is making her fortune as fast as she can, that she may get out of Havana.

Bought some *yerbillo crudo*—grass-cloth raw—very nice; and a pair of earrings—the jewelry being the only thing which is rather cheaper than otherwise; also that indispensable article, a black mantilla; also some cambric. Upon the whole, the result of my investigation: found white French lace and muslin rather cheap—but as for their silks, satins, calicoes, &c., *Caramba!!!* As it only lasted two hours I give my opinion for the present with due diffidence.

We went in the evening to the theatre of Tacón, to the Captain-General's box. It is certainly a splendid house, large, airy, and handsome. The play was the *Campanero de San Pablo,* in five acts translated from the French—which, though generally liked, appears to me a complicated and unnatural composition with some interesting scenes and a very peculiar contempt for the unities, seeing that eighteen years pass between the first and second act. Not being a judge of Spanish acting, I can but say that most of it seemed to me very bad. The favourite and chief actress, a good-looking overgrown dame, all fat and dimples, kept up a constant sobbing and heaving of her chest, yet never getting rid of an eternal smirk upon her face. The best actor was he who represented *El Ciego,* the blind man, though the blind man went immediately after recovering his sight to a masked ball, and seemed quite at home. Upon the whole it was excessively tiresome—and a bolero, danced afterwards by two Spanish damsels in black and silver, was very refreshing.[38]

Thursday: November 21st, 1839

This day was dedicated to viewing the great works of the *Intendente*—the railroad and the water filterers. At nine o'clock we went to the depot, where we found the *Intendente,* the countess, and the young gentleman of the bedchamber waiting for us, with a tail of hangers-on. Also the Conde de la Reunión and others. The countess was dressed in silk, with *white satin shoes!,* a white crape bonnet, a blonde fichu, and lapis lazuli earrings set in diamonds—equally beautiful and misplaced. I could not help thinking how much prettier and more graceful would have been the national mantilla, which she would probably have worn had she been going with Habaneras. It is a foolish narrow-mindedness to contemn any dress which is peculiar to a country—but, as the grand object in Havana is to dress *à la française,* the diamonds and white satin of a morning only tend to prove how the love of show predominates even in the best of them. In the morning the generality wear no stockings—slippers with holes in them—no stays, of course—and the gown wide open behind so as to show rather more chemise than is strictly *comme il faut.* Part of this I take from eyesight, part from unimpeachable authority. They smoke large cigars in their own rooms, but not in society, at least not before me—although I have been asked whether I smoked or preferred taking snuff.

The country through which the railroad passes is flat and rather monotonous. Nevertheless, the quantity of wild flowers of every colour, which appear for the most part like convolvuluses, as we glanced past them—the orange trees covered with fruit, but especially the clumps of palm and cocoa, the plantain with its gigantic leaves, the fresh green coffee plant, the fields of sugar cane of a still brighter green somewhat resembling Indian corn, the naked Negroes, their low wooden huts, and still more the scorching sun on the twentieth of November—all was new to us, and sufficient to remind us of the leagues of ocean we had traversed that separated us from our household gods, though this is but a halt on our voyage.

We got out at the pueblo where the cars stopped and sat for some time in the depot—and listened with much amusement to the story of a very fat, comfortable man, who was *cured by lightning* in the following manner. He was in the last stage of a consumption when, one hot July day, he was knocked down by a thunderbolt. A ball of fire, which entered his side, ran all through him and came out at his arm. At the place where the ball came out an immense ulcer was formed, and when it dispersed he found himself in perfect health, and has continued so ever since!!! In this case the "bottled lightning" demanded by Mrs. Nickleby's admirer would be rather a valuable remedy.[39]

Having re-entered the cars, we were taken to the waterworks, where we again got out to view the contrivance by which the *Intendente* has supplied Havana with clean water, and of which he and his are excessively proud.[40] Having walked about and admired it in every possible shape and way, we re-entered the cars and returned to the Havana depot —where half the *volantes* had not yet arrived. I returned in that of the *Intendenta,* with her and the little count—and, as she came home with me, I tuned up the harp and played some airs to her, such as "The Last Rose of Summer," &c.

The captain of the *Jasón* called—a nice little clean-looking man, quite a gentleman, nephew of the *General de la Marina*—by name Estrada. As all his family have been in the navy for a very long period, he has, though good-looking, a slight resemblance to a fish; that is to say, he resembles a fish more than any other animal.

At four o'clock we went to Zamora's who gave us a very abundant and very Spanish dinner, after showing us all through his house, from which there is a most beautiful view of the country—and of the sea and of Havana. The interior is unfurnished-looking even more than usual. Except in the very large houses there is but one floor habitable. The upper rooms and the entresol are bad. There were a number of gentlemen, amongst others the Marqués de Selva Alegre, whose wife, now at Madrid, is said to be about the most beautiful woman in Spain.[41] In the evening we went to the Marquis de Peñalver's, who had engaged La Pantanelli to come and sing to us. She is good-looking—a little masculine in appearance, but not in manner—looks very respectable and good. She sung extremely well: "Ah! mai più," and from *La Donna de Caritea*.[42] Mlle Peñalver sung one or two things but they sounded poor after *un vrai maître.*

One would think we had now done enough for one day—but no—we must needs pay a visit to a lady, a friend of Calderón's, and a very excellent woman apparently. Her brother, a priest, paid us a visit the other day in full canonicals, with various orders, one military. He is a little dry, active old man, seventy-eight years old. His manner of sleeping for the last twenty years is peculiar. He sits down in an armchair over which hangs, from the roof to the floor, a mosquito curtain in the form of a sack—which envelops him, chair and all. This machine stands in the middle of the room and, that he may have a constant draught of air, every door and window are thrown back, wide open. Add to this that he is in full dress.

Friday: November 22nd, 1839

Went out in the *volante* to make two visits of a different description—and was much astonished to find that the boys who drive the *volantes*, and the little niggers who act as footmen, know nearly as little of the streets and numbers as I do. The ladies whom I have asked do not know the name of the street they live in.

The shops all have most seducing names, such as *La Maravilla, La Esperanza, El Deseo*, &c.—of which three, I can affirm that the first is a marvel of dearness, that *La Esperanza* holds out false hopes, and that the third is well named inasmuch as you may there desire everything and get nothing.[43]

At length we discovered the house where I was to make my first visit—to a Havana girl, Miss Morell, brought up in Philadelphia, married to a Havana merchant [named] Fernández—a beauty and a friend of Calderón's. She kept me waiting at least half an hour, and, when she came, I found that her beauty had evaporated—though rather good-looking than otherwise.[44]

I then went to visit the other, an American of good family in her own country, the granddaughter of Jefferson, her husband a doctor and rather vulgar. She goes into no society, probably because she cannot go into the best, and does not speak a word of Spanish after a three years' residence. As they live *fuera*—out of the walls[45]—the difficulty of finding her nearly made me abandon the attempt, although I knew the street and number. I was first taken by mistake to Schenley's former house which seems very good. At last found Mrs. M., and must do her the justice to say that she had a small garden full of flowers, and both books and flowers on her table.[46]

This being the day of a great ball given us by the Countess de Fernandina, we went early to dress, and about eight o'clock arrived there.

This morning I received a very handsome set of gold ornaments given me by the master of the house. Many beautiful souvenirs have been sent us, amongst others: a gold cup from the Count de Santovenia, who also sent Calderón a beautiful model of the Royal Palace in Madrid, one of the most beautiful and ingenious pieces of workmanship possible, carved in wood with astonishing accuracy and delicacy; two drinking cups, of a kind of terra cotta used for keeping water cool, from Mme de Montalvo. Such being the Spanish habit of making presents.

The ball was really superb, the whole house, about twelve large rooms, thrown open—of which some might be eighty feet in length. There was a splendid sitting supper, quantities of refreshments and the whole picked aristocracy of Havana, such as it is. Diamonds on every head, and some gowns decidedly from Paris. Jewels and orders on every man, magnificent lustres and mirrors, and a capital band of music in the gallery.

We were met on the staircase by the *conde*, and I was led to a sofa beside La Fernandina. The Captain-General Ezpeleta, who rarely goes to a ball but who came to this one on our account, was introduced to me, and sat down and made himself very agreeable in very good French. He is a Spaniard and much more of a gentleman than any of them—quiet in his manners, the only individual in a plain dress, and without a single order.

About one hundred couple stood up in each Spanish country dance, but the rooms are so immense and so judiciously lighted that it was not very warm. Waltzes, quadrilles, and these long Spanish dances succeeded each other. The peculiarities of the ball—at least which distinguish it from an English or French ball, are: First, that all the women sat ranged in chairs placed against the wall, no man sitting, or even speaking to them —decidedly no flirtations going on overtly. Second, no woman walked about or left her seat, except to dance. Third, almost all were brown, and some nearly black. Almost all the girls have fine eyes and beautiful figures, but without colour, or much animation—some handsome—none with a good *tournure*—very few with grace—all with rich dresses—few dressed with taste.

The *Intendenta* looked as usual—not pretty but nice-looking. The woman who has most an air of fashion is decidedly La Fernandina. She had, moreover, the finest diamonds, particularly her necklace of diamonds which is *undeniable*.

One fact is remarkable—the dancers among the gentlemen were chiefly old men and little boys of ten. There were not more than half a dozen young men in all. I danced a Spanish dance with Herrera, a French set of quadrilles with the Count de Sald——,[47] aide-de-camp to the Captain-General, and various others with partners whose names I know not; one with an Englishman of the name of Tennant,[48] and [one] with a brother-in-law of La Fernandina's, who is the image of *Harris*;[49] and a waltz with Pepe Zamora—who waltzes like a German. And by the way, during a waltz the ladies sit on their chairs against the wall, the gentlemen all cluster like bees in the middle of the floor, and the waltzers waltz round them. By this means, however, they have an immense circle. I was taken to supper by the *Intendente*, and then dancing recommenced.

When the ball was nearly over, walking through the rooms after supper, we were amused to see numbers of the Negroes and Negresses helping themselves plentifully to the sweetmeats, uncorking and drinking fresh bottles of champagne, and devouring everything on the supper tables, without the slightest concern for the presence of either master or mistress; in fact, behaving like a multitude of spoilt children, who are sure of meeting with indulgence, and presume upon it. The countess told us she had an old slave to whom she offered freedom; he refused it, and is now the master of other slaves, himself a slave.

Towards four in the morning the *conde* handed me downstairs to a large suite of rooms, containing an excellent library of several thousand volumes. Here coffee, cakes, &c., were prepared in the most splendid Sèvres porcelain and gold plate. We stayed to the last, because the ball was given to us—and left the house, at last, to the music of the Spanish national hymn, which struck up as we passed through the gallery. The fête was altogether a beautiful one—and we went to bed much admiring and much fatigued.[50]

Saturday: November 23rd, 1839

Tomorrow being the day fixed for our departure—should the wind not prove contrary or the north wind, the dreaded *norte*, not blow—there is some bustle and some preparation, as our equipage must go on board the *Jasón*. We have spent the day in receiving farewell visits.

We expected hospitality and a good reception but certainly all our expectations have been surpassed. Visits, dinners, and parties have so occupied our time that to write has been next to impossible.[51] I do not pretend to form any judgment of Havana. We have seen it too much *en beau*. Of the country we have, from the same reason, seen little, and the people we are only acquainted with in full dress, which is not the way to judge of them truly.

Wrote letters home—received visits of adieu. Received a very pretty bouquet of gold and pearls from the *Intendenta*.[52]

There are great doubts as to the sailing of the *Jasón* as there are some fears of a contrary wind, a *norte*, which they seem to dread here like a wild beast. Received a visit from the *General de la Marina* and the captain. They seem to doubt our sailing on Sunday. Took leave of old General Montalvo—and many others.

We also went to the theatre, where everyone predicts we shall not get off tomorrow. The play was *Le Gamin de Paris,* translated.[53] Paid a parting visit to La Fernandina in her box. Took leave of various people who all doubt our going tomorrow. After our return, I paid a very late *visite d'adieu* to the Peñalvers who live close by us. And now, at two in the morning, I finish my letter sleepily.

My next letter will be dated on board the *Jasón*. Chocolate and bed. Tired to death.

3

Havana to Veracruz on a Man-of-War

Sunday: November 24th, 1839
On board the Spanish Brig of War *Jasón*

This morning at six o'clock, together with Captain Estrada, the commander of the *Jasón*, we breakfasted on chocolate at the Casa Hechavarría. The wind being fair, we repaired shortly after in *volantes* to the wharf, accompanied by our hospitable host and several of our acquaintances; got on board a boat; looked our last of the Captain-General's palace and the Intendencia—in short of the city of Havana, where we had arrived as strangers and which now in twelve days had begun to assume a familiar aspect, and to appear interesting in our eyes by the mere force of human sympathy—and were transported to the ship, where a line of marines with guns reversed, drawn up to receive us, presented arms as we entered. The morning was beautiful; little wind, but fair. We took leave of our friends, waved our handkerchiefs to the balconies in return for signals from scarcely-distinguishable figures, passed beneath the red-tinted Cabaña and the stately Morro, and were once more upon the deep—with a remembrance behind, and a hope before us. Our *bergantina* is a very handsome vessel, with twenty-five guns, five officers, a doctor, chaplain, and purser, and one hundred and fifty men.

We find the commander very attentive, and a perfect gentleman, like almost all of his class. He is a little man and, though very young in appearance, is past forty and has been twenty-nine years in the service. He is rather doleful-looking—and I doubt whether he has much liking for his profession, the only circumstance which can make it tolerable. Of the officers, the first lieutenant Espaleta is a gentlemanly good-natured man, but he also I suspect would prefer terra firma to the boundless sea. The second, Queveda, an impudent, good-looking devil-me-care sort of person, not much of a gentleman, appears to me very much l'étoffe of which to form a good sailor. The next, Solís, is a hard weather-beaten man without teeth—who puts on a wig when he breakfasts in our cabin. The fourth is a younger daredevil—whose name not knowing I shall christen *bonnet rouge,* one of which he wears—always laughing, scolding, eating, or at something, and apparently very clever. The doctor is old and gray; the purser good-natured and pursy; the chaplain a monk with a monkish face; and the pilot a huge man like a tame porpoise. There are besides two poor middies, one of whom—a long, pale, sad-looking stripling —would certainly rather be at home. The other seems harder and resigned. There appears to be much more confusion and noise and less discipline on board this ship than on board an English man-of-war—but this may be Spanish manners. The ship looks "a mighty maze, *and quite* without a plan."[1]

Monday: November 25th, 1839

The weather delightful, and the ship going smoothly at the rate of about five miles an hour. The accommodations in a brig not designed for passengers are of course not good—but a little foreknowledge on our part might have made it so. There is a large cabin for the officers, separated from a very small cabin, belonging to the captain, which he has given up to us. A red curtain on one side screens the captain's stateroom—ditto on the other screens ours, which contains a cot swung for me, and a mattress on the ground for El Señor Ministro. The Duchess lies on a mattress outside.

About seven o'clock Calderón rises, wakening everybody as if there were something very important to be done. However nobody rises. At eight enters our Ursa Major, a marine sentinel transformed into a lady's page, whom we are taking to Mexico as porter, [and who] answers by a grunt to the name of José. He brings two cups of very delicious chocolate. He is followed by Fruto, the captain's familiar, an unhappy-looking victim, pale, lank, and lean, with the physiognomy of a Methodist parson, and in general appearance like a weed that has grown up in one night. He tremblingly, and with most rueful countenance, carries a small plate of sugar-biscuits. These originals having vacated the cabin, I proceed to dress myself, an operation of some difficulty and even danger; and having succeeded to a certain extent—*tant bien que mal*—I repair upstairs, armed with veil, book and fan, and sit on deck till ten o'clock, when Fruto's lamentable announcement of breakfast takes us down again. As the captain has a French cook the comestibles are decidedly good, and if the *artiste* were a little less of an oil and more of a water painter he would be faultless and I individually would prefer his style. No doubt he modifies his compositions to suit the taste of his patrons. The breakfast consists of various dishes of fish, flesh and fowl, with sauces corresponding —Bordeaux and sherry, oranges, grapes, guayaba, and coffee.[2]

A very long interval between breakfast and dinner has to be filled up by reading, writing, sitting, or walking upon deck—as suits the taste of the individual—or by drinking orangeade, or by sleeping, or by any other ingenious resource for killing time. At five o'clock we have an excellent and superabundant dinner in our cabin, at which no one joins us but the captain and one of the officers; and after dinner on deck till bedtime —nine o'clock or ten—walking about, or gazing on the sky or sea, or listening to the songs of the sailors.

Tuesday: November 26th, 1839

Little wind, but a day of such abominably cruel *balances*, as they call them, that one is tempted to finish it by jumping overboard into the sea. All night the same, everything broken or breaking—people rolling on the floor—and *some*, who shall be nameless, in a horrid humour. *Paciencia*. Even the cannons disgorge their balls, which fall out by their own weight.

Wednesday: November 27th, 1839

Balances.

Thursday: November 28th, 1839

A beautiful day, perfect weather though very warm; the sky blue, without one cloud. Today we are on the sound, and have lain to about noon to let the sailors fish, thereby losing an hour or so of fair wind, and catching a preposterous number of fish of an immense size. It was more slaughter than sport. The water was so clear that we could see the fish rush and seize the bait as fast as it was thrown in. Sometimes a huge shark would bite the fish in two, so that the poor finny creature was between Scylla and Charybdis. These fish they call *cherna* and *pargo*—so pronounced, how spelt and translated history sayeth not. We ate some of them at dinner, and they were pronounced very good. At length a shark, in its wholesale greediness, seized the bait and, feeling the hook in its horrid jaw, tugged most sharkily to get off, but in vain. Twelve sailors tugged him into the ship. When he seemed with open maw to look out for the legs of the men, they rammed the butt end of a harpoon down his throat, which put a stop to all further proceedings on his part. He was said to be quite young, perhaps the son and heir of doting parents. The juvenile monster had, however, already cut three rows of teeth.

We are sometimes amused in the evening, when upon deck, by a little drummer who invariably collects all the sailors round him and spins them long, endless stories of his own invention, to which they listen with intense interest. On he goes, without a moment's hesitation, inventing everything most improbable and wonderful, of knights and giants and beautiful princesses, and imprisoned damsels, and poor peasants becoming great kings. He is a little ugly, active fellow, with a turned-up nose, a merry eye and a laughing mouth. Amongst his axioms is the following verse, which he sings with great expression:

> *Hasta los palos del monte*
> *Tienen su destinación,*
> *Unos nacen para santos*
> *Y otros para hacer carbón.*

Which may be translated so:

> Even the mountain-trees
> Have their allotted goal,
> For some are born for saints
> Whilst others serve for coal.

Friday: November 29th, 1839

Beautiful day, fair wind, great heat, and more fishing. At least thirty large fish were caught this morning—also an infant shark, a grandchild who had wandered forth to nibble, and met an earthly grave, at least a wooden one. We have too little wind, but that little—good. A dreadful reptile called an *alacrán*—scorpion—haunts the ship. It is about three inches long—black—with a number of legs—a long tail curled upwards —and a sort of snout with a venomous sting attached to it. This amiable creature—said not to be poisonous—has made several appearances in our cabin.[3] *Au reste,* the ship is the perfection of cleanness. No bad smell offends the olfactory nerves, in which respect it has over the *Norma* and all packets a singular advantage. This, and having it all to ourselves, and the officers being such perfect gentlemen and all so kind and attentive, makes our voyage so far a mere pleasure trip.

One fish we saw today had the colour and hardness of white marble —it looks like a petrefaction. We had some of the Countess de Villanueva's cocoanuts, of which she sent us a great supply, pierced this morning, and not having seen fresh cocoas before, felt much admiration and wonder at finding that they each contained two or three tumblers of fresh and delicious water. The milky rind is said to be unwholesome—it may be so to our perverted constitutions, but cannot be so to the Savage.

Saturday: November 30th, 1839

Fine day but rather more *balances*. The hatred of all these Spanish officers to the Habana is almost equal to that of the Habaneros for General Tacón—at least of the *grands seigneurs*. But their hatred does him honour. He punished crime in the highest rank; dealt unsparingly with the owners of the orders and crosses; imprisoned some; banished others; forced to leave Cuba the father of the Marqués de A., a ruffian who had in his pay a band of mulattoes who murdered at his will. In some cases he may have gone too far, and treated them with even more contempt than they deserved. On the occasion of a dispute with the *Intendente* about some papers, he ordered apartments to be prepared for him in the Morro—but the *Intendente* gave up the papers, and preferred remaining at home. Of the good he has done the city—by cleaning the streets, by rendering it possible for people to walk there in safety, by building a superb theatre, by planting and laying out a public promenade—of these everyone can judge. But his contempt of the nobles seems to have been unbounded and his disgust openly shown. In return they speak of him as "the wild beast," the "infirm old brute," and "General Tacón of unlucky memory," &c. They hate the theatre he built, the walk he planted, the fountain he constructed.[4]

One anecdote related to me by the commander is worthy of preserving. It did not occur in the time of Tacón—unfortunately. The father of the present Conde de S. V. was the founder of his family—made his immense fortune and bought his title. At his death [he] left both to his brother. The present count, his nephew, the son of another brother, got possession of this will and *forged another*—by which he left the title and immense wealth to himself. To this he added several strokes of policy. The *Intendente* had owed the deceased a sum of $150,000—in the will he *forgave this debt*, left legacies to the servants and those whom he feared—and then took possession as the heir. Meanwhile the brother hearing of this fraud came to Havana to commence a lawsuit, but, being poor and having to travel some distance in search of counsel, he was overtaken on the road, and *assassinated*. Yet no man stands higher in Havana than the Conde de S. V.! On these and similar instances—as well as on the upstart nature of the titles, and the pride and pomp of the titled—they seem to found a very fervent dislike to Her C[atholic] M[ajesty]'s Crown Jewel.

Sunday: December 1st, 1839

No hay novedad. Little wind, but fair. It is very warm, and horribly monotonous. The heat is intense. We are now about thirty leagues from Veracruz and, if the wind blows a little fresher, may reach it tomorrow. This is Sunday, but the chaplain is too seasick to say mass which I regret.

Monday: December 2nd, 1839

An unpleasant variety—a *norte!* A small one like the shark—but the very name gave me a *thrill.* I knew it was coming on only by the face of the first lieutenant when he looked at the barometer. His countenance fell as many degrees as the instrument. It is very slight, but our entry into port will be delayed for on the coast these winds are most devoutly dreaded. It has rained all day, and we have been rather stewed in the cabin. Notwithstanding the rolling of the ship, by way of variety I attempted a game at chess with the captain, but after having tried two games we gave up in despair, a *balance* having at the most interesting period of each overturned the board and left the victory undecided— somewhat after the fashion of Homer's goddess when she enveloped the contending armies in a cloud.

Tuesday: December 3rd, 1839

Contrary wind. First a little *norte,* and then a wind from the land. Fifteen leagues from Veracruz—yet, when we shall reach it, *quién sabe?* The Duchess has abandoned herself to tears and black despair, and as it rains the heavens keep company with her grief. I had last night a wretched dream—the fulfillment of which may heaven avert!

Wednesday: December 4th, 1839

Had another disagreeable dream—about home. Yesterday evening a south wind, and the Spanish proverb says truly

> *Sur duro,*
> *Norte seguro.*

> A south wind strong,
> The norther ere long.

The wind is contrary and we are now making preparations for retracing our steps. Went this morning on deck. The sky was covered with watery clouds, yet we could see the Cofre de Perote and the peak of Orizaba, which are thirty leagues inland! The latter, called by the Mexicans Citlaltepetl or the mountain of the star, from the fire which used to burn on its lofty summit, rises 19,551 feet above the level of the sea. Covered with perpetual snows, and rising far above clouds and tempests, it is the first mountain which the navigator discovers as he approaches these shores.[5]

But the south wind continues and we are obliged to turn our back to the coast. Everybody begins to grow impatient. The Duchess was taken ill, and declared she had got the yellow fever. [We] sent for the doctor who, very sick himself, and holding by the table to keep himself from falling, told her without looking at her that there was nothing the matter with her—and desired her to *keep quiet*. Not so bad that advice, when the ship was rolling about. At the same moment, he pitched headforemost out of the cabin, showing practically how much easier precept is than example. However she is better this morning—and in *such* a humour! *Ach! Guten Himmel*—What a charming *demoiselle de compagnie,* to enliven the monotony of a sea voyage!

As the wind is blowing from the land we gradually retreat, and are now about thirty leagues from Veracruz. As we shall no doubt have a norther after this, which may last at least three days, our promised land is still at some distance. One should certainly not put to sea without a stock of patience.

Thursday: December 5th, 1839

The weather is charming, but the southwest wind holds most implacably, and the barometer has fallen five or six degrees, which, added to other signs of the times known to navigators, causes all hands to prepare for the dreaded enemy. Most faces look pretty lugubrious this morning. I doubt our seeing Veracruz for several days to come.

Friday: December 6th, 1839

A *norte!* Job never was on board a ship. Not a very severe *norte,* but what they call a *norte chocolatero;* that is to say its shock tore a sail in two as one might tear a sheet of paper.

The most ingenious person I see is the master of the sails, the *couturière.* He sews most excessively quick and well. The sailors seem very confused and want ensemble. Towards evening the wind calmed, but the ship, tossed upon a horribly swelled sea, became a mortal purgatory. Still, the wind is lulled, though Humboldt and others say that a *norte* must last forty-eight hours, and we have only had it for twenty-four. We shall see.

Saturday: December 7th, 1839

A most horrible night! My hammock, which I had foolishly preferred to a bed, not only swung up and down but, not having room to swing in, threw me furiously against the wall, till perfectly exhausted and fearing a broken head, I jumped out of it and rolled on the floor. Today there is a comparative calm, so-called, a faint continuation of the *norte,* which is an air with variations. Everything now seems melancholy and monotonous, to express [which] would be impossible. We have been tossed about during four days in sight of Veracruz, and are now further from it than before. The officers begin to look dirty and miserable; even the cook with difficulty preserves his equilibrium.

Sunday: December 8th, 1839

A *norte! Caramba!* When we shall arrive, no one can even hazard a conclusion. But all faces are longer—the sea is called "a dog's life"— and they do not even shave. I have been reading Humboldt in Spanish. Wish it were in English or French—like it much.[6]

The sky is watery, and covered with shapeless masses of reddish clouds. This is a great day amongst all Spanish Catholics, *La Virgen de la Concepción*, the patroness of Spain and the Indies; but no mass today, the padre sick and the *norte* blowing. What a succession of long faces —walking barometers!

Monday: December 9th, 1839

Yesterday the wind held out false hopes to us. In the evening everyone brightened up, but *cautiously*—for the wind, though little of it, was blowing from the right quarter. The rain was over, the evening fine and "hope, the charmer," began to smile upon us.[7] The greater was our disappointment when the breeze died away, when the wind veered to the north, and when once more the most horrible rolling seized the unfortunate *Jasón*, as if it were possessed by a demon. The night was really horrible. Finding it impossible to lie in my hammock, I stretched myself on the floor, where during a night that seemed interminable we were tossed up and down, knocked against the furniture, bruised, and otherwise maltreated.[8]

This morning the wind is decidedly bad. There is little of it, but that little from the north, so that the termination of our voyage appears as far off now as it did eight days ago. The faces of all on board are calmly lugubrious. Little said. A few Spanish shrugs interchanged with ominous significance. The great point after all is: It is not a case of danger—at least so we trust—only one of dreadful ennui.

Tuesday: December 10th, 1839

Contrary wind. As it appears that there is only one particular wind during which they are not afraid to approach the coast—namely *la brisa*, the breeze which usually follows the norther but has not done so as yet —we may be here all winter. It appears besides that they have very little knowledge of the coast—which makes them the more timid. The most disagreeable part of it is the want of occupation.

The weather is beautiful, though very sultry, especially during the calms which intervene between the *nortes*. With books it would be very different; one might take patience, but I have read and re-read backwards and forwards everything I possess or can find—reviews, magazines, all of Humboldt I can get, even an odd volume of the *Barber of Paris* infamously translated into English-*Turkish letters* in Spanish—*purporting* to be the translation of a continuation of Montesquieu's *Lettres Persanes,* so *very* Turkish that the lover in the disguise of a gardener brings the vizier's daughter a bouquet and she condescendingly receives him lying in bed *à l'Espagnole!*[9] I am now reduced to a very well-written perhaps but very serious Spanish work on the truth of Christianity.

This evening, to the joy of all on board, arose the long-desired *brisa* or breeze. The ship went slowly but steadily on her course, at first four, then eight knots an hour.[10] The captain, however, looked doubtingly, and indeed towards morning the wind again changed to the south, and our hopes died away.

Wednesday: December 11th, 1839

Contrary wind—a south, expected to be followed by a *norte seguro.* So it was in the morning early. But now, at eleven a.m., it is nearly calm and very sultry—whilst to increase, if possible, our weariness, a long range of lofty mountains stretches along the horizon, from Punta Delgada to the Cofre de Perote, and on till they seem to sink into the ocean. Behind the Cofre rises the snow-crowned summit of Orizaba, now like a white cloud, but this morning tinged with a rosy light by the rays of the rising sun. The sea is tranquil and the horizon clear; nevertheless the enemy is looked for. There are a few white and feathery clouds flickering about in the sky, and there is an uneasy swell in the waves. At three o'clock out burst the norther which, like the flaming sword, guarding the issues of paradise,

> Waved over by that flaming brand; the gate
> With dreadful faces thronged and fiery arms[11]

seems to warn off all vessels from approaching these ironbound shores. Eleven days within a few hours' distance of the coast! Last night the cabin and beds were full of large winged insects which the sailors call *cucarachas*—like cockchafers—as big as sparrows—which they seem very fond of, which is more than I am. "*Gustibus non est disputandum.*" I wonder whether we shall spend our Xmas here! Ennui of itself does not kill—since prisoners have languished in dungeons for years.

Thursday: December 12th, 1839

Contrary wind. *Norte* and *balances.*

Friday: December 13th, 1839

Contrary wind. South. Constant rolling.

Saturday: December 14th, 1839

Contrary wind—south—prospect of a *norte*. We were not more than four leagues from the mountains this morning—and we are further from hope than we were fourteen days ago! Captain, officers, sailors—all seem nearly disheartened.

Sunday: December 15th, 1839

Disgust and other causes have made me abandon my *diario*—therefore I must now trust to memory and go back in the spirit to Sunday the fifteenth when the impatience of all men was nearly at its height. That day we caught the most beautiful fish I ever beheld, of the dolphin species—the Cleopatra of the ocean, about four feet long, apparently entirely composed of gold, and studded with turquoises. It changed colour in dying. Wind always contrary.

Monday: December 16th, 1839

Contrary winds—and no event worthy of record.

There is a proverb which the sailors are repeating to each other, not very encouraging: "*Este es el viaje del Orinoco; que el que no se murió, se volvió loco.* This is the voyage of the Orinoco, in which he who did not die became crazy."

Tuesday: December 17th, 1839

Spoke a *goleta*, which came close up by our vessel, and seemed to have a miserable set on board, amongst others a charming pair from Havana who keep baths there, and had been cooling themselves for some little time in prison, on account of having murdered a Negro. The wind continues contrary. I shall fold up this sea-scrawl, and write no more till we reach Veracruz.[12]

4

Veracruz: First Mexican Impressions

Wednesday: December 18th, 1839
Veracruz

This morning the sanguine hoped and the desponding feared, for the wind, though inclining to *la brisa,* seemed unlikely to prove sufficiently strong to enable us to reach Veracruz—this being the twenty-fifth day since we left Havana: a voyage that, with a steamer, might be performed in three days, and with a sailing vessel and a fair wind is made in six or seven. But about noon the aspect of things became more favourable. The breeze grew stronger, and with it our hopes.

At last appeared in view, faintly, certain spires beside the low sandy land, which for some time we had anxiously watched, and at length we could distinguish something like houses and churches, and the fort of San Juan de Ulúa, of warlike memory.[1] By slow but sure degrees we

drew nearer to the shore, until Veracruz, in all its ugliness, became visible to our much-wearied eyes.

We had brought a pilot from Havana to guide us to these dangerous coasts, but, though a native of these parts, it seemed that a lapse of years had blunted his memory, for we had nearly run upon the rocks. A gun was therefore fired for a pilot and another shortly came out, who at sight of the Spanish flag waxed enthusiastic, and—pointing out the castle to our ignorant friend—exclaimed, alluding to the desperate struggle made by the Spaniards to defend this their last stronghold at the end of the war: "*We*, although but a handful of men, defended ourselves for years like soldiers, and now these Frenchmen took it in three days!" And, walking about in a transport of patriotic despair, he seemed to forget his actual duty in the tide of remembrances which the sight of Spanish colours and a Spanish crew had called forth.[2]

Anything more melancholy, *délabré*, and forlorn than the whole appearance of things as we drew near cannot well be imagined. On one side the fort, with its black and red walls; on the other the miserable, black-looking city, with hordes of large black birds, called *zopilotes*, hovering over some dead carcass, or flying heavily along in search of carrion. Still, as the goal of our voyage, even its dreary aspect was welcome, and the very hills of red sand by which it is surrounded, and which look like the deserts of Arabia, appeared inviting.

A boat, full of cocked hats, was soon seen approaching from the city, containing the consul, an oldish Spaniard in full uniform with a face full of mystery, like a silly old crow dressed in regimentals, and other authorities. Calderón having sent for and obtained permission from the Governor to permit the *Jasón*, contrary to established usages, to anchor beneath the castle, a salute of twenty guns was fired from our ship. Being upon deck, I was nearly suffocated with smoke and powder. A salute of the same number of cannon was then returned from the

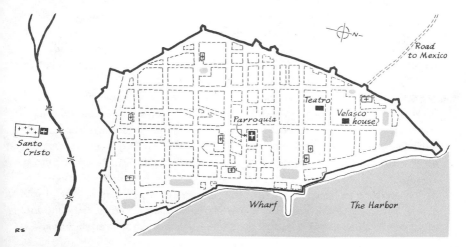

castle, in honour of the first Spanish man-of-war that has appeared in this port since the Revolution.

And now we prepared, before the sun went down, to leave our watery prison. The captain's boat being manned, and the officers having taken leave of us, we—that is, Calderón, and the captain, and I, and my French maid the Duchess, with Finette, her French poodle—got into it. Then came a salute of twenty guns from the *Jasón* in our honour, and off we rowed amidst clouds of smoke. Then the fort gave us welcome with the same number of guns, and amidst all this cannonading we were rowed up to the wharf.

A singular spectacle the wharf presented. A crowd, as far as the eye could reach, of all ages and sexes and kinds of Vera-Cruzians (and a Vera-Curious set they appeared to be) were assembled to witness His Excellency's arrival. Some had no inexpressibles; and others, to make up for their neighbours' deficiencies, had two pair—the upper slit up the side of the leg, Mexican fashion. All had large Mexican hats, with silver or bead rolls, and every tinge of dark complexion, from the pure Indian upwards. Some dresses were entirely composed of rags, clinging together by the attraction of cohesion; others were nearly whole and had only a few holes to let in the air. All were crowding, jostling, and nearly throwing each other into the water, and gazing with faces of intense curiosity.

But a plume of coloured feathers was seen towering above the copper-coloured crowd—and an extraordinary biped was seen advancing with giant strides. It looked like an immense golden eagle mounted upon an elephant. As it came nearer it proved to be a man, an aide-de-camp from the governor, General Guadalupe Victoria. He was an enormous immensely tall man, in a showy uniform all covered with gold, with colossal epaulets and a towering plume of rainbow-coloured feathers, a face the colour of burnished gold—a nose that was *not* like the tower of Lebanon looking towards Damascus[3]—but like a wide gate thrown open—a mouth so large that when it opened you were glad to see the entrance guarded by a row of immense and innumerable ivory portals—a sort of railing. This mighty personage brought to Calderón the welcome and congratulations of the general, and those Spanish offers of service and devotion which sound agreeably, whatever be their true value.

And now we began to move forward through the crowd, which formed a line on either side to let us pass, and entered the streets of Veracruz, which were crowded, balconies and all, and even roofs, with curious faces. The houses appeared like Havana, *en laid*—less actual dirt on the streets. The guard formed as we passed, and struck up a march. The principal street is wide and clean, and we reached the house of Señor Velasco, a rich merchant, formerly vice-consul, where we are to reside, escorted to the door by the whole population.[4] What they thought of us I cannot say, but I imagine at least that my poor *French bonnet* is

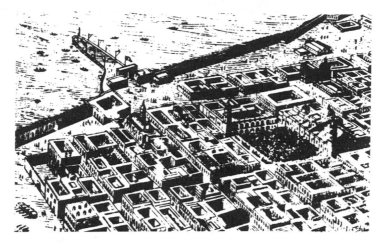

the *only* bonnet, French or otherwise, within the precincts of the City of the True Cross.[5]

We entered the house of Velasco, and were received with great hospitality by his wife, a good motherly woman who takes care of her house, feeds her children, and smokes her cigar like a good Christian. She received us very kindly, and without any Havana *showoffosity*, gave us very comfortable rooms—and was most good-natured, as was Velasco, and kind all the while we stayed. She has a number of good-looking children—the eldest pretty. They go to a *school*—what sort of school it must be one can scarcely imagine!

The house is immensely large and airy, built in a square, Havana fashion, as they all are, but with that unfurnished, melancholy, *gaping* look, which as yet this style of house has to me—and which makes one feel *triste* and lonely—though admirably adapted to the climate.

A guard of honour, sent by General Victoria, trotted into the courtyard, whose attendance Calderón declined with thanks—which is a pity, as it would have amused them and us. Calderón observed that his mission had for object to terminate the coolness hitherto existing between two families of brothers; that between members of the same family there was nothing to fear, and all compliments were unnecessary.

I found a baddish German piano in the drawing room, on which I played, glad to put my fingers once more on notes after a month's abstinence. The little girl seemed to have a natural taste for music. A number of uninteresting men came in the afternoon to visit Calderón. We were received by this family with so much real kindness that we soon found ourselves perfectly at home. We had a plentiful supper—cookery the worst of Spanish, Vera-Cruzified, but loads of it—fish, meat, wine, and chocolate, fruit and sweetmeats. A taste of the style was enough for me, garlic and oil enveloping meat, fish and fowl, with pimentos and plantains, and all kinds of curious nasty fruit, which I cannot yet endure.[6] Bed was not unwelcome, and most comfortable beds we had, with mosquito curtains, and sheets and pillows all trimmed with rich lace, so universal in Spanish houses that it is not, as with us, a luxury. But the mosquitoes had entered in some unguarded moment, and they and the heat were decidedly inimical to a sound sleep.

Thursday: December 19th, 1839

I opened my eyes this morning on the painting of a very lovely Madonna, which hung unvalued and ill-framed in one corner of our room. At eight, rose and dressed, and went to breakfast. The remembrance of Veracruz cookery is excruciating to my feelings. I would rather not think of it—I would rather think of [the] lovely Madonna, but veracity compels me to return to breakfast. One custom is remarkable in this part of "the republic" as they call it. Here, when there are two guests whom they wish to distinguish, the gentleman is placed at the head of the table, and *his* lady beside him—which is very amusing. Thus Calderón and I always sat together. Upon the whole this place is the most *arrière* I have yet seen.

To me nothing earthly can exceed the exceeding sadness of the aspect of this city and its environs—mountains of moving sand, formed by the violence of the north winds, and which, by the reflection of the sun's rays, must greatly increase the suffocating heat of the atmosphere. The scene may resemble the ruins of Jerusalem, though without its sublimity. The houses seem blackened by fire; there is not a carriage on the streets— nothing but the men with the wide open trousers slit up the side of the leg, immense hats, and blankets or sarapes, merely a closed blanket, more or less fine, with a hole for the head to go through; and the women with *rebozos*, long coloured cotton scarfs, or pieces of ragged stuff, thrown over the head and crossing over the left shoulder. Add to this the *zopilotes* cleaning the streets, disgusting but useful scavengers. These

valuable birds have black feathers, with gray heads, beaks, and feet. They fly in troops and at night perch upon the trees. They are not republican, nor do they appear inclined to declare their independence, having kings, to whom it is said they pay so much respect that if one of the royal species arrives at the same time with a plebeian *zopilote*, in sight of a dead body, the latter humbly waits till the sovereign has devoured his share before he ventures to approach.

A few ladies in black gowns and mantillas called this morning, and various men. It is agreed I believe that we shall go on Sunday. We find the weather very sultry. This place which now seems like Purgatory must in summer, with the addition of the *vómito* (as they here call the fever), be truly a chosen city![7]

The principal street where we live is the street, very long and wide and not very dirty, and seems to have many good houses in it. Nearly opposite is so clean and large and well-looking a house—so distinguished from all in the street—and where we saw beautiful flowers as we passed the door, that I inquired the name of its owner. I find it belongs to an English merchant, Jamison and something from Ireland.[8]

There is much deliberation as to the mode in which we are to travel to Mexico.[9] Some propose a coach; some, and these are nearly all, advise us to go in *literas;* others advise us to take the diligence. While in this indecision, we had a visit this morning from a very remarkable-looking character, Don Miguel de Serez, agent for the diligence office in Mexico, a tall, swarthy, energetic-looking Mexican. He evidently recommends the diligence and offers, by accompanying us, to ensure our safety from

accidents. He appears right. The diligence goes in four days, if it does not break down. The coach takes any time we choose over that; the *literas*, nine or ten days bumping slowly on mules with a sedan-chair motion.[10] The diligence has food and beds provided for it at the inns—the others nothing. A sneaking Scotchman of the name of Bell, who came with Serez, and who is enough to disgust one with one's country, so sneaking and so roguish is his expression, first recommended a coach and then the diligence. I am in favour of the diligence.

The couple from Havana, whom we passed in the *goleta*—fresh from prison—had the insolence to come in the morning and ask leave to go in the same diligence, "under the protection *del Embajador de España*." We should set off in select company.

Calderón called this morning on General Victoria. Found His Excellency in a large hall without furniture or ornament of any sort, without even chairs, and altogether in a style of more than republican simplicity. He has just returned the visit, accompanied by his colossal aide-de-camp, the Golden Eagle.

General Guadalupe Victoria is perhaps the last man in a crowd whom one would fix upon as likely to be the owner of the above high-sounding cognomen, which in fact is not his original but his assumed name—*Guadalupe* being adopted by him in honour of the renowned image of the Virgin of that name, and *Victoria*, with less humility, to commemorate his success in battle. He is an honest, plain, down-looking, common sort of citizen, lame and tall, very much at a loss what to say, and concluding every sentence with "*Eso es* [That is so]"—pronounced in a stupid dull tone, looking down at his boots. Very good-natured he may be, but courtier or orator he is certainly not, a man of undeniable bravery, capable of supporting almost incredible hardships, humane, and who has always proved himself a sincere lover of what he considers liberty, without ever having been actuated by ambitious or interested motives.[11]

It is said that his defects were indolence, want of resolution, and too much reliance on his own knowledge. He is the only Mexican president who finished as chief magistrate the term prescribed by the laws. It is

alleged, in proof of his simplicity, though I think it is too absurd to be true, that having received a dispatch with the two-headed eagle on the seal, he remarked to the astonished envoy who delivered it: "Our arms are very much alike, only I see that His Majesty's eagles have two heads. I have heard that some of that species exist here, in *tierra caliente*, and shall have one sent for." He strongly recommends us to avoid broken bones by going in *literas*, at least as far as Jalapa.

The general is not married, but appears rather desirous of entering the united state—and speaks a good deal of it. As he never looks up, anyone wishing to make an impression on him must sit on a level with his boots. Having stumbled about for some time in search of his cocked hat, it was handed to him by the Golden Eagle, and he took his leave.[12]

We walked out this evening to take a look of the environs with Señor Velasco, the commander of the *Jasón*, and several young ladies of the house. We walked in the direction of an old church, St. Christophe or Nicholas, where it is or was the custom for young ladies desirous of being married to throw a stone at the saint, their fortune depending upon the stone's hitting him—so that he is in a lapidated and dilapidated condition. Oh, Veracruz! Such environs! The surrounding houses black with smoke of powder or with fire—the streets deserted—a view of melancholy bare red sandhills all round—not a tree, or shrub, or flower, or bird, except the horrid black *zopilote*, or police officer. All looks as if the prophet Jeremiah had passed through the city denouncing woe to all the dwellers thereof. It is enough to make one feel homesick. Such a melancholy, wholly deserted-looking burial ground as we saw![13]

War and revolutions have no doubt done their work, yet I find difficulty in believing those who speak of Veracruz as having been a gay and delightful residence in former days, though even now those who have resided here for any length of time, even foreigners, almost invariably become attached to it; and as for those born here, they are the truest of patriots, holding up Veracruz as superior to all other parts of the world.[14]

The city was founded by the Viceroy Count de Monterrey at the end of the sixteenth century, and ought not to be confounded, as it sometimes is, with either of the two colonies founded by the first Spaniards. Built in front of the island of San Juan de Ulúa, it has one interesting recollection attached to it, since on these same arid shores Cortés disembarked more than three centuries ago. Unlike the green and fertile coast which gladdened the eyes of Columbus, the Spanish conqueror beheld a bleak and burning desert, whose cheerless aspect might well have deterred a feebler mind from going further in search of the paradise that existed behind.

We came home, and found the officers of the *Jasón* sitting like fish out of water, waiting to see us. Two or three indefinite sort of young ladies with indefinite manners were there. One played a thing they call a harp— it is a sort of harp-lute—a small light instrument without pedals, so light that they can lift it with one hand; and yet the music she brings from it is surprising, one air after another, played quite monotonously, without the least expression but with great ease and a certain execution—and with the additional merit of being self-taught.

I imagine that there must be a great deal of musical taste thrown away here. There are pianos in almost every house, and one lady who came to see me today had been extremely well taught and played with great taste —but her mother was an Englishwoman, which accounts not for her taste, but for her having had energy enough to learn. The women alone got up a sort of quadrille, and an attempt at a waltz. Having no dancing masters, they can only learn by what they *hear*. All they want is *teaching,* but in the meantime their dancing is rather too funny. On the balcony this evening it was delightful, and the moon is a universal beautifier.[15]

Saturday: December 21st, 1839

We walked about the city yesterday, and returned visits. [We] found the streets quiet but much cleaner than Havana. Some few tolerably handsome churches, one we went into very good. I have not seen one carriage on the street, of any sort.

The actors or *cómicos* came in the morning to offer us the centre box in the theatre, it being the benefit night of Doña Inocencia Martínez from Madrid, a favourite of the public and, in fact, a pretty woman, and a good comic actress. Velasco put down several ounces in passing.[16] The theatre is small and ugly and, they say, generally deserted, but last night it was crowded. The drop-scene, remarkably funny, represents *les beaux-arts.* The *arts* are so fat that their condition here must be flourishing. We were, however, agreeably disappointed in the performance, which amused me more than anything I saw at the Havana. The play, somewhat improbable—turning upon the Lady Abbess of a convent going to a masked ball!—was the *Segunda Dama Duende,* nearly a translation from the *Domino Noir*. [It] was good and very amusing, full of excellent *coups de théâtre.* Doña Inocencia in her various characters as domino,

servant girl, abbess, &c., was very handsome, and acted well and with great spirit.[17] Moreover, she and her sister, with two Spaniards, danced the *jota aragonesa* in perfection, and I wondered much as we returned home that anything so decent should have been seen in Veracruz.

Tomorrow, Sunday, is the day fixed for our departure, and I never shall have left a city with more good will, though really this house is excellent, a whole suite of rooms to ourselves and everything that we can want is given us, and neither ceremony nor *gêne* of any sort. The weather is certainly beautiful. The heat may be a little oppressive—too warm to walk in the middle of the day—but the evenings are cool and delightful.

We had a visit yesterday from the English and French consuls. The former is rather a nice man, something like Trueman. He is to be pitied, living in such a place.[18] The French consul assured us we shall have our arms broken and our teeth knocked out if we persist in our plan of taking the diligence—but all things balanced, we think it preferable to every other conveyance.

Another visit in the evening from General Guadalupe and *l'Aigle d'Or.* [The general] was very civil and amiable, offering very cordially every service and assistance in his power. We are to rise tomorrow at two, being invited to breakfast with General Santa Anna at his country seat called Manga de Clavo, a few leagues from this.[19]

A good many men to take leave. We have been sitting on the balcony till very late, enjoying the moonlight and refreshing breeze from the sea, and as we rise before daybreak our rest will be short.

Travelling makes us acquainted with strange bedfellows—Shakespeare.[20] I do not think there is anything in this world that could induce me to live here. The more I see, the more I become convinced of this fact, that the further we recede from civilization, the less happy we are. To live amongst people, however kind, with whom you have not one thought in common *must* be melancholy. To a person brought up in England and accustomed to European society, a place where the trace of a *book* is not to be seen—where the women spend their time in perfect idleness, smoking—idleness without grace—and where you can find no subject on which to converse—[causes] an aridness of feeling which is as *triste* as it would be to settle among the red sand hills in the neighbourhood.

5

Up to Puebla by Diligence

At two o'clock in the morning we rose by candlelight, with the pleasant prospect of quitting Veracruz and of seeing Santa Anna. We got into two boxes called carriages, drawn by mules, [which] were at the door to convey us to Manga de Clavo. Señor Velasco, Calderón, the commander of the *Jasón*, and I being encased in them, we set off half-asleep. By the faint light, as we passed through the gates,[1] we could just distinguish on either side as the carriages ploughed their way along, nothing but sand—sand—as far as the eye could reach: a few leagues of Arabian desert.

At length we began to see symptoms of vegetation, occasional palm trees and flowers—and to go along through a crossroad with wood on each side. By the time we had reached Santa Fe, a small Indian village of huts —but a pretty scene—where we stopped to change mules, the light had broke in, and we seemed to have been transported, as if by enchantment, from a desert to a garden. It was altogether a picturesque and striking scene: the huts, clean and pretty, composed of bamboo and thatched with palm leaves; the Indian women with their long black hair standing at the doors with their little half-naked children; the mules rolling themselves

on the ground according to their favourite fashion; snow-white goats browsing amongst the palm trees. The air was so soft and balmy, the first fresh breath of morning, the dewdrops still glittering on the broad leaves of the banana and the palm—and all around so silent, cool, and still.

The huts, though poor, were clean; no windows, but a certain subdued light makes its way through the leafy canes. We procured some tumblers of new warm milk, and, having changed mules, pursued our journey—now no longer through hills of sand, but across the country, which, though flat, was now pretty and fertile, the road passing through a wilderness of trees and flowers, the glowing productions of *tierra caliente*. We arrived about five at Santa Anna's *quinta*, Manga de Clavo, having in fact been passing for leagues through his property, a natural garden.

The house outside is pretty, slight-looking, and kept in nice order.[2] We were received by an aide-de-camp in uniform and by several hangers-on, and conducted into a large, cool, good-looking, uncarpeted, agreeable apartment, with little furniture, into which shortly entered *Mme la Générale*, the Señora de Santa Anna. *Figurez-vous* a tall, thin, lank, lean, ugly female, and at that early hour of six in the morning, dressed to receive us in clear white muslin with two embroidered flounces —short—silk stockings and white satin shoes, a blond fichu covered with

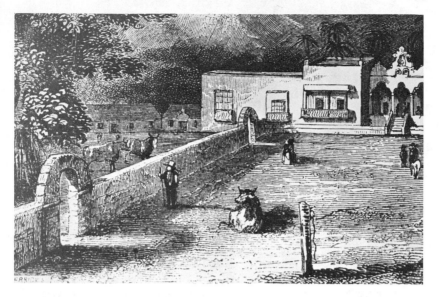

blue flowers, a pair of very splendid diamond earrings, a magnificent diamond brooch, and a diamond ring the size of a small watch on each finger. She was very civil, and introduced her daughter Miss Guadalupe de Santa Anna, the miniature of her mamma in every respect—dress, features, satin shoes, only coral instead of diamonds, and pink flowers instead of blue.

In a little while entered the General Santa Anna himself, a gentlemanly, good-looking, quietly-dressed, rather melancholy-looking person, with one leg, apparently a good deal of an invalid, and to us decidedly the best looking and most interesting figure in the group. He has a sallow complexion, fine dark eyes, soft and penetrating, and an interesting expression of face. Knowing nothing of his past history, one would have said a philosopher, living in dignified retirement—one who had tried the world and found that all was vanity, one who had suffered ingratitude and who, if he were ever persuaded to emerge from his retreat, would only do so, Cincinnatus-like, to benefit his country. It is strange, and a fact worthy of notice in natural history, how frequently this expression of philosophic resignation, of placid sadness, is to be remarked on the countenances of the most cunning, the deepest, most ambitious, most designing and most dangerous statesmen I have seen. [They have] a something that would persuade the multitude that they are above the world, and engage in its toils only to benefit others—so that one can hardly persuade oneself that these men are not *saints*. Witness Van Buren—but, above all, witness the melancholy and philosophic Santa Anna.

Calderón gave him a letter from the Queen, written under the supposition of his still being president, with which he seemed much pleased,

but to which he merely made the innocent observation, "How very well the Queen writes!"[3]

It was only now and then that the expression of his eye was startling, especially when he spoke of his leg, which is cut off below the knee. He speaks of it frequently, like Sir John Ramorny of his bloody hand, and when he gives an account of his wound, and alludes to the French on that day, his countenance assumes that air of bitterness which Ramorny's may have exhibited when speaking of Harry the Smith.[4] Otherwise he was quiet and gentlemanly in his manners. Yet here sat with this *air de philosophe* perhaps one of the worst men in the world—ambitious of power—greedy of money—and unprincipled—having feathered his nest at the expense of the republic—and waiting in a dignified retreat only till the moment comes for putting himself at the head of another revolution.

He made himself very agreeable, spoke a great deal of the United States, and of the persons he had known there, and in his manners was altogether a more polished hero than I had expected to see. To judge from the past, he will not long remain in his present state of inaction, besides having within him, according to Zavala, "a principle of action forever impelling him forward."[5]

En attendant, breakfast was announced. The Señora de Santa Anna led me in by the tips of the fingers. Calderón was placed at the head of the table, I on his right, Santa Anna opposite, the Señora on my right. The breakfast was very handsome, consisting of innumerable Spanish dishes: meat and vegetables, fish and fowl, fruits and sweetmeats—all served in white and gold French porcelain, with coffee, wines, &c. After breakfast the Señora, having dispatched an officer for her cigar case, which was gold with a diamond latch, offered me a cigar, which I having declined, she lighted her own, a little paper *"cigarrito,"* and the gentlemen followed her good example.

We then proceeded to look at the grounds round the house, the outhouses and offices; at the General's favourite war horse, an old white charger, probably a sincerer philosopher than his master; at several gamecocks, guarded with especial care, cockfighting being a favourite recreation of Santa Anna's; and at his *litera,* which is handsome and comfortable. There are no gardens, but, as he observed, the whole country, which for twelve leagues square belongs to him, is a garden. The appearance of the family says little for the healthiness of the locale; and indeed its beauty and fertility will not compensate for its insalubrity. He is yellow and she and Guadalupe are green. She has in bed a child who has had a cold for six months.

As we had but a few hours to spare, the General ordered round two carriages, both very handsome, and made in the United States, one of which conveyed Calderón and me, and Santa Anna and Mme de Santa Anna, who upon the whole looks like an old and unhappy chambermaid *endimanchée.*[6] In the other were the little girl Guadalupita, and the officers, in which order we proceeded through rather a pretty country to the highroad, where the diligence with the Duchess and our guide, Don Miguel de Serez, were to overtake us. The diligence not having arrived, we got down and sat on a stone bench in front of an Indian cottage, inhabited by one of their tenantry, where we talked—while Guadalupe ate apples in surprising quantities, and complained of the tightness of the white frock into which she had been squeezed for the occasion. Calderón and the General remained moralizing in the carriage.

Shortly after, and just as the sun was beginning to give us a specimen of his power, our lumbering escort of Mexican soldiers galloped up (orders having been given by the government that a fresh escort shall be stationed every six leagues) and announced the approach of the diligence. We were agreeably disappointed to see a good-looking new coach, made in the United States, drawn by ten good-looking mules and driven by a smart Yankee coachman. Our party consisted of ourselves and the Duchess, Don Miguel de Serez, Estrada (the captain of the *Jasón*), and Solís (his first lieutenant), who accompany us to Mexico. The day was delightful, and everyone apparently in good humour, as anyone would be who had left Veracruz behind him. We took leave of General Santa Anna, his lady, and the lovely Guadalupe; also of our hospitable entertainer Señor Velasco; got into the diligence—doors shut—all right—lash up the mules, and now for Mexico!

Gradually, as in Dante's *Commedia,* after leaving Purgatory, typified by Veracruz, we seemed to draw nearer to Paradise. The road is difficult, as the approach to Paradise ought to be, and the extraordinary jolts were sufficient to prevent us from being too much enraptured with the beauty of the scenery, which increased as we advanced. At Santa Fe and Zopilote we changed mules; and at Tolome, one of the sites of the civil war, came to the end of Santa Anna's twelve leagues of property.

We arrived at Puente Nacional, formerly Puente del Rey, celebrated as the scene of many an engagement during the Revolution, and by occupying which Victoria frequently prevented the passage of the Spanish troops, and that of the convoys of silver to the port. Here we stopped a short time to admire the beautiful bridge thrown over the river Antigua, with its stone arches, which has been sketched by Mrs. Ward—badly, Calderón says, though it is very long since I saw the book.[7] We were accompanied by the commander of the fort. It is now a peaceful-looking scene. We walked to the bridge, pulled branches of large white flowers, and greatly admired all that surrounded us—the rapid river dashing over the rocks, and the fine, bold scenery. The village is a mere collection of huts, with some fine trees.

It was difficult to believe, as we journeyed on, that we were now in the midst of December. The air was soft and balmy. The heat, without being intense or oppressive, was like that of an English July morning. The road lay through a succession of woody country: trees covered with every variety of blossom, and loaded with the most delicious tropical fruits; flowers of every colour filling the air with fragrance; beautiful creepers turning around the trees; and the most fantastical profusion of parasitical plants intertwining the branches and flinging their bright blossoms over every bough. Palms, cocoas, oranges, lemons succeeded one another, and

at one turn of the road, down in a lovely green valley, we caught a glimpse of an Indian woman, with her long hair, resting under the shade of a lofty tree, beside a running stream—an Oriental picture. Had it not been for the dust and the jolting, nothing could have been more delightful.[8]

As for Don Miguel, with his head out of the window, now desiring the coachman to go gently, now warning us to prepare for a jolt, now making the amiable to the Duchess and singing little ends of French songs in hopes of putting her in a good humour, now pointing out everything worth looking at, and making light of all difficulties, he was the very best conductor of a journey I ever met with. His hat of itself was a curiosity to us: a white beaver with immense brim, lined with thick silver tissue, with two large silver rolls and tassels round it as a band.

One fact must be observed by all who travel in Mexican territory. There is not one human being or passing object to be seen that is not in itself a picture, or which would not form a good subject for the pencil. The Indian women with their long black plaited hair, and little children slung to their backs, their large straw hats, and short petticoats of two colours— the long strings of *arrieros* with their droves of loaded mules and swarthy, wild-looking faces[9]—the chance horseman who passes with his sarape of many colours, his high ornamented saddle, Mexican hat, silver stirrups and enormous leathern boots—all is picturesque. Salvator Rosa and Hogarth might have travelled in this country to advantage, hand in hand; Salvator for the sublime, and Hogarth taking him up where the sublime became the ridiculous.[10]

At La Calera we had a distant view of the sea. Occasionally we stopped to buy oranges fresh from the trees, pineapples, and *granaditas*, which are like Brobdingnagian gooseberries, the pulp enclosed in a very thick, yellow or green rind, and very refreshing—pretty to look at, but requiring habit to like, as all new fruits do.

It was about seven in the evening when, very dusty, rather tired, but very much enchanted with the beauty of all we had seen, we arrived at Plan del Río. Here the diligence passengers generally stop for the night, that is, sleep for a few hours on a hard board and rise at midnight to go on to Jalapa. But to this arrangement I for one made vociferous objections, and strongly insisted upon the propriety and feasibility of sleeping at Jalapa that night. Don Miguel, the most obsequious of Dons, declared it should be exactly as the Señora ordered.

Accordingly it was agreed that we should wait for the moon and then pursue our journey, and meanwhile we walked out a short way to see the bridge, the river, and the wood. The bridge consists of a single large arch thrown over the river and communicating with a great highroad, formerly paved, but now going to ruin.

We returned to the inn, which is a small row of houses or rather of rooms, built of brick and prettily situated, not far from the water. Here we had the luxury of water and towels, which enabled us to get rid of a certain portion of dust before we went to supper.

The diligence from Jalapa had just deposited at the inn a German with his wife and child, he bearing so decidedly the stamp of a German musician that we at once guessed his calling. They are, I believe, from Mexico, from whence the fine arts seem to be taking their flight, and gave a most woeful account of the road between this and Jalapa.

We had a very tolerable supper, to which Don Miguel did peculiar justice: soup, fish, fowls, steak, and *frijoles,* all well stuffed with garlic and oil. The jolting had given me too bad a headache to care for much more than coffee. We were strongly advised to remain the night there and sleep, but lazy people know too well what it is to rise in the middle of the night, especially when they are very tired. We waited however for the moon, and then packed ourselves once more into the diligence, sufficiently refreshed by our rest to encounter new fatigues.

The moon was very bright, and most of the party prepared themselves for sleep with cigars in their mouths, not a very easy matter, for the roads were infamous, a succession of holes and rocks. As we were gradually ascending, the weather became cooler, and from cool began to grow cold, forcing people to look out for their cloaks and shawls. We could now discern some changes in the vegetation, or rather a mingling of the trees of a colder climate with those of the tropics, especially the Mexican oak, which begins to flourish here. Fortunately, at one part of the road, the moon enabled us to see the captain of the escort lying on the ground fast asleep, his horse standing quietly beside him, he having probably fallen off while asleep, and continued his nap. The soldiers shook him up with some difficulty.

At Corral Falso we changed mules, and from the badness of the road continued to go very slowly. Here José for some reason was put into the diligence—and a more delightful sight I shall never see, than his falling asleep on the shoulder of the Duchess, who holds him in abhorrence and shook him off as she would a mangy dog—notwithstanding which, little aware of his danger, he continually let his head drop upon her, till her rage knew no bounds.[11]

The cold increased greatly, and at last by the moonlight we had a distant view of the peak of Orizaba, with his white nightcap on (excuse the simile, suggested by extreme sleepiness), the very sight enough to make one shiver.

As we approached Jalapa, the scene was picturesque. The escort had put on their sarapes, which all looked white in the moonlight, and with their high helmets and feathers kept galloping along, dashing and skirmishing amongst the trees and bushes. Orizaba and the Cofre de Perote shone white in the distance, while a delicious smell of flowers, particularly of roses, gave token of the land through which we were passing.

It was nearly two in the morning when we reached Jalapa, tired to death, and shivering with cold. Greatly we rejoiced as we rattled through its mountainous streets, and still more when we found ourselves in a nice clean inn, with brick floors and decent small beds, and everything prepared for us. The sight of a fire would have been too much comfort; however, they gave us some hot tea, and very shortly after—I at least can answer for myself that I was in bed and enjoying the most delicious sound sleep that I have had since I left New York.

Monday: December 23rd, 1839
Perote

This morning, the diligence being at our disposal, we did not rise by break of day, but on the contrary continued to sleep till near eight o'clock. We were waited on by such a nice, civil, clean, and delightful little old woman (Mexican) that I should like to have bought her and carried her off with me. Calderón sent for a Jalapa barber to shave him, and meanwhile all the authorities of the town were ranged in the passage to give him welcome, as soon as he should present himself at the door.

They gave us a delicious breakfast. Such fresh eggs and fresh butter, and good coffee and well-fried chickens, &c. Moreover, such good bread and such peculiarly excellent water[12] that we fell very much in love with Jalapa.

After breakfast we walked out, accompanied by some of the authorities of the place. The town consists of little more than a few steep streets, very old, with some large and excellent houses, the best as usual belonging to English merchants, and many to those of Veracruz, who come to live in or near Jalapa during the reign of the *vómito*. There are some old churches, a very old convent of Franciscan monks,[13] and a well-supplied market place. Everywhere there are flowers—roses creeping over the old walls, Indian girls making green garlands for the Virgin and saints, flowers in the few shops, flowers at the windows, but, above all, everywhere one of the most splendid mountain views in the world.

Nothing can be prettier in its way than Jalapa—so old and gray and rose-becovered, with a sound of music issuing from every open door and

window, and its soft and agreeable temperature presents, even in a few hours, a series of agreeable impressions not easily effaced.

And still more beautiful was the country. The Cofre de Perote, with its dark pine forests and gigantic *chest* (a rock of porphyry which takes that form), and the still loftier snow-white peak of Orizaba tower above all the others, seeming like the colossal guardians of the land. The intervening mountains, the dark cliffs and fertile plains, the thick woods of lofty trees clothing the hills and valleys; a glimpse of the distant ocean; the surrounding lanes shaded by fruit trees: aloes, bananas, *chirimoyos*, mingled with the green liquidambar, the flowering myrtle, and hundreds of plants and shrubs and flowers of every colour and of delicious fragrance, all combine to form one of the most varied and beautiful scenes that the eye can behold.

But we returned to our inn, for it was near noon, and the veil of clouds that earlier in the morning enveloped Orizaba had passed away, leaving its white summit environed by a flood of light.

After having taken leave of the Jalapeños (and, amongst others, of Mr. Brian, an Englishman and friend of Mrs. Ashburnham's) we again found ourselves *en route*.[14] Such a view of the mountains as we gradually ascended the steep road! And such flowers and blossoming trees on all sides! Large scarlet blossoms, and hanging purple and white flowers, and trees covered with fragrant bell-shaped flowers like lilies, which the people here call the *floripundio*, together with loads of double pink roses that made the air fragrant as we passed; and here and there a church, an old ruined convent, or more rarely a white hacienda or farmhouse. We had the advantage of clear weather, not always to be found at Jalapa, especially when the north wind, blowing at Veracruz, covers this city and its environs with a dense fog.

We stopped at a small village to change horses (for on leaving Jalapa our mules were exchanged for eight strong white horses), and here Don Miguel made us enter a very pretty house belonging to some female friends of his, [to whom he] undertook to present us, who have a house half-inn and half a dwelling house—indefinite sort of women, one of whom was very handsome, with a tasteful white turban. The curiosity of this place is a rock behind the house, covered with roses, clove carnations, and every variety of bright flower-tree, together with oranges, lemons, limes, and cedrats, all growing out of the rock. The ladies were very civil, though I dare say surprised at our admiration of their December flowers. [They] gave us orangeade and cake, with large cedrats and oranges from the trees—and moreover gave me such a delicious bouquet of roses and carnations—so that we were not a little indebted to them. If a delightful climate and perpetual flowers can go far to make people happy, they have so far the requisites. Together with the unknown scarlet and purple blossoms which the captain of the escort had gathered for me, the diligence inside looked like an arbour.

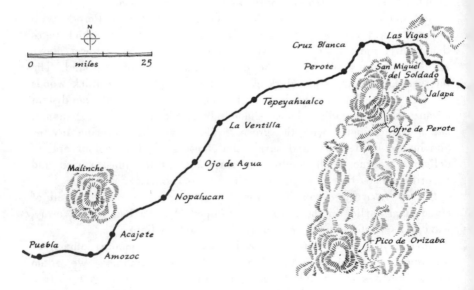

We continued our journey, the road ascending towards the tableland through the most beautiful mountainous country. At one striking point of view we got out of the diligence and looked back upon Jalapa, and round upon a panorama of mountains. Gradually the vegetation changed: fine, fresh-looking European herbage and trees succeeded the less hardy though more brilliant trees and flowers of the tropics; the banana and *chirimoyo* gave place to the strong oak, and higher still these were interspersed with the dark green of the pine.

At San Miguel del Soldado we stopped to take some refreshment.[15] The country became gradually more bleak, and before arriving at the village of Las Vigas nearly all trees had disappeared but the hardy fir, which flourishes amongst the rocks. The ground for about two leagues was covered with lava and great masses of calcined rock, so that we seemed to be passing over the crater of a volcano. This part of the country is deservedly called the *mal país,* and the occasional crosses with their faded garlands that gleam in these bleak volcanic regions give token that it may have yet other titles to the name of "evil land." The roses and carnations that I had brought from Jalapa were still unwithered, so that in a few hours we had passed through the whole scale of vegetation.

The road became steep and dreary, and after passing Cruz Blanca, excepting occasional cornfields and sombre pine forests, the scene had no objects of interest sufficient to enable us to keep our eyes open. The sun was set. It grew dusk, and by the time we reached Perote, our second nightly stoppingplace, most of us [were] fast asleep—in that cold, jolting sort of uncomfortable sleep, into which one falls in a carriage.

[We were] very cold and quite stupefied, and too sleepy to be hungry, in spite of finding a large tolerable supper which was provided for us. The inn was dirty, very unlike that of Jalapa. Having with some difficulty procured a room to the satisfaction of the Duchess—who is rather famous for making difficulties—and rooms for ourselves, we got into very miserable beds. How everybody slept I cannot say, but I slept very badly. We were quite ready to get up by the light of an unhappy-looking specimen of grease which the landlord brought to the door about two in the morning.

Tuesday: December 24th, 1839
Puebla

There are some scenes which can never be effaced from our memory, and such a one was that which took place this morning at Perote at two o'clock, the moon and the stars shining bright and cold.

When I was dressed, I went into the kitchen where Calderón, the officers of the *Jasón*, Don Miguel, and the Mexican captain of the last night's escort were assembled by the light of one melancholy sloping candle, together with a suspicious-looking landlord and a few sleepy Indian women with bare feet, tangled hair, copper faces and *rebozos*. They made us some chocolate, but with goat's milk—horrid in general and rancid in particular.

It appeared that all parties were at a standstill, for, by some mistake in the orders, the fresh escort had not arrived, and the escort of the preceding night could go no further. Don Miguel, with his swarthy face and great sarape, was stalking about, rather out of humour, while the Mexican captain was regretting, in very polite tones, with his calm, Arab-looking, impassive face, that his escort could proceed no further. He seemed to think it extremely probable that we should be robbed; believed, indeed had just heard it asserted, that a party of *ladrones* were looking out for *El Señor Ministro*; regretted that he could not assist us, though quite at our service; and recommended us to wait until the next escort should arrive.

To this advice Don Miguel, our conductor, would by no means listen. He was piqued that any detention should occur—his honour was at stake —and yet aware that it was unsafe to go on. He had sworn to take us safely, and in four days, to Mexico, and it was necessary to keep his word. I admired the sarape of the captain. *"Está a la disposición de usted, Señorita."* Calderón proposed that two of the soldiers armed should accompany the diligence upon mules, as probably a couple of these animals might be procured. The captain begged to observe that, though entirely at our disposal, two men could be of no manner of use—as, in case of attack, resistance, except with a large escort, was worse than useless. Nevertheless it was remarked by some ingenious person that they should go on mules, and ride in front, as if they were a great num- ber—armed to the teeth—and that the robbers seeing two might imagine that there were more behind. In short there were various opinions. One proposed that they should go on the coach, others that they should go *in* it. Here I put in a word, begging that they might ride on mules or go outside, but by no means within. Don Miguel declared that the Señorita had only to order.

At length we all collected before the door of the inn, and a queer group we must have made by the light of the moon, and a nice carica- ture, I thought to myself, our friend Mr. Glass[16] would have made of us had he been there.

The diligence with eight white horses and a Yankee coachman, origi- nally no doubt called Brown, but now answering to the mellifluous ap- pellation of *Bruno;*[17] Emilie with a French cap and loaded with sun- dry mysterious-looking baskets; I with a cloak and bonnet; Calderón with a Greek cap, cloak, and cigar in his mouth; the captain of the *Jasón* also with cloak and cigar, and very cold; the lieutenant Solís in his navy uniform and epaulettes, taking it coolly; Don Miguel, with his great sarape and silver hat—(seven people belonging to five different coun- tries)—the Mexican captain, with his pale, impassive face and mous- taches, enveloped in a very handsome sarape, and surrounded by the lazy tired soldiers of the last night's escort; dirty-looking soldiers lounging on the ground, wrapped in their blankets; the Indian women and the host of the dirty inn; and the bright moon and starry sky lighting up the whole. The figures in the foreground, and the lofty snow-clad mountains, and the dismal-looking old town of Perote itself that looked gray and sulky at being disturbed so early, with its old castle of San Carlos,[18] and cold, sterile plains.

Meanwhile, two soldiers with their cloaks and arms had climbed up outside of the coach. The captain remarked that they could not sit there. Bruno made some reply, upon which the captain very coolly drew his sword, and was about to put a very decided impediment to our journey by stabbing the coachman when Don Miguel, with his two eyes and his cigar all shining angrily, rushed in between them.

High words ensued between him and the captain, and the extreme coolness and precision with which the captain spoke was very amusing. It was as if he were rehearsing a speech from a play. "I always speak frankly," said Don Miguel in an angry tone. "And I," said the captain in a polite, measured voice, "am also accustomed to speak my mind with extreme frankness. I regret, however, that I did not at the moment perceive the Señora at the door; otherwise—" &c.

At length the two little men, who with their arms and sarapes looked like bundles of ammunition, and who, half asleep, had been by some zealous person, probably by our friend Bruno, tumbled upon the diligence like packages, were now rolled off it, and finally tumbled upon mules—and we got into the coach. Don Miguel, with his head out of the window to be ready for all things and placing his broad back before us, certainly [was] not very easy in his mind. Before setting off he called up the two bundles and gave them directions as to their line of conduct in a *stage* whisper: "If you see them, shout for help—but the best news you can give us is that you have killed them." The two bundles trotted off, primed with valour, while we, very cold and (I answer for myself) rather frightened, proceeded on our way. The earliness of the hour was probably our salvation, as we started two hours before the usual time and thus gained a march upon the gentlemen of the road.

We arrived at Santa Gertrudis, where we changed horses, *sin novedad ninguna.* We were certainly not very sorry, however, to see a company of lancers at full gallop, with a very good-looking officer at their head, coming along the road—though when I first heard the sound of horses' hoofs clattering along and, by the faint light, discerned the horsemen, enveloped as they were in a cloud of dust, I felt sure that they were a party of robbers. The captain made many excuses and apologies for his delay, and proceeded to inform us that the alcaldes of Tepeyahualco, La Ventilla, and of some other villages whose names I forget, had for twenty days prepared a breakfast in expectation of His Excellency's arrival—whether twenty breakfasts, or the same one cold, or *réchauffé,* we may never know.

The captain had a very handsome horse, which he showed off and caused to *caracolear* by the side of the diligence, and put at my disposal with a low bow every time I looked at it. He discoursed with Calderón of robbers and wars, and of the different sites which these gentry most affected. Calderón asked him if he were married. To a second wife, he said. Calderón asked him how he had managed to get rid of the first. He said she was shot by going to the war with him, yet his second wife always followed him also.

After [we had] arrived at Tepeyahualco, having passed over a succession of sterile plains covered with scanty pasture, a very fat alcalde advanced to meet the diligence and made a speech to Calderón offering

him the said twenty days' breakfast, which he with many thanks declined. Who ate that breakfast is buried in the past. Whether the alcalde
was glad or sorry did not appear. He vanished with a profusion of bows,
and was followed by a large, good-looking Indian woman who stood
behind him while he made his discourse. Perhaps they ate together the
long-prepared feast—*quién sabe?*—which was at least one of the many
tributes paid to the arrival of the first messenger of peace from the
mother country.

At La Ventilla, however, we descended rather hungry to breakfast,
and found several authorities waiting to give Calderón a welcome. Here
the captain presented us with a basket of fruit—delicious *chirimoyas*,
a natural custard which we liked even upon first trial, *granaditas*, bananas, *zapotes*, also a fruit resembling a sweet turnip. We were obliged to
eat and praise—though, except the *chirimoyas*, all seemed bad to me.
They also made us taste pulque; and on a first impression it appears to
me that as nectar was the drink in Olympus, we may fairly conjecture
that Pluto cultivated the maguey in his dominions. I should regret to
attempt describing the smell—the reverse of roses we may say. The taste
and smell combined took me so completely by surprise that I am afraid
my look of horror must have given mortal offense to the worthy alcalde,
who considers it the most delicious beverage in the world; and in fact
it is said that when one gets over the first shock it is very agreeable.
The difficulty must consist in getting over it.[19]

After having breakfasted pretty well, hunger making even chile and
garlic supportable, and taking with us the captain's fruit we continued
our route. He said the robbers had grown very daring, and there were

six desperate ones against whom he and his lancers were going next
day. The next stage being very dangerous our escort was to be doubled.

We had been gradually ascending into the mountains since we left
Perote; the country had become more bleak and dreary, and we had
again got into the *mal país*, barren, dreary and mountainous, where
nothing is to be seen but a few fir trees and pines covering the hills,
dark and stunted, black masses of lava, and an occasional white cross to
mark either where a murder has been committed or where a celebrated
robber has been buried. Of each Don Miguel gave us a succinct account. Some lines of *Childe Harold* suit this scene as if written for it:

> And here and there, as up the crags you spring,
>   Mark many rude-carved crosses near the path:
> Yet deem not these devotion's offering—
>   These are memorials frail of murderous wrath,
> For wheresoe'er the shrieking victim hath
>   Pour'd forth his blood beneath the assassin's knife
> Some hand erects a cross of mouldering lath;
>   And grove and glen with thousand such are rife,
> Throughout this purple land, where law secures not life.[20]

The ground now became black with lava, and we found ourselves passing over the crater of a volcano. The whole scene was wild and grand,
yet dreary and monotonous, presenting the greatest contrast imaginable
to our first day's journey. The only signs of life to be met with, the
only human beings to be seen, were the long strings of *arrieros* with
their droves of loaded mules, and an occasional miserable Indian hut,
with a few half-naked men, women, and children.

At one small wild-looking inn near Santa Gertrudis where, very cold
and miserable, we stopped, Don Miguel made us some hot wine which
was most merciful. The tavern-keeper, for it was no more than a spirit
shop, if not a robber certainly had all the appearance of one; so wild,
melancholy, and with such a sinister expression of countenance. He was

decidedly a figure for Salvator, who never drew a more bandit-looking figure, as he stood there with his blanket and slouched hat, and a knife in his belt, tall and thin and muscular, with his sallow visage and his sad, fierce eyes. However, he showed us the marks on his door where a band of twenty robbers had broken in one night and robbed some travelling merchants, who were sleeping there, of forty thousand dollars.

Calderón asked him how the robbers treated the women and what they did with [them] when they fell into their power. "*Las saludan,* &c.," said he, "and sometimes carry them off to the mountains, but rarely, and chiefly when they are afraid of their giving information against them."[21]

At Ojo de Agua, where we changed horses, we saw the sleeping place which those who travel in private coach or *litera* must submit to, unless they bring their own beds along with them, and a stock of provisions besides—a common room like a barn, with some wooden planks, where all must herd and sleep together who choose. Neither chair, nor table, nor food to be had. It was a solitary-looking house standing lonely on the plain, with a few straggling sheep nibbling the brown grass in the vicinity. A fine spring of water from which it takes its name, and Orizaba, which seems to have travelled forward and stands in bold outline against the sapphire sky, were all that we saw there worthy of notice.

We changed horses at Nopalucan, Acajete and Amozoc,[22] all small villages, with little more than the *posada* and a few poor houses, and all very dirty. The country, however, improves in cultivation and fertility, though the chief trees are the sombre pines. Very dusty, still accompanied by our two escorts, which had a very grandiloquent effect, we entered about four o'clock Puebla de los Angeles, the second city to Mexico

(after Guadalajara) in the republic, where we found very fine apartments prepared for us in the inn, and where, after a short rest and a fresh toilet, we went out to see what we could of the city before it grew dusk, before it actually became what it now is, *Christmas Eve!*

It certainly does require some time to become [used] to the style of building adopted in the Spanish colonies which has outside so much the air of a barn or a ruined house that the eye must get very much accustomed before it can see anything but dreariness and desolation. There is something at first sight exceedingly desolate-looking in these great wooden doors, like those of immense barns, the large iron-barred windows, the great ill-paved courtyards, even the flat roofs, the ruined look of the houses outside; and then the streets where, though this is a fête day, nothing but peasants and beggars set foot—all is totally different from what we are accustomed to admire in other countries. The whole gives the idea of a total absence of comfort, so that, though Puebla may be a very good-looking town of its kind, it did not please me. Yet the streets of Puebla are clean and regular, the houses large, the cathedral magnificent, and the plaza spacious and handsome.

The cathedral was shut, and is not to be opened till midnight mass, which I regret the less as we must probably return here some day.

The dress of the Poblana peasants is pretty, especially on fête days. A white muslin chemise, or shift, trimmed with lace and embroidery round the skirt, and plaited very beautifully round the neck, and sleeves; a petticoat shorter than the shift, made of stuff or foulard and divided into two colours, the lower part made generally of a scarlet and black stuff, a manufacture of the country, and the upper part of white or yellow satin, with a satin vest of some bright colour, and all brochéed with gold or silver, open in front, and turned back. This vest may be worn or omitted, as suits the taste of the wearer. It is without sleeves, but has straps; the hair plaited in two with ribbon behind and the plaits turned up and fastened together by a diamond ring; long earrings, and all sorts of chains and medals and clinking things worn round the neck. A long, broad, coloured sash, something like an officer's belt, tied behind after going twice or thrice round the waist, into which is stuck a silver cigar case. A small coloured handkerchief like a broad ribbon, crossing over the neck, is fastened in front with a brooch, the ends trimmed with silver and going through the sash. Over all is thrown a coloured *rebozo*, not over the head, but thrown on like a scarf; and they wear silk stockings, or more commonly no stockings, and white satin shoes trimmed with silver.[23]

This is on holidays. On common occasions the dress is the same, but the materials are more common, made of coloured woolen stuff, at least the vest with silver is never worn; but the shift which comes below [the] petticoat is still trimmed with lace, and the shoes are white satin.

We dined about five. It was Christmas Eve! Christmas Eve in Puebla! Who'd have said it once? The handsomest building is the cathedral, and the best-looking part of the city is the plaza, which seems generally the case. Various citizens who came to welcome Calderón accompanied us, but we could not enter the cathedral till midnight—and, as we were to leave Puebla of the Angels at four in the morning, Calderón would not let me go to midnight mass, which I much wished. In fact I had a great desire to see *something,* and proposed going to the theatre, where there is to be a *nacimiento,* a representation in figures of various events connected with the Birth of Christ, such as the Annunciation, the

Holy Family, the Arrival of the Wise Men of the East, &c.—but it was said after some deliberation that it *would not do*. In short I could arrange nothing, and had to sit listening to the polite conversation of several dozen Spaniards and Mexicans who had come to congratulate Calderón on his arrival. [They] were ranged round the room, which to do it justice was a wonderfully handsome room, furnished with chairs and sofas of scarlet stuff, having belonged to a rich man who died or [went] broke. Finding that people were all too stupid to do anything and tired of polite conversation, I went to bed.

Wednesday: Christmas Day, 1839

It is now about three o'clock, but I was awakened an hour ago by the sounds of the hymns with which they were ushering in Christmas morning. I went to the window and saw, by the faint light, bands of women or girls all dressed in white, and singing in chorus through the streets.

We have just taken some chocolate, and amidst a profusion of bows and civilities from the landlord are preparing to set off for Mexico!

6

The Capital Welcomes Spain's First Envoy

Xmas Day! 1839
Plazuela de Buenavista, Mexico

We set off from Puebla at four in the morning—or it might be five—
as we purposely made some delay, not wishing to enter Mexico too
early. In so doing we acted contrary to the advice of Don Miguel, who
was always right in these matters. The day was very fine when we set
off, though rain was predicted. Don Miguel had been at the theatre the
night before and also at a ball. At the theatre there was a *nacimiento,*
or representation in figures of the birth of our Saviour, and the audience
was composed entirely of *gentuza,* the common people, who were drinking brandy and smoking. It was therefore as well that I did not go.

The country was now flat but fertile, no longer arid, and had on the
whole more of a European look than any we had yet passed through.
At Río Prieto, San Martín, and Puente de Texmelucan we changed
horses.

At Río Prieto, a small village, I found that I had been sitting very
comfortably with my feet in a basket of *chirimoyas,* and that my

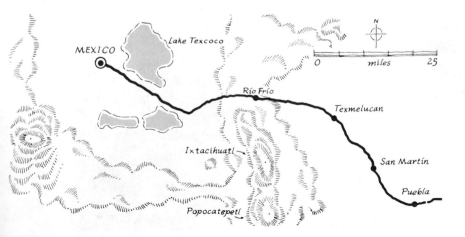

brodequins, white muslin gown, and cloak were all drenched with the milky juice and then made black by the dirty floor of the diligence. With no small difficulty we got down a carpet bag[1] to find another white gown, to the great amusement of an Indian woman who was very curious to know if my gown was the *last fashion!* She admired it very much and said it was *muy guapa*, very pretty. Here we got good hot coffee, and it being Christmas Day found everyone cleaned and dressed for church or mass.

At Río Frío, which is about thirteen leagues from Mexico, and where there is a pretty good *posada* in a valley surrounded by woods, we stopped to dinner. The inn is kept by a Bordelaise and her husband, who wish

themselves in Bordeaux twenty times a day. In front of the windows some Indians were playing at a curious and very ancient game, a sort of swing on foot—capital exercise, and very funny. [It resembles] *El Juego de los Voladores*, the Game of the Flyers, much in vogue amongst the ancient

Mexicans.[2] Our French hostess gave us a good dinner, especially excellent fried potatoes, and jelly of various sorts, regaling us with plenty of stories of robbers and robberies and horrid murders all the while.

On leaving Río Frío, the road became more hilly and the scenery more woody. At last we entered the tract known by the name of the Black Forest, a great haunt for banditti, and a beautiful specimen of forest scenery—a succession of lofty oaks, pines, and cedars, with wild flowers lighting up their gloomy green. Leagues of this wood belong to a rich merchant of Mexico, of the name of Landa.[3] I consider this one of the prettiest parts of the journey. But I confess that the impatience which I felt to see Mexico, the idea that in a few hours we should actually be there, prevented me from enjoying the beauty of the scenery, and made the road appear interminable.

But at length we arrived at the heights on which we look down upon the superb valley of Mexico, celebrated in all parts of the world, with its framework of magnificent mountains, its snow-crowned volcanoes, great lakes, and fertile plains—all surrounding the favoured city of Montezuma, the proudest boast of his conqueror, once of Spain's many diadems the brightest. But the day had overcast, nor is this the most favourable road for entering Mexico. The innumerable spires of the distant city were faintly seen. The volcanoes were enveloped in clouds, all but their snowy summits, which seemed like marble domes towering into the sky.[4] But as we strained our eyes to look into the valley, it all appeared to me rather like a vision of the Past than the actual breathing Present. The curtain of Time seemed to roll back a few centuries, and to discover to us the great panorama of Mexico that burst upon the eye of Cortés when

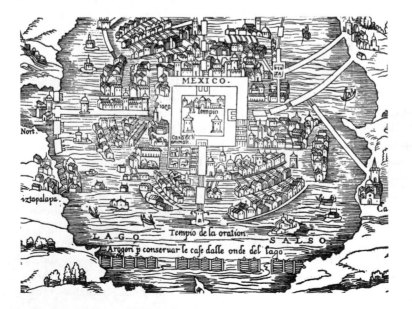

he first set foot upon these shores and first looked down upon the tableland; the king-loving, God-fearing conqueror, his loyalty and religion so
blended after the fashion of ancient Spain that it were hard to say
where the one began and the other ended or which sentiment exercised
over him the greater sway. What a scene to burst upon the first eyes that
beheld it![5] The great city of Tenochtitlan, standing in the midst of the
five great lakes, upon verdant and flower-covered islands, a western
Venice, with thousands of boats gliding swiftly along its streets and its
long lines of low houses diversified by the multitude of its pyramidal
temples, the *teocalli*, or houses of [the gods]—canoes covering the mirrored lakes—the lofty trees, the flowers, and the profusion of water now
so wanting to the landscape—the whole fertile valley enclosed by its
eternal hills and snow-capped volcanoes—what scenes of wonder and of
beauty to burst upon the eyes of these wayfaring men!

Then the beautiful gardens surrounding the city, the profusion of
flowers and fruit and birds—the mild bronze-coloured Emperor himself
advancing in the midst of his Indian nobility, with rich dress and unshod
feet, to receive his unbidden and unwelcome guest—the slaves and the
gold and the rich plumes, all to be laid at the feet of "His most sacred
Majesty." What pictures are called up by the recollection of the simple
narrative of Cortés,[6] and what wonder if in the enthusiasm of the
moment he should unintentionally have exaggerated on some occasions?
He is blamed for cruelty—for injustice—but the first cruelty and the first
injustice consisted in his entering these unknown lands, and disturbing
an inoffensive people. Once considering it his duty to God and his King
to subdue them, where was his alternative?[7] And how forcibly [these
pictures] return to the mind now when, after a lapse of three centuries,
we behold for the first time the city of palaces raised upon the ruins of
the Indian capital. It seemed scarcely possible that we were indeed so
near the end of our long and arduous journey, and in the midst of so
different a scene, only two months minus two days since leaving New
York and stepping aboard the *Norma*. How much land and sea we had
passed over since then! How much we had seen! How many different
climates, even in the space of the last four days!

But my thoughts which had wandered three centuries into the past
were soon recalled to the present by the appearance in the distance of an
officer in full uniform at the head of his troop, who came out by order of
the government to welcome Calderón, the bearer of the olive-branch from
ancient Spain. [He] had been on horseback waiting for us since the
day before. As it was beginning to rain, the officer, a young man,
Colonel Miguel Andrade, accepted our offer of taking shelter in the
diligence. We had now an immense troop galloping along with the
diligence and had not gone far before we perceived that—in spite of the
pouring rain, and that it was already beginning to grow dusk—there were
innumerable carriages and horsemen forming an immense crowd, all

coming out to welcome us. Shortly after, the diligence was stopped, and we were requested to get into a very splendid carriage all crimson and gold, into which the officer got also. [It had] the arms of the republic, the eagle and nopal, embroidered in gold on the roof inside, and [was] drawn by four handsome white horses. The carriage cost ten thousand dollars. In the midst of this immense procession—the troops, carriages, horsemen, and crowd all following—we made our entry into the city of Montezuma.

Before arriving at the city, everything became arid and flat. On each side, where the waters of the *lagunas,* covered with their gay canoes, once surrounded the city, forming canals through its streets, we now see half-drained melancholy marshy lands, little enlivened by great flights of wild duck and waterfowl. But the bleakness of the natural scenery was concealed by the gay appearance of the procession—the scarlet and gold uniforms, the bright-coloured sarapes, the dresses of the gentlemen (most, I believe, Spaniards), with their handsome horses, high Mexican saddles, gold-embroidered *anqueras* generally of black fur, their Mexican hats ornamented with gold, richly furred jackets, pantaloons with hanging silver buttons, stamped-leather boots, silver stirrups, and graceful *mangas* with black or coloured velvet capes.

At last we arrived at the gates of Mexico. Here the troops halted, and three enthusiastic cheers were given as we passed. It was now nearly dusk, and the rain was pouring in torrents, yet at the gates we met more carriages full of ladies and gentlemen, who joined the cavalcade. We found that a house in the suburbs at Buenavista had been taken and furnished for us *provisoirement* by the kindness of the Spaniards, especially of a rich merchant who accompanied us in the carriage, Don Manuel Martinez del Campo; consequently we passed all through Mexico before reaching our destination, always in the midst of the procession, on account of which and of the ill-paved streets, which seemed very bad, we went slowly. Through the rain and the darkness we got an occasional faint lamp-light glimpse of high buildings, churches, and convents. Arrived at length in the midst of torrents of rain, Calderón got out of the carriage and returned thanks to the multitude for his reception, giving several ounces to the sergeant for the soldiers. We then entered the house, accompanied by Don Manuel, the Mexican officer, and by a large party of Spaniards.

We found the house very nice, especially considering that it had been furnished for us in eight-and-forty hours. We also found an excellent supper smoking on the table, to which more especially did justice the poor little officer who had been on horseback since the dawn of morning, without breakfast. Amongst others was a New Orleans gentleman, good-looking but rather like an adventurer, who on the strength of having met Calderón in the United States made himself very much at home, and was profuse in his offers of service.[8]

Meanwhile the diligence containing the Duchess, Don Miguel, and the luggage had not yet arrived, and I became seriously apprehensive, not of any danger that might have occurred, but of the humour in which Her Grace would probably arrive. Nor were my fears unfounded, for no sooner did she about nine o'clock flounce in, than she declared her intention of setting off for New Orleans the next morning, and was fortunately so very outrageous that she gave me an opportunity of speaking my mind, which appears from its rarity to have had a good effect upon her, as she has been a perfect *godsend* ever since. It appears that the robbers had mingled with the crowd, and followed the diligence in hopes of plunder—insomuch that Don Miguel was obliged to procure two carriages, one for the servants, while into another he put the luggage, mounting in front himself to look out—all which had taken time. The poor man was drenched with rain, and once in his life quite worn out— "No *es verdad?"* as he says at the end of all his sentences. I gave him half a tumbler of sherry which he stood much in need of. We found that much of this confusion and difficulty, which was chiefly caused by the storm and darkness, would have been avoided had we left Puebla some hours sooner. However, "All's well that ends well."

At last all the Spaniards kindly took themselves off, and we were left alone—with Estrada, to whom we have given a room in the house.

Thursday: December 26th, 1839

[Last night] I thought of Christmas in Merrie England, and of our family gatherings in the olden time, and, as if one had not travelled enough in the body, began travelling in the mind, away to far different, and distant, and long-gone-by scenes; fell asleep at length with my thoughts in Scotland; and wakened in Mexico!

By daylight we find our house very pretty, with a large garden adjoining, full of flowers, and rosebushes in the courtyard, but being unfortunately all built on the ground floor it is very damp, and enjoys a very bad reputation as to health. The master of the house is said to have *died* of *living* here—the Baron de Norman to have suffered two years' rheumatism from the same cause; in short it is probable that we must take another house.[9]

The weather was very fine, rather cool, insomuch that carpets and even "a bit taste o' fire" would have been agreeable. The former we shall soon procure, but there are neither chimneys nor grates, and I have no doubt that a fire would be disagreeable for more than an hour or so in the morning.

The house stands alone, with a large court before it, and opposite to it passes the great stone aqueduct which supplies the city with water, a

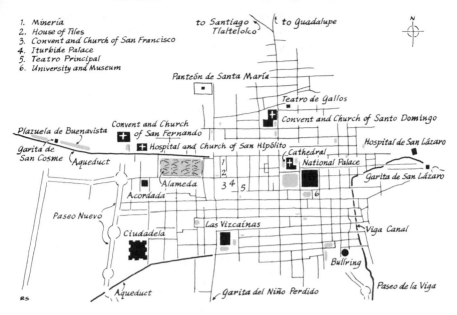

1. Minería
2. House of Tiles
3. Convent and Church of San Francisco
4. Iturbide Palace
5. Teatro Principal
6. University and Museum

to Santiago Tlaltelolco
to Guadalupe

N

Panteón de Santa María

Teatro de Gallos

Convent and Church of Santo Domingo

Plazuela de Buenavista
Convent and Church of San Fernando

Garita de San Cosme
Aqueduct
Hospital and Church of San Hipólito
Cathedral
National Palace
Hospital de San Lázaro
Garita de San Lázaro

Alameda
Acordada
Paseo Nuevo
Ciudadela
Las Vizcaínas
Viga Canal

Aqueduct
Garita del Niño Perdido
Bullring
Paseo de la Viga

magnificent work of the Spaniards, though not more so, probably, than those which supplied the ancient Tenochtitlan. Behind it we see nothing but several oldish houses, with trees, so that we seem almost in the country. To the right is one large building, with a garden and olive-ground, where the English legation formerly lived, a palace in size, since occupied by Santa Anna, and which now belongs to Señor Pérez Gálvez—a house which we shall be glad to have if the proprietor will consent to let it.

But what attracts our attention above all are the most curious and picturesque groups and figures that ever were seen here below—which we see from the windows. The men bronze colour and nearly naked, with nothing but a piece of blanket or a sarape half thrown over them, carrying lightly on their heads earthen basins, precisely the colour of their own skin, so that they look altogether like figures of terra cotta, these basins filled with sweetmeats or white pyramids of grease (*mantequilla*) or bread; the women with the invariable *rebozo,* short petticoats of two colours, sometimes all rags, yet with a lace border appearing on their undergarment, no stockings, and dirty white satin shoes, rather shorter than their small brown feet; gentlemen on horseback with their high Mexican saddles and handsome sarapes—gilt stirrups—a sort of half military coat, and the large shining black or white beaver hat with the silver rolls. Add to this the lounging *léperos* with next to nothing on, moving bundles of rags, coming to the window and begging with a most piteous but false sounding whine, or lying under the arches and lazily inhaling the air and the sunshine, or sitting at the door for hours basking in the sun or under the shadow of the wall; Indian women, with their tight petticoat of dark stuff and tangled hair, plaited with red ribbon, laying down their baskets to rest, and meanwhile deliberately *examining* the long black hair of their copper-coloured, half-naked offspring. We had enough to look at from the window for the present.

Several visitors came early—gentlemen, both Spaniards and Mexicans. Señor de Gorostiza, ex-Minister of the Treasury, decidedly the ugliest man to be seen anywhere, with a hump on his back and a smile of most portentous hideosity, yet celebrated for his *bonnes fortunes.* [He has] much pretension to be a *beau garçon*—*au reste* very pleasant—extremely witty and agreeable, and with some celebrity as a dramatic writer.[10] Soon after, Count Cortina,[11] formerly attached to the [Royal] Bedchamber in Spain, with a very rich *mother*, himself very extravagant—married to a pretty Andalusian—now entirely Mexicanized, his heart where his interests are. He is very gentlemanlike and distinguished-looking, though certainly not handsome, with good manners, speaks good French, [is] extremely eloquent in conversation and altogether a pleasant man in society. I hear him called *inconsecuente* and capricious, but he has welcomed Calderón, who knew him intimately in Madrid, with all the warmth of ancient friendship. [He is] apparently devoted to Calderón.[12]

We are told that a great serenade has been for some time in preparation, to be given to Calderón, the words, music, and performance by the young Spaniards resident here.

Made some changes in our rooms.

Friday: December 27th, 1839

A day or two must elapse before I can satisfy my curiosity by going out, while the necessary arrangements are making concerning carriage and horses, or mules, servants, &c., our vehicles from the United States not having yet arrived. [It is not] difficult to foresee, even from once passing through the streets, that only the more solid-built English carriages will stand the wear and tear of a Mexican life, and that the comparatively flimsy coaches which roll over the well-paved streets of New York will not endure for any length of time.

Meanwhile we have constant visits, but chiefly from gentlemen and from Spaniards, for there is one piece of etiquette, entirely Mexican— nor can I imagine from whence derived—by which it is ordained that all new arrivals, whatever be their rank, foreign ministers not excepted, must in solemn print give notice to every family of any consideration in the capital that they have arrived, and offer themselves and their house to their *disposición;* failing in which etiquette the newly arrived family will remain unnoticed and unknown. Our cards to this effect are consequently being printed under the auspices of Count C[ortin]a.

I have, however, received the visits of some ladies who have kindly waived this ceremony in my favour; and, amongst others, from the old Dowager and the young Countess of Cortina. The old countess, immensely rich and once very handsome, retains some *beaux restes,* but rather a hard expression—a very distinguished woman, of great natural talent, one of the true ladies of the old school of whom not many specimens now remain in Mexico. [She] was dressed in black velvet, black blonde lace mantilla, diamond earrings and brooch, rouge *à discrétion,* corked eyebrows, &c.[13] The young countess Paulita is extremely pretty, lively, and amiable, a true Andalusian both in beauty and wit. [She was] also in black, with a blonde mantilla—a nice little smart peasant-looking face, with a good-natured, half-wicked expression, a good little figure, but all smothered up with an ill-made gown and an ill-put-on mantilla. She had a pretty little daughter with her—Joaquina—with curled hair— whose good black eyes will certainly produce a kindling effect on the next generation—but spoilt to a *horrid* degree.[14]

They were both extremely kind and cordial; if there are many such persons in Mexico we shall have no reason to complain. I hope I am not seeing the cream before the milk!

The Mexican visits pass in length all that one can imagine of a visit, never lasting less than one hour, and sometimes extending over a whole day. And gentlemen, at least, arrive at no particular time. If you are going to breakfast, they go also—if to dinner, the same—if you are dressing, no matter—if you are ill, *raison de plus* for coming to see you in bed—if you are asleep, they wait till you awaken—if you are out—*à la bonne heure*— they believe you and call again, for they do not dream that you could possibly not want to see them. In this case they pity *you* and promise to come back again, and *so they do.* An indifferent sort of man, whose name I did not even hear, arrived yesterday a little after breakfast, sat still, and walked in to a late dinner with us! These should not be called visits, but visitations, though I trust they do not often occur to that extent. An open house and an open table for your friends, which includes every passing acquaintance; these are merely Spanish habits of hospitality transplanted.

Had a visit from Señor Zamora and his wife, very civil and obliging people—perpetually saying *"Eso es,"* in concert, always agreeing with each other, and with you, and with all the world, almost to the extent of Polonius to Hamlet. Our conversation reminded me of that the whole time they were here. She was a widow—plain—and with money—had been married according to the *horrible* practice prevailing here to her own uncle!!! for thirteen years. His name was *Cristo.*

I have just brought from the garden a lapful of pink roses, clove carnations, and sweet peas. Rosetta could not sing here—

For June and December will never agree.

The weather is lovely, the air fresh and clear, the sky one vast expanse of bright blue, without a single cloud. Early this morning it was cool, but now by ten o'clock the air is as soft and balmy as on a summer day with us.

Saturday: December 28th, 1839

The day of the memorable serenade. I stayed at home to receive visits— though as yet few ladies have called, it being the custom here for all foreigners de faire part de leur arrivée. After dinner, however, some ladies paid me a visit, amongst others the wife and daughter of the Spanish consul, Señor Murphy, who were accompanied by the sister of Count Agreda, whom I took to be a fat married woman of thirty-five, and who turns out to be a fat girl of eighteen. I invited them to stay to the serenade —and considering that they and a few gentlemen arrived about six o'clock, and that the serenade would not begin till twelve, it may be supposed that their visit was long enough and that our conversation, however agreeable it might be, would scarcely hold out that time. So we sat and talked and by nine o'clock we were all nearly overcome by sleep—till I proposed that we should all take a sleep—and, suiting the action to the word, I lay down and covered my face, nearly dead with sleep.

By ten I believe we were already in a refreshing slumber when we were awakened by the sound of crowds assembling before the door, and hundreds of carriages arriving and stopping. But not knowing what style of people they were, we could not invite any of them in as I proposed, thinking that it would be much more amusing—which seemed very inhospitable, as the night, though fine, was cold and chilly. About eleven Paulita Cortina and the count arrived, and the Señora de Gorostiza, a remarkably handsome vulgar woman, a Spaniard, looking nearly as young as her daughters; also the pretty daughters of the proprietress of this house, who was a beauty and is married to her third husband; and a lively little fat talkative woman, Fermina de Lehmann, all Spanish; and who, some on that account, and others from their husbands having been former friends of Calderón's, have not waited for the ceremony of receiving cards. Gradually, however, several Mexican ladies in rebozos, whom we had sent out to invite, came in. Others remained in their carriages, excusing themselves on the plea of their not being en toilette. We had quantities of men, till the room was crowded.

The night was wonderfully cold for Mexico. About midnight arrived a troop of Mexican soldiers, carrying torches, and a multitude of musicians, both amateur and professional, chiefly the former—about sixty or seventy—and men carrying music stands, violins, violoncellos, French horns, &c., &c., &c.—together with an immense crowd, mingled with numbers of léperos into the bargain, so that the great space in front of the house as far as the aqueduct, and all beyond and along the street as far as we could see, was covered with people and carriages. We threw open the windows, which are down to the ground, with large balconies and wide iron bar gratings. It was a very curious sight by the torch light. The Mexican troops holding lights for the musicians; and they of various countries, Spanish, German, and Mexican; the *léperos* with their ragged sarapes, and wild faces, and eyes that gleamed in the light of the torches;[15] the ladies within and the crowd without—all formed a very amusing *spectacle*.

At last the musicians struck up in full chorus a hymn, very well sung, accompanied by the whole orchestra. Then various instrumental pieces, all very well played—overtures and pieces from different operas. The voices were fine, and the instrumental music so good, I could hardly believe that almost all were amateur performers.

A hymn which had been composed for the occasion, and of which we had received an elegantly-bound copy in the morning, was particularly effective. The music was composed by Señor Retes, and the words by Señor Covo, both Spaniards. And at the end of what seemed to be the first act, in the midst of deafening applause from the crowd, Calderón made me come to the window and return thanks in beautiful impromptu Spanish![16] He then at the end of another chorus desired me to step out and say, "Viva la República Mexicana!"—which I did with some assistance from him. Then came shouts from the multitude of *"Viva la España!"* *"Viva el Ministro de España!"* *"Viva Isabel Segunda!"* "Viva Cristina!" "Viva Espartero!" Great and continued cheering. Then Calderón gave in return, *"Viva la República Mexicana! Viva Bustamante!"* and the shouting was tremendous. At last an Andalusian in the crowd shouted out, *"Viva todo el mundo!* (Long live everybody!)," which piece of wit was followed by general laughter—and finished the *vivas.*[17]

After hot punch and cigars had been handed about out of doors, a necessary refreshment in this cold night—which seemed to give general satisfaction, the music again struck up, and the whole ended with the national hymn of Spain with appropriate different words, sung in chorus.[18] The performance and the voices were upon the whole remarkably good, especially for amateurs, which all those who sung were. A young Spanish girl whose fine voice is celebrated here was then entreated by those within, and beseeched by those without, to sing alone the hymn composed in honour of Calderón, which she naturally did not like to do before such an immense crowd. However, being persuaded, she consented at last, and in a fine clear voice like a clarion, accompanied by the orchestra, sung it beautifully, each verse alone, and joined in chorus by the whole crowd. I give you a copy:[19]

Patriotic Hymn which various Spaniards resident in Mexico dedicate to His Excellency Señor Don Angel Calderón de la Barca, Minister

Plenipotentiary and Envoy Extraordinary from Her Catholic Majesty to the Republic, to celebrate his arrival in this Capital.

Our holy laws
Will be acknowledged,
And kings will tremble
At the power of Spain;
And should a tyrant grasp
The sceptre of opprobrium,
From his infamous hand
We shall cause it to fall.
Let us triumph, my friends, &c.

Health to *Isabella,*
Health to *Christina;*
Whom Heaven has destined
To save the country;
And may he freely crown
The white forehead
Of the innocent princess
He swore to protect.
Let us triumph, my friends, &c.

And thou, messenger
Of peace and joy,
Hear the pure voice
Of our loyalty;
Hear the accents
Which we raise to Heaven;
Hear what we cry,
Country! Liberty!
Let us triumph, my friends, &c.

Thou, *Calderón,* shalt be
The worthy symbol
Of grateful reunion,
Of eternal friendship,
Which already has changed,
In both worlds,
Insane discord
Into concord and fraternity.
Let us triumph, my friends, &c.

The music by Señor Don J. N. de Retes; the words by Señor Don Juan Covo.

CHORUS

Let us triumph, my friends,
Let us triumph at length,
And let the country of the Cid
Breathe freely again.

The august *Christina,*
The ornament of Spain,
Imprinted the most tender kiss
On the cheek of *Isabel.*
And "Reign," she said to her,
"Not now over slaves,
But over brave Iberians,
Over a faithful people!"
Let us triumph, my friends, &c.

Where is the perfidious
Army of Carlos?
A celestial thunderbolt
Has turned it to dust—
A thunderbolt which plunged
The wicked one into the abyss—
A thunderbolt which *Liberty*
Launched against Carlism.
Let us triumph, my friends, &c.

Of the brave chief,
Of the good, the valiant,
Let us gird the forehead
With myrtle and laurel.
Thy brave right hand,
Heroic warrior,
Thy right hand, *Espartero,*
Subdued the disloyal one.
Let us triumph, my friends, &c.

The air was rent with *vivas!* and *bravos!* as the Señorita de F_____ concluded.[20] Her voice was beautiful and, after the first moment of embarrassment, she sang with much spirit and enthusiasm. This was the finale of the serenade. When all was over the serenaders were invited in, and were in such numbers that the room would scarcely hold them all. More cigars, more punch, and returning of thanks. About three o'clock the crowd began to disperse, and at length, after those Spanish leave-taking which are really no joke, had ended, Captain Estrada, Calderón, and I—all three excessively cold and shivering, having passed the night at the open window—consoled ourselves with hot chocolate and punch, and went to dream of sweet-sounding harmonies. Altogether it was a scene which I would not have missed for a great deal.

The enthusiasm caused by the arrival of *El Señor Ministro*, the first minister from Spain, seems gradually to increase. The actors are to give him a *función extraordinaria* at the theatre—the matadors are to give him a bullfight extraordinary, with fireworks. Much jealousy is said to be excited amongst the other diplomats, which after all is natural enough. But in all this you must not suppose there is any personal compliment. It is merely intended as a mark of good will towards the first representative of the Spanish monarchy who brings from the mother country the formal acknowledgement of Mexican independence.[21]

"RECEIVED WITH
GREAT ETIQUETTE"

7

A Visit to the President

Sunday: December 29th, 1839
Plazuela de Buenavista,[1] Mexico

I made my debut in Mexico by going to mass in the cathedral. We drove through the Alameda, near which we live, and admired its noble trees, flowers, and fountains, all sparkling in the sun. We met but few carriages there, an occasional gentleman on horseback, and a few solitary-looking people resting on the stone benches—also plenty of beggars, and the *forçats* in chains watering the avenues.[2] We passed through the Calle San Francisco, the handsomest street in Mexico both as to shops and houses (containing, amongst others, the richly-carved but now half-ruined palace of Iturbide),[3] and which terminates in the great square where stand the cathedral and the palace. The streets were crowded, it being a holiday; and the purity of the atmosphere, with the sun pouring down upon the bright-coloured groups, and these groups

so picturesque, whether of soldiers or monks, peasants or veiled ladies; the very irregularity of the buildings, the number of fine churches and old convents, and everything on so grand a scale, even though touched by the finger of time or crushed by the iron heel of revolution, that the attention is constantly kept alive and the interest excited.

The carriage drew up in front of the cathedral, built upon the site of part of the ruins of the great temple of the Aztecs: of that pyramidal temple constructed by Ahuizotl, the sanctuary so celebrated by the Spaniards, and which comprehended with all its different edifices and sanctuaries the ground on which the cathedral now stands, together with part of the plaza and streets adjoining.[4]

We are told that within its enclosure were five hundred dwellings, that its hall was built of stone and lime, and ornamented with stone serpents. We hear of its four great gates, fronting the four cardinal points of its stone-paved court, great stone stairs, and sanctuaries dedicated to the gods of war; of the square destined for religious dances, and the colleges for the priests, and seminaries for the priestesses; of the horrible temple whose door was an enormous serpent's mouth; of the temple of mirrors and that of shells; of the house set apart for the emperor's prayers; of the consecrated fountains, the birds kept for sacrifice, the gardens for the holy flowers, and of the terrible towers composed of the skulls of the victims—strange mixture of the beautiful and the horrible!

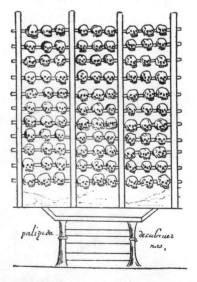

We are told that five thousand priests chanted night and day in the great temple, to the honour and in the service of the monstrous idols who were anointed thrice a day with the most precious perfumes, and that of these priests the most austere were clothed in black, their long hair dyed with ink, and their bodies anointed with the ashes of burnt scorpions and spiders. Their chiefs were the sons of kings.

It is remarkable, by the way, that their god of war was said to have been born of a woman, a *holy virgin,* who was in the service of the temple, and that when the priests, having knowledge of her disgrace, would have stoned her, a voice was heard saying, "Fear not, mother, for I shall save thy honour and my glory"—upon which the god was born, with a shield in his left hand, an arrow in his right, a plume of green feathers on his head, his face painted blue, and his left leg adorned with feathers! Thus was his gigantic statue represented.[5]

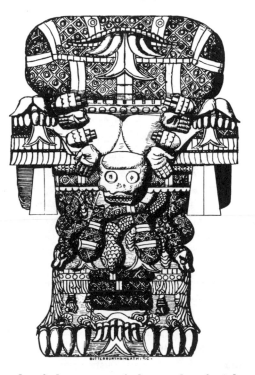

There were gods of the water, of the earth, of night, fire, and hell; goddesses of flowers and corn; there were oblations offered of bread and flowers and jewels, but we are assured that from twenty to fifty thousand human victims were sacrificed in Mexico alone! That these accounts are exaggerated, even though a bishop is among the narrators, we can scarcely doubt; but if the tenth part be the truth, let the memory of Cortés be sacred.[6] While on one side he exterminated with the sword, on the other, with the cross, he stopped the shedding of innocent blood that flowed from human victims; planted the cathedral on the ruins of the temple which had so often resounded with human groans; and in the place of their huge blood-smeared idols enshrined the mild form of the Virgin.

Meanwhile we entered the Christian edifice, a very handsome building, though it has been added to in very bad taste. [It] covers an immense space of ground, is of the Gothic form, with two lofty ornamented
towers, and is still immensely rich in gold, silver, and jewels.[7] The
interior is handsome—a good deal of bad taste and some good paintings.
A balustrade running through it, which was brought from China, is
said to be very valuable, but seems to me more curious than beautiful.
It is a composition of brass and silver.

No one can enter with a bonnet. A mantilla or *rebozo* is necessary.
Not a soul was in the sacred precincts this morning but miserable
léperos in rags and blankets—all ready to steal your handkerchief or anything possible, the cathedral or any church being a favourite place for
that amusement—mingled with women in ragged *rebozos*. At least, a
sprinkling of ladies with mantillas was so very slight that I do not think
there were half a dozen in all.

The floor is thick with dirt and dust, upon which you kneel with
a feeling of horror, and an inward determination to effect as speedy a
change of garments as possible on your return home. Besides, many of
my Indian neighbours were generally engaged half the time in an occupation too disgusting to be named, which I must leave to your
imagination; in fact, relieving their hair from the pressure of the colonial system, or rather, eradicating and slaughtering the colonists who
swarm there in greater numbers than the emigrant Irish in the United
States.[8]

The service was a mass muttered by the priest to himself with his
back turned to the crowd.

I was not sorry to find myself once more in the pure air after mass; and
have since been told that except on peculiar occasions and at certain

hours few ladies perform their devotions in the cathedral. I shall learn all these particulars in time.

We saw as we passed out the Aztec Calendar, a round stone covered with hieroglyphics, which is still preserved and fastened on the outside of the cathedral.

We afterwards saw the Stone of Sacrifices, now in the courtyard of the university, with a hollow in the middle, in which the victim was laid while six priests, dressed in red, their heads adorned with plumes of green feathers (they must have looked like macaws), with gold and green earrings, and blue stones in their upper lips, held him down, while the chief priest cut open his breast, threw his heart at the feet of the idol, and afterwards put it into his mouth with a golden spoon. They then cut off his head, to make use of it in building the tower of skulls, ate some parts of him, and either burnt the rest or threw it to the wild beasts who were maintained in the palace.

These interesting particulars occurred to us as we looked at the stone, and we were not sorry to think that it is now more ornamental than useful.[9]

After leaving the cathedral, Calderón made me fasten on his orders in the carriage, as this was the day appointed for his presentation to the

President, and we drove to the palace—an immense and handsome but ill-kept building—where I left him and the captain and returned home.[10]

Calderón and Estrada returned very much amused with their presentation. [Calderón] was received with great etiquette, a band of music playing in the court, the President in full uniform, surrounded by all his ministers and aides-de-camp, seated upon a throne under a velvet dais, his feet upon a tabouret—the whole being probably the same as was used by the viceroys. *Viva la República!* He seemed extremely embarrassed and ill at ease in this position.[11]

Calderón made a discourse to him and he made one in return, both of which are to be found, by anyone who is curious in these matters, in the *Diario* of the 30th December.[12]

Whilst I am writing a horrible *lépero*, with great leering eyes, is looking at me through the windows, and performing the most extraordinary series of groans, displaying at the same time a hand with two long fingers, probably the other three tied in.

"Señorita! Señorita! For the love of [the] most Holy Virgin! For the sake of the most pure blood of Christ! By the miraculous Conception!—"

The wretch! I dare not look up, but I feel that his eyes are fixed upon a gold watch and seals lying on the table. That is the worst of a house on the ground floor.

There come more of them! A paralytic woman mounted on the back of a man with a long beard. A sturdy-looking individual who looks as if, were it not for the iron bars, he would resort to more effective measures, is holding up a *deformed foot*, which I verily believe is merely fastened back in some extraordinary way. What groans! What rags! What a chorus of whining! This concourse is probably owing to our having sent them some money yesterday. I try to take no notice, and write on as if I were deaf. I must walk out of the room, without looking behind me, and send the porter to disperse them. There are no bell ropes in these parts.

I come back again to write, hardly recovered from the start that I have just got. I had hardly written the last words when I heard a footstep near me and, looking up, lo! there was my friend with *the foot*, standing within a yard of me, his hand stretched out for alms! I was so frightened that for a moment I thought of giving him my watch, to get rid of him. However, I glided past him with a few unintelligible words, and rushed to call the servants, sending him some money by the first person who came. The porter, who had not seen him pass, is now dispersing the crowd. What vociferous exclamations! [Emilie] has come in and drawn the curtains, and I think they are going off.[13]

In the evening, I was taken to visit the President. The palace is an immense building, containing besides the apartments of the President and his ministers all the chief courts of justice. It occupies one side of the square, but is no way remarkable in its architecture. At the end of every flight of steps that we mounted we came upon lounging Mexican sol-

diers in their yellow cloaks, and women in *rebozos*, standing about. We passed through a sort of hall filled with soldiers with helmets and cloaks. In the antechamber we were received by several aides-de-camp in uniform who conducted us into a very well-furnished room, where we sat for some time, till an officer came to lead us into the reception room, which is a really very handsome apartment, about a hundred feet long, and fitted up with crimson and gold, also well lighted. The President, General Bustamante, now in plain clothes, gave us a very cordial reception.

He looks like a little old New York merchant or doctor—fat and pursy— a good man with an honest, benevolent face, frank and simple in his manners and not at all like a hero. His conversation was not brilliant; I do not know apropos to what, I suppose to the climate, but it turned the whole time upon *medicine*. Indeed, I believe he was a doctor, and a very bad one he must have been. He seems remarkably ignorant and amiable—was a very brave soldier—and makes a very unenergetic and stupid president, though probably an honester one than Santa Anna, who was an energetic rogue—and *is*.

There cannot be a greater contrast, both in appearance and reality, than between him and Santa Anna. There is no lurking devil in his eye. All is frank, open, and unreserved. It is impossible to look in his face without believing him to be an honest and well-intentioned man. An unprincipled but clever writer has said of him that he has no great capacity or superior genius; but that, whether from reflection or from slowness of comprehension, he is always extremely calm in his determinations; that before entering into any project he inquires and considers deeply as to whether it be just or not; but that once convinced that it is or appears to be so, he sustains his ground with firmness and

constancy. He adds that it suits him better to obey than to command, for which reason he was always so devoted a servant of the Spaniards and of Iturbide.[14]

He is said to be a devoted friend, is honest to a proverb, and personally brave, though occasionally deficient in moral energy. He is therefore an estimable man, and one who will do his duty to the best of his ability, though whether he has severity and energy sufficient for those evil days in which it is his lot to govern, may be problematical.[15]

Having made a sufficiently long visit to His Excellency **General Bustamante, we took our leave—and went to pay a visit to the old Countess Cortina.** [She] has a magnificent house of immense size, with suites of large rooms, of which the drawing room is particularly handsome. But although there are cabinets inlaid with gold, fine paintings, and hundreds of rich and curious things, our European eyes are struck with the usual numerous inconsistencies here in dress, servants, &c.—in all of which there is a want of keeping very remarkable. Yet this house, and the one adjoining which also belongs to the family, are palaces in vastness, and the countess receives me more as if I were her daughter than a person with whom she has been acquainted but a few days.[16]

We passed through numbers of rooms, beautifully painted, and found her, Paulita, and the count in a little ill-furnished miserable room, with two candles—the countess with an old *rebozo* and a pair of diamond earrings, Paulita bundled up in shawls and fur, and curling Joaquina's hair—everything looking poor, dirty, and uncomfortable.

We were shown through the house, which is immense and handsome, by the light of one candle. It seemed impossible that the house could belong to the people. In the drawing room, of which the floor, roof and walls are beautifully painted, the subjects religious, there was one of the finest of Broadwood's grand pianos, which nobody ever touches—and a good deal of good music—all the operas, &c. These people would be just as happy in an Indian hut. All seems of very little use or pleasure to them. To sit smoking in an old *rebozo,* any room is good enough. They are, however, very kind and the count is a perfect gentleman.[17]

There are an extraordinary number of street cries in Mexico, which begin at dawn and continue till night, performed by hundreds of discordant voices, impossible to understand at first; but Señor_____[18] has been giving me an explanation of them, until I begin to have some distinct idea of their meaning.

At dawn you are awakened by the shrill and desponding cry of the *carbonero,* the coal-man: *"Carbón, señor,"* which, as he pronounces it, sounds like *"Carbosiu!"*

Then the grease-man takes up the song. *"Mantequilla!* Lard! Lard! At one real and a half."[19]

"Salt beef! Good salt beef! *Cecina buena!"* interrupts the butcher in a hoarse voice.

"Hay sebo-o-o-o-o-o?" This is the prolonged and melancholy note of the woman who buys kitchen stuff, and stops before the door.

Then passes by the *cambista,* a sort of Indian she-trader or exchanger, who sings out, *"Tejocotes por venas de chile?"* A small fruit which she proposes exchanging for hot peppers. No harm in that.

A kind of ambulating peddler drowns the shrill treble of the Indian cry. He calls aloud upon the public to buy needles, pins, thimbles, shirt buttons, tape, cotton balls, small mirrors, &c. He enters the house, and is quickly surrounded by the women, young and old, offering him the tenth part of what he asks, and which, after much haggling, he accepts.

Behind him stands an Indian with his tempting baskets of fruit, of which he calls out all the names, till the cook or housekeeper can resist no longer—and, putting her head over the balustrade, calls him up with his bananas, and oranges, and *granaditas*, &c.[20]

A sharp note of interrogation is heard, indicating something that is hot, and must be snapped up quickly before it cools. *"Gorditas de horno, calientes?* Little fat cakes from the oven, hot?" This is in a female key, sharp and shrill.[21]

Gor - di - tas   de hor - no   ca - lien - tes

Follows the mat seller. "Who wants mats from Puebla? Mats of five yards?"

These are the most matinal cries. At midday the beggars begin to be particularly importunate, and their cries, and prayers, and long recitations, form a running accompaniment to the other noises.

Then above all rises the cry of "Honey cakes! Cheese and honey? *Requesón* and good honey?" (*Requesón* being a sort of hard curd, sold in cheeses.)

Then come the *dulce* men, the sellers of sweetmeats, of meringues, which are very good, and of all sorts of candy. *"Caramelos de esperma! Bocadillo de coco!"*

Then the lottery men, the messengers of Fortune, with their shouts of, "The last ticket, yet unsold, for half a real!" A tempting announcement to the lazy beggar, who finds it easier to gamble than to work, and who may have that sum hid about his rags.

Towards evening rises the cry of *"Tortillas de cuajada?* Curd cakes?" —or "Do you take nuts?"—succeeded by the night-cry of "Chestnuts hot and roasted!" and by the affectionate venders of ducks: "Ducks, oh my soul, hot ducks!" "Maize cakes," &c., &c.

As the night wears away, the voices die off, to resume next morning in fresh vigour.[22]

Tortillas, which are the common food of the people, and which are merely maize cakes mixed with a little lime, and of the form and size of what we call scones, I find rather good when very hot and fresh-baked, but insipid by themselves. They have been in use all through this country since the earliest ages of its history, without any change in the

manner of baking them excepting that, for the noble Mexicans in former days, they used to be kneaded with various medicinal plants supposed to render them more wholesome.[23] They are considered particularly palatable with chile, to endure which, in the quantities in which it is eaten here, it seems to me necessary to have a throat lined with tin.

In unpacking some books today, I happened to take up *Sartor Resartus* which, by a curious coincidence, opened of itself, to my great delight, at the following passage:

> "The simplest costume," observes our Professor, "which I anywhere find alluded to in History, is that used as regimental, by Bolivar's Cavalry, in the late Columbian wars. A square Blanket, twelve feet in diagonal, is provided (some were wont to cut-off the corners and make it circular) : in the centre a slit is effected eighteen inches long; through this the mother-naked Trooper introduces his head and neck: and so rides shielded from all weather, and in battle from many strokes (for he rolls it about his left arm) ; and not only dressed, but harnessed and draperied."

Here then we find the true "Old-Roman contempt of the superfluous," which seems rather to meet the approbation of the illustrious Professor Teufelsdröckh.[24]

8

Chapultepec—
Opening of Congress—Shrine of Guadalupe

Monday: December 30th, 1839
Plazuela de Buenavista, Mexico

A great ball is to be given on the eighth of January in the theatre for the benefit of the poor, which is to be under the patronage of the most distinguished ladies of Mexico. After great deliberation amongst the lady-patronesses it is decided that it shall be a *bal costumé*. Calderón wishes me to wear a Poblana or Mexican dress, which I before described to you, in compliment to the Mexicans, and I am about looking for models. As I am told that the Señora de Gorostiza wore it at a fancy ball some years ago in London, when her husband was minister there, I have sent my maid Emilie to learn all the particulars from her—and we have bought foulards, satin, &c. to make it.

We called today on a family nearly related to the Cortinas,[1] and who have been already most excessively kind to us: Señor Adalid, Cortina's cousin, who is married to a daughter of Don Francisco Tagle, a very distinguished Mexican. We found a splendid, very large, very handsome house—but always with the same uninhabited look—the walls and roof beautifully painted in the old Spanish style which, when well executed, has an admirable effect.[2]

The lady of the house, Conchita Adalid, his second wife, who is only nineteen, I took a fancy to at first sight. She is not regularly beautiful —not very, but rather pretty—delicate in health, and with a bad figure, or at least dreadfully ill-dressed—but has lovely dark eyes and eyebrows with fair complexion and fair hair, and a beautiful expression of the most perfect goodness, with very amiable manners. I was very much astonished by hearing her sing several very difficult Italian songs beautifully with a fine voice and with great expression and wonderful facility. She has a fine contralto, which has been cultivated; but some Spanish ballads and little songs of the country she sang so delightfully, and with so much good nature and readiness, that had it not been a first visit I should have begged her to continue during half the morning.[3] Fine voices are said to be extremely common, as is natural in a country peopled from Spain; and the opera, while it lasted, contributed greatly to the cultivation of musical taste.

In the evening we went to the theatre with the Cortinas, to their box. Anything so disgusting I never saw. Such actors! Such a theatre! Dark, dirty, redolent of bad odours; the passages leading to the boxes so dirty, so ill-lighted, that one is afraid in the dark to pick one's steps through them. Such darkness—horrible odours—dirtiness—are probably unequalled in theatrical annals.[4]

The acting was nearly of a piece. The ugliness of the chief actress, who is Mexican and a favourite, and the faces she makes are equally remarkable. [She] dresses well, bears a high reputation for good conduct, [but] is perfectly wooden and never frightened out of her proprieties in the most tragical scenes. I am sure there is not a fold deranged in her dress when she goes home. [She] is so ugly that she is enough to frighten the orchestra.[5] Besides, she makes such grimaces, and has a most remarkable trick of pursing up her mouth into a smile, and frowning at the same time with tears in her eyes as if personifying an April day, that she is really remarkable. I should like to hear her sing "Said a smile to a tear."

The coolness with which they act is curious—standing talking to each other and sitting with perfect sang-froid.

There was no applause, and half the boxes were empty, whilst those who were there seemed merely to occupy them from the effect of habit, and because this is the only evening amusement. The prompter spoke so loud that as "Coming events cast their shadows before,"[6] every word was made known to the audience in confidence, before it came out upon the stage officially.

The whole pit smoked, the galleries smoked, the boxes smoked, the prompter smoked—a long stream of curling smoke ascending from his box, giving something oracular and Delphic to his prophecies. And more than all, the ladies smoked—so that sociability could go no further. *Il ne manquait* but that the actors should smoke—which they did, men and women in the side-scenes most devoutly. In nearly all the boxes, there were one or two ladies smoking! This is all of a piece—

"The force of *smoking* could no further go."[7]

The theatre is certainly unworthy of this fine city.

Tuesday: December 31st, 1839

We have spent the day in visiting the celebrated castle of Chapultepec, a short league from Mexico, the most haunted by recollections of all the traditionary sites of which Mexico can boast.

Could these hoary cypresses speak, what tales might they not disclose, standing there with their long gray beards and outstretched venerable arms, century after century, already old when Montezuma was a boy, and still vigorous in the days of Bustamante! There has the last of the Aztec emperors wandered with his dark-eyed harem. Under the shade of these gigantic trees he has rested, perhaps smoked his "tobacco mingled with amber,"[8] and fallen to sleep, his dreams unhaunted by visions of the stern traveller from the far east, whose sails even then might be within sight of the shore. In these tanks he has bathed. Here were his gardens, and his aviaries, and his fishponds. Through these now tangled and deserted woods he may have been carried by his young nobles in his open litter, under a splendid dais, stepping out upon the rich stuffs which his slaves spread before him on the green and velvet turf.

And from the very rock where the castle stands, he may have looked out upon his fertile valley and great capital, with its canoe-covered lakes and outspreading villages and temples, and gardens of flowers, no care for the future darkening the bright vision!

Tradition says that now these caves and tanks and woods are haunted by the shade of the conqueror's Indian love, the far-famed Doña Marina, but I think she would be afraid of meeting with the wrathful spirit of the Indian emperor.[9]

We set off early with Count Cortina, in a carriage accompanied by

four armed horsemen—passing over a fine paved road divided by a great and solid aqueduct of nine hundred arches, one of the two great aqueducts by which fresh water is conveyed to the city, and of which the two sources are in the hill of Chapultepec and in that of Sante Fe, at a much greater distance. The day was beautiful—rather oppressive in the sun. The castle, situated on a lofty hill covered with trees and shrubs, is a striking and noble object.

When we arrived, the sleepy soldiers, who were lounging before the gates, threw them open to let the carriage enter, and we drew up in front of the great cypress known by the name of "Montezuma's Cypress," a most stupendous tree—dark, solemn, and stately, its branches unmoved as the light wind played amongst them, of most majestic height, and forty-one feet in circumference—which cannot be spanned by eight men with their arms extended. A second cypress, standing near and of almost equal size, is even more graceful. They, and all the noble trees, coeval with Montezuma, which adorn these speaking solitudes, are covered with a creeping plant, resembling gray moss, hanging over every branch like long gray hair, giving them a most venerable and druidical look.

We wandered through the noble avenues, and rested under the trees, and walked through the tangled shrubberies, bright with flowers and coloured berries, and groped our way into the cave, and stood by the large clear tank, and spent some time in the old garden; and then got again into the carriage, that we might be dragged up the precipitous ascent on which stands the castle, the construction of which aroused the jealousy of the government against the young count whose taste for the picturesque had induced him to choose this elevated site for his summer palace. The castle itself, modern though it be, seems like a tradition! The Viceroy Gálvez, who built it, is of a bygone race![10] (The

Vice-Queen Gálvez was celebrated for her beauty and goodness and was universally adored in Mexico—a sister of hers, who still survives and who paid me a visit the other day, says that her beauty chiefly consisted in the exceeding fairness of her complexion, very few *blondes* having then been seen in this part of the world.)[11]

We were received by a Mexican governor—a fine, old military-looking Spaniard—who rarely resides there, and who received us with great politeness and very civilly led us through all the rooms and conducted us everywhere. The apartments are lonely and abandoned, the walls falling to ruin; the glass of the windows and the carved work of the doors has been sold; and standing at this great height, exposed to every wind that blows, it is rapidly falling into decay—like all the other great works in this country. The interior was never finished; yet, even as it stands, it cost the Spanish government three hundred thousand dollars. When we look at its strong military capabilities and commanding position, fortified with salient walls and parapets towards Mexico, and containing on its northern side great moats and subterranean vaults capable of holding a vast supply of provisions, the jealousy of the government and their suspicions that it was a fortress masked as a summer retreat are accountable enough.[12]

The road to it is pretty, but Chapultepec is not a *show place*. One must go there early in the morning, when the dew is on the grass, or in the evening, when the last rays of the sun are gilding with rosy light the snowy summits of the volcanoes; and dismount from your horse, or step out of your carriage, and wander forth without guide or object, or fixed time for return.

From the gallery or terrace that runs round the castle the view forms the most magnificent panorama that can be imagined. The whole valley of Mexico lies stretched out beneath as in a map: the city itself, with its innumerable churches and convents;[13] the country houses, woods and fields; the two great aqueducts which cross the plain; the avenues of elms and poplars which lead to the city; the villages, lakes and plains which surround it; the frame of noble mountains. To the north the magnificent cathedral of Our Lady of Guadalupe, to the south the villages of San Agustín, San Angel, and Tacubaya, which seem imbosomed in trees, and look like an immense garden. And if in the plains below there are many uncultivated fields and many [of] the finest buildings falling into decay and ruin, the roads broken up, the finest trees cut down, and the whole population in rags—yet, with its glorious enclosure of mountains, above which tower the two mighty snow-tipped volcanoes Popocatepetl and Ixtacihuatl, the Gog and Magog of the valley, off whose giant sides great volumes of misty clouds were rolling, and with its turquoise sky forever smiling on the scene, the whole landscape as viewed from this height is one of nearly unparalleled beauty.

Wednesday: January 1st, 1840

New Year's Day!

The birth of the young year is ushered in by no remarkable signs of festivity in the city. More ringing of bells, more chanting of mass, gayer dresses amongst the peasants in the streets, and more carriages passing along, and the ladies within rather more dressed than apparently they usually are when they do not intend to pay visits.

In passing through the plaza this morning our carriage suddenly drew up to a side and stopped, and the servants took off their hats. At the same moment the whole population—men, women, and children, venders and buyers, peasant, gentleman, and señora, priest and layman, woman with rebozo or señorita with mantilla—fell on their knees, and a more picturesque sight I never beheld. Presently an old coach came slowly along through the crowd, with the mysterious *Eye* painted on the panels, drawn by piebald horses, and with some priests within carrying the Host—bearing the divine symbols. On the balconies, in the shops, in the houses, and on the streets, everyone knelt while it passed, the little bell giving warning of its approach.[14]

It is the custom for them to get into the first carriage they meet, and if in their progress they meet a gentleman's carriage it is expected that he shall get out and the priests take it. However, they did not meet us, as we were then before the door of the palace, where we went to see the opening of congress, the two houses being included in this building.

The house of representatives, though not large, is handsome and built in good taste. Opposite to the presidential chair is a full-length representation of Our Lady of Guadalupe. All round the hall, which is semicircular, are inscribed the names of the signers and heroes of independence, and that of the Emperor Agustín Iturbide is placed at the beginning, on the right of the presidential chair, with his sword hanging on the wall; while on the left of the chief magistrate's seat there is a vacant space, perhaps destined for the name of another emperor. This—the Virgin—the multitude of priests with their large shovel hats,[15] who compose a large proportion of the members—and the entrance of the President in full uniform, announced by music and a flourish of trumpets and attended by his staff, rendered it as anti-republican-looking an assembly as I ever beheld. The utmost decorum and tranquillity prevailed. The President made a speech in a low and rather monotonous tone and very unenergetic voice, which in the diplomats' seat, where we were, was scarcely audible. No ladies were in the house, myself excepted—which I am glad I was not aware of before going, or I should perhaps have stayed away.

Yesterday I received visits from the gentlemen of the diplomatic corps, who are not in great numbers here. England, Belgium, Prussia, and the United States are the only countries at present represented, Spain excepted. The French minister has not arrived yet, but is expected in a few days.[16]

I was not sorry to hear English spoken once more, and to meet with so gentlemanly a person as the minister who for the last fourteen years has represented our island in the republic. His visit, and a large packet of letters just received from Paris and the United States, have made me feel as if the distance from home were diminished by one half.

Thursday: January 2nd, 1840

This morning a very handsome dress was forwarded to me—said to be sent *through* [Atocha], our New Orleans friend, with the compliments of a lady whom I do not know, the wife of General Barrera; with a request that if I should go to the fancy ball as a Poblana peasant I may wear this costume.[17] It is a Poblana dress, and very superb, consisting of a petticoat of maroon-coloured merino, with gold fringe, gold bands and spangles; an under petticoat, embroidered and trimmed with rich lace, to come below it. The first petticoat is trimmed with gold bands up the sides, which are slit open, and tied up with coloured ribbon. With this must be worn a chemise, richly embroidered round the neck and sleeves, and trimmed with lace; a satin vest, open in front, and embroidered in gold; a silk sash tied behind, the ends fringed with gold, and a small silk handkerchief which crosses the neck, with gold fringe, &c. Moreover, the New Orleans gentleman has promised to send two Poblana ladies to show me how to plait the hair, wear the *rebozo*, &c., &c. So the dress Emilie has half made goes for nothing—but I think this is the handsomer of the two.

There is in this city a *doctor* who is my aversion. I have a kind of creeping fear whenever I see him. He wears a half-military dress, rides a handsome horse, is good-looking, and seems very obliging—but he has a cold, stony look, compressed bloodless lips, a hollow voice—and something about him that makes me think he would poison or do anything dreadful, for money.

The actors have just called to inform Calderón that their *función extraordinaria* at the theatre in honour of his arrival is to be given on the third, that a box is prepared for him, and that the play is to be *Don John of Austria—in five acts!*[18]

Friday: January 3rd, 1840

Having sat through *five acts* in the Mexican theatre, we came home very tired and exhausted. I almost excused the ladies for smoking. As for the prompter, his box was in a cloud—one might have imagined another Jupiter. The shape of the prompter's box, by a strange association of ideas, made me feel homesick by reminding me of ———— a Boston hood! I could have fancied beneath it the musical face of old Mary Otis.[19] And can I be so far gone, as to feel *homesick* in thinking of Boston! After all we are but human vegetables.

We went with the Cortinas, not knowing what box the actors had prepared for us. At the end of the first act some alcaldes, the prefect, and other dignitaries came round in much precipitation and carried off Calderón to a large box in the centre which had been prepared for us—and installed him amongst the authorities.

The theatre looked much more decent than before, being lighted up in Calderón's honour. The dirtiness of the boxes was concealed by draperies of silk hung all round the theatre [for] the occasion. The ladies also were in full dress—and except toward the end no cigars were lighted by them—and the boxes crowded, so that one could scarcely recognize the house.

The play was *awfully* long, lasting from eight o'clock till one in the morning. I felt terribly afraid of falling asleep, as the top of the box only reaches the knees, and I might have made a descent into the pit.

Fortunately the grimaces made by the actress kept me awake. We reached home at half past one—and were refreshed by hot chocolate.[20]

Saturday: January 4th, 1840

This morning we drove out to see the cathedral of Our Lady of Guadalupe; Calderón went in one carriage with Count Cortina, and Paulita and I in another, driven by Señor Adalid who is a celebrated whip; the carriage open, with handsome white horses, *frisones* as they here call the northern horses, whether from England or the United States, and which are much larger than the spirited little horses of the country.

As usual, we were accompanied by four armed outriders. The day was beautiful, rather warm in the sun. Adalid is a first-rate coachman. We met nothing but *arrieros*, peasants, *léperos*, and soldiers.

We passed through miserable suburbs, ruined, dirty, and with a commingling of odours which I could boldly challenge those of Cologne to rival. After leaving the town, the road is not particularly pretty, but is for the most part a broad, straight avenue, bounded on either side by trees.[21]

At Guadalupe, on the hill of Tepeyac, there stood in days of yore the temple of Tonantzin, the goddess of earth and of corn, a mild deity who rejected human victims and was only to be propitiated by the sacrifices of turtledoves, swallows, pigeons, &c. She was the protectress

of the Totonac Indians. The spacious church which now stands at the foot of the mountain is one of the richest in Mexico. Paulita and I, contrary to the precepts of St. Paul, had to take off our bonnets before entering the cathedral—no bonnets being permitted within the precincts of a church. Having put on veils, we entered this far-famed sanctuary, and were dazzled by the profusion of silver, gold, and diamonds with which it is ornamented. Before the high altar, Paulita immediately popped down upon her knees, crossing herself. I followed her example.

There were a few women with *rebozos* kneeling about, and *léperos* on their knees counting their beads, and in the midst of an *Ave María Purísima* suddenly turning round and throwing themselves and their rags in your way with a *"Por el amor de la Santísima Virgen!"* &c. And if this does not serve their purpose, they appeal to your domestic sympathies. From men they entreat relief "By the life of the Señorita"; from women, "By the life of the little child!" From children it is "By the life of your mother!" And a mixture of piety and superstitious feeling makes most people, women at least, draw out their purses.

The divine painting of the Virgin of Guadalupe represents her in a blue cloak covered with stars, a garment of crimson and gold, her hands clasped, and her foot on a crescent supported by a cherub. The painting is coarse, and only remarkable on account of the tradition attached to it.

We then went to visit a small chapel covered by a dome, built over a boiling spring—also supposed to be holy—whose waters possess miraculous qualities—and had again to take off our bonnets. It is a building of which the walls are all plastered over with little daubs of

Virgins and saints. [We] bought crosses and medals which have touched the holy image, and pieces of white ribbon marked with the measure of the Virgin's hands and feet. [We] took a drink of the water, which is cold, having only the appearance of boiling. It is not bad, but has a taste of iron.

We climbed (albeit very warm) by a steep path up to the top of the hill, where there is another smaller church or chapel, from which there is a superb view of Mexico; and beside it, a sort of monument in the form of the sails of a ship, erected by a grateful Spaniard to commemorate his escape from shipwreck, which he believed to be owing to the intercession of Our Lady of Guadalupe.[22]

We then returned to the village to call on the bishop, the Ilustrísimo Señor Campos, whom we found in his canonicals, and who seems a stupid-looking good little old man, but no conjurer; although I believe he had the honour of bringing up his cousin, Señor Posada, destined to be Archbishop of Mexico. We found him quietly seated in a large, simply furnished room, and apparently buried over some huge volumes, so occupied that he did not perceive us and was not at first aware of our entrance.

After we had sat a little, Calderón praised a very bad painting of the Virgin of Guadalupe hung on the wall, upon which he observed that he was not quite sure whether it was a resemblance or not, as Our Lady did not appear very often, not so often as people supposed. Then folding his hands, and looking down, he proceeded to recount the history of the miraculous appearance of the Virgin of Guadalupe to an Indian, relating with the utmost naïveté all she said and did, pretty much as follows:

> In 1531, ten years and four months after the conquest of Mexico, the fortunate Indian whose name was Juan Diego, and who was a native of Cuautitlán, went to the suburb of Tlaltelolco to learn the Christian doctrine which the Franciscan monks taught there. As he was passing by the mountain of Tepeyac, the Holy Virgin suddenly appeared before him and ordered him to go, in her name, to the bishop, the Ilustrísimo Don Fray Francisco Juan de Zumárraga, and

to make known to him that she desired to have a place of worship erected in her honour on that spot.[23]

The next day the Indian passed by the same place, when again the Holy Virgin appeared before him, and demanded the result of his commission. Juan Diego replied that in spite of his endeavours he had not been able to obtain an audience of the bishop.

"Return," said the Virgin, "and say that it is I, the Virgin Mary, the Mother of God, who sends thee."

Juan Diego obeyed the divine orders, yet still the bishop would not give him credence, merely desiring him to bring some sign or token of the Virgin's will.

He returned with this message on the twelfth of December, when for the third time he beheld the apparition of the Virgin. She now commanded him to climb to the top of the barren rock of Tepeyac, to gather the roses which he should find there, and to bring them to her. The humble messenger obeyed, though well knowing that on that spot were neither flowers nor any trace of vegetation. Nevertheless, he found the roses, which he gathered and brought to the Virgin Mary who, throwing them into his *tilma*, said:

"Return, show these to the bishop, and tell him that these are the credentials of thy mission."

Juan Diego set out for the episcopal house, which stood on the ground occupied by the hospital now called San Juan de Dios, and, when he found himself in the presence of the prelate, he unfolded his *tilma* to show him the roses, when there appeared imprinted on it the miraculous image which has existed for more than three centuries.[24]

When the bishop beheld it, he was seized with astonishment and awe, and conveyed it in a solemn procession to his own oratory, and shortly after this splendid church was erected in honour of the patroness of New Spain.[25]

It was a curious thing to hear, in this nineteenth century, a bishop with the utmost seriousness recounting a tissue of the greatest absurdities —and not to a parcel of old women, upon whom he might have wished to impose, but to Calderón and Count Cortina, &c. Calderón listened with the most edified and edifying countenance possible—and when it was done, the bishop continued:

"From all parts of the country people flock in crowds to see Our Lady of Guadalupe, and esteem it an honour only to have a sight of her. What then must be *my* happiness, who can see her most gracious Majesty every hour and every minute of the day!" (I who had not been listening very attentively thought he was speaking of the Queen of Spain, and pricked up my ears for a new miracle.) "I would not quit Guadalupe for any other part of the world, nor for any temptation that could be held out to me." And the pious man remained for a few minutes as if wrapt in ecstasy. That he was sincere in his assertions there could be no doubt.[26]

As evening prayers were about to begin, and we wished to hear the organ, we now rose to accompany the wise man to the cathedral. His old woman opened the door for us as we passed out.

"Have my chocolate ready by four o'clock when I return," said the bishop.

"*Sí, padrecito!*" said the old woman, dropping upon her knees, in which posture she remained for some minutes.

As we passed out along the street, to our no small amazement, the sight of the reverend man had the same effect. All fell on their knees as he passed, precisely as if the Host were carried by, or the shock of an earthquake were felt—never was despotic monarch more glorified. Arrived at the door of the cathedral, he took leave of us and gave us his hand, or rather his pastoral amethyst, to kiss. Paulita kissed his hand on which was the immense amethyst ring. I did the same, but through my veil.

The organ sounded fine as it pealed through the old cathedral, and the setting sun poured his rays in through the Gothic windows with a rich and glowing light. The church was crowded with people of the village, but especially with *léperos*.

The Cortinas came home and dined with us. Count C[ortin]a promised to send me tomorrow a box of mosquitoes' eggs, of which they make tortillas and which are considered a great delicacy. Considering mosquitoes as small winged *cannibals*, I was greatly shocked at the idea, but they pretend that these which are from the *laguna* are a superior race of creatures which do not sting. In fact the Spanish historians mention that the Indians used to eat bread made of the eggs which the fly called *axayacatl* laid on the rushes of the lakes, and which they (the Spaniards) found very palatable.[27]

9

"All Mexico in a State of Shock"

Monday: January 6th, 1840
Plazuela de Buenavista, Mexico

Yesterday (Sunday), a great day here for visiting after mass is over.
We had a concourse of Spaniards, all of whom seemed anxious to know
whether or not I intended to wear the Poblana dress at the fancy ball, and
seemed wonderfully taken up about it.

Two indefinite looking young Poblana ladies or women of Puebla,
brought by Señor Atocha of New Orleans, came to proffer their services
in giving me all the necessary particulars, and dressed the hair of
Josefa, a little Mexican girl, to show me how it should be arranged;
mentioned several things still wanting, and told me that everyone was
very much pleased at the idea of my going in a Poblana dress. I thought
everybody had very little to do and was rather surprised that *everyone*
should trouble themselves about it.

About twelve o'clock the President, in full uniform, attended by his
aides-de-camp, paid me a visit, and sat pottering and talking for about
half an hour, making himself very amiable as usual and as agreeable
as he could. Shortly after came more Spaniards, and just as we were in
hopes that the visiting was over, and were going to dinner, we were
told that the Secretary of State, the Ministers of War and of the
Interior, and others, were all in the drawing room. In solemn array they
came, and what do you think was the purport of their visit? To inform
us that all Mexico was in a state of *shock* at the idea of my going
in a Poblana dress, and to adjure me, by all that was most alarming,
to discard the idea!

They assured us that all Poblanas were *femmes de rien*—now this is
what I call a sweeping clause on the part of the Ministry—that they
wore no stockings, and that *la Ministra de España* should by no
means wear, even for one evening, such a dress. They evidently thought
I was going with *bare legs,* &c. I tried to soften them. I brought in my
dresses, showed their length and their decency, but in vain—they were

not to be convinced. Meanwhile, a deputation from the chief ladies of Mexico, whom we do not even know, waited upon Calderón to the same effect, and requested that, as a stranger, I should be informed of the reasons which rendered the Poblana dress objectionable in this country, especially on any public occasion like this ball. It had become a matter of *state*. Some on the other side said it was all jealousy—a fear that after such a popular act Calderón's influence in Mexico would be too strong. In short I was obliged to yield, informing the cabinet council that, as they had spoke too late, I feared—in this land of procrastination—it would be difficult for me to procure another dress for the fancy ball; for you must know that our luggage is still toiling its weary way, on the backs of mules, from Veracruz to the capital. Against this, they protested with equal solemnity—and, with very sage faces, they walked off like men who had performed a solemn duty, and were determined to abide by the consequences.[1]

Early this morning, this being the day of the "bullfight extraordinary," placards were put up, as I understand, on all the corners of the streets announcing it, accompanied by a portrait of Calderón! Count Cortina came soon after breakfast and paid us a visit, accompanied by Bernardo, the first matador, an Andalusian, whom he brought to present to us. I send you the white satin note of invitation, with its silver lace and tassels, to show you how beautifully they can get up such things here. The matador is a handsome but heavy-looking man, though said to be active and skillful.[2] I shall write you an account of my *first bullfight*.

Just as I was dressing for the bullfight, a note marked *reservada* (private) was put into my hands, which for its insolence I insert. The contents appeared to me more odd than pleasant. It was addressed to Calderón, but, he being out, I opened it and was in a great rage in consequence. I translate it for your benefit:

Monday

The dress of a Poblana is that of a woman of no character.[3] The lady of the Señor Don Angel Calderón de la Barca is a señorita in every sense of the word. However much she may have compromised herself, she ought neither to go as a Poblana, nor in any other character but her own. So says to the Señor Calderón, José Arnáiz, who esteems him as much as possible.

I have since heard that the writer, Don José Arnáiz, is an old man and a sort of privileged character who interferes in everything, whether it concerns him or not.

Towards the afternoon there were great fears of rain, which would have caused a postponement of the combat; however, it kept off and the day cleared up, the bulls little knowing how much their fate depended upon the clouds.

A box in the centre, with carpeting and silver lamps, had been prepared for us, which not knowing, we went with our friends the Cortinas into their box adjoining. The scene, to me especially who have not seen the magnificence of the Madrid arena, appeared beautiful and was animating and brilliant in the highest degree. Fancy an immense circle or amphitheatre, with four great tiers of boxes all round and a range of uncovered seats in front, the whole crowded almost to suffocation; the boxes crowded with ladies in full dress, and the seats below by gaily dressed and most enthusiastic spectators; two regiments with bands of music, playing beautiful airs from the Norma [and other] operas; an extraordinary variety of brilliant costumes, all lighted up by the eternally deep blue sky; ladies and peasants, and officers in full uniform—the whole I thought very brilliant. You may conceive that it must have been altogether a varied and curious spectacle.

About half past six, a flourish of trumpets announced the President, who came in uniform with his staff and took his seat to the music of *"Guerra! Guerra! I bellici trombi!"*[4] Shortly after, the matadors and picadors in rich dresses, the former on foot, the latter on horseback, made their entry into the arena, saluting all round, and were received with great cheering.

Bernardo's dress of blue and silver was very superb, and cost him five hundred dollars. The signal was given—the gates were then thrown open, and a bull sprang into the arena; not an immense fierce-looking animal, as they say they are in Spain, but a small, angry, wild-looking beast, with a troubled eye.

> Thrice sounds the clarion; lo! the signal falls,
>   The den expands, and Expectation mute
> Gapes round the silent circle's peopled walls.
>   Bounds with one lashing spring the mighty brute,
> And, wildly staring, spurns, with sounding foot
>   The sand, nor blindly rushes on his foe;
> Here, there, he points his threatening front, to suit
>   His first attack, wide waving to and fro
> His angry tail; red rolls his eye's dilated glow.[5]

A picture equally correct and poetical. That first *pose* of the bull is
superb! Pasta, in her Medea, did not surpass it.[6]

Meanwhile the matadors and the *banderilleros* shook their coloured
scarfs at him—the picadors poked at him with their lances. He rushed
at the first—who left their scarfs on the ground and sprung over the
railing [of the] arena—galloped after the others, and, sticking the horses,
threw the riders and made the horses roll in the dust (both, however,
almost instantly recovering their equilibrium, in which there is no
time to be lost). Then the matadors would throw fireworks, crackers
adorned with streaming ribbons, which stuck on his horns and, as he
tossed his head, enveloped him in a blaze of fire. Occasionally the
picador would catch hold of the bull's tail and, passing it under his
own right leg, wheel his horse round, force the bullock to gallop backwards after the horses—round and round the circle—and throw him on
his face.

Maddened with pain, streaming with blood, stuck full of lances or
darts, and covered with fireworks, the unfortunate beast went galloping
round and round plunging blindly at man and horse, and frequently
trying to leap the barrier, but driven back by the waving hats and
shouting of the crowd. At last, as he stood at bay and nearly exhausted,
the matador ran up and gave him the mortal blow, considered a peculiar
proof of skill. The bull stopped, as if he felt that his hour were come,
staggered, made a few plunges at nothing, and fell. The matador gave
another finishing stroke, and the bull expired.

The trumpets sounded, the music played. Four horses immediately
galloped in tied to a yoke; the music struck up a military air. The bull
was fastened to the yoke and swiftly dragged out of the arena. This last
part had a fine effect, reminding me of a Roman sacrifice. In a similar
manner eight bulls were *done to death*. The scene is altogether fine, the
address is amusing, but the wounding, bleeding, and tormenting of the
bull is horrid and sickening—and as here the tips of his horns are

blunted, one has much more sympathy for him than for his human adversaries.

It cannot be good to accustom a people to such bloody sights. Yet let me confess that, though at first I covered my face and could not look, little by little I grew so much interested in the scene that I could not take my eyes off it, and I can easily understand the pleasure taken in these barbarous diversions by those accustomed to them from childhood.[7]

The bullfight having terminated amidst loud and prolonged cheering from the crowd, a tree of fireworks, erected in the midst of the arena, was lighted. Amidst a blaze of coloured light appeared first the arms of the republic—the Mexican eagle surmounting the cactus or nopal—and, above, a full-length portrait of Calderón represented by a figure in a blue and silver uniform! Down fell the Mexican arms with a crash at the feet of Calderón while he remained burning brilliantly and surrounded by fireworks, in the midst of tremendous shouts and cheers.

Thus terminated this *función extraordinaria* given in his honour, and, when all was over, we went to dine at the old Countess Cortina's. An ill-regulated, ill-dressed dinner—cookery entirely Spanish, though performed by a Parisian cook. The plate looks as if it had so come out of the mine, formed by a freak of nature in a shape resembling spoons and forks.[8] Various men, major domos and otherwise, served at table, and then sat down at table. Old women with *rebozos* assisted them. Everything was confused and ill-served—plenty of it—and quantities of horrid Mexican fruit and ice. After dinner played on the piano and, being rather tired, was glad to get home at last.

Tuesday, January 7th, 1840

The house in which we live is decidedly damp. Otherwise it is convenient and pretty, with a large uncultivated garden filled with roses, sweet peas, and carnations—the most familiar-looking things I have seen in this strange land. [It is] also tenanted by sundry ducks and geese. One of the latter I firmly believe to be the soul of C. M. transmigrated into a Mexican goose—so furious it is in its attacks on me. Today it tore my veil, and even swam across a pond to recommence hostilities in the afternoon.[9]

I should have dined today at Pakenham's, the English minister, but the dampness of the house, or the change of climate, has given me a sort of fever and I must to bed. I enclose the note of Pakenham as being that of a celebrated character:

Mexico 5 January

My dear Sir
The short stay which the Commander of the Jason makes in Mexico leaves me but few days to choose from, to request the favor of His company at dinner—Wednesday is the day of the Ball at the Theatre, and Thursday being the Eve of His departure, might perhaps not be convenient to Him—You will therefore I trust excuse the shortness of the notice in my requesting you to do me the favor to dine here on Tuesday next, at five o'clock.

I feel that I take a great liberty in proposing to Madame Calderon to dine at a Batchelors House, but if she will be so kind as to join the party I shall feel greatly honored—

Am I right in addressing Senor de Estrada as the Captain of the Jason?—

You see that I already address you with the same freedom as if we had been Colleagues of many years standing—

I am, my dear Sir, with great regard,

Yours very faithfully
R. Pakenham[10]

So far as I have seen, he is decidedly the best of the diplomats, who indeed here are not over-numerous: M. de Gerolt, Prussian chargé and his wife—Baron de Norman and his sister, de braves Belges—(they of France have not yet come)—ourselves, and England. Voilà tout—the rest are represented by sundry consuls and vice-ditto of whom I know nothing. I regret much that I cannot dine with P. but the ball tomorrow must be considered. Emilie is running up what she calls a Roman dress.

Thursday: January 9th, 1840

Yesterday was the day of the ball at the theatre. Although, owing either to the change of climate, or to the dampness of the house, I have been obliged to keep my room since the day of the bullfight, I thought it advisable—though feeling excessively ill and feverish—to make my appearance there, in case the old women of the cabinet should think I had taken the pet about the Poblana dress.

Having discarded the costume of the light-headed Poblanas, I adopted that of a virtuous Roman *contadina*, simple enough to be run up in one day: a white skirt, red bodice, with blue ribbons, hair plaited, and a white lace veil put on square behind. Apropos to which headdress, it is very common amongst the Indians to wear a piece of stuff folded square and laid flat upon the head, in this Italian fashion; and, as it is not fastened, I cannot imagine how they trot along without letting it fall.

We went to the theatre about eleven, and found the entrée, though crowded with carriages, very quiet and orderly. The *coup d'oeil* on entering was extremely gay, and certainly very amusing. The ball, ostensibly given for the benefit of the poor, was under the direction of several lady patronesses—Paulita Cortina, Mmes Gorostiza, Guerrero,[11] and others—but such was the original dirtiness and bad condition of the theatre that to make it decent these ladies unfortunately expended all the proceeds of the ball. As it was, and considering all the various drawbacks, the arrangements were very good.

Handsome lustres had superseded the beastly lanterns with their tallow candles, the boxes were hung with bright silk draperies, and a canopy of the same drawn up in the form of a tent covered the whole ballroom. The orchestra, perched up upon a sort of scaffolding, also was tolerably good. All the boxes were filled with ladies, remarkable for presenting an endless succession of China crape shawls of every colour and variety, and a monotony of diamond earrings; while in the theatre itself, if ever a ball might strictly be termed a *fancy* ball, this was that ball. Of

Swiss peasants, Scotch peasants, and all manner of peasants, there were a goodly assortment; as also of Turks, Highlanders, and men in plain clothes. But, being public, it was not of course select, and amongst many well-dressed people there were hundreds of women who, assuming no particular character, had exerted their imagination and the natural taste with which heaven had blessed them to make themselves as absurd as possible—and had succeeded.[12] One, for example, would have a scarlet satin petticoat, and over it a pink satin robe, trimmed with scarlet ribbons to match. Another, a short rich blue satin dress, beneath which appeared a handsome purple satin petticoat; the whole beautifully trimmed with green or yellow ribbons to look fanciful. They looked like signs of the zodiac. *All* had diamonds and pearls—many ill-mounted —old and young and middle-aged, including little children of whom there were many. I did not see one without earrings, necklace, and brooch.

The lady patronesses were very elegant. The Señora de Guerrero wore a literal headdress in the form of a net entirely composed of large pearls and diamonds, which in themselves are a fortune. Paulita de Cortina, as Madame de la Vallière in black velvet looking pretty as usual. But the cold of the house obliged her to muffle up in furs and boas, so that one could not much distinguish what her dress was meant to be. Some good diamonds—and her hair all hanging out of curl, which had a penitential effect. The Señora de G[orostiz]a as a full-blown Mary, Queen of Scots, in black velvet and pearls in wonderful profusion, with a splendid diamond necklace, was extremely handsome. She wore a mistaken cap, introduced here by the Albini in the character of the Scottish Queen, but which, though pretty in itself, is a complete deviation from the beautiful simplicity of the real Queen Mary cap. She certainly looked as if she had considerably passed forty without knowing Fotheringay.[13]

I was introduced to various ladies who are only waiting to receive our cards of *faire part* before they call.[14]

It is the most difficult thing in the world to find out a person's name. "Who is this lady to whom Count C[ortina] introduced me?" asked I of a widow—"fat, fair, and forty"—beside whom I was seated.[15]

"That is Manuelita."

"Manuelita *who?*"

"A daughter of the Count de Peñasco."

"But what is her other name?"

"Manuelita Sánchez y Flores."

"Señora de Flores?"

"No—de Peñasco."

"Then she is married to a Peñasco?"

"Oh, no—to Don Manuel."

"To whom?"
"To Manuelito."
"Manuelito *who*?"
"—de Agreda."
"Then, after all, her name is the Señora de Agreda."
"Yes—Manuelita Sánchez y Flores Peñasco de Agreda."
I have never yet managed to get a more direct answer.[16]

Amongst the girls, the best dresses that I observed were [those of] the Señoritas de Frauenfeld—the one handsome with the figure and face of a Spanish peasant; the other much more graceful and intelligent looking, though with less actual beauty.[17] However, so many of the most fashionable people were in their boxes that I am told this is not a good occasion on which to judge of the beauty or style of toilette of the Mexican women; besides which, these fancy balls being uncommon, they would probably look better in their usual costume.

Upon the whole, I saw few striking beauties, little grace, and very little good dancing. The Mexican women are decidedly neither pretty nor graceful, and their dress is *awful*. The French modistes who come here, and who are in fact the very *scum* of the earth, persuade them into all sorts of follies. Their gowns have all a *hunchy*, loaded look, all velvet or satin. The diamonds, though superb, were frequently ill-set. As to a plain white muslin, the dirtiest *lépera* wears an embroidered one. The dresses, compared with the actual fashion, are made *excessively, incredibly* short, and sticking [out] all round at the bottom like hoops —so that when they *stoop! Caramba!*[18]

Their feet, naturally small, are squeezed nearly double, Chinese fashion, into little ill-made shoes still smaller—so that they look in front like little horses' hoofs. Of course they can neither dance nor walk.

Their heads are dressed by rascally Frenchmen, who make them pay *an ounce* each hairdressing! And as they wear no curls, their hair all being the straight Indian kind, the *coiffeurs* have an easy time on't.

In colour they are (nearly all) *brown*, hair and eyes black—both good—and the latter sometimes superb, but with no expression. The rest of the features regular enough—very often bad teeth—the face round —the figure short, rather broad and almost invariably fat. Lovely hands and good arms, perfect models for a sculptor, the hands especially; the feet painfully small. Very few good complexions.

They are a peculiar contrast to the ladies of the U.S. with their pretty faces and their long scraggy figures. I have seen nothing here approaching to a beauty—and not above half a dozen who can be called pretty. There is much more beauty among the lower classes, only they are too dirty to admire very close. As they take more exercise, their figures are more svelte and graceful, their complexions a deeper and healthier brown, their teeth dazzling white—and they are taller. I do not speak of the unmixed Indian women, who are as ugly and squalid as possible.

The dancing at this ball was unique—but especially the *waltzing!* I never saw anything to equal it in absurdity, unless it were the galloping. The way in which they *padded* round on the middle of the foot, the state of fatigue caused by this unusual exertion, the marvellous dresses composed of all the colours of the rainbow—the whole effect was amusing to a degree.[19]

There were few *gentlemen* in fancy-dresses. There was one intended for a Scotch Highlander! Oh the nefarious *brute!*—and people pointing him out to me as a countryman. Such a disgusting object mine eyes never opened upon. How I wished that Sir William Cumming, Macleod of Macleod, or some veritable Highland chieftain in the true dress could have seen the nasty, fat, miserable creature—and suddenly have appeared to annihilate him, and show the people here what the dress really is![20] There was also a lady in tartan satin with a hat and plumes, *reckoned* remarkably well-dressed *à l'Ecossaise,* and so correct!

There were numbers of awful, unfortunate children—whose dress in this country is pitiable. They are even *more* overloaded than the ladies— bundled up in long satin or velvet dresses, covered with blonde and jewels, and with artificial flowers in their hair. [They] look like little old wizened dowager duchesses.

The ballroom was excessively cold—the nights here being cool. The ancient *smell* of the theatre had not been at all obliterated; nor indeed do I think that "all the perfumes of Arabia" could have overpowered it.[21] To warm myself I danced a set of quadrilles, but the dancing and figures were so absurd and, upon the whole, the dancers were such a queer set, that I found one trial more than enough.

Having walked about—and examined and admired all the varieties of fancy costumes—I, being perished with cold and nearly frozen, went to old Countess Cortina's box on the pit tier, where I found Mme Adalid and procured a cloak. They pointed out to me the most dis-tinguished persons in the boxes, amongst others the family of the Escandóns, who seem very handsome, with brilliant colours and fine teeth—to one of whom (Luz by name), Pakenham is said to have been engaged off and on these ten years. She was dressed in black velvet and diamonds and, at a distance, looked pretty.[22] We remained at the ball until about three in the morning. A man came to the box to offer us refreshments, which we declined—though after all I confess that a cup of hot chocolate would not have been amiss. There was supper somewhere, but I believe attended only by gentlemen.

I had the satisfaction in passing out to see numerous ladies on their partners' arms, and, all bedizened as they were with finery, stop under the lamps, and light their cigars!—cool and pretty.

We returned home, I very cold and by no means feeling agreeably.

Thursday: January 16th, 1840

I have passed nearly a week in a slight fever, shivering, shaking, and hot. I was attended by a Mexican doctor, who seems as ignorant and harmless a creature as ever lived. He was sent me by Gorostiza. Knowing the nature of the tribe here, I took care to have him paid every day as he went out, to prevent his composing a bill—whereat he looked rather blank. Every day he went through the same ceremony, felt my pulse, and ordered me some little innocent mixture, which I never took. But what he especially gave me was a lesson in polite conversation. Every day we had the following dialogue as he rose to take leave:

"*Señora!* (This by the bedside.) I am at your disposal."

"Many thanks, sir."

"*Señora!* (This at the foot of the bed.) Know me for your most humble servant."

"Many thanks. Good morning, sir."

"*Señorita!* (Here he stopped near another bed, bowing.) I kiss your feet."

"Sir, I kiss your hand."

"Madam! (This near the door.) My poor house, and all in it, myself, though useless, all I have, belongs to you."

"*Muchísimas gracias.* Many thanks, *señor.*"

He turns round and opens the door, again turning round as he does so:

"Adieu, madam! Your servant."

"Adieu, sir."

He goes out, half opens the door again, and puts in his head:

"*Muy buenos días, señorita!*"

"*Adiós*"—till the unfortunate patient, exhausted, can say no more.

This civility, so lengthened out, as if parting were such "sweet sorrow," between doctor and patient, seems rather misplaced.[23]

It is here considered more polite to say *señorita* than *señora*, even to married women, and the lady of the house is generally called by her servants "*La Niña*," the little girl, even though she should chance to be over ninety. This last custom is still more common in Havana, where the old Negresses who have always lived in the family, and are accustomed to call their young mistress by this name, never change whatever be her age.

I have received a packet of letters from home which have given me new life and done me more good than the old doctor's visits. All are well—Mamma and Lydia safely arrived.[24] One must be as far off as this to know what letters are, and what those who invented writing deserve. The captain left us yesterday, half killed with rheumatism, owing to the dampness of the house. [He] has taken charge of a box of chocolate stamped with various figures, and of some curious *dulces* for New Brighton.

Our cards, or *faire parts*, giving the Mexicans the tardy information of our arrival having been sent out some days ago, our room is filled with visitors, morning, noon, and night. This custom is rather a singular one—but, being universal, it is as well to submit to it. I copy one, that you may have a specimen of the style, which looks for all the world like that of a shop-advertisement, purporting that Don Angel makes wigs, dresses hair and so forth, while Doña Francisca washes lace and does up fine linen.

> Don Angel Calderón de la Barca, Envoy Extraordinary and Minister Plenipotentiary from Her Catholic Majesty near the Republic of Mexico, and his Lady, Doña Francisca Erskine Calderón de la Barca, inform you of their arrival in this capital, and put themselves at your disposal, in the Street of Buenavista, No. 2.[25]

We are employing all our leisure time in searching for another house. The rents in Mexico are tremendous—nothing decent or tolerable to be had under three thousand dollars per annum, unfurnished.[26] There is also the still more extraordinary custom of paying a sum called *traspaso* —frequently to the amount of fourteen thousand dollars, taking your chance, a very faint one, of having the same *traspaso* repaid you by the next person who takes the house.[27]

The inns are said to be awful—no ladies go there.

We have been several times to see the house of the Marquesa de Uluapa, who died of a cancer, for which reason the Mexicans are afraid either to take the house or to buy the furniture. The house they wish to sell—and, if they cannot sell it, to let it to us, expecting meanwhile that we shall wait for their decision, which we have no mind to do. The *marquesa*, who was *une femme galante*, had furnished her house with a good deal of taste, and some of it we shall probably take. One room newly furnished, with crimson satin with gold-coloured stamp, and curtains of pale straw-coloured silk, we shall probably buy the contents of—and of course be cheated. Another room is furnished with yellow satin, and crimson silk curtains, which they say had just been put up when the *marquesa* took her illness. Another room is furnished with fawn-coloured damask—but faded.[28]

A house which I greatly prefer, but which, being near our present one, is considered rather out of town, is an immense new handsome house, just finished and to be let, dear, but without *traspaso*—with a small garden, also new, and belonging to a General Gual. Moreover,

as the agent of the *marquesa* gives no decided answer, we are not going
to wait here, to be kilt with rheumatism.

Saturday, February 1st, 1840

I have now been visited by and have visited the greatest part of the
Aristocracy of Mexico—and, although the length of the visits is something
a little out of the way, the amusement of the ladies' dresses has not
yet entirely lost the charm of novelty. Since the days of the viceroys,
I imagine such a display of diamonds and pearls, silks, satins, blondes
and velvets, in which the ladies have paid their first visits of etiquette,
has not gladdened the eyes of the republic. My eyes are scarcely yet
accustomed to the [sight].

A few of the dresses I shall record for your benefit, not as being
richer than the others, but because I happen to remember them best.

The Marquesa de San Román, an old lady of seventy, who has
travelled a great deal in Europe and is very distinguished for talents
and information. She has the Grand Cross of María Luisa of Spain,
hates the present state of things, is of a noble Venetian family, and aunt
to the Duke of Canizzaro.[29] Her dress was a very rich black Genoa
velvet, black blonde mantilla, and a very splendid parure of diamonds—
earrings, necklace, &c.—black satin shoes, rouge and corked eyebrows
à *discrétion*. She seems in exceedingly delicate health. She and her
contemporaries are fast fading away, the last records of the days of
viceroyalty. In their place a new race have started up whose manners
and appearance have little of the *vieille cour* about them; chiefly, it is
said, wives of military men, sprung from the hotbeds of the revolutions,
ignorant and full of pretension, as parvenus who have risen by chance
and not by merit must be.

I continue my list after the fashion of the *Court Journal:*

Countess de Santiago.[30] Underdress of rich purple satin, gown of
black blonde, diamond earrings, five or six large diamond brooches
fastening the mantilla of black blonde, necklace of large pearls, and
diamond *sévigné*. White satin shoes, short sleeves, eight large diamond
rings.

The Señora García, the wife of a monk.[31] Dress of white satin, gown
of white blonde, white blonde mantilla, pearls, diamonds, and white
satin shoes.

Mme Subervielle, black velvet dress, white blonde mantilla, pearls,
diamonds, short sleeves, and white satin shoes.[32]

The Señora de Adalid. Fawn-colored satin dress, black blonde mantilla,
diamonds and lapis lazuli, and black satin shoes.

The Señora Barrera, the wife of General Barrera. He was a common soldier of a viceroy, she an uncommonly bad *couturière*. They are equally rich and vulgar, and have the handsomest house in Mexico.[33] Dress of purple velvet, embroidered to the knees in gold and all over with flowers of white silk; short sleeves, and corsage embroidered in gold; white satin shoes and *bas à jour* [openwork stockings]; a deep flounce of Mechlin appearing below the velvet dress which was very short. A mantilla of black blonde, fastened by three diamond aigrettes. Diamond earrings touching her shoulders, of extraordinary size. A diamond collar of immense value, and beautifully set. A necklace of pear pearls, valued at twenty thousand dollars. A diamond *sévigné*. A gold chain going three times round the neck, and touching her knees. On every finger two diamond rings the size of small watches. In her hand a handkerchief entirely covered with gold embroidery, and trimmed with broad Mechlin.

As no other dress was equally magnificent, with her I conclude my description for the present, only observing that no Mexican lady, married or single, has yet paid me her first morning visit without diamonds. Those who have none scarcely go into society or, on the occasion of a ball, such as the last, sell all they have to obtain them.

The usual carriage dress of the ladies, black silk gown and black mantilla, would in itself be pretty, but that the gown is ill made and the mantilla ungracefully put on, so as to make the shoulders appear high and the waist thick. The jewels in the morning are bad taste—but they have few other opportunities for displaying them, and they consider a visit here as an affair of great etiquette. Were it not on the occasion of some such morning visit, the diamonds would be in their cases, wasting

their serene rays in darkness. It is not worse taste than is shown in England at a morning Drawing-Room.

The worst taste they show is in the dirty, untidy state in which most of them are in their own houses in the morning—without stays, slipshod, uncombed hair, dirty gown and *rebozo*—so that one is generally, if not very intimate, kept waiting an hour while the lady of the house performs her toilette on your account, when she hastily puts on a fine gown, sticks on a quantity of pearls and diamonds, satin shoes, &c., and then makes her appearance.

They certainly all appear to greatest advantage with the mantilla. A bonnet entirely disfigures them. They are not accustomed to wear it, and in consequence look awkward in one. Moreover, their style of features and complexion do not suit it, *et de plus*, there is no doubt that a mantilla, *gracefully* put on, as I suppose the Spanish women arrange it, is a thousand times prettier even than a *Herbaut*.[34] If the Parisians wore mantillas, what a lovely dress it would be!—but the climate would make it difficult except in spring and summer.

We dined the other day in the house of Gerolt, the Prussian chargé, who looks as if he thought his wife had condescended much too far in marrying him—and she seems quite of the same opinion. They know best. The dinner was diplomatic, very good and well served. We played and waltzed in the evening—and on the whole had rather an agreeable *affair.* Mme de G. looks as if she had been born and bred in the Castle of Indolence, and when she is particularly *ennuyée* is always taken ill, and leaves the room. "*Nous avons tous nos petites faiblesses* [we all have our little weaknesses]," as the man said when he boiled his grandmother's head in a pipkin.

Last night an attempt was made to break into the house, but our fine little bulldog Hercules, a present from Señor Adalid,[35] kept his ground so well, and barked so furiously, that the servants were awakened, even the porter, the soundest slumberer amongst them; and the robbers escaped without doing further mischief than inflicting a severe wound on the poor animal's paw, which has made him for the present quite lame. Apropos to which matters, a peculiarly atrocious and most cruel murder, of which I have just been hearing the particulars, was committed not very long ago in this neighbourhood, upon Mr. Mairet, the Swiss consul. He was also a leather merchant, and one morning, having sent out his porter on some commission, he was told that three gentlemen who had come in a carriage wished to see him on business. He begged them to walk into his room, and there entered a general in uniform, a younger officer, and a monk. He began to talk with them on business, when suddenly the general, seizing hold of him whilst the others went to secure the door, exclaimed: "We have not come to hear about your goods; we want your money."

The poor man, astounded at perceiving what customers he had to deal with, assured them he kept but little money in the house, but proceeded instantly to open his private drawers, purse, &c., and empty their contents, amounting in fact to a trifle of some few hundred dollars. Finding that he had indeed no more to give them, they prepared to depart, when the *monk* said: "We must kill him, or he will recognize us."

"No," said the officers, "leave him alone and come along. There is no danger."

"Go on," said the monk, "I follow"; and, turning back, stabbed the consul to the heart. The three then re-entered the carriage and drove off at full speed.

A few minutes afterwards the porter, returning, found his master bathed in blood, and rushing out for help to a neighbouring gambling-house, gave the alarm. Several gentlemen ran to his assistance, but he died an hour after, having given all the particulars of the dress and appearance of his murderers, and that of their carriage. By these tokens they were soon afterwards discovered, and by the energy of the governor, then Count C[ortin]a, they were arrested and hanged upon the trees in front of our house, together with a *real* Mexican colonel who had kindly lent the ruffians his carriage for the occasion! It is seldom that crime here meets with so prompt a punishment.[36]

Our friend, Count Cortina, when governor of Mexico, was celebrated for his energy in *el perseguimiento de los ladrones* (persecuting the robbers), as it is called. It is said upon one occasion his zeal carried him rather far. Various robberies having been committed in the city, he had received a hint from the government that the escape of the perpetrators was considered by them as a proof that he had grown lukewarm in the public service. A few days afterwards, riding in the streets, he perceived a notorious robber who, the moment he observed himself recognized, darted down another street with the swiftness of an arrow. The governor pursued him on horseback; the robber made all speed towards the square, and rushed into the sanctuary of the cathedral. The count galloped in after him and dragged him from his place of refuge near the altar. This violation of the church's sanctity was, of course, severely reprimanded, but, as the governor remarked, they could no longer accuse him of want of zeal in the discharge of his duty.

He took as his porter the captain of a gang of robbers, ordering him to stand at the door and to seize any of his former acquaintances who might pass, his own pardon depending on his conduct in this respect. Riding out one day to his country place with his lady, this man accompanying them as a servant, they were overtaken by a messenger who desired the return of the count to the city upon some urgent and important business. It was already dusk, yet the count, trusting to the honour of the robber, ordered him to conduct his lady to the hacienda, and she, alone on horseback with this alarming guide, performed her journey in safety.

Before I conclude this letter, I must tell you that I received a visit this morning from a very remarkable character, well known here by the name of La Güera Rodríguez, or *The Fair Rodríguez*. [She] is the celebrated beauty mentioned by Humboldt as the most beautiful woman he had seen in the whole course of his travels forty or fifty years ago. Considering the lapse of time which has passed since that distinguished traveller visited these parts, I was almost astonished when her card was sent up with a request for admission, and still more so to find that in spite of years and of the furrows which it pleases Time to plough in the loveliest faces, La Güera retains a profusion of fair curls without one gray hair, a set of beautiful white teeth, very fine eyes—but plenty of rouge and wrinkles. Even her lips are painted red, and she looks rather like a Poblana, since the ministry (who ought to know) say they are all no better than they should be. She certainly still retains *de beaux restes* and much pretension to beauty and great vivacity.[37]

I found La Güera very agreeable, a great talker, and a perfect living chronicle. She must have been more pretty than beautiful—lovely hair, complexion and figure, and very gay and witty. She is lately married to her third husband, and had three daughters, all celebrated beauties: the Countess de Regla, who died in New York and was buried in the cathedral there; the Marquesa de Guadalupe, also dead; and the Marquesa de Aguayo, now a handsome widow, to be seen every day in the Calle San Francisco, standing smiling in her balcony—fat and fair.[38]

We spoke of Humboldt and, talking of herself as of a third person, she related to me all the particulars of his first visit, and his admiration of her; that she was then very young, about eighteen,[39] though married and the mother of three children; and that when he came to visit her mother she was sitting sewing in a corner where the baron did not perceive her until, talking very earnestly on the subject of cochineal, he inquired if he could visit a certain district where there was a plantation of nopals.[40]

"To be sure," said La Güera from her corner, "we can take M. de Humboldt there today."

Whereupon he, first perceiving her, stood amazed, and at length exclaimed: *"Válgame Dios!* [God protect me!] Who is that girl?"[41]

Afterwards he was constantly with her, and, she says, more captivated by her wit than by her beauty, considering her a sort of western Madame de Staël. Now as the fame of that star certainly had never reached the ears of the rebozoed Mexicanas, we must fairly infer that this compliment was paid her by Humboldt himself; all which leads me to suspect that the grave traveller was considerably under the influence of her fascinations, and that neither mines, mountains, geography, geology, geometry, petrified shells nor *alpenkalkstein* had occupied him to the exclusion of a slight *stratum* of flirtation. So I have caught him—it is a comfort to think that "sometimes even the great Humboldt nods!"[42]

As a celebrated character I insert her card[43]—but she is never called by any other name than La Güera Rodríguez:

Her sister, the Marquesa de Uluapa, lately dead, is said to have been also a woman of great talent and extraordinary conversational powers; she is another of the ancient *noblesse* who has dropped off. The physician who attended her in her last illness for three months, a Frenchman of the name of Plane, in great repute here, has sent in a bill to her executors of $14,000!!!!!! The doctors here are with few exceptions the most rascally and the most ignorant of all the sons of Galen. Indeed this bill of Plane's excited no great astonishment, though the family refuse to pay it, and there is a lawsuit in consequence.

This is a terrible place to be ill in—where your life and purse are equally exposed to the attacks of the medical robbers. The stories of gross ignorance and barefaced imposition are innumerable—and the French out-Mexicanize the Mexicans in these respects. The extortions of medical men in Mexico, especially of foreign physicians, have arrived at such a height that a person of moderate fortune must hesitate before putting himself into their hands. A rich old lady in delicate health, and with no particular complaint, is a surer fund for them than a silver mine.[44]

One of La Güera's stories is too original to be lost. A lady of high rank having died in Mexico, her relatives undertook to commit her to her last resting place, habited according to the then prevailing fashion in her most magnificent dress, the dress in fact which had been bought for her wedding. This dress was a wonder of luxury, even in Mexico. It was entirely composed of the finest lace, and the flounces were made of a species of point which cost fifty dollars a *vara* (the Mexican yard). Its equal was unknown. It was also ornamented and looped up at certain intervals with bows of ribbon very richly embroidered in gold. In this dress the Condesa de _____ was laid in her coffin, thousands of dear friends crowding to view her beautiful *costume de mort*, and at length she was placed in her tomb, the key of which was entrusted to the sacristan.

From the tomb to the opera is a very abrupt transition; nevertheless, both have a share in this story. There was in Mexico a company of French dancers, a twentieth-rate ballet, and the chief danseuse was a little

French damsel, remarkable for the shortness of her robes, her coquetry, and her astonishing pirouettes. On the night of a favourite ballet, Mademoiselle Estelle made her entrée in a succession of pirouettes and, poising on her toe, looked round for approbation, when a sudden thrill of horror, accompanied by a murmur of indignation, ran round the assembly. Mademoiselle Estelle was equipped in the very dress in which the defunct countess had been buried! Lace, point flounces, gold ribbons; there was no mistaking it! Imagine the feelings of the relatives. Hardly had the curtain dropped immediately after the opera when the little danseuse found herself surrounded by certain competent authorities, questioning her very severely as to where and how she had obtained her dress. She replied that she knew nothing of it, but that she had bought it at an extravagant price from a French modiste in the city! She had rifled no tomb, but honestly paid down golden ounces in exchange for her lawful property. To the modiste's went the officers of justice. She also pleaded innocent. She had bought it of a man who had brought it to her for sale, and had paid him much more than *à poids d'or*, as indeed it was worth. By dint of further investigation and inquiry, this man was identified. It was the sacristan of San _____. Shortsighted sacristan! He was arrested and thrown into prison, and one benefit resulted from his cupidity since, in order to avoid throwing temptation in the way of future sacristans, it became the custom, after the body had lain in state for some time in magnificent robes, to substitute a plain dress before putting the coffin into the vault. A poor vanity after all.

I was told by a lady here that on the death of her grandchild he was not only enveloped in rich lace, but the diamonds of three *condesas* and four *marquesas* were collected together and put upon him: necklaces, bracelets, rings, brooches, and tiaras, to the value of six hundred thousand dollars.[45] The street was hung with draperies, and a band of music played, whilst he was visited by all the titled relatives of the family—poor little thing, in all his dead splendour. Yet his mother mourned for him as for all her blighted hopes, and the last hopes of a noble house. Grief shows itself in different ways; but I think the more it shows itself, the less it is grief.[46]

10

"Settled at Last"

Tuesday: February 25th, 1840
San Fernando, Mexico

A lapse in my Journal. Since writing we have changed our house, having been engaged for some time past in the disagreeable occupations first of finding, then of furnishing, and lastly of entering into a new [one]. We came in on the thirteenth [of] February and have been in the delightful confusion caused by a déménagement—at all times a bore but in Mexico almost an impossibility.

We were very anxious to hire [the house] of the Marquesa de Uluapa, which is pretty, well situated, and has a garden; but the agent, after making us wait for his decision more than a fortnight, informed us that he had determined to sell it. We next endeavoured to procure a house not far from our present residence, a palace in fact, which I mentioned to you before as having been occupied at one time by Santa Anna and at another by the English legation, but the present proprietor cannot be prevailed upon to let it, on the plea that the English legation under Mr. Ward had made such a gachis in the house that they were afraid to let it again. It is a very handsome house, with a beautiful garden and olive-ground—what a sad unreal looking tree that is—but it is not a very secure abode, except with a guard of soldiers.[1]

After searching Mexico, we at length came to the determination of taking up our quarters here. It is a handsome new immensely large house, built by an old man called General Gual, and has the fault of being only too large.[2]

Built in a square like all Mexican houses, the ground floor, which has a stone-paved court, contains about twenty large rooms, besides out-houses, coach house, stables, pigeon house, large garden house, &c. The second story where the principal apartments are, the first floor being chiefly occupied by servants, has the same number of rooms, with coal room, wood room, room for making chocolate, bath room, and water everywhere. Below in the court is a fountain. In the garden there is

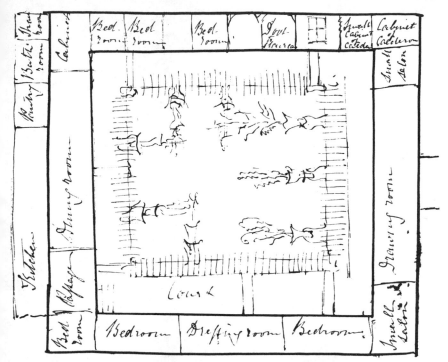

another fountain. On the *azotea,* to which there is a good staircase, there is also water. The *azotea* is excellent, and very spacious, and were the house our own and not a hired one we might build a *mirador,* and otherwise ornament it, but to build and plant for another is too heroic.[3]

The great defect in all these houses is their want of finish; the great doors that will not shut properly, and the great windows down to the ground (which in the rainy season will certainly admit water), making these residences appear something like a crossbreed between a palace and a barn—the splendour of the one, the discomfort of the other.

I will not inflict upon you the details of all our petty annoyances caused by procrastinating tradesmen. Suffice it to say that the Mexican *mañana* (tomorrow), if properly translated, means *never.* As to prices, I conclude we pay for being foreigners and diplomats, and will not believe in a first experience.

However, we are settled at last, and find the air here much purer than in the heart of the city, while the maladies and epidemics so common there are here almost unknown. The distance is inconvenient for those who have no carriage, but our visitors here are so numerous that there we should be overwhelmed, and never have a moment to ourselves.

Behind this house is a very small garden, bounded on one side by the great wall which encloses in part the orchard of the old monastery of San Fernando, within whose vast precincts only seven or eight Carmelite monks now linger. From the window [it] looks a little like that—

—but I have no time just now but to scratch it so with a pen. It is worthy of a sketch, or of being taken by the Daguerreotype.

It is an immense building, old and gray and timeworn, with church adjoining, and spacious lands appertaining to it. At all times it is picturesque, but by moonlight or sunset it forms a most olden-time vision.

When I walk sometimes alone in this high-walled garden by twilight, when the convent bells are tolling, and the convent itself, with its iron-barred Gothic windows and its gray-green olive trees that look so unreal and lifeless, is tinged by the last rays of the sun, the whole seems like a vision, or a half-remembered sketch, or a memory of romance.[4]

Then the sun sets [opposite] the snow-crowned mountains with a bright fiery red, covering their majestic sides with a rosy glow, while great black clouds come sailing along like the wings of night; and then is the hour for remembering that this is Mexico, and in spite of all the evils that have fallen over it, the memory of the romantic past hovers there still. I feel much inclined to call back the old romantic feelings of my youth. But the dark clouds sail on, and envelop the crimson tints yet lingering and blushing on the lofty mountains, and like monstrous night-birds brood there in silent watch; and gradually all the landscape—mountains and sky, convent and olive trees—looks gray and sad, and seems to melt away in the dim twilight.

Then the bright moon rises and flings her silver veil over the mountains, and lights up the plains, glittering and quivering upon the old gray stones, and a sound of military music is heard in the distance far and faint. And all the bells are tolling: from old San Fernando that repeats himself like a sexagenarian; from the towers of the cathedral that stands where Montezuma's Indian temple once reared its head and echoed perhaps to the groans of human victims; from many a distant church and convent—and, above the far-off distant rumbling of carriages and the hum of the city, are heard the notes of a hymn, now rising, now falling on the ear as a religious procession passes along to some neighbouring temple.

But it grows late—a carriage enters the courtyard—a visit. The romance is ended. Men and women are the same everywhere, whether enveloped in the graceful mantilla, or hid by *rebozo*, or *entouré* by a French bonnet; whether wrapt in Spanish cloak, or Mexican sarape, or Scottish plaid.

The manners of the ladies here are extremely kind, but Spanish etiquette and compliments are beyond measure tiresome. First, after having embraced in succession each lady who enters, according to the Mexican fashion—which after all seems cordial to say the least of it— I put the oldest lady, or lady of most consequence, on my right-hand side on the sofa, here a point of etiquette of great importance.[5] The lamps are lighted; the other ladies are seated round on chairs. I begin to make conversation, putting and answering these questions, the following dialogue being *de rigeur:*

"*Cómo está usted?* How are you? *Está usted buena?* Are you well?"

"*Mil gracias, y usted?* At your service; and you?"

"*Estoy sin novedad, para servir a usted.* Without novelty, at your service."

"*Me alegro, y usted?* I am rejoiced; and how are you, señora?"

"*A la disposición de usted, y usted?* At your disposal; and you?"

"*Buena, mil gracias; y el señor?* A thousand thanks; and the señor?"

"*Sin novedad, para servir a usted.* At your service, without novelty," &c., &c., &c.

This occupies three minutes. Besides, before sitting down, there comes:

"*Siéntese usted, señora.* Pray be seated."

"*Pase usted.* Pass first, señorita."

"*No, señorita, pase usted.* No, madam, pray pass first."

"Vaya, sin cumplimiento. Well, to oblige you, without further ceremony; I dislike compliments and etiquette."

And it is a fact that there is no real etiquette but the most perfect *laissez aller* in the world. All these are mere words, tokens of good will.

If it is in the morning, there is the additional question of, "How have you passed the night?" And the answer, "In your service."

Then comes a dead silence, and then I begin to spin conversation. Even in Mexico the weather affords a legitimate theme for the opening for a conversational battery, but this is chiefly when it rains or looks dull which, occasioning surprise, gives rise to observation. If they mention its being fine, it must be superhuman. Besides, a slight change in the degree of heat or cold, which we would not observe, they comment upon.

Then comes the question not so easily answered. *"Cómo le parece a usted México, señora?* [How do you like Mexico, señora?]"—a jealous and curious inquiry made by all the inhabitants of every country in the great Western Hemisphere. Very natural, but useless, because what stranger who does not wish to hurt their feelings can tell them the exact truth? I praise the climate—there one can be enthusiastic with truth. The beauties of the country, with a cautious remark that it is a pity that they are not more cultivated. Chapultepec—no fear of displeasing there. The magnificence of the churches—more tender ground. Here it is as well to change the subject and speak of the smallpox which is raging; of music, for which there is some taste; of the departed opera —here again you are in danger of stumbling;[6] on the theatre—but it is as well [to] abuse it, as they all agree, and to abuse something makes you seem more honest, besides giving you an opportunity of venting your spleen which may be in danger of bursting forth from compression, like a steam boiler.

But the Mexican visit is over, perhaps in two hours, perhaps in three. You must re-embrace the ladies or at least shake hands, and follow them out through the open court to the top of the staircase; and again you must pay compliments.

"Madam, you know that my house is at your disposal."

"A thousand thanks, madam. Mine is at yours, and though useless, know me for your servant, and command me in everything that you may desire." &c., &c., &c., &c.

"Adiós, muy buenas noches. I hope you may pass a good night," &c., &c., &c.

She is at the top of the stair—but alas! at the bottom of the first landing-place she again turns round to catch the eye of the lady of the house, and you must be prepared to nod and bow and mutter more complimentary humbug.[7]

All the ladies address each other and are addressed by gentlemen by their Christian names, and those who have paid me more than one or two visits use the same familiar mode of address to me. Amongst women I rather like this, but it somewhat startles my idea of the fitness of things to hear a young man address a married woman as María, Antonia, Anita, &c. However, things must be taken as they are meant, and as no familiarity is intended, none should be supposed.[8]

But these visitors are gone, and now into the open court the consolatory moon is shining. All clouds have passed away, and the blue of the sky is so blue as almost to dazzle the eyes even in the moonlight. And every star shines out bright, golden, and distinct, so that it seems a sin to sleep and to lose so lovely a sight. But for a true night view, mount upon the *azotea*, and see all Mexico sleeping at your feet: the whole valley and the city itself floating in moonlight; the blue vault above gemmed with stars; and the lofty frame of mountains all bathed in silver, the white volcanoes seeming to join earth and sky. Here even Salvator's genius were insufficient and would fail. We must call up the ghost of Byron. "The mind grows drunk with beauty." The pencil can do nothing here. The poet alone might give a faint idea of a scene so wondrously beautiful.[9]

Wednesday: February 26th, 1840

We went yesterday with Mr. Murphy, the consul,[10] his wife and daughter, and a little curate called Padre Meca to visit the archbishop's palace at Tacubaya, a pretty village about four miles from Mexico where we have already been several times—a favourite ride of ours in the morning. The country round Mexico, if not always beautiful, has the merit of being curious and original. On the road to Tacubaya, which goes by Chapultepec, you pass through large tracts of country almost entirely uncultivated, though so near the city, or covered by the mighty maguey plant, the American agave, which will flourish on the most arid soil and, like a fountain in a desert place, furnishes the poorest Indian with the beverage most grateful to his palate. It seems to be to them what the reindeer is to the Esquimaux, fitted by nature to supply all his wants. The maguey and its produce, pulque, were known to the Indians in the most ancient times, and the primitive Aztecs may have become as intoxicated on their favourite *octli*, as they called it, as the modern Mexicans do on their beloved pulque.[11]

It is not often that we see the superb flower with its colossal stem, for the plant that is in blossom is a useless beauty. The moment the experienced Indian becomes aware that his maguey is about to flower, he

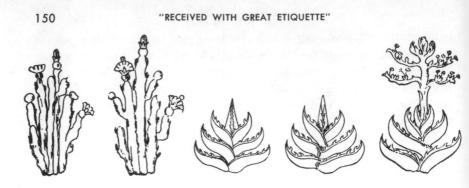

cuts out the heart, covers it over with the side leaves of the plant, and all the juice which should have gone to the great stem of the flower runs into the empty basin thus formed, into which the Indian thrice a day, and during several months in succession, inserts his *acocote* or gourd, a kind of siphon, and, applying his mouth to the other end, draws off the liquor by suction—a curious-looking process. First it is called honey-water, and is sweet and scentless, but easily ferments when transferred to the skins or earthen vases where it is kept. To assist in its fermentation, however, a little old pulque, *madre pulque*, as it is called, which has fermented for many days, is added to it, and in twenty-four hours after it leaves the plant you may imbibe it in all its perfection.[12] It is said to be the most wholesome drink in the world, and remarkably agreeable when one has overcome the first shock occasioned by its rancid odour.

At all events, the maguey is a source of unfailing profit, the consumption of pulque being enormous, so that many of the richest families in the capital owe their fortune entirely to the produce of their magueys. When the owners do not make the pulque themselves, they frequently sell their plants to the Indians. A maguey, which costs a real when first planted, will when ready to be cut sell for twelve or eighteen dollars —a tolerable profit, considering that it grows in almost any soil, requires little manure, and, unlike the vine, no very special or periodical care. They are planted in rows like hedges and, though the individual plant is handsome, the general effect is monotonous.

Of the fibres is made an excellent strong thread called *pita*, of which *pita* they make a strong brownish paper, and might make cloth if they pleased.[13] There is, however, little improvement made by the Mexicans upon the ingenuity of their Indian ancestors in respect to the maguey. Upon paper made of its fibres the ancient Mexicans painted their hieroglyphical figures. The strong and pointed thorns which terminate the gigantic leaves, having the force of daggers, they used as nails and pins; and amongst the abuses, not the uses of these, the ancient sanguinary priests were in the habit of piercing their breasts and tearing their arms with them, in acts of expiation. Besides, there is a very strong

brandy distilled from pulque which has the advantage of producing intoxication in an infinitely shorter period.[14]

Together with the maguey grows another immense production of nature, the *órganos*, which resembles the barrels or pipes of an organ, and
being covered with prickles, the plants growing close together and about
six feet high, makes the strongest natural fence imaginable, besides being
covered with beautiful flowers.

There is also another very curious prickly plant, the nopal, which
generally accompanies these and bears the tuna, a most refreshing fruit,
but not ripe at this season. The plant looks like a series of flat green
embroidered pincushions, growing together and stuck full of little
green needles, with large yellow flowers springing from their sides. But
where these plants grow, there seems little other vegetation.

But though the environs of Mexico are flat and not beautiful, though
there are few trees, whole tracts of land lying uncultivated, uninhabited
haciendas, ruined churches in all directions, and occasional large monasteries forming the centre of some scattered Indian village, still—with its
so lovely climate and ever-smiling sky, the wild flowers luxuriating everywhere, the profusion of roses and sweet peas in the deserted gardens, the
occasional clumps of fine trees, particularly the graceful *árbol de Perú*
(*schinus molle*, the Peruvian pepper tree), its bending branches loaded
with bunches of coral-coloured berries, the old orchards with their blossoming fruit trees, the conviction that everything necessary for the use
of man can be produced with scarcely any labour, but above all the
eternal and magnificent mountains which meet the view wheresoever
the eye turns—all contributes to render the landscape one which it is
impossible to pass through with indifference.

A magnificent ash tree (the Mexican *fresno*), the pride of Tacubaya,
which throws out its luxuriant branches, covering a large space of
ground, was pointed out to us as having a tradition attached to it. It had
nearly withered away when the Ilustrísimo Señor Fonte, the last of the

Spanish archbishops, gave it his solemn benediction, and prayed that its vigour might be restored. Heaven heard his prayer; new buds instantly shot forth, and the tree has since continued to thrive luxuriantly.

Tacubaya is a scattered village, rather arid and *triste,* containing some pleasant country houses and some old gardens with stone fountains. The word country house must not, however, be understood in the English acceptance of the word—or even in the U.S. meaning. The house, which is in fact merely used as an occasional retreat during the summer months, is generally a large empty building, with innumerable lofty rooms communicating with each other, and totally unfurnished or containing the scantiest possible supply of furniture. One room will contain a stock of *perones;*[15] another may boast of a deal table and a few chairs; you will then pass through five or six or as many as ten quite empty; then you will arrive at two or three with green painted wooden bedsteads and a bench; the walls always bare or ornamented with a few old pictures of saints and Virgins, and bare floors ornamented with nothing. To this add a kitchen and outhouses, a garden running to waste and overrunning with flowers, with stiff stone walks and a fountain in the middle, an orchard and an olive-ground perhaps; such are most of the haciendas or country houses that I have yet seen.

One of the best is that of the Countess Cortina, which seems to be the handsomest in Tacubaya. [It] is remarkable for commanding from its windows one of the most beautiful views imaginable of Mexico, the volcanoes, and Chapultepec. From her *azotea* there is also a magnificent view of the whole valley of Mexico. As her garden is kept in pretty good order, and she has an excellent billiard table and even the luxury of an untuned upright piano in one of the rooms, and a mahogany table, but above all a most agreeable society in her own family—and her house the very centre of hospitality—one might certainly with books, horses, &c. spend many hours there pleasantly enough without regretting the absence of the luxurious furniture which, in Mexico, seems entirely confined to the town houses.[16] The countess herself assured me that she had twice completely furnished her house, but as in two revolutions all her furniture and everything was thrown out of the windows and destroyed, she was resolved in future to confine herself to *le stricte nécessaire.*

We went to see a house and garden which has fallen in chance succession to a poor woman who, not being able to occupy her unexpected inheritance, is desirous of selling it. The garden and grounds are a deserted wilderness of sweets.

We were joined by several monks from a neighbouring convent, and with them went to visit the archbishop's palace. *Chemin faisant,* Padre Meca informed us that he was formerly a merchant, a married man, and a friend of Iturbide's. He failed, his wife died, his friend Iturbide was shot; and he joined a small community of several priests who lived re-

tired in the convent of La Profesa which, with its church, is one of the richest in Mexico.

The padres took us to visit the palace of the last Spanish archbishop.[17] The *Arzobispado* is a large, handsome, but deserted building, commanding the same fine view as from the house of the countess, and with a beautiful garden and a fine immense olive-ground, of which the trees were brought from Europe. The garden was filled with large double pink roses, and bunches of the *mille-fleur* rose, which are disposed in arches, a favourite custom here, also with a profusion of sweet peas and jessamine, and a few orange trees. The gardener gave us some beautiful bouquets, and we lingered here till sunset, admiring the view. There is no point from which Mexico is seen to such advantage. It is even a finer prospect than that from Chapultepec, since it embraces the castle itself, one of the most striking features in the landscape.

But just as the sun sunk behind the mountains a sudden change took place in the weather, which had been beautiful. The wind rose, great masses of dark clouds came driving over the sky, and the rain fell in torrents, forcing us to make a hasty retreat to our carriages. And, having omitted to take any precautions and this road not being particularly safe at night, we were probably indebted for our safe return more to "good luck than good guidance"; or perhaps we owed it in part to the padre, for the robbers are shy of attacking either soldiers or priests, the first from fear, the second from awe. The padre took a late dinner with us.

Talking of robbers and robberies, rather a fertile theme of conversation, Señor _____ told me the other day that in the time of a former president it came to pass that a certain gentleman went to take his leave at the palace previous to setting off for Veracruz. He was received by the president, then S. A.,[18] who was alone with his aide-de-camp, General _____, and mentioned to him in confidence that he was about to take a considerable sum of money with him, but that it was so well concealed in the lining of a certain trunk, which he described, that even if attacked by robbers it was impossible that they should discover it, and that therefore he did not think it necessary to take an escort with him. The next day this confidential gentleman left Mexico in the diligence. Not far from the gates the coach was attacked and, strange to say, the robbers singled out the very trunk which contained the money, opened it, ripped up the lining, and, having possessed themselves of the sum therein concealed, departed. It was a singular coincidence that the captain of the robbers, though somewhat disguised, bore a striking general resemblance to the President's aide-de-camp! These coincidences will happen.

My chief occupation lately has consisted in returning visits; and it is certain that, according to our views of the case, there is too wide a distinction between the full-dress style of toilet adopted by the ladies when they pay visits and the undress in which they receive their visitors at home. To this there are some, nay many, exceptions, but *en masse* this is the case.

On first arriving in Mexico one cannot fail—especially if arrived from the United States where an ugly woman is a phoenix—to be struck at the first glance with the general absence of beauty and grace.[19] It is only by degrees that handsome faces begin to dawn upon us. It is however to be remarked that beauty which has not the advantage of colour is always less striking and takes a longer time before it makes an impression on us. The brilliant complexion and fine figure of an English beauty strike every eye. The beauty of expression and finely chiselled features of a Spanish woman steal upon us like a soft moonlight; while a Frenchwoman, however plain she appears to us when she enters the room, says so many agreeable things, has so graceful a manner, so charming a *tournure*, such a piquant way of managing her eyes and even her mouth, that we are very apt to think her a beauty after half an hour's acquaintance, and even lose our admiration for the more quiet and highbred but less graceful *Anglaise* who at first astonished and delighted us.

The beauty of the Mexican women here consists in splendid black eyes, fine dark hair, a beautiful arm and hand, and very small, well-made feet. Their defects are that generally speaking they are too short and too fat, that their teeth are apt to be bad, and their complexion not the clear olive of the Spaniards, nor the glowing brown of the Italians, but a bilious-looking yellow. Their manner of stuffing the foot into a shoe half an inch shorter ruins the foot and destroys their grace in walking, and consequently their grace in every movement. This fashion is fortunately beginning to fall into disuse. It is therefore evident that when a *Mexicana* is by any chance endowed with white teeth and a fine complexion, when she has not grown too fat, and when she does not torture her small foot to make it smaller, she must be extremely handsome.

The general carelessness of their dress in the morning is, however, another great drawback to beauty. It is a fact that nowhere but in England does a woman dress herself on first rising, as she may be seen and visited during the whole day. A demi-toilette *a la française* is perhaps more tasteful, but the half is apt to lead to a quarter, and the quarter to nothing at all. A woman without stays, with uncombed hair and *rebozo*—not in a demi-toilette, but apparently pretty much as she has slept—has need to be very lovely if she retain any attraction at all. Fortunately this indolence is to a certain extent going out of fashion, especially among the younger part of the community, owing perhaps to their more frequent intercourse with foreigners, though it will probably be very long before the morning at home is not considered a privileged time and place for deshabille. Notwithstanding, I have made many visits where I have found the whole family in a perfect state of order and neatness but I have observed that there the fathers and, what is more important, the mothers, had travelled in Europe and established a new order of things on their return.

Upon the whole, the handsomest women here are not Mexicans, that is, not born in the capital but in the provinces. From Puebla and Jalapa and Veracruz, we see many distinguished by their brilliant complexions and fine teeth, and who are taller and more graceful than those born in the city of Mexico; precisely as in Spain, where the handsomest women in Madrid are said to be those born out of it.[20]

The common Indians, whom we see every day bringing in their fruit and vegetables to market are, generally speaking, very plain, with a humble, mild expression of countenance, very gentle, and wonderfully polite in their manners to each other. But occasionally, in the lower classes, one meets with an Indian woman and sees a face and form so beautiful that we might suppose such another was the Doña Marina who enchanted Cortés; with eyes and hair of extraordinary beauty, a complexion dark but glowing, svelte and well-made figure, with the Indian beauty of teeth like the driven snow, together with small feet and beautifully shaped hands and arms, however embrowned by sun and toil. In these cases it is more than probable that, however Indian in her appearance, there must have been some intermarriages in former days between her progenitors and the descendants of the conquerors.

We also occasionally observe very handsome *rancheritas*, wives or daughters of the farmers, riding in front of their farm servants on the

same horse, with the fresh white teeth and fine figures which are preserved by the constant exercise that country women must perforce take,
whatever be their natural indolence; while the early fading of beauty in
the higher classes, the decay of teeth, and the over-corpulency so common amongst them are no doubt the natural consequences of want of
exercise and of injudicious food, added perhaps to the effects of the
climate. There is no country in the world where so much animal food
is consumed, and there is no country in the world where so little is required. The consumers are not the Indians, who cannot afford it, but
the better classes, who generally eat meat three times a day. This, with
the quantities of chile and sweetmeats, in a climate which everyone
complains of as being irritating and inflammatory in the highest degree,
must when combined with want of exercise produce those nervous complaints which are here so general, and for which constant hot baths are
the universal and agreeable remedy—but these, as is well known, while
they soothe, also debilitate. But want of exercise is an extremely good
conservative for the eyes—and one great cause of the beauty of the
Mexican eyes is their being so little used, and never by candlelight.

In point of amiability and warmth of manner, there can be no other
women who can possibly compete with those in Mexico, and it appears
to me that women of all other countries must appear cold and stiff by
comparison. To strangers this is an unfailing charm, and it is much to
be hoped that whatever advantages they may derive in some respects
from their intercourse with foreigners they may never lose this graceful
cordiality, which forms so agreeable a contrast with English and American frigidity.[21]

Friday: February 28th, 1840

How do the Mexican ladies occupy their time? They do not read—
they do not write—they do not go into society. For the most part they do
not play—they do not draw—they do not go to the theatre—nor have
they balls, or parties, or concerts—nor do they lounge in the shops of a
morning, or promenade in the streets—nor do they ride on horseback.
What they do not do is clear, but what do they do?

Calderón received an invitation some weeks ago to attend the *honras*
of the daughter of the Marquis of Salvatierra,[22] that is, the celebration
of a mass to be sung for the repose of her soul. M_____ was observing
today that[23] if this Catholic doctrine be firmly believed, and that if
the prayers of the church are indeed availing to shorten the sufferings
of those who have gone before us [and] to relieve those whom we love

from thousands of years of torture, it is astonishing how the rich do not become poor, and the poor beggars, in furtherance of this object; and that, if the idea be purely human, it showed a wonderful knowledge of human nature on the part of the inventor, as what source of profit could be more sure?

Certainly no expense was spared on this occasion. San Agustín, in itself a beautiful church to which I went alone, Calderón not being able to accompany me, was fitted up for the occasion with extraordinary splendour.[24] The walls and pillars were covered with draperies of rich crimson velvet. Innumerable wax candles were lighted, and an invisible band of music had a fine effect, playing during the intervals of the deep-rolling organ. All the male relatives of the family, dressed in deep mourning, occupied the high-backed chairs placed along one side of the church, the floor of which was covered with a carpet, on which various veiled and mourning figures were kneeling, surrounded by *léperos,* who seem to find mass their chief amusement. I knelt down beside the former.[25]

The chanting, the solemn music, and the prayers, considering the motive of the service, appeared to me very impressive—yet more joyous than sad, perhaps from the pervading feeling that each note, as it rose to heaven, carried some alleviation to the spirit of the young and beloved one for whose repose they prayed, and brought her nearer to the gates of the Holy City.

The poor girl whose *honras* we have celebrated was just twenty when she died—they lived next door to us [at] our first house—so that we were shocked to learn that she had expired on the night of our great serenade (we, of course, not even dreaming of her illness), actually to the sound of that gay music, and amidst the shouting and clapping of hands of thousands!

All the monks of San Agustín with their white hoods and sandalled feet assisted at the ceremony. [They] were ranged near the altar, each carrying a lighted torch. When the service was over they, with the Archbishop at their head, marched out of the church, while we mysterious people remained kneeling. I then followed the crowd, and found at the gate a confusion of carriages and people, rather embarrassing for a *lone female.* However, one of the mourning relations who knew me stepped out with offers of service. As the Archbishop passed, all the gentlemen kissed the hand on which glittered the large pastoral amethyst. He stopped when he came to me and said: "Señora, estoy a los pies de usted"; to which I muttered: "Beso la mano de usted"; and then returned home, our carriage forming one of a file of at least one hundred.[26]

We found on our table another invitation to a very splendid mass which is to be performed in San Francisco on account of the death of a friend of ours, a senator of distinguished family. The style of these invitations is as follows: a device is engraved on the paper, such as a tomb and cypress, and below is printed

José María Adalid,
José Gómez de la Cortina, and Basilio Guerra,
brothers and uncle of the
Senator Don Agustín Torres Torija,
who died on the twenty-eighth of last month
request you to assist at the suffrage of the funeral honours which,
by the desire of his wife, Doña Josefa Adalid, will be celebrated
in the church of San Francisco on the morning of the eighth
of this month of February, 1840 at nine o'clock.[27]

Beside this invitation was a piece of information of a different description:

General Almonte and [Dolores Q]uesada beg to inform
you that they have contracted matrimony, and have
the honour of offering themselves to your disposal.
M_____ Street, No. 24. Mexico, 1840.[28]

Here, as in Spain, a lady after her marriage retains her maiden name; and, though she adds to it that of her husband, she is more commonly known by her own.

From ignorance of another Mexican custom I made rather an awkward blunder the other day, though I must observe in my justification that I had lately been in the agonies of searching for servants, and had just filled all the necessary departments pretty much to my satisfaction. Therefore, when the porter of the Señora de _____ brought me the compliments of his mistress, and that she begged to inform me that she had another servant at my disposal (*otra criada a mi disposición*), I returned for answer that I was greatly obliged but had just hired a *recamerera* (chambermaid). At this the man, stupid as he was, opened his great eyes with a slight expression of wonder. Fortunately, as he was turning away I bethought me of inquiring after the señora's health, and his reply, that "she and the baby were coming on very well," brought the truth suddenly before me—that the message was merely the etiquette used on informing the friends of the family of the birth of a child—a conviction which induced me slightly to alter the style of my answer. *Experientia docet!*

LIFE IN THE CAPITAL

11

Seeing and Being Seen

[Late February, 1840]¹
San Fernando, Mexico

The street in which we live forms part of the Calle de Tacuba, the ancient Tlacopan, one of the great causeways by which ancient Mexico communicated with the continent. The other two were Tepeyac (now Guadalupe) and Ixtapalapa, by which last the Mexican emperor and his nobles went out to receive Cortés on his entrance to Tenochtitlan.

The ancient city was divided into four districts, and this division is still preserved, with a change from the Indian names to those of San Pablo, San Sebastián, San Juan, and Santa María. The streets run in the same direction as they did in former times. The same street frequently changes its name in each division, and this part of the Calle de Tacuba is occasionally called the Plazuela del Zopilote, San Fernando, and the Puente de Alvarado, which is the most classic of the three, as celebrating the valour of a hero.

A ditch, crossed by a small bridge near this, still retains the name of El Salto de Alvarado, in memory of the famous leap given by the valiant Spaniard, Pedro de Alvarado, on the memorable night called the *noche triste* of the first of July, 1520, when the Spaniards were forced to retreat from Mexico to the mountains of Tepeyac.²

On that "sad night"—the rain falling in torrents, the moon and the stars refusing their light, the sky covered with thick clouds—Cortés commanded the silent march of his troops. Sandoval, the unconquerable captain, led his vanguard; and the stern hero Pedro de Alvarado brought up the rear. A bridge of wood was carried by forty soldiers to enable the troops to pass the ditches or canals, which must otherwise have impeded their retreat. It is said that in choosing the night for this march Cortés was guided by the counsels of an astrologer.

Be that as it may, the first canal was happily passed by means of the portable bridge. The sentinels who guarded that point were overcome; but the noise of the struggle attracted the attention of the vigilant priests,

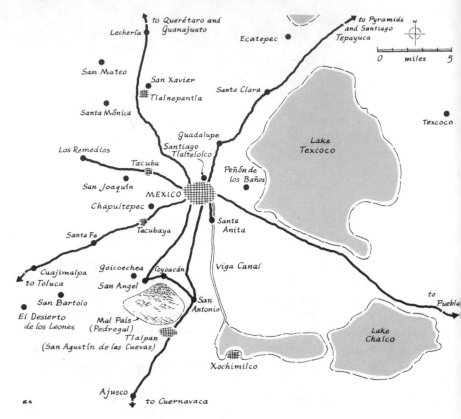

who in the silence of the night were keeping watch in the temple. They blew the holy trumpets, cried to arms, and awakened the startled inhabitants from their slumbers.

In a moment the Spaniards were surrounded by water and by land. At the second canal, which they had already reached, the combat was terrible. All was confusion, wounds, groans, and death; and the canal became so choked with dead bodies that the rear guard passed over them as over a bridge. We are told that Cortés himself swam more than once over the canal, regardless of danger, cheering on his men, giving out his orders—every blow aimed in the direction of his voice—yet cool and intrepid as ever, in the midst of all the clamour and confusion and darkness. But arrived at the third canal, Alvarado, finding himself alone and surrounded by furious enemies, against whom it was in vain for his single arm to contend, fixed his lance in the bottom of the canal and, leaning against it, gave one spring to the opposite shore.

An Aztec author and contemporary of Cortés says that when the Indians beheld this marvellous leap, and that their enemy was safe, they bit the dust (*comieron tierra*); and that the children of Alvarado, who was ever after known as "Alvarado of the leap," proved in the course of

a lawsuit before the judges of Texcoco, by competent witnesses, the truth of this prowess of their father.[3]

In a hitherto unpublished manuscript which has come to light this year in an annual called the *Mosaico Mexicano*, there are some curious particulars concerning the *noche triste*. It is said that the alarm was given by an old woman who kept a stall; and mention is made of the extraordinary valour of a lady called María de Estrada, who performed marvellous deeds with her sword and who was afterwards married to Don Pedro Sánchez Farfán.[4] It is also said that when the Indians beheld the leap they called out: "Truly this man is the offspring of the Sun"; and that this manner of tearing up the ground and eating earth by handfuls was a common Indian mode of expressing admiration.[5] However, Mexico is so rich in traditions that when I particularize this one it is only because we live on the site where the event took place.

Thursday: February 27th, 1840

We went a few days ago to see some effects which are for sale, belonging to a *cura* who died lately, Calderón having heard that he has left some good paintings amongst them. It is not a sale by auction, but anyone who likes goes to buy. We went in the evening, and found there no one but the agent (a man as big as Daniel Lambert),[6] an old woman or two, and the Padre Lyón—a Jesuit, *capellán* of the Capuchin nuns, whose face, besides being handsome, looks the very personification of all that is good, and so mild, dignified, and even holy. What a fine study for a painter his head would be! If there were many such, instead of the hundreds of narrow-minded, intolerant bigots—some sincere and others interested—who fill the pulpits and the convents, the converts to the Catholic faith would be more numerous even than they are. But it is strange that in this age, when all old things seem done away, the old religion is assuming more power daily. The innumerable sects of Protestantism, and the intolerance of each towards the other, is no doubt one of the chief causes of this fact. As for *Mexico,* I believe that the Catholic religion is the sole curb which prevents the most frightful excesses both in rich and poor. We are accustomed to consider its spirit of mystery and despotism as inconsistent with that of republicanism. But whether this be so or not, it is certain that Mexico is a republic only in name—a land of monks, marquises, and military—a land where the lower classes lick the dust before their superiors, kneel to a priest, and crouch to a soldier—a people gentle, superstitious and lazy, living *au jour la journée,* not troubling their heads with politics, stealing and even murdering when they consider it expedient—but chiefly contented to lie basking in the sun, eating tortillas, getting drunk upon pulque, and in the evening going to the Viga, strumming on a guitar, crowning themselves with poppies, and making love to the dirty, bronze-coloured beauties of their own class.[7] A more decided contrast to the cautious, moral, industrious, money-loving, time-saving, incredulous, conceited, independent Yankees probably exists not under the sun. But as to Padre Lyón, he is a monk amongst a thousand.[8]

The old *cura* or priest who died, and who had brought over various valuables from Spain, had a sister who was a leper and who died in the hospital of San Lázaro. As she took her malady in the house, and the priest died soon after—though I believe it was of gout in the stomach—there exists the same prejudice as in the case of the Marquesa de Uluapa, and his house, which is very large and fine, will probably not let. *En attendant,* the executors ask for it six thousand dollars per annum! —a preposterous rent. This dreadful scourge is by no means wholly unknown here; and though it is ordained that all who are afflicted by it shall be shut up in [the] hospital [of San Lázaro], I have met two persons, and one of these in society, who have the disease.[9]

The goods of the defunct, which were for sale, were ranged upon long tables in a very large apartment, where people go to look. There were Virgins and saints, surplices, candlesticks and snuffer trays; boxes of all sorts and sizes. Among other things there was a necklace and earrings of emeralds and diamonds—dreadfully ill-mounted, but not dear. Perhaps they belonged to his sister the leper. There were several tolerable paintings, especially one of the Annunciation. There was the death of San José, a nameless saint, &c.—all religious subjects, as may be supposed. The two last [mentioned] Calderón bought; one, [the Annunciation], I greatly coveted, and Padre Lyón proposed to the agent that it should be presented to me. There was also a standard—or at least two large pieces of embroidered velvet—on which were the arms of Castile, said to have been hung on a portrait of Queen Cristina when she entered Madrid. The agent begged Calderón to buy it, asking at the same time an impossible price for it.

The padre also showed me a large box full of relics from Jerusalem, which he said were not to be profaned by *selling*, but that I might choose whatever I liked; so I returned home with various *Agnus Deis*, crucifixes, and rosaries.

The next day a messenger from Padre Lyón brought me the painting of the Annunciation which I had admired so much, and which is a sketch of Bayeu, a Valencian painter, from his own painting of the Annunciation in the royal chapel of Aranjuez;[10] also the embroidered velvet, begging my acceptance of both. We have since wished to show our sense of the padre's politeness; but he will neither accept presents, nor will he visit anyone but such as in the hour of need require his spiritual services. In the house of sickness and by the bed of death he is ever to be found, but chiefly if it is also the abode of poverty. In the house of the rich man he rarely visits, and then only when his presence has been requested—when he has been called in to administer spiritual consolation to the sick or the dying. But in the dwelling of the lowly, in the meanest and most wretched hovels, he has never to be sought. The guardian and friend of the poor, his charities are equally extensive and judicious.

Saturday: February 29th, 1840

I have now been several Sunday evenings at the Paseo. Yesterday, being a fête day, [it] was very full of carriages and consequently more

brilliant and amusing than usual. This *paseo* is the Mexican Prado or Hyde Park, while the Viga which begins later may be reckoned as the Kensington Gardens of the metropolis, only, however, as succeeding to the other, for there is no walking. Though a few ladies in black gowns and mantillas do occasionally venture forth on foot very early to shop or to attend mass, the streets are so ill-kept, the pavements so narrow, the crowd so great, and the multitude of *léperos* in rags and blankets so annoying, that all these inconveniences, added to the heat of the sun in the middle of the day, form a perfect excuse for their nonappearance on the streets of Mexico.

The Paseo, called *de Bucareli* after a viceroy of that name, is a long and broad avenue bordered by the scattered trees which he planted, and where you encounter several stone fountains whose sparkling waters look cool and pleasant, one ornamented with a gilded statue of Victory. Here, every evening, but more especially on Sundays and fête-days, which last are nearly innumerable, from four o'clock until six or seven may be seen two long rows of carriages filled with ladies, crowds of gentlemen on horseback riding down the middle between these car-riages, soldiers at intervals attending to the preservation of public order, and multitudes of common people and *léperos* mingled with some well-dressed gentlemen on foot. The carriages are for the most part extremely handsome—European coaches with fine horses and odd liveries, mingled with carriages made here, some in the old Mexican fashion, heavy and

covered with gilding, or a modern imitation of an English carriage, strong, but somewhat clumsy and ill-finished. Various hackney coaches, drawn by mules, are seen among the finer equipages, some very tolerable, and others of extraordinary form and dimensions, which bear tokens of having belonged in former days to some noble Don.[11]

Horses, as being more showy, are more fashionable in these public promenades than mules, but the latter animal requires less care and is capable of undergoing more fatigue than the horse. Most families have both mules and horses in their stable, and for those who visit much this is necessary.

The carriages, of which the most fashionable seems to be the *carretela*, open at the sides, with glass windows, are filled with ladies in full toilet, dressed in silks and satins, without mantillas, their heads uncovered and, generally, *coiffées* with flowers or jewels; but the generality, being close coaches, nothing is seen but an indistinct vision, and a passing greeting with the fingers or the fan from one lady to another, as their carriages pass. The whole scene, on the evening of a fête, is exceedingly brilliant, but very monotonous. The gentlemen equestrians, with their Mexican saddles and occasionally fine horses and handsome Mexican dresses, apparently take no notice of the ladies as they pass. But they are generally well aware to whom each carriage belongs and consequently when it behooves them to make their horses caracole or curvet, and otherwise show off their horsemanship to advantage.[12]

When the carriages have made two or three turns, they draw up at different stations in a semicircle a little off the road, and with most solemn faces the inmates sit, as if their padre had condemned them to a gentle penance for two hours, and view the passers-by. Occasional streams of smoke may be seen curling from the carriages—proving that the fair occupants are not denied some consolation—but chiefly, it must be confessed, from the most old-fashioned equipages and from the hackney coaches. Smoking amongst ladies in the higher classes is going very much out of fashion, and is rarely practiced openly except by elderly, or at least by married ladies. In a secondary class, indeed, young and old inhale the smoke of their *cigarritos* without hesitation, but when a custom begins to be considered *vulgar*, it will hardly subsist another generation. Unfeminine as it is, I do not think it looks ungraceful to see a pretty woman smoke.[13]

This *paseo* commands a fine view of the mountains, but I greatly prefer the Viga,[14] which is now the Sunday place of resort and begins to be the fashionable promenade. It has the advantage of being bordered by a canal shaded by trees—which leads to the *chinampas*, and is constantly covered with Indians in their canoes, bringing in fruit and flowers and vegetables to the Mexican market. Early in the morning it is a pretty sight to see them in these canoes, gliding along in a perfect bower of green branches and flowers—their heads dressed with poppy-garlands—dancing, singing, or fighting. Last Sunday one woman stabbed three drunk men, but no one seems to think much of *that*.

In the Alameda, it is very agreeable to walk; but, though I have gone there frequently in the morning, I have met but three ladies on foot, and of these, two were foreigners. Of public promenades [it] is perhaps the prettiest and shadiest, and for an hour or two after dinner may be seen a few carriages rolling along under the trees. But as to *walking*, it is considered wholly unfashionable, immoral, and vulgar. After all, everybody has *feet*, but only ladies have carriages, and a mixture of aristocracy and laziness prevents the Mexican dames from ever profaning the soles of their feet by a contact with their mother earth.[15]

Here then are two amusements for the Mexican ladies—smoking, and rolling in their carriages for an hour or two. But this will not fill up their day, especially as for the most part they rise at six, and go to bed about ten or eleven.[16]

Yesterday on returning from an evening drive—having left Calderón and several gentlemen, who had dined with us, taking coffee and smoking upon the balcony—I found that by good fortune I had escaped being witness of a murder which took place before our door. These gentlemen had for some time observed below some men and women of the lower class, talking and apparently amusing themselves, sometimes laughing, and at other times disputing and giving each other blows. Suddenly one of the number, a man, darted out from amongst the others, and tried to escape by clambering over the low wall which supports the arches of the aqueduct. Instantly, and quite coolly, another man followed him, drew his knife, and stabbed him in the back. The man fell backwards with a groan, upon which a woman of the party, probably the murderer's wife, drew out her knife and gave the wounded man three or four stabs to the heart to finish him—the others, meanwhile, neither speaking nor interfering, but looking on with folded arms and their usual placid smile of indifference.

At the same moment they perceived in the distance some soldiers riding down the street, whereupon, afraid of being seen, the man and woman who had committed the murder tried to enter and take shelter in our house. But fortunately the porter had time to lock them out, and, covered with blood as they were, the soldiers took them up. As this is an everyday occurrence, it excited no sensation whatever. Yesterday I saw a dead man lying near the *Lonja* (the Exchange)[17] and nobody took any notice of him.

"You have been engaged in a disagreeable business," said I to Count Cortina who had come to pay us a visit the other day, and was still in full uniform, having just returned from the execution of one of his own soldiers who had stabbed a comrade.

"Yes," said he, with an air of peculiar gaiety, "we have just been shooting a little *tambour*."[18]

We were invited one Sunday lately to a *día de campo* (a day in the country), a very common amusement here in which, without any peculiar arrangement or etiquette, a number of people go out to some country place in the environs and spend the day in dancing, breakfasting, walking about, &c. This was given at Tacubaya by Don B[asili]o Guerra, a senator who is shortly going upon a pilgrimage to the Holy Sepulchre. We set off about eight in the morning and arrived at Tacubaya in an hour or so—Calderón and other gentlemen on horseback; Paulita I called for. Now the difference between our ideas and theirs on the subject of dress is that, whereas I had my hair dressed and no bonnet, they, because it was a dress occasion, had mounted small bonnets, made by French modistes here, which are considered full dress.

We found about fifty ladies and as many gentlemen arrived. The house is an immense barn—about forty rooms, with bare walls and floors and a few benches and two or three beds—and as usual a garden full of weeds and flowers and a fountain. First the ladies all sat round on benches, and the gentlemen walked about. The music consisted of a band of guitars, from which the performers, five or six common men who had, of course, learned by ear, contrived to draw wonderfully good music and, in the intervals of dancing, played airs from the *Norma, Straniera,* and *Puritani.* The taste for music is certainly universal, the facilities wonderful, the science nearly at zero.[19]

The Mexicans, like their country, remain uncultivated. Of their general talents I can say nothing. Their native *esprit,* generally speaking, seems mediocre—nor do they seem to have much of that native wit for which the common Spaniards are said to be remarkable. But a taste for music they decidedly have, and natural fine voices.

After the ladies had sat, the gentlemen walked, and the musicians played, quadrilles were proposed. The ladies in general wore neither diamonds nor pearls, but appeared in a sort of demi-toilette which, had their dresses been longer and well made, would have been pretty and a vast improvement upon the velvets and blonde and jewelry. But the short petticoats, short waists, and tight shoes were all most inimical to grace. Luz Escandón and P[aulita] Cortina were pretty well dressed.[20]

Mexican women, when they sit, have from their extreme tranquillity rather an air of dignity, and the most perfect repose of feature. For this reason they are always to be seen to most advantage on their sofas, in their carriages, or in their boxes at the theatre.

The dancing is shocking, but I believe there are no masters, et que voulez-vous? Nature does not teach us to dance quadrilles. She does, however, occasionally give a natural grace, which the Mexican ladies have not. Their movements seem fettered. They walk and dance upon the middle of their little Chinese feet. And, being for the most part fat, this, with the extreme shortness of their petticoats, produces an odd effect. Besides, unaccustomed to take exercise, it is not so easy, after a year's repose, to start up and waltz. Probably all they require is example, but the few who go abroad and see how they "manage these matters in France"[21] are soon overpowered by the multitude on their return, dread to lose their popularity by introducing outlandish fashions, and very shortly become re-Mexicanized.

Quadrilles and waltzes succeeded each other, and sauteuses—oh!—all this on Sunday, by the way, when all good Presbyterians are at the kirk, and all decent Episcopalians at church—and for that matter when every Catholic church is full.

Breakfast was announced. There were immensely long tables covered with Mexican cookery, which I find very bad.[22] There was fish, meat and fowl, but all ill-dressed—that is, according to European notions—ham, tongue, vegetables, sweetmeats, fruit of every description—a real Mexican feast.

A great many toasts were given and a great quantity of champagne drank—until a number of young men, chiefly Spaniards, got so drunk that when we rose they all surrounded Calderón, embracing him and entreating in the most affectionate manner their dear minister to stay and drink with them—to enforce which they hid his hat.[23] He escaped from them with some difficulty, and appeared soon after in the garden without a hat, in a very hot sun.

After walking in the garden we went on foot to Countess Cortina's, whose house is the best here; admired the view from her azotea; heard Retes, the musical Apollo of the Mexican ladies, play on the piano, which he does with much execution;[24] and played several games at billiards, in which I distinguished myself for want of skill. We then returned to Guerra's, where the dancing lasted till eight o'clock.

We danced a great deal, quadrilles, waltzes, and Spanish country-dances, walked about in the garden and orchard in the evening, and returned to dance again to the music of the indefatigable guitars. I was tired to death, and was thankful when I heard an order for the carriages. It was dusk when all set off, much about the same time, to bear each other company. Paulita returned with me. I took her home, and refused her entreaties to take an armed man on horseback with me to San Cosme. However, feeling rather afraid in consequence of her warnings, it being very late and I alone, I twisted my fur tippet and shawl together over my arm so as to look like a figure, and made it bob its head up and down, so that the passers-by might think there were two people in the carriage. Whether in consequence or not of this ingenious device I know not, but I arrived in safety, and found Calderón already at home.

The following day, the Countess C[ortin]a having been kind enough to procure an order for permission to visit the Colegio Vizcaíno, which I was anxious to see, we went there with a large party [including] the Countesses Cortina, old and young.

This college, founded by the gratuitous charities of Spaniards, chiefly, as the name imports, from the province of Biscay, is a truly splendid institution. It is an immense building of stone, solid and handsome, in the form of a square, with a court in the middle, on the model, they say, of the marble palace of Madrid. [It] possesses in the highest degree that air of solidity and magnificence which distinguishes the Mexican edifices and which, together with the width and regularity of the streets, the vastness of the public squares, the total absence of all paltry ornament, the balconies with their balustrades and window gratings of solid iron and bronze, render Mexico in spite of its inefficient police one of the noblest-looking cities in the world.

The object of this college is to provide for the education of the children of Spaniards, especially for the descendants of Biscayans in Mexico, a certain number being admitted upon application to the directors. There are female teachers in all the necessary branches, such as reading, writing, sewing, arithmetic, &c. But besides this there is a part of the building with a separate entrance from the street where the children of all the poor, of whatever country, indiscriminately who choose to send them, are educated gratis. These spend the day there and go home in the evening. The others are kept upon the plan of a convent, and never leave the institution while they belong to it; but the building is so large and airy, with its great galleries and vast court and fine fountains, garden and spacious *azotea*, that the children seem very well off. There are *portières* and sisters, pretty much as in a convent, together with an old respectable *rectora;* and the most perfect order and cleanliness prevail through the whole establishment.

We first visited the poor scholars, passing through two immense halls where they sat with their teachers, divided into classes, sewing, writing, reading, embroidering, or casting up accounts—which last accomplishment must, I think, be sorely against the Mexican genius. One of the teachers made one of her pupils, a little girl, present me with a chain made of her own hair which she had just completed. Great order and decorum prevailed.

Among the better classes, the permanent scholars in the upper part of the institution, there are some who embroider astonishingly well—surplices, altar hangings; in short, all the church vestments, in gold or silk. In the room where these are kept are the confessionals for the pupils. The priests are in a separate room, and the penitents kneel before the grating which communicates with it and separates the two apartments. We visited their sleeping rooms which are scrupulously neat and clean, with two green painted beds in each, and a small parlour off it, and frequently ornamented with flowers and birds. The girls are taught to cook and iron, and make themselves generally useful, thus being fitted to become excellent wives to respectable men in their own rank of life.

We then visited the chapel which is extremely rich and handsome, encrusted with gilding, and very large. The pupils and their teachers attend mass in the gallery above, which looks down upon the chapel and is separated by a grating before it. Here they have the organ, and various shrines, saints, *nacimientos*, &c. We were afterwards shown into an immense hall devoted to a different purpose, containing at one end a small theatre for the pupils to act plays in.

All the walls of the long galleries are covered with old paintings on holy subjects, but many of them falling to pieces from damp or want of care. The building seems interminable, and after wandering up and down all through it for several hours and visiting everything —from the old garden below where they gave me a large bunch of roses and carnations, to the *azotea* above which looks down upon every street and church and convent in Mexico—we were not sorry to rest on the antique high-backed chairs of a large handsome apartment, of which the walls were hung with the portraits of the different Spanish directors of the college in an ancient court costume. Here we found that the directors had prepared a beautiful collation for us—fruits, ices, cakes, custards, jellies, wines, &c., all in great profusion and remarkably good.

Rested and refreshed, we proceeded to visit the pupils at their different classes. At the writing class various specimens of that polite art were presented to us. That of the elder girls was absurdly bad, probably from their having entered the college late in life. That of some of the younger ones seemed much more tolerable. It is not long since writing was permitted to form part of a lady's education in Mexico. We saw some really beautiful specimens of embroidery.

Having returned to the hall and theatre, where there was a piano, some of our party began to sing and play. The Señora Gargollo sang an Italian air remarkably well. She is evidently a scientific musician. The Señorita Heras played with a great deal of execution one of Herz's most difficult *combinations*—one of those terribly difficult pieces which Dr. Johnson wished were impossible.[25] A tolerably pretty girl, who is engaged, and placed there by her *novio* to keep her out of harm's way till he is prepared to give her his hand, sang a duet from Norma with another young lady, which I accompanied. Both had fine voices, but no slightest notion of what they were singing.

My friend Paulita C[ortina], who has no voice at all, sung some of the innumerable and amusing verses of the *Jota Aragonesa* and other Spanish ballads so funnily as to amuse everybody. [They] seem to have neither end nor beginning—all gay and all untranslatable, or at least losing their point and wit when put into an English dress. Such as:

> A poor man met with a sixpence,
> And for joy he gave up the ghost,
> And in the troubles of death,
> Even his sixpence was lost.
>
> . . . . .
>
> The woman who loves two at once,
> Knows what is discreet and right,
> Since if one of her candles goes out,
> Still the other remains alight.
>
> &c.

It is impossible to see any building of this size kept more perfectly clean and neat; generally the case here in all establishments which are under petticoat government. Many of these old Spanish institutions are certainly on a magnificent scale, though now for the most part neglected and falling to ruin; nor has any work of great consequence been attempted since the independence.[26]

We have had in our house various reports of robbers and frights, some true, some exaggerated, and some wholly false. We had to get up in the night at each passing noise in the house. When Calderón went out I waited in trembling for his return—and one evening, when all were in bed but me, an attempt to open the door of the room in which I sat nearly threw me into a fit. While things were in this state, a visit from the governor of Chapultepec put all things right. He came to propose that we should have two Spanish soldiers armed to live in the house. Consequently two picked old *militaires* from the *Inválidos* have taken up their quarters downstairs. They spend their time in cleaning their guns, making shoes, eating, and sleeping; but as yet have had no occasion to prove their valour. Perhaps the fact of there being soldiers in the house will be sufficient to frighten off the more ordinary robbers.[27]

12

The Viga and the Floating Gardens

Monday: March 16th, 1840
San Fernando, Mexico

We are now in Lent in the midst of prayer, churchgoing, and fasting.
The carnival was not very gay, with the exception of a few public
masked balls and very brilliant *paseos*.[1]

It would be difficult to find in any country a more beautiful promenade
than the Viga, or rather a more beautiful promenade than it might be
made. But even as it is, with its fine shady trees and canal, along
which the lazy canoes are constantly gliding, it would be difficult, on a
fine evening in sunset, especially on the evening of a fête day, to find
anywhere a prettier or more characteristic scene. Which rank of society
shows the most taste in their mode of enjoyment on this occasion must
be left to the scientific to determine: the Indians, with their flower
garlands and guitars, lying in their canoes, and dancing or singing

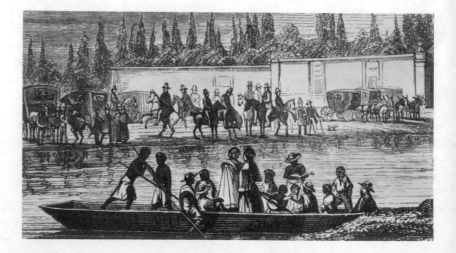

after their own fashion as they glide along the water, inhaling the soft breezes; or the ladies who, shut up in their close carriages, parade along in full dress and silence for a given space of time, feasting their eyes upon the equestrian feats of the *caballeros* who scarcely if ever even salute them as they pass, and never venture to address them, acknowledging by a gentle movement of their fingers the salutations of their fair friends from the recesses of their coaches—and seeming to think that the soles of their small feet would be contaminated by a contact with their mother earth, or their dignity compromised were the airs of heaven to blow too freely on their faces—though the soft breeze, laden with balm, steals over the sleepy water and the last rays of the sun are gilding the branches of the trees with a broken and flickering light.

Then at certain intervals of time each carriage slowly draws up beside its neighbour (as in the other *paseo*); the elegant *carretela* beside the plebeian hackney coach; the splendid equipage of the millionaire beside the lumbering and antique vehicle whose fashion hath now departed. There sit the inmates in solemn silence, as if the business of life were done and it was now their turn to watch the busy world from the loopholes of their retreat, and see it rolling along whilst they take their rest. The gentlemen also draw up their prancing steeds, though not within hail of the carriages; but they in the fresh air and under the green trees have as much advantage over the señoras as the wandering friar has over the cloistered nun.

Yet enter the Viga about five o'clock, when freshly watered, and the soldiers have taken their stand to prevent disturbances and two long lines of carriages are to be seen going and coming as far as the eye can reach, and hundreds of gay plebeians are assembled on the sidewalks with flowers and fruit and *dulces* for sale, and innumerable equestrians in picturesque dresses, and with spirited horses, fill up the interval between the carriages, and the canoes are covering the canal, the Indians singing and dancing lazily as the boats steal along, and the whole under the blue and cloudless sky, and in that pure clear atmosphere; and could you only shut your eyes to the one disagreeable feature in the picture, the innumerable *léperos* busy in the exercise of their vocation, you would believe that Mexico must be the most flourishing, most enjoyable, and most peaceful place in the world, and moreover the wealthiest; not a republic, certainly, for there is no well-dressed *people;* no connecting link between the blankets and the satins, between the poppies and the diamonds.

As for the carriages, many would not disgrace Hyde Park, though there are some that would send a shiver all along Bond Street; but the very contrast is amusing, and upon the whole, both as regards horses and equipages, there is much more to admire than to criticize.

There, for example, is the handsome carriage of the rich General Barrera,[2] who has one of the handsomest and finest houses in Mexico; his wife wears a velvet turban twisted with large pearls, and has at this moment a cigar in her mouth. She is not pretty, certainly, but her jewels are superb, and worth—it would be dangerous to calculate too nearly. How he made his fortune, partly by gambling, and partly by even less honourable means—by taking advantage of the ruin of others, by keeping a theatre which is a haunt of infamy and vice, clad in their lowest garb, and partly by erecting a cockpit—let some abler chronicler relate.

Or look at this elegant *carretela*, with its glass sides all opened, giving to view a constellation of fair ones, and drawn by handsome gray *frisones*. These ladies are remarkable as having a more European air than most others, brighter colours, longer and simpler dresses, and Paris bonnets. Apparently they are not Mexicans, or perhaps they have visited foreign parts. It is remarkable that the horses of the gentlemen all appear peculiarly unmanageable every time they pass this carriage. Another handsome, plain carriage, containing the family of one of the ministers—mother and daughters all beautiful, with Spanish eyes and dark glowing complexions—followed close by a hackney coach containing women with *rebozos*, and little children with their faces and fingers all bedaubed with candy. Some of the coachmen and footmen wear Mexican dresses, and others have liveries.

But here come three carriages *en suite*, all with the same crimson and gold livery, all luxurious, and all drawn by splendid white horses. Is it the President? Certainly not; it is too ostentatious. Were it in Europe, it might be royalty, but that even royalty goes in simpler guise when it condescends to mingle in the amusements of its subjects. In the first carriage appear the great man himself and his august consort, in silence and rather withdrawing from the plebeian gaze. There is here much crimson and gold, much glass and well-stuffed cushions, much comfort and magnificence combined. Two handsome northern steeds, white and prancing, draw this commodious chariot. Next passes a splendid coach containing the royal children and servants, and then a third, equally magnificent, in which are the babies and nurses.[3]

Nor is this all. By the side of the first carriage rides an elderly gentleman who at first sight might be mistaken for a *picador*, but that only in his accoutrements, for he does not ride well enough. He wears a magnificent Mexican dress all covered with gold embroidery; his hat with gold rolls is stuck jauntily on one side, contrasting oddly enough with his uneasy expression of countenance, evidently caused by a certain degree of inward trepidation of which he cannot wholly repress the outward sign while managing his highbred steed, and with his feet pressing against his silver stirrups, cautiously touching him with a whip which has a large diamond in the handle.

But the chief wonder of his whole equipment, and that which has probably procured him such a retinue of little ragged and shouting boys, is his saddle. This extraordinary piece of furniture, which cost the owner five thousand dollars, is entirely covered with velvet, richly embossed in massive gold; he sometimes appears with another, inlaid with pure silver.

His whole appearance is the most singular imaginable as he prances along by the side of his august relative's equipage, and must be seen to be conceived, and the perturbation of spirit in which he must return when it begins to grow dusk, and he reflects at once upon his own value, and the desire for appropriation so common amongst his countrymen, must necessarily balance the enjoyment which his vanity receives from the admiration of the little boys and *léperos* in the *paseo*. How he and his have risen from nothing, making their fortune by the most highhanded smuggling—how their fortune is now colossal, while their meanness is indescribable, and how, having introduced more than half a million of contraband goods, the law ventured to take cognizance of their proceedings, but without the slightest possibility existing of their being able to bring the offenders to justice—this is only one of the thousand instances of corruption that are bringing disgrace and ruin upon this unfortunate country.

But just as these millionaires pass by, an old hackney coach in their wake attracts our attention, exactly the sort of quaint old vehicle in which it sometimes pleases Lady Morgan to introduce her heroines.[4] In it are six figures, closely masked, and their faces covered with shawls. After many conjectures, it is impossible to guess what they may be or whether they are men or women. It *was* impossible, but as the carriages return, the wind suddenly blows aside the shawls of two of the party, and discloses the white gowns of the _____ friars! *O tempora! O mores!*[5]

There were three masked balls at the theatre, of which we only attended one. We went about ten o'clock to a box on the pit tier, and, although a *pronunciamiento* (the fashionable term here for a revolution) was prognosticated, we found everything very quiet and orderly, and the ball very gay and crowded. As we came in and were giving our tickets, a number of masks came springing by, shrieking out our names in their unearthly voices. Captain Gore, brother of Lord Arran, came to our box; also a scion of *La jeune France*, M. Mercier, who condescendingly kept his hat on during the whole evening. In a box directly above us were the French legation, who arrived lately.[6] Amongst the women the dresses were for the most part dominoes, adopted for greater concealment, as it was not considered very creditable to be there.

There were also several in men's attire, chiefly French modistes, generally a most disreputable set here, and numerous men dressed as women. There were masked Poblanas without stockings, and with very short petticoats; knights in armour; innumerable dresses probably borrowed from the theatre; and even more than the usual proportion of odd figures. The music was very good, and the dancers waltzed and *galloped* and flew round the room like furies. There was at least no want of animation.

Hundreds of masks spoke to us, but I discovered no one. One in a domino was particularly anxious to direct my attention to the Poblana dress, and asked me if it would have done for me to attend the fancy ball in such a costume. Very angry at his absurdity, I began to explain how I should have dressed, when I recollected the folly of explaining anything to a creature whom I did not know. Calderón stepped out of the box to walk amongst the crowd, at which various masks showed great signs of joy, surrounding and shaking hands with him.

The boxes were filled with ladies, and the scene was very amusing. Señor Matuti,[7] whose box we occupied, ordered in cakes and wine, and about one o'clock we left the ballroom and returned home, one of our old soldiers acting as lackey.

I paid a visit the other day, which merits to be recorded. It was to the rich Señora de Agüero,[8] whose first visit I had not yet returned. She was at home, and I was shown into a very large drawing room, where to my surprise I found the lamps, mirrors, &c. covered with black crape, as in cases of mourning here. I concluded that some one of the family was dead, and that I had made a very ill-timed first visit. However I sat down, when my eyes were instantly attracted by *something awful* placed directly in front of the sofa where I sat. There were six chairs ranged together, and on these lay stretched out a figure, apparently a dead body, about six feet long, enveloped in black cloth, the feet alone visible from their pushing up the cloth. Oh, horror! Here I sat, my eyes fixed upon this mysterious apparition, and lost in conjecture as to whose body it might be. The master of the house? He was very tall, and being in bad health might have died suddenly. My being received argued nothing against this, since the first nine days after a death the house is invariably crowded with friends and acquaintances, and the widow or orphan or childless mother must receive the condolences of all and sundry in the midst of her first bitter sorrow. There seems to be no idea of grief wishing for solitude.

Pending these reflections I sat uneasily, feeling or fancying a heavy air in the apartment, and wishing most sincerely that some living person would enter. I thought even of slipping away but feared to give offense, and in fact began to grow so nervous that, when the Señora de Agüero entered at length, I started up as if I had heard a pistol. She wore a coloured muslin gown and a blue shawl; no signs of mourning!

After the usual complimentary preface I asked particularly after her husband, keeping a side glance on the mysterious figure. He was pretty well. Her family? Just recovered from the smallpox, after being severely ill.

"Not dangerously?" said I, hesitatingly, thinking she might have a *tall son*, and that she alluded to the recovery of the others.

"No"; but her sister's children had been alarmingly ill.

"Not *lost* any, I hope?"

"None."

Well, so taken up was I that conversation flagged, until at last I happened to ask the lady if she were going to the country soon.

"Not to remain. But tomorrow we are going to convey a *Santo Cristo* (a figure of the Crucifixion) there, which has just been made for the chapel"—glancing towards the figure—"for which reason this room is, as you see, hung with black."

I never felt so relieved in my life, and thought of *The Mysteries of Udolpho*.[9]

The houses being so large and the servants not drilled to announce visitors—besides that the entresols are frequently let to other families —it is a matter of no small difficulty for a stranger to pioneer him or her self into the presence of the people of the house. The mistakes that I have made!—for not being aware of this fact concerning the entresols, which are often large and handsome, and the porter having begged me to walk up. I generally stopped at the first landing-place, and then *walked up* to the first door that I saw. I did walk in one morning upon two gentlemen, who seemed marvellously startled by my visit. They looked like two medical students, and were engaged before a table, heaven knows how—dissecting, I imagine. I inquired for the Señora Zamora, which astonished them still more, as well it might. However, they were very civil, and rushed downstairs to call up the carriage. After that adventure I never entered a house unaccompanied by a footman, until I had learnt my way through it.[10]

We had a pleasant dinner party a few days ago at the Prussian minister's, and met the Casa Flores family there. The Condesa de Casa Flores has been a long while in Europe, and in the best society, and is now entirely devoted to the education of her daughters—giving them every advantage that Mexico can afford in the way of masters, besides having at home a Spanish governess to assist her, an excellent woman whom they regard as a second mother.[11]

Though there is very little going on in Mexico at present, I amuse myself very well; there is so much to see, and the people are so kind and friendly. Having got riding horses, we have been making excursions all round the country, especially early in the morning, before the sun is high, when the air is delightfully cool and refreshing. Sometimes we go to the Viga at six in the morning, to see the Indians bringing in their flowers and vegetables by the canal. The profusion of sweet peas, double poppies, bluebottles, stock, gillyflower, and roses, I never saw equalled. Each Indian woman in her canoe looks as if seated in a floating flower garden.

The same love of flowers distinguishes them now as in the time of Cortés, the same which Humboldt remarked centuries afterwards. In the evening these Indian women, in their canoes, are constantly crowned with garlands of roses or poppies. Those who sit in the market, selling their fruit or their vegetables, appear as if they sat in bowers formed of fresh green branches and coloured flowers. In the poorest village church the floor is strewed with flowers, and before the service begins fresh nosegays are brought in and arranged upon the altar. The baby at its christening, the bride at the altar, the dead body in its bier, are all adorned with flowers. We are told that in the days of Cortés a bouquet of rare flowers was the most valuable gift presented to the ambassadors who visited the court of Montezuma, and it presents a strange anomaly, this love of flowers having existed along with their sanguinary worship and barbarous sacrifices.[12]

We went the other evening on the canal, in a large canoe with an awning, as far as the little village of Santa Anita,[13] and saw for the first time the far-famed *chinampas*, or floating gardens—which have now become fixtures, and are covered with vegetables intermingled with flowers, with a few poor huts beside them occupied by the Indians who bring these to the city for sale. There were cauliflowers, chile, tomatoes, cabbages, and other vegetables, but I was certainly disappointed in their beauty. They are, however, curious on account of their origin. So far back as 1245, it is said, the wandering Aztecs or Mexicans arrived first at Chapultepec, when, being persecuted by the princes of Xaltocan, they took refuge in a group of islands to the south of the lake of Texcoco. Falling under the yoke of the Texcocan kings, they abandoned their

island home and fled to Tizapán where, as a reward for assisting the chiefs of that country in a war against other petty princes, they received their freedom, and established themselves in a city to which they gave the name of Mexicalcingo—from Mejitli, their god of war—now a collection of strong barns and poor huts. But they did not settle there, for to obey an oracle they transported themselves from this city to the islands east of Chapultepec to the western side of the lake of Texcoco. An ancient tradition had long been current amongst them that wherever they should behold an eagle seated upon a nopal whose roots pierced a rock, there they should found a great city. In 1325 they beheld this sign, and on the spot, in an island in the lake, founded the first house of God—the *teocalli,* or great temple of Mexico.[14]

During all their wanderings, wherever they stopped, the Aztecs cultivated the earth, and lived upon what nature gave them. Surrounded by enemies and in the midst of a lake where there are few fish, necessity and industry compelled them to form floating fields and gardens on the bosom of the waters.

They weaved together the roots of aquatic plants, intertwined with twigs and light branches, until they had formed a foundation sufficiently strong to support a soil formed of the earth which they drew from the bottom of the lake; and on it they sowed their maize, their chile, and all other plants necessary for their support. These floating gardens were about a foot above the water, and in the form of a long square. Afterwards, in their natural taste for flowers, they not only cultivated the useful but the ornamental, and these small gardens multiplying were covered with flowers and aromatic herbs, which were used in the worship of the gods, or were sent to ornament the palace of the emperor.

The *chinampas* along the canal of the Viga are no longer floating gardens, but fixed to the mainland in the marshy grounds lying between the two great lakes of Chalco and Texcoco. A small trench full of water separates each garden; and, though now in this marshy land they give but a faint idea of what they may have been when they raised their flower-crowned heads above the clear waters of the lake, and when the Indians in their barks, wishing to remove their habitations, could tow along their little islands of roses, it is still a pretty and a pleasant scene.[15]

We bought numerous garlands of roses and poppies from the Indian children, both here and at Santa Anita, a little village where we landed, and as we returned towards evening we were amused by the singing and dancing of the Indians. One canoe came close up to ours, and kept beside it for some time. A man was lying lazily at the bottom of the boat tingling his guitar, and one or two women were dancing monotonously and singing at the same time to his music. Sundry jars of pulque and earthen dishes with tortillas and chile and pieces of *tasajo*—long festoons of dried and salted beef—proved that the party were not without their solid comforts, in spite of the romantic guitar and the rose and poppy garlands with which the dancing nymphs were crowned. Amongst others they performed "*El Palomo*, The Dove," one of their most favourite dances. The music is pretty, and I send it you with the words, the music from ear; the words are given me by my friend the Señora Adalid, who sings all these little Indian airs in perfection.

If we may form some judgment of a people's civilization by their ballads, none of the Mexican songs give us a very high idea of theirs. The words are generally a tissue of absurdities, nor are there any patriotic songs which their newborn freedom might have called forth from so musical a people. At least I have as yet only discovered one air of which the words bear reference to the glorious *Grito de Dolores*, and which asserts in rhyme that on account of that memorable event the Indian was able to get as drunk as a Christian! The translation of the "*Palomo*" is as follows:

"What are you doing, little dove, there in the wineshop? Waiting for my love until Tuesday, my life. A dove in flying hurt her little wing.

If you have your dove I have my little dove too. A dove in flying
all her feathers fell off. Women pay badly; not all, but some of them.
Little dove of the barracks, you will tell the drummers when they beat
the retreat to strike up the march of my loves. Little dove, what are
you doing there leaning against that wall? Waiting for my dove till
he brings me something to eat." At the end of each verse the chorus
of *"Palomita, palomo, palomo."*[16]

Yet, monotonous as it is, the air is so pretty, the women sang so
softly and sleepily, the music sounded so soothingly as we glided along
the water, that I felt in a pleasant half-dreamy state of perfect contentment and was sorry when, arriving at the landing-place, we had to
return to a carriage and civilized life, with nothing but the garlands of
flowers to remind us of the *chinampas*.[17]

Unfortunately these people generally end by too frequent applications
to the *jarro* of pulque, or, what is worse, to the pure spirit known by
the name of *chinguirito*—the consequence of which is that, from music
and dancing and rose-becrowning, they proceed to quarrelling and jealousy and drunkenness, which frequently terminates in their fighting,
stabbing each other, or throwing each other into the canal. "The end
crowns the work."[18]

Noble as this present city of Mexico is, one cannot help thinking
how much more picturesque the ancient Tenochtitlan was, and how
much more fertile its valley must have been, on account of the great

lakes. Yet even in the time of Cortés these lakes had no great depth of water, and still further back, in the time of the Indian emperors, navigation had been so frequently interrupted in seasons of drought that an aqueduct had been constructed in order to supply the canals with water.

After this, the Spaniards, like all new settlers, hewed down the fine trees in this beautiful valley, both on plain and mountain, leaving the bare soil exposed to the vertical rays of the sun. Then their well-founded dread of inundation caused them to construct the famous *Desagüe* of Huehuetoca, the drain or subterranean conduit or channel in the mountain for drawing off the waters of the lakes, thus leaving marshy lands or sterile plains covered with carbonate of soda where formerly were silver lakes covered with canoes. This last was a necessary evil, since the Indian emperors themselves were sensible of its necessity and had formed great works for draining the lakes, some remains of which works still exist in the vicinity of the Peñón.[19] The great *Desagüe* was begun in 1607, when the Marquis of Salinas was viceroy of Mexico; and the operations were commenced with great pomp, the Viceroy assisting in person, mass being said on a portable altar, and fifteen hundred workmen assembled—while the marquis himself began the excavation by giving the first stroke with a spade.[20] From 1607 to 1830 eight millions of dollars were expended, and yet this great work was not brought to a conclusion. However, the limits of the two lakes of Zumpango and San Cristóbal, to the north of the valley, were thus greatly reduced, and the lake of Texcoco, the most beautiful of all the five, no longer received their contributions. Thus the danger of inundations has diminished, but water and vegetation have diminished also, and the suburbs of the city, which were formerly covered with beautiful gardens, now present to the eye an arid expanse of efflorescent salt.

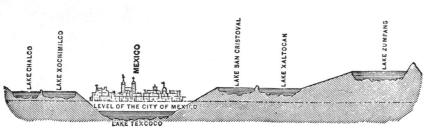

The plains near San Lázaro especially, in their arid whiteness, seem characteristic of the unfortunate victims of leprosy enclosed in the walls of that hospital.[21]

We rode out the other day by the *barrio*, or ward, of Santiago, which occupies part of the ancient Tlaltelolco, which once constituted a separate state, had kings of its own, and was conquered by a Mexican monarch, who made a communication by bridges between it and Mexico. The great market mentioned by Cortés was held here, and its boundaries are still pointed out, whilst the convent chapel stands on the height where Cortés erected a battering engine when he was besieging the Indian Venice.[22]

13

Pleasant Excursions

[Lent], 1840
San Fernando, Mexico

Early this morning we rode to the convent of San Joaquín, belonging to friars of the Carmelite order, passing through Tacuba—the ancient Tlacopan—once the capital of a small kingdom whose monarch, Tetle-panquetzaltzin (short and convenient name), Cortés caused to be hung on a tree for a supposed or real conspiracy.[1]

The number of carts, the innumerable Indians loaded like beasts of burden, their women with baskets of vegetables in their hands and children on their backs, the long strings of *arrieros* with their loaded mules, the droves of cattle, the flocks of sheep, the herds of pigs, render it a work of some difficulty to make one's way on horseback out of the gates of Mexico at an early hour of the morning—but it must be confessed that the whole scene is lively and cheerful enough to make one forget that there is such a thing as care in the world. There is an indifferent, placid smile on every face, and the bright blue sky smiling over them all; dogs bark and asses bray, and the Indian, with near a mule's load on his back, drags his hat off to salute a bevy of his bronze-coloured countrymen nearly equally laden with himself, and they all show their teeth and talk their liquid Indian and pass on.[2]

These plains of Tacuba, once the theatre of fierce and bloody conflicts, and where during the siege of Mexico Alvarado of the leap fixed his camp, now present a very tranquil scene. Tacuba itself is now a small village of mud huts, with some fine old trees, a few very old ruined houses, a ruined church, and some traces of a building which Adalid assured us had been the palace of their last monarch—whilst others declare it to have been the site of the Spanish encampment.[3]

San Joaquín, also a poor village, contains the fine convent and immense walled garden and orchard belonging to the rich monks of the Carmelite order. As Calderón knows the prior, he sent in our names, and I was admitted as far as the sacristy of the convent church.[4]

The prior received us with the utmost kindness: he is a good-looking man, extremely amiable and well-informed, and still young. The gentlemen were admitted into the interior of the convent, which they describe as being a very large handsome building, clean and airy, with a fine old library chiefly composed of theological works; to the garden, which is immensely large and, though not much cultivated, full of flowers; and to the great orchard, celebrated for the profusion and excellence of its fruit. There is a mirador in the garden which can be seen from the road, and from which there is a very extensive view. I was very anxious for admittance only to the garden, and pleaded the *manly* appearance of my riding-hat, which would prevent all scandal were I seen from a distance. But the complaisance of the good prior would not go quite so far as that, so I sat in the sacristy and conversed with a good-natured old monk with a double chin, whilst the others wandered through the grounds. They afterwards gave us a very nice breakfast, simple but good: fish from the lake, different preparations of eggs, *riz au lait,* coffee and fruit. The monks did not sit down with us, nor would they partake of anything themselves.

We went in the evening to see a pretty hacienda called Los Morales (The Mulberry Trees), belonging to a Spaniard, which has a nice garden with a bath in it, and where they bestowed a quantity of beautiful flowers on us.[5]

The other day we set off early, together with the Belgian and French ministers and their families, in carriages, to visit a beautiful deserted hacienda, called El Olivar, belonging to the Marquis of Santiago.[6] The house is perfectly bare, with nothing but the walls; but the grounds are a wilderness of tangled flowers and blossoming trees, rosebushes, sweet peas, and all manner of fragrant flowers. We passed an agreeable day, wandering about, breakfasting on the provisions brought with us, arranging large bouquets of flowers, and firing at a mark, which must have startled the birds in this solitary and uncultivated retreat. We had a pleasant family dinner at the Escandóns' and passed the evening at the Baron de Cyprey's. The gentlemen returned late, it being the day of a diplomatic dinner at the English minister's.

The Countess del Valle[7] has just sent me a beautiful bird with the most gorgeous plumage of the brightest scarlet and blue. It is called a *guacamaya,* and is of the parrot species, but three times as large, being about two feet from the beak to the tip of the tail. It is a superb creature but very wicked, gnawing not only its own pole, but all the doors, and com-

mitting great havoc amongst the plants, besides trying to bite everyone who approaches it. It pronounces a few words very hoarsely and indistinctly, and has a most harsh, disagreeable cry. In fact it presumes upon its beauty to be as unamiable as possible.

I prefer some beautiful little hummingbirds (*chupamirtos* as they are called here) which have been sent me, and which I am trying to preserve alive. But I fear the cold will kill them—for, though we see them occasionally here, hanging by their beaks upon the branches of the flowers like large butterflies and shaking their brilliant little wings so rapidly that they seem to emit sparkles of coloured light, still this is not their home; properly speaking, they belong to the *tierra caliente*. These little birds are of a golden green and purple, and are so tame that whilst I am writing I have two on my shoulder and one perched on the edge of a glass, diving out its long tongue for sugar and water. Our livestock is considerable: we have guinea fowls, who always remind me of old maiden ladies in half-mourning, and whose screaming notes match those of the *guacamaya;* various little green parrots; a scarlet cardinal; one hundred and sixty pigeons in the pigeon house; and three fierce dogs in conspicuous situations.

I received a very polite letter today from the Señora de Santa Anna, and, as it was enclosed in a few lines from Santa Anna himself, I send you his *autograph*—for I doubt much whether we have seen the last of that illustrious personage, or whether his philosophic retirement will endure forever.

I have been endeavouring lately to procure permission from Señor Posada, who is shortly to be consecrated archbishop, to visit the convents of nuns in Mexico. Señor Cañedo, Secretary of State, our particular friend, has been kind enough to interest himself in the matter, though with indifferent hopes of success.[8] A few days ago he sent me his correspondence with Señor Posada, who observes that the vice-queens alone had the privilege of the *entrée,* and seems to hesitate a good deal as to the advisableness of granting a permission which might be considered a precedent for others. However, I think he is too amiable to resist our united entreaties. I hold out as an argument that, Calderón being the *duplicado* of the Queen herself, my visit is equal to that of the vice-queen, which argument has at least amused him. His consecration is fixed for the thirty-first of May.

Don Pedro Fonte, the last archbishop named in the time of the Spanish dominion, having renounced the mitre, three illustrious churchmen were proposed to fill the vacant place: this Don Manuel Posada, Don Antonio Campos, and Dr. Don José María de Santiago. The first was chosen by the Mexican government, and was afterwards proclaimed in the Roman Consistory last December, with the approbation of Gregory XVI. They are now only waiting for the pontifical bulls which are daily expected from Rome; and it is said that the ceremony, which will take place in the cathedral, will be very magnificent.

Friday: April 3rd, 1840

Accompanied by the Belgian minister, we spent yesterday in visiting the Minería, the Botanic Garden, the Museum, &c., all which leave a certain disagreeable impression on the mind, since, without having the dignity of ruins, they are fine buildings neglected. The Minería, or School of Mines, the work of the famous architect and sculptor Tolsá, is a magnificent building, a palace whose fine proportions would render it remarkable amongst the finest edifices of any European country. All is on a great scale—its noble rows of pillars, great staircases, large apartments, and lofty roofs—but it reminds one of a golden aviary containing a few common sparrows. Several rich Spaniards contributed more than six hundred thousand dollars to its construction. We were

shown through the whole of this admirable building by the director, who occupies a very handsome house attached to it. But however learned the professors may be—and amongst them is the scientific Señor del Río, now very old but a man of great learning and research—the collection of minerals, the instruments, and models are all miserable and ill kept.[9]

The Botanic Garden, within the palace, is a small ill-kept enclosure where there still remain some rare plants of the immense collection made in the time of the Spanish government—when great progress was made in all the natural sciences, four hundred thousand dollars having been expended in botanical expeditions alone. Courses of botanical lectures were then given annually by the most learned professors, and the taste for natural history was universal.

El *árbol de las manitas* (the tree of the small hands) was the most curious which we saw in the garden. The flower is of a bright scarlet in the form of a hand, with five fingers and a thumb; and it is said that

there are only three of these trees in the republic. The gardener is an old Italian, who came over with one of the viceroys, and, though now one hundred and ten years old, and nearly bent double, possesses all his faculties.[10]

The garden is pretty from the age of the trees and luxuriance of the flowers, but melancholy as a proof of the decay of the science in Mexico. The palace itself, now occupied by the President, formerly belonged to Cortés, and was ceded by his descendants to the government. In exchange they received the ground formerly occupied by the palace of the Aztec kings, and built on it a very splendid edifice, where the state archives are kept, and where the Monte Pío (the office where money is lent on plate, jewels, &c.) now is—the director of which is Don Francisco Tagle, whose apartments within the building are very elegant and spacious.[11]

The Museum—within the University, and opposite the palace, in the plaza called del Volador—contains many rare and valuable works, many curious Indian antiquities, but they are ill arranged.[12] On the walls are the portraits of the vice-kings, beginning with Hernán Cortés. We spent a long while here examining these antiquities; but we have seen nothing in Mexico to equal the beauty of the colossal equestrian statue in bronze of Charles IV placed on a pedestal of Mexican marble, which stands in the court of the University, but formerly adorned the middle of the square.[13]

It is a magnificent piece of sculpture, the masterpiece of Tolsá, remarkable for the noble simplicity and purity of its style, and was made at the expense of an ex-viceroy, the Marquis of Branciforte. We also saw the goddess of war lying in a corner of the court, beside the Stone of Sacrifices which we had already been shown.[14]

Today we have been visiting the academy of painting and sculpture, called the Academy of Fine Arts, of which I unfortunately recollected having read Humboldt's brilliant account, in my forcibly prolonged studies on board the *Jasón*, and that he mentions its having had the most favourable influence in forming the national taste. He tells us that every night, in these spacious halls well illuminated by Argand lamps, hundreds of young men were assembled, some sketching from the plaster casts or from life, and others copying designs of furniture, candelabras, and other bronze ornaments; and that here all classes, colours, and races were mingled together, the Indian beside the white boy and the son of the poorest mechanic beside that of the richest lord. Teaching was gratis, and not limited to landscape and figures, one of the principal objects being to propagate amongst the artists a general taste for elegance and beauty of form, and to enliven the national industry. Plaster casts, to the amount of forty thousand dollars, were sent out by the King of Spain; and as they possess in the Academy various colossal statues of basalt and porphyry, with Aztec hieroglyphics, it would have been curious—as the same learned traveller remarks—to have collected these monuments in the courtyard of the Academy and compared the remains of Mexican sculpture, monuments of a semibarbarous people, with the graceful creations of Greece and Rome.[15]

Let no one visit the Academy with these recollections or anticipations in his mind. That the simple and noble taste which distinguishes the Mexican buildings, their perfection in the cutting and working of their stones, the chaste ornaments of the capitals and relievos, are owing to the progress they made in this very Academy, is no doubt the case. The remains of these beautiful but mutilated plaster casts, the splendid engravings which still exist, would alone make it probable; but the present disorder, the abandoned state of the building, the nonexistence of these excellent classes of sculpture and painting, and above all the low state of the fine arts in Mexico at the present day, are amongst the sad proofs, if any were wanting, of the melancholy effects produced by years of civil war and unsettled government.

The Holy Week is now approaching, and already Indians are to be seen bringing in the palm branches and the flowers for the altars, and they are beginning to erect booths and temporary shops, and to make every preparation for the concourse of people who will arrive next Sunday [week] from all the different villages and ranchos, far and near.

14

Holy Week

Tuesday: April 21st, 1840
San Fernando, Mexico

On the morning of Palm Sunday I went to the cathedral, accompanied by Mademoiselle de Cyprey, daughter of the French minister. We found it no easy matter to make our way through the crowd, but at last, by dint of patience and perseverance, and changing our place very often, we contrived to arrive very near the great altar. There we had just taken up our position when a disinterested man gave us a friendly hint that, as the whole procession, with their branches, must inevitably squeeze past the very spot where we were, we should probably be crushed or suffocated. Consequently we followed him to a more convenient station, also close to the altar and defended by the railing, where we found ourselves tolerably well off. Two ladies, to whom he made the same proposition, and who rejected it, we afterwards observed in a sad condition, their mantillas nearly torn off and the palm branches sweeping across their eyes.

In a short time, the whole cathedral presented the appearance of a forest of palm trees (*à la* Birnam wood), moved by a gentle wind; and under each tree a half-naked Indian, his rags clinging together with wonderful pertinacity; long, matted, dirty black hair both in men and women, bronze faces and mild unspeaking eyes—or all with one expression of eagerness to see the approach of the priests. Many of them had probably travelled a long way, and the palms were from *tierra caliente*, dried and plaited into all manner of ingenious ways. Each palm was about seven feet high, so as far to overshadow the head of the Indian who carried it; and whenever they are blessed, they are carried home to adorn the walls of their huts. The priests arrived at length, in great pomp and also carrying palm branches. For four mortal hours we remained kneeling or sitting on the floor, and thankful we were when it was all over and we could make our way once more into the fresh air.

From this day, during the whole week, all business is suspended, and but one train of thought occupies all classes, from the highest to the lowest. The peasants flock from every quarter, shops are shut, churches are opened; and the Divine Tragedy enacted in Syria eighteen hundred years ago is now celebrated in land then undiscovered, and by the descendants of nations sunk in paganism for centuries after that period.

But amongst the lower classes the worship is emphatically the worship of her who herself predicted, "From henceforth all nations shall call me blessed."[1] Before her shrines, and at all hours, thousands are kneeling. With faces expressive of the most intense love and devotion, and with words of the most passionate adoration, they address the mild image of the Mother of God. To the Son their feelings seem composed of respectful pity, of humble but more distant adoration; while to the Virgin they appear to give all their confidence, and to look up to her as to a kind and bountiful queen, who—dressed in her magnificent robes and jewelled diadem, yet mourning in all the agony of her divine sorrows—has condescended to admit the poorest beggar to participate in her woe, whilst in her turn she shares in the afflictions of the lowly, feels for their privations, and grants them her all-powerful intercession.

On Holy Thursday nothing can be more picturesque than the whole appearance of Mexico. No carriages are permitted and the ladies, being on foot, take the opportunity of displaying all the riches of their toilet. On this day velvets and satins are your only wear. Diamonds and pearls walk the streets. The mantillas are white or black blonde; the shoes white or coloured satin. The petticoats are still rather short, but it would be hard to hide such small feet, and such still smaller shoes. "*Il faut souffrir pour être belle*," but *à quoi bon être belle?* if no one sees it. As for me I *ventured* upon a lilac silk of Palmyre's, and a black mantilla.

The whole city was filled with picturesque figures. After the higher señoras were to be remarked the common women, chiefly in clear white very stiffly starched muslins—some very richly embroidered, and the petticoat trimmed with lace—white satin shoes, and the dresses extremely short, which on them looks very well. A *rebozo* is thrown over all. Amongst these there were many handsome faces, but in a still lower and more Indian class, with their gay-coloured petticoats, the faces were sometimes beautiful, and the figures more upright and graceful; also they invariably walk well, whilst many of the higher classes, from tight shoes and want of custom, seem to feel pain in putting their feet to the ground.[2]

But none could vie with the handsome Poblana peasants in their holiday dresses, some so rich and magnificent that, remembering the warning of our ministerial friends, I am inclined to believe them more showy than respectable. The pure Indians, with whom the churches and the whole city is crowded, are as ugly as can be imagined: a gentle, dirty, and much-enduring race. Still, with their babies at their backs,

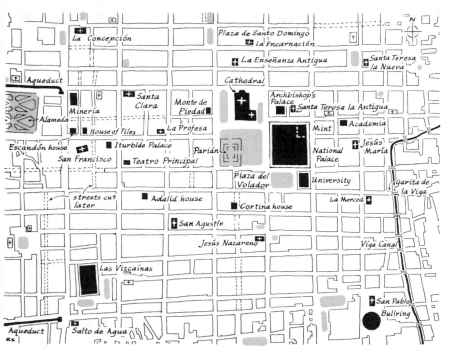

going along at their usual gentle trot, they add much to the general effect of the *coup-d'œil.*

We walked to San Francisco about ten o'clock, and, the body of the church being crowded, went upstairs to a private gallery with a gilded grating belonging to the Countess de Santiago, and here we had the advantage of seats, besides a fine view of the whole. This church is very splendid, and the walls were hung with canvas paintings representing different passages of our Saviour's life (his entry into Jerusalem, the woman of Samaria at the well, &c.) which, with the palm trees, had a cool and oriental effect.

Before the altar, which was dazzling with jewels, was a representation of the Lord's Supper, not in painting, but in sculptured figures as large as life, habited in the Jewish dresses. The bishops and priests were in a blaze of gold and jewels. They were assisted during the ceremony by the young Count of Santiago. The music was extremely good, and the whole effect impressive.[3]

We visited several churches in the course of the day, and continued walking until four o'clock, when we went to dine with our friends the Adalids.[4] After dinner one of their coachmen, a handsome Mexican in a superb dress all embroidered in gold, was called upstairs to dance the *jarabe* to us with a country girl. The dance is monotonous, but they acquitted themselves to perfection.

We then continued our pilgrimage through the city, though, as the sun had not yet set, we reserved our chief admiration until the churches should be illuminated. One, however, we entered at sunset, which was worthy of remark—Santo Domingo. It looked like a little paradise, or a story in the Arabian Nights. All the steps up the altar were covered with pots of beautiful flowers, orange trees loaded with fruit and blossom, and rosebushes in full bloom, glasses of coloured water, and all kinds of fruit. Cages full of birds, singing delightfully, hung from the wall, and really fine paintings filled up the intervals. A gay carpet covered the floor, and in front of the altar, instead of the usual representation of the Saviour crucified, a little Infant Jesus, beautifully done in wax, was lying amidst flowers with little angels surrounding him. Add to this the music of *Romeo and Juliet* and you may imagine that it was more like a scene in an opera than anything in a church.[5] But certainly, as the rays of the setting sun streamed with a rosy light through the stained windows, throwing a glow over the whole—birds, and flowers, and fruit, paintings and angels—it was the prettiest and most fantastic scene I ever beheld, like something expressly got up for the benefit of children.

We did not kneel before each altar for more than three minutes, otherwise we should never have had time even to enter the innumerable churches which we visited in the course of the night. We next went to Santa Teresa la Nueva, a handsome church belonging to a convent of strict nuns, which was now brilliantly illuminated; and here, as in all the churches, we made our way through the crowd with extreme difficulty. The number of *léperos* was astonishing, greatly exceeding that of well-dressed people. Before each altar was a figure, dreadful in the extreme, of the Saviour as large as life, dressed in purple robe and crown of thorns, seated on the steps of the altar, the blood trickling from his wounds—each person, before leaving the church, devoutly kneeling to kiss his hands and feet. The nuns, amongst whom is a sister of Señor Adalid, sung behind the grating in the gallery above, but were not visible.[6]

One of the churches we visited, that of Santa Teresa called the *Antigua,* stands upon the site formerly occupied by the palace of the father of the unfortunate Montezuma. It was here that the Spaniards were quartered when they took Montezuma prisoner, and here Cortés found and appropriated the treasures of that family.[7] In 1830 a bust of stone was found in the yard of the convent, which the workmen were digging up. Don Lucas Alamán, then Minister of Exterior Relations, offered a compensation to the nuns for the curious piece of antiquity, which they gladly gave up to the government on whose account he acted. It is said to be the idol goddess of the Indians, Centeotl, the goddess of medicine and medicinal herbs, also known by the name of Temazcalteci, or the "Grandmother of the Baths." A full account is given of her in one of the numbers of the *Mosaico Mexicano,* as also of a square stone found in the same place, beautifully carved and covered with hieroglyphical characters.[8]

In the evening, towards the hour when the great procession was expected, we went to the balconies of the Academia,[9] which command a fine view of the streets by which it was to pass. Till it arrived we amused ourselves by looking over the *beaux restes* of former days, the collections of painting and sculpture, the fine plaster-casts that still remain, and the great volumes of fine engravings. It was dark when the procession made its appearance, which rendered the effect less gaudy and more striking. The Virgin, the saints, the Holy Trinity, the Saviour in different passages of his life, imprisonment and crucifixion were carried past in succession, represented by figures magnificently dressed, placed on lofty scaffoldings of immense weight, supported by different bodies of men. One is carried by the coachmen, another by the *aguadores* (water carriers), a third by the *cargadores* (porters), a Herculean race.

First arrived the favourite protectress of all classes, the Virgin of Dolores, surmounted by a velvet canopy, seated on a glittering throne, attired in her sable robes, her brow surmounted by glittering rays and contracted with an expression of agony; of all representations of the Virgin, the only one which is always lovely, however rudely carved, with that invariably beautiful face of terrible anguish. Then followed the Saviour bearing the cross; the Saviour crucified, the Virgin supporting the head of her dying son; the Trinity (the Holy Spirit represented by a dove); all the apostles, from St. Peter with the keys to Judas with the moneybag; and a long train of saints, all brilliantly illuminated and attended by an amazing crowd of priests, monks, and laymen. However childish and superstitious all this may seem, I doubt whether it be not as well thus to impress certain religious truths on the minds of a people too ignorant to understand them by any other process. By the time the last saint and angel had vanished, the hour was advanced, and we had still to visit the illuminated churches. Being recommended to divest ourselves of our ornaments before wandering forth amongst the crowd, a matter of some moment to the Señora Adalid who wore all her diamonds, we left our earrings, brooches, &c., in charge of the person who keeps the Academia, and recommenced our pilgrimage.

Innumerable were the churches we visited that evening: the cathedral, La Enseñanza, Jesús María, Santa Clara, Santa Brígida, San Hipólito, La Encarnación, the five churches of San Francisco, &c., &c., a list without an end—kneeling for a short space of time before each blazing altar, for the more churches one visits, the more meritorious is the devotion.[10]

The cathedral was the first we entered, and its magnificence struck us with amazement. Its gold and silver and jewels, its innumerable ornaments and holy vessels, the rich dresses of the priests, all seemed burning in almost intolerable brightness. The high altar was the most magnificent; the second, with its pure white marble pillars, the most imposing.

The crowd was immense, but we made our way slowly through it to the foot of each altar, where the people were devoutly kissing the Saviour's hand or the hem of his garment; or beating their breasts before the mild image of Our Lady of Grief. Each church had vied with the other in putting forth all its splendour of jewelry, of lights, of dresses, and of music.

In the church of Santa Clara—attached to the convent of the same name, small but elegant, with its pillars of white marble and gold—one voice of angelic sweetness was singing behind the grating alone, and in the midst of a most deathlike stillness. It sounded like the notes of a nightingale in a cage. I could have listened for hours, but our time was limited and we set off anew. Fortunately the evening was delightful, and the moon shining brightly.[11] We visited about twenty churches in succession. In all the organ was pealing, the blaze of light overpowering, the magnificence of jewels and crimson velvet and silver and gold dazzling, the crowd suffocating, the incense blinding.

The prettiest effect in every church was caused by the orange trees and rosebushes, which covered the steps of the altars up to where the magnificence of the altar itself blazed out; and the most picturesque effect was produced by the different orders of monks in their gowns and hoods, either lying on their faces or standing ranged with torches like figures carved in stone.

In the passage leading to most of the churches was a table, at which several ladies of the highest rank sat collecting alms for the poor. The fair *quêteuses* had not been very successful, and that chiefly amongst the lower classes. The fatigue was terrible, walking for so many hours on that bad pavement with thin satin shoes, so that at length our feet seemed to move mechanically—and we dropped on our knees before each altar like machines touched by a spring, and rose again with no small effort.

Of all the churches we entered that night, the cathedral was the most magnificent, but the most beautiful and tasteful was San Francisco. The crowd there was so dense that we were almost carried off our feet, and

were obliged, in defiance of all rule, to take the arms of our *caballeros*.
Still, it was worth the trouble of making our way through it to see such a
superbly illuminated altar. It was now eleven o'clock, and the crowd was
breaking up as the churches are shut before midnight. On one corner of
the middle aisle, near the door, was the representation of a prison from
which issued a stream of soft music, and at the window was a figure of
Christ in chains, his eyes bandaged and a Jew on each side; the chains
hanging from his hands, and clanking as if with the motion of his arms.
The rush here was immense. Numbers of people were kneeling before
the window of the prison, and kissing the chains and beating their breasts
with every appearance of contrition and devotion. This was the night
before the Crucifixion, and the last scene of the Holy Thursday.

We reached home hardly able to stand. I never felt more dazzled,
bewildered, and sleepy; but I was awakened by finding a packet of letters from home, which brought back my thoughts—or rather carried them
away to very different lands.

On Good Friday, a day of sorrow and humiliation, the scene in the
morning is very different. The great sacrifice is complete—the Immortal
has died a mortal death. The ladies all issue forth in mourning, and the
churches look sad and wan after their last night's brilliancy. The heat
was intense. We went to San Francisco, again to the *tribuna* of the
Countess de Santiago, to see the Adoration and Procession of the Cross,
which was very fine.

But the most beautiful and original scene was presented towards sunset in the great square, and it is doubtful whether any other city in the
world could present a *coup d'œil* of equal brilliancy. Having been
offered the *entrée* to some apartments in the palace, we took our seats on

the balconies, which commanded a view of the whole. The plaza itself, even on ordinary days, is a noble square, and but for its one fault—a row of shops called the Parián, which breaks its uniformity—would be nearly unrivalled.[12] Every object is interesting. The eye wanders from the cathedral to the house of Cortés (the Monte Pío), and from thence to a range of fine buildings with lofty arcades to the west. From our elevated situation, we could see all the different streets that branch out from the square covered with gay crowds pouring in that direction to see another great procession, which was expected to pass in front of the palace. Booths filled with refreshments, and covered with green branches and garlands of flowers, were to be seen in all directions, surrounded by a crowd who were quenching their thirst with orgeat, *chía*,[13] lemonade, or pulque.

The whole square, from the cathedral to the *portales* and from the Monte Pío to the palace, was covered with thousands and tens of thousands of figures, all in their gayest dresses, and as the sun poured his rays down upon their gaudy colours they looked like armies of living tulips. Here was to be seen a group of ladies, some with black gowns and mantillas; others, now that their churchgoing duty was over, equipped in velvet or satin, with their hair dressed—and beautiful hair they have; some leading their children by the hand, dressed—alas! how they were dressed! Long velvet gowns trimmed with blonde, diamond earrings, high French caps befurbelowed with lace and flowers, or turbans with plumes of feathers. Now and then the head of a little thing that could hardly waddle alone might have belonged to an English dowager duchess in her opera box. Some had extraordinary bonnets, also with flowers and feathers, and as they toddled along, top-heavy, one would have thought they were little old women—till a glimpse was caught of their lovely little brown faces and black eyes. Now and then a little girl, simply dressed with a short frock and long black hair plaited down and un-covered, would trip along, a very model of grace amongst the small caricatures. The children here are generally beautiful, their features only too perfect and regular for the face "to fulfill the promise of its spring." They have little colour, with swimming black or hazel eyes and long lashes resting on the clear pale cheek, and a perfect mass of fine dark hair of the straight Spanish or Indian kind plaited down behind.

As a contrast to the señoras, with their overdressed beauties, were the poor Indian women, trotting across the square, their black hair plaited with dirty red ribbon, a piece of woolen cloth wrapped round them, and a little mahogany baby hanging behind, its face upturned to the sky and its head going jerking along somehow without its neck being dislocated. The most resigned expression on earth is that of an Indian baby.

All the groups we had seen promenading the streets the day before were here collected by hundreds: the women of the shopkeeper class, or it may be lower, in their smart white embroidered gowns, with their white satin shoes, and neat feet and ankles, and *rebozos* or bright shawls thrown over their heads; the peasants and countrywomen, with their short petticoats of two colours, generally scarlet and yellow (for they are most anti-Quakerish in their attire), thin satin shoes and lace-trimmed chemises; or bronze-coloured damsels, all crowned with flowers, strolling along with their admirers, and tingling their light guitars. And above all, here and there a flashing Poblana, with a dress of real value and much taste, and often with a face and figure of extraordinary beauty, especially the figure—large, and yet *élancée*, with a bold coquettish eye, and a beautiful little brown foot shown off by the white satin shoe, the petticoat of her dress frequently fringed and embroidered in real massive gold, and either a *rebozo* shot with gold or a bright-coloured China crape shawl coquettishly thrown over her head. We saw several whose dresses could not have cost less than five hundred dollars.

Add to this motley crowd, men dressed *à la Mexicaine,* with their large ornamented hats and sarapes, or embroidered jackets, sauntering along smoking their cigars; *léperos* in rags; Indians in blankets; officers in uniform; priests in their shovel hats; monks of every order; Frenchmen exercising their wit upon the passers-by; Englishmen looking cold and philosophical; Germans gazing through their spectacles, mild and mystical; Spaniards seeming pretty much at home, and abstaining from remarks—and it may be conceived that the scene at least presented variety. Sometimes the tinkling of the bell announced the approach of *Nuestro*

Amo. Instantly the whole crowd are on their knees, crossing themselves devoutly. Two men who were fighting below the window suddenly dropped down side by side. Disputes were hushed, flirtations arrested, and to the busy hum of voices succeeded a profound silence. Only the rolling of the coach wheels and the sound of the little bell were heard.

No sooner had it passed than the talkers and the criers recommenced with fresh vigour. The venders of hot chestnuts and cooling beverages plied their trade more briskly than ever. A military band struck up an air from *Semiramis;* [14] and the noise of the innumerable *matracas* (rattles), some of wood and some of silver, with which everyone is armed during the last days of the holy week, broke forth again as if by magic, while again commenced the sale of the Judases, fireworks in the form of that archtraitor which are sold on the evening of Good Friday and let off on Saturday morning. Hundreds of these hideous figures were held above the crowd by men who carried them tied together on long poles. An ugly misshapen monster they represent the betrayer to have been. When he sold his Master for thirty pieces of silver, did he dream that in the lapse of ages his effigies should be held up to the execration of a Mexican mob, of an unknown people in undiscovered countries beyond the seas? A secret bargain, perhaps made whisperingly in a darkened chamber with the fierce Jewish rulers, but now shouted forth in the ears of the descendants of Montezuma and Cortés!

But the sound of a distant hymn rose on the air, and shortly after there appeared advancing towards the square a long and pompous retinue of mitred priests, with banners and crucifixes and gorgeous imagery, conducting a procession in which figures representing scenes concerning the death of our Saviour were carried by on platforms, as they were the preceding evening. There was the Virgin in mourning at the foot of the cross—the Virgin in glory—and more saints and more angels—St. Michael and the dragon, &c., &c.—a glittering and innumerable train. Not a sound was heard as the figures were carried slowly onwards in their splendid robes, lighted by thousands of tapers which mingled their unnatural glare with the fading light of day.

As the *Miserere* was to be performed in the cathedral late in the evening, we went there, though with small hopes of making our way through the tremendous crowd. Having at length been admitted through a private entrance, per favour, we made our way into the body of the church; but the crowd was so intolerable that we thought of abandoning our position, when we were seen and recognized by some of the priests and conducted to a railed-off enclosure near the shrine of the Virgin, with the luxury of a Turkey carpet. Here, separated from the crowd, we sat down in peace on the ground. The gentlemen were accommodated with high-backed chairs beside some ecclesiastics, for men may sit on chairs or benches in church, but women must kneel or sit on the ground. Why?

"Quién sabe? Who knows?" is all the satisfaction I have ever obtained on that point.

The music began with a crash that awakened me out of an agreeable slumber into which I had gradually fallen; and such discordance of instruments and voices, such confusion worse confounded, such inharmonious harmony, never before deafened mortal ears. The very spheres seemed out of tune, and rolling and crashing over each other. I could have cried *Miserere!* with the loudest; and in the midst of all the undrilled band was a *music master,* with violin-stick uplifted, rushing desperately from one to the other, in vain endeavouring to keep time, and frightened at the clamour he himself had been instrumental in raising, like Phaeton entrusted with his unmanageable coursers.[15] The noise was so great as to be really alarming, and the heat was severe in proportion. The calm face of the Virgin seemed to look reproachfully down. We were thankful when, at the conclusion of this stormy appeal for mercy, we were able to make our way into the fresh air and soft moonlight through the confusion and squeezing at the doors, where it was rumoured that a soldier had killed a baby with his bayonet. A bad place for poor little babies— decidedly.

Outside in the square it was cool and agreeable. A military band was playing airs from the *Norma,* and the womenkind were sitting on the stones of the railing, or wandering about and finishing their day's work by a quiet flirtation *au clair de la lune.*

It was now eleven o'clock, and the *pulquerías* were thrown open for the refreshment of the faithful, and though hitherto much order had prevailed it was not likely to endure much longer; notwithstanding which, we had the imprudence to walk unattended to our own house at San Fernando. In the centre of the city there seemed no danger. People were still walking, and a few still drinking at the lighted booths; but when we arrived at the lower part of the Alameda all was still, and as we walked outside under the long shadows of the trees I expected every moment to be attacked, and wished we were anywhere, even on the silvery top of Popocatepetl! We passed several crowded *pulquerías,* where some were drinking and others drunk. Arrived at the arches, we saw from time to time a suspicious blanketed figure half hid by the shadow of the wall. A few doors from our own domicile was a pulque shop filled with *léperos,* of whom some were standing at the door shrouded in their blankets. It seemed to me we should never pass them, but we walked fast and reached our door in safety. Here we thundered in vain. The porter was asleep and for nearly ten minutes we heard voices within, male and female, ineffectually endeavouring to persuade the heavy-headed Cerberus to relinquish his keys. It would have been a choice moment for our friends had any of them wished to accost us; but either they had not observed us, or perhaps they thought that Calderón, walk-

ing so late, must have been armed—or perhaps, more charitable construction, they had profited by the solemnities of the day.

We got in at last, and I felt thankful enough for shelter and safety,
and as wearied of the day's performances as you may be in reading a
description of them.

Next morning, *Sábado de Gloria*, I could not persuade myself to go
as far as the plaza, to see the Iscariots explode. At a distance we listened
to the hissing and crackling of the fireworks, the ringing of all the bells,
and the thundering of artillery—and knew by the hum of busy voices,
and the rolling of carriages, that the Holy Week was numbered with
the past.[16]

We hear that it is in contemplation amongst the English here, headed
by their minister, to give a ball in the Minería to celebrate the marriage
of Queen Victoria, which will be turning these splendid halls to some
account.

I have some intention of giving a series of weekly soirées, but am
assured that they will not succeed, because hitherto such parties have
failed. As a reason is given the extravagant notions of the ladies in point
of dress, and it is said that nothing but a ball where they can wear
jewels and a toilet therewith consistent will please them; that a lady of
high rank, who had been in Madrid, having proposed simple *tertulias*
and white muslin dresses, half the men in Mexico were ruined that
year by the embroidered French and India muslins bought by their wives
during this reign of simplicity—the idea of a plain white muslin, a dress
worn by any *lépera*, never having struck them as possible. Nevertheless
we can but make the attempt.[17]

We propose going next week to Tulancingo, where our friends the
Adalids have a country place; from thence we proceed to visit the mines
of Real del Monte.

Thursday: April 23rd, 1840

On Monday we gave a *tertulia* which, notwithstanding all predic-
tions, went off remarkably well, and consisted of nearly all the pleasantest
people in Mexico. We had music, dancing, and cards, and at three in
the morning the German cotillon was still in full vigour. Everyone was
disposed to be amused, and moreover the young ladies were dressed very
simply, most of them in plain white muslins. There was but a small
sprinkling of diamonds, and that chiefly among the elderly part of the
community. Still, it is said that the novelty alone induced them to come,
and that weekly soirées will not succeed. We shall try. Besides which,
the lady of the French minister proposes being *at home* on Wednesday
evenings; the lady of the Prussian minister takes another evening; I, a
third, and we shall see what can be effected.

15

A Convent from Inside

Friday: April 24th, 1840
San Fernando, Mexico

The Archbishop has not only granted me permission to visit the convents, but permits me to take two ladies along with me—of which I have been informed by the minister, Señor Cañedo,[1] in a very amiable note just received, enclosing one from Señor Posada which I translate for your edification:

To His Excellency Señor Don J. de D. Cañedo.

April 24th, 1840

My dear Friend and Companion:
The Abbess and Nuns of the Convent of the Encarnación are now prepared to receive the visit of our three pilgrims, next Sunday, at half past four in the afternoon, and should that day not suit them, let them mention what day will be convenient.

Afterwards we shall arrange their visit to the Concepción, Enseñanza Antigua, and Jesús María, which are the best, and I shall let you know, and we shall agree upon the days and hours most suitable. I remain your affectionate friend and *Capellán,*

Manuel Posada

Monday: April 27th, 1840

Accordingly, on Sunday afternoon, we drove to the Encarnación, the most splendid and richest convent in Mexico, excepting perhaps La Concepción.[2] If it were in any other country I might mention the surpassing beauty of the evening, but as—except in the rainy season, which has not yet begun—the evenings are always beautiful, the weather leaves no room for description. The sky always blue, the air always soft, the flowers always blossoming, the birds always singing, Thomson never could have written his *Seasons* here.[3]

We descended at the convent gate, were admitted by the portress, and were received by several nuns, their faces closely covered with a double crape veil. We were then led into a spacious hall, hung with handsome lustres, and adorned with various Virgins and saints magnificently dressed. Here the eldest, a very dignified old lady, lifted her veil—the others following her example—and introduced herself as the *madre vicaria*, bringing us many excuses from the old abbess who, having an inflammation in her eyes, was confined to her cell. She and another reverend mother, and a group of elderly dames—tall, thin, and stately—then proceeded to inform us that the Archbishop had, in person, given orders for our reception and that they were prepared to show us the whole establishment.

The dress is a long robe of very fine white cassimere, a thick black crape veil, and long rosary. The dress of the novices is the same, only that the veil is white. For the first half-hour or so, I fancied that along with their politeness was mingled a good deal of restraint, caused perhaps by the presence of a foreigner, and especially of an Englishwoman. My companions they knew well, the Señorita [Escandón] having even passed some months there. However this may have been, the feeling seemed gradually to wear away. Kindness or curiosity triumphed; their questions became unceasing; and before the visit was concluded I was addressed as "*mi vida*, my life," by the whole establishment.

Where was I born? Where had I lived? What convents had I seen? Which did I prefer, the convents in France or those in Mexico? Which were largest? Which had the best garden? &c., &c. Fortunately I could, with truth, give the preference to their convent, as to spaciousness and magnificence, over any I ever saw.[4]

The Mexican style of building is peculiarly advantageous for recluses, the great galleries and courts affording them a constant supply of fresh air—while the fountains sound so cheerfully, and the garden in this climate of perpetual spring affords them such a constant source of enjoyment all the year round, that one pities their secluded state much less here than in any other country.

This convent is in fact a palace. The garden, into which they led us first, is kept in good order, with its stone walks, stone benches, and an ever-playing and sparkling fountain. The trees were bending with fruit, and they pulled quantities of the most beautiful flowers for us: sweet peas and roses, with which all gardens here abound, carnations, jasmine, and heliotrope. It was a pretty picture to see them wandering about, or standing in groups in this high-walled garden, while the sun was setting behind the hills, and the noise of the city was completely excluded, everything breathing repose and contentment. Most of the halls in the convent are noble rooms. We visited the whole, from the refectory to the *botica*, and admired the extreme cleanness of everything, especially of the immense kitchen, which seems hallowed from the approach even of a particle of dust. This circumstance is partly accounted for by the fact that each nun has a servant, and some have two; for this is not one of the strictest orders. The convent is rich; each novice at her entrance pays five thousand dollars into the common stock. There are about thirty nuns and ten novices.

The prevailing sin in a convent generally seems to be pride, the

Pride that apes humility;[5]

and it is perhaps nearly inseparable from the conventual state. Set apart from the rest of the world they, from their little world, are too apt to look down with contempt which may be mingled with envy, or modified by pity, but must be unsuited to a true Christian spirit.

The novices were presented to us—poor little entrapped things! who really believe they will be let out at the end of the year if they should grow tired, as if they would ever be permitted to grow tired! The two eldest and most reverend ladies are sisters—thin, tall, and stately, with high noses, and remains of beauty. They have been in the convent since they were eight years old (which is remarkable, as sisters are rarely allowed to profess in the same establishment), and consider La Encarnación as a small piece of heaven upon earth. There were some handsome faces amongst them, and one whose expression and eyes were singularly lovely, but truth to say these were rather exceptions to the general rule.

Having visited the whole building, and admired one virgin's blue satin and pearls, and another's black velvet and diamonds, sleeping holy infants, saints, paintings, shrines, and confessionals—having even climbed up to the *azotea*, which commands a magnificent view—we came at length to a large hall decorated with paintings and furnished with antique high-backed armchairs, where a very elegant supper, lighted up and ornamented, greeted our astonished eyes: cakes, chocolate, ices, creams, custards, tarts, jellies, blancmangers, orange and lemonade, and other profane dainties, ornamented with gilt paper cut into little flags, &c. I was placed under a holy family, in a chair that might have served for a pope; the Señora Adalid and the Señorita Escandón on either side. The elder nuns, in stately array, occupied the other armchairs, and looked like statues carved in stone. A young girl, a sort of *pensionnaire*, brought in a little harp without pedals and, while we discussed cakes and ices, sung different ballads with a good deal of taste. The elder nuns helped us to everything, but tasted nothing themselves. The younger nuns and the novices were grouped upon a mat *à la Turque*, and a more picturesque scene altogether one could scarcely see: the young novices with their white robes, white veils and black eyes; the severe and dignified *madres* with their long dresses and mournful-looking black veils and rosaries; the veiled figures occasionally flitting along the corridor; ourselves in contrast, with our *worldly* dresses and coloured ribbons; and the great hall lighted by one immense lamp that hung from the ceiling. I felt transported three centuries back, and half afraid that the whole would flit away and prove a mere vision, a waking dream.

A gossiping old nun, who hospitably filled my plate with everything, gave me the enclosed *flag* cut in gilt paper, which, together with her custards and jellies, looked less unreal. They asked many questions in regard to Spanish affairs, and were not to be consoled for the defeat of Don Carlos, which they feared would be an end of the true religion in Spain.

After supper, to try the organ we proceeded upstairs to the choir where the nuns attend public worship, and which looks down upon the handsome convent church. I was set down to a sonata of Mozart's, the servants blowing the bellows. It seems to me that I made more noise than music, for the organ is very old, perhaps as old as the convent, which dates three centuries back. However, the nuns were pleased and, after they had sung a hymn, we returned below. I was rather sorry to leave them, and felt as if I could have passed some time there very contentedly; but it was near nine o'clock, and we were obliged to take our departure; so, having been embraced very cordially by the whole community, we left the hospitable walls of the Encarnación.[6]

Tuesday: April 28th, 1840

Last evening we were sitting at home very quietly about ten o'clock —Calderón, Monsieur Mercier of the French legation, and I—when Emilie rushed into the room all dishevelled. "Come quickly, sir! Robbers are breaking open the kitchen door!" A succession of feminine shrieks in the distance added effect to her words. Calderón jumped up, ran for his pistols, gave one to Monsieur Mercier, called up the soldiers, but no robbers appeared. The kitchen door was indeed open, and the trembling *galopina* attested that, being in the kitchen alone, dimly lighted by one small lamp, three men, all armed, had entered, and had rushed out again on hearing her give the alarm. We somewhat doubted her assertions, but the next morning found that the men had in fact escaped by the *azotea*, a great assistance to all Mexican depredators. At the end of this row of houses the people ran out and fired upon them, but without effect. The house of the old Countess of San Francisco has been broken into, her porter wounded—report says killed—and her plate carried off.[7] In the meantime our soldiers watch in the kitchen, a pair of loaded pistols adorn the table, a double-barreled gun stands in the corner, and a bulldog growls in the gallery. This little passing visit to us

was probably caused by the arrival of some large boxes from London, especially of a very fine harp and piano, both Erard's, which I had the pleasure of seeing unpacked this morning and which, in spite of jolting and bad roads, have arrived in perfect condition.

Thus far I had written, it being now the evening and I sitting alone, when a succession of shrieks arose even more awful than those which alarmed us last night. At the same time the old *galopina*, her daughter, and a French girl who lives here rushed shouting along the gallery— not a word they said comprehensible, but something concerning "a robber in black, with men at his back, who had burst open the door." At the noise the whole household had assembled. One ran this way, one ran that. A little French *teinturier*, who it appeared had been paying the maids a polite visit, seized the loaded gun; the footman took a pistol and hid himself behind the porter; Emilie, like a second Joan of Arc, appeared with a rusty sabre; the soldiers rushed up with their bayonets; the coachman stood aloof with nothing; the porter led up the rear, holding a large dog by the collar—but no robber appears, and the girls are all sobbing and crying because we doubt their having seen one. *Galopina* the younger, shedding tears in torrents, swears to the man. *Galopina* the elder, enveloped in her *rebozo*, swears to any number of men; and the *recamerera* has cried herself into a fit between fear and indignation.

Such is the agreeable state of things about nine o'clock this evening, for one real attempt to enter the house invariably gives rise to a thousand imaginary attacks and fanciful alarms.

After many attempts at walking, I have very nearly abandoned it, but take a great deal of exercise both on horseback and in the carriage— which last, on account of the ill-paved condition of the streets, affords rather more exercise than the former.

I drove out this morning in an open carriage with the Señorita Escandón to her country house at San Agustín, the gambling emporium. But the famous annual fête does not take place till Whitsunday, and the pretty country villas there are at present abandoned. We walked in the garden till the sun became insupportable. The fragrance of the roses and jasmine was almost overpowering. There are trees of *mille-fleur* roses; heliotrope and honeysuckle cover every pillar; and yellow jasmine trails over everything.

Found on my return an anonymous letter, begging me to "beware of my cook!" and signed *Fernández*. Having shown it to some gentlemen who dined here, one thought it might be a plan of the robbers to get rid of the cook, whom they considered in their way; another, with more probability, that it was merely a plan of the attentive Señor Fernández to get the cook's place for himself.

We went lately to pay a visit to the celebrated Virgen de los Remedios —the *Gachupina*, the Spanish patroness and rival of Our Lady of Guadalupe. This Virgin was brought over by Cortés, and, when he displaced the Indian idols in the great temple of Mexico, caused them to be broken in pieces, and the sanctuary to be purified, he solemnly placed there a crucifix and this image of the Virgin—then kneeling before it, gave solemn thanks to Heaven which had permitted him thus to adore the Most High in a place so long profaned by the most cruel idolatries.

It is said that this image was brought to Mexico by a soldier of Cortés' army called Villafuerte, and that the day succeeding the terrible *noche triste* it was concealed by him in the place where it was afterwards discovered. At all events, the image disappeared and nothing further was known of it until, on the top of a barren and treeless mountain, in the heart of a large maguey, she was found by a fortunate Indian. Her restoration was joyfully hailed by the Spaniards. A church was erected on the spot. A priest was appointed to take charge of the miraculous image. Her fame spread abroad. Gifts of immense value were brought to her shrine. A treasurer was appointed to take care of her jewels; a *camarista* to superintend her rich wardrobe. No rich dowager died in peace until she had bequeathed to Our Lady of los Remedios her largest diamond, or her richest pearl.

In seasons of drought she is brought in from her dwelling in the mountain, and carried in procession through the streets. The viceroy himself on foot used to lead the holy train. One of the highest rank drives the chariot in which she is seated.[8] In succession she visits the principal convents, and as she is carried through the cloistered precincts the nuns are ranged on their knees in humble adoration. Plentiful rains immediately follow her arrival. Señor Adalid, who accompanied us, has on several occasions filled the office of her coachman, by which means he has seen the interior of most of the convents in Mexico. It is true that there came a time when the famous curate Hidalgo, the prime mover of the Revolution, having taken as his standard an image of the Virgin of Guadalupe, a rivalry arose between her and the Spanish Virgin; and, Hidalgo having been defeated and forced to fly, the image of the Virgen de los Remedios was conducted to Mexico dressed as a general, and invoked as the Patroness of Spain. Later still, the Virgin herself was denounced as a *gachupina!*—her general's sash boldly torn from her by the valiant General Tornel, who also signed her passport, with an order for her to leave the republic.[9] However, she was again restored to her honours, and still retains her treasurers, her *camarista,* and sanctum sanctorum.

Being desirous of seeing this celebrated image, we set off one fine afternoon in a carriage of Adalid's, drawn by six unbroken horses, accompanied by him and his lady—and performed four leagues of bad road in an incredibly short space of time. The horses themselves were in an evident state of astonishment, for after kicking and plunging and, as they imagined, running away, they found themselves driven much faster than they had the slightest intention of going; so after a little while they acknowledged, in Adalid's capital coachman, *une main de maître.*

The mountain is barren and lonely, but the view from its summit is beautiful, commanding the whole plain. The church is old and not very remarkable, yet a picturesque object as it stands in its gray solitariness with one or two trees beside it, of which one without leaves was entirely covered with the most brilliant scarlet flowers. Señor Adalid having been the Virgin's coachman, the Señora Adalid being the daughter of her *camarista,*[10] and Calderón the minister from the land of her predilection, we were not astonished at the distinguished reception which we met with from the reverend padre, the guardian of the mountain.

The church within is handsome; and above the altar is a copy of the original Virgin. After we had remained there a little while we were admitted into the sanctum, where the identical Virgin of Cortés, with a large silver maguey, occupies her splendid shrine. The priest retired and put on his robes, and then returning, and all kneeling before the altar, he recited the Credo. This over, he mounted the steps and, opening the shrine where the Virgin was encased, knelt down and removed her in his arms. He then presented her to each of us in succession, everyone kissing the hem of her satin robe. She was afterwards replaced with the same ceremony.

The image is a wooden doll about a foot high, holding in its arms an infant Jesus, both faces evidently carved with a rude penknife; two holes for the eyes and another for the mouth. This doll was dressed in blue satin and pearls, with a crown upon her head and a quantity of hair fastened on to the crown. No Indian idol could be much uglier. As she has been a good deal scratched and destroyed in the lapse of ages, Calderón observed that he was astonished they had not tried to restore her a little. To this the padre replied that the attempt had been made by several artists, each one of whom had sickened and died. He also mentioned, as one of her miracles, that living on a solitary mountain she had never been robbed; but I fear the good padre is somewhat *oblivious*, as this sacrilege has happened more than once. On one occasion, a crowd of *léperos* being collected, and the image carried round to be kissed, one of them, affecting intense devotion, bit off the large pearl that adorned her dress in front, and before the theft was discovered he had mingled with the crowd and escaped. When reminded of the circumstance, the padre said it was true, but that the thief was a *Frenchman*. After taking leave of the Virgin, we visited the padre in his own old house, attached to the church, where his only attendant, as usual among padres, is an old woman.[11]

We then made our way on foot down a steep hill, stopping to admire some noble stone arches, the remains of an aqueduct built by the Spaniards for conveying water from one mountain to the other; and with an Indian for our guide visited a newly discovered though anciently opened mine, said to be of silver, which had until lately been covered with rubbish. We groped through it, and found vaults and excavations and a deep pit of water. Calderón got some Indians to break off pieces of stone for him, which were put into a sack and sent home for examination. We were so tired of our walk down this steep and mountainous path, that on our return I mounted a horse with a man's saddle, belonging to one of the servants, and contrived to keep on while it climbed up the perpendicular ascent. As this seemed rather a selfish proceeding while the others walked, I invited the Señora Adalid to mount also in front, which she did; and, the path being almost perpendicular, my head nearly touched the ground, which certainly made the seat not over-safe or easy. However, we reached the top of the mountain in safety, though somewhat exhausted with laughing, and were driven home with the speed of a rail-car.[12]

TO THE SILVER MINES

16

Life on the Great Pulque Haciendas

Wednesday: May 6th, 1840
Hacienda of Santiago

Before the setting in of the rainy season, we accepted of the invitation of our friends the Adalids[1] to visit their different haciendas, as in a short time the roads will become nearly impassable.

The country in May is perhaps at its highest beauty, or even a little earlier as already the great blow of roses is nearly over; *au reste* there are roses all the year round, though more in December than in July. And this, by the way, is rather a source of disappointment to the unwary traveller. He arrives in December, and finds the gardens full of flowers. "If this be the case in December," says he to himself, "what will it be in May?" May comes—the roses are over, and the chief flowers in the gardens are dahlias and marigolds, our autumnal flowers; September, and these autumnal flowers still bloom, and with them you have mignonette and roses, and then pinks and jasmine and other flowers. In fact there seems to be no particular season for anything.

The weather at present is neither warm nor cold, but colder here than in Mexico, and when it does not rain it is lovely. Already there has been much rain, and the torrents are so swelled that there was some doubt as to whether our carriages could pass them.

Yesterday at five in the morning we left Mexico, in a coach once the property of Charles X. *"Sic transit,"* &c.; and a most luxurious travelling carriage is that of his ex-majesty; entirely covered with gilding save where the lilies of France surmount the crown (sad emblems of the fallen dynasty!); lined with white satin with violet-coloured binding, the satin cushions most excellently stuffed; large, commodious, and with a movement as soft as that of a gondola.[2]

A Frenchman bought it on a speculation, and brought it here for sale. In former days, from its gilded and showy appearance, it would have brought any price; but the taste for gaudy equipages has gone by since the introduction of foreign—and especially of English—carriages; and the present proprietor, who bought it for its intrinsic good qualities, paid but a moderate sum for it. In this carriage, drawn by six strong horses, with two first-rate coachmen and several outriders well armed, we went along at great speed. The drivers, dressed Mexican fashion with all their accoutrements smart and new, looked very picturesque. Jackets and trousers of deerskin, the jackets embroidered in green with hanging silver buttons, the trousers also embroidered and slit up the side of the leg, trimmed with silver buttons, and showing an under-pair of unbleached linen. These, with the postilions' boots, and great hats with gold rolls, form a dress which would *faire fureur* if some adventurous Mexican would venture to display it on the streets of London.

We left the city by the gate of Guadalupe, and passed by the great cathedral, our road lying over the marshy plains once covered by the waters of Lake Texcoco. To the east lay the great lake, its broad waters shining like a sheet of molten silver, and the two great volcanoes—the rising sun forming a crown of rays on the white brow of Popocatepetl.

To describe once for all the general aspect of the country on this side of the valley of Mexico, suffice it to say that there is a universal air of dreariness, vastness, and desolation. The country is flat, but always enlivened by the surrounding mountains, like an uninteresting painting in a diamond frame; and yet it is not wholly uninteresting. It has a character peculiar to itself: great plains of maguey, with huts with uncultivated patches that have once been gardens, still filled with flowers and choked with weeds; the huts themselves, generally of mud yet not unfrequently of solid stone, roofless and windowless, with traces of having been fine buildings in former days; the complete solitude, unbroken except by the passing Indian—certainly as much in a state of savage nature as the lower class of Mexicans were when Cortés first traversed these plains—with the same character, gentle and cowardly, false and cunning, as weak animals are apt to be by nature, and indolent and improvident as men are in a fine climate; ruins everywhere—here a viceroy's country palace, serving as a tavern, where the mules stop to rest and the drivers to drink pulque—there a whole village crumbling to pieces; roofless houses, broken-down walls and arches, an old church, the remains of a convent. For leagues, scarcely a tree to be seen, then a clump of the graceful *árbol de Perú*, or one great cypress—long strings of mules and asses, with their drivers—pasture fields with cattle—then again whole tracts of maguey, as far as the eye can reach; no roads worthy of the name, but a passage made between fields of maguey, bordered by crumbling-down low stone walls, causing a jolting from which not even the easy movement of Charles X's coach can save us. But the horses go at full gallop, accustomed to go through and over everything.

The first village we saw was Santa Clara, to our left, lying at the foot of some dark hills, with its white church and flat-roofed or noroofed houses. There being no shade, frequently not a tree for leagues, the sun and dust were disagreeable, and became more so as the day advanced. Here it came to pass that, travelling rapidly over these hot and dusty plains, the wheels of our carriage began to smoke. No house was in sight—no water within ken. It was a case of difficulty; when suddenly Adalid recollected that not far from thence was an old rancho, a deserted farmhouse, at present occupied by robbers; and, having ordered the coachman to drive to within a few hundred yards of this house, he sent a servant on horseback with a *medio* (fourpence) to bring some water, which was treating the robbers like honourable men. The man galloped off, and shortly returned with a can full of water, which he carried back when the fire was extinguished.[3]

Meanwhile we examined, as well as we could, the external appearance of the robbers' domicile, which was an old half-ruined house, standing alone on the plain, with no tree near it. Several men with guns were walking up and down before the house—sporting-looking characters, but rather dirty—apparently either waiting for some expected *game*, or going in search of it. Women with *rebozos* were carrying water, and walking amongst them. There were also a number of dogs. The well-armed men who accompanied us, and the name of Adalid—so well known in these parts that once, when his carriage was surrounded by robbers, he merely mentioned who he was and they retreated with many apologies for their mistake—precluded all danger of an attack; but woe to the solitary

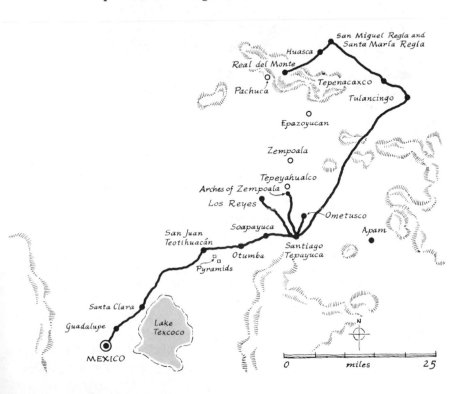

horseman or unescorted carriage that may pass thereby! Nor, indeed, are they always in the same mood; for Señor Adalid's houses have been frequently attacked in his absence, and his hacienda at Santiago once stood a regular siege, the robbers being at length repulsed by the bravery of his servants.

We set off again *au grand galop*, drivers and outriders giving, from time to time, the most extraordinary shrieks to encourage the horses and to amuse themselves, wild and shrill enough to frighten any civilized quadruped. The road grew more picturesque as we advanced, and at length our attention was arrested by the sight of the two great pyramids, which rise to the east of the town of San Juan Teotihuacán, which are mentioned by Humboldt, and have excited the curiosity and attention of every succeeding traveller. These huge masses were consecrated to the sun and moon, which, in the time of Cortés, were there represented by two vast stone idols covered with gold. The conquerors made use of the gold, and broke the idols in pieces, by order of the first bishop of Mexico.

Unfortunately our time was too limited to give them more than a passing observation. Fragments of obsidian, in the form of knives and of arrows, with which the priests opened the breasts of their human victims, are still to be found there; and numerous small idols, made of baked clay, are to be seen both there and in the plains adjoining. The Indians rather dislike to guide travellers to these pyramids, and their reluctance to do so has increased the popular belief of the existence of great concealed treasures near or in them.

The whole plain on which these great pyramids stand was formerly called Micaotli, or the Pathway of the Dead; and the hundreds of smaller pyramids which surround the larger ones (the Temples of the Sun and Moon) are symmetrically disposed in wide streets, forming a great burial plain, composed perhaps of the dust of their ancient warriors—an Aztec or Toltec Père Lachaise, or rather a roofless Westminster Abbey. So few of the ancient *teocallis* now remain, and these being nearly the only traces now existing of that extraordinary race, we regretted the more not being able to devote some time to their examination.[4] Fanaticism and policy induced the Spanish conquerors to destroy these heathen temples; and when we recollect that at the time of the Reformation in civilized England the most splendid Catholic edifices were made level with the ground—in compliance with the ferocious edict of John Knox, "Ding down the nests, and the rooks will fly off" —we can have little wonder or blame to bestow upon Cortés, who, in the excitement of a siege, gave orders for the destruction of these bloodstained sanctuaries.

In the afternoon we arrived at San Juan, a pretty village boasting of an inn, a schoolhouse, an avenue of fine trees, and a stream of clear water. It is true that the inn is a Mexican *posada,* bearing as much resemblance to what is generally called an inn as an hacienda does to an English country house; [and] the schoolhouse, a room with a mud floor and a few dirty benches occupied by little ragged boys and girls; but the avenue is pretty, the grass as green as emeralds, and the water crystal. We walked out while they changed horses—of which Señor Adalid had fresh relays of his own prepared all along the road— and entered the schoolhouse, attracted by the noise and the invitingly open door. The master was a poor, ragged, pale, careworn looking young man, seemingly half-dinned with the noise, but very earnest in his work. The children, all speaking at once, were learning to spell out of some old bills of Congress. Several moral sentences were written on the wall in very independent orthography. Calderón having remarked to the master that they were ill-spelt, he seemed very much astonished, and even inclined to doubt the fact. I thought it was one of those cases where ignorance is bliss, and fear the observation may have cost the young man a night's rest.

A row of grinning skulls was ranged round the wall of the churchyard, and the sexton, who gave us admittance to the church, taking up one to show it off, it all crumbled into dust, which filled the air like a cloud.

At the *posada* they gave us rancid sheep's milk, cheese, and biscuits so hard that Calderón asked the host if they were made in the same year with the church; at which he seemed mightily pleased, and could not stop laughing till we got into the carriage.

Soon after leaving San Juan we were met by the Señora de Adalid, in an open carriage, coming with her children to meet us. And, though she had travelled since sunrise from her hacienda, she appeared as if freshly dressed for an evening party: her dress, amber-coloured crape trimmed with white blonde, short sleeves, and *décolletée;* a set of beautiful Neapolitan strawberry-coral, set in gold; straw-coloured satin shoes, and a little China crape shawl embroidered in bright flowers—her hair dressed and uncovered.

We stopped at their hacienda of Soapayuca, an old house standing solitarily in the midst of great fields of maguey. It has a small deserted garden adjoining, amongst whose tangled bushes a pretty little tame deer was playing, with its half-startled look and full wild eye. We found an excellent breakfast prepared, and here, for the first time, I conceived the possibility of not disliking pulque. We visited the large buildings where it is kept, and found it rather refreshing, with a sweet taste and a creamy froth upon it, and with a much less decided odour than that which is sold in Mexico.[5]

This hacienda is under the charge of an *administrador,* to whom **Adalid** pays a large annual sum, and whose place is by no means a sinecure, as he lives in perpetual danger from robbers. He is captain of a troop of soldiers, and, as his life has been spent in "persecuting robbers," he is an object of intense hatred to that free and independent body, and has some thoughts of removing to another part of the country where he may be more tranquil. He gave us a terrible account of these night attacks, of the ineffectual protection afforded him by the government, and of the nearly insuperable difficulties thrown in the way of any attempt to bring these men to justice. He lately told the President that he had some thoughts of joining the robbers himself, as they were the only persons in the republic protected by the government. The President, however, is not to blame in this matter. He has used every endeavour to check these abuses; and difficulties have been thrown in his way from very unexpected sources.

Apropos to which, the **French** consul told us the other day that some time ago, having occasion to consult Judge _____ upon an affair of importance, he was shown into an apartment where that functionary was engaged with some suspicious-looking individuals—or rather who were above suspicion, their appearance plainly indicating their calling. On the table before him lay a number of guns, swords, pistols, and all sorts of arms. The judge requested Monsieur de _____ to be seated, observing that he was investigating a case of robbery committed by these persons. The robbers were seated, smoking very much at their ease, and the judge was enjoying the same innocent recreation. When his cigar became extinguished, one of these gentlemen taking his from his mouth handed it to the magistrate, who relighted his *puro* (cigar) at it, and returned it with a polite bow. In short, they were completely *hand in glove.*

In the evening we reached Santiago, where we now are, about eighteen leagues from Mexico—a large house in a wild-looking country, standing in solitary state, with hills behind and rocks before it, and surrounded by great uncultivated plains and pasture fields. Everything is *en grande* in this domain. There is a handsome chapel and sacristy; a *plaza de toros;*

hundreds of horses and mules; and, between *dependientes* and hangers-on, we sat down, thirty or forty people, to dinner.[6]

Thursday: May 7th, 1840

The very day of our arrival, Bernardo the matador, with his men, arrived from Mexico, bringing their superb dresses with them, for the purpose of giving us a country bullfight. As an hacienda of this kind is an immense empty house, without furniture or books, all the amusement is to be found either out of doors or in large parties in the house; and the unostentatious hospitality which exists in this and some other of the old families is a pleasing remnant of Spanish manners and habits—now falling into disuse, and succeeded by more pretension to refinement, and less of either real wealth or sociability.

In the evening here, all assemble in a large hall, the Señora de Adalid playing the piano, while the whole party—agents, *dependientes*, major-domo, coachmen, matadors, picadors, and women servants—assemble and perform the dances of the country: *jarabes, aforrados, enanos, palomos, zapateros,* &c., &c. It must not be supposed that in this apparent mingling of ranks between masters and servants there is the slightest want of respect on the part of the latter; on the contrary, they seem to exert themselves, as in duty bound, for the amusement of their master and his guests. There is nothing republican in it, no feeling of equality; as far as I have seen, that feeling does not exist here, except between people of the same rank. It is more like some remains of the feudal system, where the retainers sat at the same table with their chief, but below the salt.[7]

The dances are monotonous, with small steps and a great deal of shuffling, but the music is rather pretty, and some of the dancers were very graceful and agile; and, if it were not invidious to make distinctions, we *might* particularize Bernardo the matador, the head coachman, and a handsome peasant girl with a short scarlet and yellow petticoat and a foot and ankle *à la Vestris.*[8] They were all very quiet, but seemed in a state of intense enjoyment; and some of the men accompanied the dancers on the guitar.

First the player strikes up in quick time, and the dancer performs a quick movement; then the musician accompanies the music with his voice, and the dancer goes through some slow steps. Such is the case in the *"Aforrado"* (or "Lining"), a curious *nom de tendresse,* expressive, I suppose, of something soft and well wadded. The words are as follow:

1.

Aforrado de mi vida!
  Cómo estás, cómo te va?
Cómo has pasado la noche,
  No has tenido novedad?

2.

Aforrado de mi vida!
  Yo te quisiera cantar,
Pero mis ojos son tiernos,
  Y empezarán a llorar.

3.

De Guadalajara vengo,
  Lidiando con un soldado,
Sólo por venir a ver
  A mi jarabe aforrado.

4.

Y vente conmigo,
  Y yo te daré
Zapatos de raso,
  Color de café.

Of these poetical sublimities, a translation at once literal and metrical would, we think, damp the spirit of a Coleridge.

1.

Lining of my life!
How are you, how do you do?
How have you passed the night,
Have you met with nothing new?

2.

Lining of my life!
To you I should like to sing,
But that my eyes are weak,
And tears might begin to spring.

3.

From Guadalajara fighting,
With a soldier I came on,
My well-lined *sweet syrup!*
I came to see you alone.

4.

And come then with me,
And I will give thee
Such fine shoes of satin,
The colour of *tea.*

It is *coffee,* but you will excuse the poetical licence. The music married to this "immortal verse" I have learned by ear, and shall send you.

In the *"Enanos"* (the "Dwarfs") the dancer *makes himself little* every time the chorus is sung.

1.

Ah! qué bonitos
Son los enanos,
Los chiquititos
Y mexicanos.

2.

Sale la linda,
Sale la fea,
Sale el enano,
Con su zalea.

3.

Los enanitos
Se enojaron,
Porque a las enanas
Las pellizcaron.

There are many more verses, but I think you will find these quite satisfactory. "Ah! how pretty are the dwarfs, the little ones, the Mexicans! Out comes the pretty one, out comes the ugly one, out comes the dwarf, with his jacket of [sheep]skin. The little he-dwarfs were angry, because someone pinched the she-dwarfs."[9]

There is another called the *"Toro,"* of which the words are not very interesting; and the *"Zapatero"* (or "Shoemaker") was very well danced by a gentleman who accompanied himself, at the same time, on the guitar.[10]

Yesterday morning we set off in a burning sun, over a perfect Egyptian desert, to visit the famous arches of Zempoala, a magnificent work, which we are told had greatly excited the admiration of Mr. Poinsett when in this country. This aqueduct, the object of whose construction was to supply these arid plains with water, was the work of a Spanish Franciscan friar, and has never been entirely concluded. We travelled about six leagues, and sat there for hours, looking up at the great stone arches, which seem like a work of giants.[11]

In the afternoon, we all rode to the *plaza de toros.* The evening was cool and our horses good, the road pretty and shady, and the plaza itself a most picturesque enclosure, surrounded by lofty trees. Chairs were placed for us on a raised platform; and the bright green of the trees, the flashing dresses of the toreadors, the roaring of the fierce bulls, the spirited horses, the music and the cries—the Indians shouting from the trees up which they had climbed—all formed a scene of savage grandeur, which for a short time at least is interesting.

Bernardo was dressed in blue satin and gold; the picadors in black and silver; the others in maroon-coloured satin and gold. All those on foot

wore knee breeches and white silk stockings, a little black cap with ribbons, and a plait of hair streaming down behind. The horses were generally good and, as each new adversary appeared, seemed to participate in the enthusiasm of their riders. One bull after another was driven in roaring, and as here they are generally fierce, and their horns not blunted as in Mexico, it is a much more dangerous affair. The bulls were not killed, but were sufficiently tormented. One stuck full of arrows and fireworks, all adorned with ribbons and coloured paper, made a sudden spring over an immensely high wall, and dashed into the woods. I thought afterwards of this unfortunate animal, how it must have been wandering about all night, bellowing with pain, the concealed arrows piercing its flesh, and looking like gay ornaments:

> So, when the watchful shepherd, from the blind,
> Wounds with a random shaft the careless hind,
> Distracted with her pain, she flies the woods,
> Bounds o'er the lawn, and seeks the silent floods—
> With fruitless care; for still the fatal dart
> Sticks in her side, and rankles in her heart.[12]

If the arrows had stuck too deep, and the bull could not rub them off against the trees, he must have bled to death. Had he remained, his fate would have been better, for when the animal is entirely exhausted they throw him down with a lasso and, pulling out the arrows, put ointment on the wounds.

The skill of the men is surprising; but the most curious part of the exhibition was when a coachman of Adalid's—a strong, handsome Mexican—mounted on the back of a fierce bull, which plunged and flung himself about as if possessed by a legion of demons, and forced the animal to gallop round and round the arena. The bull is first caught by the lasso, and thrown on his side, struggling furiously. The man mounts while he is still on the ground. At the same moment the lasso is withdrawn, and the bull starts up, maddened by feeling the weight of his unusual burden. The rider must dismount in the same way, the bull being first thrown down, otherwise he would be gored in a moment. It is terribly dangerous, for if the man were to lose his seat, his death is nearly certain; but these Mexicans are superb riders. A monk, who is attached to the establishment, seems an ardent admirer of these sports, and his presence is useful in case of a dangerous accident occurring, which is not unfrequent.

The amusement was suddenly interrupted by sudden darkness and a tremendous storm of rain and thunder, in the midst of which we mounted our horses and galloped home.

Friday: May 8th, 1840
Tulancingo

Another bullfight last evening! It is like pulque; one makes wry faces at it at first, and then begins to like it. One thing we soon discovered, which was that the bulls, if so inclined, could leap upon our platform, as they occasionally sprang over a wall twice as high. There was a part of the spectacle rather too horrible. The horse of one of the picadors was gored, his side torn up by the bull's horns, and in this state, streaming with blood, he was forced to gallop round the circle.

We spent one day in visiting Ometusco, an hacienda belonging to the Señora [Torres] Torija situated in the plains of Apam, and famous for the superior excellence of its pulque. The *órganos*, the nopal, and great fields of maguey constitute the chief vegetation for many miles round. The hacienda itself, a fine large building, stands lonely and bleak in the midst of magueys. A fine chapel, left unfinished since her husband's death, attracted our attention by its simple architecture and unpretending elegance.[13] It is nearly impossible to conceive anything more lonely than a residence here must be; or in fact in any of the haciendas situated on these great plains of Otumba and Apam.

This morning we set off for Tulancingo, in four carriages-and-six containing the whole family, ourselves, maids, and children, padre and nursery governess—relays being placed all along the road, which we traversed at full gallop. But in crossing some great pasture fields, the drivers of two of the carriages began to race; one of the horses fell and threw the postilion; the carriage itself was overturned, and, though none of the inmates were injured, the poor *mozo* was terribly wounded in his head and legs. No assistance being near, he changed places with one of the men on horseback, and was brought on slowly.

About three in the afternoon, we arrived at Tulancingo, rather an important city in its way, and which has been the theatre of many revolutionary events—with various streets and shops, a handsome church, alcaldes, a prefect, &c. There appear to be some few good houses and decent families, and clean, small shops, and there are pretty, shady walks in the environs; and, though there are also plenty of miserable dwellings and dirty people, it is altogether rather a civilized place. The house of the Adalids, which stands within a courtyard and is *the* house *par excellence,* is very handsome, with little furniture, but with some remnants of luxury. The dining hall is a noble room, with beautiful Chinese paper, opening into a garden which is the boast of the republic, and is indeed singularly pretty and kept in beautiful order, with gravel walks and fine trees, clear tanks and sparkling fountains, and an extraordinary profusion of the most beautiful flowers—roses especially. There is something extremely oriental in its appearance, and the fountains are ornamented with China vases and Chinese figures of great value. Walking along under arches formed by rosebushes, a small column of water spouted forth from each bush, sprinkling us all over with its shower. But the prettiest thing in the garden is a great tank of clear water, enclosed on three sides by a Chinese building, round which runs a piazza with stone pillars, shaded by a drapery of white curtains. Comfortable well-cushioned sofas are arranged along the piazza, which opens into a large room where one may dress after bathing. It is the prettiest and coolest retreat possible, and entirely surrounded by trees and roses. Here one may lie at noonday, with the sun and the world completely shut out. They call this an English garden, than which it rather resembles the summer retreat of a sultan.

When we arrived, we found dinner laid for forty persons, and the table ornamented, by the taste of the gardener, with pyramids of beautiful flowers.[14]

I have now formed acquaintance with many Mexican dishes: *mole* (meat stewed in red chile), boiled nopal, fried bananas, green chile, &c. Then we invariably have *frijoles* (brown beans stewed), [and] hot tortillas—and, this being in the country, pulque is the universal beverage. In Mexico, tortillas and pulque are considered unfashionable, though both are still to be met with occasionally in some of the best old houses. They have here a most delicious species of cream cheese, made by the Indians, and ate with virgin honey. I believe there is an intermixture of goats' milk in it; but the Indian families who make it, and who have been offered large sums for the receipt, find it more profitable to keep their secret.

Every dinner has *puchero* immediately following the soup, consisting of boiled mutton, beef, bacon, fowls, *garbanzos* (a white bean), small gourds, potatoes, boiled pears, greens, and any other vegetables—a piece of each put on your plate at the same time, and accompanied by a sauce of herbs or tomatoes.

As for fruits, we have *mameyes, chirimoyas, granaditas,* white and black *zapotes*—the black, sweet, with a green skin and black pulp, and with black stones in it—the white resembling it in outward appearance and form, but with a white pulp, and the kernel, which is said to be poisonous, very large, round, and white. It belongs to a larger and more leafy tree than the black *zapote,* and grows in cold or temperate climates; whereas the other is a native of *tierra caliente*. Then there is the *chicozapote,* of the same family, with a whitish skin and a white or rose-tinged pulp (this also belongs to the warm regions); the *capulín,* or Mexican cherry; the mango, of which the best come from Orizaba and Córdoba;

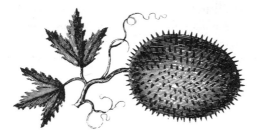

the *chayote,* &c.[15] Of these I prefer the *chirimoya, zapote blanco, granadita,* and mango; but this is a matter of taste.

Tuesday: May 12th, 1840

We have spent some days here very pleasantly; riding amongst the hills in the neighbourhood, exploring caves, viewing waterfalls, and climbing on foot or on horseback, wherever foot or horse could penetrate. No habits to be worn in these parts, as I found from experience, after being caught upon a gigantic maguey, and my gown torn in two. It is certainly always the wisest plan to adopt the customs of the country one lives in. A dress either of stuff (such as merino) or of muslin, as short as it is usually worn, a *rebozo* tied over one shoulder, and a large straw hat is about the most convenient costume that can be adopted.

The horses are small but strong, spirited, and well-made; generally un-shod, which they say makes the motion more agreeable; and almost all, at least all ladies' horses, are taught the *paso*, which I find tiresome for a continuance, though a good *paso* horse will keep up with others that gallop, and for a longer time.[16]

The great amusement here in the evening is playing at *juegos de prendas*, games with forfeits, which I recommend to all who wish to make a rapid improvement in the Spanish tongue. Last night, being de-sired to name a forfeit for the padre, I condemned him to dance the *jarabe*, of which he performed a few steps in his long gown and girdle, with equal awkwardness and good nature.

We met today the prettiest little *ranchera*, a farmer's wife or daughter, riding in front of a *mozo* on the same horse—their usual mode—dressed in a short embroidered muslin petticoat, white satin shoes, a pearl neck-lace and earrings, a *rebozo*, and a large round straw hat. The ladies sit their horse on a contrary side to our fashion.[17] They have generally adopted English saddles, but the farmers' wives frequently sit in a sort of chair, which they find much more commodious.

Some country ladies, who attended mass in the chapel this morning, were dressed in very short clear white muslin gowns, very much starched, and so disposed as to show two underpetticoats also stiffly starched and trimmed with lace; their shoes coloured satin. Considered as a costume of their own, I begin to think it rather pretty. The oldest women here or in Mexico never wear caps; nothing but their own gray hair, sometimes cut short, sometimes turned up with a comb, and not unusually tied behind in a pigtail. There is no attempt to conceal the ravages of time.

It appears to me that amongst the young girls here there is not that desire to enter upon the cares of matrimony which is to be observed in many other countries. The opprobrious epithet of "old maid" is unknown. A girl is not the less admired because she has been ten or a dozen years in society; the most severe remark made on her is that she is "hard to please." No one calls her *passée*, or looks out for a new face to admire. I have seen no courting of the young men either in mothers or daughters: no matchmaking mammas, or daughters looking out for their own in-terests. In fact, young people have so few opportunities of being to-gether that Mexican marriages must be made in heaven, for I see no opportunity of bringing them about upon earth![18] The young men, when they do meet with young ladies in society, appear devoted to and very much afraid of them. I know but one lady in Mexico who has the reputation of having manoeuvred all her daughters into great marriages; but she is so clever, and her daughters were such beauties, that it can have cost her no trouble. As for flirtation, the name is unknown, and the thing.

I have been taking lessons in the Indian dances from Doña Rosita; they are not ungraceful, but lazy and monotonous.

On every door in this house there is a printed paper to the following effect:

> *Quién a esta casa da luz? Jesús.*
> *Quién la llena de alegría? María.*
> *Y quién la abraza en' la fe? José.*
> *Luego bien claro se ve*
> *Que siempre habrá contrición,*
> *Teniendo en el corazón,*
> *A Jesús, María, y José.*

Who gives light to this house? Jesus.
Who fills it with joy? Mary.
Who kindles faith in it? Joseph.
Then we see very clearly
That there will always be contrition,
Keeping in our hearts,
Jesus, Mary, and Joseph.

These are written in verse, and below:

The most illustrious Bishop of Monte-Rey, Don Fray José de Jesús María Belaunzarán, hereby ordains and grants, along with the Bishops of Puebla, Durango, Valladolid and Guadalajara, two hundred days of indulgence to all those who devoutly repeat the above ejaculation, and invoke the sweet names of Jesus, Mary, and Joseph.

The people here have certainly a poetical vein in their composition. Everything is put into verse—sometimes doggerel, like the above (in which *luz* rhyming with *Jesús* shows that the *z* is pronounced here like an *s*), occasionally a little better, but always in rhyme.

We went this evening to visit the Countess del Valle who has a house in the village.[19] Found her in bed, feverish, and making use of simple remedies, such as herbs, the knowledge and use of which have descended from the ancient Indians to the present lords of the soil.

The Spanish historians who have written upon the conquest of Mexico all mention the knowledge which the Mexican physicians had of herbs. It was supposed by these last that for every infirmity there was a remedy in the herbs of the field; and to apply them, according to the nature of the malady, was the chief science of these primitive professors of medicine. Much which is now used in European pharmacy is due to the research of Mexican doctors—such as sarsaparilla, jalap, friars' rhubarb, mechoacan, &c., various emetics, antidotes to poison, remedies against fever, and an infinite number of plants, minerals, gums, and simple medicines. As for their infusions, decoctions, ointments, plasters, oils,

&c., Cortés himself mentions the wonderful number of these which he saw in the Mexican market for sale. From certain trees they distilled balsams, and drew a balsamic liquid both from a decoction of the branches and from the bark steeped in water. Bleeding and bathing were their other favourite remedies. The countrypeople breathed a vein with a maguey-point, and when they could not find leeches substituted the prickles of the American hedgehog.

Besides bathing in the rivers, lakes, tanks, and fountains, they used a bath which is still to be seen in many Indian villages, and which they call the *temazcalli*. It is made of unbaked bricks; its form is that of a baker's oven, about eight feet wide and six high; the pavement rather convex, and lower than the surface of the soil. A person can enter this bath only on his knees. Opposite the entry is a stone or brick stove, its opening towards the exterior of the bath, with a hole to let out the smoke. Before the bath is prepared, the floor inside is covered with a mat, on which is placed a jar of water, some herbs, and leaves of corn. The stove is then heated until the stones which unite it with the bath become red-hot. When the bather enters the entry is closed, and the only opening left is a hole at the top of the vault, which, when the smoke of the oven has passed through, is also shut. They then pour water upon the red-hot stones, from which a thick vapour arises, which fills the *temazcalli*.

The bather then throws himself on the mat and, drawing down the steam with the herbs and maize, wets them in the tepid water of the jar, and if he has any pain applies them to the part affected. This having produced perspiration, the door is opened and the well-baked patient comes out and dresses. For fevers, for bad colds, for the bite of a poisonous animal, this is said to be a certain cure; also for acute rheumatism.[20]

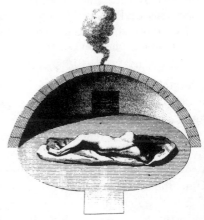

For the cure of wounds, the Spaniards found the Mexican remedies most efficacious. Cortés himself was cured by one of their doctors of a severe wound in the head, received at Otumba, through which we lately passed. For fractures, for humours, for everything, they had their remedy; sometimes pulverizing the seeds of plants, and attributing much of their efficacy to the superstitious ceremonies and prayers which they used while applying them, especially those which they offered up to Tzapotlatenan, the goddess of medicine.

A great deal of this knowledge is still preserved amongst their descendants and considered efficacious. For every illness there is an herb, for every accident a remedy. Baths are in constant use, although these *temazcallis* are confined to the Indians. In every family there is some knowledge of simple medicine, very necessary in haciendas especially, where no physician can possibly be procured.

There is a hill upon Adalid's property said to contain much buried treasure. There are many traditions here of this concealed Indian wealth, but very little gold has been actually recovered from these mountain tombs. Buried gold has occasionally come to light—not by researches in the mountains, for few are rash enough to throw away their money in search of what would probably prove an imaginary treasure—but by accident, in the ruins of old houses, where the proprietors had deposited it for safety in some period of revolution, perhaps no later than at the time of the Spanish expulsion.

Some years ago an old and very poor woman rented a house in the environs of Mexico, as old and wretched as herself, for four reals a week. It had an old broken-down stone patio (inner courtyard), which she used to sweep now and then with her little old broom. One day she observed two or three stones in this patio larger and more carefully put together than the others, and the little old woman, being a daughter of Eve by some collateral branch, poked down and picked and worked at the stones until she was able to raise them up—when, lo and behold, she discovered a can full of treasure: no less than five thousand dollars in gold! Her delight and her fright were unbounded; and, being a prudent old lady, she determined in the first place to leave the house, and next to carry in her treasure, *poquito a poquito* (little by little), to a room in Mexico, keeping the old house as a sort of bank. She did so; took a nice room, and instead of sleeping on a *petate* (mat), as she had hitherto done, brought herself a little bedstead, and even a mattress—two chairs and a small table—and treated herself not only to chocolate, but to a few bottles of good wine! Such extraordinary luxury could not fail to excite suspicion. She was questioned by her neighbours, and at length entrusted her secret to their keeping. Nevertheless, my informant assures me that notwithstanding this she was not robbed, and was allowed to enjoy her good fortune in peace. It is difficult to credit such a miracle in this land of picking and stealing, but my authority is beyond impeachment.

Whilst I write on these irrelevant matters, I am warned that the coaches are at the door, and that we are about setting off for Tepenacaxco, another hacienda of Señor Adalid's, a few leagues from this.

17

Visit to the Mines; A Stormy Journey

May, 1840
Hacienda of Tepenacaxco

This is a fine wild scene. The house stands entirely alone; not a tree near it. Great mountains rise behind it, and in every other direction as far as the eye can reach are vast plains, over which the wind comes whistling fresh and free, with nothing to impede its triumphant progress. In front of the house is a clear sheet of water, a great deep square basin for collecting the rain. These *jagüeyes*, as they are called, are very common in Mexico, where there are few rivers, and where the use of machines for raising water is by no means general as yet.

There is no garden here, but there are a few shrubs and flowers in the inner courtyard. The house inside is handsome, with a chapel and a patio, which is occasionally used as a *plaza de toros*. The rooms are well fitted up, and the bedroom walls are covered with a pretty French paper, representing scenes of Swiss rural life. There are great outhouses, stables for the mules and horses, and stone barns for the wheat and barley, which, together with pulque, form the produce of this hacienda.[1]

We took a long ride this morning to visit a fine lake where there are plenty of wild duck and turtle. The gentlemen took their guns and had

tolerable sport. The lake is very deep, so that boats have sailed on it, and several miles in circumference, with a rivulet flowing from it. Yet with all this water the surrounding land, not more than twenty feet higher, is dry and sterile and the lake is turned to no account, either from want of means or of hydraulic knowledge. However, Calderón having made some observation on this subject, the proprietor of the lake and of a ruined house standing near, which is the very picture of loneliness and desolation, remarked in reply: that from this estate to Mexico the distance is thirty-six leagues; that a load of wheat costs one real a league; and moreover [that] the *alcabala*, the duty, has to be paid at the gates of Mexico, so that it would bring no profit if sent there—while in the surrounding district there is not sufficient population to consume the produce. So these unnecessary and burdensome taxes, the thinness of the population, and the want of proper means of transport impede the prosperity of the people, and check the progress of agriculture.

I had a beautiful horse, but half-broke, which took fright and ran off with me. I got great credit for keeping my seat so well, which I must confess was more through good fortune than skill. The day was delightful, the air exhilarating, and the blue sky perfectly cloudless as we galloped over the plains; but at length the wind rose so high that we dismounted, and got into the carriage. We sat by the shores of the lake, and walked along its pebbly margin, watching the wild duck as they skimmed over its glassy surface, and returned home in a magnificent sunset; the glorious god himself a blood-red globe, surrounded by blazing clouds of gold and crimson.

In the evening a troop of asses were driven across the plain, and led round to the back of the house; and we were all called out in haste, and each desired to choose one of the long-eared fraternity for our particular use. Some had saddles, and some had none, but we mounted to the number of thirty persons, followed by a cavalcade of little ragged boys armed with sticks and whips. My ass was an obstinate brute, whom I had mistakenly chosen for his sleek coat and open countenance; but, by dint of being lashed up, he suddenly set off at full gallop, and distanced all the others. Such screaming and laughing and confusion!—and so much difficulty in keeping the party together! It was nearly dark when we set off; but the moon rose, her silver disk lighting up the hills and the plains; the wind fell, and the night was calm and delightful. We rode about six miles to a pretty little chapel with a cross that gleamed amongst the trees in the moonlight, by the side of a running stream. Here we dismounted, and sat by the brink of the little sparkling rivulet, while the deep shadows came stealing over the mountains, and all around was still, and cool, and silent; all but the merry laughter of our noisy cavalcade.

We returned about eleven o'clock, few accidents having occurred. Doña Rosita had fallen once. Doña Manuelita had crushed her foot against her neighbour's ass. The padre was shaken to a jelly, and a learned senator who was of the party declared he should never recover from that night's jolting.[2]

Tomorrow we shall set off for Real del Monte.[3]

Sunday: May 17th, 1840
Huasca

After mass in the chapel we left Tepenacaxco about seven o'clock, and travelled (I believe by a short cut) over rocks and walls, torrents and fields of maguey, all in a heavy carriage with six horses. Arriving in sight of walls, the *mozos* gallop on and tear them down. Over the mountain torrents or barrancas they dash boldly, encouraging the horses by the wildest shrieks.

We stopped at San Miguel, a country house belonging to the Count de Regla, the former proprietor of the mines which we were about to visit —the most picturesque and lovely place imaginable, but entirely abandoned, the house comfortless and out of repair.[4] We wandered through paths cut in the beautiful woods, and by the side of a rivulet that seems to fertilize everything through which it winds. We climbed the hills, and made our way through the tangled luxuriance of trees and flowers; and, in the midst of hundreds of gaudy blossoms, I neglected them all upon coming to a grassy slope covered with daisies and buttercups. We even found some hawthorn bushes. It might be English scenery, were it not that there is a richness in the vegetation unknown in England. But all these beautiful solitudes are abandoned to the deer that wander fearlessly amongst the woods, and the birds that sing in their branches.

While we were still far from the house, a thunderstorm came on. When it rains here, the windows of heaven seem opened, and the clouds pour down water in floods; the lightning also appears to me peculiarly vivid, and many more accidents occur from it here than in the north. We were drenched in five minutes, and in this plight resumed our seats in the carriage, and set off for Huasca (a village where we were to pass the night) in the midst of the pelting storm. In an hour or two the horses were wading up to their knees in water, and we arrived at the pretty village of Huasca in a most comfortless condition. There are no inns in these parts, but we were hospitably received by a widow lady, a friend of Adalid's.

The Señora de Adalid, in clear muslin and lace, with satin shoes, was worse off than I in *mousseline de laine* and brodequins.[5] Nevertheless, I mean to adopt the fashion of the country tomorrow, when we are to rise at four to go on to Real del Monte, and try the effect of travelling with clear gown, satin petticoat, and shoes ditto—because, "when one is in Rome," &c.

The storm continues with such unabated violence that we must content ourselves with contemplating the watery landscape from the windows.

Monday: May 18th, 1840
Hacienda of Tepenacaxco

Rose in Huasca at four o'clock; dressed by candlelight, took chocolate, and set off for Real del Monte. After we had travelled a few leagues, tolerably cold, we rejoiced when the sun rose and, dispelling the mist, threw his cheerful light over mountain and wood. The trees looked green and refreshed after their last night's bath; the very rocks were sparkling with silver. The morning was perfectly brilliant, and every leaf and flower was glittering with the raindrops not yet dried. The carriage ascended slowly the road cut through the mountains by the English company, a fine and useful enterprise; the first broad and smooth road I have seen as yet in the republic. Until it was made, hundreds of mules daily conveyed the ore from the mines over a dangerous mountain path to the hacienda of Regla, a distance of six or seven leagues. We overtook wagons conveying timber to the mines of Real, nine thousand feet above the level of the sea.

The scenery was magnificent. On one side mountains covered with oak and pine, and carpeted by the brightest-coloured flowers; goats climbing up the perpendicular rocks and looking down upon us from their vantage ground; fresh clear rivulets flinging themselves from rock to rock; and here and there little Indian huts perched amongst the cliffs. On the other, the deep valley with its bending forests and gushing river; while far above we caught a glimpse of Real itself, with its sloping roofs and large church, standing in the very midst of forests and mountains.

We began to see people with fair hair and blue eyes; and one individual, with a shock of fiery red hair and an undeniable Scotch twang, I felt the greatest inclination to claim as a countryman. The Indians here looked cleaner than those in or near Mexico, and were not more than half naked.

The whole country here, as well as the mines, formerly belonged to the Count de Regla, who was so wealthy that, when his son, the [father of the] present count, was christened, the whole party walked from his house to the church upon ingots of silver. The countess, having quarreled with the Vice-Queen, sent her in token of reconciliation a white satin slipper, entirely covered with large diamonds. The count invited the King of Spain to visit his Mexican territories, assuring him that the hoofs of His Majesty's horse should touch nothing but solid silver from Veracruz to the capital. This might be a bravado; but a more certain proof of his wealth exists in the fact that he caused two ships of the line, of the largest size, to be constructed in Havana at his expense, made of mahogany and cedar, and presented them to the King.[6] The present count was, as I already told you, married to the beautiful daughter of the Güera Rodríguez.

We arrived at Real del Monte about nine o'clock and drove to the director's house, which is extremely pretty, commanding a most beautiful and extensive view, and where we found a large fire burning in the grate—very agreeable, as the morning was still somewhat chill—and which had a look of home and comfort that made it still more acceptable. We were received with the greatest cordiality by the director, Mr. Rule, and his lady, and invited to partake of the most delicious breakfast that I have seen for a long while: a happy *mélange* of English and Mexican. The snow-white tablecloth, smoking tea urn, hot rolls, fresh eggs, coffee, tea, and toast looked very much *à l'Anglaise*, while there were numbers of substantial dishes *à l'Espagnole,* and delicious fresh cream cheeses, to all which our party did ample justice.

After breakfast we went out to visit the mines, and it was curious to see English children—clean and pretty, with their white hair and rosy cheeks, and neat straw bonnets—mingled with the little copper-coloured Indians. We visited all the different works: the apparatus for sawing, the turning-lathe, foundry, &c.; but I regretted to find that we could not descend into the mines. We went to the mouth of the shaft called the Dolores, which has a narrow opening, and is entered by perpendicu-

lar ladders. The men go down with conical caps on their heads, in which is stuck a lighted tallow candle. In the great shaft, called Terreros, they descend by means of these ladders to the depth of a thousand feet, there being platforms at certain distances on which they can rest.[7]

We were obliged to content ourselves with seeing them go down, and with viewing and admiring all the great works which English energy has established here: the various steam engines, the buildings for the separation and washing of the ore, the great stores, workshops, offices, &c. Nearly all the workmen are British, and of these the Scotch are preferred. Most of the miners are Indians, who work in companies, and receive in payment the eighth part of the proceeds. The director gave us some specimens of silver from the great heaps where they lie, sparkling like genii's treasure.

Although I have not descended into these mines, I might give you a description of them by what I have heard, and fill my paper with arithmetical figures by which you might judge of the former and the present produce. I might tell you how Don Lucas Alamán went to England and raised, as if by magic, the enthusiasm of the English;[8] how one fortune after another has been swallowed up in the dark, deep gulf of speculation; how expectations have been disappointed, and how the great cause of this is the scarcity of quicksilver, which has been paid [for] at the rate of one hundred and fifty dollars per quintal in real cash, when the same quantity was given at credit by the Spanish government for fifty dollars; [and] how heaps of silver lie abandoned, because the expense of acquiring quicksilver renders it wholly unprofitable to extract it. And I might repeat the opinion of those persons by whom I have heard the subject discussed, who express their astonishment that such being the case an arrangement is not made with the country which is the almost exclusive possessor of the quicksilver mines—by which it might be procured at a lower rate, and this great source of wealth not thrown away. But for all these matters I refer you to Humboldt and Ward, by whom they are scientifically treated, and will not trouble you with superficial remarks on so important a subject.[9]

In fact, I must confess that my attention was frequently attracted from the mines, and the engines, and the works of man, and the discussions arising therefrom, to the stupendous natural scenery by which we were surrounded: the unexplored forests that clothe the mountains to their very summits, the torrents that leaped and sparkled in the sunshine, the deep ravines, the many-tinted foliage, the bold and jutting rocks. All combine to increase our admiration of the bounties of nature to this favoured land, to which she has given "every herb bearing seed," and "every tree that is pleasant to the sight, and good for food,"[10] while her veins are rich with precious metals—the useful and the beautiful offered with unsparing hand.

We were obliged to leave Real about two o'clock, having a long journey to perform before night, as we had the intention of returning to sleep at Tepenacaxco. We took leave of our hospitable entertainers and again resumed our journey over these fine roads—many parts of which are blasted from the great rocks of porphyry—and, as we looked back at the picturesque colony glistening in the sun, could hardly believe the prophecies of our more experienced drivers that a storm was brewing in the sky which would burst forth before evening. We were determined not to believe it, as it was impossible to pass by the famous hacienda and ravine of Regla without paying them at least a short visit.

This stupendous work of the Mexican miners in former days is some

leagues to the south[11] of Real del Monte, and is said to have cost many millions of dollars. One should view it as we did, in a thunderstorm, for it has an air of vastness and desolation, and at the same time of grandeur, that shows well amidst a war of the elements. Down in a steep barranca, encircled by basaltic cliffs, it lies: a mighty pile of building, which seems as if it might have been constructed by some philosophical giant or necromancer—so that one is not prepared to find there an English director and his wife, and the unpoetic comforts of roast mutton and potatoes!

All is on a gigantic scale: the immense vaulted storehouses for the silver ore; the great smelting furnaces and covered buildings where we saw the process of amalgamation going on; the water wheels—in short, all the necessary machinery for the smelting and amalgamation of the metal. We walked to see the great cascade, with its rows of basaltic columns, and found a seat on a piece of broken pillar beside the rushing river, where we had a fine view of the lofty cliffs covered with the wildest and most luxuriant vegetation: vines trailing themselves over every broken shaft; moss creeping over the huge disjointed masses of rock, and trees overhanging the precipitous ravine. The columns look as if they might have been the work of those who, on the plains of Shinar, began to build the city— and the tower whose top was to reach to heaven.[12]

But, as we sat here, the sky suddenly became overcast; great black masses of cloud collected over our heads, and the rumbling of thunder in the distance gave notice of an approaching storm. We had scarcely time to get under shelter of the director's roof, when the thunder began to echo loudly amongst the rocks, and was speedily followed by torrents of rain. It was a superb storm: the lightning flashed amongst the trees, the wind howled furiously, while

> Far along
> From peak to peak, the rattling crags among
> *Leapt* the live thunder.[13]

After resting and dining amidst a running accompaniment of plashing rain, roaring wind, and deep-toned thunder, we found that it was in vain to wait for a favourable change in the weather; and certainly, with less experienced drivers, it would have been anything but safe to have set off amidst the darkness of the storm, down precipitous descents and over torrents swelled by the rain.

The Count de Regla, who, attracted by the plentiful supply of water in this ravine, conceived the idea of employing part of his enormous fortune in the construction of these colossal works, must have had an imagination on a large scale. The English directors, whose wives bury themselves in such abysses, ought to feel more grateful to them than any other husbands towards their sacrificing better halves. For the men—occupied all day amongst their workmen and machinery, and returning late in the evening to dine and sleep—there is no great self-immolation. But a poor

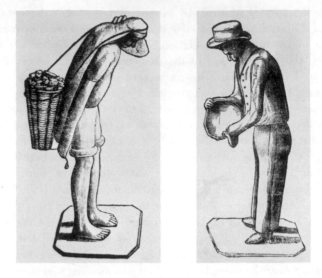

woman, living all alone in a house fenced in by gigantic rocks, with no other sound in her ears from morning till night but the roar of thunder or the clang of machinery, had need for her personal comfort to have either a most romantic imagination, so that she may console herself with feeling like an enchanted princess in a giant's castle, or a most common-place spirit, so that she may darn stockings to the sound of the waterfall, and feel no other inconvenience from the storm, but that her husband will require dry linen when he comes home.[14]

As for us, we were drenched before reaching the carriage, into which the water was pouring; and when we set off once more amidst the rapidly increasing darkness, and over these precipitous roads, we thought that our chance of reaching the proposed haven that night was very small. After much toil to the horses, we got out of the ravines and found ourselves once more on the great plains, where the tired animals ploughed their way over fields and ditches and great stones, and among trees and tangled bushes—an occasional flash of lightning our only guide. Great was our joy, when, about eleven o'clock, a man riding on in advance shouted out that the lights of Tepenacaxco were in sight; and still more complete our satisfaction when we drove round the tank into the courtyard of the hacienda. We were received with great applause by the inmates, and were not sorry to rest after a very fatiguing yet agreeable day.

Thursday: May 21st, 1840
San Fernando, Mexico

We left Tepenacaxco the day before yesterday. Our journey was very dangerous in consequence of the great rains which had swelled the torrents—especially as we set off late, and most of it was performed by night. In these barrancas, carriages and horsemen have been frequently swept away and dashed in pieces over the precipices. But to make our situation more disagreeable, we had scarcely set off before a terrible storm of thunder and rain again came on with more violence than the night preceding. It grew perfectly dark, and we listened with some alarm to the roaring torrents, over which—especially over one, not many leagues from Soapayuca where we were to spend the night—it was extremely doubtful whether we could pass. The carriage was full of water, but we were too much alarmed to be uneasy about trifles. Amidst the howling of the wind and the pealing of thunder, no one could hear the other speak. Suddenly, by a vivid flash of lightning, the dreaded barranca appeared in sight for a moment, and almost before the drivers could stop them, the horses had plunged in.

It was a moment of mortal fear such as I shall never forget. The shrieks of the drivers to encourage the horses—the loud cries of *Ave María!*—the uncertainty as to whether our heavy carriage could be dragged across—the horses struggling and splashing in the boiling torrent —and the horrible fate that awaited us should one of them fall or falter! The Señora Adalid and I shut our eyes and held each other's hands, and certainly no one breathed till we were safe on the other side. We were then told that we had crossed within a few feet of a precipice over which a coach had been dashed into fifty pieces during one of these swells, and of course everyone killed; and that, if instead of horses we had travelled with mules, we must have been lost.[15] You may imagine that we were not sorry to reach Soapayuca, where the people ran out to the door at the sound of carriage wheels, and could not believe that we had passed the barranca that night—as two or three horsemen who had rode in that direction had turned back, and pronounced it impassable.[16]

Lights and supper were soon procured, and by way of interlude a monstrous bull, of great fame in these parts, was led up to the supper table for our inspection with a rope through his nose—a fierce brute, but familiarly called *el chato* (the flatnose), from the shortness of his horns. The lightning continued very vivid, and they told us that a woman had been struck there some time before, while in the chapel by night.

We rose at four o'clock the next morning and set off for Mexico. The morning, as usual after these storms, was peculiarly fresh and beautiful; but the sun soon grew oppressive on the great plains. About two o'clock we entered Mexico by the Guadalupe gate. We found our house in *statu quo;* agreeable letters from Europe; great preparations making for the English ball—to assist at which we have returned sooner than we otherwise should, and for which my *femme de chambre* has just completed a dress for me, very much to her own satisfaction.[17]

BALLS AND MASSES

18

Consecration of the Archbishop

Monday: May 25th, 1840
San Fernando, Mexico

The English ball at the Minería has passed off with great éclat. Nothing could be more splendid than the general effect of this noble building, brilliantly illuminated and filled with a well-dressed crowd. The President and *corps diplomatique* were in full uniform, and the display of diamonds was extraordinary. We ladies of the *corps diplomatique* tried to flatter ourselves that we made up in elegance what we wanted in magnificence!—for in jewels no foreign ladies could attempt to compete with those of the country.

The daughter of Countess _____, just arrived from Paris, and whose acquaintance I made for the first time, wore pale blue, with garlands of pale pink roses, and a parure of most superb brilliants. The Señora de Agüero's head reminded me of that of the Marchioness of Londonderry, in her opera box.[1] The Marquesa de Vivanco had a *rivière* of brilliants of extraordinary size and beauty, and perfectly well set. Madame Subervielle wore a very rich blonde dress, *garnie* with plumes of ostrich feathers, a large diamond fastening each plume. One lady wore a diadem which _____ said could not be worth less than a hundred thousand dollars. Diamonds are always worn plain or with pearls; coloured stones are considered trash, which is a pity, as I think rubies and emeralds set in diamonds would give more variety and splendour to their jewels. There were a profusion of large pearls, generally of a pear shape. The finest and roundest were those worn by the Señora Barrera.

There were many blonde dresses, a great fashion here. I know no lady without one. Amongst the prettiest and most tastefully-dressed girls were the Escandóns, as usual. Many dresses were overloaded, a common fault in Mexico; and many of the dresses, though rich, were old-fashioned; but the *coup d'œil* was not the less brilliant, and it was somewhat astonishing in such a multitude not to see a single objectionable person. To be sure, the company was all invited.

On entering the noble court, which was brilliantly illuminated with coloured lamps hung from pillar to pillar, and passing up the great staircase, we were met at the first landing by Mr. Pakenham, in full uniform, and other English gentlemen—the directors of the ball, who stood there to receive the ladies. His Excellency led me upstairs to the top of the ballroom, where chairs were placed for the President, ladies of the *diplomaties,* cabinet ministers, &c. The music was excellent, and dancing was already in full force. And though there were assembled what is called *all Mexico,* the rooms are so large that the crowd was not disagreeable, nor the heat oppressive. Pictures of Queen Victoria were hung in the different large halls. The supper tables were very handsome; and in fact the ball altogether was worthy of its object, for *Messieurs les Anglais* always do these things well when they attempt them.

The President took me to supper.[2] The company walked in to the music of "God Save the Queen." After we had sat a little while, the President demanded silence, and, in a short speech, proposed the health of Her Majesty Queen Victoria, which was drank by all the company standing. After supper, we continued dancing till nearly six in the morning; and when we got into the carriage it was broad daylight, and all the bells were ringing for mass![3]

This is the best ball we have seen here, without any exception; and is said to have cost eleven thousand dollars. There were certainly a great number of pretty faces at this fête, many pretty girls whom we had not seen before, and whom the English secretaries had contrived to *unearth.* Fine eyes are a mere *drug*—everyone has them: large, dark, full orbs, with long silken lashes. As for diamonds, no man above the rank of a *lépero* marries in this country without presenting his bride with at least a pair of diamond earrings, or a pearl necklace with a diamond clasp. They are not always a proof of wealth, though they constitute it in themselves. Their owners may be very poor in other respects. They are considered a necessary of life, quite as much so as shoes and stockings.

Tuesday: June 2nd, 1840

On the 15th of April, the pontifical bulls arrived from Rome, confirming the election of the Señor Posada to the archiepiscopal dignity; and on Sunday last, the 31st of May, the consecration took place in the cathedral with the greatest pomp. The presiding bishop was the Señor Belaunzarán, the old Bishop of Linares. The two assistant bishops were the Señor Madrid, a young good-looking man who, having been banished from Mexico during the revolution, took refuge in Rome where he obtained the favour of the Pope (who afterwards recommended him to an episcopal see in Mexico), and the Doctor Morales, formerly

Bishop of Sonora.[4] His *padrino* was the President, General Bustamante, who in his capacity presented his godson with the splendid pastoral ring, a solitary diamond of immense size.

All the diplomatic body and the cabinet went in full uniform, chairs being placed for them on each side of the *crujía* (the passage leading to the altar). A dispute upon the subject of precedence arose between an excellency of the diplomatic corps and the Secretary of State, which seems likely to have disagreeable consequences.[5] I had the pleasure of kneeling beside these illustrious persons for the space of three or four hours, for no seats were placed for the wives either of the diplomats or of the cabinet.

But the ceremony though long was very superb, the music fine, the quantity of jewels on the dresses of the bishops and priests, and on the holy vessels, &c., enormous. The bishops were arrayed in white velvet and gold, and their mitres were literally covered with diamonds. The gold candlesticks and golden basins for holy water, and golden incensories, reminded me of the description of the ornaments of the Jewish tabernacle in the days of Moses: of the "candlesticks of pure gold, with golden branches"; and "the tongs and snuff-dishes of pure gold"; or of the temple of Solomon, where the altar was of gold, and the table of gold, and the candlesticks, and the snuffers, and the basins, and the spoons, and the censers were of pure gold.[6]

The pontifical vestments, destined for the elected primate, were all prepared: sandals, amice, surplice, girdle, pectoral cross, stole, gown, vestment with open sleeves (the *dalmática*), crosier, mitre, pontifical ring, &c. Magnificent chairs were prepared for the bishops near the altar, and the President in uniform took his place amongst them. The presiding bishop took his seat alone, with his back to the altar, and the Señor Posada was led in by the assisting bishops—they with their mitres, he with his priest's cap on. Arrived before the presiding bishop, he uncovered his head, and made a profound obeisance. These three then took their places on chairs placed in front; and the ceremony having begun, in case you should wish to have some idea of it, I shall endeavour to give it you, for I was so situated that although the cathedral was crowded to excess, I could see and hear all that passed. Let me premise, however, that there was not one *lépero*, as they are always excluded on such occasions.

Posada and his assistant bishops rose and uncovered their heads; and the Bishop Morales, turning to the presiding bishop, said: "Most reverend father, the holy Catholic Mother Church requests you to raise this presbyter to the charge of the archbishopric."

"Have you an apostolical mandate?"

"We have."

"Read it."

An assistant priest then read the mandate in a loud voice; upon which they all sat down, the consecrator saying, "Thanks be to God!" Then Posada, kneeling before him, took an oath upon the Bible, which the bishop held, concluding with these words: "So may God help me, and these his holy gospels."

Then, all sitting down and resuming their mitres, the examination of the future archbishop took place. It was very long, and at its conclusion Posada knelt before the presiding bishop and kissed his hand. To this succeeded the confession, everyone standing uncovered before the altar, which was then sprinkled with incense. Then followed the mass, chanted.

The assistant bishops then led out the Señor Posada to the chapel, where they put on his sandals, and where he assumed the pectoral cross, amice, surplice, &c. and, arriving at the altar, read the office of the mass. He was then conducted again before the consecrating bishop, who was seated with his mitre, and after saluting him reverently, he sat down. Then the bishop, addressing him, said: "It is the duty of the bishop to judge, interpret, consecrate, ordain, offer, baptize, and confirm."

All then rose, and the bishop prayed that the newly-elected primate might receive the grace of heaven. All the bishops and priests then prostrated themselves while the litanies were sung. The presiding bishop, rising, took the crosier and prayed three times for a blessing on the chosen one, thrice making on him the sign of the cross; and they continued to sing the litanies, at the conclusion of which they all arose, took their seats, and resumed their mitres, Posada alone kneeling before the bishop.

The Bible was then placed upon his shoulders, while he remained prostrated, and the bishop, rising up, pronounced a solemn benediction upon him, while the hymn of *"Veni Creator Spiritus"* was sung in full chorus. Then the bishop, dipping his hand in the holy chrism, anointed the primate's head, making on it the sign of the cross, saying, "Let thy head be anointed and consecrated with the celestial benediction, according to the pontifical mandate." The bishop then anointed his hands, making in the same manner the sign of the cross, and saying, "May these hands be anointed with holy oil; and, as Samuel anointed David a king and a prophet, so be thou anointed and consecrated." This was followed by a solemn prayer.

Then the crosier was blessed, and presented to the elected archbishop with these words: "Receive the pastoral crosier, that thou mayest be humanely severe in correcting vices, exercising judgment without wrath, &c." The blessing of the ring followed with solemn prayer, and, being sprinkled with holy water, it was placed on the third finger of the right hand, the bishop saying, "Receive the ring, which is a sign of faith; that, adorned with incorruptible faith, thou mayest guard inviolably the spouse of God, His Holy Church."

The Bible, being then taken off the shoulders of the prostrate prelate, was presented to him with an injunction to receive and to preach the gospel. Finally the bishop bestowed on him the kiss of peace; and all the other bishops did so in their turn. Posada then retired, and, his head and hands being washed, he soon after returned with the assistant bishops, carrying two lighted wax tapers, which he presented to the presiding bishop, together with two loaves and two small barrels of wine, reverently kissing his hand. After this, the presiding bishop washed his hands and mounted the steps of the altar, and the new primate received the sacrament.

The mitre was then blessed and placed upon his head, with a prayer by the bishop, that thus, with his head armed and with the staff of the gospels, he might appear terrible to the adversaries of the True Faith. The gloves were next consecrated and drawn on his hands, the bishop praying that his hands might be surrounded by the purity of the new man; and that as Jacob, when he covered his hands with goatskins, offered agreeable meats to his father, and received his paternal benediction, so he, in offering the Holy Sacrament, might obtain the benediction of his Heavenly Father. The Archbishop was then seated by the consecrating bishop on his pontifical throne, and at the same moment the hymn *"Te Deum laudamus"* was chanted. During the hymn the bishops, with their jewelled mitres, rose and, passing through the church, blessed the whole congregation, the new Archbishop still remaining near the altar, and without his mitre. When he returned to his seat, the assistant bishops, including the consecrator, remained standing till the hymn was concluded.

The presiding bishop, then advancing, without his mitre, to the right hand of the Archbishop, said: "May thy hand be strengthened! May thy right hand be exalted! May justice and judgment be the preparation of thy See!"

Then the organ pealed forth, and they chanted the hymn of *"Gloria Patri."* Long and solemn prayer followed; and then all, uncovered, stood beside the gospels at the altar.

The Archbishop rose, and with mitre and crosier, pronounced a solemn blessing on all the people assembled. Then, while all knelt beside the altar, he said: "For many years." This he repeated thrice; the second time in the middle of the altar, the third at the feet of the presiding bishop. Then, all rising, the Archbishop bestowed on each the kiss of peace, and the ceremony concluded.

When everything was over, our carriage not being visible amongst the crowd of vehicles, I returned home in that of the British minister, with him and his attachés—after which they and Calderón returned to dine with the new archbishop in his palace.

A dish of sweetmeats was sent me from his table, which are so pretty (probably the chef-d'œuvre of the nuns) that I send them to you, to preserve as a memorial of the consecration of the first Mexican archbishop—perhaps of the last![7]

19

On the Subject of Mexican Servants

Wednesday: June 3rd, 1840
San Fernando, Mexico

You ask me to tell you how I find the Mexican servants. Hitherto I had avoided the ungrateful theme, from very weariness of it.

Throughout the whole Republic of Mexico there is one never-failing source of complaint amongst families of the better class: *the badness of the servants*. An unfailing source of complaint amongst Mexicans, among foreigners it is naturally much worse, and at their first arrival especially they find this a serious evil.

We hear of their addiction to stealing, their laziness, drunkenness, dirtiness, together with a host of other vices. That these complaints are just there can be no doubt, but that the evil might be remedied, if not entirely, at least to a great extent, is equally certain.

In the first place, servants are constantly taken without being required to bring a character recommendation from their last place; and in the next, good character recommendations are constantly given, whether from indolence or a mistaken kindness, to servants who do not deserve them. A servant who has lived in six or seven—or a dozen—different houses, staying about a month in each, is not thought the worse of on that account. As the love of finery is inherent in them all, even more so than in other daughters of Eve, a girl will go to service merely to earn sufficient to buy herself an embroidered shift or chemise, and if, in addition to this, she can pick up a pair of small old satin shoes, she will tell you she is tired of working, and is going home to rest (*para descansar*) —nor will she go to service again, until her finery begins to wear out, and any few reals she may have over are spent. So little is necessary when one can contentedly live on tortillas and chile, sleep on a mat, and dress in rags!—and it must be hard indeed if the young lady has not an admirer who will spend a penny at each fête to buy her a glass of pulque.

A woman, a decent old creature, who came to the house to wash shortly after our arrival in this country, left us at the end of a month *"para descansar"*—because *she was tired.* Soon after, she used to come with her six children, they and herself all in rags, and beg the gardener to give her any *odds and ends* of vegetables he could spare. My maid asked her why, being so poor, she had left a good place where she got twelve dollars a month. "Jesus!" said she, "if you only knew the pleasure of doing nothing!"

I wished to bring up a little girl as a servant, having her taught to read, sew, dress hair, &c. A child about twelve years old, one of a large *very poor* family who subsisted entirely upon charity, was procured for me; and I promised her mother that she should be taught to read, taken regularly to church, and instructed in all kinds of work. She was rather pretty, and very intelligent, though extremely indolent; and, though she had no stockings, would consent to wear nothing but dirty white satin shoes, too short for her foot. Once a week her mother—a tall, dirty, slatternly woman with long tangled hair and a cigar in her mouth—used to come to visit her, accompanied by a sister, a friend, a friend's friend, and a train of six or seven girls, her daughters. I would order them some dinner, after which they would all light their cigars and, together with the little Josefita, sit, and howl, and bemoan themselves—roaring, crying, and lamenting her sad fate in being obliged to go out to service. After these visits Josefita was fit for nothing. If desired to sew, she would sit looking so miserable, and doing so little, that it seemed better to allow her to leave her work alone. Then, sitting on a mat, her hands folded, her eyes fixed on nothing, she would remain for hours perfectly contented.

According to a promise I had made, I took her several times to see her mother, but one day, being occupied, I sent her alone in the carriage, with charge to the servants to bring her safely back. In the evening she returned, accompanied by her whole family, all crying and howling: "For the love of the Most Holy Virgin, *Señora mía! Por la Purísima Concepción!*" &c., &c., &c. I asked what had happened, and after much difficulty discovered that their horror was occasioned by my having sent her alone in the carriage. It happened that the Countess C.[1] was in the drawing room at the time, and to her I related the cause of the uproar. To my astonishment she assured me that the woman was in this instance perfectly right, and that it was very dangerous to send a girl of twelve years old from one street to another in the power of the coachman and footman. Finding from such good authority that this was the case, I begged the woman to abstain from seeing her daughter, which only left her miserable and discontented, oftener than once a month—when, if she could not come herself, I should send her under proper protection. She agreed; but one day, having given Josefita permission to spend the night at her mother's, I received next morning from that worthy individual a very dirty note, nearly illegible, informing me that her daughter with many thanks was tired of learning to read and sew, and therefore would not trouble me any longer. After calling down the protection of the Virgin upon me [it] concluded: ". . . but with much sorrow I must take my child from the most illustrious protection of Your Excellency, for she needs to rest herself (*es preciso que descanse*), and is tired for the present of working." The woman then returned to beg, which she considered infinitely less degrading than working.

Against this nearly universal indolence and indifference to earning money, the heads of families have to contend, as also against thieving and dirtiness—yet I think there is a remedy much easier than it appears. If on the one hand, no one were to receive a servant into their house without respectable references, especially from their last place, and if their having remained one year in service in the same house were considered necessary to their being received into another, unless from some peculiar circumstances—and if on the other hand it were considered as unjust and dangerous, as it really is, to recommend to another a servant who has been found guilty of stealing as being "*muy honrado* (very honest)"—some improvement might soon take place.

We received a porter into our house who brought a certificate of being "*muy honrado*," not from his last place, but from one before it. He was a well-dressed, sad-looking individual; and at the same time we hired his wife as washerwoman, and took his brother as valet to our attaché, thus having the whole family under our roof, wisely taking it for granted that he being recommended as particularly honest, his relations were "all honourable men." An English lady happened to call on me, and a short time after I went to return her visit—when she informed me that the person who had opened the door for her in my house was a notorious thief and a gambler, and moreover that the police had been in search of him for six weeks. He had come to her house upon the same recommendation which he brought to ours. She had feared sending a servant to warn us of our danger lest, guessing the purport of her message, he might rob the house before leaving it. We said nothing to the man that night, but he looked even paler and more miserable than usual, probably suspecting what must be the result of Mrs. Dunlap's visit.[2]

The next morning Calderón sent for him and told him he must leave the house, at the same time paying him a month's wages, that the poor wretch might not be tempted to steal from immediate want. His face turned perfectly livid, as if he were going to faint, but he said nothing, only bowed and went away. About half an hour after, he came back and asked to speak with Calderón. He confessed to him that the crime of which he concluded he was accused he had in fact committed; that he had been tempted to a gambling house while he had in his pocket a large sum of money belonging to his master. After losing his own money, he was tempted to try his fortune with what was not his own. He lost the whole sum, and in despair went on, then pawned a valuable shawl worth several hundred dollars, with which also he had been entrusted. Having lost everything, he then wrote to the porter in his master's house, confessing what he had done, and in despair made his escape from Mexico. He remained in concealment for some time, till, hearing that we wanted a porter, he ventured to present himself to the housekeeper[3] with his former certificate [of] character. He declared himself thoroughly repentant—that this was his first and last crime. I had little doubt that it was, but who can trust the good resolutions of a gambler! We were obliged to send him away, especially as the other servants already had some suspicions concerning him; and everything stolen in the house for years to come would have been laid at his door.

The gentleman who had recommended him afterwards confessed that he always had strong suspicions of this man's honesty, and knew him to be so determined a gambler that he had pawned all he possessed, even his wife's clothes, to obtain money for that purpose. Now, as a porter in Mexico has pretty much at his disposal the property and even the lives of the whole family, it is certainly most blamable to recommend to that situation a man whose honesty is more than doubtful.

We afterwards procured two soldiers from the *Inválidos*, old Spaniards, to act in that capacity, who had no other *faiblesse* but that of being constantly drunk. We at length found two others who only got drunk alternately, so that we considered ourselves very well off. It is evident enough that the faults in these instances are on both sides—in the person who gives a good character to a thief, and in those who are contented to take a servant into their house without a recommendation from his *last* place, or as still more frequently happens, without any at all—knowing probably that the truth will not be told.

We had a long series of *galopinas*, as the kitchen maids here are called, and the only one who brought a first-rate character with her robbed the housekeeper of fifty dollars. The money, however, was recovered, and was found to have been placed by the girl in the hands of a rich and apparently respectable coach maker. He refunded it to the rightful owner, and the *galopina* was punished by a month's imprisonment. It would certainly have been but justice had he shared it with her.

As to the accusation of *dirtiness*, a quality too inherent in *la gentuza mexicana*, it is impossible for any experience to reconcile one to it. One of the most disagreeable customs of the women servants is that of wearing their long dirty hair hanging down at its full length, matted, uncombed, always in the way, and, especially in kitchen maids, appearing to be always suspended over the soup. Now for my part, I cannot imagine why the Mexican ladies, who complain of this custom, should permit it. Long flowing hair sounds very picturesque, but when it is very dirty, a receptacle for all that is most horrible, it is not a pretty picture. One would rather read of it than see it. As to their general dirtiness of person, if cleanliness were reckoned an essential in a servant, no doubt she would be clean for her own advantage.

The *rebozo*, in itself graceful and without doubt extremely convenient, has the disadvantage of being the greatest cloak for all untidiness, uncombed hair, and raggedness that ever was invented. Even in the better classes it occasions much indolence in the toilette—much laziness and untidiness—but in the common people its effect is overwhelming. When the *rebozo* drops off, or is displaced by chance, we see what they would be without it! But if they had not this ready cover, the probability is that they would be really a little cleaner, and their dress more decent.

As for the blanket or sarape—which Carlyle admires so much in his Philosophy of Clothes when speaking of the dress of Bolívar's men— it is both convenient and graceful, especially on horseback; but though no doubt exclusively Indian in its origin, the custom of covering the lower part of the face with it is taken from the Spanish cloak. The opportunity which both sarape and *rebozo* afford for concealing large knives about the person, as also for enveloping both face and figure so as to be scarcely recognizable, is no doubt the cause of many of those murders which take place amongst the lower orders in moments of excitement and drunkenness. If they had not these knives at hand, their rage would probably cool, or a fair fight would finish the business —and if they could not wear these knives concealed, I presume they would be prohibited from carrying them.

As for taking a woman cook in Mexico, one must have strong nerves, a stronger stomach, and a good appetite to eat what she dresses, however palatable, after having seen her. One look at her flowing locks, one glance at her *rebozo, et c'est fini.* And yet the Mexican servants have their good qualities, and are a thousand times preferable to the foreign servants one finds in Mexico, especially to the French. Bringing them out with you is a hazardous experiment. In ten days they begin to fancy themselves ladies and gentlemen—the men have *Don* tacked to their name—and they either marry and set up shops, or behave so unbearably that one is too thankful to get rid of them.[4] A tolerable French cook may occasionally be had, but you must pay [for] his services their weight in gold—and wink at his insolence, extortions, and robberies. There are one or two French restaurants, which will send you in a very good dinner at an extravagant price; and it is common in foreign houses, especially amongst the English, to adopt this plan whenever they give a large entertainment.

The Mexican servants have some never-failing good qualities—and over [the foreigners] one immense advantage. They are the perfection of civility: humble, obliging, excessively—and constantly—good-tempered, and very easily attached to those with whom they live. And if that *rara avis,* a good Mexican housekeeper, can be found—and that such may be met with I from experience can testify—then the troubles of the ménage rest upon her shoulders, and, accustomed as she is to the amiable weaknesses of her *compatriotes,* she is neither surprised nor disturbed by them.

As for wages, a good porter has from fifteen to twenty dollars per month; a coachman from twenty to thirty. Many houses keep two or even three coachmen: one who drives from the box, one who rides postilion, and a third for emergencies. Our friend Adalid—who has many horses, mules, and carriages—has four, and pays forty dollars per month to his head coachman, the others in proportion.[5] A French cook has about thirty dollars; a housekeeper from twelve to fifteen; a major-domo about twenty or more; a footman six or seven; *galopina* and chambermaid five or six; a gardener from twelve to fifteen. Sewing girls have about three reals per diem.[6] Porter, coachman, and gardener have their wives and families in the house, which would be an annoyance were the houses not so large. The menservants generally are much cleaner and better dressed than the women.[7]

One circumstance is to be remarked and is remarkable: that, dirty as the women servants are, and notwithstanding the enormous size of Mexican houses and Mexican families, the houses themselves are, generally speaking, the perfection of cleanliness. This must be due either to a good housekeeper, which is rarely to be found, or to the care taken by the mistress of the house herself. That private houses should be clean, while churches and theatres are dirty, only proves that ladies know how to manage these matters better than gentlemen, so that one is almost inclined to wish with Miss Martineau that the Mexican police were entirely composed of *spare old women*.[8]

Friday: June 12th, 1840

I have formed an acquaintance with a very amiable and agreeable nun in the convent of the Santa Teresa, one of the strictest orders. I have only seen her twice, through a grating. She is a handsome woman of good family, and, it is said, of a remarkably joyous disposition, fond of music and dancing, and gay society. Yet at the age of eighteen, contrary to the wishes of all her family, she took the veil, and declares she has never repented of it. Although I cannot see her, I can hear her voice, and talk to her through a turning wooden screen, which has a very mysterious effect. She gives me an account of her occupations and of the little events that take place in her small world within; whilst I bring her news from the world without. The common people have the greatest veneration for the holy sisterhood, and I generally find there a number of women with baskets, and men carrying parcels or letters; some asking their advice or assistance, others executing their commissions, bringing them vegetables or bread, and listening to the sound of their voice with the most eager attention. My friend, the Madre Adalid, has promised to dress a number of wax figures for me, in the exact costume of all the different nuns in Mexico, beginning with that of her own convent.

I have now seen three nuns take the veil; and, next to a death, consider it the saddest event that can occur in this nether sphere. Yet the frequency of these human sacrifices here is not so strange as might at first appear. A young girl who knows nothing of the world; who, as it too frequently happens, has at home neither amusement nor instruction, and no society abroad; who from childhood is under the dominion of her confessor, and who firmly believes that by entering a convent she becomes sure of heaven; who moreover finds there a number of companions of her own age, and of older women who load her with praises and caresses—it is not, after all, astonishing that she should consent to insure her salvation on such easy terms.

Add to this the splendour of the ceremony, of which she is the sole object, the cynosure of all approving eyes. A girl of sixteen finds it hard to resist all this. I am told that more girls are smitten by the ceremony than by anything else, and am inclined to believe it, from the remarks I have heard made on these occasions by young girls in my vicinity. What does she lose? A husband and children? Probably she has seen no one who has touched her heart. Most probably she has hitherto seen no men, or at least conversed with none but her brothers, her uncles, or her confessor. She has perhaps also felt the troubles of a

Fanny Calderón de la Barca

A. Calderón de la Barca

Journal. Volume 1ˢᵗ

October 27ᵗʰ 1839

Ship Norma

This morning at 10 o'clock, we left New York — and got on board the steam-boat Hercules to be conveyed to our ship with its nautical name. The morning foggy and rainy, so that all prognosticated we should not go. Nevertheless all were mistaken. "Where there's a will, there's a way." We took leave of our friends who had come to see us off — Bodisco who is about taking a part in El Si de las Niñas — Kramer — who tried to look sentimental, and brought tears into his eyes, by some process he must have learned in St Petersburgh — "The tear forgot as soon as shed." Judge Patterson — Marqueta Harrison and Suarez, who looked like a stale lemon — and Freeman who appeared on the scene to increase the effect at the last moment — also General Alvear &c &c — Richmond — a Nobleman — Jane & Mary Jones — accompanied us as far as the Ship — Luggage hoisted in — The Steam-boat towed us some distance. Houghton came in a boat, and made later

Top left, Fanny Calderón de Barca, *née* Frances Erskine [I]is.

Top right, Her husband, [Ángel] Calderón de la Barca.

At right, Opening page of [Fan]ny Calderón de la Barca's [Mex]ican Journals.

Below, The walled city of [Ver]acruz.

[5] *Above,* "The fort of Juan de Ulúa, of warlike m ory."

[6] *At left,* Tiled dome of parochial church in Veracr

[7] *Below left,* General G dalupe Victoria, former p dent of Mexico.

[8] *Below right,* Don Dio de Velasco, the Calderóns' in Veracruz.

Above left, The Calderóns
[ ]t here: Don Dionisio's house.

[ )] *Above right,* Puente Naci-
[ ]l, historic bridge spanning
Antigua.

[ ] *At right,* "Arrieros with
[ ]r . . . loaded mules and
[ ]rthy, wild-looking faces."

[ )] *Below,* "There is not one
[ ]an being or passing object
[ ]e seen that is not in itself
[ ]icture . . ."

[13] *At left,* Jalapa: "Greatly we rejoiced as we rattled through its mountainous streets." [14] *Below,* "At San Miguel del Soldado we stopped to take some refreshment."

[15] *Above,* An hacienda on the road to Puebla. [16] *At left,* Popocatepetl before the days of photography.

[17, 18, 19, 20] "The great square where stand the cathedral and the palace."

[21] *Top,* Evening promenade before the cathedral.
[22] *Above left,* Buttresses of the cathedral façade.
[23] *At right,* Interior of the cathedral.
[24] *Below,* Its choir screen.

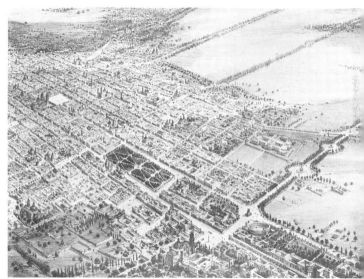

25] *Above,* The Sagrario façade.

26] *At right,* The capital looking southeast: The Calderóns' house was one of those at the lower right.

27] *Below,* Their neighborhood, looking west.

28] *Bottom,* San Fernando: "An immense building, old and gray and timeworn, with church adjoining."

[29] *Top,* The Alameda: "Of public promenades
. . . perhaps the prettiest and shadiest."

[30] *Center,* The busy Calle de Tacuba (the Minería
on the left, the Alameda beyond).

[31] *Above,* Street venders and customers.

[32] *At right,* Street criers in Holy Week.

[33, 34] *Top,* Scenes in the great square. [35] *Center left,* A lady on her balcony.
[36] *Center right,* "Holies, with their ragged blankets." [37] *Above,* An *azotea*
use.

[38] *Top,* The bull ring, with San Pablo beyond. [39] *Center,* Plazuela de Guardiola: The House of Tiles, with the convent of San Francisco on the right. [40] *Above left,* Church of San Francisco. [41] *Above right,* Its interior.

[42] *Top,* Within the convent of San Francisco. [43] *Center,* The plaza and church of Santo Domingo. [44, 45] *Above left and right,* Mass in honor of the Virgin of Covadonga.

[46] *Top,* "Presently an old coach came slowly along through the crowd, with the mysterious *Eye* painted on the panels . . ."

[47] *Second from top,* "The peasant and the *marquesa* kneel side by side . . ."

[48] *Above,* The *Posadas:* ". . . A procession was formed, two by two, which marched all through the house . . ."

[49] *At left,* Colegio de las Vizcaínas: "An immense building of stone, solid and handsome."

Mexican ménage. The society of men! She will still see her confessor, and she will have occasional visits from reverend padres and right reverend bishops.

Some of these convents are not entirely free from scandal. Amongst the monks, there are many who are openly a disgrace to their calling— though I firmly believe that by far the greater number lead a life of privation and virtue. Their conduct can, to a certain extent, be judged of by the world; but [as to] the pale nuns, devout and pure, immured in the cloister for life, kneeling before the shrine, or chanting hymns in the silence of the night, a veil both truly and allegorically must shade their virtues or their failings. The nuns of the Santa Teresa and of other strict orders, who live sparingly, profess the most severe rules, and have no servants or boarders, enjoy a universal reputation for virtue and sanctity. They consider the other convents worldly, and their motto is, "All or nothing; the world or the cloister." Each abbess adds a stricter rule, a severer penance than her predecessor, and in this they glory. My friend Madre Adalid frequently says: "Were I to be born again, I should choose, above every lot in life, to be a nun of the Santa Teresa, but of no other convent."[9]

It is strange how, all the world over, mankind seems to expect from those who assume religion as a profession a degree of superhuman perfection. Their failings are insisted upon. Every eye is upon them to mark whatsoever may be amiss in their conduct. Their virtues, their learning, their holy lives—nothing will avail them, if one blot can be discovered in their character. There must be no moral blemish in the priesthood. In the Catholic religion, where more is professed, still more is demanded, and the errors of one padre or one ecclesiastic seem to throw a shade over the whole community to which they belong.

20

"Last Look of This Wicked World"

Thursday: June 4th, 1840
San Fernando, Mexico

Some days ago, having received a message from *my nun* that a girl
was about to take the veil in her convent, I went there about six
o'clock. Knowing that the church on these occasions is apt to be crowded
to suffocation, I proceeded to the *reja*, and—speaking to an invisible
within—requested to know in what part of the church I could have a
place. Upon which a voice replied:

"*Hermanita* (my sister), I am rejoiced to see you. You shall have a
place beside the godmother."

"Many thanks, *hermanita*. Which way shall I go?"

Voice: "You shall go through the sacristy. José María!"

José María, a thin, pale, lank individual with hollow cheeks, who
was standing near like a page in waiting, sprang forward: "*Madrecita,*
I am here!"

Voice: "José María—that lady is the Señora de Calderón. You will
conduct Her Excellency to the front of the grating, and give her a
chair."[1]

After I had thanked the *voice* for her kindness in attending to me on a
day when she was so much occupied with other affairs, the obsequious
José María led the way, and I followed him through the sacristy into the
church where were already a few kneeling figures, and thence into the
railed-off enclosure—destined for the relatives of the future nun—where I
was permitted to sit down in a comfortable velvet chair. I had been there
but a little while when the aforesaid José María reappeared, picking his
steps as if he were walking upon eggs in a sickroom. He brought me a
message from the Madre Adalid that the nun had arrived, and that the
madrecita wished to know if I should like to give her an embrace before
the ceremony began. I therefore followed my guide back into the sacristy,
where the future nun was seated beside her godmother, and in the midst
of her friends and relations, about thirty in all.

She was arrayed in pale blue satin, with diamonds, pearls, and a crown of flowers. She was literally smothered in blonde and jewels; and her face was flushed as well it might be, for she had passed the day in taking leave of her friends at a fête they had given her, and had then, according to custom, been paraded through the town in all her finery. And now her last hour was at hand.

When I came in she rose and embraced me with as much cordiality as if we had known each other for years. Beside her sat the *madrina,* also in white satin and jewels; all the relations being likewise decked out in their finest array. The nun kept laughing every now and then in the most unnatural and hysterical manner, as I thought—apparently to impress us with the conviction of her perfect happiness—for it is a great point of honour amongst girls similarly situated to look as cheerful and gay as possible: the same feeling, though in a different degree, which induces the gallant highwayman to jest in the presence of the multitude when the hangman's cord is within an inch of his neck; the same which makes a gallant general, whose life is forfeited, command his men to fire on him; the same which makes the Hindu widow mount the funeral pile without a tear in her eye, or a sigh on her lips. If the robber were to be strangled in a corner of his dungeon; if the general were to be put to death privately in his own apartment; if the widow were to be burnt quietly on her own hearth; if the nun were to be secretly smuggled in at the convent gate like a bale of contraband goods—we might hear another tale.

This girl was very young, but by no means pretty—on the contrary, rather *disgraciée par la nature*—and perhaps a knowledge of her own want of attractions may have caused the world to have few charms for her.

But José María cut short my train of reflections by requesting me to return to my seat before the crowd arrived, which I did forthwith. Shortly after, the church doors were thrown open, and a crowd burst in, everyone struggling to obtain the best seat. Musicians entered, carrying desks and music books, and placed themselves in two rows, on either side of the enclosure where I was. Then the organ struck up its solemn psalmody, and was followed by the gay music of the band. Rockets were let off outside the church, and, at the same time, the *madrina* and all the relations entered and knelt down in front of the grating which looks into the convent, but before which hung a dismal black curtain. I left my chair and knelt down beside the godmother.

Suddenly the curtain was withdrawn, and the picturesque beauty of the scene within baffles all description. Beside the altar, which was in a blaze of light, was a perfect mass of crimson and gold drapery—the walls, the antique chairs, the table before which the priests sat, all hung with the same splendid material. The bishop wore his superb mitre and robes of crimson and gold, the attendant priests also glittering in crimson and gold embroidery.

In contrast to these, five-and-twenty figures, entirely robed in black from head to foot, were ranged on each side of the room prostrate, their faces touching the ground, and in their hands immense lighted tapers. On the foreground was spread a purple carpet bordered round with a garland of freshly gathered flowers, roses and carnations and heliotrope, the only things that looked real and living in the whole scene. In the middle of this knelt the novice, still arrayed in her blue satin, white lace veil and jewels, and also with a great lighted taper in her hand.

The black nuns then rose and sang a hymn, every now and then falling on their faces and touching the floor with their foreheads. The whole looked like an incantation, or a scene in *Robert le Diable.*[2] The novice was then raised from the ground and led to the feet of the bishop, who examined her as to her vocation, and gave her his blessing —and once more the black curtain fell between us and them.

In the *second act,* she was lying prostrate on the floor, disrobed of her profane dress and covered over with a black cloth, while the black figures kneeling round her chanted a hymn. She was now dead to the world. The sunbeams had faded away, as if they would not look upon the scene, and all the light was concentrated in one great mass upon the convent group.

Again she was raised. All the blood had rushed into her face, and her attempt at a smile was truly painful. She then knelt before the bishop and received the benediction, with the sign of the cross, from a white hand with the pastoral ring. She then went round alone to embrace all the dark phantoms as they stood motionless, and, as each dark shadow clasped her in its arms, it seemed like the dead welcoming a new arrival to the shades.

But I forget the sermon, which was delivered by a fat priest who elbowed his way with some difficulty through the crowd to the grating, panting and in a prodigious heat, and ensconced himself in a great arm chair close beside us. He assured her that she "had chosen the good part, which could not be taken away from her"; that she was now one of the elect, "chosen from amongst the wickedness and dangers of the world" (picked out like a plum from a pie). He mentioned with pity and contempt those who were "yet struggling in the great Babylon"; and compared their miserable fate with hers, the Bride of Christ, who, after suffering a few privations here during a short term of years, should be received at once into a kingdom of glory. The whole discourse was well calculated to rally her fainting spirits, if fainting they were, and to inspire us with a great disgust for ourselves.[3]

When the sermon was concluded, the music again struck up. The heroine of the day came forward, and stood before the grating to take her last look of this wicked world. Down fell the black curtain. Up rose the relations, and I accompanied them into the sacristy. Here they coolly lighted their cigars, and very philosophically discoursed upon the exceeding good fortune of the new-made nun, and on her evident delight and satisfaction with her own situation. As we did not follow her behind the scenes, I could not give my opinion on this point. Shortly after, one of the gentlemen civilly led me to my carriage, and *so it was.*[4]

As we were returning home, some soldiers rode up and stopped the carriage, desiring the coachman to take the other side of the aqueduct, to avoid the body of a man who had just been murdered within a few doors of our house.

In the convent of the Incarnation, I saw another girl sacrificed in a similar manner. She was received there without a dowry, on account of the exceeding fineness of her voice. She little thought what a fatal gift it would prove to her. The most cruel part of all was that, wishing to display her fine voice to the public, they made her sing a hymn alone, on her knees, her arms extended in the form of a cross, before all the immense crowd: *"Ancilla Christi sum* (The Bride of Christ I am)." She was a good-looking girl, fat and comely, who would probably have led a comfortable life in the world, for which she seemed well fitted, most likely without one touch of romance or enthusiasm in her composition; but, having the unfortunate honour of being niece to two *chanoines,* she was thus honourably provided for without expense in her nineteenth year. As might be expected, her voice faltered and, instead of singing, she seemed inclined to cry out. Each note came slowly, heavily, tremblingly; and at last she nearly fell forward exhausted, when two of the sisters caught and supported her.

I had almost made up my mind to see no more such scenes—which, unlike pulque and bullfights, I dislike more and more upon trial—when we received an invitation which it was not easy to refuse, but was the more painful to accept, being acquainted, though slightly, with the victim.[5] I send you the printed note of invitation.

On Wednesday, the _____ of this month, at six o'clock in the evening, my daughter, Doña María de la Concepción Navarrete will assume the habit of a nun of the choir and the black veil in the Convent of Our Lady of the Incarnation. I have the honour to inform you of this, entreating you to co-operate with your presence in the solemnity of this act, a favour which will be highly esteemed by your affectionate servant, who kisses your hand.

María Josefa de Navarrete[6]

Mexico, June _____, 1840

Having gone out in the carriage to pay some visits, I suddenly recollected that it was the very morning of the day in which this young girl was to take the veil, and also that it was necessary to inquire where

I was to be placed—for, as to entering the church with the crowd on one of these occasions, it is out of the question; particularly when, the girl being as in the present case of distinguished family, the ceremony is expected to be peculiarly magnificent. I accordingly called at the house, was shown upstairs, and to my horror found myself in the midst of a "goodlie companie" in rich array, consisting of the relations of the family to the number of about a hundred persons. The bishop himself in his purple robes and amethysts, a number of priests, the father of the young lady in his general's uniform[7]—she herself in purple velvet, with diamonds and pearls, and a crown of flowers, the corsage of her gown entirely covered with little bows of ribbon of divers colours, which her friends had given her, each adding one, like stones thrown on a cairn in memory of the departed. She had also short sleeves and white satin shoes.

Being very handsome, with fine black eyes, good teeth, and fresh colour—and above all with the beauty of youth, for she is but eighteen —she was not disfigured even by this overloaded dress. Her mother, on the contrary—who was to act the part of *madrina*, who wore a dress facsimile, and who was pale and sad, her eyes almost extinguished with weeping—looked like a picture of misery in a ball dress. In the adjoining room long tables were laid out, on which servants were placing refreshments for the fête about to be given on this joyous occasion.

I felt somewhat shocked, and inclined to say with Paul Pry, "Hope I don't intrude."[8] But my apologies were instantly cut short, and I was welcomed with true Mexican hospitality, repeatedly thanked for my kindness in coming to see the nun, and hospitably pressed to join the family feast. I only got off upon a promise of returning at half past five to accompany them to the ceremony, which, in fact, I greatly preferred to going there alone.

I arrived at the hour appointed, and being led upstairs by the Senator Don José Cacho,[9] found the morning party, with many additions, lingering over the dessert. There was some gaiety, but evidently forced. It reminded me of a marriage feast previous to the departure of the bride, who is about to be separated from her family for the first time. Yet how different in fact this banquet, where the mother and daughter met together for the last time on earth!

At stated periods, indeed, the mother may hear her daughter's voice speaking to her as from the depths of the tomb; but she may never more fold her in her arms, never more share in her joys or in her sorrows, or nurse her in sickness; and when her own last hour arrives, though but a few streets divide them, she may not give her dying blessing to the child who has been for so many years the pride of her eyes and heart.

I have seen no country where families are so knit together as in Mexico, where the affections are so concentrated, or where such devoted respect and obedience are shown by the married sons and daughters to their parents. In that respect they always remain as little children. I know many families of which the married branches continue to live in their father's house, forming a sort of small colony, and living in the most perfect harmony. They cannot bear the idea of being separated, and nothing but dire necessity ever forces them to leave their *fatherland*. To all the accounts which travellers give them of the pleasures to be met with in European capitals they turn a deaf ear. Their families are in Mexico—their parents, and sisters, and relatives—and there is no happiness for them elsewhere. The greater therefore is the sacrifice which those parents make, who from religious motives devote their daughters to a conventual life.

_____, however, was furious at the whole affair, which he said was entirely against the mother's consent, though that of the father had been obtained; and pointed out to me the confessor whose influence had brought it about. The girl herself was now very pale, but evidently resolved to conceal her agitation, and the mother seemed as if she could shed no more tears—quite exhausted with weeping. As the hour for the ceremony drew near, the whole party became more grave and sad, all but the priests who were smiling and talking together in groups. The girl was not still a moment. She kept walking hastily through the house, taking leave of the servants, and naming probably her last wishes about everything. She was followed by her younger sisters, all in tears.

But it struck six, and the priests intimated that it was time to move. She and her mother went downstairs alone, and entered the carriage which was to drive them through all the principal streets, to show the nun to the public according to custom, and to let them take their last look—they of her, and she of them.

As they got in, we all crowded to the balconies to see her take leave of her house, her aunts saying, "Yes, child, *despídete de tu casa*, take leave of your house, for you will never see it again!" Then came sobs from the sisters, and many of the gentlemen, ashamed of their emotion, hastily quitted the room. I hope, for the sake of humanity, I did not rightly interpret the look of constrained anguish which the poor girl threw from the window of the carriage at the home of her childhood.

They drove off, and the relations prepared to walk in procession to the church. I walked with the Count [de] Santiago; the others followed in pairs.[10]

The church was very brilliantly illuminated, and as we entered the band was playing one of *Strauss's* waltzes![11] The crowd was so tremendous that we were nearly squeezed to a jelly in getting to our places. I was carried off my feet between two fat señoras in mantillas and shaking diamond pendants, exactly as if I had been packed between two movable feather beds.

They gave me, however, an excellent place, quite close to the grating, beside the Countess de Santiago—that is to say, a place to kneel on. A great bustle and much preparation seemed to be going on within the convent, and veiled figures were flitting about, whispering, arranging, &c. Sometimes a skinny old dame would come close to the grating, and, lifting up her veil, bestow upon the pensive public a generous view of a very haughty and very wrinkled visage of some seventy years' standing —and beckon into the church for the major-domo of the convent (an excellent and profitable situation by the way), or for padre this or that. Some of the holy ladies recognized and spoke to me through the grating.

But at the discharge of fireworks outside the church the curtain was dropped, for this was the signal that the nun and her mother had arrived. An opening was made in the crowd as they passed into the church; and the girl, kneeling down, was questioned by the bishop, but I could not make out the dialogue which was carried on in a low voice. She then passed into the convent by a side door, and her mother, quite exhausted and nearly in hysterics, was supported through the crowd to a place beside us, in front of the grating. The music struck up; the curtain was again drawn aside. The scene was as striking here as in the convent of the Santa Teresa, but not so lugubrious. The nuns, all ranged around and carrying lighted tapers in their hands, were dressed in mantles of bright blue, with a gold plate on the left shoulder.[12] Their faces, however, were covered with deep black veils. The girl, kneeling in front, and also bearing a heavy lighted taper, looked beautiful with her dark hair and rich dress, and the long black lashes resting on her glowing face. The churchmen near the illuminated and magnificently-decked altar formed, as usual, a brilliant background to the picture. The ceremony was the same as on the former occasion, but there was no sermon.

The most terrible thing to witness was the last, straining, anxious look which the mother gave her daughter through the grating. She had seen her child pressed to the arms of strangers, and welcomed to her new home. She was no longer hers. All the sweet ties of nature had been rudely severed, and she had been forced to consign her, in the very bloom of youth and beauty, at the very age in which she most required a mother's care, and when she had but just fulfilled the promise of her childhood, to a living tomb. Still, as long as the curtain had not fallen, she could gaze upon her, as upon one on whom, though dead, the coffin lid is not yet closed.

But while the new-made nun was in a blaze of light—and distinct on the foreground, so that we could mark each varying expression of her face—the crowd in the church, and the comparative faintness of the light probably made it difficult for her to distinguish her mother; for, knowing that the end was at hand, she looked anxiously and hurriedly into the church, without seeming able to fix her eyes on any particular object; while her mother seemed as if her eyes were glazed, so intently were they fixed upon her daughter.

Suddenly, and without any preparation, down fell the black curtain like a pall, and the sobs and tears of the family broke forth. One beautiful little child was carried out almost in fits. Water was brought to the poor mother; and at last, making our way with difficulty through the dense crowd, we got into the sacristy.

"I declare," said the Countess _____ to me, wiping her eyes, "it is worse than a marriage!" I expressed my horror at the sacrifice of a girl so young, that she could not possibly have known her own mind. Almost all the ladies agreed with me, especially all who had daughters, but many of the old gentlemen were of a different opinion. The young men were decidedly of my way of thinking, but many young girls, who were conversing together, seemed rather to envy their friend—who had looked so pretty and graceful, and "so happy," and whose dress "suited her so well"—and to have no objection to "go, and do likewise."

I had the honour of a presentation to the bishop, a fat and portly prelate with good manners, and well besuiting his priestly garments.[13] I amused myself, while we waited for the carriages, by looking over a pamphlet which lay on the table containing the ceremonial of the veil-taking. When we rose to go, all the ladies of the highest rank devoutly kissed the bishop's hand; and I went home, thinking by what law of God a child can thus be dragged from the mother who bore and bred her, and immured in a cloister for life, amongst strangers, to whom she has no tie, and towards whom she owes no duty. That a convent may be a blessed shelter from the calamities of life, a haven for the unprotected, a resting place for the weary, a safe and holy asylum, where a new family and kind friends await those whose natural ties are broken and whose early friends are gone, I am willing to admit; but it is not in the flower of youth that the warm heart should be consigned to the cold cloister. Let the young take their chance of sunshine or storm; the calm and shady retreat is for helpless and unprotected old age.

A.N.M., to whom I described one of these ceremonies, wrote some verses suggested by my account of them, which I send you.[14]

21

The Gambling Tables of San Agustín

Monday: June 15th, 1840
San Fernando, Mexico

Since my last letter we have been at San Agustín de las Cuevas, which, when I last saw it, was a deserted village—but which during three days in the year presents the appearance of a vast beehive or anthill.

San Agustín! At the name how many hearts throb with emotion! How many hands are mechanically thrust into empty pockets! How many visions of long-vanished golden ounces flit before aching eyes! What faint crowing of wounded cocks! What tinkling of guitars and blowing of horns come upon the ear! Some indeed there be, a fortunate few, who can look round upon their well-stored hacienda and easy rolling carriages, and remember the day when, with threadbare coat and stake of three modest ounces, they first courted Fortune's favours; and who, being then indigent and enjoying an indifferent reputation, found themselves at the conclusion of a few successive San Agustíns the fortunate proprietors of gold, and land, and houses—and moreover with an unimpeachable fame, for he who can fling gold dust in his neighbour's eyes prevents him from seeing too clearly. But these favourites of the blind goddess are few and far between; and they have for the most part, with a view to greater security, become holders or sharers of banks at San Agustín, thus investing a part of their fortune in a tolerably secure fund—more so decidedly, if we may believe the newspaper reports, than in the Bank of the United States at this present writing.[1]

Time, in its revolutions whirling all things out of their places, has made no change in the annual fête of San Agustín. Fashions alter. The graceful mantilla gradually gives place to the ungraceful bonnet. The old painted coach, moving slowly like a caravan, with Guido's Aurora painted on its gaudy panels, is dismissed for the London-built carriage. Old customs have passed away. The ladies no longer sit on the doorsills,

eating roast duck with their fingers, or with the aid of tortillas—
Montezuma's forks.[2] Even the *chinampas* have become stationary, and
have occasionally joined the continent. But the annual fête of San
Agustín is built on a more solid foundation than taste, or custom, or
floating soil. It is founded upon that love of gambling which is said
to be a passion inherent in our nature, and which is certainly im-
pregnated with the Mexican constitution—in man, woman, and child
from the President down to the *lépero*. The beggars gamble at the
corners of the streets or under the arches; the little boys gamble in
groups in the villages; the coachmen and footmen gamble at the doors
of the theatre while waiting for their masters.

But while their hand is thus *kept in* all the year round, there are
three days sacredly set apart annually in which every accommodation
is given to those who are bent upon ruining themselves or their neighbours; whilst every zest that pleasure and society can afford is held out to
render the temptation more alluring. As religion in this country is called
in to sanctify everything, right or wrong, as the robber will plant a
cross at the mouth of his cave, and the pulque shops do occasionally
call themselves "*Pulquerías* of the Most Holy Virgin," so this season of
gambling is fixed for the fête of *Pascua* (Whitsunday), and the churches
and the gambling houses are thrown open simultaneously.

The village is in itself pretty and picturesque; and, as a stone at its
entry informs us, was built by the active Viceroy Revillagigedo with the
product, as Cuevas assured us, of two lotteries.[3] It is charmingly situated
in the midst of handsome villas and orchards, whose high walls, over-
topped by fruit trees, border the narrow lanes. At this season the trees
are loaded with the yellow *chabacano* and the purple plum, already
ripe—while the pear trees are bending under the weight of their fruit.
The gardens are full of flowers: the roses in their last bloom covering
the ground with their pink leaves, and jasmine and sweet peas in
profusion making the air fragrant. The rainy season has scarce set in,
though frequent showers have laid the dust and refreshed the air. The
country villas are filled with all the gayest and most distinguished in
Mexico, and every house and every room in the village has been hired
for months in advance.[4] The ladies are in their most elegant toilettes,
and looking forward to a delightful whirl of dancing, cockfighting,
flirting, gambling, dining, dressing, and driving about.

The highroad leading from Mexico to San Agustín is covered with
vehicles of every description: carriages, diligences, hackney coaches, carts,
and *carretelas*. Those who are not fortunate enough to possess any
wheeled conveyance come out on horse, ass, or mule—single, double, or
treble if necessary. And many hundreds, with visions of silver before
their eyes and a few *tlacos* (pence) hid under their rags, trudge out on
foot. The President himself, in carriage and six, and attended by his
aides-de-camp, sanctions by his presence the amusements of the fête. The

Mexican generals and other officers follow in his wake, and the gratifying spectacle may not unfrequently be seen of the President leaning from his box in the *plaza de gallos*, and betting upon a cock with a coatless, bootless, hatless, and probably worthless ragamuffin in the pit. Everyone, therefore, however humble his degree, has the pleasure, while following his speculative inclinations, of reflecting that he treads in the steps of the magnates of the land—and, as Sam Weller would say, "Vot a consolation that must be to his feelings!"[5]

At all events, nothing can be gayer than the appearance of the village, as your carriage makes its way through the narrow lanes into the principal plaza amidst the assembled crowd of coaches and foot-passengers— though the faces of the people bear evidence that pleasure alone has not brought them to San Agustín. All around the square are the gambling houses where, for three nights and three days, every table is occupied. At the principal *montes* nothing is played but gold, but, as there is accommodation for all classes, so there are silver tables in the inferior houses, while outside are rows of tables on which are heaps of copper, covered with a ragged awning, and surrounded by *léperos* and blanketed Indians, playing *monte* in imitation of their betters, though on a scale more suited to their fortunes.[6]

Having left Mexico early in the morning, we stopped to breakfast at San Antonio, a noble hacienda about four leagues from Mexico belonging to the Dowager Marquesa de Vivanco, where we breakfasted with a large party. It is a fine solid mass of building, and as you enter the courtyard, through a deep archway, the great outhouses, stables, and especially the granary look like remains of feudalism, they are on so large and magnificent a scale.[7]

It is an immense and valuable property, producing both maize and maguey, and the hospitality of the family, who are amongst our earliest friends here, is upon as large a scale as everything that belongs to them. We had a splendid breakfast, in a fine old hall, and stayed but a short time to visit the gardens and the chapel, as we were anxious to arrive at San Agustín in time for the cockfight.

It is singular that, while San Agustín is situated in the midst of the most fertile and productive country, there should lie opposite to it—and bounded as it were by the graceful Peruvian trees and silver poplars which surround a small church on the other side of the highroad—a great tract of black lava, sterile, bleak, and entirely destitute of vegetation, called the Pedregal. This covers the country all along to San Agustín and to the base of the mountain of Ajusco, which lies behind it, contrasting strangely with the beautiful groves and gardens in its neighbourhood, and looking as if it had been cursed for some crime committed there.[8] The highroad, which runs nearly in a direct line from the hacienda to San Agustín, is broad and in tolerable repair; but, before arriving there, it is so little attended to that during the rainy season it might be passed in canoes; yet this immense formation of ferruginous lava and porphyritic rock lies conveniently in its vicinity. A large sum, supposed to be employed in mending the road, is collected annually at the toll, close to San Antonio. For each carriage two dollars are asked, and for carts and animals in proportion. The proprietor of this toll or *portazgo* is also the owner of the *plaza de gallos,* where a dollar is paid for entry—the sums produced by which go exclusively to enrich the same individual. The government has no advantage from it.

The last day of the fête is considered the best, and it is most crowded on that day, both by families from Mexico and by foreigners who go solely for pleasure, though they are apt [to] succumb before the temptation so generally held out and not unfrequently [are] tempted to do a little business on their own account. In fact, the temptations are great; and it must be difficult for a young man to withstand them.

We went to the *gallos* about three o'clock. The plaza was crowded and in their boxes the ladies in their gay dresses looked like a gay parterre of different coloured flowers. But while the ladies in their boxes did honour to the fête by their brilliant toilette, the gentlemen promenaded round the circle in jackets, high and low being on the same *curtailed* footing, and certainly in a style of dress more befitting the exhibition. The President and his suite were already there, also several of the foreign ministers.[9]

Meanwhile the cocks crowed valiantly, bets were adjusted, and even the ladies entered into the spirit of the scene, taking bets with the gentlemen *sotta voce* in their boxes, upon such and such favourite animal. As a small knife is fastened to the leg of each cock, the battle seldom lasted long, one or another falling every few minutes in a pool of blood. Then there was a clapping of hands, mingled with the loud and triumphant crowing of some unfortunate cock, who was giving himself airs previous to a combat where he was probably destined to crow his last. It has a curious effect to European eyes to see young ladies of good family, looking in everything else peculiarly feminine and gentle, sanctioning by their presence this savage diversion. It is no doubt the effect of early habit, and you will say that at least it is no worse than a bullfight, which is certain. Yet, cruel as the latter is, I find something more *en grande,* more noble, in the

Ungentle sport that oft invites
The Spanish maid, and cheers the Spanish swain[10]

—in the roaring of the "lord of lowing herds," the galloping of the fine horses, the skill of the riders, the gay dresses, the music and the agile matador; in short, in the whole pomp and circumstances of the combat, than when one looks quietly on to see two birds peck each other's eyes out, and cut each other to pieces. Unlike cockpits in other countries, attended by blacklegs and pickpockets and gentlemanly roués, by far the

largest portion of the assembly in the pit was composed of the first young men in Mexico, and, for that matter, of the first old ones also. There was neither confusion, nor noise, nor even loud talking, far less swearing, even amongst the lowest of those assembled in the ring; and it is this quiet and orderly behaviour which throws over all these incongruities a cloak of decency and decorum, that hides the real impropriety even from themselves—and so completely that even foreigners who have lived here a few years, and who were at first struck with astonishment by these things, are now quite reconciled to them.

As far as the company went, it might have been the House of Representatives in Washington: the ladies in the gallery listening to the debates, and the members in the body of the house surrounding Messrs. Wise and _____, or any other two vehement orators—applauding their biting remarks and cutting sarcasms, and encouraging them to crow over each other.[11] The President might have been the speaker, and the *corps diplomatique* represented itself.

We had an agreeable dinner at the Escandóns' and afterwards accompanied them to the Calvario, a hill where there was a ball *al fresco*[12] which was rather amusing, and then paid a visit to the family of General Morán, who has a beautiful house and gardens in the neighbourhood. We found a large party assembled, and amongst them the President. Afterwards, accompanied by the French minister and the ladies of our party, we went to take a view of the gambling tables, and opened our eyes at the heaps of gold, which changed owners every minute. I saw Carrera, a millionaire, win and lose a thousand ounces, apparently with equal indifference.[13] A little advocate, having won two thousand five hundred ounces, wisely ordered his carriage and set off for Mexico, with the best *fee* he had ever received in his life.

Ladies do not generally look on at the tables, but may if they please, and especially if they be strangers. Each gambling room was well fitted up, and looked like a private apartment.

We then returned home and dressed for the ball, which is given in the evening in the *plaza de gallos*. We first went upstairs to a box, but I afterwards took the advice of M. de Cyprey and came down to see the dancers. There were ladies in full dress, and gentlemen in white jackets—rather inconsistent. The company, though perfectly quiet and well-behaved, were not very select, and were, on that account, particularly amusing. Madame de Cyprey and I walked about, and certainly laughed much more than we should have done in a more distinguished society.

About two in the morning we returned to Mexico, and, as I this moment receive a note from the American minister[14] informing me that the packet from Veracruz is about to sail, I shall send off my letters now. Should we still be here next year, I shall then give you a more detailed description of the fête, of the ball, both at Calvario and in the cockpit, and also of the "high life below stairs" gambling, at which the scenes are *impayable*.[15]

In one respect the fashions of San Agustín are altered from what they were a few years ago, when the señoras used to perform five elaborate and distinct toilettes daily: the first in the morning, the second for the cockfight, the third for the dinner, the fourth for the ball on the hill of Calvary, and the fifth for the ball in the evening. I am told that as they danced in the open air on the hill with all their diamonds and pearls on, in the midst of an immense concourse of people, a great many jewels were constantly lost, which the *léperos* used afterwards to search for, and pick up from the grass: a rich harvest. Though they still dress a great deal, they are contented with changing their toilet twice or, at the most, three times in the course of the day.

Upon the whole, these three days are excessively amusing and, as all ranks and conditions are mingled, one sees much more variety than at a ball in the city.

On their way home Calderón and Señor Cuevas discussed the effects likely to be produced on the morals of the people by this fête. Señor Cuevas, like nearly all the wisest men here, persists in considering gambling an innocent amusement, and declares that at all events this fête ought never to be done away with. In his opinion it conduces to the happiness of the people, gives them an annual pleasure to look forward to, and, by the mingling of all ranks which then takes place, keeps up a good feeling between the higher and lower orders. Calderón asked him why, if such was the case, the government did not at least endeavour to draw some advantage from it, after the manner of the Count de Revilla-gigedo—why, as the bank by the nature of the game has (besides a great capital which swallows up all the smaller ones) an immense profit, amounting to twenty-five percent, they do not make the bankers pay four or five percent and charge half a dollar or more to each individual who enters to gamble—with which money they might beautify the village, make a public *paseo*, a good road, a canal to Mexico, &c. I thought that whatever the government might feel on this subject, neither the bankers nor the gamblers would relish the insinuation.

I shall write in a few days by the Baron de Norman, minister from Belgium, who leaves Mexico in a fortnight.[16]

22

Approach of the Rainy Season

Wednesday: June 17th, 1840
San Fernando, Mexico

As we dine nearly every Sunday with the Countess de la Cortina at
Tacubaya, where she keeps open house to all her friends, we have had
the pleasure of becoming intimately acquainted with her son-in-law,
Señor Gutiérrez Estrada, who with his amiable wife has lately returned
from Europe.[1]

A great dinner was given us the other day by General Morán and his
lady, the Marquesa de Vivanco, at San Agustín. We went early that we
might have time to walk about the garden, which is beautiful, and to
visit an artificial cave there—which we found lighted up with coloured
lamps and where a most fascinating species of cold milk punch, with
cakes, was served to the company.[2] The dinner would certainly have
been superb in any country. The family has travelled a great deal in
Europe (perforce, the general having been exiled for several years) and
is amongst the oldest and richest in Mexico. The dowager *marquesa* has
a most patriarchal family of daughters and granddaughters, and of the
large party assembled at table nearly all were composed of its different
members. In the evening we had a pleasant dance under the trees.[3]

Thursday: June 18th, 1840[4]

Day of the Corpus Christi, in which the Host is carried through the
city in great procession, at which the President in full uniform, the
Archbishop, and all the ministers, &c., assist. In former days this ceremony took place on Holy Thursday; but, finding that on account of the
various ceremonies of the Holy Week it could not be kept with due
solemnity, another day was set apart for its celebration.[5] We went to a
window in the square to see the procession, which was very brilliant—

all the troops out, and the streets crowded. Certainly, a stranger entering Mexico on one of these days would be struck with surprise at its apparent wealth. Everything connected with the church is magnificent.

This evening the Señora Adalid came after it was dark, in a Poblana dress which she had just bought to wear at a *Jamaica* which they are going to have in the country—a sort of fair, where all the girls disguise themselves in peasants' dresses and go about selling fruit, lemonade, vegetables, &c. to each other—a very ancient Mexican amusement. This dress cost her some hundred dollars. The top of the petticoat is yellow satin; the rest, which is of scarlet cashmere, is embroidered in gold and silver. Her hair was fastened back with a thick silver comb, and her ornaments were very handsome—coral set in gold. Her shoes white satin, embroidered in gold; the sleeves and body of the chemise, which is of the finest cambric, trimmed with rich lace; and the petticoat, which comes below the dress, shows two flounces of Valenciennes. She looks beautiful in this dress, which will not be objected to in the country, though it might not suit a fancy ball in Mexico.[6]

Saturday: June 20th, 1840

Being invited yesterday to a fête at San Antonio, we left Mexico about eight o'clock by the great causeway leading to San Agustín.[7] The day was peculiarly brilliant, but the rainy season is now announcing its approach by frequent showers towards evening.

We found a large party assembled, and about twelve o'clock sat down to a most magnificent breakfast of about sixty persons. Everything was solid silver, even the plates. (A vast capital is sunk in diamonds and plate in this country, no good sign of the state of commerce.) The ladies in general were dressed in white embroidered muslins, over white or coloured satin, and one or two Paris dresses shone conspicuous. There was one specimen of real Mexican beauty, the Señora Cuevas—a face perhaps more Indian than Spanish, very dark, with fine eyes, beautiful teeth, very long dark hair, and full of expression.[8]

The house, which is immensely large, is furnished, or rather unfurnished, in the style of all Mexican haciendas. After breakfast we had music, dancing, walking, and billiard playing. Some boleros were very gracefully danced by a daughter of the *marquesa*, and they also showed us some dances of the country.[9] The fête terminated with the most beautiful supper I almost ever saw. A great hall was lighted with coloured lamps, the walls entirely lined with green branches, and hung with fresh garlands of flowers most tastefully arranged. There was a great deal of gaiety and cordiality, of magnificence without ceremony, and riches without pretension.

Although warned by various showers that a bad night would probably set in, and although it was too likely that the hospitality within the house would be extended to our coachmen—and even though the whole party were strongly pressed by the *marquesa* to pass the night there, so that it was with difficulty we resisted her entreaties to remain—we did, in the face of all this, set off at twelve o'clock at night to return to Mexico: about seven carriages together, with various gentlemen riding. Though very dark there was no rain, and we flattered ourselves it would keep fair till we reached the city. The Minister of the Interior, who is married to a daughter of the *marquesa,* Calderón and I, and La Güera Rodríguez set off in one carriage.[10] Some carriages had lamps, others had none. Some had six horses—we had six mules, and an escort of dragoons.

We had not gone two miles before a thunderstorm came on, and the black clouds which had been gathering above our heads burst forth in torrents of rain. The wind was tremendous. All the lamps were extinguished. The horses waded up to their knees in mud and water. Suddenly there was a crash, followed by loud cries. A carriage was overturned, in which were the Señora Lombardi and a party of gentlemen.[11] In the midst of this awful storm, and perhaps still more bewildered by generous liquor, their coachman had lost his way and lodged them all in a ditch. The poor señora was dreadfully bruised, her head cut, and her wrist dislocated. In the darkness and confusion she was extricated with difficulty, and placed in another carriage.

Our mules stood still. As far as the noise of the storm would allow us to hear, we made out that our coachman also had lost the road. Two dragoons rode up to direct him. One fell, horse and all, into a deep ditch—where he remained till the next morning. Another carriage came ploughing its way behind us. Another exclamation in the darkness! A mule had fallen and broken his traces, and plunged into the water. The poor animal could not be found.

Never was there such a chapter of accidents. We were the only carriage load which escaped entirely, owing chiefly to the sobriety of the coachman. Very slowly, and after sundry detentions, we arrived in Mexico towards morning, very tired but with neither broken bones nor bruises.

Saturday: June 27th, 1840

I was awakened this morning by hearing that two boxes had arrived from New York containing books, letters, &c.—all very acceptable. We also received a number of old newspapers by post, for which we had to pay eighteen dollars! Each sheet costs a real and a half—a mistaken source of profit in a republic, where the general diffusion of knowledge

is of so much importance—for this not only applies to the introduction
of French and English, but also of Spanish newspapers. Señors Gutiérrez
Estrada and Cañedo used every effort to reduce this duty on newspapers,
but in vain. The post office opposes its reduction, fearing to be deprived
of an imaginary rent—imaginary because so few persons, comparatively,
think it worth their while to go to this expense.

There is but one daily newspaper in Mexico, *la gaceta del gobierno* (the
government paper), and it is filled with orders and decrees. An opposition paper, the *Cosmopolita,* is published twice a week; also a
Spanish paper, the *Hesperia.* Both (especially the latter) are well written.
There is also the *Mosquito,* so called from its stinging sarcasms. Now
and then another with a new title appears, like a shooting star, but from
want of support, or from some other motive, is suddenly extinguished.[12]

Enlightened individuals like Don Lucas Alamán and Count Cortina
have published newspapers, but not for any length of time. Count
Cortina (especially) edited a very witty and brilliant paper called the
Zurriago (the *Scourge*), and another called the *Mono* (the *Ape*)—and
in many of his articles he was tolerably severe upon the incorrect Spanish
of his brother editors, of which no one can be a better judge, he having
been a member of the *Academia de la Lengua* in Spain.

The only kind of monthly review in Mexico is the *Mosaico Mexicano,*
whose editor has made his fortune by his own activity and exertions.
Frequently it contains more translations than original matter; but from
time to time it publishes scientific articles, said to be written by Don J. M.
Bustamante, which are very valuable,[13] and occasionally a brilliant
article from the pen of Count Cortina. General Orbegoso, who is of
Spanish origin, is also a contributor.[14] Sometimes, though rarely, it
publishes *documentos inéditos* (unedited documents)—connected with
Mexican antiquities, and Mexican natural history and biography—which
are very important; and now and then it contains a little poetical gem, I
know not whether original or not, but exceedingly beautiful. So far as it
goes, this review is one great means of spreading knowledge, at least
amongst the better classes. But I understand that the editor, Don Ignacio
Cumplido, a very courteous, intelligent man, complains that it does not
pay.[15]

There are no circulating libraries in Mexico. Books are at least double
the price that they are in Europe. There is no diffusion of useful knowledge amongst the people, neither cheap pamphlets nor cheap magazines
written for their amusement or instruction. But this is less owing to
want of attention to their interests on the part of many good and enlightened men than to the unsettled state of the country, for the blight of
civil war prevents the best systems from ripening.

Fortunately there is an English society here, a kind of book club, who, with their minister, have united in a subscription to order from England all the new publications—and, as Calderón is a member of this society, we are not so *arrierés* in regard to the literature of the day as might be supposed. Like all English societies, its basis is a good dinner, which each member gives in turn once a month, after which there is a sale of the books that have been read, and propositions for new books are given in to the president. It is an excellent plan, and I believe is in part adopted by other foreigners here. But Germans of a certain class do not seem to be sufficiently numerous for such an undertaking, and the French in Mexico, barring some distinguished exceptions, are apt to be amongst the very worst specimens of that people which *"le plaisant pays de France"* can furnish forth.[16]

We went lately to a ball given by a young Englishman, which was very pretty, and where nearly all the English were collected. Of families there are not more than half a dozen resident here, the members of whom form a striking contrast in complexion to the *Mexicanas*. With very few exceptions (and these in the case of English women married to foreigners) they keep themselves entirely aloof from the Mexicans, live quietly in their own houses into which they have transplanted as much English comfort as possible, rarely travel, and naturally find Mexico the dullest of cities.

Calderón has gone to dine with the English minister, and I am left alone in this large room, with nothing but a hummingbird to keep me company—the last of my half dozen. It looks like a large blue fly, and is perfectly tame, but will not live many days.

I was startled by a solemn voice saying, *"Ave María Purísima!"*—and, looking up, there stood in the doorway a "friar of orders grey,"[17] bringing some message to Calderón from the head of the convent of San Fernando, with whose monks Calderón has formed a great intimacy, chiefly in consequence of the interest which he has taken in the history of their missions to California.[18]

In fact, when we hear the universal cry that is raised against these communities for the inutility of their lives, it is but just that exceptions should be made in favour of those who, like the monks of San Fernando, have dispersed their missionaries over some of the most miserable parts of the globe and who—undeterred by danger, and by the prospect of death—have carried light to the most benighted savages.

These institutions are of a very remote date. A learned Jesuit monk, Eusebius Kühn, is said to have been the first who discovered that California was a peninsula. In 1683 the Jesuits had formed establishments in Old California,[19] and for the first time it was made known that the country—which had until then been considered an El Dorado, rich in all precious metals and diamonds—was arid, stony, and without water or earth fit for vegetation; that where there is a spring of water it is to be found amongst the bare rocks, and where there is earth there is no water. A few spots were found by these industrious men uniting these advantages, and there they founded their first missions.

But the general hatred with which the Jesuits were regarded excited suspicion against them, and it was generally supposed that their accounts were false, and that they were privately becoming possessed of much treasure. *A visitador* (surveyor) was sent to examine into the truth and, though he could discover no traces of gold or silver, he was astonished by the industry and zeal with which they had cultivated the barren and treeless waste. In a few years they had built sixteen villages, and when they were expelled in 1767, the Dominican friars of Mexico took their place.[20]

Until these missions were established, and in every part of the peninsula which is not included in the territory of the missions, the savages were the most degraded specimens of humanity existing. More degraded than the beasts of the field, they lay all day upon their faces on the arid sand, basking in the heat. They abhorred all species of clothing, and their only religion was a secret horror that caused them to tremble at the idea of three divinities, belonging to three different tribes, which divinities were themselves supposed to feel a mortal hatred and to wage perpetual war against each other.[21]

Undeterred by the miserable condition both of human and of vegetable nature, these missionaries cultivated the ground, established colonies, made important astronomical observations, and devoted themselves to science, to agriculture, and to the amelioration of the condition of these wretched savages.

In New California, the missions were under the charge of thirty-six Franciscan friars, under whom the most extraordinary progress in civilization took place; since, in little more than thirty years, upwards of thirty-three thousand Indians were baptized, and eight thousand marriages had taken place. The soil being fertile and the climate more benign than in the other California, in eighteen missions established there, they cultivated corn, wheat, maize, &c.,[22] and introduced vegetables and fruit trees from Spain; amongst these, the vine and the olive, from which excellent wine and oil were made all through that part of the country.

Amongst the monks destined to these distant missions were those of San Fernando. There, banished from the world, deprived of all the advantages of civilization, they devoted themselves to the task of *taming* the wild Indians. [They] introduced marriage amongst them, taught them to cultivate the ground, together with some of the most simple arts, assisted their wants, reproved their sins, and transplanted the beneficent doctrines of Christianity amongst them—using no arms but the influence which religion and kindness united with extreme patience had over their stubborn natures, and making what Humboldt, in speaking of the Jesuit missions, calls "a pacific conquest" of the country.[23]

Many were the hardships which these poor men endured: changed from place to place; at one time ordered to some barren shore where it was necessary to recommence their labours; at another, recalled to the capital by orders of the prelate—in conjunction with the wishes of their brethren, among whom there was a species of congress, called by them a *capítulo*. No increase of rank, no reward, no praise inspired their labours; their only recompense was their intimate conviction of doing good to their fellow creatures.

In the archives of the convent there still exist papers proving the hardships which these men underwent, [and] the zeal with which they applied themselves to the study of the languages of the country (and when we are informed that in the space of one hundred and eighty leagues nineteen different languages are spoken, it was no easy task)—and containing their descriptions of its physical and moral state, more or less well written, according to their different degrees of instruction or talent.

It frequently happened that marketable goods and even provisions had to be sent by sea to those missionaries who lived in the most savage and uncultivated parts of the peninsula; and a curious anecdote on this subject was related to Calderón by one of these men who is now a gardener by profession. It happened that someone sent to the monks, amongst other things, a case of fine Málaga raisins; and one of the monks, whose name I forget, sowed a number of the dried seeds. In process of time they sprouted up, became vines, and produced fine grapes, from which the best wine in California was made.

When the independence was declared—and that revolutionary fury, which makes a merit of destroying every establishment, good or bad, which is the work of the opposite party, broke forth—the Mexicans, to prove their hatred to the mother country, destroyed these beneficent institutions; thus committing an error as fatal in its results as when in 1828 they expelled so many rich proprietors—who were followed into exile by their numerous families, and by their old servants who gave them, in these times of trouble, proofs of attachment and fidelity belonging to a race now scarcely existing here except amongst a few of the oldest families.[24]

The result has been that—the frontiers being now unprotected by the military garrisons or *presidios* which were established there, and deserted by the missionaries—the Indians are no longer kept under subjection, either by the force of arms or by the good counsels and persuasive influence of their padres. The Mexican territory is, in consequence, perpetually exposed to their invasions. Whole families are massacred by the savages, who exchange guns for rifles, which they already know how to use, and these evil consequences are occasionally and imperfectly averted at a great expense to the republic. Bustamante has indeed been making an investigation lately as to the funds and general condition of these establishments, with the intention of re-establishing some similar institutions; but as yet I believe that nothing decisive has been done in this respect.[25]

Near the convent there is a beautiful garden—where we sometimes walk in the morning—cultivated by an old monk who, after spending a laborious life in these distant missions, is now enjoying a contented old age among his plants and flowers. Perhaps you are tired of my *prosing* (caused by the apparition of the old lay brother) and would prefer some account of him in verse.

> An aged monk in San Fernando dwells,
>   An innocent and venerable man;
> His earlier days were spent within its cells,
>   And end obscurely as they first began.
> Manhood's career in savage climes he ran,
>   On lonely California's Indian shore—
> Dispelling superstition's deadly ban,
>   Or teaching (what could patriot do more?)
> Those rudiments of peace, the gardener's humble store.

> Oft have I marked him, silent and apart,
>   Loitering near the sunny convent-gate,
> Rewarded by tranquillity of heart
>   For toils so worthy of the truly great;
> And in my soul admired, compared his state
>   With that of some rude brawler, whose crude mind
> Some wondrous change on earth would fain create;
>   Who after flatt'ring, harassing mankind,
> Gains titles, riches, pomp, with shame and scorn combined.

23

Mexican Women Appraised

Sunday: July 5th, 1840
San Fernando, Mexico

Yesterday morning we had a visit from the President, with two of his officers. He was riding one of the handsomest black horses I ever saw. On going out we stopped to look at a wax figure of Iturbide on horseback, which he considers a good resemblance, and which was sent me as a present some time ago. He ought to be a good judge, as he was a most devoted friend of the unfortunate Agustín I, who, whatever were his faults, seems to have inspired his friends with the most devoted and enthusiastic attachment.

In the prime of life, brave and active, handsome and fond of show, he had all the qualities which render a chief popular with the multitude —"but popularity, when not based upon great benefits, is transient; it is

founded upon a principle of egotism, because a whole people cannot have personal sympathies."[1] Ambition led him to desert the royal cause which he had served for nine years. And vanity blinded him to the dangers that surrounded him in the midst of his triumphs, even when proclaimed Emperor by the united voice of the garrison and city of Mexico—when his horses were taken from his carriage, and when amidst the shouts of the multitude his coach was dragged in triumph to the palace. His great error, according to those who talk of him impartially, was indecision in the most critical emergencies, and his permitting himself to be governed by circumstances, instead of directing these circumstances as they occurred.

I could not help thinking, as the general stood there looking at the waxen image of his friend, what a stormy life he himself has passed— how little real tranquillity he can ever have enjoyed—and wondering whether he will be permitted to finish his presidential days in peace, which, according to rumour, is doubtful.[2]

Wednesday: July 8th, 1840

I had the honour of a long visit this morning from His Grace the Archbishop. He came about eleven o'clock, after mass, and remained till dinner time—sitting out all our Sunday visitors, who are generally numerous as it is the only day of rest for *employés* and especially for the cabinet.

Amongst our visitors were: Señor Cañedo [Minister of Foreign Relations], who is extremely agreeable in conversation, and as an orator famed for his sarcasm and cutting wit; he has been particularly kind and friendly to us ever since our arrival. General Almonte, Minister of War, a handsome man and pleasant, and an officer of great bravery— very unpopular with one party and especially disliked by the English, but also a great friend of ours.[3] Señor Cuevas, Minister of the Interior, married to a daughter of the Marquesa de Vivanco, an amiable and excellent man, who seems generally liked, and is also most friendly to us.[4]

All these gentlemen are praised or abused according to the party of the person who speaks of them—but I, not interfering in Mexican politics, find them amongst the most pleasant of our acquaintances.

However, were I to choose a situation here, it would undoubtedly be that of Archbishop of Mexico, the most enviable in the world to those who would enjoy a life of luxury, indolence, tranquillity, and universal adoration. He is a pope without half the trouble, or a tenth part of the responsibility. He is venerated more than the Holy Father is in enlightened Rome, and, like kings in the good old times, can do no wrong. His salary amounts to about one hundred thousand dollars, and a revenue might be made even by the sweetmeats alone which are sent him by all the nuns in the republic. His palace in town, his well-cushioned carriage, well-conditioned horses and sleek mules, himself and all around him, seem the very perfection of comfort. In fact, *comfort*, which is unknown amongst the profane of Mexico, has taken refuge with the Archbishop; and, though many drops of it are shed on the shaven heads of all bishops, curates, confessors, and friars, still, in his illustrious person it concentrates as in a focus. He himself is a benevolent, goodhearted, good-natured, portly, and jovial personage, with the most *laissez-aller* air and expression conceivable. He looks like one on whom the good things of this world have fallen in a constant and benignant shower, which shower hath fallen on a rich and fertile soil. He is generally to be seen leaning back in his easy carriage, dressed in purple, with amethyst cross, apparently chewing a piece of tobacco, and making in a kind of mechanical way the sign of the cross to the people as he passes. He seems engaged in a kind of pleasant, half-sleepy reverie, and his countenance wears an air of the most placid and insouciant content. He enjoys a good dinner, good wine, and ladies' society, but just sufficiently to make his leisure hours pass pleasantly, without stomach-aches from the first, headaches from the second, or heartaches from the third.[5] So does his life seem to pass on like a deep untroubled stream, on whose margin grow sweet flowers, on whose clear waters the bending trees are reflected, but on whose placid face no lasting impression is made.

I have no doubt that his charities are in proportion to his large fortune; and when I say that I have no doubt of this, it is because I firmly believe there exists no country in the world where charities, both public and private, are practiced on so noble a scale—especially by women, who are directed by the priests. I am inclined to believe that, generally speaking, charity is a distinguishing attribute of a Catholic country. But to return to the Archbishop.

The Archbishop is said to be a man of good information, and was at one time a senator. In 1833, being comprehended in the law of banishment caused by the political disturbances which have never ceased to afflict this country since the independence, he passed some time in the United States, chiefly in New Orleans—but this, I believe, is the only cloud that has darkened his horizon, or disturbed the tranquil current of his life. His consecration, with its attendant fatigues, must have been a black-letter day in the prelate's life, a wearisome overture to a pleasant drama, a hard stepping-stone to glory, especially when we consider that he had to remain on all fours, with the heavy Testament on his back during a great part of the ceremony. As to the rest, he is very unostentatious, and his conversation is far from austere. On the contrary, he is one of the best-tempered and most cheerful old men in society that it is possible to meet with.

I send you, by the Mexican commissioners,[6] who are kind enough to take charge of a box for me, the figure of a Mexican *tortillera*, by which you may judge a little of the wonderful facility with which the Indians work in wax. The perfection of their models in that and in *trapo* (rags),[7] and especially the expression which they give even to the *faces* of these last, all proves that they have a natural taste for sculpture—and above all the most extraordinary facility for imitation, certainly the lowest species of genius, and in which (as in numerous other instances) they resemble the Chinese. The incredible patience which enabled the ancient Mexicans to work their statues in wood or stone with the rudest instruments has descended to their posterity. With a common knife and a piece of hard wood, an uneducated man will produce a fine piece of sculpture. There is no imagination. They do not leave the beaten track, but continue on the models which the Spanish conquerors brought out with them, some of which, however, were very beautiful.[8]

In wax, especially, their figures have been brought to great perfection. Everything that surrounds them they can imitate, and their wax portraits are sometimes little gems of art; but in this last branch, which belongs to a higher order of art, there are no good workmen at present.

Apropos to which, a poor artist brought some tolerable wax portraits here for sale the other day, and amongst others that of a celebrated general. Calderón remarked that it was fairer than the original, as far as he recollected. "Ah!" said the man, "but when His Excellency *washes his face*, nothing can be more exact."

A valuable present was sent lately by a gentleman here to the Count de Tepa in Spain: twelve cases, each case containing twelve wax figures, each figure representing some Mexican trade or profession or employment. There were men drawing the pulque from the maguey, Indian women selling vegetables, *tortilleras*, venders of ducks, fruit men, lard sellers, the postman of Huachinango loaded with parrots, monkeys, &c. (more of everything than of letters), the Poblana peasant, the *rancherita* on horseback before her farm servant, the gaily dressed *ranchero*—in short, a little history of Mexico in wax.[9]

You ask me how the Mexican women are educated. In answering you, I must put aside a few brilliant exceptions, and speak *en masse*—the most difficult thing in the world, for these exceptions are always rising up before me like accusing angels, and I begin to think of individuals when I should keep to generalities.

Generally speaking, then, the Mexican señoras and señoritas write, read, and play a little—sew, and take care of their houses and children. When I say they read, I mean they know how to read; when I say they write, I do not mean that they can always spell; and when I say they play, I do not assert that they have generally a knowledge of music. Example is better than precept. The adjoining letter will show better than a thousand homilies how the first-rate young ladies are educated.

I believe it is little better in Spain.[10] In fact, if we compare the education of women in Mexico with that of girls in England or in the United States, we should be inclined to dismiss the subject as nonexistent. It is not a comparison, but a contrast.

Belonging to countries where the lowest of the lower classes can generally write and read, we should naturally consider a country where the *highest of the higher* classes can do no more, as totally without education. But we must, in justice, compare the women of Mexico with those of the mother-country; and when we consider the acquirements of the fair in old Castile, we shall be apt to be less severe upon their *far niente* descendants.

In the first place, the climate inclines everyone to indolence, both physically and morally. One cannot pore over a book when the blue sky is constantly smiling in at the open windows; then, out of doors after ten o'clock, the sun gives us due warning of our tropical latitude and, even though the breeze is so fresh and pleasant, one has no inclination to walk or ride far. Whatever be the cause, I am convinced that it is impossible to take the same exercise with the mind or with the body in this country, as in Europe or in the northern states.

Then as to schools, there are none that can deserve the name, and no governesses—and their mothers are naturally content with seeing their children equal themselves. Young girls can have no emulation, for they never meet. They have no public diversion, and no private amusement. There are a few good foreign masters, most of whom have come to Mexico for the purpose of making their fortune—by teaching, or marriage, or both—and whose object naturally is to make the most money in the shortest possible time, that they may return home and enjoy it. The children generally appear to have an extraordinary disposition for music and drawing, yet there are few girls who are proficients in either, especially in the former.[11]

When very young they occasionally attend the miserable schools where boys and girls learn to read in common, or any other accomplishment that the old woman can teach them; but at ten in this precocious country they are already considered too old to render it safe for them to attend these promiscuous assemblages, and a master or two is got in for drawing or music until at fourteen their education is complete. I greatly shocked a lady in this city the other day by asking her if her daughter went to school. "Good heavens!" said she, "she is near eleven years old!"[12]

It frequently happens and is remarkable that the least well-informed girls are the children of the cleverest men who, keeping to the customs of their forefathers, are content if they confess regularly, attend church constantly, and can embroider and sing a little. Nothing more seems to be required of them. Where there are more extended ideas, it is chiefly amongst some few families who have travelled in Europe, and have seen the superiority of women and the different education of women in foreign countries. Of these the fathers occasionally devote a short portion of their time to the instruction of their daughters, perhaps during their leisure evening moments, but it may easily be supposed how very little influence such a desultory system of things can have upon the minds of the children.

I do not think there are three married women, or as many girls above fourteen in all Mexico, who, with the exception of their mass book on Sundays and fête days, ever open a book in the whole course of the year. They thus greatly simplify the system of education in the United States, where parties are frequently divided [and feelings] run high between the advocates for solid learning and those for superficial accomplishments—seeming to think that nothing can amalgamate the solid beef of science with the sweet sauce of *les beaux arts*.[13]

Here the road lies in a direct line, by which—leaving science on the right and art on the left—the blissful path of ignorance is steadily pursued. But in Spain the path is flowery; here it is bleak and arid as the plains of Apam. It is not all work and no play, but no work and no play, and the Mexican *Jenny* is a very dull girl indeed. It is the greater pity, [in] that they have a great aptitude for imitation. Their talent for imitation is an Indian gift; [the Indians] in their turn probably inherit it from their Chinese ancestors, as they may also their mode of torturing the feet to make them small, and their occasionally obliquely cut eyes.

But if a Mexican girl is ignorant she rarely shows it. They have generally *de grandes dispositions* for music and various other accomplishments—and the greatest possible tact, never by any chance wandering out of their depth or by word or look betraying their ignorance or that they are not well-informed on the subject under discussion.

The Mexican women are never graceful, yet they are rarely awkward, and always self-possessed. Their mode of walking, owing to the tightness of their shoes and the want of habit, is a mixture of tottering and waddling. In a large society they are extremely quiet, but when off ceremony their voices are generally loud and high—and most speak through their nose.

They have plenty of natural talent, and where it has been thoroughly cultivated, no women can surpass them. Of what is called literary society, there is of course none—

No bustling Botherbys have they to show 'em
That charming passage in the last new poem.[14]

There is a little annual lying beside me called *Calendario de las Señoritas Megicanas* of which the preface by Galván, the editor, is very amusing:

To none—he says—better than to Mexican ladies, can I dedicate this mark of attention (*obsequio*). Their graceful attractions well deserve any trouble that may have been taken to please them. Their bodies are graceful as the palms of the desert; their hair, black as ebony or golden as the rays of the sun, gracefully waves over their delicate shoulders; their glances are like the peaceful light of the moon. The Mexican ladies are not so white as the Europeans, but their whiteness is more agreeable to our eyes. Their words are soft, leading our hearts by gentleness, in the same manner as in their moments of just indignation they appall and confound us. Who can resist the magic of their song, always sweet, always gentle, and always natural? Let us leave to foreign ladies (*las ultramarinas*) these affected and scientific manners of singing; here nature surpasses art, as happens in everything, notwithstanding the cavillings of the learned.

And what shall I say of their souls? I shall say that in Europe the minds are more cultivated, but in Mexico the hearts are more amiable. Here they are not only sentimental, but tender; not only soft, but virtuous; the body of a child is not more sensitive (*no es más sensible el cuerpo de un niño*), nor a rosebud softer. I have seen souls as beautiful as the borders of the rainbow, and purer than the drops of dew. Their passions are seldom tempestuous, and even then they are kindled and extinguished easily; but generally they emit a peaceful light, like the morning star, Venus. Modesty is painted in their eyes, and modesty is the greatest and most irresistible fascination of their souls. In short, the Mexican ladies, by their manifold virtues, are destined to serve as our support whilst we travel through the sad desert of life.

Well do these attractions merit that we should try to please them; and in effect a new form, new lustre, and new graces have been given to the *Almanac of the Mexican Ladies,* whom the editor submissively entreats to receive with benevolence this small tribute due to their enchantments and their virtues![15]

There are in Mexico a few families of the old school, people of high rank but who mingle very little in society—who are little known to the generality of foreigners, and who keep their daughters entirely at home that they may not be contaminated by bad example. These select few, rich without any ostentation, are certainly doing everything that is in their power to remedy the evils occasioned by the want of proper schools, or of competent instructresses for their daughters. Being nearly all allied by birth, or connected by marriage, they form a sort of *clan;* and it is sufficient to belong to one or other of these families to be hospitably received by all. They meet together frequently, without ceremony, and whatever elements of good exist in Mexico are to be found amongst them. The fathers are generally men of talent and learning, and the mothers women of the highest respectability to whose name no suspicion can be attached.

But, indeed, it is long before a stranger even suspects the state of morals in this country, for—whatever be the private conduct of individuals—the most perfect decorum prevails in their outward behaviour. But indolence is the mother of vice, and not only to little children might Doctor Watts have asserted that

Satan finds some mischief still,
For idle hands to do.[16]

They are besides extremely *leal* to each other, and, with proper *esprit de corps,* rarely gossip to strangers concerning the errors of their neighbours' ways—indeed, if such a thing is hinted at, deny all knowledge of the fact. Besides, so long as outward decency is preserved, and the person most interested takes no notice, habit has rendered them perfectly indifferent as to the *liaisons* existing amongst their particular friends. They who live in a house of glass [should] beware of throwing stones at their neighbours. I have heard ladies, who I believe were honourable exceptions to these remarks, declare in a whisper their disgust at the conduct of so-and-so, who had *affichéed* herself so publicly with such a one—but lament the impossibility of breaking with her on account of her having such a *méchante langue.* This cowardice seems incomprehensible unless it may arise from the fact that the few who would wish to be severe, perhaps on account of their young daughters, would find their visiting list diminished to half-a-dozen in consequence. As long as a woman attends church regularly, is a patroness of charitable institutions, and gives no scandal by her outward behaviour, she may do pretty much as she pleases. As for flirtations in public, they are unknown.

I must, however, confess that this indulgence on the part of women of unimpeachable reputation is sometimes carried too far. I was lately at a marriage feast given to celebrate the wedding of the sister of the lady of Don Lucas Alamán with a Spaniard. The fête was given at the hacienda of the Conde de Peñasco, celebrated for his love of *les beaux arts,* his gallery, &c. His first wife having died some time ago, he has recently married a young lady—very handsome—of low birth and doubtful reputation. This new countess was looking very splendid, dressed in rose colour, with a profusion of diamonds. After dinner we adjourned to another room, where I admired the beauty of a little child who was playing about on the floor. "Yes, she is very pretty. I have a little girl just that age," said the countess, "and a boy a year older."

"Indeed!" said I, rather astonished, seeing that she has been married about six months.

"Yes," said she. "My little girl is very pretty, quite French—not in the least Mexican—and indeed I myself am much more Spanish in my feeling than Mexican."

I was rather surprised, but concluded she had been a widow, and some time after she rose up made the inquiry of an old New Orleans lady (sister of the last vice-queen) who was sitting near me if the *condesa* had been a widow.

"Oh, no!" said she, "she was never married before. She alludes to the children she had before the count became acquainted with her!"

Amiable naïveté! And yet Mme Alamán, one of the most prudish women in Mexico,[17] was actually *faisant la cour* to this woman, and loading her with attentions and caresses. Don Lucas was *aux petits soins* with her. *Ainsi va le monde au Mexique.* I must say, however, that this was a singular instance.

The Mexicans, particularly the women, have the most *cariñoso* tone of voice, and there are no women more affectionate and caressing in their manners. In fact, a foreigner, especially if he be an Englishman and a shy man, and accustomed to the coldness and reserve of his fair country-women, need only live a few years here and understand the language, and become accustomed to their peculiar style of beauty, to find the Mexican señoritas perfectly irresistible.[18]

And that this is so may be judged of by the many instances of Englishmen married to the women of this country, who—whatever they may be in their conduct towards their own countrymen—almost invariably make excellent wives to foreigners, particularly to Englishmen. But when an Englishman marries here, he ought to settle here, for it is very rare that a *Mexicaine* can live happily out of her own country. They miss the climate—they miss that warmth of manner, that universal cordiality by which they are surrounded here. They miss the *laissez-aller* and absence of all etiquette in habits, toilet, &c. They miss their *cigars.* They find themselves surrounded by women so differently educated as to be doubly strangers to them, strangers in feeling as well as in country and in language. A very few instances there are of girls married very young, taken to Europe, and introduced into good society, who have acquired European ways of thinking, and even prefer other countries to their own; but this is so rare as scarcely to form an exception. They are true patriots, and the visible horizon bounds all their wishes. In England especially they are most completely out of their native element. A language nearly impossible for them to acquire, a religion which they consider heretical, outward coldness covering inward warmth, a climate where there is a perpetual war between sun and fog, universal order [and] neatness, etiquette carried to excess, what to them must appear an insupportable stiffness and order in the article of the toilet—*rebozos* unknown and cigars undreamt of except by the masculine gender—the whole must form a contrast to them the most disagreeable and insupportable imaginable. They feel like exiles from paradise, and live but in hopes of a speedy return.

As to the colleges for young men, although various projects of reform

have been made by enlightened men in regard to them, especially by
Don Lucas Alamán and afterwards by Señor Gutiérrez Estrada—and
though to a certain extent many of these plans were carried into effect—
it is a universal source of complaint among the most distinguished
persons in Mexico that, in order to give their sons a thorough education,
it is necessary to send them abroad.

"REVOLUTION IN MEXICO!"

24

The President Seized in His Bed

Wednesday: July 15th, 1840
San Fernando, Mexico

Revolution in Mexico!—or *pronunciamiento*, as they call it.[1]
The storm, which has for some time been brewing, has burst forth at last. Don Valentín Gómez Farías and the banished General Urrea have "pronounced" for federalism. At two this morning, joined by the fifth battalion and the regiment of *comercio*, they took up arms, set off for the palace, surprised the President in his bed, and took him prisoner.[2]

Our first information was a message, arriving on the part of the government, desiring the attendance of our two old soldiers, who put on their old uniforms and set off quite pleased. Next came our friend Don Manuel del Campo, who advised us to haul out the Spanish colours that they might be in readiness to fly on the balcony in case of necessity.[3] Little by little, more Spaniards arrived with different reports as to the state of things. Some say that it will all end in a few hours—others, that it will be a long and bloody contest. Some are assured that it will merely terminate in a change of ministry—others, that Santa Anna will come on directly and usurp the presidency. At all events, General Valencia, at the head of the government troops, is about to attack the *pronunciados*, who are in possession of the palace.

The firing has begun! People come running up the street. The Indians are hurrying back to their villages in double-quick trot. As we are not in the centre of the city, our position for the present is very safe, all the cannon being directed towards the palace. All the streets near the square are planted with cannon, and it is pretended that the revolutionary party are giving arms to the *léperos*.

The cannon are roaring now. All along the street people are standing on the balconies, looking anxiously in the direction of the palace,[4] or collected in groups before the doors, and the *azoteas* which are out of the line of fire are covered with men.

They are ringing the tocsin—things seem to be getting serious.

Nine o'clock, p.m.

Continuation of firing without interruption.

I have spent the day standing on the balcony, looking at the smoke, and listening to the different rumours. Gómez Farías has been proclaimed president by his party.

The streets near the square are said to be strewed with dead and wounded. There was a terrible thunderstorm this afternoon. Mingled with the roaring of the cannon, it sounded like a strife between heavenly and earthly artillery. We shall not pass a very easy night, especially without our soldiers. Unfortunately there is a bright moon, so night brings no interruption to the firing and slaughter.

Thursday: July 16th, 1840

Our first news was brought very early this morning by the wife of one of our soldiers, who came in great despair to tell us that both her husband and his comrade are shot, though not killed—that they were amongst the first who fell; and she came to entreat Calderón to prevent their being sent to the hospital.

It is reported that Bustamante has escaped, and that he fought his way, sword in hand, through the soldiers who guarded him in his apartment. Almonte at all events is at the head of his troops. The balls have entered many houses in the square. It must be terribly dangerous for those who live there, and, amongst others, for our friend Señor Tagle, director of the Monte Pío, and his family.

They have just brought the government bulletin, which gives the following statement of the circumstances:[5]

Yesterday at midnight Urrea, with a handful of troops belonging to the garrison and its neighbourhood, took possession of the National Palace, surprising the guard and committing the *incivility* of imprisoning His Excellency the President, Don Anastasio Bustamante, the Commander in Chief, the *Mayor de la Plaza*, and other chiefs. Don Gabriel Valencia, chief of the *plana mayor* (the staff), General Don Antonio Mozo, and the Minister of War, Don Juan Nepomuceno Almonte, reunited in the citadel, prepared to attack the *pronunciados* who, arming the lowest populace, took possession of the towers of the cathedral and of some of the highest edifices in the centre of the city.[6]

Although summoned to surrender, at two in the afternoon firing began and continued till midnight, recommencing at five in the morning, and only ceasing at intervals. The colonel of the sixth regiment, together with a considerable part of his corps who were in the barracks of the palace, escaped and joined the government troops, who have taken the greatest part of the positions near the square and the palace.

His Excellency the President, with a part of the troops which had pronounced in the palace, made his escape on the morning of the sixteenth, putting himself at the head of the troops who have remained faithful to their colours, and at night published the following proclamation:[7]

The President of the Republic to the Mexican Nation

Fellow Citizens: The seduction which has spread over a very small part of the people and garrison of this capital, the forgetfulness of honour and duty, have caused the defection of a few soldiers, whose misconduct up to this hour has been thrown into confusion by the valiant behaviour of the greatest part of the chiefs, officers, and soldiers, who have intrepidly followed the example of the valiant general-in-chief of the *plana mayor* of the army. *The government was not ignorant of the machinations that were carrying on; their authors were well known to it, and it foresaw that the gentleness and clemency which it had hitherto employed in order to disarm them would be corresponded to with ingratitude.*

This line of policy has caused the nation to remain headless (*acéfala*) for some hours, and public tranquillity to be disturbed; but, my liberty being restored, the dissidents, convinced of the evils which have been and may be caused by these tumults, depend upon a reconciliation for their security. The government will remember that they are misled men, belonging to the great Mexican family, but not for this will it forget how much they have forfeited their rights to respect; nor what is due to the great bulk of the nation. Public tranquillity will be restored in a few hours; the laws will immediately recover their energy, and the government will see them obeyed.

Anastasio Bustamante

Mexico, July 16th, 1840

A roar of cannon from the palace, which made the house shake and the windows rattle, and caused me to throw a blot over the President's good name, seems the answer to this proclamation.

Friday: July 17th, 1840

The state of things is very bad. Cannon planted all along the streets, and soldiers firing indiscriminately on all who pass. Count C[ortin]a slightly wounded, and carried to his country house at Tacubaya.

Two Spaniards have escaped from their house, into which the balls were pouring, and have taken refuge here. The Escandón family have kept their house, which is in the very centre of the affray, cannons planted before their door, and all their windows already smashed. Indeed, nearly all the houses in that quarter are abandoned. We are living here like prisoners in a fortress. The Countess del Valle, whose father was shot in a former revolution, had just risen this morning when a shell entered the wall close by the side of her bed and burst in the mattress.[8]

As there are two sides to every story, listen to the proclamation of the chief of the rebels:

Señor Valentín Gómez Farías to the Mexican People

Fellow Citizens: We present to the civilized world two facts which, while they will cover with eternal glory the Federal army and the heroic inhabitants of this capital, will hand down with execration and infamy, to all future generations, the name of Gen-

eral Bustamante; this man without faith, breaking his solemnly pledged word after being put at liberty by an excess of generosity; for, having promised to take immediate steps to bring about a negotiation of peace upon the honourable basis which was proposed to him, he is now converted into the chief of an army, the enemy of the Federalists; and has beheld, with a serene countenance, this beautiful capital destroyed, a multitude of families drowned in tears, and the death of many citizens—not only of the combatants, but of those who have taken no part in the struggle. Amongst these must be counted an unfortunate woman *enceinte,* who was killed as she was passing the palace gates under the belief that, a parley having come from his camp, the firing would be suspended, as in fact it was on our side. This government, informed of the misfortune, sent for the husband of the deceased, and ordered twenty-five dollars to be given him; but the unfortunate man, though plunged in grief, declared that twelve were sufficient to supply his wants. Such was the horror inspired by the atrocious conduct of the ex-government of Bustamante, that this sentiment covered up and suffocated all the others.

Another fact, of which we shall with difficulty find an example in history, is the following: The day that the firing began, being in want of some implements of war, it was necessary to cause an iron case to be opened, belonging to Don Stanislaus Flores, in which he had a considerable sum of money in different coin, besides his most valuable effects. Thus, all that the government could do was to make this known to the owner, Señor Flores, in order that he might send a person of confidence to take charge of his interests, making known what was wanting, that he might be immediately paid. The pertinacity of the firing prevented Señor Flores from naming a commissioner for four days, and then, although the case has been open and no one has taken charge of it, the commissioner has made known officially that nothing is taken from it but the implements of war which were sent for.[9] Glory in yourselves, Mexicans! The most polished nation of the earth, illustrious France, has not presented a similar fact.

The Mexicans possess heroic virtues, which will raise them above all the nations in the world. This is the only ambition of your fellow citizen,

Valentín Gómez Farías

God, Liberty, and Federalism.
Mexico, July 17th, 1840

Besides this, a circular has been sent to all the governors and commandants of the different departments from the "Palace of the Federal Provisional Government," to this effect:

The Citizen José Urrea, with the greater part of the garrison of the capital and the whole population, pronounced early on the morning of this day for the re-establishment of the Federal system, adopting in the interim the Constitution of 1824, whilst it is reformed by a Congress which they are about to convoke to that effect; and I, having been called, in order that at this juncture I should put myself at the head of the government, communicate it to Your Excellency, informing you at the same time that the object of the Citizen Urrea, while[10] re-establishing the Federal system, has been to reunite all the Mexicans, by proclaiming toleration of all opinions and respect for the lives, properties, and interests of all.

God, Liberty, and Federalism.

Valentín Gómez Farías

National Palace of Mexico, July 15th, 1840

Saturday: July 18th, 1840

There is a great scarcity of provisions in the centre of the city, as the Indians, who bring in everything from the country, are stopped. We have laid in a good stock of *comestibles*, though it is very unlikely that any difficulties will occur in our direction.

While I am writing, the cannon are roaring almost without interruption, and the sound is anything but agreeable—though proving the respect entertained by Farías for "the lives, properties, and interests of all." We see the smoke, but are entirely out of the reach of the fire.

I had just written these words, when the Señora Marran, who lives opposite, called out to me that a shell has just fallen in her garden, and that her husband had but time to save himself. The cannon directed against the palace kill people in their beds, in streets entirely out of that direction—while this ball, intended for the citadel, takes its flight to San Cosme! Both parties seem to be *fighting the city* instead of each other; and this manner of firing from behind parapets, and from the tops of houses and steeples, is decidedly safer for the soldiers than for the inhabitants. It seems also a novel plan to keep up a continual cannonading by night and to rest during a great part of the day. One would think that were the guns brought nearer the palace, the affair would be sooner over.

Late last night a whole family came here for protection, the Señora Barbachano, with _____, nurse and baby, &c. She had remained very quietly in her own house, in spite of broken windows, till the bullets whizzed past her baby's bed.[11]

This morning everything remains as it was the first day—the President in the citadel, the rebels in the palace. The government [forces] are trying to hold out until troops arrive from Puebla. In an interval of firing, the English secretary contrived to make his way here this morning.

The English minister's house is also filled with families, it being a little out of the line of fire. Those who live in the square and in the Calle San Francisco are most exposed, and the poor shopkeepers in the Parián are in a state of great and natural trepidation. I need not say that the shops are all shut.

Sunday: July 19th, 1840

Dr. Plane, a famous French physician, was shot this morning as he was coming out of the palace, and his body has just been carried past our door into the house opposite.[12]

The Señorita _____ having imprudently stepped out on her balcony, her house being in a very exposed street, a pistol ball entered her side and passed through her body. She is still alive, but it seems impossible that she can recover.[13]

The prior of San Joaquín, riding by just now, stopped below the windows to tell us that he fears we shall not remain long here in safety, as the *pronunciados* have attacked the convent of La Concepción, at the end of the street.[14]

My writing must be very desultory. Impossible to fix one's attention on anything. We pass our time on the balconies, listening to the thunder of the cannon, looking at the different parties of troops riding by, receiving visitors, who in the intervals of the firing venture out to bring us the last reports—wondering, speculating, fearing, hoping, and excessively tired of the whole affair.

Gómez Farías, the prime mover of this revolution, is a distinguished character—one of the *notabilities* of the country—and has always maintained the same principles, standing up for "rapid and radical reform." He is a native of Guadalajara, and his literary career is said to have been brilliant. He is also said to be a man of an ardent imagination and great energy. His name has appeared in every public event. He first aided in the cause of independence; then, when deputy for Zacatecas, showed much zeal in favour of Iturbide; was afterwards a warm partisan of the federal cause, [and] contributed to the election of General Victoria; afterwards, to that of Pedraza; took an active part in the political changes of '33 and '34; detests the Spaniards; and during his presidency endeavoured to abolish the privileges of the clergy and troops—suppressed monastic institutions—granted absolute liberty of opinion—abolished the laws against the liberty of the press—created many literary institutions. Whatever were his political errors, and the ruthlessness with which in the name of liberty and reform he marched to the attainment of his object without respect for the most sacred things, he is generally allowed to be a man of integrity and, even by his enemies, an enthusiast who deceives

himself as much as others. Now, in the hopes of obtaining some uncertain and visionary good, and even while declaring his horror of civil war and bloodshed, he has risen in rebellion against the actual government, and is the cause of the cruel war now raging, not in the open fields or even in the scattered suburbs, but in the very heart of a populous city.[15]

This morning all manner of opinions are afloat. Some believe that Santa Anna has started from his retreat at Manga de Clavo and will arrive today—will himself swallow the disputed oyster (the presidential chair), and give each of the combatants a shell apiece; some that a fresh supply of troops for the government will arrive today; and others that the rebels must eventually triumph.

Among the reports which I trust may be classed as doubtful is that General Urrea has issued a proclamation promising *three hours' pillage* to all who join him. Then will be the time for testing the virtues of all diplomatic *drapeaux*.

In the midst of all, here comes another:

Address of His Excellency, Señor Don Valentín Gómez Farías, charged provisionally with the government of Mexico, and of the General-in-Chief of the Federal army, to the troops under his command.

Companions in Arms: No one has ever resisted a people who fight for their liberty and who defend their sacred rights. Your heroic endeavours have already reduced *our unjust aggressors* almost to complete nullity. Without infantry to cover their parapets, without artillery to fire their pieces, without money, without credit, and without support, they already make their last useless efforts.

On our side, on the contrary, all is in abundance (*sobra*), men, arms, ammunition, and money, and above all the invincible support of opinion—while the parties which adhere to our *pronunciamiento* in all the cities out of the capital, and the assistance which within this very city is given by every class of society to those who are fighting for the rights of the people, offer guarantees which they will strictly fulfill to all the inhabitants of the country, natives as well as foreigners. Our enemies, in the delirium of their impotence, have had recourse to their favourite weapon, calumny. In a communication directed to us, they have had the audacity to accuse you of having attacked some property. Miserable wretches! No, the soldiers of the people are not robbers. The cause of liberty is very noble, and its defense will not be stained by a degrading action. This is the answer given to your calumniators by your chiefs, who are as much interested in your reputation as in their own.

Soldiers of the people! Let valour, as well as all other civic virtues, shine in your conduct, that you may never dim the renown of valiant soldiers and of good citizens.

Valentín Gómez Farías
José Urrea

We hear that two shells have fallen into the house of Señor Lasquetti, who has a pretty wife and a number of children, and that his *azotea* is occupied by the federalist troops. Fortunately these grenades burst in the patio of his house, and no one was injured. The chief danger for those who are not actually engaged in this affair is from these bullets and shells, which come rattling into all the houses. We have messages from various people whom we invited to come here for safety that they would gladly accept our offer, but are unwilling to leave their houses exposed to pillage, and do not dare to pass through the streets. So our numbers have not increased as yet.

You may suppose that, although this is Sunday, there is no mass in the churches. The prior of San Fernando, who has just sent us round some colossal cauliflowers and other fine vegetables from his garden, permits us to come to his convent for safety should anything occur here. I am afraid he would lodge the womankind in some outhouse.

I had written thus far when we received a visit from the Baron de Norman, Belgian minister, who, living in a very exposed situation near the palace, requests us to receive his secretary of legation, M. de Pryse, who is dangerously ill of typhus fever—as the doctors, no doubt warned by the fate of poor Dr. Plane, fear to pass into that street, which is blocked up by troops and cannon.

Some people fear a universal sacking of the city, especially in the event of the triumph of the federalist party. The ministers seem to have great confidence in their *flags*—but I cannot help thinking that a party of armed *léperos* would be no respecters of persons or privileges!

As yet our position continues very safe. We have the Alameda between us and the troops; the palace, the square, and the principal streets being on the other side of the Alameda; and this street, a branch of the great Calle de Tacuba, stretching out beyond it.[16] I write more to occupy my thoughts than in hopes of interesting you, for I am afraid that you will almost be tired of this *revolutionary* letter. As a clever Mexican, the Marquis of Apartado, says: "Some years ago we gave forth cries (*gritos*)—that was in the infancy of our independence. Now we begin to *pronounce* (*pronunciamos*). Heaven knows when we shall be old enough to speak plain, so that people may know what we mean!"

Sunday evening

Monsieur de Pryse has arrived, and is not worse. We have unexpectedly had twelve persons to dinner today. The news tonight is that the government troops have arrived, and that a great attack will be made by them tomorrow on the rebels in the palace, which will probably bring matters to a conclusion. Some of our guests are sitting up, and others lying down on the sofa without undressing. I prefer being comfortable, so good night.

Monday: July 20th, 1840

We were astonished this morning at the general tranquillity, and concluded that, instead of having attacked the rebels, the government was holding a parley with them—but a note from the English minister informs us that a skirmish has taken place between the two parties at one of the gates of the city, in which the government party has triumphed. So far the news is good.

Our street has a most picturesque and lively appearance this morning. It is crowded with Indians from the country, bringing in their fruit and vegetables for sale, and establishing a temporary market in front of the church of San Fernando. Innumerable carriages drawn by mules are passing along, packed inside and out, full of families hurrying to the country with their children and movables. Those who are poorer are making their way on foot—men and women carrying mattresses, and little children following with baskets and bird cages. Carts are passing, loaded with chairs and tables and beds, and all manner of old furniture, uprooted for the first time no doubt since many years. All are taking advantage of this temporary cessation of firing to make their escape. Our stables are full of mules and horses sent us by our friends in the centre of the city, where all supplies of water are cut off.

Another physician, a Spaniard, has just been shot!

Every room at San Cosme and in all the suburbs is taken. In some rooms are numbers of people, obliged to sleep upon mats, too glad to have escaped from the danger to care for any inconvenience. A quantity of plate and money and diamonds were sent here this morning, which we have been hiding in different parts of the house; but they say that in cases of pillage the plunderers always search the most *impossible* places, pulling up the boards, brick floors, &c., ripping up the mattresses, and so on. So I believe there is no use in concealing anything.[17]

Near us lives a celebrated general, on whose political opinions there seems much doubt, as he has joined neither party and has become invisible ever since this affair commenced. He is a showy, handsome man, with a good deal of superficial instruction, and exceedingly vain of his personal advantages. I am quite sure that, having allowed him to be a fine-looking man, he would forgive me for saying that his character is frivolous, and that his principles, both moral and political, are governed entirely by that which best suits his own advantage.[18]

The Count de Breteuil, secretary to the French legation, mounted his horse last evening and, like a true young Frenchman, set off to pay a visit to a pretty girl of his acquaintance—passing through the most dangerous streets, and particularly conspicuous by his singular dress, good looks, and moustaches. He had not gone far before he was surrounded by some dozen of *léperos* with knives, who would, no doubt, have robbed and dispatched him but that, in tearing off his sarape, they discovered his uniform—and, not being very skilled in military accoutrements, concluded him to be an officer on the part of the government. They, being on the federalist side, hurried with their prize to the palace where he was thrown into prison, and obliged to remain until some of the officers came to see the prisoner, and recognized him, much to their astonishment.

We are now going to dine with what appetite we may, which is generally pretty good.

Ten o'clock, p.m.

We ventured out after dinner to take a turn in the direction opposite the city, and met various parties of ladies—who, as they cannot use their carriages at present, were thankful to escape from their temporary and crowded dwellings, and were actually taking exercise on foot—when we were encountered by people full of the intelligence that the great attack on the palace is to be made this evening, and were advised to hurry home. We were also assured that a party of *léperos*, headed by their long-bearded captain, an old robber by the name of Castro, had passed the night before our door. Before we could reach home the firing began, and we have passed several hours in a state of great suspense, amidst the roaring of the cannon, the shouting of the troops, the occasional cries of those who are wounded, and, to make everything appear more lugubrious, the most awful storm of thunder and rain I almost ever heard.

The Señora de **Barbachano**'s brother is a captain in the government service, and he and his regiment have distinguished themselves very much during these last few days; consequently she is dreadfully uneasy tonight.[19]

The gentlemen seem inclined to pass the night in talking. We think of lying down, and sleeping if we can. I hope nothing will happen in the night, for everything seems worse in the darkness and consequent confusion.

Tuesday: July 21st, 1840

After passing a sleepless night, listening to the roaring of cannon and figuring to ourselves the devastation that must have taken place, we find to our amazement that nothing decisive has occurred. The noise last night was mere skirmishing, and half the cannons were fired in the air. In the darkness there was no mark. But, though the loss on either side is so much less than might have been expected, the rebels in the palace cannot be very comfortable, for they say that the air is infected by the number of unburied dead bodies lying there. Indeed there are many lying unburied on the streets, which is enough to raise a fever, to add to the calamitous state of things.

The government bulletin of today expresses the regret of the supreme magistrate at seeing his hopes of restoring peace frustrated, and publishes the assurances of fidelity which they have received from all the departments, especially from Puebla, Querétaro, and Veracruz—in spite of the extraordinary dispatches which had there been received from [Gómez] Farías, desiring them to recognize Urrea as Minister of War and Don Manuel Crescencio Rejón as Minister of the Interior, "which communications," says the commandant of Querétaro, "produced in my soul only indignation and contempt towards their miserable authors."

The account of the yesterday's affair is as follows:

> The *pronunciados* in the palace, knowing that the infantry which was to come from Puebla to the assistance of the government was expected to arrive yesterday, endeavoured to surprise it near the gate of Saint Lazarus with a column of infantry of two hundred in number and some cavalry; but the brave Colonel Torrejón, with eighty dragoons, beat them completely—killing, wounding, and taking many prisoners and pursuing them as far as the Archbishop's palace.[20] The supreme government, appreciating the distinguished

services and brilliant conduct of the aforesaid colonel, has given him the rank of general of brigade.[21]

The President in today's proclamation, after declaring that "the beautiful capital of the republic is the theatre of war," says that "nothing but consideration for the lives and properties of the inhabitants has been able to restrain the enthusiasm of the soldiers of the nation, and to prevent them from putting forth their whole force to dislodge the rebels from the different points of which they have possessed themselves."

The President adds that this revolt is the more inexcusable, as his administration has always been gentle and moderate; that he has economized the public treasure [and] respected the laws, and that citizens of whatever opinion had always enjoyed perfect tranquillity under his rule; that constitutional reforms were about being realized, as well as the hopes of forming by them a bond of union between all Mexicans. He concludes by reproaching those revolutionary men who thus cause the shedding of so much innocent blood.

The commander-in-chief, General Valencia, writing perhaps under some inspiring influence, is more figurative in his discourse.

"Soldiers of Liberty!" he exclaims, "Anarchy put out its head, and your arms drowned it in a moment." This would have been a finer figure in the days of the great lakes. And again he exclaims:

Mexicans! My heart feels itself wounded by the deepest grief, and all humanity shudders in contemplating the unsoundable chaos of evils in which the authors of this rebellion have sunk the incautious men whom they have seduced, in order to form with their dead bodies the bloody ladder which was to raise them to their aggrandizement! Already the Mexican people begin to gather the bitter fruits with which they have always been enticed by these men who, while blazoning forth their humanity and philanthropy, gorge themselves on the blood of their brothers, and strike up songs to the sad measures of sobs and weeping. The cruel creatures abandon their wounded, without giving the least alleviation of their pain!

These tropes are very striking. All is brought before us as in a picture. We see anarchy raising his rascally head above the water (most likely adorned with a liberty cap), and the brave soldiers instantly driving it down again. We behold Gómez Farías and Urrea rushing up a ladder of dead bodies. And then the Lucrezia Borgia kind of scene that follows!— alluring their victims with bitter fruit (perhaps with sour grapes), drinking blood, and singing horridly out of tune to a running bass of sobs! The teeth of humanity are set on edge only by reading it. Well may His Excellency add: "I denounce them before their fellow citizens; I present them to the nations of the world as an inimitable model of ferocity and barbarity!"[22]

This morning General Almonte sent [us] a few lines from the citadel

—where he and the President are—in which he speaks with confidence of speedily putting down the rebels. Calderón returned many affectionate messages, accompanied by a supply of cigars.

They say that the greatest possible bravery is shown by the boys of the military college, who are very fine little fellows, and all up in arms on the side of the government. A strong instance of maternal affection and courage was shown by the Señora Gorostiza this morning. Having received various reports concerning her son who belongs to this college— first that he was wounded; then that the wound was severe; then that it was slight—and being naturally extremely uneasy about him, she set off alone and on foot at five o'clock in the morning, without mentioning her intention to anyone, carrying with her a basket of provisions. [She] passed across the square and through all the streets planted with cannon, made her way through all the troops into the citadel; had the satisfaction of finding her son in perfect health, and returned home—just as her husband and family had become aware of her absence.[23]

General Valencia is said to have a large party amongst the soldiers who are in favour of his being named president. It is said that he was seen riding up and down in the lines in a most *spirited* manner, and rather unsteady in his saddle.[24]

Some rumours there are that Santa Anna has arrived at Perote; but, as he travels in a litter, he cannot be here for some days, even should this be true.

There seems no particular reason to believe that this will end soon, and we must remain shut up here as patiently as we can. In the intervals of firing the gentlemen go out, but they will not hear of our doing so, except sometimes for a few minutes in the evening—and then either firing or thunder sends us back. Various people, and especially the Countess Cortina, have invited us to their country places; but, besides that we are in the safest part of the city, and have several guests, Calderón does not think it right for him to leave Mexico. They say that house rents will rise hereabouts, on account of the advantages of the locale in cases of this sort.

Amongst other announcements, the government has published that the rebels have demanded that the jewels, together with the service of gold and silver belonging to the Holy Cathedral Church, shall be given up to them—and threaten to seize the whole by force should their demand not be acceded to within two hours. "It is very probable that they will do so," adds the bulletin, "thus adding a new crime to all they have committed."

It is now evening and again they announce an attack upon the palace, but I do not believe them, and listen to the cannon with tolerable tranquillity. All day families continue to pass by, leaving Mexico. The poor shopkeepers are to be pitied. Besides the total cessation of trade, one at least has been shot and others plundered. A truce of two hours was granted this afternoon to bury the dead who were carried out of the palace.

Two of our colleagues ventured here this morning.

Wednesday: July 22nd, 1840

The government bulletin of this morning contains a letter from Santa Anna, dated Manga de Clavo, nineteenth of July, informing the President, with every expression of loyalty and attachment to the government, that according to his desire he will set off this morning in the direction of Perote "at the head of a respectable division."

Various other assurances of fidelity from Victoria, from Galindo,[25] &c. are inserted with the remark that the Mexican public will thus see the uniformity and decision of the whole republic in favour of order, and especially will receive in the communication of His Excellency, Santa Anna, an unequivocal proof of this unity of sentiment, notwithstanding the assurances given by the rebels to the people that Santa Anna would either assist them, or would take no part at all in the affair. It must be confessed, however, that His Excellency is rather a dangerous umpire.

The governor Vieyra published a proclamation today, declaring "Mexico in a state of siege."[26] It seems to me that we knew that already.

Upon the whole, things are going on well for the government. Parties of *pronunciados* have been put down in various places. The wounded on both sides have been carried to the hospital of San Andrés. A battery is now planted against the palace in the Calle de Pláteros, where they are at least near enough to do more execution than before.[27]

One circumstance worthy of notice has been published today. The rebels, as you may recollect, declared that they had permitted the President to leave the palace on condition of his taking conciliatory measures, and that he had agreed to favour their pretensions. Now here is Bustamante's own letter, written in the palace when surrounded by his enemies, a proof if any were wanting of his exceeding personal bravery and perfect coolness in the midst of danger. There is something rather *Roman* in these few lines:

Ministers: I protest that I find myself without liberty and without defense, the guards of the palace having abandoned me. Under these circumstances, let no order of mine which is contrary to the duties of the post I occupy be obeyed—since, although I am resolved to die before failing in my obligations, it will not be difficult to falsify my signature. Let this be made known by you to the Congress, and to those generals and chiefs who preserve sentiments of honour and fidelity.

National Palace, July 15th, 1840.

Anastasio Bustamante[28]

The following propositions are made to the government by the rebels:

Article 1st. It not having been the intention of the citizen José Urrea, and of the troops under his command, to attack in any way the person of the President of the Republic, General Anastasio Bustamante, he is replaced [i.e., Bustamante is placed again] in the exercise of his functions.

2nd. Using his faculties as President of the Republic, he will cause the firing to cease on the part of the troops opposed to the citizen Urrea, who on his side will do the same.

3rd. The President shall organize a ministry deserving of public confidence, and shall promise to re-establish the observance of the Constitution of 1824, convoking a Congress immediately for the express purpose of reform.

4th. Upon these foundations peace and order shall be re-established, and no one shall be molested for the opinions which he has manifested, or for the principles he may have supported, all who are in prison for political opinions being set at liberty.

Almonte, in the name of the President, rejected these conditions but offered to spare the lives of the *pronunciados,* in case they should surrender within twenty-four hours. The chiefs of the opposite party hereupon declared the door shut to all reconcilement, but requested a suspension of the hostilities, which was granted.

Adalid is going to drive me out during this suspension, in an open cab, to call on the Cortina family. The Lasquettis have left their house, their position having become too dangerous.

Another letter from General Almonte this morning. Nothing decisive. The streets continue blocked up with cannon, the roofs of the houses and churches are covered with troops, the shops remain closed, and the streets deserted. People are paying ounces for the least morsel of room in the suburbs, on the San Cosme side of the city.

Thursday: July 23rd, 1840

Yesterday the Archbishop invited the chiefs of the *pronunciados* to a conference in his archiepiscopal palace, in order that he might endeavour, in his apostolical character, to check the effusion of blood. The conference took place, and the rebels requested a suspension of hostilities whilst the prelate should communicate its results to the President, which was granted by the generals-in-chief. But the *pronunciados* broke the truce, and endeavoured to surprise the President and Almonte in the citadel, passing over the parapets in the Calle de Monterilla. They were repulsed with slaughter, and a fierce cannonading was kept up all night. They have now requested a parley, which is granted them.

In the midst of all, there is a communication from the governor of Morelia, giving an account of the routing of a band of robbers who had attacked an hacienda.

We went to Tacubaya, and met with no other danger but that of being drenched wet—as a daily watering of the earth, short but severe, now takes place regularly.

The new propositions of the *pronunciados* are these:

1st. The forces of both armies shall retire to occupy places out of the capital.

2nd. Both the belligerent parties shall agree that the constitutional laws of 1836 shall remain without force.

3rd. A convention shall be convoked, establishing the new constitution, upon the basis fixed in the Constitutive Act, which will begin to be in force directly.

4th. The elections of the members of the convention will be verified according to the laws by which the deputies of the Constituent Congress were directed.

5th. His actual Excellency, the President, will form a provisional government, he being the chief, until the foregoing articles begin to take effect.

6th. No one shall be molested for political opinions manifested since the year '21 until now. Consequently the persons, employments and properties of all who have taken part in this or in the past revolutions shall be respected.

7th. That the first article may take effect, the government will facilitate all that is necessary to both parties.

The government has refused these second propositions, and at the same time makes known to the Mexican world that various deserters from the opposite party assure them that the *pronunciados*, including the principal chiefs, are occupied in destroying everything within the palace—that the general archives and those of the ministers are torn in pieces, and that the dispatches are taken to make cartouches, and so on. They end by accusing them of being all united with the most noted robbers and public highwaymen, such as a Ricardo Teo, a José Polvorilla, a Román Chávez, a Juan Vega, a Rosas, a Garcilazo, and others. I put down the names of these Mexican Dick Turpins and Paul Cliffords, in case we should meet them some *beau jour*.[29]

More forces have arrived from Puebla and Toluca. Santa Anna is expected to reach Puebla tonight, and again General Valencia holds out an invitation to repentance to the "deceived men in the palace."

Saturday: July 25th, 1840

A letter is published today from Santa Anna to General Victoria, assuring him that, whatever personal considerations might have detained him in his country seat, he accepts with pleasure the command of the division going to Perote, and will in this, as in all things, obey the orders of the supreme government.

Firing, with short intervals, continued all yesterday, during the night, and this morning. Two mortars are placed in front of the old Acordada,[30] in the direction of the palace, but as yet they have not been used. There is a crowd of people examining them.

Things remain nearly in the same position as before, except that there are more deserters from the revolted party. A proclamation was issued by Urrea accusing the government of all the evils that afflict the city, and of all the bloodshed caused by this civil war. Amongst other things, they complain of the death of Dr. Plane who was shot in the Calle del Seminario, and, according to them, by the government troops. General Valencia answers this time without figures, and with good reason, that the responsibility of these misfortunes must be with those who have provoked the war.

In the bulletin of today the government [leaders] praise their own moderation in having taken off the duties[31] from all provisions entering the capital, in order that the price might not become too high—an advantage in which the *pronunciados* themselves participate; [and] mention their exertions to supply the city with water, and their permission given to the *pronunciados* to send their wounded to the hospital of San Andrés. They deny that the government has any share in the evils that afflict the whole population, their endeavour having ever been to preserve tranquillity and order. "But when a handful of factious men have taken possession of part of the city, no choice is left them but to besiege and combat them until they surrender, and not to abandon the peaceful citizens to pillage and vengeance." They declare that they might already have subdued them, and are only held back by the fear of involving in their ruin the number of innocent persons who occupy the circumjacent houses.

The policy of this moderation seems doubtful, but the sincerity of the President is unimpeachable. They continue to observe upon the absurdity of this handful of men pretending to impose laws upon the whole republic, when already the body of the nation have given unequivocal proofs that they have no desire that the questions relative to their political institutions should be decided by the force of arms.

While the *pronunciados* declare on their side that "information of *pronunciamientos* everywhere" has been received by them; the government remarks that eleven days have now elapsed, which has given full time to all the departments to declare themselves in favour of those who call themselves their representatives; but, on the contrary, nothing has been received but assurances of fidelity and of support to the government cause.

I believe that the English packet will be detained till the conclusion of this affair, but should it not be so, you need not feel any uneasiness in regard to us. Our house is full of people, money, jewels, and plate—our stables of horses and mules. Amongst the diamonds are those of the Señora **Lasquetti**, which are very fine—and there are gold rouleaus enough to set up a bank at San Agustín.

Santa Anna seems in no hurry to arrive. People expect him tomorrow, but perhaps he thinks the hour has not come for him.

Sunday: July 26th, 1840

The proclamation of the governor of the department of Jalisco is published today, in which he observes:

> The nation cannot forget that this Urrea who has brought so many evils upon his country—this faithful friend of Monsieur Carlos Baudin, and of the French squadron which invaded our territory, for whom he procured all the fresh provisions which they required[32]— is the same man who now escapes from prison to figure at the head of a tumultuous crowd, whose first steps were marked by the capture of His Excellency the President.

Firing continues, but without any decided result. It is a sound that one does not learn to hear with indifference. There seems little doubt that ultimately the government will gain the day, but the country will no doubt remain for some time in a melancholy state of disorder. Bills are fastened today on the corners of the streets, forbidding all ingress or egress through the military lines from six in the evening till eight in the morning. Gentlemen who live near us now venture in towards evening, to talk politics or play at whist, but generally in the middle of a game some report is brought in which drives them back to their houses and families with all possible haste.

Señor _____, a young Spaniard who is living with us, returning here late last night was challenged by the sentinels at the corner of the street with the usual *"Quién vive?"*—to which, being in a brown study, he mechanically replied, *"Spain!"* Fortunately the officer on duty was a man of common sense and humanity, and, instead of firing, warned him to take better care for the future.

Last night the Archbishop paid a visit to the President in the convent of San Agustín, to intercede in favour of the *pronunciados.* The mortars have not yet played against the palace, owing it is said to the desire of the general-in-chief to avoid the further effusion of blood.

The tranquillity of the sovereign people during all this period is astonishing. In what other city in the world would they not have taken part with one or other side? Shops shut, workmen out of employment, thousands of idle people subsisting heaven only knows how—yet no riot, no confusion, apparently no impatience. Groups of people collect on the streets, or stand talking before their doors, and speculate upon probabilities—but await the decision of their military chiefs as if it were a judgment from heaven from which it were both useless and impious to appeal.

Monday: July 27th, 1840

"Long live the Mexican Republic! Long live the Supreme Government!"

Thus begins the government bulletin of today, to which I say "Amen!" with all my heart, since it ushers in the news of the termination of the revolution. And what particularly attracts my attention is that instead of the usual stamp (the eagle, serpent, and nopal) we have today a shaggy pony: flying as never did mortal horse before—his tail and mane in a most violent state of excitement, his four short legs all in the air at once, and on his back a man in a jockey cap furiously blowing a trumpet, from which issues a white flag on which is printed "News!" *in English!*—and apparently in the act of springing over a milestone on which is inscribed, also in English, "100 *to New York"!*[33]

> We have—says the government—the grateful satisfaction of announcing that the revolution of this capital has terminated happily. The rebellious troops having offered in the night to lay down arms upon certain conditions, His Excellency the Commander-in-Chief has accepted their proposals with convenient modifications which will be verified today, the empire of laws, order, tranquillity, and all other social guarantees being thus re-established, &c.

> Cuevas, Minister of the Interior, publishes a circular addressed to the governors of the departments to the same effect, adding that "in consideration of the inhabitants and properties which required the prompt

termination of this disastrous revolution, the guarantees of personal safety solicited by the rebels have been granted, but none of their pretensions have been acceded to, the conspiracy of the 15th having thus had no other effect but to make manifest the general wish and opinion in favour of the government, laws, and legitimate authorities." A similar circular is published by General Almonte.

Having arrived at this satisfactory conclusion, which must be as agreeable to you as it is to us, I shall close this long letter, merely observing in apology—as Madame de Staël said in answer to the remark that "women have nothing to do with politics"—"That may be, but when a woman's head is about to be cut off, it is natural she should ask: *'Why?'*" So it appears to me that when bullets are whizzing about our ears, and shells falling within a few yards of us, it ought to be considered extremely natural, and quite feminine, to inquire into the cause of such phenomena.[34]

25

Quiet after the Cannonading

Tuesday: July 28th, 1840
San Fernando, Mexico

Today is published the plan which was formed by the federalists for
the "political regeneration of the republic."[1] They observe that it is six
years since the federal plan, adopted freely by the nation in 1824, was
replaced by a system which monopolizes all advantages in favour of a
few; that evils had now arrived at that height in which the endeavours
of a few men, however illustrious, could have no effect in remedying
them, rendering it necessary for all Mexicans to unite in one combined
and energetic force to better their situation; that salvation can only be
hoped for from the nation itself, &c.

They then proceed to lay their plan, consisting of ten articles, before the public:

The *first* restores the constitution of '24, the national interests to
be reformed by a congress composed of four deputies from each
state.

By the *second*, the reformed constitution is to be submitted to the
legislatures of the states for approbation.

By the *third*, they engage to respect the Catholic religion, the form
of popular government—representative and federal—the division of
powers, political liberty of the press, the organization of a military
and naval force, and the equality of rights between all the inhabitants
of the nation.

By the *fourth* article, a provisional government is to be established
in the capital, whose functions are to be limited exclusively to the
direction of the external relations of the republic.

By the *fifth*, this provisional government is to be vested in a Mexican, reuniting the requisites for this employment, as established in
the constitution of '24.

By the *sixth*, the republic promises to give back the ten percent added to the duties of consumption to those who have paid it until now.

By the *seventh*, in eight months after the triumph of the present revolution, all interior customhouses are to be suppressed and henceforth no contributions shall be imposed upon the internal circulation of goods, whether foreign or domestic.

By the *eighth*, they promise to confirm all the civil and military employments of those who do not oppose this political regeneration.

By the *ninth*, the army is to be paid with great punctuality.

By the *tenth*, a general amnesty is promised to all who have committed political errors since the independence; and the names of [Gómez] Farías and Urrea are followed by a goodly list of major generals, colonels, &c.

There is also published a letter from [Gómez] Farías, indignantly denying the report of the federal party's having threatened to seize the cathedral jewels and plate—accompanied by one from the Archbishop himself, not only denying the circumstance but expressing his satisfaction with the conduct of the federalist party in regard to all the convents which they had occupied, and the respect which they had shown towards all things pertaining to the church.[2]

On the night of the twenty-sixth the articles of capitulation were signed on both sides, a letter from General Andrade having been received by General Valencia to the effect that—as General Urrea had abandoned the command of the troops and left it in his hands—he, in the name of the other chiefs and officers, was ready to ratify the conditions stipulated the preceding night.[3]

This was at three in the morning, and about eight o'clock the capitulation was announced to the *pronunciados* in the different positions occupied by them; and they began to disperse in different directions, in groups of about a hundred, crying, *"Viva la Federación!"* At a quarter before two o'clock, General Manuel Andrade marched out, with all the honours of war, to Tlalnepantla, followed by the *pronunciados* of the palace.

This morning, at eleven, *Te Deum* was sung in the cathedral, there being present the Archbishop, the President, and all the authorities. The bells, which have preserved an ominous silence during these events, are now ringing forth in a confusion of tongues. The palace being crippled with balls, and in a state of utter confusion, the President and his ministers occupy cells in the convent of San Agustín.

The federalists have marched out upon the following conditions:

1st. Their lives, persons, employments, and properties are to be inviolably preserved.

2nd. General Valencia engages to interpose his influence with the government by all legal means, that they may request the chambers to proceed to reform the constitution.

3rd. All political events which have occurred since the 15th up to this date are to be totally forgotten, the forces who adhered to the plan of the 15th being included in the agreement.

4th. A passport out of the republic is to be given to whatever individual, comprehended in this agreement, may solicit it.

5th. The troops of the *pronunciados* are to proceed to wherever General Valencia orders them, commanded by one of their own captains, whom he shall point out and who must answer for any disorders they may commit.

6th. General Valencia, and all the other generals of his army, must promise on their honour before the whole world to keep this treaty, and see to its exact accomplishment.

7th. It only applies to Mexicans.

8th. Whenever it is ratified by the chiefs of both parties, it is to be punctually fulfilled—hostilities being suspended until six in the morning of the 27th, which gives time to ratify the conditions.

The President may exclaim, "One such victory more, and I am undone!"[4] Orders are issued by General Valencia to the effect that until the federalist troops have marched out of the city no group passing five in number will be permitted in the streets; that until then there is to be no trading through the streets; that at three o'clock the eating houses may be thrown open, but not the taverns till the next day; and that the police and alcaldes of the different wards are held responsible for the accomplishment of these orders, and may make use of armed force to preserve order.

The governor enforces these orders with additions. People must turn in at nine o'clock, or give an account of themselves, [and] must give up all their guns, carbines, &c. to the alcalde, under a heavy penalty; and none, excepting military men, may go on horseback from five in the evening until six in the morning during five days.[5]

General Valencia makes a pathetic address to his soldiers, and foretells that henceforth all mothers, wives, and old men will point them out as they pass, saying, "There go our deliverers!" And [he] adds: "I grow proud in speaking to you."

"Inhabitants of this beautiful capital!" he says again, "the aurora of the 15th of July was very different from that of the 27th; *that* prognosticated destruction, *this* rises announcing happiness. *Never again will you hear the crash of cannon, but to celebrate the triumphs of your country, or to solemnize your civic functions.*"

May your words be prophetic, and especially may you yourself assist in their accomplishment.[6]

Wednesday: July 29th, 1840

Our guests have left us, all but Monsieur de Pryse[7] who, although recovered, cannot yet be moved. All money, plate, and jewels in our charge are restored to their rightful owners; and the Spanish colours, which have never been hoisted, return to their former obscurity. I reopen the piano, uncover and tune the harp, and, as we have been almost entirely shut up during thirteen days of heavenly weather, feel rejoiced at the prospect of getting out again.

As yet, I have not seen the state of things in the city, but the *Cosmopolita* of today says:

I should wish to have the pen of Jeremiah to describe the desolation and calamities of this city, which has been the mistress of the new world. In the days of mourning that have passed we have not been able to fix our eyes on any part of it where we have not encountered desolation, weeping, and death. The palace has become *a sieve,* and the southern bulwark is destroyed; that part of the *portal* which looks towards the Monterilla is ruined; the finest buildings in the centre have suffered a great deal; innumerable houses at great distances from it have been also much injured by stray balls.[8]

Persons of all ages, classes, and conditions, who interfered in nothing, have been killed, not only in the streets, but even their own apartments. The balls crossed each other in every direction, and the risk has been universal. The city has been in the dark during these days, without patrol or watch; and many malefactors have taken advantage of this opportunity to use the murderous poniard without risk, and with the utmost perfidy.

At the break of day horrible spectacles were seen, of groups of dogs disputing the remains of a man, a woman, and a child.[9]

The *Cosmopolita* goes on to insist upon the necessity of forming a new ministry and of a reform in the two houses.

Saturday: August 1st, 1840

Have just come in from a drive through the city. The palace and houses near it are certainly in a melancholy condition. The palace, with

its innumerable smashed windows and battered walls, looks as if it had become stone blind in consequence of having the smallpox. Broken windows and walls full of holes characterize all the streets in that direction, yet there is less real damage done than might have been expected after such a furious firing and cannonading.

To read the accounts published, and of the truth of which we had auricular demonstration, one would have expected to find half the city in ruins. Here is the sum total of the firing, as published:

> On the 15th, firing from two o'clock till the next day. On the 16th, continual firing till one o'clock; suspension till four o'clock; firing from that hour, without intermission, till the following day. 17th, firing from morning till night. 18th, firing from before daybreak till the evening. 19th, continual firing; constant emigration of families these last four days. 20th, continual firing all day; skirmish at the gate of San Lázaro. 21st, firing continued, though less hotly, but in the night with more vigour than ever. 22nd, day of the junta in the Archbishop's palace; firing began at eleven at night, and lasted till morning. 23rd, firing till midday; parley. 24th, formidable firing, terrible attack, and firing till morning. 25th, firing till the evening. 26th, firing from six in the morning till two o'clock; capitulation that night.

As "every bullet has its billet," they must all have lodged somewhere.[10] Of course, nothing else is talked of as yet, and everyone has his own personal experiences to recount. Some houses have become nearly uninhabitable—glass, pictures, clocks, plaster, all lying in morsels about the floor, and air holes in the roofs and walls, through which these winged messengers of destruction have passed. Ladies and children escaped, in many instances, by the *azoteas*, going along the street from one roof to another, not being able to pass where the cannon was planted. The Señora _____, with her six beautiful boys, escaped in that way to her brother's house, in the evening, and in the very thick of the firing. I was in her drawing room today, which has a most forlorn appearance: the floor covered with heaps of plaster, broken pictures, bullets, broken glass, &c., the windows out, and holes in the wall that look as if they were made for the pipe of a stove to fit into.

The soldiers of both parties, who have occupied the roofs of the houses, behaved with great civility, their officers on many occasions sending to the family with a request that they would complain of any insolence that might be shown by the men. But no civility could insure the safety of the dwellers in these houses.

The poor nuns have been terribly frightened, and have passed these stormy nights in prayers and hymns, which those who live near their convents say were frequently heard at midnight, in the intervals of firing.

I went to see the Countess del Valle, and she showed me the great hole in the wall by her bedside, through which the shell made its *entrée*. The fragments are still lying there, so heavy that I could not lift them.[11] All the windows at the head of that street are broken in pieces. The shops are reopened, however, and people are going about their usual avocations, pretty much as if nothing had happened; and probably the whole result of all this confusion and destruction will be—a change of ministry.

Santa Anna, finding that he was not wanted, has modestly retired to Manga de Clavo, and has addressed the following letter to the Minister of War:

> The triumph which the national arms have just obtained over the horrible attempts at anarchy, communicated to me by Your Excellency in your note of the 27th, is very worthy of being celebrated by every citizen who desires the welfare of his country, always supposing that the public vengeance (*la vindicta pública*) has been satisfied; and in this case, I offer you a thousand congratulations.
>
> This division, although filled with regret at not having participated on this occasion in the risks of our companions in arms, is rejoiced at so fortunate an event, and hopes that energy and a wholesome severity will now strengthen order forever, and will begin an era of felicity for the country. The happy event has been celebrated here in the fortress, and in Tepeyahualco, where the first brigade had already arrived (and which I have ordered to countermarch), with every demonstration of joy. I anxiously desire to receive the details which Your Excellency offers to communicate to me so that, if the danger

has entirely ceased, I may return to my hacienda, and may lay down the command of those troops which Your Excellency orders me to preserve here.

With sentiments of the most lively joy for the cessation of the misfortunes of the capital, I reiterate to Your Excellency those of my particular esteem.

God and Liberty.

Antonio López de Santa Anna[12]

Perote, July 29, 1840

The houses of congress are again opened. The ministers presented themselves in the chamber of deputies, and a short account of the late revolution was given by General Almonte—who by the way was never taken prisoner, as was at first reported. He had gone out to ride early in the morning, when General Urrea, with some soldiers, rode up to him and demanded his sword, telling him that the President was arrested. For all answer, Almonte drew his sword and, fighting his way through them, galloped to the citadel. Urrea, riding back, passed by Almonte's house and, politely taking off his hat, saluted the ladies of the family, hoped they were well, and remarked on the fineness of the weather. They were not a little astonished when a short time after they heard what had happened.

Madame de Cyprey and her daughter were out riding when the firing began on the morning of the revolution, and galloped home in consternation.

Friday: August 7th, 1840

A long discussion today in congress on the propriety of granting extraordinary powers to the President; also a publication of the dispatches written by Gómez Farías during the revolution. He speaks with the utmost confidence of the success of his enterprise. In his first letter he observes that General Urrea, with the greater part of the garrison and people of the capital, have pronounced for the re-establishment of the federal system, and have, by the most fortunate combination of circumstances, got possession of the palace, and arrested the President. That troops have been passing over to them all day, and that the triumph of the federalists is so sure he has little doubt that the following morning will see tranquillity and federalism re-established. The different accounts of the two parties are rather amusing.

It is said that Gómez Farías is concealed in Mexico.[13]

Saturday: August 8th, 1840

Paid a visit today where the lady of the house is a leper, though it is supposed that all who are afflicted with this scourge are sent to the hospital of San Lázaro.

We rode before breakfast this morning to the old church of La Piedad,[14] and on our return found a packet containing letters from London, Paris, New York, and Madrid. The arrival of the English packet, which brings all these *nouveautés*, is about the most interesting event that occurs here.

FAMILIAR SIGHTS
AND FRIENDLY FACES

26

"This Awful Penance"

Sunday: August 30th, 1840
San Fernando, Mexico

In the political world nothing very interesting has occurred, and as yet there is no change of ministry.

Yesterday morning Calderón set off in a coach-and-six for the valley of Toluca, about eighteen leagues from Mexico, with a rich Spaniard, Señor Mier de Terán, who has a large hacienda there.[1]

Last Sunday morning, being the first Sunday since the revolution,[2] we had forty visitors—ladies and gentlemen, English, French, Spanish, and Mexican. Such varieties of dresses and languages I have seldom seen united in one room; and so many anecdotes connected with the *pronunciamiento* as were related—some grave, some ludicrous—that [they] would form a volume! The Baron de Norman having just left this for your part of the world, you will learn by him the last intelligence of it and of us.[3]

As there is a want of rain the Virgen de los Remedios was brought into Mexico, but as there is still a slight ripple on the face of the lately-troubled waters, she was carried in privately—for all reunions of people are dreaded at this juncture. I had just prepared pieces of velvet and silk to hang on the balconies, when I found that the procession had gone by a back street after sunset.

I went lately to visit the nuns of the Encarnación, to inquire how they stood their alarms—for their convent had been filled with soldiers, and they had been in the very heart of the firing. I was welcomed by a figure covered from head to foot with a double black crape veil, who expressed great joy at *seeing* me again and told me she was one of the *madres* who received us before. She spoke with horror of the late revolution, and of the state of fear and trembling in which they had passed their time—soldiers within their very walls, and their prayers interrupted by volleys of cannon. Thanks to the intercession of the Virgin no accident had occurred, but she added that had the Virgin of los

Remedios been brought in sooner these disorders might never have taken place.

I went from thence to the convent of Santa Teresa, where I saw no one, but discoursed with a number of *voices*—from the shrill treble of the old *madre priora,* to the full cheerful tones of my friend the Madre Adalid. There is something rather awful in sending one's voice in this way into an unknown region, and then listening for a response from the unseen dwellers there. I have not yet been inside this convent, but now that affairs are settled for the present I trust that the Archbishop will kindly grant his permission to that effect.

The rainy season is now at its height; that is, it rains severely every evening, but in the morning it is lovely. The disagreeable part of it is that the roads are so bad it is difficult to continue our rides in the environs. Horse and rider, after one of these expeditions, appear to have been taking a mud bath. It is very amusing to stand at the window about four o'clock, and see everyone suddenly caught in the most tremendous shower. In five minutes the streets become rivers; and canoes would be rather more useful than carriages. Strong porters (*cargadores*) are in readiness to carry well-dressed gentlemen or women, who are caught in the deluge, across the streets. Coachmen and footmen have their great-coats prepared to draw on; and strapped behind their saddles all horsemen have their sarapes—in which, with their shining leather hats, they can brave the storm. Trusting to an occasional cessation of rain, which sometimes takes place, people continue to go out in the evening, but it is downright cruelty to coachman and animals unless the visit is to a house with a porte-cochere—which many of the houses have, this amongst others.

Tuesday: September 1st, 1840

Had a dispute this morning with an Englishman who complains bitterly of Mexican insincerity. I really believe the chief cause of this complaint amongst foreigners consists in their attaching the slightest value to the common phrase, *"Está a la disposición de usted."* Everything is placed at your disposal—house, carriage, servants, horses, mules, &c., &c., &c.—the lady's earrings, the gentleman's indispensables, the children's shoes.[4] You admire a diamond ring—it is perfectly at your service; a shawl, the same; a horse—ditto. Letters are dated "from your house (*de la casa de usted*)." Some from ignorance of the custom, and some few others from knavery, take advantage of these offers which are mere expressions of civility—much to the confusion and astonishment of the polite *offerer,* who has no more intention that you should accept than you have of being believed when, from common etiquette, you sign yourself the very humble servant of the very most despicable bore. It is a mere habit, and to call people who indulge in it insincere reminds me of the Italian, mentioned somewhere by Lady Blessington,[5] who thought he had made a conquest of a fair Englishwoman—though somewhat shocked by her forwardness—because in an indifferent note to him she signed herself *"Truly yours."* Shall I ever forget the crestfallen countenance of a Mexican gentleman who had just purchased a very handsome set of London harness when, hearing it admired by a Frenchman, he gave the customary answer, "It is quite at your disposal"—and was answered by a profusion of bows and thanks, and a ready acceptance of the offer!—the only difficulty with the Frenchman being as to whether or not he could carry it home under his cloak, which he did.

If all these offers of service, in which it is Mexican etiquette to indulge, be believed in—"Remember that I am here but to serve you"—"My house and everything in it is quite at your disposal"—"Command me in all things"—we shall of course be disappointed by finding that, notwithstanding these reiterated assurances, we must hire a house for ourselves, and even servants to wait on us. Take these offers *"au pied de la lettre"* and you will no doubt consider them the most insincere people under the sun. But take these expressions at what they are worth, and I believe we shall find that people here are pretty much on an average with their neighbours.

Tuesday: September 8th, 1840

A good deal of surmise, because four Texian vessels are cruising in the bay off Veracruz.[6]

There is also a good deal of political talk, but I have no longer Madame de Staël's excuse for interfering in politics, which by the way is a subject on which almost all Mexican women are well informed—possessing practical knowledge, the best of all, like a lesson in geography given by travelling. I fear we live in a Paradise Lost, which will not be Regained in our day.

My attention is attracted, while I write, by the apparition of a beautiful girl in the opposite balcony, with hair of a golden brown hanging in masses down to her feet. This is an uncommon colour here, but the hair of the women is generally very long and fine. It rarely or never curls. We were amused the other day in passing by a school of little boys and girls, kept in a room on the first floor of Señor _____'s house, to see the schoolmistress, certainly not in a very elegant dishabille, marching up and down with a spelling book in her hand, her long hair hanging down and trailing on the floor a good half-yard behind her—while every time she turned she switched it round like a court train.

You ask me about this climate for Kate.[7] For one who, like her, is in perfect health, I should think it excellent; and even an invalid has only to travel a few hours and he arrives at *tierra caliente*. This climate is that of the tropics, raised some [seven] thousand feet above the level of the sea; consequently there is an extreme purity and thinness of the atmosphere, which generally affects the breathing at first. In some it causes an oppression on the chest. On me, it had little effect, if any; and, at all events, the feeling goes off after the first month or so. There is a general tendency to nervous irritation and to inflammatory complaints, and during September and October, on account of the heavy rains and the drained lakes on which part of the city is built, there is said to be a good deal of ague.

Since the time of the cholera in 1833, which committed terrible ravages here, there has been no other epidemic. The smallpox indeed has been very common lately, but it is owing to the carelessness of the common people, or rather to their prejudice against having their children vaccinated.[8]

The nervous complaints of the ladies are an unfailing source of profit to the sons of Galen, for they seem to be incurable. Having no personal experience of these evils, I only speak from what I see in others.

It appears to me that the only fault of the climate consists in its being monotonously perfect, which is a great drawback to easy and polite conversation. The evening deluge is but a periodical watering of the earth, from which it rises like Venus from the sea, more lovely and refreshed than ever.

Calderón has returned from Toluca, after an absence of eight days.

Everyone is hurrying to the theatre just now, in spite of the rain, to see some Spaniards who are performing *tours de force* there.

Wednesday: September 16th, 1840

Celebration of the Day of Independence—anniversary of the *Glorioso Grito de Dolores* of September the sixteenth, 1810—of the revolution begun thirty years ago by the curate of the village of Dolores in the province of Guanajuato. "It is very easy," says Zavala—and it is about his most sensible remark—"to put a country into combustion, when it possesses the elements of discord; but the difficulties of its reorganization are infinite."[9]

A speech was made by General Tornel in the Alameda. All the troops were out—plenty of officers, monks, priests, and ladies, in full dress. We did not go to hear the speech, but went to the Escandóns' house[10] to see the procession, which was very magnificent. The line of carriages was so deep that I thought we should never arrive.

After all was over, we walked in the Alameda, where temporary booths were erected and the trees were hung with garlands and flowers. The *paseo* in the evening was extremely gay, but I cannot say that there appeared to be much enthusiasm or public spirit. They say that the great difficulty experienced by the junta named on these occasions for the preparation of the festivities is to collect sufficient funds.[11]

Saturday: September 19th, 1840

We went yesterday to San Angel, one of the prettiest villages in the environs of Mexico, and spent the day at the hacienda of Señor Tagle, which is in the neighbourhood.

The rain has rendered the roads almost impassable, and the country round Mexico must be more like Cortés' description of it at this season than at any other period. Near the hacienda one part of the road, which is entirely destroyed, the owner of the house wished to repair; but the Indians, who claim that part of the land, will not permit the innovation— though he offered to throw a bridge over a small stream, which passes there, at his own expense.

Thursday: September 24th, 1840

We passed a pleasant day at Tacubaya, and dined with Monsieur [de] Siry, who gave a fête in consequence of its being his wife's saint's day.[12]

Sunday: September 27th, 1840

Great fête, being the anniversary of the day on which the army called the *trigarante* (the three guarantees) entered Mexico with Iturbide at its head. The famous Plan of Iguala (so called from having first been published in that city) was also called the plan of the three guarantees— freedom, union, and religion—which were offered as a security to the Spaniards, against whom so many cruelties had been exercised.[13]

We have had ringing of bells and firing all the morning, and in the evening there is to be a bullfight, followed by the exhibition of the *tours de force* of these Spaniards, commonly called here *"Los Hércules,"* who have just come to offer us a box in the plaza.

This Plan of Iguala was certainly the only means by which Spain could have continued to preserve these vast and distant possessions. The Treaty of Córdoba, which confirmed it,[14] was signed in that city between the

Spanish General O'Donojú and Don Agustín Iturbide, in August, 1821, and consisted of seventeen articles:

By the first, Mexico was to be acknowledged as a free and independent nation, under the title of the Mexican Empire.

By the second, its government was to be a constitutional monarchy.

By the third, Ferdinand VII, Catholic King of Spain, was [to be] called to the throne of Mexico; and, should he renounce or refuse the throne, it was [to be] offered to his brother the Infante Don Carlos, and, under the same circumstances, to each brother in succession.

By the fourth, the emperor was to fix his court in Mexico, which was to be considered the capital of the empire.

By the fifth, two commissioners named by O'Donojú were to pass over to the Spanish court, to place the copy of the treaty and of the accompanying exposition in His Majesty's hands, to serve him as an antecedent until the Cortes should offer him the crown with all formality; requesting him to inform the Infantes of the order in which they were named; interposing his influence in order that the emperor of Mexico should be one of his august house, for the interest of both nations, and that the Mexicans might add this link to the chain of friendship which united them with the Spaniards.

By the sixth, a junta of the first men in Mexico—first by their virtues, position, fortune, &c.—was to be named, sufficient in number to insure success in their resolutions by the union of so much talent and information.

By the seventh, this junta takes the name of Administrative Provisional Junta.

By the eighth, O'Donojú was named member of this junta.

By the ninth, this junta was to name a president.

By the tenth, it was to inform the public of its installation, and of the motives which had caused it to meet.

By the eleventh, this assembly was to name a regency, composed of three persons, to compose the executive power and to govern in the name of the monarch, until his arrival.

By the twelfth, the junta was then to govern comformably to the laws, in everything which did not oppose the Plan of Iguala, and till the Cortes had formed the constitution of the state.

By the thirteenth, the regency, as soon as they were named, were to proceed to the convocation of the Cortes, according to the method decreed by the provisional junta.

By the fourteenth, the executive power was to reside in the regency —the legislative in the Cortes—but until the reunion of the Cortes, the legislative power was to be exercised by the junta.

By the fifteenth, all persons belonging to the community—the system of government being changed, or the country passing into the power of another prince—were perfectly at liberty to transport themselves and their fortunes wherever they chose, &c., &c.

By the sixteenth, this does not hold good in regard to the military or public *employés* disaffected to the Mexican independence; they will leave the empire within the term prescribed by the regency, &c., &c.

By the seventeenth and last, as the occupation of the capital by the peninsula troops is an obstacle to the realization of the treaty, this difficulty must be vanquished; but, as the chief of the imperial army desires to bring this about, not by force but by gentler means, General O'Donojú offers to employ his authority with the troops, that they may leave the capital without any effusion of blood, and by an honourable treaty.

This treaty was signed by Iturbide and O'Donojú. Had this Plan of Iguala taken effect, what would have been the result in Mexico?—what its present condition?[15]

This being Sunday and a fête day, a man was murdered close by our door in a quarrel brought about probably through the influence of pulque, or rather of *chinguirito.*

If they did not so often end in deadly quarrel, there would be nothing so amusing as to watch the Indians gradually becoming a little intoxicated. They are at first so polite: handing the pulque jar to their fair companions (fair being taken in the general or *Pickwickian* sense of the word); always taking off their hats to each other; and, if they meet a woman, kissing her hand with an humble bow as if she were a duchess. But these same women are sure to be the cause of a quarrel, and then out come these horrible knives—and then, *Adiós!*

It is impossible to conceive anything more humble and polite than the common countrypeople. Men and women stop and wish you a good day, the men holding their hats in their hands, and all showing their white teeth, and faces lighted up by careless good nature. I regret to state, however, that today there are a great many women quite as tipsy as the men, returning home after the fête—and increasing the distance to their village, by taking a zigzag direction through the streets.

Señor Cañedo, Secretary of State, has formally announced his intention of resigning. Certainly the situation of premier in Mexico, at this moment, is far from enviable—and the more distinguished and clearheaded the individual, the more plainly he perceives the impossibility of remedying the thickly-gathering evils which crowd the political horizon.[16]

"Revolution," says Señor de _____, "has followed revolution since the independence; no stable government has yet been established. Had it been so, Mexico would have offered to our eyes a phenomenon unknown until now in the world—that of a people, without previous preparation, passing at once to govern themselves by democratical institutions."[17]

Monday: September 28th, 1840

We drove out to the Peñón, a natural boiling fountain, where there are baths which are considered a universal remedy—a pool of Bethesda[18] —but an especial one for rheumatic complaints.

The baths are a square of low stone buildings, with a church—each building containing five or six empty rooms, in one of which is a square bath. The idea seems to have been to form a sort of dwelling house for different families, as each bath has a small kitchen attached to it. Like most *great ideas* of Spanish days, it is now in a state of perfect desolation, though people still flock there for various complaints. When one goes there to bathe, it is necessary to carry a mattress to lie down on when you leave the bath, linen, a bottle of cold water, of which there is not a drop in the place and which is particularly necessary for an invalid in case of faintness—in short, everything that you may require. A poor family live there to take charge of the baths, and there is a small tavern where they sell spirits and pulque; and occasionally a padre comes on Sunday to say mass in the old church.

We were amused by meeting there with General **Barrera** and his family, who had brought with them a whole coach load of provisions, besides mattresses, sheets, &c.

The road to the Peñón crosses the most dreary plain imaginable. Behind the baths are two volcanic hills; and the view of Mexico and of the great volcanoes from this is magnificent. It is the most solitary of buildings; not a tree to be seen in its environs—these volcanic rocks behind—Mexico fronting it—the great lakes near it—to the right Guadalupe—to the left San Angel, San Agustín, and the mountains which bound the valley. The Indian family who live there are handsome savages; and the girl who attended me at the bath spoke an extraordinary jargon—half Spanish, half Indian—but was a fine specimen of savage good looks. The water is extremely warm, and my curiosity to try its temperature was very soon satisfied.

These boiling springs are said to contain sulphate of lime, carbonic acid, and muriate of soda—and the Indians make salt in their neighbourhood precisely as they did in the time of Montezuma, with the difference, as Humboldt informs us, that then they used vessels of clay and now they use copper caldrons. The solitary-looking baths are ornamented with odd-looking heads of cats or monkeys, which grin down upon you with a mixture of the sinister and facetious, rather appalling.[19]

The Señora de Barrera insisted on my partaking of her excellent luncheon after the bath. We could not help thinking, were these baths in the hands of some enterprising and speculative Yankee, what a fortune he would make; how he would build a hotel à la Saratoga, would paper the rooms, and otherwise beautify this uncouth temple of boiling water.

There is an indescribable feeling of solitude in all houses in the environs of Mexico, a vastness, a desolation, such as I never before experienced in the most lonely dwellings in other countries. It is not sad —the sky is too bright, and nature too smiling, and the air we inhale too pure for that. It is a sensation of being entirely out of the world, and alone with a giant nature, surrounded by faint traditions of a bygone race; and the feeling is not diminished when the silence is broken by the footstep of the passing Indian, the poor and debased descendant of that extraordinary and mysterious people who came, we know not whence, and whose posterity are now "hewers of wood and drawers of water" on the soil where they once were monarchs.[20]

In Chapultepec especially, near as it is to a large and populous city, the traditions of the past come so strongly upon the mind that one would rather look for the apparition of a whole band of these inky-haired, adder-anointed priests of Montezuma, than expect to meet with the benevolent-looking Archbishop, who, in purple robes, occasionally walks under the shade of the majestic cypresses.

All Mexicans at present, men and women, are engaged in what are called the *desagravios*, a public penance performed at this season in the churches, during thirty-five days. The women attend church in the morning, no men being permitted to enter, and the men in the evening, when women are not admitted. Both rules are occasionally broken.

The penitence of the men is most severe, their sins being no doubt proportionably greater than those of the women—though it is one of the few countries where they suffer for this, or seem to act upon the principle that "if all men had their deserts, who should escape whipping?"[21]

Today we attended the morning penitence at six o'clock, in the church of San Francisco; the hardest part of which was their having to kneel for about ten minutes with their arms extended in the form of a cross, uttering groans—a most painful position for any length of time. It was a profane thought, but I dare say so many hundreds of beautifully-formed arms and hands were seldom seen extended at the same moment before. Gloves not being worn in church, and many of the women having short sleeves, they were very much seen.

But the other night I was present at a much stranger scene, at the discipline performed by the men—admission having been procured for us by certain means, *private but powerful*. Accordingly, when it was dark, enveloped from head to foot in large cloaks—and without the slightest idea of what it was—we went on foot through the streets to the church of San Agustín. When we arrived a small side door apparently opened of itself, and we entered—passing through long vaulted passages and up steep winding stairs, till we found ourselves in a small railed gallery looking down directly upon the church.

The scene was curious. About one hundred and fifty men, enveloped in cloaks and sarapes, their faces entirely concealed, were assembled in the body of the church. A monk had just mounted the pulpit, and the church was dimly lighted, except where he stood in bold relief, with his gray robes and cowl thrown back—giving a full view of his high bald forehead and expressive face.

His discourse was a rude but very forcible and eloquent description of the torments prepared in hell for impenitent sinners. The effect of the whole was very solemn. It appeared like a preparation for the execution of a multitude of condemned criminals. When the discourse was finished they all joined in prayer with much fervour and enthusiasm, beating their breasts and falling upon their faces. Then the monk stood up, and in a very distinct voice read several passages of scripture descriptive of the sufferings of Christ. The organ then struck up the *Miserere*, and all of a sudden the church was plunged in profound darkness—all but a sculptured representation of the Crucifixion, which seemed to hang in the air illuminated. I felt rather frightened, and would have been very glad to leave the church, but it would have been impossible in the darkness.

Suddenly a terrible voice in the dark cried, "My brothers! When Christ was fastened to the pillar by the Jews, he was *scourged!*" At these words, the bright figure disappeared, and the darkness became total. Suddenly, we heard the sound of hundreds of scourges descending upon the bare flesh. I cannot conceive anything more horrible. Before ten minutes had passed, the sound became *splashing*, from the blood that was flowing.

I have heard of these penitences in Italian churches, and also that half of those who go there do not really scourge themselves; but here, where there is such perfect concealment, there seems no motive for deception.[22] Incredible as it may seem, this awful penance continued, without intermission, for half an hour! If they scourged *each other*, their energy might be less astonishing.

We could not leave the church, but it was perfectly sickening; and had I not been able to take hold of the Señora Adalid's hand, and feel something human beside me, I could have fancied myself transported into a congregation of evil spirits. Now and then, but very seldom, a suppressed groan was heard, and occasionally the voice of the monk encouraging them by ejaculations, or by short passages from scripture. Sometimes the organ struck up, and the poor wretches, in a faint voice, tried to join in the *Miserere*. The sound of the scourging is indescribable. At the end of half an hour a little bell was rung, and the voice of the monk was heard calling upon them to desist—but such was their enthusiasm that the horrible lashing continued louder and fiercer than ever.

In vain he entreated them not to kill themselves; and assured them that heaven would be satisfied, and that human nature could not endure beyond a certain point.

No answer but the loud sound of the scourges, which are many of them of iron, with sharp points that enter the flesh. At length, as if they were perfectly exhausted, the sound grew fainter, and little by little ceased altogether. We then got up in the dark, and with great difficulty groped our way in the pitch darkness through the galleries and down the stairs, till we reached the door, and had the pleasure of feeling the fresh

EL PERICO

air again. They say that the church floor is frequently covered with blood after one of these penances, and that a man died the other day in consequence of his wounds.

I then went to the house of the Prussian minister, where there was a *réunion,* and where I found the company comfortably engaged in eating a very famous kind of German salad—composed of herrings, smoked salmon, cold potatoes, and apples (salmagundi?) and drinking hot punch. After the cold, darkness, and horrors of the church, this formed rather a contrast; and it was some time before I could shake off the disagreeable impression left by the *desagravios* and join in the conversation.

Along with this you will receive some Mexican airs, which I have written by ear from hearing them played, and of some of which I gave you the words in a former letter.[23]

27

"*Like an Old Resident*"

Saturday: October 3rd, 1840
San Fernando, Mexico

Yesterday being Calderón's fête day we had a dinner and small *soirée*, and, according to custom, visits the whole day.[1] A very agreeable guest from Havana, Don Joaquín Arrieta, arrived to spend a few weeks with us.[2] We had rather a pleasant party, and some good singing. But just as dancing had begun, Calderón took me aside and showed me a little friendly note which he had received while at dinner from General Tornel, in which he informs him that the robbers would in all probability attack our respective houses that night; that he had taken his precautions and advises Calderón to do the same, in the understanding that, if necessary, they should mutually assist each other. A pleasant piece of intelligence! The thing got whispered about, and some of the ladies looked a little blank at the information; but there could be no risk while so many persons were collected. About one they went away, and Calderón sent for some soldiers to keep watch all night. Nothing happened, as no doubt the robbers found out what precautions had been taken. The intended attack had been discovered by a servant of the general's, who heard them discussing the matter in the back room of a pulque shop.

We have been obliged to procure two old soldiers as porters, in lieu of the two who were shot in the revolution—for though not killed, they are entirely disabled for the present.

Mexico appears particularly quiet just now, and, whatever storms may be preparing, no symptoms are visible to the uninitiated eye. The palace has got in its glass eyes again, and externally is almost entirely repaired; but it is not yet fit for the residence of the President, who still *holds his court* in the convent of San Agustín.

I have been driving about with our Havana friend, like an old resident, showing the beauties of Mexico to a stranger. We have been in the Minería, museum, botanical garden, Biscay College,[3] &c., all of which can bear revision.

The museum especially, which—owing to the want of arrangement and classification in the antiquities, and the manner in which they are crowded together in the different rooms of the university—appears at first undeserving of much attention, improves upon acquaintance. It is only since the year '25 that it was established by the government, and various plans have been since made for enriching and arranging it, and also for transporting it to the old building of the Inquisition. But as yet nothing essential has been carried into effect.[4]

It contains upwards of two hundred historical manuscripts, some in hieroglyphical characters anterior to the conquest, and many in the different ancient languages of the country. Of the ancient sculpture, it possesses two colossal statues and many smaller ones, besides a variety of busts, heads, figures of animals, masks, and instruments of music or of war, curiously engraved, and indicating the different degrees of civilization of the different nations to whom they belonged. A great many of the

vases of *tecal*,[5] and of the candlesticks in clay, curiously worked, were drawn from excavations in the Isle of Sacrifices near Veracruz, from Oaxaca, &c.—and from the suburbs of Mexico.

There is also a collection of very ancient medals, to the number of six hundred, a bronze bust of Philip V, and about two hundred Mexican paintings—comprehending two collections of the portraits of the Spanish viceroys, [also] many of the celebrated Cabrera's[6]—and various dresses, arms, and utensils from both the Californias.

In the cabinet of natural history there is a good collection of minerals, and some very fine specimens of gold and silver. But in the animal or vegetable branch of natural history there is a great deficiency, and altogether the museum is not worthy of a country which seems destined by nature to be the great emporium of all natural science.

Of course we have revisited old Chapultepec and Our Lady of Guadalupe, with her legend and holy well. In the morning we have rode to Tacubaya and the environs, and the weather at that early hour has the most indescribable freshness, caused by the evening rains. Everything looks bright and sparkling. The Peruvian trees, with their bending green branches and bunches of scarlet berries, glitter with the heavy raindrops, and even the hoary cypresses of Chapultepec sparkle with water in all their gigantic branches. Little pools have become ponds, and ditches rivulets, and frequently it is rather wading than riding, which is not so pleasant.

Saturday: October 24th, 1840

Last evening we had a very pretty ball in the house of the French minister, where all the Paris furniture was very effective. There were as usual plenty of diamonds, and some handsome dresses—mine white satin, with flowers.

Sunday: October 25th, 1840

The whole world is talking of a pamphlet written by Señor Gutiérrez Estrada, which has just appeared and seems likely to cause a greater sensation in Mexico than the discovery of the gunpowder plot in England. Its sum and substance is the proposal of a constitutional monarchy in Mexico, with a foreign prince (not named) at its head, as the only remedy for the evils by which it is afflicted. The pamphlet is written merely in a speculative form, inculcating no sanguinary measures or sudden revolution, but the consequences are likely to be most disastrous to the fearless and public-spirited author. Even those who most question his prudence in taking this step agree that in this, as well as in every other political action of his life, he has acted from thorough conviction and from motives of the purest patriotism, unalloyed by one personal feeling; indeed, entirely throwing behind him every consideration of personal or family interest, which even the best men allow to have some weight with them on such occasions.[7]

In a political review of Mexico—written some years ago by a Mexican who deals fearlessly and, it would seem, impartially with the characters of all the leading men of that period—I find some remarks on Señor Gutiérrez Estrada, which you will place more faith in as coming from a less partial source than from persons so attached as we are to him and his family. In speaking of the conduct of the administration, he says:

Señor Gutiérrez Estrada was one of the few who remained firm in his ideas and, above all, true to his political engagements. This citizen is a native of the state of Yucatán, where his family, who are distinguished in every point of view, reside. It is unnecessary to say that Gutiérrez received a thorough and brilliant education, as it is sufficient to have conversed with him to discover this fact; nor that he knew how to turn it to account in the career of public service to which he devoted himself, and in which he has remained pure and unblemished in the midst of a corrupt class. From the first he was destined to the European legations, on account of his fluency in speaking and writing both English and French; and he is one of the few who have employed their time usefully in the capitals of the Old World. Flexible by nature, honourable by education, and expeditious in business, his services have been perfect, and above all, loyal and conscientious.[8]

He goes on to say that, "notwithstanding the gentleness of his temper, his political conscience is so firm and pure, that he will never yield in what he considers his obligation, *even when it interferes with the most intimate friendships, or most weighty considerations.*"

One would think that the writer had foreseen the present emergency. I have not yet read the pamphlet which the friends of the author consider an equal proof of his noble independence, bold patriotism, and vast information—being, to say the truth, much more interested in its domestic effects than its public results, or even in its intrinsic merits.[9]

Monday: October 26th, 1840

Soldiers were sent to the house of the Countess de la Cortina to arrest her son-in-law, but in compliance with the entreaties of his family he had gone into concealment. I found them in great affliction, but they are so accustomed to political persecution from one party or another, particularly the countess, that her courage has never deserted her for a moment. He is accused in congress—[and] in the senate house. A proclamation is made by the President, anathematizing his principles—even the printer of the pamphlet is thrown into prison.[10] Nothing else is spoken of, and the general irritation is so terrible that it is to be hoped his place of concealment is secure—otherwise the consequences may be fatal.

On pretend that many distinguished men here hold the same opinions, but their voices—even were they to venture to raise them—could not stem the tide of public indignation. The most offended are naturally the military men.[11] In short, Señor Gutiérrez—who has been passing four years abroad, in countries where hundreds of obscure scribblers daily advocate republicanism, or any wild theory that strikes their fancy, with the most perfect security—was probably hardly aware of the extraordinary ferment which such a pamphlet was likely to produce at the present juncture.

Tuesday: October 27th, 1840

A few days before Señor Arrieta left us, we went up the canal in a canoe, as far as Santa Anita, to show him all that remains of the *chinampas*. It is as pleasant a way of passing an evening as any that I know of here.

We drove lately to Mexicalcingo, where there is a cave in which there is a figure of our Saviour, which they pretend has lately appeared there.

The excitement concerning the pamphlet seems rather to increase than diminish, but Señor Gutiérrez has many devoted friends, and the place of his retreat is secure. There is little doubt that he will be forced to fly the country.[12]

Thursday: October 29th, 1840

Señor Don Javier Echeverría, Minister of the Treasury, has sent in his resignation. Being a man of large private fortune, extremely simple in his habits, and the most amiable of men in domestic life, I believe that no minister has ever thrown off with more unaffected satisfaction the burden of state affairs, or will enjoy his retreat from public life with more true philosophy.[13]

I have been so much interested in the affairs of the C[ortin]a family that I have forgotten to tell you of my having obtained permission from the Archbishop to visit the Santa Teresa, accompanied by one young married lady, who has a sister there. The Archbishop desired that our visit should be kept a secret; but it has *oozed* out by some means or other —probably through the nuns themselves—and exposed him to so much inconvenience and such a torrent of solicitations from those ladies who, having daughters or sisters amongst the nuns, are naturally most desirous to see them, that I fear notwithstanding his good nature he will put a veto on all my future applications. You will think I pass my time in convents, but I find no other places half so interesting, and you know I always had a fancy that way.

In some of these convents there still exist, buried alive like the inmates, various fine old paintings; amongst others, some of the Flemish school, brought to Mexico by the monks at the time when the Low Countries were under Spanish dominion. Many masters also of the Mexican school, such as Enríquez,[14] Cabrera, &c., have enriched the cloisters with their productions, and employed their talent on holy subjects, such as the lives of the saints, the martyrs, and other Christian subjects.

Everywhere, especially, there are *Cabreras*, an artist somewhat in the Luca Giordano style—the same monotony, facility, and *"fa presto Luca!"*[15] All his pictures are agreeable, and some strikingly beautiful. Occasionally he copies from the old masters, but rarely. Ximenes[16] and Enríquez are not so common, and some of their productions are very good, and deserve to be better known than I imagine they are in Europe. They are a branch of the Spanish school, and afford striking proofs of the extraordinary talent of the Mexicans for the fine arts, as well as of the facilities which the mother country afforded them.

But it is in the convent of the Profesa that the finest paintings are, and there I cannot enter! The galleries are full of paintings, the most part by Cabrera; and Calderón speaks with enthusiasm of one exceedingly beautiful painting, in the sacristy of the chapel, said to be an original Guido, being a representation of Christ tied to the pillar and scourged—in which the expression of pure divinity and suffering humanity is finely blended, and well contrasted with savage cruelty in the countenances of his executioners. But most of these paintings are neglected, and so falling to decay that it is pitiable to look at them.[17]

The Santa Teresa, however, has few ornaments. It is not nearly so large as the Encarnación, and admits but twenty-one nuns. At present there are, besides these, but three novices.[18] Its very atmosphere seems holy, and its scrupulous and excessive cleanness makes all profane dwellings appear dirty by comparison.

We were accompanied by a bishop, Señor Madrid, the same who assisted at the Archbishop's consecration—a good-looking man, young and tall, and very splendidly dressed.[19] His robes were of purple satin, covered with fine point lace, with a large cross of diamonds and amethysts. He also wore a cloak of very fine purple cloth lined with crimson velvet, crimson stockings, and an immense amethyst ring.

When he came in we found that the nuns had permission to put up their veils, rarely allowed in this order in the presence of strangers. They have a small garden and fountain, plenty of flowers, and some fruit; but all is on a smaller scale, and sadder than in the convent of the Incarnation. The refectory is a large room, with a long narrow table running all round it—a plain deal table, with wooden benches; before the place of each nun, an earthen bowl, an earthen cup with an apple in it, a wooden plate and a wooden spoon; at the top of the table a grinning skull, to remind them that even these indulgences they shall not long enjoy.

In one corner of the room is a reading desk, a sort of elevated pulpit, where one reads aloud from some holy book, whilst the others discuss their simple fare. They showed us a crown of thorns, which on certain days is worn by one of their number, by way of penance. It is made of iron, so that the nails—entering inwards—run into the head and make it bleed. While she wears this on her head, a sort of wooden bit is put into her mouth, and she lies prostrate on her face till dinner is ended; and while in this condition her food is given her, of which she eats as much as she can, which probably is none.

We visited the different cells, and were horror-struck at the self-inflicted tortures. Each bed consists of a wooden plank raised in the middle, and on days of penitence crossed by wooden bars. The pillow is wooden, with a cross lying on it which they hold in their hands when they lie down. The nun lies on this penitential couch, embracing the cross, and her feet hanging out as the bed is made too short for her upon principle. Round her waist she occasionally wears a band with iron points turning inwards; on her breast, a cross with nails of which the points enter the flesh—of the truth of which I had melancholy ocular demonstration. Then, after having scourged herself with a whip covered with iron nails, she lies down for a few hours on the wooden bars, and rises at four o'clock. All these instruments of discipline, which each nun keeps in a little box beside her bed, look as if their fitting place would be in the dungeons of the Inquisition. They made me try their *bed and board,* which I told them would give me a very decided taste for early rising.

Yet they all seem as cheerful as possible,[20] though it must be confessed that many of them look pale and unhealthy. It is said that when they are strong enough to stand this mode of life they live very long; but it frequently happens that girls who come into this convent are obliged to leave it from sickness, long before the expiration of their novitiate.

I met with the girl whom I had seen take the veil, and cannot say that she looked either well or cheerful though she assured me that "of course, in doing the will of God," she was both. There was not much beauty amongst them generally, though one or two had remains of great loveliness. My friend the Madre A[dalid] is handsomer on a closer view than I had supposed her, and seems an especial favourite with old and young.[21] But there was one whose face must have been strikingly beautiful. She was as pale as marble, and, though still young, seemed in very delicate health. But her eyes and eyebrows as black as jet—the eyes so large and soft, the eyebrows two pencilled arches—and her smiles, so resigned and sweet, would have made her the loveliest model imaginable for a Madonna.

Again, as in the Incarnation, they had taken the trouble to prepare an elegant supper for us. The bishop took his place in an antique velvet chair; the Señora Adalid and I were placed on each side of him. The room was very well lighted, and there was as great a profusion of custards, jellies, and ices as if we had been supping at the most profane *café*. The nuns did not sit down, but walked about, pressing us to eat —the bishop now and then giving them cakes, with permission to eat them, which they received laughing. They have the most humble and caressing manners, and really appear to be the most amiable and excellent women in the world. They seem to make no ostentation of virtue, but to be seriously impressed with the conviction that they have chosen the true road to salvation; nor are there in them any visible symptoms of that spiritual pride from which few devotees are exempt.

After supper a small harp was brought in, which had been sent for by the bishop's permission. It was terribly out of tune, with half the strings broke; but we were determined to grudge no trouble in putting it in order and giving these poor recluses what they considered so great a gratification. We got it into some sort of condition at last, and when they heard it played they were vehement in their expressions of delight. The Señora [Adalid], who has a charming voice, afterwards sang to them, the bishop being very indulgent and permitting us to select whatever songs we chose—so that when rather a profane canticle, "The Virgin of the Pillar (*La Virgen del Pilar*)," was sung he very kindly

turned a deaf ear to it, and seemed busily engaged in conversation with an old *madre*, till it was all over.[22]

We were really sorry to leave them, particularly as it is next to impossible that we shall ever see them again; and it seemed as if in a few hours a friendship had been formed between us and these recluses, whose sensations are so few they must be the more lasting. The thoughts of these poor women cost me a sad and sleepless night. They have sent me some wax figures dressed in the costumes of the different orders, beginning with their own. They wear the coarsest and hardest stuff next their skin, in itself a perpetual penance.

In these robes they are buried, and one would think that, if any human being can ever leave this world without a feeling of regret, it must be a nun of the Santa Teresa—when, her privations in this world ended, she lays down her blameless life and joins the pious sisterhood who have gone before her, dying where she has lived, surrounded by her companions, her last hours soothed by their prayers and tears, sure of their vigils for the repose of her soul, and above all sure that neither pleasure nor vanity will ever obliterate her remembrance from their hearts.

At matins, at vespers, at the simple board, at the nightly hymn, she will be missed from their train. Her empty cell will recall her to their eyes; her dust will be profaned by no stranger's footstep and, though taken away, she still seems to remain amongst them.

As for the monasteries, not only no woman can enter, but it is said (with what truth I know not) that, a vice-queen having insisted on the privilege of her vice-royalty to enter, the gallery and every place which her footsteps desecrated were unpaved. This was very Saint Senanus like, and *peu galant*, to say the least.[23]

The finest convent of monks in Mexico is that of San Francisco, which from alms alone has an immense annual rent. According to Humboldt, it was to have been built upon the ruins of the temple of Huitzilopochtli, the god of war; but, those ruins having been destined for the foundation of the cathedral, this immense convent was erected where it now stands in 1531. The founder was an extraordinary man, a great benefactor of the Indians, and to whom they owed many useful mechanical arts which he brought them from Europe. His name was Fray Pedro de Gante—his calling that of a lay friar—and his father was the Emperor Charles V![24]

Of the interior of this convent I am enabled to give you a partial description—but whether from hearsay, in a vision, or by the use of my natural eyes, I shall not disclose.

It is built in the form of a square, and has five churches attached to it. You enter a gate, pass through the great, silent, and grass-grown court—up the broad staircase, and enter the long, arched cloisters, lighted by one dim lamp, where everything seems to breathe a religious repose.

The padre prior, with his bald head and pale, impressive face, seated alone in his cell—with plain but decent furniture, a thick and richly-clasped volume before him, a single lamp on his table, on the wall a crucifix—would have made a fine study for a painter. By such men the embers of learning and of science were nursed into a faint but steady flame, burning through the long gloomy night of the dark ages, unseen by profane eyes—like the vestal fire in pagan temples.

A small room, opening into his little parlour, contains his bed, on which is a mattress—for the padres do not perform such acts of self-denial and penitence as the cloistered nuns—and I am assured that his cigars are genuine Havana.

Beggars [are] lounging within the courtyard—a group of monks [are] talking together within the walled enclosure.

Change the scene to the monastery of San Agustín and you might fancy yourself in the days of one of Walter Scott's romances—in the *mélange* of soldiers and friars—for here His Excellency the President has his temporary abode; and the torchlight gleams brightly on the swarthy faces of the soldiers, some lying on the ground enveloped in their cloaks, others keeping guard before the convent gate.

This convent is also very large, but not so immense as that of San Francisco. The padre prior is a good little old man, but has not the impressive, ascetic visage of the guardian of the other convent. His room is as simple, though not in such perfect order; and his bed is also furnished with a comfortable mattress. An air half military, half monkish, pervades the convent—aides-de-camp of the President passing along the galleries, their uniforms contrasting with the dark robe of a passing monk, returning at nightfall to his cell.

The President had an alarm the night preceding, the prisoners in the jail having broken out. A serious affray had been expected, and everything was prepared for putting the person of the President in safety. The back stairs and secret passages in these old convents lead to excellent hiding places, and have been put to frequent use during revolutions. In the *old* Monte Pío there is a communication with a convent of nuns, and in cases of pillage the jewels used to be carried by a private staircase out of Monte Pío, and placed under the care of the nuns of Santa Brígida.[25]

The convent of La Profesa is also a fine and spacious building but, excepting that it has a greater number of good paintings than the others, when you have seen one, you have seen all—and I believe none are as large as that founded by the illegitimate scion of the imperial Charles, who himself ended his days in a similar retreat.[26]

28

A Second Visit to Santiago

Tuesday: November 3rd, 1840
Hacienda of Santiago

Yesterday, the second of November, a day which for eight centuries has been set apart in the Catholic church for commemorating the dead —the day emphatically known as the *Día de Muertos*—the churches throughout all the republic of Mexico present a gloomy spectacle, darkened and hung with black cloth, while in the middle aisle is a coffin, covered also with black and painted with skulls and other emblems of mortality. Everyone attends church in mourning, and considering the common lot of humanity, there is perhaps not one heart over the whole Catholic world which is not wrung that day in calling up the memory of the departed.[1]

After early mass we set off for Santiago, where we intend to spend a week to be present at the *herraderos*—the marking of the bulls with a hot iron with the initials of the proprietor's name; stamping them with the badge of slavery—which is said to be an extraordinary scene, to which all rancheros and Indians look forward with the greatest delight. We had a very pleasant journey here, leaving Mexico at six in the morning and travelling at the usual rate, with *seven* horses and plenty of *mozos*. Indeed, no one attempts a journey of any length into the country without at least six horses or mules.

Near Soapayuca, while they were changing horses, we went to mass in the picturesque church of San Cristóbal. The magnificence of these places of worship is extraordinary. Here was this country church crowded with *léperos*, the officiating priests, Indians with bare feet; yet the building large and rich, hung with black cloth, and lighted with great tapers which threw their gloomy rays on as much of the rich gilding that encrusted the walls as the dark pall left visible.

We got into the carriage a basket of that most refreshing of fruits, the tuna, which grow wild in abundance all over the country. The first time I unwarily pulled them off the trees I got my fingers full of the innumerable little prickles which cover the skin, and which it is very difficult to get rid of. The Indians have great dexterity in gathering and peeling them. There is the green and the red tuna; the last the prettiest to look at, but not nearly so agreeable a fruit as the other.

When we arrived at Santiago we sat down to dinner to the number of about fifty persons, and in the room next to us was a party still larger, of lower degree—for all the world has come to be present at this annual festivity.

Friday: November 6th, 1840

The next morning we set off early to the *plaza de toros*. The day was fresh and exhilarating. All the country people from several leagues round were assembled, and the trees up to their very topmost branches presented a collection of bronze faces and black eyes, belonging to the Indians who had taken their places there as comfortably as spectators in a one-shilling gallery. A platform opposite ours was filled with the wives and daughters of agents and small farmers, little *rancheras* with short white gowns and *rebozos*. There was a very tolerable band of music, perched upon a natural orchestra. Bernardo and his men were walking and riding about, and preparing for action.[2] Nothing could be more picturesque than the whole scene.

Seven hundred bulls were driven in from the plains, bellowing loudly so that the air was filled with their fierce music. The universal love which the Mexicans have for these sports amounts to a passion. All their money is reserved to buy new dresses for this occasion—silver rolls or gold linings for their hats, or new deerskin pantaloons and embroidered jackets with silver buttons. The accidents that happen are innumerable, but nothing damps their ardour. *It beats fox hunting!*

The most striking part of the scene is the extraordinary facility which these men show in throwing the lasso. The bulls—being all driven into an enclosure—one after another, and sometimes two or three at a time, were chosen from amongst them and driven into the plaza, where they were received with shouts of applause if they appeared fierce and likely to afford good sport; or of irony if they turned to fly, which happened more than once.

Three or four bulls are driven in. They stand for a moment, proudly reconnoitring their opponents. The horsemen gallop up, armed only with the lasso, and with loud insulting cries of *"Ah toro!"* challenge them to the contest. The bulls paw the ground, then plunge furiously at the horses, frequently wounding them at the first onset. Round they go in fierce gallop, bulls and horsemen, amidst the cries and shouts of the spectators.

The horseman throws the lasso. The bull shakes his head free of the cord, tosses his horns proudly, and gallops on. But his fate is inevitable. Down comes the whirling rope, and encircles his thick neck. He is thrown down struggling furiously, and repeatedly dashes his head against the ground in rage and despair. Then, his legs being also tied, the man with the hissing red-hot iron, in the form of a letter, brands him on the side with the token of his dependence on the lord of the soil.

Some of the bulls stand this martyrdom with Spartan heroism and do not utter a cry; but others, when the iron enters their flesh, burst out into long bellowing roars that seem to echo through the whole country. They are then loosened, get upon their legs again, and like so many branded Cains are driven out into the country, to make way for others.

Such roaring, such shouting, such an odour of singed hair and *biftek au naturel,* such playing of music, and such wanton risks as were run by the men!

I saw a toreador, who was always foremost in everything, attempting to drag a bull by the horns, when the animal tossed its head and with one jerk of one horn tore all the flesh off his finger to the very bone. The man coolly tore a piece off a handkerchief, shook the blood off his finger with a slight grimace, bound it up in a moment, and dashed away upon a new venture. One Mexican—extraordinarily handsome, with eyes like an eagle, but very thin and pale—is, they say, so covered from head to foot with wounds received in different bullfights that he cannot live long. Yet this man was the most enthusiastic of them all. His master tried to dissuade him from joining in the sport this year; but he broke forth into such pathetic entreaties, conjuring him "by the life of the Señorita," &c., that he could not withhold his consent.

After an enormous number of bulls had been caught and *labelled,* we went to breakfast. We found a tent prepared for us, formed of boughs of trees intertwined with garlands of white moss, like that which covers the cypresses at Chapultepec, and beautifully ornamented with red blossoms and scarlet berries. We sat down upon heaps of white moss, softer than any cushion. The Indians had cooked meat under the stones for us—which I found horrible, smelling and tasting of smoke. But we had also boiled fowls, and quantities of burning chile; hot tortillas; *atole* (or *atolli*, as the Indians call it), a species of [gruel] made of very fine maize and water, and sweetened with sugar or honey;[3] *embarrado*, a favourite composition of meat and chile, very like *mud* as the name imports, which I have not yet made up my mind to endure; quantities of fresh tunas, *granaditas*, bananas, aguacates, and other fruits—besides pulque *à discrétion*.

The other people were assembled in circles under the trees, cooking fowls and boiling eggs in a gypsy fashion in caldrons at little fires made with dry branches; and the band, in its intervals of tortillas and pulque, favoured us with occasional airs.

After breakfast we walked out amongst the Indians, who had formed a sort of temporary market, and were selling pulque, *chia,* roasted chestnuts, yards of baked meat, and every kind of fruit. We then returned to see a great bullfight, which was followed by more *herraderos*—in short, spent the whole day amongst the *toros*, and returned to dinner at six o'clock, some in coaches, some on horseback.

In the evening, all the people danced in a large hall; but at eleven o'clock I could look on no longer, for one of these days in the hot sun is very fatiguing. Nevertheless, at two in the morning these men, who had gone through such violent exercise, were still dancing *jarabes*.

Sunday: November 8th, 1840

For several days we lived amongst bulls and Indians, the *herraderos* continuing, with variation of *colear*, riding the bulls, &c. Not the slightest slackening in the eagerness of the men. Even a little boy of ten years old mounted a young bull one day, and with great difficulty and at a great risk succeeded in forcing him to gallop round the circle. His father looked on, evidently frightened to death for the boy, yet too proud of his youthful prowess to attempt to stop him.[4]

At night when I shut my eyes I see before me visions of bulls' heads. Even when asleep I hear them roaring, or seem to listen to the shouts of "*Ah toro!*" The last day of the *herraderos*, by way of winding up, a bull was killed in honour of Calderón, and a great flag was sent streaming from a tree, on which flag was inscribed in large letters, "*Gloria al Señor Ministro de la Augusta Cristina!*"—a piece of gallantry which I rewarded with a piece of gold.

The animal when dead is given as a present to the toreadors, and this bull, cut in pieces, they bury with his skin on in a hole in the ground previously prepared with a fire in it—which is then covered over with earth and branches. During a certain time it remains baking in this natural oven, and the common people consider it a great delicacy (in which I differ from them).

Yesterday we climbed to the top of a steep mountain, which cost us as much labour as if it had been that steep path which "leads to fame." Fortunately, it has a good deal of wood, and we had an occasional rest in the shade. We mounted the hill on horseback as far as horses could go; but the principal part could only be performed on foot. Most of the party remained half way. We reached the top, swinging ourselves up by the branches in places where it was nearly perpendicular. We were rewarded, first by the satisfaction one always has in making good one's intentions, and next by a wonderfully fine and extensive view. Our return was more agreeable, as the weather, except in the heat of the noonday sun, is very cool in this part of the country. The hills are covered chiefly with tunas, low firs, and numbers of shrubs with flowers and berries.

Met on our return a horseman who came to announce the arrival of a guest, Señor H[aro] from Puebla, who proved a pleasant addition to our society.[5]

Monday: November [9th], 1840

We went out early this morning on horseback and breakfasted at an hacienda five leagues distant from Santiago belonging to the widow of [Adalid]'s agent, a good-looking, respectable woman who, alone in this solitary place, brings up her eight children as she best can. This may really be called solitude. From one year to the other she never sees a human being except an occasional Indian. She is well off and everything in her house is clean and comfortable. She herself manages the farm and educates her children to the best of her abilities, so that she never finds time to be dull. She expected us, and gave us breakfast (we being about twenty in number), consisting of everything which that part of the country can afford; and the party certainly did justice to her excellent fare. She gave us pulque fermented with the juice of the pineapple, which is very good.

When the sun had gone down a little we rode to the fine hacienda of Los Reyes belonging to Señor A[dalid], where he is making and projecting alterations and improvements. When we left Los Reyes it began to rain, and we were glad to accept the covering of sarapes as we galloped over the plains. We had a delightful ride. Towards evening the rain ceased, and the moon rose brightly and without a cloud; but we were certainly tired enough when we got home, having rode in all ten leagues.

Wednesday, November [11th], 1840

These two days have been passed in seeing the mules marked.[6] They are even more dangerous than the bulls, as they bite most ferociously while in their wild state. When thrown down by the lasso they snore in the most extraordinary manner, like so many aldermen in an apoplectic nap.

This is, perhaps, the most useful and profitable of all Mexican animals. As beasts of burthen and for draught, they are in use over the whole republic, and are excellent for long journeys, being capable of immense fatigue, particularly in those arid, hilly parts of the country where there are no roads. Those which go in droves can carry about five hundred pounds weight, going at the rate of twelve or fourteen miles a day, and in this way they can perform journeys of more than a thousand miles.[7] For constant use they are preferable to horses, being so much less delicate, requiring less care, and enduring more fatigue. A good pair of carriage mules will cost from five hundred to a thousand dollars.

After dinner we saw some of these wild creatures that had just been caught put into a carriage, each wild mule harnessed with a civilized one—and such kicking and flinging up of heels I never witnessed. However, the *mozos* can manage anything, and in about half an hour, after much alternate soothing and lashing, they trotted along with the heavy coach after them, only rearing and plunging at decent intervals.

Thursday: November 12th, 1840
San Fernando, Mexico

We have passed ten days in the country, taking constant exercise, and have been obliged to return home rather sooner than we should have wished in order to mark Queen Isabel's Day with a diplomatic dinner.

Though less is now said on the subject of the pamphlet than when we left this, the irritation seems to continue as before. Señor Gutiérrez remains concealed, communicating only with his family and a few devoted friends; a most disagreeable position, and one which it is impossible for him to endure long.[8]

Friday: November 20th, 1840

Our dinner has *gone off* as well as could be expected.[9] The party were twenty-six in number, consisting of His Grace the Archbishop, their excellencies of the cabinet and the *corps diplomatique,* together with Count Cortina, the Valencias, and Gorostizas.

The gentlemen were in full uniform—the ladies *en grande toilette* —the Archbishop in his robes. We had a band of music in the gallery, and walked in to the sound of the *Norma,* precedence being given to the Archbishop who took me—or rather whom I took, as I found some difficulty in getting my arm into his robes. I believe no blunders in etiquette were committed. The dinner lasted three and a half mortal hours. The Archbishop proposed the health of Her Majesty the Queen, which was drank standing—the band performing "God save the Queen." I was dreadfully tired (though in a very agreeable position), and have no doubt everyone else was the same, it being eleven when we returned to the drawing room.[10]

The Archbishop's familiars, two priests who always accompany him, respectable *black guards,* were already in waiting. As for him, he was as kind and agreeable as usual and, after coffee, took his departure to the sound of music.

29

Young Relatives from Home

Saturday: November 21st, 1840
San Fernando, Mexico

We received a few days since an invitation to attend the sumptuous mass annually given by the Asturian Brotherhood in honour of the Virgin of Covadonga in the church of Santo Domingo. The invitation —being printed on blue satin, with gold lace and tassels—seems worthy

of a place in a box of wax figures which will be sent by the next packet.

The church was superbly decorated, and only well-dressed people were admitted. Calderón was carried off to a post of honour near the altar, and a padre gave me a velvet chair. The music was beautiful, but too gay for a church. There were violins and wind instruments, and several amateur players. Some pieces from the *Cheval de Bronze* were very well played.[1] The sermon, preached by Guerrero, a *chanoine* who has some reputation as an orator, contained a prudent degree of praise of the Spaniards—and even of a king, could that king be a Pelayo.[2]

In the evening we dined at the Prussian minister's—a pleasant party.

Yesterday we went to Chapultepec—Calderón and I, M. de Gerolt, and M. de Nebel—to take views with the daguerreotype, which Calderón had the pleasure of receiving some time ago from Boston, from our friend Mr. Prescott.[3] While they were working in the sun I, finding that the excessive heat had the effect of cooling my enthusiasm, established myself with a book under Montezuma's cypress, which felt very romantic. The poetry of the scene, however, was greatly weakened by the arrival of a party of *forçats* in chains who are working in the castle, which I believe there is some intention of having transformed into a military college. They are so insolent that, forgetting they are guarded and chained in couples, I felt glad to see that the servants were within call.

Our weekly *soirées* have begun and so far are very successful. There are now three *tertulias* in the week at the houses of the diplomats. We have generally music, cards, and plenty of dancing, and everyone seems pleased—the best proof of which they give by generally staying till two or three in the morning.

Saturday: November 28th, 1840

You may imagine my joy at the arrival of Kate and Alex in health and safety at three o'clock today. They have had a good journey from Veracruz, suffering from nothing but the cold, which they felt especially at Perote. As they arrived on the day of a *soirée* they did not make their appearance, being tired. I have now an excuse for revisiting all my old haunts, and the first week or two must pass in sight-seeing.[4]

Monday: November 30th, 1840

We dined yesterday at Tacubaya, where the Cortina family, particularly the ladies of the family, are in a state of the greatest uneasiness.

I had just written these words when I began, to my great astonishment, to rock up and down—chair, table, and myself. Suddenly the room—the walls—all began to move, and the floor to heave like the waves of the sea! At first, I imagined that I was giddy, but almost immediately saw that it was an earthquake. We all ran, or rather staggered as well as we could, into the gallery, where the servants were already ranged on their knees, praying and crossing themselves with all their might.

The shock lasted above a minute and a half, and I believe has done no injury, except in frightening the whole population, and cracking a few old walls. All Mexico was on its knees while it lasted, even the poor madmen in San Hipólito, which Alex had gone to visit in company with Señor Adalid. I have had a feeling of seasickness ever since. They expect a return of the shock in twenty-four hours. How dreadful a severe earthquake must be! How terrible it is to feel this heaving of the solid earth, to lose our confidence in its security, and to be reminded that the elements of destruction which lurk beneath our feet are yet swifter and more powerful to destroy than those which are above us.

I cannot help laughing yet at the recollection of the face of a poor little clerk who had just entered the house with a packet of letters for Calderón. He did not kneel, but sat down upon the steps as pale as death, looking as "creamed faced" as the messenger to Macbeth; and, when the shock was over, he was so sick that he ran out of the house without making any remarks.[5] The scarlet *guacamaya*, with a loud shriek, flew from its perch and performed a zigzag flight through the air, down to the troubled fountain in the court.

Your friend the Honourable Mr. Bertie arrived the other day, looking very ill—having had the yellow fever at Havana very severely, a peculiar piece of bad fortune at this season.[6]

All the furniture we ordered from the United States arrived some time ago, a mass of legs and arms. Tables, wardrobes, &c. were, I believe, all sold for the mahogany at Veracruz. The mirrors also arrived *in powder*. This must be owing to bad packing, since our most delicate things from London, such as crystal, porcelain, &c., have arrived in excellent condition.

Thursday: December 3rd, 1840

Have had many visits today, this being my *día de fiesta*. Amongst others the President was here. This custom of keeping people's *días* gives one a great deal of trouble, but the omission is considered rather a breach of politeness.[7]

Saturday: December 12th, 1840

This being the anniversary of the day of the miraculous apparition of Our Lady of Guadalupe, the cathedral and village will be crowded with Indians from all parts of the country. Alex and Mr. Bertie have driven over there, but from all accounts the crowd will be so great that we are not tempted to accompany them.

We have a *soirée* this evening, and have had two pleasant parties this week at the other houses. Tomorrow we intend going with a large party to the Desierto, where some gentlemen are to give a breakfast. I understand that there are to be twenty-three people on horseback, and eighteen in carriages, and our *trysting place* is by the great fountain with the gilt statue, in the Paseo de Bucareli; the hour, half-past seven. They say the Desierto is a beautiful place, but being seven leagues from Mexico, we shall probably all return as tired as possible.

Tuesday: December 15th, 1840

The morning of our party to the Desierto was beautiful. Here one need not fear those *contretemps* in regard to the weather which in England so often render a party of pleasure painful—unless, indeed, one chooses to select an evening in the rainy season for an expedition.

We met by the fountain at the hour appointed, some in carriages and some on horseback. Of the latter I formed part. The road leads along the aqueduct by Chapultepec, and through Tacubaya, and is the highroad that goes to Toluca. The first part, after passing Tacubaya, is steep, bleak, and uninteresting. Plantations of maguey and occasional clumps of Peruvian trees are the only vegetation, and Indian huts the only traces of human life. But after a tedious ascent, the view looking back upon Mexico—with all her churches, lakes, and mountains—is truly magnificent. The road also begins to wind through a fertile and wooded country. About noon we reached an inn where travellers stop who are going to Toluca, and where we halted to collect our scattered forces. Hanging up by a hook in the entry, along with various other dead animals, polecats, weasels, &c., was the ugliest creature I ever beheld. It seemed a species of dog, with a hunch back, a head like a wolf, and no neck—a perfect monster. As far as I can make out it must be the *itzcuintepotzotli*, mentioned by some old Mexican writers.[8] The

people had brought it up in the house, and killed it on account of its fierceness. This inn stands in the valley of Cuajimalpa, and is about a league from the Desierto.

There is no longer any road there, but a steep and winding path through the beautiful woods. Therefore those who had come in coaches were now obliged to proceed on donkeys, with Indian guides. The beauty of the scenery is indescribable. The path winds, ascending through a wilderness of trees and flowering shrubs, bathed by a clear and rapid rivulet; and every now and then, through the arched forest trees, are glimpses of the snowy volcanoes and of the distant domes and lakes of Mexico.

The ruins of the old Carmelite convent, standing on the slope of a hill, are surrounded by noble forests of pine, and oak, and cedar—[with] long and lofty forest aisles, where the monks of former days wandered in peaceful meditation. But they removed from this beautiful site to another, said to be equally beautiful and wilder, also called the Desierto, but much farther from Mexico; and this fertile region (which the knowing eye of a Yankee would instantly discover to be full of capabilities in the way of machinery) belongs to no one, and lies here deserted in solitary beauty. Some poor Indians live amongst the ruins of the old cloisters, and the wild deer possess the undisputed sovereignty of the woods.[9]

It is said that a benighted traveller who had lost his way in these solitudes, and was miraculously saved from dying of cold, founded this rich convent of Carmelite monks in gratitude to heaven for his deliverance, bequeathing his desire that all travellers who passed that way should receive hospitality from the convent. Certainly no place more fitted for devotion could have been selected than this mountain retreat; and when the convent bell tolled at evening, calling the monks to prayer and wakening the echoes of the silent hills, its deep notes must have been all in unison with the solemn scene.

But the sight of a very magnificent *déjeuner a la fourchette* spread under the pine trees, the uncorking of champagne bottles and Scotch ale, the savoury odour of soups and *fricandeaus*, the bustling attendance of English waiters, put to flight all romantic fancies. We remembered that we were hungry, that we had ridden seven leagues[10] and had not breakfasted; and no order of friars could have done more justice to the repast than we did.

But the component parts of a party of pleasure must be very curiously selected, the mosaic of the society very nicely fitted, or it will inevitably terminate unpleasantly; and the elements of discord are more dangerous, their effects more lasting, than even the coughs and colds and rheumatisms produced by those watery elements, sworn foes to all picnics and gypsy parties in our foggy island.[11]

About four o'clock we remounted our horses and retraced our path through the woods; and who could ruminate on petty disputes, or complain of trifling accidents, or not forget any disagreeable individuals who might have been found among our numerous party, when the splendid panorama of Mexico burst upon us—with all its mountains, lakes, and plains, its churches and towers and gardens, bathed in a flood of golden light, the rich crimson clouds of sunset resting upon the snow of the volcanoes—while the woods through which our horses picked their steps, over stones and streamlets, were fragrant with blossoming shrubs and wild roses?

When we reached the inn where the carriages had been left, we remounted our horses, and—as it was growing dusk, and the whole party had not yet collected together—we thought it advisable for the equestrian part of the expedition to ride forward. So, leaving the carriages with their escort, we set off for Mexico—Calderón, I, Alex, and a servant—at full gallop, and hardly drew our bridles till we reached the city, tired as you may suppose after our fourteen leagues' ride.

Sunday: December 20th, 1840

Our yesterday evening's *tertulia* was very crowded, and there was a great deal of music and dancing. These weekly *soirées* are decidedly successful, and the best families in Mexico unite there without etiquette, which we were told it was impossible to bring about.

Perhaps it is that I am getting accustomed to the Mexican style of face, but it appeared to me that there was a great deal of beauty assembled; and as for fine voices, they are as common in Mexico as they are rare in England.

A rich senator, Don Basilio Guerra, made a vow to the Virgin some years ago that he would cause a splendid mass to be performed annually in the cathedral, at his own expense, in honour of our Saviour's birth, on the morning of Christmas Eve. This mass is performed entirely by amateurs, most of the young ladies in Mexico who have fine voices taking a part in it. I was *drawn in*, very unwillingly, to promise to take a trifling part on the harp, the accompaniment to the *Incarnatus*.

Preparations have long been going on for this solemnization, and various rehearsals have taken place amongst the amateur singers, in the evening, before large audiences in the Minería. The whole thing promises well.

Wednesday: December [23rd], 1840[12]

Calderón has gone with Señor Zurutuza (a Spanish gentleman) to Cuernavaca, in *tierra caliente*, to spend a few days at his estate in the neighbourhood—which at this season will be delightful.[13]

This morning we rode to San Joaquín, where we met the prior on horseback, on his way to Mexico to confess the old prioress of the convent of Santa Teresa. He turned back, and accompanied us during all the rest of our ride. He rode with us to Tacuba, round the traces of the ruins, and to the fine old church and dismantled convent, where we dismounted and—having taken off our riding hats—accompanied the prior through the deserted cloisters into the old church. I imagine we must have looked very picturesque, I in my riding habit and the sandalled friar in his white robes, kneeling side by side on the broken steps of the altar. He is so pleasant and well-informed that he is a particularly agreeable companion.[14]

30

Second Christmas: A Year in Mexico

Friday: December 25th, 1840
San Fernando, Mexico

Christmas Day! One year this evening since we made our entry into
Mexico.

What a different aspect everything has assumed to us in one year!
Then every object was new, every face that of a stranger. Now we
are surrounded by familiar sights and sounds, and above all by friendly
faces. But, though novelty, which has its charms and also its *désagré-
ments*, has gone, nothing in Mexico ever appears commonplace. Everything is on a large scale, and everything is picturesque. Then there is
so much interest attached to its old buildings, so much to see—even
though there are no *sights* and no show places, unless we are to put
in that class the Minería, museum, cathedral, university, and botanic

garden, usually visited by travellers—that, at whatever period we may leave it, I feel convinced we shall regret some point of interest that we have left unvisited.

Some days ago coloured cards printed in gilt letters were sent round, inviting all the senator's friends to the [annual Christmas] mass, in this form:

José Basilio Guerra requests that you will honour him with your presence and that of your family, in the solemn function of Kalends and Mass, with which he annually makes a humble remembrance of the Birth of the Saviour, which festivity will take place on the morning of the 24th of this month, at nine o'clock, in the Parish Church of the Sagrario[1] of the Holy Cathedral.

Mexico, December, 1840

By nine we were all assembled in the choir: Don Basilio in his uniform, dark blue and gold; we in mantillas. The church looked very splendid and, as usual on these occasions, no *léperos* were admitted; therefore the crowd was very elegant and select. The affair went off brilliantly. Four or five of the girls, and several of the married women, have superb voices; and not one of all those who sang in chorus has a bad voice. The finest I almost ever heard is that of the Señorita [Cepeda y] Cosío. Were she to study in Italy I venture to predict that she might rival Grisi. Such depth, power, extension, and sweetness, with such richness of tone in the upper notes, are very rarely united. She sang a solo in such tones that I thought the people below must have felt inclined to applaud. There are others whose voices are much more cultivated and who have infinitely more science. I speak only of the raw material.[2]

The orchestra was really good, and led by a first-rate musician. I was thankful when my part of the entertainment was over and I could give my undivided attention to the others. The celebration lasted four hours, but there was rather a long sermon. You will shortly receive a detailed account of the whole, which is to be published in the Mexican annual called *The Ladies' Guide*.

In the evening we went to the house of the Marquesa de Vivanco to spend Christmas Eve. On this night all the relations and intimate friends of each family assemble in the house of the *head of the clan* —a real gathering, and in the present case to the number of fifty or sixty persons.

This is the last night of what are called the *Posadas*, a curious mixture of religion and amusement, but extremely pretty. The meaning is this: At the time that the decree went forth from Cæsar Augustus that "all the world should be taxed," the Virgin and Joseph, having come out of Galilee to Judæa to be inscribed for the taxation, found

Bethlehem so full of people who had arrived from all parts of the world that they wandered about for nine days without finding admittance in any house or tavern, and on the ninth day took shelter in a manger where the Saviour was born. For eight days this wandering of the Holy Family to the different *posadas* [inns] is represented, and seems more intended for an amusement to the children than anything serious.

We went to the *marquesa's* at eight o'clock, and about nine the ceremony commenced. A lighted taper was put into the hand of each lady and a procession was formed, two by two, which marched all through the house—the corridors and walls of which were all decorated with evergreens and lamps, the whole party singing the litanies. Kate walked with the dowager *marquesa*, and a group of little children dressed as angels joined the procession. They wore little robes of silver or gold lamé, plumes of white feathers, and a profusion of fine diamonds and pearls—in *bandeaux*, brooches, and necklaces—white gauze wings, and white satin shoes embroidered in gold.

At last the procession drew up before a door, and a shower of fireworks was sent flying over our heads—I suppose to represent the descent of the angels, for a group of ladies appeared dressed to represent the shepherds who watched their flocks by night upon the plains of Bethlehem. Then voices, supposed to be those of Mary and Joseph, struck up a hymn in which they begged for admittance, saying that the night was cold and dark, that the wind blew hard, and that they prayed for a night's shelter. A chorus of voices from within refused admittance. Again those without entreated shelter, and at length declared that she at the door, who thus wandered in the night and had not where to lay her head, was the Queen of Heaven! At this name the doors were thrown wide open, and the Holy Family entered singing.[3]

The scene within was very pretty: a *nacimiento*. Platforms, going all round the room, were covered with moss, on which were disposed groups of wax figures, generally representing passages from different parts of the New Testament, though sometimes they begin with Adam and Eve in paradise. There was the Annunciation—the Salutation of Mary to Elizabeth—the Wise Men of the East—the Shepherds—the Flight into Egypt. There were green trees and fruit trees, and little fountains that cast up fairy columns of water, and flocks of sheep, and a little cradle in which to lay the Infant Christ. One of the angels held a waxen baby in her arms. The whole was lighted very brilliantly, and ornamented with flowers and garlands. A padre took the baby from the angel, and placed it in the cradle, and the *Posada* was completed.

We then returned to the drawing room—angels, shepherds, and all —and danced till supper time. The supper was a show for sweetmeats and cakes.

Today, with the exception of there being service in all the churches,

Christmas is not kept in any remarkable way. We are spending this evening alone, and very quietly. Tomorrow we have a *soirée*. I have letters from Calderón from Cuernavaca, delighted with the beauties of *tierra caliente,* and living amongst roses and orange trees. I hope that in January we shall be able to go there, in case anything should occur to induce us to leave Mexico before next winter.

Sunday: December 27th, 1840

We had a very crowded party last evening, I think the best we have had yet, a fact which I mention because I triumph in my opinion that these weekly parties would succeed in Mexico having proved correct.

I have lately been engaged in search of a *cook,* with as much pertinacity as Japhet in search of his father, and with as little success as he had in his preliminary inquiries.[4] One, a Frenchman, I found out had been tried for murder; another was said to be deranged; a third, who announced himself as the greatest *artiste* who had yet condescended to visit Mexico, demanded a salary which he considered suitable to his abilities. I tried a female Mexican in spite of her flowing hair. She seemed a decent woman and tolerable cook, and, although our French housekeeper and prime minister had deserted us at our utmost need,[5] we ventured to leave the house and to spend the day at Tacubaya. On our return, found the whole establishment unable to stand! Cook tipsy —soldiers ditto—*galopina* slightly intoxicated—in short, the house taking care of itself—no *standing force* but the coachman and footman, who have been with us some time and appear to be excellent servants. I am, however, promised a good Mexican housekeeper and trust that some order will be established under her government; also a Chinese cook with a *celestial* character.

Letters from Spain, announcing the speedy arrival of a secretary of legation and another attaché.[6]

Friday: January 1st, 1841

A happy New Year to all! We began it by attending early mass in San Francisco, about the cleanest church in Mexico, and that most frequented by the better classes. There you may have the good fortune to place yourself between two well-dressed ladies, but you are equally likely to find your neighbour a beggar with a blanket—besides, the floor is nearly as dirty as that of the cathedral.

As to the universal dirtiness of the lower classes of Mexicans, one might write a volume upon it, were the subject not too disagreeable. But if a stranger wishes to see it in perfection, let him go to church—and, of all churches, let him select the cathedral.

This dirtiness is certainly one of the greatest drawbacks to human felicity in this beautiful country. It pervades everything, destroying the most noble works of God, degrading the most beautiful productions of man. The streets, the churches, the theatres, the market place, and the people—all are contaminated by this evil. The market place is indeed full of flowers and green branches and garlands, the same love of flowers distinguishing the Indians as in the time of Cortés—the same which Humboldt admires centuries afterwards. But the dirtiness of those who sell the flowers and weave the garlands! It seems as if the very roses must be contaminated by them—and the effect of what would otherwise be the prettiest possible picture is completely destroyed. In the theatre a series of villainous suffocating odours affect the olfactory nerves, especially in the dimly-lighted corridors which lead to the boxes—which is anything but agreeable.

The custom of kneeling on the floor in church is both fitting and devout, but there surely can be no reason why the floor of a sacred building should not be kept scrupulously clean, or why the lower classes should not be obliged to dress themselves with common decency and cleanness. Those who are unable to do so from poverty—though probably there are not half a dozen people in Mexico who do not wear rags merely from indolence—should certainly have a place set apart for them. Were this order given, it is probable that, in a wonderfully short period, that appearance of squalid poverty would disappear. On [the] occasion of any peculiar fête, the church is washed and beggars are excluded, and then indeed the cathedral and these noble edifices seem fitting temples wherein to worship God.

On other days, in addition to the *léperos* (especially in the cathedral), the poor Indian women are in the habit of bringing their babies and baskets of vegetables with them to church, and the babies on their part are in the habit of screaming, as babies generally do when they consider themselves neglected. It appears to me that a very little trouble might remedy nearly all these evils: the churches kept clean; neither men nor women admitted who are not at least covered with decency—for the most ragged are generally strong, stout men who prefer begging to working, or half-naked women who think themselves degraded by doing anything to better their condition except asking for alms. As for the babies it is more difficult, the poor woman having come in from her village and perforce brought her progeny with her, but the vegetables might be amended; and as for the dogs which wander up and down and about the church during the time of divine service, they might, I think, be induced to remain outside if proper measures were employed. All these might be brought to order by proper regulations.

Notwithstanding all these drawbacks, I have sometimes compared in my own mind the appearance of a fashionable London chapel with that of a Mexican church on the occasion of a solemn fête, and the comparison is certainly in favour of the latter.

The one—light, airy, and gay, with its velvet-lined pews, its fashionable polite preacher, the ladies a little sleepy after the last night's opera, but dressed in the most elegant morning toilet, and casting furtive glances at Lady _____'s hat and feathers, and at Mrs. _____'s cashmere shawl or lovely ermine pelisse, and then exchanging whispered greetings or a few fashionable nothings at the door while their livery servants let down the steps of their gay equipages.

The other—solemn, stately, and gloomy, and showing no distinction of rank. The floor covered with kneeling figures—some enveloped in the *rebozo*, others in the mantilla, but all alike devout, at least in outward seeming. No showy dress, or gay bonnet, or fashionable mantle to cause the eye of the poor to wander with envy or admiration. All seem to think that they are alike in the sight of heaven; the peasant and the *marquesa* kneel side by side with scarcely any distinction of dress; and each one appears occupied with their own devotions, their own solemn thoughts, without observing either their neighbour's dress or degree of devoutness.

There can be no doubt as to which appear the most likely to have their ideas concentrated upon the one subject which ought to occupy them. Religious feeling may be equally strong in the frequenters of both places of worship; but, as long as we possess senses which can be affected by external objects, the probabilities of the most undivided devotional feeling are in favour of the latter. The eye will wander—the thoughts will follow where it leads. In the one case it rests on elegant forms and fashionable toilets—in the other it sees nothing but a mass of dark and kneeling figures, or a representation of holy and scriptural subjects.[7]

However, one consequence of the exceeding dirtiness of the Mexican churches and of the number of *léperos* who haunt them—as much in the way of their calling as from devotion—is that most of the principal families here have small chapels in their houses, and have engaged the services of a padre to say mass for them at home.[8]

There is a small chapel in the house of General Barrera, the handsomest house in Mexico,[9] where there is a Virgin carved in wood, one of the most exquisite pieces of sculpture that can be seen. The face is more than angelic—it is divine—but a divine nature suffering mortal anguish.

Wednesday: January 27th, 1841

On the first of February we hope to set off on an expedition to *tierra caliente*, from which Calderón returned some time ago.[10] We have, by good fortune, procured an excellent Mexican housekeeper, under whose auspices everything has assumed a very different aspect, and to whose care we can entrust the house when we go.

Nothing remarkable has occurred here lately—the usual routine of riding on horseback, visiting in carriage, walking very rarely in the Alameda, driving in the Paseo, dining at Tacubaya, the three weekly *soirées*— varied by a diplomatic dinner in the house of the _____ minister, and by the dinner of the English club who met here yesterday, [followed] by a sale of books after dinner, in which the president of the society fined me five dollars for keeping a stupid old poem past the time—upon which I *moved* that the poem should be presented to me, which was carried *nem. con.*[11]

We have been strongly advised not to attempt this journey, and the stories of robbers and robberies related by credible persons are not encouraging. Robbers, bad roads, horrible heat, poisonous animals—many are the difficulties prognosticated to us. The season is already rather advanced, but it has been impossible for us to set off sooner. Our next letters will be written either during our journey, should we find the opportunity, or after our return.

A JOURNEY THROUGH

THE SUGAR COUNTRY

31

To Cuernavaca
and the Hacienda of Atlacomulco

Tuesday: February 2nd, 1841
Hacienda of Atlacomulco

A quiet day in a hospitable country house, too sunny to go out and nothing else to do, are temptations sufficient to induce me to sit down and give you an account of our proceedings during these last two days.

Yesterday, the first of February, at four in the morning, very sleepy, we set off in the diligence which we had taken for ourselves; our sole luggage, two portmanteaus and a carpet bag; our dresses, dark strong calico gowns, large Panama hats, *rebozos* tied on like scarfs, and thick green *barège* veils. A government escort of four soldiers with a corporal, renewed four times, accompanied us as far as Cuernavaca, which is about eighteen leagues from Mexico and the entrance, as it were, to *tierra caliente*. These are supposed sufficient to frighten away three times the number of robbers, whose daring, however, has got to such a height that no diligence now arrives from Puebla without being robbed. Six robberies have happened there in the last fortnight, and the road to Cuernavaca is said to be still more dangerous.

We took chocolate before starting, and carried with us a basket of cold meat and wine, as there is nothing on the road that can be called an inn. When we set off it was cool, almost cold; the astral lamps were out, and the great solar lamp was not yet lighted.

> But soon, like lobster boiled, the morn,
> From black to red began to turn.[1]

By the time we had reached San Agustín [de las Cuevas], where we changed horses, the sun had risen, enabling us to see all the horrors of the road which, after leaving that beautiful village with its trees and gardens, winds over the mountain amongst great volcanic rocks—a toilsome ascent— and passes by the village of Ajusco, a miserable robbers' nest. Yet the

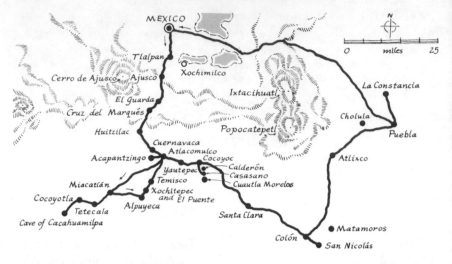

view, as we looked back from this barren tract while the sun was breaking over the summits of the mountains, was very grand in its mixture of fertility and wildness, in its vast extent of plains and villages with their groves and gardens, and in its fine view of Mexico itself, white and glittering in the distance. The mountain of Ajusco, clothed with dark forests of pine, frowned on our right, and looked worthy of its brigand haunted reputation.

At El Guarda, a collection of miserable huts, we changed horses, and declined some suspicious-looking *frijoles* in dirty saucers which were offered to us—a proof both that we were young travellers in this country, and that we had not exhausted our basket of civilized provender.

The road wound round through a succession of rocks and woods till we reached Cruz del Marqués—the marquis being of course Cortés, while the cross, it is said, was planted there by him to mark the limits of his territory, or rather of that which the Indian emperor had assigned him.[2] About two o'clock the heat became intense, and we began to see and to feel symptoms of our approach to *tierra caliente*.

We arrived at the Indian village of Huitzilac, which is rather pretty, with cane cottages and a good many flowering trees; and from the eminence on which it is situated the *hot land* is visible.

The diligence now began galloping down the rocky and stony descent. The country looked even more arid than before; the vegetation more dried up. Not a tree—but here and there, at long intervals, a feathery cocoa or a palm, and occasionally some beautiful, unknown wild flowers. But the heat, the dust, the jolting! When at length we rattled through Cuernavaca, and stopped before the quiet-looking inn, it was with joy that we bade adieu, for some time at least, to all diligences, coaches, and carriages—having to trust for the future to four-legged conveyances, which we can guide as we please.

Cuernavaca (cow's horn), the ancient Quauhnahuac,[3] was one of the thirty cities which Charles V gave to Cortés, and [which] afterwards formed part of the estates of the Duke of Monteleone, representative of the family of Cortés, as Marquis of the Valley of Oaxaca. It was celebrated by the ancient writers for its beauty, its delightful climate, and the strength of its situation—defended on one side by steep mountains, and on the other by a precipitous ravine through which ran a stream which the Spaniards crossed by means of two great trees that had thrown their branches across the barranca, and formed a natural bridge.[4]

It was the capital of the Tlahuica nation, and after the conquest Cortés built here a splendid palace, a church, and a convent of Franciscans—believing that he had laid the foundation of a great city. And in fact, its delicious climate, the abundance of the water, the minerals said to exist in the neighbourhood, its fine trees, delicious fruits, and vicinity to the capital all combined to render it a flourishing city. It is, however, a place of little importance, though so favoured by nature; and the conqueror's palace is a half-ruined barrack, though a most picturesque object, standing on a hill behind which starts up the great white volcano.

There are some good houses, and the remains of the church which Cortés built, celebrated for its bold arch;[5] but we were too tired to walk about much, and waited most anxiously for the arrival of horses and men from the sugar estate of Don Anselmo Zurutuza, at Atlacomulco, where we were to pass the night.

The house where the diligence stopped was formerly remarkable for the fine garden attached to it, and belonged to a wealthy proprietor. We sat down amongst the fruit trees by the side of a clear tank, and waited there till the arrival of our horses and guides.[6] It was nearly dusk when they came. The sun had gone down, the evening was cool and agreeable, and, after much kicking and spurring and loading of mules and barking of dogs, we set off over hill and dale, through pretty wild scenery, as far as we could distinguish by the faint light, climbing hills and crossing streams for two leagues—till at length the fierce fires, pouring from the sugar oven chimneys of Atlacomulco, gave us notice that we were near our haven for the night. We galloped into the courtyard, amongst dogs and Negroes and Indians, and were hospitably received by the *administrador* (the agent). Greatly were we divided between sleep and hunger; but hunger gained the victory, and an immense smoking supper received our most distinguished attention.

This morning, after a refreshing sleep, we rose and dressed at eight o'clock—late hours for *tierra caliente*—and then went out into the coffee plantation and orange walk. Anything so lovely! The orange trees were covered with their golden fruit and fragrant blossom; the lemon trees, bending over, formed a natural arch which the sun could not pierce. We laid ourselves down on the soft grass, contrasting this day with the preceding. The air was soft and balmy, and actually heavy with the fragrance of the orange blossom and starry jasmine. All round the orchard ran streams of the most delicious clear water, trickling with sweet music, and now and then a little cardinal, like a bright red ruby, would perch on the trees. We pulled bouquets of orange blossom, jasmine, lilies, double red roses, and lemon leaves—and wished we could have transported them to you, to those lands where winter is now wrapping the world in his white winding sheet.

The gardener, or coffee planter—such a gardener!—Don Juan by name, with an immense black beard, Mexican hat, and military sash of crimson silk, came to offer us some orangeade; and, having sent to the house for sugar and tumblers, pulled the oranges from the trees, and drew the water from a clear tank, overshadowed by blossoming branches and cold as though it had been iced. There certainly is no tree more beautiful than the orange, with its golden fruit, shining green leaves, and lovely white blossom with so delicious a fragrance. We felt this morning as if Atlacomulco was an earthly paradise.

It belongs in fact to the Duke of Monteleone, and is let by his agent, Don Lucas Alamán, to Señor Zurutuza.[7] Its average annual produce of sugar is about thirty thousand *arrobas* (an *arroba* containing twenty-five pounds). The sugar cane was unknown to the ancient Mexicans, who made syrup of honey and also from the maguey, and sugar from the stalk of maize. The sugar cane was introduced by the Spaniards from the Canary Islands to Santo Domingo, from whence it passed to Cuba and Mexico. The first sugar canes were planted in 1520, by Don Pedro de Atienza. The first cylinders were constructed by Gonzalo de Velosa, and the first sugar mills built by the Spaniards at that time were worked by hydraulic wheels and not by horses. M. de Humboldt, who examined the will of Cortés, informs us that the conqueror had left sugar plantations near Coyoacán, in the valley of Mexico, where now, owing it is supposed to the cutting down of the trees, the cold is too great for sugar cane or any other tropical production to thrive.[8]

There are few Negroes on these sugar plantations. Their numbers have not increased since their introduction. We observed but one old Negro, said to be upwards of a hundred, who was working in the courtyard as we passed; the generality of the workmen are Indians.[9]

As for the interior of these haciendas, they are all pretty much alike, so far as we have seen: a great stone building, which is neither farm nor country house (according to our notions), but has a character peculiar to itself—solid enough to stand a siege—with floors of painted brick, large deal tables, wooden benches, painted chairs, and whitewashed walls; one or two painted or iron bedsteads, only put up when wanted; numberless empty rooms; kitchen and outhouses. The courtyard a great square, round which stand the house for boiling the sugar (whose furnaces blaze day and night), the house with machinery for extracting the juice from the cane, the refining rooms, the places where it is dried, &c.—all on a large scale. ——

If the hacienda is, as here, a coffee plantation also, then there is the great mill for separating the beans from the chaff. And sometimes also there are buildings where they make brandy. Here there are four hundred men employed—exclusive of boys—one hundred horses, and a number of mules. The property is generally very extensive, containing the fields of sugar cane, plains for cattle, and the pretty plantations of coffee, so green and springlike—this one containing upwards of fifty thousand young plants, all fresh and vigorous, besides a great deal of uncultivated ground, abandoned to the deer and hares and quails, of which there are [a] great abundance.[10]

For four months in the year the "hot land" or *tierra caliente,* with all [its] delightful productions, must be a paradise, and it has the advantage over the coasts in being quite free from the scourge of yellow fever. But the heat in summer, and the number of poisonous insects, are great drawbacks. Of these, the *alacranes,* or scorpions, which haunt all the houses, are amongst the worst. Their bite is poisonous and, to a child, deadly—which is one of the many reasons why these estates are left entirely to the charge of an agent, and, though visited occasionally by the proprietor, rarely lived in by the family. The effects are more or less violent in different constitutions. Some persons will remain for eight days in convulsions, foaming at the mouth, and the stomach swelled as if by dropsy; others, by immediate remedies, do not suffer much. The chief cures are brandy, taken in sufficient quantities to stupefy the patient, guaiacum, and boiled silk, which last is considered the most efficacious. In Durango they are particularly numerous and venomous, so that a reward is given for so many *head* of scorpions to the boys there, to encourage them to destroy them. The Señora _____, who lives there, feels no inconvenience from their bite, but the scorpion who bites her immediately dies! It is pretended that they prefer dark people to fair, which is to suppose them very discriminating. Though as yet there have been few seen in the houses, I must confess that we feel rather uneasy at night, and scrupulously examine our beds and their environs before venturing to go to sleep. The walls being purposely whitewashed, it is not

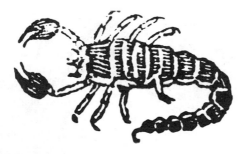

difficult to detect them; but, where the roofs are formed of beams, they are very apt to drop through.[11]

There are other venomous reptiles, for whose sting there is no remedy, and if you would like to have a list of these interesting creatures, according to the names by which they are known in these parts, I can furnish you with one from the best authority. These, however, are generally to be found about outhouses, and only occasionally visit your apartments. There is the *chicaclino,* a striped viper, of beautiful colours; the *coralillo,* a viper of a coral colour, with a black head; the *vinagrillo,* an animal like a large cricket. You can discover it, when in the room, by its strong smell of vinegar. It is orange-coloured, and taps upon the person whom it crawls over, without giving any pain, but leaving a long train of deadly poison. I have fancied that I smelt vinegar in every room since hearing this. [There is] the *salamanquesa,* whose bite is fatal (it is shaped like a lizard); the *eslaboncillo,* which throws itself upon you and, if prevented from biting you, dies of spite; the *cencoatl,* which has five feet, and shines in the dark. So that fortunately a warning is given of the vicinity of these animals in different ways; in some by the odour they exhale, in some by the light they emit, and in others, like the rattlesnake, by the sound they give out.[12]

Then there is a beautiful black and red spider, called the *chinclaquili,* whose sting sends a pain through all your bones, the only cure for which is to be shut up for several days in a room thick with smoke. There are also the *tarántula* and *casampulga* spiders. Of the first, which is a shocking looking soft fat creature covered with dark hair, it is said that the horse which treads on it instantly loses its hoof—but this wants confirmation. Of the scorpions, the small yellowish-coloured ones are the most dangerous, and it is pretended that their bite is most to be apprehended at midday. The workmen occasionally eat them, after pulling out the sting. The flesh of the viper is also eaten roasted, as a remedy against eruptions of the skin. Methinks the remedy is worse than the disease.[13]

But to banish this *creeping* subject, which seems not at all in unison with the lovely scenes that surround us—an Eden where no serpent should enter—we have been riding this evening to a beautiful little Indian village called Acapantzingo, than which I never beheld anything

prettier in its way. Some few houses there are of stone, but the generality are of cane, and each cottage is surrounded by its fruit trees, and by others covered with lilac or white blossoms, and twined with creepers. The lanes or streets of the village are cleanly swept, and shaded by the blossoming branches that overhang them—while every now and then they are crossed by little streams of the purest water. I think I never knew what really delicious water was till I came here. The Indians, both men and women, looked clean—and altogether this is the prettiest Indian village we have yet seen.

As we are very anxious to visit the celebrated cave of Cacahuamilpa, near the [town of that name],[14] and also to see as much of *tierra caliente* as possible, we have determined, though with regret, to leave our pleasant quarters at Atlacomulco tomorrow morning, at two o'clock, a.m. As there are no inns, we are furnished with letters of recommendation to the proprietors of the chief haciendas in these parts. Formerly, there was so much hospitality here that an annual sum (three thousand dollars, it is said) was assigned by the proprietors to their agents for the reception of travellers, whether rich or poor, and whether recommended or not.

Our plan of visiting the cave has been nearly frustrated by the arrival of General C_____s, a neighbouring proprietor, who assured us that we were going to undertake an impossibility; that the barrancas, by which we must pass to arrive at the cave, were impassable for women—the mountain paths being so steep and perpendicular that men and horses had frequently fallen backwards in the ascent, or been plunged forward over the precipices in attempting to descend. We were in despair, when it was suggested that there was another though much longer road to the cave, by which we might ride; and though our time is at present very precious we were too glad to agree to this compromise.

Calderón and A[lex] have returned from a shooting expedition, in which they have not been very successful; and, though I have only recounted to you the beginning of our adventures, I must stop here and take a few hours' rest before we set off on our *matinal* expedition.

32

Cross Country to the Cave of Cacahuamilpa

Friday: February 5th, 1841
Hacienda of Cocoyotla

On the morning of the third of February we rose about half past two, and a little after three, by the light of the stars and the blaze of the sugar fires, our whole party were assembled on horseback in the courtyard. We were about twelve in number. Don Juan, the coffee planter, and Don Pedro, a friend of his, were deputed by the agent to act as our guides. Four or five well-armed *mozos* (farm servants) were our escort, together with our Mexican boy; and we had mules to carry our luggage, which was compressed into the smallest possible compass.

The morning was perfectly enchanting, and the air like balm, when we set off by this uncertain light; not on roads (much to our satisfaction), but through fields and over streams, up hills and down into valleys, climbing among stones—the horses picking their way like goats. I certainly never felt or imagined such an atmosphere. The mere inhaling it was sufficient pleasure.

When the light gradually began to dawn, so that we could discern each other's faces and make sure that we were not a party of shadows—for, besides the obscurity, a mixture of sleepiness and placid delight had hitherto kept us all silent—we looked round on the landscape as little by little it assumed form and consistency. The fires from the hacienda were still visible, but growing pale in the beams of morning, vanishing like false visions from before the holy light of truth. As we rode along we found that the scenery on the hilly parts was generally bleak and sterile, the grass dried up and very little vegetation; but, wherever we arrived at a valley sheltered from the sun's rays, there we found a little rivulet trickling through it, with water like liquid diamonds bathing the trees and the flowers—the loveliest blossoming trees, mingled with bananas, oranges, and lemons, and interspersed with bright flowers, forming a natural garden and orchard.

One tree, with no leaves on it, is covered with white starry flowers, and looks at a distance as if it had been covered with snow which had melted off the branches, leaving only occasional white tufts. Another is bending with lilac blossoms, which hang in graceful clusters—another with flowers like yellow balls. Then there are scarlet wild flowers, that seem as if they were made of wax or shining coral, and quantities of white jasmine trailing on the grass, and throwing itself over the branches of the trees. There is one beautiful tree with flowers like immense white lilies, and buds that look like shut lily blossoms in white wax.

Leaving these beautiful and fertile lands that adorn the slopes and bases of the hills, you mount again up the steep paths, and again you find the grass dried up and no vegetation but stunted nopals or miserable-looking blue-green magueys. Yet sometimes in the most desert spot, a little sheltered by a projecting hill, you come upon the most beautiful tree, bending with rich blossoms, standing all alone—as if through ambition it had deserted its lowly sisters in the valley and stood in its exalted station, solitary and companionless.

As for the names of these tropical trees, they are almost all Indian, and it is only *botanically* that they can be properly distinguished. There is the *floripundio,* with white odoriferous flowers hanging like bells from its branches, with large, pointed, pale green leaves; the *yoloxochitl,* signifying flower of the heart, like white stars with yellow hearts, which when shut have the form of one, and the fragrance of which is delicious; the *izguixochitl,* whose flowers look like small white musk roses; another with a long Indian name, which means the flower of the raven, and is white, red, and yellow. The Indians use it to adorn their altars, and it is very fragrant as well as beautiful.[1]

After six hours' good riding, our guides pointed out to us the formidable barrancas at some distance, and expressed their opinion that—with great caution, our horses being very sure-footed—we might venture to pass them, by which means we should save three leagues, and be enabled to reach an hacienda within six leagues of the cave that night; and after some deliberation it was agreed that the attempt should be made. These barrancas (the word literally means a ravine or gully) are two mountains, one behind the other, which it is necessary to cross by a narrow path that looks like a road for goats.

We began the ascent in silence and some fear, one by one, till the horses were nearly perpendicular. It lasted about twenty minutes; and we then began to descend slowly, certainly not without some danger of being thrown over our horses' heads. However, we arrived in safety at the end of the first mountain and, this being accomplished, drew up to rest our horses and mules beside a beautiful clear stream bordered by flowering trees. Here some clearheaded individual of the party proposed that we should open our hamper, containing cold chicken, hard eggs, sherry, &c.—observing that it was time to be hungry. His suggestion was agreed to without a dissenting voice and, a napkin being spread under a shady

tree, no time was lost in proving the truth of his observation. A very ingenious contrivance for making a wineglass, by washing an eggshell in the stream, is worthy of record. When we had demolished the cold chicken, the *mozos* surrounded the cold meat, and, after gathering branches covered with beautiful flowers, with which we ornamented our horses' heads and our own hats, we prepared to ascend the second mountain. This is as steep or nearly as steep as the first; but we were already confident in the sure-footedness of our horses, and even able to admire the view as we ascended single file. After much rain, this path must of course be completely impassable.[2]

The day had now become oppressively warm, though it was not later than eleven o'clock; and, having passed the hills, we came to a dusty high road which, about twelve, brought us to the hacienda of Miacatlán, belonging to the family of Pérez Palacios. We were overtaken on the road by the eldest son of the proprietor, who cordially invited us in and introduced us to the ladies of his family and to his father, a fine, noble-looking old gentleman.[3] As we were excessively tired, hot, and dusty, we were very glad to spend a few hours here during the heat of the sun; and after joining the family at breakfast—consisting of the most extraordinary variety of excellent dishes, with a profusion of fine fruits and curious sweetmeats (amongst which was that ethereal-looking production called angel's hair, *cabello de ángel*)—we were glad to lie down and rest till four o'clock.

This hacienda is very productive and valuable, and has a silver mine on it.[4] There is also every variety of fine fruit, especially the largest cedrats I ever saw which, although they have not a great deal of flavour, are very refreshing.

With all their beauty and fertility, there is something very lonely in a residence on these estates which are so entirely shut out of the world— not so much for the proprietors themselves, who are occupied in the care of their interests, but for the female part of the family.

We left this hospitable mansion about four o'clock, rested and refreshed, the proprietor giving K[ate] a horse of his instead of her own, which was tired. The sun was still powerful when we and our train remounted, but the evening had become delightfully cool by the time that we had reached the beautiful village of San Francisco de Tetecala, lying amongst wooded hills, its white houses gleaming out from amidst the orange trees, with a small river crossed by bridges running through it. Many of the houses were tolerably large and well built. It was a fête day, and the musical bells ringing merrily. The people were clean and well-dressed, and were assembled in crowds in an enclosure looking at a bull-fight, which must be hot work in this climate, both for man and beast.

But when the moon rose serenely and without a cloud, and a soft breeze, fragrant with orange blossom, blew gently over the trees, I felt as if we might have rode on forever, without fatigue, and in a state of the most perfect enjoyment. It were hard to say whether the first soft breath of morning, or the languishing and yet more fragrant airs of evening, were most enchanting. Sometimes we passed through a village of scattered Indian huts, with little fires of sticks lighted in their courts, glowing on the bronze faces of the women and children; and at the sound of our horses' hoofs a chorus of dogs, yelping with most discordant fury, would give us loud notice of their total disapprobation of all night travellers. Sometimes a decided smell of boiled sugar was mingled with the fragrance of the orange blossom and jasmine, reminding us of those happy days of yore when the housekeeper, in all her glory, was engaged in making her annual stock of jellies and jams.

Once we were obliged to dismount that our horses might make an *ugly leap* over a great ditch guarded by thorny bushes, and amongst trees where the moon gave us no light.

About ten o'clock symptoms of weariness began to break out amongst us, spite of moonbeams and orange buds, when down in a valley we saw the sugar fires of Cocoyotla, the hacienda to which we trusted for our next place of shelter, darting out their fierce red tongues amongst the trees. We knocked for admittance at the great gate, and it was some time before the people within would undo the fastenings, which they did with great caution and after carefully reconnoitring us—afterwards giving for excuse that a party of thirty robbers had passed by the night before, and that they thought we might have been some of these *night-errants*.[5] We sent in our credentials to the proprietor (an old gentleman married to a young wife) who, living on the road to the cave, is by no means pleased at his house being turned into a *posada* for all and sundry, and complained bitterly of a party of Englishmen who had passed by some time before: "And the only *Spanish* word they could say was *vater*, by which they meant *agua. Caramba!*" However, he was very hospitable to us, and pressed us to remain there the following day and rest ourselves and our horses, after our fourteen leagues' march, previous to going on to the cave.

A very good supper and a very sound sleep were refreshing, and the whole of the next day we spent in wandering about or sitting lazily amongst the magnificent orange trees and cocoas of this fine hacienda. Here the orange trees are the loftiest we had yet seen—long ranges of noble trees, loaded with fruit and flowers. At the back of the house is a small grove of cocoas, and a clear running stream passing through beautiful flowers and refreshing everything in its course. Indeed, all through *tierra caliente*, except on the barren hills, there is a profusion of the most delicious water—here at once a necessity and a luxury.

These sugar estates are under high cultivation, the crops abundant, the water always more than sufficient both for the purposes of irrigation and for machinery, which A[lex] considers equal to anything he has seen in Jamaica. They produce annually from thirty to fifty thousand *arrobas* of sugar. The labourers are free Indians, and are paid from two and a half to six and a half reals per day.[6] I believe that about one hundred and fifty are sufficient for working on a large estate.

Bountiful nature, walking on the traces of civil war, fills up the ravages caused by sanguinary revolutions, and these estates in the valley of Cuernavaca, which have so frequently been theatres of bloodshed and have so often changed proprietors, remain in themselves as fertile and productive as ever.

In the evening we visited the *trapiche*, as they call the sugarworks: the sugar boilers, warehouses, storerooms, and engines. The heat is so intense among these great boilers that we could not endure it for more than a few minutes, and pitied the men who have to spend their lives in this work. They make *panoja* on this estate, cakes of coarse sugar, which the common people prefer to the refined sugar.

Just as we were preparing to retire for the night, an animal on the wall attracted our attention, close by Kate's bed, and—gentle reader!—it was a scorpion! We gave a simultaneous cry, which brought Señor Silva[7] into the room, who laughed at our fears, and killed our foe; when lo!— just as our fright had passed away—another, a yellowish-coloured, venomous-looking creature, appeared stealing along the wall. The lady of the house came this time, and ordered the room and the beds to be searched. No more could be discovered, but it was difficult to sleep in peace after such an apparition.[8]

At three the next morning we rose, and set off by moon and starlight for the cave. The morning was lovely as usual, and quite cool. We passed a great deal of barren and hilly road till we reached some plains, where we had a delightful gallop, and arrived early at a small rancho, or farmhouse, where we were to procure guides for the cave. Here we added four Indians, and the master of the house, Benito, to our party, which was afterwards increased by numbers of men and boys, till we formed a perfect regiment. This little rancho, with its small garden, was very clean and neat. The woman of the house told us she had seen no ladies since an English *ministra* had slept there two nights. We concluded this must have been Mrs. Ashburnham, who spent two days in exploring the cave.[9]

We continued our ride over loose stones and dry, rocky hills where, were the horses not sure-footed, and used to climb, the riders' necks would no doubt suffer. Within about a quarter of a mile of the cave, after leaving on our right the pretty village of Cacahuamilpa, we found ourselves in a place which I consider much more dangerous than even the barrancas near Miacatlán: a narrow path overhanging a steep precipice and bordering a perpendicular hill, with just room for the horse's feet, affording the comfortable assurance that one false step would precipitate you to the bottom. I confess to having held my breath as, one by one, and step by step, no one looking to the right or the left, our gowns occasionally catching on a bush, with our whole train we wound slowly down this narrow descent. Arrived near the mouth of the cave, we dismounted, and climbed our way among stones and gravel to the great mountain opening. But an account of the cave itself must be reserved till our return to Atlacomulco.

33

A Marble Dream

Sunday: February 7th, 1841
Hacienda of Atlacomulco

The cave of Cacahuamilpa, whose actual wonders equal the fabled descriptions of the palaces of Genii, was until lately known to the Indians alone—or, if the Spaniards formerly knew anything about it, its existence was forgotten amongst them.[1] But, although in former days it may have been used as a place of worship, a superstitious fear prevented the more modern Indians from exploring its shining recesses—for here, it was firmly believed, the evil spirit had his dwelling and, in the form of a goat with long beard and horns, guarded the entrance of the cavern. The few who ventured there and beheld this apparition brought back strange tales to their credulous companions, and even the neighbourhood of the enchanted cave was avoided, especially at nightfall.

The chain of mountains into whose bosom it leads is bleak and bare, but the ravine below is refreshed by a rapid stream that forms small waterfalls as it tumbles over the rocks, and is bordered by green and flowering trees. Amongst these is one with a smooth, satin-like bark, of a pale golden colour, whose roots have something snakish and witch-like in their appearance, intertwining with each other, grappling as it were with the hard rock, and stretching out to the most extraordinary distance.[2]

We arrived at the entrance of the cave, a superb portal, upwards of seventy feet high and one hundred and fifty wide, according to the computation of a learned traveller—the rocks which support the great arch so symmetrically disposed as to resemble a work of art. The sun was already high in the heavens, shining with intense brightness on the wild scenery that surrounded us, the rocks and trees and rushing waters. A sensation of awe came over us as we stood at the mouth of the cave, and, turning from day to night, strained our eyes to look down a deep descent into a gigantic vaulted hall, faintly lighted by the red embers of a fire which the Indians had kindled near the entrance. We made our way down a declivity of, it may be, one hundred and fifty feet, surrounded by blocks of stone and rock, and remained lost in astonishment at finding ourselves in this gloomy subterranean palace, surrounded by the most extraordinary, gigantic, and mysterious forms—which it is scarcely possible to believe are the fantastic productions of the water which constantly trickles from the roof.

I am shocked to confess it—I would prefer passing it over—but we had tasted nothing that morning, and we had rode for eight hours and were dying of hunger! Moreover we travelled with a cook, a very tolerable native artist, but without sentiment—his heart in his stewpan—and he, without the least compunction, had begun his frying and broiling operations in what seemed the very vestibule of Pharaoh's palace. Our own *mozos* and our Indian guides were assisting his operations with the utmost zeal; and in a few minutes—some sitting round the fire and others upon broken pyramids—we refreshed ourselves with fried chicken, bread, and hard eggs before proceeding farther on our exploring expedition. Unromantic as this proceeding was, we looked, Indians and all, rather awful, with no other light than the ruddy glare of the fire flickering upon the strange, gigantic forms in that vast labyrinth; and, as to what we felt, our valour and strength of mind were increased sevenfold.

Twenty-four huge pine torches were then lighted, each man carrying one. To [Kate] and me were given lighted wax candles, in case by accident anyone should go astray from his companions and lose his way, as would too certainly happen in the different windings and galleries and compartments of the cave, and be alone in the darkness! We walked on in awe and wonder, the guides lighting up the sides of the cavern with their torches. Unfortunately, it is indescribable—as in the fantastic forms of the clouds, everyone sees some different creation of his fancy in these stupendous masses. It is said that the first *sala*—for travellers have pretended to divide it into halls, and a very little imagination may do so— is about two hundred feet long, one hundred and seventy wide, and one hundred and fifty in height—a noble apartment. The walls are shaded with different colours of green and orange; great sheets of stalactites hang from the roof; and white phantoms, palm trees, lofty pillars, pyramids, porches, and a thousand other illusions surround us on all sides. One figure, concerning which all agree, is a long-haired goat, the Evil One in that form. But someone has broken the head, perhaps to show the powerlessness of the enchanted guardian of the cave.

Some say that there are no living animals here, but there is no doubt that there are bats; and an exploring party who passed the night here not only heard the hissing of the rattlesnake, but were startled by the apparition of a fierce leopard, whose loud roarings were echoed amongst the vaults, and who, after gazing at them by the light of the torches, stalked majestically back into the darkness.

We passed on into the second *sala,* collecting as we went fragments of the shining stones, our awe and astonishment increasing at every step.

Sometimes we seemed to be in a subterranean Egyptian temple. The architecture was decidedly Egyptian, and the strange forms of the animals resembled those of the uncouth Egyptian idols—which, together with the pyramids and obelisks, made me think that perhaps that ancient people took the idea of their architecture and of many of their strange shapes from some natural cave of this description, just as nature herself suggested the idea of the beautiful Corinthian pillar.

Again, we seemed to enter a tract of country which had been petrified. Fountains of congealed water, trees hung with frozen moss, pillars covered with gigantic acanthus leaves, pyramids of ninety feet high losing their lofty heads in the darkness of the vault and looking like works of the preadamites; yet no being but He who inhabits eternity could have created them. This second hall, as lofty as the other, may be nearly four hundred feet in length.

We then passed into a sort of double gallery, separated by enormous pyramidal formations—stalagmites, those which are formed by water dropping on the earth. The ground was damp, and occasionally great drops trickled on our heads from the vaults above. Here Gothic shrines, odd figures—some that look like mummies, others like old men with long beards—appall us like figures that we see in some wild dream. These are intermingled with pyramids, obelisks, baths that seem made of the purest alabaster, &c. A number of small round balls, petrifactions of a dead white, lie about here, forming little hollows in the ground. Here the cave is very wide—about two hundred feet, it is said.

When we left this double gallery we came to another vast corridor, supported by lofty pillars covered with creeping plants, but especially with a row of the most gigantic cauliflowers, each leaf delicately chiseled and looking like a fitting food for the colossal dwellers of the cavern. But to attempt anything like a regular description is out of the question. We gave ourselves up to admiration, as our torches flashed upon the masses of rock, the hills crowned with pyramids, the congealed torrents that seem to belong to winter at the north pole, and the lofty Doric columns that bring us back to the pure skies of Greece. But amongst all these curious *accidents* produced by water, none is more curiously exquisite than an amphitheatre, with regular benches, surmounted by a great organ whose pipes, when struck, give forth a deep sound. It is really difficult not to believe that some gigantic race once amused themselves in these petrified solitudes, or that we have not invaded the sanctuary of some mysterious and superhuman beings. It is said that this cavern has been explored for four leagues, and yet that no exit has been discovered. As for us, I do not know how far we went: our guides said a league. It seemed impossible to think of time when we looked at these great masses, formed drop by drop, slowly and rarely and at distant intervals falling, and looked back upon the ages that must have elapsed since these gigantic formations began.

At length, on account of the loose stones, the water, and the masses of crystal rock that we had to climb over, our guides strongly recommended us to return. It was difficult to turn away our eyes from the great unformed masses that now seemed to fill the cave as far as the eye could reach. It looked like the world in chaos—nature's vast workshop, from which she drew the materials which her hand was to reduce to form and order. We retraced our steps slowly and lingeringly through these subterranean palaces, feeling that one day was not nearly sufficient to explore them, yet thankful that we had not left the country without seeing them.

The skeleton of a man was discovered here by some travellers, lying on his side, the head nearly covered with crystallization. He had probably entered these labyrinths alone—either from rash curiosity or to escape from pursuit—lost his way, and perished from hunger. Indeed, to find the way back to the entrance of the cave is nearly impossible without some clue to guide the steps amongst these winding galleries, halls, and issues, and entries, and divided corridors. Though there are some objects so striking that they may immediately be recognized, such as the amphitheatre for instance, there is a monotony even in the variety! And I can imagine the unfortunate man wandering amongst obelisks and pyramids and alabaster baths and Grecian columns; amongst frozen torrents that could not assuage his thirst, and trees with marble fruit and foliage, and crystal vegetables that mocked his hunger; and pale phantoms with long hair, and figures in shrouds that could not relieve his distress—and then his cries for help, where the voice gives out an echo as if all the pale dwellers in the cave answered in mockery—and then, his torch becoming extinguished, [his] lying down, exhausted and in despair near some inhospitable marble porch, to die.

As we went along, our guides had climbed up and placed wax candles on the top of all the highest points, so that their pale glimmering light pointed out the way to us on our return. The Indians begged they might be left there "on account of the blessed souls in purgatory," which was done. As we returned, we saw one figure we had not observed before, which looks something like a woman mounted on an enormous goat. To one hall, on account of its beauty, some travellers have given the name of the "Hall of Angels." It is said that by observation the height of the stalagmites might determine the age of their formation, but where is the enterprising geologist who would shut himself up in these crystal solitudes sufficiently long for correct observation?

I never saw or could have imagined so beautiful an effect as that of the daylight in the distance, entering by the mouth of the cave—such a faint misty blue, contrasted with the fierce red light of the torches, and broken by the pillars through which its pale rays struggled. It looked so pure and holy that it seemed like the light from an angel's wings at the portals of the *città dolente*.[3] What would that poor traveller have given to have seen its friendly rays! After climbing out and leaving the damp, cool, subterraneous air, the atmosphere felt dry and warm as we sat down to rest at the mouth of the cavern, surrounded by our Indian torchbearers. Truly, nature is no coquette. She adorns herself with greater riches in the darkest mountain cave than on the highest mountain top.[4]

We were sitting in thoughtful silence—ourselves, Indians and all, in a circle—when we saw, stumping down the hill in great haste and apparently in great wrath, an Indian alcalde with a thick staff in his hand, at whose approach the Indians looked awe-struck. He carried in his brown hand a large letter, on which was written in great type: *"Al Señor dominante de esta caravana de gente* (To the Commander of this caravan of people)"! This missive set forth that the justice of peace of the [town of Cacahuamilpa] begged to know by what right, by whose authority, and with what intentions we had entered this cave, without permission from government; and desired the *Señor dominante* to appear forthwith before the said justice for contempt of his authority. The spelling of the letter was too amusing. The Indians looked very much alarmed, and, when they saw us laugh, still more astonished. Calderón wrote with a pencil in answer to the summons that he was the Spanish minister, and wished good day to the alcalde, who plodded up the hill again, very ill pleased.

We now took leave of this prodigious subterranean palace and again put ourselves *en route*. Once more we wound our way round the brink of the precipice, and this time it was more dangerous for us than before —for we rode on the side next it, our gowns overhanging the brink, and, if caught by a branch there, might have been dragged over. Our two guides afterwards said that, if alone, they would have dismounted—but that, as the ladies said nothing, they did not like to propose it!

Some day, no doubt, this cave will become a show place, and measures will be taken to render the approach to it less dangerous; but, as yet, one of its charms consists in its being unhackneyed.[5] For long after, its recollection rests upon the mind, like a marble dream. But, like Niagara, it cannot be described; perhaps even it is more difficult to give an idea of this underground creation than of the emperor of cataracts— for there is nothing with which the cave can be compared.

Meanwhile, we had rather a disagreeable ride, in all the force of the sun's last rays, back to the rancho. No one spoke—all our thoughts were wandering amongst marble palaces, and uncouth, gigantic, half-human forms.

But our attention was again attracted by the sudden reappearance of our friend the alcalde, on the brow of the hill, looking considerably indignant. He came with a fresh summons from the judge of Cacahuamilpa, which lay white and glittering in the valley below. Calderón endeavoured gravely to explain to him that the persons of ambassadors were not subject to such laws, which was Greek and Hebrew to him of the bronze countenance. "If it were a *consul,* indeed, there might be something in that." At last our guide, the ranchero [Don Miguel Benito], promised to call upon the judge in the evening, and explain the matter to his satisfaction; and again our alcalde departed upon his bootless errand—bootless in every sense, as he stalked down the hill with his bare bronze supporters. As we passed along, a parcel of soldiers in the village were assembled in haste, who struck up an imposing military air to give us some idea of their importance.

When we arrived at the rancho, we found that a message had come from the judge prohibiting Don [Miguel] Benito from accompanying strangers to the cave in future, which would be hard upon the old man, who makes a little money by occasionally guiding strangers there. Calderón has therefore written on the subject to the prefect of the department.[6]

In the cool of the evening, we had a delightful ride to Cocoyotla. The air was soft and fragrant. The bells of the villages were ringing amongst the trees, for every village, however poor, has at least one fine church—and all the bells in Mexico, whether in the city or in the villages, have a mellow and musical sound, owing, it is said, to the quantity of silver that enters into their composition.

It was late when we arrived at Cocoyotla, but we did not go to rest without visiting the beautiful chapel, which we had omitted to do on our last visit. It is very rich in gilding and ornaments, very large and in good taste.[7]

We supped, and threw ourselves down to rest for a few hours, and set off again at three o'clock, by the light of a full moon. Our greatest difficulty in these hurried marches is to get our things in and out of our portmanteaus, and to dress in time in the dark. No looking glasses of course—we arrange our hair by our imagination. Everything gets broken, as you may suppose—the mules that carry our trunks cantering up and down the hills to keep up with us, in most unequal measure.

The moon was still high, though pale, when the sun rose, like a youthful monarch impatient to take the reins from the hands of a mild and dying queen. We had a delightful gallop, and soon left the fires of Cocoyotla far behind us.

After riding six leagues, we arrived at six in the morning at the house of the Pérez Palacios. We should have gone further while it was cool; but their hospitality, added to a severe fit of toothache which had attacked Calderón, induced us to remain till four o'clock, during which time we improved our acquaintance with the family. How strange and even melancholy are those glimpses which travellers have of persons whom they will probably never meet again; with whom they form an intimacy, which owing to peculiar circumstances seems very like friend-

ship—much nearer it certainly than many a long acquaintanceship which we form in great cities, and where the parties go on *knowing each other* from year to year, and never exchanging more than a mere occasional and external civility.

It was four o'clock when we left Miacatlán and we rode hard and fast till it grew nearly dark, for our intention was to return to our headquarters at Atlacomulco that night—and we had a long journey before us, especially as it was decided that we should by no means attempt to recross the barrancas by night, which would have been too dangerous. Besides, an eclipse of the moon was predicted[8] and, in fact, as we were riding across the fields, she appeared above the horizon, half in shadow—a curious and beautiful spectacle. But we should have been thankful for her entire beams, for after riding for hours we discovered that we had lost our way and, worse still, that there were no hopes of our finding it. Not a hut was in sight—darkness coming on—nothing but great plains and mountains to be distinguished, and nothing to be heard but bulls roaring round us. We went on, trusting to chance—and where chance would have led us it is hard to say—but by good fortune our advanced guard stumbled over two Indians, a man and a boy, who agreed to guide us to their own village, but nowhere else.

After following them a long and weary way, all going at a pretty brisk trot, the barking of hundreds of dogs announced an Indian village, and by the faint light we could just distinguish the cane huts snugly seated amongst bananas and with little enclosed gardens before each.[9] Our cavalcade drew up before a hut, a sort of tavern or spirit shop, where an old half-naked hag, the *beau idéal* of a witch, was distributing *firewater* to the Indians, most of whom were already drunk. We got off our horses and threw ourselves down on the ground too tired to care what they were doing, and by some means a cup of bad chocolate was procured for us. We found that we had entirely lost our way, and it was therefore agreed that, instead of attempting to reach Atlacomulco that night, we should ride to the village of El Puente, where our conductors knew a Spanish family of bachelor brothers who would be glad to *harbour* us for the remainder of the night. We then remounted and set off somewhat refreshed by our rest and by the bad chocolate.

It was late at night when we entered El Puente, after having crossed in pitch darkness a river so deep that the horses were nearly carried off their feet; yet they were dancing in one place, playing cards on the ground in another, dogs were barking as usual, and candles lighted in the Indian huts. We were very well received by the Spaniards, who gave us supper and made us take their room, all the rest of the party sleeping upon mattresses placed on the floor of a large empty apartment.[10]

We slept a few hours very soundly, rose before daylight, wakened the others who, lying on the ground rolled up in their sarapes, seemed to be sleeping for a wager, and remounted our horses, not sorry at the prospect of a day's rest at Atlacomulco. It was dark when we set off, but by the time we reached the hacienda of Señor [Felipe] Neri del Barrio—whose family is amongst the most distinguished of the old Spanish-Mexican stock[11]—the sun had risen and had lighted up the bright green fields of sugar cane and the beautiful coffee plantations that look like flowering myrtles. We stopped to take a tumbler of milk fresh from the cow; declined an invitation to go in, as we were anxious to finish our journey while it was cool; and after a hard ride galloped into the courtyard of Atlacomulco, which seemed like returning home.

We spent a pleasant, idle day, lying down and reading while the sun was high, and in the evening sauntering about under the orange trees. We concluded with a hot bath.

Monday: February 8th, 1841[12]

Before continuing our journey, we determined to spend one more day here—which was fortunate, as we received a large packet of letters from home, forwarded to this place, and we have been reading them stretched under the shade of a natural bower formed by orange boughs, near a clear, cold tank of water in the garden.

Tomorrow we shall set off betimes for the hacienda of Cocoyoc, the property of Don Juan Goríbar, with whom Calderón was acquainted in Mexico. After visiting that and some other of the principal estates, we shall continue our ride to Puebla, and, as we shall pass a few days there, hope to have leisure to write again from that city.

34

Around the Volcanoes

[Tuesday to Monday: February 9th to 15th, 1841]
Atlacomulco to Puebla

On the ninth of February we took leave of Atlacomulco and the
hospitable *administrador,* and—our party being diminished by the absence of Don Pedro who was obliged to go to Mexico—we set off as
usual by starlight, being warned of various *bad bits* on the road, where
the ladies at least were advised to dismount.

The country was wild and pretty, mountainous and stony. When the
light came in we separated and galloped about in all directions. The air
was cool and laden with sweetness. We came, however, to a pretty lane
where those of our escort who were in front stopped, and those who
were behind rode up and begged us to keep close together, as for many
leagues the country was haunted by robbers. Guns and pistols being
looked to, we rode on in serried ranks, expecting every moment to hear
a bullet whiz over our heads.

Here were the most beautiful wild
flowers we have yet seen: some purple,
white, and rose colour in one blossom,
probably the flower called *oceloxochitl,*
or viper's head; others bright scarlet;
others red, with white and yellow
stripes, and with an Indian name, signifying the tiger's flower; some had rose-
coloured blossoms; others were of the
purest white.[1]

We came at last to a road over a
mountain, about as bad as anything we
had yet seen. Our train of horses and
mules, and men in their Mexican
dresses, looked very picturesque winding up and down these steep crags; and

here again, forgetful of robbers, each one wandered according to his own fancy—some riding forward, and others lingering behind to pull branches of these beautiful wild blossoms. The horses' heads were covered with flowers of every colour, so that they looked like victims adorned for sacrifice. Calderón indulged his botanical and geological propensities, occasionally to the great detriment of his companions, as we were anxious to arrive at some resting place before the sun became insupportable.

As for the robbers, these gentlemen—who always keep a sharp lookout and rarely endanger their precious persons without some sufficient motive, and who, moreover, seem to have some magical power of seeing through stone walls and into portmanteaus—were no doubt aware that our luggage would neither have replenished their own nor their *ladies'* wardrobes, and calculated that people who travel for pleasure are not likely to carry any great quantity of superfluous coin. Besides this, they are much more afraid of these honest, stout, well-armed farm servants, who are a fine race of men, than even soldiers.

We arrived about six o'clock at the village of Yautepec, remarkable for its fine old church[2] and lofty trees, especially for one magnificent wide-spreading ash tree in the churchyard. There were also many of those pretty trees with the silvery bark, which always look as if the moon were shining on them.

The road began to improve, but the sun became very oppressive about nine o'clock when we arrived at a pretty village, which had a large church and a *venta* (tavern), where we stopped to refresh ourselves with water and some very well-baked small cakes. The village was so pretty that we had some thoughts of remaining there till the evening, but as Don Juan [the coffee planter] assured us that one hour's good gallop would carry us to Cocoyoc, the hacienda of Don Juan Goríbar, we determined to continue. We had a dreadful ride in the hot sun, till we arrived at a pretty Indian village on the estate, and shortly after entered the courtyard of the great hacienda of Cocoyoc, where we were most hospitably welcomed by the proprietor and his family.[3]

We were very tired owing to the extreme heat, and white with dust. A fresh toilet, cold water, an hour's rest, and an excellent breakfast did wonders for us. Soon after our arrival, the sugarhouse, or rather the cane rubbish, took fire, and the great bell swung heavily to and fro summoning the workmen to assist in getting it under. It was not extinguished for some time, and the building is so near the house that the family were a little alarmed. We stood on the balcony, which commands a beautiful view of Popocatepetl, watching the blaze. After a hard battle between fire and water, water carried the day.[4]

In the evening we drove to the orange grove, where three thousand lofty trees are ranged in avenues, literally bending under the weight of their golden fruit and snowy blossom. I never saw a more beautiful sight. Each tree is perfect, and lofty as a forest tree. The ground under their broad shadows is strewed with thousands of oranges, dropping in their ripeness, and covered with the white, fragrant blossoms. The place is lovely, and everywhere traversed by streams of the purest water. We ate a disgraceful number of oranges, limes, guayabas, and all manner of fruits, and even tasted the sweet beans of the coffee plants.

We spent the next morning in visiting the coffee mills, the great brandy works, sugarhouses, &c., all which are in the highest order; and in strolling through the orange groves, and admiring the curious and beautiful flowers, and walking among orchards of loaded fruit trees— the calabash, papaw, mango, tamarind, citron—also *mameyes, chirimoyos,* custard apples, and all the family of the *zapotes,* white, black, yellow, and *chico; chayotes,* cocoas, *cacahuates,* aguacates, &c., &c., &c., a list without an end.[5]

Besides these are an infinity of trees covered with the brightest blossoms; one, with large scarlet flowers, most gorgeous in their colouring, and one whose blossoms are so like large pink silk tassels that, if hung to the cushions of a sofa, you could not discover them to be flowers. What prodigality of nature in these regions! With what a lavish hand she flings beauty and luxury to her tropical children!

In the evening we drove to Casasano, an hacienda about three leagues from Cocoyoc, and passed by several other fine estates, amongst others, the hacienda of Calderón.[6] Casasano is an immense old house, very dull looking, the road to which lies through a fine park for cattle, dotted with great old trees, but of which the grass is very much burnt up.[7]

Each hacienda has a large chapel attached to it, at which all the workmen and villagers in the environs attend mass, a padre coming from a distance on Sundays and fête days. Frequently there is one attached to the establishment.

We went to see the celebrated water tank of Casasano, the largest and most beautiful reservoir in this part of the country—the water so pure that, though upwards of thirty feet deep, every blade of grass at the bottom is visible. Even a pin, dropped upon the stones below, is seen shining quite distinctly. A stone wall, level with the water, thirty feet high, encloses it, on which I ventured to walk all round the tank—which is of an oval form—with the assistance of our host, going one by one. A fall would be sufficiently awkward, involving drowning on one side and breaking your neck on the other. The water is beautiful—a perfect mirror, with long green feathery plants at the bottom.[8]

The next morning we took leave of our friends at three o'clock, and set off for Santa Clara, the hacienda of Don Eusebio García. Señor Goríbar made me a present of a very good horse, and our ride that day was delightful, though the roads led over the most terrible barrancas. For nine long leagues, we did nothing but ford rivers and climb steep hills, those who were pretty well mounted beating up the tired cavalry.

But, during the first hours of our ride, the air was so fresh among the hills that, even when the sun was high, we suffered little from the heat; and the beautiful and varied views we met at every turn were full of interest.

Santa Clara is a striking, imposing mass of building, beautifully situated at the foot of three bold, high rocks, with a remarkably handsome church attached to it.[9] The family were from home, and the agent was a philosopher, living upon herb tea, quite above the common affairs of life. It is a fine hacienda, and very productive, but sad and solitary in the extreme, and as K[ate] and I walked about in the courtyard after supper, where we had listened to frightful stories of robbers and robberies, we felt rather uncomfortably dreary, and anxious to change our quarters. We visited the sugarworks, which are like all others, the chapel, which is very fine, and the shop where they sell spirituous liquors and calicoes.

The hills looked gray and solemn. The sun sunk, gloomy, behind them, his colour a turbid red. So much had been said about robbers that we were not sure how our next day's journey might terminate. The *administrador's* own servant had turned out to be the captain of a band, whom the robbers, from some mysterious motive, had murdered a few days before!

As we intended to rise before dawn, we went to bed early, about nine o'clock, and were just in the act of extinguishing a melancholy-looking candle, when we were startled by the sight of an *alacrán* on the wall. A man six feet high came at our call. He looked at the scorpion, shook his head, and ran out. He came back in a little while with another large man—he with a great shoe in his hand, and his friend with a long pole. While they were both hesitating how to kill it, Don Juan came in, and did the deed. We had a melancholy night after this, afraid of everything, with a long unsnuffed candle illuminating the darkness of our large and lonely chamber.

The next morning, the twelfth of February, before sunrise, we took our leave in the darkness of Santa Clara and the philosopher.[10] The morning, wonderful to relate, was windy and almost cold. The roads were frightful, and we hailed the first gray streak that appeared in the eastern sky, announcing the dawn, which might enable us at least to see our perils. Fortunately it was bright daylight when we found ourselves crossing a barranca so dangerous that, after following for some time the precipitous course of the mountain path, we thought it advisable to get off our horses, who were pawing the slippery rock without being able to find any rest for the soles of their feet. We had a good deal of difficulty in getting along ourselves on foot among the loose, sharp stones, and the horses, between sliding and stumbling, were a long while in accomplishing the descent. After climbing up the barranca, one of them ran off along the edge of the cliff, as if he were determined to cut the whole concern, and we wasted some time in catching him.

It was the afternoon when we rode through the lanes of a large Indian village, and shortly after arrived at Colón, an hacienda belonging to Don Antonio Orría. He was from home, but the good reception of the honest *administrador*—the nice, clean, cheerful house, with its pretty painted chairs, good beds, the excellent breakfasts and dinners, and the *good will* visible in the whole establishment—delighted us very much, and decided us to pitch our tent here for a day or two. Some Spaniards, hearing of Calderón's arrival, rode over from a distance to see him, and dined with us. There was a capital housekeeper, famous for her excellent cakes and preserves. We had also the refreshment of a warm bath, and felt ourselves as much at home as if we had been in our own house.

The next morning we rode through the great sugar-cane fields to the hacienda of San Nicolás, one of the finest estates in the republic, eighteen leagues long and five wide, belonging to Señor Zamora, in right of his wife. It is a productive place, but a singularly dreary residence. We walked out to see all the works, which are on a great scale, and breakfasted with the proprietor, who was there alone. We amused ourselves by seeing the workmen receive their weekly pay (this being Saturday), and at the mountains of copper piled up on tables in front of the house.[11]

There is a feeling of vastness, of solitude and of dreariness in some of these great haciendas, which is oppressive. Especially about noon, when everything is still, and there is no sound except the incessant buzz of myriads of insects, I can imagine it like what the world must have been before man was created.

Colón, which is not so large as San Nicolás, has a greater air of life about it; and in fact we liked it so well that, as I observed, we seemed inclined to consider it, not as a *colon*, but a *full stop*. You must not expect more vivacious puns in *tierra caliente*.[12]

We rode back from San Nicolás in the afternoon, accompanied by the proprietor, and had some thoughts of going to Matamoros in the evening to see the *Barber of Seville* performed by a strolling company in open air, under a tree!—admittance twenty-five cents.[13] However, we ended by remaining where we were, and spent the evening in walking about through the village—surrounded by barking dogs, the greatest nuisance in these places—and pulling wild flowers—and gathering castor oil nuts from the trees. A begging Franciscan friar, from the convent of San Fernando, arrived for his yearly supply of sugar which he begs from the different haciendas for his convent, a tribute which is never refused.

We left our hospitable entertainer the next morning, with the addition of sundry baskets of cake and fruit from the housekeeper. As we were setting off, I asked the *administrador* if there were any barrancas on this road. "No," said he, "but I have sent a basket full with one of the boys, as they are very refreshing." I made no remark, concluding I should find out his meaning in the course of the journey, but keeping a sharp lookout on the mysterious *mozo* who was added to our train. When the light became stronger, I perceived that he carried under his sarape a large basket of fine *naranjas* (oranges), which no doubt the honest *administrador* thought I was inquiring after.

It rained when we left Colón, a thick misty drizzle, and the difference of the temperature gave us notice that we were passing out of *tierra caliente*. The road was so straight and uninteresting, though the surrounding country was fertile, that a few barrancas would really have been enlivening.

At Colón we took leave of our conductor, Don Juan—who returned to Atlacomulco—and got a new director of our forces, a handsome man—y-clept Don Francisco, who had been a Spanish soldier. We had an uncomfortable ride in a high wind and hard rain, the roads good but devoid of interest, so that we were glad when we learnt that Atlixco, a town where we were to pass the night, was not far off. Within a mile or two of the city we were met by a tall man on horseback, with a pink turban and a wild, swarthy face, who looked like an Abencerrage[14]— and who came with the compliments of his master, a Spanish gentleman, to say that a house had been prepared for us in the town.

Atlixco is a large town, with a high mountain behind it crowned by a white chapel, a magnificent church at the base—the whole city full of fine churches and convents, with a plaza and many good houses. The numerous pipes, pointed all along the roofs, have a very threatening and warlike effect; one seems to ride up the principal street under a strong fire. We found that Don Fernando _____, pink turban's master, not considering his own house good enough, had on hearing of our expected arrival hired another, and furnished part of it for us! This is the sort of wholesale hospitality one meets with in this country. Our room looked out upon an old Carmelite monastery, where Calderón, having a recommendation to the prior, paid a visit and found one or two good paintings. Here also we saw the famous cypress mentioned by Humboldt, which is seventy-three feet in circumference.[15]

The next morning we set out with an escort of seven *mozos*, headed by Don Francisco, and all well armed—for the road from Atlixco to Puebla is the robbers' highway *par excellence*.

This valley of Atlixco, as indeed the whole department of Puebla, is noted for its fertility and its abundant crops of maguey, wheat, maize, *frijoles, garbanzos*, barley, and other vegetables—as well as for the fineness of its fruits, its *chirimoyas*, &c. There is a Spanish proverb, which says:

> *Si a morar en Indias fueres,*
> *Que sea donde los volcanes vieres.*[16]

"If you go to live in the Indias, let it be within sight of the volcanoes"—for it appears that all the lands surrounding the different volcanoes are fertile, and enjoy a pleasant climate. The great Cordilleras of Anáhuac cross this territory, and amongst these are the Mountain of the Malinche, Ixtacihuatl, Popocatepetl, and the Peak of Orizaba.

The Malinche, a corruption by the Spaniards of the Indian name Malintzin, signifying Doña María or Marina, is supposed to be called after Cortés' Indian Egeria, the first Christian woman of the Mexican empire. Though given to Cortés by the Tabascan Indians, it seems clear that she was of noble birth, and that her father was the lord of many cities. It is pretended that she fell into a tributary situation through the treachery of her mother, who remarried after the death of her first husband, and who, bestowing all her affection on the son born of this second marriage, determined in concert with her husband that all their wealth should pass to him. It happened, in furtherance of their views, that the daughter of one of their slaves died, upon which they gave out that they had lost their own daughter. [They] affected to mourn for her and, at the same time, privately sold her, after the fashion of Joseph's brethren, to some merchants of Xicalango, who in their turn disposed of her to their neighbours, the Tabascans, who presented her to Cortés.

That she was beautiful and of great talent, versed in different dialects, the devoted friend of the Spaniards, and serving as their interpreter

in their negotiations with the various Indian tribes, there seems no doubt. She accompanied Cortés in all his expeditions. He followed her advice and, in the whole history of the conquest, Doña Marina (the name given to the beautiful slave at her Christian baptism) played an important part. Her son, Martín Cortés, a knight of the order of Santiago, was put to the torture in the time of Philip II on some unfounded suspicion of rebellion.[17] It is said that when Cortés, accompanied by

Doña Marina, went to Honduras, she met her guilty relatives who, bathed in tears, threw themselves at her feet, fearful lest she might avenge herself of their cruel treatment—but that she calmed their fears, and received them with much kindness. The name of her birthplace was Painala, a village in the province of Coatzacoalcos. After the conquest, she was married to a Spaniard named Juan de Jaramillo.[18]

But I have wandered a long way from the Sierra Malinche. The two great volcanoes, but especially Popocatepetl, the highest mountain in New Spain, seem to follow the traveller like his guardian spirit wherever he goes.[19] Orizaba, which forms a boundary between the departments of Puebla and Veracruz, is said to be the most beautiful of mountains on a near approach—as it is the most magnificent at a distance—for, while its summit is crowned with snow, its central part is girded by thick forests of cedar and pine, and its base is adorned with woods and sloping fields covered with flocks, and dotted with white ranchos and small scattered villages—forming the most agreeable and varied landscape imaginable.

Ixtacihuatl means white woman; Popocatepetl, the mountain that throws out smoke. They are thus celebrated by the poet Heredia:[20]

Eternal snow crowns the majestic heads
Of Orizaba, Popocatepetl,
And of Ixtacihuatl the most pure.
Never does winter with destructive hand
Lay waste the fertile fields where from afar
The Indian views them bathed in purple light
And dyed in gold, reflecting the last rays
Of the bright sun, which, sinking in the west,
Poured forth his flood of golden light, serene
Midst ice eternal, and perennial green;
And saw all nature warming into life,
Moved by the gentle radiance of his fires.

The morning was really cold and, when we first set out, Popocatepetl was rolled up in a mantle of clouds. The road led us very near him. The wind was very piercing, and K[ate] was mounted on a curate's pony, evidently accustomed to short distances and easy travelling. We had been told that it was *"muy proprio para señora* (very much suited to a lady)," an encomium always passed upon the oldest, most stupid, and most obstinate quadruped that the haciendas can boast. We overtook and passed a party of cavalry, guarding some prisoners, whom they were conducting to Puebla.

As the sun rose, all eyes were turned with amazement and admiration to the great volcano. The clouds parted in the middle, and rolled off in great volumes like a curtain withdrawn from a high altar. The snowy top and sides of the mountain appeared, shining in the bright sun, like a grand dome of the purest white marble. But it cannot be described. I thought of Sinai, of Moses on the Mount, when the glory of the Lord was passing by; of the mountain of the Transfiguration, something too intolerably bright and magnificent for mortal eye to look upon and live. We rode slowly, and in speechless wonder, till the sun, which had crowned the mountain like a glory, rose slowly from its radiant brow, and we were reminded that it was time to ride forwards.

We were not far from the ancient city of Cholula, lying on a great plain at a short distance from the mountains, and glittering in the sunbeams, as if it still were the city of predilection as in former days when it was the sacred city, "the Rome of Anáhuac."

It is still a large town, with a spacious square and many churches, and the ruins of its great pyramid still attest its former grandeur; but of the forty thousand houses and four hundred churches mentioned by Cortés, there are no traces. The base of this pyramid, which at a distance looks like a conical mountain, is said by Humboldt to be larger than that of any discovered in the old continent, being double that of Cheops.[21] It is made of layers of bricks mixed with coats of clay and contains four stories. In the midst of the principal platform, where the Indians worshipped Quetzalcoatl, the god of the air (according to some the patriarch

Noah, and according to others the apostle Saint Thomas!—for *doctors differ*), rises a church dedicated to the Virgen de los Remedios, surrounded by cypresses, from which there is one of the most beautiful views in the world. From this pyramid, and it is not the least interesting circumstance connected with it, Humboldt made many of his valuable astronomical observations.

The treachery of the people and priests of Cholula, who, after welcoming Cortés and the Spaniards, formed a plan for exterminating them all —which was discovered by Doña Marina, through the medium of a lady of the city—was visited by him with the most signal vengeance. The slaughter was dreadful; the streets were covered with dead bodies, and houses and temples were burnt to the ground. This great temple was afterwards purified by his orders, and the standard of the cross solemnly planted in the midst.

Cholula, not being on the direct road to Puebla, is little visited, and as for us our time was now so limited that we were obliged to content ourselves with a mere passing observation of the pyramid, and then to hurry forward to Puebla.

We entered that city to the number of eighteen persons, eighteen horses, and several mules—and passed some people near the gates who were carrying blue-eyed angels to the chosen city, and who nearly let them drop in astonishment on seeing such a cavalcade. We were very cold and felt very tired as we rode into the courtyard of the hotel, yet rather chagrined to think that the remainder of our journey was now to be performed in a diligence. Having brought my story up to civilized life, and it being late, I conclude.

35

Four Days in Puebla

[Wednesday: February 17th, 1841]
Puebla

You will be surprised when I tell you that notwithstanding our fatigue we went to the theatre the evening we arrived, and sat through a long and tragical performance, in the box of Don Antonio Haro—one of the richest citizens of Puebla, who, hearing of our arrival, instantly came to invite us to his house, where he assured us rooms were prepared for our reception.[1] But, being no longer in savage parts where it is necessary to throw yourself on the hospitality of strangers or to sleep in the open air, we declined his kind offer and remained at the inn—which is very tolerable, though we do not see it now *en beau* as we did last year, when we were expected there.

The theatre is clean and neat, but dull, and we were much more looked at than the actors, for few foreigners (ladies especially) remain here for any length of time, and their appearance is somewhat of a novelty.[2] Our toilet occasioned us no small difficulty now that we were again in polished cities, for you may imagine the condition of our trunks, which two mules had galloped with over ninety leagues of plain and mountain, and which had been opened every night. Such torn gowns, crushed collars, ruined pelerines! One carpet bag had burst and discharged its contents of combs, brushes, &c. over a barranca, where some day they may be picked up as Indian antiquities and sent to the museum, to be preserved as a proof that Montezuma's wives brushed their hair. However, by dint of a washerwoman and sundry messages to *peluqueros* (hairdressers), we were enabled to *turn out* something like Christian travellers.

The first night we could not sleep on account of the innumerable ants, attracted probably by a small garden, with one or two orange trees in it, into which our room opened.

The next morning we had a great many visitors and, though there is here a good deal of that provincial pretension one always meets with out

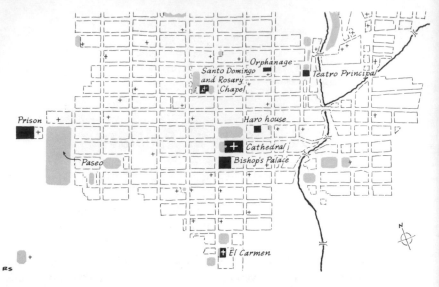

of a capital, we found some pleasant people amongst them. The Señora Haro came in a very handsome carriage, with beautiful northern horses, and took us out to see something of the town. Its extreme cleanness after Mexico is remarkable. In that respect it is the Philadelphia of the republic, with wide streets, well paved; large houses of two stories, very solid and well-built; magnificent churches, plenty of water—and withal a dullness which makes one feel as if the houses were rows of convents, and all the people, except beggars and a few business men, shut up in performance of a vow.

The house of Don Antonio Haro is, I think, more elegantly furnished than any in Mexico. It is of immense size, and the floors beautifully painted.[3] One large room is furnished with pale blue satin, another with crimson damask, and there are fine inlaid tables, handsome mirrors, and everything in very good taste.

He and his wife are both very young—she not more than nineteen, very delicate and pretty, and very fair; and in her dress, neatness, and house she reminds me of a Philadelphian, always with the exception of her diamonds and pearls.[4] The ladies smoke more, or at least more openly, than in Mexico; but they have so few amusements they deserve more indulgence. There are eleven convents of nuns in the city, and taking the veil is as common as being married.

We dined at the Señora Haro's; found her very amiable, and heard a young lady sing who has a good voice, but complains that there are no music masters in Puebla.

The fine arts, however, are not entirely at a standstill here; and in architecture, sculpture, and painting there is a good deal, comparatively speaking, worthy of notice.[5] There used to be a proverb amongst the

Mexicans, that "if all men had five senses, the Poblanos had seven."
They are considered very reserved in their manners—a natural consequence of their having actually no society.

Formerly, Puebla rivalled Mexico in population and in industry. The
plague, which carried off fifty thousand persons, was followed by the
pestilence of civil war, and Puebla dwindled down to a very secondary
city. But we now hear a great deal of their cotton factories, and of the
machines, instruments, and workmen brought from Europe here, already
giving employment to thirty thousand individuals.

In the evening we drove to the new *paseo*, a public promenade where
none of the public were to be seen, and which will be pretty when the
young trees grow.[6]

Friday: February 19th, 1841[7]

Calderón went out early and returned the visit of the celebrated Don
M[iguel] Ramos Arizpe, now an old man and canon of the cathedral,
but formerly deputy in the Spanish Cortes—and the most zealous supporter of the cause of independence. It is said that he owed the great
influence which he had over men of a middling character rather to his
energetic, some say his domineering, disposition than to genius; that
he was clearheaded, active, dexterous, remarkable for discovering hidden
springs and secret motives, and always keeping his subordinates zealously
employed in his affairs.[8]

Calderón also visited the bishop, Señor Vásquez, who obtained from Rome the acknowledgement of independence.[9]

We set out after breakfast with several gentlemen who came to take us to the cotton factories, &c. We went first to visit the factory established at the mill of Santo Domingo, a little way out of the city, and called *La Constancia Mexicana* (Mexican Constancy). It was the first established in the republic, and deserves its name from the great obstacles that were thrown in the way of its construction, and the numerous difficulties that had to be conquered before it came into effect.

In 1831, a junta for the encouragement of public industry was formed, but the obstacles thrown in the way of every proposal were so great that the members all abandoned it in despair, excepting only the Señor Don Esteban Antuñano, who was determined himself to establish a manufactory of cotton, to give up his commercial relations, and to employ his whole fortune in attaining this object.

He bought the mill of Santo Domingo for $178,000, and began to build the edifice, employing foreign workmen at exorbitant prices. In this he spent so much of his capital that he was obliged to have recourse to the Bank of Avío for assistance. This bank (*avío* meaning pecuniary assistance, or advance of funds) was established by Don Lucas Alamán, and intended as an encouragement to industry. But industry is not of the nature of a hothouse plant to be forced by artificial means; and these grants of funds have but created monopolies, and consequently added to the general poverty.

Machinery, to the amount of 3,840 spindles, was ordered for Antuñano from the United States, and a loan granted him of $178,000, but of which he never received the whole. Meanwhile his project was sneered at as absurd, impossible, ruinous; but—firmly resolved not to abandon his enterprise—he contented himself with living with the strictest economy, himself and his numerous family almost suffering from want, and frequently unable to obtain credit for the provisions necessary for their daily use.

To hasten the arrival of the machinery, he sent an agent to the north to superintend it, and to hire workmen; but the commercial house to which he was recommended, and which at first gave him the sums he required, lost their confidence in the agent, and redemanded their money, so that he was forced to sell his clothes in order to obtain food and lodging. In July, 1833, the machinery was embarked at Philadelphia, and in August arrived at Veracruz, to the care of Señor Paso y Troncoso, who never abandoned Antuñano in his adversity and even lent him unlimited sums; but much delay ensued, and a year elapsed before it reached Puebla. There, after it was all set up, the ignorant foreign workmen declared that no good results would ever be obtained; that the machines were bad, and the cotton worse. However, by the month of January, 1835,[10] they began to work in the factory, to which was given the name of Mexican Constancy. A mechanist was then sent to the north to procure a collection of new machinery; and, after extraordinary delays and difficulties, he embarked with it at New York in February, 1837.

He was shipwrecked near Cayo Hueso, and, with all the machinery he could save, returned to the north in the brig *Argos;* but on his way there he was shipwrecked again, and all the machinery lost! He went to Philadelphia to have new machines constructed, and in August re-embarked in the *Delaware*. Incredible as it may seem, the *Delaware* was wrecked off Cayo Alcatraces, and for the third time the machinery was lost, the mechanist saving himself with great difficulty![11]

It seemed as if gods and men had conspired against the cotton spindles; yet Antuñano persevered. Fresh machinery was ordered; and though by another fatality it was detained, owing to the blockade of the ports by the French squadron, seven thousand spindles were landed, and speedily put in operation.

Others have followed the example of Señor Antuñano, who has given a decided impulse to industry in Puebla, besides a most extraordinary example of perseverance, and a determined struggle against what men call *bad luck*, which persons of a feeble character sink under, while stronger minds oppose till they conquer it.

It was in his carriage we went, and he accompanied us all over the building. It is beautifully situated, and at a distance has more the air of a summer palace than of a cotton factory. Its order and airiness are delightful, and in the middle of the court, in front of the building, is a large fountain of the purest water. A Scotchman, who has been there for some time, says he has never seen anything to compare with it, and he worked six years in the United States.

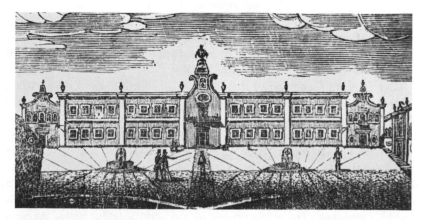

Antuñano is unfortunately very deaf, and obliged to use an ear trumpet. He seems an excellent man, and I trust he may be ultimately successful.[12] We came out covered with cotton, as if we had been just unpacked, and were next taken to visit a very handsome new prison, which they are building in the city, but whether it will ever be finished, or not, is more doubtful. We also visited the Foundling Hospital, a large building, where there are more children than funds. They were all clean and respectable looking, but very poor. Antuñano presented them with two hundred dollars, as a memorial, he said, of our visit.[13]

Calderón then went to the convent of El Carmen to see the paintings of the Life of the Virgin, supposed to be original works of Murillo, particularly the Ascension and Circumcision, but which are ill-arranged and have suffered greatly from neglect, many of them being torn. Indeed, in some of them are large holes made by the boys, who insisted that the Jewish priest was *the devil*. There is a Descent from the Cross, which is reckoned a fine painting; and it is a pity that these works should be shut up in this old convent, where there are about half a dozen old monks, and where they serve no purpose, useful or ornamental.[14] Were they removed to the Mexican museum, and arranged with care, they would at least serve as models for those young artists who have not the means of forming their taste by European travel. Zendejas as a painter and Cora as a sculptor, both natives of Puebla, are celebrated in their respective arts, but we have not yet seen any of their works.[15]

Calderón also visited the bishop and saw his paintings and library (which we hope to do tomorrow), and from thence went to the college, the rector of which was attaché in Spain to the minister Santa María.[16]

We dined again in the house of Señor H[ar]o. The manner in which his floors are painted is pretty and curious. It is in imitation of carpets, and is very rich in appearance and very cool in reality. A great many of the floors here are painted in this way, either upon canvas with oil colours or upon a cement, extended upon the bricks of which the floor is made, and prepared with glue, lime, or clay, and soap.

Señor H[ar]o has four young and pretty sisters, all nuns in different convents. As there are no other schools but these convents, the young girls who are sent there become attached to the nuns, and prefer remaining with them forever to returning home.

After dinner, accompanied by Don M[iguel] Ramos Arizpe, whom Calderón formerly knew intimately in Madrid,[17] and by various other ecclesiastics, we visited the boast of Puebla, the cathedral—which we did not do when we passed through the city on our arrival last year. To my mind, I have never seen anything more noble and magnificent. It is said that the rapid progress of the building was owing to the assistance of two angels, who nightly descended and added to its height, so that each morning the astonished workmen found their labour incredibly advanced. The name given to the city, Puebla de los Angeles, is said to be owing to this tradition.

It is not so large as the cathedral of Mexico, but it is more elegant, simpler, and in better taste.[18] Sixteen columns of exquisite marble, adorned with silver and gold, form the tabernacle (in Mexico called *el ciprés*). This native marble, called Puebla marble, is brought from the quarries of Totimehuacán and Tecali, at two and seven leagues from the city. The floor of the cathedral is of marble—the great screens and high-backed chairs of richly carved cedar. Everything was opened to show us: the tombs where the bishops are buried; the vault where a martyr lies, supposed to have been miraculously preserved for centuries, the gift of a pope to a bishop of Puebla. The figure appears to be of wax, enclosing the skeleton of the martyr, and has the most angelic countenance I ever beheld. It is loaded with false emeralds and diamonds.

We were also shown the jewels, which they keep buried, in case of a revolution. The *custodia*, the gold stand in which they carry the Host, is entirely encrusted with large diamonds, pearls, emeralds, amethysts, topazes, and rubies. The chalices are equally rich. There are four sets of jewels for the bishop. One of his crosses is of emeralds and diamonds, another of topazes and diamonds—with great rings of the same belonging to each.

In the evening we went with the M_____ family, who have been very civil to us, to the theatre where we saw a comedy better acted and more amusing than the tragedy which they murdered two nights before.[19]

We went early the next morning to the bishop's palace, to see his fine library and collection of paintings, where there were a few modern originals and many fine copies of the old masters.[20]

We then went with the Señora H[ar]o to return the visits of the ladies who had called on us. The young ladies invariably complain that they have neither music, nor drawing, nor dancing masters. There is evidently a great deal of musical taste among them, and—as in every part of Mexico, town or country—there is a piano (*tal cual*) in every house; but most of those who play are self-taught, and naturally abandon it very soon for want of instruction or encouragement.

We are now going to dine out, and in the evening we go to a concert in the theatre, given by the Señora Cesari and Mr. Wallace.[21] As we must rise at three, to set off by the diligence, I shall write no more from this place. Our next letters will be from Mexico.

36

Tales of Robbery and Murder

Saturday: February 20th, 1841
San Fernando, Mexico

We went to the concert with our friends the H[ar]os.[1] The music
was better than the instruments, and the Señora Cesari looked handsome, as she always does, besides being beautifully dressed in white with
Paris wreaths.

We took leave of our friends at the door of the hotel at one in the
morning, and lay down for two hours—in the full expectation of being
robbed the following day, a circumstance which has now grown so common that when the diligence from Puebla arrives in safety it excites
rather more sensation than when it has been stopped. The governor[2]
had ordered us an escort to Mexico, to be stationed about every six
leagues, but last week the escort itself—and even the gallant officer at
its head—were suspected of being the plunderers. Our chief hope lay in
that well-known miraculous knowledge which they possess as to the value
of all travellers' luggage, which no doubt not only makes them aware
that we are mere pilgrims for pleasure and not fresh arrivals laden with
European commodities, but also renders them perfectly familiar with the
contents of our well-shaken portmanteaus; so that we trusted that a
sarape or two, a few rings and earrings, and one or two shawls would
not prove sufficient to tempt them.

We got into the diligence in the dark, half asleep, having taken all
the places but three which were engaged before we came—some sleepy
soldiers on horseback, ready to accompany us, and a loaded gun sticking
out of each window. Various beggars, who are here innumerable, already surrounded us. It is, by the way, a remarkable circumstance that,
notwithstanding the amazing numbers of the *léperos* in Puebla, the
churches there are kept scrupulously clean, from which Mexico might
take a hint with advantage.

Puebla is one of the few cities founded by the Spanish colonists, instead of being built upon the ruins of former greatness. It was founded

in the sixteenth century, on the plains of Acajete, in a site occupied only by a few huts belonging to the Cholula Indians. It is surrounded by productive corn estates, and the landscape, when the light visited our eyes, was fertile though flat.

The two finest views of Puebla may be seen from the towers of the cathedral and from an *azotea* in the street of San Agustín. The land-scape is extremely varied and very éxtensive.

To the north we see the mountain of Tlaxcala—the Matlalcueyetl, better known as the Malinche—next it the hill and temple of Guadalupe and the mountain of the Pinar, crowned by its white church. Other churches and convents adorn the slopes of the mountains—the church of Loreto, the Temple of Calvary, &c. The Malinche is fertile, but these inferior mountains are sterile and bare.[3]

To the west lie the great volcanoes, and between them we can dis-tinguish the difficult and steep road by which Cortés undertook his first march to Mexico. We also see the city and pyramid of Cholula, the hill of San Nicolás, and that of San Juan, where General Bustamante encamped in 1832 when he went out against Santa Anna; near it the farmhouses of Posadas and Zavaleta, the one celebrated by a battle, the other by a treaty.[4]

To the east, but at a greater distance than the other mountains, rises the Peak of Orizaba—the Star Mountain—the side now seen, that which rises over the tableland of Mexico. Its other side descends rapidly to the burning plains of Veracruz, and is the first distinguishable land dis-cerned by those who approach these coasts. Even at this distance, its snowy summit is seen contrasting with its fertile woods and pleasant villages. It has what mortals rarely possess united, a warm heart with a clear, cold head.

We were awakened at a *posada* by their bringing us some hot coffee. A man with a white nightcap on having poked his head in at the win-dow, in defiance of a loaded musket, I concluded he was a *lépero* and sleepily told him I had nothing for him, in the phrase of the country to importunate beggars: *"Perdone usted, por Dios!* (Excuse me, for God's sake!)" But he proved to be a gentleman who merely came to put himself and his property at our disposal, at that early hour of the morning.

When we entered the Black Forest, and passed through the dark pine woods, then the stories of robbers began—just as people at sea seem to take a particular pleasure in talking of shipwrecks. Every cross had its tale of murder; and, by the way, it seems to me that a work written with *connaissance de cause,* and entitled *History of the Crosses*—though it might not equal the *History of the Crusades*—would be quite as in-teresting and much more romantic than the *Newgate Calendar.*[5] The difficulty would consist in procuring authentic information concerning them. There were a lady and two gentlemen in the diligence, and the lady seemed to be very much *au fait* as to their purport and history. Under one her own servant was buried, and she gave rather a graphic account of his murder. He was sitting outside, on the top of the diligence. The party within were numerous but unarmed. Suddenly a number of robbers with masks on came shouting down upon them from amongst the pine trees. They first took aim at the poor *mozo*, and shot him through the heart. He fell, calling in piteous tones to a padre who was in the coach, entreating him to stop and confess him, and groaning out a farewell to his friend the driver. Mortal fear prevailed over charity both in priest and layman, and the coachman, whipping up his horses, passed at full gallop over the body of the murdered man, so that, the robbers being on foot, the remainder of the party escaped.

Whilst we were listening to tales of blood and murder, our escort took leave of us, supposing that we should meet another immediately, whereas we found that we had arrived at the most dangerous part of the road and that no soldiers were in sight. We certainly made up our minds to an attack this time, and got ready our rings and watches—not to hide, but to give—for we womenkind were clearly of opinion that, in case of an attack, it was much better to attempt no defense, our party having only two guns amongst them.

There was a diligence some way behind us, full of people, and belonging to another line—driven by a Yankee coachman so drunk that he kept his seat with difficulty. In defiance of all remonstrances, [he] persisted in driving the coach at a gallop close by the brink of the great precipice along which the road wound, so that the poor passengers were exposed to a double danger.

Suddenly our escort appeared at the top of the hill, and the officer, riding up, excused himself to Calderón for the delay, which had arisen from their having been engaged in a skirmish with the robbers in that very place. Two he said were taken, and he had marched them off to Puebla—where they will probably be let off in a few days, after a form of trial. Four had escaped and had hid themselves amongst the trees and rocks, but could not, according to his calculations, be very far off. However, we were quite reassured by the arrival of the soldiers, and the sight of Río Frío was very reviving. We got a very tolerable dinner from the Bordelaise in the forest valley; and, although the next part of the road is reckoned very insecure, we had no longer any apprehension, as, besides having an escort, the fact that some of the robbers had been taken a few hours before made it very unlikely that they would renew their attempts that day.

This pestilence of robbers, which infests the republic, has never been eradicated. They are in fact the growth of civil war. Sometimes in the guise of insurgents, taking an active part in the independence, they have independently laid waste the country and robbed all whom they met. As expellers of the Spaniards, these armed bands infested the roads between Veracruz and the capital, ruined all commerce, and—without any particular inquiry into political opinions—robbed and murdered in all directions.

In 1824 a law was proposed in congress which should subject all armed bands of robbers to military judges, in order to shorten proceedings—for many of those who had been apprehended and thrown into prison found some opportunity to escape while their trial was pending, and many had been imprisoned four or five times for the same offense yet never brought to justice. In this law were included both robbers by profession and those bodies of insurgents who were merely extempore amateurs.

But whatever measures have been taken at different times to eradicate this evil its causes remain, and the idle and unprincipled will always take advantage of the disorganized state of the country to obtain by force what they might gain by honest labour. Count Cortina says gravely that he cannot imagine why we complain of Mexican robbers, when the city of London is full of organized gangs of ruffians whom the laws cannot reach, and when English highwaymen and housebreakers are the most celebrated in the world. Moreover, that Mexican robbers are never unnecessarily cruel, and in fact are very easily moved to compassion. This last assertion may occasionally hold good, but their cruelties to travellers are too well known to bear him out in it as a general remark.[6]

As a proof of their occasional moderation, I may mention that the ladies of the F[agoag]a family,[7] at the time of their emigration, were travelling from Mexico with a padre when they were met by a party of robbers or insurgents who stopped the coach, and commenced pillaging. Amongst other articles of value they seized a number of silver dishes.

The padre observed to them that as this plate did not belong to the ladies, but was lent them by a friend, they would be obliged to replace it, and requested that one might be left as a pattern. The reasonable creatures instantly returned a dish and a cover!

Another time, having completely stripped an English gentleman and his servant and tied them both to a tree, observing that the man appeared particularly distressed at the loss of his master's spurs, they politely returned and laid the spurs beside the gentleman.

About four o'clock, though nearly blinded with dust, we once more looked down upon the valley of Mexico—and at five, during our last change of horses, we were met by Don Manuel del Campo and the English courier Beraza, who had rode out to meet us and accompanied us on their fine horses as far as the *garita*.[8] Here we found our carriage waiting, [and we] got in and drove through Mexico, dusty as we were, and warlike as we seemed, with guns at the windows. In the Calle San Francisco, the carriage was stopped by Mr. Ward, secretary to the English legation, who invited us to a grand masked and fancy carnival ball to be given on Monday, it being now Saturday. On our return home we found everything in good order. Had some difficulty in procuring ball dresses in time.[9]

[Monday: February 22nd, 1841]

On Sunday we had a number of people to dinner, by chance—it being Spanish fashion to dine at a friend's house without invitation. This evening we go to the ball.

The ball was in the theatre, and very brilliant, but too many of the first people on these occasions keep their boxes, and do not dance—yet it was wonderfully select for so large an assembly.

When we arrived, we were led upstairs by some of the commissioners, those who had charge of the ball, to the E[scandón]s' box, whom we found, as usual, elegantly dressed—the married ladies of the family with diamonds, the younger ones in white crape and gold. I had a black silk mask, but finding myself universally recognized saw no particular advantage in keeping it on, and promptly discarded it. We took a few turns in the ballroom, and afterwards returned to the box.

There were some capital figures in masks, and some beautiful ball dresses, and, though there were a number of dominoes and odd figures, I could not help remarking the great improvement in toilet which had taken place since the fancy ball of last year. One or two girls, especially the Señorita Marran, wore ball dresses which could only have proceeded from the fingers of a Parisian modiste. Madame de _____, dressed as a peasant, and with a mask, was known everywhere by her small foot and pretty figure. But it is impossible to look on at a ball very long, not mingling with it, without growing tired; and not even the numerous visitors to our box could prevent us from feeling much more sleepy than during many a moonlight ride through the lovely lanes of *tierra caliente*.

Next night there was a public masked ball, but we did not attend it. We feel much the better for our journey, and only hope that some day Calderón may have leisure sufficient to enable us to take another ride through some other part of the country.

This being near Lent,[10] we shall have no *soirées* for six weeks, though balls are occasionally given during that time of fasting. The house has become very comfortable in the way of servants: our housekeeper, a treasure; the coachman and footman, excellent; the cook, tolerable; the soldiers, rarely tipsy more than once a week and generally only one at a time; the others, decent—so that we have nothing to complain of.

Kate has established a henhouse near the stable, and any old Indian woman who brings her a *manojo* (several hens tied together) is sure to be received with open arms.

One of our first visits on our return was to Tacubaya, where we were sorry to find the Countess Cortina very much indisposed, and her court-yard filled with carriages, containing visitors making inquiries.

I shall now send off my letters by the packet, that you may see we are safely re-established in Mexico.

37

Distinguished Men of Mexico

Saturday: February 27th, 1841
San Fernando, Mexico

H_____ in his last letter asks what distinguished men we have in Mexico—and with a tone of doubt as to their being very numerous.[1] Distinguished in what way? As generals, as statesmen, as men of literature? It seems to me that a country where we have known Bustamante, Santa Anna, General Victoria, Posada, Gómez Pedraza, Gutiérrez Estrada, Count Cortina, Gorostiza, Don Carlos Bustamante, Quintana Roo, General Morán, Don Lucas Alamán, General Almonte, Señor Cañedo, Don Francisco Tagle, Señor [Felipe] Neri del Barrio, Señor Fagoaga, Don [Miguel] Valentín, the Count de Casa Flores, &c., &c., is not so destitute of distinguished men as he supposes.[2]

The preceding are, I confess, strung together as they occur to me, without order or regularity: soldiers, statesmen, and literary men—some on one side of politics, some on another—but all men of note, and men who have acted, or suffered, or been distinguished in one way or another in the revolutions of the last thirty-two years. And there is not one amongst those I have mentioned who, if he were to write merely his personal history, would not by so doing write the history of these civil wars.

The three first, as principal figures in every revolution, are already historical: Bustamante as an honest man and a brave soldier; Santa Anna as an acute general, active and aspiring, whose name has a *prestige* (whether for good or for evil) that no other possesses; General Victoria, a plain, uneducated, well-intentioned man, brave and enduring.[3]

A passage in [Victoria's] life is well known, which ought to be mentioned as an *offset* to the doubtful anecdote of the two-headed eagle. When Iturbide, alone, fallen and a prisoner, was banished from Mexico —and when General Bravo, who had the charge of conducting him to Veracruz, treated him with every species of indignity—Victoria, the sworn foe of the Emperor during his prosperity, now (when orders were given

50] *Above*, Church of the convent of Corpus Christi (facing the Alameda).

51] *At right*, The great doorway of the Cortina House.

52, 53] *Below and bottom*, The principal court of the national palace: In peace and in revolution.

[54] *Top,* The gate of San Lázaro (July 20, 1840). [55] *Center,* Revolution
damage: "Desolation, weeping, and death" (July 29, 1840). [56] *Above l[eft]*
"The mantillas are white or black. The petticoats . . . rather short, but it would
hard to hide such small feet . . ." [57] *Above right,* "The handsome Poblana pe[

[58] For the *paseo*.

[59] For the country.

[60] For a *tertulia*.

[61] "Pantaloons with . . . silver buttons."

[62] *Above*, "Riding . . . on the same horse, their usual mode."
[63] *At right*, Outriders and coachman.

[64] *At left*, "We have dered *mangas* . . . They warm and convenient for ing in the country."

At right, President Anastasio
[Bu]stamante.

Below left, Juan de Dios Ca-
[ñedo,] Minister of Foreign Rela-
[tions.]

Below right, Juan Nepomu-
[ceno] Almonte, Minister of War.

Bottom left, Francisco Javier
[Ech]everría, Minister of the Trea-
[sury.]

Bottom right, Luis Gonzaga
[Cuev]as, Minister of Interior Affairs.

[71] General Mariano Po

[70] General Antonio López de Santa Anna.

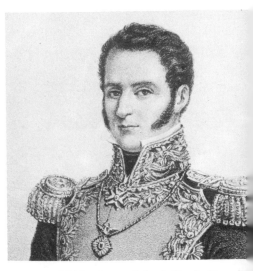

[72] General Gabriel Valencia.

[73] General José María Tornel.

4] José Gómez de la Cortina.

[75] Francisco Manuel Sánchez de Tagle.

Richard Pakenham, British Minister.

[77] Manuel Eduardo Gorostiza.

[78] José María Gutiérrez Estrada.

[79] General José María Morán.

[80] Manuel Posada, Archbishop of Mexico.

[81] Carlos María de Bustamante.

[82] *Top left*, Andrés Quintana Roo.
[83] *Top right*, Francisco Fagoaga.

[84] Miguel Ramos Arizpe.

[85] "Having got riding horses, we have been making excursions all

[86] *At left,* The Viga canal: "Constantly covered with Indians in their canoes, bringing in fruit and flowers and vegetables."
[87] *Below,* The woods of Chapultepec: "Already old when Montezuma was a boy."

[88] *Above,* Tacubaya: View from the summer palace of the archbishops.
[89] *At right,* Guadalupe and the hill of Tepeyac.

[90] *At left,* The Chapel of the Well at Guadalupe.
[91] *Below,* San Agustín de las Cuevas: The ball on the hill of El Calvario.

Above, Gambling at *monte:* "e was neither fighting, nor "ing, nor high words."

At right, ". . . The cocks "d valiantly, bets were ad- ", and even the ladies en- into the spirit of the scene

[94] *Left,* The great gate at the hacienda of Santiago. [95] *Right,* Country bull rin

[96] "The famous arches of Zempoala, a magnificent work."

[97] "Lonely . . . haciendas situated on these great p

him to see Iturbide embarked) surrounded him with attentions and loaded him with respectful distinctions; so that Iturbide himself, moved with gratitude, after expressing his warm esteem for the general's consistent conduct, presented him with his watch as a memorial of his grateful admiration.[4]

As for Don Manuel Gómez Pedraza, he has occupied too distinguished a place in the political occurrences of this country not to be generally known. An officer in the time of the Spanish government, he was distinguished for his severe discipline and strict moral conduct. In the time of Iturbide he was military commandant of Huasteca, and supported the Emperor, who afterwards made him commander-general of Mexico. In 1827 he was Minister of War during the presidency of Victoria, and was distinguished for his extraordinary activity, which quality was greatly wanting in that general. In 1828 he and Guerrero were announced as candidates for the presidency, and after a terrible political tempest Gómez Pedraza was elected. The fermentation that succeeded [and] the fury of the two parties (the *Guerreristas* and *Pedrazistas,* which were mingled with *Iturbidistas*) was increased by the arrival of Santa Anna at Perote with eight hundred men. Having shut himself up in the fortress, [Santa Anna] declared for Guerrero, and published a manifesto which set forth that general as a hero—and his rival as a hypocrite. Then came the famous revolution of the Acordada, and both [Gómez] Pedraza and Guerrero disappeared. [Gómez] Pedraza left the republic, and after another revolution, hearing that "the constitution and laws were re-established," returned to Veracruz—but was met by an order which prohibited him from disembarking. He then set sail for New Orleans. Another change brought him back; and at this present juncture he lives in tranquillity—together with his lady, a person of extraordinary talent and

learning, daughter of the *licenciado* (jurisconsult) Señor Azcárate. Such are the disturbed lives passed by the "children of the soil."[5]

Of Gutiérrez Estrada, now far from his household gods and languishing under unjust persecution, I have already spoken.

Count Cortina is a gentleman and a scholar, a man of vast information, and a protector of the fine arts. His conversation is a series of electric sparks, brilliant as an *ignis fatuus*, and bewildering as a will-o'-the-wisp. I have seldom heard such eloquence, even in trifles; and he writes with as much ease as he speaks. We have seen three clever pieces of his lately, showing his versatile genius: one upon earthquakes, one upon the *devil*, and one upon the holy fathers of the church! The first [is] in the form of a pamphlet, addressed to a lady, giving a scientific explanation of the causes of these phenomena, interspersed with compliments to her *beaux yeux;*[6] the second is a burlesque poem; and the third, a grave and learned dissertation.

Don [Manuel] Eduardo Gorostiza, though a native of Veracruz, is the son of a Spanish officer, and when very young went to Spain, where he was known politically as a liberal. He was distinguished as a writer of theatrical pieces, which have been and still are very popular; and those which he merely translated he had the merit of adapting to the Spanish stage, and *Castilianizing* in grace and wit. One of his pieces, which we saw the other evening at the theatre—*Contigo, Pan y Cebolla* (With Thee, Bread and Onions)—is delightful.[7] Besides occupying a place in the cabinet of Mexico, he has been chargé d'affaires in Holland, and minister at the Court of St. James. In conversation he is extremely witty and agreeable, and he has collected some good paintings and valuable books in the course of his European travels.[8]

The reputation of Don Carlos Bustamante, deputy from Oaxaca, is altogether literary. He has made many researches in Mexican antiquities; and has published a *History of the Discovery of America*, written by Padre Vega, which was unknown before; also the *Gallery of Mexican Princes; Tezcoco in the Last Days of Its Last Kings;* &c.[9] He lately sent me his *Mornings in the Alameda*, a book intended to teach Mexican young ladies the history of their own country. I have read but a few pages of it, but was struck with the liberality of his remarks in regard to the Spaniards, which—coming from such a source—are so much more valuable and worthy of credit than any that can be made by a foreigner, that I am tempted to translate the passage to which I allude:[10]

The Spanish government founded colleges and academies in the reign of the wise Charles III; it established that of Fine Arts, which it enriched with the most beautiful statues, which you can still see when you visit it. ("Their transportation," he says in a note, "cost seventy thousand dollars.") He sent excellent workmen, and imitated his predecessor Philip II, who sent to Mexico whatever could not find a place in the works of the Escorial. Of his wisdom, we have proofs in those magnificent temples which attract the attention of travellers, such as the cathedral of Mexico, San Agustín, Santo Domingo of Oaxaca, and others.

Spain did no more, because she could do no more. And Spain gave to this America a constitution which these Mexicans themselves who pride themselves most on their learning are unacquainted with —an analysis of which was made by the learned Padre Mier in the *History of the Revolution*, which he printed in London—a constitution in which are made manifest the good intentions of the Austrian monarchs, and their earnest desire to render the Indians happy— especially true in the case of the great Philip IV, whose autograph law is preserved, which I have read with respect and tears,[11] prohibiting the bad treatment of the Indians.

In short, this America, if it were considered in a state of slavery under the Spanish dominion, was at least on a level with the Peninsula itself. Read over the frightful list of taxes which oppressed the Spaniards, and compare it with those that were imposed upon us, and you will find that theirs is infinitely greater than ours.

These truths being granted, remark the progress which the colonies had made in sciences and arts—and this truth, which escaped from the agreeable pen of the canon Beristáin,[12] will be found confirmed: Mexico (he says) was the sunflower of Spain. When in Spain's principal universities there were no learned men to fill the mathematical chairs, Mexico could boast of Don Carlos de Sigüenza y Góngora; when in Madrid there was no one who had written a good epic poem, in Mexico the *Bernardo* was composed—&c., &c.[13]

The next on my list is Don Andrés Quintana Roo, the best modern poet of Mexico, a native of Yucatán—and who came to the capital when very young, to study law. He is said to possess immense learning, and was enthusiastic to fanaticism in the cause of independence—insomuch that he and his wife Doña Leona Vicario, who shared in his ardent love of liberty, braved every danger in its cause, suffered imprisonment, escaped from the Inquisition, from the hands of robbers, endured every privation, so that their history would form a romance. He is now devoted to literature and, though he occasionally launches forth some political pamphlet, he is probably wearied of revolutions. [He] possesses all the calmness of a man whose first years have been spent in excitement and troubles, and who at length finds consolation in study alone—the well of science proving to him the waters of Lethe, in which he drinks the oblivion of all his past sorrows.[14] And it is very much the case, in Mexico at present, that the most distinguished men are those who live most retired—those who have played their part on the arena of public life, have seen the inutility of their efforts in favour of their country, and have now retreated into the bosom of their families, where they endeavour to forget public evils in domestic retirement and literary occupation.

Amongst these may be reckoned Don Lucas Alamán, who passed many years in Europe, and in 1820 was deputy to the Spanish Cortes. Shortly after his return, he became Minister of Foreign Relations, which high office he has filled during various seasons of difficulty. He is a man of learning, and has always been a protector of art and science. In

conversation he is more reserved, less brilliant, and more minute than Count Cortina—always expressing his opinion with caution, but very ready and able to give information on anything in this country unconnected with politics.[15]

General Morán, now infirm, and long since retired from public service, is universally respected both as a military man and a gentleman. He is married to a daughter of the late Marquis de Vivanco, general of division who long held out against the independence, and, when the colonial system was dissolved, would never go further than to desire a prince of royal birth in Mexico. General Morán has been exiled several times, and his health has not held out against bodily and mental suffering—but he is ending his days in a tranquil retirement in the midst of his family.[16]

Of General Almonte[17] and of Señor Cañedo,[18] who are figuring in public life in our own day, I have frequently written.

Señor [Felipe] Neri del Barrio and the Count de Casa Flores, married to sisters—ladies of high birth, the eldest a countess in her own right —are, as well as their families, all that is most distinguished in Mexico.[19]

Señor Fagoaga, who is now in bad health, I know only by reputation. He is [younger] brother of the Marquis of Apartado, and of the cele brated Don José María Fagoaga, with whose family we have the pleasure of being very intimate.[20] Calderón says that he is a man of great taste and a thorough gentleman, and that his house, which is one of the handsomest in Mexico, possesses that ornament so rare in this country—well-chosen paintings.[21]

Don José [Miguel] Valentín, who has figured in the political world, and who was curate of Huamantla, is one of the kindest and best old men I have ever met with: so severe to himself, so indulgent to others—so simple in worldly matters, so learned in everything else—so sincere, good, and charitable. He is a universal favourite with young and old, being cheerful [and] fond of music and of gay conversation—in proportion as he is wise and learned in his observations, and serious in his conversation when the occasion requires it. Doctor Valentín as an ecclesiastic, and Padre Lyón as a monk, are models.[22]

As for Don Francisco [Sánchez de] Tagle, he is a gentleman of the old school, and his name figures in all the political events which have taken place since the independence, of which he was one of the signers. He is very rich, possessing—besides a profitable maguey estate near Mexico—enormous property bounding Texas, and being also the keeper of the Monte Pío, formerly the house of Cortés, a palace, in which he and his family live. He is a man of great learning and information, and too distinguished not to have suffered personally in political convulsions. Whether he would choose the same path, with his present experience of a Mexican republic, he is too wise to mention. He and his family are amongst our most intimate friends, and with a few exceptions all those whom I have mentioned have been here since our return, which is one of the reasons why their names occurred first to my memory—for there are still many distinguished persons remaining.[23]

Nearly all these, at least all who are married, have had the good fortune to unite themselves with women who are either their equals or superiors—if not in education, [then] in goodness, elevation of sentiment, and natural talent. They, as well as every Mexican, whether man or woman, not under forty, have lived under the Spanish government. [They] have seen the revolution of Dolores of 1810, with continuations and variations by Morelos, and paralyzation in 1819; the revolution of Iturbide in 1821; the Cry of Liberty (*Grito de Libertad*) given by those generals, "*beneméritos de la patria*," Santa Anna and Victoria in 1822; the establishment of the federal system in 1824; the horrible revolution of the Acordada, in which Mexico was pillaged, in 1828; the adoption of the central system in 1836; and the last revolution of the federalists in 1840. Another is predicted for next month, as if it were an eclipse of the sun.

In nineteen years, three forms of government have been tried, and two constitutions, the reform of one of which is still pending in the chambers. *"Dere is notink like trying!"* (as the old *perruquier* observed when he set out in a little boat to catch the royal yacht, still in sight of Scottish shores, with a new wig of his own invention—which he had trusted to have been permitted to present to his most gracious majesty George IV!)

THE END OF
CALDERON'S MISSION

38

News from Spain

Tuesday: March 30th, 1841
Hacienda of Goicoechea, San Angel

It is a long while since I last wrote, but this week has been employed in moving into the country and making arrangements for the sale of our furniture, in consequence of our having received official news from Spain of the nomination of a new envoy extraordinary and minister plenipotentiary to the republic of Mexico. As, on account of the yellow fever at Veracruz, we shall not wish to pass through that city later than May, it is necessary to be in readiness to start when the new minister arrives.[1]

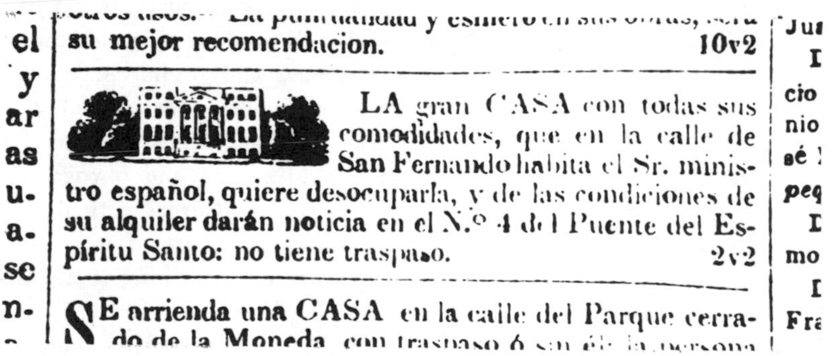

el
y
ar
as
u-
a-
se
n-

su mejor recomendacion.   10v2

LA gran CASA con todas sus comodidades, que en la calle de San Fernando habita el Sr. ministro español, quiere desocuparla, y de las condiciones de su alquiler darán noticia en el N.° 4 del Puente del Espíritu Santo: no tiene traspaso.   2v2

SE arrienda una CASA en la calle del Parque cerrado de la Moneda, con traspaso ó sin él: la persona

Jui
I
cio
nio
sé !
peq
I
mo
I
Frá

On Thursday last we came out to this place, within three leagues of Mexico, where Don Francisco Tagle has kindly lent us his unoccupied country house. As we had an infinity of arrangements to make, much to bring out, and much to leave, and *all Mexico* to see, you will excuse this long silence. Our house in town we leave to the guardianship of the housekeeper; the other servants follow us here.

This house is very large, and has a fine garden and orchard full of fruit, with pretty walks all through it, and a sort of underwood of roses and sweet peas. It is a great pulque hacienda and—besides what is sent into Mexico for sale—the court is constantly filled with the half-naked Indians from the village who come to have their *jarros* filled with that inspiring beverage. Then there is Doña Bárbara (the guardian of the pulque), a Spanish *administrador,* a number of good-looking Indian women, and babies *à discrétion.* There is a small chapel, a piazza with handsome pillars going all round the interior courtyard of the house, a billiard table, and plenty of good rooms. In front of the house are the maguey fields, and the *azotea* commands a beautiful view of the neighbouring villages—San Angel, Coyoacán, Mixcoac, &c.—with their woods and gardens, as well as of the city itself with [the distant] lakes and volcanoes.[2]

As Calderón's affairs take him to Mexico nearly every day, we feel a little lonely in this large house, even though perfectly comfortable; and, besides the extreme stillness and solitude, it is not considered safe for us to walk out alone. Consequently the orchard must bound our wishes. And, of course, being prohibited from going further, we have the greatest desire to do so! In the evening, however, when our *caballeros* return, we frequently walk down to the village—where the English minister has also a house.

In the first place, San Angel is pretty in its own way: with its fields of maguey, its scattered houses that all look like the *beaux restes* of better days, its market place, parish church, church of El Carmen with the monastery and high-walled gardens adjoining; with its narrow lanes, Indian huts, profusion of pink roses, its little bridge, and clusters and avenue of trees; its houses here and there for *temperamento* (constitution), as they call those where Mexican families come to reside in summer, with their grated windows, and gardens, and orchards; and then its distant view of Mexico, with its cathedral towers, and volcanoes, and lofty mountains, and scattered churches, and long lines of trees; and nearer, the pretty villages of Coyoacán and Mixcoac; and always everywhere the old church, and broken arch, and ancient cross with its faded flower garlands, to mark a murder, or erected as an act of piety—all is so characteristic of Mexico that the landscape could belong to no other part of the known world.[3]

There is the half-naked Indian with his blanket, extracting the pulque from the maguey; the *ranchera* with her *rebozo* and broad-brimmed hat, passing by upon her ass; the old *lépero* in rags, sitting basking in the sun upon the stone seat before the door; the poor Indian woman, with her matted hair and brown baby hanging behind her, refreshing herself by drinking three *tlacos* (halfpence) worth of pulque from a *jarrito* (little earthen jar); the portly and well-looking *padre prior del Carmen* (the Carmelite prior), sauntering up the lane at a leisurely pace; all the little ragged boys, down to the merest urchin that can hardly lisp, dragging off their large, ragged, well-holed hats, with a *"Buenos días, padrecito* (Good morning, little father)!"—the father replying with a benevolent smile, and a slight sound in his throat intended for a *Benedicite;* and all that would be dull in any other climate brightened up and made light and gay by the purest atmosphere, and sunshine, and bluest sky, and softest air, that ever blew or shone upon a wicked world.

We are now approaching the Holy Week once more—in Mexico a scene of variety in the streets and of grandeur and splendour in the churches; but here in the country it is a play, a sort of melodrama, in which the sufferings, death, and burial of Christ our Saviour are represented to the naked eye by living figures in pantomime. We have heard a great deal of these representations, and are glad to have the opportunity of seeing them, which we intend to do in the village of Coyoacán where they are particularly curious. Besides this, our friends the Adalids have a house there for the season, and—as the city of Cortés' predilection—it is classic ground.[4] Meanwhile, for about ten days before, the whole country has been overrun with Pharisees, Nazarenes, Jews—and figures of the Saviour are carried about in procession; all this in preparation for the Holy Week, a sort of overture to the drama.

The first evening we arrived here there was a representation of the Pharisees searching for Christ. The Pharisees were very finely dressed, either in scarlet stuff and gold, or in green and silver, with helmets and feathers. They are mounted upon horses which are taught to dance and rear to the sound of music, so that upon the whole they look like performers at Astley's.[5]

They came on with music, riding up the lanes until they arrived in front of this house which, being the principal place hereabouts, they came to first, and where the Indian workmen and servants were all collected to see them. They were accompanied by crowds of ragged Indians on foot—men, women, and children. They rode about for some time, as if in search of Christ, until a full-length figure of the Saviour appeared, dressed in purple robes, carried on a platform by four men, and guarded on all sides by soldiers.

It is singular that, after all, there is nothing ridiculous in these exhibitions; on the contrary, something rather terrible. In the first place, the music is good, which would hardly be the case in any but a Mexican village; the dresses are really rich, the gold all real—and the whole has the effect of confusing the imagination into the belief of its being a true scene.

The next evening the same procession passed, with some additions, always accompanied by a crowd of Indians from the villages—men, women, and children. Bonfires were made before the door of the hacienda, which were lighted whenever the distant music was heard approaching, and all the figures in the procession carried lighted lamps. The Saviour was then led up to the door, and all the crowd went up to kiss his feet. The figure which is carried about this evening is called Our

Saviour of the Column, and represents the Saviour tied to a pillar, bleeding, and crowned with thorns. All this must sound very profane, but the people are so quiet, seem so devout, and so much in earnest, that it appears much less so than you would believe.

The cross was planted here in a congenial soil. And, as in the pagan East the statues of the divinities frequently did no more than change their names from those of heathen gods to those of holy Christian saints —and image worship continued, though the mind of the Christian was directed from the being represented to the true and only God who inhabits eternity—so here the poor Indian still bows before visible representations of saints and virgins, as he did in former days before the monstrous shapes representing the unseen powers of the air, the earth, and the water. But he, it is to be feared, still lifts up his thoughts no higher than the rude image which a rude hand has carved.

The mysteries of Christianity, to affect his untutored mind, must be visibly represented to his eyes. He kneels before the bleeding image of the Saviour who died for him, before the gracious form of the Virgin of Grief who intercedes for him; but he believes that there are many Virgins, of various gifts and possessing various degrees of miraculous power, and also of different degrees of riches, according to the quality and number of the diamonds and pearls with which they are endowed— one even who is the rival of the other—one who will bring rain when there is drought, and one to whom it is well to pray in seasons of inundation.

Mexico owes much of its peculiar beauty to the religious or superstitious feelings of its inhabitants. At every step we see a white cross gleaming amongst the trees, in a solitary path, or on the top of some rugged and barren rock—a symbol of faith in the desert place. And wherever the footsteps of man have rested, and some three or four have gathered together, there—while the ruined huts proclaim the poverty of the inmates —the temple of God rises in comparative splendour.

It is strange, yet well authenticated, and has given rise to many theories, that the symbol of the cross was already known to the Indians before the arrival of Cortés. In the island of Cozumel, near Yucatán, there were several; and in Yucatán itself there was a stone cross; and there an Indian, considered a prophet among his countrymen, had declared that a nation bearing the same as a symbol should arrive from a distant country!

More extraordinary still was a temple dedicated to the Holy Cross by the Toltec nation in the city of Cholula. Near Tulancingo also there is a cross engraved on a rock with various characters, which the Indians by tradition attribute to the apostle Saint Thomas. In Oaxaca also there existed a cross which the Indians from time immemorial had been accustomed to consider as a divine symbol. By order of the Bishop Cervantes it was placed in a sumptuous chapel in the cathedral. Information concerning its discovery, together with a small cross cut out of its wood, was sent to Rome to Paul V, who received it on his knees, singing the hymn *"Vexilla Regis prodeunt . . ."*[6]

If anyone wishes to try the effect of strong contrast, let him come direct from the United States to this country; but it is in the villages especially that the contrast is most striking. Travelling in New England, for example, we arrive at a small and flourishing village. We see four new churches, proclaiming four different sects—religion suited to all customers. These wooden churches or meeting-houses are all new, all painted white, or perhaps a bright red. Hard by is a tavern with a green paling, as clean and as new as the churches, and there are also various smart *stores* and neat dwelling houses—all new, all wooden, all clean, and all ornamented with thin Grecian pillars. The whole has a cheerful, trim, and flourishing aspect. Houses, churches, shops, and taverns, all are of a piece. They are suited to the present emergency, whatever that may be, though they will never make fine ruins. Everything proclaims prosperity, equality, consistency; the past forgotten, the present all in all, and the future taking care of itself. No delicate attentions to posterity, who can never repay them anything. No beggars. If a man has even a hole in his coat, he must be lately from the Emerald Isle.

Transport yourself in imagination from this New England village of _____ near Boston to that of Saint _____, it matters not which, not far from Mexico. Then "Look on this picture, and on that."[7] The Indian huts, with their half-naked inmates, and little gardens full of flowers; the huts themselves either built of clay, and invariably in ruins, or the half-ruined *beaux restes* of some great stone building. At a little distance a handsome hacienda, like a deserted palace, built of solid masonry, with its inner patio surrounded by stone pillars, with thick walls and iron-barred windows that might stand a siege. Here a ruined arch and cross, so solidly built that one cannot but wonder how the stones ever crumbled away. There, rising in the midst of old faithful-looking trees, the church, gray and ancient, but strong as if designed for eternity; with its saints and virgins, its martyrs and relics, its gold and silver and precious jewels, whose value would buy up all the spare lots in the New England village; the *lépero* with scarce a rag to cover him, kneeling on that marble pavement.

Or leave the enclosure of the church, and mark the high stone wall that bounds the road for more than a mile; the fruit trees overtopping it, high though it be, with their loaded branches. This is the convent orchard. And that great Gothic pile of building that stands in its hoary majesty—surmounted by the lofty mountains whose cloud-enveloped summits, tinged by the evening sun, rise behind it—what could so noble a building be but the monastery, perhaps of the Carmelites, because of its exceeding rich garden and well-chosen site, for they of all monks are richest in this world's goods. Also we may see the handsome but heavy-looking padre-prior riding slowly from under the arched gate up the village lanes, the Indians coming from their huts and doing him lowly reverence as he passes.

Here, everything reminds us of the past; of the conquering Spaniards, who seemed to build for eternity, impressing each work with their own solid, grave, and religious character; of the triumphs of Catholicism; of the days of papal power; and of the Indians when Cortés first startled them from their repose and stood before them like the fulfillment of a half-forgotten prophecy. It is the present that seems like a dream, a pale

reflection of the past. All is decaying and growing fainter, and men seem trusting to some unknown future which they will never see.

The one [—the United States—] a democracy, where the sovereign people tyrannize over the small aristocracy, who privately affect to despise and publicly adulate them: a hard-working, independent, and stiff-necked generation as they are. Here [—in Mexico—] there is no people, nor is there any country where there is a more complete distinction of classes than in this self-styled republic. One government has been abandoned, and there is none in its place; one revolution follows another, yet the remedy is not found.

Still they dream on, as if waiting like the Jews for some fancied deliverer. Let them beware. Some day, when they have dreamt on—it may be a half a century longer—they will be rudely awakened from their sleep, and find their cathedral turned into a large meetinghouse and all painted white—the silver railing melted down, the silver transformed into dollars—the Virgin's pearls sold to the highest bidder—the floor washed, which it greatly requires—and perhaps, round the whole, a nice new wooden paling, freshly done in green. And all this will be performed by some of the artists from the *wide-awake* republic further north.

Just as I wrote these words, a shower of crackers startled me from the profane ideas in which I was indulging, and the prancing of the horses of Jews and Pharisees, and the crackling of bonfires, warn me that it is time to take an evening stroll—that the sun is down, and the air refreshing. However, as to crackers and rockets, the common people enjoy them by day as much as by night. It is their favourite method of commemorating any event, civil or religious.

"What do you suppose the Mexicans will be doing now?" said King Ferdinand to a Mexican who was at the Spanish court, shortly after the final success of the revolutionists.

"Letting off rockets, Your Majesty," answered the Mexican.

"Well—I wonder what they are doing now in Mexico!" said the King in the afternoon.

"*Tirando cohetes*—letting off rockets, Your Majesty."

"What will your countrymen be doing now?"

"The same thing, Your Majesty. Still letting off rockets."[8]

Yesterday we drove into Mexico to see how matters stood in our house, and received a number of visitors in our deserted apartments.

Just before we left Mexico for this place, three very magnificent aides-de-camp brought us an invitation from General Valencia to attend a ball to be given by him and other officers, in the theatre, to the President on the occasion of His Excellency's being declared "*benemérito de la patria*."[9] We did not go, as we were setting off for the country, but Calderón, being requested, as were the other ministers, to send the colours of his nation, did so, and today there is much talk in Mexico, besides a paragraph in the newspapers, connected with these matters. It appears that the *drapeaux*, whether by accident or design, were improperly placed—and these faults in etiquette are not uncommon here. The English minister, having observed that his *drapeau* was placed in a subordinate rank and finding that his warnings beforehand on the subject, and his representations on seeing it, were neglected, cut it down and left the ballroom, followed by all the English who were there.[10]

39

Holy Week in Coyoacán

[Thursday–Friday: April 8th–9th, 1841]
Hacienda of Goicoechea, San Angel

As we were told that these ceremonies, though pretty much the same in all the villages, are particularly curious in Coyoacán (now pronounced Cuyacán), we went there early in the morning on Holy Thursday. [Coyoacán] is almost like a continuation of the village of San Angel, but there are more trees in it, and almost every house has its garden, or at least its inner court full of orange trees.

Here, after the total destruction of the ancient Tenochtitlan, Cortés took up his residence for several months. Here he founded a convent of nuns, and in his testament he desired to be buried in this convent, "in whatever part of the world I may finish my days."[1] The conqueror's last wishes in this respect were not held sacred. At the time of the conquest, Coyoacán, together with Tacubaya, &c., stood upon the margin of the lake of Texcoco—most of the houses built within the water upon stakes, so that the canoes entered by a low door. This was undoubtedly the favourite retreat of Cortés, and it is now one of the prettiest villages near Mexico. Its principal church is extraordinarily handsome—one of the finest village churches we have yet seen.[2]

One of the prettiest places in the village belongs to an order of monks called the Padres Camilos. It consists of a house and garden where those monks go by turns to enjoy the country air and taste the *dolce far niente* of their own hacienda. Comfortable padres! There is one room looking into the garden, and opening into a walk bordered by rose-bushes, which is *such* a place for a siesta!—cool, retired, fragrant. A comfortable hammock is slung across the room—not a hammock with nothing in it, but with a good cool mattress—and here the good padre may lie with one eye opened to the roses, and the other closed in inward meditation. However, its whole merit consists in being cleanly and neatly kept, for it is a large, empty house, and the garden, so called, is little more than a pasture field—with nice gravel walks cut through it, bordered with fine rosebushes, and beautified by a clear fountain.[3]

We went to the Adalids' house, which is halfway between San Angel and Coyoacán—Conchita driving me herself in an open *carretela* with white *frisones* (northern horses) which, compared with the spirited little Mexican steeds, look gigantic.[4]

We went first to see the church, which was very magnificently illuminated, and ornamented with loads of flowers and fruit (especially oranges), and thronged with ragged *léperos* and blanketed Indians. We then set off to endeavour, if possible, to find a place in the crowd, who had hurried off to see *el prendimiento* (the taking of Christ), and to hear the curate preach an appropriate sermon in a portable pulpit amongst the trees.

We made our way through the patient, bronzed, and blanketed crowd, not without sundry misgivings as to the effect of *evil communication;*[5] and at length reached the procession, all ranged on the grass under the trees in a pretty and secluded little grove—in two long rows fronting each other, each person carrying a lamp surmounted by a plume of coloured feathers, very ingeniously made of coloured spun glass. They were all dressed in the costume of Pharisees, Jews, Romans, &c.

The image of the Saviour was shortly after carried through on a platform to the sound of music—followed by the eleven disciples—and was placed in a kind of bower amongst the trees, supposed to give a representation of the garden of Gethsemane. A portable pulpit, covered with shining stuff, was carried in and placed beneath a tree just outside of this enclosure, and, soon after, the curate arrived and mounted into his place. A number of little ragged boys, who had climbed up on the very topmost branches of the trees to have a good view, were *piked* down with lances by the Jews, notwithstanding their seemingly just remonstrances that they were doing no harm. But when—in answer to their *"Qué hacemos?* (What are we doing?)"—the Jews observed, "The Señor *Cura* will be angry," they tumbled down one on the top of the other like ripe apples— and then stood watching for the first convenient opportunity of slipping up again. But if ever there was a patient, good-natured, *laissez-aller* mob, this was it.

The curate began his sermon by an account of the sufferings and persecution of Christ; of the causes and effects of his death; of the sinfulness of the Jews, &c. He talked for about half an hour, and his sermon was sensible enough and adapted to his audience. He described the agony of Christ when in the garden to which he often resorted with his disciples, and the treachery of Judas who knew the place, and who, *"having received a band of men and officers from the chief priests and Pharisees, cometh thither with lanterns and torches and weapons."*[6] As [the curate] went on describing minutely the circumstances of his *prendimiento,* [the] one who represented the spy, with a horrible mask like a pig's face, was seen looking through the trees to where the Saviour was concealed; and shortly after, Judas, his face covered with a black crape, and followed by a band of soldiers, glided stealthily through the procession.

"And now," said the curate, "observe what the traitor does. He hath given them a sign, saying, '*Whomsoever I shall kiss, that same is he: hold him fast.*' He goes up to his master—he approaches the sacred person of the Lord."

Meanwhile Judas was advancing and here went forward and embraced the Saviour.

"It is done! He betrays the Son of man with a kiss," cried the preacher. "The horrible act of treachery is completed. *And forthwith he came to Jesus, and said, 'Hail, master,' and kissed him. But now, Jesus, knowing all things that should come upon him, went forth, and said unto them, 'Whom seek ye?' They answered him, 'Jesus of Nazareth.' Jesus saith unto them, 'I am he.'*"

As the curate said these words, they all answered, "Jesus of Nazareth," and fell upon their faces on the ground.

"Mark," cried the curate, "the power of the Word! They came out to take him with swords and with staves, but at the sound of the divine voice they acknowledge the power of God, and fall at his feet. But it is only for a moment. Behold, now they tie his hands, they buffet him, they smite him with the palms of their hands, they lead him off to the high priest."

All this was acted in succession, though sometimes the curate had to repeat the same thing several times before they recollected what to do.

"And already, in anticipation of the iniquitous sentence, behold what is written." This alluded to a paper fastened high upon a pole, which a man held above the heads of the crowd, and on which was written, "Jesus of Nazareth, King of the Jews, condemned to death by Pontius Pilate, President of Upper Galilee."

And now, escorted by Judas and the multitude, the Saviour was borne through the crowd, in conclusion of the *prendimiento*. The curate wound up his discourse by an exhortation to them all to abstain from sin, which had been the cause of this horrible event.

I regret to state that, at this very moment, a man poked his hand into Adalid's pocket, who turned very sharply round and asked him what he was doing. "*Nada, señorito* (Nothing, sir)," said he with an innocent smile, showing two rows of teeth like an ivory railing, but at the same time disappearing pretty swiftly amongst the crowd—who now all began to move and to follow the procession, the band striking up a *galope*.

In the evening we returned to San Angel, and visited the lighted churches there. As it was late when we entered the *parroquia* (parish church), the lights were nearly all extinguished, and a few alone of the devout were still kneeling before a figure of our Saviour in chains.

On Good Friday we set off early for Coyoacán, though very tired after our yesterday's work—and rather afraid of the sun, which at present in the middle of the day is insupportable, and even by ten o'clock disagreeable. The whole enclosure of the church, and for a great distance round, was covered with people, and there were even a few carriages full of well-dressed persons who had come from the different neighbouring haciendas—amongst others, the family of the Marquesa de Vivanco. The padre Iturralde, who has some reputation for eloquence, was expected to preach three sermons at Coyoacán that day, besides one in the village of Mixcoac.[7]

By the time we arrived the sun was pouring down his beams like molten lead. Our carriage was open, and under every tree was a crowd—so there were small hopes of finding shade. Women were selling fruit, and booths with ices and *chía* were erected all down the lane leading from the church.

The procession was passing by as we arrived, and the curate had already preached one sermon, I believe at one of the stations where it is said the Saviour fell while carrying his cross on the road to Calvary.

The image of the Saviour was now carried forward on a platform, with the heavy cross appearing to weigh him down; and on the same platform was Simon the Cyrenian, assisting him to bear the weight. The Cyrenian was represented by an old man, with hair as white as snow, dressed in scarlet cloth—who, in a stooping posture and without once moving his body, was carried about for hours in the whole force of the sun, the rays pouring down upon his uncovered head. For a long while we had believed him to be a wooden figure dressed up, and when he came near he greatly excited our surprise and compassion. If he survives this day's work it will be a miracle. I can now almost give faith to Adalid's assertion that in some of the villages the man who represents Judas actually hangs himself, or is hanged upon a tree! The Saviour was dressed in crimson velvet, with the crown of thorns. Behind was a figure of the Virgin in deep mourning, carried by Indian women.

The procession consisted of the same men on horseback as we had seen on foot the preceding day—of the Spy, the Pharisees, the Jews, Judas the Betrayer, and the mob. Some had helmets and feathers, some armour. Some wore wreaths of green and gold leaves. One very good-looking man, who looked like a gigantic woman—with long curls and a gold crown, and a splendid mantle of scarlet and gold—was intended for a Roman. By his crown he probably meant to personify the Roman Cæsar.

At last, however, room was made and we got two chairs a little in the shade under a tree, and near the pulpit where the padre was to preach. His sermon, or rather discourse, was very good, and appeared to be extemporary. He made an address to the Virgin, as she was carried by and stopped near the pulpit, and another to the Saviour—during all which time the audience was breathlessly attentive, notwithstanding the crying of children and the barking of dogs. It was supposed that they were now leading Christ before the judgment seat of Pilate, and the next scene was to be the delivery of the sentence.

When the curate's discourse was finished, the procession passed on; the Indian women began to sell their nuts and oranges; and the band struck up in the distance, playing an air to which, when last I heard it, Ducrow's horses were dancing![8]

We next proceeded in a fiery sun, which made its way through our mantillas, to search for a convenient place from which to hear the padre's next sermon, and to see the next scene in the sacred drama. The padre, who was walking under the shade of a lilac silk parasol, insisted compassionately upon resigning it to me. The Señora Adalid did not seem to feel the heat at all. At last, not being able to get through the crowd, we got up on the low *azotea* of a house adjoining the church—beside which the pulpit was placed—but here the sun was perfectly overwhelming.

The padre's sermon was really eloquent in some passages, but lasted at least an hour, during which time we admired the fortitude of the unfortunate Cyrenian, who was dreeing a penance of no ordinary kind. The sun darted down perpendicularly on the back of his exposed head, which he kept bent downwards, maintaining the same posture the whole time, without flinching or moving. Before the sermon was over I could stand the heat no longer, and went in under cover, feeling as if my brains were all melted into a hot and liquid jelly.

At last the procession began to move towards the pulpit, where it shortly after formed itself as before into two lines—upon which I emerged into the sun. In a few moments a man with a helmet and feathers, mounted on a fiery horse, galloped furiously through the ranks, and holding a paper on the point of his lance, brought the sentence pronounced by Pontius Pilate. Arrived at the pulpit, he handed it up to the priest, who received it with a look of horror, opened it, tried to read it, and threw it to the ground with an air of indignation. The messenger galloped back more furiously than he came—and, his horse bolting at the end of the lines, occasioned a laugh amongst the spectators. Then followed the parting address to the Saviour, whose bearers now brought him up to the pulpit, followed by the mournful figure of the Virgin. Reflections on the event concluded this act.

We returned in the afternoon to see the descent from the cross, which was to be performed within the church. The church was crowded, and a black curtain hung before the altar. The padre now recapitulated all that had taken place, and described the Saviour's parting with his mother at the foot of the cross—addressing the Virgin who stood at the side of the church in her sable mourning robes not far from the altar, and interrupting his sermon to pray for her intercession with her Divine Son. I observed all the women in tears as he described the Virgin's grief, the torments of the crucifixion, the indignities that the Saviour had suffered.

All at once he exclaimed in a loud voice: "Draw back the veil, and let us behold him!" The curtain was drawn, and the Saviour crucified appeared. Then the sobs of the women broke forth. They clasped their hands, beat their breasts, and groaned, while the soldiers who stood below the cross clashed their swords, and one of them struck the body with a lance. At the same time the Virgin bowed her head, as if in grief. Unfortunately I was near enough to see how this was effected, which peep behind the scenes greatly diminished the effect.

Then the soldiers mounted a ladder beside the crucifix, and took down the body, to bear it away. As it came by the pulpit, the priest seized its hands and showed the marks of the nails, at the same time breaking out into exclamations of grief. The soldiers stood below, impatiently clashing their swords; the women sobbed violently; the procession passed out—and we returned to the Adalids' house.

In the evening the Procession of the Angels took place. Figures dressed in silk and gold, with silver wings, were carried by on platforms —the music playing as they went. The body of the Saviour lay in a sort of glass hearse, carried by men chanting a dirge, and followed by the Virgin. This procession was really pretty, but had an odd, unnatural effect amongst the fresh green trees, the smell of incense mingling with the fragrance of the flowers, and the gaudy silk and gold and plumes of feathers gilded by the soft setting sun, as they flashed along under the broken arches.

I climbed up upon an old stone cross near the church as they passed by, and had a beautiful view. Everything looked gaudy when near, but as the procession wound along under the arch and through the green lanes, and the music came fainter upon the ear, and the beating of the drums and the tolling of the bells and the mournful chant were all blended into one faint and distant harmony, the effect was beautiful. I thought of the simple service of the Scottish kirk, and of the country people coming out after a sermon, with their best Sunday gowns on, and their serious, intelligent faces, discussing the merits of their minister's discourse—and wondered at the contrasts in the same religion. There are many ways of worshipping God—and here the Catholic ceremonies have found a congenial soil.

When it grew later, as the evening was cool and pleasant, we walked through the fields up to the church of La Concepción, where the procession was again to pass, and sat down on the grass till we heard it coming.[9] As the body was carried by, all went upon their knees. At night commenced the *pésame*, or condolence to the Virgin, in the church. She stood on her shrine, with her head bowed down; and the music, hymns, and prayers were all addressed to her—while the sermon, preached by another *cura*, was also in her honour.

I plead guilty to having been too sleepy to take in much more than the general tenor of the discourse. The musicians seemed to me to be playing "Sweet Kitty Clover," with variations. If "Sweet Kitty Clover" is genuine Irish, as who can doubt, how did these Indians get hold of it? Did Saint Patrick go round from the Emerald Isle by way of Tipperary? But, if he had, would he not have killed the *alacranes,* and *chicaclinos,* and *coralillos,* and *vinagrillos?* This requires consideration.[10]

In the *Ora pro nobis,* we were struck with the fineness of the rustic voices. But music in this country is a sixth sense. It was but a few days before leaving Mexico that—sitting alone at the open window, enjoying the short twilight—I heard a sound of distant music: many voices singing in parts, and coming gradually nearer. It sounded beautiful, and exactly in unison with the hour and the scene. At first I concluded it to be a religious procession; but it was not a hymn—the air was gayer. When the voices came under the window, and rose in full cadence, I went out on the balcony to see to whom they belonged. It was the *forçats*—returning from their work to the Acordada!—guarded by soldiers, their chains clanking in measure to the melody, and accompanied by some miserable-looking women.

We left the church feeling very tired and sleepy, and walked towards the booths where, in the midst of flowers and evergreens, they were still selling ices, and lemonade, and *chia.* We sat down to rest in the cleanest of these leafy bowers, and then returned to [the centre of] Coyoacán. There was no drunkenness, or quarrelling, or confusion of any sort. An occasional hymn, rising in the silence of the air, or the distant flashing of a hundred lights, alone gave notice that the funeral procession of the Saviour had not yet halted for the night—but there was no noise, not even mirth. Everything was conducted with a sobriety befitting the event that was celebrated. That some of the curate's horses were stolen that night is only a proof that bad men were out, and took the opportunity of his absence from home to plunder his stables.

We were told an anecdote concerning Simon the Cyrenian, which is not bad. A man was taken up in one of the villages as a vagrant, and desired by the justice to give an account of himself—to explain why he was always wandering about, and had no employment. The man, with the greatest indignation, replied: "No employment! I am *substitute Cyrenian* at Coyoacán in the Holy Week!" That is to say, he was to be substituted in the Cyrenian's place, should anything occur to prevent that individual from representing the character.

40

On the Subject of Indians

Friday: April 23rd, 1841
Hacienda of Goicoechea, San Angel

We went to Mexico yesterday to see a balloon ascend from the Plaza de Toros, with an aeronaut and his daughter—French people, I believe. The scene was really beautiful. The plaza was filled with well-dressed people, and all the boxes crowded with ladies in full toilet. The President was there with his staff, and there were two bands of music. The day was perfectly brilliant, and the streets crowded with handsome carriages, many of them open. The balloon swayed itself up and down in the midst of the plaza like a living thing. Everything seemed ready for the ascent, when it was announced that there was a hole in the balloon, and that consequently there could be no ascent that day. The people bore their disappointment very good-humouredly, although it was conjectured that the *air traveller* had merely proposed to himself to get their money without the slightest intention of performing his voyage.

One amusing circumstance was that some penny-a-line rhymer had written an account of the ascent of the balloon—and, when we came out, the plaza was full of men selling these verses which the people were all buying and reading with roars of laughter.[1]

The first of May being San Felipe, there will be a ball at the French minister's, to which we shall probably go.[2]

Sunday: April 25th, 1841

We have just returned from a ride to San Bartolo, an Indian village four leagues from this. The road to it [is] nearly impassable—rocky, arid, and uninteresting, with the exception of the loveliness of the distant landscape. We went with a large party, some on horses, some on asses, others on mules, and one adventurous Jehu driving himself in a four-wheeled carriage with a pair of horses, over a road formed of ruts, stones, holes, and rocks—where, I will venture to say, no carriage ever made its appearance before. Even the horses and asses got along with difficulty. In spite of large straw hats and green veils, we were burnt the colour of red Indians. In the middle of the day we find the sun intolerable at present—and, owing to the badness of the roads, we did not reach our destination until twelve or one o'clock.[3]

San Bartolo is a small, scattered Indian village with a church, and is remarkable for its beautiful spring of water that jets cold and clear from the hard rock, as if Moses had but just smote it; for its magnificent tall pine trees; for the good looks and cleanness of the Indian women, who are forever washing their long hair in the innumerable clear streamlets formed by the spring; and for the most beautiful view of Mexico that I think I have yet seen—which is particularly favourable owing to the thick, dark screen of pine wood in the foreground, and the fine distinct view of the *laguna*—giving to the view wood and water, which it generally wants.

Our dinner was carried by Indians, who had trotted off with it at daydawn—but who had taken the wrong road, and did not arrive till long after us. We dined under the pine trees by the side of the stream, but surrounded by crowds of gaping Indians in too close vicinity to be agreeable. Some of the young women were remarkably handsome, with the most beautiful teeth imaginable, laughing and talking in their native tongue at a great rate as they were washing in the brooks—some their hair and others their clothes.

The men looked as dirty as Indians generally do and by no means on a level with these handsome damsels, who are so much superior to the common race of Indians near Mexico that one would think they had some intermixture of Spanish blood in their veins. A sister of the woman who takes charge of the hacienda where we live is one of the most beautiful creatures I ever beheld. Large eyes, with long dark lashes, black hair nearly touching the ground, teeth like snow, a dark but glowing complexion, a superb figure, with fine arms and hands, and small beautifully formed feet. All that is best of Indian and Spanish, "of dark and bright," seems united in her.[4] Calderón says he has seen peasant women in Andalusia in the same style of beauty, and quite as handsome. She is only nineteen. Such beauties as these startle one every now and then in some remote village. She belongs, no doubt, to the mestizos—the descendants of whites and Indians, the handsomest race in Mexico.

You ask if the castes in Mexico are distinct. There are seven supposed to be so:[5] 1st, the *gachupines,* or Spaniards born in Europe; 2nd, the creoles, that is, whites of European family born in America; 3rd, the mestizos; 4th, the mulattoes, descendants of whites and Negroes, of whom there are few; 5th, the *zambos,* descendants of Negroes and Indians, the ugliest race in Mexico; 6th, the Indians; and 7th, the remains of the African Negroes.[6]

Of pure Indians, Humboldt in his day calculated that there existed two millions and a half in New Spain (without counting mestizos), and they are probably very little altered from the inferior Indians as Cortés found them. The principal families perished at the time of the conquest. The priests, sole depositaries of knowledge, were put to death—the manuscripts and hieroglyphical paintings were burnt—and the remaining Indians fell into that state of ignorance and degradation from which they have never emerged.

The rich Indian women preferred marrying their Spanish conquerors to allying themselves with the degraded remnant of their countrymen: poor artisans, workmen, porters, &c., of whom Cortés speaks as filling the streets of the great cities, and as being considered little better than beasts of burden—nearly naked in *tierra caliente,* dressed pretty much as they now are in the temperate parts of the country, and everywhere with nearly the same manners, and habits, and customs as they now have, but especially in the more distant villages where they have little intercourse with the other classes.

Even in their religion, Christianity—as I observed before—seems to be formed of the ruins of their mythology. And all these festivities of the church, these fireworks and images and gay dresses, harmonize completely with their childish love of show, and are in fact their greatest source of delight. To buy these they save up all their money, and when you give a penny to an Indian child it trots off to buy [fire]crackers, as another would to buy candy. Attempts have been made by their curates to persuade them to omit the celebration of certain days, and to expend less in the ceremonies of others; but the indignation and discontent which such proposals have caused have induced them to desist in their endeavours.

Under an appearance of stupid apathy they veil a great depth of cunning.[7] They are grave and gentle and rather sad in their appearance, when not under the influence of pulque. But when they return to their villages in the evening, and have taken a drop of comfort, their white teeth light up their bronze countenances like lamps, and the girls especially make the air ring with their laughter, which is very musical. I think it is Humboldt who says that their smile is extremely gentle, and the expression of their eyes very severe. As they have no beard, if it were not for a little moustache, which they frequently wear on the upper lip, there would be scarcely any difference between the faces of men and women.

The Indians in and near the capital are, according to Humboldt, either the descendants of the former labourers, or are remains of noble Indian families who, disdaining to intermarry with their Spanish conquerors, preferred themselves to till the ground which their vassals formerly cultivated for them. It is said that these Indians of noble race, though to the vulgar eye undistinguishable from their fellows, are held in great respect by their inferior countrymen.[8] In Cholula particularly there are still caciques with long Indian names; also in Tlaxcala—and, though barefoot and ragged, they are said to possess great hidden wealth.

But it is neither in or near the capital that we can see the Indians to perfection in their original state. It is only by travelling through the provinces that we can accomplish this; and, should the lateness of the season oblige us to remain here any time after another minister arrives, we may probably take a longer journey in some different direction from *tierra caliente*, where we may see some tribes of the indigenous Mexicans. Certainly no visible improvement has taken place in their condition since the independence. They are quite as poor and quite as ignorant and quite as degraded as they were in 1808, and—if they do raise a little grain of their own—they are so hardly taxed that the privilege is as nought.[9]

Sunday: May 2nd, 1841

We returned from Mexico this morning, having gone in to attend the ball given at the French minister's on the day of Louis-Philippe. It was very pretty, and we stayed till it was very late. We met with such a cordial reception from all our friends, whom we have not seen for a month, that we are tempted to believe ourselves as much missed in Mexico as they say we are. The Señora L[asquetti] and the E[scandón]s were amongst the best-dressed Mexican ladies last night; the latter in white crape and diamonds, and the other in black blonde over rose colour, also with diamonds. The Señora [Adalid], who went with us, looked very pretty in a white blonde dress—with a small black velvet turban rolled round with large diamonds and pearls.[10] There were a great number of small crimson velvet turbans, and an amazing number of black blonde dresses. There were certainly some very pretty women. The *corps diplomatique* went in uniform.

Friday: May 7th, 1841

Avecilla, a favourite Spanish actor, died a few days ago, and, as Calderón took several boxes on the night of a play given for the benefit of his widow, we went in to the theatre on Saturday last.[11]

We are now looking out for another house in Mexico, for when the rainy season begins we shall find this too far from the city for Calderón—who is obliged to be there constantly.

We ventured to take a walk alone yesterday morning through the lanes, down to San Angel and Coyoacán, for which piece of imprudence we were severely reprehended. And today it appears that two women had been robbed and ill-treated on the road near here—so we are too ready to subscribe to the renewal of our sentence of imprisonment in the house and orchard, when we have no gentlemen with us. But it must be confessed that it takes greatly from the charms of a country life not to be able to walk out fearlessly.

The quietness and stillness of this place is incredible. There is actually not a sound in the air, not a sight but a ragged Indian. The garden is in great beauty. The apricots are ripe and abundant. The roses are in full blow—and there is a large pomegranate tree at the gate of the orchard, which is one mass of ponceau blossom. It is much warmer in the middle of the day this summer than it was last.

We spent a pleasant day lately at a great hacienda a few leagues from this, belonging to a Spanish millionaire, on occasion of a shooting party. We went there to breakfast, and afterwards set off on horseback, sitting sideways on *men's* saddles, to see the sport. It would have been very agreeable but for the heat. The sportsmen were not very successful. [They] saw a flight of rose-coloured flamingoes who sailed over their heads unhurt [and] killed some very handsome birds called *trigueros* with beautiful yellow plumage, and some ducks. The *trigueros* are considered a delicacy.

We rode with the *administrador* all round the estate, which is very productive and profitable. He told us that they sell in Mexico, annually, fifteen thousand dollars' worth of corn, and ten thousand dollars' worth of milk—sending in this produce in canoes by the canal which passes this way. We dismounted from our horses in a green meadow covered with daisies and buttercups which, from association, I prefer to the tuberoses and pomegranate blossom which now adorn the gardens. The Señor [Carrera] gave us an excellent dinner *à l'Espagnole*,[12] after which I made an attempt to fire at some birds—which shook their tails, and flew away in the most contemptuous manner.

The new secretary of legation, Señor Tavira, and the new attaché, Señor G[araycochea], have just arrived in Mexico.[13]

Monday: May 10th, 1841

The Baron and Madame de Cyprey, with their secretary, the Count de B[reteuil], came out yesterday morning unexpectedly to breakfast, and spent the day with us.

Thursday: May 13th, 1841

We went out with Calderón last evening to take a walk, when a man rushed by us in a state of great agitation; and on going further we met some workmen who told us that an Indian labourer had stabbed a man in the next field, and that he had died before a padre could be procured. We heard the cries of his wife and children, and Alex, crossing the ditch that bordered the field, went to see the man. He was a master workman, or director, and had found fault with one of the men for his idleness. High words ensued, and the labourer (probably the man who had passed us) drew his knife and stabbed him. He was lying stone dead, with his hand half cut through in his efforts to defend himself. A[lex] asked an *administrador*, who was standing near, what would be done to the guilty man. "Probably nothing," said he, shrugging his shoulders, "we have no judges to punish crime." This rencontre, as you may believe, took away from us all inclination to pursue our rambles.[14]

There is a pretty farmhouse in the village, in which we took shelter the other day from a shower of rain. The farmers are civil and respectful, a superior kind of people, with good manners rather above their station. The daughters are good-looking, and the house clean and neat. One of the girls gave me an account of a nocturnal visit which the robbers paid them last winter. She showed me the little room where she was alone and asleep when her mother and sister, who slept in the chamber adjoining, being wakened by the breaking in of their door, sprang out of the window to make their escape—and she was left in the house alone. She jumped out of bed and bolted the door (her room had no other egress), and there she held a parley with these night visitors, promising to unlock every drawer and closet if they would wait till she put on her clothes, and would do her no personal injury. The agreement was made, and they kept their word. They cleared the house of every article it contained, leaving nothing but the blanket in which the girl had wrapped herself. All their clothes, household utensils, money, everything was carried off with astonishing precision; and, having made her swear not to move till they had time to leave the village, they paid her no further attention. The other women, who had given the alarm, found no one inclined to move in the middle of the night against a party whose numbers their fears had probably magnified.

The *administrador* gave us an amusing account this evening of a visit which a band of no less than thirty robbers once ventured to pay this strong and well-defended hacienda. He was living there alone— that is, without the family—and had just barred and bolted everything for the night, but had not yet locked the outer gate when, looking out from his window into the courtyard by moonlight, he saw a band of robbers ride up to the door. He instantly took his measures and, seizing the great keys, ran up the little stair that leads to the *azotea*—locking the gate by which he passed—and, calling to the captain by name (for the robbers were headed by a noted chieftain), requested to know what he wanted at that hour of the night. The captain politely begged him to come downstairs and he would tell him; but the agent, strong in the possession of his great keys, and well knowing the solidity of the iron-barred windows, continued his parley in a high tone.

The captain rode round, examined everything with a practiced eye, and found that it would require a regular siege to make good his entry. He threatened, entreated, observed that he would be content with a small sum of money, but all in vain. There stood the sturdy *administrador* on the housetop, and there sat the captain on his horse below, something like the fox and the crow. But the agent with the keys was wiser than the crow and her cheese, for no cajoling would induce him to let them out of his grasp; and, worse than all, shooting him would have done them no good. At last the captain, finding himself entirely outwitted, took off his hat, politely wished the agent a very good night, drew off his men, and departed.

Another time, being also alone, he was attacked in broad daylight by two men who came under pretense of buying pulque. But having time to get hold of a sword he overpowered one, which frightened the other, upon which they both began to laugh and assured him it was mere experiment to see what he would do—a perfect jest, which he pretended to believe, but advised them not to try it again as it was too good a joke to be repeated.

Señor Adalid pointed out to us the other day a well-known robber captain, who was riding on the highroad with a friend. He had the worst looking, most vulgar and most villainous face I ever saw—a low-lived and most unpoetic looking ruffian, fat and sallow.

We saw a horribly ugly man today, and were told he was a *lobo*, the name given here to the *zambos*—the race produced by the mixture of Indians and Negroes, who are the most frightful human beings that can be seen, almost monstrous. La Güera Rodríguez told us that on an estate of hers a certain woman of that race was in the habit of attending church, and that she was so fearfully hideous the priest had been obliged to desire her to remain at home and abstain from attending mass, as her ugliness distracted the attention of the whole congregation![15]

We spent yesterday at the house of the English minister at San Angel, where he gave us and the _____ minister and his family a beautiful breakfast. How consistent everything looks in a good English house!—so handsome without being gaudy—the plate so well cleaned, the servants so well trained.

Monday: May 24th, 1841

A dinner given by Pakenham on the Queen's birthday, to which none of the ministers of the country were invited. Much speculation in consequence. For the first time heard P[akenham] abused by Mexicans the other day.[16]

A *pronunciamiento* is predicted. Signs before a moral earthquake. *Veremos* [we shall see].

Tuesday: June 8th, 1841

It is almost impossible, even after a two years' experience of Mexico, not to indulge in constant exclamations upon the beauty of the weather.[17] [In] the tropics the heat is trying to a European constitution, and oranges and jasmine will not compensate for scorpions and *alacranes* —even though one may pass a pleasant life there, and without much danger of being stung, for four months in the year. But in these temperate and higher regions, which are the tropics raised many thousand feet above the level of the sea, what can be more delicious than the climate, which seems to realize the perpetual spring of Elysium? Here there is neither scorching heat nor blighting cold. Here every natural production may grow. The air is soft and balmy. The sky is one vast turquoise, with light and pearly clouds floating over it. The earth yields spontaneously her fruit and flowers, and, though poverty exists, the evils of cold and hunger are lightly felt.

But what is the effect of this charming climate on the character and condition of the inhabitants? Bad enough to prove the sad truth, that man in his fallen state is not fitted for paradise. Since enough to support life can be had with little trouble, no trouble is taken to procure more. Since little clothing is necessary, the common people wear little or none, and a bed *al fresco* is as pleasant as sleeping on a piece of mat on a brick or mud floor—which last arrangement is quite satisfactory to the common servants in Mexico. Since begging is easier than working, the strong man begs, and, if he finds it more convenient, robs. The earth yields so much spontaneously, that a great part of the country remains uncultivated. The softness of the climate enervates both body and mind, and particularly of the better classes who have no motive to exertion, and who enjoy life much less than those who labour under the blue canopy and have the advantage of the fresh air.

The Indians lie in the shade and tingle their guitars, drink pulque and crown themselves with poppies, and laugh, or occasionally fight. The lady sits in her armchair and smokes, with no view but the opposite houses, and amidst a reunion of odours that might rival those of Cologne. Great moral energy would be necessary to counteract the physical influence of the climate, and neither education nor necessity teach or impart it.

The evil begins with the government, and goes downwards. The most flagrant abuses are passed over—either from indolence or corruption, for the one leads to the other. A president who has neither time nor perhaps opportunity to ameliorate the state of the nation, which he is called upon to govern, turns his brief authority to his present enjoyment and future profit. The well-known honesty of the actual President must place him above such a reproach, but he is not the less incapacitated by his own mildness and by the force of circumstances from taking the active measures which alone can save the country in its present precarious state.

A few officers, who are little more than military robbers—men of circumstance risen upon the ruins of some military revolution—soldiers of fortune, risen from the ranks and enriched by chance or plunder—are these the stuff of which to form patriots who have their country's good at heart? Such circumstances may produce an Iturbide—but a Washington, never. Priests, who ought to be devoted to the duties of their holy calling, sit in Congress, take their share in its debates, and meddle in politics. Formerly there were warrior-priests, men who exchanged the mitre for the helmet, the cassock for the saddle, when occasion made it necessary. But these were dark and sanguinary ages when men did all but sleep with their foot in the stirrup and their hand on the sword. The pope who declared the celibacy of churchmen necessary to an undivided heart, and who would have been right had he issued his bull in the golden age, what would he reply to those who complain that politics may occupy the thoughts to the exclusion of religion, more than wife, or children, or domestic economy? He might say that the priest should be there to soothe the fiery passions of worldly men, to influence their debates with mildness and to temper their worldly maxims with the pure doctrines of Christianity. If this be so, it is well.

We were sitting under an apple tree the other day trying to tame the fiercest little deer I ever saw, who was butting and kicking with all his might, when a large packet of letters was brought us, the reading of which insured us an agreeable afternoon.

We continue to lead a very quiet life here, occasionally taking a short ride in the evening, and making acquaintance with the neighbouring villages—the prettiest of which is Tizapán, a most rural and leafy spot, where there are fine fruit trees, plenty of water, and good-looking peasant girls. Sometimes we go to San Antonio to see the Vivanco family; occasionally to San Agustín, where they are preparing for the great fête.

We are in treaty for a house in Mexico, having now given up all idea of passing through Veracruz this summer. We are in hopes of having that of the late Marquesa de San Román, who died some time ago, but the delays that take place in any transaction connected with a house in Mexico, and the difficulty of obtaining a decisive answer, are hard trials of patience.

We generally have a number of visitors from Mexico on Sunday, and those who come in carriages may be considered as real friends, for they decidedly risk their necks, not to mention their carriage springs, at a *bad bit* on the road—which the owners, who are Indians, will not allow anyone to mend for them, and will not mend themselves. When we reach it, we are obliged regularly to get out of the carriage, go about a hundred yards on foot, and then remain in much anxiety at the top of the hill, till we see whether or not the carriage arrives unbroken—which it rarely does. A few dollars would make it perfectly safe.

Our chief visitors during the week are from the Carmelite convent of San Angel. The old *padre guardián* is about eighty. Each convent has a prior, but the *padre guardián* exercises authority over all the convents of his order as well as over his own.

There are many excellent houses and fine gardens in San Angel, and a number of families from Mexico are now there for the season. Tacubaya and all the environs are beginning to be occupied, and Mexico looks warm and deserted. But there are so few incidents in our quiet life among the magueys that I shall write no more till we return from San Agustín after the fête.

If you wish to hear how we pass our time, you must know that we generally rise about six and go out into the orchard and stroll about, or sit down with a book in a pleasant arbour at the end of one of the walks, which is surrounded by rosebushes and has a little stream of water running past it. Nor do we ever enter the orchard unarmed with a long pole, for its entrance is guarded by a flock of angry geese, hissing like the many-headed Hydra that watched over the golden apples of the Hesperides.

At eight we breakfast, and by nine the sun is already powerful enough to prevent us from leaving the house. We therefore sit down to read or

write, and do occasionally take a game at billiards. Calderón generally rides to Mexico but, if not, goes up to the *azotea* with a book, or writes in his study until four o'clock when we dine.

After dinner we walk into the village, if we have any attendant esquire. If not, we go to the *azotea* and see the sun set behind the volcanoes, or walk in the garden till it is dark, and then sit down in the front of the house and look at the lights in Mexico. Then we have tea or chocolate, and the candles are lighted, and the last Indian workman has gone off to his village, and the house is barred in—and we sit down to read, or write, or talk, or sometimes we play billiards by lamplight. And then indeed the silence and the solitude make us feel as if the world were completely shut out. I never experienced such perfect stillness. Even the barking of a dog sounds like an event. Therefore, expect no amusing letters from this place, for though we are very comfortable there are no incidents to relate.

The Indians come in the morning to drink pulque (which, by the way, I now think excellent, and shall find it very difficult to live without!) ;[18] a little child from the village brings us some bouquets of flowers, which

the Indians have a pretty way of arranging in a pineapple or pyramidal form; the Chinese cook, with his little slits of eyes, passes by with meat and fruit which he has been buying at the market of San Angel; the prior saunters in to see how we are; a chance visitor comes on horseback from Mexico, with a long sword by his side, as if he were going to fight the Saracens. And excepting that a padre came last Sunday and said mass to us in the pretty little chapel of the hacienda, which saved us the trouble of going down to the village, and moreover took chocolate with us afterwards, there has been nothing to vary the usual routine of our country life.

41

Dancing, Gambling, and Prayers

One year since I last wrote of San Agustín!

An entire year has fled swiftly away on rushing pinions, to add its unit to the rolling century. And again, on a bright morning in June, we set off for the hospitable San Antonio, where we were invited to breakfast and to pass the night on the second day of the fête. We found a very brilliant party assembled: the family with all its branches; the ex-Minister Cuevas, with his handsome sister-in-law; La Güera Rodríguez, with one of her beautiful granddaughters (daughter of the Marquis of Guadalupe), now making her first appearance in Mexico; and various other agreeable people.[1]

The first day of the fête a rumour was afloat that an attack was to be made upon the banks by the federal party; that they expected to procure the sinews of war to the extent of a million of dollars, and then intended to raise a *grito* in Mexico—taking advantage of the temporary absence of the President and his principal officers. The plan, whether true or false, was very feasible; but, if there was any truth in it, the discovery has been made in time, for nothing has occurred.

San Agustín appeared even gayer and more crowded than it was last year. We spent the day at the Escandóns', and went with them to a box in the plaza to see the cockfight, which I had no particular pleasure, I must confess, in witnessing again, but went for the sake of those who had not seen it before. The general *coup d'œil* was exceedingly gay, and the improvement in the dress of the ladies since last year very striking. There were neither diamonds nor pearls, or at least but a sprinkling—neither amongst the most fashionable. There were various Paris bonnets and even gowns—and perhaps the difference most to be remarked in general between these ladies and those at a morning dress-concert, for example, in London consists (putting aside, of course, the difference of complexion) in a look [these] generally had of being *dressed for the occasion* and an absence of perfect ease in consequence—not more so perhaps than English ladies would have who were compelled by fashion to wear mantillas for the first time. It is a pity that the bonnet is usurping its place both here and in Spain, and especially with a style of features which suit the mantilla, and generally look coarse under a bonnet.

The ladies of our party wore dresses and bonnets as simple, fresh, and elegant as could be seen in any part of the world. A young and titled heiress, newly arrived from her distant estates, wore pink satin with a white hat and feathers, and we observed that, according to the ancient San Agustín fashion, she changed her dress four or five times a day.[2] One box looked like a veritable parterre of flowers.

But the ladies may dress, and may smile, and may look their very best—they are little thought of this day in comparison with the one all-powerful, all-pervading object. It is even whispered that one cause of the more than usual crowd at San Agustín this year is that many failures are expected in mercantile houses, and that the heads of these houses or their agents are here on the desperate hope of retrieving their falling fortunes.

A good deal of play on a small scale goes on in the private houses among those who do not take much part in the regular gambling, but all are interested more or less—even strangers, even ladies, even ourselves. We returned to the house at which we were staying, where private *monte,* in which the ladies took a part, filled up the interval between the cock-fight and the ball on the hill of Calvario. Occasional news was brought in and received with deep interest—of the state of the banks, of the losses or gains of the different individuals, or of the result of the *vacas* (a sort of general purse, into which each puts two or three ounces). [This was supplied] by different stragglers from the gambling houses, who had themselves only ventured a few ounces and preferred the society of the ladies to that of the *monte* players. These were generally foreigners, and chiefly English.

We found the road to the Calvario—where, as usual, there was a ball in the afternoon—blocked up with carriages, and the hill itself covered with gay figures who were dancing as well as the tremendous crowd would permit. This was really tolerably republican.

The women generally were dressed as the better classes of Mexicans used to be years ago—and not so many years either, and as many in the country still are—in blonde dresses, with very short petticoats, open silk stockings, and white satin shoes. And such a collection of queer bonnets certainly never has been seen since the days when *les Anglaises pour rire* first set foot on Gallic shores.[3] Some were like small steeples, others resembled helmets, some were like sugar loaves, and most seemed to have been sat upon for convenience sake, all the way out. Amidst these there was a good sprinkling of pretty French bonnets and some well-made Herbauts and Paris dresses—but they belonged to the more fashionable classes. The scene was amusing from its variety, but we did not remain long, being afraid of rain. As we looked back, the crowd on the hill presented the appearance of a bed of butterflies dancing with black ants —which I presume were the men.

We returned to the Escandóns' house, where prayers and *monte* amused us till dinnertime. The dinner was very splendid: French cookery and good wines. There were about twenty-eight persons at table; some of them—Señores Casa Flores, [Felipe] Neri del Barrio, &c.—looked as if they had rather lost than otherwise. After dinner we returned to music and *monte,* and conversation on the events and probabilities of the day, till it was time to prepare for the ball at the plaza. As we were *ultra-fashionables,* or what is here called *"señoritas de mucho tono,"* we did not dress, intending to go to a box—which saves the trouble of dressing— and look down upon the natives. But when we arrived not a box was to be had for love or money, the crowd was so great and there were so many people of *tono* besides ourselves who wished to do the same thing. So we were obliged to content ourselves with hiding on the third row of benches on the floor, after persuading at least a dozen of very good-natured ladies to turn out in order to let us in. We were afterwards joined by the French minister and his wife. The ball looked very gay, and was prodigiously crowded, and exceedingly amusing.

There were people of all classes: modistes and carpenters, shopboys, tailors, hatters, and hosiers—mingled with all the *haut ton* of Mexico. Every shopboy considered himself entitled to dance with every lady, and no lady considered herself as having a right to refuse him, and then to dance with another person. The Señora de _____,[4] a most highbred, ladylike, and dignified person, danced with a stableboy in a jacket and without gloves, and he appeared particularly gratified at the extraordinary opportunity thus afforded him of holding her white gloves in his dirty brown paws. These fellows very naturally pick out the best ladies as their partners, and, strange as it may seem, there is certainly nothing in their behaviour that the most fastidious can complain of. They are perfectly polite, quiet, and well-mannered—and, what is more remarkable, dance and go through a quadrille quite as well as anybody else. The ball was quietness itself, until near the end when the wind instruments were suddenly seized with a fit of economy—the time they were paid for having probably expired—and stopped short in the midst of a waltz; upon which the gentlemen waltzers shouted out *"Viento! Viento!* [Wind! Wind!]" at the fullest extent of their voices, clapping their hands, refusing to dance, and entirely drowning the sound of some little jingling guitars which were patiently twanging on, until the windy gentlemen—the hired sons of Æolus—had to resume their labours.

There were some pretty faces among the secondary class of small shopkeepers, but their beauty is not striking, and takes a long time to discover—especially *fagotées* as they are in their ill-made, overloaded dresses. Amongst the prettiest of the ladies were Mme P. Cuevas and a daughter of the Marquis of Guadalupe—a granddaughter of La Güera's —but neither of them were *sobresaliente* [surpassing].

On the third night of the fête, Calderón and I, having left the ballroom about ten o'clock, walked out in the direction of the copper-tables which filled the middle of the square and were covered with awnings. It is a sight that, once seen, can never be forgotten. Nothing but the pencil of Hogarth, or the pen of Boz, could do justice to the various groups there assembled. It was a gambling *fête-champêtre*, conducted on the most liberal scale.

On each table were immense heaps of copper—great mountains— and occasionally a tolerable sprinkling of silver. There was a profusion of evergreens, small tin lamps dripping with oil, and sloping tallow candles shedding grease upon the board. Little ragged boys acting as waiters —their rags fluttering in the night breeze—were busily engaged in handing round pulque and *chia* in cracked tumblers. There was, moreover, an agreeable tinkling produced from several guitars, and even the bankers condescended to amuse their guests with soothing strains. The general dress of the company consisted of a single blanket, gracefully disposed in folds about the person, so as to show various glimpses of a bronze skin. To this some added a pair of Mexican pantaloons, and some a shirt of a doubtful colour—sufficiently torn to afford free entrance to the fresh air. There were many with large hats, most of which had crowns or parts of crowns. Generally speaking, however, the head was uncovered, or covered only with its native thatching of long, bushy, tangled black hair. This might be out of compliment to the ladies, of whom there were several, and who ought in politeness to have been mentioned first. Nothing could be simpler than their costume, consisting of a very dirty and extremely torn shift, with short sleeves, a shorter petticoat, and a pair of shoes—generally of dirty satin—also generally a *rebozo*, and the long matted hair hanging down like so many Eves in paradise. "They call this place a paradise," a Spanish soldier in Mexico wrote to his father; "and so it ought to be, it is so full of *Adams*."

There was neither fighting, nor swearing, nor high words. I doubt whether there be as much decorum at Crockford's; indeed, they were scrupulously polite to each other.[5] At one table, the person who held the bank was an enormously fat gentleman, one half of whose head was bound up with a large dirty white handkerchief, over which a torn piece of hat was stuck, very much to one side. He had a most roguish eye, and a smile of inviting benignity on his dirty countenance. In one hand he held and tingled a small guitar, while he most ingeniously swept in the copper with the other. He had a blanket carelessly thrown over one shoulder, and was altogether a superior-looking personage. By his side sat two wretched-looking women with long matted hair, their elbows on the table, and their great eyes fixed upon the cards with an expression of the most intense anxiety. At another table the *banker* was a very pretty little Indian woman, rather clean, comparatively speaking, and who appeared to be doing business smartly. A man stood near her—leaning against one of the wooden poles that supported the awning—who attracted all our attention. He had literally nothing on but a torn blanket— his head uncovered, and his feet bare—and was glaring upon the cards with his great dark, haggard-looking eyes, his brown face as pale as death, and with an expression bordering on despair. It needed no one to tell us that on the table was his last stake. What can such a man do but go upon the road? And what do those deserve who encourage these unfortunate people in this frightful vice—frightful from the consequences which it must eventually produce?

I have heard it mentioned, as a strong circumstance in favour of the Mexican character, that there is neither noise nor disturbance in these reunions; none of that uproar and violence that there would be in an English mob, for example. The fact is certain, but the inference is doubtful. The Indians are a people degraded, and accustomed to endure. They are gentle and cunning, and their passions are not easily roused, at least to open display; but once awakened, it is neither to uproar that these passions will be excited, nor by fair fight that they will be assuaged. In England a boxing match decides a dispute amongst the lower orders; in Mexico, a knife—and a broken head is easier mended than a cut throat. Despair must find vent in some way; and secret murder, or midnight robbery, are the fatal consequences of this very calmness of countenance, which is but a mask of nature's own giving to her Indian offspring.

Another reason for their calmness is the *habit* of gambling, in which they have indulged from childhood, and which has taught them that neither high words nor violence will restore a single dollar once fairly lost; and, in point of fairness, everything is carried on with the strictest honour, as among gamblers of high degree.

While "high life below stairs" is thus enacting, and these people are courting fortune and losing their money in the fresh air, the gentlemanly gamblers are seated before the green cloth-covered tables—with the gravity befitting so many cabinet councils, but without their mystery, for there is no concealment. Doors and windows are thrown open and even ladies may pass in and out, and look on at the game, if they please.

The heaps of ounces look tempting, and make it appear a true El Dorado. Nor is there any lack of creature comforts to refresh the flagging spirits. There are supper-spread tables, covered with savoury meats to appease their hunger, and with generous wines to gladden their hearts; and the gentlemen who surrounded *that* board seemed to be playing, instead of *monte*, an excellent knife and fork.

You must not suppose that those who hold gambling tables are the less considered on that account; on the contrary, as the banks generally win, they are amongst the richest, and consequently the most respected men in Mexico. After all, a gold ounce is a gold ounce, and in a republic we must not look to *origin*. These bankers are frequently Spaniards, who have found gambling the readiest steppingstone to fortune. Señor _____ explained to me one plan of those who hold the banks, a sort of *hedging*, by which it is next to impossible that they can lose. For example, one of these gentlemen proposes to his friends to take a share in a *vaca* or general purse, into which each person puts two or three ounces. Having collected several hundred ounces, they go to play at *his* bank. If they win, he receives his share of course; and if they lose, his bank wins the whole. It is in fact proceeding upon the principle of "Heads I win, tails you lose."[6]

At the tables not a word is spoken. The heaps of gold change masters; but the masters do not change countenance. I saw but one person who looked a little out of humour, and he was a foreigner. The rich man adds to his store, and the man of small fortune becomes a beggar—without making an exclamation. He is ruined, but "makes no sign."[7]

The ladies who have collected ounces, and made purses, send their friends and admirers to the tables to try their luck for them; and in some of the inferior houses the señoras of a lower class occasionally try their fortune for themselves. I saw one of these, who had probably lost, by no means "taking it coolly." She looked like an overcharged thundercloud— but whether she broke forth in anger or in tears, thunder or rain, we did not stay to see.

In short, it is an all-pervading mania, and custom has done so much that—as man is "a bundle of habits"—the most moral persons in this country or those who have most pretensions to be so (always excepting one or two ladies who express their opinions strongly against it), see nothing in it to condemn, and are astonished at the effect which such a scene produces on a stranger who views it for the first time. And, indeed, after a few years' residence here, a foreigner almost becomes blinded to these abuses, by the veil of decorum with which they are covered.

"*Los pobres!*" said the good-natured President to a foreign gentleman who made some remark on the subject. "It amuses them."

We returned the same night to San Antonio in the brightest, most beautiful moonlight possible, and in perfect safety—it being on the highroad to Mexico—and therefore guarded by soldiers. We heard the next morning that a nephew of General Barrera's who had ventured upon going by a crossroad to his house at Mixcoac, was attacked, robbed of the money he had won at the fête, and severely wounded. This, being the natural consequence of gambling—the *morale* to the story, as it were—excited neither surprise nor remark. The robbers who, in hopes of plunder, flock down at the time of the fête like *zopilotes* seeking carrion, hide themselves among the barren rocks of the Pedregal, rendering all crossroads insecure, and making it impossible to travel, except on the highroad which is guarded, without a strong escort.[8]

An anecdote on the subject of gambling at San Agustín—which is too curious not to be recorded, although but one amongst a thousand of the same description—was related to us this morning by a member of the cabinet. A very rich Spaniard, possessed of many haciendas and much land, attended the fête at San Agustín, and—having won three thousand ounces—ordered the money to be carried in sacks to his carriage, and prepared to return to Mexico along with his wife. His carriage was just setting off when a friend of his came out of an adjoining house, and requested him to stay and breakfast with him before going. Much pressed, he at length got out of his carriage, along with his wife—leaving the money and intending to proceed to Mexico immediately after breakfast. But after breakfast, there being a *monte* table in the house, at which some of his acquaintances were playing, he was induced to put down two ounces, which he lost. He continued playing and losing, until he had lost his three thousand ounces, which were sent for and transferred to the winners. He still continued playing with a terrible infatuation, till he had lost his whole fortune. He went on blindly, staking one hacienda after another, lands and property of all sorts, until the sun—which had risen upon him a rich and prosperous man—set, leaving him a beggar! It is said that he bore this extraordinary and sudden reverse with the utmost philosophy and equanimity. He left a son, whom we have seen at San Agustín, a poor man who earns a scanty livelihood by dealing cards as croupier at different gambling-houses—a sad fate for one born in prosperity and affluence.

Tuesday: June 29th, 1841

No particular occurrence has taken place since the fête: a visit from the new secretary of legation and the attaché, a diplomatic dinner at the English minister's, much going and coming and writing on the subject of a house in Mexico, a correspondence concerning the sale of our furniture, mules, &c., &c. A good deal of interest excited by a bet between two English gentlemen, as to whether it were possible for one of them to ride from Mexico to San Angel in twenty minutes, which feat he performed, starting from the gate called El Niño Perdido, and reaching the old church of San Angel within the given time.[9] These I think are the most remarkable circumstances that have taken place

We are now in treaty for the furnished apartments of the director of the Casa de Moneda (the mint),[10] a great building next the palace—from which upwards of one thousand three hundred millions of coined gold and silver have issued since the beginning of the sixteenth century. The house is a palace in extent and solidity; and the residence of the

director is very spacious and handsome, besides having the great
advantage of being furnished. We expect to return to Mexico in a few
days.

Tuesday: July 6th, 1841
Casa de Moneda, Mexico

Here we are, re-established in Mexico for a short time at least—and
not without difficulty has it been accomplished.

We left the country with some regret, as this is the pleasantest time of
the year for being there, and everything was looking green and beautiful.
We came in, ourselves in a loaded carriage, and in advance: fourteen
asses loaded with boxes, four Indians with ditto, and two enormous loaded
carts—one drawn by four, and another by eight mules. We were a regular
caravan, as our friend the alcalde called us. Imagine the days of packing
and unpacking consequent thereupon!

On the thirtieth of June, the victory gained by the government over
the federalist party was celebrated with great éclat. The President was
presented with a diamond cross, valued at six thousand dollars, and
General Valencia with a splendid jewel-hilted sword of great value.[11]

"Yesterday at dawn," says the newspaper of the day, "a general pealing
of the bells, accompanied by the customary salvos, announced to the
capital that it was the day of rewards and of universal joy.

"At twelve o'clock His Excellency the President of the Republic went
to the palace to fulfill the formality of closing the sessions, and to receive
from the hands of the president of the chamber of deputies the diploma
and the cross of honour mentioned in the decrees of the second of March
and second of May of this year.

"An immense multitude occupied the galleries; and the president of
he chamber of deputies, Licenciado Don José María Bravo, addressed
His Excellency General Bustamante in the following speech:

Citizen General, and illustrious President: Nations never forget the
distinguished services that are done for them, nor fail to reward those
heroic actions performed for the common good. Sooner or later they
show themselves grateful and reward, as they ought, their good and
valiant servants. The Mexican nation has not forgotten yours, and its
congress has ever borne in mind those which you performed for it at
that happy period when the unfortunate hero of Iguala, causing the
voice of freedom to resound to the remotest lands of the Mexican
territory, gave a terrible lesson to those who wish to subdue weak nations, with no other title than that of strength.[12] You were one of the
first and most valiant chiefs, who, placed by his side, assisted in this
important and happy work; you it was who showed to the tyrant in

the fields of Juchi, Atzcapotzalco, and others, that the sword of the Mexicans, once unsheathed for liberty and justice, fights without softening or breaking; and knows how to triumph over its enemies, even when superior forces oppose it. You it was, in short, who with intrepid valour co-operated in re-establishing a liberty which, torn from the ancient children of the soil, was converted by their oppressors into a hard and shameful tyranny. History has already consecrated her pages to you; she will record to posterity your heroic deeds, and congress has already busied itself in rewarding such useful services.

If some Mexicans, erring in their opinions, by a fatality in this country, have disowned them, making an attempt against your personal liberty, notwithstanding the dignity of the first magistrate, trampling upon laws and overturning order, they have at length been obliged to respect you; and your valour, firmness, and decision have made them preserve the consideration due to an ancient chief of our independence, and to a first magistrate who has known how to set an example of subordination to the laws, and to give with dignity lessons of valour and of honourable conduct.

A diploma and a cross are the rewards which the sovereign congress has decreed for these services and merits. Do not regard in the one the effaceable characters in which it is written, nor be dazzled by the brilliancy of the other. See in both a proof of your country's gratitude, and, engraving it in your soul, continue to give testimonies to your country that she is the first object of your care; that your watchings, fatigues, and labours are dedicated only to procure for her those benefits which may bring about the durable and solid peace that she so much desires, and for which you would, if necessary, sacrifice yourself on her altars. Do not forget that today she shows herself grateful, and that this is the day decreed by the august national representative body, to put you in possession of the title and insignia which manifest her gratitude.

I, in the name of the congress, congratulate you on this fortunate event, and having the honour to fulfill the desire of the sovereign power, place in your hands this diploma of deserving reward from your country, and give you possession of this cross.

"His Excellency, having received the diploma and cross above mentioned, with his native modesty replied thus:

In hearing, by the organ of the august national representation, the great encomiums with which it favours me, putting me at the same time in possession of these precious gifts, my soul overflows with ineffable pleasure, and is overwhelmed with the deepest gratitude.

My satisfaction and my glory are immense. What could I have done, that thus the generous hand of the representatives of the Mexican people should load me with honours? Have my trifling services been able to fix the attention of the country, on whose altars have been sacrificed so many and such illustrious heroes of liberty?

My glory would have been yet greater, had I, like them, descended to the sepulchre, when the sun of victory brightened the existence of this sovereign and independent nation, to the glory of the Universe. The honours which I receive today are certainly great; but I should have preferred them before the never-sufficiently mourned catastrophe of the immortal Iturbide. Let us throw a thick veil over so irreparable a loss.

It is true that, surviving such great misfortunes, I have been enabled to consecrate my existence and my vigilance to the peace, order, and felicity of this beloved country. But how difficult is the conduct of those who govern in the midst of the conflict of civil dissensions! In these, my conscience has chosen, and my resolution has never vacillated between ignominy and honour.

Do I, on this account, deserve the national gratitude and munificence manifested by such distinguished rewards?

I return for them to the representatives of the nation my frankest gratitude; fixing my mind only on the grandeur and benevolence of the sovereign power which rewards me in the sacred name of the country. I shall preserve till death these precious objects which render my name illustrious as a soldier and as a supreme magistrate.

They will stimulate me more and more every day to all kinds of sacrifices, even to the giving up my life should it be necessary; that I may not be unworthy of the favourable conception and of the recompense with which the worthy representatives of so magnanimous a nation have today honoured me.

Receive, gentlemen, this frank manifestation of my sentiments, and of my fervent vows for the felicity of the republic, with the most sincere protestations of my eternal gratitude.

"The liveliest emotions of satisfaction"—I still quote from the *Diario*—"followed this expressive discourse. Joy was painted on every countenance. The frank satisfaction which everyone felt gave to this act a solemnity which words are incapable of describing. . . .

"His Excellency, accompanied by the corporations and by a brilliant and numerous concourse, then passed to the hall of the court-martial, to put in possession of His Excellency General Don Gabriel Valencia the sword of honour which the august national representation had granted him for his loyal and valiant conduct in the affair of July of 1840.

"His Excellency the President began this ceremony by expressing his sentiments to His Excellency [General Valencia], *jefe de la plana mayor* (head of the staff), in these terms:

Citizen General: In this day, the most flattering of my life, in which the august representatives of the nation have just put me in possession of the rewards granted to my small services, I fulfill the law which imposes upon me the grateful task of presenting you with the sword of honour, with which their munificence has also chosen to remunerate yours.

Receive it as the distinguished reward of your loyalty, and of the valour with which you fought at that memorable period, from the

15th to the 26th of July of 1840, defending with bravery the constitution and supreme powers of the Republic.

I congratulate myself with you, not doubting that you will always employ the edge of this steel in defense of the honour, of the sacred rights, and of the laws of this country. Yes, general of this beloved country, to whom we owe all kinds of sacrifices; yes, of this beloved mother, who now more than ever reclaims the fraternal union of all her children, to resist the internal and external enemies who oppose her felicity and aggrandizement.

Let us pledge ourselves to respond thankfully to the generosity with which the representatives of the nation have rewarded us, and let us march united in the same path which honour and duty traced out for us, in that day of honourable memory for the defenders of the laws.

Eternal praise to the brave soldiers and citizens who co-operated with us in the establishment of order!

"To which General Valencia replied:

That a correspondent reward should follow an heroic action is natural; but to remunerate a service which does not go beyond the sphere of ordinary things, such as mine in the affair of the 15th to the 26th of July of 1840, by such a noble distinction as the sword of honour with which Your Excellency has deigned to gird me, in the name of the national congress—of this the magnanimity of the sovereignty is alone capable; and so it is that I remain annihilated by a present worthy of the ages of the Roman senate and republic. What did I do, Your Excellency, in those days, that any one of my countrymen would not have done better? Nothing, sir; so that, in receiving this sword of honour, my confusion equals my doubt as to my place in the gratitude of the congress which has given it to me, of Your Excellency who has deigned to present it to me, and of my worthy countrymen who bestowed it that I might wear it.

In this condition, Your Excellency, of content and satisfaction, I can say no more, but that I hope Your Excellency will manifest to congress my eternal gratitude; that Your Excellency will receive my noble acknowledgments, and my companions the assurance that every time I put it on I shall remember the names of all and each of them who accompanied me on the 15th of July of 1840, together with the pleasure that to them I owe so great a mark of respect.

"Amongst the congratulations which were given to His Excellency the President, there was circulated in print the following"—very remarkable —"document, which we copy in full:

CONGRATULATION from [His Excellency General Valencia,] the head of the army staff, to His Excellency the President on his receiving the decoration of the cross of honour from congress.

God said, the first day of the creation of the world, when it was in a state of chaos, "Let there be light, and there was light." And God saw his work and pronounced it good! With how much more reason ought the garrison of Mexico to do so every day in which, by any action, the 15th of July of 1840 is celebrated—in which, by their strength and heroic valour, that passage of Genesis was politically repeated in this capital. Society arose in chaos. Its President is taken. Authorities no longer exist, and those who ought to save them are converted into their oppressors.

God said, "Let there be light," and there was light! The honourable troops, reunited in the citadel, in the midst of chaos, said, "Let order be re-established; let the supreme magistrate be set at liberty, and let things resume their proper march." Order *was* re-established, Your Excellency was set free, and the political body followed the regular path, without which no society exists. So it is that those worthy troops who thus said, thus undertook, and thus accomplished, today also resemble the Creator of the world (*hoy también asemejan al Criador del mundo*) in his content, when satisfied with his work.

The cross which has been worthily placed on Your Excellency's breast this day reflects in such a unique manner upon the hearts of the valiant men of that period (*reflecta de un modo tan singular sobre los corazones de los valientes de aquella época*) that their souls are expanded in contemplating it, by the honour which results to them from it.

May Your Excellency be happy one and a thousand times, with such a noble and worthy decoration. Let Your Excellency receive in it the sincere congratulations of the garrison of Mexico, which figures in each stone of this cross, like the stars in the firmament.

"This ceremony being concluded, the two rewarded generals presented themselves on the principal balcony of the palace, in front of which passed the brilliant column of honour; at its head marched the commandant-general, Don Valentín Canalizo; and the brilliancy, neatness, and elegance which all the corps of the garrison displayed is above all praise.

"When the regiment had passed, a sumptuous collation was served in one of the halls of the ministry of war, in which elegance, good taste, and propriety rivalled one another; while repeated toasts showed the most sincere joy, united with the most patriotic and fraternal sentiments.

"Rain having begun to fall at about three in the afternoon, the *paseo* was on this account not so crowded as might have been expected; nevertheless, the military bands were present, and at six in the evening their Excellencies Generals Bustamante and Valencia, having presented themselves there, were received with *vivas* and universal joy.

"At night the chiefs and officers of the *plana mayor* gave a ball in the college of the Minería; and the theatre of New Mexico dedicated its entertainment to His Excellency the President. . . .

"Nothing disturbed the joy of this day: one sentiment alone of union and cheerfulness overflowed in the capital, proving to those illustrious generals the unanimous applause with which Mexicans see their country reward the distinguished services of their children, who are so deserving of their love and gratitude."

The above is the account published in the *Diario* of the celebration of the putting down of the federalist party in the famous *pronunciamiento* of last year.

It is peculiarly remarkable in all its details when we consider all the circumstances of that revolution: the manner in which the President suffered himself to be surprised, the shameful want of military skill displayed by the soldiers, and the disgraceful peace by which the federalists were suffered to march out of the palace *tambour battant* and colours flying—moreover, the desertion of several of the most *loyal* regiments to the rebellious party.

Notwithstanding the ineffable joy which, according to the *Diario*, is generally felt on this occasion, there are many who doubt the policy of this celebration—the peculiar time chosen for presenting the President with a cross valued at $6,000, and General Valencia with a sword of equal price—a time when the troops are unpaid, when the soldiers wounded at this very *pronunciamiento* are refused their pensions, when the widows and orphans of others are starving and without a hope that the government will be able or willing to afford them the least assistance. "At the best," say those who cavil on the subject, "it was a civil war—a war between brothers—a subject of regret and not of glory—of sadness and not of jubilee."

As for General Valencia's congratulation to the President, in which he compares the "honourable troops" to the Supreme Being, the re-establishment of order in Mexico to the creation of the world from chaos, it is chiefly incomprehensible. Perhaps he is carried away by his joy and gratitude, and personal affection for Bustamante—perhaps he has taken a leaf from a translation of *Bombastes Furioso*, [which] it is not unlike.[13] Had it been the address of an enthusiastic multitude to the Duke of Wellington at the termination of the battle of Waterloo, could hyperbole and even profanity have reached the height of the speech addressed by Valencia to the President? Can *bathos* and absurdity go further!

It is said that the President, not quite understanding it, but having apparently a confused idea that they were comparing him to God, said two or three times: "Como Dios! No tanto—no tanto—oh no [Like God! That's too much—Oh no!]" The whole speech resembles c little the excellent rules of Captain Marryat's for writing a fashionable novel: "If you had understood one particle, that particle I would have erased!" The enthusiasm for Valencia was so great that his principal officers acted as coachmen and footmen to his carriage.

One thing is certain: the whole affair had a brilliant appearance; and the handsome carriages, fine horses, gaily dressed officers and soldiers—together with the military music and the crowds of people collected—produced an imposing effect.

42

In Apartments at the Mint

Tuesday: July 13th, 1841
Casa de Moneda, Mexico

We little expected to be still here at the opening of the new Italian opera, and had consequently given up our box. Señor Roca, who went to Italy to bring out the requisites, has arrived at the end of a wonderfully short period with the singers, male and female, the new dresses, decorations, &c.—and the first opera, *Lucia di Lammermoor*, was given last week.

The theatre is the former Teatro de Gallos—the cocks' theatre—an octagonal circus which has been fitted up as elegantly as circumstances would permit, and as the transition from the crowing of cocks to the soft notes of *Giulietta* rendered necessary. Juliet to sing where cocks did crow—"It is the nightingale that sings so late!"

The new company who have come over with Roca are *said* to be firstrate—in which case they would probably not have chosen this distant scene of action.

The *prima donna assoluta* is the Signora Anaide Castellan de Giampietro, born in Paris, bred in Milan. The *prima donna soprano* is the Signora Amalia Luzio de Ricci; and the *altra prima* and *seconda donna* is called Signora [Luigia] Branzanti. The first tenor is Signor Emilio Giampietro, husband of the prima donna; and the second tenor is the Signor Alberti Bozetti. The first bass is Signor Antonio Tommasi, and the *buffo* bass Signor Luigi Spontini.[1]

L_____ is proné-ing them to such an extent—and public expectation has been so much excited—that the public will probably be disappointed and the first evening at least be a failure to a certain extent. He declares the prima donna to resemble Persiani, and the tenor to be superior to Rubini! The Mexican audience, if not very experienced, is decidedly musical; and they have already had a pretty good opera here, have heard Madame Albini, la Cesari, García (the father of Malibran), and the *beaux restes* of Galli; therefore can compare.[2]

The first evening the Castellan made her appearance as Lucia. She is about twenty: slight and fair, with black hair, rather *graziosa*, and with a very sweet, clear, and pure young voice, also very correct—but rather wanting in fullness and power. The tenor Giampietro rests upon his wife's laurels. He looks well, but little more can be said in his praise —a handsome stick, with a disagreeable voice that sounds as if it were poured through a gigantic comb. Of the others, Tommasi is the best. [He] has some good notes, and a fine figure. The rest are 0. The theatre is extremely well got up, the dresses are new and very rich, and the decorations and scenery remarkably good. On the whole it is a wonderful opera for Mexico. The public, however, was evidently disappointed. They had prepared for wonders, and were not satisfied with a tolerable performance. The applauses were few and far between. The Castellan was not called for, and the following day a certain degree of discontent pervaded the aristocracy of the capital. The remarks were manifold: the Castellan was no actress—the tenor was a horror—they had been deceived—and so on.

At the second representation of the same opera, matters mended. The Castellan was more at ease—things went better. [Her] voice was appreciated. Applauses were loud and long, and at the end of the opera she and Roca, the director, were called for, and received with enthusiasm. She seems likely to become a favourite.

The director of the orchestra, Wallace, quarrelled with the director who was brought from Italy, and still more with the second director— a Negro or Chinese—and, finding he could make nothing of any of them, gave up the concern.

Last evening we had *Giulietta e Romeo*, in which La Ricci and La Cesari made their appearance, the former as Giulietta, the latter as Romeo.[3] The Ricci is a thin young woman, with a long, pale face, black eyes and hair, long bony neck and arms, and large hands; extremely pretty, it is said, off the stage, and very ineffective on it; but both on and off with a very distinguished air. Her voice is extensive, but wanting cultivation, and decidedly *pea-hennish*; besides that, she is apt to go out of tune. Her style of dress was excessively unbecoming to her style of beauty and her figure. She wore a tight white gown, a tight blue satin peaked body, low, with long tight blue sleeves. Her chest is hollow and her back is round—and her arms looked like two blue posts. To me she appears a failure, though she was rather applauded than otherwise. The public were indulgent, but it was evident that they were disappointed.

La Cesari, highly married, leading the life of a lady, and having had a child—and who for the last three years has not appeared upon the stage— came out as Romeo, with tunic and mantle, white silk stockings, hat and feathers, &c. In short, after having lost to a certain extent her voice— grown older, accustomed to domestic comfort, and unaccustomed to admirers—[she] had to put herself into tights and white silk stockings, tunic, mantle, hat, and feathers, &c., to enact the part of Romeo. She was dreadfully frightened and ill at ease, and it required all the applause with which the audience greeted the *entrée* of their former favourite to restore her to self-possession. She looked remarkably well—tall, handsome, beautifully made, rather pale, with fine dark eyes, dark hair, and *moustaches*. Her acting was greatly superior, as much so as was her beauty, to that of any of the others. She has more knowledge of the theatre—more science, taste, grace, and energy—than any of them; but her voice unfortunately was but the *beaux restes* of better days—a sweet, soft contralto, out of use and without any force. To a certain extent applause revived her, but it was evident that the voice is feeble— or out of use. One consideration, however, is that the theatre, hitherto used for cocks to crow in, is very badly constructed for the voice—and must have an exceedingly bad effect upon the fullness and tone.

On the whole, it seems very doubtful whether the opera will endure long. Were we going to remain here, I should trust that it might be supported, for, with all its faults and drawbacks, it is decidedly the best public exhibition in Mexico. The *coup d'œil* was exceedingly pretty, as all the boxes were crowded, and the ladies were in full dress.

Tuesday: July 20th, 1841

As we are living in the mint, the directors have called on us; and this morning they came to invite us to descend into the lower regions, to see some silver coined. We went all over this immense establishment, a fine picture of decayed magnificence, built about one hundred and ten years ago by the Spaniards. Dirty, ill-kept, the machinery rude, the workmen half-naked and discontented, the directors discontented, its fine vaulted roofs, that look like the interior of a cathedral, together with that *grandiose* style which distinguished the buildings of the Spaniards in Mexico, form a strange contrast with the occupants.

We saw the silver bars stretched out, the dollars cut and whitened and stamped. And in one place we saw the machines for *coining false money*, which have been collected in such numbers that there is hardly room for them! We saw the place where the silver and gold is tested, and a room with medals, amongst which are some ancient Greek, Roman, Persian, and English, but especially Spanish, and many of the time of Charles III. When we were looking at [these], an old director exclaimed: "Would to heaven that those days would return!"—without doubt the general feeling.

This old man had been forty-four years in the Casa de Moneda, and had lived under six viceroys. He told me he was a boy when his father sent him with a commission to the Viceroy Revillagigedo, and that he went very much frightened, but was so kindly received that he was very soon at his ease. He described to me the flourishing condition of the mint in those days, which coined twenty-seven millions annually, and was a royal house. He said that the viceroys used to praise them and to thank them for their exertions—whereas now they met with nothing but insults—that the house was then kept in the most beautiful order, the principal officers wearing a uniform, &c.

Hereupon another little old gentleman took up the theme, and improved upon it; and told us that, on one occasion, they had one million three hundred thousand dollars' worth of gold in the house; and described how the Vice-Queen Iturrigaray came to see it, and sat down and looked round her in amazement at the extraordinary quantity of wealth she saw accumulated around her.[4] This little old gentleman had been thirty years there in the mint, and seemed as though he had never been anywhere else—as if he were part and parcel in it, and had been coined, and beat out, and clipped there.

Hearing him, a fat man, rather unclipped-looking than otherwise, began to bewail the state of the times, till it was a chorus universal, where all sang in one key. The first man had a very large, hanging underlip, with a kind of tragi-comic countenance, as if, miserable or not, he had determined to make the best of it. He made two or three lugubrious puns. The second, who seemed bred to the mint (though by his account the mint was not *bread* to him) was horribly and insatiably curious, as a man born in a mint might be.

We passed about three hours in a mixture of admiration for the past and disgust for the present—and we were reconducted to our domicile by the poor *employés* who seemed to think that a Spanish minister was the next best to a Spanish viceroy, of anything they had seen for some time. If their well-*mint* efforts could put a Spanish king on the throne, [they] would certainly not be very long in bringing it about.

> The Past is nothing; and at last,
> The Future will but be the Past,

says Lord Byron. Here the Past is everything; and the Future—? Answer it who can. I suspect that [it] will be vastly different—Amen.[5]

I was assured by the directors, while wondering at the number of machines for false coining which had been collected, that there are twice that number now in full force in Mexico—but that they belong to such distinguished personages the government is afraid to interfere with them! Besides this, there is now no sufficient punishment for this crime, which in the days of the Spanish government was considered a capital offense. They informed me that many of these personages are amongst our visiting acquaintances—and illustrated, as one well known, General _____!

A lady here is said to have exclaimed with much simplicity on hearing her husband accused of false coining, "I really wonder why they make so much noise about it. It seems to me that my husband's copper is as good as any other!"[6]

One may live a long while in Mexico, if not given to *chismes* [gossip], without discovering the secret crimes that disgrace it. I have heard an account today, and from *too* good authority, of the private life of General A. *qui fait frémir la nature*—and [it] is the more extraordinary as the individual in question appears in his countenance the very impersonation of honesty—frank, open, manly and handsome. The very least of the crimes imputed to him is the murder of his sister's husband. The others are too horrible to have been enacted by the most accursed by fate in Grecian fable.[7]

Saturday: July 24th, 1841

We went last evening to the opera, which was a repetition of *Lucia* —as it appears they dare not venture, in the face of public disapprobation, to repeat *Giulietta e Romeo* as yet.

As we were passing through the great square near the cathedral, the carriage suddenly stopped, the coachman and footman uncovered their heads, and an immense procession went passing by towards the cathedral, with lights and military music. There were officers in full uniform, with their heads uncovered, a long file of monks and priests, and a carriage carrying the Host—surrounded by several hundreds of people on foot, all bearing lighted torches. A band of military music accompanied the whole. We were very much astonished at this magnificent procession, it not being a fête day. When at length, being able to pass along, we arrived at the opera, we were informed that they were carrying the *viaticum* to General Barrera,[8] who—in the midst of a dangerous illness—had gone out that morning on horseback and immediately on his return home was seized with a vomiting of blood. His case is considered hopeless.

And so for him, then, these great cathedral bells are tolling heavily; for him, the torches and the pompous procession, the sandalled monks, and the officers in military array; while two bands of music are playing at his door and another in front of the cathedral; and in the midst of these sounds of monkish hymn and military music, his soul, alone and unattended, is preparing to wing its flight—whither?

His ill-gotten wealth—his splendid house—what are they now to him? Memorials of the dross for which he may have risked his immortal soul. "But what art thou that judgest?"[9] If we are to be judged by our *opportunities*, who can say how much severity may be lessened in the case of a common soldier, surrounded by examples of triumphant vice, raised from nothing by energy without principle, uneducated, and with models of successful villainy forever before his eyes? Here he was too rich and too high to be judged. He has gone or is about to go— before a different tribunal.

But meanwhile the sweet music of *Lucia* drove all other from our ears, if not from our thoughts. In a house, not many hundred yards off, they are administering the Host to a dying man, while here La Castellan, with her pretty French graces, and charming voice, is trying to draw forth tears from our eyes for fictitious sorrows.

There is not an expression of regret for General Barrera. On the contrary, he seems to go on his way unlamented, and the talk is of the *pleitos* [controversies] there will probably be between the children of his first wife and his widow and his creditors.

The theatre was pretty well filled, though there were some empty boxes—sights more hideous in the eyes of actors than toothless mouths. We sat with Madame la Baronne de Cyprey and Madame Schneider, a pretty little German, but *sans tournure*.[10] In our box was a little French- man, bent upon travelling prodigiously, the Baron de Froissac.

Nearly opposite to us was Madame Mangino, niece of the wife of the Príncipe de la Paz, Madame Tudó. She is a handsome woman with a fine Bohemian cast of face, so dark in complexion, with such glittering teeth, brilliant eyes, and dark hair. Moreover, very *comme il faut*. She does not seem too enchanted with Mexico. Having spent her life on the continent of Europe, and much in Paris, it is rather a change of its kind.[11]

La Castellan sang very well—never better—with much clearness, preci- sion, and facility. She is certainly graceful and on the stage pretty. Except in her method of singing, there is nothing Italian about her. [She is] more French than Italian. Her style suits *Lucia*, but I doubt her having *l'air noble* sufficient for a Norma or a Semiramis.[12] The bass improves upon further acquaintance, but the handsome tenor is nought. [He] sings out of tune and is an unredeemable and handsome stick. The audience seemed to me both indulgent and discriminating. They applauded the pretty prima donna *con furor;* they praised the bass a good deal when he deserved it, and the tenor whenever they possibly could—but where he sang false, as he did in his dying song in the last scene, nothing could extort from them a solitary *viva*. This discrimination makes their applause worth having, and it does not proceed either from experience or cultivation but from a *musical instinct*.

News has come in that the general, though still ill and in great danger, is not dead—and is likely to recover. La Güera, who is a living chronicle, has just been here, and has given me his history.

He was a small *tailor* in this city, and, wishing to marry a woman with money, he got himself made a halberdier in the palace—it being in the palmy days of the viceroys—so that his duty was to mount guard on the staircase. Dressed in his soldier's uniform, and knowing (as it appears) the *faiblesses* of the feminine heart, he now presented himself before his belle—who had before slighted him. The uniform and pike were irresistible, and with her money he commenced tailoring on a larger scale, until at length he got a contract from [the] government for supplying the officers' uniforms. The lady, the steppingstone to his fortune, died—leaving our tailor in a state of widowed blessedness, in which the fates did not permit him long to continue. He fell a victim to a predilection for clean and finely-sewed linen. A pretty sewing girl, hearing of this inclination, bought at a French shop a shirt of wonderful fineness, sewed and embroidered in the most minute and tasteful fashion, *all adown* the front—and, having made her way to our hero, presented it to him with many blushes as being the workmanship of her own fair fingers. She came—*he* saw—she conquered! From a sewing girl she became the wife of the military tailor. Fortune favours the cunning.

The government was now irretrievably in debt to this great man. Instead of money, of which they had none, he asked for glory, a mere drug in the Mexican market. He became a captain—a colonel—at length a general. The Marquis of Apartado, in want of money or actuated by caprice, sold him his palace—family diamonds, and pearls, &c.—for the smallest sum possible, and went to Paris. The general also embarked first in the profitable trade of smuggling—and then took to coining the money of the realm on his own account.

Thus has he thriven until the ripe age of seventy—when inexorable Death has given him a rough summons. Perhaps the noisy reception he met with has induced him to withdraw for the present. What with trumpets and drums, fife and clarion, it seems as if the inexorable had been induced to beat a retreat.

In a visit we made the other day we were shown a piece of embroidery, which—from its splendour and good taste—is worthy of comment, though by no means uncommon here. We went to call on the wife of Peña y Peña, a judge, and he and Madame Peña y Peña showed us all through their beautiful house, which looks out on the Alameda.[13] In one of the rooms, their daughter was engaged on a piece of embroidery for the altar of the chapel. The ground was the very richest and thickest white satin; the design was a garland of vine leaves, with bunches of grapes. The vine leaves were beautifully embroidered in fine gold, and the grapes were composed of real amethysts. I can conceive nothing richer and more tasteful than the general effect.

The gold embroidery done in Mexico is generally very beautiful, and there are many ladies who embroider in great perfection. There is an amazing quantity of it used in the churches, and in military uniforms. I have also seen beautiful gold-embroidered ball dresses, but they are nearly out of fashion.

Sunday: July 25th, 1841

This being the day of Santiago, the patron saint of Spain, Calderón was invited by the padres of San Francisco to attend mass at nine o'clock in the church there. Calderón was invited by the padres as minister, and wore his crosses and orders.

We were shown to the *tribuna* (gallery) of the Countess de Santiago, where we were alone, and where they gave us chairs, and put down a piece of carpet. Calderón and the rest of the legation were placed in the body of the church, in velvet chairs—and lighted tapers were put in their hands. The saint was carried in procession, all carrying tapers —through the church—going out by the principal door—making the tour of the streets—and returning by a side door. Calderón and the secretaries walked in the procession carrying lighted tapers.

The music was pretty good, and one soprano voice especially was very fine. The prettiest thing was twelve little boys placed on crimson velvet benches, on either side of the altar, representing pilgrims of Galicia (of which Santiago is the capital).[14] [They were] handsome little fellows, belonging to respectable families, dressed in robes of dark green, or crimson, or violet coloured velvet, with falling lace collars, and the necks ornamented with gold and silver shells—a large black pilgrim's hat fastened on behind and hanging down, and in their hands staffs with gold bells.[15] They were beautiful children, and all behaved with becoming gravity and decorum during the ceremony, walking seriously and with much dignity in the procession.

After the *función* we went out to Santiago, an old church near Mexico, where from time immemorial the Indians annually come in great procession on this day—and sell their fruit, flowers, pulque, &c. All the waste ground near the church was covered with green booths, where Indian men and women were established with their goods for sale. There was an immense crowd of carriages and horsemen, and people on foot. The troops were drawn out, escorting the procession to the church.[16]

But though the scene was curious, as the remnant of an old established ceremony, and the Indians—with their booths and flowers, and great show of fruit—were all very picturesque, the sun was so intense that after wandering about for some time, and buying tunas and nuts and peaches, we returned home, together with the Güera Rodríguez, who was in our carriage with us, and who was all the time lamenting the state of the times and giving us a lively description of what this fête used to be in former days.[17]

Except amongst the present race of soldiers raised by revolution to be colonels and generals, it seems to me that there is scarcely a dissentient voice of regret amongst the Mexicans for the old days of viceroyalty. Foreigners of course tell a different tale, but I speak of Mexicans as I find them.[18]

Had a visit the same morning from the Señora Mangino, whom I think even handsomer by daylight than she appeared to be at the opera—not always the case with dark beauties.

Monday: July 26th, 1841

Another representation of Vaccai's *Giulietta e Romeo*, with the second appearance of La Ricci. Music and Ricci were considered a failure. It is true that her voice is harsh and untutored. The Señora Cesari made the handsomest of Romeos, as usual, but was ill, and out of spirits and voice—and towards the end an announcement was made that, being suddenly indisposed, her grand aria in the last act would be omitted. Shortly after followed announcement number two: "In spite of the illness of the Señora Cesari, desirous of pleasing the public, she will sing as she can."[19] The first piece of news was received in ominous silence; the second with a slight applause.

The opera as a whole was coldly received; the boxes and pit were nearly empty, and La Ricci seems unlikely to gain any favour with the public—though it must be confessed that she certainly looked better, was more becomingly dressed, and both sang and acted better than the first time.

We spent the other evening at Mme de Cyprey's. Nobody there, though her *soirée* night, but little Mme de Cussac and the Baron of Ditto.[20] It seems to me they are very *mauvais genre*, both man and wife. She is an odd little forward, noisy thing—a constant talker and laugher, always looking at herself in the glass. He looks a horrid roué, and vulgar—and covered with hair. I like neither of them, and doubt their being anything in France. Nobody seems to know what they have come for—which in fact is nobody's business. But when I said to her the other night that she at least had come for her amusement, and not like *nous autres* diplomats per order, she answered with her quick pert voice: *"Pas tout à fait, Madame, pas tout à fait.* [Not entirely, Madame, not entirely.]"

Late in the evening the Castellan with her tenor came in. They had come from a dinner given by a rich curate to the whole *corps opératique,* from the prima donna down to the *joueur du basson,* and even to the tailor who makes the opera dresses, and his wife. This rich padre, it is said, spends a great part of his fortune in entertaining actors and singers —about $20,000 per annum *obsequiando los cómicos!*—a noble employ-ment for an ecclesiastic's money.

The Castellan informed us that she could not sing without Roca's permission, an agreement being made between him and the *artistes* that whoever sung at a private house should lose a month's salary. A messenger was immediately dispatched to mollify Mr. Roca, in the person of an idiot named Labatte, who returned shortly with an affir-mative from Roca—which seemed greatly to please La Castellan. She immediately sat down to the piano to sing, and gave us with much expression the romance in *Robert le Diable*—*"Grâce, grâce pour moi!"* —very well indeed as to voice, but too laboured and theatrical for a small room. I prefer her voice in the theatre.

Her face, though perhaps not strictly pretty, is very charming. Having had her hair cut short in consequence of an illness, she wears a close crop which suits her very well. She is excessively white—her face pale, and her eyebrows and hair black as jet. She has a beautiful mouth and teeth, and altogether a feminine and graceful air. Her eyes are not large and she is too thin, and her nose is rather long. *Con todo,* she looks so young and sweet—with such a musical expression in her face —that the severest critic ought to be disarmed on looking at her. She also sung [from] *Nina Pazza per Amore* and various other *canciones,* all with great enthusiasm and expression.[21] Her husband the tenor is ugly and awkward, but seems a good stupid creature, and lost in admiration of the star that has fallen to his lot. A prima donna always seems to choose a horror for a husband. He looks like a good stupid country Scotch schoolmaster.[22] He looks neither like an actor nor a roué, but a good simple creature devoted to her. When Mme de C[yprey] bid her put her shawl on over her head, and not be a coquette, *"Oh, non, Madame!"* said he, with a most deprecating air, *"Anaïs n'est pas coquette."*

We returned home by moonlight, the most flattering medium through which Mexico can be viewed. By moonlight Mexico is a splendid city —with its broad and silent streets, and magnificent old buildings, whose decay and abandonment are softened by the faint silvery light; its ancient churches, from which the notes of the organ occasionally come pealing forth, mingled with faint blasts of music borne on the night wind from some distant procession; or with the soft music of a hymn

from some neighbouring convent. The white-robed monk—the veiled female—even the ragged beggar, add to the picture; by daylight his rags are too visible.

Frequently, as the carriages roll along to the theatre, or as, at a late hour, they return from it, they are suddenly stopped by the appearance of the mysterious, slow, heavy coach in which the divine symbols are carried—with its piebald mules, and figure of the *Eye* surrounded by rays of light on its panels. A melancholy apparition, for it has come from the house of mourning, probably from the bed of death. Then, by the moonlight, the kneeling figures on the pavement seem as if carved in stone. Mexico at night—and the environs of Mexico at the first dawn of morning—these are the hours for viewing both to advantage, and for feeling how

All but the spirit of man is divine.[23]

In front of our house—I should say of *the Mint*—is the Archbishop's palace, where an old man has greatly excited our curiosity. Whether as a penance or not we do not know, but beside the wall of the *Arzobispado* this old man, wrapped in his sarape, kneels from sunset till midnight, or later. We have frequently gone out at nine in the evening and left him kneeling there—and on returning at one in the morning have found him in the same position, kneeling still. He asks no alms, but kneels there silent and motionless, hour after hour, apparently performing some vow. Either the pavement must wear out his knees, or vice-versa, his knees must wear out the pavement.

We made a call this evening on the Archbishop in his own palace, an enormously large building—a sort of street, like this Casa de Moneda. He received us very cordially—and looked very comfortable without his robes of state, in a fine cloth dressing gown, lined with violet-coloured silk.

An old soldier belonging to us, having taken it into his wise head that a small empty room, next a large empty one in which he sleeps, is haunted, has for his consolation bought the following document. It is difficult to believe that in this age such a paper can be sold and bought. At the top is a large cross.

Copy of the Writing which was found in the Holy Sepulchre of Our Lord Jesus Christ, which the Holy Pontiff has in his oratory and which King Philip IV has on a plaque of silver. It declares that Santa Brígida and Santa Isabel Queen of Hungary, having made supplication to Our Lord Jesus Christ, He desired those saints to have knowledge of His Holy Passion, and appeared to them, and said to them the following words:

Know ye, my dear daughters, that the soldiers who seized me were 201; they who carried me off as prisoner were 25; they gave me 110 blows in order to raise me; they gave me 80 wounds in the mouth, and 150 in the chest; and they gave me 5,670 lashes tied to a column; they left on my body 101 wounds and 1600 mortal gashes. I fell with the Holy Cross three times, and the blood which I spilled was 300,670 drops.

Whatever person shall recite *seven Pater Nosters* and seven *Ave Marias* over a period of twelve years, until the number equals the number of drops of blood which I spilled, I grant him five graces— The first, remission of all his sins. The second, he shall be free from the punishments of purgatory. The third, if he should die before completing the twelve years, it shall be as if he had completed them. The fourth, I shall descend from heaven to earth to receive joyfully his soul in my arms with those of his relatives. The fifth, those who carry this document with them shall be free of the Devil and shall not die an evil death. And in whatever house he shall possess it, he will not have diabolical visions. Four days before his death, my Most Holy Mother will descend to accompany and console him. The woman who shall carry this document with her, being with child, shall bring forth without danger.[24]

The clause concerning diabolical visions is the important part to the soldier. On the other side of the paper, the same is repeated *in verse.*

The effect produced upon the ignorant Indians by this easy method of absolution may be conceived. The most hardened ruffian will find time to say seven *Pater Nosters* and seven *Ave Marias* daily, even before lying down with his blood-stained hands to rest, after depositing in safety the spoil seized from the unfortunate traveller. And with faith in this precious production, his conscience will be as easy as though he had returned from supplying the wants of an unfortunate and virtuous family. Is there no medium between this degrading superstition and the hardened contempt for sacred things which permits the alcalde of _____ to address the head of the Catholic church as though his epistle were intended for the *sous-préfet* of a petty village?

Sunday: August 1st, 1841

We had a visit last evening from one of the directors of the mint, a curious and most original genius, a Mexican, who has served twenty-eight years in that and other capacities, and who, after lamenting the decay of everything since the days of the Spanish government, and speaking of the different viceroys he had seen, proceeded to give us

various anecdotes of the Viceroy Revilla-gigedo, the most honoured for his justice, renowned for his energy, and feared for his severity, of the whole dynasty.[25]

Our friend was moved to enthusiasm by the sight of an old-fashioned but very handsome musical clock, which stands on a table in the drawing room, and which he says was brought over by this viceroy, and was no doubt considered a miracle of art in those days.

Some of the anecdotes he told us are already generally known here, but his manner of telling them was very interesting, and he added various particulars which we had not heard before. Besides, the stories themselves seem to me so curious and characteristic that, however much they lose by being tamely written instead of *dramatized* as they are by him, I am tempted to give you one or two specimens. But my letter is getting beyond all ordinary limits, and your curiosity will no doubt keep cool till the arrival of another packet.[26]

43

Calderón's Successor Arrives

Tuesday, August 3rd, 1841
Casa de Moneda, Mexico

A lady of fortune, owing to some combination of circumstances, found herself in difficulties, and in immediate want of a small sum of money. Don _____ being her *compadre*[1] and a respectable merchant, she went to him to state her necessities—and offered him a case of valuable jewels as security for repayment, provided he would advance her the sum of eight hundred dollars. He agreed to do so, and the bargain was instantly concluded without any written document, the lady depositing her jewels and receiving the sum.

At the end of a few months, her temporary difficulties being ended, she went to her *compadre's* house to repay the money, and to receive back her jewels. The man readily received the money, but declared to his astonished *comadre* that, as to the jewels, he had never heard of them—and that no such transaction had taken place. The señora, indignant at the merchant's treachery, instantly repaired to the palace of the Vice-King, hoping for justice from this Western Solomon, though unable to conceive how it could be obtained. She was instantly received by Revillagigedo, who listened attentively to her account of the circumstances.

"Had you no witnesses?" said the count.

"None," replied she.

"Did no servant pass in or out during the transaction?"

"No one. The affair was strictly private between us two."

The Viceroy reflected a moment. "Does your *compadre* smoke?"

"No, sir," said the lady, astonished at this apparently irrelevant question, and perhaps the more so as the count's aversion to smoking was so well known that none of his smoking subjects ventured to approach him without being sufficiently washed and perfumed to deaden any odour of the fascinating weed which might lurk about their clothes or person.

"Does he take snuff?" said the Viceroy.

"Yes, Your Excellency," said his visitor, who probably feared that for once His Excellency's wits were woolgathering.

"That is sufficient," said the Viceroy. "Retire into the adjoining chamber and *keep quiet*—your jewels shall be restored." His Excellency then dispatched a messenger for the merchant, who immediately presented himself.

"I have sent for you," said the Viceroy, "that we may talk over some matters in which your mercantile knowledge may be of use to the state."

The merchant was overwhelmed with gratitude and joy; while the Viceroy entered into conversation with him upon various affairs connected with his profession. Suddenly the Viceroy put his hand first in one pocket, then in the other, with the air of a man who has mislaid something.

"Ah!" said he, "my snuffbox. Excuse me for a moment while I go to fetch it from the next room."

"Sir!" said the merchant, "permit me to have the honour of offering my box to Your Excellency."

His Excellency received it as if mechanically—holding it in his hand and talking—till, pretexting some business, he went out, and, calling an officer, desired him to take that snuffbox to the merchant's house, asking his wife as from him, by that token, to deliver to the bearer a case of jewels which he had there. The Viceroy returned to the apartment where he had left his flattered guest, and remained in conversation with him until the officer returned, and, requesting private speech of the Viceroy, delivered to him the jewel case which he had received from the merchant's wife.

Revillagigedo then returned to his fair complainant and, under pretense of showing her some rooms in the palace, led her into one where, amongst many objects of value, the jewel case stood open. No sooner had she cast her eyes upon it than she started forward in joy and amazement. The Viceroy requested her to wait there a little longer, and returned to his other guest.

"Now," said he, "before going further, I wish to hear the truth concerning another affair in which you are interested. Are you acquainted with the Señora de _____ ?"

"Intimately, sir—she is my *comadre*."

"Did you lend her eight hundred dollars on such a date?"

"I did."

"Did she give you a case of jewels in pledge?"

"Never," said the merchant, vehemently. "The money was lent without any security—merely as an act of friendship—and she has invented story concerning some jewels, which has not the slightest foundation."

In vain the Viceroy begged him to reflect, and not, by adding falsehood treachery, force him to take measures of severity. The merchant with oaths persisted in his denial. The Viceroy left the room suddenly, and returned with the jewel case in his hand—at which unexpected apparition the astonished merchant changed colour, and entirely lost his presence of mind. The Viceroy ordered him from his presence, with a severe rebuke for his falsehood and treachery, and an order never again to enter the palace. At the same time he commanded him as a punishment to send him, the next morning, eight hundred dollars with five hundred more—which he did, and which were, by the Viceroy's order, distributed among the hospitals. His Excellency is said to have added a severe reprimand to the lady, for having made a bargain without writing.

Another story which I recollect is as follows: A poor Indian appeared before the Viceroy, and stated that he had found in the street a bag full of golden ounces, which had been advertised with the promise of a handsome reward to the person who should restore them to the owner; that, upon carrying them to this Don _____ _____, [the latter] had received the bag, counted the ounces, extracted two, which he slipped into his pocket; and had then reproached the poor man with having stolen part of the money, had called him a thief and a rascal, and, instead of rewarding him, had driven him from the house.

With the Viceroy there was no delay. Immediate action was his plan. Detaining the Indian, he dispatched an officer to desire the attendance of Don _____ with his bag of ounces. He came, and the Viceroy desired him to relate the circumstances, his practiced eye reading his falsehood at a glance.

"May it please Your Excellency, I lost a bag containing gold. The Indian, now in Your Excellency's presence, brought it to me in hopes of a reward, having first stolen part of the contents. I drove him from the house as a thief, who, instead of recompense, deserves punishment."

"Stop," said the Viceroy, "there is some mistake here. How many gold ounces were there in the bag you lost?"

"Twenty-eight."

"And how many are here?"

"But twenty-six."

"Count them down. I see it as you say. The case is clear, and we have all been mistaken. Had this Indian been a thief, he would never have brought back the bag, and stolen merely two ounces. He would have kept the whole. It is evident that this is not your bag, but another which this poor man has found. Sir, our interview is at an end. Continue the search for your bag of gold; and as for you, friend, since we cannot find the true owner, sweep up these twenty-six pieces and carry them away. They are yours." So saying, His Excellency bowed out the mortified cheat and the overjoyed rustic. (Mr. _____ says that this story, he thinks is taken from something similar in an oriental tale. However, it may have occurred twice.)

A horrible murder took place in 1789, during the viceroyaltyship of Revillagigedo, which is remarkable in two particulars: the trifling circumstances which led to its discovery; and the energy displayed by the Viceroy, contrasting so strongly with the tardy execution of justice in our days.

There lived in Mexico at that period, in the street of Cordobanes, No. 15, a rich merchant of the name of Don Joaquín Dongo. A clerk named José Joaquín Blanco, who had formerly been in his service—having fallen into vicious courses and joined in companionship with two other young men, Felipe Aldama and Baltazar Quintero, gamblers and cockfighters (with reverence be it spoken!) like himself—formed, in concert with them, a plan for robbing his former master.

They accordingly repaired to the house one evening when they knew that Dongo was from home, and, imitating the signal which Blanco knew the coachman was in the habit of making to the porter when the carriage returned at night, the doors were immediately thrown open, and the robbers entered. The pastor was their first victim. He was thrown down and stabbed. A postman, who was waiting with letters for the return of the master of the house, was the next murdered, and then the cook, and so on, until eleven lay weltering in their blood. The wretches then proceeded to pick the locks of the different bureaus, guided by Blanco, who, in his former capacity, had made himself *au fait* of all the secrets of the house. They obtained twenty-two thousand dollars in specie, and about seven thousand dollars' worth of plate and jewels.

Meanwhile, the unfortunate master of the house returned home, and at the accustomed signal the doors were opened by the robbers, and, on the entrance of the carriage, instantly relocked. Seeing the porter bathed in blood—and dead bodies lying at the foot of the staircase—he comprehended at once his desperate situation, and, advancing to Aldama who stood near the door, he said: "I see that my life is in your hands; but, for God's sake, show some mercy, and do not murder me in cold blood. Say what sums of money you want. Take all that is in the house, and leave me, and I swear to keep your secret."

Aldama consented, and Dongo passed on. As he ascended the stairs, stepping over the body of the postman, he encountered Quintero, and to him he made the same appeal, with the same success—when Blanco, springing forward, held his sword to Quintero's breast and, swearing a great oath, exclaimed: "If you do not stab him, I will kill you on the spot." Conceive, for one moment, the situation of the unfortunate Dongo, surrounded by the murdered and the murderers, in his own house, at the dead of night, and without a hope of assistance! The suspense was momentary. Thus adjured, Quintero stabbed him to the heart.

The murderers then collected their spoil, and, it being still dark, two of them got into Dongo's carriage—the third acting as coachman—and so drove swiftly out of the gates of the city, till, arriving at a deserted spot not far from a village, they turned the carriage and mules adrift and buried their treasure, which they transported afterwards to a house in the

Calle de la Aguila (the Street of the Eagle), No. 23; and went about their usual avocations in the morning as if nothing had occurred.

Meanwhile, the public consternation may be conceived when the morning dawned upon this bloody tragedy. As for the Viceroy, he swore that the murderers should be discovered, and hanged before his eyes, that day week.

Immediately the most energetic measures were taken, and the gates of the city shut, to prevent all egress. Orders were given through all the different districts of the capital that every guest, or visitor, or boarder— whether in inn, or lodging, or private house—should have their names given up to the police, with an account of their condition, occupation, motives for living in Mexico, &c. Strict cognizance was taken in all the villages near the capital, of every person who had passed through, or entered, or left [each] village within a certain space of time. All the roads near the capital were scoured by parties of soldiers. Every hidden place was searched by the police; every suspected house entered. The funeral of the ill-fated Dongo and of the other victims took place the following day; and it was afterwards remembered that Aldama was there amongst the foremost, remarking and commenting upon this horrible wholesale butchery, and upon the probabilities of discovering the murderers.

It happened that a country family from a neighbouring village, hearing of all these doings in Mexico, and with that love of the marvellous which characterizes persons uneducated, or unaccustomed to the world, determined to pay a visit to the capital, and to hear, at the fountain head, all these wonderful stories, which had probably reached them under a hundred exaggerated forms. No sooner had they entered their lodgings than they were visited and examined by the police, and their deposition taken down as to their motives for visiting the capital, their place of birth, &c. As a gratuitous piece of information, one of them mentioned that, passing by a French barber's shop (probably with his eyes opened wide in the expectation of seeing horrible sights), he had observed a man talking to the barber, who had a stain of blood upon his *queue* (hair being then worn powdered and tied behind).

Trifling as this circumstance appears to us, the Viceroy ordered that the person who mentioned it should instantly conduct the police officers to the shop where he had observed it. The shop being found, the barber was questioned as to what persons he had been conversing with that morning, and mentioned about half a dozen—amongst others Aldama, who did not bear a very good reputation. Aldama was sent for, confronted with the man who gave the information, identified as the same, and, the stain of blood being observed, he was immediately committed to prison upon suspicion. Being questioned as to the cause of the stain, he replied that, being at a cockfight—on such a day, at such an hour—the blood from one of the dying cocks, which he held, had spurted up and stained the collar of his shirt and his hair. Inquiries being made at the cockpit, this was corroborated by several witnesses, and, extraordinary as it is, it is most probable that the *assertion was true.*

But meanwhile, the mother of Blanco, deeply distressed at the dissolute courses of her son, took the resolution (which proves more than anything else Revillagigedo's goodness, and the confidence which all classes had in him) to consult the Viceroy as to the means of converting the young man to better habits. It seems as if the hand of an avenging Providence had conducted this unfortunate mother to take a step so fatal to her son. She told the Viceroy that she had in vain attempted to check him, that his days and nights were spent with profligate companions in gambling houses and in cockpits, and that she feared some mischief would come some day from his fighting and swearing and drinking; that, but a few days since, he had come home late, and that she had observed that his stockings were *dabbled in blood;* that she had questioned him upon it, and that he had answered surlily he had got it in the cockpit.

The woman's narration was hardly concluded before Blanco was arrested and placed in a separate cell of the same prison with Aldama. Shortly after, Quintero—only as being the intimate friend and companion of both parties—was taken up on suspicion and lodged in the same prison, all being separately confined, and no communication permitted between them.

It seems as if Quintero, perhaps the least hardened of the three, was struck with the conviction that, in the extraordinary combination of circumstances which had led to the arrest of himself and his companions in villainy, the finger of God was too distinctly visible to permit a doubt of ultimate discovery to rest upon his mind—for he confessed at once and, declaring that he saw all denial was useless, gave a circumstantial account of the whole. He begged for nine days' grace to prepare himself for death, but the Viceroy would grant but three.

Aldama then made his confession, and at the same time avowed to the priest that he was guilty of a previous murder which took place when he was alcalde of a village near Mexico—before the time of Revillagigedo —and for which he had been tried and acquitted: He being alcalde, the postman of the village was in the habit of passing by his house, giving him an account of whatever money he had collected, &c. One evening this man stopped at Aldama's, and told him he was entrusted with a sum of fifteen hundred dollars to carry to a neighbouring village. At twelve o'clock he left the house of Aldama, who—taking a short cut across the fields—reached the postman by this other direction, stabbed him, and carried back the money. Next day, when the murder was made known, the alcalde, in his robes of justice, visited the body, and affected to institute a strict search for the murderer. Nevertheless he was suspected and arrested, but escaped by bribery, and shortly after, leaving the village, came to the wider theatre of Mexico.

The murderers, having thus made their confession, were ordered to prepare for death. A scaffold, erected between the central gate of the palace and that which is now the principal gate of the city guards, was hung with black to denote that the criminals were of noble blood. An immense crowd were assembled; and the Viceroy, standing on the balcony of his palace, witnessed the execution in the great square, the *very day week* that the murders were committed.[2]

The streets were then kept in the most perfect order, both as to paving and lighting; and on one occasion, having rode all through the city, as was his custom, to observe whether everything was in order for the approaching Holy Week, he observed that several parts of the different streets were unpaved and out of repair; whereupon, sending for the head of the police, he desired that these streets should be paved and in order before the Holy Week, of which it wanted but a few days. The officer declared the thing to be impossible. The Viceroy ordered it to be done, on the penalty of losing his place. Early on the morning of Palm Sunday, he sent to know if all was in readiness; and, as the bells tolled for early mass, the last stone was laid on the Calle San Francisco, which completed the work.[3]

It is said he frequently went about incognito, attended by one or two aides-de-camp, by which means, like another Haroun Al Raschid, he was enabled to discover and correct hidden abuses. By his orders, no monk could be out of his convent after vespers. Walking one evening along the streets, he encountered a monk in the Calle San Francisco, taking his pleasure long after the appointed hour. The Viceroy walked directly to the convent; and, on making himself known, was received by the abbot with all due respect.

"How many monks have you in your convent, father?" asked the Viceroy.

"Fifty, Your Excellency."

"There are now only forty-nine. Call them over, see which is the missing brother, and let his name be struck out."

The list was produced—the names called over, and only forty-five monks presented themselves. By order of the Viceroy, the five who had broken through the rules were never again admitted into the convent. Alas! Could His Excellency behold the monks of these days, drinking pulque and otherwise diverting themselves—strolling along the streets with an *Indita* tucked under their arm![4]

One more anecdote of this, our hero the "immortal Revillagigedo," and I have done. It was very late at night, when not far from the Garita del Niño Perdido—the gate of the city called "The Lost Child," in commemoration of that period when "the child Jesus tarried behind in

Jerusalem," and his parents sought for him sorrowing—His Excellency encountered a good-looking damsel, walking briskly and alone, at these untimely hours; yet withal quiet and modest in her demeanour. Wishing to try the temper of her steel (or brass), he left his officers a little way behind; and perhaps they were not astonished—"Oh! by no means, not at all, certainly not!"—when they saw the grave and severe Revillagigedo approach the fair maiden somewhat familiarly, and request permission to accompany her in her rambles, a proposal which was indignantly rejected.

"*Anda!* (Come!)" said His Excellency. "Give over these airs—you, a *mujercilla*, strolling about in search of adventures."

Imagine the feelings of His Excellency on receiving forthwith in reply a tremendous and well-applied box on the ear! The staff rushed forward, and were astonished to find the Viceroy with a smiling countenance, watching the retreating steps of the adventurous damsel.

"What! Your Excellency—such insolence!—such audacity! such——"

"Come, come," said the Viceroy, "she has proved herself worthy of our favour. Let instant inquiry be made as to her birth and parentage, and as to her reasons for being on the streets at this hour. They must be honest ones."

The result proved the Viceroy correct in his opinion. She was a poor girl, supporting a dying mother by giving music lessons, and obliged to trudge on foot from house to house at all hours; and amongst her scholars was the daughter of an old lady who lived out of the gates of the city, and from whose house, being that of her last visited pupil, she had frequently to return alone late at night. On being informed of these particulars, His Excellency ordered her a pension of three hundred dollars per annum, to be continued to the day of her death, and it is said she is still alive, though very old. This is making one's fortune by a *coup de main*, or by a *lucky hit!*[5]

Friday: August 6th, 1841

This morning we had some very good music—Madame Castellan and the tenor, and Madame Cesari having passed some hours here, together with Madame la Baronne de Cyprey and a few other gentlemen and ladies. La Castellan was very amiable, and sang beautifully, but looked pale and fatigued. She has been very effective lately in the *Sonnambula*. Madame Cesari was in great beauty.

About an hour after they had gone, the new minister and his family made their *entrée* into Mexico.[6] It is now, however, too late for us to return till the autumn, as there is a great deal of fever at Veracruz; nor do we entirely give up hopes, as soon as Calderón shall be at leisure, of making another journey on horseback, into the interior. There are, however, rumours of another *pronunciamiento*, and, should this be the case, our present quarters next to the palace will be more distinguished than agreeable.

I have always had a curiosity to know why the Calle del Indio Triste was so called. We are on visiting terms with two or three *houses* in that street, and never pass those large black letters, which tell the passenger that this is the street of "The Sad Indian," without my imagination figuring to itself that here some tragedy connected with the conquest must have taken place. It was therefore with great joy that I fell upon an article in the *Mosaico Mexicano* purporting to give an explanation of this melancholy title-page to an otherwise tolerable (in the way of houses) but very ill-paved street—where, amongst other handsome edifices, is the house of a rich Spaniard (Señor R[ubi]o), remarkable for its beautiful entrance and elegant *salons*.[7]

It appears that there are different traditions respecting it. One, that shortly after the conquest a rich cacique lived there, who acted as a spy on his Indian brethren, and informed the viceroy of all their plans and combinations against the government; but that on one occasion, having failed to inform his patrons of an intended mutiny, they seized this pretext for sequestrating his property; that afterwards, poor, abandoned, and despised, he sat down in the corner of the street, weeping his misfortune and meeting with no pity, until at length he abstained from all food for some days, and was found dead in the corner of the street, sitting in the same melancholy posture; that the viceroy declared his wealth crown property, and, with the intention of striking terror into the hearts of the malcontents, caused a stone statue to be made representing the weeping Indian; [and] that this statue was placed at the corner of the street, with its back to the wall, and so remained until, the house being pulled down, the statue was sent to the museum, where it now is—the street retaining the name of the Sad Indian.

But there is another tradition mentioned concerning the origin of the name, more interesting and even more probable. It appears that the ground now occupied by this street is the site of the palace of Axayacatl, the father of Montezuma, last Emperor of Mexico. In this spacious and magnificent palace the Spaniards were received and lodged, and, according to Torquemada,[8] each in a separate apartment. There were a multitude of idols in this dwelling, and, though they had no separate temple, various feasts were dedicated to them. After the conquest they were for the most part broken and destroyed, and it was only lately that, by accident, the head of the god of the waters, beautifully worked in serpentine marble, was discovered there. Still, one statue had been preserved, that of an Indian, said to have been placed there by the Aztecs as a memorial of their sorrow at the death of Montezuma, to whom, on account of his misfortunes, they gave the name of *"el Indio triste."* This

was afterwards placed at the corner of the new building erected there by the Spaniards, and gave its name to the street. It is a melancholy-looking statue, whomsoever it may represent, of an Indian in a sitting posture, with a most dejected and forlorn air and countenance. The material is basaltic stone.[9]

Wednesday: August 11th, 1841

Calderón has just returned from seeing the general archives, which are all in confusion and going to ruin. Don Ignacio Cubas, who has the charge of them, has written various works—the History of the Viceroys—the Californias, &c.—which were robbed or destroyed in the last *pronunciamiento*.[10] He related the story of Revillagigedo and the jewels, only differing from *my* friend's narrative in that he says it was not a jewel case, but a diamond bracelet. He assured Calderón that Mexico in Indian means "below this," alluding to the population who, according to tradition, are buried beneath the Pedregal.[11]

Wednesday: August 18th, 1841

News has arrived that General Paredes *pronounced* in Guadalajara on the eighth of the month! Strange rumours are afloat, and it is generally supposed that Santa Anna is or will be the prime mover of the great changes that are predicted. By many, however, it is talked of as very trifling, as a mere movement that will soon be put down. The plan which Paredes has published is essentially military, but announces a congress, which renders it very popular in the departments.[12] It has been adopted by the departments of Zacatecas, Durango, and Guanajuato.

Meanwhile, everything continues here as usual. We have been several times at the opera; the *paseos* are very crowded; and we had a musical *soirée* the other evening which was very gay but, from the signs of the times, will probably be our last in Mexico.

Sunday: August 29th, 1841

This morning Calderón took his farewell audience of the President at ten o'clock. At two the new minister was received and presented his credentials.[13]

Monday: August 30th, 1841

These few last days have chiefly been spent in paying visits of ceremony with the Señora [Oliver].[14]

Nevertheless, we spent an hour last evening in the beautiful cemetery a little way out of the city, which is rather a favourite haunt of ours, and is known as the Panteón de Santa María. It has a beautiful chapel attached to it, where daily mass is said for the dead, and a large garden filled with flowers. Young trees of different kinds have been planted there, and the sight of the tombs themselves, in their long and melancholy array of black coffins, with gold-lettered inscriptions, even while it inspires the saddest ideas, has something soothing in its effect. They are kept in perfect order, and the inscriptions, though not always eloquent, are almost always full of feeling, and sometimes extremely touching.[15] There is one near the entrance which is pathetic in its native language, and though it loses much in the translation, I shall transcribe it:

Here lie the beloved remains of Carmen and José Pimentel y Heras. The first died the 11th of June, 1838, aged one year and eleven months; the second on the 5th of September of 1839, in the sixteenth month of his existence; and to their dear memory maternal love dedicates the following—

EPITAPH

Babes of my love! My Carmen and José!
Sons of your cherished father, Pimentel.
Why have you left your mother's side? For whom?
What motives have ye had to leave me thus?
But hark! I hear your voice—and breathlessly
I listen. I hear ye say: "To go to heaven!
Mother! We have left thee to see our God!"
Beloved shades! If this indeed be so,
Then let these bitter tears be turned to joy.
It is not meet that I should mourn for ye,
Since me ye have exchanged for my God.
To Him give thanks! And in your holy songs,
Pray that your parents' fate may be like yours.[16]

REVOLUTION AGAIN:
SANTA ANNA RETURNS

44

Manifestoes and the Roaring of Cannon

Monday: August 30th, 1841
Casa de Moneda, Mexico

News has arrived that Veracruz has *pronounced itself*. It is said that Santa Anna has really and truly "put his *fut* in it" this time. If he had been spared *two*, he would have been in it long ago, but it is awkward for a revolutionary chief not to be able to mount his horse without assistance—or, if on foot, to be obliged to *hop* instead of running away. However, it is said that he too has *pronounced* himself—and that he has arrived at least as far as Jalapa, some accounts say Perote.

Bustamante, it is said, is determined to die fighting at the worst. His preparations of all kinds are made. His *cross*, "in each stone of which the garrison of Mexico figures like the stars of the firmament" —his money in gold, and other valuables—he has sent out of San Agustín, to the house of a friend.[1] It is said he will go out to meet Santa Anna.

There is a good deal of excitement this evening in Mexico.

Tuesday: August 31st, 1841

This afternoon the clouds, gathered together in gloomy masses, announced a thunderstorm, and at the same time a certain degree of agitation apparently pervading the city was suddenly observable from our balconies. Shops were shutting up; people rushing in all directions, heads at all the windows, and men looking out from the *azoteas;* but, as these symptoms were immediately followed by a tremendous storm of thunder and lightning and splashing rain, we took it for granted that the cause was very simple. But these elements of nature are wielded by the Hand that called them forth, and can stay them at His will; and the sun breaking forth smilingly and scattering the clouds made us feel that the storm had but refreshed the parched earth and cleared the sultry atmosphere. Not so with the storm which has been brooding in the hearts of a handful of ambitious men, and which has burst forth at last, its bolts directed by no wise or merciful power, but by the hands of selfish and designing and shortsighted mortals.

The storm, though short, had not passed away when we saw soldiers on the palace roof and news was brought us of a new *revolution in Mexico!* The troops in the citadel have revolted—*pronounced* themselves. Next comes the intelligence that Bustamante with troops and cannon has sallied out to attack the citadel. As yet, we hear no firing, and conclude there may be a parley. It is said that General Valencia, he who pronounced (but two short months ago!) the high-flown and brilliantly flattering speech to the President on [his] receiving the cross of honour, has now *pronounced* himself in a very different and much clearer manner. Listen to him now:

> Soldiers! The despotism of the Mexican government, the innumerable evils which the nation suffers, the unceasing remonstrances which have been made against these evils, and which have met with no attention, have forced us to take a step this evening which is not one of rebellion, but is the energetic expression of our resolution to sacrifice everything to the common good and interest. The cause which we defend is that of all Mexicans; of the rich as of the poor; of the soldier as of the civilian. We want a country, a government, the felicity of our homes, and respect from without; and we shall obtain all; let us not doubt it. The nation will be moved by our example. The arms which our country has given us for her defense we shall know how to employ in restoring her honour—an honour which the government has stained by not acknowledging the total absence of morality and energy in the actual authorities. The army which made her independent shall also render her powerful and free. The illustrious General Santa Anna today marches to Puebla, at the head of our heroic companions at Veracruz, while upon Querétaro, already united to the valiant General Paredes, the brave General Cortázar now begins his operations.
>
> In a few days we shall see the other forces of the republic in motion, all co-operating to the same end. The triumph is secure, my friends, and the cause which we proclaim is so noble that, conquerors, we shall be covered with glory; and, happen what may, we shall be honoured by our fellow citizens.[2]

In this manifesto, which is mere declamation, there is no plan. I appears that no one particularly counted upon General Valencia, an that, whether fearing to be left out in the events which he saw approach ing, or apprehensive of being arrested by the government who suspecte him, he has thought it wisest to strike a blow on his own accoun Pacheco, who commanded the citadel, together with Generals Lombardi and Salas, who had been ordered out to march with their respecti regiments against the *pronunciados,* are now in the citadel, and in a state of revolt. The two last had but just received money for the payment of their troops on the preceding day.[3]

So far as the citadel is concerned, we are well enough off—but if the rebels take the palace, as they did last time, we shall have rather dangerous nextdoor neighbours.

Today, a conference took place amongst all the members of the *corps diplomatique* in regard to a letter addressed them by the Secretary of State Camacho on the subject of introducing goods.[4] However, the approaching *pronunciamiento* is driving all other things for the present out of everyone's head. The shops are shut up—the opera adjourned.

8 o'clock.

The cannonading has begun—that horrid sound of last year. What a country! What a government! Valencia is positively at the head of the rebels in the citadel—the traitor! It is raining hard. We shall probably not learn the news till the morning. The soldiers are shutting the doors downstairs as we are lodged in the important Casa de Moneda. I wish well to Bustamante—he is a brave old man, and has justice on his side.

Nothing further, but that the President has sallied forth on horseback from San Agustín, and was received with repeated *vivas* by the people collected in the square.

[Thursday]: September [2nd], 1841

This revolution is like a game at chess, in which kings, castles, knights, and bishops are making different moves, while the pawns are looking on or taking no part whatever. To understand the state of the board, it is necessary to explain the position of the four principal pieces: Santa Anna, Bustamante, Paredes, and Valencia.

The first move was made by Paredes, who published his plan, and pronounced on the eighth of August at Guadalajara.[5] About the same time, Don Francisco Morphy, a Spanish broker who had gone to Manga de Clavo, was sent to Guadalajara and had a conference with Paredes, the result of which was that the plan of that general was withdrawn, and it was supposed that he and Santa Anna had formed a combination.[6] Shortly after, the *Censor de Vera Cruz,* a newspaper entirely devoted to Santa Anna, pronounced in favour of the plan of Paredes, and Santa Anna, with a few miserable troops and a handful of cavalry, arrived at Perote. Here he remains for the present, kept in check by the government [through] General Torrejón.

Meanwhile Paredes, with about six hundred men, left Guadalajara and marched upon Guanajuato; and there a blow was given to the government party by the defection of General Cortázar, who thought fit thus to show his grateful sense of having just received the rank of general of brigade with the insignia of this new grade, which the President put on with his own hands. Another *check to the President*.

Once begun, defection spread rapidly, and Paredes and Cortázar, having advanced upon Querétaro, found that General Juvera, with his garrison, had already *pronounced* there at the moment that they were expected in Mexico to assist the government against Valencia. Paredes, Cortázar, and Juvera are now united, and their forces amount to two thousand two hundred men.

Meanwhile, General Valencia, pressed to declare *his plan*, has replied that he awaits the announcement of the intentions of Generals Paredes and Santa Anna; and, for his own part, only desires the dismissal of General Bustamante.

This, then, is the position of the three principal *pronounced* chiefs on this second day of September of the year of our Lord 1841: Santa Anna in Perote, hesitating whether to advance or retreat, and, in fact, prevented from doing either by the vicinity of General Torrejón; Paredes in Querétaro, with the other revolted generals; Valencia in the citadel of Mexico, with his *pronunciados*; while Bustamante, with General Almonte and Canalizo, the *mark* against which all these hostile operations are directed, is determined, it is said, to fight to the last.[7]

Mexico looks as if it had got a general holiday. Shops shut up—and all business is at a stand. The people, with the utmost apathy, are collected in groups, talking quietly; the officers are galloping about; generals in a somewhat party-coloured dress, with large gray hats, striped pantaloons, old coats, and generals' belts, fine horses, and crimson-coloured velvet saddles. The shopkeepers in the square have been removing their goods and money. An occasional shot is heard, and sometimes a volley succeeded by a dead silence. The Archbishop shows his reverend face now and then upon the opposite balcony of his palace, looks out a little while, and then retires.[8] The chief effect, so far, is universal idleness in man and beast—the soldiers and their quadrupeds excepted.

The position of the President, however, is not so bad as at first sight it might appear, or as it will be if his enemies are permitted to unite. He has upwards of two thousand men, twelve pieces of ordnance, and though his infantry are few and he has little artillery, he has good cavalry. Valencia has twelve hundred men, twenty-six pieces of ordnance, with good infantry, and almost all the artillery. The rebels have possessed themselves of the Acordada, and given liberty to those who were imprisoned for political opinions—a good loophole for the escape of criminals.

Those who understand these matters say that the principal object of the government should be to reduce the rebels to the citadel only, and to occupy all the important points in the neighbourhood—San Diego, San Hipólito, San Fernando, &c.—but as yet this has not been done, and the *pronunciados* are gradually extending and taking possession of these points.[9]

Friday: September 3rd, 1841

They are now keeping up a pretty brisk fire between San Agustín and the citadel. This morning the streets were covered with coaches, filled with families leaving the city.

Saturday: September 4th, 1841

Things are becoming more complicated. The rebels now occupy San José, Salto del Agua,[10] the college of Vizcaínas (from which all the

poor girls and their teachers have fled), Regina, San Juan de la Penitencia, San Diego, and San Fernando—a long line of important points. The President's line begins at San Francisco, continuing by La Concepción; but, without a map of the city, you will not understand the position of the two parties. However, every turret and belfry is covered with soldiers, and the streets are blocked up with troops and trenches.

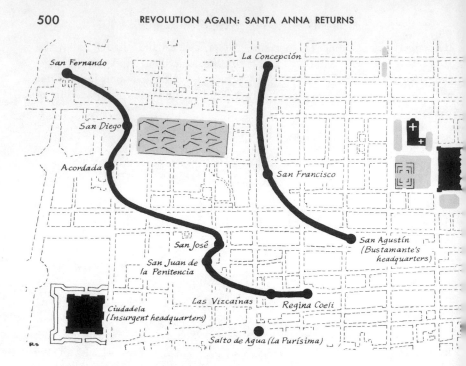

From behind these turrets and trenches they fire at each other, scarcely a soldier falling but numbers of peaceful citizens—shells and bombs falling through the roofs of the houses, and all this for *"the public good."*

The war of July [last year] had at least a shadow of pretext; it was a war of party, and those who wished to re-establish federalism may have acted with good faith. Now there is neither principle, nor pretext, nor plan, nor the shadow of reason or legality. Disloyalty, hypocrisy, and the most sordid calculation are all the motives that can be discovered; and those who then affected an ardent desire for the welfare of their country have now thrown aside their masks, and appear in their true colours; and the great mass of the people, who, thus passive and oppressed, allow their quiet homes to be invaded, are kept in awe neither by the force of arms, nor by the depth of the views of the conspirators, but by a handful of soldiers who are themselves scarcely aware of their own wishes or intentions, but that they desire power and distinction at any price.[11]

It is said that the federalists are very much elated, hoping for the eventual triumph of their party, particularly in consequence of a proclamation by Valencia, which appeared two days ago and is called "the plan of the Comicios." [It is] said to be written by General Tornel, who has gone over to the citadel, and who, having a great deal of classical learning, talks in it of the Roman *Committees* (the *Comicios*). Since then the revolution has taken the name of liberal, and is supported by men of name—the Pedrazas, Balderas, Riva Palacio, and others —which is of great importance to Valencia, and has given force and consistency to his party.[12] Besides this, the *pronunciados* have the advantage of a free field from the citadel out to Tacubaya, where it is said that certain rich bankers, who are on their side, are constantly supplying the citadel with cartloads of copper, which they send in from thence.

Meanwhile, we pass our time very quietly. In the morning we generally have visitors very early, discussing the probabilities, and giving us the last reports. Sometimes we venture out when there is no firing, which is much less constant and alarming than it was last year. So far we continue to have visitors in the evening, and Señor Blanco and I have been playing duets on the harp and piano, even though Mexico is declared "in a state of siege."[13] The Prussian minister, who was here this morning, does, however, strongly recommend us to change our quarters, and to remove to Tacubaya—which will be so troublesome that we are inclined to delay it until it becomes absolutely necessary.

Sunday: September 5th, 1841

We went upon the *azotea* this afternoon, to have a good view of the city. There were people on almost all the balconies, as on a fête day. A picturesque group of friars of the order of La Merced, in their white robes, had mounted up on the belfry of their church, and were looking out anxiously.[14] The palace roof next our own had soldiers on it. Everything at that moment was still and tranquil; but the conduct of the people is our constant source of surprise. Left entirely uncurbed, no one to direct them, thousands out of employment, many without bread, they meddle with nothing, do not complain, and scarcely seem to feel any interest in the result. How easily might such a people be directed for their good! It is said that all their *apathetic sympathies* are in favour of Bustamante.

Some say that Santa Anna will arrive today—some that the whole affair will be settled by treaty. But neither reports nor bulletins can be depended on, as scarcely anyone speaks according to his true feelings or belief, but according to his political party.

It appears that the conduct of congress in this emergency has given little satisfaction. They affect to give a declaration of the national will, and are as ambiguous as the Delphic Oracle; and it is said that their half measures, and determination not to see that public opinion is against them and that a thorough change can alone undermine this military revolution, will contribute more than anything to its eventual triumph.

The President has made use of the extraordinary powers which have been granted him by the *Poder Conservador* (Conservative Power, a singular and intermediate authority introduced into the Mexican constitution) to abolish the ten percent on consumption, and to modify the personal contribution, reducing it to the richer classes alone.[15] This concession has apparently produced no effect. It is said that the government troops continue to desert, convinced that a revolution in which Santa Anna takes part must triumph. Four new generals have been made by the President.

Monday: September 6th, 1841

We went out to Tacubaya, and found it impossible to procure a room there, far less a house. This is also the case in Guadalupe, San Joaquín— in fact in every village near Mexico. We are in no particular danger, unless they were to bombard the palace.

There was a slight shock of an earthquake yesterday.

Friday: September 10th, 1841

On the seventh, the President offered an amnesty to the *pronunciados*. Whatever might have been the result, the evening concluded with a terrible thunderstorm, mingled with the roaring of cannon, which had a most lugubrious effect. Many people were killed on the street.

We had gone out in the morning, but met the ex-Minister Echeverría, who strongly advised us to return home directly, as balls were falling and accidents happening all round. Soon after, a proclamation was issued by General Valencia, purporting that, if the President would not yield, he would bombard the palace; and that, if the powder which is kept there were to blow up, it would ruin half the city. This induced us to look at home, for if the palace is bombarded the Casa de Moneda cannot escape, and if the palace is blown up the Casa de Moneda will most certainly keep it company.

When the proclamation came out in the morning, various were the opinions expressed in consequence. Some believed it to be a mere threat, and others that it would take place at eleven at night. An old supernumerary soldier who lives here (one of those who were disabled by the last revolution) assured us that we had better leave the house, and, as we refused on the plea of having no safer house to go to, he walked off to the *azotea*, telling us he would *let us know* when the first bomb fell on the palace, and that then we must go perforce.

In the evening we went downstairs to the large vaulted rooms where they are making cannon balls, and where the vaults are so thick and solid that it was thought we should be in safety, even if General Valencia really kept his word.[16] We sat up that night till twelve o'clock, listening anxiously, but nothing happened; and now, in consequence of a deputation which has been sent to the citadel by certain foreigners of distinction (though unknown to the government), we are no longer afraid of any sudden assault of this kind, as General Valencia has promised, in consideration of their representations, not to proceed to these last extremities unless driven to them for his own defense.[17]

In listening to the different opinions which are current, it would seem that Bustamante, Santa Anna, and Valencia are all equally unpopular; and that the true will of the nation, which congress was afraid to express, was first for the immediate convocation of a constitutional congress, and second, that they should not be governed by Santa Anna— yet that Bustamante should renounce, and a provisional president be named.

Santa Anna writes complaining that Bustamante—by assuming extraordinary powers, commanding the army, and yet continuing [as] president—is infringing the constitution. But, as he is coming on to destroy it entirely, this is being rather particular.[18]

It is reported that the typhus fever is in the citadel, but there are many floating rumours, which are not to be depended upon. There is evidently a great deal of consternation beginning to be felt amongst the lower classes. Foreigners generally are inclined towards Santa Anna, Mexicans to Bustamante; but all feel the present evils. The *léperos* seem to swarm in greater numbers than ever, and last evening two small shops were broken into and robbed. In vain the President publishes manifestoes that the shops may be opened; they remain carefully shut, all commerce paralyzed, and everyone, who has the means to do so, leaving the city.

We hear that the shells from the citadel have destroyed part of the beautiful house belonging to Judge Peña y Peña, in front of the Alameda.

Saturday: September 11th, 1841

We have just received private information from the government that they will shortly require this house for arms and ammunition and troops —coupled with still more private advice to provide for our safety by leaving it. We shall therefore gladly accept the kind invitation of the Fagoaga family to remove to their hacienda of San Xavier, about three leagues from this. We had at first declined this invitation, owing to its distance from the city—inconvenient for us, who are only waiting for the first opportunity to leave it; but, besides that after the most diligent search in all the surrounding villages we cannot find a single unoccupied room, we are very glad to spend our remaining days in Mexico with so distinguished a family.[19] I shall therefore write little more at present on the subject of the revolution, which now that we have lived some time in Mexico, and have formed friendships there, fills us with feelings entirely different from those which the last produced: with personal sentiments of regret, private fears and hopes for the future, and presentiments of evil which owe more than half their sadness to individual feelings.

Sunday: September 12th, 1841

We are now in the midst of all the confusion occasioned by another removal—surrounded by trunks and boxes and *cargadores,* and at the same time by our friends (all those who have not taken flight yet) taking leave of us.

A great cannonading took place last night, but without any important result. The soldiers, in the daytime, amuse themselves by insulting each other from the roofs of the houses and convents. Yesterday, one of the President's party singled out a soldier in the citadel, shot him, and then began to dance the *Enanos*—and in the midst of a step, *he* was shot, and rolled over dead.

We shall write again from San Xavier.

45

Refuge in the Country

Thursday: September 16th, 1841
Hacienda of San Xavier

After a morning of fatigue, confusion, bustle, leave-taking, &c., &c., a coach with four mules, procured with the utmost difficulty, drove up to the door: the coach old and crazy, the mules and harness quite consistent, and the postilions so tipsy that they could hardly keep their seats. But we had no time to be particular and climbed in amidst bows and handshakings, and prophecies of breaking down and of being robbed by a band of *forçats*, headed by a Spaniard, who are said to be scouring the country—who are *said* to be, for just now seeing is believing, and few reports are worth attending to. However, we took two servants on horseback by way of escort, and rattled off, the coach creaking ominously, the postilions swinging from side to side—and our worthy housekeeper, whom we were carrying off from the smoking city, screaming out her last orders to the *galopina* concerning a certain green parrot which she had left in the charge of that tenderhearted damsel, who, with her *rebozo* at her eyes, surrounded by directors of the mint, secretaries of legation, soldiers, and porters, had enough to do to take charge of herself.

The city looked very sad as we drove through the streets, with closed shops, and barred windows, and cannon planted, and soldiers riding about. At every village we passed, the drivers called for brandy [and] tossed off a glassful, which appeared to act like a composing draught, as they gradually recovered their equilibrium.[1] We were glad to arrive at San Xavier, where we received a most cordial welcome, and to be removed, at least for a while, from sights and sounds of destruction. A great part of the road to Tlalnepantla, the village near which San Xavier is situated, leads through traces of the ruins of the ancient Tenochtitlan.

This part of the country is extremely pretty, being a corn and not a maguey district. Instead of the monotonous and stiff magueys, whose heads never bend to the blast, we are surrounded by fields of waving corn. There are also plenty of trees: poplar, ash, and elm—and one flourishing specimen of the latter species, which we see from the windows in front of the house, was brought here by Mr. Poinsett.

The hacienda, which is about three leagues from Mexico, is a large irregular building in rather a low situation, surrounded by dark blue hills. It belongs to the Señoras de Fagoaga, of the family of the Marquis de Apartado: *millionaires*, being rich in haciendas and silver mines; very religious, very charitable, and, what is less common here, extremely learned—understanding French, English, German, and even Latin. Their education they owe to the care of their father, one of the most distinguished men in Mexico, who was banished twice—once for liberal opinions, and the second time for supporting the Plan of Iguala, in fact, for not being liberal enough.[2] In these emigrations his family accompanied him, travelled over a great part of Europe, and profited by their opportunities. They returned here when the independence was accomplished, hoping for peace, but in vain. Constant alarms and perpetual revolutions have succeeded one another ever since that period.[3]

The hacienda has the usual quantum of furniture belonging to these country houses—and it is certainly no longer a matter of surprise to us that rich proprietors take little interest in embellishing them. A house which will in all probability be converted once a year into a barrack is decidedly better in a state of nature than encumbered with elegant furniture. This house has been entirely destroyed in that way more than once, and the last time that it was occupied by troops was left like an Augean stable.

We have here the luxury of books. My room opens into a beautiful chapel, covered with paintings representing saints and Virgins holding lilies, where mass is said occasionally, though the family generally attend mass in the village church of Tlalnepantla. Before the house is a small flower garden filled with roses and peculiarly fine dahlias, pomegranate trees, and violets, which, though single, have a delicious fragrance. This stretches out into an immense vegetable garden and orchard, terminating in a shrubbery, through which walks are cut, impervious to the sun at noonday. There is also a large reservoir of water, and the garden, which covers a great space of ground, is kept in good order. There are beautiful walks in the neighbourhood, leading to Indian villages, old churches, and farms; and all the lanes are bordered with fruit trees.[4]

Tlalnepantla, which means in Indian *between lands*—its church having been built by the Indians of two districts—is a small village with an old church, ruined remains of a convent where the curate now lives, a few shops, and a square where the Indians hold market (*tianguis*, they call it) on Fridays.[5] All along the lanes are small Indian huts, with their usual mud floor, small altar, earthen vessels, and collection of daubs on the walls (especially of the Virgin of Guadalupe), with a few blest palm leaves in the corner—occupied, when the men are at work, by the Indian woman herself, her sturdy scantily-clothed progeny, and plenty of yelp-ing dogs. Mrs. Ward's sketch of the interior of an Indian hut is perfect, as all her Mexican sketches are.[6] When the women are also out at their work, they are frequently tenanted by the little children alone. Taking refuge from a shower of rain yesterday in one of these mud huts, we found no one there but a little bronze-coloured child, about three years old, sleeping all alone on the floor with the door wide open; and, though we talked loud, and walked about in the cottage, the little thing never wakened.

A second shower drove us for shelter to a farmhouse, where we en-tered a sort of oratorio attached to the house: a room which is not consecrated, but has an altar, crucifix, holy pictures, &c. The floor was strewed with flowers, and in one corner was an old stringless violoncello, that might have formed a pendant to the harp of Tara. However, the most remarkable object of the rancho is its proprietress, a tall, noble-looking Indian, Doña Margarita by name, a mountaineer by birth, and now a rich widow possessing lands and flocks, though living in apparent poverty. The bulk of her fortune she employs in educating poor orphans. Every poor child who has no parents finds in her a mother and protec-tress; the more wretched, or sick, or deformed, the more certain of an asylum with her. She takes them into her house, brings them up as her own children, has them bred to some useful employment, and, when they are old enough, married. If it is a boy, she chooses him a wife from amongst the girls of the mountains, where she was born, who she says are "less corrupted" than the girls of the village. She has generally from twelve to twenty on her hands, always filling up with new orphans the vacancies caused in her small colony by death or marriage. There is nothing picturesque about these orphans, for, as I said before, the most deformed and helpless, and maimed and sick, are the peculiar objects of Doña Margarita's care; nevertheless, we saw various healthy, happy-looking girls, busied in various ways, washing and ironing, and sewing, whose very eyes gleamed when we mentioned her name, and who spoke of her with a respect and affection that it was pleasant to witness. Truly, this woman is entitled to happy dreams and soft slumbers! The remainder of her fortune she employs in the festivals and ceremonies of the church —in fireworks, in ornaments for the altars, &c.

Sunday: September 19th, 1841

Every day a messenger arrives from Mexico, bringing news of the *pronunciamiento*, which is eagerly waited for, and read with intense interest. It is probable, now, that affairs will soon come to a crisis. A step has been taken by the President which is considered very imprudent by those who are looking on in this great game. General Torrejón, who with nine hundred good soldiers kept Santa Anna in awe at Perote, has been sent for to Mexico, Bustamante wishing to reunite his forces. These troops, together with those of Codallos (the governor of Puebla), bring up his army to three thousand five hundred, or some say to four thousand men, all effective, and of whom nine hundred are good cavalry. Bustamante being now at the head of the army, Echeverría exercises the executive power, according to the constitution, in his capacity of president of the Council of State (*Consejo de Estado*), the Mexicans having no vice-president.[7]

Santa Anna, who had until now remained in Perote with his unorganized troops, no officers on whom he could depend, and a handful of miserable cavalry, has moved forwards to Puebla. Arrived there, his numbers were increased by one hundred men of the tobacco customs (brought him by Señor Manuel Escandón, who with a rich Spanish banker went out to meet him), forty horsemen seduced from the escort of Codallos, and a company of watchmen![8] As yet, no movement has taken place or seems likely to take place in his favour in Puebla. Señor Haro is named governor of that city[9] in the place of Codallos, who was sent for to join the President in Mexico; and Puebla, which used to be the great theatre of revolutions, has remained on this occasion in the most perfect neutrality, declaring for neither one party nor the other—probably the wisest course to pursue at this juncture. Everyone is of opinion that five hundred troops sent by Bustamante would instantly put this mongrel army of Santa Anna's to flight—for, though he has collected about a thousand men, he has not three hundred good soldiers.

On the other hand, General Paredes is marching in this direction with General Cortázar, his orders from Santa Anna no doubt being to keep the President in play, and to divert his attention by treaties or preliminaries of treaties whilst [Santa Anna] continues to march with caution towards the capital.

The great event to be dreaded by the government is a junction of the *pronunciado* forces. As long as they are separate, it is in no immediate danger; but, like the bundle of rods, what can easily be broken separately will assume strength when joined together. I make no further excuse for talking about politics. We talk and think of little else.

Monday: September 20th, 1841[10]

Yesterday (Sunday) we were startled by the intelligence that Generals Canalizo and Noriega had arrived at the village in the middle of the night, with a large troop, and that General Bustamante himself had made his appearance there at five in the morning—so that the peaceful little Tlalnepantla had suddenly assumed a warlike appearance. As it lies on the direct road to Guanajuato there could be no doubt that they were marching to meet Paredes. Calderón immediately walked down to the village to pay his respects to the President, who was lodged at the curate's, and meanwhile General Noriega came to the hacienda to see the ladies. Calderón found the President very much fatigued, having passed fourteen days and nights under arms, and in constant anxiety. General Orbegoso was with him.[11]

After breakfast we went down to the village to see the troops, who were resting there for a few hours. The cavalry occupied the square, the horses standing, and the men stretched asleep on the ground, each soldier beside his horse. The infantry occupied the churchyard. Dreadfully fatigued, they were lying, some on the grass and others with their heads pillowed on the old tombstones, resting as well as they could with their armour on. Before they started, the curate said mass to them in the square. There was a good deal of difficulty in procuring the most common food for so many hungry men. Tortillas had been baked in haste, and all the hens in the village were put in requisition to obtain eggs for the President and his officers.

We sat down in a porch to see them set off, a melancholy sight enough, in spite of drums beating and trumpets sounding. An old soldier, who came up to water his own and his master's horse, began to talk to us of what was going on, and seemed anything but enthusiastic at the prospects of himself and his comrades, assuring us that the army of General Paredes was double their number. He was covered with wounds received in the war against Texas, and expressed his firm conviction that we should see the Comanche Indians on the streets of Mexico one of these days, at which savage tribe he appeared to have a most devout horror—describing to a gaping audience the manner in which he had seen a party of them devour three of their prisoners.

About four o'clock the signal for departure was sounded, and they went off amidst the cheers of the people.

Tuesday: September 21st, 1841

Great curiosity was excited yesterday afternoon when news was brought us that Bustamante, with his generals and troops, had returned, and had passed through the village on their way back to Mexico! Some say that this retrograde march is in consequence of a movement made in Mexico by General Valencia—others that it has been caused by a message received from General Paredes.

We paid a visit in the evening to the old curate, who was pretty much in the dark, morally and figuratively, in a very large hall, where were assembled a number of females, and one tallow candle. Of course all were talking politics, and especially discoursing of the visit of the President the preceding night, and of his departure in the morning, and of his return in the afternoon, and of the difficulty of procuring tortillas for the men, and eggs for the officers.

Wednesday: September 22nd, 1841

We have received news this morning of the murder of our porter, the Spaniard whom we brought here from Havana. He had left us, and was employed as porter in a *fábrica* (manufactory), where the wife and family of the proprietor resided. Eight of General Valencia's soldiers sallied forth from the citadel to rob this factory, and poor José, the most faithful and honest of servants, having valiantly defended the door, was cruelly murdered. They afterwards entered the building, robbed, and committed dreadful outrages. They are selling printed papers through the streets today, giving an account of it. The men are taken up and, it is said, will be shot by orders of the general; but we doubt this, even though a message has arrived requiring the attendance of the padre who confesses criminals—a Franciscan monk, who, with various of his brethren, is living out here for safety at present.[12]
The situation of Mexico is melancholy.

Thursday: September 23rd, 1841

News has arrived that General Paredes has arrived at the Lechería, an hacienda belonging to this family, about three leagues from San Xavier; and that from thence he sent one of the servants of the farm to Mexico, inviting the President to a personal conference. The family take this news of their hacienda's being turned into military quarters very philosophically—the only precaution on these occasions being to conceal the best horses, as the *pronunciados* help themselves, without cere- mony, to these useful quadrupeds, wherever they are to be found.

Saturday: September 25th, 1841

This morning General Bustamante and his troops arrived at Tlalne- pantla, the President in a coach. Having met Calderón on the road, he stopped for a few moments and informed him that he was on his way to meet General Paredes at the Lechería, where he hoped to come to a composition with him.

We listened all day with anxiety, but hearing no firing concluded that some arrangement had in fact been made. In the evening we walked out on the highroad, and met the President, the governor, and the troops all returning. What securities Bustamante can have received, no one can imagine, but it is certain that they have met without striking a blow. It was nearly dusk as they passed, and the President bowed cheerfully, while some of the officers rode up and assured us that all was settled.

Sunday: September 26th, 1841

Cavalry, infantry, carriages, cannons, &c., are all passing through the village. These are the *pronunciados*, with General Paredes, following to Mexico. Feminine curiosity induces me to stop here, and to join the party who are going down to the village to see them pass.

We have just returned after a sunny walk, and an *inspection* of the *pronunciados*—they are too near Mexico now for me to venture to call them the *rebels*. The infantry, it must be confessed, was in a very ragged and rather drunken condition—the cavalry better, having *borrowed* fresh horses as they went along. Though certainly not point-device in their accoutrements, their good horses, high saddles, bronze faces, and picturesque attire had a fine effect as they passed along under the burning sun.

The sick followed on asses, and amongst them various masculine women, with sarapes or *mangas*, and large straw hats tied down with coloured handkerchiefs, mounted on mules or horses. The sumpter mules followed, carrying provisions, camp beds, &c.—and various Indian women trotted on foot in the rear, carrying their husbands' boots and clothes. There was certainly no beauty amongst these feminine followers of the camp, especially amongst the mounted Amazons, who looked like very ugly men in a semi-female disguise.

The whole party are on their way to Tacubaya, to join Santa Anna! The game is nearly up now. *Check from two knights and a castle*—from Santa Anna and Paredes in Tacubaya, and from Valencia in the citadel. People are flying in all directions, some from Mexico, and others from Guadalupe and Tacubaya.

It appears that Santa Anna was marching from Puebla, feeling his way towards the capital in fear and trembling. At Río Frío, a sentinel's gun having accidentally gone off, the whole army were thrown into the most ludicrous consternation and confusion. Near Ayotla the general's brow cleared up, for here he was met by commissioners from the government, Generals Orbegoso and [Quijano].[13] In a moment the quick apprehension of Santa Anna saw that the day was his own. He gave orders to continue the march with all speed to Tacubaya, affecting to listen to the proposals of the commissioners, amusing them[14] without compromising himself, and offering to treat with them at Mexicalcingo. They returned without having received any decided answer, and without on their part having given any assurance that his march should not be stopped; yet he has been permitted to arrive unmolested at Tacubaya, where Paredes has also arrived, and where he has been joined by General Valencia—so that the three *pronunciado* generals are now united there to dispose of the fate of the republic.[15]

The same day General Almonte had an interview with Santa Anna, who said with a smile, when he left him, *"Es buen muchacho* (He is a good lad)—he may be of service to us yet."[16]

The three *allied sovereigns* are now in the archbishop's palace at Tacubaya, from whence they are to dictate to the President and the nation. But they are, in fact, chiefly occupied with their respective engagements and respective rights. Paredes wishes to fulfill his engagements with the departments of Guanajuato, Jalisco, Zacatecas, Aguascalientes, Querétaro, &c. In his *plan* he promised them religious toleration, permission for foreigners to hold property, and so on—the last, in fact, being his favourite project. Valencia, on his side, has his engagements to fulfill with the federalists, and has proposed Señor [Gómez] Pedraza as an integral part of the regeneration—one whose name will give confidence now and forever to his party. General Santa Anna has engagements *with himself.* He has determined to command them all, and allows them to fight amongst themselves, provided he governs. Paredes is, in fact, furious with Valencia, accusing him of having interfered when not wanted, and of having ruined his *plan* by mingling it with a revolution with which it had no concern. He does not reflect that Valencia was the person who gave the mortal wound to the government. Had he not revolted, Santa Anna would not have left Perote, nor Paredes himself have passed on unmolested.

The Conservative Body [or Power] has been invited to go to Tacubaya but has refused. The majority desire the election of Paredes, or of any one who is not Santa Anna or Valencia; but Paredes himself, while drawing no very flattering portrait of Santa Anna, declares that he is the only man in the republic fit for the presidency—the only man who can make himself obeyed—in short, the only one capable of taking those energetic measures which the safety of the republic requires. He flatters himself that he, at the head of his division, will always keep Santa Anna in check—as if Cortázar, who deserted Bustamante in a moment of difficulty, could be depended on!

Meanwhile they are fortifying Mexico; and some suppose that Busta mante and his generals have taken the rash determination of permitting all their enemies to unite, in order to destroy them at one blow.

Tuesday: September 28th, 1841

There being at present an armistice between the contending parties, a document was published yesterday, fruits of the discussion of the allied powers at Tacubaya. It is called *"las bases de Tacubaya"* and—being published in Mexico by General Almonte—many expected and hoped that a new *pronunciamiento* would be the consequence.[17] But it has been quietly received, and the federalists welcome it as containing the foundations of federalism and popularity.

There are thirteen articles, which are as follows:

By the first—It is the will of the Nation that the so-called Supreme Powers (*Poderes Supremos*), established by the Constitution of 1836, have ceased—excepting the Judicial, which will be limited in its functions to matters purely judicial, according to the existing laws.

By the second—A Junta is to be named, composed of two deputies from each Department, chosen by His Excellency the General-in-Chief of the Mexican Army, Don Antonio López de Santa Anna, in order that they may be entirely free to appoint the person who is to hold the Executive power provisionally.

By the third—This person is immediately to assume the Executive power, taking an oath in the presence of the Junta to act for the welfare of the Nation.

By the fourth—The provisional Executive shall in two months convoke a new Congress, which, with ample powers, shall engage to reconstitute the Nation, as appears most suitable to them.

By the fifth—This Congress extraordinary shall re-unite in six months after it is convened, and shall solely occupy itself in forming the Constitution.

By the sixth—The provisional Executive shall answer for his acts before the first Constitutional Congress.

By the seventh—The provisional Executive shall have all the powers necessary for the organization of all the branches of the Public Administration.

By the eighth—Four ministers shall be named, of Foreign and Home Relations, of Public Instruction and Industry, of Treasury, and of War and Marine.

By the ninth—Each Department is to have two trustworthy individuals to form a Council, which shall give judgment in all matters on which they may be consulted by the Executive.

By the tenth—Till this Council is named, the Junta will fulfill its functions.

By the eleventh—Till the Republic is suitably organized, the authorities in the Departments which have not opposed, and will not oppose, the national will, shall continue.

By the twelfth—The General-in-Chief [Santa Anna] and all the other generals promise to forget all the political conduct of military men or citizens during the present crisis.

By the thirteenth—When three days have passed after the expiration of the present truce, if His Excellency the General-in-Chief of the government troops [Bustamante] does not adopt these *bases,* their accomplishment will be proceeded with; and we declare, in the name of the Nation, that this general, and all the troops who follow him, and all the so-called authorities which counteract this national will, shall be held responsible for all the Mexican blood that may be uselessly shed, which shall be upon their heads.

Wednesday: September 29th, 1841

To the astonishment of all parties, Bustamante and his generals *pronounced* yesterday morning for the federal system, and *this* morning Bustamante has resigned the presidency.[18] His motives seem not to be understood, unless a circular, published by General Almonte, can throw any light upon them:

> Without making any commentary—he says, speaking of the document of Tacubaya—upon this impudent document, which proposes to the Mexican nation a military government, and the most ominous of dictatorships in favour of the false defender of public liberty, of the most ferocious enemy of every government that has existed in the country, I hasten to send it to you, that you may have it published in this state, where surely it will excite the same indignation as in an immense majority of the inhabitants of the capital, who, jealous of the national glory, and decided to lose everything in order to preserve it, have spontaneously proclaimed the re-establishment of the federal system, the whole garrison having followed this impulse. There is no medium between liberty and tyranny; and the government, relying on the good sense of the nation, which will not see with indifference the slavery that is preparing for it, puts itself in the hands of the states, resolved to sacrifice itself on the altars of the country, or to strengthen its liberty forever.
>
> I enclose the renunciation which His Excellency Don Anastasio Bustamante makes to the presidency—&c.

Sunday: October 3rd, 1841

Though a very democratic crowd collected, and federalism was proclaimed in Mexico, it appears that no confidence in the government was inspired by this last measure. Some say that had Bustamante alone declared for the federal system, and had sent some effective cavalry to protect the *pronunciados* of that party all through the country, he might have triumphed still. Be that as it may, General Canalizo pronounced for federalism on the second of October, but this is not followed up on the part of the Generals Bustamante and Almonte—while the vice-president Echeverría[19] has retired to his house, blaming Almonte for having published an official document without his knowledge. Everything is in a state of perfect anarchy and confusion. The *léperos* are going about armed, and no one remains in Mexico but those who are obliged to do so. It is said that in Tacubaya great uneasiness prevailed as to the result of this new movement, and Santa Anna offered an asylum there to the congress and Conservative Body, although by the ultimatum from Tacubaya, published on the twenty-seventh, the constitution of '36 was concluded and of course these authorities were politically dead.

Tuesday: October 5th, 1841

For the last few days we have been listening to the cannon, and, even at this distance, the noise reverberating amongst the hills is tremendous. The sound is horrible! There is something appalling, yet humbling, in these manifestations of man's wrath and man's power, when he seems to usurp his Maker's attributes, and to mimic His thunder. The divine spark kindled within him has taught him how to draw these metals from the earth's bosom; how to combine these simple materials, so as to produce with them an effect as terrible as the thunderbolts of heaven. His earthly passions have prompted him so to wield these instruments of destruction as to deface God's image in his fellow men. The power is so divine—the causes that impel him to use that power are so paltry! The intellect that creates these messengers of death is so near akin to divinity—the motives that put them in action are so poor, so degrading even to humanity!

On the third, there was a shower of bombs and shells from the citadel, of which some fell into the palace, and one in our late residence, the mint. An engagement took place in the Viga; and though Bustamante's

party were partially victorious it is said that neither has much reason to boast of the result.

General Espinosa, an old insurgent, arrived at the village last night and sent to request some horses from the hacienda, which were sent him with all convenient speed that he might not, according to his usual plan, come and take them. In exchange for some half dozen farm horses in good condition, he sent half a dozen lean, wretched-looking quadrupeds, the bones coming through their skin—skeletons fit for dissection.

News has just arrived to the effect that last night, at three o'clock, Bustamante suddenly left the city, drawing off all his troops from the turrets, and leaving General Orbegoso in the palace, with one hundred men. It was generally reported that he had marched into the interior, to bring about a federal revolution, but it appears that he has arrived at Guadalupe, and there taken up his quarters.

A loud cannonading has been kept up since ten o'clock, which keeps us all idle, looking out for the smoke, and counting the number of discharges.

Wednesday: October 6th, 1841

A messenger has brought the intelligence that there had been more noise and smoke than slaughter, the cannons being planted at such distances that it was impossible they could do much execution. Numerous bulletins are distributed: some violently in favour of Bustamante and federalism, full of abuse and dread of Santa Anna; others lauding that general to the skies, as the saviour of his country.[20]

The *allied forces* being in numbers double those of Bustamante, there is little doubt of the result.

Thursday: October 7th, 1841

A capitulation. Santa Anna is triumphant.[21] He made his solemn entry into Mexico last evening, Generals Valencia and Canalizo being at the head of the united forces. Not a solitary *viva* was heard as they passed along the streets; nor afterwards, during his speech in congress. *Te Deum* was sung this morning in the cathedral, the Archbishop in person receiving the new president.[22]

We have just returned from Mexico, where we went in search of apartments, and with great difficulty have found rooms in the hotel of the Calle [de] Vergara; but we shall remain here a day or two longer. There is no great difference in the general appearance of the city, except that the shops are all reopened, and that most of the windows are broken. Immediately after the morning ceremony, Santa Anna returned to the archbishop's palace at Tacubaya, which residence he prefers to the president's palace in Mexico. His return there, after his triumphant entry into the capital, was very much *en roi:* a retinue of splendid coaches with fine horses, going at full speed, the general's carriage drawn by four beautiful white horses belonging to Don Francisco Morphy (the very same that were sent to bring us into Mexico); brilliant aides-de-camp; and an immense escort of cavalry.

Thus concludes the Revolution of 1841, though not its effects.[23]

The new ministry, up to this date, are Señor Gómez Pedraza for Foreign and Home Relations; Castillo, *un petit avocat* from Guadalajara, said to be a furious federalist and Latin scholar, for Public Instruction; General Tornel for War and Marine; and Señor Dufoo for the Treasury.[24] Valencia proposed Paredes for the War Department, but he declined, saying, "No, no, General. I understand you very well—you want to draw me off from my division."[25]

Those who know Bustamante best, even those who most blame him for indecision and want of energy, agree in one point: that the true motives of his conduct are to be found in his constant and earnest desire to spare human life.[26]

46

Back to the Capital

The revolution lasted upwards of thirty-five days, and during that time, though I have written of little else, we have been taking many rides in the environs of this hacienda, some of which were very interesting. We are also making the most of our last few days of Mexican country life.

On Thursday we went on horseback with a large party to visit the mill of Santa Mónica, an immense hacienda, which tradition, I know not with what truth, supposes to have been in former days the property of Doña Marina; a gift to her from Cortés. At all events, at a later period it belonged to the Augustine monks; then to a Mexican family who lost their fortune from neglect or extravagance. It was bought by the present proprietor for a comparatively trifling sum, and produces him an annual rent of thirty-five thousand dollars upon an average. The house is colossal, and not more than one-third of it occupied. The granaries, of solid masonry, contain fourteen thousand loads of corn— they were built about two hundred and fifty years ago.[1]

From all the neighbouring haciendas, and even from many distant estates, the corn is sent to this mill, and is here ground, deposited, and sold on account of the owner [with] a certain portion deducted for the proprietor of Santa Mónica. It seems strange that they should have no windmills here, in a country colonized by Spain, where according to Cervantes they were common enough.

The house is in a commanding situation, and the views of the mountains, especially from the upper windows, are very grand. In some of the old unoccupied apartments are some good copies of old paintings, the copies themselves of ancient date. There is the angel announcing to Elizabeth the birth of Saint John; a Holy Family, from Murillo; the destruction of Sodom and Gomorrah, which is one of the best, particularly the figures in the foreground of Lot and his family. Lot's wife stands in the distance, a graceful figure just crystallized, her head turned in the direction of the doomed city. I looked into every dark corner in hopes of finding some old daub representing Doña Marina, but without success.[2] There is the strangest contrast possible between these half-abandoned palaces and their actual proprietors. We had beautiful riding horses belonging to the hacienda, and enjoyed everything but the exceeding heat of the sun, as we galloped home about one o'clock.

As a specimen of rather a remarkable anachronism, we were told that a justice in the village of Tlalnepantla, speaking the other day of General Bustamante, said, "Poor man—he is persecuted by all parties, just as Jesus Christ was by the *Jansenists,* the *Sadducees,* and the *Holy Fathers of the Church!*" What a curious *olla podrida* the poor man's brain must be!

In the midst of the revolution, we were amused by a very peaceful sight—all the nurses belonging to the Cuna, or Foundling Hospital,[3] coming from the different villages to receive their monthly wages. Amongst the many charitable institutions in Mexico, there appears to me (in spite of the many prejudices existing against such institutions) none more useful than this. These otherwise unfortunate children, the offspring of abject poverty or guilt, are left at the gate of the establishment, where they are received without any questions being asked; and, from that moment, they are protected and cared for by the best and noblest families in the country.

The members of the society consist of the first persons in Mexico, male and female. The men furnish the money; the women give their time and attention. There is no fixed number of members, and amongst them are the ladies in whose house we now live. The president is the Dowager Marquesa de Vivanco. When the child has been about a month in the Cuna, it is sent with an Indian nurse to one of the villages near Mexico. If sick or feeble, it remains in the house under the more immediate inspection of the society. These nurses have a *fiadora,* a responsible person who lives in the village, and answers for their good conduct. Each nurse is paid four dollars per month, a sufficient sum to induce any poor Indian with a family to add one to her stock. Each lady of the society has a certain number under her peculiar care, and gives their clothes which are poor enough, but according to the *village fashion.* The child thus put out to nurse is brought back to the Cuna when weaned, and remains under the charge of the society for life; but, of the hundreds and tens of hundreds that have passed through their hands, scarcely one has been left to grow up in the Cuna. They are constantly adopted by respectable persons, who, according to their inclination or abilities, bring them up either as favoured servants or as their own children; and the condition of a *huérfano,* an orphan—as a child from the hospital is always called—is perfectly upon a level with that of the most petted child of the house. The nurses in the Cuna are paid eight dollars per month.

Upwards of a hundred nurses and babies arrived on Sunday, taking up their station on the grass under the shade of a large ash tree in the courtyard. The nurses are invariably bronze; the babies generally dark, though there was a sprinkling of fair English or German faces amongst them with blue eyes and blonde hair, apparently not the growth of Mexican land. Great attention to cleanliness cannot be hoped for from this class, but the babies looked healthy and contented. Each nurse had to present a paper which had been given her for that purpose, containing her own name, the name of the child, and that of the lady under whose particular charge she was. Such as: "María Josefa—baby Juanita de los Santos—belonging to the Señora Doña Matilde F[agoag]a,[4] given on such a day to the charge of María Josefa."

Constantly the nurse had lost this paper, and it was impossible for her to remember more than her own name; as to who gave her the baby, or when she got it, was entirely beyond her powers of calculation. However, then stepped forward the *fiadora* Doña Tomasa, a sensible looking village dame, grave and important as became her situation, and gave an account of the nurse and the baby, which, being satisfactory, the copper was swept into the nurse's lap, and she and her baby went away contented. It was pleasant to see the kindness of the ladies to these poor women; how they praised the care that had been taken of the babies; admired the strong and healthy ones, which indeed nearly all were; took an interest in those who looked paler, or less robust; and how fond and proud the nurses were of their charges; and how little of a hired, mercenary, *hospital* feeling existed among them all.

A judge in the village, who comes here frequently, a pleasant and well-informed man, amused us this evening by recounting to us how he had once formed a determination to become a monk, through sudden fear. Being sent by [the] government to Toluca, some years ago, to inquire into the private political conduct of a Yorkino,[5] he found that his only means of remaining there unsuspected, and also of obtaining information, was to lodge in the convent of the Carmelite friars. The padres accommodated him with a cell, and assisted him very efficaciously in his researches. But the first night, being alone in his cell, the convent large and dreary and the wind howling lugubriously over the plains, he was awakened at night by a deep sepulchral voice, apparently close at his ear, tolling forth these words:

> *Hermanos, en el sepulcro acaba*
> *Todo lo que el mundo alaba!*

> My brothers, all must finish in the tomb!
> Of all that men extol, this is the doom.

Exceedingly startled, he sprang up, and opened the door of his cell. A dim lamp faintly illuminated the long vaulted galleries, and the monks, like shadows, were gliding to midnight prayer. In the dreariness of the night, with the solemn words sounding in his ears like a warning knell, he came to the satisfactory conclusion that all was vanity, and to the determination that the very next day he would retire from the world, join this holy brotherhood, and bind himself to be a Carmelite friar for life. The day brought counsel, the cheerful sunbeams dispelled the gloom, even within the old convent, and his scruples of conscience melted away.

There are old villages and old churches in this neighbourhood that would delight an antiquary. In the churchyard of the village of San Andrés is the most beautiful weeping ash I ever saw. We took shelter from the sun yesterday under its gigantic shadow, and lay there as under a green vault. We saw today, near another solitary old church, one of the Indian oven-baths, the *temezcallis*, built of bricks, in which there is neither alteration nor improvement since their first invention, heaven alone knows in what century.

Saturday: October 9th, 1841

We rode last evening to another estate belonging to this family, called San Mateo, one of the prettiest places on a small scale we have seen here. The road, or rather path, led us through fields covered with the greatest profusion of bright yellow sunflowers and scarlet dahlias, so tall that they came up to our horses' ears. The house is built in the cottage style (the first specimen of that style we have seen here), with a piazza in front, large trees shading it, and a beautiful view from the height on which it stands. It has rather an English than a Spanish look. No one lives there but the agent and his wife—and a fierce dog.[6]

Monday: October 11th, 1841

This morning we rose at five, mounted our horses, and, accompanied by Señor E[scandón][7] together with the *administrador* and the old gardener, set off to take our last long ride from San Xavier—for this evening we return to Mexico. The morning was fine and fresh, the very morning for a gallop, and the country looked beautiful.

We rode first to the Lechería, where Generals Bustamante and Paredes had their last eventful conference, having passed on our way various old churches and villages, and another hacienda also belonging to this family, whose estates seem countless. The Lechería is a large unoccupied house, or occupied only by the *administrador* and his family. It is a fine building, and its courtyard within is filled with flowers; but, having neither garden nor trees near, it seems rather lonely, and must have been startled to find itself the rendezvous of contending chieftains. It is surrounded by fertile and profitable fields of corn and maize.[8] We stayed but a short time in the house, and, having observed with due respect the chamber where the generals conferred together, remounted our horses and rode on. I have no doubt, by the way, that their meeting was the most amicable imaginable. I never saw a country where opponent parties bear so little real ill will to each other. It all seems to evaporate in words. I do not believe that there is any real bad feeling subsisting at this moment, even between the two rival generals, Bustamante and Santa Anna. Santa Anna usurped the presidency, partly because he wanted it, and partly because, if he had not, someone else would; but I am convinced that, if they met by chance in a drawing room, they would give each other as cordial an *abrazo* (embrace), Mexican fashion, as if nothing had happened.[9]

Our road led us through a beautiful tract of country, all belonging to the Lechería, through pathways that skirted the fields where the plough had newly turned up the richest possible soil, and which were bordered by wild flowers and shady trees. For miles our path lay through a thick *carpeting* of the most beautiful wild flowers imaginable; bright scarlet dahlias, gaudy sunflowers, together with purple, and lilac, and pale straw-coloured blossoms, to all which the gardener gave but the general name of *mirasoles* (sunflowers). The purple convolvulus threw its creeping branches on the ground, or along whatever it could embrace; while all these bright flowers, some growing to a great height, seemed, as we rode by them, to be flaunting past us in their gay colours, like peasants in their holiday dresses. The ground also was enamelled with a little low inquisitive-looking blossom, bright yellow, with a peeping brown eye; and the whole, besides forming the gayest assemblage of colours and groups, gave to the air a delicious fragrance.

But at last we left these fertile grounds and began to ascend the hills, part of which afford pasture for the flocks, till, still higher up, they become perfectly arid and stony. Here the whole landscape looks bleak and dreary, excepting that the eye can rest upon the distant mountains of a beautiful blue, like a peep of the promised land from Mount Nebo. After having rode four leagues, the latter part over this sterile ground affording but an insecure footing for our horses, we descried, low down in a valley, an old sad-looking building with a ruined mill and some trees. This was the object of our ride: the *Molino Viejo* (Old Mill), another hacienda belonging to these rich lady proprietors, and profitable on account of the fine pasturage which some of the surrounding hills afford. Nothing could look more solitary. Magdalene might

have left her desert, and ended her days there without materially better-
ing her situation. The only sign of life is a stream that runs round a very
productive small orchard in front of the house, while on a hill behind
are a few maguey plants—and on the *mirador*, in front of the house,
some creepers have been trained with a good deal of taste. There are
bleak hills in front, hills with a scanty herbage behind it, and everywhere a stillness that makes itself felt; while—strange circumstance in
this country!—there is not even a church within a league and a half.
There has been a chapel in the house, but the gilded paintings are falling from the wall, the altar is broken, and the floor covered with dried
corn. The agent's wife, who sits here all alone, must have time to collect
her scattered thoughts, and plenty of opportunity for reflection and self-
examination. Certain it is, she gave us a very good breakfast, which we
attacked like famished pilgrims; and shortly after took our leave.

The heat on the shadeless hills had now become intense. It is only
on such occasions that one can fully appreciate the sufferings of Regulus.
We returned by the *carriage road*, a track between two hills, composed
of ruts and stones, and large holes. On the most barren parts of these
hills, there springs a tree which the Indians call *güizache;*[10] it resembles
the savine, and produces a berry of which ink is made. The road was
bordered by bushes, covered with white blossoms, very fragrant. We
galloped as fast as our horses would carry us, to escape from the sun,
and passed a pretty village on the highroad, which is a fine broad causeway in good repair, leading to Guanajuato. We also passed San Mateo,
and then rode over the fields fast home, where we arrived looking like
broiled potatoes.

We had a conversation with _____ this morning on the subject of the
ejercicios, certain religious exercises, to which in Mexico men as well
as women annually devote a certain number of days, during which they
retire from the world to a religious house or convent, set apart for that
purpose, of which some receive male and others female devotees. Here
they fast and pray and receive religious instruction, and meditate upon
religious subjects during the period of their retreat. A respectable merchant, who in compliance with this custom lately retired for a few days
to one of these religious establishments, wrote on entering there to his
head clerk, a young man to whom he was much attached, informing
him that he had a presentiment that he would not leave the convent
alive, but would die by the time his devotional exercises were completed,
[and] giving him some good advice as to his future conduct, together
with his last instructions as to his own affairs. He ended with these
words: *"hasta la eternidad!*—until eternity!"* The letter produced a strong
effect on the mind of the young man; but still more when the merchant
died at the end of a few days, as he had predicted, and was carried from
the convent to his grave.

Tuesday: October 12th, 1841
Fonda in the Calle de Vergara, Mexico

We reached Mexico last evening and took up our quarters in an inn
or hotel—kept by an English woman, and tolerably clean though of
course not very agreeable.[11] A number of *pronunciado* officers are also
here, amongst others General _____, who I hope will be obliged to go
soon that we may have his parlour; [also] a mysterious English couple,[12]
a wounded colonel, an old gentleman (a fixture in the house), &c.
There is a *table d'hôte*, but I believe no ladies dine there. Invitations
to take up our quarters in private houses have been pressed upon us with
a kindness and cordiality difficult to resist.

Though politics are the only topic of interest at present, I think you
will care little for having an account of the Junta of Representatives,
with its chiefly military members, or of the elections. Considering by
whom the members are chosen, and the object for which they are
elected, the result of their deliberations is, as you may suppose, pretty
well known beforehand. Military power is strengthened by every act,
and all this power is vested in the commanders-in-chief. New batches of
generals are made, in order to reward the late distinguished services of
the officers, and colonels by hundreds. Eleven generals were created in
the division of Paredes alone. Money has been given to the troops in the
palace with orders to purchase new uniforms, which it is said will be
very brilliant. There appears, generally speaking, a good deal of half-
smothered discontent, and it is whispered that even the revolutionary
bankers are half repentant and look gloomy. The only opposition paper
is *Un Periódico Más* (*One More Periodical*)—the others are all ministerial.[13]

In the south there has been some trouble with Generals Bravo and
Alvarez,[14] who wish that part of the country to govern itself until the
meeting of congress. There was some talk of putting Valencia at the
head of the troops which are destined to march against them, but there
are now negotiations pending, and it is supposed there will be some
agreement made without coming to bloodshed.

It is said that orders were sent to General Almonte to leave the republic, and that he answered the dispatch with firmness, refusing to
acknowledge the authority of Santa Anna. General Bustamante, who is
now in Guadalupe, intends to leave the scene of his disasters within a
few months. Calderón paid him a visit lately, and, though scarcely recovered from his fatigues both of body and mind, he appears cheerful
and resigned, and with all the tranquillity which can be inspired only

by a good conscience and the conviction of having *done his duty to the best of his abilities.*

As for us personally, this revolution has been the most inconvenient revolution that ever took place, doing us all manner of mischief: stopping the sale of our furniture; throwing our affairs into confusion; overthrowing all our plans; and probably delaying our departure until December or January.[15] But in these cases, everyone must suffer more or less; and meanwhile we are surrounded by friends and by friendly attentions. It will be impossible for us to leave Mexico without regret. It requires nothing but a settled government to make it one of the first countries in the world. Santa Anna has much in his power. *Reste à savoir* how he will use that power. Perhaps in these last years of tranquillity, which he has spent on his estate, he may have meditated to some purpose.

It is singular how, in trying to avoid small evils, we plunge into unknown gulfs of misery; and how little we reflect that it might be wiser to

Bear those ills we have,
Than fly to others that we know not of.[16]

Everyone has heard of the abuses that produced the first revolution in Mexico—of the great inequality of riches, of the degradation of the Indians, of the high prices of foreign goods, of the Inquisition, of the ignorance of the people, the bad state of the colleges, the difficulty of obtaining justice, the influence of the clergy, and the ignorance in which the Mexican youth were purposely kept. Which of these evils has been remedied? Foreign goods are cheaper, and the Inquisition *is not*—but this last unchristian institution had surely gradually lost its power before the days of the last viceroy. But in the sacred name of *Liberty,* every abuse can be tolerated.[17]

O fatal name, misleader of mankind,
   Phantom, too radiant and too much adored!
Deceitful Star, whose beams are bright to blind,
   Although their more benignant influence poured
The light of glory on the Switzer's sword,
   And hallowed Washington's immortal name.
Liberty! Thou when absent how deplored,
   And when received, how wasted, till thy name
Grows tarnished; shall mankind ne'er cease to work thee shame?

Not from the blood in fiercest battle shed,
   Nor deeds heroical as arm can do,
Is the true strength of manly freedom bred,
   Restraining tyranny and license too,
The madness of the many and the few.
   Land, whose new beauties I behold revealed,
Is this not true, and bitter as 'tis true?

The ruined fane, the desolated field,
The ruffian-haunted road, a solemn answer yield.

Where look the loftiest Cordilleras down
   From summits hoary with eternal snow
On Montezuma's venerable town
   And storied vale, and Lake of Mexico;
These thoughts the shade of melancholy throw
   On all that else were fair, and gay, and grand
As nature in her glory can bestow.
   For never yet, though liberal her hand,
So variously hath she adorned, enriched one land.

What boots it that from where the level deep
   Basks in the tropic sun's o'erpow'ring light
To where yon mountains lift their wintry steep,
   All climes, all seasons in one land unite?
What boots it that her buried caves are bright
   With wealth untold of gold or silver ore?
While, checked by anarchy's perpetual blight,
   Industry trembles 'mid her hard-earned store,
While rapine riots near in riches stained with gore?

O sage regenerators of mankind!
   Patriots of nimble tongue and systems crude!
How many regal tyrannies combined,
   So many fields of massacre have strewed
As you, and your attendant cutthroat brood?
   Man works no miracles; long toil, long thought,
Joined to experience, may achieve much good,
   But to create new systems out of nought,
Is fit for Him alone, the universe who wrought.

But what hath such an hour of such a day
   To do with human crimes, or earthly gloom?
Far wiser to enjoy while yet we may,
   The mockbird's song, the orange flower's perfume,
The freshness that the sparkling fountain showers.
   Let nations reach their glory or their doom,
Spring will return to dress yon orange bowers,
And flowers will still bloom on, and bards will sing of flowers.

Thursday: October 21st, 1841

In pursuance of the last-mentioned advice, we have been breakfasting today at Tacubaya, with the Prussian minister and his family, and enjoying ourselves there in Madame [von Gerolt]'s garden.[18] We have also just returned from the Marquesa de Vivanco's, where we had a pleasant evening, and met General Paredes, whom I like very much: a real soldier, thin, plain, blunt, and all hacked with wounds.[19]

Saturday: October 23rd, 1841

Calderón has been dining at the English minister's, where he met all the great actors in the present drama, and had an agreeable party. We are now thinking of making our escape from this hotel, and of taking a horseback journey into Michoacán, which shall occupy a month or six weeks. Meantime I am visiting, with the Señorita Fagoaga,[20] every hospital, jail, college, and madhouse in Mexico!

Tuesday: October 26th, 1841

Today they are celebrating their independence. All the bells in all the churches, beginning with the cathedral, are pealing—cannon firing—rockets rushing up into the air—Santa Anna in the Alameda, speechifying—troops galloping—little boys running—*Te Deum* chanting—crowds of men and women jostling each other—the streets covered with carriages, the balconies covered with people—the Paseo expected to be crowded. I have escaped to a quiet room, where I am trying to find time to make up my letters before the packet goes. I conclude this just as the dictator, with his brilliant staff, has driven off to Tacubaya.[21]

47

The Warmth of Mexican Charity

Thursday: November 4th, 1841
Fonda in the Calle de Vergara, Mexico

A great *función* was given in the opera in honour of His Excellency. The theatre was most brilliantly illuminated with wax lights. Two principal boxes were thrown into one for the President and his suite, and lined with crimson and gold, with draperies of the same. The staircase leading to the second tier, where this box was, was lighted by and *lined* all the way up with rows of footmen in crimson and gold livery.

A crowd of gentlemen stood waiting in the lobby for the arrival of the hero of the fête. He came at last in regal state, carriages and outriders at full gallop: himself, staff, and suite in splendid uniform. As he en-

tered, Señor Roca presented him with a libretto of the opera, bound in red and gold. We met the great man *en face*, and he stopped and gave us a cordial recognition. Two years have made little change in him in appearance. He retains the same interesting, resigned, and rather melancholy expression; the same quiet voice, and grave but agreeable manner; and surrounded by pompous officers, he alone looked quiet, gentlemanly and high-bred.

The theatre was crowded to suffocation: boxes, pit, and galleries. There was no applause as he entered. One solitary voice in the pit said "*Viva Santa Anna!*"—but it seemed checked by a slight movement of disapprobation, scarcely amounting to a murmur. The opera was *Belisarius*—considered apropos to the occasion—and was really beautifully *montée:* the dresses new and superb, the decorations handsome.[1] They brought in real horses, and Belisarius entered in a triumphal chariot drawn by white steeds; but for this the stage is infinitely too small, and the horses plunged and pranced so desperately that Belisarius wisely jumped out and finished his aria on foot. The two prima donnas acted together the wife and daughter of the hero—both about the same age, and dressed very well. But the Castellan's voice is not suited to the opera, and the music, beautiful as it is, was the least effective part of the affair. The generals in their scarlet and gold uniforms sat like peacocks surrounding Santa Anna, who looked modest and retiring, and as if quite unaccustomed to the public gaze! The boxes were very brilliant—all the diamonds taken out for the occasion. His Excellency is by no means indifferent to beauty—*tout au contraire*—yet I dare say his thoughts were this night of things more warlike and less fair.

Let all this end as it may, let them give everything whatever name is most popular, the government is now a military dictatorship. Señor _____ calls this revolution "the apotheosis of egotism transformed into virtue," and it must be confessed that in most of the actors it has been a mere calculation of personal interests.

Wednesday: November 10th, 1841

We went some days ago, with our friends from San Xavier, to visit the hospital of San Juan de Dios, at San Cosme. We found that, being at present under repair, it has but two occupants: old women, who keep each other melancholy company. The building is very spacious and handsome, erected of course during the Spanish dominion, and extremely clean—an observation worthy of note when it occurs in Mexican public buildings. There is a large hall, divided by square pillars, with a light and cheerful aspect, where the patients sleep; and a separate apartment for women. The rooms are all so clean, airy, and cheerful that one forgets it is a hospital. In this respect, the style of building here is superior to all others, with large airy courtyards and fountains, long galleries and immense apartments, with every window open. There is no part of Europe where, all the year round, invalids can enjoy such advantages; but, also, there are few parts of Europe where the climate would permit them to do so.[2]

The following day we visited another hospital, that known as the Hospital de Jesús—hallowed ground, for here the mortal remains of

Cortés were deposited. And, though rescued from desecration by a distinguished individual during a popular tumult, so that they no longer repose in the sanctuary of the chapel, there still exists, enshrined here, that over which time and revolutions have no power—his *memory*.[3]

The establishment, as a hospital, is much finer—and the building infinitely handsomer—than the other. The director, a physician, led us first to his own apartments, as the patients were dining, and afterwards showed us through the whole establishment. The first large hall, into which we were shown, is almost entirely occupied by soldiers who had been wounded during the *pronunciamiento*. One had lost an arm, another a leg, and they looked sad and haggard enough, though they seemed perfectly well attended to—and, I dare say, did anything but *bless* the revolutions that brought them to that state, and with which they had nothing to do—for your Mexican soldier will lie down on his mat at night, a loyal man, and will waken in the morning and find himself a *pronunciado*. Each one had a separate room, or at least a compartment divided by curtains from the next, and in each was a bed, a chair, and a small table—this on one side of the long hall. The other was occupied by excellent hot and cold baths.

We then visited the women's apartment, which is on a similar plan. Amongst the patients is an unfortunate child of eight years old, who in the *pronunciamiento* had been accidentally struck by a bullet, which entered her left temple and came out below the right eye, leaving her alive. The ball was extracted, and a portion of the brain came out at the wound. She is left blind, or nearly so, having but a faint glimmering of light. They say she will probably live, which seems impossible. She looks like a galvanized corpse—yet must have been a good-looking child. Notwithstanding the nature of her wound, her reason has not gone; and as she sat upright in her little bed, with her head bandaged and her fixed and sightless eyes, she answered meekly and readily to all the questions we put to her. Poor little thing! She was shocking to look at; one of the many innocent beings whose lives are to be rendered sad and joyless by this revolution. The doctor seemed very kind to her.

At the end of the women's apartment in this hospital there is a small chapel where mass is said to the invalids. It is only remarkable as having over the altar an image of the Purísima, brought from Spain by Cortés. We went all through the building, even to the enclosure on the *azotea* where dead bodies are dissected; and on which *azotea* was a quantity of wool—taken from the mattresses of those who die in the hospital—which is left in the sun during a certain period before it is permitted to be used again. The whole establishment struck us as being healthy, cleanly, and well-conducted.

We then visited the fine old church, which has but one broad aisle with a handsome altar, and near it is the small monument under which the bones of the conqueror were placed. The sacristy of the church is remarkable for its ceiling, composed of the most intricately and beautifully carved mahogany: a work of immense labour and taste, after the Gothic style. The divisions of the compartments are painted blue and ornamented with gilding. In the centre of the apartment is an immense circular table, formed of one piece of mahogany—for which large sums have been refused.[4]

A curious accident happened to Señor [Muñoz] in this last *pronunciamiento*. He had already lost his leg in the first one, and was limping along the street when he was struck by a ball. He was able to reach his house, and called to his wife to tell her what had occurred. Her first impulse was to call for a doctor, when he said to her very coolly: "Not this time—a carpenter will do better." He had been shot in his *wooden leg!*[5]

We went in the evening to visit the Cuna, which is not a fine building but a large, healthy, airy house. At the door, where there are a porter and his wife, the babies are now given in. Formerly they were put in at the *reja*, at the window of the porter's lodge, but this had to be given up in consequence of the tricks played by boys or idle persons, who put in dogs, cats, or dead animals. As we were going upstairs, we heard an old woman singing a cheerful ditty in an awfully cracked voice; and, as we got a full view of her before she could see us, we saw a clean, old body sitting, sewing and singing, while a baby rolling on the floor in a state of perfect ecstasy was keeping up a sort of crowing duet with her. She seemed delighted to see these ladies, who belong to the Junta, and led us into a large hall where a score of nurses and babies were performing a symphony of singing, hushing, crying, lullabying, and other nursery music. All along the room were little green painted beds, and both nurses and babies looked clean and healthy.

The [Fagoaga]s[6] knew every baby and nurse and directress by name. Some of the babies were remarkably pretty, and when we had admired them sufficiently we were taken into the next hall, occupied by little girls of two, three, and four years old. They were all seated on little mats at the foot of their small green beds: a regiment of the finest and healthiest children possible—a directress in the room sewing. At our entrance, they all jumped up simultaneously, and surrounded us with the noisiest expressions of delight. One told me in a confidential whisper that "Manuelita had thumped her own head, and had a pain in it"—but I could not see that Manuelita seemed to be suffering any acute agonies, for she made more noise than any of them. One little girl sidled up to me and said in a most insinuating voice, "*Me llevas tú?* Will you take me away with you?"—for even at this early age they begin to have a glimmering idea that those whom the ladies choose from amongst them are peculiarly favoured.

We stayed some time with them, and admired their healthy, happy, and well-fed appearance; and then proceeded to the apartment of the boys: all little things of the same age, sitting ranged in a row like senators in congress, and strange to say much quieter and graver than the female babies. But this must have been from shyness, for before we came away we saw them romping in great style. The directresses seem good respectable women, and kind to the children, who, as I mentioned before, are almost all taken away and brought up by rich people before they have time to know that there is anything peculiar or unfortunate in their situation. After this adoption, they are completely on a level with the other children of the family. An equal portion is left them and, although their condition is never made a secret of, they frequently marry as well as their adopted brothers and sisters.

Those who are opposed to this institution are so on the plea that it encourages and facilitates vice. That the number of children in the hospital is a proof that much vice and much poverty do exist, there is no doubt; that, by enabling the vicious to conceal their guilt, or by relieving the poor from their burthen, it encourages either vice or idleness is scarcely probable. But even were it so, the certain benefits are so immense, when laid in the balance with the possible evils, that they cannot be put in competition. The mother who leaves her child at the Cuna, would she not abandon it to a worse fate if this institution did not exist? If she does so to conceal her disgrace, is it not seen that a woman will stop at no cruelty to obtain this end?—[such] as exposure of her infant, even murder—and that, strong as maternal love is, the dread of the world's scorn has conquered it? If poverty be the cause, surely the misery must be great indeed which induces the poorest beggar or the most destitute of the Indian women (whose love for their children amounts to a passion) to part with her child; and, though it is suspected that the mother who has left her infant at the Cuna has occasionally got herself hired as a nurse that she may have the pleasure of bringing it up, it seems to me that no great evil can arise, even from that.

These orphans are thus rescued from the contamination of vice, from poverty, perhaps from the depths of depravity; perhaps their very lives are saved, and great sin is prevented. Hundreds of innocent children are thus placed under the care of the first and best ladies in the country, and brought up to be worthy members of society.[7]

Another day we devoted to visiting a different and more painful scene —the Acordada, or public jail—a great solid building, spacious and well ventilated. For this there is also a junta, or society of ladies of the first families, who devote themselves to teaching the female malefactors. It is painful and almost startling to see the first ladies in Mexico familiarly conversing with and embracing women who have been guilty of the most atrocious crimes—especially of murdering their husbands, which is the chief crime of the female prisoners. There are no bad faces amongst them; and probably not one who has committed a premeditated crime. A moment of jealousy during intoxication, violent passions without any curb suddenly aroused and as suddenly extinguished, have led to these frightful results.

We were first shown into a large and tolerably clean apartment, where were the female prisoners who are kept apart as being of a more *decent family* than the rest. Some were lying on the floor, others working— some were well dressed, others dirty and slovenly. Few looked sad, most appeared careless and happy, and *none* seemed ashamed. Amongst them were some of the handsomest faces I have seen in Mexico. One good-looking common woman, with a most joyous and benevolent countenance, and lame, came up to salute the ladies. I inquired what she had done. "Murdered her husband, and buried him under the brick floor!" Shade of Lavater![8] It is some comfort to hear that their husbands were generally such brutes they deserved little better! Amongst others confined here is the wife, or rather the widow, of a governor of Mexico, who made away with her husband. We did not see her, and they say she generally keeps out of the way when strangers come. One very pretty and coquettish little woman, with a most intellectual face and very superior-looking, being in fact a relation of Count _____'s, is in jail on suspicion of having poisoned her lover. A beautiful young creature, extremely like Mrs. _____ of Boston, was among the prisoners. I did not hear what her crime was. We were attended by a woman who has the title of *presidenta*, and who, after some years of good conduct, has now the charge of her fellow prisoners—but she also murdered her husband! We went upstairs, accompanied by various of these distinguished criminals, to the room looking down upon the chapel, in which room the ladies give them instruction in reading, and in the Christian doctrine. With the time which they devote to these charitable offices, together with their numerous devotional exercises, and the care which their houses and families require, it cannot be said that the life of a Mexican señora is an idle one—nor, in such cases, can it be considered a useless one.[9]

We then descended to the lower regions where—in a great, damp, vaulted gallery—hundreds of unfortunate women of the lowest class were occupied in *travaux forcés*—not indeed of a very hard description. These were employed in baking tortillas for the prisoners. Dirty, ragged, and miserable-looking creatures there were in these dismal vaults, which looked like purgatory and smelt like—heaven knows what! But, as I have frequently had occasion to observe in Mexico, the sense of smell is a doubtful blessing. Another large hall near this, which the prisoners were employed in cleaning and sweeping, has at least fresh air, opening on one side into a court where poor little children, the saddest sight there, were running about—the children of the prisoners.

Leaving the side of the building devoted to the women, we passed on to another gallery, looking down upon an immense paved court with a fountain, where were several hundreds of male prisoners, unfortunately collected together without any reference to the nature of their crime: the midnight murderer with the purloiner of a pocket handkerchief; the branded felon with the man guilty of some political offense; the debtor with the false coiner—so that many a young and thoughtless individual whom a trifling fault, the result of ignorance or of unformed principles, has brought hither must leave this place wholly contaminated and hardened by bad example and vicious conversation. Here there were indeed some ferocious, hardened-looking ruffians—but there were many mild, good-humoured faces—and I could see neither sadness nor a trace of shame on any countenance. Indeed they all seemed much amused by seeing so many ladies. Some were stretched full-length on the ground, doing nothing; others were making rolls for hats, of different coloured beads such as they wear here, or little baskets for sale; whilst others were walking about alone, or conversing in groups. This is the first prison I ever visited, therefore I can compare it with no other; but the system must be wrong which makes no distinctions between different degrees of crime.[10] These men are the same *forçats* whom we daily see in chains, watering the Alameda or Paseo, or mending the streets.

Several hundreds of prisoners escaped from the Acordada in the time of the *pronunciamiento*—probably the worst amongst them—yet *half the city* appears to be here now. We were shown the row of cells for criminals whom it is necessary to keep in solitary confinement, on account of disorderly behaviour—also the apartments of the directors.

In passing downstairs, we came upon a group of dirty-looking soldiers busily engaged in playing at cards. The alcalde, who was showing us through the jail, dispersed them all in a great rage, which I suspected was partly assumed for our edification. We then went into the chapel, which we had seen from above, and which is handsome and well kept. In the sacristy is a horrid and appropriate image of *the bad thief*. We were also shown a small room off the chapel, with a confessional, where the criminal condemned to die spends the three days preceding his execution with a padre chosen for that purpose. What horrid confessions, what lamentations and despair that small dark chamber must have witnessed! There is nothing in it but an altar, a crucifix, and a bench. I think the custom is a very humane one.

We felt glad to leave this palace of crimes, and to return to the fresh air.

The following day we went to visit San Hipólito, the insane hospital for men, accompanied by the director, a fine old gentleman who has been a great deal abroad, and who looks like a French marquis of the *ancien régime*. I was astonished, on entering, at the sweet and solitary beauty of the large stone courts, with orange trees and pomegranates now in full blossom, and the large fountains of beautifully clear water.[11] There must be something soothing in such a scene to the senses of these most unfortunate of God's creatures. They were sauntering about, quiet and for the most part sad; some stretched out under the trees, and others gazing on the fountain; all apparently very much under the control of the *administrador*, who was formerly a monk—this San Hipólito being a dissolved convent of that order. The system of giving occupation to the insane is not yet introduced here.

On entering we saw rather a distinguished-looking, tall and well-dressed gentleman, whom we concluded to be a stranger who had come to see the establishment, like ourselves. We were therefore somewhat startled when he advanced towards us with long strides, and in an authoritative voice shouted out, "Do you know who I am? I am the Deliverer of Guatemala!" The *administrador* told us he had just been taken up, was a Frenchman, and in a state of furious excitement. He continued making a tremendous noise, and the other madmen seemed quite ashamed of him. One unhappy-looking creature, with a pale, melancholy face, and his arms stretched out above his head, was embracing a pillar, and when asked what he was doing, replied that he was "making sugar."

We were led into the dining hall, a long airy apartment provided with benches and tables, and from thence into a most splendid kitchen—high, vaulted, and receiving air from above—a kitchen that might have graced the castle of some feudal baron, and looked as if it would most surely last as long as men shall eat and cooks endure. Monks of San Hipólito! How many a smoking dinner, what viands steaming and savoury must have issued from this noblest of kitchens to your refectory next door.

The food for the present inmates, which two women were preparing, consisted of meat and vegetables, soup and sweet things, excellent meat, and well-dressed *frijoles*. A poor little boy, imbecile, deaf and dumb, was seated there cross-legged in a sort of wooden box—a pretty child, with a fine colour, but who has been in this state from his infancy. The women seemed very kind to him, and he had a placid, contented expression of face, but took no notice of us when we spoke to him. Strange and unsolvable problem, what ideas pass through the brain of that child!

When we returned to the dining hall the inmates of the asylum, to the number of ninety or a hundred, were all sitting at dinner, ranged quietly on the benches, eating with wooden spoons out of wooden bowls. The poor hero of Guatemala was seated at the lower end of the table, tolerably tranquil. He started up on seeing us, and was beginning some furious exclamations, but was prevented by his neighbour who turned round with an air of great superiority, saying, "He's *mad!*"—at which the other smiled with an air of great contempt and, looking at us, said, "He calls *me* mad!" The man of the pillar was eyeing his soup, with his arms, as before, extended above his head. The director desired him to eat his soup, upon which he slowly and reluctantly brought down one arm, and ate a few spoonfuls. "How much sugar have you made today?" asked the director. "Fifty thousand kingdoms!" said the man.

They showed us two men of very good family, and one old gentleman who did not come to dinner with the rest, but stood aloof in the court-yard with an air of great superiority. He had a cross upon his breast, and belongs to an old family. As we approached he took off his hat, and spoke to us very politely; then, turning to the director, "*Y por fin*," said he, "*Cuándo saldré?* When shall I leave this place?" "Very soon," said the director, "You may get your trunks ready." He bowed and appeared satisfied, but continued standing in the same place, his arms folded, and with the same wistful gaze as before.

The director told us that the two great causes of madness here are love and drinking (mental and physical intoxication); that the insanity caused by the former is almost invariably incurable, whereas the victims of the latter generally recover, as is natural. The poor old gentleman with the cross owes the overthrow of his mind to the desertion of his mistress. We saw the chapel where a padre says mass to these poor creatures—"the innocents," as they are called here. They do not enter the chapel, for fear of their creating any disturbance, but kneel outside in front of the iron grating, and the *administrador* says it is astonishing how quiet and serious they appear during divine service.

As we passed through the court there was a man busily employed in hanging up various articles of little children's clothes, as if to dry them—little frocks and trousers—all the time speaking rapidly to himself, and stopping every two minutes to take an immense draught of water from the fountain. His dinner was brought out to him (for he could not be prevailed on to sit down with the others), and he ate it in the same hurried way, dipping his bread in the fountain, and talking all the time. The poor madman of the *sugar-kingdoms* returned from dinner and re-sumed his usual place at the pillar, standing with his arms above his head, and with the same melancholy and suffering expression of face.

The director then showed us the room where the clothes are kept: the straw hats, and coarse dresses, and the terrible straight waistcoats made of brown linen, that look like coats with prodigiously long sleeves, and the *botica* where the medicines are kept, and the secretary's room where they preserve the mournful records of entry and death—though often of exit. All round the court are strong stone cells, where the furious are confined. He took us into an empty one, where a Franciscan friar had been lodged. He had contrived to pull down part of the wall, and to make a large hole into his neighbour's cell adjoining. Fancy one mad-man seeing the head of another appear through a hole in his cell! The whole cell was covered with crosses of every dimension, drawn with a piece of coal. They had been obliged to remove him into another in the gallery above, where he had already begun a new work of destruction. I was afterwards told by the padre P[inzó]n, the confessor of con-demned criminals, and who is of the same order as this insane monk,[12] that this poor man had been a merchant and had collected together about forty thousand dollars with which he was travelling to Mexico when he was attacked by robbers, who not only deprived him of all he possessed, but gave him some severe wounds on the head. When somewhat recovered, he renounced the world, and took his vows in the convent of San Francisco. Shortly after, he became subject to attacks of insanity, and at last became so furious that the superior was obliged to request an order for his admission to San Hipólito.

The director then led us to the gallery above, where are more cells and the terrible *Cuarto Negro,* the Black Chamber: a dark, round cell, about twelve feet in circumference, with merely a slit in the wall for the admission of air. The floor is thickly covered with straw, and the walls are entirely covered with soft stuffed cushions. Here the most furious madman is confined on his arrival, and whether he throws himself on the floor, or dashes his head against the wall, he can do himself no injury. In a few days, the silence and the darkness soothe his fury, he grows calmer, and will eat the food that is thrust through the aperture in the wall. From this he is removed to a common cell, with more light and air; but, until he has become tranquil, he is not admitted into the court amongst the others.

From this horrible, though I suppose necessary, den of suffering we went to the apartments of the *administrador,* which have a fine view of the city and the volcanoes; and saw a Virgin, beautifully carved in wood, and dressed in white satin robes embroidered with small diamonds. On the ground was a little dog, dying, having just fallen off from the *azotea*—an accident which happens to dogs here not unfrequently.

We then went up to the *azotea,* which looks into the garden of San Fernando and of our last house, and also into the barracks of the soldiers who, as _____ observed, are more dangerous madmen than those who are confined. Some rolled up in their dirty yellow cloaks, and others standing in their shirt sleeves, and many without either, they were as dirty looking a set of military heroes as one would wish to see. When we came downstairs again, and had gone through the court, and were passing the last cell—each of which is only lighted by an aperture in the thick stone wall—a pair of great black eyes glaring through upon a level with mine startled me infinitely. The eyes, however, glared upon vacancy. The face was thin and sallow, the beard long and matted, and the cheeks sunken. What long years of suffering appeared to have passed over that furrowed brow! I wish I had not seen it.

We afterwards went to the college of Vizcaínas, that K[ate] might see it—my third and last visit. What a palace! What courts and fountains! We went over the whole building as before, from the *azotea* downwards, and from the porter's lodge upwards. Many of the scholars, who went out during the revolution, have not yet returned. K[ate] was in admiration at the galleries, which look like long vaulted streets, and at the chapel, which is certainly remarkably rich.

Having stopped in the carriage on the way home at a shoemaker's, we saw *Santa Anna's leg* lying on the counter, and observed it with due respect, as the prop of a hero. With this leg, which is fitted with a very handsome boot, he reviews his troops next Sunday—putting his *best foot foremost*, for generally he merely wears an unadorned wooden leg. The shoemaker, a Spaniard, whom I can recommend to all customers as the most impertinent individual I ever encountered, was arguing in a blustering manner with a gentleman who had brought a message from the general, desiring some alteration in the boot—and wound up by muttering, as the messenger left the shop, "He shall either wear it as it is, or review the troops next Sunday without his leg!"[13]

We have ordered *mangas* to wear in our intended journey, which is now nearly decided on—nothing tolerable to be had under seventy or eighty dollars. They are made of strong cloth—with a hole in the middle for putting the head through—with black velvet capes, fringed either with silk or gold, and are universally lined with strong calico. They are warm and convenient for riding in the country. I have seen some, richly embroidered, which cost five hundred dollars.[14]

It is as I prophesied: now that we are about leaving Mexico, we fancy that there still remain objects of interest which we have not seen. We have paid a visit, probably a last visit, to Our Lady of Guadalupe, and certainly never examined her cathedral with so much attention, or lingered so long before each painting and shrine, or listened with so much interest to the particulars of its erection, which were given us by Señor _____ whose authority in these matters is unimpeachable.[15]

It appears that the present sacristy of the parochial church dates back to 1575, and was then a small chapel where the miraculous image was kept, and where it remained until the beginning of the next century, when a new church was built to which the image was solemnly transported. Even when enclosed in the first small sanctuary its fame must have been great, for, by orders of the archbishop, six dowries of three hundred dollars each, to be given to six orphans on their marriage, were annually drawn from the alms offered at her shrine. But in 1629 Mexico suffered a terrible inundation which destroyed a large part of the city, and the excellent Archbishop Don Francisco Manzo, while devoting his time and fortune to assist the sufferers, also gave orders that the Virgin of Guadalupe should be brought into Mexico and placed in the cathedral there— then of very different dimensions from the present noble building, occupying, it is said, the space which is now covered by the principal sacristy. When the waters retired, and the Virgin was restored to her own sanctuary, her fame increased to a prodigious extent. Copies of the divine image were so multiplied that there is [today] probably not an Indian hut throughout the whole country where one does not exist. Oblations and alms increased a thousand fold. A silver throne, weighing upwards of three hundred and fifty marks—and beautifully wrought, chiefly at the expense of the viceroy, [the] Count of Salvatierra—was presented to her sanctuary, together with a glass case (for the image), considered at that time a wonder of art.

At the end of the century a new temple, the present sanctuary, was begun; the second church was thrown down, but not until a provisional building (the actual parish church) was erected to receive the image. The new temple was concluded in 1709, and is said to have cost from six to eight hundred thousand dollars collected from *alms alone*, which were solicited in person by the viceregal archbishop, Don Juan de Ortega y Montáñez.[16] Two private individuals in Mexico gave, respectively, thirty and fifty thousand dollars towards its erection.

The interior is of the Doric order, and has three aisles, divided by eight pillars, upon which (and the walls) rest fifteen vaults, the centre one forming the dome of the edifice. The temple runs from north to south, and has three great doors, one fronting Mexico, and two others at the sides. Its length is 184 feet, and its width 124. In the four external angles of the church are four lofty towers, in the midst of which rises the dome. Three altars were at first erected, and in the middle one, destined for the image, was a sumptuous tabernacle of silver gilt, in which were more than three thousand two hundred marks of silver, and which cost nearly eighty thousand dollars. In the centre of this was a piece of gold, weighing four thousand and fifty *castellanos* (an old Spanish coin, the fiftieth part of a mark of gold), and here the image was placed, the linen on which it is painted secured and backed by a silver sheet of great value. The rest of the temple had riches corresponding. The candlesticks, vases, railing, &c., contain nearly fourteen thousand marks of silver, without counting the numerous holy vessels, cups and chalices, adorned with jewels. One golden lamp weighed upwards of two thousand two hundred *castellanos*—another seven hundred and fifty silver marks.

In 1802 some part of the walls and arches began to give way, and it was necessary to repair them. But first, under the direction of the celebrated sculptor Tolsá, a new altar was erected for the image. His first care was to collect the most beautiful marbles of the country for this purpose—the black he brought from Puebla, and the white, gray, and rose-coloured, from the quarries of San José Vizarrón. He also began to work at the bronze ornaments, but, from the immense sums of money necessary to its execution, the work was delayed for nearly twenty years. Then, in 1826, it was recommenced with fresh vigour. The image was removed meanwhile to the neighbouring convent of the Capuchinas, and the same year the altar was concluded and the Virgin brought back in solemn procession, in the midst of an innumerable multitude. This great altar, which cost from three to four hundred thousand dollars, is a concave hexagon, in the midst of which rise two white marble pillars, and on each side two columns of rose-coloured marble, of the composite order, which support the arch. Between these are two pedestals, on which are the images of San Joaquín and Santa Ana, and two niches, containing San José and St. John the Baptist. Above the cornices are three other pedestals, supporting the three Saints—Michael, Gabriel, and Raphael; and above St. Michael, in the midst of cherubim and seraphim, is a representation of the Eternal Father. The space between the upper part of the altar and the roof is covered with a painted crimson curtain, held by saints and angels. The tabernacle, in the centre of the altar, is of rose-coloured marble, in which the image is deposited, and all the ornaments of the altar are of gilt bronze and calamine.

Besides the collegiate and the parish churches, there are at Guadalupe the church of the Capuchin nuns, and the churches of the Hill and the Well—all in such close conjunction that the whole village or city (as it calls itself) seems altogether some religious establishment or confraternity, belonging to these temples and churches united in the worship of the Virgin, and consequent upon the "Miraculous Apparition" manifested to the chosen Indian, Juan Diego.

I regret not having known till lately that there exists in Mexico a convent of *Indian nuns;* and that each nun, when she takes the veil, wears a very superb Indian dress—the costume formerly worn by the *cacicas,* or ladies of highest rank.[17]

I went some days ago with the Señorita Fagoaga to visit the house for insane women in the Calle de Canoa, built in 1698 by the rich congregation of El Salvador.[18] The institution is now in great want of funds, and is by no means to be compared with the establishment of San Hipólito. The directress seems a good kindhearted woman who devotes herself to doing her duty, and who is very gentle to her patients, using no means but those of kindness and steadiness to subdue their violence. But what a life of fear and suffering such a situation must be! The inmates look poor and miserable, generally speaking, and it is difficult to shake off the melancholy impression which they produce on the mind.

We were particularly struck by the sight of one unfortunate woman of the better class, who, with her long hair all dishevelled and eyes sparkling with a wild light, stood at the open window of her cell, where for the present they are obliged to confine her, and who poured forth the most piteous lamentations and adjured everyone who passed, in the most pathetic terms, to restore her husband and children to her. One girl was singing cheerfully, one or two women were sewing, but most of them were sitting crouched on the floor with a look of melancholy vacancy. The poor are admitted gratis, and the richer classes pay a moderate sum for their board.

To turn to a very different theme—we continue to go to the opera, certainly the most agreeable amusement in Mexico, and generally to the _____ minister's box, in the centre. Last evening *Belisario* was repeated, but with less splendour than on its representation in honour of Santa Anna.

We expect to leave this on the sixteenth, going in a diligence as far as Toluca where a Mexican officer, Colonel Iniestra, has kindly promised to meet us with mules and horses.[19] M. le Comte de Breteuil and Mr. Ward, secretaries of the French and English legations, have made arrangements for accompanying us as far as Valladolid; with which agreeable travelling companions we may reasonably expect a pleasant journey.[20]

Last Sunday was the festival of All Saints, on the evening of which day we walked out under the *portales* with M. and Madame de _____, _____ minister and his wife, to look at the illumination[21] and at the numerous booths filled with *sugar skulls*, &c.—temptingly ranged in

grinning rows, to the great edification of the children. In general there are crowds of well-dressed people on the occasion of this fête, but the evening was cold and disagreeable and, though there were a number of ladies, they were enveloped in shawls, and dispersed early. The old women at their booths, with their cracked voices, kept up the constant cry of "Skulls, *niñas*, skulls!"—but there were also animals done in sugar, of every species, enough to form specimens for a Noah's ark.

Sunday: November 14th, 1841

We leave this the day after tomorrow, and shall write from our first halting place; and, as on our return we shall do little more than pass through Mexico, we are *almost* taking leave of all our friends. Were I to tell you all the kindness and hospitality and cordial offers of service that we receive, and the manner in which our rooms (albeit the rooms of an inn) are filled from morning till night, it would seem an exaggeration. One acquaintance we have made lately whom we like so much that we have been vociferously abusing the system of *faire part* in this city, since, owing to the mistake of a servant, we have until now been deprived of the pleasure of knowing her. The mistake is rectified at the eleventh hour. The lady is the Señora de Gómez Pedraza, one of the most accomplished and well-informed women in Mexico; and, though our friendship has been short, I trust it may be enduring.[22]

Two evenings since, we went with the Señora de Casa Flores to an amateur concert—and I question whether in any capital of Europe so many good amateur voices could be collected. I do not speak of the science or cultivation, though the hostess, the Señora A[dalid], has a perfect method.[23]

But yesterday we spent a most agreeable evening in a delightful family reunion at the house of Señor [Felipe] Neri del Barrio. It was strictly limited to the family relations, and was, I believe, his *jour de fête*. If all Mexican society resembled this, we should have too much regret in leaving it. The girls handsome, well educated, and simple in their manners and tastes—the countess a model of virtue and dignity. Then so much true affection and love of home amongst them all! So much wealth and yet good taste and perfect simplicity visible in all that surrounds them! Mexico is not *lost* as long as such families exist and, though they mingle little in society, the influence of their virtues and charities is widely felt.[24]

This morning Calderón had an audience of the new president. He also paid a visit to General Bustamante, who is still at Guadalupe, and preparing for his departure. He will probably sail in the *Jasón*, the man-of-war which brought us to Veracruz, and it is probable that we shall leave the republic at the same period.

The Dowager Marquesa de Vivanco, who in consequence of ill health has not left her house for months, was among our visitors this morning.

Today Count C[ortin]a dined here, and brought for our inspection the splendid sword presented by congress to General Valencia, with its hilt of brilliants and opals—a beautiful piece of workmanship, which does credit to the Mexican artificers. He was particularly brilliant and eloquent in his conversation today—whether his theories are right or wrong, they are certainly *entrainant*.[25]

Our next letters will probably be dated from Toluca.

FIVE WEEKS ON HORSEBACK

IN MICHOACAN

48

Toluca, and to the Mines of Angangueo

Tuesday: November 16th, 1841
Toluca

In vain would be a description, with the hopes of bringing them before you, of our last few days in Mexico!—of the confusion, the bustle, the visits, the paying of bills, the packing of trunks, the sending off of heavy luggage to Veracruz, and extracting the necessary articles for our journey—especially yesterday when we were surrounded by visitors and *cargadores,* from half past seven in the morning till half past eleven at night.

Our very last visitors were the families of Cortina and Escandón. The new president, *on dit,* is turning his sword into a ploughshare. Preferring a country to a city life, nearly every Sunday he names the house in which he desires to be *fêted* the following week—now at the villa of Señor _____ at Tacubaya—now at the hacienda of Señor _____ at San Agustín. As yet the diplomatic corps do not attend these assemblies, not having been officially received; but we hear that there is singing and dancing, and other amusements, and that His Excellency is extremely amiable and *galant.*

By six o'clock this morning several of our friends—Señors C[añed]o, M[atuti], Robles, A[lmont]e, &c.[1]—were assembled to accompany us to

the diligence, which unfortunately we had not been able to secure for ourselves, for at this moment the whole world is in motion, going to attend the great annual fair of San Juan de los Lagos which begins on the fifth of December, and to which Toluca is the direct road.[2] Fortunately, the diligence had broken down the preceding evening, and it was necessary to repair it; otherwise we should have left behind various important articles, for, in the confusion of our departure, everyone had left some requisite item at the hotel: Calderón his gun; Kate her bag; I *everything*—and more especially the book with which I intended to beguile the weary hours betweeen Mexico and Toluca. Our servant boy ran—Señor Robles mounted his horse, and most good-naturedly galloped between the diligence office and the hotel—until, little by little, all the missing articles were restored.

We climbed into the coach, which was so crowded that we could but just turn our heads to groan an adieu to our friends. The coach rattled off through the streets—dashed through the Alameda—and gradually we began to shake down and, by a little arrangement of cloaks and sarapes, to be less crowded. A padre with a very Indian complexion sat between Kate and me; and a horrible, long, lean, bird-like female, with immense red goggle eyes, coal-black teeth, fingers like claws, a great goitre, and drinking brandy at intervals, sat opposite to us. There were also various men buried in their sarapes. Satisfied with a cursory inspection of our companions, I addressed myself to *Blackwood's Magazine.* But the road which leads towards the Desierto, and which we before passed on horseback, is dreadful, and the mules could scarcely drag the loaded coach up the steep hills. We were thrown into ruts, horribly jolted, and sometimes obliged to get out, which would not have been disagreeable but for the necessity of getting in again.

The day and the country were beautiful, but impossible to enjoy either in a shut coach. We were rather thankful when—the wheels sticking in a deep rut—we were forced to descend and walk forwards for some time. We had before seen the view from these heights, but the effect never was more striking than at this moment. The old city, with her towers, lakes, and volcanoes, lay bathed in the bright sunshine. Not a cloud was in the sky—not an exhalation rose from the lake—not a shadow was on the mountains. All was bright and glittering, and flooded in the morning

light; while in contrast rose to the left the dark, pine-covered crags behind which the Desierto lies.

At Santa Fe we changed horses, and found there an escort which had been ordered for us by General Tornel: a necessary precaution in these robber-haunted roads. We stopped to breakfast at Cuajimalpa where the inn is kept by a Frenchman, who is said to be making a large fortune, which he deserves for the good breakfast he had prepared for us by orders of the Count de Breteuil and Mr. Ward—who had preceded us early in the morning on horseback, enviable fate! We had whitefish from the river of Lerma, which crosses the plains of Toluca, fresh and well dressed, and without that taste of *mud* which those from the Mexican *laguna* occasionally have; also hot cutlets, potatoes, coffee, &c.

After leaving this inn, situated in a country formed of heaps of lava and volcanic rocks, the landscape becomes more beautiful and wooded. It is, however, dangerous on account of the shelter which the wooded mountains afford to the knights of the road, and to whose predilection for these wild solitudes the number of crosses bore witness. In a woody defile there is a small clear space, called Las Cruces, where several wooden crosses point out the site of the famous battle between the curate Hidalgo and the Spanish General Trujillo.[3]

An object really in keeping with the wild scenery was the head of the celebrated robber Maldonado, nailed to the pine tree beneath which he committed his last murder. It is now quite black, and grins there, a warning to his comrades and an encouragement to travellers. From the age of ten to that of fifty when he expiated his crimes, he followed the honourable profession of free trader. The padre who was in the coach with us told us that he heard his last confession. That grinning skull was once the head of a man, and an ugly one too, they say; but stranger still it is to think that that man was once a baby, and sat on his mother's knee, and that his mother may have been pleased to see him cut his *first tooth*. If she could but see his teeth now! Under this very head, and as if to show their contempt for law and justice, the robbers lately eased some travellers of their luggage. Those who were robbed, however, were false coiners, rather a common class in Toluca, and two of these ingenious gentlemen were in the coach with us (as we afterwards learnt), and were returning to that city. These, with the brandy-drinking female, composed our select little party!

The scenery without was decidedly preferable to that within, and, the leathern sides of the vehicle being rolled up, we had a tolerable view. What hills covered with noble pines! What beautiful pasture fields, dotted with clumps of trees, that looked as if disposed for effect, as in an English park!—firs, oaks, cedars, and elms. [Once] arrived at the town or village of Lerma, famous for its manufacture of spurs and standing in a marshy country at the entrance of the valley of Toluca, all danger of the robbers is passed—and, with the danger, much of the beauty of the scenery. But we breathed more freely on another account, for here she of the goggle eyes and goitre descended with her brandy bottle, relieving us from the oppressive influence of the sort of *day*mare, if there be such a thing, which her presence had been to us.

The valley of Toluca was now before us, its volcano towering in the distance.[4] The plains around looked cold and dreary, with pools of transparent water, and swamps filled with various species of waterfowl. The hacienda of San Nicolás, the property of Señor Mier de Terán, a Spaniard, was the only object that we saw worthy of notice before we reached Toluca. This hacienda, formerly the property of the Carmelite monks, is a valuable estate. Not a tree is to be seen here, or in the valley— a great extent of which is included in it—but it is surrounded by vast fields of maguey and maize; it is traversed by a fine river, and is one of the most profitable estates in the country.[5] The labourers here are in general the Otomí Indians, a poor and degraded tribe.

Here we dismissed our escort, which had been changed every six leagues, and entered Toluca about four o'clock, passing the *garita* without the troublesome operation of searching to which travellers in general are subject. We found tolerable rooms in an inn—at least there were two or three wooden chairs in each, and a deal table in one—Mr. Ward and the Count de Breteuil looking out for us. Colonel Iniestra had not yet made his appearance.

Toluca, a large and important city, lies at the foot of the mountain of San Miguel de Totocuitlapilco, and is an old, quiet, good-looking, respectable-seeming place, about as sad and solitary as Puebla. The streets, the square, and the churches are clean and handsome. To the south of the city lie extensive plains covered with rich crops; and about ten miles in the same direction is the volcano. We walked out in the afternoon to see the Alameda—passing under the *portales*, handsomer and cleaner than those of Mexico—and sat down on a stone bench beside a fountain, a position which commanded a beautiful view of the distant hills and of the volcano, behind which the sun was setting in a sea of liquid flame, making it look like a great pearl lying amongst melted rubies. The Alameda has not been much ornamented, and is quite untenanted; but walks are cut through the grass, and they were making hay. Everything looked quiet and convent-like, and a fine fresh air passed over the new-mown grass, inclining to cold, but pleasant.[6]

The volcano is scooped out into a natural basin, containing, in the very midst of its fiery furnace, two lakes of the purest, coldest and most transparent water. It is said that the view from its summit, the ascent to which is very fatiguing, but has been accomplished, is beautiful and extensive. On the larger lake travellers have embarked in a canoe, but I believe it has never been crossed, on account of the vulgar prejudice that it is unfathomable, and has a whirlpool in the centre. The volcano is about fifteen thousand feet above the level of the sea and [more than six] thousand above Toluca. It is not so grand as Popocatepetl, but a *respectable* volcano for a country town—*"muy decente* (very decent),*"* as a man said in talking of the pyramids that adorn the wonderful cavern of Cacahuamilpa.

We ordered supper at the inn, and were joined by the *comandante* of Toluca, Don Miguel Andrade, the officer who came out to meet us when we arrived in Mexico. I regret to state that such a distinguished party should have sat down, six in number, to fowl and *frijoles*, with only three knives and two forks between them. The provident travellers had, however, brought good wine; and if our supper was not very elegant, it was at least very gay. Colonel Iniestra arrived about ten o'clock; but it is agreed that the animals require one day's rest, and we shall consequently spend tomorrow at Toluca.

Wednesday: November 17th, 1841

We have spent this day in arranging our route, in which we are guided not by the most direct, but the most agreeable; in walking through the city, which, in the time of federalism, was the capital of the state; in climbing some of the steep roads cut through the hills at whose base it lies; and in admiring the churches and convents, and broad, well-paved streets with their handsome houses, painted white and red. It is decided that the first night of our pilgrimage we shall request hospitality at the hacienda of the ex-Minister Echeverría—La Gavia, which is about ten leagues of very bad road from Toluca, which is sixteen from Mexico.[7] All these important arrangements being made, and a sketch of our journey traced out, we are about retiring to rest in the agreeable prospect of not entering any four- or two-wheeled vehicle—be it cart, carriage, coach, or diligence—till we return here.

Friday: November 19th, 1841
Hacienda of La Gavia

To get *under weigh* the first morning was a work of some difficulty: mules to be loaded; horses to be fitted with saddles; and one mule lame, and another to be procured; and the trunks found to be too heavy, and so on. We rose at five, dressed by candlelight, took chocolate, put on our *mangas*, and then planted ourselves in the passage looking down upon the patio to watch the proceedings and preparations.

Colonel Andrade arrived at seven with a trooper, to accompany us part of the way, and we set off while it was cool, without waiting for the rest of the party. Toluca looked silent and dignified as we passed through the streets—with its old convents and dark hills. The road, after leaving the city, was stony and mountainous; and, having reached a small rancho with an old oratorio beside it, we halted to wait for our travelling companions. Colonel Andrade amused us with an account of his warfare against the Comanches, in which service he has been terribly wounded. Singular contrast between these ferocious barbarians and the mild Indians of the interior! He considers them an exceedingly handsome, fine-looking race, whose resources, both for war and trade, are so great that were it not for their natural indolence, the difficulties of checking their aggressions would be formidable indeed.[8]

Colonel Andrade, being obliged to return to Toluca, left us in charge of his trooper, and we waited at the rancho for about half an hour, when our party appeared with a long train of mules and *mozos*—the

gentlemen dressed Mexican fashion as well as their men, the best dress in the world for a long equestrian journey. Colonel Iniestra had stayed behind to procure another mule and, there being two roads, we, as generally happens in these cases, chose the worst—which led us for leagues over a hilly country, unenlivened by tree, shrub, bush, or flowers. The sun was already high, and the day intensely hot. We passed an occasional poor hut—a chance Indian passed us, showed his white teeth, and, in spite of the load on his back, contrived to draw his hat off his matted locks and give us a mild good morrow—but for the rest, from Dan to Beersheba, from Toluca to La Gavia, all was barren.

By twelve o'clock we might have fancied ourselves passing over the burning plains of Mesopotamia, notwithstanding an occasional cold breeze which swept across us for a moment, serving only to make us feel the heat with greater force. Then barranca followed barranca. The horses climbed up one crag, and slid down another. By two o'clock we were all starving with hunger, but nothing was to be had. Even Nebuchadnezzar would have found himself at a nonplus. The Count de Breteuil contrived to buy some *granaditas* and parched corn from an Indian, which kept us quiet for a little while; and we tried to console ourselves by listening to our *arrieros*, who struck up some wild songs in chorus, as they drove the wearied mules up the burning hills.

Every Indian that we met assured us that La Gavia was "*cerquita, quite near*"—"*detrás lomita*, behind the little hill"—and every little hill that we passed presented to our view another little hill, but no signs of the much-wished-for dwelling. A more barren, treeless, and uninteresting country than this road (on which we have unanimously revenged ourselves by giving it the name of "the road of the three hundred barrancas") led us through, I never beheld. However, "it's a long lane that has no turning," as we say in Scotland, and between three and four La Gavia was actually in sight—a long, low building, whose entrance appeared to us the very gates of Eden. We were all, but especially me—who had ridden with my veil up, from a curiosity to see where my horse was going—burnt to the colour of Pawnee Indians.

We were most cordially welcomed by Señor Echeverría and his brothers-in-law, and soon refreshed by rest and an excellent dinner. Fortunately Kate and I had no mirrors; but each gave such a flattering description of the other's countenance that it was quite graphic.

This beautiful hacienda, which formerly belonged to the Count de Regla, whose possessions must have been royal, is thirty leagues in length and seventeen in width—containing in this great space the productions of every climate, from the fir-clad mountains on a level with the volcano of Toluca, to the fertile plains which produce corn and maize; and lower down, to fields of sugar cane and other productions of the tropics.[9]

We retired to rest betimes, and early this morning rode out with these gentlemen, about five leagues through the hacienda. The morning was bright and exhilarating, and, our animals being tired, we had fresh, strong little horses belonging to their stud, which carried us delightfully. We rode through beautiful pine woods and beside running water—contrasting agreeably with our yesterday's journey—and were accompanied by three handsome little boys, children of the family, the finest and manliest little fellows I ever saw, who, dressed in a complete Mexican costume, like three miniature rancheros, rode boldly and fearlessly over everything.[10] There was a great deal of firing at crows and at the wild duck on a beautiful little lake, but I did not observe that anyone was burthened with too much game. We got off our horses to climb through the wooded hills and ravines, and passed some hours lying under the pine trees, listening to the gurgling of the little brook, whose bright waters make music in the solitude; and, like the soldiers at the *pronunciamiento*, but with surer aim, pelting each other from behind the parapets of the tall trees, with fir tops. About ten o'clock we returned to breakfast, and, Colonel Iniestra having arrived, we are now preparing to continue our journey this afternoon.

Saturday: November 20th, 1841
Angangueo

We left La Gavia at four o'clock, accompanied by our hospitable hosts for some leagues, all their own princely property, through great pasture fields, woods of fir and oak, hills clothed with trees, and fine clear streams. We also passed a valuable stone quarry, and were shown a hill belonging to the Indians, presented to them by a former proprietor.

We formed a long train, and I pitied the mistress of El Pilar, our next halting-place, upon whom such a regiment was about to be unexpectedly quartered. There were Calderón, Kate, and I, and a servant; the Count de Breteuil and his servant; Mr. Ward and his servant; Colonel Iniestra and his men; mules, *arrieros*, spare mules, and led horses; and all the *mozos* armed—forming altogether a formidable gang.[11] We took leave of the Echeverría family when it was already growing dusk, and when the moon had risen found we had taken a great round, so that it was late at night when we arrived at El Pilar, a small hacienda situated in a wild-looking, solitary part of the country. A servant had been sent forward to inform the lady of the establishment of our approach, and we were most kindly received. The house is clean and pretty, and, tired as we were, the *sala*, boasting of an old piano, tempted us to try a waltz while they were preparing supper. The man who waited at table, before he removed the things, popped down upon his knees, and recited a long prayer aloud. The gentlemen had one apartment prepared for them; we another, in which—nay, even in the large four-posted and well-curtained bed allotted to us—Madame Iturbide had slept when on her way to Mexico before her coronation. The Señora M_____ also showed us her picture, and spoke of her and the Emperor with great enthusiasm.[12]

This morning we rose by candlelight at five o'clock, with the prospect of a long ride—having to reach the *Trojes* of Angangueo, a mining district (*trojes* literally mean granaries), fourteen leagues from El Pilar. The morning was cold and raw, with a dense fog covering the plains, so that we could scarcely see each other's faces, and found our *mangas* particularly agreeable.

We were riding quickly across these ugly, marshy wastes, when a curious animal crossed our path, a *zorillo*, or *epatl*, as the Indians call it, which Buffon mentions under the generic name of *moufettes*. It looks like a brown and white fox, with an enormous tail, which it holds up like a great feather in the air. It is known not only for the beauty of its skin, but for the horrible and pestilential odour with which it defends itself when attacked, and which poisons the air for miles around. Notwithstanding the warnings of the *mozos* as to its peculiar mode of defense, the gentlemen pursued it with guns and pistols, on horseback and on foot, but fired in vain. The beast seemed bulletproof, turning, doubling, winding, crossing pools, hiding itself, stopping for a moment as if it were killed, and then trotting off again with its feathery tail much higher than its head—so that it seemed to be running backwards. The fog favoured it very much. It was certainly wounded in the paw and, as it stopped and seemed to hesitate, the sportsmen thought they had caught him. But a minute afterwards away went the waving tail amongst the pools and the marshy grass—the *zorillo* no doubt accompanying it, though we could not see him—fortunately without [his] resorting to any offensive or defensive measures.[13] While they were chasing the *zorillo*, and we had rode a little way off that we might not be accidentally shot in the fog, an immense wolf came looming by in the mist, with its stealthy gallop, close by our horses, causing us to shout for the sportsmen. But our numbers frightened it, besides which it had but just breakfasted on a mule belonging to the hacienda, as we were told by the son of the proprietress of El Pilar, who, hearing all this distant firing, had ridden out to inquire into its cause, supposing that we might have lost our way in the fog and were firing signals of distress.

We continued our journey across these plains for about three leagues, when the sun rose and scattered the mist; and, after crossing a river, we entered the woods and rode between the shadows of the trees, through lovely forest scenery interspersed with dells and plains and sparkling rivulets. But by the time we left these woods, and made our way up amongst the hills, the sun was riding high in the heavens, the pastures and green trees disappeared, and, though the country was still fertile and the soil rich, its beauties lay hid in the valleys below. Kate's horse received a sort of *coup de soleil*, shivered and trembled, and would not go on—so she mounted another, and one of the *mozos* led hers slowly by a different road to a village, to be watered.

About one o'clock we began to wish for breakfast, but the mules which carried the provisions had taken a different path and were not in sight, so that, arriving at an Indian hut close by a running stream, we were unanimous in dismounting, and at least procuring some tortillas from the inmates. At the same time, the Count de Breteuil very philan-thropically hired an old discoloured-looking horse, which was grazing peaceably outside the hut, and, mounting the astonished quadruped, who had never in his wildest dreams calculated upon having so fine a chevalier on his back, galloped off in search of more solid food, while we set the Indian women to baking tortillas. He returned in about half an hour with some bones of boiled mutton—tied up in a handkerchief! —some salt, and thick tortillas, called *gorditas,* and was received with immense applause. Everything vanished in an incredibly short space of time, and we resumed our journey with renewed vigour.

Towards the afternoon we entered the state of Michoacán, by a road (destined to be a highway) traced through great pine forests, after stopping once more to rest at Las Millas, a few huts, or rather wooden cages, at the outskirts of the wood.[14] Nothing can be more beautiful or romantic than this road, ascending through these noble forests whose lofty oaks and gigantic pines clothe the mountains to their highest summits—sometimes so high that, as we look upwards, the trees seem diminished to shrubs and bushes, the sun darting his warm, golden light between the dark green extended branches of these distant forest pyra-mids, so that they seem to be basking in the very focus of his rays. Untrodden and virgin as these forests appear, an occasional cross, with its withered garland, gives token of life, and also of death; and green and lonely is the grave which the traveller has found among these Alpine solitudes, under the shadows of the dark pine, on a bed of fragrant wild flowers, fanned by the pure air from the mountain tops. The flowers which grow under the shade of the trees are beautiful and gay in their colours. Everywhere there are blue lupines, marigolds, dahlias, and innumerable blossoms with Indian names. Sometimes we dismounted and walked up the steepest parts, to rest our horses and ourselves. But, as it was impossible to go fast on these stony paths, it became entirely dark before Angangueo was in sight; and the road, which for a great part of the way is remarkably good, now led us down a perpendicular descent amongst the trees, covered with rocks and stones, so that the horses stumbled, and one, which afterwards proved to be blind of one eye and not to see very clearly with the other, fell and threw his rider, who was not hurt.

It was near eight o'clock (and we had been on horseback since six in the morning) when, after crossing a shallow stream, we saw the fires of the furnaces of Angangueo, a mining village, at the foot of some wild hills. We rode past the huts, where the blazing fires were shining on the swarthy faces of the workmen, the road skirting the valley, till we reached the house of Don Carlos Heimbürger, a Polish gentleman at the head of the German mining establishment. This house, the only one of any consequence at Angangueo, is extremely pretty, with a piazza in front—looking down upon the valley, which at night seems like the dwelling of the Cyclops—and within, a very picture of comfort. We were welcomed by the master of the house, and by Madame Backhausen, a pretty and accomplished German lady, the wife of a physician who resides there. We had already known her in Mexico, and were glad to renew our acquaintance in this outlandish spot. One must have travelled fourteen leagues, from morning till night, to know how comfortable her little drawing room appeared—with its well-cushioned red sofas, bright lights, and vases of flowers—as we came in from the cold and darkness; and how pretty and *extra*-civilized she looked in her black satin gown—not to mention the excellent dinner and the large fires, for they have chimneys in this part of the world. In a nice little bedroom, with a cheerful fire, the second time I have seen one in two years, I indite these particulars, and shall continue from our next place of rest.[15]

49

Through Morelia and Pátzcuaro to Uruapan

Thursday: November 25th, 1841
Morelia

As the house was so agreeable, and our next day's journey short, we could not prevail upon ourselves to leave the *Trojes* before nine o'clock; and even then, with the hopes of spending some time there on our return to see the mining establishment: the mills for grinding ore, the horizontal water wheels, &c., &c.—and, still more, the beautiful scenery in the neighbourhood.

That you may understand our line of march, take a map of Mexico and you will see that Michoacán, one of the most beautiful and fertile territories in the world, is bounded on the north by the river Lerma, afterwards known by the name of Río Grande, also by the department of Guanajuato; to the east and northeast it bounds that of Mexico; and to the west, that of Guadalajara. It lies on the western slope of the Great Cordillera of Anáhuac. Hills, woods, and beautiful valleys diversify its surface; its pasture grounds are watered by numerous streams—that rare advantage under the torrid zone—and the climate is cool and healthy. The Indians of this department are the Tarascos, the Otomí, and the Chichimeca Indians; the first are the most civilized of the tribes, and their language the most harmonious. We are now travelling in a northwesterly direction, towards the capital of the state, Valladolid

—or Morelia, as it has been called since the independence, in honour of the curate Morelos, its great supporter.

We had a pleasant ride of nine leagues through an open pasture country, meeting with nothing very remarkable on our journey but an Indian woman seated on the ground, her Indian husband standing beside her. Both had probably been refreshing themselves with pulque —perhaps even with its homeopathic extract, mezcal.[1] But the Indian was sober and sad, and stood with his arms folded and the most patient and pitying face, while his wife, quite overcome with the strength of the potation and unable to go any further, looked up at him with the most imploring air, saying repeatedly, *"mátame, Miguel, mátame* (kill me, Miguel, kill me)"—apparently considering herself quite unfit to live.

About five o'clock we came in sight of the pretty village and old church of Taximaroa;[2] and, riding up to the *mesón* or inn, found two empty dark rooms with mud floors—without windows, in fact without anything but their four walls—neither bench, chair, nor table. Although we travel with our own beds,[3] this looked rather uninviting—especially after the pleasant quarters we had just left—and we turned our eyes wistfully towards a pretty small house upon a hill, with a painted portico, thinking how agreeably situated we should be there! Colonel Iniestra thereupon rode up the hill and, presenting himself to the owner of this house, described our forlorn prospects—and he kindly consented to permit us all to sup there and, moreover, to receive the ladies for the night. For the gentlemen he had no room, having but one spare apartment, as one of his family was a great invalid and could not be moved. Accordingly, our travelling luggage was carried up the hill, the horses and mules and servants were quartered in the village, the gentlemen found lodging for themselves in a bachelor's house, and we found ourselves in very agreeable quarters—on a pretty piazza with an extensive view, and one large room containing a table and some benches at our service.

Meanwhile, M. de Breteuil rushed through the village, finding eggs and hens and tortillas; and then, returning, he and Mr. Ward produced the travelling stores of beef and tongue, and set about making mustard and drawing bottles of wine—to the great wonderment and edification of the honest proprietor. Even a clean tablecloth was produced, a piece of furniture which he had probably never seen before, and now eyed wistfully, doubtless taking it for a *sheet*. We had a most amusing supper, some performing dexterously with penknives and others using tortillas as forks. We won the heart of the *bourgeois* by sending a cup of tea to his invalid, and inviting him to partake of another, which he seemed to consider a rare and medicinal beverage. About nine o'clock the gentlemen departed to their lodgings, and our beds were erected in the large room where we had supped—the man assuring us that he was quite pleased to have us under his roof and liked our company extremely well, adding, "*Me cuadra mucho la gente decente*—I am very fond of decent people."

We left Taximaroa at six o'clock, having spent rather a disturbed night in consequence of the hollow coughs with which the whole family seemed afflicted, at least the poor invalid on one side of our room and the master of the house on the other. The morning was so cold that every *manga* and sarape was put in requisition.

Our ride this day was through superb scenery, every variety of hill and valley, water and wood, particularly the most beautiful woods of lofty oaks, the whole with scarcely a trace of cultivation and for the most part entirely uninhabited. Our numbers were augmented by Colonel Iniestra's troop, who rode out from Morelia to meet him. We had a long journey, passed by the little village of San Andrés, and stopped to eat tortillas in a very dirty hut at Pueblo Viejo,[4] surrounded by the dirtiest little Indian children. Throughout the whole ride the trees and flowering shrubs were beautiful, and the scenery so varied that, although we rode for eleven hours in a hot sun, we scarcely felt fatigued—for wherever there are trees and water and fresh green grass, the eye is rested. In this and in our last few days' journey, we saw a number of blue birds, called by the common people *guarda-bosques*, wood guardians.

About half past five we entered a winding road, through a natural shrubbery, leading to Queréndaro, the fine hacienda of Señor Pimentel, a senator. When we arrived the family were at dinner, and we were invited to join them; after which we went out to see the hacienda, and especially the handsome and well-kept stables where the proprietor has a famous breed of horses, some of which were trotted out for our inspection—beautiful, spirited creatures—one called *Hilo de Oro*, Golden Thread, another, *Pico Blanco*, White Mouth, &c. In the inner courtyard are many beautiful and rare flowers, and everything is kept in great order.[5]

At nine o'clock the following morning we left Queréndaro, and rode on to San Bartolo, a vast and beautiful property belonging to Señor Don Joaquín Gómez of [Morelia]. The family were from home, with the exception of [the owner's] son and nephew, who did the honours of the house with such cordial and genuine hospitality that we felt perfectly at home before the day was over.

I think the Mexican character is never seen to such advantage as in the country, amongst these great landed proprietors of old family, who live on their own estates, engaged in agricultural pursuits and entirely removed from all the party feeling and petty interests of a city life. It is true that the life of a country gentleman here is that of a hermit, in the total absence of all society in the nearly unbroken solitude that surrounds him. For leagues and leagues there is no habitation but his own. The nearest miserable village may be distant half a day's journey, over an almost impassable road. He is "monarch of all he surveys," a king amongst his farm servants and Indian workmen.[6] Nothing can

exceed the independence of his position, but to enjoy this wild country life he must be born to it. He must be a first-rate horseman, and addicted to all kinds of country sport; and if he can spend the day in riding over his estate, in directing his workmen, watching over his improvements, redressing disputes and grievances, and can sit down in the evening in his large and lonely halls, and philosophically bury himself in the pages of some favourite author, then his time will probably not hang heavy on his hands.

As for the *young master* here, he was up with the lark—he was on the most untractable horse in the hacienda, and away across the fields with his followers, chasing the bulls as he went—he was fishing—he was shooting—he was making bullets—he was leagues off at a village, seeing a country bullfight—he was always in a good humour, and so were all who surrounded him—he was engaged in the dangerous amusement of *colear*—and by the evening it would have been a clever writer who had kept *his* eyes open after such a day's work. Never was there a young lad more evidently fitted for a free life in the country.

There was a generous, frank liberality apparent in everything in this hacienda, that it was agreeable to witness; nothing petty or calculating.[7] Señor _____, lame through an accident, and therefore unable to mount his horse, or to go far on foot, seemed singularly gentle and kind-hearted. The house is one of the prettiest and most cheerful we have seen yet; but we passed a great stone building on the road, which the proprietor of San Bartolo is having constructed for one of his family, which, if it keeps its promise, will be a palace when finished.

The principal produce of this hacienda is *pimiento*, the capsicum. There is the *pimiento dulce* and the *pimiento picante*, the sweet fruit of the common capsicum, and the fruit of the bird pepper capsicum. The Spaniards gave to all these peppers the name of *chile*, which they borrowed from the Indian word *quauhchilli*, and which, to the native Mexicans, is as necessary an ingredient of food as salt is to us. At dinner we had the greatest variety of fine fruit, and pulque, which is particularly good in this neighbourhood. They also make here a quantity of excellent cheese.

After dinner they proceeded to amuse us with the *colear* of the bulls, of which amusement the Mexicans throughout the whole republic are passionately fond. They collect a herd, single out several, gallop after them on horseback; and he who is most skillful catches the bull by the tail, passes it under his own right leg, [and] turns it round the high pummel of his saddle—and, wheeling his horse round at right angles by a sudden movement, the bull falls on his face. Even boys of ten years old joined in this sport. It is no wonder that the Mexicans are such *centaurs*, seeming to form part and parcel of their horses, accustomed as they are from childhood to these dangerous pastimes. This is very dangerous, since the horse's legs constantly get entangled with those of the falling bull, which throws both horse and rider. Manifold are the accidents which result from it, but they are certainly not received as warnings. And after all, such sports, which are mere games of skill [or] trials of address—and where there is nothing bloody nor even cruel, saving the thump which the bull gets and the mortification which he no doubt feels, but from both of which he soon recovers—are manly and strengthening, and help to keep up the physical superiority of that fine race of men, the Mexican rancheros.

The next day we parted from our travelling companions, the Count de Breteuil and Mr. Ward, who are on their way to the fair of San Juan [de los Lagos], and are from thence going to Tepic, even to the shores of the Pacific Ocean. Unfortunately our time is limited, and we cannot venture on so distant an expedition, but we greatly regretted separating from such pleasant *compagnons de voyage*. We spent the morning in walking about the hacienda, seeing cheese made, and visiting the handsome chapel, the splendid stone granaries, the great mills, &c. We also hope to spend some time here on our return.

By letters received this morning from Mexico, we find that Señor Gómez Pedraza has left the ministry. As we had but six leagues to ride in order to reach Morelia, we did not leave San Bartolo till four in the afternoon, and enjoyed a pretty ride through a fertile and well-wooded country, the road good and the evening delightful. As the sun set, millions and tens of millions of ducks, in regular ranks and regiments, darkening the air, flew over our heads, changing their quarters from one lake to another.[8] Morelia is celebrated for the purity of its atmosphere and the exceeding beauty of its sky, and this evening upheld its reputation. Toward sunset the whole western horizon was covered with myriads of little lilac and gold clouds, floating in every fantastic form over the bright blue of the heavens. The lilac deepened into purple, blushed into rose colour, brightened into crimson. The blue of the sky assumed that green tint peculiar to an Italian sunset. The sun himself appeared a globe of living flame. Gradually he sank in a blaze of gold and crimson, while the horizon remained lighted as by the flame from a volcano. Then his brilliant retinue of clouds, after blazing for a while in borrowed splendour, melted gradually into every rainbow hue and tinge—from deep crimson to rose colour and pink and pale violet and faint blue, floating in silvery vapour until they all blended into one soft gray tinge which swept over the whole western sky. But then the full moon rose in cloudless serenity, and at length we heard faintly, then more distinctly, and then in all its deep and sonorous harmony, the tolling of the cathedral bell, which announced our vicinity to a great city.

It has a singular effect, after travelling for some days through a wild country, seeing nothing but a solitary hacienda or an Indian hut, to enter a fine city like Morelia, which seems to have started up as by magic in the midst of the wilderness, yet bearing all the traces of a venerable old age. By moonlight it looked like a panorama of Mexico, with a fine square, *portales*, cathedral, broad streets, and good houses. We rode through the city to the house of Colonel Iniestra, where we now are; but, as we intend to continue our journey to its furthest limits without stopping, we are now, after a night's rest, preparing to resume our ride. They are saddling the horses, strapping on the sarapes

behind the saddles, taking down and packing up our *lits de voyage,* and loading the mules—all which is a work of time. On our return we hope to remain here a few days, to see everything that is worthy of notice.

[Saturday: November 27th, 1841]
Pátzcuaro

Accompanied by several gentlemen of Morelia, who came early in the morning to see Calderón, we set off for the warm baths of Cointzio; and, as we rode along, the hill of Las Bateas was pointed out to us, where, by order of the curate Morelos, two hundred Spaniards were murdered in cold blood to revenge the death of his friend, the curate Matamoros, who was taken prisoner and shot by orders of Iturbide. Horrible cruelty in a Christian priest![9]

It is singular that the great leaders of the independence should have been ecclesiastics: the curate Hidalgo, its prime mover; the curates Morelos and Matamoros, the principal chiefs. Hidalgo, it is said, had no plan, published no manifesto, declared no opinions—but rushed from city to city at the head of his men, displaying on his colours an image of the Virgin of Guadalupe, and inciting his troops to massacre the Spaniards. Morelos was an Indian, uneducated but brave and enterprising, and considered the mildest and most merciful of these soldier priests![10]

Matamoros, equally brave, was better informed. Both were good generals, and both misused the power which their position gave them over the minds of the unenlightened populace.

When Morelos became generalissimo of the revolutionary forces, he

Below, Hidalgo; *at right,* Morelos.

took a step fatal to his interests, and which led to his ultimate ruin. He formed a congress, which met at Chilpancingo, and was composed of lawyers and clergymen: ignorant and ambitious men, who employed themselves in publishing absurd decrees and impossible laws, in assigning salaries to themselves, and giving each other the title of *Excellency.* Disputes and divisions arose amongst them; and, in 1814, they published an absurd and useless document in the village of Apatzingán, to which they gave the name of the "Mexican Constitution."[11] The following year Morelos was defeated in an engagement which took place in the environs of Tezmalaca, taken prisoner, led to Mexico, and, after a short trial, degraded from his ecclesiastical functions and shot in the village of San Cristóbal Ecatepec, seven leagues from the capital. The revolutionary party considered him as a martyr in the cause of liberty, and he is said to have died like a true hero. The appellation of Morelia, given to the city of Valladolid, keeps his name in remembrance—but her blood-stained mountain is a more lasting record of his cruelty.[12]

A vile action is recorded of a Spaniard, whose name, which deserves to be branded with infamy, escapes me at this moment. The soldiers of Morelos having come in search of him, he, standing at his door, pointed out his brother, who was in a room inside the house, as the person whom they sought—and escaped himself, leaving his brother to be massacred in his place. We contrasted the conduct of this miserable wretch with the noble action of the Prince de Polignac, under similar circumstances.[13]

At half past ten, after a pleasant ride of about five leagues, we arrived at the natural hot springs of Cointzio. The place is quite wild, the scenery very striking. The building consists of two very large baths, two very damp rooms, and a kitchen. The baths are kept by a very infirm old man, a martyr to intermittent fever, and two remarkably handsome girls, his daughters, who live here completely alone and—

except in summer, when the baths are resorted to by a number of *canónigos* and occasional gentlemen from Morelia—"waste their sweetness on the desert air."[14] The house, such as it is, lies at the foot of rocky hills, covered with shrubs, and pouring down streams of hot water from their volcanic bosoms. All the streams that cross your path are warm. You step by chance into a little streamlet, and find the water of a most agreeable temperature. They put this water in earthen jars to cool, in order to render it fit for drinking, but it never becomes fresh and cold. It contains muriatic acid, without any trace of sulphur or metallic salt. I think it is Humboldt who supposes that in this part of Mexico there exists, at a great depth in the interior of the earth, a fissure running from east to west for 137 leagues, through which, bursting the external crust of the porphyritic rocks, the volcanic fire has opened itself a passage at different times, from the coasts of the Mexican Gulf as far as the South Sea. The famous volcano of Jorullo is in this department, and boiling fountains are common in various parts of it.

We stopped here to take a bath, and found the temperature of the water delicious, about the ordinary temperature of the human body. The baths are rather dark, being enclosed in great stone walls, with the light coming from a very small aperture near the roof. A bird, that looked like a wild duck, was sailing about in the largest one, having made its entry along with the water when it was let in. I never bathed in any water which I so much regretted leaving.[15]

After bathing we waited for the arrival of our mules, which were to follow us at a gentle pace, that we might have breakfast, and continue our journey to Pátzcuaro, a city nine leagues further. But several hours passed away, and no mules appeared; and at length we came to the grievous conviction that the *arrieros* had mistaken the road, and that we must expect neither food nor beds that night—for it was now too late to think of reaching Pátzcuaro.

In this extremity, the gentlemen from Morelia—suffering from their politeness in having escorted us—[and] the two damsels of the bath (naiads of the boiling spring), pitying our hungry condition, came to offer their services. One [damsel] asked me if I should like "to eat a *burro* in the meantime?" A *burro* being an *ass*, I was rather startled at the proposition, and assured her that I should infinitely prefer waiting a little longer before resorting to so desperate a measure. "Some people call them *pecadoras* (female sinners)!" said her sister. Upon this, the gentlemen came to our assistance, and burros or *pecadoras* were ordered forthwith. They proved to be hot tortillas with cheese in them, and we found them particularly good.

It grew late, but no mules arrived; and at length the young ladies and their father rushed out desperately, caught an old hen that was wandering amongst the hills, killed, skinned, and put it into a pot to boil—baked some fresh tortillas—and brought us the spoil in triumph! One penknife was produced, the boiling pan placed on a deal table in the room off the bath, and—everyone surrounding the fowl, a tough old creature who must have clucked through many revolutions—we ate by turns, and concluded with a comfortable drink of lukewarm water.

We then tried to beguile the time by climbing amongst the hills at the back of the house—by pushing our way through the tangled briers—by walking to a little lake, where there were ducks and waterfowl and, close to the margin, a number of fruit trees. We returned to the baths—the mules had not been heard of—there was no resource but patience. Our Morelian friends left us, to return home before it should grow dusk; and, shortly after, an escort of twenty-three lancers, with a captain, arrived by orders of the governor, Don Pánfilo Galindo, to accompany us during the remainder of our journey. They looked very picturesque, with their lances and little scarlet flags, and gave a very formidable aspect to the little portico in front of the baths, where they deposited all their military accoutrements—their saddles, guns, sarapes, &c. The captain had with him his wife and daughter, and a baby of about two years old, which, during all the time they were with us, was constantly carried by one of the soldiers, with the utmost care, in front of his horse.

Meanwhile, the moon rose and we walked about disconsolate in front of the baths—fearing greatly that some accident might have overtaken our unescorted mules and servants—that the first might be robbed —and that the drivers might be killed. But it was as well to try to sleep, if it were only to get over the interminable night; and at length some clean straw was procured, and spread in a corner of the damp floor. There Kate and I lay down in our *mangas*. Calderón procured another corner—Colonel Iniestra a third—and then and thus we addressed ourselves seriously to repose, but in vain. Between cold and mosquitoes and other animals, we could not close our eyes, and were thankful to rise betimes, shake the straw off, and resume our march.

The road was pretty and flowery when the light came in, and we gradually began to open our eyes—after taking leave of our fair hostesses and their father. When I say *the road*, you do not, I trust, imagine us riding along a dusty highway. I am happy to say that we are generally the discoverers of our own pathways. Every man his own Columbus. Sometimes we take short cuts, which prove to be long rounds;

> Over hill, over dale,
> Thorough bush, thorough brier;[16]

through valley and over stream; and this kind of journey has something in it so independent and amusing that, with all its fatigues and inconveniences, we find it delightful—far preferable even to travelling in the most commodious London-built carriage, bowling along the Queen's highway with four swift posters at the rate of twelve miles an hour.

Arrived at some huts, we stopped to make inquiries concerning the mules. Two loaded mules, the peasants said, had been robbed in the night, and the men tied to a tree, on the low road leading to Pátzcuaro. We rode on uneasy enough, and at another hut were told that many robbers had been out in the night, and that amongst others a woman had been robbed, and bound hand and foot. The road now became bleak and uninteresting, the sun furiously hot, and we rode forward with various misgivings as to the fate of the party—when, at a cluster of huts called El Correo, we came up with the whole concern. The *arrieros* had forgotten the name of Cointzio and, not knowing where to go, had stopped here the previous night, knowing that we were bound for Pátzcuaro, and must pass that way. They had arrived early, and missed the robbers.

We stopped to breakfast at some huts called La Puerta de Chapultepec, where we got some tortillas from a half-caste Indian, who was in great distress because his wife had run off from him for the fourth time with "another gentleman!" He vowed that though he had taken her back three times, he never would receive her more; yet I venture to say that, when the false fair one presents herself, she will find him placable, he is evidently in such distress at having no woman to take care of his house.

After leaving Chapultepec the scenery improves, and at length we had a beautiful view of the hills at the foot of which—close by the opposite shore of the Lake of Pátzcuaro—lies the ancient city of Tzintzuntzan, formerly capital of the independent kingdom of Michoacán, an important city, and called, in the time of Cortés, Huitzitzila. It was formerly the residence of the monarch, King Caltzontzi—an ally of Cortés—who, with his Indian subjects, assisted [Cortés] in his Mexican war.[17] It is now a poor Indian village, though it is said that some remains of the monarch's palace still exist. Apropos to which, we have several times observed, since we entered this state, large stones lying in fields, or employed in fences, with strange hieroglyphic characters engraved on them, some of which may be curious and interesting.

The view as we approach Pátzcuaro, with its beautiful lake, studded with little islands, is very fine. The bells were tolling and they were letting off rockets for some Indian festival, and we met parties of the natives who had been keeping the festival upon pulque or *mezcal* (a strong spirit) and were stumbling along in great glee. We came up to an old church that looks like a bird's, nest amongst the trees, and stands at the outskirts of the city. Here, it is said, his majesty of Michoacán came out to meet his Spanish ally, when he entered this territory.[18]

Pátzcuaro is a pretty little city with sloping roofs, situated on the shores of the lake of the same name—and in front of the little Indian village of Janitzio, built on a beautiful small island in the midst of the lake. Calderón says that Pátzcuaro resembles a town in Catalonia. It is entirely unlike any other Mexican city. We made a great sensation as we entered with our lancers and mules, tired and dust-becovered as we were, and brought all the *Patzcuaranians* to their balconies. We passed churches bearing the date of 1580![19]

We went to the largest and best house in the town, that of Don Miguel Acha, a friend of Colonel Iniestra's.[20] He was from home, but we were most hospitably entertained by his wife, who received us without any unnecessary ceremony or compliments, and made us quite at home. We walked out with her by moonlight to see the square and the *portales*, which is a promenade in the evening, and were followed by crowds of little boys, strangers being rather an uncommon spectacle here.[21] The only foreign lady, Doña Pepita says, who ever was here in her recollection was a Frenchwoman, to whom she was very much attached—the daughter of a physician, and whose husband was murdered by the robbers.

This morning the weather being cold and rainy, and our quarters too agreeable to leave in any violent haste, we agreed to remain until tomorrow and have spent a pleasant day in this fine large house, with Doña Pepita and her numerous and handsome children. We have not been able to visit the lake, or the Indian islands, on account of the weather, but we hope to do so on our return from Uruapan, our next destination. Our hostess is a most agreeable person—lively, kindhearted, and full of natural talent. We did not expect to meet such a person in this corner of the world.

The first bishop of Michoacán, Vasco de Quiroga—who died in Uruapan—was buried in Pátzcuaro, and the Indians of this state still venerate his memory. He was the father and benefactor of these Tarascan Indians, and went far to rescue them from their degraded state. He not only preached morality, but encouraged industry amongst them by assigning to each village its particular branch of commerce. Thus one was celebrated for its manufacture of saddles, another for its shoes, a third for its *bateas* (painted trays), and so on. Every useful institution of which some traces still remain amongst them is due to this excellent prelate—an example of what one good and zealous and well-judging man can effect.[22]

We have been taking another stroll by moonlight,[23] the rain having ceased; we have lingered over a pleasant supper, and have wished Doña Pepita good night. Yet let me not forget, before laying down my pen, to celebrate the excellence of the whitefish from the lake!—so greatly surpassing in excellence and flavour those which we occasionally have in Mexico. These no doubt must have constituted "the provisions" which, according to tradition, were carried by regular running posts from Tzintzuntzan to Montezuma's palace in Mexico, and with such expedition that, though the distance is about one hundred leagues, they were placed, still smoking, on the Emperor's table!

Tuesday: November 30th, 1841
Uruapan

We went to mass at six o'clock, and then took leave of the Señora Acha, who gave us a cordial invitation to spend some days with her on our return. It was about eight o'clock when we left Pátzcuaro and mounted the hills over which our road lay—and stopped to look down on the beautiful lake, lying like a sheet of silver in the sun, and dotted with green islands.

Two disagreeable personages were added to our party. Early in the morning intelligence was brought that a celebrated robber named Morales, captain of a large band, had been seized along with one of his companions—and permission was requested to take advantage of our large escort in order that they may be safely conducted to Uruapan, where they are to be shot, being already condemned to death. The punishment of hanging is not in use in Mexico.

The first thing therefore that we saw, on mounting our horses, was the two robbers, chained together by the leg, guarded by five of our lancers, and prepared to accompany us on foot. The companion of Morales was a young, vulgar-looking ruffian, his face livid, and himself nearly naked; but the robber captain himself was equal to any of Salvator's brigands, in his wild and striking figure and countenance. He wore a dark-coloured blanket, and a black hat—the broad leaf of which was slouched over his face, which was the colour of death— while his eyes seemed to belong to a tiger or other beast of prey. I never saw such a picture of fierce misery. Strange to say, this man began life as a shepherd; but how he was induced to abandon this pastoral occupation, we did not hear. For years he has been the scourge of the country, robbing to an unheard of extent (so that whatever he may have done with them, tens of thousands of dollars have passed through his hands), carrying off the farmers' daughters to the mountains, and at the head of eighty ruffians committing the most horrible disorders. His last crime was murdering his wife in the mountains, the night before last, under circumstances of barbarity too shocking to relate— and, it is supposed, assisted by the wretch now with him. After committing the crime, they ran to hide themselves in an Indian village, as the Indians, probably from fear, never betray the robbers. However, their horror of this man was so great that perfect *hate* cast out their fear, and collecting together they seized the ruffians, bound them, and carried them to Pátzcuaro, where they were instantly tried and con- demned to be shot—the sentence to be executed at Uruapan.

The sight of these miserable wretches, and the idea of what their feelings must be, occupied us as they toiled along, each step bringing them nearer to their place of execution. And we could not help thinking what wild wishes must have sometimes throbbed within them, of break- ing their bonds, and dashing away from their guards—away through the dark woods, over mountain and river, down that almost perpendicular precipice, over the ravine, up that green and smiling hill, and into these gloomy pine woods, in whose untrod recesses they would be secure from pursuit. And then their despair when they felt the heavy clanking chain on their bare feet, and looked at the lances and guns that surrounded them, and knew that—even if they attempted to fly, could they be insane enough to try it—a dozen bullets would stop their career forever. Then horror and disgust at the recollection of their savage crimes took the place of pity, and not even _____'s sugges- tion that the robber chief might have killed his wife in a transport of jealousy could lessen our indignation at this last most barbarous murder of a defenseless woman.

But these thoughts took away half the pleasure of this most beautiful journey, through wild woods, where for leagues and leagues we meet nothing but the fatal *cross;* while through these woods of larches, cedars, oaks, and pines are bright vistas of distant pasture fields, and of lofty mountains covered with forests. Impossible to conceive a greater variety of beautiful scenery—a greater *waste* of beauty, if one may say so—for not even an Indian hut was to be seen, nor did we meet a single passing human being, nor a trace of cultivation.

As we came out of the woods we heard a gun fired amongst the hills, the first token of human life that had greeted us since we left Pátzcuaro. This, Señor _____ told us, was the signal gun usually fired by the Indians on the approach of an armed troop, warning their brethren to hide themselves. Here the Indians rarely speak Spanish, as those do who live in the neighbourhood of cities. Their language is chiefly the harmonious Tarascan.

Towards the afternoon we came to a path which led us into a valley of the most surpassing beauty, entirely carpeted with the loveliest blue, white, pink, and scarlet wild flowers, and clothed with natural orchards of peach and apricot trees in full bloom, the grass strewed with their rich blossoms. Below ran a sparkling rivulet, its bright gushing waters leaping over the stones and pebbles that shone in the sun like silver. Near this are some huts called Las Palomas, and it was so charming a spot that we got off our horses and halted for half an hour; and while they prepared breakfast for us, a basket of provisions from Pátzcuaro having been brought on by the provident care of Doña Pepita, we clambered out amongst the rocks and luxuriant trees that dipped their leafy branches in the stream, and pulled wild flowers that would grace any European garden.

Having breakfasted in one of the huts, upon fowl and tortillas, on which memorable occasion two penknives were produced (and I still wonder why we did not bring some knives and forks with us, unless it be that we should never have had them cleaned), we continued our journey: and this mention of knives leads me to remark that all common servants in Mexico, and all common people, eat with their fingers! Those who are rather particular roll up two tortillas and use them as knife and fork, which, I can assure you from experience, is a great deal better than nothing, when you have learnt how to use them.

Our road after this, though even wilder and more picturesque, was very fatiguing to the horses: up and down steep rocks, among forests of oak and pine—through which we slowly wended our way—so that it was dark when we descended a precipitous path leading to a small Indian village, or rather encampment, called Curu.[24] It was now too late to think of reaching Uruapan, or of venturing to climb by night the series of precipices called the Cuesta de Curu, over which we should have had to pass. But such a place as Curu for Christians to pass the night in! A few miserable huts filled with Indians, and not, so far as we could discern, even an empty shed where we might rest under cover. However, there was no remedy. The *arriero* had already unloaded his mules, and was endeavouring to find some provender for them and the poor horses. It was quite dark, but there was a delicious fragrance of orange blossoms, and we groped our way up to the trees, and pulled some branches by way of consolation.

At length an old wooden barn was discovered, and there the beds of the whole party were put up! We even contrived to get some boiling water, and to have some tea made—an article of luxury which, as well as a teapot, we carry with us. We sat down upon our trunks, and a piece of candle was procured and lighted and, after some difficulty, made to stand upright on the floor. The barn, made of logs, let the air in on all sides, and the pigs thrust their snouts in at every crevice, grunting harmoniously. Outside, in the midst of the encampment, the soldiers lighted a large fire, and sat round it roasting maize. The robbers sat amongst them, chained, with a soldier mounting guard beside them. The fire, flashing on the livid face of Morales, who, crouched in his blanket, looked like a tiger about to spring—the soldiers, some warming their hands at the blaze, some lying rolled in their sarapes, and others devouring their primitive supper—together with the Indian women bringing them hot tortillas from the huts—the whole had a curious and picturesque effect. As for us, we also rolled ourselves in our *mangas*, and lay down in our barn, but passed a miserable night. The pigs grunted, the mosquitoes sung, a cold air blew in from every corner; and, fortunately, we were not until morning aware of the horrid fact that a whole nest of scorpions, with their tails twisted together, were reposing above our heads in the log wall. Imagine the condition of the unfortunate slumberer on whose devoted head they had descended *en masse!* In spite of the fragrant orange blossom, we were glad to set off early the next morning.

[Monday: November 29th, 1841]
Uruapan

On leaving the fascinating village of Curu we began to ascend La Cuesta, and travelled slowly four leagues of mountain road, apparently inaccessible—but the sure-footed horses, though stepping on loose and nearly precipitous rocks, rarely stumbled. The mountain of Curu is volcanic, a chaos of rent rocks, beetling precipices, and masses of lava that have been disgorged from the burning crater. Yet from every crag and crevice of the rock spring the most magnificent trees twisted with flowering parasites, shrubs of the brightest green, and pale delicate flowers whose gentle hues seem all out of place in this savage scene. Beside the forest oak and the stern pine, the tree of the white blossoms— the graceful *floripundio*—seems to seek for shelter and support. Creepers that look like scarlet honeysuckles, and flowering vines of every variety of colour, hang in bright garlands and festoons, entwining the boughs of the trees—adorning, but not concealing, the masses of bare rock and the precipitous crag that frowns amidst all this luxury of vegetation. The whole scene is "horribly beautiful."[25]

As we wound through these precipitous paths, where only one can go at a time, our train stretched out to an immense distance, and the scarlet streamers and lances of the soldiers looked very picturesque, appearing and then vanishing amongst the rocks and trees. At one part, looking back to see the effect, I caught the eye of the robber Morales, glaring with such a frightful expression that, forgetful of his chains, I whipped up my horse, in the greatest consternation, over stones and rocks. He and the scene were in perfect unison.

At length we came to the end of this extraordinary mountain forest and, after resting the tired horses for a little while in a grove of pines and yellow acacias, entered the most lovely little wood, a succession of flowers and shrubs and bright green grass, with vistas of fertile cornfields bordered by fruit trees—a peaceful scene, on which the eye rests with pleasure, after passing through these wild, volcanic regions.

On leaving the woods, the path skirts along by the side of these fields, and leads to the valley where Uruapan, the gem of Indian villages, lies in tranquil beauty. It has indeed some tolerable streets and a few good houses, but her boast is in the Indian cottages—all so clean and snug, and tasteful, and buried in fruit trees.[26]

We rode through shady lanes of trees, bending under the weight of oranges, *chirimoyas, granaditas, plátanos,* and every sort of delicious fruit. We found that through the kindness of Señor Izazaga, the principal person here, the curate's house had been prepared to receive us—an old unfurnished house next the church, and at present unoccupied, its owner being absent. We found the whole family extremely kind and agreeable: the father a well-informed, pleasant old gentleman; the mother still beautiful, though in bad health; and all the daughters pretty and unaffected. One is married to a brother of Madame Iturbide's.[27] They made many apologies for not inviting us to their own house, which is under repair; but as it is but a few steps off we shall spend most of our time with them. It seems strange to meet such people in this secluded spot! Yet, peaceful and solitary as it appears, it has not escaped the rage of civil war, having been burnt down four different times by insurgents and by Spaniards. Señor Izazaga, who belongs to [Morelia], has taken an active part in all the revolutions, having been the personal friend and partisan of Hidalgo. His escapes and adventures would fill a volume.[28]

I could not help taking one last look of the robbers, as we entered this beautiful place, where Morales at least is to be shot. It seemed to me that they had grown perfectly deathlike. The poor wretches must be tired enough, having come on foot all the way from Pátzcuaro.

[Tuesday: November 30th, 1841][29]

This place is so charming we have determined to pitch our tent in it for a few days. Our intention was to proceed twenty leagues further, to see the volcano of Jorullo. But, as the road is described to us as being entirely devoid of shade and the heat almost insupportable, with various other difficulties and drawbacks, we have been induced, though with great regret, to abandon the undertaking—which it is as tantalizing to do, as it is to reflect that yesterday we were but a short distance from a hill which is but thirty leagues from the Pacific Ocean.

In 1803 M. de Humboldt and M. Bonpland ascended to the crater of this burning mountain, which was formed in September, 1759. Its birth was announced by earthquakes, which put to flight all the inhabitants of the neighbouring villages; and, three months after, a terrible eruption burst forth which filled all the inhabitants with astonishment and terror, and which Humboldt considers one of the most extraordinary physical revolutions that ever took place on the surface of the globe.

Flames issued from the earth for the space of more than a square league. Masses of burning rock were thrown to an immense height, and through a thick cloud of ashes, illuminated by the volcanic fire, the whitened crust of the earth was seen gradually swelling up. The ashes even covered the roofs of the houses at Querétaro, forty-eight leagues distant—and the rivers of San [Pedro] and Cuitumba sank into the burning masses. The flames were seen from Pátzcuaro; and from the hills of Aguazarca was beheld the birth of this volcanic mountain—the burning offspring of an earthquake—which, bursting from the bosom of the earth, changed the whole face of the country for a considerable distance round.

And now, the glee
Of the loud hills shakes with its mountain-mirth,
As if they did rejoice o'er a young earthquake's birth.[30]

Here the earth returned that salutation, and shook, though it was with fearful mirth, at the birth of the young volcano.

In a letter written at the time of this event to the bishop of Michoacán by the curate of the neighbouring village, he says that the eruption finished by destroying the hacienda of Jorullo, and killing the trees, which were thrown and buried in the sand and ashes vomited by the mountain. The fields and roads were, he says, covered with sand, the crops destroyed, and the flocks perishing for want of food, unable to drink the pestilential water of the mountains. The rivulet that ran past his village was swelled to a mighty river, that threatened to inundate it; and he adds that the houses, churches, and hospitals are ready to fall down from the weight of the sand and the ashes—and that "the very people are so covered with the sand, that they seem to have come out of some sepulchre."[31]

The great eruptions of the volcano continued till the following year, but have gradually become rarer, and at present have ceased.[32]

Having now brought our journey to its furthest limits, I shall conclude this letter.

50

Uruapan and Return to Morelia

Wednesday: December 1st, 1841
Uruapan

The dress of the Indian women of Uruapan is pretty, and they are altogether a much cleaner and better looking race than we have yet seen. They wear *enaguas*, petticoats of black cotton with a narrow white and blue stripe, made very full and rather long; over this, a sort of short chemise made of coarse white cotton, and embroidered in different coloured silks. It is called the *sutunacua*. Over all is a black *rebozo*, striped with white and blue, with a handsome silk fringe of the same colours. When they are married, they add a white embroidered veil, and a remarkably pretty coloured mantle, the *huipilli*—which they seem to pronounce *güipil*. The hair is divided, and falls down behind in two long plaits, fastened at the top by a bow of ribbon and a flower. In this dress there is no alteration from what they wore in former days, saving that the women of a higher class wore a dress of finer cotton with more embroidery—and a loose garment over all, resembling a priest's surplice, when the weather was cold. Among the men, the introduction of trousers is Spanish—but they still wear the *maxtlatl*, a broad belt with the ends tied before and behind, and the *tilmatli*, or *tilma* as they now call it, a sort of square short cloak, the ends of which are tied across the breast or over one shoulder. It is on a coarse *tilma* of this description that the image of the Virgin of Guadalupe was found painted.

Yesterday being the festival of San Andrés, the Indians were all in full costume and procession, and we went into the old church to see them. They were carrying the saint in very fine robes, the women bearing coloured flags and lighted tapers, and the men playing on violins, flutes, and drums. All had garlands of flowers to hang on the altars—and for these lights and ornaments, and silk and tinsel robes, they save up all their money. They were playing a pretty air, but I doubt its being original. It was not melancholy and monotonous, like the generality of Indian music, but had something wild and gay in it: it was probably

Spanish. The organ was played by an Indian. After mass we went upstairs to try it, and wondered·how, with such miserable means, he had produced anything like music.

In the patio between the curate's house and the church are some very brilliant large scarlet flowers, which they call here *flor del pastor*— the shepherd's flower, a beautiful kind of euphorbia—and in other places *flor de nochebuena*, flower of Christmas Eve.[1]

Last evening we walked out in the environs of this Garden of Eden, by the banks of the river Marqués, amidst a most extraordinary union of tropical and European vegetation—the hills covered with firs and the plains with sugar cane. We walked amongst bananas, shaddocks, *chirimoyos*, and orange trees; and but a few yards higher up, bending over and almost touching them, were groves of oak and pine. The river pursues its bright unwearied course through this enchanting landscape, now falling in cascades, now winding placidly at the foot of the silent hills and among the dark woods, and in one part forming a most beautiful natural bath—by pouring its waters into an enclosure of large, smooth, flat stones, overshadowed by noble trees.[2]

A number of the old Indian customs are still kept up here, modified by the introduction of Christian doctrines—in their marriages, feasts, burials, and superstitious practices. They also preserve the same simplicity in their dress, united with the same vanity and love of show in their ornaments, which always distinguished them. The poorest Indian woman still wears a necklace of red coral, or a dozen rows of red beads. And their dishes are still the *xicalli*, or, as they were called by the Spaniards, *jicaras*, made of a species of gourd, or rather a fruit resembling it, and growing on a low tree—which fruit they cut in two, each one furnishing two dishes. The inside is scooped out and a durable varnish given it by means of a mineral earth, of different bright colours, generally red. On the outside they paint flowers, and some of them are also gilded. They are extremely pretty, very durable and ingenious. The beautiful colours which they employ in painting these *jicaras* are composed not only of various mineral productions, but of the wood, leaves, and flowers of certain plants, of whose properties they have no despicable knowledge.[3] Their own dresses, manufactured by themselves of cotton, are extremely pretty, and many of them very fine.

We rode out early this morning, and—passing through the lanes bordered with fruit trees, and others covered with blossoms of extraordinary beauty, of whose names I only know the *floripundio*—ascended into the pine woods, fragrant and gay with wild thyme and bright flowers, the river falling in small cascades among the rocks. After riding along these heights for about two leagues, we arrived at the edge of a splendid valley of oaks. Here we were obliged to dismount and to make our way on foot—

] *Top,* Provincial dinner
y. (Courtesy of the Museo
ional de Historia, Cha-
epec.)

] *Above left,* Bells at the
enda of Tepenacaxco.

0] *Above right,* San Miguel
a: "The most picturesque
luvely place imaginable."

1] *At right,* San María Re-
"Down in a steep barranca
a mighty pile of building."

[102] The sugarworks of Atlacomulco.

[103] *Above left,* C
Marqués.
[104] *Above right,*
yard of the hacienda
coyotla.
[105] *At left,* Entr
the cave of Cacahua

106] *Top left,* A window at the
[haci]enda of Temisco.

107] *Top right,* Ruins of the
[dwel]ling at Casasano.

[10]8, 109] *Above and at right,*
[Sa]nta Clara . . . at the foot of
[th]e bold, high rocks, with a re-
[mar]kably handsome church at-
[tach]ed to it."

[110, 111] *Above and at right,* San Nicolás: "One of the finest estates in the republic."

[112] *At left,* "The num[ber] pipes, pointed all alon[g] roofs, have a very threa[tening] and warlike effect . . ."

[113] *Below,* Atlixco[: a] large town, with a high [moun]tain behind it crowned [with a] white chapel."

[114] *Above,* Home of the Calderóns' Puebla friend, Antonio Haro y Tamariz.

[115] *At left,* Puebla's famous Rosary chapel, an example of Mexican exuberance.

SAN ANGEL

16] *Left,* The hacienda of Goicoechea where the Calderóns lived for two months.
17] *Right,* The domes of El Carmen.

[118] Holy Week in the country: "The image of the Saviour . . . carried through on a platform to the sound of music." (Courtesy of the Museo Nacional de Historia, Chapultepec.)

HACIENDA OF SANTA MONICA

[119] Chapel and outbuildings.

[120] The superb entrance to the

[121] *At left*, Patio at La Lechería.

122] *Top,* "All along the lanes are
ll Indian huts, with their usual mud
, small altar, earthern vessels, and
ction of daubs on the walls
ecially of the Virgin of Guada-
) . . .''

123] *Second from top,* "Mules to be
ed; horses to be fitted with sad-
"

124, 125] *Above and at right,* La
ia: The hacienda dwelling and
ch.

[126] *Top,* Angangueo: mining village at the foot some wild hills."

[127] *Center,* A handsome building at the hacienda of Bartolo.

[128] *At left, Colear:* ". . who is most skillful catches bull by the tail . . . and, wh ing his horse around . . . bull falls . . ." (Courtesy of Museo de América, Mad

9] *At right,* "A fine city
. as by magic in the midst
he wilderness." (Courtesy of
Museo Nacional de Historia,
pultepec.)

0] *Below left,* The cathe-
: "That splendid building."

1] *Below right,* "We toiled
hrough winding staircases
he belfry . . ."

2] *Bottom left,* "The Ala-
a, a broad, straight walk
shaded by fine trees—un-
which are stone benches."

3] *Bottom right,* "A fine
duct of solid masonry, with
and elegant arches."

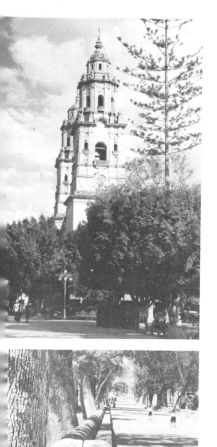

[134] *At left,* The hot springs of Cointzio: "Two ver large baths, two very damp rooms, and a kitchen."

PATZCUARO

[135] *Upper at right,* "A pretty little city with sloping roofs . . . entirely unlike any other Mexican city."
[136] *Lower at right,* "Its beautiful lake, studded with little islands."
[137] *Below,* ". . . We embarked in a long canoe formed of the hollow trunk of a tree . . ."
[138] *Bottom,* "The chief food of these islanders . . . is the whitefish, for which the lake is celebrated . . ."

JANITZIO

?, 140] *Top and center,* "En-
? peopled by Indians who
le little with the dwellers on
mainland."

?] *At right,* Celebrating the
of the Dead.

[142] Falls of the Tzaráracua: ". . . The river comes thundering and boiling . . . jets of water issuing from every crevice."

[143] Tampico, point of final departure: ". . . I could have fancied myself in a New England village . . ."

down the longest, steepest, and most slippery of paths, winding in rapid descent through the woods—with the prospect of being repaid for our toil by the sight of the celebrated falls of the Tzaráracua.

After having descended to the foot of the oak-covered mountain, we came to a great enclosure of lofty rocks—prodigious natural bulwarks— through a great cavern in which the river comes thundering and boiling into the valley, forming the great cascade of the Tzaráracua, which in the Tarascan language means *sieve*. It is a very fatiguing descent, but it is worth while to make the whole journey from Mexico to see anything so wildly grand. The falls are from fifty to sixty feet high, and of great volume. The rocks are covered with shrubs and flowers, with small jets of water issuing from every crevice. One lovely flower, that looks as if it were formed of small white and rose-coloured shells, springs out of the stones near the water. There are rattlesnakes among the woods, and wild boars have occasionally been seen. The Señoritas Izazaga, when children two or three years ago, wandering among these mountain paths, saw an immense rattlesnake coiled up, and, tempted by its gaudy colours, were about to lift it when it suddenly wakened from its slumber, uncoiled itself, and swiftly glided up the path before them—its rattle sounding all the way up amongst the hills.

We sat beside the falls for a long while, looking at the boiling, hissing, bubbling, foaming waters—rolling down headlong with such impetuous velocity that one could hardly believe they form part of the same placid stream which flows so gently between its banks when no obstacles oppose it—and at all the little silvery threads of water that formed mimic cascades among the rocks. But at length we were obliged to recommence our toilsome march up the slippery mountain.[4] We were accompanied by several officers—amongst others, by the commandant of Uruapan.

Señor Izazaga says that they are at present occupied here, at the instigation of a Frenchman named Guénot, in planting a large collection of mulberry trees (which prosper wonderfully well in this climate) for the propagation of silkworms. But they have no facilities for transport, and at what market could the silk be sold? There are a thousand improvements wanting here, which would be more profitable than this speculation.[5] They have sugar, corn, maize, minerals, wood, cotton, water for machinery: every valuable and important produce, all requiring their more immediate attention.

We had a pleasant ride home and, when we got back amongst the lanes leading to the village, stopped every moment to admire and wonder at the rare and beautiful blossoms on the trees; and pulled branches of flowers off them, more delicate and lovely than the rarest exotics in an English hothouse.

Thursday: December 2nd, 1841

This morning the weather was damp and rainy, but in the afternoon we took a long walk, and visited several Indian cottages: all clean, and the walls hung with fresh mats, the floors covered with the same, and all with their kitchen utensils of baked earth neatly hung on the wall, from the largest size in use to little dishes and *jarritos* in miniature, which are only placed there for ornament. We also went to purchase *jícaras*, and to see the operation of making and painting them, which is very curious. The flowers are not painted, but inlaid. We were fortunate in procuring a good supply of the prettiest, which cannot be procured anywhere else. We bought a very pretty *sutunacua*, and a black *rebozo*. The women were not at all anxious to sell their dresses, as they make them with great trouble, and preserve them with great care.

We had a beautiful walk to the Magdalena,[6] about a mile from the village. Every day we discover new beauties in the environs. And one beauty we saw on entering a small rancho—where they were painting *jícaras* at a table while a woman lay in the shaking fever in a bed adjoining, which was quite consistent with the place. This [beauty] was a lady, the proprietress of a good estate some leagues off, who was seated on her own trunk, outside the door of the rancho. She was a beautiful woman in her prime (the gentlemen said *passée*) and perhaps at eighteen she may have been more charming still, but now she was a model for a Judith—or rather for a Joan of Arc—even though sitting on her own luggage. She was very fair, with large black eyes, long eyelashes, and a profusion of hair as black as jet. Her teeth were literally dazzling—her lips like the reddest coral—her colour glowing as the down upon a ripe peach. Her figure was tall and full, with small, beautifully formed hands, and fine arms. She rose as we came in, and begged us to be seated on a bench near the door; and, with the unceremoniousness of travellers who meet in outlandish places, we entered into conversation with her. She told us her name, and her motives for travelling, and gave us an account of an adventure she had had with robbers, of which she was well fitted to be the heroine. It appears that she was travelling with her two sons, lads of fifteen and sixteen, when they arrived at this rancho to rest for the night—for by this time you will understand that those who travel hereabouts must trust to chance or to hospitality for a night's lodging. To their surprise, they found the farmers gone, their dogs gone, and the house locked. They had no alternative but to rest as they could, among their luggage and mules, in the yard in front of the house. In the middle of the night they were attacked by robbers. The boys instantly took their guns, and fired, but without effect. Still, in the darkness, the robbers probably imagined that there were more people and more arms, and when she, dragging a loaded musket off one of the horses, prepared to join in the engagement, the cowardly ruffians took flight—a good half dozen, before a woman and two boys. She was particularly indignant at the farmers, these *malditos rancheros,* as she called them, who she said had been bribed or frightened into withdrawing their dogs and themselves.

We returned home, after a long walk, in the dark and in the midst of all the howling, yelping, snarling, barking dogs—which rushed out as we went by, from every cottage in Uruapan.

After supper they sent for a clever Indian girl who understands Spanish as well as her native idiom, and who translated various Castilian words for us into the original Tarascan, which sounds very liquid and harmonious.[7]

Tomorrow we shall leave Uruapan and this hospitable family, whose kindness and attention to us we never can forget. It seems incredible that we have only known them a few days. We have, however, the hopes of seeing them again as we pass through [Morelia], where they intend removing in a few days.

Saturday: December 4th, 1841
Pátzcuaro

We left Uruapan yesterday morning at eleven o'clock, accompanied part of the way by Señor Izazaga and other gentlemen, amongst whom was Madame Iturbide's brother.

We are now returning to Morelia, but avoided Curu and the rocks, both to save our animals and for the sake of variety. We rode through large tracts of land, all belonging to the Indians. The day was agreeable and cloudy, and the road as usual led us through beautiful scenery, monotonous in description, but full of variety in fact. Though nearly uninhabited, and almost entirely uncultivated, it has pleased nature to lavish so much beauty on this part of the country that there is nothing melancholy in its aspect—no feeling of dreariness in riding a whole day, league after league, without seeing a trace of human life. These forest paths always appear as if they must, in time, lead to some habitation; the woods, the groves, the clumps of trees seem as if they had been disposed, or at least beautified, by the hand of art. We cannot look on these smiling and flowery valleys and believe that such lovely scenes are always untenanted—that there are no children occasionally picking up these apricots—no village girls to pluck these bright, fragrant flowers. We fancy that they are out in the fields, and will be there in the evening, and that their hamlet is hid behind the slope of the next hill; and it is only when we come to some Indian hut, or cluster of poor cabins in the wilderness, that we are startled by the conviction that this enchanting variety of hill and plain, wood and water, is for the most part unseen by human eye, and untrod by human footstep.

We had no further adventure during this day's journey than buying bread and cheese, from sheer hunger, at a little wooden tavern by the roadside, whose shelves were covered with glittering rows of bottles of brandy and *mezcal*.

At some of the Indian huts also we bought various bunches of *plátanos*, that most useful of fruits, and basis of the food of the poor inhabitants of all the tropical climates. It has been said that the banana is not indigenous in America, and that it was brought over by a friar to Santo Domingo. If so, its adopted country agrees with it better than its native land; but I believe there are many traditions which go to prove that it did already exist in this hemisphere before the sixteenth century, and that the Spaniards did no more than increase the number of the already indigenous species. Its nutritive qualities, and the wonderful facility with which it is propagated, render it at once the most useful of trees and the greatest possible incentive to indolence. In less than one year after it is planted the fruit may be gathered, and the proprietor has but to cut away the old stems and leave a sucker, which will produce fruit three months after. There are different sorts of bananas, and they are used in different ways: fresh, dried, fried, &c. The dried plantain, a great branch of trade in Michoacán, with its black shrivelled skin and flavour of smoked fish or ham, is exceedingly liked by the natives. It is, of all Mexican articles of food, my peculiar aversion.

About four o'clock we arrived at the small village of Ziracuaretiro, a collection of Indian cottages with little gardens, surrounded by orange and all manner of fruit trees. As we had still one or two hours of day-light, and this was our next halting place, we wandered forth on foot to explore the environs, and found a beautiful shady spot, a grassy knoll sheltered by the surrounding woods, where we sat down to rest and to inhale the balmy air, fragrant with orange blossom. We were amused by a sly-looking Indian of whom Calderón asked some questions, and who was exceedingly talkative, giving us an account of his whole *ménage*, and especially praising beyond measure his own exemplary conduct to his wife—from which I infer that he beats her, as indeed all Indians consider it their particular privilege to do. (An Indian woman, who complained to a padre of her husband's neglect, mentioned, as the crowning proof of his utter abandonment of her, that he had not given her a beating for a whole fortnight.) Someone asked [the Indian] if he allowed his wife to govern him. "Oh! no," said he, "that would be the mule leading the *arriero!*"

There was nothing to be seen in the village, of which it hardly deserves the name, but a good-looking old church which two old women were sweeping out; but they told us they rarely had mass there, as the padre lived a long way off. The alcalde permitted us and our escort to occupy his house, consisting of three empty rooms with mud floors; and about seven the next morning we were again on horseback and again *en route* for Pátzcuaro, a pretty ride of eleven or twelve leagues. We breakfasted at the village of Ajuno in a clean hut, where they gave us quantities of tortillas and chile, baked by some very handsome *tortilleras*. A number of women were carrying about a Virgin all covered with flowers, to the sound of a little bell.

It was about four o'clock when we arrived at the hills near Pátzcuaro. Here we dismounted from our horses, and remained till it was nearly dusk, lying on the grass and gazing on the lake, as the shadows of evening stole slowly over its silver waters. Little by little the green islands became indistinct; a gray vapour concealed the opposite shores, and like a light breath spread gradually over the mirrored surface of the lake.[8] Then we remounted our horses and rode down into Pátzcuaro, where we found the Señora Acha, as before, ready to receive us; and where, our mules being disabled, we proposed remaining one or two days.

Sunday: December 5th, 1841

We have been spending a quiet day in Pátzcuaro, and went to mass in the old church, which is handsome and rich in gilding.[9] At the door is printed in large letters: "For the love of God, all good Christians are requested not to spit in this holy place."

If we might judge from the observation of one morning, I should say that the better classes in Pátzcuaro are fairer and have more colour than is general in Mexico; and, if this is so, it may be owing partly to the climate's being cooler and damper, and partly to their taking more exercise—there being no carriages here, whereas in Mexico no family of any importance can avoid having one.

We were very anxious to see some specimens of that mosaic work which all ancient writers upon Mexico have celebrated, and which was nowhere brought to such perfection as in Pátzcuaro. It was made with the most beautiful and delicate feathers, chiefly of the *picaflores*, the humming-birds, which they called *huitzitzilin*. But we are told that it is now upwards of twenty years since the last artist in this branch lived in Pátzcuaro; and, though it is imitated by the nuns, the art is no longer in the state of perfection to which it was brought in the days of Cortés.

We are told that several persons were employed in each painting, and that it was a work requiring extraordinary patience and nicety, in the blending of the colours, and in the arrangement of the feathers. The sketch of the figure was first made, and, the proportions being measured, each artist took charge of one particular part of the figure or of the drapery. When each had finished his share, all the different parts were reunited, to form the picture. The feathers were first taken up with some soft substance with the utmost care, and fastened with a glutinous matter upon a piece of stuff. Then the different parts, being reunited, were placed on a plate of copper, and gently polished till the surface became quite equal, when they appeared like the most beautiful paintings or, according to these writers, more beautiful from the splendour and liveliness of the colours—the bright golden, and blue, and crimson tints—than the paintings which they imitated. Many were sent to Spain, and to different museums both in Europe and Mexico, but the art is now nearly lost, nor does it belong to the present utilitarian age. Our forefathers had more leisure than we, and probably we have more than our descendants will have, who, for aught we know, may by extra high-pressure be able to

Put a girdle round about the earth in forty minutes.[10]

We, however, saw some few specimens of saints and angels, very defective in the sketch, but beautiful in the colouring, and quite sufficient to prove to us that there was no exaggeration in these accounts.[11]

Tuesday: December 7th, 1841

We rode yesterday to the shores of the lake, where we embarked in a long canoe formed of the hollow trunk of a tree, and rowed by Indians— a peculiarly ugly race, with Tartar-looking faces. The lake was very placid, clear as one vast mirror, and covered with thousands of wild ducks, white egrets, cranes, and herons—all those waterfowl who seem to whiten their plumage by constant dipping in pools and marshes and lakes. On the opposite shore, to the right, lay the city of Tzintzuntzan; and on a beautiful island in the midst of the lake, the village of Janitzio, entirely peopled by Indians who mingle little with the dwellers on the mainland, and have preserved their originality more than any we have yet seen.[12] We were accompanied by the prefect of Pátzcuaro, whom the Indians fear and hate in equal ratio, and who did seem a sort of Indian *Mr. Bumble;* and after a long and pleasant row we landed at the island, where we were received by the village alcalde, a half-caste Indian who sported a pair of bright blue merino pantaloons!—I suppose to distinguish himself from his blanketed brethren. The island is entirely surrounded by a natural screen of willow and ash trees, and the village consists of a few scattered houses with small cultivated patches of ground, the alcalde's house, and an old church.

We walked, or rather climbed, all over the island, which is hilly and rocky, and found several great stones entirely covered with ancient carving. Moved by curiosity, we entered various caverns where idols have been found, and amongst others one large cave, which we had no sooner groped our way into than I nearly fell down suffocated by the horrible and most pestilential atmosphere. It appears that it is the sleeping place of all the bats in the island—and heaven forbid that I should ever again enter a bat's bedchamber! I groped my way out again as fast as possible, heedless of idols and all other antiquities, seized a *cigarrito* from the hand of the astonished prefect, who was wisely smoking at the entrance, lighted it, and inhaled the smoke, which seemed more fragrant than violets after that stifling and most unearthly odour.[13]

The chief food of these islanders, besides the gourds and other vegetables which they cultivate, is the whitefish, for which the lake is celebrated—and, while we were exploring the island, the Indians set off in their canoes to catch some for us. These were fried at the alcalde's, and we made a breakfast upon them which would have rejoiced the heart of an epicure.

We then went to visit the church; and, though the cottages are poor, the church is, as usual, handsome. Amongst other curiosities there is a Virgin, entirely covered with Indian embroidery. The organist's place is hereditary in an Indian family, descending from father to son. The long-haired Indian who played it for us has such a gentle expression and beardless face that he looks like a very young woman.

Some of the Indians here are very rich, and bury their money; and one called Agustín Campos, who has beautified the church, as we read on an inscription carved on a stone outside, has thirty thousand dollars, is much respected, and has the addition of *Don* to his name, yet wears a coarse blanket like his fellow men.[14]

We stayed some hours on the island, and went into some of the huts,

where the women were baking tortillas—one Indian custom, at least, which has descended to these days without variation. They first cook the grain in water with a little lime, and when it is soft peel off the skin; then grind it on a large block of stone, the *metate*, or, as the Indians (who know best) call it, the *metatl*. For the purpose of grinding it, they use a sort of stone roller, with which it is crushed and rolled into a bowl placed below the stone. They then take some of this paste and clap it between their hands till they form it into light round cakes, which are afterwards toasted on a smooth plate—called the *comalli* (*comal* they call it in Mexico)—and which ought to be eaten as hot as possible.[15]

On our return we had the variety of a slight storm, which ruffled the placid surface of the lake, and caused the rowers to exert all their strength to bring the canoe to port before it should become more violent.

This morning we walked all through Pátzcuaro—which can boast of many good houses, a square and *portales*—and ended by going to visit the convent of Santa Catarina.[16] We saw some of the nuns, who wear white dresses and, instead of veils, the black Indian *rebozo*. They were common-looking women, and not very amiable in their manners, but we did not go further than the outside entry.

On our return we met a remarkable baby in arms, wearing an enormous white satin turban, with a large plume of white feathers on one side, balanced on the other by huge bunches of yellow ribbons and pink roses. It also wore two robes, a short and a long one, both trimmed all round with large plaitings of yellow satin ribbon. It was evidently very much admired as it passed along. Tomorrow, our mules having recovered, we set off for [Morelia].

Thursday: December 9th, 1841
Morelia

About half past seven we left Pátzcuaro, which, considering that we had a long day's journey before us, was scarce early enough. We regretted very much taking leave of the Señora Acha, who has been so kind to us, and whom we can certainly never hope to see again.

I observe that in these long days' journeys we generally set off in silence, and sometimes ride on for hours without exchanging a word. Towards the middle of the day we grow more talkative, and again towards evening we relapse into quiet. I suppose it is that in the morning we are sleepy, and towards evening begin to grow tired—feeling sociable about nine o'clock a.m., and not able to talk for a longer period than eight or ten hours.

It was about four in the afternoon when we reached Cointzio, where we were welcomed by the damsels of the baths, whose father is now still more of an invalid than before. It is a lonely life that these poor girls lead here, nor should I think their position a very secure one. Their poverty, however, is a safeguard to a certain extent, and there are few robbers in this country in the style of Morales. We were tempted to stop here and take a bath, in consequence of which it was dark when we set off for Morelia. The horses, unable to see, took enormous leaps over every little streamlet and ditch, so that we seemed to be riding a steeplechase in the dark. Our gowns caught upon the thorny bushes, and our journey might have been traced by the tatters we left behind us. At length we rode the wrong way, up a stony hill, which led us to a wretched little village of about thirty huts, each hut having ten dogs on an average according to the laudable custom of the Indians. Out they all rushed simultaneously, yelping like three hundred demons, biting the horses' feet, and springing round us. Between this canine concert, the kicking of the horses, the roar of a waterfall close beside us, the shouting of people telling us to come back, and the pitch darkness, I thought we should all have gone distracted. We did, however, make our way out from amongst the dogs, redescended the stony hill—the horses leaping over various streamlets that crossed their path—turned into the right road, and entered the gates of Morelia without further adventure between nine and ten o'clock.

Saturday: December 11th, 1841

We have passed the last few days very agreeably in this beautiful city, seeing everything worthy of notice, and greatly admiring the wide and airy streets, the fine houses, the handsome public buildings, but especially the cathedral, the college, and the churches. It has also a fine square, with broad piazzas occupying three of its sides, while the cathedral bounds it to the east. There is a crowded market in the plaza, and a fine display of fruit and vegetables. The population is said to be a little upwards of fifteen thousand, but one would suppose it to be much greater. Living and house rent is so cheap here that a family who could barely exist upon their means in Mexico may enjoy every luxury at [Morelia]. The climate is delightful, and there is something extremely cheerful in the aspect of the city, in which it differs greatly from Toluca. We received visits from various Morelians, amongst others, from Don Cayetano Gómez, the proprietor of San Bartolo.[17]

We went one evening to the Alameda, a broad, straight walk, paved with flat stones, shaded by fine trees—under which are stone benches—and bounded by a low stone wall. Several ladies were sitting there, whom we joined—and, amongst others, a remarkably pretty Poblana, married into the Gómez family.[18] The Alameda is crossed by a fine aqueduct of solid masonry, with light and elegant arches. We drove to the *paseo*, a broad, shady road where we met but few carriages; and the same evening we went out on foot to enjoy the music of a very good military band, which plays occasionally for the amusement of the citizens.[19]

It is not to be supposed that when Mexico can boast of so little society, there should be much in a provincial town. Besides, this city has the pretension of being divided into cliques, and there are "first people," and "second-rate people," and "families in our set," and so on— so that, some of the ladies being musicians, one set will get up a concert, another a rival concert, and, there not being a sufficient musical society to fill two concerts, both fall to the ground. There is a neat little theatre, but at present no company. Some of the houses are as handsome as any in Mexico, but there is no city which has fallen off so much since the independence as Morelia, according to the accounts given us by the most respectable persons.[20]

We had a visit from the bishop, Señor Portugal, one of the most distinguished men here—or in fact in the whole republic of Mexico—a man of great learning, gentle and amiable in his manners, and in his life a model of virtue and holiness. He was in the cabinet when Santa Anna was President, concerning which circumstance an amusing story was told us, for the correctness of which I do not vouch—but the narrator, a respectable citizen here, certainly believed it. Señor Portugal had gone, by appointment, to see the President on some important business, and they had but just begun their consultation when Santa Anna rose and left the room. The minister waited—the President did not return. The time passed on, and still the minister continued expecting him, until at length he inquired of an aide-de-camp in waiting if he could inform him how soon the President might be expected back. "I hardly know," said the officer, "for His Excellency has gone to visit *Cola de Plata* (Silver Tail)." "And who may *Cola de Plata* be?" said the minister. "A favourite cock of His Excellency's, wounded this morning in a fight which he won, and to whose care he is now personally attending!" The bishop soon after sent in his resignation.[21]

Accompanied by several of our friends, including one of the canons of the cathedral, we visited that splendid building the second day of our arrival. It is still wonderfully rich, notwithstanding that silver to the amount of thirty-two thousand marks has been taken from it during the civil wars. The high altar is dazzling with gold and silver; the railing which leads from it to the choir is of pure silver, with pillars of the same metal; the two pulpits, with their stairs, are also covered with silver; and the general ornaments, though numerous and rich, are disposed with good taste, are kept in good order, and have nothing tawdry or loaded in their general effect. The choir itself is extremely beautiful; so also is the carved screen before the organ, the doors of the first being of solid silver, and those of the other of richly carved wood. There is also an

immense silver font, and superb lamps of silver.[22] We particularly admired some fine paintings, chiefly by Cabrera, and especially a Madonna and Child, in which there is that most divine expression in the face of the Virgin, the blending of maternal love with awe for the divinity of the Child. Four of these paintings, it is said, were sent here by a Spanish king, as far back as Philip II. These four are colossal in size, and are finely painted, but little cared for or appreciated, and placed in a bad light.

We were shown two saints, sent from Rome, loaded with false jewels, but carefully preserved in their respective shrines. All the holy vessels and priests' dresses and jewels were taken out for our inspection. The sacramental *custodia* cost thirty-two thousand dollars, and the richest of the dresses eight thousand. There is a lamb made of one pearl, the fleece and head of silver—the pearl of great size and value.

We toiled up through winding staircases to the belfry; and it required the beautiful and extensive landscape spread out before us to compensate us for this most fatiguing ascent. The bells are of copper, and very sonorous. The *canónigo* pointed out to us all the different sites which had been the scenes of bloody battles during the revolutionary war. The

facilities for obtaining provisions and the mountainous character of the country are amongst the causes that have rendered this province the theatre of civil war. The padre afterwards took us into a large apartment, a sort of office, hung round with the portraits of all the bishops of Michoacán—one bearing so striking a resemblance to our friend Don Francisco Tagle that we were not surprised to find that it was in fact the portrait of one of his family who had occupied the episcopal see of Michoacán; and below it were the Tagle arms, referring to some traditionary exploit of their ancestors. They represent a knight killing a serpent, and the motto is: *Tagle se llamó el que la sierpe mató y con la Infanta casó.* (Tagle was the name of him who killed the serpent, and married the Princess.)[23]

The same evening we visited a lady who possesses a most singular and curious collection of works in wax—and, more extraordinary still, they are all her own workmanship. Every fruit and every vegetable production is represented by her with a fidelity which makes it impossible to distinguish between her imitations and the works of nature. Plates with bread, radishes, and fish—dishes of fowls, and chile, and eggs—baskets full of the most delicious looking fruit—lettuces, beans, carrots, tomatoes, &c.—all are copied with the most extraordinary exactness. But her figures show much greater talent. There are groups for which an amateur might offer any price, could she be prevailed upon to offer these masterpieces for sale. There is a Poblana peasant on horseback before a ranchero, looking back at him with the most coquettish expression—her dress perfection, from the straw hat that half shades her features to the beautiful little ankle and foot in the white satin shoe, the short embroidered petticoat and the *rebozo* thrown over one shoulder. [Also] a handsome Indian selling pulque and brandy in her little shop, with every variety of liquor temptingly displayed, in rows of shining bottles, to her customers—the grouping and colouring perfect, and the whole interior arrangement of the shop imitated with the most perfect exactness. There is also a horrid representation, frightfully correct, of a dead body in a state of corruption, which it makes one sick to look at, and which it is inconceivable that anyone can have had pleasure in executing. In short, there is scarcely anything in nature upon which her talent has not exercised itself.

Yesterday we visited the Seminario, or college, a fine spacious old building, kept in good repair.[24] The rector conducted us over the whole establishment. There is a small well-chosen library, containing all the most classic works in Spanish, German, French, and English; and a larger library, containing Greek and Latin authors, theological works, &c. [Also there was] a large hall, with chemical and other scientific apparatus, and a small chapel where there is a beautiful piece of sculpture in wood: the San Pedro, by a young man, a native of Morelia, so exquisitely wrought that one cannot but regret that such a genius should be buried here—should not at least have the advantage of some years' study in Italy, where he might become a second Canova.

One must visit these distant cities, and see these great establishments, to be fully aware of all that the Spaniards bestowed upon their colonies, and also to be convinced of the regret for former times which is felt amongst the most distinguished men of the republic—in fact, by all who are old enough to compare what has been with what is.

I ought not to omit, in talking of the natural productions of [Morelia], to mention that it is famous for *fleas*. We had been alarmed by the miraculous stories related to us of these vivacious animals, and were rejoiced to find ourselves in a house from which, by dint of extreme care, they are banished. But in the inns and inferior houses they are said to be a perfect pestilence, sometimes literally walking away with a piece of matting upon the floor, and covering the walls in myriads. The nuns, it is said, are or were in the habit of harnessing them to little carriages, and of showing them off by other ingenious devices.[25]

We rode out in the evening to meet our friends from Uruapan—who were expected to arrive yesterday—I upon a very formidable and handsome cavalry horse, rather above his work, which some expected to run away, and others to throw me off, and which might have done both but, being a noble creature, did neither. We did not meet our friends who, having been delayed upon the road, only arrived this evening. We have therefore decided to remain here till tomorrow afternoon, when we shall continue our journey homewards by San Bartolo.

51

Friends Revisited; Toluca in Commotion

Tuesday: December 14th, 1841
Anagueo

After taking leave of all our hospitable friends in Morelia, we set off in the afternoon, and had a delightful ride to San Bartolo. Fortunately the following day (Sunday) was that of the Virgin of Guadalupe, one of the greatest festivals here—so that we had an opportunity of seeing all the people from the different villages, who arrived in the courtyard by daybreak, and held a market in front of the hacienda.

Various were the articles for sale, and picturesque the dresses of the sellers. From cakes, chile, *atole*, and groundnuts, to *rebozos* and bead rosaries, nothing was omitted. In one part of the market the sturdy rancheros were drinking pulque and devouring hot cakes; in another, little boys were bargaining for nuts and bananas. Countrywomen were offering low prices for smart *rebozos;* an Indian woman was recommending a comb, with every term of endearment, to a young country girl who seemed perfectly ignorant of its use, assuring her customer that it was an instrument for unravelling the hair, and making it beautiful and shining, and enforcing her argument by combing through some of the girl's tangled locks.

Before breakfast we went to mass in the large chapel of the hacienda. We and the family went to the choir; and the body of the chapel was filled with rancheros and their wives. It is impossible to see anywhere a finer race of men than these rancheros—tall, strong, and well made, with their embroidered shirts, coarse sarapes, and dark blue pantaloons embroidered in gold.[1] After mass, the marketing recommenced, and the *rebozos* had a brisk sale. A number were bought by the men for their wives, or *novias*, at home—which reminds me of a story of Julia Fagoaga's of a poor Indian woman in their village who desired her husband to buy a petticoat for her in Mexico, where he was going to sell his vegetables. She particularly impressed upon him that she wished it to be the *colour of the sky*, which at sunrise, when he was setting off, wa of a flaming red. He returned in the evening bringing, to her great indignation, a petticoat of a dusky gray—which happened to be the colour of the sky when he made his purchase.

In the evening we rode through the fields, the servants and the young master of the house amusing themselves as they went by the chasing and *colear* of the bulls. They have one small, ugly, yellow-coloured bull, which they call tame, and which the *mozos* ride familiarly. They persuaded me to try this novel species of riding, a man holding the animal's head with a rope; but I thought that it tossed its horns in a most uncomfortable and alarming manner, and very soon slipped off. We stopped during our ride at a house where the proprietors make a small fortune by the produce of their numerous beehives, and walked along the banks of a fine clear river, winding through beautiful and verdant groves.

The next morning by six o'clock we were again on horseback, and took leave of San Bartolo. We rode by Indaparapeo—a considerable village, with sloping shingle roofs—and about ten reached Queréndaro, breakfasted with Señor Pimentel, and then continued our journey towards San Andrés where we were to pass the night. We had a horse with us which occasionally fell down on the road, shivering all over, groaning,

and apparently dying; but which had twice recovered from these fits. But this day, having stopped beside a running stream to water our horses, the unfortunate beast fell again, and, when we had remounted and were riding forward, a servant galloped after us to tell us that the horse was dead at last—so we left him to his lonely grave by the river's side. Great, therefore, was our amazement when, some time after, we perceived him trotting along the road at a great rate in pursuit of his party, apparently quite recovered.

We passed the night at San Andrés, a poor *venta*, but clean, consisting of three empty rooms, a spirit shop, and a kitchen. Our escort slept in the piazza, rolled in their sarapes. Our beds were stuck up in the empty rooms, and we got some supper upon fowl and tortillas. We were interested by the melancholy air of a poor woman who sat aloof on the piazza, uncared for, and noticing no one. We spoke to her, and found that she was insane, wandering from village to village, and subsisting on charity. She seemed gentle and harmless, but the very picture of misery, and quite alone in the world, having lost all her family. But God tempers the wind to the shorn lamb."[2] We saw her again in the morning before we set off, and saw her get some breakfast in the kitchen. The poor people of the *venta* seemed kind to her. They who dwell in comfortable houses, surrounded by troops of friends, and who repine at their lot, would do well to compare it with that of such a being.

This morning we left San Andrés, and have had a pleasant ride— in spite of a hard-trotting horse which fell to my lot. Impossible to conceive more beautiful scenery than that which we passed through today. Some of the hills have a singular formation, each large hill appearing composed of a variety of smaller ones, of a pyramidal shape.

We rode through Taximaroa without stopping, and breakfasted at a rancho where the whole family were exceedingly handsome. The ranchero himself was a model for a fine-looking farmer, hospitable and well-bred—knowing his place, yet without any servility. The *rancherita*, who was engaged in the kitchen, was so handsome that we made every possible excuse for going to look at her.

About four o'clock we once more crossed the hills and came down upon the plains by which we left Angangueo; and passed over a river, as red as blood, that looked as if hostile armies had been engaged in fierce combat by its banks, and their bodies rolled in the tide. This ensanguined hue is, however, caused not by warlike steel but by peaceful copper[3]—not peaceful in its effects, by the way, at this moment, for the whole country, more or less, is in commotion on the subject of copper coin.

You must know that some few years ago the value of copper was suddenly reduced by law to one half, causing a great loss to all, but much distress to the poor. The intrinsic value of the copper, however, bore so little relation to the value given to it that it was a very productive business to counterfeit it, of which many unprincipled individuals availed themselves to such an extent that it had almost become an openly exercised branch of industry all through the republic. When Santa Anna became provisional president, he ordered that all the copper coin—whose currency was now reduced to six or eight percent below par—should be given in to certain deposits which he named, promising to repay it in genuine coin of real value. But this naturally caused a still greater depreciation, bringing it down as low as sixty percent, and still greater discontent, the people having little faith in the promise. And, in fact, the payment could not be made at the appointed time because there were not sufficient coining machines; and, as the few new cents that did circulate were said not to contain their real value the distress became greater than ever. The merchants refused to receive copper, and there was no silver or small change. In the meantime, in many of the large haciendas, the proprietors have given checks to the workmen, with which they have been able to buy what they required at the shops which are attached to these haciendas.

The amount of the copper in circulation cannot be calculated, foit is almost all counterfeit. It is supposed, however, to be at least from eight to nine millions of dollars. You may easily imagine the fortunes that will be made (and, as they say, are being made) by those of the government party who are buying up for sixty [percent] what will be paid [for] by favour of the government at the rate of a hundred.[4]

We rode up the hills that lead to the house of Don Carlos Heimbürger, and were again hospitably received by him and his German friends. Nothing can have a finer effect than the view from the piazza of his house in the evening, looking down upon the valley. The piazza itself has a screen of green creepers, which have the effect of a curtain of a theatre half drawn up. Behind the house rises a dark frowning hill in the form of a pyramid. In front is the deep ravine, with the huts of the workmen, and while the moon throws her quivering beams over the landscape the metallic fires of livid blue light up the valley. There is something wild and diabolic in the scene; and, as the wind howls round the valley with a dismal sound, it seems as if one were looking on at some unholy, magical incantation—so that it is pleasant to return after a while to the comfortable rooms and cheerful fires within, which have so homely and domestic an air. We hope to spend tomorrow here, and the following day go on to Toluca, from whence I shall continue my letter.

Sunday: December 19th, 1841
Toluca

The next day we visited the works which are like all others, excepting that here they do not use quicksilver to extract the silver from the lead, but do so by the process of oxidation, by the means of a reverberatory furnace.[5] The people generally have an unhealthy appearance, as nearly all have who are engaged in these works, the air being loaded with particles of metal. After visiting the mills and the sheds where the process of oxidation is carried on, and admiring the metallic riches of these mountains, we left the hot and poisoned atmosphere and walked up the mountains—clothed with a hardy vegetation, with every noble tree and flowering shrub—and pursued our course till we came to a fine waterfall which plunges from a great height over the gigantic rocks.

The scenery here is rude and wild. The great rocks are covered with hardy trees: the pine, the cedar, the oak, and the flowering laurel. The river, after dashing down in this noble cascade, runs brawling amongst the forest-clothed hills till it reaches the plains, and flows on placidly. We spent an agreeable day wandering amongst the mountains; and, when we returned, sat on the piazza to watch the moon as her broad disk rose over the valley, and the fierce blue lights that made her mild fires grow pale.

All Germans are musical, and the gentlemen in this house did not belie the national reputation. After dinner, a bright fire blazing, doors and windows shutting out the cold air that whistled along the hills, they struck up in chorus some of the finest national airs, particularly the "Hymn to the Rhine," so that it seemed an illusion that we were in this wild mining district inhabited only by the poorest Indians— and we were transported thousands of miles off, across the broad Atlantic, even to the land where

> The castled crag of Drachenfels
> Frowns o'er the broad and winding Rhine.[6]

We also amused ourselves by examining Madame Backhausen's Album; and, if those milk-and-water volumes belonging to young ladies—where young gentlemen write prettinesses—be called Albums, some other name should be found for a book where some of the most distinguished artists in Germany have left proofs of their talent, and where there is not one page which does not contain something striking and original. Nothing pleased me so much as the fanciful illustration of the beautiful legend of Lorelei, which Madame Backhausen read to us with great feeling. We became too comfortable here for hardy equestrian travellers, and had we stayed much longer should have begun to complain of tough fowls, beds in barns, and other inconveniences which we had hitherto laughed at; but we tore ourselves away from our Capua,[7] and on the morning of the sixteenth set off for El Pilar.

Don Carlos Heimbürger, M. and Mme Backhausen, &c., accompanied us for seven leagues, all through the woods. We had a delightful ride, the day was cool and cloudy, and we were, besides, constantly shaded by the noble forest trees. But we had not reached Las Millas before the sky was overcast, the clouds became black and gloomy, and at length broke out in rain. We galloped fast, for the day—besides being rainy —was cold, and in the afternoon reached Las Millas. Here we break-fasted in the little portico, which we preferred to the interior of the cottage—chiefly upon tortillas and boiled *tejocotes*, a fruit which grows in great abundance, and resembles a small apple. Here again were two Indian girls of admirable beauty, *dans leur genre*, baking tortillas.

We were now obliged to part from our kind German friends, and to ride across the plains. But we had not gone more than halfway when the clouds burst forth in torrents, pouring their fury on our devoted heads, so that in five minutes we were all drenched as if we had fallen into a river. We took shelter for a little while under a solitary spreading tree, but the storm increased in violence and it was advisable to gallop forwards in order to arrive at El Pilar before it became dark. Suddenly, the most beautiful rainbow I ever beheld smiled out from amongst the watery clouds. It formed a complete and well-defined arch of the most brilliant colours in the heavens, reflected by another on the plains, which, uniting with it, blended its fainter hues with the light of the heavenly bow.

We arrived at El Pilar tired and drenched, and greatly in need of the hospitable reception which was given to us by its mistress.

The following morning we set off early for La Gavia, feeling some regret that our journey was drawing to a close. Some of us who rode in front found ourselves surrounded by several suspicious-looking, well-armed men on horseback, who, under pretense of asking some questions, rode very close to us and then stopped and faced round on their horses—but there was no danger, our escort being at a short distance, and when they observed its approach they bestowed no further attention upon us.

Don Javier Echeverría had returned to Mexico, but we were cordially welcomed by his brother-in-law, Don Manuel Gorospe, and so kindly pressed to remain some days that nothing but our limited time would have induced us to set off next morning for Toluca.[8] Here we arrived last night, having performed our journey by a different and more agreeable road than that of the "three hundred barrancas." We entered Toluca by moonlight, and found that respectable city all in commotion on the subject of copper—presenting a very different aspect from the quiet and conventual air of repose which distinguished it little more than a month ago. Yesterday Colonel Iniestra, who has accompanied us during all this journey, left us to return to Michoacán, having thus brought us back in safety to the point from which we started.

We are spending a very tiresome day in the inn, which, however, is a more decent place and belongs to a better line of coaches than the other. We have been enlivened by several visits, amongst others, from the commandant, and from an aide-de-camp of General Valencia's.

For the first time since we left it, we have news from Mexico.[9] Santa Anna, dit-on, is now dictator or king, in all but the name—affecting more than royal pomp, yet endeavouring by his affability to render himself popular. Above all, he has made known his determination of not seizing an inch of ground belonging to the clergy, which seizure of church property was the favourite idea of Paredes and the progresistas. This resolution he has not printed, probably in order not to disgust that party, but his personal declaration to the Archbishop and the padres of the Profesa, and in a letter to the bishop of Puebla, is not only that he will leave their property untouched, but that, were he out of power, he would draw his sword in their defense—for the reason that, good or bad, he is a sincere Catholic. This has done much to re-establish him in the good opinion of the clergy, and it is said that in every convent in Mexico monks and nuns are now wearying heaven with prayers in his behalf.[10] In short, the conquerors and the conquered, those of the Progress and those of the Dictatorship, seem all—barring a few noble exceptions—actuated by one motive: personal interest.

Count Cortina is restored to the command of his battalion *del Comercio,* which has been re-established—it having deserted to the federalists in the last revolution. It appears that the President's favourite plan is to have thirty thousand men under arms, and there is little doubt that he will bring this about. Sixteen new generals have been created, and General Tornel is made a general of division. The Señora Valencia has given a ball, at which she and other ladies appeared with trains, rehearsing, as it would seem, before the court drawing rooms. I was told, and by good authority, that the present sent by Santa Anna to the lady of the commander-in-chief on her birthday was a box containing three general's belts, with a request that she would bestow them on those whom she considered most deserving of them; and that the lady herself buckled the sashes on her favoured knights, in her own boudoir. Thus was valour rewarded by the hand of beauty; and

> Thus should desert in arms be crowned.[11]

Meanwhile the master of the house presents himself with a disturbed and gloomy countenance, and doubts much whether we can have any dinner today because no one will sell anything, either for copper or silver. Moreover [he] hints darkly that they expect a copper *pronunciamiento* tomorrow, and observes that the shops are shut up.

Since we could get no dinner, we went out to take a walk; and methinks the *Tolucanos* have a fierce and agitated aspect. We attempted to go to mass this morning, but there was a congregation of *léperos* who filled not only the church but the whole enclosure and the street beyond, so that we could not even approach the church door. Unfortunately we cannot get a diligence until the twenty-first.

They have brought us at last, I will not say dinner—but something to eat.

Monday: December 20th, 1841

This morning the firing of squibs, the beating of drums, the shouting and confusion on the streets announced that the ragamuffin population of Toluca had turned out; and, going to the balcony, I very nearly received the salutation of

> A sky-
> Rocket in my eye.

Orders have been given out by the alcalde that copper shall be received in payment by the merchants, some of whom have declared they will only receive silver. A large mob has collected before the alcalde's door, with shouts of *"Viva la plata! Muera el cobre!* (Long live silver! Death to copper!)"—apostrophizing these useful metals as if they were two generals.

The merchants have issued a declaration that, during three days only, they will sell their goods for copper (of course at an immense advantage to themselves). The Indians and the poorer classes are now rushing to the shops and buying goods, receiving in return for their copper about half its value. If Santa Anna keeps his word the *patriotism* of the merchants will be rewarded.

Calderón has just had a visit from one of the merchants, who wishes his conduct to be represented in a proper light in Mexico.

Wednesday: December 22nd, 1841
Calle de Cadena, Mexico

With much joy we stepped into the diligence early yesterday morning, accompanied by the commandant of Toluca, and retraced our road to Mexico; for, though Toluca is a fine city with clean, airy houses, wide, well-paved streets, and picturesque in its situation, there is something sad and deserted in its appearance—an air of stagnation that weighs upon the spirits—and the specimens we have seen of its lower orders are not inviting.

We had rather an agreeable journey, as the day was cool, and we had the diligence to ourselves. We breakfasted again at Cuajimalpa, took leave of the interesting *itzcuintepotzotli,* still hanging from its hook— and again ascended the eminence from which Mexico suddenly bursts upon the view, and, after a short absence, with all the charms of novelty. Before we arrived at Tacubaya we were met by a carriage containing Señor A[dalid] and his lady, who insisted on our leaving the diligence and carried us off to their own house, where we now are.[12] On the second of January we expect to take our final departure from the "great city of the lake."

Tuesday: December 28th, 1841

Another old year about to chime in! Another Christmas passed away! But during these last few days it has been all in vain to attempt finishing my letter, between making arrangements for our journey, receiving and returning visits, going to the opera, and seeing and revisiting all that we had left unseen or wished to see again before leaving this. People seem determined that we shall regret them, and load us with kindness and attentions—the more flattering that now at least they are entirely personal, and cannot proceed from any interested motive. We have reason to think them both steady and sincere in their friendship.

General Morán has died, universally regretted.[13] He has been embalmed according to the system of Gannal, and his funeral was performed with extraordinary magnificence—the troops out, the foreign ministers and the cabinet following on foot, the former in full uniform, and a great train of carriages reaching along the whole Calle San Francisco, from the church to the square. The body, dressed in a general's uniform, was carried upon a splendid bier, and was so perfectly embalmed that he seemed not dead, nor even asleep, but lying in an attitude of repose.[14] The expense of this operation will probably prevent its ever becoming very common; and certainly there are but few cases where it can be advisable to adopt it. An *embalmed dynasty* might be a curious sight. To trace the features of a royal line—from Charlemagne to Charles X, from Alfred to William IV—would be a strange study. Mary of Scotland and Elizabeth, lying in the repose of death, yet looking as they lived and hated centuries back, might be a curious piece of antiquity. A Hernan Cortés, a Washington, a Columbus, a Napoleon— men whose memory for good or for evil will survive time and change— it would be a strange and wondrous thing if we could look on their features as they were in life. But it is to be trusted that this method of successfully wrestling with the earth, for what it claims as its due, will not generally prevail—or at the end of a few centuries the embalmed population would scarce leave room for their living and breathing descendants. Nor is it an agreeable idea that one might, in a lapse of ages, grace the study of an antiquary, or be preserved amongst the curiosities of a museum. I would stuff birds and beasts, and preserve them in cabinets, but not the remains of immortal man. *Dust unto dust;* and the eye of faith turned from the perishing remains to the spirit which has gone to the God who gave it.[15]

The *función* performed in the general's honour within the church was as magnificent as ecclesiastic and military splendour could render it. We were in the gallery above. The bier, placed on a lofty scaffolding, covered with black velvet and lighted with wax tapers, was placed near the altar. The music was solemn and impressive. Every respect has been shown to the deceased general, by Santa Anna's orders. Excepting the *corps diplomatique* and the officers, all within the church were in deep mourning.

The chief difficulty we have in arranging our affairs here consists in the perfect impossibility of persuading any tradesman to keep his word. They name the day, the hour, the minute at which they are to be with you, or at which certain goods are to be sent to you. They are affronted if you doubt their punctuality, and the probability is you never hear of them or their goods again. If they are not exact for their own interest, they will not be so for yours; and, although we have had frequent proofs of this carelessness, we are particularly annoyed by it now that we are within a few days of our departure. During our residence here we have had little to do with shops and shopkeepers, having found it more convenient and economical to send to Paris or even to the United States for all articles of dress. Now, though everything must still be comparatively dear, the *bad times* have caused a great reduction in prices— and, dear as all goods are—they would be still dearer were it not for the quantity that is smuggled into the republic. There are an amazing number of French shopkeepers: French tailors, hatters, shoemakers, apothecaries, &c.—but especially French modistes, and *perruquiers*. The charges of the former are exorbitant; the latter are little employed except by gentlemen. There are also many Spanish shops, some German, and a few English, but I think the French preponderate.

We went some time ago to see the Monte Pío, which is under the auspices of Señor Tagle, and it is melancholy enough to see the profusion of fine diamonds and pearls that are displayed in these large halls. After a certain time has elapsed without their being redeemed the pledged articles are sold—gold and silver, in whatever form, by the weight, but jewels for their intrinsic value. There is a sale once a week. We were shown privately the jewels of the Virgen de los Remedios, which are very superb.

There is a small theatre lately established, called the Theatre of New Mexico, where there is a Spanish company, the same whom we saw two years ago in Veracruz. They are drawing away various persons from the principal theatre. Their object seems to be to make people laugh, and they succeed. On Christmas Eve we went there to see the *gracioso* (harlequin), in a woman's dress, dance the *Trípili,* an old Spanish dance, accompanied with singing. They introduced some appropriate lines concerning the late troubles about the *copper,* which were received with great applause. Just as they were concluding the *Trípili* a young gentleman in the pit, I do not know whether Mexican or Spanish, rose and—waving his hand after the manner of a man about to make an address, and requesting attention—kindly favoured the audience with some verses of his own, which were received with great good nature, the actors bowing to him, and the pit applauding him. It seemed to me a curious piece of philanthropy on his part.

At midnight we went to the church of Santa Clara to attend what is called the *Misa del Gallo,* the Cock's Mass, which is private

LA MISA DEL GALLO.

—only respectable persons being admitted by a private entrance, for midnight mass in Mexico takes place with shut doors as all nightly reunions are dreaded. Santa Clara being attached to the convent of that name, we remained after mass to see the white-robed sisters receive the sacrament from the hands of a priest, by the small side door that opens from the convent to the church. The church was lighted, but the convent was in darkness; and, looking in through the grating, we could only distinguish the outline of their kneeling figures, enveloped in their white drapery and black veils. I do not think there were a dozen persons in the church besides ourselves.[16]

A good deal of interest has been excited here lately about the Texian prisoners taken in the Santa Fe expedition, the first detachment of whom have arrived, after a march of nearly two thousand miles, and are now lodged in the convent of Santiago about two miles from the centre of the city. As their situation is represented to be very miserable, and as it is said that they have been stripped of their hats, shoes, and coats, some of the Mexican families—and amongst others that of Don Francisco Tagle —regardless of political enmity, have subscribed to send them a supply of linen and other necessary articles, which they carried out there themselves. Being invited to accompany them to Santiago, I did so; and we found the common men occupying the courtyard, and the officers, the large hall of the convent. So far they have been treated as prisoners of war generally are, but it is said to be the intention of Santa Anna to have them put in chains, and sent out to sweep the streets with the miserable prisoners of the Acordada. Colonel Cooke, who was presented to me, seemed to treat the whole affair very lightly, as the fortune of war, and had evidently no idea that any such fate was in store for them —seeming rather amused by the dress of the monks, whom he now saw for the first time. In the Mexicans generally, there seems very little if any vindictive feeling against them; on the contrary, a good deal of interest in their favour, mingled with some curiosity to see them. The common men appeared more impatient and more out of spirits than the officers. We shall probably know nothing more of their fate before leaving Mexico.[17]

We had some intention of paying a last visit to the museum before we went; and Don José María Bustamante, a friend of ours, professor of botany and considered a man of learning, was prepared to receive us, but we were prevented from going.[18] I must, however, find time to answer your question as to the population. The Mexican republic is supposed to contain upwards of seven millions of inhabitants; the capital, two hundred thousand. Their number cannot be exactly fixed, as there has for some time been no general census: a labour in which a commission, with Count Cortina at its head, has been employed for some time past, and the result of which will be published shortly. All other questions must be replied to *de vive voix*.

I must now conclude my last letter written from this place; for we are surrounded by visitors—day and night—and, to say the truth, feel that it is only the prospect of returning to our family which can counterbalance the unfeigned regret we feel at leaving our friends in Mexico.[19] My next letter will most probably be dated from Veracruz.

FAREWELL TO MEXICO

52

Revised Impressions

Thursday: January 6th, 1842
Veracruz

Having concluded our arrangements for leaving Mexico on the second of January, we determined, as the diligence started long before daybreak, not to attempt taking any rest that night. We went out early and took leave of the Dowager Marquesa de Vivanco, who was confined to the house by illness, and whose kindness to us has been unremitting ever since our arrival. It is a sad thing to take leave of a person of her age, and in her delicate state of health, whom there is scarcely a possibility of our ever seeing again. Some days before, we parted also from one of our oldest friends here, the [Dowager] Countess Cortina. The last day, besides the Spaniards who have been our constant friends and visitors ever since we came here, we had melancholy visits of adieu from Señor Gómez Pedraza and his lady, from the families of Echeverría, of Fagoaga, Cortina, Escandón, Casa Flores, and many whose names are unknown to you. Amongst others was the Güera Rodríguez.[1]

About eight o'clock, accompanied even to the door of the carriage by a number of ladies who were with us to the last—and amongst these were Paulita Cortina and Luz Escandón—we broke short all these sad partings and, with the A[dalid]s and the family of the French minister, set off for the Theatre of New Mexico. I can imagine your surprise at such a finale, but it was the only means left us of finishing a painful scene, and of beguiling the weary hours yet remaining before the diligence started, for it was in vain to think of rest or sleep that night.

The theatre was very crowded, the play an amusing piece of *diablerie*, called the *Pata de Cabra* (The Goat's Foot), badly got up, of course, as its effect depends upon scenery and machinery. I believe it was very entertaining, but I cannot say we felt inclined to enter into the spirit of it.[2] The family of General V[alenci]a were there, and—this being the day of a great diplomatic dinner given by Santa Anna—various officers and diplomats came in late and in full dress. I was informed by one

of the company that six colonels stood the whole time of dinner behind
His Excellency's chair! I wonder what French officer would do as much
for Louis Philippe. *Vogue la galère!*[3]

From the theatre, which concluded about one, we drove to the house
of the French minister—where we spent a very grave half-hour—and
then returned home with a very splendid *brioche*, of generous proportions, which Madame la Baronne de Cyprey had kindly prepared for our
journey.[4]

Arrived at the Adalids', we sat down to supper, and never was there a
sadder meal than this, when for the last time we sat at the hospitable
board of these our earliest and latest Mexican friends. We were thankful when it was all over and we had taken leave, and when, accompanied to the inn by Señor Adalid and other gentlemen, we found
ourselves fairly lodged in the diligence on a dark and rather cold
morning—sad, sleepy, and shivering. All Mexico was asleep when we
drove out of the gates. The very houses seemed sunk in slumber. So
terminated our last Mexican *New Year's Day*.

When we reached the eminence from which is the last view of the
valley, the first dawn of day was just breaking over the distant city; the
white summits of the volcanoes were still enveloped in mist, and the
lake was veiled by low clouds of vapour that rose slowly from its surface.
And this was our last glimpse of Mexico!

The diligence is now on a new and most fatiguing plan of travelling
night and day after leaving Puebla—so that, starting from Mexico at
four o'clock on the morning of the second of January, it arrives in
Veracruz early on the morning of the fifth, saving a few hours and
nearly killing the travellers.[5] The government had granted us escorts for
the whole journey, now more than ever necessary.

It was five in the afternoon when we reached Puebla, and we set off
again by dawn the next morning. We had just left the gates—and our
escort, which had rode forward, was concealed by some rising ground—
when, by the faint light, we perceived some half dozen mounted cavaliers
making stealthily up to us across the fields. Their approach was first
discerned by a Spanish lady who was with us, and who was travelling
with strings of pearl and valuable diamonds concealed about her person,
which made her peculiarly sharp-sighted on the occasion. "*Ladrones!*"
said she, and everyone repeated "*Ladrones!*" in different intonations.
They rode across the fields, came up pretty close to the diligence, and
reconnoitred us. I was too sleepy to be frightened, and reconnoitred
them in return with only one eye open. The coachman whipped up his
horses, the escort came in sight, and the gentlemen struck into the fields
again. The whole passed in a minute or two. The soldiers of the escort
came riding back to the diligence; and the captain, galloping up to the
window, gave himself great credit for having "frightened away the robbers."

We arrived at Perote when it was nearly dusk, supped, and started again at eleven o'clock at night. We passed a horrible night in the diligence, and were thankful when daybreak showed us the beautiful environs of Jalapa. It is singular that on a second impression, returning by this road, the houses appear handsomer than they did before, and nature less beautiful. I conclude that this is to be accounted for simply from the circumstance of the eye having become accustomed both to the works of nature and of man which characterize this country. The houses, which at first appeared gloomy, large, and comfortless, habit has reconciled us to, and experience has taught us that they are precisely suited to this climate of perpetual spring. The landscape, with its eternal flowers and verdure, no longer astonishes and bewilders us, as when we first arrived from a country where, at that season, all nature lies buried in snow. Besides, in our last journey through Michoacán, we have passed among scenes even more striking and beautiful than these. Then the dresses, which at first appeared so romantic—the high, Moorish-looking saddle, the gold-embroidered *manga*, the large hat shading the swarthy faces of the men, the coloured petticoat and *rebozo*, and long black hair of the women—though still picturesque, have no longer the charm of novelty, and do not attract our attention. The winter also has been un-usually severe for Mexico, and some slight frosts have caused the flowers of this natural garden to fade; and, besides all this, we were tired and sleepy and jolted, and knew that we had but an hour or two to remain, and had another day and night of purgatory in prospect.

Still, as we passed along the shady lanes—amongst the dark *chirimoyos*, the green-leaved bananas, and all the variety of beautiful trees entwined with their graceful creepers—we were forced to confess that winter has little power over these fertile regions, and that in spite of the leveller, *Habit*, such a landscape can never be passed through with indifference.

Arrived at Jalapa, we refreshed ourselves with the luxury of a bath, having to pass through half the city before we reached the bathing establishment, from which there is the most beautiful view of wood, water, and mountain that it is possible to behold. The baths are the property of a lady who has a cotton factory and a good house in the city, and fortunate she is in possessing a sufficient portion of worldly goods since, as she informed us, she is the mother of twenty children! She herself, in appearance, was little more than thirty. We then returned to breakfast, and shortly after left Jalapa.

I will not inflict upon you a second description of the same journey: of Plan del Río, with its clear river and little inn; of Puente del Rey, with its solid majestic bridge thrown over the deep ravine, through which rushes the impetuous Antigua—or of how we were jolted over the road leading to Paso de Ovejas, &c. Suffice it to say that we passed a night which, between suffocating heat, horrible jolting, and extreme fatigue, was nearly intolerable. Stopping to change horses at Santa Fe, we saw, by the light of the torches which they brought to the door, that we were once more among bamboo huts and palm trees. Towards morning we heard the welcome sound of the waves, giving us joyful token that our journey was drawing to a close; yet, when we entered Veracruz and got out of the diligence, we felt like prisoners who have been so long confined in a dungeon they are incapable of enjoying their liberty— we were so thoroughly worn out and exhausted. How different from the agreeable kind of fatigue which we used to feel after a long day's journey on horseback!

Breakfast and a fresh toilet had, however, their due influence. We were in an hotel, and had hardly breakfasted when our friend Don Dionisio Velasco, with some other gentlemen, arrived and, kindly reproaching us for preferring an inn to his house, carried us and our luggage off to his fine airy dwelling where we now are, and where a good night's rest has made us forget all our fatigues.

As we must remain here for one or two days, we shall have time to see a little more of the city; and already, upon a second survey—sad and dilapidated as it now appears—I can more readily imagine what it must have been in former days, before it was visited by the scourge of civil war. The experience of two Mexican revolutions makes it more easy for us to conceive the extent to which this unfortunate city must have suffered in the struggle made by the Spaniards to preserve the castle their last bulwark in this hemisphere. San Juan de Ulúa, in spite of the miserable condition in which it now is, remains a lasting memorial of the great works which, almost immediately after their arrival on these shores, were undertaken by the Spanish conquerors.

In 1582, sixty-four years after they had set foot on Aztec soil, they began this fortress, in order to confirm their power. The centre of the space which it occupies is a small island where the Spaniard Juan de Grijalva arrived, one year before Cortés reached the Mexican continent. Having found the remains of two human victims there, they asked the natives why they sacrificed men to their idols; and, receiving for answer that it was by orders of the kings of Acolhua, the Spaniards gave the island the name of Ulúa, by a natural corruption of that word.[6]

It is pretended that the fortress cost forty millions; and, though this

immense sum is no doubt an exaggeration, the expense must have been very great when we consider that its foundations are below the water, and that for nearly three centuries it has resisted all the force of the stormy waves that continually beat against it. Many improvements and additions were gradually made to the castle; and, in the time of the viceroys, a first-rate engineer paid it an annual visit to ascertain its condition, and to consider its best mode of defense in case of an attack. In 1683, however, Veracruz was sacked by the English corsair Nicholas Agramont, incited by one Lorencillo who had been condemned to death for murder in Veracruz, and had escaped to Jamaica. Seven millions of dollars were carried off, besides three hundred persons of both sexes, whom the pirates abandoned in the island of Sacrificios when they re-embarked.[7]

In 1771 the viceroy, then the Marquis de la Croix, remitted a million and a half of dollars to the governor in order that he might put the castle in a state of defense, and the strong bulwarks which still remain attest the labour that has been bestowed upon it. The outer polygon, which looks towards Veracruz, is three hundred yards in extent. To the north it is defended by another of two hundred yards, whilst a low battery is situated as a rear guard in the bastion of Santiago—and on the opposite front is the battery of San Miguel. The whole fortress is composed of a stone which abounds in the neighbouring island, a species of coral, excellent for building, *piedra múcara*.

In 1822 no stronghold of Spanish power remained but this castle, whose garrison was frequently reinforced by troops from Havana. Veracruz itself was then inhabited by wealthy and influential Spaniards. Santa Anna then commanded in the province, under the orders of Echávarri, the captain general, and with instructions from Iturbide relative to the taking of the castle. The commandant was the Spanish General Don José Dávila. It was not, however, till the following year, when Lemaur succeeded Dávila in the command of the citadel, that hostilities were begun by bombarding Veracruz.[8] Men, women, and children then abandoned the city. The merchants went to Alvarado, twelve leagues off, whilst those who were driven from their houses by a shower of balls sought a miserable asylum amongst the burning plains and miserable huts in the environs. Some made their way to Jalapa, thirty leagues off; others to Córdoba and Orizaba, equally distant. With some interruptions, hostilities lasted two years, during which there was nearly a constant firing from the city to the castle, and from the castle to the city.

The object of General Barragán, now commander-in-chief, was to cut off all communication between the garrison of the castle and the coasts, and to reduce them to live solely upon salt provisions—fatal in this warm and unhealthy country. In 1824 the garrison, diminished to a mere handful, was replaced by five hundred men from the [Spanish] peninsula; and very soon these soldiers, shut up on the barren rocks, surrounded by water, and exposed to the dangers of the climate, without provisions and without assistance, were reduced to the most miserable condition. The next year, Don José Copinger succeeded Lemaur, and continued hostilities with fresh vigour.

This brave general, with his valiant troops, surrounded by the sick and the dying, provisions growing scarcer every day and those that remained corrupt and unfit to eat, yet resolved to do his duty and hold out to the last. No assistance arrived from Spain. A Mexican fleet was stationed off the island of Sacrificios and other points, to attack any squadron that might come from thence, while the north winds blew with violence, keeping back all ships that might approach the coasts. "Gods and men," says a furious republican (Zavala), "the Spaniards had to contend with; having against them hunger, sickness, the fire and balls of the enemies, a furious sea covered with reefs, a burning atmosphere, and above all, being totally ignorant as to whether they should receive any assistance."[9]

The Minister of the Treasury, Esteva, then came from Mexico and proposed a capitulation; and the Spanish general agreed that, should no assistance arrive within a certain time, he would give up the fortress, evacuating it with his whole garrison, and with the suitable honours. The Spanish succours arrived a few days before the term was expired, but the commander of the squadron, seeing the superiority in point of numbers of the Mexican fleet, judged it prudent to return to Havana to augment his forces. But it was too late. On the [nineteenth of November, 1825], the brave General Copinger, with the few troops that remained to him, marched out of the fortress, terminating the final struggle against the progress of revolution, but upholding to the last the character for constancy and valour which distinguished the sons of ancient Spain.[10]

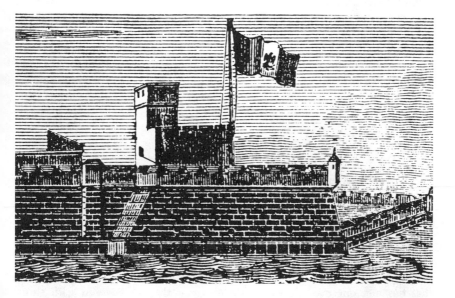

Of its last assault by the French squadron in 1838, there is no need to say anything. Every newspaper, as you will remember, gave an account of the capitulation of what the French gazettes called "San Juan de Ulúa, the St. Jean d'Acre of the new world, which our mariners saluted as the Queen of the Seas, *vierge sans tache*, &c."[11]

We have just had a visit from General Bustamante, who, with his aide-de-camp, a son of General Calderón (formerly governor of Jalapa), intends shortly to sail in the *Jasón* for Havana.[12] We have also had a visit from the commander of that vessel, Captain Puente, who succeeded our friend Captain Estrada, and who has been kindly endeavouring to make arrangements for taking us also, not having before been aware of our intentions of leaving Veracruz at this period.[13] But although we should have much pleasure in returning by the vessel that brought us we fear that, without putting the officers to great inconvenience, it will be impossible for them to accommodate so many, for we know the *carte du pays.* It is therefore probable that we shall go by the English packet, which sails on the eighth—but unfortunately goes round by Tampico, not very agreeable at this season.

We went to mass this morning, which was said to be particularly crowded in consequence of the general desire to catch a glimpse of the ex-President.

I find, personally, one important change in taste if not in opinion. Veracruz cookery, which two years ago I thought detestable, now appears to me delicious! What excellent fish!—and what incomparable *frijoles!* Well, this is a trifle; but after all, in trifles as in matters of moment, how necessary for a traveller to compare his judgments at different periods, and to correct them! First impressions are of great importance, if given only as such; but, if laid down as decided opinions, how apt they are to be erroneous! It is like judging of individuals by their physiognomy and manners, without having had time to study their character. We all do so more or less, but how frequently we find ourselves deceived!

Friday: January 7th, 1842

We went to the theatre last evening. In the boxes there were only a lady and gentleman, besides our party. The pit, however, was full—but there are no good actors at present. We have been walking about today, notwithstanding the heat, purchasing some necessary articles from French modistes and French perfumers, most of whom, having got over the fever, are now very well satisfied to remain here and make their fortune. We afterwards walked down to the mole, and saw the pleasantest sight that has met our eyes since we left Mexico—the sea covered with ships. It was refreshing to look again on the dark blue waves, after so long an absence from them. Commodore **López** of Mexico, who was present, pointed out the *Jasón,* and the *Tyrian,* Captain Griffin, lying out in the harbour—and strongly recommended us to go in the latter, as did the English consul, with proper patriotism. We have requested him to take our berths when he goes to visit the captain on board this evening.

No sooner has this been done beyond recall, than we find that comfortable arrangements have been made for taking us in the *Jasón,* which goes direct to Havana. It is now too late, so we can only regret our precipitation. There is another beautiful Spanish vessel just arrived, the *Liberal,* Captain Rubalcava, who, with Captain Puente of the *Jasón,* has been to see us this evening. If the wind holds fair, the packet sails tomorrow—but the experienced predict a norther.

The symptoms of this terrible wind, which blows in the Mexican Gulf from the autumnal to the vernal equinox, are known not only to the sailors, but to all those who have lived some time in this city. The variation in the barometer is the surest sign. A land breeze from the northwest first blows gently, then varies to the northeast, then changes to the south. The heat is then suffocating, and the summits of all the great mountains appear cloudless and distinct against the deep blue sky, while round their base floats a veil of semi-transparent vapour. Suddenly the tempest bursts forth, and all are instantaneously relieved—all but the poor mariners! The air becomes refreshed—clouds of dust come sweeping along the streets, driving away, as it were, the pestilential atmosphere. Then there is no fever in Veracruz.

All communication is cut off between the castle and the city, and between the city and all foreign shipping. Sometimes the norther lasts three or four days, sometimes even twelve. If it turns to a southerly breeze, the tempest generally returns; if it changes to the east or northeast, the breeze generally lasts three or four days—and the ships in the port take advantage of this interval to escape, and gain the high seas. These gales are particularly dreaded off the coasts of Tampico.

Saturday: January 8th, 1842

We sail in a few hours, the *norte* not having made its appearance, so that we expect to get clear of the coast before it begins. The *Jasón* sails in a day or two, unless prevented by the gale. We only knew this morning that it was necessary to provide mattresses and sheets, &c., for our berths on board the packet. Fortunately, all these articles are found ready made in this seaport town.

We have just received a packet of letters, particularly acceptable as bringing us news of home before our departure. I have also received two agreeable *compagnons de voyage* in the shape of books: Stephens' *Central America,* and Washington Irving's *Life of Margaret Davidson,* opportunely sent me by Mr. Prescott.[14]

Our next letters will be written either at sea, or from Tampico.

53

To Havana by Way of Tampico

Saturday: January 15th, 1842
On board H. B. M. Packet Ship *Tyrian*

On the eighth, having taken leave of the family of our friend Señor Velasco, and of General Bustamante whom we hope to see again in Havana, we went out in a little boat, accompanied as far as the packet by several gentlemen, and in a short time were standing on deck—looking our last at Veracruz, and its sandbanks, and *zopilotes*, and frowning castle—as the shores gradually receded from our view, while the *Tyrian* was making the best of her time to get clear of reefs and rocks before the arrival of the norther. We regretted to find that, instead of being one of the new line of English packets, the *Tyrian* was the last of the old line: small, ancient, and incommodious, and destined to be paid off on her return to England. Captain Griffin, the commander, who looks like an excellent, gentlemanly man, is in wretched health, and in a state of acute suffering. There were no passengers but ourselves, and a young Mexican guiltless of any acquaintance with salt water up to this date.

The very next morning out burst the norther, and with loud howling swept over the ocean, which rose and tossed to meet the coming storm. Surely no wind ever had a voice so wildly mournful. How the good ship rolled, and groaned, and creaked, and strained her old timber joints! What rocking, thumping, falling, banging of heads at the low entry of the cabin!—water falling into berths, people rolling out of them. What fierce music at night, as the wind, like a funeral dirge, swept over the ocean, the rain falling in torrents, and the sky covered with one dark, lugubrious pall! And how lonely our ship seemed on the world of waters!

But the next day the storm waxed fiercer still, and the night was worse than the day. The waves that dashed over the deck made their way into the cabin. At one time we thought the ship had struck, and even the captain believed that a mast had fallen. It was only a huge wave that broke over the deck with a sound like thunder, drowning the wretched hens and ducks—who little thought, when they left their comfortable English poultry yard, they were destined to be drowned off Tampico— and drenching the men. Our little lamp, after swinging to and fro for some time, went out and left the cabin in darkness. Impossible to sleep of course, and for the *first time* at sea I confess to having felt afraid. Each time that the ship rolled upon her side on the slope of a huge billow it seemed impossible that she could ever right again, or that she could avoid receiving the whole contents of the next great watery mountain that came roaring on.

On the morning of the eleventh there was still no abatement of the storm. All was dark and dreary. The norther continued to blow with unrelenting fierceness, and the ship to rock and roll amongst a tumult of foaming billows. The nights in this pitch darkness seemed interminable. The berths being constantly filled with water, we dragged our mattresses on the floor, and lay there wishing for the dawn. But the dawn brought no relief. The wind howled on like a fierce wild beast, roaring for its prey. I had made my way every day upstairs, and by dint of holding on, and with a chair tied with strong ropes, had contrived to sit on deck. But this day I retreated under cover behind the helmsman, when lo! a large wave burst over the ship, found me out in my retreat, and, nearly throwing down several stout sailors in its way, gave me the most complete salt-water bath I have had since I left New York. All that night we were tossed about in storm and darkness.

On the thirteenth the wailing of the norther grew fainter, and towards night it died away. On the fourteenth it veered round, and the coast of Tamaulipas appeared in sight faintly.

This morning opened with a slight norther; nevertheless, they have hung out the packet flag and cast anchor, in expectation of the pilot boat. Meanwhile all is at a standstill, *morally* speaking, for we are rolling so that it is scarce possible to write comprehensibly. We see the sad-looking shores of Tampico, long, low, and sandy, though to the south stretching out into gloomy, faintly-seen woods. We can distinguish the distant yellow sand and the white surf breaking furiously over the *bar*. The day is gloomy but not cold. A slight rain accompanies the light north wind. Sea gulls are flying in circles round the ship and skimming the surface of the waves. The master looks impatient and anxious, and prognosticates another week of northers. Vessels, they say, have been detained here thirty days, and some even three months! No notice is taken of our signal—a sign that the bar is impassable.

Sunday: January 16th, 1842

The ship has rolled and pitched all night, and today we remain in the same predicament.

Tuesday: January 18th, 1842
Tampico

Yesterday morning the wind was much lighter, and a pilot boat came out early, in which the captain set off with his dispatches—and we, being assured that we might cross the ominous bar in safety, hired for forty dollars a boat with ten sailors and a pilot, too glad at the prospect of touching the solid earth, even for one day. Having got into this boat and being rowed out to the bar, we found that there the sea was very high, even though the day was calm. The numerous wrecks that have taken place here have given this bar a decidedly bad reputation. Great precaution is necessary in crossing it, constant sounding, and calm weather. It is formed by a line of sandhills under the water, whose northern point crosses that to the southward, and across which there is a passage, whose position varies with the shifting sands, so that the pilots are chiefly guided by the surf.

Perched upon a sandbank was a regiment of enormous white pelicans, of thoughtful and sage-like physiognomy, ranged in a row as if to watch how we passed the bar. Over many a drowning crew they have screamed their wild sea dirge, and flapped their great white wings. But we crossed in safety, and in a few minutes more the sea and the bar were behind us, and we were rowing up the wide and placid river Pánuco —an agreeable change. We stopped at the house of the commandant, a large, tall individual who marched out and addressed us in English, and proved to be a native of the United States.

We stopped at a collection of huts, to let our sailors breakfast, where there is the house of a celebrated character, Don Leonardo Mata, a colossal old pilot, but who was from home at present. We amused ourselves by wandering along the beach of the river and making a collection of beautiful shells, which we left at the old pilot's house, to be kept there till our return. A sort of garden, attached to the house, is appropriately ornamented with the figurehead and anchor from a wreck. We got into our boat again and glided along the shores: on one side low and marshy, with great trees lying in the water; on the other also low, but thickly wooded and with valuable timber, such as logwood and ebony, together with cedars, India-rubber trees, limes, lemons, &c.

On the bare trunk of a great tree, half buried in the water, sat an amiable-looking alligator, its jaws distended in a sweet, unconscious grin as if it were catching flies, and not deigning to notice us, though we passed close to it. A canoe with an Indian woman in it was paddling about at a very little distance. All these beautiful woods to the right contain a host of venomous reptiles, particularly the rattlesnake. Cranes and herons were fluttering across the surface of the river, and the sportsmen brave the danger of the reptiles for the sake of shooting these and the beautiful rose-coloured spoonbills and pheasants that abound there.

The approach to Tampico is very pretty, and about two miles from it on the wooded shore, in a little verdant clearing, is a beautiful *ranchito*—a small farmhouse, white and clean, with a pretty piazza. In this farm they keep cows and sell milk, and it looks the very picture of rural comfort, which always comes with double charm when one has been accustomed to the sight of the foaming surges and the discomforts of a tempest-tossed ship. The sailors called it "El Paso (the pass) de Doña Cecilia"; which sounded delightfully romantic. The proprietress, this Doña Cecilia, who lives in such peaceful solitude, surrounded by mangroves, with no other drawback to her felicity but snakes and alligators, haunted my imagination. I trusted she was young, and lovely, and heartbroken: a pensive lay nun who had retreated from the vanities and deceits of the world to this secluded spot, where she lived like a heroine upon the produce of her flocks, with some "neat-handed Phillis" to milk the cows and churn the butter, while she sat rapt in contemplation of the stars above or the snakes below. It was not till after our arrival at Tampico that I had the mortification to discover that the interesting creature, the charming recluse, is seventy-eight—and has just buried her seventh husband! I accept the account doubtingly, but henceforth shall endeavour to picture her to my mind as an ancient enchantress, dwelling amongst serpents, and making her venomous charms of

> Adder's fork, and blind-worm's sting,
> Lizard's leg, and owlet's wing.[1]

As you approach Tampico, the first houses that meet the eye have the effect of a number of coloured bandboxes—some blue, some white —which a party of tired milliners have laid down amongst the rushes. On leaving the boat and walking through the town, though there are some solid stone dwellings, I could have fancied myself in a New England village: neat "shingle palaces," with piazzas and pillars—nothing Spanish—and, upon the whole, an air of cleanness and cheerfulness astonishing to me who have fancied Tampico an earthly purgatory. We afterwards heard that these houses were actually made in the United States and sent out here.[2]

There are some good-looking *stores;* and, though there is certainly little uniformity in the architecture of the houses, considering the city was built only sixteen years ago, I consider it a slandered place. In 1825 there were but a few Indian huts here, and any little commerce there was concentrated itself in Pueblo Viejo, which stands on the shores of a lake some miles off.

We were taken to the house of the Spanish consul, a fine, airy, stone building, with a gay view from the windows—the very first house that was built in the place. Its owner, Don José de la Lastra,[3] Spanish vice-consul, is not here himself, but we were kindly received by Don José de Gómez Mira, the consul. In the evening, all the principal Spaniards in the place came to see Calderón; and, having arrived here yesterday morning as perfect strangers, without the probability of finding anyone whom we knew, we find ourselves surrounded by the most unexpected and gratifying attentions. As to what is called society, there is literally none in Tampico. Those who live here have come in the hope of making their fortune; and the few married men who are amongst them have been unwilling to expose their wives to the unhealthy climate, the plague of mosquitoes and *jejenes,* the intermittent fevers—which are more to be dreaded here than the yellow fever—and the nearly total deprivation of respectable female society. The men, at least the Spaniards, unite in a sort of club and amuse their leisure evenings with cards and billiards, but the absence of ladies' society must always make it dull. Riding and shooting in the neighbourhood are their out-of-door amusements, and there is excellent sport along the river, which may be enjoyed when the heat is not too intense.

Our captain, who has paid us a visit this evening with several Englishmen, expects to get off tomorrow. We stayed at home in the morning on account of the heat, and wrote letters, but in the afternoon we made the most of our time, walking about the city, in which there is not much to see. There are many comfortable-looking large houses, generally built according to the customs of the country whereof the proprietor is a native. Were it not for the bar, which is a terrible obstacle—not only from the danger in crossing it, but from the detention that it causes, vessels having been stopped outside for months—Tampico would become a most flourishing port. Besides that the depth of water can permit vessels of burden to anchor near the town, there is an interior navigation up the country, for upwards of forty leagues.[4]

The banks of the river are described as being very beautiful, which we can easily believe from what we have already seen. But for its beauties after passing Tampico—its wooded shores dotted with white ranchos, its large cattle farms, and its picturesque old Indian town of Pánuco—we must trust to hearsay. The country in the vicinity is described as being a wilderness of rare trees, matted together with graceful and flowering creepers, the wild haunts of birds of bright and beautiful plumage. But our ardour to visit these tangled shrubberies was damped by the accounts of myriads of *jejenes* and *garrapatas*—little insects that bury themselves in the skin, producing irritation and fever—of the swarming mosquitoes, the horrid caymans that bask on the shore; and, worse than all, the venomous snakes that glide amongst the rank vegetation. Parrots and butterflies and fragrant flowers will not compensate for these.

We have just been hearing a curious circumstance connected with poisonous reptiles, which I have learned for the first time. Here, and all along the coasts, the people are in the habit of inoculating themselves with the poison of the rattlesnake, which renders them safe from the bite of all venomous animals. The person to be inoculated is pricked with the tooth of the serpent—on the tongue, in both arms, and on various parts of the body—and the venom introduced into the wounds. An eruption comes out, which lasts a few days. Ever after, these persons can handle the most venomous snakes with impunity; can make them come by calling them; have great pleasure in fondling them—and the bite of these persons is poisonous! You will not believe this, but we have the testimony of seven or eight respectable merchants to the fact. A gentleman who breakfasted here this morning says that he has been vainly endeavouring to make up his mind to submit to the operation, as he is very much exposed where he lives, and is obliged to travel a great deal on the coast. [He says] that when he goes on these expeditions he is always accompanied by his servant, an inoculated Negro, who has the power of curing him, should he be bit, by sucking the poison from the wound. He also saw this Negro cure the bite given by an inoculated Indian boy to a white boy with whom he was fighting, and who was the stronger of the two. The stories of the eastern jugglers, and their power over these reptiles, may perhaps be accounted for in this way. I cannot say that I should like to have so much *snaky* nature transferred into my composition, nor to live amongst people whose bite is venomous.

We have just returned from a moonlight walk to the Glorieta, a public promenade which they are making here, where there are some stone benches for the promenaders—close to which some public-spirited individuals had dragged the carcass of a horse, which obliged us to retrace our steps with all convenient speed.

As for provisions in this place, if we may judge by the specimens we have seen in this house, they are both good and abundant. We had especially fine fish, and a variety of vegetables. Tomorrow—alas!—we return to the packet, much refreshed, however, by two pleasant days on shore, and consoling ourselves for our prolonged voyage by the reflection that, had we gone direct to Havana, we should not have seen Tampico; and, as La Fontaine's travelling pigeon says,

He who sees little, little can he say;
But when my travels I describe some day,
And say, "That chanced to me—there I have been"—
The pleasure you will feel will be so great
You will believe, while hearing me relate,
That all these wonders you yourself have seen.[5]

Wednesday: January 19th, 1842
On board H. B. M. Packet Ship *Tyrian*

Once more on board our floating prison. A *norte* is expected this evening, but at least it will now be in our favour, and will drive us towards Havana.

Our Spanish friends concluded their cordial and disinterested kindness by setting off with us by daybreak this morning in a large boat with Spanish colours unfurled, crossing the bar with us, coming on board, and running no small risk in recrossing it, with every prospect of a norther before their eyes. We stopped at the house of the *"Marine Monster,"* Don Leonardo Mata, before crossing the bar, took up our shells, and had the felicity of making his acquaintance. He is a colossal old man, almost gigantic in height, and a Falstaff in breadth—gruff in his manners, yet with a certain clumsy good nature about him. He performs the office of pilot with so much exclusiveness, charging such high prices, governing the men with so iron a sway, and arranging everything so entirely according to his own fancy, that he is a complete sovereign in his own small way—the *tyrant of Tampico*. He has in his weatherbeaten face such a mixture of bluffness and slyness—with his gigantic person, and abrupt half-savage manners—that altogether I conceive him to be a character who might have been worthy [of] the attention of Walter Scott, had he chanced to encounter him. Old and repulsive as he is, he has lately married a pretty young girl—a subject on which he does not brook raillery. One amiable trait the old tyrant has in his character: his affection for his old mother, who is upwards of ninety, and who resides at Mahón, and to whom he is constant in his attentions. At one time he was in the habit of sending her small sums of money; but, as they were frequently lost, he sent her five hundred dollars at once by a safe conveyance. The old woman, he said, was so frightened by seeing such a quantity of money in her hut that she could not sleep, and at length entrusted it to a *friend*, who carried it off altogether. Since then he has assigned her fifteen dollars a month, upon which the old woman lives in what she considers great luxury.

We took leave of our friends an hour or two ago, but do not expect to set sail till the afternoon, as they are discharging the quicksilver which our vessel brought, and loading the silver which we carry away.[6] Three young Englishmen came on board this morning, to see the packet, and are making a disagreeable visit, being perfectly overwhelmed by seasickness.[7]

Thursday: January 20th, 1842

Last night arose a furious norther. Today it continues; but as it is driving us towards our desired haven, and away from these dangerous coasts, we need not complain. As usual on these occasions, I find myself alone on the deck, never suffering from the universal prostrator of landsmen. By way of variety I have been sitting in the cabin, holding on to the leg of a table, and trying to read Stephens, with as much attention as circumstances will permit. All further attempts at *writing* must be delayed!

Sunday: January 30th, 1842

On the twenty-first the norther continued with unabated violence, the wild wind and the boiling waves struggling on the agitated bosom of the ocean—great billows swelling up one after the other and threatening to engulf us—the ship labouring and creaking as if all its timbers were parting asunder, and the captain in such a state of intense suffering that we were in great apprehension for his life. Horrible days, and yet more horrible nights! But they were succeeded by fine weather, and at length we had the consolation of seeing the moon, smiling placidly down upon us, like a harbinger of peace. On the evening of the twenty-sixth the full moon rose with a troubled countenance, her disk obscured by angry clouds. She shook them off, but still looked turbid and superb. A gloomy cloud, black as night, still stretched over her like a pall—thickly veiling yet not entirely obscuring her light—and soon after she appeared, riding serenely in the high heavens, mildly triumphant. Of all who sing the praises of the moon, who should love her blessed beams from his inmost heart like the seaman? Then the angry clouds dispersed, the north wind blew freshly, but not fiercely, as if even his blustering fury were partly soothed by the influence of her placid light; the studding sails were set, and the *Tyrian* bounded on her course, eight knots an hour.

The next day the wind died away, and then blew lightly from the opposite quarter. We were about two hundred and fifty miles from Havana, but were then driven in the direction of Yucatán. The two following days we had contrary wind, but charming weather. We studied the chart, and read, and walked on deck, and played at drafts, and sat in the moonlight. The sea was covered with flying fish, and the "Portuguese men-of-war," as the sailors call the independent little nautilus, sailed contemptuously past us in their fairy barks, as if they had been little steamers. A man fell overboard but, the weather being calm, was saved immediately.

We have been tacking about and making our way slowly towards Havana, in a zigzag line. Yesterday evening the moon rose in the form of a large heart, of a red gold colour. This morning, about four o'clock, a fine fresh breeze sprung up from the northeast, and we are going on our course at a great rate, with some hopes of anchoring below the Morro this evening. Today being Sunday, we had prayers on deck, which the weather had not before permitted—the sailors all clean and attentive, as English sailors are. Last night they sang "Rule Britannia," with great enthusiasm.[8]

Monday: January 31st, 1842
Havana

Last evening we once more saw the beautiful bay of Havana, once more passed the Morro—and our arrival was no sooner known than the Captain-General, Don Gerónimo Valdés,[9] sent his *falúa* to bring us to the city, and even wished us to go to his palace; but Don Bernardo Hechavarría, who gave us so hospitable a reception on our first visit, came on board and kindly insisted on taking us to his house, where we found everything as elegant and comfortable as before, and from whence I now write these few lines.[10]

In the midst of our pleasure at being once more on dry land, surrounded by our former friends, and at receiving letters from home, we were shocked and distressed to hear of the unexpected death of our friend, the Señora de Gutiérrez Estrada, who had followed her husband to Havana in his exile. What a blow to him, to her mother, to all her friends![11]

I shall send off this letter by the first opportunity, that you may know of our safe arrival.

54

With Friends in Cuba; Home by Steamer

Sunday: February 27th, 1842
Havana

It has been very agreeable for us to return here as private individuals, and to receive the same attentions as when we came in a public situation, but now with more real friendliness. Having arrived at the time of the carnival, we have been in the midst of masked balls—which are curious to see for once—[and] of operas, dinners, and every species of gaiety. But returning so soon, I shall enter into no details. The weather is beautiful, and this house, situated on the bay, receives every sea breeze as it blows. The Elssler is still attracting immense and enthusiastic crowds, and is now dancing at the theatre of Tacón, where she is seen to much more advantage than in the other.[1]

We have been breakfasting in the luxurious *quintas* in the neighbourhood, driving in the Paseo every evening in an open *volante*, attending the opera—in short, leading so gay a life that a little rest in the country will be agreeable; and we have accepted with pleasure the invitation of Count and Countess Fernandina to spend some time at La Angosta, one of his country places, a sugar and coffee estate. General Bustamante arrived in the *Jasón* a few days after us, they having sailed later. They had been very anxious concerning the fate of the *Tyrian* in these northern gales off Tampico.

We have received letters from our Mexican friends, and learn, with great sorrow, of the death of the Dowager Marquesa de Vivanco and the Señora Acha of Pátzcuaro, also the *murder* of a Spanish physician, with whom we were intimately acquainted, at his distant hacienda.

Sunday: March 13th, 1842
La Angosta

We have spent a most agreeable fortnight at La Angosta, and have also visited the Count and Countess Villanueva in their plantation near this.[2] General Bustamante was here for a day or two. Lord Morpeth also passed a few days with us—so that altogether we have had a pleasant party.[3] We have been delighted with the elegant hospitality, without ostentation or etiquette, which we have met with here. But we shall now return so soon that I shall reserve all particulars till we meet.[4]

Thursday: April 28th, 1842
On board the Steamship *Medway*

With a warning of only three hours we came on board this splendid steamer, eight days ago, after taking a hurried leave of our kind friends —at least of all those who are now in Havana, for the Count and Countess de Fernandina, and the Count and Countess de Villanueva are still in the country.[5] Don Bernardo Hechavarría and his family accompanied us to the ship in the government *falúa*. General Bustamante, with his young aide-de-camp, together with Señor Gutiérrez Estrada, and various other gentlemen, hearing of our sudden departure, came out in boats to take leave of us. Alas! those leave-takings.

We had the agreeable surprise of finding that we were acquainted with all our fellow passengers. There are our particular friends the Escandóns, the padre Fúrlong,[6] and Mr. Geanes, all from Mexico; M. Duflot de Mofras, who was attached to the French legation in Mexico, and is now returning from a mission to California;[7] Mr. Bryant and Miss Lee of Boston, &c. We came on board on the evening of the twentieth, but did not leave the harbour till the morning of the twenty-first. The day was beautiful and, as we passed out, we could distinguish the waving of many handkerchiefs from the balconies. In this floating palace with large airy berths, a beautiful cabin, an agreeable society, books, a band of music, ices, &c.—not to mention that important point, an excellent and goodhearted captain—we have passed our time as pleasantly as if we were in the most splendid hotel.

On the twenty-third we went out in a little boat, in the middle of the night, to Nassau, in New Providence, to buy some of those beautiful specimens of shell flowers for which that place is celebrated. We set off again at three in the morning of the twenty-fourth, on which day, being Sunday, we had prayers on board. The weather was beautiful and, even with contrary wind, the *Medway* went *steaming* on her course at the rate of nine knots an hour.

On the twenty-fifth we lay off Savannah. A pilot came on board, and we went up the river in a boat to the city, where we passed an agreeable day, and in the evening returned to the ship. Crowds of people from Savannah went out to see the steamer. The next day we ca anchor off Charleston, and again a pilot came on board—but the day was stormy and gloomy, and only two of the passengers went on shore. We have now had several days of bad weather—wind and rain, and one night a storm of thunder and lightning—yet down in the cabin there is scarce any motion, and we have been sitting reading and writing as quietly as if we were in our own rooms. After two years and a half of spring and summer, we feel the cold very much.

Friday: April 29th, 1842

We are now passing the Narrows. Once more the green shores of Staten Island appear in sight. We left them two years and six months ago, just as winter was preparing to throw his white shroud over the dolphin hues of the dying autumn—the weather gloomy and tearful. Now the shores are covered with the vegetation of spring, and the grass is as green as emeralds. I shall write no more, for we must arrive today, and I shall be the bearer of my own dispatches.

The day is bright and beautiful. The band is playing its gayest airs. A little boat is coming from the Quarantine. In a few minutes more we shall be *at home!*

First Appearance of Life in Mexico; Early Comments; Subsequent History

It is plain from the record that William Hickling Prescott, who admired *Life in Mexico* not only as the product of a friend but also as a valuable piece of work, had much to do with its appearance in print. His generous preface gave solid sponsorship to a quasi-anonymous book by a then unknown author:

> The present work is the result of observations made during a two years' residence in Mexico, by a lady, whose position there, made her intimately acquainted with its society, and opened to her the best sources of information in regard to whatever could interest an enlightened foreigner. It consists of letters written to the members of her own family, and, *really,* not intended originally,—however incredible the assertion,—for publication. Feeling a regret that such rich stores of instruction and amusement, from which I have so much profited, myself, should be reserved for the eyes of a few friends only, I strongly recommended that they should be given to the world. This is now done, with a few such alterations and omissions as were necessary in a private correspondence; and although the work would derive more credit from the author's own name, than from anything which I can say, yet as she declines prefixing it, I feel much pleasure in making this statement by way of introduction to the public.

In spite of the date 1843 on the book's title page, we know from a letter Prescott wrote on December 31, 1842—in which he referred to the book's having "just been published"—that the first American edition of *Life in Mexico* actually appeared during the last few days of 1842. Final loose ends must have been knotted with all speed, as shown by a letter in the New York Public Library written in Fanny's own hand to her American publishers, Little and Brown. This indicates that a corrected copy of the table of contents and "the remainder of the manuscript— together with a glossary" were not delivered until the second week of December. (The glossary of Spanish words, added so late on the advice of the learned George Ticknor, is not included in the present edition.

Its equivalent is incorporated, together with additional foreign words and phrases, in alphabetical order in the index.)

Life in Mexico in its first American edition consists of two smallish volumes, each with an engraved frontispiece. The typography is handsome, with well-spaced lines and ample margins. Judging by the pragmatic standard of the supply in today's old book market, the edition could not have been a large one.

Supplementing his preface, Prescott also gave the book a warm and unqualified send-off by means of a signed review in the January issue of the *North American Review*. One notes that he made the identity of the author ("Madame C_____ de la B_____" according to the title page) crystal clear by naming her husband and his office, though Fanny herself remained merely her husband's "accomplished wife."

Comments passed by a number of other prominent Americans were likewise favorable. Alexander Everett, former United States minister to Spain and evidently one of the book's first readers, wrote his wife on January 1, 1843, that it was "piquant, characteristic, and altogether first rate." (His more reserved younger brother Edward Everett—American minister to England—some months later noted his enjoyment of *Life in Mexico* in his diary, but added: "It must be admitted however that much of the amusement is purchased by the invasion of the Sanctity of private life.") The rising young Boston lawyer Charles Sumner was an enthusiast: "It will have a great run," he predicted to a friend. And in far-away Spain an aging diplomat with an international literary reputation—Washington Irving—recommended the "lively work" to his niece.

One published American review of the book is of especial interest in view of the deteriorating relationship between the United States and Mexico which culminated in war three years later. The *United States Magazine and Democratic Review* for February 1843 said: "These volumes are beautifully printed, admirably written, full of wit, sprightliness, good feeling, and solid information, on a topic of intense interest, with which the great mass of us have very little acquaintance, and concerning which we have the most vague and erroneous notions. They deserve a more extended notice than we can now give them. They must and will be read, and so far as read will tend to dissipate many of our errors concerning our Mexican neighbors, whom we are in the ungenerous habit of under-rating, and increase our respect for them."

Arrangements for a British edition of *Life in Mexico* had been initiated late in the summer of 1842 when Prescott wrote Charles Dickens (whom he had met during the latter's triumphal visit to Boston the winter before) to ask his help in placing the book with a London publisher. Dickens obliged by making arrangements with his own publisher, then Chapman and Hall. On the first day of December Prescott was able to inform Dickens that Volume I of the American edition was on its way to him—presumably in the form of printed, unbound sheets. The rest of the material, including the two engravings used in the American edition, followed soon thereafter.

The British publishers incongruously determined to issue the work as a part of their "Foreign Library," described as "a series of translations of popular and interesting foreign works." They must have acted with dispatch, for the first half of *Life in Mexico*—called Part I—was out in time for reviewers to begin their extensive discussion of it by January 28, 1843. Part II seems to have appeared about three weeks later.

Printed on somewhat tightly filled pages, and minus the two engravings of the American edition, the first English edition is a less distinguished example of book-making than its Boston predecessor. In addition, it contains a substantially greater number of typographic errors.

We have never seen, nor do we know of the existence even, of an example of the first English edition in precisely the form in which it initially came from the press: in paper wrappers, unbound, in two separate parts, though with continuous pagination. However, Mr. C. L. Hindle of the Bodleian Library at Oxford, who kindly answered our inquiry on the subject made long ago, pointed out that in accordance with the prevailing practice of the day, *Life in Mexico*'s two parts would have been divested of their paper wrappers by the process of binding. In any case, not long after the issuance of the second portion, Chapman and Hall was offering *Life in Mexico* bound as one volume in cloth and bearing the words "Foreign Library II" on the spine. (By this time, as may be seen from an advertisement in the April first issue of the *Athenæum*, the author's full name was being used in promoting the book.)

In general the public reception of the British edition was enthusiastic. The *Athenæum* of January 28 and the *Examiner* of the same date, possessed only of Part I, were highly pleased. The former called upon "all to do admiring homage to the lively talents of Madame Calderon de la Barca," and after Part II became available went on with comment and excerpts for three more issues. The *Examiner* liked the "uncommonly spirited, lively, and amusing" style, but deplored the author's "effort to set everything forth somewhat too picturesquely." The *Spectator*, reviewing Part I on February 4, liked the spontaneity of *Life in Mexico*, but the author's use of blanks for some names came in for sharp adverse comment: "Mr. Prescott should have attended to this when he undertook the responsibility of giving the book to the world."

The *Illustrated London News* for February 11 also approved of the new book. It reported that speculation was rife as to whether the author was English or American, and guessed that she was Scottish. *John Bull* for March 11 announced: "These two gay and sparkling volumes are the production of Madame CALDERON DE LA BARCA, the lady of the first Ambassador credited by Spain to Mexico after the recognition of the independence of the latter by the mother country." The reviewer added this comment: "She does not, we are happy to say, aim at depth, and is consequently infinitely truer and more natural, and in fact, more profound, than they who do."

But all was not favorable. A sharply negative note was struck in the April issue of the *Foreign and Colonial Quarterly Review*, whose staff members were evidently determined not to be caught in the trap of a possible literary hoax. *Life in Mexico* was "a work elaborated at home, from rude notes of the time, aided by a vivid imagination. . . . We well know that many a traveller has passed over many miles on paper, by the aid of a good map, a good general history, and a fertile brain. . . . Ladies . . . are fond of embroidery. Our ancestresses embroidered on silk or satin . . . Now we embroider, some on canvass, some few on silk, some more on paper . . ." The author, according to the reviewer, was said to be French.

In the summer of 1843, Fanny Calderón de la Barca was visiting in Scotland and could hardly have missed the comments in the July issue of the *Edinburgh Review* (in which, one notices, she was identified as "a Scottish lady," though not by name). The friendly tone must have pleased the author, but she may or may not have been amused over the fact that her "feats of personal strength" filled the editors with amazement. They went on to say that "all this seems the lady's very element, and gone through with a hearty honest good-will, which makes the reader long to have been one of her party. Her curiosity is as prodigious as her endurance." In an evident riposte to the charge by the *Foreign and Colonial Quarterly Review* that *Life in Mexico* was bogus, the *Edinburgh Review* added: "Some have gone so far as to pronounce her work altogether an article of fictitious manufacture—Paris-made, we believe. A more genuine book, in air as well as reality, it would be difficult to find."

Other comments of 1843 which we have encountered include material in the *Literary Gazette*, which liked the book on the whole but thought that "a little more repose" would have been agreeable, and that the use of initials rather than full names and frequent French phrases was unfortunate; the *Monthly Review*, which applauded the "freshness of spirit" but deplored what it termed the cabalistic symbols that concealed identities; and *Chambers's Edinburgh Journal*, which gravely observed that the book was graphic but rather light, and expressed worry over the love of frivolity evidently so rampant in Mexico. (How, it wondered, could such a nation possibly hang together?)

The sharpest British remarks regarding *Life in Mexico* appeared some two years later in the *Quarterly Review*, a magazine which had given it a passing kind word in December 1843. Prim disapproval of the book, and more especially of its author, was expressed by a lady reviewer who in June 1845 undertook to analyze the work of twelve recent travel books written by women. *Life in Mexico* was admittedly a brilliant book, she said, but it was *un-English;* there was nothing *domestic* about it. "This is very striking and picturesque writing, and would do admirably under Basil Hall's or any other man's name, but, to our feeling, there is neither a woman's hand nor heart in it." Forgetting that Fanny's attendance at bullfights was an essential part of her job as the Spanish minister's wife, the reviewer compared her unfavorably with a more sensitive lady traveler who had fled a Spanish bull ring in horror. Without doubt, the author of *Life in Mexico* "would stand a public execution as well." The book made it plain, the reviewer asserted, that Fanny had not only abandoned her own nationality but also had become a Catholic. "We feel that it is not only tropical life we are leading, but with the exception of an occasional trait of Scotch shrewdness, and, we must say it, of Yankee vulgarity, a tropical mind which is addressing us."

In Mexico, the book's reception was wholly critical. On April 28 (four months after *Life in Mexico*'s initial appearance in Boston), the recently established semi-weekly newspaper *El Siglo Diez y Nueve* (The Nineteenth Century) spoke of the "public anxiety" regarding the contents of the new book—two or three copies of which had arrived and were circulating—and announced its plan to issue serially a Spanish translation. Names of persons would be presented exactly as in the original, whether complete, partial, or concealed by blanks. Annotations would be provided to point out those statements considered to be exaggerated or unfounded. Also, comment would be welcome from individuals who might consider themselves unjustly dealt with or who might wish to point out errors in the book, provided, of course, that they expressed themselves with decency and moderation. With this by way of explanation, *"Carta 1"* (Letter 1) was printed in full in the same issue.

Two days later the government-supported newspaper, the *Diario del Gobierno de la República Mexicana,* came out with an editorial of extraordinary bitterness. This not only censured the editors of the *Siglo* for venturing to put into Mexican hands the "unjust, passionate, virulent diatribes" dealt out by the Señora Calderón in return for the exquisite and benevolent hospitality with which she and her husband had been treated, but also went on to upbraid her husband who, it was averred, must have had a hand in the more serious parts of the book, thus betraying his trust as a diplomat and surrendering himself to vile passions and the detraction of highly respected persons. The editors of the *Siglo* were warned that they could be called to judgment for any injuries they might publish. On the following day the same editorial was repeated with minor changes.

Nothing further appeared in the *Siglo*'s next three issues, but on May 9 there was printed a long letter signed by Juan Covo, the Spanish author of the hymn of welcome with which the Calderóns were serenaded soon after their arrival. He did not read English well enough, said Covo, to judge the book in detail but neither, he surmised, did most of those who were discussing it "in every house and on every corner." Convinced that few understood its real character, he pointed out that *El Siglo* proposed to see to it that everyone interested could in fact find out what was in the book, and have access to its columns for discussion and corrections. He suggested that a newspaper supported by the government had no business to indulge in personal grudges. He decried the insults and "criminal accusations" leveled against Calderón, whom he stoutly defended against any possible charge of diplomatic indiscretion. Less warm, one notes, was his defense of the book's author, his esteemed friend "the poor señora, who in an unhappy hour conceived the idea of publishing her letters."

On May 11, the *Diario*, now slightly on the defensive, explained that the opinions expressed in the matter were those of its editors, published on their own responsibility and not dictated by governmental authority. "It is very strange," it said, "that while Sra. Calderón's book was passing from hand to hand no one expressed himself angered by the diatribes it contains," but "hardly has the *Diario* ventured a few preliminary remarks in defense of the honor of the Republic when heavens and earth are stirred up." There was bitter reference to Fanny's "disdain" and Calderón was again charged with a share of responsibility in the matter: Just as Adam was granted superiority over Eve, so Calderón must have granted permission to his wife to amuse herself at the expense of the Mexican people.

On the following day, May 12, the *Diario* continued the attack. It termed the words of Calderón's defender Covo outrageously insolent, and Señor Covo himself as one who had gone beyond the limits of decency. As to the *Siglo*'s plan of publishing the letters in sequence, it was predicted that "on the day that they are in the hands of everyone, there will hardly be a Mexican who reads them who will not feel the blood boil in his veins with the most righteous indignation." The book's author was termed the new Mrs. Trollope, and the suspicion that her husband aided her was again reiterated. "We want only justice for Mexico, and that her circumstances be not disfigured or corrupted by ruinous passions. . . . The men, great and small, who have been the uncalled-for objects of Sra. Calderón's hatred and wrath care little about that, because they are known in their country; and the reputation that they enjoy need not be damaged by the caprice of a foreign woman . . ."

On May 14, the *Siglo* presented "Letter 2," which in its original form dealt briefly with the Calderóns' experiences in Havana. Accompanying it was an editorial repeating the offer to correct any "erroneous facts and unfounded accusations against the nation." Its next issue, May 21, offered "Letter 3," covering the voyage from Havana to Mexico. "Letter 4"—the first to deal with Mexico—appeared on May 26. A writer in the *Diario* voiced caustic comment on this chapter and its author, alleging many insults to Veracruz, its inhabitants, and their clothes. (Would the Scots be pleased, asked the *Diario*'s commentator, if Mexican visitors were to make public their amusement over Scotland's soldiery, costumed like ballet dancers?)

The next installment in the *Siglo* would have dealt with no less a person than General Santa Anna who, at the time these heated discussions were taking place, was president and in effect dictator of Mexico. This fifth letter did not appear. The *Siglo*'s project of publishing a complete Spanish translation of *Life in Mexico* so soon after its original appearance was apparently abandoned. An article in the *Diario* of June 20 pointing out the negligible value of Madame Calderón's book and comparing it unfavorably with another travel work—now forgotten—closed the government paper's successful campaign of suppression.

Life in Mexico has been reissued many times since the appearance of these two first editions.

The earliest such reissue was made by its original British publishers, Chapman and Hall—apparently to keep up with a continuing demand. It bore the same date of 1843 as its predecessor, but some copies included advertisements bound in at the back with dates as late as 1847. This second British edition, reset from start to finish, corrected some of the earlier errors but introduced a few new ones. The original two-page glossary was compressed to one page, and the main text reduced one page in length by shrinking the space devoted to the "Mexican Airs," making a total of 436 rather than 437 pages. While the differences are trivial, it may be of some interest that this edition has until now served as the basis for all, save one, of the full-length twentieth-century versions of *Life in Mexico* in English. (See, for example, the passage near the end of "Letter the Forty-Fifth" which describes the triumphant entry of General Santa Anna somewhat bafflingly as *en Rio*, rather than *en Roi* as the author had it in the two original editions of her work.)

The next appearance of *Life in Mexico* was an abridgement, brought out by the London and Belfast firm of Simms and M'Intyre in 1852, as Volume V in their series called "The Bookcase." Surviving family materials indicate that Fanny Calderón de la Barca, following her conversion to the Catholic faith in 1847, would not have authorized a reissue without minor modifications in some of her passages dealing with religious matters. As no such revisions were made in this 1852 version, it was probably printed without her knowledge or approval, and presumably without compensation.

Life in Mexico had been long out of print when, in 1907, it was made available once more by "The Aztec," a bookshop in the Mexican capital dealing also in antiquities and curios. This version was based on a reprinting of the text of the first English edition. A few years later, in 1913, *Life in Mexico* was brought out by Everyman's Library, and inclusion in that famous series brought it to the attention of a wide public. For the first time it was accompanied by supplementary material, in the form of an introduction by Henry Baerlein, an English journalist and novelist familiar with Mexico. Subsequently the book was reissued from the same plates under the sponsorship of the Junior League of Mexico City.

Although a translation of *Life in Mexico* into Spanish was undertaken by the Mexican diplomat Victoriano Salado Alvarez, only a part of his work was printed. The first full-length published translation in Spanish was that made by Enrique Martínez Sobral, issued in two volumes in 1920, with a preface by Manuel Romero de Terreros, Marqués de San Francisco. In this version the names of a few of the more easily identified characters were filled in. In view of the tempest produced in 1843 by the then-new book, it may be of interest to note that excerpts of the translation by Martínez Sobral were brought out in 1944 by the Mexican government, issued through its Secretaría de Educación Pública (as No. 14 in an inexpensive series entitled Biblioteca Enciclopédica Popular). A subsequent complete Mexican edition of the same translation was accompanied by a preface by Artemio de Valle-Arizpe.

In June 1959 there appeared in Mexico a new Spanish translation by Felipe Teixidor—soon reissued as a large two-volume edition with a prologue and many illustrations. The first to be annotated, it constituted a landmark in the history of the book.

In 1965, selections translated by Emilio Cecchi were published in Italy under the title of *Vita in Messico.*

In the meantime, in 1952, there appeared in Mexico an English version illustrated with sixteen plates of the period. Incomplete, though without a statement to that effect, it appears to have been largely based on the old condensation of 1852, with some supplementation from the full text.

After an absence of some years from Everyman's Library, *Life in Mexico* was again included in the series. An introduction by Manuel Romero de Terreros, Marqués de San Francisco, was substituted for that earlier used. In 1960 the book was issued in paperback by Doubleday & Company.

Procedure Used in
the Preparation of This Edition

In earlier editions the chapters of the book were assigned a uniform system of designations, running from "LETTER THE FIRST" through "LETTER THE FIFTY-FOURTH." We have retained the same basic organization of material and numerical sequence, but have substituted a brief descriptive title for each chapter. In addition, we have grouped chapters under a number of broad headings which conform to the logical flow of principal events.

Full dates, each including the day of the week, have been provided on a consistent basis wherever known, in place of the more random procedure originally employed. At the start of each chapter the place is always given; for subsequent dates within any chapter the place is indicated only when it differs from that previously mentioned. The editors assume sole responsibility for the wording of all headings, though these are based on the author's statements. Heading material in slightly differentiated type has been drawn directly from the author's hitherto unpublished journals. Heading material in brackets is based on supposition, supported by internal evidence.

Throughout we have tried to standardize the author's not always consistent spelling, forms of abbreviation, capitalization, etc., while still using some of her characteristic British forms. In deference to consistency and modern usage, and to aid comprehension, we have taken the liberty of adjusting punctuation. This was particularly necessary in passages from the Journal, which was punctuated largely with dashes. Similarly, we have not always followed the sometimes lavish underscoring of the Journal. We have broken up some of the longer paragraphs (and occasionally longer sentences), especially when conversation is presented or when dealing with material from the Journal, which was written in almost uninterrupted blocks under each date. In some few instances, the sequence of paragraphs has been altered, usually to conform more closely to the sequence of material in the Journal. A few, but not all, grammatical errors have been corrected. The Spanish version of some quoted material has been omitted. Occasional words added by the editors (with the exception of "and" and "or," as noted below) have been placed in brackets.

For geographic names in Mexico we have followed modern usage as verified, with the co-operation of Mexican authorities, by the American Geographical Society and published in its *Index to Map of Hispanic America*, Volume II. For a few places not to be found in this document, we have depended on local usage insofar as it could be determined.

The interweaving of the newly available material from the Journal with the previously printed text has inevitably presented special problems requiring judgment. The resolution of these has been guided by the policy that historical accuracy and human interest should, when necessary, take precedence over literary form. In general, the first English edition has been used as a base, with passages from the Journal added or substituted at appropriate points, set off in slightly differentiated type. In some cases the precise sequence of words has been altered where valid reasons for such modification appeared to exist. Whenever Journal material and previous text were not identical, a full combination of the two was provided insofar as practicable. Where, however, the resulting wording would have been redundant, that wording which appeared more informal, revealing, or spontaneous has generally been employed. This procedure was followed even where differences appeared minor or trivial. Where no basis for choice seemed to exist, or where the use of wording from the Journal would have resulted in an unacceptably awkward construction, we have kept to the wording of the previously published text. (The second chapter is an exception, as explained in the notes.)

It must be recognized that, in combining Journal material with text, slight adjustments in wording have sometimes been necessary or desirable for mechanical reasons to insure a grammatical result and general readability. The introduction of the word "and" has sometimes been essential in order to be able to combine wording from both the Journal and the text. Similarly the word "or" has occasionally been required. Sometimes, in combining Journal and text, it was found that they employed different tenses or verb forms. In such cases it was obviously necessary at times to choose one or the other for consistent use throughout the resulting passage. Where, as a result of combining material, sentences of too great length or complexity resulted, we have divided them into parts. In a few cases it has been necessary to omit a non-redundant word or two of no special significance. There has been no censorship.

Our strong endeavor throughout has been to preserve with accuracy the author's intent and spirit, and especially the full flavor of her first impressions. Except for certain mechanical adjustments of the type noted in the previous paragraph, every effort has been made to insure that the words (as well as the thoughts) are strictly her own. In a few significant instances where wording from text and Journal differed to such a degree that they could not sensibly be meshed in the manner described, both "before and after" wording is presented through the aid of notes.

Occasional adjustments of the specific types mentioned have not been differentiated. To have done so would, in most cases, have proved confusing and extremely burdensome to the reader. (How, for example, would a change of tense, made necessary by a merging of Journal with text, be indicated?) In the few cases where the addition of words other than "and" and "or" were required such added words are shown in brackets. (Occasional words added to material derived from the Journal are without exception shown in brackets.) Should any reader wish to know the exact nature of the adjustments made, other than in passages from the Journal, he may determine them through comparison with an earlier edition.

The name of the author's husband, which was printed "C_____n" throughout the original text, has in this edition been spelled out in full as "Calderón." The slightly differentiated type face previously mentioned has also been used for all personal names and identifications derived from the marked first American edition of *Life in Mexico* which we have termed the Singer copy (see note 16, pages 679–680).

To show the style of the Journal and to illustrate the editorial procedures that have been employed as here described, we present the text of the opening page of the first English edition followed by the corresponding portion of the Journal—the merging of which has resulted in the opening text of this edition.

LIFE IN MEXICO

THIS morning, at 10 o'clock, we stepped on board the steamboat Hercules, destined to convey us to our packet with its musical name. The day was foggy and gloomy, as if refusing to be comforted, even by an occasional smile from the sun. All prognosticated that the Norma would not sail to-day, but "where there's a will," &c. Several of our friends accompanied us to the wharf; the Russian Minister, the Minister of Buenos Ayres, Mr. _____, who tried hard to look sentimental, and even brought tears into his eyes by some curious process; Judge _____, Mr. _____, and others, from whom we were truly sorry to part.

The Norma was anchored in one of the most beautiful points of the bay, and the steamboat towed us five miles, until we had passed the Narrows. The wind was contrary, but the day began to clear up, and the sun to scatter the watery clouds.

Still there is nothing so sad as a retreating view. It is as if time were visibly in motion; and as here we had to part from _____, we could only distinguish, as through a misty veil, the beauties of the bay; the shores covered to the water's edge with trees rich in their autumnal colouring; the white houses on Staten Island—the whole gradually growing fainter, till like a dream, they faded away.

The pilot has left us, breaking our last link with the land. We

JOURNAL

This morning at 10 o'clock, we left New York—and got on board the steam-boat Hercules—to be conveyed to our ship with its musical name—The morning foggy and rainy—so that all prognosticated we should not go—Nevertheless all were mistaken—"Where there's a will, there's a way"—We took leave of our friends who had come to see us off—*Bodisco*—who is about taking a part in *El Si de las Niñas*—Kramer—who tried to look sentimental, and brought tears into his eyes, by some process he must have learned in St. Petersburgh—"The tear forgot as soon as shed." Judge Patterson—Mariquita Harmony and Suarez, who looked like a stale lemon—and Trueman who appeared on the scene, to increase the effect at the last moment—also General Alvear &c &c.—Richmond—A. Norman—Jane & Mary Jones—accompanied us as far as the Ship—Luggage hoisted in—

The Steam-boat towed us some distance—Stoughton came in a boat, and made the amiable. His motto is—"Welcome the coming, speed the parting guest."

Acknowledgments

The list of those to whom we are indebted is long, and the cumulative magnitude of our debt is great. We regret that some of those who aided us do not survive to receive our thanks today. Our record of acknowledgments would be still longer if, over the years during which we have worked, with many interruptions, on Fanny Calderón de la Barca and her book, we had kept a more consistent roster of the names of all those who helped us in various ways. Our humble apologies to unnamed collaborators.

First, and by far most important, we wish to express our unending sense of obligation to the composer Mary Howe of Washington, D.C., whose long and effective life closed in 1964. Without her generosity this edition of *Life in Mexico* would never have been undertaken. As great-granddaughter of Richmond Inglis Macleod, older sister of the childless Fanny Calderón de la Barca, Mary Howe had inherited various family documents and memorabilia, including the portrait of Fanny reproduced in this volume, and the two manuscript journals which have made possible its augmented text. Mrs. Howe's kindness was unbounded, and not the least of the pleasures of working on this book was coming to know her, her husband Walter Bruce Howe, and her three children— Dr. Bruce Howe, Dr. Calderon Howe, and Mrs. Molly Lynn—as well as her niece, Mrs. Leonid Ourusoff, inheritor of Angel Calderón de la Barca's likeness which is also reproduced in this volume. (Introduction to this gifted family stemmed from the long-ago kindness of Justice Oliver Wendell Holmes, then next-door neighbor of Mrs. Calderon Carlisle, Mrs. Howe's mother.)

We are also under great obligation to a generous member of another branch of the Inglis family: Mrs. R. Lucien Patton of Ligonier, Pennsylvania, a descendant of Fanny's younger sister, Harriet Inglis Addison. Among various inherited possessions made available to us by Mrs. Patton was a copy of the two-volume first American edition of *Life in Mexico* which contains handwritten identifications of many of the persons whose names Fanny left blank or partially blank in her published book. Its significance for our work is obvious. (To the impersonal but effective hand of *The New York Times Book Review*, which brought our efforts to Mrs. Patton's attention, our thanks are also due.)

Another descendant of Harriet Inglis Addison—her grandson Santiago Fernández Giménez of Ciboure, near St. Jean-de-Luz, France—was a delightful and informative correspondent. We acknowledge his aid with gratitude.

Still another Inglis family connection—though, as he explained, it would be necessary to go back to the fourteenth century to establish the link—was extraordinarily helpful to us: Mr. John Alexander Inglis of Edinburgh and Auchindinny House, Midlothian, enthusiastic researcher into the genealogical records of the Inglis family. Our indebtedness to him and, for personal reasons to his daughter Mrs. Edward Dalmahoy, is large. As the result of inquiry made for us by Mr. Inglis, we have likewise benefited from the aid of another valued Edinburgh correspondent: Mr. R. L. Lindsay, Writer to the Signet, whose legal firm is descended from that initiated in the eighteenth century by Laurence Inglis, Fanny's grandfather.

Numerous others, not to be named here, have helped us with material regarding the non-Mexican days of the author of this book. We gratefully proffer them a collective salute. The facts they have made available to us, with proper credit, will appear in a later biography of Fanny Calderón de la Barca—as material on her change-filled life far exceeds appropriate limitations for the introduction to this volume. Most of the acknowledgments that follow therefore relate to Mexico and the period of Fanny's life there.

Needless to say, the dedicated zeal of librarians and library aides has most fundamentally served to facilitate our work. Within the United States the Library of Congress has been by far our greatest resource. Long have we drawn on its superb riches—and, while living in Washington during four war years, enjoyed the coveted privilege of the weekend withdrawal of certain categories of books, for which we were indebted to the Librarian of Congress, Archibald MacLeish. The library's Hispanic Foundation, for obvious reasons, had the most to offer us. Our great appreciation is due to its personnel, including Dr. Howard F. Cline, Francisco Aguilera, and Mrs. Concha Romero James. From Elizabeth Wilder of the library's Archive of Hispanic Culture we received various thoughtful suggestions. We are similarly grateful to many others at the Library of Congress who have helped us either in person or through correspondence, and we wish to thank also those administrative authorities who allocated study space for our use during many visits to Washington after 1944 and who made it possible for us to do photographic work.

In Washington we also benefited from the admirable service at the National Archives, particularly in relation to its files of diplomatic correspondence.

The Newberry Library of Chicago has been an especially enjoyable haven for work. In our use of the rich Mexican materials of its Ayer Collection we were the recipients of the efficient kindness of Frederick Hall.

The Massachusetts Historical Society numbers among its many treasures the remarkable international correspondence of William Hickling Prescott. This includes a number of letters to and from Fanny Calderón de la Barca and her husband. We are grateful to Roger Wolcott, editor of the scholarly *Correspondence of William Hickling Prescott, 1833–1847*, and to Allyn B. Forbes and Stephen T. Riley, successive directors, for their co-operation and permission to quote numerous passages from that book and also from certain unpublished materials. To Denys P. Myers, Marshall Swan, and Miss Shirley E. Wood, who at various times helped by searching out and copying pertinent material on our behalf, we offer our thanks.

We are obligated to various members of the staff of the New York Public Library; to Miss Carolyn E. Jakeman of Harvard's Houghton Library; to the Boston Public Library and to the Dartmouth College Library (for copies of letters written by Fanny Calderón de la Barca and her husband); and to the Deering Library of Northwestern University (with special reference to Spanish plays).

Among those in the field of history and in government service who have been so kind as to answer inquiries or to make suggestions in person are: Dr. H. W. L. Dana, Dr. Powrie V. Doctor, Dr. Lewis U. Hanke, Dr. Roland D. Hussey, Dr. Irving A. Leonard, Father Charles Ronan, S.J., and E. Wilder Spaulding. We have had especially good reason for repeated thanks to Dr. Frederick Starr of the University of Chicago: we never knew him, but became the fortunate owners by purchase of most of his well-chosen small library of nineteenth-century books on Mexico.

Arthur Edwards processed most of the large number of photographs from which those actually used in this book were drawn; and Raleigh Spinks drew the maps from Howard T. Fisher's pencil drawings. The onerous task of proofreading was aided by H. Frederick Willkie, II.

Others who have helped directly or made suggestions on one phase or another of our project include both friends and courteous correspondents: Richard S. Barnes, Joan Ryerson Brewster, Mary Brown, William T. Davis, John Gay, Mary Norris Lloyd, I. P. Earle, Charles Gauld, Pierre Long, Thatcher P. Luquer, George and Louise Massey, Samuel Eliot Morison, Marjorie Peters, Rosamond Forbes Pickhardt and her father Edward W. Forbes, Ralph Fletcher Seymour, John J. Slocum, Hector M. Sosa, and Victor Wolfgang von Hagen. Most particularly we wish to thank Herbert Weinstock, the editors' all-patient editor, to whose knowledge of Mexico, practical wisdom in general, and unerring help on details of varied scope, a large debt is owing.

644 ACKNOWLEDGMENTS

Several people have helped us in the specialized task of trying to identify Fanny's numerous literary and musical references. We owe grateful thanks particularly to Dr. Walter McIntosh Merrill, but also to Mrs. Kenneth J. Conant, J. Christopher Herold, and Dr. and Mrs. Daniel Lyons Leary.

We wish to acknowledge the aid rendered in long-past years by two secretaries to Howard T. Fisher from whose stellar competence we have greatly benefited: Miss Else Petersen and Mrs. Myles Boylan. We also take this opportunity to thank for numerous courtesies Mrs. H. M. Fraser, for many years secretary to Mr. and Mrs. Walter Bruce Howe.

Before proceeding to foreign fields, we must name one among the various members of our own large family group who have co-operated in our undertaking: Ruth Fisher Rhetts—originally a full partner in the venture which has resulted in this book. She participated in launching the enterprise, in early explorations in Mexico, and in the initial gathering of books, maps, and other valuable background material, both in the United States and Mexico.

Among foreign, but non-Mexican sources, we gratefully acknowledge aid by Dr. Henry Meikle of the National Library of Scotland; C. L. Hindle of the Bodleian Library; H. Sellers of the British Museum; and Mrs. O. D'Arcy Hart, who went through many of the dispatches of Richard Pakenham on our behalf in the Public Record Office in London. Mr. Robert Crichton, of Scottish Oils, Ltd. (the firm which occupies the former country property of William Inglis, Fanny Calderón de la Barca's father), was extremely generous with information. In Spain we have profited from the invaluable and meticulous aid of Professor Demetrio Nalda of Madrid, who prosecuted various inquiries for us, including work in Spanish governmental archives. We are likewise indebted to Doña Pilar Fernández Vega, Director of the new Museo de América in Madrid, and to Doña María Luisa Vázquez de Parga, its secretary; and to Dr. John Van Horne, formerly with the United States Embassy in Madrid. Dr. Miguel Querol Gavaldá of the Instituto Español de Musicología kindly identified and wrote down the words and music of one of the songs mentioned by Fanny. And our long-time friend Ester Pérez de King made various valuable suggestions. In Argentina, birthplace of Angel Calderón de la Barca, Dr. Gustavo Martínez Zuviría of the Biblioteca Nacional and Señor Hector C. Quesada, director of the Archivo de la Nación, were generous and informative correspondents. In 1943 we were recipients of material of great interest furnished through the courtesy of the Archivo Nacional de Cuba.

It is difficult to separate into categories the names of the many persons in Mexico who have taken time and trouble to help us. Some of this help, no doubt, was extended more to the memory of Fanny Calderón de la Barca than to her North American editors, but all of it was enthusiastically given. In theory, the list of those to whom we are indebted could be divided into: officials of governmental departments; anthropologists, historians and others knowledgeable about Mexico's nineteenth-century past; descendants of people mentioned by Fanny; those encountered in retracing Fanny's journeyings; and good Mexican friends of long standing upon whose interest and limitless patience we have imposed time and again. But in practice, all these categories have constantly tended to overlap—and to be augmented by kind but nameless informants who, for example, might appear in a library, museum, or churchyard to offer brief, solid advice, and then quickly disappear forever. Some of those whose names we did succeed in obtaining will not remember us, but their suggestions on where to look and whom to see have been, nonetheless, invaluable. Some we know only as the generous answerers to letters written in regrettable Spanish. To all we give our heartfelt thanks.

In the city of Mexico, we were fortunate in having done most of our work at the Biblioteca Nacional a good many years ago, before the commencement of its extensive remodeling program which made necessary the inactive storage of its less used but, for our purposes, more valuable collections. We were granted permission by its director, Juan B. Iguíniz, to take photographs and in general were given every facility for work. We look back on several periods of study there with gratitude.

The Hemeroteca Nacional de México—possessor of many old annuals and periodicals of the 1840's as well as old newspapers—was a pleasant hunting ground. Similarly, our brief forays in the library of the Secretaría de Relaciones Exteriores and to the Archivo General de la Nación were made fruitful by the courtesy of various staff members. We may also mention the Benjamin Franklin Library as a useful source of information.

We are much indebted to several officials of the Instituto Nacional de Antropología e Historia for information and suggestions. Among them are the architect Señor Jorge Enciso, who at the time of our inquiries was head of the Dirección de Monumentos Coloniales, and the architect Señor Lauro E. Rosell, of the same office; also Señorita Hilda Colar of the Museo de Arte Colonial. Our thanks likewise go to Licenciado Joaquín Cortina Goríbar for permission to publish photographs of paintings in the Museo Nacional de Historia at Chapultepec.

Among many kind and well-informed individuals in the capital who have helped us in person or by mail we mention: Doña Guadalupe Adalid; Mrs. Perry Allen; Dr. Arturo Arnáiz y Freg of the Universidad Nacional Autónoma; the architect Bernabé León de la Barra and his brother Don Luis; Don Manuel Campero, Marqués de Apartado; Miss Alice Dugas; Señor Rafael Espinosa; Señor Santiago Espinosa de los Monteros; Doña Natalia Franco; Don Luis Gutiérrez Cañedo, owner of the portrait of Juan de Dios Cañedo; Doña Carlota Adalid, Viuda de Lazo; the *presbítero* José Juan Martínez; Dr. John Paddock of the University of the Americas; Don Manuel Romero de Terreros, Marqués de San Francisco; the Hon. A. A. M. Stols of the Netherlands Embassy; the Hon. Rafael Heliodoro Valle; and Licenciado Ricardo José Zevada, Director General of the Banco Nacional de Comercio Exterior and likewise president of Impulsora Minera de Angangueo.

We wish to thank particularly our long-time friend Carlos Iturbe for his enthusiasm and practical help extended over many years, and we likewise remember with especial warmth and gratefulness the aid of the late Vica de Iturbe.

Felipe Teixidor, recent translator of *Life in Mexico* into Spanish and the first to annotate its text, belongs in a special category in this list of acknowledgments. That we do not agree with every statement made, or every identification of characters assumed, in his text and notes for *La Vida en México* is of little importance as compared with our admiration and lasting respect for his total product, a constant challenge to us and at times a valuable source of information (acknowledged in our notes in each specific instance).

Among the many persons outside of the capital who assisted us we may mention: Doña Esta O. de Dávila of Cuernavaca; Don Ricardo de Velasco of Veracruz and, more recently, Mr. St. John Bargas, United States consul in Veracruz; Señorita Clotilde Schondube of Oaxaca; Señora Trinidad González, Viuda de Desentis and her daughter Señora María Carmen Desentis de Soto, of Tulancingo; the Olvera brothers of the hacienda of Tepenacaxco; Don Jorge Palomino y Cañedo of San Miguel de Allende and likewise Mrs. Helen Wale of the same city; and, in the Puebla area, Señor Nicolás Fraile Churumbel, Señor Guillermo Grüneberg, Licenciado Miguel López and his wife Doña Marcela Artasánchez de López, and Señor Eloy Pellón. At the hacienda of La Gavia we were welcomed by the spirited Doña Dolores García Pimentel, Viuda de Riba; and we are likewise indebted to La Gavia's present owner Señor José Ramón Albarrán y Pliego, and to Señor Hector Medina Neri of Toluca. At Angangueo we remember with great pleasure the interest and aid of Roger W. Loveless and William L. Parker, and we are much indebted to Mr. and Mrs. Parker for subsequent informative letters. The Mendizábal brothers at Queréndaro were most kind. In Morelia, we benefited from the cordiality of Doña María and Doña Soledad Iturbide, descendants of Cayetano Gómez of the hacienda of San Bartolo. In Pátzcuaro, we received help from their nephew Felipe Oseguera e Iturbide and his wife Doña Pamela; and earlier from Don Luis Ortiz Lazcano. We remember with especial gratitude and sorrow the more than thirty-year friendship of José Francisco Peralta, who aided in many ways. On the island of Janitzio, José Campos and his wife Severiana were lively vacation companions as well as careful informants.

Various Mexicans have unwittingly been our hosts, at least briefly. For example, Doña María Campero de Bustos, Duquesa de Huete, whose foreman did the honors at her lonely hacienda of Santiago; or Señor

Carlos Novoa, whose caretaker, deviating not an instant in watchful loyalty to his post, permitted a glimpse but not entrance into the high-walled garden in Tlalpan where Fanny and her husband were fêted in 1841.

Remembrance of faithful gatekeepers brings us to our last but essential category: rural Mexicans of modest means and backgrounds who —familiar with every crossroad and landmark of their native districts— directed us to places sought. Some were small children, competently guarding family flocks of goats or cattle. Some were men wise not only as to roads and their status under varying weather conditions but also as to cars and their clearances. Some were local ancients, proud of their unique remembrances of old times. Like their more sophisticated urban countrymen, all of them shared the national endowment of calm, structured courtesy. We thank them all. *¡Viva México!*

Bibliography

This listing provides information regarding bibliographical sources cited by the editors, plus a selection from other publications which proved useful in preparing this edition. (Some works served solely as sources for illustrations.) Materials unrelated to Mexico or Cuba and general reference works have not been included, except in a few instances where it was thought that their inclusion might prove of interest to others.

Material is arranged alphabetically according to the principal name of the author or editor. Anonymous books, newspapers, periodicals, etc. are indexed under the first significant word of the title.

Alamán, Lucas. *Historia de Méjico.* México, 1942. 5 vols. Edited by Carlos Pereyra. (The first edition of this work, published 1849–52 in Mexico, was the source of the half-tone portrait of President Bustamante reproduced in this volume.)

Album Mejicano; Tributo de Gratitud al Civismo Nacional. Méjico, 1843.

Album Mexicano, El. México, 1849. Vols. I and II.

Alcaraz, Ramón. See Ramsey, Albert C.

Alexander, James Edward. *Transatlantic Sketches.* London, 1833. 2 vols.

Almanach de Gotha; annuaire généalogique, diplomatique et statistique. Gotha, volumes for 1838–43.

American Geographical Society. *Index to Map of Hispanic America,* 1:1,000,000, Vol. II: *Geographical Names in Mexico.* Washington, 1944.

Apuntador, El. Semanario de Teatros, Costumbres, Literatura y Variedades. México, 1841.

Archivo Histórico Diplomático Mexicano. Núm. 22. *El Tratado de Paz con España.* Prólogo de Antonio de la Peña y Reyes. México, Publicaciones de la Secretaría de Relaciones Exteriores, 1927.

Arnáiz y Freg, Arturo. See Mora, José María Luis.

Arróniz, Marcos. *Manual de Biografía Mejicana.* Paris, 1857.

Arróniz, Marcos. *Manual del Viajero en México*. Paris, 1858.

Ashton, Helen. *Letty Landon*. New York, 1951.

Ateneo Mexicano, El. México, 1844–45. 2 vols. in one.

Atl, Dr. See Murillo, Gerardo.

Atúnez, Francisco. *Los Alacranes en el Folklore de Durango*. Aguascalientes, 1950.

Bacourt, Adolphe de. *Souvenirs of a Diplomat*. New York, 1885.

Baird, Joseph Armstrong, Jr. *The Churches of Mexico, 1530–1810*. Berkeley and Los Angeles, 1962.

Bancroft, Hubert Howe. *A Popular History of the Mexican People*. San Francisco, 1887.

Bancroft, Hubert Howe. *History of Mexico*. San Francisco, 1890. 6 vols. (Vol. V, 1824–61.)

[Barinetti, Carlo.] *A Voyage to Mexico and Havanna*. New York, 1841.

Beaufoy, Mark. *Mexican Illustrations*. London, 1828.

Bellemare, Louis de. *Vagabond Life in Mexico*. New York, 1856. (Written under pseudonym of Gabriel Ferry.)

Benítez, José R. *Morelia*. México, 1936. (*Monografías Mexicanas de Arte*.)

Bishop, William Henry. *Old Mexico and Her Lost Provinces*. New York, 1883.

Blanchard, P. and A. Dauzats. *San Juan de Ulúa; ou Relation de l'expédition française au Mexique*. Paris, 1839.

Bocanegra, José María. *Historia de México Independiente, 1822–1846*. México, 1897. 2 vols.

Boletín Oficial. Nos. 1–16. Aug. 31–Sept. 10, 1841. México, [1841].

Bolton, Herbert Eugene. *Rim of Christendom; a Biography of Eusebio Francisco Kino, Pacific Pioneer*. New York, 1936.

Bosch García, Carlos. *Problemas Diplomáticos del México Independiente*. México, El Colegio de México, 1947.

Botsford, Florence Hudson. *Folk Songs of Many Peoples*. New York, 1922.

Bradley, Hugh. *Havana, Cinderella's City*. Garden City, New York, 1941.

Brand, Donald R., assisted by José Corona Núñez. *Quiroga, A Mexican Municipio*. Washington, 1951. (Smithsonian Institution, Institute of Social Anthropology, Pub. No. 11.)

Brenner, Anita. *Idols behind Altars*. New York, 1929.

Brockway, Wallace, and Herbert Weinstock. *The Opera, a History of Its Creation and Performance: 1600–1941*. New York, 1941.

Bullock, William. *Six Months' Residence and Travels in Mexico*. London, 1824.

Bullock, W. H. *Across Mexico in 1864–65*. London and Cambridge, 1866.

Bustamante, Carlos María de. *Apuntes para la Historia del Gobierno del General D. Antonio López de Santa-Anna, desde Principios de Octubre de 1841 hasta 6 de Diciembre de 1844.* México, 1845.

Bustamante, Carlos María de. *El Gabinete Mexicano durante el Segundo Período de la Administración del Exmo. Señor Presidente D. Anastasio Bustamante, hasta la Entrega del Mando al Exmo. Señor Presidente Interino D. Antonio López de Santa-Anna.* México, 1842. 2 vols. in one.

Bustamante, Carlos María de. *Mañanas de la Alameda de México.* México, 1835–36. 2 vols.

Bustamante, Carlos María de. *El Nuevo Bernal Díaz, ó sea, Historia de la Invasión de los Anglo-Americanos en México.* México, 1847. 2 vols. in one.

Calderón de la Barca, Angel. See *Relaciones Diplomáticas Hispano-Mexicanas.*

[Calderón de la Barca, Frances Erskine Inglis.] *The Attaché in Madrid.* New York, 1856.

Calderón de la Barca, Frances Erskine Inglis. *Life in Mexico.* For a discussion of various editions, see page 629 ff. For obvious reasons, the editions most useful in the preparation of this volume were the first American edition, the first English edition, and the two translations into Spanish, especially that by Felipe Teixidor.

Caldwell, Robert Granville. *The Lopez Expeditions to Cuba, 1848–1851.* Princeton, New Jersey, 1915.

Calendario de Galván para el Año de 1836. Mégico, n.d. Also volumes for 1837–41, 1844–47, 1850, 1852, 1855.

Calendario Manual para el Año de 1839, Arreglado por las Tablas de Ontiveros. México, [1838]. Also volumes for 1840–42.

Calendario de las Señoritas Megicanas, para el Año 1838, Dispuesto por Mariano Galván. Mégico, [1837]. Also volumes for 1839–41.

Callcott, Wilfrid Hardy. *Church and State in Mexico, 1822–1857.* Durham, North Carolina, 1926.

Callcott, Wilfrid Hardy. *Santa Anna; the Story of an Enigma Who Once Was Mexico.* Norman, Oklahoma, 1936.

Campos, Rubén M. *El Folklore Musical de las Ciudades.* México, 1930. (Publicaciones de la Secretaría de Educación Pública.)

Campos, Rubén M. *El Folklore y la Música Mexicana.* México, 1929. (Publicaciones de la Secretaría de Educación Pública.)

Cantero, Justo Germán. *Los Ingenios: Colección de Vistas de los Principales Ingenios de Azucar de la Isla de Cuba.* Habana, 1867.

Carpenter, William W. *Travels and Adventures in Mexico.* New York, 1851.

Carreño, Alberto María. "Hernán Cortés y el Descubrimiento de Sus

Restos." In *Academia Mexicana de la Historia, Memorias,* VI (Oct.–Dec. 1947), 301–403.

Carreño, Alberto María, editor. *Jefes del Ejercito Mexicano en 1847.* México, 1914.

Carson, W. E. *Mexico, the Wonderland of the South.* New York, 1910.

Caruso, John Anthony. *The Liberators of Mexico.* New York, 1954.

Caso, Alfonso. *The Aztecs, People of the Sun.* (Illustrated by Miguel Covarrubias and translated by Lowell Dunham.) Norman, Oklahoma, 1958.

Castillo Negrete, Emilio del. *Galería de Oradores de México en el Siglo XIX.* México, 1877–80. 3 vols.

Chavero, Alfredo. See Muñoz Camargo, Diego; Riva Palacio, Vicente.

Clavijero, Francisco Javier. *Historia Antigua de Mégico.* (Translated by José Joaquín de Mora from the Italian.) London, 1826. 2 vols.

Clavijero, Francisco Javier. *The History of Mexico.* (Translated by Charles Cullen from the Italian.) Richmond, Virginia, 1806. 3 vols.

Conkling, Alfred R. *Appletons' Guide to Mexico.* New York, 1884.

Conte, Augusto. *Recuerdos de un Diplomático.* Madrid, 1901–3. 3 vols. (Vol. I.)

Cortés, Hernán. See Day, A. Grove; MacNutt, Francis Augustus.

Corti, Egon Caesar (Count). *Maximilian and Charlotte of Mexico.* (Translated from the German by Catherine Alison Phillips.) New York and London, 1928. 2 vols.

Cortina, José María Justo Gómez de la. See Gómez de la Cortina.

Cosmopolita, El. Aug. 7, 1839–June 29, 1842.

Cossío, José Lorenzo. *Guía Retrospectiva de la Ciudad de México.* México, 1941.

Cotner, Thomas E., editor, and Carlos E. Castañeda, co-editor. *Essays in Mexican History.* Austin, Texas, 1958. (The Institute of Latin American Studies, University of Texas.)

Covarrubias, Miguel. *Mexico South.* New York, 1946.

Cruz, La. Periódico esclusivamente religioso. México, 1855–58 (Vols. I–VII).

Cuevas, Gabriel. *El Glorioso Colegio Militar Mexicano en un Siglo (1824–1924).* México, 1937.

Cuevas, Mariano (S.J.). *Historia de la Nación Mexicana.* México, 1940.

Curtis, William Eleroy. *The Capitals of Spanish America.* New York, 1888.

Day, A. Grove, editor. *Fernando Cortés: Despatches from Mexico to Charles V.* New York, 1935.

Decaen, José. See *México y Sus Alrededores.*

Decorme, Gerardo (S.J.). *Historia de la Compañía de Jesús en la República Mexicana durante el Siglo XIX.* Guadalajara, 1914. 2 vols.

Delgado, Jaime. *España y México en el Siglo XIX.* Madrid, Consejo

Superior de Investigaciones Científicas, Instituto Gonzalo Fernández de Oviedo, Vol. 1 and 2, 1950; Vol. 3, 1953.

Demarest, Donald, and Coley Taylor. *The Dark Virgin.* Freeport, Maine, and New York, 1956.

Despachos Generales. See *Relaciones Diplomáticas,* etc.

Despatches from U.S. Ministers to Mexico, Aug. 1, 1840–May 19, 1842. Roll #11, Microfilm Copy #97, United States Archives.

Diario de la Habana. Nov.–Dec. 1839; Jan.–April 1842.

Diario de los Niños: Literatura, Entretenimiento e Instrucción. Méjico, 1839–40. Vols. 1–3.

Diario del Gobierno de la República Mexicana. México, Nov. 1839– Dec. 1842; April–June 1843.

Díaz del Castillo, Bernal. *The Discovery and Conquest of Mexico, 1517–1521.* (Edited by Genaro García, and translated by A. P. Maudslay.) New York, 1956.

Diplomatic Correspondence of the United States, Inter-American Affairs, 1831–1860. (Selected and arranged by William R. Manning.) Volume VIII—*Mexico, 1831–1848 (Mid-Year), Documents 3128–3771.* Washington, 1937. (Carnegie Endowment for International Peace.)

Documentos de la Guerra de Independencia. (Biblioteca Enciclopédica Popular, Núm. 74.) México, Secretaría de Educación Pública, 1945.

[Donaldson, (Sir) Stuart Alexander.] *Mexico Thirty Years Ago.* London, 1865.

Duflot de Mofras, Eugène. *Duflot de Mofras' Travels on the Pacific Coast.* (Translated, edited, and annotated by Marguerite Eyer Wilbur.) Santa Ana, California, 1937. 2 vols.

Ellis, Powhatan. See *Despatches from U.S. Ministers to Mexico.*

Estrada, Genaro. *Las Figuras Mexicanas de Cera en el Museo Arqueológico de Madrid.* Madrid, Museo Arqueológico Nacional (Cuadernos Mexicanos de la Embajada de México en España), 1934.

Evans, Albert S. *Our Sister Republic.* Hartford, Connecticut, 1870.

Fernández, Justino. *Uruapan.* México, 1936.

Fernández Ledesma, Enrique. *Viajes al Siglo XIX.* México, 1933.

Ferry, Gabriel. See Bellemare, Louis de.

Flandrau, Charles. *Viva Mexico!* New York, 1935.

Fossey, Mathieu de. *Le Mexique.* Paris, 1857.

Foster, George M., assisted by Gabriel Ospina. *Empire's Children: The People of Tzintzuntzan.* Mexico, 1948. (Smithsonian Institution, Institute of Social Anthropology, Pub. No. 6.)

Frost, John. *The History of Mexico and Its Wars.* New Orleans, 1887.

Frost, John. *Pictorial History of Mexico and the Mexican War.* Philadelphia, 1850.

Gadow, Hans. *Through Southern Mexico.* New York and London, 1908.

Galindo y Villa, Jesús. "El Panteón de San Fernando y el Futuro Panteón Nacional." In *Anales del Museo Nacional,* Ser. 2, IV, 337–552.

Gallo, Eduardo L., editor. *Hombres Ilustres Mexicanos.* México, 1873–74. 4 vols.

Gamboa, Fernando. *Posada, Printmaker to the Mexican People.* Chicago, 1944.

García, Genaro. "Leona Vicario, Heroína Insurgente." In *Anales del Museo Nacional,* Ser. 3, I, 257–457.

García, Rubén. *Rincones y Paisajes del México Maravilloso.* México, Secretaría de Educación Pública, 1950.

García Carraffa, Alberto and Arturo. *Enciclopedia Heráldica y Genealógica Hispano-Americana.* Madrid, 1919–63. 88 vols. In progress.

García Cubas, Antonio. *Atlas Pintoresco e Histórico de los Estados Unidos Mexicanos.* México, 1885.

García Cubas, Antonio. *Cuadro Geográfico, Estadístico, Descriptivo, e Histórico de los Estados Unidos Mexicanos.* (Text for *Atlas Pintoresco.*) México, 1885.

García Cubas, Antonio. *El Libro de Mis Recuerdos.* México, 1945.

García Icazbalceta, Joaquín. *Don Fray Juan de Zumárraga, Primer Obispo y Arzobispo de México.* México, 1881.

García Icazbalceta, Joaquín. *La Ultima Palabra sobre la Maravillosa Aparición de La Sma. Virgen de Guadalupe: Folleto Escrito y Publicado por Orden de S. S. I. El Sr. Arzobispo D. Pelagio Antonio de Labastida y Dávalos.* México, 1896.

García Loya, Diego. *Mosaic of Mexican History.* Mexico, 1958.

García Pimentel y Elguero, Luis. *Don Joaquín García Icazbalceta como Católico.* México, 1944.

Gardiner, C. Harvey. *Foreign Travelers' Accounts of Mexico, 1810–1910.* (Reprinted from Vol. VIII—Jan. 1952, No. 3—of *The Americas.*) Washington.

Gardiner, C. Harvey, editor. *Mexico, 1825–1828: The Journal and Correspondence of Edward Thornton Tayloe.* Chapel Hill, North Carolina, [1959].

Gómez de la Cortina, José María Justo. *Poliantea.* Prólogo y Selección de Manuel Romero de Terreros. México, 1944. (Biblioteca del Estudiante Universitario, Núm. 46.)

Gómez de la Cortina, José María Justo. "Terremotos: a la Señorita Doña * * *." In *El Mosaico Mexicano,* IV (1840), 545–53.

Gómez Farías, Valentín. *Alocución del Presidente Interino a Sus Conciudadanos.* México, 15 de julio de 1840.

Gómez Farías, Valentín. *Plan para la Regeneración Política de la República.* [México], 19 de julio de 1840.

Gómez de Orozco, Federico. "El Desierto de los Leones." In *Anales del Museo Nacional*, Ser. 4, I, 280–91.

Gómez de Orozco, Federico. *Doña Marina, La Dama de la Conquista*. México, 1942. (Vidas Mexicanas, Núm. 2.)

Gómez Pedraza, Manuel. "Don Miguel Ramos Arizpe." In *Museo Mexicano*, II, 105–10.

González Obregón, Luis. *México Viejo*. México, 1945.

González Obregón, Luis. *The Streets of Mexico*. (Translated by Blanche Collet Wagner.) San Francisco, 1937.

Gosnell, Charles F. *Spanish Personal Names*. New York, 1938.

Gouverneur, Marian. *As I Remember. Recollections of American Society during the Nineteenth Century*. New York and London, 1911.

Grant, Isabel Frances. *The Macleods, the History of a Clan, 1200–1956*. London, [1959].

Gruening, Ernest. *Mexico and Its Heritage*. New York, 1936.

Gualdi, Pedro. *Monumentos de Méjico*. Méjico, 1841.

Guía de Forasteros en la Ciudad de Mégico, para el Año de 1854. Mégico, [1854?].

Guía de Forasteros en la Siempre Fiel Isla de Cuba para el Año de 1839. Habana. (Also for 1840–42.)

Guía Nobiliaria de España. Madrid, 1932.

Gutiérrez de Estrada, José María. *Carta Dirigida al Escmo. Sr. Presidente de la República, sobre la Necesidad de Buscar en una Convención el Posible Remedio de los Males que Aquejan a la República*. México, 1840.

Hall, Basil. *Extracts from a Journal, Written on the Coasts of Chili, Peru, and Mexico, in the Years 1820, 1821, 1822*. Edinburgh, 1824. 2 vols.

Hardy, Robert William Hale. *Travels in the Interior of Mexico, in 1825, 1826, 1827, & 1828*. London, 1829.

Haven, Gilbert. *Our Next-Door Neighbor: A Winter in Mexico*. New York, 1875.

Hazard, Samuel. *Cuba with Pen and Pencil*. Hartford, Connecticut, 1871.

Hernández, Francisco. *Historia Natural de Nueva España*. México, Universidad Nacional de México, 1959. 2 vols. (Vols. II and III of *Obras Completas* of Hernández. Translated by José Rojo Navarro.)

Hesperia, La. Vol. I (March 15–Dec. 26, 1840). México.

Humboldt, Alexander von. *Ensayo Político sobre Nueva España*. (Tr. al castellano por Vicente González Arnao.) Paris, 1836. 5 vols.

Humboldt, Alexander von. *Essai politique sur l'île de Cuba*. Paris, 1826. 2 vols.

Humboldt, Alexander von. *Political Essay on the Kingdom of New*

Spain. (Translated from the original French by John Black.) London, 1814. 4 vols.

Humboldt, Alexander von. *Selections from the Works of the Baron de Humboldt, Relating to the Climate, Inhabitants, Productions, and Mines of Mexico.* (With Notes by John Taylor.) London, 1824.

Humboldt, Alexander von. *The Island of Cuba.* (Translated from the Spanish, with Notes and a Preliminary Essay by J. S. Thrasher.) New York, 1856.

Iguíniz, Juan B. *Bibliografía Biográfica Mexicana.* México, 1930. Vol. I. (Monografías Bibliográficas Mexicanas, Núm. 18.)

Ilustración Mexicana, La. Vols. I–V (1851–56). México.

Instituto Nacional de Antropología e Historia, Dirección de Monumentos Coloniales. *Edificios Coloniales e Históricos de la República Mexicana Que Han Sido Declarados Monumentos.* México, 1939.

Kelemen, Pál. *Baroque and Rococo in Latin America.* New York, 1951.

Kendall, George Wilkins. *Narrative of the Texan Santa Fé Expedition.* New York, 1844. 2 vols.

Kilham, Walter H. *Mexican Architecture of the Vice-Regal Period.* New York and London, 1927.

Kollonitz, (Countess) Paula. *The Court of Mexico.* (Translated by J. E. Ollivant.) London, 1867.

Kubler, George. *Mexican Architecture of the Sixteenth Century.* New Haven, 1948. 2 vols.

Latrobe, Charles Joseph. *The Rambler in Mexico.* London, 1836.

Leclercq, Jules. *Voyage au Mexique de New-York à Vera-Cruz.* Paris, 1885.

Leduc, Alberto, and Luis Lara y Pardo. *Diccionario de Geografía, Historia y Biografía Mexicanas.* México, 1910.

Leicht, Hugo. *Las Calles de Puebla.* Puebla, [1930?].

Lempriere, Charles. *Notes in Mexico in 1861 and 1862.* London, 1862.

León, Nicolás. *Las Castas del México Colonial ó Nueva España.* México, 1924. (Publicaciones del Departamento de Antropología Anatómica, Museo Nacional de Arqueología, Historia y Etnografía, Núm. 1.)

León, Nicolás. "Los Indios Tarascos del Lago de Pátzcuaro." In *Anales del Museo Nacional,* Ser. 5, I, 149–68 and following.

Leonard, Irving A. "Cortés' Remains—and a Document." In *The Hispanic American Historical Review,* XXVIII (Feb. 1948), 53–61.

Lerdo de Tejada, Miguel M. *Apuntes Históricos de la Heróica Ciudad de Vera-Cruz.* México, 1858. 3 vols.

Liceo Mexicano, El. Vols. I and II. México, 1844.

Linati, C[laudio]. *Costumes et mœurs de Mexique.* London, 1830.

Litografía en México en el Siglo XIX, La. México, Ediciones Facsimilares de la Biblioteca Nacional de México, 1934. (Texto de Manuel Toussaint.)

Löwenstern, Isidore. *Le Mexique.* Paris, 1843.

Lucero y Noticioso. Habana. Issues for December 1839.

Lummis, Charles F. *The Awakening of a Nation.* New York and London, 1898.

Macedo Enciso, Miguel. *Manual del Magueyero.* México, 1950.

MacNutt, Francis Augustus. *The Five Letters of Relation from Fernando Cortes to the Emperor Charles V.* New York and London, 1908. 2 vols.

Maissin, Eugène. *The French in Mexico and Texas (1838–1839).* Salado, Texas, 1961. (Translated from the French and edited by James L. Shepherd, III.)

Malo, José Ramón. *Diario de Sucesos Notables (1832–1864).* México, 1948. 2 vols. (Arreglados y anotados por el P. Mariano Cuevas, S.J.)

Manning, William R. See *Diplomatic Correspondence of the United States,* etc.

Mañón, Manuel. *Historia del Teatro Principal de México.* México, 1932.

María y Campos, Armando de. "Half Century of Bull-Fighting." In *Mexican Art and Life,* Mexico, April 1939 (No. 6). Unpaged.

Mariscal, Federico E. *La Patria y la Arquitectura Nacional.* México, 1915.

Mariscal, Mario. *Reseña Histórica del Archivo General de la Nación, 1550–1946.* México, Secretaría de Gobernación, 1946.

Marroqui, José María. *La Ciudad de México.* México, 1900–3. 3 vols.

Mason, R. H. *Pictures of Life in Mexico.* London, 1851. 2 vols.

Mayer, Brantz. *Mexico as It Was and as It Is.* New York, 1844.

Mayer, Brantz. *Mexico, Aztec, Spanish and Republican.* Hartford, [Connecticut], 1852. 2 vols. in one.

Maza, Francisco de la. "Los Restos de Hernán Cortés." In *Cuadernos Americanos,* Vol. XXXII (March–April 1947), 153–74.

McNair, James B. *Sugar and Sugar-making.* Chicago, 1927. (Chicago Natural History Museum, Popular Series No. 13.)

McSherry, Richard. *El Puchero.* Philadelphia, 1850.

Menninger, Edwin. *Flowering Trees of the World.* New York, [1962].

México a Través de los Siglos. See Riva Palacio, Vicente.

México y Sus Alrededores. Colección de monumentos, trajes y paisajes dibujados al natural y litografiados por los artistas mexicanos C. Castro, J. Campillo, L. Auda y G. Rodríguez, bajo la dirección de Decaen. México, 1855–56; also 1864.

Mora, José María Luis/Ensayos, Ideas y Retratos. Prólogo y selección de Arturo Arnáiz y Freg. México, Universidad Nacional Autónoma, 1941. (Biblioteca del Estudiante Universitario, Núm. 25.)

Mora, José María Luis. *Méjico y Sus Revoluciones*. Paris, 1836. 3 vols.

Mora, José María Luis. *Obras Sueltas de José María Luis Mora, Ciudadano Mejicano*. Paris, 1837. 2 vols.

Morales Díaz, Carlos. *Quien es Quien en la Nomenclatura de la Ciudad de México*. México, 1962.

Moreno de Guerra y Alonso, Juan. *Guía de la Grandeza*. Madrid, 1924.

Mosaico Mexicano, El. México, I. Cumplido, Vols. 1–7 (1837–42).

Mosquito Mexicano, El. México, Vols. VIII–IX.

Muñoz Camargo, Diego. *Historia de Tlaxcala*. México, 1947. (Alfredo Chavero, editor.)

Murillo, Gerardo. *Las Artes Populares en México*. México, 1922. 2 vols. (Publicaciones de la Secretaría de Industria y Comercio.)

Murray, (Hon.) Amelia Matilda. *Letters from the United States, Cuba and Canada*. New York, 1856.

Murray, Charles Augustus. *Travels in North America during the Years 1834, 1835 & 1836*. London, 1839. 2 vols.

Museo Mexicano, El. Vols. I–IV (1843–44).

Museo Nacional de Artes e Industrias Populares. *La Charrería*. México, 1954.

Museo Popular. Vol. I (1840). México.

Nebel, Carl. *Voyage pittoresque et archéologique dans la partie la plus intéressante du Mexique*. Paris, M. Moench, 1836. Reissued in 1839 (Paris y Méjico, Impr. de P. Renouard) under the title of *Viaje Pintoresco y Arqueolojico sobre la parte mas interesante de la República Mejicana, en los Años Transcurridos desde 1829 hasta 1834*. Reissued in Spanish in 1840 (Paris y México); and in French in 1845 (Paris).

Norman, Benjamin Moore. *Rambles by Land and Water*. New York and New Orleans, 1845.

Núñez y Domínguez, José de Jesús. *Historia y Tauromaquia Mexicanas*. México, 1944.

Ober, Frederick A. *Travels in Mexico*. Boston, 1884.

O'Gorman, Helen. *Mexican Flowering Trees and Plants*. Mexico, 1961. (Edited by Ella Wallace Turok.)

Olavarría y Ferrari, Enrique. *Reseña Histórica del Teatro en México*. México, 1895. 2 vols.

Olavarría y Ferrari, Enrique. See Riva Palacio, Vicente.

Oliver, Pedro Pascual de. See *Relaciones Diplomáticas Hispano-Mexicanas*.

Orozco y Berra, Manuel, editor. *Apéndice al Diccionario Universal de Historia y de Geografía*. México, 1855. Vols. I–III (VIII–X de la obra).

Ortega y Pérez Gallardo, Ricardo. *Historia Genealógica de las Familias Más Antiguas de México*. México, 1908. 3 vols.

Pakenham, Richard. Various despatches written between 1840 and 1841. Public Record Office, London. Manuscript.

Palacios, Enrique Juan. *Puebla, Su Territorio y Sus Habitantes*. México, 1917.

Palomino Cañedo, Jorge. *La Casa y Mayorazgo de Cañedo de Nueva Galicia*. México, 1947.

Parkes, Henry Bamford. *A History of Mexico*. Boston, 1938.

Periódico Más, Un. México, 1841.

Peterson, Frederick A. *Ancient Mexico*. New York, 1961.

Pezuela, Jacobo de la. *Ensayo Histórico de la Isla de Cuba*. Nueva York, 1842.

Pimentel, Francisco. *Obras Completas*. (Jacinto and Fernando Pimentel, editors.) México, 1904. 5 vols.

Poinsett, Joel Roberts. *Notes on Mexico*. London, 1830.

Pol, Ferrán de. *Cuernavaca*. México, 1948. (Colección Anáhuac de Arte Mexicano, Vol. 11.)

Polk, James. *The Diary of James K. Polk during His Presidency, 1845 to 1849*. Chicago, 1910. (Chicago Historical Society's Collections— Vol. VIII. Edited and annotated by Milo Milton Quaife.)

Prescott, William H. *History of the Conquest of Mexico*. Philadelphia, 1893. 3 vols.

Prescott, William H. See Wolcott, Roger.

Priestley, Herbert Ingram. *The Mexican Nation, a History*. New York, 1923.

Prieto, Guillermo. *Memorias de Mis Tiempos*. Paris-México, 1906. 2 vols. (Vol. I: 1828–40; Vol. II: 1840–53.)

Ramírez, José Fernando. *Mexico during the War with the United States*. Edited by Walter V. Scholes, and translated by Elliott B. Scherr. Vol. XXIII, The University of Missouri studies No. 1. Columbia, Missouri, 1950.

Ramírez Aparicio, Manuel. *Los Conventos Suprimidos en Méjico*. Méjico, 1861.

Ramsey, Albert C., editor and translator. *The Other Side: or, Notes for the History of the War between Mexico and the United States*. (From the text in Spanish edited by Ramón Alcaraz.) New York and London, 1850.

Relaciones Diplomáticas Hispano-Mexicanas (1839–1898). Serie I, *Despachos Generales*. México, El Colegio de México. Vol. I, 1949; Vol. II, 1952.

Révérend, Albert (Vicomte). *Titres, Anoblissements, et Pairies de la Restauration, 1814–1830*. Paris, 1909. 6 vols.

Rincón Gallardo y Romero de Terreros, Carlos (Duque de Regla, Marqués de Guadalupe). *El Libro de Charro Mexicano*. México, 1946.

Rippy, J. Fred. *Historical Evolution of Hispanic America*. New York, 1933.

Riva Palacio, Vicente, editor. *México a Través de los Siglos*. Barcelona, [1887–89]. 5 vols.
Vol. I: Alfredo Chavero, *Historia Antigua y de la Conquista*
Vol. II: Vicente Riva Palacio, *El Vireinato*
Vol. III: Julio Zárate, *La Guerra de Independencia*
Vol. IV: Enrique Olavarría y Ferrari, *México Independiente*
Vol. V: José María Vigil, *La Reforma*

Rivera Cambas, Manuel. *Los Gobernantes de México*. México, 1872–73. 2 vols.

Rivera Cambas, Manuel. *México Pintoresco, Artístico y Monumental*. México, 1880. 3 vols.

Rives, George Lockhart. *The United States and Mexico, 1821–1848*. New York, 1913. 2 vols.

Robertson, William Parish. *A Visit to Mexico, by the West India Islands*. London, 1853. 2 vols.

Robertson, William Spence. *Iturbide of Mexico*. Durham, North Carolina, 1952.

Robinson, Fayette. *Mexico and Her Military Chieftains*. Philadelphia, 1847.

Robinson, William Davis. *Memoirs of the Mexican Revolution*. London, 1821. 2 vols.

Rodríguez, Gustavo A. *Doña Marina*. México, 1935. (Secretaría de Relaciones Exteriores, Monografía Histórica.)

Romero, José Guadalupe. *Noticias para Formar la Historia y Estadísticas del Obispado de Michoacán*. México, 1862. 2 vols. in one.

Romero, Matías. *Geographical and Statistical Notes on Mexico*. New York and London, 1898.

Romero Flores, Jesús. *Geografía del Estado de Michoacán*. México, 1931.

Romero de Terreros, Manuel (Marqués de San Francisco). *Antiguas Haciendas de México*. México, 1956.

Romero de Terreros, Manuel (Marqués de San Francisco). *Bocetos de la Vida Social en la Nueva España*. México, 1944.

Romero de Terreros, Manuel (Marqués de San Francisco). *Cosas Que Fueron*. México, 1925.

Romero de Terreros, Manuel (Marqués de San Francisco). *La Casa de los Azulejos*. México, 1925.

Romero de Terreros, Manuel (Marqués de San Francisco). *La Corte de Agustín I, Emperador de México*. México, 1921.

Romero de Terreros, Manuel (Marqués de San Francisco). *El Conde de Regla, Creso de la Nueva España*. México, 1943.

Romero de Terreros, Manuel (Marqués de San Francisco). *Los Condes de Regla*. Méjico, 1909.

Rosell, Lauro E. *Iglesias y Conventos Coloniales de México*. México, 1961.

Ruiz, Eduardo. *Michoacán, Paisajes, Tradiciones y Leyendas*. México, 1935.

Ruxton, George F. *Adventures in Mexico and the Rocky Mountains*. New York, 1848.

Sahagún, Bernardino de. *Historia General de las Cosas de Nueva España*. (Carlos María de Bustamante, editor.) México, 1829–30. 3 vols.

Salado Alvarez, Victoriano. *La Vida Azarosa y Romántica de Don Carlos María de Bustamante*. Madrid, 1933.

Salas León, Antonio. *Pátzcuaro: Cosas de Antaño y Ogaño*. Pátzcuaro, 1941.

Santa Cruz y Mallen, Francisco Xavier (Conde de San Juan de Jaruco y de Santa Cruz de Mopox). *Historia de Familias Cubanas*. La Habana, 1940. 5 vols.

Santamaría, Francisco J. *Diccionario General de Americanismos*. México, 1942. 3 vols.

Sartorius, Christian. *Mexico. Landscapes and Popular Sketches;* also entitled *Mexico and the Mexicans*. (Edited by Dr. Thomas Gaspey.) London, 1859.

Scholes, Walter V. See Ramírez, José Fernando.

Shepard, A. K. *The Land of the Aztecs*. Albany, 1859.

Shepherd, James L., III. See Maissin, Eugène.

Sierra, Justo, editor. *Mexico, Its Social Evolution*. Mexico, 1900. 2 vols.

Siglo Diez y Nueve, El. Vols. I and II (Oct. 8, 1841–July 31, 1842).

Simpson, Lesley Byrd. *Many Mexicos*. New York, 1941.

Sketch of the Customs and Society of Mexico, in a Series of Familiar Letters; and a Journal of Travels in the Interior, during the Years 1824, 1825, 1826. London, 1828.

Smart, Charles Allen. *Viva Juárez!* Philadelphia and New York, 1963.

Smith, E. Kirby. *To Mexico with Scott*. Cambridge, Massachusetts, 1917.

Smith, Justin H. *The War with Mexico*. New York, 1919. 2 vols.

Sosa, Francisco. *Biografías de Mexicanos Distinguidos*. México, 1884.

Stuart-Wortley, (Lady) Emmeline Charlotte Elizabeth (Manners). *Travels in the United States, etc., during 1849 and 1850*. New York, 1851. 2 vols. (Vol. II.)

Suárez de Tangil y de Angulo, Fernando (Conde de Vallellano). *Nobiliario Cubano*. Madrid, 1929. 2 vols.

Tayloe, Edward Thornton. See Gardiner, C. Harvey.

Teja Zabre, Alfonso. *Guide to the History of Mexico*. Mexico, 1935.

Terry, T. Philip. *Terry's Mexico*. Mexico, 1909.

Tharp, Louise Hall. *The Peabody Sisters of Salem*. Boston, 1950.

Toor, Frances. *A Treasury of Mexican Folkways*. New York, 1947.

Torquemada, Juan de. *Monarquía Indiana*. Madrid, 1723. 3 vols.

Torrea, Juan Manuel. *135 Años de Labor Diplomática al Servicio de México, desde el Dr. Manuel de Herrera (1821) hasta el Lic. Luis Padilla Nervo*. México, Publicaciones de la Academia Nacional de Historia y Geografía, 1956.

Toussaint, Manuel. *Arte Colonial en México*. México, 1948.

Toussaint, Manuel. *Pátzcuaro*. México, 1942.

Toussaint, Manuel. See *Litografía en México* . . .

Trollope, Frances. *Domestic Manners of the Americans*. (Edited by Donald Smalley.) New York, 1949.

Tylor, Edward B. *Anahuac*. London, Re-issue of 1861.

Unión, La. Periódico Político y Literario. México, Nov. 11, 1840–Aug. 28, 1841.

Vaillant, George C. *Aztecs of Mexico*. Garden City, New York, 1941.

Valadés, José C. *Alamán, Estadista e Historiador*. México, 1938.

Valdés, Octaviano. "Fray Francisco de Tembleque." In *The Americas*, Vol. III (Oct. 1946), 223–33.

Valencia, Gabriel. *El General en Gefe del Ejército de Operación sobre los Sublevados de Esta Capital a Sus Conciudadanos*. [México], 20 de julio de 1840.

Valle, Rafael Heliodoro. *Iturbide, Varón de Dios*. México, 1944.

Valle-Arizpe, Artemio de. *Calle Vieja y Calle Nueva*. México, 1949.

Valle-Arizpe, Artemio de. *Historia de la Ciudad de México según los Relatos de Sus Cronistas*. México, 1939.

Valle-Arizpe, Artemio de. *El Palacio Nacional de México*. México, 1936.

Valle-Arizpe, Artemio de. *Por la Vieja Calzada de Tlacopan*. México, 1937.

Van Horne, John. *El Bernardo of Bernardo de Balbuena*. Urbana. (University of Illinois Studies in Language and Literature, Vol. XII, Feb. 1927, No. 1.)

Velázquez Chávez, Agustín. *Tres Siglos de Pintura Colonial Mexicana*. México, 1939.

Victoria Gómez, Felipe. *Guadalupe Victoria, Primer Presidente de México*. México, 1952.

Vigil, José María. See Riva Palacio, Vicente.

Vilar y Pascual, Luis. *Diccionario Histórico, Genealógico y Heráldico de las Familias Ilustres de la Monarquía Española*. Madrid, 1859–66. 8 vols.

Ward, Henry George. *Mexico in 1827*. London, 1828. 2 vols.

Wauchope, Robert. *Lost Tribes & Sunken Continents*. Chicago, 1962.

Weismann, Elizabeth Wilder. *Mexico in Sculpture, 1521–1821*. Cambridge, Massachusetts, 1950.

Weiss y Sánchez, Joaquín. *Arquitectura Cubana Colonial*. Habana, 1936.

West, Robert C. *Cultural Geography of the Modern Tarascan Area*. Washington, 1948. (Smithsonian Institution, Institute of Social Anthropology, Pub. No. 7.)

[Wheat, Marvin.] *Travels on the Western Slope of the Mexican Cordillera*. San Francisco, 1857.

Wilson, Robert A. *Mexico: Its Peasants and Its Priests*. New York, 1856.

Wolcott, Roger, editor. *The Correspondence of William Hickling Prescott, 1833–1847*. Cambridge, Massachusetts, 1925. (Publication of the Massachusetts Historical Society.)

Zamacois, Niceto de. *Historia de Méjico, desde Sus Tiempos Más Remotos hasta Nuestros Días*. Barcelona-Méjico, 1876–82. 18 vols. in 20.

Zárate, Julio. See Riva Palacio, Vicente.

Zavala, Lorenzo de. *Ensayo Histórico de las Revoluciones de Mégico, desde 1808 hasta 1830*. Paris, 1831 (Vol. I); New York, 1832 (Vol. II).

Zevada, Ricardo J. *"Angangueo"/Breves Notas sobre Sus Luchas y Realizaciones*. Angangueo, Michoacán, [México], 1963. Mimeographed.

Zurriago, El. Periódico Científico, Literario e Industrial. México, Vol. I, 1839.

Background and Editorial Notes

1. To Havana on a Merchant Packet

[1] The Young Maidens' Consent, a comedy (1806) by Leandro Fernández de Moratín, sometimes called the Spanish Molière. Bodisco perhaps acted the part of Don Diego, the kind elderly uncle, who gives up his arranged marriage with a young girl in favor of his handsome nephew.

As explained in our introduction, wording in slightly differentiated type is from Fanny Calderón de la Barca's private journals. (For information on the editorial procedures used in preparing this edition of Life in Mexico, see page 637ff.)

[2] From Thomas Gray's "Ode on a Distant Prospect of Eton College."

[3] Many of the Calderóns' well-wishers can be identified. Alexander de Bodisco was the Russian minister to the United States and George Krehmer was his first secretary of legation. Carlos María de Alvear had long been minister from Argentina, then known as Buenos Aires. The presence of these diplomats in New York may perhaps have been due to the well-known fact that foreign representatives did not much care for the unripe little capital city on the Potomac and managed to spend large blocks of time elsewhere.

Richmond Inglis Macleod was Fanny's beloved older sister who, with her widowed mother, was the mainstay of the family boarding school then being conducted at Belmont House in New Brighton on Staten Island. Alexander Norman Macleod (bearing the same name as his father) and Jane Macleod, then about twenty-two and twenty, were Richmond's two oldest children.

Suárez was probably Leonardo S. Suárez; he and Harmony & Company are listed in a New York directory of the time as merchants at 63½ Broadway. Francisco Stoughton, mentioned in the next paragraph, is shown in the same source as Spanish consul in New York.

[4] From the translation by Alexander Pope, with others, of the Odyssey, XV, line 83.

[5] The Sandy Hook lighthouse, built in 1764, partly from the proceeds of a lottery, still stands as the oldest light tower in the United States. (The Highlands of Navesink show in the background of the cut.)

[6] Maria Napoleona Albini, born in Italy in 1808, daughter of a prosperous merchant of Modena, had begun her career at thirteen. She achieved success not only at various opera houses in Italy, Madrid, and Paris, but also in the New World. (From articles in El Museo Mexicano, I, 536; and Museo Popular, I, 114–16.)

Mme Albini was described by another writer as somewhat hefty but graceful, possessed of an enchanting smile and real acting talent which reinforced the effect of her fine voice. In her rendition of the title role of Bellini's Norma she had aroused among Mexicans during her stay in 1836 an enthusiasm approaching delirium. (Mathieu de Fossey, Le Mexique, pp. 241, 536–37.)

Fanny in picking up by ear the name of the prima donna's Italian husband spelled it wrong in her Journal, as she would occasionally misspell other names in the course of her notes. The editors have corrected her spelling without comment whenever more reliable information has been available. (For her published text, Fanny invented a mythical "M. B———" to serve as the owner of the spectacular moustaches.)

[7] Nicholas P. Trist (1800–74) had been a student of Jefferson's, and married his granddaughter. When he was United States consul in Havana a number of charges were made against him, among them failure to support the rights of American citizens and connivance in the outlawed slave trade. Following an investigation he was cleared; the comment expressed here was evidently made before his exoneration.

In 1847 Trist would be sent by President Polk as emissary with peace proposals to end the war with Mexico. Polk and his cabinet later regretted the terms that Trist was empowered to offer and sent a message recalling him. Trist, however, in the belief that breaking off negotiations nearly completed would invite anarchy in Mexico and an indefinite prolongation of hostilities, continued his work with Mexican representatives and signed the treaty that was subsequently ratified by both sides.

[8] Fanny herself as well as her *Life in Mexico* would be denounced some three and a half years later by an irate Mexican newspaper writer who drew an analogy between her work and that of Frances Trollope, British author of *Domestic Manners of the Americans* which had presented in 1832 a highly unflattering view of social life in the United States. (*Diario del Gobierno de la República Mexicana*, April 30, 1843.) For more about the commotion this book first engendered in Mexico, see page 629ff.

[9] "Everything begins to stink, even the eau de cologne!" In her published text this remark was attributed by Fanny to a non-existent Frenchwoman. Fanny explains most of her *Spanish* terms, and in her book provided a brief glossary. In this edition, foreign words not readily guessed or elsewhere translated will be found in the index (with phrases entered under the first significant word).

The *Norma*, according to the shipping news in the *Diario de la Habana* of the following November 13, was an American-owned vessel of 292 tons carrying twenty-one passengers on her present voyage. Only Calderón de la Barca and Mme Albini were named.

[10] "Rotten pot" is a classic Spanish dish of various kinds of meat and vegetables cooked together.

[11] "Between keeping silence and trumpeting." Apparently the phrase is applied to someone who wishes to attract attention without seeming to do so.

[12] The description of the quarrel as revised for publication was more delicately put: ". . . and they ended by applying to each other epithets which, however much they might be deserved, were certainly rather strong."

[13] A reference to Bird's-Nest, Mme Albini's bewhiskered husband.

[14] Emilie Martin, who hereafter will occasionally be referred to as the Duchess, had been in Fanny's employ for over a year. It seems a fair guess that the decision to take this difficult handmaiden to Mexico—where Calderón might have continued as minister for many years—rested on the belief that her capabilities outweighed her known shortcomings.

[15] This reference seems to imply a pillar of society from Havana. "C. T. Catlin, Esq., New Brighton" was one of several persons listed as willing to provide particulars regarding the Inglis family's school on Staten Island.

[16] *Les Enfants d'Edouard* was a play (1833) dealing with the supposed murder in the Tower of London of the dead Edward IV's sons in 1483 at the behest of their guardian and uncle, who ruled as Richard III. *Curiosities of Literature*, a highly entertaining hodgepodge of information by Isaac D'Israeli (the statesman's father), reached its ninth edition in 1834. The book by Irving, according to a reference made to it a little later, was his *History of the Life and Voyages of Christopher Columbus*, which first appeared in 1828.

[17] A reference unknown to the editors. The immediately previous quotation is from *Romeo and Juliet*, Act IV, Scene 1. Along with other writers of her day, Fanny Calderón de la Barca enjoyed quoting. She did so in her Journal for her own amusement, and she later added other quotations for the benefit of her public. To provide background for the heroine of these memoirs—to know what she read and what she liked, what theatrical and musical performances she experienced—we have tried, not always with success, to identify her references.

[18] This allusion seems to be to the opening lines of one of the odes of Horace (III, iii). C. E. Bennett's translation reads: "The man tenacious of his purpose in a righteous cause is not shaken from his firm resolve . . . not by the face of threatening tyrant, not by Auster, stormy master of the restless Adriatic, not by the mighty hand of thundering Jove. Were the vault of heaven to break and fall upon him, its ruins would smite him undismayed." The quotation from Thomas Carlyle which follows is from his then quite recent *Sartor Resartus*, Book I, Chapter III.

[19] The Calderóns' passage was to consume sixteen and a half days. One of the few footnotes in Fanny's own printed text explains the Spanish phrase thus: "The most precious jewel in the Spanish crown, the name given to Cuba." There remained to Spain after the loss of its vast mainland holdings in the western hemisphere only Cuba and Puerto Rico.

[20] *The Pirate*, by the prolific Captain Frederick Marryat, appeared in 1836. Fanny had perhaps already read—she refers to it later—his *Japhet, in Search of a Father*, also published in 1836, a novel *not* concerned with the sea or seafaring men.

21 Donizetti's *Roberto Devereux, Conte d'Essex* had been first produced at the Teatro San Carlo in Naples in October 1837.

22 During the prior January the French painter Louis Jacques Mandé Daguerre had startled the world with the announcement of success, after years of effort, in fixing photographic images as permanent pictures upon copper plates. Prodded into action by the news, William Henry Fox Talbot, a Scottish painter who had also been working for some time upon the same problem, presented a few days later to the Royal Society a report entitled (at least in its printed form): *Some account of the art of photogenic drawing, or the process by which natural objects may be made to delineate themselves without the aid of the artist's pencil.* A more extensive report called *An account of the process employed in photogenic drawing* followed three weeks later. It was undoubtedly one or both of these documents that Calderón was undertaking to translate.

Daguerre, and the heirs of his deceased co-worker Joseph Nicéphore Niepce, were handsomely pensioned by the French government in consideration of Daguerre's revealing the following August the details of his invention for the benefit and free use of all mankind. Even before the disclosure Calderón had written to his good friend the historian William Hickling Prescott on August 2, 1839—when he had been named Spanish envoy to Mexico but was still in the United States—expressing great interest in the new development: "In any case and wherever I may be do not fail to inform me of whatever may come to your notice about it, since besides being useful to me on my travels it is probable that knowledge of these things will be a long time in reaching Mexico."

The description of the process was rushed across the Atlantic in the *British Queen*, one of the first transatlantic steamships, and on September 27, 1839, exactly one month before the Calderóns' departure from New York, the first photograph taken in America showed a view of Broadway, including the Astor house and St. Paul's church.

While Daguerre stole the show with a more perfected technique—his invention would dominate commercial photography for many years—Talbot's process was to prove more significant for the long-term future of photography. With Daguerre's system publicized through lectures, exhibited samples, and glowing reports in the New York press, it is not clear why Calderón selected Talbot's report for translation rather than Daguerre's. Perhaps he had started to work upon it before Daguerre's announcement arrived, or perhaps he intended to cover both. So far as we can determine, his translation was never published. But, as will appear, Calderón would attempt in the following year the role of pioneering photographer in Mexico.

(Heinrich Schwarz, *David Octavius Hill*, pp. 14–15; Roger Wolcott, editor, *The Correspondence of William Hickling Prescott, 1833–1847*, p. 85; Carleton Mabee, *The American Leonardo, A Life of Samuel F. B. Morse*, pp. 228–29.)

23 *Cinq-Mars; ou une conjuration sous Louis XIII* was an historical novel (1826) by Count Alfred Victor de Vigny. *Jacob Faithful* (1834) was one of Captain Frederick Marryat's stories of the sea.

24 From the Nineteenth Psalm, verse 2.

25 Fanny took both these quotations from Shakespeare's *Tempest*, Act I, Scene 1.

26 The vessel could have stopped and searched the American-owned *Norma* by virtue of a British-American agreement of 1824 aimed at an end to slave trading—already an act of piracy by American law. Pressured by various humanitarian groups, Great Britain (which early in the previous century enjoyed a monopoly on carrying slaves to Spanish colonies) had assumed leadership in abrogating the trade. Spain, upon receiving a payment of £400,-000 from Great Britain, had likewise agreed to stop importing slaves.

Slaves continued to be brought into Cuba, nevertheless. An Englishman who had been in Havana during this general period commented on the large importations that slipped through in spite of British efforts at policing, while another writer whose visit was within a year of the Calderóns' not only saw slavers at the docks but also boarded one recently arrived. (Charles Augustus Murray, *Travels in North America during the Years 1834, 1835, & 1836*, II, 267–78; Carlo Barinetti, *A Voyage to Mexico and Havanna*, pp. 136–37.) A modern writer cites the estimate that 250,000 slaves were brought into Cuba between 1820 and 1850. (Hugh Bradley, *Havana, Cinderella's City*, p. 278.)

27 A paraphrase of lines from *Hamlet* in Act III, Scene 2.

28 L. E. L. was the pen name of Laetitia Elizabeth Landon, an English writer of popular novels and flowery poetry, and editor of ladies' annuals. Her sudden death of a little over a year before was still a matter of wide speculation. She had met and married George Maclean, governor of the Gold Coast (now Ghana), in west Africa, while he was in England to testify at an inquiry into his administration. He was completely cleared of all charges and they sailed in the brig *Maclean* to Cape Coast Castle. She died soon, and suddenly, apparently of poison, on the morning of the very day the *Maclean* was to return to England, taking back the only other white woman in the colony, the steward's wife, who had

been serving her as maid and companion. At the inquest it was brought out that since before her marriage she had possessed and used, for a supposedly ailing heart and attacks of "spasms," drugs of varying potency bottled in somewhat similar containers. A prompt verdict of death by misadventure was reached by the local officials and she was buried the night following her death under the courtyard of the castle. Rumors of suicide or of murder by a discarded local mistress of the governor flourished; and about a year after the time Fanny wrote her Journal a medical investigator was sent out to Africa—but no evidence contrary to the established verdict was uncovered. By the time Fanny prepared *Life in Mexico* for publication she either had modified her original opinion as a result of the investigation or hesitated to add to the gossip. What she presented in print was limited to these few words: "It does not seem to me at all astonishing that the remedies which she took in England without injury should have proved fatal to her in that wretched climate." A biography of L. E. L. by Helen Ashton entitled *Letty Landon* appeared in 1951.

[29] The peak of Matanzas, presumably called *pan* from its shape like a loaf, rises to a height of more than a thousand feet. In contrast to the low sandy shore to the east, it provides a striking landmark for sailors.

[30] Morro Castle, first used in 1597 although much altered later, had been constructed as part of a plan to protect the far-spread holdings of Spain. The Morro at San Juan in Puerto Rico, Morro Castle in Havana, and fortifications in Santo Domingo and on the Isthmus of Panama had all been designed by the same Italian-born military engineer, Bautista Antonelli; so, also, had the island fortress which the Calderóns would later see as they reached Veracruz. (George Kubler, *Mexican Architecture of the Sixteenth Century*, I, 207 and fn.)

[31] Calderón's dispatches to his government, now available in two entirely separate printed works, offer a valuable supplement to Fanny's account. As will shortly appear, the Calderóns were guests of Don Bernardo Hechavarría, no advance plans apparently having been confirmed as to where they would stay. In a dispatch written a few days later Calderón reports on his Cuban welcome "after a long and laborious passage." In language that sounds somewhat guarded he then acknowledges indebtedness to his host, who "came on board and obliged me to follow him to his house where he has entertained me with a prodigal magnificence which it has cost me considerable difficulty to restrain." (*Relaciones Diplomáticas Hispano-Mexicanas (1839–1898), Serie I, Despachos Generales*, I, 1839–1841, 12–13.)

[32] General Juan José Montalvo, who in his younger days had fought the French in Spain, was a sugar planter of great wealth. Don Ramón was second of the general's six sons in the family's roster of ten children. (Fernando Suárez de Tangil y de Angulo, Conde de Vallellano, *Nobiliario Cubano*, I, 179–90.)

[33] Don Bernardo Hechavarría, holder of a financial post of some importance in the colonial administration, lived, according to an official directory of the time, at the Calle de Cuba No. 153—which faced directly on the bay. He and his brother Prudencio, who will appear shortly, were both trained as lawyers and were both Gentlemen of the Royal Bedchamber. (*Guía de Forasteros en la Siempre Fiel Isla de Cuba*, 1839.) Bernardo would be made a *marqués* some years later, but his title and line died out with his only granddaughter. (Francisco Xavier de Santa Cruz y Mallen, *Historia de Familias Cubanas*, III, 210.)

Not only was Fanny in the position, as soon will be evident, of initially not much liking life with her Havana hosts, but she was psychologically quite unprepared for what she was to encounter in a tropical Spanish colony long accustomed to a mixture of racial stocks. Her astonishment over unfamiliar physical and social situations quickly mellowed, however, during her twelve-day visit. In spite of all she confided to her Journal at this time, when the Calderóns returned through Havana two years later, they elected to stay with the Hechavarrías in preference to being guests of the Captain-General.

(The cut on page 17 showing a *volante* and the cuts on pages 23 and 26 are enlarged segments from the frontispiece of Volume II of the first American edition of *Life in Mexico*.)

[34] Lace of the type known as blonde, originally made only of unbleached natural-color silk, may also be either white or black. Fanny will often note the use of blonde lace for mantillas and dresses.

2. A Glimpse of Spanish Colonial Life

[1] The preparation of this chapter has differed from that of others: instead of starting with Fanny's previously published text and enriching it with material from the Journal, we have reversed the procedure. For, contrary to her published statement that "the last few days have been spent in such a round of festivity, that not a moment has been left for

writing," she managed to write at great length. Of her twelve days in Havana, not one went by without a copious entry in her Journal. But for print she omitted most of what she first set down, and reorganized the remainder. She struck out the great bulk of her adverse comment, and salved her conscience by the statement: "I do not pretend to form any judgment of Havana. We have seen it too much *en beau*."

The heavy censoring was due, no doubt, to more than the wish to avoid an overload of sharp comment at the beginning of her book. By the time she returned through Havana two years later and encountered once more its generous, showy hospitality—which was then clearly for them and not for her husband's office—she had become accustomed to Latin ways and manners, and the memory of their first visit was perhaps tempered by her two years' experience in Mexico.

[2] In addition to the many titled Spanish-born officials on the scene, there were at this time some twenty-five Cuban *marqueses* and thirty *condes*, most of them heads of families of enormous wealth. More than half of the patents of nobility had been granted since 1816, and bearers of older titles sometimes loftily referred to families more recently honored as "sugar nobility."

[3] Fanny in readying herself for her husband's new post had evidently read the Mexican memoirs of the much-traveled South Carolinian who became first United States minister to Mexico, Joel R. Poinsett. What Poinsett wrote after making a round of ceremonial visits in Mexico in the autumn of 1822 was: "Remember, when you take your leave of a Spanish grandee, to bow as you leave the room, at the head of the stairs, where the host accompanies you, and after descending the first flight, turn round, and you will see him expecting a third salutation, which he returns with great courtesy, and remains until you are out of sight; so that as you wind down the stairs, if you catch a glimpse of him, kiss your hand, and he will think you a most accomplished cavalier. This is the only ceremony to undergo, for your reception will be cordial and friendly." (*Notes on Mexico*, p. 86.) And on his following page Poinsett added: "If you take to the house, the oftener you go the more welcome you are, and you are treated by all the family with kindness and familiarity."

[4] The Condesa de Villanueva was born María Teresa de Ugarte in 1797. The Calderóns would spend much of their time with the Villanuevas on their return later to Cuba.

[5] Both the identity of Mrs. S. and the source of the quotation are unknown to the editors. It is possible that Mrs. S. was the second wife of Captain E. W. H. Schenley, Fanny's twice-widowed brother-in-law whose first bride had been the short-lived Catherine Inglis. Schenley lived in Havana for a period in the 1830's as a British official concerned with the suppression of the slave trade. But whether his second wife died there we do not know.

[6] Fanny's guess as to the age of the Condesa de Fernandina—"the Chieftainess" or "the Boss" as her nickname might be translated—was close to the mark. She had been born Teresa de Garro y Risel forty-six years before. Her husband, José María de Herrera y Herrera, who was distinguished from almost all the nobility of Cuba by being a grandee of Spain as well as a count, was fifty-two.

Fanny would later write her friend Prescott that the countess was "full of revolutionary and reformatory projects"—and that her diamonds were worth $300,000. (Wolcott, *Correspondence of . . . Prescott*, p. 286.)

[7] The piece which so frightened the usually poised Fanny must have been that advertised in the *Diario de la Habana* as *Los Ladrones Nocturnos* (The Nocturnal Thieves).

[8] The *General de la Marina* was Manuel de Cañas. Calderón in his dispatch of November 23 from Havana explained that he decided to accept this offer without previous authorization on the ground that it seemed more suitable for the Queen's representative to appear at Veracruz in a ship bearing the almost-forgotten flag of a Spanish naval vessel rather than by ordinary passenger ship. (*Despachos Generales*, I, 13.)

[9] *Lucia di Lammermoor* was only four years old and New York had not yet heard it. According to Havana press notices, the soprano was "T. Rossi." One is tempted to guess that she was a relative of the famous Elisa Rossi who sang both *Lucia di Lammermoor* and *Roberto Devereux* in Italy under Donizetti's own direction. Montresor was presumably Gian Battista Montresor, who had earlier been well received in other roles in New York.

[10] Cláudio Martínez de Pinillos, second Conde de Villanueva, husband of the lady who had captured Fanny's interest and affection, was second in importance only to the Captain-General of Cuba. He was described by a visiting Englishman of the period as a man of integrity and ability, and the first native-born Cuban ever to hold such high office. (Benjamin Moore Norman, *Rambles by Land and Water*, p. 67.)

[11] The Conde de Santovenia, born in Seville and a lawyer by training, was José Martínez de Campos y de la Vega. (Santa Cruz y Mallen, *Historia de Familias Cubanas*, II, 278.) On Fanny's return to Havana two years later she described him in a letter to her friend Prescott as "a rich *soltero* [bachelor], whom a young girl had the good taste to re-

fuse the other day, though considered the greatest *parti* in Havana." (Wolcott, *Correspondence of . . . Prescott*, p. 286.) The count did marry some twelve years later.

The number of adult Peñalvers in Havana at this time as listed in genealogical works, and the complexities of their interrelationships, have made it impossible for us to identify Fanny's pleasant dinner companion with surety, but a likely guess is that he was José María Peñalver y Cárdenas. Domingo Herrera was a cousin of the Conde de Fernandina.

[12] Prudencio Hechavarría, brother of the Calderóns' host, had been among those Cubans who, a few years earlier, argued in the Spanish press that Cuba should share in Spanish political reforms. (Jacobo de la Pezuela, *Ensayo Histórico de la Isla de Cuba*, p. 587.)

Fanny later fastens to Don Prudencio the nickname of Mirabeau—referring, perhaps, to the French statesman's oratorical and literary powers and his reputed self-assurance.

[13] Tenochtitlan was the pre-Spanish name for the great Aztec city on the site of which Mexico's capital stands. Fanny hastily set down the improvisation in Spanish in her Journal, and the translation here given is necessarily free in a few places in view of difficulties in interpreting her handwriting.

As noted by Fanny, the improvisation also dealt with the termination the previous summer of the Carlist War in Spain through victories won by the Queen's forces under General Baldomero Espartero.

[14] In her Journal, Fanny placed an asterisk after the word "pretty" and then entered this note at the bottom of the page: "Since writing the above I have changed my mind."

[15] María Cristina was the Queen Regent, widow of Ferdinand VII and acting at this time on behalf of her little daughter Isabel II, whose younger sister was the Infanta Luisa Fernanda, referred to in the next paragraph.

[16] The beautiful Duchess of Sutherland was Mistress of the Robes to Queen Victoria. The Marchioness of Normanby was one of the Queen's Bedchamber Women. They and other Whig ladies in the Queen's household had been during the previous May the center of a resounding political broil. After a reverse in Parliament, Lord Melbourne and his cabinet resigned and Sir Robert Peel as the new prime minister interviewed the Queen on the formation of his cabinet. The youthful Queen—she was just short of twenty—flatly refused Peel's request that she replace her principal ladies with the wives of Tories. Peel declined to form a cabinet under the circumstances and Melbourne remained in power until 1841.

A brother of the Duchess of Sutherland—Viscount Morpeth—will appear fleetingly at the end of this book.

[17] Santiago de la Cuesta y Manzanal was created first Conde de la Reunión de Cuba in 1824. (Santa Cruz y Mallen, *Historia de Familias Cubanas*, III, 125–26.) He was almost certainly the same Señor Cuesta who, many years earlier, had been host to the great geographer Alexander von Humboldt during his visit to Cuba.

Here and later Fanny seems to use the word *merchant* as synonymous with the modern term *businessman*. It is plain from newspapers and other sources of the time that prosperous merchants, who were also the bankers of this period, ranked high socially, and were intermingled with the aristocracy.

[18] Both of these buildings survive as a part of Cuba's heritage of colonial architecture.

[19] What Fanny heard sung was almost certainly not an adaptation, but the actual words of the finale to Act II of Bellini's *I Puritani*, first performed early in 1835. The ample singable tune in march time, together with its rousing theme of honor, death, and freedom, inevitably acquired widespread political significance. Not many years later when Cuba openly chafed under Spanish rule, the song as written was apparently banned there. In Washington a young lady, unaware of its implications, innocently called for the inflammable song at an evening gathering, and later described its fiery rendition by a young Cuban in the presence of the then Spanish minister, who courteously applauded the performance. (Marian Gouverneur, *As I Remember*, pp. 234–35.)

[20] Another source speaks of San Felipe as a small church with handsome altars, and as having attached to it a large library of religious works. (Samuel Hazard, *Cuba with Pen and Pencil*, p. 125.) The convent of San Felipe—of which presumably the church and library were a part—appears on maps of the time.

In her Journal Fanny added: "The Cathedral is large—with an altar all gilt—".

[21] A group portrait of the Montalvos, done a good many years before Fanny visited Havana, is reproduced in a Cuban genealogical work. The general's attractive-looking wife, Doña María Antonia Calvo de la Puerta, is shown garbed in a high-waisted Empire dress; in her arms she holds the child then her youngest, and round her are disposed her father, her husband, and a flock of children. The Montalvos had ten children altogether, nine of whom ultimately married and produced children. (Suárez de Tangil, *Nobiliario*

Cubano, I, 179–90.) The Montalvo house, according to a guide of the time, was on the Calle de Cuba, No. 150.

[22] Hortense de Beauharnais, daughter of Napoleon's Empress Josephine by her first husband, was for a short time Queen of Holland as unhappy wife to Louis Bonaparte, who ostensibly ruled it under his older brother Napoleon. She had died two years before.

[23] The traveler-scientist Humboldt—who was interested in almost everything in the New World, and collected statistics, climbed mountains, descended into mines, observed, and recorded—noted that the Peruvian Indians were able in the middle of the night to distinguish among Indians, Negroes, and Europeans by their respective smells. (*A Political Essay on the Kingdom of New Spain,* translated by John Black, I, 245.)

[24] The Marquesa de Arcos, who earlier lent Fanny a harp, was María Matilde Calvo, married to Ignacio Francisco Peñalver y Peñalver, third *marqués.* Born in 1804, and therefore almost exactly Fanny's age, she was the mother of a daughter already taking part in adult society.

[25] As may be remembered, the earlier impromptu offered at the Hechavarría party in the Calderóns' honor was by Don Prudencio Hechavarría, brother of Don Bernardo, at whose house they were staying. From this fact, and later statements by Fanny on November 19, it seems clear that Don Prudencio was also author of the toasts which follow. The first of them was offered in the name of Doña Antonia, hostess at the dinner, and the second apparently in the name of her husband, General Juan Montalvo.

For her Journal Fanny hurriedly set down these improvisations in Spanish and, as before, the translation here given is necessarily free in part. It may, however, serve to recreate the atmosphere of the long-ago Havana dinner party. The first, second, fifth, and sixth lines, as Fanny heard them addressed to her in Spanish, ran:

> *A ti, blonda ninfa de la Caledonia*
> *Amiga entusiasta del gran Walte Scot . . .*
> *Que tu Angel dichoso, con lazo de flores,*
> *En ti, dulce Fani, produzca un botón . . .*

[26] We can only speculate as to why Fanny herself did not call her husband by his first name of Angel (pronounced approximately Ahn'-hel), but instead used the first part of his *last* name. As Calderón in his signature seems never to have written out his first name, to ignore it may have been his own preference. (Fanny in writing her husband's name did not bother with the accent mark. We use it, however, for the sake of consistency.)

[27] The six exclamation points seem to be the comment of the fourteen-months-wed Fanny on this public expression of good wishes for a fertile future. The lasso or rope of flowers may have been a reference to the custom, still current, of thus encircling a couple during the marriage ceremony. The six *lustres* or glories of love (plural *loves* in the Spanish original) were perhaps the Montalvos' six sons. If so, their four daughters seem not to have counted. But while Fanny's handwriting in this case is clear, one cannot help but wonder whether the word *lustres* had not been used—a term meaning, in the singular, a period of five years. In such case the translation might be: "And like Juan and Antonia, with thirty years of loving,/May you have grandchildren to cradle!!!!!!" (The Calderóns would have no children.)

In the poem to Calderón that follows, Anáhuac is an old term for Mexico's great central plateau. The eagle perched on the nopal symbolizes Mexico, and the lion obviously personifies Spain.

[28] "Happen what may—it's only the first step that's hard." The second phrase is said to have been the Marquise du Deffand's retort to the Cardinal de Polignac's relation of the tradition that St. Denis of France, after having been decapitated by the Roman governor, walked two leagues carrying his head in his hands. Just as Fanny regarded the Habaneros as exotic, she seems sensibly to have realized that she was equally a subject for fascinated scrutiny.

[29] Lorenzo Papanti, the husband whom Mme Papanti had left behind her, was a Boston institution. He continued teaching into old age, and as this book goes to press there still survive hardy Boston elders who remember being drilled during childhood by the dancing master who came to the United States at about the same time as the Inglis family.

[30] "Lay on, Macduff,/And damn'd be him that first cries, 'Hold, enough!' "—*Macbeth,* Act V, Scene 8.

[31] Fanny's informant is not borne out by the official Cuban statistics of 1846 regarding the racial composition of the island's population. The then captain-general reported the total population at close to 900,000, of whom almost half were listed as white, with one-sixth shown as "free Blacks." (*Diario de la Marina,* cited by Robert Granville Caldwell, *The Lopez Expeditions to Cuba, 1848–1851,* p. 19 fn.) What does not show, of course, in

such general figures is how many Cubans had some African ancestry. As Fanny sensed, the colonial Spanish attitude toward race (in spite of theoretical stratification) seems in reality to have been far from rigid.

32 The official termed *Regente* for Cuba was, according to the *Guía de Forasteros* for 1839, Señor Fermín Gil de Linares. The name of the family at whose house the gifted child was encountered was left a blank in Fanny's Journal.

33 November 19 was not the birthday of the nine-year-old Queen Isabel II, who had been born October 10, 1830, but rather the feast day of St. Elizabeth (Isabel in Spanish) of Hungary, her patron.

34 The governor or Captain-General was Joaquín Ezpeleta y Enrile. He would in fact very soon be replaced by another official.

35 The mother of the *Intendenta* was the widowed Doña María de los Angeles Risel de Ugarte. The little count, who was precociously attending a grown-up dinner party, was about eight, and was named Cláudio after his father. An only child, he died unmarried in 1858, and the family title descended to another branch of the family. (Santa Cruz y Mallen, *Historia de Familias Cubanas*, II, 383–84.)

36 "Here the great nobles call each other *thou* and *thee*." The startling degree to which the custom of intermarriage reached during this period may be illustrated by the Peñalver family whose members, with few exceptions, when they did not marry a Montalvo, a Cárdenas, or a Calvo, intermarried among themselves. The Marqués de Casa Peñalver was, in 1839, Sebastián Peñalver, the third *marqués*. He was married to a Peñalver cousin, sister of the more recently ennobled Nicolás Peñalver, Conde de Peñalver. This Nicolás Peñalver married his own niece María Peñalver—and this niece was, moreover, a Peñalver on her mother's side too, and was the widow of his brother. The head of still another branch, Juan Crisóstomo Peñalver, Conde de San Fernando de Peñalver (whose father had likewise married his own Peñalver niece), was a bachelor at this time; he would subsequently marry a Montalvo and acquire many civic honors. The Marqués de los Arcos, mentioned with his wife a few pages earlier, was Ignacio Francisco Peñalver y Peñalver, son of Peñalver first cousins.

Domingo de la Herrera y Herrera, mentioned in passing, was the product of three generations of Herrera-Herrera marriages.

37 Another foreign lady who visited Havana in the mid-nineteenth century remarked that the ownership of a *volante* was a social necessity for every family which could afford one and for many which could not. She noted that in the house of a family of modest means the *volante* when not in use might be kept in the nearly empty drawing room, to serve as a sofa. (Lady Emmeline Stuart-Wortley, *Travels in the United States, etc., during 1849 and 1850*, II, 207–8.)

38 A quick look at the text of this melodrama laid in the reign of Charles II of England —translated from the French of Joseph Bouchardy by Eugenio de Ochoa (Madrid, 1839) —reveals that it has 52 scenes. The eighteen-year interval between the prologue and first act provides time for a number of mysterious political fugitives to emigrate to America, where the youthful hero and heroine are born, and for some of them to return to England after the Restoration. Maria, brought up as foster-daughter of Tom, the humble blind bell ringer of St. Paul's cathedral, is kidnapped and shut up in *la quinta de Vindsor* because she stands in the way of the ambitious Lord Bedfort's plans for his son, who loves her. Many characters, including the king himself, and a gifted young eye surgeon, thicken the plot. It is resolved when Tom, his sight restored, recognizes in the wicked Lord Bedfort a former would-be regicide whom he had known as Villiams Smith. Some of those who seemed to be of low degree are found to be of high degree, and vice versa.

39 "Bring in the bottled lightning, a clean tumbler, and a corkscrew," ordered the demented gentleman in question after he had descended the Nicklebys' chimney to pay a call; he then requested a thunder sandwich. (Charles Dickens, *Nicholas Nickleby*, Chapter XLIX.) The book had been published that same year.

40 The water system, finished in 1835, brought water in an iron pipe from Almendares to Havana. The railroad was a slightly later project. It went southward across the island toward Batabanó, about twenty-five miles, and by the time of Fanny's visit connected eastward to Güines. (Pezuela, *Ensayo Histórico de . . . Cuba*, pp. 603–5.)

Cubans had good reason to be proud of their railroad, as it antedated rail construction in the mother country by some ten years.

41 Zamora, later referred to as Pepe Zamora, was presumably José Zamora—formerly a high official in Havana, who undertook to help the Calderóns' friend Prescott to obtain documents needed in preparation for writing his *Conquest of Mexico*. (Wolcott, *Correspondence of . . . Prescott*, pp. 111–12.)

[42] A reference to the aria sung by Elvira in *I Puritani*, Act II. It begins, *"Qui la voce sua soave,"* and continues, *"Ah! mai più li rivedrò . . ."* The other reference is to *Caritea, Regina di Spagna* (Caritea, Queen of Spain) by Giuseppe Saverio Mercadante, first produced in 1826.

[43] A century-later writer on Havana explains that shops bore poetic names because Spanish law taxed more heavily those which advertised under the names of their proprietors. (Bradley, *Havana, Cinderella's City*, p. 287.) In any case, the tradition of charming names for shops has survived in smaller cities and towns in Mexico.

[44] Although Fanny spelled the fading beauty's name with one "l", it seems likely that she was a connection of the Morell family on whose sugar estate two of the three gifted Peabody girls of Salem, Massachusetts—Mary, later wife to Horace Mann, and Sophia, who married Nathaniel Hawthorne—spent the year 1834. Mary acted as tutor to the family's two small sons. Just before sailing for home, the girls enjoyed a short visit with a wealthy three-generation Fernández family in their handsome house in Havana. (Louise Hall Tharp, *The Peabody Sisters of Salem*, pp. 73–74, 97–98.)

[45] Havana's system of fortifications included stout walls as protection against attack by land. Before the nineteenth century, however, the city had outgrown its walls, and long before the time of the Calderóns' visit various suburbs had grown up outside.

[46] Captain E. W. H. Schenley, as already indicated, had been married years before to Fanny's older sister Catherine Inglis. The lady called on was evidently Septimia Randolph Meikleham, granddaughter of Thomas Jefferson and seventh daughter of Thomas Mann Randolph, once governor of Virginia, and his wife Martha Jefferson. Her Scottish-born husband, David Scott Meikleham, kinsman to Sir Walter Scott, was listed in the Cuban *Guía de Forasteros* for 1840 as *profesor de medicina*, his name spelled Mechlehem. He died in New York, and his widow with her children lived in Washington for many years. (Gouverneur, *As I Remember*, p. 357.)

[47] As written in Fanny's Journal this name cannot be deciphered with certainty.

[48] Perhaps S. C. Tennant who, according to advertisements in the local press, was providing Cuban sugar planters with rollers, pumps, and steam engines with the potency of eight horses. (*Noticioso y Lucero*, November 12, 1839.)

[49] This we assume was Alexander Norman Macleod—whom Fanny, in accordance with Scottish custom, calls by the name of the property of which he had formerly been laird, the island of Harris. As explained in the introduction, he was the estranged husband of Fanny's older sister Richmond, and was making his life in Jamaica.

[50] Another British traveler, Sir James Edward Alexander, also describes dining with the Fernandinas. He admired the splendid house and the large library, but he noted that as they dined gamecocks ran under the table and that old favored servants peered in at the company from other rooms. He characterized the count as intelligent and his wife as handsome and accomplished. (*Transatlantic Sketches*, I, 379–80.) The Fernandinas' address is given in a directory of the time as the Calle de Mercaderes No. 95.

[51] As we have seen, throughout her entire stay in Havana, Fanny was busy making daily additions to her Journal. But this paragraph is what she stated in her published text, apparently to account for the heavy censorship of her Journal material.

[52] This piece of jewelry (which Fanny's gift from her friend seems to have been) would be mentioned in a roundabout way by Alexander Everett in a letter he wrote to his wife from Havana on February 9, 1841. In speaking of the enthusiasm engendered by the Austrian-born dancer Fanny Elssler, he says: "It is now intended to present her with an elegant garland of artificial flowers, wrought in gold, diamonds and other precious stones —similar, I suppose, to the bouquet which was presented to her namesake, my fair friend, Madame Calderon de la Barca, on her visit to the island on her way to Mexico." (Unpublished letter of Alexander H. Everett, in the Massachusetts Historical Society.)

[53] A comedy in two acts by Jean-François-Alfred Bayard, first presented in 1838.

3. Havana to Veracruz on a Man-of-War

[1] Paraphrased from Pope's *Essay on Man*, Epistle I. "All this scene of man;/A mighty mazel but not without a plan."

Fanny implies here some familiarity with operations on an English man-of-war. The sponsor for her presentation to George IV as a young girl in Edinburgh in 1822 was recorded as Lady Beresford, presumably the wife of Admiral Sir John Poo Beresford, who from 1820 to 1823 was Naval Officer Commanding at Leith and on the coast of Scotland. If so, Fanny may have been in fact a guest on board a British naval vessel.

2 The naval commandant in Havana may well have ordered the *Jasón* stocked in the Calderóns' honor with more and better food than its officers ordinarily enjoyed. Two years later the *Jasón* would carry, as a courtesy, Mexico's fallen former president—Anastasio Bustamante—from Veracruz to Havana on his way to exile. Appended as a part of the diplomatic correspondence on the matter was a list of extra supplies laid on for the journey: they included not only such staples as chocolate, beans, rice, a hundred onions and what seems to the modern housekeeper a stupendous quantity of oil, but also fresh fruits and vegetables, colonies of chickens, thirty dozen eggs, raisins, shelled almonds, twenty-four-pound Westphalian hams, and a variety of wines, beer, and rum. (*Despachos Generales,* I, 306–8.)

3 The *alacrán* which Fanny in her Journal called an insect and then scratched out and inflated to a reptile is neither. It is a scorpion, and scorpions, along with spiders, are arachnids. Contrary to what Fanny's informants said, *alacranes* are venomous. The suggestion that they were not was perhaps advanced to allay feminine fears.

4 These anecdotes were presumably passed on to Fanny by the officers of the *Jasón*, and therefore represent a pro-Tacón point of view. An officer in a French squadron which visited Havana earlier in 1839, not long after Tacón's departure, likewise spoke of him with admiration. Tacón, he said, not only put a stop to graft and crime but also succeeded in bringing down the island's high mortality rate. His vigorous administration made him enemies and he was the victim of unfounded accusations made by detractors who succeeded in getting him recalled to Spain. (Eugène Maissin, *The French in Mexico and Texas (1838–1839),* translated and edited by James L. Shepherd, III, pp. 218–20.)
A modern writer (Bradley, *Havana, Cinderella's City,* pp. 293–99) takes the other side. Tacón did clean up Havana and rid it of petty peculation, he says, but was a merciless tyrant who reserved all the really succulent graft for himself.

5 The figure now accepted for the height of Orizaba (which Fanny, writing from ear, originally called Orizavel) is approximately 18,700 feet. On the North American continent only Mount McKinley in Alaska is higher.

6 Fanny is almost certainly referring here to that section of Humboldt's monumental series of reports on his explorations and observations in South and North America which dealt with Mexico—the *Essai politique sur le royaume de la Nouvelle-Espagne.* Her volume in Spanish must have been the translation by Vicente González Arnao, under the title of *Ensayo Político sobre Nueva-España,* of which three editions had appeared by the time she encountered the work on shipboard. She seems not merely to have read and re-read it, but almost to have committed it to memory. Like other travelers before and after her, she would paraphrase Humboldt in some of her later discussions.

7 From *Pleasures of Hope,* Part I, 1, 41, by Thomas Campbell.
"But Hope, the charmer, linger'd still behind."

8 Fanny by no means exaggerated the violence of the storm. The Veracruz newspaper *El Censor* for December 20, 1839, later reported that Calderón requested permission of the local commandant to allow the *Jasón* to remain in the port to permit repairs of injuries sustained on the unlucky passage.

9 Fanny was reading—in what version we do not know—a work by the French army officer Germain-François Poulain de Saint-Foix. This incident may be found in his *Essais historiques sur Paris et autres œuvres* (edition of 1776, Vol. VI entitled *Lettres Turques,* pp. 64–65). The story first appeared in 1732, about a decade after the publication of Montesquieu's *Lettres Persanes.*

10 Nautically-minded readers will note that correctly speaking this speed should have been given simply as eight knots.

11 From near the close of Book XII, the final book, of Milton's *Paradise Lost.*

12 This last sentence, which gives the impression that Fanny is about to fold up the sheets upon which she has written, seems to have been added to give verisimilitude to the plan of presenting her *Life in Mexico* as composed purely from a series of letters. That she used real letters for parts of her book seems clear. Certainly, however, this early portion, for which the parallel Journal survives, is based primarily on a revision and expansion of what she there set forth. According to a letter from Calderón to Prescott of the following March, Fanny was so completely occupied during her early Mexican months that she had "not even found time to send two letters to her family." (Wolcott, *Correspondence of . . . Prescott,* p. 112.)

4. Veracruz: First Mexican Impressions

1 The great polygonal-shaped island fortress of San Juan de Ulúa, now connected to the mainland, had been built in the sixteenth century. The present city of Veracruz was

established under its protection on the opposite shore. The fortress, a romantic-appearing complex of walls, moats, and damp dungeons, is now a colonial monument. (See Plate 5.)

[2] The local pilot, evidently a Spanish combatant who had remained in Mexico after the War of Independence, was referring to the final bitter defense of the island fortress as the last toe-hold of Spanish power in Mexico. Fanny will later tell how, in 1825, the Spanish garrison had been finally starved into surrender.

The French capture of the fortress occurred only the year before the Calderóns' arrival, in 1838. It was an action of the brief so-called Pastry War, which took its name from the previous destruction during civil disturbances of property of French citizens, including a pastry shop. The French contended that Mexican officials had been dilatory in considering their claims and that forced loans had been exacted from resident Frenchmen. The total sum in dispute mounted to some 600,000 pesos. In January 1838 the French minister, his demands unsatisfied, left Mexico, and French naval vessels blockaded Veracruz through the spring and summer. Meetings between French and Mexican representatives proved inconclusive, and the French dispatched more ships under the one-armed Admiral Charles Baudin, a veteran of Trafalgar. San Juan de Ulúa was fired upon with notable efficiency on November 27, 1838, and the Mexican garrison at the castle was forced to capitulate. Through mediation initiated by the British minister to Mexico, Richard Pakenham—whom the Calderóns will soon know—a settlement was effected.

[3] "Thy neck is as a tower of ivory; thine eyes like the fishpools in Heshbon, by the gate of Bath-rabbim: thy nose is as the tower of Lebanon which looketh toward Damascus." (Song of Solomon, 7:4.)

[4] A dispatch Calderón sent back to Spain a few days later described Dionisio José de Velasco as a man of honor and a leading Spanish merchant of Veracruz, who had acted without recompense as Spanish vice-consul. The consul who had rowed out to meet them—one of several Spanish officials whose service antedated Calderón's arrival—is identified in the dispatch as Miguel Ruiz Sáinz. (Jaime Delgado, *España y México en el Siglo XIX*, II, 142.)

When one of the editors was in Veracruz some years ago he enjoyed meeting a descendant of Don Dionisio, Señor Ricardo de Velasco. Through his courtesy the house where Fanny spent her first rather despondent days in Mexico was identified (see Plate 9) at the Avenida de la Independencia No. 27. (Nearly opposite at No. 30 stood the house whose flourishing condition Fanny will shortly admire.) Don Dionisio de Velasco himself, the Calderóns' kindly host, was saluted via his portrait, a family possession (Plate 8).

[5] What they thought of Fanny is not recorded. The difference in the journalistic approach of a mid-nineteenth-century Mexican paper and a newspaper of today is well illustrated by the account of their arrival in the Veracruz newspaper *El Censor*. There was no mention of Fanny or her stylish bonnet or of her maid or of the poodle Finette; Calderón's arrival alone constituted the news.

[6] As the reader will discover, two years in Mexico would change Fanny's views on many things, including Veracruz cookery.

The French minister stationed in Washington complained, in September 1841, in similar vein about the cuisine of the United States: "But that is the painful side of travelling in America: it is impossible to eat the atrocious things they serve to you—tough meat, spiced, and stewed in the most awful sauces; impossible to get a cutlet, or even an egg." (Adolphe de Bacourt, *Souvenirs of a Diplomat*, p. 241.)

[7] The prospect of painful death by the *vómito negro*—the black vomit, or yellow fever—dominated the thinking of every traveler to Veracruz during the warm months. Foreigners were known to be especially vulnerable. The modern reader, equipped with hindsight, hears the unrealized word *mosquito* buzzing insistently through long-ago discussions of the mysterious malady. The observant Humboldt had even put into print his belief that yellow fever was *not* passed directly from one person to another. He cited the fact that some of the most cautious departing travelers—who, to avoid personal contacts, hurried across the fever belt to the coast and passed quickly through Veracruz at night in a litter—later died of the dread disease at sea. (*Political Essay on . . . New Spain*, IV, 176.)

H. G. Ward also recorded in his *Mexico in 1827* (II, 244–45) various speculations about the "seeds" of yellow fever, which were thought to be related to the action of the sun on wet, low-lying, rank tropical vegetation. He noted that it was rarely contracted by the crews of ships anchored offshore at Veracruz; moreover that, when isolated cases did occur on shipboard, the pestilence seldom spread.

The Cuban doctor Carlos Juan Finlay held as early as 1881 that mosquitoes were the transmitters of yellow fever and even named the particular variety (*Stegomyia fasciata*, now termed *Aëdes aegypti*), which bites by day as well as by night—and which insists on clean, standing water in which to breed. Finlay later convinced Walter Reed, but it was not until the famous experiments on heroic volunteers in 1900 that Finlay, Reed, and their associates were vindicated.

W. Bullock, a traveler who in the 1820's enjoyed the best of health during the "sickly season," quoted in full the confident advice of his own English physician on how to avoid yellow fever. He cautioned his charge to guard against sunstroke ("wear always a light silk umbrella"), to keep his feet dry and his bowels "comfortably open," to wear flannel next to his skin, and not to worry should prickly heat appear (as a good showing of heat rash was almost positive insurance against seizure by other complaints). He then more pertinently directed: "You ought most carefully to avoid sleeping in low, damp, or marshy places. . . . never, if you can avoid it, in bed-rooms, the windows of which are in a direction that admits the *land wind*, more especially if that wind blow over neighbouring marshes or swamps." Smoking, the doctor observed, seemed to be an efficacious preventive, especially in the rainy season when the air was oppressive and when diseases were rife. Anticipating the modern theory of psychosomatic causes of some illnesses, he went on to urge his charge to maintain a state of good cheer: "Avoid all the depressing passions, and be not too anxious about any object. You have nothing to fear from an attack of illness in Mexico. . . . The only complaints by which you may be invaded are fever, dysentery, and diarrhœa, and, perhaps, cholera morbus." (*Six Months' Residence and Travels in Mexico,* pp. 512–17.)

[8] Newspaper advertising of the period refers to the mercantile firm of Jamison Ledward y Compañía.

[9] In conformity with Mexican custom Fanny throughout uses the single word Mexico to designate Mexico City. It will usually be clear from the context whether she refers to the country or to the capital.

[10] Travel by *litera* is described in a slightly later account by a visiting Englishman. He and his young daughter faced each other in one *litera*. They carried a stock of Huntley and Palmer biscuits, by means of which, plus cold roast chickens, they sustained themselves en route. Their mules, changed frequently for the uphill climb, were pressed on by stinging exhortations from the drivers—"Ah! mules without shame!"—and they reached Jalapa in thirty-six hours, as against diligence time of about twenty-four. (William Parish Robertson, *A Visit to Mexico, by the West India Islands,* I, 264–75.)

[11] General Guadalupe Victoria was born in 1785 in what is now the state of Durango, and had been baptized José Miguel Ramón Adaucto Fernández y Félix. (Felipe Victoria Gómez, *Guadalupe Victoria,* pp. 8, 9.) He fought doggedly in the War of Independence until, during the darkest days of the struggle, the reprisals visited by Spanish troops on settlements which sheltered him forced him to hide for more than two years in wild country. According to tradition, more than a thousand men were detailed to track him down, and at times he could hear the voices of his pursuers. It was said that at one point, as he lay ill and close to death, he was able to save himself by catching and drinking the blood of one of the vultures which had perched by him waiting for his last breath. When, near the end of the war, his friends sought him out and found him gaunt and half-clothed, he had become a legend. (W. Bullock, *Six Months . . . in Mexico,* p. 455; Ward, *Mexico in 1827,* I, 228–34.) Chosen as Mexico's first president in 1824, Victoria made an honest and undynamic head of state. When the Calderóns met him he was *comandante general* or governor of the department of Veracruz.

[12] Victoria, who had been married and widowed, would find a new wife in 1841. (Victoria Gómez, *Guadalupe Victoria,* p. 179.)

The shades of opinion that combine to make up the composite portrait of a public man are well illustrated in the case of Victoria. One touch to his portrait was added as late as 1959 by the publication of material written in the 1820's by a young Virginian named Tayloe, who was private secretary to Joel R. Poinsett, the first United States minister to Mexico. To Tayloe, the Mexican president appeared to be in poor health, and the young foreigner felt also that Victoria was dominated by those who advised him. (C. Harvey Gardiner, editor, *Mexico, 1825–1828: The Journal and Correspondence of Edward Thornton Tayloe,* p. 72.) A history written about a generation after Fanny's time pointed out that Victoria, in an effort to achieve a just balance in politics, chose for his cabinet men of widely varying viewpoints. These officials, who were strong personalities, disagreed among themselves, and the conduct of public affairs was hampered by the ensuing conflicts. (Vicente Riva Palacio, editor, *México a Través de los Siglos,* IV, 141–42.) Not long before the Calderóns came to Mexico, Victoria had been one of the two commissioners named by his country to conclude the treaty with the French that closed the unfortunate Pastry War. The French Admiral Baudin was reported as being strongly impressed by the straightforwardness and good sense of the former Mexican president. (Maissin, *The French in Mexico and Texas,* p. 93.)

Although the Frenchman just cited had called him "old General Victoria," he was only fifty-four when Fanny saw him in 1839. His health had begun to deteriorate, however, and just a year after the Calderóns met him he suffered a serious apoplectic stroke. He died in

March 1843. (*La Hesperia*, December 23, 1840; Manuel Rivera Cambas, *Los Gobernantes de México*, II, 130.) A likeness of Victoria appears as Plate 7.

[13] This expedition was almost certainly to the still surviving small church of Santo Cristo del Buen Viaje, whose name seems to have sounded to Fanny like Saint Cristophe. Old maps show it as lying a short distance outside the city walls to the south, just beyond the Arroyo Tenoya. Adjoining it was a cemetery which even before the Calderóns' time was being abandoned, as too near the city, in favor of a new and more distant one begun in 1830. (Miguel M. Lerdo de Tejada, *Apuntes Históricos de la Heróica Ciudad de Vera-Cruz*, III, map opposite p. 10, and pp. 36–37.) In today's expanded city, Santo Cristo faces on the Plaza Gutiérrez Zamora.

[14] As already explained, Veracruz had been battered from the fortress of San Juan de Ulúa while the Spanish still held it, and damaged again by the French during the brief Pastry War. In 1833 it suffered frightful human loss in a cholera epidemic: out of some 16,000 inhabitants it was said that only 5,000 remained. (Charles Joseph Latrobe, *The Rambler in Mexico*, p. 299.) Today's yellow-fever-free Veracruz, with a reputation for the enjoyment of living, has more than passed the hundred thousand mark.

[15] The moon was at the full on Friday, December 20, according to the *Calendario Manual para el Año de 1839 de Ontiveros*. The weathered dome of the *parroquia* is shown as Plate 6.

[16] One learns from other sources that an ounce, or *onza*, was a gold piece worth between fifteen and sixteen dollars in silver—and Don Dionisio's contribution was, therefore, a handsome sum.

[17] Fanny was evidently familiar with *Domino Noir*, a work by the prolific playwright and opera librettist Augustin-Eugène Scribe. Its heroine Doña Angela, cousin to the Queen of Spain, is somehow not irrevocably an abbess, and after various escapades and disguises ends up as a bride.

The first production of the play in its Spanish form—by Ventura de la Vega, a young Argentine-born dramatic writer—had been given in Madrid just a year before. A Mexican theatrical reviewer of the Calderóns' time explained that not only had the story been adapted from Scribe, but also that Scribe had drawn his plot from *La Dama Duende* (The Fairy Lady), written by the early seventeenth-century dramatist Pedro Calderón de la Barca. Thus the author of the play Fanny saw, in adapting Scribe's adaptation, gave credit to the Spanish source by calling his work the second of its name, or *Segunda Dama Duende*. (*El Apuntador*, pp. 348–49.)

[18] From the *Almanach de Gotha* for 1840 we learn that the British consul was F. Giffard, and that the French consul was I. Gloux. Trueman was mentioned on Fanny's opening page, but who he was we do not know.

[19] A league—a term still in some use in country areas of Mexico—was reckoned as 2.63 miles.

A biographer of Santa Anna explains that the name Manga de Clavo, meaning Clove Spike, was reminiscent either of Mexico's old colonial trade with the East or of a local effort to produce cloves. (Wilfrid Hardy Callcott, *Santa Anna; The Story of an Enigma Who Once Was Mexico*, p. 56.)

[20] "Misery acquaints a man with strange bedfellows. I will here shroud till the dregs of the storm be past." Thus says Trinculo in Act II, Scene 2 of *The Tempest*.

5. Up to Puebla by Diligence

[1] Unlike inland Mexican cities, which typically were not fortified, Veracruz still retained, even at this late date, its old inheritance of encircling walls. The architectural historian George Kubler explains that "in the sixteenth-century world, Mexico was unique by virtue of the pacific appearance of its cities. . . . In Europe, the century was marked by unparalleled activity in the arts of war, but in America, the Spanish colonies developed pacifically excepting at their sea-girt periphery." (*Mexican Architecture of the Sixteenth Century*, I, 207.)

The term *gates* will be encountered later in descriptions of the capital, but they refer not to military fortifications but to *garitas* or stopping points at which an internal duty called the *alcabala* was levied on goods entering the city. In times of strife, because the city gates were on roads and roads were convenient for approach, skirmishes often in fact took place at such points.

[2] One of the editors visited Manga de Clavo a good many years ago. Ruined roofless walls, pointed out as being those of the hacienda buildings, were heavily overgrown with

lush vegetation which included trees of substantial size. The cut is of a nameless hacienda depicted in a book of this period, but it may serve to suggest how Manga de Clavo perhaps looked.

3 Antonio López de Santa Anna (see cut, and Plate 70) was a far more complex personality than General Victoria, the other former chief of state whom the Calderóns had just met in Veracruz. Among his many gifts was a sure ability to capitalize on events. A professional soldier from the age of fourteen, he had established himself as a national hero in 1829 by his victory over the meager forces of an ill-planned expedition sent by Spain to reconquer Mexico. Not long after, he precipitated a successful revolution against his government and was duly elected president at the age of thirty-eight.

In April 1836—a few weeks after his annihilation of the revolted Texans at the Alamo in San Antonio—Santa Anna was defeated and captured at San Jacinto. This denouement and his subsequent willingness to work for the Texan cause (on behalf of which he even traveled to the United States), tarnished his reputation. Yet it was not long before the persuasive Santa Anna once more became a national hero through his skillful exploitation of a crippling leg wound received in brief action against the French at Veracruz in December 1838.

When the Calderóns met him a year later at his hacienda of Manga de Clavo, he was a restive ex-president still short of his forty-fifth birthday, with an impressive record for heading insurrections at opportune moments. Calderón, in his first dispatch written from Mexico, mentioned his hesitation in calling on Santa Anna lest he offend the government authorities in the capital, but he decided that "the perpetual revolutions of this wretched country" might well return the enigmatic general to power and that any initial courtesy shown him could be considered a good hedge for the future. (*Despachos Generales*, I, 18.) Calderón's letter from the Queen of Spain resulted from the fact that Santa Anna had for several months earlier in the year acted as provisional president by decree of congress during an absence of the regularly elected president and the illness of the head of the council of state.

Santa Anna combined undeniable organizing ability, shrewdness, audacity, and a sense of timing with a willingness to take on whatever shade of political opinion might, at any given moment, lead most surely to advancement. Sometimes, for reasons of his own, he would work with men of stature and integrity. Similarly, there were times when men of principle supported Santa Anna in the belief that he was the one leader through whose popular appeal a sound program might be put into effect. But his own motives were seldom other than egocentric; and the recurrent grasp of this self-styled Napoleon of the West upon the government and the purse strings of his country was a continuing misfortune for Mexico.

4 "See—this gauntlet is empty . . ." is one of Sir John Ramorny's bitter references to his mutilation in *The Fair Maid of Perth*, Sir Walter Scott's novel laid in the time of Robert III of Scotland. Henry Gow the Smith, or armourer, crippled his adversary in one mighty blow, struck in defense of the story's heroine.

5 It seems likely that the Calderóns owned a copy of Lorenzo de Zavala's *Ensayo Histórico de las Revoluciones de Mégico*, which had appeared in 1831. Calderón mentions Zavala's work in a dispatch and in writing to Prescott, and Fanny quotes or paraphrases from it on several occasions—particularly from Chapter VIII of the first volume, rich in characterizations of important Mexicans. Her estimate of former President Victoria is apparently drawn in part from this source (I, 149); and the present quotation about Santa Anna, rather freely translated, occurs two pages later (I, 151).

6 The Señora de Santa Anna, born Inés de la Paz García, had married at fourteen. In spite of Fanny's likening her to an old dressed-up-for-Sunday chambermaid, she was not yet twenty-nine. She was, in fact, younger by several years than the fresh-skinned Fanny who would pass her thirty-fifth birthday—considered by her as her thirtieth—the very next day upon the road.

Santa Anna's wife had the reputation of being devoted to her husband and to her family, and was evidently held in genuine public esteem. She died only a few years later. Less than six weeks after her death Santa Anna took as his bride a pretty, vapid girl of fifteen.

7 The book referred to is *Mexico in 1827* by H. G. Ward, illustrated with drawings by his wife. (For a photograph of the bridge, see Plate 10.) Ward's clear sedate descriptions, enlivened with touches of cautious humor, still make good reading, and are cited in these notes from time to time.

The Wards emerge from their book as a young couple who thoroughly enjoyed the Mexican scene. Henry George Ward, who had previously spent four years in Spain and knew its language well, was sent first to Mexico in 1823 as a member of a commission to investigate the state of affairs following the achievement of independence in 1821. He returned home in a few months, was married in 1824 to Emily Elizabeth Swinburne, and was sent out again in January 1825 at the age of about twenty-eight to negotiate a treaty with Mexico. By the time they reached Veracruz, Mrs. Ward was approaching her first confinement and was in consequence carried in a *litera* up to the capital. They took a beautiful house in Mexico—one which the Calderóns would soon try to rent.

[8] Fanny's remarks about the road are a good deal milder than those of most travelers. A United States diplomat who came to Mexico about two years later described it as being in places simply a washed-out gully dammed at frequent intervals by rock piles up to two feet high to turn off the water. His coach, he maintained, did not roll but jumped from dam to dam and rock to rock, and the angle of ascent in many places he estimated as no less than 45°. (Brantz Mayer, *Mexico as It Was and as It Is*, p. 36.)

An intrepid female traveler of a few years later, Lady Emmeline Stuart-Wortley, discussed the least incommodious way of poising oneself while being jolted over perilous roads at full gallop. Some, she said, screwed their mouths into tight buttonholes, while others opened them wide. The latter plan she recommended as saving the teeth from being rammed together and "played upon like castanets." (*Travels . . .* , II, 236.)

[9] The muleteers might be wild-looking, but according to other chroniclers they constituted a resourceful and notably trustworthy part of the national economy: they and the strings of mules they drove conveyed practically all of Mexico's freight. As compared with the river transportation of flatter lands it was an expensive system and entailed heavy increases in cost to the final consumers of goods.

"Stout, hardy, and honest men," said the United States minister Waddy Thompson in referring to *arrieros* a few years later. "Courteous, obliging, cheerful, and perfectly honest," wrote Captain G. F. Lyon, ". . . Thousands and even millions of dollars have frequently been confided to their charge, which they in many instances have defended, at the hazard of their lives . . ." "Yet this person is often poor," said Brantz Mayer, "bondless and unsecured—with nothing but his fair name and *unbroken word.*" And Charles Joseph Latrobe corroborated the simplicity of the system whose efficacy rested upon the proverbial honesty of the *arriero*: "The most precious commodities are unhesitatingly delivered to his care, merely enclosed in bags for conveyance to the coast, and the *arriero* never fails to perform his contract."

(Thompson, *Recollections of Mexico*, p. 36; Lyon, *Journal of a Residence and Tour in the Republic of Mexico in the Year 1826*, II, 236–37; Mayer, *Mexico as It Was and as It Is*, p. 18; Latrobe, *Rambler in Mexico*, p. 49.)

[10] Salvator Rosa, the seventeenth-century Neapolitan painter who specialized in the sinister and picturesque and enjoyed depicting nature in all its moods, was greatly admired in England at this time.

[11] José was, it will be remembered, the servant whom the Calderóns had engaged in Havana to serve as their porter.

[12] The quality and abundance of Jalapa water seem to have impressed travelers. It must have constituted an important economic asset, as one of Jalapa's occupations apparently was doing laundry for Veracruz—even though it was up more than four thousand feet and some seventy miles away. "I never saw linen look so well; many of the inhabitants of Vera Cruz send hither to have their washing done," said W. Bullock (*Six Months . . . in Mexico*, p. 51), who described one public washing place where 144 women could work at the same time. And Captain G. F. Lyon (*Journal . . .* , II, 196) spoke of two laundries in the open air with waist-high troughs through which water constantly flowed.

[13] Throughout her book Fanny uses the designation of monk to include friars—members of mendicant orders—and occasionally other ecclesiastics. The chaplain of the *Jasón* whom she described (p. 42) as "a monk with a monkish face" was presumably not a monk in any cloistered sense.

[14] Mrs. Ashburnham, like Emily Ward whose sketch for her husband's book has been mentioned earlier, was the wife of a British diplomat (Charles Ashburnham) formerly stationed in Mexico. Fanny would cross her path again in a remote spot.

[15] For photographs illustrative of this part of the Calderóns' route, see Plates 13, 14, and 15.

[16] Possibly this was James W. Glass, Jr., who later—although still very young—is recorded as making sketches for Prescott. (Wolcott, *Correspondence of . . . Prescott*, pp. 354–55, 356–57.)

The name is not from the Journal, but is from another source: a pleasantly worn copy of the two-volume first American edition of *Life in Mexico* containing many handwritten ink insertions where Fanny had left partial or complete blanks in her printed text. This copy is the inherited possession of Mrs. R. Lucien Patton—born Jane Singer, and a great-granddaughter of Fanny's younger sister Harriet—and she generously lent it to us, the editors. The cramped brief notations it contains may not be in Fanny's own hand, but there is no doubt that they originated with Fanny herself, perhaps by way of her niece (Mrs. Patton's grandmother) who as a young girl enjoyed a long eventful visit with the Calderóns in 1854. Material from this source, like that from the Journal, is in the present edition printed in slightly differentiated type. Our notes show when the "Singer copy" is the sole basis for identifications. (Names in brackets are neither from the Journal nor from the Singer copy, but indicate the editors' best guesses.)

Those names which were entered in *both* the Journal and the Singer copy tally in every instance, with one exception. The Calderóns' fellow passenger on the *Norma* (p. 8), given as Mr. Smith in the Journal, was remembered as Mr. Wilson in the Singer copy.

[17] The stagecoach line, established by North Americans, had recently been acquired by Mexican capital. The new owner would soon be numbered among the Calderóns' good friends. The line's Yankee coachmen were evidently retained; other accounts of travel of this time and for a number of years later specifically mention them. (Mayer, *Mexico as It Was and as It Is*, pp. 12 and 36; Thompson, *Recollections of Mexico*, p. 10; Albert M. Gilliam, *Travels in Mexico during the Years 1843 and 44*, p. 50.)

[18] Like San Juan de Ulúa in Veracruz and many other fine historic buildings, the fortress of San Carlos de Perote survives under the protection of the Mexican government's Instituto Nacional de Antropología e Historia, Dirección de Monumentos Coloniales. San Carlos, formerly equipped with a moat and drawbridge, long served as a place of safekeeping for silver on its way to the coast. In post-independence times an important use seems to have been as a place of incarceration for unsuccessfully rebellious military leaders and even former presidents forcibly supplanted by another regime.

[19] Writers on Mexico from Humboldt on have discussed pulque, the fermented juice of the maguey plant, and have described it in various ways: reminiscent of putrid meat, said one; like an alcoholic starch solution, said another; "matchlessly horrible," said Lady Emmeline Stuart-Wortley (*Travels . . .* , II, 236). But most voyagers who remained for a time came to like pulque, although they might not go so far as George F. Ruxton, who declared that when fresh it was "brisk and sparkling, and the most cooling, refreshing, and delicious drink that ever was invented for thirsty mortal . . ." (*Adventures in Mexico and the Rocky Mountains*, p. 70.)

Fanny's gradually changing views on pulque show why some of her initial critical comments on people and things should be considered only as preliminary impressions. As time went on Fanny would find pulque possible, tolerable, admirable, and finally almost indispensable.

[20] This is a complete quotation of stanza XXI of Canto I. A footnote to it in *The Works of Lord Byron in Verse and Prose* (published in 1836) discusses the daily casual killings, particularly of foreigners, in Lisbon in the year 1809 and cites Byron's own escape from attack by virtue of his being armed.

[21] The verb *saludar* provides wide latitude in meaning. It may be translated as to greet, salute, accost, express contentment or joy by words or actions.

[22] In general the spelling of geographical locations has been modified to conform to modern usage. Our guide has been the series of large detailed maps of Mexico issued in sections in 1932 by the American Geographical Society of New York with the co-operation of Mexican authorities. For places not appearing in the published index to these maps we have had to depend on local usage so far as it could be determined.

[23] A lissome Poblana, or woman of Puebla, wearing a costume that tallies closely with this description, is portrayed in Plate 57. One notes that what Fanny has termed the skirt or shift is the longer garment, worn underneath what she calls the petticoat. Later, in describing the dress of country ladies, she will mention under-petticoats deliberately arranged so as to show below the hem of the outer garment.

6. The Capital Welcomes Spain's First Envoy

[1] For reasons of diplomatic dignity, perhaps, Fanny's comfortable-sounding carpet bag was transformed for publication into a trunk.

[2] In her Journal Fanny makes no note of the similarity of the swinging game she saw at Río Frío to the ancient Game of the Flyers, performed from a pole of great height. The comparison she added for print is her first culling from a well-known book she evidently encountered later. She almost certainly owned a copy, as she draws on it frequently for historical and anthropological background. The author of the book—whose name she never gives, although she sometimes credits "old writers"—was Francisco Javier Clavijero, a Veracruz-born Jesuit. Originally published in Italian in 1780, the work appeared in Spanish in 1826 under the title of *Historia Antigua de Mégico*. An amusing subsequent

error Fanny will make in paraphrasing from Clavijero makes it plain that it was this Spanish edition (translated by José Joaquín de Mora) which she used.

Clavijero's discussion of the ceremonial game was part of his Book VII dealing with education, art, language, and recreation among the ancient Mexicans. Fanny was apparently unaware that the traditional game survived in its original hazardous form among Indians in eastern Mexico. (It still survives today in various parts of Mexico, and was performed regularly at the Mexican pavilion of the 1964–65 New York world's fair.)

³ Perhaps José María de Landa y Urquiza. His wife was a member of the prominent Escandón family, whose members the Calderóns would soon come to know.

⁴ A year later the Calderóns again approached the valley of Mexico from Puebla, and Fanny must have revised her text here in the light of her second experience. On this first occasion she wrote in her Journal that the volcanoes had their "heads . . . lost in the clouds." (For a rendition of Popocatepetl before the days of photography, see Plate 16.)

⁵ The cut shows an absent artist's fanciful concept of the Aztec capital—based on a conqueror's description.

Fanny presented, on the title page of her published book, the following lines from Robert Southey's long romantic poem of 1805 entitled *Madoc*, in which an Aztec city is described: ". . . Thou art beautiful! / Queen of the Valley! thou art beautiful, / Thy walls, like silver, sparkle to the sun; / Melodious wave thy groves . . ."

⁶ Fanny seems to have read the bland bold words of the conqueror himself. Prescott and others have spoken with admiration of the effectiveness of Cortés' small but vivid vocabulary and economical style in describing the amazing events he reported to "*Vuestra Sacra Majestad*," his youthful monarch Charles V (who in the Spanish succession was Charles I).

Montezuma and Cortés exchanged ceremonious greetings. Cortés gave Montezuma a necklace—of glittering glass beads. Montezuma, after conducting the Spaniards to the quarters they were to occupy, placed around the neck of Cortés a necklace made of mother of pearl and golden shrimps.

⁷ This whole passage in which Fanny in spirit leaves the diligence and transports herself to the time of Cortés she took from *another* volume of her Journal (having deleted in her printed version her thoughts, reinstated here, concerning the possible basic injustice of the conquest).

This other Journal she entitled 3d Volume—/Mexican Anecdotes—including Love—murder—/robbery and other peculiarities (with the last word underscored). It is not primarily a chronological record, and there is nothing to establish exactly when it was begun. It does, however, contain a few dates which, together with its content, indicate that it was started some time in the spring of 1841 when the Calderóns were living quietly on an hacienda outside the capital.

⁸ In a subsequent entry in her Journal, Fanny identifies their self-assured caller from New Orleans as Atoche. We have assumed with confidence that this acquaintance so eager to please the Calderóns was the international intriguer Alexander Atocha, whose subsequent career was sufficiently colorful as to warrant a summary of it here, even though he soon disappears from this story. Atocha had been born in Spain, but had become a naturalized citizen of the United States, and apparently at this time was living in Mexico. A few years later, in February 1846, when war between the United States and Mexico seemed likely but no hostilities had yet occurred, Atocha appeared in Washington in the role of a friend of Santa Anna, who was then living in restless exile in Havana.

No one, including President Polk, quite trusted Atocha when he intimated that the former Mexican president favored a settlement of questions in dispute between Mexico and the United States—especially when he suggested that Santa Anna, who was confident of being able to return to power, would need to be financed on a large scale until public opinion in Mexico was amenable to the idea of parting with Mexican territory for cash or in settlement of United States claims. Atocha quoted Santa Anna as advising the United States to maintain a stiff attitude toward Mexico, and to make it clear that force would be used if necessary, because only thus could Santa Anna and other leaders justify, before the Mexican public, a pacific arrangement involving territorial transfer. But Atocha was not entirely disbelieved either. Later, on the very day war was declared, secret orders were given by President Polk to allow Santa Anna to slip past the American naval blockade of Veracruz. Apparently Polk believed that the least that Santa Anna's return to Mexico would accomplish for the United States would be increased dissension in Mexico's internal politics; and that there was a chance that Santa Anna would push for accession to United States demands. After the declaration of war, and before returning to Mexico, Santa Anna would receive secretly in Havana a United States naval officer sent especially to talk with him. The young Spanish-speaking Lieutenant Mackenzie reported that Santa Anna expounded the same line of thinking that Atocha had expressed earlier in Washington, and that he even outlined an invasion course that United States troops might profitably pursue in a campaign to be waged for the purpose of persuading the Mexican public to agree with what Santa Anna claimed to wish—the relinquishment of Mexican territory for a price.

Polk guessed wrong. Once at home, the magnetic Santa Anna quickly rallied Mexican forces, and conducted the war with energy—although frequently with faulty tactical judgment. During the war Atocha appeared in Washington twice again as an unofficial go-between, but he influenced no more important decisions. (See the entries under Alexander Atocha and Alexander Slidell Mackenzie in: Rives, *The United States and Mexico*; Justin H. Smith, *The War with Mexico*; and *The Diary of James K. Polk*, edited by Milo Milton Quaife.)

[9] This temporary home of the Calderóns was a handsome one-story building attributed to the great sculptor-architect Tolsá. Although declared a colonial monument, it was demolished in 1935 in the course of opening up a new street. One may judge where it stood by relating it to the still surviving Pérez Gálvez house at the Calle del Puente de Alvarado 52. This large building (also designed by Tolsá) is described by Fanny in the second paragraph following as the former English legation. It was apparently next the Calderóns on the east, one house nearer to the Alameda and the center of town.

The Baron de Norman, mentioned again later, was a diplomatic representative from Belgium who seems to have been sent as an observer and negotiator prior to Belgium's later formal dealings with independent Mexico.

[10] In preparing her book for the printer, as the Journal makes clear, Fanny used the curious device of leaving largely uncensored her thoughts on Señor Gorostiza's looks but fastening them to a non-existent character whom she called Señor A＿＿＿z. Her other comments about Gorostiza she left under the easily recognizable guise of G＿＿＿a.

According to others who knew him, Gorostiza did have a slight hump and carried one shoulder higher than the other—the results of a severe wound suffered in the Peninsular War. He is described as having a bulky nose under brilliant eyes, and teeth so badly occluded that they flawed his speech, but as also possessing an eloquence and charm which soon overcame the initial effect of his looks on new acquaintances. (Prieto, *Memorias . . . ,* I, 257; *Obras Completas de D. Francisco Pimentel*, V, 39–42.)

He was the youngest son of a Spanish general and the godson of a viceroy, and his mother was a descendant of the Cepeda family which had produced Saint Teresa of Avila. The colonial-born child was taken to Spain after the death in Mexico of his father, was educated in the university at Sevilla, and, like Calderón, fought for Spain against the invading French. As penalty for his liberal opinions, his property was confiscated and he was banished from Spain. He lived for a time in London, where he contributed to various magazines, including the *Edinburgh Review*. After the War of Independence he chose Mexican citizenship. He was sent by the new government twice on important diplomatic assignments; and he later had two different cabinet posts. He was exactly Calderón's age—forty-nine. Gorostiza will be discussed again, particularly as a dramatist. His likeness is shown in Plate 77.

[11] Titles of nobility had been suppressed by law in republican Mexico as deriving from the crown of Spain. Verbally at least they seem to have continued in rather widespread use. Some periodicals of the time ignored titles while others, including the government newspaper, frequently indicated title holders by the prefix *ex*. (In reporting election results, the *Diario del Gobierno* for October 2, 1840 mentions, for example, "Colonel Agustín Suárez Peredo, ex-Conde del Valle.") Perhaps when employed by the government this style of address was used to reinforce the fact that these remnants of the viceregal past had been discarded. But in the absence of the legal right to be called *conde*, how better could the bearer of such a title be distinguished from his fellow men than by being referred to as *ex-conde*?

Even today in Mexico, titles are sometimes encountered in purely social usage. Mexican genealogical studies distinguish between the actual holder of a title validated in Spain and the potential holder of a title. They refer to the former as he who *is* (or *was*) the Conde de ＿＿＿, and to the latter as he who *ought to be* (or *ought to have been*) the Marqués de ＿＿＿. It may be noted that according to Spanish usage a woman without a brother inherits her father's title.

[12] José María Justo Gómez de la Cortina, third Conde de la Cortina—"Pepe" to his friends—is surely among those in this book whom one would have liked most to know. He was about forty when the Calderóns came to Mexico, and had already made something of a literary reputation. For his portrait, see Plate 74.

Like Gorostiza, Cortina had been sent to Spain for his education, and devoted some time to his country's diplomatic service. By the time of the Calderóns' arrival he had already served in congress, had been governor of the Federal District, had held two cabinet posts, and had edited a newspaper and contributed to reviews. In 1838 he wrote a serious essay on Mexico's population and he continued his interest in the gathering of sound census figures and other statistical information as a member of a commission operating under the ministry of war. He was deeply interested in art, and with his mother formed a notable collection of paintings. He was at this time a colonel and later held the rank of brigadier general. In 1845 he would bring out a dictionary of synonyms, and in the 1850's would write a work on diplomacy. He would find time to perpetrate an occasional elaborate hoax. He was interested in various charitable causes, and he and his mother spent, lent, and gave away so much of the family's large fortune that there was little of it left for his later years. (See especially the prologue by Manuel Romero de Terreros to selections from Cortina's writings entitled *Poliantea*.)

Cortina's variety of interests perhaps served to diffuse his energies; however, he impressed the United States minister of three years later as "brave, accomplished, cordial, generous, and punctiliously honorable." (Thompson, *Recollections of Mexico*, p. 86.)

[13] Fanny came later to feel very warmly toward the widowed María Ana, Condesa de la Cortina, who was about sixty at this time. She was born a Cortina, married a Cortina cousin before she was seventeen, and, as her parents' only child, inherited their wealth and title in her own right. Some years earlier a British naval officer had written of her: "A more excellent and amiable lady does not exist . . . She is a woman of great talent and wit, although I never knew her to make an ill-natured observation. She has an excellent house, furnished in very good taste, and containing a variety of extremely good paintings." (R. W. H. Hardy, *Travels in the Interior of Mexico, in 1825, 1826, 1827, & 1828*, p. 520.)

[14] Cortina's wife, the young countess, whom Fanny began at once to call Paulita, was born Francisca de Paula Rodríguez de Rivas, daughter of a Spanish statesman of noble family. Her little daughter was María Joaquina, then five. She would in fact grow up to be a beautiful girl—as noted by an English visitor of some years later who had read *Life in Mexico* and remembered Fanny's prediction. (Robertson, *Visit to Mexico . . .* , II, 50.)

[15] Léperos as a type are discussed at some length by Guillermo Prieto in his *Memorias de Mis Tiempos* (I, 292–97). The lépero, he said, was typically a mestizo—a mixture of Indian and Spanish stock—often well endowed with both physical courage and intelligence. His life, centered around love, pulque, and quarreling, was lived almost entirely on the streets of Mexican cities (Plate 36).

Another observer wrote: "At once brave and cowardly, calm and violent, . . . the lépero can accommodate himself to every turn of fortune, as his humor or idleness inclines him. Porter, stone-mason, teamster, street-paver, hawker, the lépero is everything at different times. A thief sometimes by inclination, he practices his favorite calling everywhere, in the churches, at processions, and in the theatres; his life is only one struggle with justice . . . Lavish when he finds himself master of a little money, he is not the less resigned or courageous when he has none." (Gabriel Ferry, *Vagabond Life in Mexico*, p. 10.)

[16] This hint that Calderón coached his wife on what to say suggests that Fanny was still less than entirely at home in her husband's language. It will be remembered that earlier, when she was reading Humboldt at sea, she wished that the work had been in French instead of Spanish. Within two years, however, she would speak so well as to deceive her own husband at a fancy-dress ball into guessing her a Spanish-born stranger.

[17] Calderón sent the notebook containing the hymn to Spain and it was presented to María Cristina, the Queen Regent. (*Despachos Generales*, I, 19, 21.) The composer of the music is termed a "professor" in another example of his work which may be found in an annual of the period (*El Liceo Mexicano*, Vol. I, 1844). Fanny will later refer to him as "the musical Apollo of the Mexican ladies." He is presumably the same Juan Nepomuceno Retes mentioned as an orchestra director in *El Folklore Musical de las Ciudades* (pp. 25–26), by Rubén M. Campos.

[18] In her Journal Fanny calls it "the National Hymn of Riego." General Rafael del Riego was a leader in the struggle that in 1814 restored Ferdinand VII of Spain to the throne usurped by Napoleon's brother Joseph. In 1820 he revolted successfully against the absolutist policies inaugurated by the returned king, and forced him to accept the wartime liberal constitution of 1812. Later, he led Spanish troops against those of the Holy Alliance which entered Spain in the cause of absolutism, was captured, and hanged. As a patriotic song associated with liberal causes, Riego's hymn has at various times been outlawed in Spain.

[19] What the hymn celebrated was the recent resolution of the long and bloody Carlist War in Spain. Ferdinand VII, last Spanish king to rule Mexico, had been childless through three marriages, and his brother Carlos, married and the father of children, confidently expected to inherit the throne and was surrounded by a party of extreme royalists and ultraconservatives who had already shown their impatience to take over. But Ferdinand's childless wife died; he remarried; and his new wife, María Cristina, soon expected an heir.

Urged on by his wife, Ferdinand proclaimed the abrogation of the Salic law, which would have prevented a daughter from inheriting the throne, in favor of an older law under which the succession of his child, whether male or female, would be insured. The Carlist party was roused to fury. This was heightened when the King's child was a girl, born October 10, 1830, who was followed by a sister two years later. Carlos obtained from his brother the King, as he apparently lay dying, a signed denial of his proclamation —but Ferdinand recovered sufficiently to nullify the plans of Carlos and to make arrangements for his wife to become regent during his daughter's minority. Upon the death of Ferdinand on September 29, 1833 and the accession of Isabel II as Queen—she was not yet three years old—Carlos, who had been banished, returned and actual hostilities broke out. Civil war raged for six years.

Later the son and a grandson of Carlos would similarly contest the succession and bring on more civil strife; but this first struggle was concluded by the Convention of Vergara, signed the summer before the Calderóns reached Mexico. Baldomero Espartero was one of the generals most responsible for the victory over the Carlist forces.

20 The skeletonized name of the young Spanish girl—perhaps one of the Señoritas Frauenfeldt mentioned later—was evidently added when Fanny put her material together for publication.

21 In spite of the cryptic "Madame C_____ de la B_____" used to designate the author of the book as published, and the use throughout of "C_____n" for her husband, this and many other statements left not the slightest doubt as to the Calderóns' identity.

In gentle derision of the strictly nominal degree of anonymity adopted by Fanny, Charles Macomb Flandrau, in his classic Viva Mexico! (p. 148) termed it "a proceeding always suggestive of the manner in which the two-hundred-pound soprano of Mozart opera holds a minute, black velvet mask a foot and a half away from her face and instantly becomes invisible to the naked eye."

7. A Visit to the President

1 Not a plaza in the sense of an open square, the plazuela was, rather, a widened portion of the street built up along the ancient causeway leading westward out of what in pre-Spanish days was an island city. On the south side of the street (just east of where the Calderóns were living) was the neighborhood's most magnificent house, sometimes called the Buenavista Palace. Fanny has already mentioned this enormous residence— which Calderón would try to rent—as then belonging to the Pérez Gálvez family, and as having formerly served as the English legation. Shorn of its open grounds and gardens, it still stands today, preserved as a colonial monument, at the Calle del Puente de Alvarado 52. Its classic design is attributed to the versatile sculptor-architect Tolsá. The name Buenavista survives in the Calle Buenavista a little west, and in the Buenavista railway station a short distance north.

In 1840 and for many years thereafter the area was indeed suburban in character. Open fields and pastures lay all about and the San Cosme gate, marking the official western limit of the city, was just beyond.

2 The capital's Alameda, now a downtown oasis, was ordered set aside and planted as a public park by an early viceroy in 1593. In 1840 it lay near the city's western edge. Engravings of the time depict it as a thickly planted walled enclosure, with a carriage drive around the edge and walks through it (Plate 29).

3 This magnificent house of the viceregal period, which had served as the residence of Iturbide during his short reign as Emperor, still stands as No. 17 on the Avenida Madero —the modern name for two continuing streets Fanny knew as the Calle San Francisco and, further east, the Calle de Pláteros (Street of the Silversmiths).

4 The reader will soon encounter the other two sons of Montezuma I. All three ruled successively after his death: Axayacatl, Tizoc, and Ahuizotl. It was in the reign of the last named, from 1482 to 1502, that the great temple begun under an earlier regime was completed. Montezuma II, ruler at the time of the coming of the Spaniards, was the son of Axayacatl, and succeeded after Ahuizotl's death. (George C. Vaillant, Aztecs of Mexico, p. 103; Frederick A. Peterson, Ancient Mexico, pp. 96–105.) Fanny was not able to see what has been uncovered by excavation work in the twentieth century opposite the rear of the cathedral to the east—a fragment of the great temple of the Aztecs.

We have kept Fanny's—and Prescott's—spelling of Montezuma. The name is written in many ways, but the most usual modern Spanish rendition is Moctezuma.

5 The war and sun god whose birth is described was Huitzilopochtli. Clavijero, evidently again her source, describes him as "born of woman, but without male cooperation." His mother (Coatlicue, a statue of whom is shown in the cut) had already borne

other children. (*Historia Antigua* . . . , I, 234–35.) Instead of the name Huitzilopochtli, Fanny used Mejitli, an alternative appelation mentioned by Clavijero which we have omitted to minimize confusion.

As given by a modern writer, the myth is of interest for its explanation of the ritual of human sacrifice. In brief it runs thus: The aging mother of the gods, Coatlicue, already the mother of the moon and the stars, had become a priestess dedicated to a life of retreat and chastity. Her children, enraged at her mysterious pregnancy, planned to kill her, but her child was born just in time to save his mother by decapitating the moon and putting the stars to flight. To maintain the greatest of the gods in his daily cycle of rebirth and triumph, as well as other gods, the nourishment of blood had to be maintained—and, to obtain blood, war became for the Aztecs a form of worship with the purpose of insuring a constant flow of prisoners for human sacrifice. (Alfonso Caso, *The Aztecs: People of the Sun,* pp. 12–14.)

[6] In citing these figures on sacrifices, Fanny continues to draw from Clavijero (*Historia Antigua* . . . , I, 259 fn). Bishop Juan de Zumárraga, who wrote in 1531, is quoted by him as having estimated the annual number of human sacrifices at 20,000, while other sources raised this to 50,000. But the Dominican Bartolomé de las Casas, strong admirer of Indian cultures and zealous protector of Indian rights, held that the yearly number had not exceeded one hundred.

The truth can never be known, but George C. Vaillant, outstanding modern scholar, speaks of "great monthly sacrifices" and says that the taking of prisoners for sacrifice became one of the chief purposes of war. As the result of a two-year campaign into northern Oaxaca, "no less than twenty thousand victims, the high point of the sacrificial cult in Mexico" were sacrificed at the dedication of the great temple in Tenochtitlan. Montezuma II, he states, sacrificed 12,000 human beings on a single occasion. (*Aztecs of Mexico,* pp. 90, 103, 104, 203.)

[7] If Fanny seems conservative in her aesthetic judgment, she was not alone among Anglo-Saxon visitors of the nineteenth century. The exuberance of some of Mexico's baroque architecture, and especially its uninhibited Churrigueresque, tended to distress those unaccustomed to such bold and imaginative flights of fancy. "Excessively gaudy and in the worst possible taste," said Joel R. Poinsett from the United States (*Notes on Mexico,* pp. 98, 99) of one building; "neat and chaste" of another less ornate. "In a gaudy bad taste," was the pronouncement of a British traveler (Mark Beaufoy, *Mexican Illustrations,* p. 66), and "a thousand pities . . . so very questionable an architectural taste," the comment of another (Edward B. Tylor, *Anahuac,* p. 46).

As Fanny in preparing her text for publication struck out her reference to "bad taste," perhaps here, as in so many other instances, she may have come to enjoy what at first seemed strange.

Many minds, many hands, and more than two centuries went into the building of Mexico's cathedral: it was begun in 1563 near the site of an older church, and was not finally completed until 1813. The addition disparagingly referred to here was probably the Sagrario (Plate 25) that was built on to the cathedral to the east: "one of the finest examples of Mexican Churrigueresque," says Pál Kelemen in his *Baroque and Rococo in Latin America* (pp. 28, 29).

Mexico's cathedral has survived the opinions of foreign travelers and remains a glorious, enormous, much-loved building. Writing of the cathedral and its adjoining Sagrario, one architectural critic has said that they "form together what is easily the finest ecclesiastical group in North America, and one of the finest in the world." (Walter S. Kilham, *Mexican Architecture of the Vice-Regal Period,* p. 93.)

It is curious to find a woman of Fanny's sophistication, who had traveled through France and who knew at least something of Italy, speaking of the cathedral as Gothic, a term which she uses also several times elsewhere in her descriptions. Predominantly baroque of a conservative character, it does have a system of vaulting resting upon high piers, and perhaps this soaring construction influenced her choice of words. But her later references seem to suggest that whatever appeared old was to be considered Gothic; in other words, she used the term in the sense of un-classical, ancient, or romantic. (The superb conventual establishments built by the earliest mendicant friars who came to Mexico soon after the conquest did in fact continue unbroken the true Gothic tradition which was already dying out in Europe.)

[8] The great wave of Irish immigration to the United States was just beginning at this time. It would vastly increase a few years later following the potato famine of 1845.

These comments on Mexican dirt are part of a long discussion of the subject which Fanny took from Volume 3 of her Journal.

[9] The Calendar Stone, probably the best known of all Mexico's pre-Spanish remains, was discovered in 1790 in the course of a project to level the cathedral square and repair its underlying drainage system. (The statue of Coatlicue was similarly discovered a few

months previously.) The tremendously heavy round carving, more than twelve feet across, was made at the time of Axayacatl, who reigned from 1469 to 1481. Its superb design represents the Aztec concept of the history of the world and the universe beyond. The Calendar Stone remained where Fanny saw it—fastened near the base of the west tower of the cathedral—until 1885.

What used to be called the Stone of Sacrifices is now termed the Stone of Tizoc: it is no longer considered to have been a sacrificial block, but rather to have been a commemoration of the wars of Tizoc, who ruled between 1481 and 1486. (The cut represents scenes from its side.) Fanny saw the stone in the courtyard of the university, but evidently as late as 1823 it still remained in the cathedral square, with only its upper surface exposed to view. (W. Bullock, *Six Months . . . in Mexico*, pp. 336–38.) Both the Calendar Stone and the Stone of Tizoc are housed today in the Museo Nacional de Antropología.

[10] Calderón seems to have worn his decorations only on occasions of strict diplomatic necessity: he had consented to wear only one, it will be remembered, in Havana upon the occasion of the Queen's birthday. According to the newspaper article describing his official reception in Mexico, he was a *Caballero pensionado de la real y distinguida órden de Carlos III, Comendador de la real órden americana de Isabel la Católica, y la de Constantino de Nápoles.* (*Diario del Gobierno*, December 30, 1839.)

By the "palace" Fanny refers, of course, to what is now called the Palacio Nacional, extending all along the east side of the cathedral square.

[11] Fanny's account for the printer stated that Bustamante received Calderón standing, but she left in the give-away phrase, *his feet on a tabouret.* In his dispatch of January 1, 1840 Calderón mentions the throne, "probably of the viceroys," and the footstool. He then adds that, along with ministers, generals, and aides-de-camp, a large crowd of people was present "in various costumes, and not all clean or elegant." (*Despachos Generales*, I, 19.) For print, Fanny also omitted the fact that Calderón was accompanied by Captain Estrada of the *Jasón.*

[12] The account of Calderón's reception by the President appeared in the government paper, the *Diario del Gobierno de la República Mexicana.* Calderón enclosed a copy with his dispatch of January 1, 1840 and pointed out that it could serve as proof to treasury officials in Spain that his salary should commence (*Despachos Generales*, I, 19).

His speech and Bustamante's reply followed a predictable pattern. Calderón spoke of the re-establishment of harmony between members of the Spanish family, and of the indestructible ties of parenthood, religion, and language. He then passed on expressions of good will and friendship tendered by his Queen and his government.

Bustamante more briefly indicated his gratification over the peace treaty which had finally ended the differences between the two countries, welcomed Calderón, and once more mentioned the inherited ties between Spain and Mexico.

[13] This incident is not recorded in the Journal.

[14] The writer was Lorenzo de Zavala, whom Fanny has drawn on before. His assessment of Bustamante she found in his *Ensayo Histórico . . .* (I, 148).

Fanny must have heard Zavala called unprincipled because of his activities during the last years of his life. He had been an ardent advocate of Mexican independence and spent three years in prison for his beliefs. He held various high offices under a strongly liberal regime, but suffered political reverses. After a period spent abroad, he threw in his lot with the revolted Texans and became first vice-president of independent Texas shortly before his death in 1836.

[15] Three weeks after his first meeting with the President, Calderón reported to his chief in Spain that Bustamante was known as an honest man "without rival in personal valor," but lacking in energy and ability. (*Despachos Generales*, I, 28.)

Opinions regarding Anastasio Bustamante, especially on the conduct of his first administration as president of Mexico in the early 1830's, vary a good deal among different writers. By some he is depicted as upright, efficient, and effective; by others as ruthless and repressive. Guillermo Prieto, who knew him, reconciles these varying interpretations by presenting Bustamante as a well-meaning, single-minded man of conservative bent who admired the authoritarian Spanish system of government. Personally disinclined to harm anyone, he saw issues in terms of black and white, and when influenced by stronger men he was capable of harsh action. Prieto considered him a brave man, scrupulously honest, but politically uneducated. (The dark blot on his record was his share earlier in forcing Vicente Guerrero from the presidency—and in Guerrero's later execution.) Prieto also provides a few additional touches: Bustamante was well-set-up but somewhat heavy-figured, had rather small eyes, toed out when he walked, and spoke with great deliberation, punctuating his remarks with gentle slaps directed at his own stomach. He ate simply and was devoted to soft-boiled eggs. Interested in women at least during his younger days, he was known to have fathered various children, though remaining a bachelor. (*Memorias* . . . , II, 20–23, 32–34.)

[16] What remains of the Cortina house, following the street-opening operation for the Avenida del 20 de Noviembre, is at the Avenida República del Uruguay 94—two blocks south of the central plaza, on the northwest corner of the new intersection. In order to preserve as much as possible of the old façade, the cut-off portion was re-erected around the corner, facing the new avenue. The building today is given over to commercial occupancy, but still standing, and in everyday use, is the enormous doorway through which Fanny undoubtedly passed many times (Plate 51).

[17] A few months later Fanny would write her good friend Prescott, to whom she seems always to have expressed her views frankly, in a somewhat different vein: "He [Count Cortina] has a fine house with good paintings and has a great deal of taste. His wife Paulita is a pretty Andalusian, and they are altogether a pleasant family." (Wolcott, *Correspondence of . . . Prescott*, p. 129.)

[18] Here and elsewhere Fanny seems to have invented a mythical "Mr. Blank" to serve as the source for information perhaps gathered from many sources.

[19] A real was one-eighth of a Mexican dollar, or twelve and a half cents. It served as the source of our term *bit*, as in two bits.

[20] This was apparently added later, as Fanny seems to have forgotten that she was then living in a house whose rooms were all on the ground floor.

[21] Fanny's interest in street cries may have been stimulated by a discussion of the subject contained in an annual of the period. The editors have never seen the publication, but that it existed is evident from a brief notation about it accompanying a piece of music in a magazine then current—the *Mosaico Mexicano* (Vol. III, 1840, opposite p. 160). Some street cries, according to a notation, were sung rather than shouted, and the composer of "*Wals de las Gorditas de Horno Calientes*" concluded his parlor piano piece with a rendition of one of the cries Fanny cites.

[22] Another somewhat later book on Mexico's nineteenth-century past—*El Libro de Mis Recuerdos*, by Antonio García Cubas—also contains a discussion of street cries (pp. 204–5). Included are two not mentioned by Fanny but which she must have heard time and again, as they related to supplies necessary, then and now, to practically every self-respecting Mexican household, whether conducted in a shanty or a palace: "*Tierra para las macetas!* (Earth for flower pots!)"; and "*Alpiste para los pájaros!* (Seed for birds!)"

[23] Again, Clavijero seems to have been used as a source book (*Historia Antigua . . .* , I, 391). As will later be made clear in a more careful description of the making of tortillas, the corn before grinding is soaked and cooked in water to which a piece of lime has been added.

[24] *Sartor Resartus* by Thomas Carlyle had appeared a few years earlier. Professor Teufelsdröckh's career was devoted to "Our Clothes: Their Origin and Influence." The passage quoted occurs at the end of Chapter VII of Book I.

Lady Emmeline Stuart-Wortley, British visitor to Mexico a few years after the Calderóns, also admired the sarape (*Travels . . .* , II, 189): "A Mexican and his *sarape* seem one and indivisible, like the ancient Centaurs and their horses—inseparable and the same. The whole dress is very graceful; what a horror is a swallow-tailed coat in comparison . . ."

8. Chapultepec—Opening of Congress—Shrine of Guadalupe

[1] The near relationship was actually that of first cousins once removed (Adalid's mother and Cortina's grandmother were sisters); this connection would be further cemented in the future by the marriage of Cortina's son to one of Adalid's daughters.

[2] According to information derived from a descendant of the family, the Adalids lived at this time in the building now numbered 49 on the Calle Venustiano Carranza. The old designation of this particular block was the Calle de Cadena. Street names in the capital have been altered since the Calderóns' time, and many now bear names of men then unborn, or of memorable dates still in the future. But a few still retain their old designations. Some idea of the scale of the Adalids' handsome house may be suggested by the fact that, with the addition of a fourth story and by virtue of extensive interior remodeling, it has become a fifty-room hotel.

[3] Concepción Sánchez de Tagle de Adalid—called Conchita—only daughter among the eight children of her famous father (whose career will be discussed more fully later) was

younger than her husband by a good many years, and must have carried a large share of responsibility for a girl of nineteen. Her delicacy of health was surely temporary as, of all of Fanny's friends, she will be involved more than any other in various strenuous expeditions.

José Adalid's first wife, Doña Javiera Valdivielso, daughter of a *marqués*, had left three daughters at her death. Doña Conchita, his second wife, presented him with two more daughters—Paz and Angela—and finally with his only son, Joaquín.

One of the editors had the privilege some years ago of meeting with two granddaughters of Conchita Adalid—and of seeing her portrait in the home of the younger, Señorita Guadalupe Adalid. It showed her as a still young, slender, and attractive woman, dressed in unadorned ruby red velvet. The elder granddaughter, the widowed Señora de Lazo, remembered her grandmother well—and the beautiful contralto voice that held true and rich through the years.

4 Fanny again went to the theater with the Cortinas the second night following, but in the printed text she merged her comments concerning the two occasions, a procedure which we have retained.

5 This actress was Soledad Cordero, born in 1816. From her picture in a theatrical and literary review of the time, she was plain and prim rather than ugly. A contemporary newspaper critic complained that her soul was ice; but she appears to have enjoyed great popularity and was admired for her invincible virtue—her *"conducta inmaculada y sus virtudes privadas."* Señorita Cordero attracted, among other admirers, Ignacio Rodríguez Galván, a well-known young poet who was said to have quit Mexico on her account—though a less romatic reminiscence reported simply that he had always wanted to travel. He died of yellow fever in Havana in 1842 en route to a diplomatic assignment, and she died unmarried a few years later. (*El Apuntador*, pp. 3–5, with illustration opposite p. 3; *El Zurriago*, November 30, 1839; Prieto, *Memorias* . . . , I, 337; Pimentel, *Obras*, IV, 509.)

6 From "Lochiel's Warning" by Thomas Campbell. The source of the quotation a few lines earlier is unknown to us.

7 Paraphrased from "Under Milton's Picture," by John Dryden: "The force of Nature could no farther go."

8 A reference, probably, to Humboldt, who said (*Ensayo Político* . . . , II, 392) that the great lords among the Aztecs frequently mixed their tobacco with the resin of *liquidambar styraciflua* (sweet gum).

9 Prescott in *The Conquest of Mexico* cites this tradition in his Chapter III of Book VII and points to its source in *Life in Mexico* written by his friend. In a footnote he adds: "The fair author does not pretend to have been favored with a sight of the apparition."

Malinche—or Marina, as the Spaniards called the handsome Indian girl whose intelligence and devotion served Cortés so well—seems to have appealed strongly to Fanny, who mentions her several times. As she will later explain, Marina and other Indian women were presented to Cortés after his initial victory in Tabasco. Her native language was Aztec or Nahuatl, and from enslavement in Tabasco she had learned to speak Mayan. Cortés had earlier picked up a Spaniard who, shipwrecked years before, knew Mayan. When, therefore, Cortés landed near what is now Veracruz, he was able to communicate at once with the curious, friendly, Nahuatl-speaking native people through the combination of Marina and Jerónimo de Aguilar, the Mayan-speaking Spaniard. The existence of the emperor Montezuma in his central city of Tenochtitlan, the heavy exactions of the victorious Aztecs from their subject tribes, and the hatreds of defeated or still warring peoples toward them were thus soon made known to Cortés. With characteristic sagacity and opportunism he laid plans to use these bitter resentments to his own advantage, and began to acquire the Indian allies with whose aid in materials and men he would achieve the conquest.

Plate 87 shows the woods of Chapultepec on a festive occasion.

10 There were two Condes de Gálvez, father and son, who served as viceroys of New Spain. It was the second, Bernardo de Gálvez (after whom Galveston in Texas is named), who was the builder of Chapultepec.

11 The vice-queen had been born Felícitas Saint Maxent of New Orleans. (Her husband, before being appointed viceroy, served as captain-general of Louisiana and Florida.) He died in Mexico after a brief term of office and his young widow soon afterward gave birth to her second child, a daughter. In token of respect and affection for her parents the infant was given a magnificent baptism by officials of the capital. (Manuel Romero de Terreros, *Ex Antiquis*, pp. 59–65.)

12 Chapultepec's military strength would before long undergo a tragic test. In September 1847 the castle was, with heavy losses, successfully assaulted by United States troops. Among its defenders were heroic cadets of the military college which established quarters there at the end of 1841.

[13] A writer of the same period says that there were in the capital, in addition to the cathedral, fifty-six churches and thirty-eight monastic establishments—of which twenty-three were for men and fifteen for women. (Latrobe, *Rambler in Mexico*, pp. 107, and 156 fn.) In referring to convents Fanny followed local usage: a convent in these pages means an establishment devoted to those vowed to a communal religious life, whether a group of men or of women.

[14] Other writers of the time have also described the carrying of the Host through the streets to bring to one nearing death the sacrament of extreme unction. (See Plate 46.) If the sufferer were prominent, the procession would be a long one and would include not only priests and friends but also officials, and might be attended by a band. Waddy Thompson, United States minister shortly after Fanny's time, witnessed and described (*Recollections of Mexico*, p. 102) the extraordinary procession of thousands of people, headed by the Archbishop, who accompanied the Host as it was carried to the bedside of the gravely ill Señora de Santa Anna.

[15] A North American visitor of the period, Albert M. Gilliam, was so forcibly struck by the size of the priests' hats that he contrived to measure one. Its longest diameter was twenty-eight inches. (*Travels in Mexico* . . . , p. 78.)

The Chamber of Deputies in which Fanny heard the President speak was burned in 1872. It was a part of the national palace.

[16] Calderón's dispatch of January 22, 1840 discusses some of the diplomatic representatives stationed in the capital. From this and other sources we learn a little of the personalities of the Calderóns' small official circle:

The affable, competent Pakenham of Great Britain had been longest on the ground. The Belgian representative, Baron Florent de Norman (who was not a resident minister plenipotentiary), seems to have been stationed for some time in Mexico preliminary to the drawing up of a treaty with his country. He would soon leave. Baron Friedrich von Gerolt, referred to as Prussian minister, served at this time rather in the capacity of chargé d'affaires. Calderón said he was well liked, friendly to him, and well paid. Like Calderón, Gerolt was an enthusiastic amateur geologist and botanist. He had won a determined battle against Popocatepetl; undeterred by having contracted a severe case of snow blindness during his first attempt to scale the great volcano, he and others climbed to its top in April 1834, and Gerolt even descended into its crater. The United States minister, Powhatan Ellis, is unaccountably absent both from Calderón's dispatches and from Fanny's pages, in which he will be mentioned only once. (However, in correspondence with Prescott, the Calderóns refer by name to Ellis, who seems to have taken responsibility for forwarding their letters to the United States.)

Also on the scene, according to Calderón, were consuls representing the interests of several other countries.

The French minister, the Baron Alleye de Cyprey, was at this time on the way, but would not arrive in the capital until February. He was destined to generate most of the diplomatic excitement during the Calderóns' stay and for some time afterward. Even before the Baron's arrival Calderón had some idea of what to expect, having prudently made inquiries through friends in the French legation in Washington. Calderón informed his chief that the Baron was said to be capable, but easily offended. (*Despachos Generales*, I, 29–30, 33.) That this was an understatement will soon be evident.

[17] General Barrera, whose shrewd, unscrupulous rise to eminence Fanny will record later in her Journal, was a supplier of army uniforms rather than a soldier. The Señora de Barrera, Fanny later explains, was his ambitious second wife.

[18] From the French of Casimir Delavigne, said Fanny herself in one of her rare footnotes.

[19] Presumably the stepmother of Harrison Gray Otis, Boston statesman who had been helpful to the Inglis family.

[20] A cursory glance at the text of the play—first produced in 1835—evokes sympathy for the entrapped guests of honor. There were ten scenes in Act I, fourteen in Act II, twenty-four in Act III, fifteen in Act IV, with a final eight in Act V.

[21] The road to Guadalupe followed the route of one of the ancient causeways connecting from the mainland to the pre-conquest island city.

[22] Guadalupe—surrounded by a multitude of visitors—is shown in Plate 89. Behind, one may identify the chapel crowning the hill, with the sail-shaped monument nearby, while on the right is the Chapel of the Well (shown larger in Plate 90).

[23] Mexico's first bishop and later archbishop—ascetic in his personal life, practical, and charitable—had been a fearless defender of the rights of the conquered. During a dark period of corrupt and repressive government, Zumárraga wrote a careful report in which he detailed the brutalities being practiced against Indians. To make sure it would

reach Spain he journeyed himself to Veracruz to arrange with a sailor on a ship leaving the port for its ingenious concealment (in a cake of wax in a barrel of oil) and subsequent delivery to the highest authorities. He and other Franciscans founded the center for the education and religious training of Indians at Santiago Tlaltelolco, to which Juan Diego was bound. (Kubler, Mexican Architecture of the Sixteenth Century, I, 9–11; Lesley Byrd Simpson, Many Mexicos, pp. 38–40.)

The bishop has been the subject of a biography, Don Fray Juan de Zumárraga, published in Mexico in 1881, by Joaquín García Icazbalceta, in which the writer demolished the persisting legend accepted by Prescott and others that Zumárraga had collected together and burned a great store of Indian manuscripts. Unquestionably he was zealous in destroying Indian idols, and he is known to have had burned to death for heresy a cacique of Texcoco—for which action he was reprimanded by his superiors.

24 The fabric, apparently not sized or prepared to receive paint, is made of vegetable fiber, probably maguey, according to the Catholic Encyclopedia. It is formed of two strips, each about 18" by 70", held together by stitching.

25 The church the Calderóns visited was not the original sixteenth-century shrine but was erected after Zumárraga's time, reaching completion in 1709. In a later chapter its history will be described in some detail; also its interior which has undergone many changes since 1840.

Fanny will shortly term Guadalupe—incorrectly—a cathedral. The venerable churchman whom they met held a bishop's rank, but in relation to the shrine of Guadalupe (which in 1840 was a colegiata and is now a basílica) he was its abbot or abad.

26 Fanny's skepticism concerning the story of Juan Diego, if known, could have seriously undermined Calderón's mission. Today, as then, affection for the Virgin of Guadalupe lies at the core of most Mexicans' feelings about their country and its varied heritage. One of the world's greatest Catholic shrines, Guadalupe is by far the most revered Mexican shrine. Fanny will later observe in modest dwellings the display of pictures of the Virgin of Guadalupe. Today the Virgin's likeness is perhaps even more omnipresent, guarding taxicabs, elevators, and shops as well as homes. It is not only the humble who are drawn to the dark Virgin: delegations of many kinds, including business and professional groups, are likely to make a pilgrimage to the historic shrine incidental to meetings and conventions in the capital; and devotion to the beloved image is not unknown among the sophisticated and well-to-do.

Calderón was of course a Catholic. What he felt—and there is no way of knowing whether he ever discussed this matter with his wife, who was dutifully concealing her Protestantism under a cloak of outward conformity—may well have been not disrespect but unwillingness to believe in the miraculous derivation of the painting which had served so effectively as the symbol of Mexico's struggle against Spain.

Of possible interest is a report by a noted Mexican historiographer, Don Joaquín García Icazbalceta (1825–1894). This was intended only for the eyes of the archbishop of Mexico, but soon after García Icazbalceta's death, without his authorization or that of the archbishop, it mysteriously appeared in print. As a Catholic layman and eminent scholar, García Icazbalceta had been asked by the archbishop to examine the available documentation concerning the painting's origin. He consented with reluctance, but, following careful study, gave his findings. He wished with all his heart, he said, that he could believe that his country had been so signally honored by the Virgin in accordance with tradition, but he personally was forced to conclude that the origin of the painting was not miraculous. He cited, among his reasons, the complete absence of any reference to the subject in the extensive writings of Bishop Zumárraga, or in the records left by other prominent churchmen to whom Zumárraga would have talked or written regarding so overwhelming an event in which he himself had participated. Surely, one so zealous in the cause of the Indians and their conversion to Christianity would have left at least some mention of such an occurrence. García Icazbalceta also pointed out the fact that a very long period had elapsed before there were any written records regarding the matter, during which time traditions presumably might have accumulated; and said that to him, the evidence of the painting itself appeared to be open to question. In short, he considered that the decision to build a shrine, named for one in Spain, had come first, and that the tradition had developed afterwards.

The image of the Virgin, García Icazbalceta suggested, had been the work of a skilled Indian painter from the nearby convent at Santiago Tlaltelolco, Franciscan center for the instruction of Indians. The story of the miraculous imprint on Juan Diego's tilma he considered to have developed as a kind of innocent oral folk drama among zealous Indian converts and others, with the story set down later by pious writers in all good faith. He had, in his younger days, believed in the painting's divine origin, but in the light of his study felt he could no longer do so. He emphasized that he did not deny the possibility of miracles, but that he spoke as a conscientious scholar who had been directed by the archbishop to investigate this particular matter. While the beloved painting of the Virgin of Guadalupe was not in his opinion the result of a miracle, it possessed inherent validity as a symbol of ancient origin. (*La Ultima Palabra sobre la Maravillosa Aparición de la Sma. Virgen de Guadalupe.*)

Belief in the divine origin of the painting rests in part upon: the durability of the apparently untreated fabric of coarse maguey fiber, perishable under ordinary circumstances; an investigation made in 1666, when a number of elderly persons were interviewed in an effort to cast light on the fading past (Juan Diego and Bishop Zumárraga both died in 1548, the bishop at the age of eighty); and statements that Bishop Zumárraga had indeed written about the miracle of the divine image, but that the writings had subsequently perished in a fire. (Donald Demarest and Coley Taylor, *The Dark Virgin,* p. 31.) The origin of the painting is recognized by the Vatican as miraculous, but belief in its miraculous derivation is not a matter of dogma. Catholics are free to hold their own opinions on the matter, as was pointed out by the succeeding archbishop of Mexico, who ordered an official printing of the controversial document. (Luis García Pimentel y Elguero, *Don Joaquín García Icazbalceta como Católico,* p. 20.)

27 Clavijero was probably Fanny's informant regarding the marsh fly whose eggs constituted a kind of caviar. (*Historia Antigua . . . ,* I, 65.) According to other accounts, the eggs might be cooked like fish roe, or pounded into a paste and baked. The mashed flies were likewise cooked and eaten.

9. "All Mexico in a State of Shock"

1 "The President and his Cabinet are a set of amiable old women." So Fanny wrote Prescott the following June. (Wolcott, *Correspondence of . . . Prescott,* p. 131.) With the benefit of hindsight, and subsequent friendship with those involved in the little affair, Fanny for print shortened and toned down her brush with Mexico's cabinet officials. As hitherto published, her text read: ". . . As to their being in the right, there could be no doubt, and nothing but a kind motive could have induced them to take this trouble; so I yielded with a good grace, and thanked the cabinet council for their timely warning . . . I was really thankful for my escape."

2 Bernardo Gaviño, Spanish by birth but Mexican by adoption, had a sure sense of publicity (according to an article by Armando de María y Campos, "Half a Century of Bull-Fighting," in *Mexican Art and Life* for April 1939), and made a practice of dedicating his performances to persons currently prominent; in the absence of a living celebrity he often invoked, at appropriate times, the memory of dead heroes.

The tall matador is also discussed at length in *Historia y Tauromaquia Mexicanas* by José de Jesús Núñez y Domínguez (pp. 109–43); and in *Calle Vieja y Calle Nueva* by Artemio de Valle-Arizpe (pp. 661–65). Both of these modern writers quote at length from Fanny's description of her first bullfight. A few years after this performance, Gaviño and his party were traveling in a sort of convoy toward Chihuahua and were attacked by savage Indians. Some seventy Mexicans were killed, but the matador's great agility in hand-to-hand fighting brought him through the battle although wounded; a few days later, however, he was back in the ring. Gaviño earned well through the years and spent well, and was known as the dean of bullfighters. He had the misfortune in his old age to lose a small fortune which had been deposited with a business house. Unwell, old, and poor, he contracted to fight in the city of Texcoco for the sum of thirty pesos. On January 31, 1886, forty-six years after the performance he dedicated to Calderón, he fought his last bull. Terribly gored, he somehow walked from the ring, survived removal to Mexico, went into delirium, and died on February 11. Gaviño, seventy-three at his death (eighty-three according to one account) must have been one of the most ageless bullfighters of all time.

3 What Señor Arnáiz really wrote was: "*El traje de poblana es de una muger . . . . .*" The dots were his and presumably indicated a word too coarse to write. Fanny pasted the note into her Journal. It was penned with thick black ink and the sand which he used to blot it in January 1840 still stands out in gritty relief on the page.

4 As printed, Fanny's quotation has defied identification. She apparently read Italian well, yet we understand that *I bellici trombi* is unusual in form—while *le bellice trombe* would mean "the warlike bugles" and would fit the text. In her Journal description of the scene, Fanny mentions only the opera *Norma,* and in consequence it seems likely that the music she heard played was from its second act: "*Guerra! guerra! le galliche selve/ Quante han querce producon guerrier/. . . Strage! strage!* (Warfare! Warfare! The hungry wolf glances not with half our rage on his prey . . . Slaughter! Slaughter!)"

[5] Stanza LXXV from Canto I of *Childe Harold's Pilgrimage*. Fanny seems to have admired Byron, and this work in particular; this is the second of a number of quotations she makes from it.

[6] The dramatic soprano Giuditta Pasta (born Giuditta Negri in Como in 1798) sang in the opera by Johann Simon Mayr, *Medea in Corinto*, rather than in the earlier and more exacting *Medée* by Cherubini. (Wallace Brockway and Herbert Weinstock, *The Opera, a History of Its Creation and Performance: 1600–1941*, p. 207.)

[7] Within a few years after the conquest the first bullfight had been held in Mexico. The bull ring of Fanny's day was *not* that shown in Plate 26 (derived from a lithograph of some years later), but was southwest of the cathedral plaza, near the beginning of the Paseo de la Viga. Close by was the still-surviving church of San Pablo, whose roof provided a vantage point for non-paying *aficionados*, who may be glimpsed in Plate 38.

[8] One occasionally sees today—as much prized items offered in Mexican antique shops—examples of the plain, prodigally heavy, hand-wrought silver pieces of the type that evidently startled Fanny at this her first meal in a great Mexican household.

[9] C. M., presumably someone in the United States, remains unidentified. The initials stand, perhaps, for Captain Morgan, mentioned some years earlier in one of Fanny's letters. If so, he was one of the several infuriated Bostonians caricatured in the pamphlet *Scenes at the Fair* who, convinced of Fanny's part in its production, descended on the family's school in wrath.

[10] A French writer of Mexican memoirs speaks of Richard Pakenham as notably thrifty during his earlier days. The British diplomat, he said, was anxious to put money by and did not even maintain a carriage; he either walked or, when transportation was absolutely essential, borrowed a carriage from one of the resident English. (Mathieu de Fossey, *Le Mexique*, p. 284.) If this report had any basis in fact, Pakenham by 1840 must have achieved his goal of financial security—for Calderón in one of his early dispatches said that Pakenham, by virtue of his long residence in Mexico (he had been secretary of legation before becoming minister in 1835), spoke perfect Spanish, frequently wore Mexican dress, lived well on his generous salary, and entertained in an open-handed manner. Calderón further characterized him as discreet, courteous, and conciliatory. (*Despachos Generales*, I, 29.) A French naval officer who met him in 1839 mentioned his "winning personality." (Maissin, *The French in Mexico and Texas*, p. 64.) But as will later be seen, Pakenham could be unflinchingly tough when aroused. His likeness, taken when he was somewhat older, is shown in Plate 76.

Fanny pasted Pakenham's note into her Journal. The un-British spelling of "honor" and "favor" is from the original.

[11] Señora de Guerrero, who seems not to appear again, was Doña Juana Martínez de Guerrero, according to an actual invitation to the ball quoted by Felipe Teixidor (*La Vida en México*, I, *Notas*, 48). The Señora de Gorostiza was Doña Juana Castilla from Spain.

[12] Ladies were admitted free, according to a notice which appeared in the *Diario del Gobierno* of January 1. Individual tickets were ten pesos, and boxes cost thirty—not inconsiderable sums in those days. While it was advertised as a costume ball (*baile de carácter*, or *de fantasía*), patrons might come in ordinary dress. It opened at nine.

[13] The Scottish queen was forty-four when she laid her head on the block at Fotheringay Castle in February 1587.

The opera singer Albini had perhaps appeared in *Maria Stuarda* by Gaetano Donizetti, first performed in Naples in 1834.

[14] The opening phrase of this sentence is as Fanny wrote it in her Journal. When she edited for publication, perhaps more conscious of her rank, she said: "Various ladies were introduced to me . . ." In a few other instances she made similar adjustments of no great consequence.

[15] "Fat, fair, and forty . . . that is all I know of her . . ." From Sir Walter Scott's *St. Ronan's Well*, Chapter VII.

[16] This conversation illustrates only a few of the possible traps awaiting foreigners in the use of Spanish surnames. Many North Americans are familiar with the custom of the double surname, in which the name of the mother follows that of the father, sometimes but not necessarily separated by *y* signifying *and*; curiously enough, even after a year of marriage to a Spaniard, Fanny shows herself as baffled on this score.

Manuelita Sánchez y Flores derived her name from her Sánchez father and her Flores mother. It may be of interest that this double name system, which in some Hispanic places and times has tended to be limited to more ceremonious usage, now proves to have a practical value with the rapid growth of cities and increasing dependence upon the telephone.

What makes for far greater complication in the understanding of Spanish names is the existence of compound surnames of various types; that is, surnames composed of two or three parts, inherited as a whole from a progenitor. Three examples already encountered are Angel Calderón de la Barca; José María Justo Gómez de la Cortina, and Antonio López de Santa Anna. In Calderón's name, Calderón was the nucleus, so to speak, by which he was informally known, although in theory the name is as indissoluble as though held together by hyphens. In Gómez de la Cortina, however, or López de Santa Anna, the Gómez and the López are old but frequently encountered names (not unlike Wilson or Thompson in English in their ancient derivation from first names). They are shared by numerous totally unrelated families, and it is therefore the second half of the name, derived perhaps originally from an estate or location, which sets it apart from others—and as the more distinctive designation, it may be the part of the name most frequently used. Thus the Calderóns' friend, in conversation, was Pepe Cortina, and Mexico's former president was called not General López but General Santa Anna.

Further complications are encountered with families belonging to the nobility, as titles more often than not differ entirely from family names.

In practice, there are many exceptions to general rules and wide latitude is given to family and individual preferences. A book entitled Spanish Personal Names by Charles F. Gosnell is designed to help English-speaking readers and librarians through the maze, but admittedly the variations involved in using and indexing Spanish family names remain difficult for foreigners. The editors have proceeded with care, and hope that they have not been guilty of errors.

To return to Fanny's example: We learn from Volume II of the Historia Genealógica de las Familias Más Antiguas de México by Ricardo Ortega y Pérez Gallardo that the lady in question was the daughter of the third Conde de Nuestra Señora de Guadalupe del Peñasco, whose title was evidently shortened for greater convenience in ordinary use to that of the Conde del Peñasco. Presumably called Manuelita by her friends, before marriage she had been Manuela Sánchez Espinosa y Flores—Sánchez Espinosa being a simplified version of her father's unusually complex family name of Sánchez Espinosa de Mora Luna y Pérez Calderón, and Flores being a shortened version of her mother's compound family name of Flores Alatorre y Sandoval. Following her marriage, she conformed to Spanish custom by adding her husband's family name on his father's side, preceded by de to indicate wife of. Her husband, called Manuelito by his friends, had the comparatively simple name of Manuel de Agreda y Pascual—Agreda from his father and Pascual from his mother. In addition, at some time, presumably later, he also bore the title of Conde de Agreda.

The final name given—Manuelita Sánchez y Flores Peñasco de Agreda—was thus pared to little more than its essentials, with Peñasco presumably inserted by Fanny's informant to identify the lady in question with her father's title.

[17] This name—not encountered in the Journal—was written out as "Frauenfeldt" in the Singer copy of Life in Mexico. (Among the graves one may see today in the Panteón de San Fernando is that of Luisa Moreno de Frauenfeld, who died in 1862—perhaps the girls' mother.)

[18] Plate 56 seems to corroborate the fact that Mexican ladies had been in the habit of wearing their dresses decidedly short. For Mexican fashions of 1839 and 1840—presumably derived from Paris—see Plates 58, 59, and 60. (The amply-skirted ladies depicted in Plate 40 are of a slightly later period.)

[19] It would be interesting to know what Fanny thought of social life in Washington, where she had recently spent a winter as a bride. A French diplomat described thus an evening party at Gadsby's hotel in December 1840: ". . . What society, my God! It made my hair stand on end to find myself amongst these men and women rivalling each other in bad manners. I have never thought of the great importance of politeness in social relations, but now I see that it is the fundamental basis and the most indispensable element. The women, ridiculously dressed, stood around the room hanging on their husbands' arms. Perhaps it was very moral, but I assure you it was very grotesque. There are no young people in the French provinces who have not better manners." (Souvenirs of a Diplomat, by the Chevalier Adolphe de Bacourt, pp. 183–84.) The same writer on his page 214 remarked that the American toilettes "are in very bad taste, and the fashion seems to be that of France twenty years ago."

[20] Macleod of Macleod was presumably John Norman Macleod, twenty-fourth chief of Siol Tormod. He had died in 1835. Fanny undoubtedly saw him and other magnificently arrayed Highlanders at the gala events of the summer of 1822 during George IV's state visit to Scotland. Seven fully equipped bodies of Highlanders came to the capital. Of one review, in which they marched with their chieftains, it was recorded that they wore not the kilt but "the belted plaid," tartan jackets and scarlet vests, and cocked

bonnets. (Isabel Frances Grant, The Macleods, the History of a Clan, 1200–1956, p. 601fn.)

At a guess, the Cumming whom Fanny remembered was Sir William Gordon Gordon-Cumming, second baronet of Altyre and Gordonstown.

[21] "Here's the smell of the blood still; all the perfumes of Arabia will not sweeten this little hand," said Lady Macbeth in the sleepwalking scene—Scene 1 of Act V—of Macbeth.

[22] The Escandón family, whom the Calderóns would come to know well, is almost always spoken of in these pages as a unit, and in consequence no one of its members is described in enough detail to emerge as a personality. The most prominent Escandón at this time was Don Manuel, then in his early thirties but already engaged in various large-scale banking and business ventures. A later British visitor to Mexico described him as able, extremely agreeable, and entirely unassuming. (Robertson, Visit to Mexico . . . , II, 156.) Another Escandón who will appear briefly in later chapters was Don Joaquín, married to a member of the Fagoaga family. But it is an unmarried sister, Doña Luz, with whom Fanny seems to have developed a close friendship. Her Journal gives no clue as to why the supposed intermittent romance between Pakenham, in his early forties at this time (and who never married), and Doña Luz Escandón was inconclusive.

[23] "Parting is such sweet sorrow,/That I shall say good-night till it be morrow"—said Juliet to Romeo from her balcony in Scene 2 of Act II.

[24] Fanny's mother was the widowed Jane Inglis. Lydia was Fanny's much younger sister. From a surviving family document, we guess that they were going to or returning from Europe.

[25] In the Journal at this point there is a small oblong blank space on the page, bounded by diagonal slits. Formerly, it must have accommodated one of the cards announcing the Calderóns' arrival. Fanny's previously published text has here been modified so as to include in full the names which she skeletonized. The omission of her maiden name of Inglis, contrary to what was then and is now Spanish custom, is puzzling.

[26] Fanny for print revised downward her Journal figure to the sum of $2,500; perhaps, therefore, this lower sum is what they paid for the somewhat outlying house which they later took—the house for which she expresses a preference in the third paragraph following. Brantz Mayer, the United States secretary of legation a year or two later, said of rents (Mexico as It Was and as It Is, p. 385): "They vary according to situation, but they are very high throughout the Capital; $500–$2,500; and even higher rates are given for the very best."

The high cost of living well in Mexico seems to have come as a surprise. Calderón, in his dispatch of January 22 to his government (Despachos Generales, I, 30–31) pointed out that much in the way of entertaining would be expected of them, and implied some worry over prospective costs. He could not have managed during the first weeks when waiting for the arrival of his salary, he said, if the Spanish merchant Manuel Martínez del Campo had not lent him the necessary funds.

[27] The traspaso—transfer charge—is explained by an earlier anonymous writer: "The origin of this, both in shops and houses, was a demand for the value of fixtures, wall paintings, and improvements, placed at the expense of the tenant, who, when he left, thus transferred them to his successor:—by degrees, the demands for central situations became so great, that these enormous premiums were given, to induce a tenant to leave; and they are estimated by every tenant as real property, which he can realize whenever he leaves the situation. The fixtures are not generally worth more than three or four hundred dollars." (A Sketch of the Customs and Society of Mexico, p. 68.)

[28] The Marquesa de Uluapa who had recently died was María Josefa Rodríguez de Velasco, married in 1796 to Antonio Manuel Cosío, Marqués de Uluapa.

[29] Many years later, Fanny herself would be decorated with the insignia of the Damas Nobles de María Luisa.

The Marquesa de San Román, born María Guadalupe de Moncada y Berrio, was the widow of Francisco Fernández de Córdoba, who had been director of the mint at the time of Humboldt's encyclopedic study of Mexican mines and economy. She was, according to an article in El Museo Mexicano (IV, 536), a competent amateur painter, and an honorary director of the Academy of Fine Arts. She died nine months after Fanny first met her.

[30] This lady was presumably Doña Ana María Ozta, second wife of José María Cervantes y Velasco, twelfth Conde de Santiago de Calimaya. She will be mentioned on several later occasions.

[31] Señora García never reappears, at least by name, and we have not attempted to identify her. Presumably her husband, with her consent, had obtained sanction from ec-

clesiastical authorities to be relieved of his marriage vows in order to devote himself to the monastic life.

[32] The name as Fanny wrote it in her Journal was Subervier, but we assume that the caller was the wife of the French consul (who acted also as consul general of the Netherlands), M. Justin Victor Subervielle.

[33] Reflecting a less critical masculine point of view, Guillermo Prieto in his memoirs mentions Señora Barrera—whom he calls Alejita, from her maiden name of Aleja Delgado —as a lively hostess, whose humble origin was not forgotten by those more highly placed. (Memorias . . . , II, 32.)

[34] Herbaut and Palmyre were among the leading Paris fashion houses of the era. (Octave Uzanne, Fashion in Paris, p. 102.) Fanny will soon, during Holy Week, appear in a creation of Palmyre's.

[35] This rather obvious identification is substantiated in the Singer copy, as is also that of Count Cortina a few paragraphs later.

[36] Other memoirs of the time also detail the murder of M. Mairet (whose name Fanny caught and recorded as Merry). Just before one of the perpetrators was about to be executed, he revealed the complicity of Colonel Juan Yáñez. The colonel's guilt was soon proved by the discovery among his effects of an incriminating paper written in cipher. The excitement caused by the murder was greatly heightened by the news that an aide-de-camp of Santa Anna was also involved. A judge who refused to lose the incriminating cipher died mysteriously, apparently of poison. Another judge was thought to have accepted a large bribe to get rid of the evidence, then to have confessed remorsefully to a priest, who persuaded him to see that justice was done. Yáñez seemed completely confident all through these protracted proceedings of going free, but finally slashed his throat with a razor in July 1839 to escape public execution. Nicolás Bravo, who only a few days earlier had temporarily assumed office as acting president, ordered his body exposed as a public example of the deserts of crime. (Mayer, Mexico as It Was and as It Is, p. 140; Thompson, Recollections of Mexico, pp. 24–26; Carlos María de Bustamante, El Gabinete Mexicano, I, 202; José Ramón Malo, Diario de Sucesos Notables, 1832–1864, I, 109–10.)

Another book of the period says that Yáñez, on the basis of information secured from the passport office on the movements of travelers, had been regularly engaged in highway robbery. (Barinetti, Voyage to Mexico and Havanna, pp. 21–22.)

[37] Her maiden name had been María Ignacia—or Ygnacia as she herself seems to have spelled it—Rodríguez de Velasco; and she was the sister of the dead Marquesa de Uluapa, whose house the Calderóns would have liked to rent.

The impact she produced in her younger days suggests that the name La Güera might better be translated as The Blonde. Beautiful and intelligent, reckless and durable, she has attained in retrospect something of the status of a legend.

[38] The loveliness of La Güera's daughters was also legendary. Their fame is said to have reached the ears of the King of Spain, who asked that the still-radiant mother and her three beautiful girls be painted together and the portrait sent to him.

María Josefa, the oldest, married the third Conde de Regla in 1812. Poinsett, later United States minister, met her in 1821 as the still very young mother of several children, and thought her beautiful, amiable, and intelligent. A few years later, depleted by the privations of a winter voyage from Veracruz to New York, she failed to recover, and died in Brooklyn in 1828. Years later one of her sons would bring her body back from St. Patrick's Cathedral to the family's hacienda of Xalpa.

María de la Paz also died young. She was said to have been angelic in appearance, but also tall, superbly built, and strong. As she came out of church one day, a street loiterer spoke to her impertinently; she countered with a slap so powerful as to knock her annoyer flat. She married in 1815 José María Rincón Gallardo, second Marqués de Guadalupe Gallardo, and had two daughters. H. G. Ward, who knew her, spoke not only of her beauty and cleverness, but also of her unaffected kindness of heart. (Mexico in 1827, II, 642.)

María Antonia—whom Fanny saw on her balcony as the "fat and fair" Marquesa de San Miguel de Aguayo—married at fifteen a widower with two young daughters, the older of whom became José Adalid's short-lived first wife. Subsequently the marquesa had three daughters of her own.

(These facts come from entries in Ortega y Pérez Gallardo's Historia Genealógica . . . ; and from a book by Manuel Romero de Terreros, a descendant of La Güera's oldest daughter: Bocetos de la Vida Social en la Nueva España, pp. 210–21.)

[39] Any number of people must have known the exact age of La Güera, renowned since the age of fourteen for beauty and independence of behavior, but she evidently could

not resist this opportunity of whittling down her age for a new and sympathetic listener. Born in November 1778, she was twenty-four, not eighteen, when Humboldt reached Mexico in 1803. She had then been married eight years and had already borne all four of her children by her first husband, whose death about two years later would end a stormy marriage. When Fanny met La Güera, she was sixty-one. She had outlived two husbands and three of her five children. (Fanny does not mention her only son; nor the daughter of her second marriage, who died in infancy.)

A Frenchman who knew and admired her in middle age termed her the most aristocratic woman of his acquaintance, and compared her to the seventeenth-century Ninon de Lenclos, whose bloom and vitality also defied the passing years. La Güera was still casting her old spell—"fort séduisante" was how he described her—even in her fifties, until 1833 when her looks apparently suffered as a result of the cholera she contracted in the great epidemic of that year. (Fossey, Le Mexique, p. 282.)

She is mentioned in several of the books of her descendant, Manuel Romero de Terreros, including La Corte de Agustín I, Emperador de México; México Virreinal; and Los Condes de Regla. In the last of these there is reproduced (opposite page 86) a head-and-shoulders miniature, rather blurred, of La Güera in youth. Although appealing in effect, this likeness does not bear the authoritative stamp of classic beauty, but portrays, rather, a face dominated by enormous eyes and framed in shoulder-length fair hair cut across her forehead in a bang. Her magic, as Fanny surmised when viewing the "beaux restes" of her looks, must have been compounded of an incandescent blend of magnificent coloring, perfection of figure, and lightness of heart.

[40] In her Journal, Fanny has the baron "asking whether he could visit the place where the cochineal plant is in great quantities." As she evidently learned later, cochineal is the name for a minute scale-insect which feeds principally on the nopal cactus. From the bodies of the females a brilliant and lasting carmine dye may be obtained. An important industry was formerly centered around the careful propagation and nurture of the insects, which were collected, killed, dried, and packed in hides for shipment. The culture was successfully transported to other warm-weather parts of the world; prices dropped, and the industry in Mexico declined even before the Calderóns' arrival. The known superiority of the Mexican product, however, served to maintain a continuing demand.

[41] In her Journal, Fanny quotes La Güera's own words in describing the scene: "Humboldt, first perceiving me, stood transfixed with amazement, and at length exclaimed: 'Who is that muchacha?'"

[42] Apparently a paraphrase of line 359 of the Ars Poetica of Horace: "Even the worthy Homer sometimes nods."

Alpenkalkstein—a word presumably plucked out of Humboldt—is translated in the English version of his work as Alpine limestone.

In his mid-thirties when La Güera had enchanted him thirty-seven years before, Humboldt in 1840 was still very much alive—a splendid-looking, vital old man, who kept his health and his wits until shortly before his death in 1859 at the age of almost ninety. He never married.

[43] The message on La Güera's thick calling card—which Fanny did in fact insert into her Journal—may be translated thus:

María Ygnacia Rodríguez de Elizalde
will have the honor of calling
today upon the Minister's Lady

[44] Fanny introduced at this point the following footnote for her printed text: "The Mexican Government has since taken this matter into consideration, and is making regulations which render it necessary for a medical man to possess a certain degree of knowledge, and to have resided a specified time in the city before he is permitted to practise; they are also occupied in fixing a certain sum for medical attendance."

The litigation between Dr. Juan Plane and the executors of the Marquesa de Uluapa—who, her only son having died without heirs, left a large sum to charity—achieved lengthy press coverage. (For example: El Cosmopolita, February 5, 1840.)

[45] This figure—one notices that Fanny in her Journal liked to use definite sums—was modified for print to "several hundred thousand dollars."

[46] That Fanny occasionally revised the vitality out of her Journal in readying her manuscript for print is nowhere better illustrated than in the last sentence of this chapter. Her printed text ran: "Grief shows itself in different ways; yet one might think that when it seeks consolation in display, it must be less profound than when it shuns it." (This anecdote opens the third volume of the Journal and was, therefore, probably gleaned a good deal later.)

10. "Settled at Last"

[1] As earlier noted, this house—which the Calderóns tried but failed to lease and which was apparently next door to their first place of residence—still survives at this time. What if anything the young Wards and their two little girls had done to make a mess of it does not appear, but in one respect at least they went further than most tenants do: they buried someone in the garden. An English writer of memoirs, Captain G. F. Lyon, after making a call on Ward, wrote of the house that it was ". . . really superb. In its extensive garden, amidst overhanging and flowering trees I saw the tomb of my much-lamented friend the Honourable Augustus Waldegrave, who unfortunately lost his life by an accident when on a shooting-party." (*Journal* . . . , II, 115–16.) The Wards probably had little choice in this matter because there existed at the time no arrangement for the interment of Protestants in Mexico. Soon afterward, however, in the implementation of a treaty negotiated by Ward, a burial ground for Protestants was established outside the San Cosme gate in the open country. Santa Anna's use of the house had been rather recent—early in 1839, when he was provisional president in the absence of Bustamante. The house apparently belonged to a daughter of the Conde de Pérez Gálvez. (Malo, *Diario de Sucesos Notables*, I, 164.) The cut on page 147 shows the view from the roof, looking east toward the city. The Calderóns' new house, on the opposite side of the street farther east, presumably did not exist at the time this representation was made.

[2] Of this house into which the Calderóns settled it can be said with absolute certainty only that it is gone, for the immediate neighborhood now contains nothing but modern construction on the north side of the street. Señor Jorge Enciso (at the time of our inquiry the head of the Dirección de Monumentos Coloniales) explained in courteous response to a letter that tradition—not, however, backed up by documentation—held that the Calderóns' house had been a large building which was demolished when the Calle Zaragoza was opened. The Calderóns' landlord was apparently Manuel Gual.

Plate 27 is an enlarged portion of a charming lithograph "taken from a balloon" about 1855. Looking west, it shows in the foreground the northwest corner of the Alameda, with the edge of the city only a little beyond. Various surviving landmarks appear: at the left, the church of San Diego, now a museum; at the right, the church of San Hipólito and, directly behind, the church of San Fernando with its then-existing convent. At the center of the picture, on the right of the street which bisects it, is a row of houses. One of these, with outbuildings and a garden behind, was unquestionably the Calderóns' Mexican home. In back of it, to the right, is a wing of the enormous old convent of San Fernando, which Fanny herself will shortly sketch from one of her windows. Plate 26 shows another air view, of about the same time, looking toward the southeast.

[3] Starting with the three rooms at the upper left of Fanny's drawing, and proceeding clockwise, her designations for the various spaces read thus: Pantry; Bath room; Store (?) room; Cabinet; Bed room; Bed room; ———; Bed room; ———; Door to staircase; ———; Small cabinet of Calderon; Cabinet of Calderon; Small salon; Drawing room; Small salon; Bedroom; Dressing room; Bedroom; Bed room; Passage (with the Kitchen behind); and Dining room. Calderón's Cabinet was presumably his office. It is not easy to draw to scale an entire establishment, and the rooms were surely deeper in proportion than shown.

In the middle is the "Court," arcaded on all four sides. Fanny has taken the liberty of folding down, for clearer representation, its iron railing complete with potted plants, the size of which seems a bit out of hand.

The side to the right, with its large drawing room, almost certainly faced south, toward the street. Carriages must have entered here (where two lines extend toward the right) and then crossed the courtyard to service quarters behind. We know from a later comment that there was a balcony on the street side.

[4] San Fernando's handsome baroque church (Plate 28) survives, fronting on a small deep plaza to its south. Nothing remains of the large conventual establishment of the Calderóns' time. Its grounds have long since been divided into blocks and built over. In 1915, when Federico E. Mariscal published *La Patria y la Arquitectura Nacional*, San Fernando was, he said (p. 33), "the most imposing ruin in the city of Mexico," although its former cells and rooms were then a maze of tenements.

[5] The embrace, or *abrazo*, as conducted between women of fashion was evidently a stylized routine in which many shades of feeling could be indicated. In theory, each lady placed one hand behind the neck and the other behind the waist of her partner. In practice, it was not required that the participants touch. Observers noted that a pair not on the warmest terms could manage all the correct motions—faces gently inclined, and arms extended in the proper manner—as much as two feet apart. In contrast, extra cordiality

called for enthusiastic pats and for a double embrace; that is, for reaffirmation by reversing the position of the arms and repeating the action. (Sir Stuart Alexander Donaldson, *Mexico Thirty Years Ago*, pp. 206–8; Isidore Löwenstern, *Le Mexique*, p. 162.)

[6] That a discussion of churches could be uncertain conversational ground for the Protestant Fanny is obvious. As to the opera, she apparently had discovered what two other accounts of the time tell us: that a by-product of the departed opera had been a feud which divided social Mexico into two rival groups—the *Albinistas*, proponents of Mme Albini (the singer encountered in the *Norma*, and the *Cesaristas*, equally fervid admirers of the contralto Mme Cesari. A duel, thoroughly satisfactory in that no one was hurt but honor preserved intact, was one of the high points of the furore. (Fossey, *Le Mexique*, pp. 241, 536–37.) The Calderóns' friend Count Cortina had been the leader of the pro-Cesari faction. (Prieto, *Memorias . . .* , I, 263–65.)

[7] Fanny prepared her final text for publication in the reserved world of Boston, more than two years after she made this Journal entry during her first days of wary conversational efforts in a strange land. By then thoroughly acclimated to the easy Latin pace, she wrote: "All this, which struck me at first, already appears quite natural, and would scarce be worth mentioning, but as affording a contrast to our slight and indifferent manner of receiving and taking leave of our guests."

[8] Apparently not only were Christian names in far more general use in Mexico than in the United States (Prescott, on terms of warmest friendship with both Calderón and Fanny for many years, never addressed her, at least in writing, other than formally), but also a more frank tone of conversation prevailed. A physician from the United States who wrote of his experiences in Mexico a few years later remarked: "I have always thought a refinement, too subtle to be commendable, pervaded society at home, in common conversation between gentlemen and ladies; such is not the case in this country; one may say anything, not absolutely indecent, that comes up naturally in his discourse." (McSherry, *El Puchero*, pp. 183–84.)

[9] Perhaps Fanny was thinking here, without remembering it exactly, of a passage (Canto IV, Stanza L) in *Childe Harold's Pilgrimage*: "We gaze and turn away, and know not where,/ Dazzled and drunk with beauty, till the heart/Reels with its fulness; . . ."

[10] Señor Murphy—whose name is entered in the Singer copy—was the Spanish consul in the capital, according to occasional mentions of him in Calderón's dispatches.

[11] Clavijero (in *Historia Antigua . . .* , I, 393) describes *octli*, or pulque, but he noted that among the ancient Aztecs drunkenness, except for special ceremonial occasions, could be punished by death. But tippling was condoned as solace for old age.

[12] A special vocabulary developed around the making and imbibing of pulque. The honey-water mentioned here—*aguamiel* in Spanish—is *tlachique* in the Aztec language, and the source for the word *tlachiquero* to signify the worker who siphons off honey-water with his *acocote* or gourd. The place where pulque is sold is a *pulquería*, and one drunk on pulque may be described as *pulqueado*—that is, pulquefied.

The mother pulque, a later visitor to Mexico thought, had the "combined odour of gasworks and drains." But before he left Mexico he was a confirmed devotee of pulque, as well as of tortillas, and wondered how he would contrive to live without them after his departure. (Tylor, *Anahuac*, p. 31.)

[13] Of the many kinds of maguey, one (the *agave atrovirens*) is of especial value for its sweet sap from which pulque is made. The amount of liquid yielded by a vigorous plant—when hollowed out at the strategic moment of its development and regularly "milked" as already decribed—may vary from 125 to 200 gallons, or even more. After this effort the plant shrivels up and dies.

The Mexicans did and do make coarse cloth from maguey fiber—for sacks, bags, and other uses. The charcoal for Fanny's kitchen was almost certainly brought to the house in paired maguey-fiber sacks, so large that they all but hid the donkeys which bore them; and whoever did the marketing for the household undoubtedly went out, like cooks and housewives ever since, armed with strong capacious bags made from the maguey.

Humboldt, in his discussion of maguey culture, speaks of the juice, at a certain period of the plant's development, as useful for cleaning wounds. (*Ensayo Político . . .* , II, 335–42.) Hans Gadow, in *Through Southern Mexico* (pp. 24–25), lists additional uses: the huge dried leaves can be employed to thatch roofs; from the root a starchy food may be prepared; and the stems may be burned for firewood. Miguel Macedo Enciso, in a modern treatise (*Manual del Magueyero*, pp. 38–46, 141–42), points out that the smaller and more tender leaves, if carefully de-spined and chopped, may be fed to cattle.

An allied product of maguey that undoubtedly reaches back to prehistoric times is the dried fibre in omnipresent use for household scouring. The wiry little wads are cheap, expendable, and effective—and completely incompatible with the limited digestive capacities of modern plumbing.

Anyone who has traveled in Mexico will have observed that the family wash of the humble is likely to be impaled for drying on the thorny-edged leaves (*pencas*) of maguey plants; that magueys are useful as boundary markers; and that the easily punctured, thickly-fleshed leaves of maguey plants growing near country gathering points offer a gratifying medium for recording initials and expressions of sentiment. Even a parasitic enemy of the maguey is useful. It is a fat succulent worm of cleanly habits whose Aztec name is *meocuil*, not to be confused with its less tasty rival maguey worm *chiloquil*. Plucked from maguey plants in April and May, fried crisp on the outside in deep fat, and conjoined with *guacamole*—an avocado-base sauce—they make a delectable dish.

[14] The reference is presumably to *mezcal*.

[15] *Perón* to some Mexicans seems to signify a type of pear; but in various parts of the country the term refers to a kind of cooking apple.

[16] The once-quiet village of Tacubaya is today entirely urbanized. A high-speed throughway bounds it on one side. At least one delightful oasis fortunately remains—the hilly Parque Lira—on the lower edge of which, facing the busy Calle Parque Lira at No. 136, there is still preserved La Casa de la Bola, the solid old house that was formerly the Cortinas' country retreat.

The change between Fanny's first impressions and her later experience is apparent here in a minor but revealing difference between her Journal and her book. Writing in her Journal, she noted that "one might with books, horses &c. pass the time there pleasantly enough." Warmed by the memory of many Sundays spent in the country at the Cortina house and her two-year friendship with the family, she later added the references to "most agreeable society" and "the very centre of hospitality."

[17] This building, dating from 1784 and formerly the summer palace of the archbishops, still stands on the Calle Ex-Arzobispado at the Avenida Observatorio. Plate 88 suggests its once-superb view, now impeded by surrounding construction.

[18] This anecdote is from Volume 3 of Fanny's Journal, where she set it down without giving any names other than the initials S.A.—standing, certainly, for Santa Anna.

[19] Mrs. Frances Trollope, whose generally unfavorable impressions of life in the United States in the 1830's are spread through her *Domestic Manners of the Americans*, unhesitatingly praised the good looks of women of the United States, but also pronounced most of them colorless, over-genteel, and completely wanting in warmth and charm. On page 267 of Donald Smalley's recent edition she put her views succinctly: "I certainly believe the women of America to be the handsomest in the world, but as surely do I believe that they are the least attractive."

[20] Of some interest is what a male British writer on Mexico at about this time thought on the always-interesting topic of national differences. George F. Ruxton, who found little that pleased him about most aspects of Mexican life, admired Mexican women and spoke up enthusiastically for the untrammeled state of their figures, so much deplored by Fanny: ". . . Although not distinguished for beauty, I never once remember to have seen a really ugly woman. Their brilliant eyes make up for any deficiency of feature, and their figures, uninjured by frightful stays, are full and voluptuous. Now and then, one does meet with a perfectly beautiful creature . . ." (*Adventures in Mexico* . . . , p. 57.)

[21] The opinion of Countess Paula Kollonitz, who saw Mexico some twenty years later as one of the Empress Carlota's attendants, reinforces what is here expressed. While cautious in generalizing on Mexican women's looks, she cited lovely eyes, teeth, and hair, and the charm of small hands and feet. She then added with more enthusiasm: "I saw some ladies whose features were so refined, their forms so gracious and charming, and their manners so noble, simple, and unrestrained, that I was filled with admiration whenever I met them." (*The Court of Mexico*, pp. 165–66.)

[22] Miguel Cervantes y Velasco, Marqués de Salvatierra (spoken of in other accounts of the time as an albino), had been a signer of Mexico's affirmation of independence from Spain, had held the rank of general of brigade, and at this time was serving in congress. He was the father of a large family. One cannot be certain of the identity of the daughter whose funeral mass will shortly be described, but it seems likely that she was Doña Manuela Cervantes y Michaus, only child of his dead first wife.

[23] Fanny herself is the speculative "M_____," a mythical character whom she invented for print. In her Journal the sentence starts with the sixth word, "if," and later she says, "It is to me astonishing."

This paragraph dealing with the funeral mass was entered by Fanny in her Journal under date of February "29th," which she then wrote over so as to read "30th." The year 1840 was, in fact, leap year.

24 The church of San Agustín, at what is now the Avenida República del Uruguay 67, was finished before the end of the seventeenth century. Various alterations were made in the 1880's when it became the Biblioteca Nacional—the national library of the University of Mexico. Over the doorway one may admire today the superb sculpture Fanny undoubtedly saw as she entered—a rigid but powerful grouping which shows the Protector Saint Augustine as both kindly and forceful, his cape extended by angels to shelter kneeling figures in monastic habits, his feet upon vanquished heretics. Among the glories of the church were its boldly carved wooden choir stalls. Some of them are preserved in the Escuela Nacional Preparatoria. (Elizabeth Wilder Weismann, *Mexico in Sculpture, 1521–1821*, pp. 84, 99.)

25 A curious contradiction between Journal and previously published text is noticeable here. For print Fanny concluded her total description of the event with: ". . . we found some difficulty in making our way through the crowds of léperos, who, though not allowed to enter the church on this occasion, were swarming at the gates." Perhaps she later learned that typically the poor and unwashed were excluded from such private functions, and altered her record to fit what was the general custom. Lauro E. Rosell notes (*Iglesias y Conventos Coloniales de México*, p. 195) that the sacristy of San Agustín formerly belonged to the Marqueses de Salvatierra and that various members of the family were interred there. Might the parents of the young girl have insisted that on this particular occasion the church be open to all, whether invited guests or not?

26 The churchman termed the "Archbishop" in Fanny's Journal, but designated as the bishop in her printed text, was Manuel Posada y Garduño. He had already been named archbishop but had not yet been formally consecrated in his new office. What he said to Fanny was, "Señora, I am at your feet," to which she replied, "I kiss your hand."

27 This invitation does not appear in the Journal. The names filled in come from notations in the Singer copy. Newspapers of the time—and information from a present-day family connection—fill in the story.

In spite of the February date, the Calderóns must have received this invitation some weeks later. It was perhaps inserted here, with a change of date, in order to round out the subject of funeral masses. From the *Diario del Gobierno* of March 30, 1840, one learns that Senator Torres Torija died on March 28. His fellow senators wanted to arrange a public funeral as a mark of respect toward their colleague, but Senator Basilio Guerra, speaking on behalf of the family, said that the relatives preferred a private ceremony.

Senator Agustín Torres Torija y Guzmán had been the husband of Doña Josefa Adalid, sister of the Calderóns' good friend. Adalid and Cortina were not, of course, brothers of the dead senator, but were his brother-in-law and cousin-in-law respectively. The wording was based, no doubt, on the generous assumption of the time that relatives of comparable age within a large family group were in effect brothers.

28 This was presumably an old announcement which Fanny somewhere encountered, as General Almonte, the Minister of War, had been married to Doña Dolores Quesada in 1839. (Prieto, *Memorias* . . . , II, 31–32.) For print Fanny disguised the bride's name as "Anna R——."

11. Seeing and Being Seen

1 In preparing this and the prior chapter for publication Fanny readjusted the sequence of her material, with the result that the events as here given are not all in strict chronological sequence. Both chapters draw extensively on the concluding portion of Volume 1 of her Journal.

2 The disaster of the *noche triste* or sad night—the night following June 30, 1520—seemed at the time an end to the Spaniards' tenuous grasp on Mexico. Until May, Cortés, by a combination of luck, intrepidity, guile, and uncomplicated belief in the righteousness of his own cause, had succeeded in maintaining his troops and his Tlaxcalan Indian allies for some months in a comparatively peaceful occupation of the Aztec capital. Cortés had been welcomed uneasily by Montezuma—who had tried unsuccessfully by means of fatally rich gifts to persuade the frightening, fire-shooting strangers against coming to his city of Tenochtitlan—but it was apparent to the Spaniards from the moment they entered the island capital on November 8, 1519, that they were walking into a potential trap.

After the first ceremonious meeting on the causeway, Cortés felt his way in a policy of dealing suavely but insistently with the vacillating Montezuma, already troubled by a long accumulation of portents of change and doom. One day, in a quietly executed stroke, Cortés seized the Indian emperor as a hostage and bore him off, shaken but making a proud pretense of acquiescence, to the palace of Axayacatl, which was occupied as headquarters by the Spanish troops. Here he was joined by his family and various functionaries. He was in general treated with great respect and was later allowed to come and go —but only when accompanied by a vigilant escort of Spanish soldiers. Thus, through possession of the person of Montezuma, the vastly outnumbered Spaniards held the key to at least the outward subordination of the Aztecs.

Cortés soon pressed for action on the Indian monarch's offer to become a vassal of Charles V—whom Montezuma associated with the legendary ruler from beyond the eastern seas who, according to Aztec tradition, would some day return to reign over Mexico. As soon as the subdued Montezuma and his chieftains had sworn formal allegiance to the crown of Spain, Cortés persuaded Montezuma to order the collection of an immense tribute in gold and jewels. In return, he promised the anxious Indian monarch to do what he had no intention of doing: to take the rich treasure and depart.

In May, Cortés left the capital with about a third of his men in order to cope with a large rival group of Spaniards who had landed on the coast—sent out from Cuba to discipline the independently acting conqueror. With typical boldness, he captured their leader and annexed the newcomers to his forces. Not long after this feat, however, he had news of disastrous developments in the capital, and hastened his return there: Alvarado, whom he had left in charge, had ruthlessly massacred some 600 Aztec nobles. Smoldering hatred among the Aztecs soon flamed into overt hostility against the returned Cortés and his united garrison. The Aztecs pulled up the bridges leading out of the city, and prepared to destroy the invaders in their palace stronghold.

The failure of various brief sorties only brought home to the Spaniards the hopelessness of any attempt to emerge openly from their trap. Montezuma, speaking from the turret that rose above the palace, urged his subjects to let the aliens leave. The answer was a storm of taunts and stones. Stunned, apparently as much by grief as by a heavy blow from a stone, the Emperor died a few days later, politely spurning to the end conversion to the faith urged upon him by his captors. (Some careful students of the conflicting accounts of these desperate days have been convinced that Montezuma was killed at the orders of Cortés.) Montezuma was mourned not only by his own entourage, but also, it was said, by the Spaniards, who had become attached to their generous, fatalistic, and once-priceless hostage. On the night following his death or on the night after—here records differ— Cortés resolved to act. He gave directions for the order of march, saw to the reckoning and transport arrangements for the King's fifth of the fabulous treasure, and, warning his men to travel light, told them to take what they wished from the gleaming piles that remained. Mass was celebrated; then the Spanish troops, with their Tlaxcalan allies, and the remaining hostages—and their ordnance, their precious horses, and their plunder— began a surreptitious abandonment of Tenochtitlan.

For the account that follows, Fanny seems to have leaned heavily upon Clavijero's *Historia Antigua de Mégico* (II, 108).

[3] Clearly Fanny is here drawing on Humboldt (*Ensayo Político . . .* , I, 350–51). His source was a document which he encountered during his Mexican sojourn, written by Diego Muñoz Camargo, a noble mestizo of Tlaxcala. In a note to this document, which was not published in its entirety until 1892, the Mexican editor concluded that the weight of evidence showed that in spite of the persisting legend Alvarado had in reality crossed the ditch on a beam. A note by another scholar explained that the Aztecs only appeared to eat dirt: actually they touched the ground, and then their mouths, to indicate respect. (Diego Muñoz Camargo, *Historia de Tlaxcala*, edited by Alfredo Chavero, with notations also by José Fernando Ramírez, pp. 221–23.)

[4] The story of the valiant María de Estrada was well known: she had been mentioned long before in Fray Juan de Torquemada's history *Monarquía Indiana* (I, 504). Prescott, in his forthcoming *Conquest of Mexico* (II, 309), would pay tribute to her and several Spanish wives who appear at this point in the conquest as sharing the hardships of the venture. (The article which Fanny read—signed simply with the initial *B*—is from the *Mosaico Mexicano*, III, 234–37.)

[5] The bright-haired Pedro de Alvarado was brave, attractive, and well-liked by the royal prisoner Montezuma—until the massacre of the Aztec nobles demonstrated his capacity for rash cruelty. By both the Tlaxcalans and the Aztec leaders he had earlier been called Tonatiuh, or the Sun.

[6] It is highly unlikely that Fanny had ever seen, in his monumental flesh, the professional fat man Daniel Lambert, who had died in 1809 before she was five. He weighed 739 pounds and measured over nine feet around the middle. What would have stuck in the mind of a child was the fact that the wall of the house in which he died had to be knocked out to permit removal of his body. Likenesses of this then heaviest known of human beings abounded. (*Notes and Queries*, 6th series, Nov. 3, 1883, VIII, 347.) A print depicting Lambert, dated 1823, is part of the collection of the Ringling Museum of the Circus at Sarasota, Florida.

7 Fanny's characterization here of what she termed the lower classes seems to have been based on observations of the *léperos,* for later she would voice admiration of the sturdy folk of the Mexican countryside. The numbers, picturesqueness, and lawlessness of the *léperos*—the floating poor of the capital—forcibly struck other foreign visitors. Brantz Mayer, United States secretary of legation at about this time, commented on their wildness and misery: "Is it wonderful, in a city with an immense proportion of its inhabitants of such a class, (hopeless in the present and the future,) that there are murderers and robbers?" (*Mexico as It Was and as It Is,* p. 42.) But the United States minister of 1842, estimating that eight out of ten men on the street fell into the category of soldier, priest, or *lépero,* gave it as his opinion that of the three groups the *lépero* was the least burdensome on the national economy. (Thompson, *Recollections of Mexico,* pp. 128, 165–66.)

8 Juan Ignacio Lyón (who as a Jesuit was a cleric, rather than a monk) was born in Yucatán of a French father and an Italian mother. Almost rejected by the Society of Jesus because of a tendency to stammer, he was accepted on the ground that his character and ability would outweigh any deficiency in the pulpit. He apparently achieved a special place as a confessor and counselor, and not many years after the Calderóns were in Mexico, high officials in the government sent representations to Rome urging that he be raised to the rank of bishop. (Gerardo Decorme, S.J., *Historia de la Compañía de Jesús en la República Mexicana durante el Siglo XIX,* I, 253–54, 405 fn; also portrait opposite II, 20.)

9 A North American, confined not long afterwards for military as well as sanitary reasons, has left a graphic first-hand description of what San Lázaro was like from the inside. Some of its inmates, he said, were voiceless, some fingerless, some noseless—and most had twisted limbs. More pleasantly, he noted that the food was ample and good, that patients' friends and relatives visited frequently, often bringing small gifts, and that they unconcernedly stayed for many hours. On holidays San Lázaro's patients put on their finery and received an especially large number of visitors, including lepers from the women's side; and music and gayety surged through the hospital. Later, after outsiders left, and the potent drink which had somehow found its way inside the walls began to take effect, Kendall found the strident hilarity of the doomed men and women, as they danced and sang, macabre in the extreme. (George Wilkins Kendall, *Narrative of the Texan Santa Fé Expedition,* II, 220–49.)

10 Francisco Bayeu y Subías, now usually ranked as a competent but not inspired painter, lived from 1736 to 1795. Fanny would refer briefly to the original of this painting in her later book about Spain, *The Attaché in Madrid* (p. 271). In her widowhood, as a member of the court, she must have seen it many times; one wonders whether it may not have provided something of a link between the later Spanish phase of her life and her younger days in Mexico, to which she never returned.

11 An Englishwoman who saw Mexico a few years later was delighted with the wide variety of vehicles seen there, and described them as "the most charming original, aboriginal, indescribable, huge nondescripts, drawn by astonished-looking mules, that do not so much seem to be trying to drag them, as attempting to race away from them with might and main, utterly scared; and they really look as if they were about to topple over, and crush everything near them." (Stuart-Wortley, *Travels . . . ,* II, 63.)

The Paseo de Bucareli, also at this time called the Paseo Nuevo (not to be confused with today's Paseo de la Reforma which, under another name, would be laid out and planted some twenty years later under Maximilian and Carlota), terminated in what was then open country at the church of La Piedad. It is now in the heart of downtown Mexico, but still bears the name of Bucareli in honor of an upright and able viceroy. The equestrian statue of Charles IV of Spain—which Fanny will mention in a later chapter—now stands where the fountain flowed in the Calderóns' time.

12 The horse for evening riding in the Paseo, one reads elsewhere, was of a type called *brazeador,* after the high action of the *brazos,* or forelegs. In the performance of the ideal parade horse, extreme showiness and much curveting were desirable, combined with the capacity to maintain, under the rider's direction, all but imperceptible progress forward, in keeping with the circumspect social atmosphere. (Ward, *Mexico in 1827,* II, 229; Mayer, *Mexico as It Was and as It Is,* p. 285.)

13 Smoking among women, as practiced in polite circles in nineteenth-century Mexico, would evidently die lingeringly. Ward noted that between his first visit to Mexico in 1824 and his second about three years later there had been a marked decline and that ladies no longer smoked publicly. (*Mexico in 1827,* II, 716.) But Albert M. Gilliam, watching carriages making the rounds of the Alameda some sixteen years later, remarked on the nonchalance with which a young lady occupant would take flint and steel from a bag and "by the friction of a blow or two, ignite a piece of spunk," light her *cigarrito,* and puff luxuriously away. (*Travels in Mexico . . . ,* p. 93.) Lady Emmeline Stuart-Wortley, visit-

ing Mexico still a few years later, wrote: "I saw no smoking among the ladies—there may have been a little, but I am inclined to think not." (*Travels* . . . , II, 119.) Some twenty years after Fanny's time, Countess Paula Kollonitz said with finality: "Cigarette-smoking by ladies is no longer considered *bon ton*." (*Court of Mexico*, p. 170.)

[14] In the Calderóns' time the Viga canal connected the *chinampas* or canal gardens with the capital. It passed some four blocks east of the southeast corner of the cathedral square and extended southward.

[15] A North American physician wrote a few years later: "But walking is not fashionable in Mexico; so the Alameda is generally relinquished to the French *modistas* (dressmakers, &c.) and others, who are too poor to breathe the aristocratic dust of the Paseo from their coach windows." (McSherry, *El Puchero*, p. 131.)

[16] Waddy Thompson, United States minister about two years later, cited the importance of constant attendance at the theater as a way of life. "How else," he quotes a Mexican lady as saying (*Recollections of Mexico*, p. 127), "could I possibly get through the evenings?" As to how upper-class women in general spent their time, he observed (p. 163): "The general routine of female life is to rise late, and spend the larger portion of the day standing in their open windows, which extend to the floor. It would be a safe bet at any hour of the day between ten and five o'clock, that you would in walking the streets see one or more females standing thus at the windows of more than half the houses. At five they ride on the Paseo, and then go to the theatre, where they remain until twelve o'clock, and the next day, and every day in the year, repeat the same routine. In this dolce far niente their whole lives pass away. But I repeat that in many of the qualities of the heart which make women lovely and loved, they have no superiors."

[17] The *Lonja*, or Merchant Exchange, was at this time in the Municipal Palace which formed the west portion of the south side of the cathedral square.

[18] In her Journal Fanny quotes Count Cortina (who was a colonel and whom she disguised for print as "Colonel _____") as saying that the little drummer was hanged.

[19] Catchy operatic airs were probably played on guitars and hummed all over Mexico following the visit of the Italian company in 1836. Fanny has already spoken of an air from *I Puritani*, sung in the San Cristóbal procession in Havana, and of music from *Norma*, played at the bullfight held in honor of Calderón—and here she mentions a third opera by Vincenzo Bellini: *La Straniera*.

[20] Fanny wrote more tactfully for print: "The E_____ family, and the young Señora de C_____ were beautifully dressed."

[21] " 'They order,' said I, 'this matter better in France' "—the opening line of *A Sentimental Journey through France and Italy*, by Laurence Sterne.

[22] For print Fanny revised this to read, "Mexican cookery, which I begin to get accustomed to"—in preparation no doubt for her subsequent admission that she had come to enjoy the once-despised Mexican cuisine.

[23] As a contrast to this episode, the United States minister of a slightly later date—who definitely was not well impressed with certain aspects of Mexican life, although attracted to many individuals—thought that nowhere had he seen a people so temperate in the use of spirits as the Mexicans. "I am sure that during my residence in Mexico I did not see a dozen men drunk, and I have seen assemblies of fifty and a hundred thousand people without one case of drunkenness. As to intemperance amongst respectable people, it is almost unknown." (Thompson, *Recollections of Mexico*, p. 150.)

[24] Juan N. de Retes was, it will be remembered, the composer of the hymn sung at the serenade welcoming Calderón to Mexico.

[25] Doña Margarita, wife of Manuel Gargollo, is mentioned in other memoirs as a distinguished matron. (Prieto, *Memorias* . . . , II, 414, 435.)

Señorita Heras, one guesses from genealogical sources, was a daughter or niece of the second Conde de Heras Soto. (The splendid house that once belonged to this family still stands on the Avenida República de Chile at its intersection with the Calle de Donceles; although given over to business uses, its exterior is protected by its status as a colonial monument.)

Henri Herz (1803–1888) is best remembered as a performer and arranger. Among his works are various *Grandes fantaisies brillantes*—complicated elaborations of well-known themes by other composers.

Fanny's allusion to Dr. Johnson—the lexicographer—is from an anecdote in *The Life of Samuel Johnson LL.D.* (Volume I in *The Works of Samuel Johnson*, p. 319 fn), by Sir John Hawkins: "I have sometimes thought that music was positive pain to him. Upon his once hearing a celebrated performer go through a hard composition, and hearing it remarked that it was very difficult, Johnson said, 'I would it had been impossible.' "

26 The building of the Colegio de las Vizcaínas, more formally termed the Colegio de San Ignacio, is a splendid example of monumentally scaled baroque. The bold design of its main doorway is shown as Plate 49. When last visited by one of the editors, parts of it at least were still in use as a school. Portraits of the three Basque founders hung downstairs in the hall, and a tablet by the great stairway recorded the approbation of Pope Clement XIII and Charles III of Spain for the purposes which the institution served. On a wall upstairs hung a list of the school's directors, from which it was apparent that the "old respectable *rectora*" whom Fanny encountered was Doña Ignacia Blanco.

The room where the visiting party was served refreshments was perhaps that more recently filled with rows of desks laden with typewriters, useful modern tools for the type of self-sufficiency taught dowerless girls in the day-school of Fanny's time. The rich chapel Fanny admired was closed.

27 This last paragraph—from an entry dated by the absent-minded Fanny as simply the "31st" (of February!)—continues in the Journal with the descriptions, already presented, of the stabbing in front of their house and the murder of the Swiss consul. On this note of violence Volume 1 of the Journal closes. As Fanny neared the end she used the inside cover down to the last fraction of an inch—suggesting that at the time she had no replacement at hand.

Volume 2, so far as is known, has not survived. We can only suppose that it may have covered, to some degree at least, the events of the next nine or ten months.

Volume 3, as already noted, is undated at its beginning. It appears from later dated passages to have been begun some time in the spring of 1841. When Fanny put her material together for the printer, she used bits of Volume 3 (especially anecdotes and general observations not keyed into specific happenings) at various points in her completed book. A few such excerpts have been used already; some will appear in the next few chapters; and others, much later.

12. The Viga and the Floating Gardens

1 Lent had begun almost two weeks before, on March 4th.

2 This name, which is left blank in both text and Journal, comes from a notation in the Singer copy, as do the other identifications provided in this chapter.

3 Opposite this description of the three carriages there is noted in pencil in the margin of the Singer copy: "The Rubios." One may read in other memoirs about Don Cayetano Rubio, a rich industrialist and banker—a tall man, irreproachably dressed, and of arrogant bearing. (García Cubas, *Libro de Mis Recuerdos*, p. 449.) And a dispatch of Calderón's dealing with the complicated affairs of the Spanish-born "C. Rubio" reveals that he was the object of strong disapproval on the part of certain Mexican officials whom Calderón consulted. (*Despachos Generales*, I, 68–72.)

4 Lady Morgan, born Sydney Owenson in 1783 and alive in Fanny's time, was a writer of slipshod but zestful novels. *The Book of the Boudoir*, which was autobiographical, opens: ". . . I stepped into my job-carriage at the hour of ten . . ."

5 With the exception of its opening paragraph, the text of this chapter so far is drawn from Volume 3 of the Journal—written, we think, a year later during the carnival period before Lent in 1841.

6 Lord Arran—the fourth Earl of the Arran Islands—was Philip Yorke Gore, born in 1801. Which of his younger brothers visited Mexico at this time we do not know. For print M. Mercier was disguised by Fanny as Monsieur de C_____. A notation at a later point in the Singer copy further identifies him as Henri Mercier of the French legation. He does not appear in the brief list of the legation staff as recorded in the *Almanach de Gotha* for 1840 and 1841; but he may have been overlooked, or he may have been an unpaid attaché.

The diplomatic corps was undoubtedly curious about the new French minister, the Baron de Cyprey, whose bellicose reputation had preceded him. As already noted, Calderón was somewhat primed through having earlier sounded out a friend in the French legation in Washington. One cause of the Baron's known sensitiveness, according to the sketchy information Calderón relayed to his chief, was slights proffered him because of his "unequal marriage." (*Despachos Generales*, I, 33.) The Baron—Isidore-Elizabeth-Jean Baptiste Alleye de Cyprey, born in September 1784 and therefore fifty-five when he reached Mexico—had been ennobled in 1830. Mme la Baronne was his second wife whom he had married in 1824, and there appears about her only the fact that before her marriage she had been "the widow Jacoby." She was evidently the stepmother of the Baron's only child Léontine who, born in 1819, must have been a young woman of twenty or twenty-one.

(Albert Révérend, *Titres, Anoblissements et Pairies de la Restauration, 1814–1830*, I, 27–28.)

[7] This name (but ending in e) was obtained from the Singer copy. A likely guess is that it was Don Juan Matuti, listed elsewhere as a founding member of a cultural organization launched in 1841. (*El Ateneo Mexicano*, I, 144.) The remaining names provided in this chapter are also from the Singer copy.

[8] Probably Doña Antonia González y Echeverría, wife of Francisco de Agüero.

[9] Fanny's own copy of *The Mysteries of Udolpho*, late-eighteenth-century thriller, still exists in the possession of a relative. Its writer, Mrs. Anne Ward Radcliffe, had been well known as a pioneer in the field of romantic, horror-filled novels.

[10] The Mexican practice of renting out portions of houses for shops and lodgings is respectably rooted in antiquity. George Kubler (*Mexican Architecture of the Sixteenth Century*, I, 204) notes that it was common even in the time of which he wrote. Today in larger Mexican cities the prosperous tend to move to purely residential areas, but in smaller cities and provincial towns *el centro* retains its ancient prestige. The downtown location is convenient and the houses themselves are often historic and architecturally superb. To rent to others, including operators of shops, their noisy lower frontage is even to well-to-do Mexican owners quite natural. They live in privacy in ample quarters above and in the patios behind—sharing the pleasant bustle of the plaza but slightly withdrawn from it.

[11] Later references to this couple, whom Fanny obviously came to like and admire, make it plain that they were Juan María Flores and his wife Manuela de Rengel, whose three daughters, according to genealogical works, were Rafaela, Magdalena, and Micaela. Confusingly enough, these sources also show that Juan María Flores was not the Conde de Casa Flores (or Flórez as the name was also spelled), but rather was a brother of the count, whose descendants in Spain bear the title today. A possible explanation would seem to be that, at the time Fanny wrote, her new acquaintance possessed the inherited right to his family's title but later gave it to a brother more closely identified with Spain.

[12] Fanny is here paraphrasing Humboldt, with whose work she had been cooped up so long on the *Jasón*. (This particular reference is from the *Ensayo Político* . . . , I, 191–92.) Prescott in his *Conquest of Mexico* quoted the first and last parts of this paragraph written by his good friend Fanny, whom he called "one of the most delightful of modern travellers." It appears in a footnote to a description of the inward march of the troops of Cortés from the coast, and their meeting with the inhabitants of Cempoalla who greeted them with garlands of flowers. (*Conquest of Mexico*, I, 312 fn.)

[13] About three miles south of the cathedral square.

[14] Fanny seems here to have summarized Humboldt's account of the Aztecs' wanderings. (*Ensayo Político* . . . , I, 313–15.) Xaltocan was an island in Lake Xaltocan, a northern extension of Lake Texcoco. Tizapán is a little south of what Fanny knew as the village of San Angel, now called Villa Obregón; Mexicalcingo, about five miles south and a little east of the center of the city of Mexico.
The origin of the Aztecs has never been clearly established, in spite of various investigations—including one made by Aztecs themselves in the time of the first Montezuma. Prior to about 1350 the valley of Mexico appears to have been simultaneously occupied by some half-dozen different groups. Frederick Peterson's *Ancient Mexico* (pp. 85–105) presents the story of the Aztecs' movements and their rise to power, first over their neighbors on the lakes, and finally (in alliance with Tlacopan and Texcoco) over large areas reaching to both oceans.

[15] Again Fanny took her data from Humboldt, at the time of whose visit to Mexico less than forty years before there were still gardens that actually floated, although their number was fast diminishing. (*Ensayo Político* . . . , I, 364–67.)

[16] An Englishman who remembered this song from his youthful visit to Mexico in the 1830's said that the dance performed to its music was the *jarabe*, and that the man and girl participating sang alternately. (Donaldson, *Mexico Thirty Years Ago*, p. 97.) He quoted the first verse in Spanish:

> Palomita, qué haces ahí
> En esa aguardientería?
> Esperando mi palomo
> Hasta el martes, vida mía.

Other writers have set down the music and at least some of the words of "El Palomo." As in the case of many folksongs, more than one version seems to have developed. That which appears in *El Libro de Mis Recuerdos* by Antonio García Cubas (pp. 210–11) is quite different in part from what Fanny recorded, but obviously the two are variants of the same song. A modern folklorist, Frances Toor, included "El Palomo" in a magazine article entitled "El Jarabe Antiguo y Moderno" (in Mexican Folkways, 1930, VI, 7).

[17] Until the early twentieth century, when the inner portion of the Viga canal was abandoned, one could travel in and out of the city of Mexico by water (Plate 86). The truck gardening area now flourishes at a point more distant from the capital, near Xochimilco. There today's visitors ride the waterways in what Fanny termed canoes, in reality large stable punts. While tawdriness may obtrude, the tree-lined canals, the festivity, and the music—some of which is spontaneous and not for hire—still combine to create an effect of great charm.

[18] Pulque, at 6¼ cents (half a real) for three quarts, was one-third the cost of milk, according to a table in an account of the time. And the price of aguardiente—or chinguirito as the ordinary potent liquor distilled from sugar cane is called—was 18¾ cents per quart, or a real and a half. (Mayer, Mexico as It Was and as It Is, p. 385.) Fanny's quotation seems to be a translation of the Latin proverb: Finis coronat opus.

[19] An isolated hill east of the city, formerly an island in Lake Texcoco, which Fanny will later visit.

[20] The Marqués de Salinas was Luis de Velasco the second, son of the just, firm viceroy of the same name. (The two Velascos, says J. Fred Rippy, in his Historical Evolution of Hispanic America, pp. 70–71, were Spain's outstanding colonial administrators during the sixteenth century.) The second Velasco was some seventy years old when he broke ground for the Desagüe of Huehuetoca: he had capably governed Mexico, then Peru, and then had retired, when the King again summoned him to administer Mexico in 1607.

[21] The theory behind the Desagüe was to reduce the level of Zumpango, the highest and northernmost of the series of lakes near the capital, by diverting some of the water that fed it to lower land beyond the rim of the valley of Mexico. Working under great pressure, an army of Indian laborers toiled to complete a tunnel four miles long through the hills, and within ten months the water drained through—to empty into the Tula River which in turn drains, via the Pánuco, to the Gulf of Mexico.

But subsequent cave-ins and stoppages gave constant trouble and complaints mounted. In 1629 more than usually heavy rains fell and the tunnel's designer, either in fear for his project or perhaps to prove its value, quietly plugged its entrance. The capital was inundated in a single night. Almost the entire city was affected and for some five years canoes had to be used as aids to transportation. Ladies' annuals of Fanny's time still commemorated that flood as a national landmark in time: the Calendario de 1840 de Ontiveros noted that it had been 4797 years since the Biblical Flood; 309 since the apparition of the Virgin of Guadalupe; 211 since the great inundation of Mexico's capital; and nineteen since the independence.

What Fanny's account does not make plain is that more than a century and a half after the original construction, between 1767 and 1789, the costly, troublesome project went through a second phase. This involved the conversion of the deteriorating tunnel into a deep open cut—a monumental operation in terms of earth dug and moved by hand, and a frightful one in terms of the lives expended in accomplishing it. At the time of Humboldt's visit in 1803 it was still being worked on to lessen the steepness of the sloping sides. (Humboldt, Ensayo Político . . . , I, 380–406; Ward, Mexico in 1827, II, 282–87; Matías Romero, Geographical and Statistical Notes on Mexico, pp. 269–80.)

The great colonial drainage project serves a use today quite unanticipated by its long-ago engineers—as roadbed for a rail line (between the capital and Querétaro, via Tula) whose track was laid along a shoulder within the now-mellowed giant cut.

[22] Tlaltelolco—after the conquest called Santiago Tlaltelolco—served as the combined city's main trading center, and its enormous busy market evoked the Spaniards' admiration upon their first peaceful entry into the Aztec capital. Prescott, who garnered his description from various ancient accounts, describes it as having whole streets devoted exclusively to one commodity. Goods of all kinds changed hands, sometimes through the medium of bags of cacao or quills filled with gold dust. There were offered not only fruits and staples, but furs, lumber, medicines, and tobacco; there were brilliant stuffs and feathers, animals, weapons, finely-wrought ornaments, jewels, and slaves. There were refreshment stands, barber shops, and an office for the equitable settlement of trading disputes. (Prescott, Conquest of Mexico, II, 125–30; Bernal Díaz del Castillo, The Discovery and Conquest of Mexico, pp. 215–17.)

In the final bitter siege of the city by the Spaniards, Tlaltelolco was its last desperately defended stronghold. The battering engine mentioned in the text (which was a catapult rather than a ramming device) failed in action, but the overall efforts of the Spaniards and their Aztec-hating allies succeeded, and this the last center of resistance crumbled. Long after the coming of the Spaniards, Tlaltelolco still retained a strong association with its pre-conquest past. It was the logical site for a school for the sons of Indian *caciques,* founded by the dedicated Franciscan friars who followed close on the military victory. To this center of learning for Indians Juan Diego was bound in December of 1531 when there appeared to him the Virgin of Guadalupe.

In mid-March of 1840 the Calderóns must have had their good friend Prescott, who was hard at work on his *Conquest of Mexico,* much in their thoughts. Calderón had just written him at some length on March 5, to report rather pessimistically on various inquiries he was pursuing on his friend's behalf. He mentioned his own heavy load of work and the fact that Fanny, in addition to settling their new "enormous house," was acting temporarily as his only secretary. He concluded by warmly urging Prescott to pay them a visit. (Wolcott, *Correspondence of . . . Prescott,* pp. 111–13.)

13. *Pleasant Excursions*

[1] Fanny does not happen to mention Tetlepanquetzaltzin's much better known companion in tragedy, Montezuma's nephew Cuauhtemoc. They were both captured by the Spaniards at the final fall of Tacuba and Tenochtitlan. Against the wishes of Cortés who, it has been said, gave in reluctantly to the cupidity of his rank and file, the Indian chieftains were tortured in an effort to extort from them knowledge of supposed hidden hoards of Aztec gold. Cuauhtemoc, stoically silent during his ordeal, finally addressed his anguished groaning companion with the often quoted rebuke: "Do you think I am taking my pleasure in my bath?" The hanging took place not at that time but some four years later in 1525 when they were accompanying Cortés as hostages on his exhausting expedition to Guatemala. Cortés learned of a conspiracy among the Indian contingent of his party to kill the Spaniards. The captive leaders, when questioned, admitted to knowledge of, but not a part in, the projected Indian rising. They and others were hanged on the branches of a ceiba tree.

A monument to the heroic Cuauhtemoc in the capital's Paseo de la Reforma honors also other Indian leaders, among them the prince of Tacuba, his named inscribed there—without the reverential ending *tzin*—as Tetlepanquetzal.

[2] This is one of several references to indigenous Indian tongues. The "liquid Indian" heard in and near the capital was almost certainly Nahuatl, the most important of the various pre-conquest languages which still survive today. Clavijero, the learned eighteenth-century Jesuit who wrote about ancient Mexico and who had studied Nahuatl, considered it—and other scholars agreed with him—a highly expressive language, "tolerably polished," and rich in poetry. (*History of Mexico,* II, 197–204.)

[3] In this and the following two chapters, names and nationality identifications which Fanny left all or partially blank in her text have been filled in from the Singer copy.

Prescott quoted the foregoing paragraph complete, with acknowledgment to its "spirited author," as a footnote to his Chapter IV of Book VI of *The Conquest of Mexico* (III, 95), in which is described the encampment of the Spaniards just prior to their final assault to regain the capital.

The recovery of the forces of Cortés during the months following the débâcle of the *noche triste* was no less epic than their earlier adventures. As they fought their way along the causeway that night they were shorn of all their firearms, many of their horses, and most of the treasure; and both Spaniards and Indian auxiliaries suffered terrible losses in numbers. Yet within a week, still exhausted from wounds and lack of food, they met and scattered a large Aztec force at Otumba. Their Tlaxcalan allies stood by them in the face of counter-offers from the Aztecs, and in friendly Tlaxcalan territory the Spaniards, including the gravely injured Cortés, nursed their wounds. Cortés persuaded the crew of a supply-laden vessel sent by authorities in Cuba (in support of the earlier expedition which he had already subdued and annexed) to join him; and later three more vessels arriving at the coast swelled his forces and bolstered his supplies. The establishment of a puppet prince in Texcoco gave Cortés not only another ally, but a potential base located within striking distance of the island city of Tenochtitlan.

Cortés welded together his mixed and sometimes quarrelsome forces in masterly fashion as he prepared to move forward his grand plan. In Tlaxcala he ordered the construction of a small fleet of compact sailing ships. Thirteen brigantines were fabricated in sections and then carried piece by piece by his indispensable Indian allies some fifty miles through mountainous territory to Texcoco for assembly and launching. Meanwhile, in anticipation of their arrival, a small stream which ran for over a mile from the city of Texcoco to the lake was widened and deepened into a canal, lined with wood and masonry, and furnished with locks.

As a result of a succession of hard-fought battles that ranged as far south as Cuernavaca, Cortés subdued, frightened, or attracted into desertion most of the former vassals of the Aztecs who ringed the lakes. He then moved in closer. Spanish forces occupied the towns of Tacuba and Coyoacán which commanded two of the causeways running to the Aztec capital. Supported by his little navy—whose value in protecting the troops from harassment by canoe as they advanced along the causeways was now demonstrated—the Spanish-Indian forces attacked. The city's vital water supply, brought by aqueduct from Chapultepec, was cut after a hot struggle. At first, the Spaniards made bold thrusts into the heart of the city, in one of which they destroyed their old quarters, the palace of Axayacatl. In a later essay Cortés was barely saved from being pulled into a boat by the almost-triumphant Aztecs who, even in this desperate hour, instead of striking to kill sought to fill their ceremonial need of taking live captives for sacrifice.

Cortés, after taking the measure of Aztec resistance under the galvanizing leadership of Cuauhtemoc, Montezuma's valorous young nephew, profited from the lessons of these spectacular but costly initial actions. As a result he adopted the policy of pressing forward slowly from a securely held base. Every concealing wall and every building, as it was wrested from the defenders, was demolished and leveled to the ground. Starving, fighting bitterly, cut off from reinforcements because the Spaniards controlled the lake by means of their sailing ships, the Aztecs fell slowly inward.

Cortés renewed his offer to Cuauhtemoc for peace and safety upon surrender of the city. Cuauhtemoc once more stonily refused. Block by block—amid pestilence, death, and the capture and sacrifice of some of the Spaniards and Indian allies—the buildings of the city were leveled and the canals filled. One of the last areas to fall was the great market of Tlaltelolco north and west of the main city—which Fanny, in the following chapter, will describe as seen over 300 years later.

The end of the two-months' siege came once again on a night of rain—August 13, 1521, feast day of San Hipólito—in frightful last-ditch carnage and the capture of Cuauhtemoc and other Indian leaders. The less important survivors who emerged from the ruins were allowed to file out across the causeways, leaving behind them, instead of the fair city Cortés and his companions had first beheld, a mass of rubble and fetid corpses.

[4] San Joaquín's garden and orchard are gone. Its remaining buildings, on the Calle Santa Cruz Cacalco, off the Calzada Legaria, are now part of a hybrid area among whose other components are a cemetery, a jail, a military shop, and a semi-rural slum. Its adjoining plaza, floored with dust, still has something of the aspect of the poor village Fanny must have seen; but clean children, carrying their books, cross it going to and from school. The church has been renovated in recent years with devotion and taste. It is ample and bare, with its fine stone construction and the brick of its vaulting exposed to view. It is adorned with one superb piece of colonial sculpture—from its original main altar—a figure of San Joaquín bearing in his arms the Virgin as a little child.

[5] The hacienda of Los Morales has disappeared in the city's growth, but the colonia or residential neighborhood built on its former land, slightly northwest of Chapultepec, bears its name.

[6] The hacienda of El Olivar was probably that known as El Olivar del Conde, located a little to the west of the capital between Tacubaya and Mixcoac. Again, the name survives. (As there was no Marqués de Santiago among the thirty-two colonial marqueses, presumably Fanny meant the conde of that title.)

[7] From genealogical sources one learns that the Countess del Valle was Doña Loreto, wife of Agustín Suárez de Peredo, Conde del Valle de Orizaba. Her brother, General Mariano Paredes, will come into sudden prominence later in the book.

[8] Juan de Dios Cañedo, Minister of Foreign Affairs, had recently turned fifty-four. He was the youngest son of a prominent Jalisco family of enormous size, which owned not only the rich hacienda of El Cabezón but also a splendid house in Guadalajara.

Calderón in one of his early dispatches to his government described Cañedo, whom he had known earlier in Madrid, as having a reputation among the diplomats of being rather unpredictable. (Despachos Generales, I, 28.) Cañedo's independent turn of mind had been demonstrated earlier by his defense of a writer imprisoned for issuing a pamphlet on religious toleration. (Pimentel, Obras, 487-88.) He has been described as a small but spirited figure, frank and festive with friends, gallant to women. A brilliant conversationalist, he was usually surrounded at parties by a circle of friends waiting expectantly for his flow of rapier-like wit. In public life he was a polished, trenchant speaker. (Prieto, Memorias . . . , II, 27-28, 62.) His likeness (Plate 66), made available through the kindness of his descendant Don Luis Gutiérrez Cañedo, is from a portrait painted in Philadelphia by Thomas Sully.

Cañedo was a widower when the Calderóns met him. His beautiful wife—Doña María Romana de la Cuesta—had died in Lima near the end of his seven-year tour of duty as Mexico's minister plenipotentiary "to the Republics of the South and the Empire of Brazil," leaving him with three small sons. (Jorge Palomino Cañedo, La Casa y Mayorazgo de Cañedo de Nueva Galicia, pp. 69-76, 94-97.)

[9] The Minería, which fronts on the busy Calle de Tacuba, a little east of the Alameda, is still a noble building—noted for the astonishing sagging visible in its side façades. (The cut showing the Minería is from the frontispiece of Volume I of the first American edition of *Life in Mexico*. It is based on a view by Pedro Gualdi, published in 1841.) The distinguished mineralogist, the Spanish-born Andrés Manuel del Río, had been a fellow-student in Europe with the great Humboldt, and possessed an international reputation in his field as a writer and translator.

[10] The supposed rarity of the *árbol de las manitas* was perhaps an exaggeration spread by the old gardener to enhance the size of his tips. According to an official of today's Conservatorio de la Flora Tropical, the tree grows freely at certain altitudes in Mexico and there are examples in Chapultepec Park. Called also "dragon's hand," it belongs to the family of Sterculiaceae, and bears the specific name of chiranthodendron pentadactylon.

The aged custodian, Juan Lázari, was evidently a shrewd entrepreneur. One account describes him as an "old badger of a functionary, who will make you up a packet of the most vulgar and ordinary garden-seeds, and charge you fifty dollars for it, with the best assurance of conscience in the world." (Latrobe, *Rambler in Mexico*, p. 168.) The Calderóns' friend Count Cortina wrote an article about Lázari when he finally died four years later, with his age reckoned at 117. He had been born, said Cortina's account, in the Papal States in 1723, migrated to Spain, and came to Mexico in 1794 as chef to the viceroy. (*Ateneo Mexicano*, 1844, I, 115.)

The fact that the old man lived on the premises enabled him, as will appear later, to play a brief role in public events.

[11] Francisco Manuel Sánchez de Tagle (Plate 75) was "a distinguished and virtuous man," as judged by the United States minister of some two years later. (Thompson, *Recollections of Mexico*, p. 128.) He was, it will be remembered, father of Fanny's young friend Conchita Adalid. The Monte Pío—more correctly, the Monte de Piedad—is Mexico's national pawnshop, an institution devoted to making loans secured by personal property on fair terms. It was one of the many good works of the fortunate and generous first Conde de Regla whose vast mining enterprises Fanny will discuss later.

In the pre-conquest city of Tenochtitlan, the great temple was slightly northeast of where the cathedral is located. On the east of the great square (or right, when facing the cathedral) was the compound containing the residence of Montezuma—on the approximate site now occupied by the national palace. Correspondingly on the west (or left) stood the palace of Axayacatl, where the Spaniards were first given hospitality and where they were later besieged. This is the site now occupied by the Monte de Piedad.

Fanny's reference to Cortés' exchanging sites (derived evidently from Humboldt's *Ensayo Político . . .*, I, 348–49) does not accord with present knowledge. Upon Cortés' decision to rebuild the Indian city for his capital, *both* of these sites—obviously destined to be important—were appropriated by him and developed with large, elaborate buildings. ". . . The incident is of interest," says George Kubler, architectural historian, "in that it demonstrates Cortés' far-sighted policy of speculative building. The only suitable edifices for governmental occupancy were his own dwellings, and the Crown depended upon his properties for proper housing of the colonial government." (*Mexican Architecture of the Sixteenth Century*, I, 190–93.)

Today, as in 1840, the national palace serves as the symbol of governmental authority. The present structure dates from the late seventeenth century. It has been remodeled many times, the third story having been added in the twentieth century. The building housing the Monte de Piedad is a splendid colonial structure built in the eighteenth century.

[12] The Plaza del Volador, which lay immediately south of the palace, is now occupied by the Supreme Court Building. The building in which the University of Mexico—oldest in the western hemisphere—was then housed was demolished in the twentieth century. It was on the east side of the Plaza del Volador.

[13] The Iron Horse, as North American visitors to Mexico like to call the great equestrian statue, now occupies its third site. As Fanny indicates, it was originally placed in the square in front of the cathedral. Following the bitterness of the struggle for independence it was relegated to the obscurity and greater safety of the University courtyard, where the Calderóns saw it. In 1852 it was moved to what was then thought of as a somewhat outlying focal point (which in the course of time has become an island in the midst of surging tides of downtown traffic). The Calderóns' friend Count Cortina would be influential in the decision to remove the statue from the courtyard in order to give it a setting more appropriate to its size and aesthetic importance. Independent Mexico had no particular wish to honor Charles IV of Spain, but, as the inscription on the statue's pedestal indicates, accorded recognition to a notable work of art.

[14] Fanny was probably referring to Coatlicue, the *mother* of the god of war, mentioned in note 5, pages 684–85.

[15] The Academy of San Carlos (at the Calle de la Academia 22) was founded in 1791 and is still today both a gallery and an art school.

The description Fanny remembered may be found in Humboldt's *Ensayo Político . . . ,* I, 232–35. Humboldt was deeply impressed by the collection of imported casts—finer and more complete, he said, in spite of difficulties involved in transport, than could be found in any part of Germany.

The Argand lamps mentioned, which burned oil, were of a superior design with a tubular wick admitting air inside as well as outside the flame.

14. Holy Week

[1] From Luke 1:48, as quoted in the Book of Common Prayer.

[2] Fanny seems to have been almost obsessed with the smallness of Mexican women's feet and their weakness for too-tight shoes. Small feet are discussed in Chapters 10, 12, 14, 40, and 50; and too-tight shoes in Chapters 6, 9, 10, 11, 14, 19, and 23. Fanny's own feet were, no doubt, considerably larger. The following anecdote, told to the editors in May 1949 by Doña Dolores García Pimentel de Riba, and later confirmed by letter, gives an authentic glimpse of the spirited Fanny in a predicament:

"I remember a story told me by my grandfather—he was Joaquín García Icazbalceta—about Madame Calderón de la Barca. He was born in 1825, so that he must have been fifteen or sixteen when it happened. She and her husband were at a country party at the house of the Escandón family outside Mexico. Some of the guests were playing battledore and shuttlecock, or some such outdoor game, and Madame Calderón, who was very active, fell into the fountain while playing and was soaked to the skin.

"Madame Calderón was tall and larger than the Mexican ladies but her hostesses managed somehow to fit her out in borrowed clothes so as to be fairly presentable. But when it came to her feet—it was impossible! She had the long English feet; and as she says in her book, the Mexican ladies who never walked further than from their carriage doors to the church and back had very small feet and wore little tight satin shoes. It was hopeless. Finally in desperation someone said to a servant, 'Fetch a pair of Don Manuel's boots!' So Madame Calderón, to everyone's amusement, wore Don Manuel Escandón's boots to lunch."

[3] The interior of San Francisco as it was during this period is shown as Plate 41. One of the elevated grilled enclosures apparent on each side was presumably the private gallery of the Condesa de Santiago.

Members of the Cervantes y Velasco family possessed three different titles. According to Lucas Alamán's *Historia de Méjico* (V, 915), José María Cervantes y Velasco during his own lifetime made over to his eldest son, José Juan Cervantes y Michaus, the title of Conde de Santiago. Evidently the latter was the "young count" whom Fanny watched during the ceremonies of Holy Thursday. The lady whom she terms the Countess de Santiago—already encountered as one of her earliest callers (p. 137)—was the young count's stepmother. Her husband will appear later briefly in these pages. He had been an army officer and like his brother Miguel, who was Marqués de Salvatierra, had been a signer of the document affirming Mexican independence on September 28, 1821.

[4] One has to guess at the meal hours whose rhythm compartmented the Calderóns' daily routine. Fanny described their shipboard meals on the Spanish *Jasón* as a cup of chocolate on arising, a large breakfast at ten, and dinner at five. Pakenham, the British minister, invited them to dine at five. Later, when living quietly in the country, Fanny will speak of their taking chocolate in the evening as a sequel to dinner at four. She does not seem to mention supper except as a special collation, or when traveling. But a young Virginian who was in Mexico fifteen years earlier ends his listing on the subject with a late evening repast: chocolate on arising; breakfast at ten; dinner at three; chocolate at six or seven; and a hot supper at ten. (*Mexico, 1825–1828: The Journal and Correspondence of Edward Thornton Tayloe*, p. 70.)

[5] Probably music from the opera *Giulietta e Romeo* by Nicola Vaccai, first produced in 1825; or possibly the older opera by Zingarelli.

[6] This church of Santa Teresa la Nueva—founded in 1701 and dedicated in 1715 and therefore new only as contrasted with the older church of Santa Teresa la Antigua—was one to which Fanny would return a good many times. Subsequent notations in the Singer copy make it clear that a nun with whom she later develops a tenuous but warm relationship was this sister of José Adalid.

[7] Santa Teresa la Antigua, on the Calle del Licenciado Verdad—a block-long street opening north from the Calle de la Moneda—is no longer a functioning church. Various

earlier writers, among them Humboldt (*Ensayo Político* . . . , II, 349–50), held that Axaya-catl's palace which served as headquarters for Cortés was near this church—at the corner of the streets now called the Avenida República de Guatemala and the Calle del Carmen. A modern authority on the city's history accounts for the confusion. While Cortés, his principal captains, and some of his troops—and also Montezuma after he was taken as a hostage—were housed in the palace built by Axayacatl (father of Montezuma) on the site now occupied by the Monte de Piedad, *other* Spaniards with their Tlaxcalan allies were housed on the site Fanny mentions. (Artemio de Valle-Arizpe, *Historia de la Ciudad de México según los Relatos de Sus Cronistas*, pp. 207–8, 214–17.)

[8] This article in the *Mosaico Mexicano* (III, 402–5), signed only with the initials C.B., was evidently written by Carlos María de Bustamante, a passionate devotee of Mexican history from the Indian point of view. This learned writer—not to be confused with President Bustamante—will be discussed in a later chapter dealing with Mexico's distinguished men. The article was accompanied by an illustration of the immense stone head, which Bustamante interpreted as representing the goddess Centeotl. The superb piece, a part of the collection of the Museo Nacional de Antropología, is today thought to represent the moon goddess Coyolxauhqui.

[9] This was the Academy of San Carlos, art museum and school, which has been discussed in the previous chapter.

[10] This recital includes only a fraction of the long list of handsome colonial churches which, in addition to the cathedral, still stand in downtown Mexico. San Francisco's large main church remains, although shorn of its former subordinate buildings. La Enseñanza, whose richly gilded interior blazes today as in Fanny's time, is at the Calle de Donceles, 104. The church of Jesús María, with bold simple pediments over twin doorways, is three blocks east of the great square, on the Calle de Jesús María at the corner of the Calle de la Soledad. Santa Clara on the Calle de Tacuba at the Calle Allende now houses a government library, as does also the church of the former convent of La Encarnación on the Calle Luis González Obregón. San Hipólito, not far from the Calderóns' house, a baroque church of strong individual character, stands a little west of the Alameda on the Avenida Hidalgo at the Calle Zarco; it is set back of a small atrium, so that the passer-by gets a good view of its unusual diagonally-placed towers—only the eastern one of which stood in the Calderóns' time, the other having been added in recent years. Among those specifically named here, only the subordinate churches of San Francisco and the church of Santa Brígida are gone. The latter was demolished in 1938, a victim of pressures on the capital's street system.

[11] The moon was at the full on that night of Holy Thursday, April 16, 1840.

[12] This flaw in the cathedral plaza is gone. Its demolition—one of the laudable accomplishments of the not wholly black Santa Anna—took place in 1843. The Parián was in effect a bazaar, housed in a solid building occupying the southwest part of the square. It may be seen in some but not all of the plates in this book which depict the plaza.

[13] "A drink made of the seed of the plant of that name," said Fanny herself in one of her own notes. One learns elsewhere that it is a kind of salvia.

[14] Fanny might well have heard Rossini's *Semiramide* in Italy during the days of her family's prosperity. For Holy Week venders, see Plate 32.

[15] Perhaps the "undrilled band" was the then very new Sociedad Filarmónica, founded the previous December by Professor José Antonio Gómez. (Enrique de Olavarría y Ferrari, *Reseña Histórica del Teatro en México*, I, 365–66.) And perhaps the same musicians again performed the *Miserere* on Good Friday a year later. "The music," said Brantz Mayer, a United States diplomat who heard it, "was execrable." (*Mexico as It Was and as It Is*, p. 151.)

[16] Easter Sunday still lay ahead, but Fanny's account reflected the Mexican—and Spanish—preoccupation with the Passion of Christ rather than the Resurrection.

Charles Joseph Latrobe, who visited Mexico a few years earlier, provides some details which can serve to round out Fanny's description. The bells rang and the carriages rolled, he said, until ten o'clock on the morning of Holy Thursday—when all shops shut, the carriages disappeared from the streets, and bells were silenced. Crowds poured through the streets on foot. In the churches a variety of gay and worldly music was played. Some fifty thousand people, he estimated, moved about the great square and in and out of the cathedral. Latrobe recorded what on Saturday morning Fanny was too exhausted to go and see. In the great square the flower-bedecked booths were taken down, and troops and artillery were drawn up in front of the palace. On the stroke of half-past nine the cathedral bell, silent for forty-eight hours, struck out; the dark shrouding in the churches was removed; organs pealed; all the other church bells rang; the artillery was fired by the troops; the Judases were exploded; and carriages rolled once more through the streets. (*Rambler in Mexico*, pp. 158–64.)

A somewhat later account shows the spectacle as still unchanged. "For three days no carriages are allowed in the streets, and no bells are rung; in their place, huge rattles are used upon the church steeples, of which (the rattles not the steeples), every child in the street has a pocket edition. At ten o'clock, on the third day, effigies of Jews and Protestants are strung across the streets and filled with fireworks. The great bell of the cathedral strikes, instantly all the smaller ones peal forth; the gates are thrown open, and horses, carriage, mules and donkeys, come rushing in together, the fireworks blaze, and whiz, and crackle, the dogs yell and howl: and for fifteen minutes there is a perfect Babel." (A. K. Shepard, The Land of the Aztecs, pp. 47–48.)

A cynical note is struck in a discussion of the conclusion of Holy Week by an anonymous writer in El Album Mexicano for 1849. He said (I, 323): "On Easter Sunday the theaters and places of public amusement open; the paseos are full of people; and contrite sinners forget the sermons of Lent and commence to do things to repent of during the holy time of the year following."

[17] H. G. Ward, familiar with Mexican society some thirteen years before, commented on the lack of informal social gatherings in the capital, as contrasted with the spontaneous hospitality offered by Mexicans when in the country.

"I have said nothing of the organization of society in Mexico, because, in fact, there is none. In the Capital, evening-parties and dinners, except upon some great occasions, are equally unknown. After the Paseo, or evening promenade, which takes place between five and seven, every body goes to the theatre, and after the theatre to bed. The Mexicans have not yet acquired the European habit of meeting frequently in small parties for the promotion of social intercourse. They accept invitations with pleasure from foreigners, but cannot divest themselves of the idea that where any thing is to be given on their side, a degree of superfluous display is requisite, which renders the frequent repetition of such entertainments impracticable. It is only in their Haciendas that they indulge without restraint in the hospitality to which they are naturally inclined." (Mexico in 1827, II, 715.)

15. A Convent from Inside

[1] Juan de Dios Cañedo was, it will be remembered, the witty and eloquent Minister of Foreign Affairs.

[2] From the Singer copy we learn that the two other ladies in the party were Señora Adalid and Señorita Escandón—presumably Doña Luz, the only woman in the family to be designated specifically by name.

The convent of La Encarnación survives in part, although much altered, as a portion of the building which is occupied by the Secretaría de Educación Pública y Bellas Artes. Its church—which the visiting party will shortly see from above—is today a library, facing on the Calle Luis González Obregón, two blocks north of the rear of the cathedral.

[3] Fanny had a possible reason for special familiarity with the poems of James Thomson (1700–48), pioneer romanticist. Her father's eccentric cousin, the eleventh Earl of Buchan, had been a fervent admirer of the Scottish poet's work. He promoted Thomson celebrations and erected a monument in Thomson's honor on his country property.

[4] A few weeks later Fanny wrote a long letter to her friend Prescott which betrayed her uneasiness under this barrage of artless inquiries from the nuns. "I pass a great part of my time in Convents and churches, which are the buildings best worth visiting in Mexico. The Archbishop as a great favour has granted me the entree of the Convents, which is never permitted. They are some of them very rich, and I spent four hours rather pleasantly with the ladies of La Encarnación, they little dreaming that a heretic was profaning their sanctuary. I kept the conversation off England and on France most strenuously. They asked me who was my Saint. San Francisco, said I. But which?, said the Abbess, while they all made a circle round me to listen. Xaviera! said I with the inspiration of despair. 'So then the Señora Ministra's name is Francisca Xaviera Calderón de la Barca!' So be it. At least there is plenty of it." (Wolcott, Correspondence of . . . Prescott, p. 130.)

Fanny was fortunate in her panicky choice of St. Francis Xavier, stout-hearted Jesuit missionary to the Orient—as she may have realized when she returned home after the convent visit and perhaps consulted her calendar. If she had, for example, chosen St. Francis de Sales, whose feast-day had been January 29, or St. Francis de Paul, whose feast-day had just passed on April 2, she would have been in hot water at once, with a need for excuses and explanations as to why she had not permitted her friends to share in her saint's-day celebration. St. Francis Xavier's day, however—December 3—she had spent safely on board the Jasón, waiting out the norther off Veracruz.

Fanny, or at least her friends, evidently took note of her obligation to St. Francis Xavier—for on the following December 3 she duly celebrated her día de fiesta.

[5] This appears in "The Devil's Thoughts" by Coleridge, and also in the poem Southey rewrote and expanded from it, "The Devil's Walk."

[6] Fanny's campaign for permission to see something of convent life must have been launched almost immediately after the Calderóns were settled in their permanent home. It was an unusual request and she knew it, but by going with strong backing to the highest ecclesiastical authority in Mexico she met with success. One may guess the root of her interest. She had a sister, Jane, concerning whom almost nothing is known except that she became a Catholic and—perhaps about this time—a nun in France. Only fourteen months older than Fanny, Jane had presumably been her closest childhood and girlhood companion. Jane's desertion—for such it must have seemed at the time to this strongly united Protestant family—undoubtedly had a powerful emotional impact upon them all. An effort better to understand her sister's motivation may have been the basis for Fanny's strong interest in the cloistered life as manifested in Mexico.

[7] The excitement of the armed robbery of this other household did not pass unnoticed in the press. At four in the morning, according to El Mosquito Mexicano of May 8, five thieves broke into No. 8 on the Calle de San Ildefonso, belonging to Doña María Dolores [Romero de] Terreros, ex-Marquesa (not Countess as Fanny wrote) de San Francisco. (The old lady, born 1765, was a marquesa in her own right; twice widowed, she seems to have been known by her maiden name rather than by that of either of her husbands.) The thieves not only made off with her silver but also chose from her possessions a pair of silk stockings and a clock. In addition they picked up—as aids for future professional efforts, no doubt—a screwdriver and a brace-and-bit.

[8] The private secretary to the first minister from the United States described such a procession in June 1825. The tiny image was ensconced in the presidential coach, and, escorted by troops and a great multitude, was driven slowly into the capital. (Mexico, 1825–1828: The Journal and Correspondence of Edward Thornton Tayloe, pp. 54–55.)

[9] Gachupín and gachupina are Mexican words meaning a native of Spain. The little Virgin of los Remedios was definitely associated with the Spanish cause, just as the Virgin of Guadalupe was invoked by those fighting for independence. Early in the struggle, on the approach of Hidalgo's insurgent forces toward the capital in October 1810, the Virgin of los Remedios was brought from her village church to the cathedral. The viceroy himself, General Francisco Xavier Venegas, went in full uniform to implore her help for the royalist cause, and to lay at her feet his staff of command. (Ward, Mexico in 1827, I, 169.)

Robert A. Wilson says (in Mexico: Its Peasants and Its Priests, p. 216) that the movement to banish the Virgin took place when Spaniards in general were being expelled from Mexico (following legislation passed at the close of 1827).

General José María Tornel—who has been characterized in various sources as a man of learning, a brave soldier, and an astute, rather vain, and not too scrupulous politician of pro-Santa Anna leanings—appears as a minor figure later in the book. Tornel disliked foreigners, especially Spaniards; and Calderón, not unnaturally, disliked Tornel.

[10] The mother of Fanny's good friend Concepción—or Conchita—de Adalid was Doña Guadalupe Lebrija de Sánchez de Tagle. She was evidently in charge of the rich wardrobe of the Virgin of los Remedios.

The trees Fanny mentions as bearing red flowers on bare branches were, surely, examples of the colorín, whose scientific name is erythrina americana.

[11] The church of La Virgen de los Remedios, northwest of the capital, was built on the site of the Indian temple in which Cortés and his exhausted followers took refuge after the retreat of the noche triste. It is set on the top of a small mountain, and the openings in the walls of its large atrium frame long views of the surrounding country.

When the editors first visited Los Remedios a good many years ago on a quiet weekday, the church was almost empty. The revered figure—dark with age as Fanny has described it—was enclosed in a glass case and could be revolved by its custodian so as to permit viewing at close range from a small room behind the altar. On a second visit, made in 1962 on a feast day, hundreds of worshippers filled the church to overflowing and hundreds more stood outside in a downpour of rain to hear the service as broadcast over a public-address system. The small historic image, still protected by its case, was bright and fresh in appearance. We subsequently learned that it had been restored in 1952 by the sculptor Juan Ramírez.

The great aqueduct mentioned in the next paragraph still stands close by.

[12] As reported (note 3, pp. 687–88), one of the editors in 1951 enjoyed meeting two granddaughters of José Adalid and his wife Conchita. The older of the two, the Señora Viuda de Lazo, remembered hearing her grandmother speak of Fanny Calderón de la Barca and their long-ago friendship. When pressed for details, Señora de Lazo could recall no specific anecdotes but, after thought, she proffered one revealing comment: "I remember my grandmother's saying that they laughed together a great deal."

16. Life on the Great Pulque Haciendas

[1] In this and the following chapter, the Singer copy is the source of various identifications for full or partial blanks left by Fanny.

[2] Fanny and her family were still living in Normandy, we believe, when Charles X, absolutist king of France from 1824, was overthrown in the summer of 1830.

[3] H. G. Ward remarked that Mexican coachmen "in general drive over, or through every thing, and look excessively surprised when an unfortunate wheel gives way, (as it usually does,) with a crash, after surviving trials which it would make an English coachmaker's hair stand on end to look at." (*Mexico in 1827*, II, 405.)

[4] Fanny was apparently drawing upon Humboldt here (*Ensayo Político* . . . , II, 347). For some reason not apparent, she describes the pyramids before reporting arrival at San Juan, although the town would seemingly have been reached first.

These remains, described by other travelers of the Calderóns' period as heavily covered over with debris and vegetation, constitute one of the largest and most widely known archaeological sites in Mexico. (Modern exploration has shown that the numerous small pyramids and mounds were not tombs.) The builders were neither Aztecs nor Toltecs, but a much earlier people, who seem to have ranged far and wide as traders and to have exercised control over a large territory. Their culture apparently reached its peak around 300 to 400 A.D. The once powerful people are believed to have themselves destroyed and buried their capital.

[5] A modern road now passes close by the large buildings of the hacienda of Soapayuca, which have obviously undergone alterations since the Calderóns' day. As, according to Fanny, it was already afternoon when they passed through San Juan, she evidently uses the term *breakfast* in the sense of a substantial lunch.

[6] Santiago (more precisely called Santiago Tepayuca) lies in isolation at the end of a wandering rock-strewn road. It exemplifies both the old and the new in today's Mexico, where the revolutionary movement of the twentieth century has all but brought an end to the hacienda system through efforts to extend land ownership to many.

Santiago's interior court is entered through a fortress-like gate in one of its major buildings (Plate 94). Though still owned by a member of the former landholding class, the establishment seemed more a production center for pulque workers with courteous independent manners than the great house of a *patrón*. The large hall in which so many dined and danced during the Calderóns' stay was probably that more recently devoted to the odoriferous processing of maguey juice. The fermented product travels to the capital in tank cars on the narrow-gauge *Servicio de Pulque* that threads its way, via numerous spurs and loops, through the still-lonely countryside. But the making of pulque, starting with the sucking device similar to that used before the conquest, is essentially unaltered by time.

According to Don Manuel Campero—members of whose family owned the hacienda for many years after it passed from the Adalids' hands—Santiago had consisted of five different ranches, as shown by a map in his possession made in 1796 for Santiago's then owner, Francisco Leandro de Viana, first Conde de Tepa.

[7] ". . . A degree of familiarity is allowed between the servants and their superiors, of which in England there is no example in any rank of life," wrote Captain Basil Hall some years earlier; he observed also that old servants sometimes talked with guests at an evening party. And in the same vein, he said: "Indeed, I never have seen in any part of the world a more amiable, or more considerate and kindly feeling of superiors towards their dependents, than exists in South America and Mexico. In those parts, also, now very few, where slaves exist, the manner in which they are treated is highly exemplary. And it may be said, generally, that in the Spanish colonies, or in places occupied by the descendants of Spaniards, the treatment of servants of every kind is milder than in most other parts of the world. This has sometimes been explained, on the supposition, that the oppression of the mother country might have taught the colonists gentleness, and indulgence to such as were dependent upon them. But experience shows, that the contrary really takes place in the world; and we must look for an explanation of the fact in the genuine goodness of the Spanish character, which, though overlaid and crushed down by a series of political and moral degradations, is still essentially excellent, and worthy of a far better destiny." (*Extracts from a Journal, Written on the Coasts of Chili, Peru, and Mexico in the Years 1820, 1821, 1822*, II, pp. 198, 217–18.)

[8] A reference, one guesses, not to one of the dancer members of the famous gifted Vestris family, but to the actress and singer Lucia Elizabeth Bartolozzi, born 1797. A Vestris by virtue of her first marriage, she was noted for good looks and a flawless figure

as well as for her superb but undisciplined contralto voice. Fanny might have seen and heard her in the early 1820's before the Inglis family's emigration to the United States.

[9] This same song with variations in wording and additional verses may be found in *El Libro de Mis Recuerdos* by Antonio García Cubas (p. 318). What Fanny gives as the second verse is shown as the chorus, with *la enana* appearing in place of *el enano*. Additional wording includes: "Make thyself little, make thyself big (*Hazte chiquito, hazte grandote*)." And another version of "*Los Enanos*" was published in the magazine *Mexican Folkways*, edited by Frances Toor, Vol. VI, No. 1 (1930), p. 20.

[10] "*El Toro*" may be found, without words, in *The Republic of Mexico in 1876*, by Antonio García Cubas—translated into English by George F. Henderson. Of course the music given may not be the same as that heard by the Calderóns.

[11] The young private secretary of the first United States minister Joel R. Poinsett recorded his visit to Mexico's greatest aqueduct (Plate 96), made with his chief some fifteen years earlier. They too visited the hacienda of Soapayuca, and breakfasted at Ometusco (to be mentioned by Fanny), which was then the property of Don Ignacio Adalid, José Adalid's father. (*Mexico, 1825–1828: The Journal and Correspondence of Edward Thornton Tayloe*, pp. 103–4.)

These arches constitute the most spectacular portion of a system that ran nearly thirty miles to convey water, plentiful near Zempoala, to dry Otumba to the south. The immense undertaking was executed over a sixteen-year period, only a generation after the conquest. Its designer—the one European involved in the project—was Francisco de Tembleque, who lived alone for many years in a hut while he supervised his Indian work force. (Kubler, *Mexican Architecture of the Sixteenth Century*, I, 117, 149, 227–28; Octaviano Valdés, "Fray Francisco de Tembleque," in *The Americas*, Vol. III—October, 1946 —pp. 223–33.)

The editors likewise looked up in wonderment at this extraordinary example of sixteenth-century hydraulic engineering. The arches, which are some 140 feet high where they cross the deepest point of their isolated valley—tenanted by browsing goats—are in almost perfect condition.

[12] This is from John Dryden's translation of the *Aeneid*, Book IV, 11, lines 95–100.

[13] Señor Adalid's sister Doña Josefa had recently been widowed by the death of her husband Senator Agustín Torres Torija y Guzmán (see p. 158). She had inherited San Miguel Ometusco, property of her father and her grandfather before her, in 1836. Ometusco was a large and valuable domain, whose identity went back to a land grant made in 1570. There were two houses identified with it: San Miguel Ometusco and San Antonio Ometusco. Both remained in the hands of descendants of the Torres-Adalid marriage into the twentieth century.

[14] Plate 98 may serve to suggest the atmosphere of this occasion.

The vases and garden figures must have come by the old Spanish colonial trade route: from China to the Philippines, from there to Acapulco via the once-a-year galleon, from Acapulco to the capital by mule or burro, and thence to the Adalids' house in Tulancingo.

This garden and its large tank—whose pool-side loggia and dressing room sound startlingly modern—had long since disappeared when we visited Tulancingo in 1951. An amiable elderly local lady, Señora Doña Trinidad González, Viuda de Desentis, who with her daughter Señora María Carmen Desentis de Soto was our informant, knew of the past existence of the garden. One fragment only survived, she explained; she was sure that the wall and a small niche and fountain remaining in the Calle Juárez were a part of the original construction.

[15] The *chayote* (illustrated in the cut) is eaten as a cooked vegetable. The text has heretofore used the misspelling *cayote*, apparently derived by Fanny from the Spanish translation of Clavijero's work (*Historia Antigua de Mégico*, I, 22). However, in the original Italian version as written by Clavijero himself, the word is correctly spelled with a "ch" (*Storia Antica del Messico*, I, 50).

[16] The *paso*, descriptions of which vary, seems to have been inculcated in the past by the use of the *anquera*, a leather covering for the horse's hindquarters. One notices it in engravings of the time. The *anquera* had a fringe, made of bits of iron that swung in motion, and this device induced the horse in training to accommodate his natural gait to an action so smooth that the iron pendants did not tickle his legs. (Museo Nacional de Artes e Industrias Populares, *La Charrería*, pp. 16–17, and illustration on p. 44.)

H. G. Ward in his *Mexico in 1827* (II, 313–14) maintains his usual clarity in discussing this gait: "The passo consists in a peculiar motion of the horse, by which the hind legs are drawn along the ground, sustaining nearly the whole weight of the body, while the fore are raised in high and graceful action; the rider, from the gentle movement of the hind quarter, is hardly moved in his seat, while the horse before appears to be going at a trot, and does in fact move at nearly the same rate."

Perhaps a good *paso* horse, such as Fanny describes, which could keep up with others going at a gallop, was using the *sobre paso* or *reparte*. This is mentioned in an anonymous book of this general period as a faster type of *paso*. The horse performing it, the writer maintained, could do twelve miles an hour. (*Sketch of . . . Mexico*, p. 208.)

17 A lady thus riding in comfort is depicted in Plate 62.

18 One avenue of tentative courtship was, apparently, through the very game of *prendas* just described. An Englishman writing about a visit made to Mexico in the 1830's recalled that even under the eyes of their elders ingenious young people could manage to bring into the payment of forfeits situations involving languishing looks, sentimental exchanges, and even brief hand-holding. (Donaldson, *Mexico Thirty Years Ago*, p. 205.)

19 The Condesa del Valle was Fanny's friend Loreto, Condesa del Valle de Orizaba, who had given her the parrot not long before.

20 Fanny probably read about the operation of *temazcallis*, and noted the graphic cross-sectional illustration reproduced, in Clavijero's *Historia Antigua de Mégico* (I, 389 and page opposite).

17. *Visit to the Mines; A Stormy Journey*

1 Tepenacaxco looked somewhat forlorn when we last saw it in the dry summer of 1962. Its main buildings were, however, still intact, grouped largely between the reservoir and the spacious walled forecourt, which must have been the site of the bullfights Fanny mentions. Plate 99 shows the gracefully framed bells of the hacienda chapel.

A North American visitor left an account of his stay in Tepenacaxco in 1881. By this time it had passed from the hands of the Adalid family, but José Adalid, although not specifically mentioned, seems to have been still remembered for hospitality and high-speed transportation. One of the two principal bedrooms, said the visitor, had cut-off corners, in three of which beds were set into niches, while the fourth formed the room's entrance. Wallpaper in this room depicted Swiss scenes, and great was his astonishment, upon returning to the United States and subsequently reading *Life in Mexico*, to realize that he had seen the same paper as that described in it forty years before. (William Henry Bishop, *Old Mexico and Her Lost Provinces*, pp. 245–62.)

Greater still was the editors' astonishment to find in 1962 the same wallpaper adorning the room where Fanny slept. The wooden floor and wainscot of the empty room were in sad disrepair and the paper tattered in numerous spots, but the boldly-scaled scenic design, with only one repeat in the entire room, depicted in fresh, bright colors Swiss peasants and cattle in a background of chalets and mountains. According to information earlier obtained for us by Don Carlos Iturbe of Mexico, the octagonal room with its niches for three beds had been fitted up for the three daughters—Josefa, Manuela, and Soledad—of José Adalid by his first marriage.

2 Who Doña Rosita and Doña Manuelita were does not appear: their names never recur.

3 For some two hundred and fifty years, Mexico's silver mines had been known as by far the richest in the world, producing more of the metal than those of all other countries combined. Among Mexican mines, those of Real del Monte were particularly famous. The best known was that acquired some hundred years before Fanny's day by a small capitalist named Pedro Romero de Terreros, whose ensuing good fortune, and munificent use of it, later gained for him the title of first Conde de Regla.

The frequent enemy of mines is water, and Don Pedro amassed his almost measureless fortune through conquering it. The property at Real del Monte, which he and a partner held together, had under prior ownership produced magnificently, yet it had been abandoned in view of the impossibility of fighting water successfully by the best means known. Don Pedro, sole owner after the death of his partner, carried out the difficult solution they had initiated. This called for the excavation of a slanting tunnel nearly two miles in length, much of it through solid rock, by means of which the rich but unworkable mine was to be emptied into a watercourse at a lower level. The project advanced slowly over the years, aided by the yield of small silver deposits encountered as work moved forward. But when the water finally drained out in 1762, the mine proved spectacularly successful, and Romero de Terreros reaped millions in profits.

As in all mining work, however, the gradual deepening of shafts and lengthening of galleries piled up costs, and round-the-clock effort was required to keep abreast of new flooding. Enormous drums revolved by relays of horses operated endless chains of hide buckets to raise the unwanted water. With the passing years, twenty-eight such drums became necessary, each demanding forty horses twenty-four hours a day. Profits declined, and by 1801 work was all but abandoned. Once again the mine's tantalizing resources lay inaccessible, under water.

But time was maturing an important new weapon not earlier available: the steam engine was at last reaching a stage of development that permitted its substitution for inadequate horse power. During the War of Independence, unsettled conditions brought almost all mining in Mexico to a halt, but shortly after 1821, by special act of congress, the way was opened for foreign investors to become joint proprietors on highly favorable terms in the exploitation of the new republic's moribund mining industry. Investors in the United States and Germany showed interest, but in Great Britain the effect of the news was to launch one of the greatest speculative crazes in the history of that country's finance.

In London in 1824, among a number of enterprises established for the purpose of growing rich quickly from the development of Mexico's silver resources, there was formed what was called The Adventurers in the Mines of Real del Monte. A Captain Vetch of the Royal Engineers was soon dispatched to Mexico—together with three hundred and fifty Cornish miners and their families—and an effort was launched to apply the most modern technical knowledge and equipment to salvaging and operating the old mine, leased by the company from the second Conde de Regla. The burro trail to the refining works at Santa María Regla was replaced with a fine, expensive new wagon road. Some 1500 tons—three shiploads—of machinery brought from England were transported up from the coast, a project in which hundreds of men and mules labored for months and some of the supervising English lost their lives to yellow fever.

Although the mine was completely inoperable when the new company took over in July 1824 and little was known concerning working conditions in Mexico, optimism was unbounded; and during the following year shares with a par value of one hundred British pounds sold in the open market for as much as sixteen thousand. In this atmosphere it is no wonder that money was spent with abandon, including large salaries to overly numerous imported administrative personnel, on a scale shocking to the Mexicans. (For example, Captain John Rule, who welcomed the Calderóns, received a yearly salary of £10,000.) The task of getting the historic mine back into operation—pumping out the water, removing tons of fallen rubble, and replacing all the timbers—proved far more burdensome than had been anticipated, and deep pessimism soon followed. H. G. Ward, not as sanguine as the first director Captain Vetch, but reassured by an on-the-spot check in 1827, predicted that within a year all doubts of ultimate success would be resolved. But his prediction was wrong and his optimism ill-founded. More than ten million dollars' worth of silver was produced, but fifteen million had been spent.

(From a variety of sources, including: Humboldt, *Ensayo Político* . . . , III, 112–13, and *Selections from the Works of the Baron de Humboldt, Relating to the Climate, Inhabitants, Productions, and Mines of Mexico*, with notes by John Taylor, pp. xi–xv; Ward, *Mexico in 1827*, II, 63, 75–78, 87–90, 97, 102, 351–66; Wilson, *Mexico: Its Peasants and Its Priests*, pp. 353–65; Manuel Romero de Terreros, *El Conde de Regla, Creso de la Nueva España*, pp. 12–17.)

[4] San Miguel Regla (like Santa María Regla, described a few pages later) was primarily a mining establishment, located near abundant water, for refining the silver-bearing ore brought down from the mines of Real del Monte.

Today the big central house is in good repair and the grounds beautifully maintained. Many North Americans as well as Mexicans have vacationed within the stout walls of San Miguel Regla, for it is now a country retreat owned by the Club Panamericano de Doctores.

The water level of the river which flows through the property has been raised through the construction of a hydroelectric dam, with the result that some of the old works have been partially flooded. The combined effect of roofless stone buildings, whose walls and varying levels have been developed into a series of terraced gardens, the pervading sound of falling water, and the partially submerged smelting works whose ghostly remains can be explored in a small boat, is unforgettable. (See Plate 100.)

[5] In other words, Fanny wore a thin wool costume and ankle-height shoes. The shoes were, perhaps, like the pair—seemingly made of soft leather, flat-heeled, and laced at the sides—illustrated as an example of fashionable footwear in the year 1840 in *The History of the Feminine Costume of the World*, by Paul Louis de Giafferi (Part XIV, "France," Plate 9).

[6] Humboldt, who tells this same story of the two ships, adds that the count also made a loan, never repaid, to his sovereign in the amount of five million francs. (*Ensayo Político* . . . , III, 243–44.) It would appear that the two ships were the *Conde de Regla* and *El Mejicano*, both mounting 114 guns and both launched (after the count's death) in 1786. The statistically-minded Humboldt mentions them in a listing of naval vessels constructed for Spain in Havana. (*The Island of Cuba*, by Alexander von Humboldt, translated by J. S. Thrasher, p. 122.) Fanny says nothing here of the count's large-scale philanthropy as

manifested in the building and endowment of charitable institutions in Querétaro and Pachuca, not to mention the Monte de Piedad in the capital.

7 "There are upon an average of about three hundred Indians constantly thus engaged in different parts of the mine," wrote Charles Joseph Latrobe, another visitor of the time who descended via the Dolores shaft to explore the workings and then came up the more than one thousand feet served by thirty-two perpendicular ladders of the Terreros shaft. ". . . The scenes presented in those gloomy caves, where they work by the red light of their tapers, with scarcely any covering, are far beyond my describing." (*Rambler in Mexico*, pp. 96–97.)

8 Lucas Alamán (already mentioned on page 196 as a former minister of foreign affairs) was, according to H. G. Ward, the principal director of the United Mexican Company, one of the seven major British speculative ventures. Although Fanny speaks of his effective salesmanship, Ward's account shows him to have been reasonably cautious as to the prospects of his enterprise. While Captain Vetch, first director in Mexico for The Adventurers in the Mines of Real del Monte, stated in his 1826 report that his company could expect to derive from its mines "a yearly return of one million and a half dollars," Don Lucas declined hazarding any positive calculation. He observed instead that "the produce of a mine could never be said to bear any exact proportion to the capital invested in it; sometimes exceeding all reasonable expectations, and at others, falling short of the most moderate estimate, particularly when confined to any given time." (*Mexico in 1827*, II, 101, 108.)

9 The unnamed "country which is the almost exclusive possessor of the quicksilver mines" was Spain. Calderón would, a short while later, undertake negotiations (apparently to prove fruitless, at least at that time) looking to the importation of Spanish mercury on a basis which might lead to benefits for both Mexico and Spain. (Delgado, *España y México en el Siglo XIX*, II, 176–82.)

In this paragraph Fanny seems well aware that she is dealing with a delicate subject of great complexity—for the discussion of which she was not well qualified—yet one likely to be of special interest to many of her readers. The English edition of *Life in Mexico*, like the American, appeared in 1843, and its large sale during the ensuing several years may have been aided by the still high level of British investor interest in Mexico.

As to the outcome of subsequent British efforts in relation to this mine, the story can be told briefly: Operations continued with uneven success until 1848. By that date, with losses exceeding a million British pounds, the company went into liquidation. In 1850 its assets were sold for $130,000, little more than the value of the imported machinery as scrap. The buyer was a Mexican company in which the Calderóns' friend Manuel Escandón was a leading figure. Almost immediately a spectacular bonanza was uncovered and within a few years profits equalled some eighty million dollars. The historic mine is still in production. (Wilson, *Mexico: Its Peasants and Its Priests*, pp. 370–71; Bishop, *Old Mexico . . .* , pp. 229–31; Terry, *Terry's Mexico*, edition of 1909, p. 423.)

10 From Genesis 1:29 and 2:9.

11 Fanny is wrong here. The ravine of Regla is to the northeast.

12 The ravine of Santa María Regla is hushed today. The rush of water—described in old accounts as a milk-white foam as it spilled through the gorge—is gone. The construction of a dam upstream (already mentioned in the note on nearby San Miguel Regla) has left only a trickle of the once mighty flow that now passes with relative quiet through electric generators.

When we first visited the tight, green little barranca, with its complex of empty and partly roofless structures of beautifully laid stone, all was silent and decayed except for the little church and part of the main residence. Plainly visible were the fireplaces presumably installed by the comfort-loving British, and, in another building, the remains of the furnaces Fanny saw. On later visits in 1957 and 1962 we found the narrow entrance heavily barred. Rumor ran that Santa María Regla had become a private week-end retreat, and that its many levels, maze-like passages, and big vaulted rooms had served as background for motion pictures. (A view from above, showing the chapel and part of the old refining works, is shown in Plate 101.)

One aspect of the ravine remains unchanged: the great polygonal basaltic columns that form its upper margin. Some are broken; some are whole. One can see now what Fanny could not—that cross-sectional pieces had been used to make a neat pavement for the channel of the former watercourse.

The Biblical reference is to Genesis 11:2–4.

13 This quotation—in which she altered the tense from *leaps* to *leapt*—Fanny took from Byron's *Childe Harold's Pilgrimage*, Canto III, Stanza XCII.

14 The process of extracting pure silver from ore, although modified in some cases by local differences or the use of varying machinery, remained essentially the same as that

invented in nearby Pachuca in 1557 by Bartolomé de Medina—and continued to hold its own even up into the early twentieth century.

The ore was broken up and separated from refuse by hand-hammering at the mine head. There it was roughly graded, and then loaded into leather sacks to be carried by burro or muleback to a fortress-like compound for extraction. Some accounts mention a preliminary dry stamping on an iron plate, followed by sifting and a re-stamping of the residue; all accounts describe the subsequent wet milling process. In this, great stones were revolved, typically by mules—or by machinery as here at Santa María Regla where water wheels provided the power. This milling process reduced the ore to a wet mud that was then hauled or sluiced to a tightly-paved courtyard where it was spread out in circular masses one or two feet thick.

Salts were next added, plus the essential mercury. The whole was then worked repeatedly by trampling mule or horse power for three to six weeks, until the quicksilver united with the silver and sank to the bottom. This mass was then washed in an incline or trough until the mud passed off and the amalgam settled into slots made for the purpose.

Here again accounts vary. H. G. Ward in his *Mexico in 1827* (II, 434–38) speaks of the amalgam's being placed in leather bags which were squeezed until all unused quicksilver was exuded through the pores of the leather. Then followed the refining process, wherein the lumpy amalgam was fired for twelve hours, during which the remaining quicksilver was first vaporized and then condensed in water—leaving the pure silver. Joel R. Poinsett in his *Notes on Mexico* (pp. 211, 217–23) omits mention of the squeezing process and speaks of the amalgam as being put directly into kettle-shaped retorts, from which the mercury was vaporized (a deadly poison in this form) and the molten, relatively pure silver cast into bars.

This classic system was wasteful in the light of today's methods, and in many cases the old slack around long-worked mines has been re-worked with profit. The story is told of an astute entrepreneur who, realizing that certain huts in a mining town had been built from adobe bricks made from mine tailings, purchased the huts, tore them down, and extracted sufficient profit from the bricks to clear a tidy sum on the transaction. (W. E. Carson, *Mexico, The Wonderland of the South*, p. 366.)

A costly aspect of mining operations in Fanny's day was the purchase and care of horses and mules. Ward noted (II, 72) that the poorer ores at mines he visited were allowed to accumulate until after a good harvest when the price of feed dropped, as only then could silver be extracted with profit.

(Other sources include Bishop, *Old Mexico* . . . , pp. 239–40; Bullock, *Six Months . . . in Mexico*, pp. 369–70; Alfred R. Conkling, *Appletons' Guide to Mexico*, pp. 267–68; Frederick A. Ober, *Travels in Mexico*, pp. 450–67.)

[15] Anxious to discover why, if their carriage had been mule-drawn, the party would surely have perished, the editors sought council with the United States Department of Agriculture. In reply it was pointed out that, while the mule is indeed sure-footed, his reputation for eccentricity and insuperable obstinacy is well founded. "He dislikes mud and water and does not work well in soft muddy ground. His 'mulishness' regarding the crossing of a stream arises not so much from an inability to swim as from a suspiciousness regarding the unknown and a mulish refusal to be forced into a tight place." (Letter of June 20, 1961, from I. P. Earle of the Animal Husbandry Research Division.) Apparently horses could be more relied upon to plunge blindly through "the boiling torrent" under the guidance of man, whereas mules would insist on doing their own thinking.

Carlos Rincón Gallardo, Marqués de Guadalupe, in a unique work on Mexican horsemanship, *El Libro de Charro Mexicano*, summed up mules (p. 45) in a single word; they are, he said, unconfiding.

[16] This area seems to have been particularly subject to dangerous flash floods. Another account mentions "ravines now dry and sandy, but in one of which a waggon of the Real del Monte transport party, containing thirty-six hundred weight of iron, was washed away by the rains; nine mules were drowned, and several men escaped with great difficulty." And again: ". . . We passed a gloomy Hacienda, near which one night twenty-one mules of the transport party employed in conveying machinery to the mines of Real del Monte, were swept away and drowned by a sudden fall of rain." (Lyon, *Journal* . . . , II, 166 and 161.)

[17] We think that Fanny planned to assist at the English ball only in the French and Spanish meaning of attending it.

There seems to have been a good deal of speculation and perhaps heartburning over who had or had not been invited. A newspaper article in *El Mosquito Mexicano* for May 22 (Vol. VIII, No. 41) criticized Pakenham for not having invited people who, although not upper-class socially, were prominent in business affairs. Was it not the case—it was asked pointedly—that the British were eager to foment commerce between England and

Mexico? Among those receiving invitations, the writer remarked, were individuals known more for their ancestry than for their education or virtues.

It would appear that the accelerated return from Real del Monte, with all its risks, was solely to be in good time for the party.

18. Consecration of the Archbishop

[1] The diamond necklace and earrings belonging to the Marchioness of Londonderry had been the gift of Alexander I, Czar of Russia, and were of extraordinary splendor. The identifications provided in this chapter are from the Singer copy.

[2] This mark of attention from the President toward Fanny was rumored to have irked the French minister, the Baron de Cyprey, who was displeased that the lady so honored had not been his own wife. Calderón, who reported this in one of his dispatches, noted that he did not believe the rumor as the baron must have been aware of the usual diplomatic rule that precedence was established solely by virtue of being on the ground longer. (*Despachos Generales*, I, 74.) Calderón's comment seems to imply that Fanny was the highest ranking among the diplomatic wives present on this occasion.

[3] A newspaper of the day—*El Cosmopolita* for May 27, 1840—describes this ball in some detail. The splendid illumination and the flowers twined around the columns of the patio were much admired. Confirming Fanny's observations, it was noted that many of the ladies wore lace dresses, white predominating. The jewels of the Señoras de Agüero, Lazquety (whose name Calderón will later spell Lasquetti), and Cervantes were remarked as being especially magnificent. The crowding hampered the dancing but, in spite of this fact, all was *"decencia, urbanidad, y buen tono."* One would hardly think, the article continued, that the country was practically in a state of civil war, and that among those present and apparently enjoying one another's company were men pitted against one another in the game of life. Perhaps it was the music which, according to the pleasant Spanish turn of phrase, exerted a powerful influence to happy the function. There was not one orchestra, but two; there was dancing until supper, served at two in the morning; and afterwards dancing and card playing continued until seven.

Another account—that in *La Hesperia* of May 28, 1840—quoted one of the toasts given, which may well have pained Calderón as Spanish minister trying to rebuild close relations between Spain and Mexico: "To the royal couple, and may their marriage be as fortunate and lasting as that of Mexico with Great Britain!"

Why the ball was held in late May instead of on February 10 when Victoria's marriage to Albert had actually taken place is not clear.

[4] José María de Jesús Belaunzarán, renowned for piety, renounced his bishopric in 1839 to live simply in a convent. Bishop Joaquín Fernández de Madrid will be encountered again on a later occasion in this book. Bishop Angel Mariano Morales had capably engaged in governmental problems both before and after the Independence, and in 1837 had been a member of the council of state. According to another source of the time, Bishop Campos, whom Fanny had met as the good little *abad* of Guadalupe, was to have taken part in the ceremony but was prevented by illness. (Bustamante, *Gabinete Mexicano*, II, 58–59.)

[5] Again it was the Baron de Cyprey, the French minister, who took umbrage and who this time drew other diplomats into what proved to be a serious row with the Mexican officials.

Calderón's dispatches and the newspapers of the day tell the story. The baron and two members of his entourage entered the cathedral after the ceremony had begun. Enraged to find that the places assigned to diplomats were inferior to the seats of honor occupied by members of the Mexican cabinet, he first muttered his displeasure to Calderón —who tried to quiet him by urging that there had been no intentional slight. Unmollified, the baron went up to Cañedo, Mexican Minister of Foreign Affairs, and made an obviously offensive remark. With all eyes upon him he then ostentatiously gathered his companions around him and stalked out.

One of the reasons for Calderón's careful explanation of the whole affair to his chief was that the agitated whispering between him and the baron was noted by observers and the baron's exit attributed to a quarrel between them. A newspaper adopted this interpretation in its report of the incident; and a denial issued on Calderón's behalf had to be hurried into print of extra-large size in the next issue of *La Hesperia*, organ of the capital's Spanish residents.

Calderón and Pakenham, as uncomfortable dinner guests of the Archbishop after the ceremony, were besieged with indignant questions from Mexican officials. Reluctantly they entered the fray by maintaining that according to international usage the French minister did have grounds for complaint in that diplomats as representatives of their sovereigns should be accorded the respect due to sovereigns at public functions. Cañedo, vexed at the baron's public snub of Mexicans, wrote him insisting on an explanation for his conduct. The baron evidently continued to rage. Calderón and Pakenham decided to back him up on the principle involved and wrote Cañedo, citing a work on diplomatic protocol and insisting that on future occasions diplomats must be accorded due consideration. The Mexicans countered by pointing out that for some time they had been conducting public ceremonies as called for by a Mexican law giving their own high officials precedence, and that Pakenham had never seen fit to object before. In addition they cited another work on international usage which sanctioned compliance with local custom. Pakenham responded that, when he had first come to Mexico, diplomats had been accorded precedence, and that the reason he had not complained about Mexico's change in protocol was that no occasion had previously arisen which demonstrated lack of respect for foreign envoys.

Further confusing the issue was Cañedo's adroit shift of emphasis to the effect that the function in the cathedral had not been an official one in which rules of protocol might apply, but was private—and that the President in inviting attendance had acted not as head of the state but rather as *padrino*, or sponsor, for the Archbishop on this great occasion.

While heat abated, the issue was not resolved, and would continue to prove vexatious. So needlessly offensive had been the Baron de Cyprey's tone in this and other matters that Calderón and Pakenham seriously considered the possibility that he might be acting under definite instructions from his government to provoke a situation which could lead to a second armed intervention from the French.

This long-forgotten episode is dealt with at some length in *Despachos Generales* (I, 72–77, 99–108, 276–79, 311–13).

According to a Frenchman long resident in Mexico, the inflammable baron was a deplorable choice as an emissary from a country which less than two years before had sent out a fleet to shell the fort guarding Veracruz. The French minister, he said, carried a cane with which he was wont to reinforce his frequent arguments, and once almost precipitated an international incident over a debt of thirty-six cents. (Fossey, *Le Mexique*, p. 285.)

The Baron de Cyprey's position in Mexico was probably an uncomfortable one from the start, for the previous September his government had recognized the independence of Mexico's former territory of Texas. (The only other country which had accorded recognition to Texas was the United States.) After signing the treaty ending the Pastry War in March 1839, the French Admiral Baudin had visited Texas and had recommended that his government enter into relations with the new republic—with the thought, apparently, that a friendly base for French ships near Mexico might be an asset for possible later contingencies. (Maissin, *The French in Mexico and Texas*, pp. 138–47.)

[6] "And the candlesticks of pure gold, five on the right side, and five on the left . . ." —I Kings, 8:49.

"And the tongs thereof, and the snuff-dishes thereof, shall be of pure gold."—Exodus, 25:38.

[7] Manuel Posada was the first archbishop of Mexico following its independence. The ceremony Fanny witnessed was final recognition of the termination of a long estrangement between independent Mexico and the Holy See.

Mexico as a nation had never wavered in loyalty to the Catholic faith implanted at the time of the conquest. Exclusive adherence to the Catholic religion had been proclaimed as one of the principles governing the newly-emerging nation. The republican constitution of 1824 reiterated Mexico's exclusive support of the Catholic faith as opposed to all others. The Vatican, nevertheless, pressured by Spain, took the position that Mexico had revolted from its lawful king, and Pope Leo XII in September 1824 instructed Mexican priests to preach obedience to Ferdinand VII. This order was not generally obeyed. The death of Leo XII in 1829 and of Pius VIII in 1830 interrupted Mexican overtures toward recognition, but with the election of Gregory XVI as pope in 1831 they were resumed.

The relationship of Mexico with the papacy was further strained by developments in 1833 instituted by Santa Anna's vice-president Valentín Gómez Farías, a political idealist who acted as chief of state during Santa Anna's long periods of absence from office. Gómez Farías began speedily to implement his conviction that the power of the church and the privileged classes stood in the way of Mexican progress. Supported by a strongly liberal congress, he put through one reform measure after another: legislation to secularize education (for a time the University of Mexico was closed as being dominated by the clergy); cessation of the enforced collection of church tithes; and a law to permit members of monastic establishments, women as well as men, to forsake their vows and take up life in the world, and which secularized certain church properties.

The storm of conflicting opinion on these and other measures became so violent that the bishop of Puebla and other Spanish-born members of the clergy were obliged to leave Mexico. Santa Anna—alert to the rising tide of unpopularity for these reforms by his vice-president—returned to more active participation in the government, reversed Gómez Farías' measures, closed down the radical congress, and by executive orders shifted to a conservative course. Gómez Farías went into hiding and left Mexico in 1835. He subsequently returned, and will assume a brief but important role in this book.

The Calderóns would later meet the churchman, Francisco Pablo Vásquez of Puebla, whose long negotiations abroad paved the way for final coveted recognition of Mexican independence by the Vatican on November 29, 1836.

(This long-protracted period of negotiations is dealt with at length in Carlos Bosch García's *Problemas Diplomáticos del México Independiente*, and in Wilfrid Hardy Callcott's *Church and State in Mexico, 1822–1857*, pp. 32–111.)

As to the meaning of Fanny's strange closing observation that Posada might also be Mexico's last archbishop, we can only guess. Calderón's dispatches make plain his conviction that Bustamante's administration was weak and that trouble lay ahead, while Fanny will later throw out a half-serious speculation on a possible future occupation of Mexico by the United States.

Archbishop Posada's likeness is shown in Plate 80, and the interior of the cathedral on a ceremonial occasion in Plate 23.

19. On the Subject of Mexican Servants

[1] We assume that Countess C., disguised by Fanny for print as the Countess S——, was probably the elder Countess Cortina.

[2] This lady, whose name is left blank in the Journal as well as in Fanny's published text, and who never appears again, is designated in a notation written into the Singer copy. Who she was we do not know, but the *Diario del Gobierno* for June 9, 1840 listed a James Dunlop among local Englishmen prominent in mercantile affairs.

The quotation "all honourable men" is, one assumes, from Shakespeare's *Julius Caesar* —Mark Antony's speech in Act III, Scene 2.

[3] In her Journal Fanny uses the term *ama de llaves*, meaning literally "mistress of the keys."

[4] Fanny's bitterness toward French domestics was perhaps colored by her dealings with Emilie—the Duchess—who, we learn later, would leave her in the lurch the following October or November. (It must be remembered that Fanny actually wrote this discussion of the servant problem about a year later than the date given.)

[5] Adalid's name is derived from the Singer copy, but might have been assumed with some assurance in view of his interest in horses and reputation for high-speed travel.

[6] A real was, it will be remembered, one-eighth of a peso or dollar. The wages reported here are in general so much higher than those listed at approximately the same time by the United States diplomat Brantz Mayer—eight to ten dollars per month for a housekeeper, for example, as against Fanny's figure of twelve to fifteen—that one surmises that either the Calderóns demanded and were willing to pay for the best, or that they were victims of the world-wide theory that foreigners should pay more. Mayer, a bachelor, was lodged with a Mexican *marquesa* whose fortunes had declined, and he may have had good information as to rates paid by less affluent Mexicans. (Mayer, *Mexico as It Was and as It Is*, p. 385.)

[7] Our guess—and we believe it a conservative one—is that more than thirty people lived in the household over which Fanny presided. In addition to the Calderóns there was the attaché recently mentioned. As he had a valet, it seems not unlikely that his chief had one also; however, no such character figures in these pages, and consequently the second valet will be dismissed from the count. So far, then, the reckoning is *four*.

The housekeeper, cook, and kitchen maids—two *galopinas* have been mentioned earlier —bring the number to *eight*. Fanny has mentioned the major-domo, or steward, who presumably served the hospitably dispensed dinners. Remembering that she had been critical of the Cortinas' ample but to her eyes informal service at table, the major-domo must have had an assistant. But to keep the count conservative, the footman whom Fanny has earlier mentioned as accompanying her in making calls is assumed to have doubled in this capacity. When we add the chambermaid and the laundress—each of whom has been previously mentioned—the number rises to *twelve*.

Fanny speaks of only one coachman instead of the two or three she gives as the usual complement for a large Mexican household. But, as she has earlier spoken of their importation of *two* carriages, there must have been at least one extra hand in the stable.

Definitely mentioned are the porter, the gardener, and the two old soldiers who acted as guards. The number has become *eighteen*.

The coachman, the porter, and the gardener, Fanny has said, had their families with them. If we allot to each a modest family, by Mexican standards, of a wife and three children, we add twelve more members to the household. However, perhaps we should remove from the reckoning the three wives and put them to work as members of the kitchen or laundry staff, already counted. But, as an offset, we must surely add in as a part of each of these subordinate families an average of one aged parent—who never, in warm-hearted Mexico, would have been permitted to live elsewhere in lonely poverty. Retaining and adding, then, our estimate of twelve extra dependents to the earlier count of *eighteen*, we arrive at a plausible total of *thirty* souls who lived under the ample roof of the Spanish legation. The number in all likelihood was considerably higher. Emilie, the Duchess, was not included on the theory that during her tenure she acted also as housekeeper. Nor was Josefita, the little girl in training—nor were house guests, some of whom, as will be seen, stayed for long periods.

[8] Harriet Martineau, well known as a British writer, translator, and reformer—and still young although very deaf—had come with her ear trumpet to the United States in 1834, and had spent some time in Boston.

[9] The Discalced Carmelites—Nuns of the Primitive Rule of St. Joseph, familiarly called Teresianas in Mexico—were founded by Teresa of Avila, extraordinary combination of dynamic executive and ascetic, joyous mystic. Not content with the comfortable atmosphere of the Carmelite convent in Spain in which she had become a nun in 1534—and which operated under the Mitigated Rule—she left it with a few companions to inaugurate nearby in 1562 a more austere branch to be governed by the ancient rigorous rule of Carmel, reinforced by additional reforms of her own. The Teresianas had two establishments in the Mexican capital, and both their churches survive.

Fanny has already referred (p. 196) to the sister of José Adalid who was a nun in the convent of Santa Teresa la Nueva. The Adalid name given here—as well as the filled-in names in the following chapter—is derived from handwritten notes in the Singer copy. Señor Adalid's cloistered sister would not in fact have been called "Madre Adalid," but rather by a new name chosen when she relinquished her worldly ties to become a Carmelite nun.

20. "Last Look of This Wicked World"

[1] A handsome old grating still stands in Santa Teresa la Nueva, its formidable iron spikes symbolic of protection to the nuns living in a world apart.

Santa Teresa, one block north and two blocks east of the cathedral, on the Calle Loreto, shares with another old colonial church the charming if slightly shabby Plaza de Loreto. Within, Santa Teresa is simple as to architecture, with unadorned red *tezontle* stone piers. In spite of somewhat cluttered furnishings, its atmosphere of sober, humble piety is all-pervasive.

As may be apparent, the godmother (or *madrina*) was not necessarily the future nun's godmother in baptism, but her sponsor for this occasion.

[2] Meyerbeer's *Robert le Diable* had first been presented in November 1831 in Paris, just after Fanny's family is believed to have emigrated to the United States. It was first heard in New York in the spring of 1834. The opera is fictional, but Robert the Devil, Duke of Normandy—although represented out of his time in the opera's story—had been a real person. The handsome, unscrupulous, and energetic duke died in the eleventh century on his way home from a penitential journey to Jerusalem. He, the tanner's daughter by whom he had a bastard son named William, and that son—who later made his mark as William the Conqueror of England—were all among Fanny's picturesque array of ancestors.

[3] After Fanny became a Catholic in 1847 she apparently regretted some of the statements she made here.

In the possession of a descendant of Fanny's great-nephew there is a copy of the first English edition of *Life in Mexico* inscribed by her in 1843 as a birthday present to her mother. Restored apparently to Fanny's possession after her mother's death (and later passing to Lydia, the youngest Inglis sister, and finally to relatives in the United States), this copy contains a few handwritten corrections, deletions, and rough revisions. Presumably made by Fanny (in 1848), these would somewhat temper the effect of the present chapter. It cannot be said with complete assurance that Fanny did in fact make all these ink-written revisions herself, but one or two corrections which appear later in the text (as, for example, the distance covered during a day's outing in Mexico) make it seem highly likely that some, at least, originated with her. In any event, these alterations seem to reflect a change in her attitude following her conversion to the Catholic faith.

Lydia, like Fanny, became a Catholic and made her life in Spain. Two years after Fanny's death, Lydia carried on a correspondence with their great-nephew Calderon Carlisle, who lived in Washington. In this she discussed her hope to bring out in the United States a new edition of *Life in Mexico*—an undertaking that did not materialize. Writing from Madrid in 1884, she said in part: "The book is corrected—that is to say, a few trifles which she [Fanny] didn't like, erased."

The marked volume (which we will refer to as the Carlisle copy, to distinguish it from the frequently cited Singer copy) was evidently sent together with a new preface, prepared in rather effusive style by an English friend of Lydia's. Calderon Carlisle must have objected to the proposed preface, because a subsequent letter from Lydia asked him to prepare one himself. Rough notes among his papers indicate that he proposed to say in part: "Madame Calderon deeply religious by nature was a protestant when she wrote the book—but became a Roman Catholic in [1847] and would never consent that a second edition of the book should be published without revision—as with the sensitiveness of a convert she magnified the importance of certain words & phrases which she had employed with reference to the Church."

In the Carlisle copy the following wording was proposed to be stricken near the beginning and middle of the present paragraph: "which was delivered by a fat priest"; "(picked out like a plum from a pie)"; "and contempt." Additional alterations were shown for the present chapter and will be noted as encountered.

That the proposed alterations were based on the memory of certain passages or a cursory review of what was said, rather than on any systematic going over of the entire text, is clear from their fragmentary nature and the absence of changes in other passages no less outspoken.

4 The following day Fanny wrote a parallel description of this same event to her friend Prescott. It incorporates one or two additional poignant touches on the induction of the homely girl into the convent of Santa Teresa: she was "led to the grating to look for the last time at all her family, who all cried *adios, adios*, and the curtain was drawn that shut her out from the world forever. The family then left the church, lighted their cigars in the Sacristy, and sat down to smoke, apparently very much pleased with the day's work." (Wolcott, *Correspondence of . . . Prescott*, p. 132.)

5 In the Carlisle copy the word "victim" was stricken and the word "lady" substituted. In the previous paragraph, "The most cruel part of all" was altered to read "The most difficult part of all." The phrase "having the unfortunate honour" was altered to "having the honour."

6 The Singer copy shows the name Navarrete written in here as the surname of the writer of the invitation; and in the body of the note, where Fanny for print disguised the name as P—e—, this is crossed out and the name Navarrete written over it.

7 Perhaps the girl's father was Martín Martínez Navarrete, a general of brigade. (*Cosmopolita*, October 24, 1840.) One who comes to mind as a possible family connection was Juan Gómez Navarrete, earlier minister of justice under Iturbide and still active in political and cultural affairs. (*La Unión*, January 6, 1841; *Ateneo Mexicano*, I, 24 and 140.)

8 From Act I, Scene 2, of *Paul Pry, A Comedy of Three Acts*, by John Poole, performed at the Haymarket Theatre in London in 1826.

9 In the Singer copy, the senator's name is written in as J. Cacho.

10 Information in genealogical works makes it possible to piece together a few more facts bearing on this occasion. José María Cacho (listed in the government newspaper as a senator at this time) was married to the senior Conde de Santiago's sister, and their daughter was married to Pedro Navarrete, who was presumably related to the nun-to-be. The solemn little procession to the church was thus led by a family connection—the Conde de Santiago—who was, one assumes, the guest of highest rank. As his partner, the count took Fanny, the wife of the envoy from Spain.

11 Not, evidently, by the "Waltz King" Johann the younger, fifteen or so at this time, but by Johann Strauss senior, himself composer of 152 waltzes.

12 This habit of the nuns of La Encarnación, together with those of other orders, is depicted in color in *México a Través de los Siglos*, edited by Vicente Riva Palacio (II, following page 712). The habit is white, with a long panel in front; over it is the blue cape which Fanny describes, with what appears to be a plaque or plate not only on one shoulder but also in front.

13 In the Carlisle copy of *Life in Mexico* the words "fat and portly prelate" were stricken.

[14] The initials A.N.M. from the Singer copy undoubtedly stand for Alexander Norman Macleod, Fanny's nephew—usually called Alex—who would later join the Calderóns in Mexico. (The Carlisle copy, with the handwritten insert "A-" here, provides further confirmation.)

Alex's fifty-line poem was included by Fanny in her published text. Here are a few excerpts: "The novice entered: to her doom she went,/ . . . /Virgin of tender years, poor innocent!/ . . . /What if thy heart should change, thy spirit fail?/ . . . /They raise a hymn which seems a funeral wail,/ . . . /A life-in-death must her long years consume./ . . . /They seemed like spectres from their place of doom,/Stealing from out eternal night's blind cave,/To meet their comrade new, and hail her to the grave."

21. The Gambling Tables of San Agustín

[1] The Bank of the United States, a private organization, previously used as the official depository of government funds, was at this time in grave financial difficulty. As will later appear, Calderón's savings were involved.

San Agustín de las Cuevas even in Fanny's time was beginning to be called by its present name of Tlalpan.

[2] Fanny had perhaps read Charles Joseph Latrobe's Rambler in Mexico, published in 1836. The author describes (p. 150) "luxuriously dressed females, chatting and smoking with their beaux," whose custom it was to pause during the course of the fashionable evening promenade in the portales or arcades and sit on "the dirty steps at the doorways of the shops."

[3] Filled-in blanks in this chapter and in the chapter which follows are derived from the Singer copy.

Luis Gonzaga Cuevas who accompanied the Calderóns to San Agustín was a member of the cabinet as Minister of Interior Affairs.

Felipe Teixidor points out, in his annotated translation of Life in Mexico (La Vida en México, I, p. 112 of his Notas), that Revillagigedo did not build the village, as Fanny thought, but only the bridge leading into it.

[4] H. G. Ward, who thoroughly enjoyed his excursion to San Agustín, said that house rent for the three special days might run from three to five hundred dollars. (Mexico in 1827, II, 298–99.)

Today Tlalpan, formerly San Agustín, still retains something of its former small-town charm in spite of its nearness to the constantly enlarging capital; and a few of its larger houses are still surrounded by the gardens for which it was once famous.

[5] Sam Weller of the Pickwick Papers—which had appeared in 1836—seems not to have said these exact words, although the cheery cynicism and turn of phrase could have been his. Perhaps Fanny had in mind Dickens' more recent Nicholas Nickleby (Chapter 21). "A good half of wot's here isn't paid for, I des-say, and wot a consolation oughtn't that to be to her feelings!" said Mr. Scaley, the bailiff, as he looked over Mme Mantalini's dressmaking establishment on the eve of seizing its fixtures for her husband's debts.

[6] An account of the coins then in use may be of interest, and we accordingly draw on a second book on Mexico written by Brantz Mayer, United States secretary of legation whose period of service overlapped that of Calderón (Mexico, Aztec, Spanish and Republican, Appendix No. 2, p. 347): 1 onza (gold)=16 dollars; 1 peso (silver)=1 dollar; 1 real (silver)=12½ cents; 1 medio (silver)=6¼ cents; 1 quartillo (copper)=3⅛ cents; 1 tlaco (copper)=1 9/16 cents. There were thus eight copper tlacos to a real, and eight reals to a peso or dollar. The ratio of silver to gold fluctuated to some degree, as will be noted.

[7] So solid was San Antonio, surrounded by walls six feet thick, and so strategic its position, that a few years after the Calderóns' time it would be occupied by Mexican troops defending their capital during the United States-Mexican War. The principal actions developed elsewhere, however—first at Contreras (also called Padierna), and then at nearby Churubusco. The village of San Agustín was occupied by United States troops and used as a supply base and hospital area.

The buildings of the hacienda of San Antonio survived in a ruined state into the twentieth century.

[8] The Pedregal lay between San Angel and San Agustín de las Cuevas. It resulted from the long-ago eruption of the mountain of Ajusco, and in the Calderóns' time was thought of as a bandit-haunted waste. It is now the site of the University of Mexico and developing residential suburbs.

[9] See Plate 93 for a cockfight scene of the period.

The opening of a cockfight, according to Waddy Thompson who soon after the Calderóns' time was minister from the United States, was prefaced by an announcement made two or three times by the master of the pit: *Ave María Purísima, los gallos vienen!* Hail, most pure Mary, the cocks are coming! (*Recollections of Mexico*, p. 132.)

[10] This is from what seems to have been one of Fanny's favorite poems, Byron's *Childe Harold's Pilgrimage*, Canto I, stanza LXXX. The quoted words that follow are from the same work, stanza LXXIV.

[11] The reference is to Henry Alexander Wise, a Democrat from Virginia, who broke with Jackson on an issue involving the United States Bank.

[12] An old lithograph of this festivity is shown as Plate 91.

[13] Waddy Thompson noted that at San Agustín "it is not genteel to bet anything but gold." He observed also that the sudden demand for gold among the élite bent on gambling at the fête caused a shift from what he described as the usual ratio of fifteen-and-a-quarter silver dollars for one gold doubloon, or *onza*, to the temporarily enhanced value of sixteen or even seventeen dollars in silver. What Fanny saw won and lost, then, was some sixteen thousand dollars. Thompson's account also mentions the unwavering composure, even on the part of those of modest means, in the face of heavy loss. The Mexican propensity for gambling was, he felt, natural in a country steeped in mining traditions. Thompson noted the complete trustworthiness of the ragged brokers in the cockpit who, during the course of betting, held large sums tossed down by various rapid-fire bettors. (*Recollections of Mexico*, pp. 132–35.)

The player for high stakes was presumably Lorenzo Carrera, mentioned more than once in Calderón's dispatches as a prominent resident Spaniard.

[14] This is Fanny's only direct reference to Powhatan Ellis, United States minister from 1839 to 1842 in Mexico (where he had served somewhat earlier as chargé d'affaires). He was a polished Virginian, and is remembered as a capable and honorable, although not brilliant, public servant.

[15] Much of this chapter up to this point is from a far fuller account of the fête written the *following* year; that is, all the general descriptions are drawn from Volume 3 of Fanny's Journal, with a few specifics added regarding her first visit. (The reference to returning "home" to dress, at the beginning of the previous paragraph, is apparently a resulting editorial inconsistency.) In preparing her text for publication Fanny could safely predict what she would do the following year, as she already had the necessary material at hand. Perhaps the phrase "should we still be here next year" was a "plant" inserted to prepare the reader for Calderón's not-too-distant recall.

[16] The baron's departure would be deferred for many weeks, apparently because of stirring events to come—of which the reader will soon be apprised.

22. Approach of the Rainy Season

[1] José María Gutiérrez Estrada, about forty at this time, was married to Loreto Cortina, sister of the Calderóns' friend Count Cortina. The *Almanach de Gotha* volumes of the late 1830's list him as Mexican minister in London, and it is presumably from this post that he and his wife had recently returned. As the reader will see, within a few months he would become the center of an intense political turmoil.

[2] This walled pleasure garden (entirely separate from the Morán family's nearby hacienda of San Antonio) still exists within today's town of Tlalpan. The artificial cave survived until recently.

[3] Doña María Loreto Vivanco, like the Calderóns' other good friend the elder Condesa de la Cortina, was the bearer of a title in her own right. Her husband José Morán (sharer of her title according to Spanish custom) had risen through merit to high army rank, and had formerly served as minister of war.

Felipe Teixidor uses as illustrations (*La Vida en México*, I, following p. 231) reproductions of portraits of General Morán and his wife, now in possession of their descendants. The Marquesa de Vivanco appears as serene and kind. Her husband the general is shown as possessor of a strong face, less handsome but more interesting than the presumably more youthful likeness shown here as Plate 79.

None of the two Morán sons or three daughters is ever referred to in these pages by a first name: it seems to have been the *marquesa* whom Fanny especially liked. She must have known fairly well, at least, the Morán daughter Doña Teodosia, married not long before to Luis Cuevas, Minister of Interior Affairs.

[4] In previous editions the entry under June 20 was placed ahead of this entry of June 18.

[5] A later United States minister to Mexico described the keeping of this holy day— celebrated on the ninth Thursday following Easter—as he saw it in 1843. The streets were canopied and between thirty and forty thousand people, among them ten thousand troops, marched in a procession headed by high dignitaries of the church, who carried a litter bearing the Host, followed by another litter on which rested the tiny figure of the Virgen de los Remedios. (Thompson, Recollections of Mexico, p. 103.)

[6] If one remembers Fanny's ire over the cabinet members' interference with her own projected public appearance as a Poblana, it is hard to know whether this last sentence was penned in all seriousness.

[7] Fanny apparently refers here to the road which in part followed the ancient causeway leading south from the capital—opposite to that leading north to Guadalupe. The corresponding road toward the west was that upon which the Calderóns resided at San Fernando.

[8] This lady was perhaps the wife of José María Cuevas—brother of the cabinet member Luis Gonzaga Cuevas and remembered as a good speaker, and an effective member of Congress (Pimentel, Obras, V, 447–48). The memorable good looks of Señora Cuevas are mentioned by another chronicler of the time, Guillermo Prieto (Memorias . . . , II, 438). She is presumably the same beauty who will subsequently be referred to at the beginning of Chapter 41.

[9] An anonymous Englishman of some years earlier gravely described the bolero as combining "the style of the minuet and the English hornpipe." The same writer was struck, as Fanny was, by the simultaneous effect of emptiness and magnificence in Mexican houses. Speaking not of a specific house, but in general, he noted "the want of chairs, tables, and a washing basin in the bedrooms, whilst the pot de chambre is of silver . . ." (Sketch . . . of Mexico, pp. 96, 89.)

[10] It seems likely that La Güera Rodríguez, who will be remembered as the vital beauty so much admired by Humboldt many years earlier, may have been more in Fanny's company and thoughts than this book indicates. "She has taken up a serious affection for me . . ." Fanny not long before had said to Prescott in a letter giving a breathless account of new experiences and friends. (Wolcott, Correspondence of . . . Prescott, p. 129.)

One wonders whether Fanny's quick grasp of the social scene might not have been aided by genealogical and biographical résumés provided by three older ladies of high social rank: the elder Countess de la Cortina, the Marquesa de Vivanco, and La Güera.

[11] Of Señora Lombardi, whose name was written into the Singer copy, we know nothing. Perhaps she was Señora Lombardo, wife of Francisco María Lombardo, who had been Minister of Foreign Affairs a few years before.

[12] The official title of the government daily was the Diario del Gobierno de la República Mexicana. The privately-owned paper called El Cosmopolita came out on Wednesdays and Saturdays, and El Mosquito Mexicano on Tuesdays and Fridays. La Hesperia, organ of the Spanish residents of Mexico—initiated March 15, 1840, less than three months after Calderón's arrival—was also a semi-weekly. In a dispatch of March 24, 1840, Calderón cited the potential usefulness of the new paper but carefully mentioned his warning to the editors that they should avoid any appearance of being spokesmen for the Spanish minister. In spite of all precautions, however, including the fact that Calderón seems almost never to have been referred to by name or office, Mexicans would more than once link him with the newspaper when issues between Spain and Mexico became prickly. Calderón's government sent him strong warning on the subject. (Despachos Generales, I, 45–46, 91–93, 171.)

La Hesperia frankly assumed its readers' interest in Spanish affairs and featured regular bulletins covering legislation and appointments in Spain. In contrast, political events in Mexico seem usually to have been handled through the liberal use of reprints from other papers. Occasional moves on the part of the Mexican government, as for example an increase in import duties, might evoke direct comment. The movements of ships were likewise reported—of special interest to the many Spaniards in Mexico who were importers or merchants. Usually included was at least one article of a literary nature, together with news of theatrical performances.

[13] José María Bustamante was a scientist learned in several fields. Although Fanny mentions his name only once again, the Calderóns seem to have come to know him well. From the accounts of three British visitors of the 1820's it would appear that he was outstanding in mineralogy, and was modest and unassuming in spite of his great learning. (Hardy, Travels . . . , p. 513; W. Bullock, Six Months . . . in Mexico, p. 330; Lyon, Journal . . . , II, 156–57. See also José C. Valadés, Alamán, p. 190.)

Confusingly enough, there also lived at this time in Mexico: a musician with the same name of José María Bustamante; a well-known botanist named Miguel Bustamante, whom Calderón must have known as both became members of a new cultural organization (the

Ateneo); and Carlos María de Bustamante, a distinguished historian and editor (whose writings will be cited in various notes). And, of course, there was also the President, Anastasio Bustamante.

14 Judging from various references to him in other works, General Orbegoso (who had earlier spelled his name with an initial H, silent in Spanish) had been a prominent figure among the political conservatives in Mexico's early post-independence days. (Riva Palacio, México a Través de los Siglos, IV, 214; Zamacois, Historia de Méjico, XI, 21–22, 154.)

15 El Mosaico Mexicano, whose subtitle was Colección de Amenidades Curiosas e Instructivas, was just what its title implied. (From the evidence of occasional dated covers bound in with the Library of Congress copies, it seems to have come out weekly for at least a large part of the period covered by the Calderóns' stay, rather than monthly.)

Some of its material certainly had its origin outside of Mexico, as Fanny indicated. There were short biographies of men of many nations, bits of history, problems in chess, and informative articles on natural history. Its breadth of scope offered something for nearly everyone. There were urgent propaganda pieces on hygiene, including one (dramatically illustrated) on the lamentable results of tight corseting. Among the many illustrations were heroes of fable, new inventions, and magnified snowflakes.

Señor Cumplido, the editor, told his readers about places as far apart as Monte Etna and Filadelfia. In spite of the increasing political tension to be noted in the Mexican newspapers over the secession of Texas from Mexico and the interest of the United States in independent Texas, Señor Cumplido devoted a good deal of friendly attention to the folklore of the United States. For example, described and pictured for Mexican readers was the timely intervention of Pocahontas on behalf of Juan Smith. Also described were Monticello, home of Tomás Jefferson, and Monte-Vernon, abode of Jorge Washington. The cupola of the latter, it was remarked (IV, 381–83), was a common attribute of houses of los ricos hacendados de Virginia.

16 A Frenchman long resident in Mexico not unnaturally presents a different story: Some few French residents were scoundrels whose bad reputations hurt all their compatriots, but some were men of education, and many were capable artisans and mechanics who passed on their skills to Mexicans. In contrast, he said, some of the Spaniards were distinguished in the fine arts but in general they were not skilled workers, and tended rather to the occupations of wine merchant, grocer, and shopkeeper; and, as to the English, they came to sell their merchandise and exploit mines, and conferred no lasting benefit on Mexico. (Fossey, Le Mexique, pp. 271–76.)

From Calderón's dispatches it is plain that at least a few Spaniards operated on a large scale as merchants or bankers.

17 From The Taming of the Shrew, Act IV, Scene 1—or perhaps from Thomas Percy's Reliques of Ancient English Poetry: "It was a friar of orders gray/Walkt forth to tell his beades . . ."

18 Fanny devotes the rest of this chapter to an account of the establishment of the then little-known California missions—a subject apparently of great interest to her. Her information seems in large part to have been derived from the Franciscan friars of San Fernando, whose predecessors had played a leading role in the pioneer undertaking. What follows here and in subsequent notes may help to clarify her somewhat involved discussion.

Spanish Franciscans had followed close on the military victories of Cortés, and within fifty years of the conquest they had established a number of conventual centers in Mexico. In 1683 a group of recently-arrived Franciscans founded a special missionary training center in Querétaro, and some fifty years later an offshoot was established in the capital. This was the Colegio Apostólico de San Fernando—whose few inmates in 1840 were Calderón's friends.

The Jesuits likewise were notable missionaries. Their field of effort included Lower California, northern Mexico, and parts of what is now the southwestern United States. As Fanny will note shortly, in 1767 all Jesuits were expelled from New Spain. To fill the difficult missionary posts thus left vacant in Lower California, the viceroy called on the Franciscan friars of the missionary college of San Fernando. Leadership fell to the capable Majorca-born friar Junípero Serra. Only a few years later, in 1772, an agreement between Franciscans and Dominicans resulted in the transfer of the Lower California missions to the latter, while the Franciscans, who had already made a beginning in Upper or New California, took the northern area as their exclusive field.

19 The early Jesuit Eusebio Francisco Kino—as Father Kühn was usually called in Spanish—was born in the Tyrolean Alps in 1645. A teacher of mathematics in Bavaria, he later was sent to Mexico, where he achieved remarkable success as a missionary. (He was not the first to discover that Lower or Old California was a peninsula, but rather reaffirmed what had long been lost sight of, and the maps he made shed much new light on the as-

tonishingly large areas he traversed.) He was devoted to his Indian charges, and once rode more than seventy-five miles in a single day to succor one of them. The great Jesuit, who was a skilled organizer, was the founder of La Paz in Lower California and of a chain of missions—one of which was San Xavier del Bac near Tucson—in the Pima country of Sonora and Arizona. He is the subject of a biography by Herbert Eugene Bolton, *Rim of Christendom.*

20 The ousting of Jesuits from the Californias and from all of New Spain was only part of a larger episode. In 1759 the Jesuits had been expelled from Portugal and in 1764 from France. Expulsion from Spain and Spanish America followed upon the edict of the Spanish king Charles III. At dawn on June 25, 1767, by secret orders sent to all parts of New Spain, Jesuits were summarily taken from their posts and dispatched from the country. (In spite of careful executive planning, the remoteness of the California Jesuits postponed their expulsion by some months.) Great popular sympathy was shown the departing fathers, and rioting broke out in various Mexican towns. In 1773 Pope Clement XIV, thinking to achieve peace within the church, and without attempting to judge the merits of the issues involved, suppressed the Society throughout the Catholic world.

Much difference of opinion has existed as to the true basis for the suppression of the Jesuits. Such factors as the rapid growth of Jesuit enlistment, the order's emphasis upon study and academic learning with resulting dominance in educational affairs, and the identification of Jesuits with the power of the papacy at a time when conflicts between the Pope and various European monarchies were frequent, are all thought to have played a part.

The feeling against the Jesuits gradually subsided. Pope Pius VII restored the order in 1814, and Ferdinand VII not long afterward issued permission for Jesuits to reorganize in Spanish dominions. Jesuits in Mexico thus reorganized as a province of their order. Then, in 1820, the liberal government which had just come to power in Spain suppressed the Society of Jesus as an organization, and put individual Jesuits under the jurisdiction of their local bishops. This decree took effect in Mexico only shortly before the achievement of independence. After Mexico's separation from Spain, debate in the new congress in favor of the re-establishment of the Jesuits ensued, but no legislative action was taken. Consequently, at the time of the Calderóns' stay in Mexico, individual Jesuits (of whom Padre Lyón, mentioned on page 163 was one) continued in a "secularized" status. (Decorme, *Historia de la Compañía de Jesús* . . . , I, 184–94, 224–29, 365–68, 382.)

21 The material in this paragraph is derived from Humboldt, whom Fanny will later credit. His wording, even more than hers, seems a description of the comatose devotees of modern beaches: "They pass whole days stretched out mouth down in the sand, enjoying the heat communicated to them by the reflection of the rays of the sun." She omitted Humboldt's indirect quotation of an understanding Spanish missionary who noted the Indians' amusement over the white men's burden of apparel: "A clothed monkey would appear less ridiculous to the people of Europe than a dressed man to the Indians of California." (*Ensayo Politico* . . . , II, 116–18.)

22 Fanny, who elsewhere speaks of corn and maize and also of corn and wheat, seems sometimes to follow British usage and sometimes that of the United States. Perhaps as a Scotswoman she was here thinking of oats, wheat, and corn.

23 The chain of Upper California missions, completed by 1823 and numbering twenty-one in all (for three were added to the eighteen listed by Humboldt, Fanny's source) stretched from San Diego six hundred miles north to a point beyond San Francisco—which about 1800 was a village of some 820 souls, according to Humboldt. (*Ensayo Politico* . . . , II, 138.)

24 Fanny is presumably echoing here her husband's natural antipathy as a Spaniard toward some of the developments in Mexico after the War of Independence, particularly toward legislation adopted in December 1827 and a more sweeping measure of March 1829, expelling Spaniards from the new republic. This move took away from Mexico in its early formative post-independence years not only a few rich Spaniards, but also a considerable number of prosperous middle-class families experienced in management and business. At the time of Calderón's mission, however, a sizable number of Spanish nationals resided in Mexico.

25 Fanny will mention the fears inspired by the fierce Comanches, and the papers a few months later will be full of news of their depredations in northern Mexico.

Mexico never regained its former hold in Upper California. The first wagon train bearing North American settlers had arrived in 1826. British and French interest in the restive area, so remote from Mexico's central control, was also strong. In 1848, after the United States-Mexican War, part of the new international border was determined by the boundary stone which a missionary from San Fernando had erected about seventy-five years earlier to establish the division between Lower and Upper California.

23. Mexican Women Appraised

[1] Fanny translates from Zavala's *Ensayo Histórico* . . . (I, 144), a work from which she has drawn various apt characterizations of public figures. The observation she cites here was made about Iturbide after his military achievements, but before he was proclaimed emperor. Later Zavala pointed out (I, 239) that Iturbide, loved as Mexico's liberator, lost public esteem when he mounted a throne.

[2] Agustín de Iturbide, crowned Emperor of Mexico before his thirty-ninth birthday and deposed before his fortieth, would have been only fifty-seven if he had still been alive.

President Bustamante had been not merely a supporter of Iturbide; he had implemented his belief in the fallen leader by launching on the exiled Iturbide's behalf, early in 1824, a revolution calling for his restoration. The movement failed, and one result of it was that the republican government issued a decree prohibiting Iturbide from returning on pain of death. He did return—so soon that he was unaware of the decree. He landed on the coast on July 15, 1824 and was shot on July 19.

In 1840 his widow was living in Philadelphia with some of her large family of children. In theory she was well pensioned by the Mexican government; in fact, as debate in congress at that time showed, the hard-up government was behind in its payments.

Iturbide's vivid personality, his courage, and the gratitude felt by his countrymen for his eminently practical services in achieving independence for Mexico combined to keep his memory green. Among the upper classes and the military, at least, his reputation in Fanny's day eclipsed that of the earlier and less successful revolutionary heroes. In 1838 Bustamante had caused Iturbide's remains to be exhumed and brought by an escort of troops to the capital. There, in a magnificent ceremony on October 27, they were placed in the cathedral of Mexico—on the west side, in the chapel dedicated to Mexico's own San Felipe de Jesús. Bustamante's heart, after his death, would be deposited in the same chapel with the bones of his friend. (Niceto de Zamacois, *Historia de Méjico*, XII, 135–46.)

As will appear, ten days after Fanny recorded this entry, Bustamante's well-known devotion to Iturbide probably saved his life.

[3] Señor Cañedo has already been mentioned (pp. 188 and 205). The reader may recall particularly his tilt with the fiery-tempered French minister (note 5, pp. 720–21).

In discussing Almonte, Fanny does not say that, unlike most of their friends who were of Spanish or predominantly Spanish descent, he was a mestizo with a strong Indian strain. Moreover, it was well known that he was the son by an Indian mother of the revolutionary warrior-priest Morelos (himself a mestizo). Like many of his contemporaries, Almonte had led a life of extraordinary variety. He faced fire in the revolution as a child, finished his education in the United States, and then was sent while still in his early twenties on diplomatic missions to London, Paris, and to South America. He fought ably in the war against Texas, in which he was captured at the battle of San Jacinto; and after his return home he continued his rise to eminence. When the Calderóns met him as Minister of War he was only thirty-six. His likeness—taken, presumably, when he was somewhat older—is shown in Plate 67.

Another chronicler has described Almonte as a superb-looking man of fine athletic physique. He was studious by nature, beautifully mannered, always flawlessly groomed. His controlled exterior was said to have masked an ardent interest in women. His ambition was boundless. (Prieto, *Memorias* . . . , II, 31–32, 63.)

[4] Calderón described Luis Gonzaga Cuevas in a dispatch as a tactful, calm official who seemed well-disposed toward him. (*Despachos Generales*, I, 28.) Other sources have described him as a shrinkingly modest man but, nevertheless, a lucid-minded, effective public servant. Previous to the time Fanny wrote, the widely traveled Cuevas had held a diplomatic post in France and had already served—as he would again later—as Minister of Foreign Affairs. Cuevas is depicted in Plate 69.

[5] In addition to respectfully removing a possible quid and waking him up a little, Fanny for publication freed the Archbishop from "indigestion" rather than "stomach-ache." She seems genuinely to have liked the genial churchman whom she probably knew well by the time she wrote this description in Volume 3 of her Journal.

Perhaps it was really caramels that Archbishop Posada was chewing. A few years later he died suddenly from stomach trouble. Carlos María de Bustamante wrote that the extremely corpulent, lethargic Archbishop (Plate 80) was not only overfond of julienne soup, but also was possessed of a childish passion for sweets. (*El Nuevo Bernal Díaz del Castillo*, II, 15.)

[6] Two Mexican commissioners, Joaquín Velázquez de León and Pedro Fernández del Castillo, would leave Mexico in August 1840 to take part in negotiations over claims of United States citizens against Mexico growing in large part out of disturbances incidental to the War of Independence. They would be balanced by two United States commissioners, with the Prussian minister to the United States serving as neutral member in the arbitration.

[7] A visitor to Mexico in the early 1880's spoke with admiration of the realistic effect achieved by *trapo* figures, and sensed their future value as a record of the past. "Another evidence of refinement of taste in the Indian is to be found in the 'rag figures,' which have a reputation that is not less than world-wide. The French, in their invasion of Mexico, went into raptures over these marvellous imitations of life . . . Upon a core of carefully-manipulated wax [the artist] moulds a skin of thin, specially-prepared cloth, tinted the exact color of the tawny people he purposes to represent. He does not draw upon his imagination for material, but imitates exactly the figures that move through the street before his workshop door." (Ober, *Travels in Mexico*, p. 322.)

[8] Modern students of Mexico's enormously rich artistic tradition would disagree with the opinion expressed here that Indian artists and artisans were solely copyists. They would point out that pre-Columbian Indian cultures have contributed generously to the world's store of great art and that the high place of post-Columbian Mexican art may be ascribed in considerable part to Indian influences.

Elizabeth Wilder Weismann, in her *Mexico in Sculpture, 1521–1821*, combines scholarship with insight in discussing this interplay between Spanish teaching and Indian interpretation, and shows many examples of artistic independence within the historic Spanish framework.

In the field of Mexican popular arts, still fresh and vital today, the Indian influence is strongly dominant.

[9] The name Tepa written into the Singer copy of *Life in Mexico* makes reasonably certain what apparently has not before been realized: that this very set of figures, minus some casualties, survives in Madrid today, in the custody of the recently established Museo de América. A pamphlet of 1934—entitled *Las Figuras Mexicanas de Cera en el Museo Arqueológico de Madrid*, by Genaro Estrada—says that the collection was donated to that museum in 1877 by Don Ignacio Muñoz de Baena y Goyeneche, Marqués de Prado Alegre. Published genealogies show that the donor had a maternal uncle, Don José de Goyeneche y Viana, who in 1829 had inherited the title of third Conde de Tepa. Related to both José Adalid and Count Cortina, he was presumably the recipient of the magnificent gift from Mexico.

According to the descriptive pamphlet, the date of 1840 is assigned to the collection by virtue of the costuming. The set now numbers 134 pieces. They vary in height from seven to fourteen inches. Most of them bear the name of their forgotten maker, Andrés García. The collection is considered to be the most complete of its kind, either in or out of Mexico. Plate 128 shows one of the spirited representations.

[10] At this point Fanny pasted into Volume 3 of her Journal an undated note, addressed to *Mi querida Fany*, and signed by her friend Luz Escandón. Its text is not quoted here because much of the brief letter, which seems to deal with practical arrangements and a deferred visit, is obscure (although somewhat more intelligible if read aloud). It illustrates the point under discussion in that, although agreeably expressed, it is unconventionally spelled and written in an unformed hand. Fanny as a former schoolteacher seems to have indicated disapprobation by placing x marks near a number of errors.

[11] The wording of this sentence in the original Journal is not restricted to children, but refers to "the extraordinary disposition of the Mexicans for music and drawing."

[12] For print, Fanny lengthened the age of innocence by a year or two, and pluralized "the old woman" teacher. She made a number of such adjustments in this chapter.

[13] For publication, Fanny was a little gentler, increasing her "three married women" to "above half a dozen," and broadening "open a book" to "read any one book through."

Here, in chronological order, is what four other observers said about the education of Mexican women. H. G. Ward wrote fifteen years earlier: "Their manners and education are just what a person acquainted with Spain would expect to find in a Spanish colony. So little is required of women in the Mother-country, that it would be hardly fair to expect any very great intellectual superiority amongst their descendants. The Mexican ladies, (with some brilliant exceptions, whom it would perhaps be invidious to name,) read and write in about the same proportion as those of Madrid; they speak, in general, no language but their own, and have not much taste for music, or knowledge of it as an art." Ward later continued: "But in return, they have no affectation or hauteur, they are kind and unpretending to the highest degree, and do the honours of their houses with perfect ease and propriety." (*Mexico in 1827,* II, 715–16.)

George F. Ruxton, an Englishman who in the 1840's found little that pleased him in Mexico, excepted Mexican women from his criticisms: "The Mexican ladies are totally uneducated, and in the presence of foreigners, conscious of their inferiority, are usually shy and reserved. This, of course, refers only to general society. In their own houses, and among themselves, they are vivacious, and unaffectedly pleasing in their manners and conversation; and in all classes is evinced a warmth of heart and sympathy which wins for the women of Mexico the respect and esteem of all strangers." (*Adventures in Mexico* . . . , pp. 56–57.)

A. K. Shepard, visiting from the United States, made comparisons in the late 1850's with what he knew at home: "Young ladies are usually educated in convents; and for accomplishments, languages, music, &c., they compare very favorably with the graduates of most flashy seminaries and fashionable boarding-schools, where execrable piano pounding and bad French and Italian are generally thought by admiring mammas to be the most important branches of a good education." (*Land of the Aztecs,* p. 77.)

Countess Paula Kollonitz, who some twenty years after Fanny's time accompanied the Empress Carlota to Mexico, admired most of the Mexican women she met, but did not hesitate to comment on their educational shortcomings. Except for the prayer book, she said, she never saw a Mexican woman with a book in her hands. Their knowledge of geography was fragmentary. "Europe to them consists of Spain, from whence they sprang; Rome, where the Pope rules; and Paris, from whence come their clothes." (*Court of Mexico,* p. 161.)

[14] From *Beppo, A Venetian Story,* by Byron, Stanza LXXII. The particular stanza is an aside, speculating on harem life.

[15] This quotation is from the *Calendario de las Señoritas Megicanas* for the year 1838. (The last word of the title was spelled by the bookbinder in its more usual form as *Mexicanas.*) It and its companion volumes, edited by Mariano Galván, are minute little annuals which contain various informative articles as well as a calendar covering holy days, saints' days, and phases of the moon. The volume for 1838 includes, for example, detailed instructions on the propagation of plants and another on the history of the sanctuary of Guadalupe. Like others of the series, it is rounded out with charmingly colored fashion drawings (see Plates 58, 59, and 60).

In the field of education, there had appeared in Mexico in 1839 the first volume of the *Diario de los Niños.* This included poetry, drawing lessons, essays on history, lessons in botany and chemistry (with diagrams), engravings depicting monuments of antiquity, and a recipe for indelible ink. The year 1841 would see the publication of the first volume of the *Semanario de las Señoritas Mexicanas,* with instructive articles on many subjects.

[16] From *Divine and Moral Songs for Children,* by Isaac Watts: Song XX, "Against Idleness," which opens with the much better-remembered lines ". . . How doth the little busy bee/Improve each shining hour . . ."

[17] This is Fanny's sole mention of Doña Narcisa Castrillo, wife of the prominent Lucas Alamán. She was just Fanny's age—thirty-five—but, having been married young, she was the mother of a large family of children. Alamán's modern biographer, who reproduced both a portrait of her and a photograph in which she figured, surmised that the plump, matronly-looking Doña Narcisa was no intellectual match for her brilliant husband. (Valadés, *Alamán,* pp. 24, 90–91, 159.) But someone who knew her remembered her as endowed with angelic kindness, and said that she and her husband headed a quiet, pious, well-regulated household. (Prieto, *Memorias* . . . , II, 236.)

The young Condesa del Peñasco, whose unconventionally acquired children prompted Fanny's discussion here, is in genealogical résumés only a name: Vicenta Irolo. One notes that she bore no children to the count, whose descendants, intertwined with the Cervantes and Cuevas families, all stem from his first marriage.

The Conde del Peñasco's private museum, referred to by Fanny as his gallery, is mentioned in other writings of the time. Albert M. Gilliam, United States consul of three years later, may have glimpsed the beautiful second wife in the course of seeing the well-known collection. He describes calling on the count, whose name he tried to spell phonetically as the Conde Paniaski. After inspecting paintings, oriental curios, cases of minerals, ancient Mexican manuscripts, and a pickled two-headed baby, Gilliam reported himself as all but overcome by the beauty of a young woman who walked by the door of the room. (*Travels in Mexico* . . . , pp. 71–73.)

[18] The same susceptible consular officer cited in the note just above found the Mexican girls irresistible, not after a few years but *pronto:* "The expression of their countenance, in general, is distinguished for its mildness and gentleness; this, added to their suavity and languishing air, makes their deportment peculiarly interesting; and, I could almost say that to see one of them is to love her." (Gilliam, *Travels in Mexico* . . . , p. 97.)

24. The President Seized in His Bed

[1] The reader will soon see why a revolution was frequently called a *pronunciamiento*. The printing press and speech-making were weapons no less to be relied upon than cannons. The ammunition consisted of such words as glory, honor, duty, and intrepidity—seduction, sedition, and machinations—execration and infamy. What will shortly be referred to as "the lowest populace" was well accustomed to overturns of government, but was equally accustomed to little in the way of tangible benefits other than possibly a brief period of lawless looting.

In theory the basic issue involved in this revolution was federalism versus centralism—Mexican names for the opposing viewpoints between liberals and conservatives, typical of many countries and times. The more liberal federalists, dominant for a while after the overthrow of the Emperor Iturbide and at other periods since, were out of power at this time. In general they wanted as the embodiment of national policy a document similar to the supplanted constitution of 1824, under which Mexican state governments wielded strong influence. (Their program of objectives during this particular revolution will be given by Fanny at the start of the next chapter.) The more conservative centralists, whose principles were embodied in the constitution of 1836, believed in a more authoritarian and centralized national government. Their constitution at this time was the law of the land, and Mexico was administered under departments rather than states, with each department headed by a military governor.

In practice, *pronunciamientos* often lacked the simplicity of a struggle based on clear-cut principles. What complicated them, and sometimes rendered them intellectually and economically meaningless, was the cynical opportunism of some of the high-ranking military figures of the day.

[2] Because of the irregularity of newspaper publication during this period of civil strife, Fanny's intimate day-by-day report has more than usual historic value, and works covering this period of Mexican history have frequently used *Life in Mexico* as a source.

General Urrea, with a notable past record for heading revolutionary endeavors, had for some months been imprisoned in the capital but on the night of July 14–15 was freed by troops friendly to his cause. A group of prominent men—among them the Archbishop—had earlier petitioned Bustamante on Urrea's behalf, not, apparently, because they agreed with Urrea's views, but because they felt that his incarceration without recourse to counsel was unfair and unhandsome treatment. (*Diario del Gobierno*, January 30, 1840; *Cosmopolita*, May 13 and 16, 1840.)

As to Gómez Farías (who, according to other accounts of the affair, did not personally take part in the seizure of the President), he has already been mentioned in note 7 on pages 721–22 as an outstanding Mexican and zealous reformer.

The interruption of the President's sleep seems to have been accomplished with true Latin suavity: "Fear not, my general, I am Urrea," said the latter; to which President Bustamante—wishing, perhaps, that he had disposed of his lively foe more securely—cried out: "You are an ungrateful rogue! If you are a man, fight with me, body to body." At this point some of the invading party proposed to shoot Bustamante forthwith, but one, whose name has been recorded as Captain Marrón, interrupted with the urgent plea: "Don't fire! He was the ally of Iturbide!" (Bustamante, *Gabinete Mexicano*, II, 62–64.)

[3] Calderón was aware early in his stay of the potential usefulness of a flag for the legation, "so necessary in moments of revolution," for he thus wrote his government in a dispatch of late January. (*Despachos Generales*, I, 31.)

Manuel Martínez del Campo was the rich Spanish merchant who, it will be remembered, had welcomed the Calderóns to the capital.

The filling in of blanks or partial blanks in this chapter derives from handwritten notations in the Singer copy.

[4] The heavy-set soldier-president, just sixty years old that week, is said to have displayed his customary coolness during his brief captivity. He inquired if Captain Marrón had saved his life only to starve him to death and, when a meal was subsequently brought, ate with matter-of-fact relish while balls (being fired by his own troops trying to recapture the palace) crashed into the room in which he sat. A ball did strike Marrón, injuring his leg so severely that it later had to be amputated. Bustamante is known to have paid the insurgent officer a pension out of his own pocket in recognition of his debt to him. (Bustamante, *Gabinete Mexicano*, II, 70–71.)

[5] By occupying the national palace, Gómez Farías and Urrea had access to the government printing press which it housed. They began at once to use this weapon by issuing a

series of bulletins, some of which Fanny will quote. Meanwhile, Bustamante's government issued its own pronouncements, and it is one of these emergency bulletins that is quoted.

6 The citadel, called by Mexicans the Ciudadela, was outside the built-up area, in what was then almost open country. It is now of course in the heart of the city, a few blocks south and slightly west of the Alameda. The massiveness of the large low structure was an asset to the troops ensconced within, and throughout the firing here described the Ciudadela served as headquarters for the government forces trying to dislodge the insurgents from the national palace. Each side also seized church towers as vantage points from which to fire.

7 The revolutionaries or *pronunciados* insisted that the President had not escaped, but had been allowed to depart from the palace with the understanding that he bore definite terms of peace from the insurgents and would work for agreement between factions. Bustamante, however, maintained that he had made no promise of any kind except to mediate in an effort to avoid needless bloodshed. (Bustamante, *Gabinete Mexicano*, II, 69; Zamacois, *Historia de Méjico*, XII, 204.)

The situation at this time inside the national palace may be judged from Plate 53.

8 Fanny's reference to the Condesa del Valle's father may be correct, but one wonders whether she may not have meant the lady's father-in-law, Andrés Suárez de Peredo, eighth Conde del Valle de Orizaba, who was attacked in the presence of his wife and daughters in a barbarous episode during the revolution of the Acordada on December 4, 1828. He bled to death on the great stone staircase of his palatial family residence— familiar to every North American visitor as the House of Tiles, on what is now called the Avenida Madero. The berserk artillery officer who led the assault (he was rumored to have been refused the hand of one of the count's daughters) roved through the house, wrecking furniture and smashing glass. Justice eventually caught up with the assassin. The place chosen for his execution was outside the House of Tiles. (Manuel Rivera Cambas, *México Pintoresco, Artístico, y Monumental*, I, 231–33; Manuel Romero de Terreros, *Residencias Coloniales de México*, pp. xxxv–vi; Luis González Obregón, *The Streets of Mexico*, p. 18.)

The no longer existing house of the Escandóns was just west of the House of Tiles.

9 Estanislao Flores and his brother Joaquín were rich merchants who owned—in addition to other properties—a large shop in the capital's central bazaar, the Parián. (Prieto, *Memorias* . . . , II, 155–56.)

10 The original Spanish is "a la vez," which in her published text Fanny rather confusingly translated as "instead of."

11 It is our guess that Señora Barbachano was Doña Guadalupe Iniestra de Barbachano, whose name appears as a subscriber to the *Mosaico Mexicano* in 1840, and to a ladies' magazine in 1841. She was presumably the wife of Manuel Barbachano from Yucatán. He and his family occupied an apartment in the entresol of the House of Tiles— the damage to which has recently been mentioned. Señor Barbachano, who had spent some years in Spain, was a member of congress. (Prieto, *Memorias* . . . , II, 314–15; Sosa, *Biografías de Mexicanos Distinguidos*, pp. 124–26.)

12 Dr. Juan Plane has been mentioned as the physician involved in litigation over his thumping fee for medical services rendered to the dying sister of La Güera Rodríguez. Because of his prominence, his death (just as he was about to return to France) provoked widespread comment, as exemplifying the number of innocent civilians who were killed in the revolution. (Fossey, *Le Mexique*, p. 518.) Dr. Plane had gone to the palace to treat the badly wounded Captain Marrón, the insurgent officer who was said to have been responsible for sparing President Bustamante's life.

13 An Englishwoman who visited Mexico during a slightly later period of civil strife was struck by the aplomb with which Mexican women carried on in the face of revolution. She observed from her hotel window a Mexican lady who continued to appear daily on her balcony in the midst of cannonading in order to water her cherished plants. Only when a flower pot was cut in two by a ball as she was bending over it did she make a dignified retreat. (Stuart-Wortley, *Travels* . . . , II, 187.)

14 This convent—whose church still stands—was just east and a little north of the Alameda.

15 Gómez Farías was a highly controversial figure in his own time and later. The words Fanny quotes near the beginning of the paragraph and some of what follows show that she was familiar with the work of a Mexican liberal in exile, whose trenchant political discussions had been issued not long before in book form: *Obras Sueltas de José María Luis Mora, Ciudadano Mejicano*. (His observations on Gómez Farías, whom he deeply admired, were part of his first volume, pp. LXXXVIII–XCI.)

Another Mexican of about this time described Gómez Farías as stubborn to the point of being unrealistic about practicable objectives, but granted him the possession of pure, unselfish patriotism. (José Fernando Ramírez, *Mexico during the War with the United States*, edited by Walter V. Scholes and translated by Elliott B. Scherr, p. 109.)

To the conservative Calderón, the leader whose ideas had helped to ignite this *pronunciamiento* was a fanatic, a demagogue, and a tyrant—for he so characterized Gómez Farías in the first of his dispatches dealing with the revolution. Calderón was convinced that a federalist triumph would mean a rise in anti-Spanish sentiment. (*Despachos Generales*, I, 125, 128.)

A modern Mexican historian, writing after his country's upheaval of the early twentieth century, ranks Gómez Farías—in view of his attempts to modernize the political and social structure of Mexico—as the real father of the later Reform movement, and a forerunner of the great liberal leader Benito Juárez. (Alfonso Teja Zabre, *Guide to the History of Mexico*, p. 293.)

[16] By "branch" Fanny presumably meant a segment, for she earlier has made it clear that their street—called both San Fernando and Puente de Alvarado—was a part of the Calle de Tacuba which extended westward, following the route of the ancient causeway.

[17] Calderón—who occasionally gives evidence of being more of a worrier than his wife—tells in a subsequent dispatch of his disquiet over the fact that Don Manuel Lasquetti had brought a large sum in gold to the Spanish legation for safekeeping during this troubled time. (*Despachos Generales*, I, 129.) Lasquetti, according to other memoirs, was a Spaniard and the nephew of a former viceroy, but had married a beautiful Mexican. (Augusto Conte, *Recuerdos de un Diplomático*, I, 294.)

[18] This was almost certainly General José María Tornel, who will be identified as the Calderóns' close neighbor by a later notation in the Singer copy. The historian Zavala had described Tornel in almost the same terms—as the possessor of a "*carácter frívolo*," and as likely to act in political matters from expediency rather than conscience. (*Ensayo Histórico . . . ,* II, 46–47.)

[19] Perhaps this was Ignacio Iniestra (at this time a captain), whom the Calderóns will come to know very well. In reviewing the events of this revolution the government newspaper refers to his effective conduct. (*Diario del Gobierno*, August 12, 1840.)

[20] Plate 54 depicts this very incident. The Garita de San Lázaro, the main city gate toward Puebla, was in open fields about a dozen blocks due east of the cathedral. A part of this old tax-collection point—which the Calderóns had passed when first entering the capital on a rainy night the previous December—still survives. It consists of arched stone *portales* on the south side of the intersection of the Calle Emiliano Zapata with the Avenida Francisco Morazán.

[21] This was Anastasio Torrejón, who, like many other officers mentioned in this book, would play a part in the coming United States-Mexican War.

[22] This pronouncement, on a single sheet, dated July 20, 1840, was issued by Valencia, who termed himself "General in Chief of the Army of Operation against the Rebels of This Capital." The editors have filled in two omissions and have taken the liberty of slightly modifying Fanny's translation.

[23] Whether the doughty mother was the wife of the statesman and dramatist, or of another Gorostiza, we do not know. The names of the cadets at this time are on record, but no Gorostiza is listed among them. Perhaps the boy was the son of a former marriage.

The cadets of the military college were a not inconsequential force in view of the relatively small bodies of troops actually involved as combatants in this revolution. The insurgents tried to woo the boys into their camp, but without success. They marched out with alacrity on behalf of the government, pulling their one cannon—a welcome asset —with them. On order of their commander, Colonel Pedro García Conde, the service of the younger cadets was limited to guarding the citadel, base for the government forces. The older ones, however, manfully held the tower of the church of Jesús Nazareno. (Gabriel Cuevas, *El Glorioso Colegio Militar Mexicano en un Siglo* (1824–1924), pp. 47–51.)

[24] Valencia (see Plate 72) is described in another source as a big-shouldered active man, humble in origin, ignorant, and on the make—but not lacking, apparently, in attractive qualities and personal bravery. (Prieto, *Memorias . . . ,* II, 213–14.) Calderón, however, reported that Valencia was considered an opportunist "who spends his life drinking, gaming, and among courtesans." (*Despachos Generales*, I, 145.)

[25] General Pánfilo Galindo was *comandante* and governor of Michoacán, with headquarters in the provincial city of Morelia. General Victoria, the former president, was, it will be remembered, *comandante* of Veracruz. News as to how various strong local leaders might cast their lots—and their troops—would be significant.

[26] Colonel Luis Gonzaga Vieyra was governor of the capital district of Mexico.

27 As the reader may recall, the two easternmost blocks of the Avenida Madero, directly across the plaza from the national palace, were formerly called the Calle de Pláteros. The hospital of San Andrés stood opposite the Minería on the north.

28 In the sequence of events this letter belongs earlier in the chapter, as it deals with the President's captivity in the national palace—apparently before he knew he would soon be set at liberty by the insurgents. The President had an ally during his brief incarceration of whom his captors were unaware: the aged gardener, Juan Lázari, whom Fanny had noticed pottering about when she made a visit to the botanic garden in the palace courtyard during a more peaceful time. Lázari is recorded as the bearer of this message from the captive Bustamante to his cabinet. (Bustamante, Gabinete Mexicano, II, 63; Zamacois, Historia de Méjico, XII, 198.)

29 Dick Turpin was a real British highwayman, executed in 1739 at York. Paul Clifford was an imaginary one, hero of the novel of the same name by Edward Bulwer Lytton, published in 1830; its first edition sold out on the day of publication.

30 The large prison called the Acordada—just west of the southwest corner of the Alameda—was only a few blocks from the Calderóns' house.

31 The alcabala, or internal duty on goods passing from one area to another, has been mentioned before. It was an extremely important source of government revenue and in consequence was slow to disappear; withdrawn at various times, it was always re-established.

A visitor from the United States decades later described the final end of the system, and recorded that on July 1, 1896 the municipal customs gates of the city of Mexico finally stood open and unguarded. (Charles F. Lummis, The Awakening of a Nation, p. 38.)

32 Urrea's dealings with the French at the time of the hostilities between France and Mexico (the Pastry War, mentioned earlier on p. 53) occurred after the capture of San Juan de Ulúa by Admiral Baudin and during the interval preceding final peace negotiations. Urrea, who was in 1838 heading a federalist uprising against the central Mexican government—just as he was at this present time in July 1840—had originally denounced French aggression. In December 1838, Baudin dispatched ships and a letter to Tampico, then held by Urrea. The French and the dissident Mexicans seem to have sounded each other out without making any commitments to work together against the central Mexican regime. But Baudin did lift his blockade of federalist-held ports, and he did obtain much-needed water and, perhaps, provisions. In addition, Urrea's federalists benefited from the revenue collected at the unblocked ports they controlled. (Maissin, The French in Mexico and Texas, pp. 65–66, 71–72; Riva Palacio, México a Través de los Siglos, IV, 433–34.)

33 A minor mystery surrounds this issue from the series of special bulletins put out by the government during the revolution (as a substitute for the Diario del Gobierno which in quieter times was printed on a press apparently located in the national palace). Felipe Teixidor reproduces the masthead from a copy. It shows the dashing pony, the rider with trumpet and streaming banner, and the milestone—but there are no captions. (La Vida en México, I, Notas, 130.)

34 It was not Mme de Staël, but an unnamed lady whom she cited (in 1797, after the Reign of Terror). Napoleon said: "Madame, I don't like women to mix in politics." The lady retorted: "You are right, general, but in a country where heads are cut off, it is natural that women should like to know why." (Considérations sur les principaux événements de la révolution françoise, II, 201—edition of 1818.)

25. Quiet after the Cannonading

1 The material here presented covers what the federalists had hoped to achieve by the revolution just ended, not what was actually accomplished. In fact, nothing was accomplished. When the revolution was over, newspapers began to catch up with events, and Fanny in the next several paragraphs does likewise. (The plan of Gómez Farías had first been issued on a single sheet, printed in the national palace on July 19, while the federalist forces held it.)

2 This letter from the Archbishop was evidently published in rebuttal to the earlier government bulletin which Fanny mentioned in her entry of July 21 (p. 308). It was in the form of a personal communication to Gómez Farías, dated July 22, 1840. El Cosmopolita published it on July 29.

A Mexican who knew the Archbishop personally spoke of him as a man not only of charity but also of good sense, as evidenced by his honest efforts to bring the contending parties together at this critical time. (José María Bocanegra, Historia de México Independiente, 1822–1846, II, 797–98.)

[3] It appears that Gómez Farías and Urrea were not included in the general amnesty. Fanny's text read "stipulated for by them." We have omitted the last three words as unclear. By "the preceding night" Fanny apparently meant earlier the same night of July 26–27.

[4] So said Pyrrhus, king of Epirus, when he defeated the Romans in 279 B.C., but with heavy losses to his own side.

[5] Only a country thoroughly experienced in revolutions could have dealt so expertly with the liquidation of one just over.

The settlement terms agreed to by both sides were printed in the Diario del Gobierno of July 28 (Vol. 17, p. 293).

One account explains the mild terms and lack of punishment for the rebels on the ground that throughout the combat it was apparent that neither side had decisive strength. The government troops could not eject the rebels from the national palace, official seat of the government; and the rebels lacked the force to effect a change of government. (Zamacois, Historia de Méjico, XII, 204–10.)

[6] General Valencia, who had no pretension to a literary education, seems to have shared the natural gift of many of his countrymen for politics. As Fanny has already noted, he had his eye on the presidency—which he never achieved, even though during the next few years about a dozen different men served as heads of the government. On July 30 he followed up with a pronouncement calculated to win more friends: "Fellow Citizens: My conduct has been circumspect, fair, moderate, and cautious, with the sole object that the country in which I first saw light might tranquillize itself; such is the wish of your fellow countryman and friend Gabriel Valencia." (Diario del Gobierno, Vol. 17, p. 302.)

[7] The young diplomat who survived typhus under Fanny's roof was sufficiently recovered within a few weeks to undertake an ocean voyage. The Diario del Gobierno for October 15, 1840 noted the recent departure of "Louis Price," secretary to the Belgian legation.

The names provided in this chapter and in that following are derived from the Singer copy.

[8] Plate 55 shows some of the havoc. It is a view looking toward the cathedral from the southwest corner of the plaza—at what is now the intersection of the Avenida del 16 de Septiembre and the Calle del Cinco de Febrero, formerly known at this location as the Monterilla. (The building in the center is the no-longer-existing Parián, mentioned by Fanny on p. 200).

[9] A careful observer of the time, Carlos María de Bustamante, reported that the total casualty list—which included a large proportion of civilians—was 177 dead and 198 wounded. (Gabinete Mexicano, II, 80.)

[10] This saying (attributed to William of Orange) seems to have been paraphrased and quoted often. Perhaps Fanny was thinking of a passage in Chapter 19 of The Pickwick Papers describing the flighty marksmanship of Mr. Winkle: "It is an established axiom that every bullet has its billet."

[11] It appears from a pamphlet written about the House of Tiles by a distinguished student of the past that the Condes del Valle owned and lived in the house until after the fall of Maximilian. (Manuel Romero de Terreros, La Casa de los Azulejos, p. 37.) Fanny must have been in and out of the famous landmark many times.

[12] As a supplement to Fanny's account of the revolution, we insert the comments of another shrewd observer—of special interest as clarifying the actual and potential role of Santa Anna in the whole affair. It is that of Richard Pakenham, British minister to Mexico, summarizing revolutionary events up to this point for the benefit of his chief, Lord Palmerston. (Dispatch dated July 29, F. O. 50/136. This unpublished Crown-copyright material in the Public Record Office, London, is reproduced by permission of the Controller of H. M. Stationery Office.)
"My Lord,
"Since I last had the honour of addressing your Lordship, occurrences of a very serious character have taken place in this Capital.
"On the morning of the 15th Inst. we were surprised by the news that in the course of the previous night the troops at the palace had revolted and seized the President, General Bustamante, the Commandant, General Filisola, and other military Authorities, proclaiming at the same time the reestablishment of the Federal Constitution of 1824. Some of the other troops forming the garrison of Mexico also joined in the revolt, so as to increase the number of the Insurgents to a force equal, if not superior to that remaining faithful to the Government; and it can hardly be doubted that if they had followed up their first success with boldness and activity, they might have made themselves masters of the whole City, and thus greatly increased their chance of effecting the object of the Revolution.

"After a few hours, however, General Valencia, the Chief of the Staff, was able to collect a sufficient force to assume the offensive; an attack was then commenced, although
not a close one, with cannon and musketry on the Palace and other positions occupied by
the Insurgents, which continued, with occasional interruptions, until the evening of Sunday
the 26th, that is to say, for eleven days and nights, when the main body of the Insurgents surrendered by capitulation.

"The number of the killed and wounded of the actual combatants may amount on both
sides to about four hundred, but a great many casualties have occurred to private individuals whom necessity or curiosity had led abroad during the combat. The damage done
to the palace and to many publick buildings and private houses is considerable, but it is
satisfactory to be able to add that the affair has been brought to a close without pillage or
other acts of violence independent of military operations; and great credit is unquestionably due to the leaders on both sides for the pains taken by them for the protection of
property and the prevention of excesses on the part of the populace or soldiery. . . .

"The persons who took the lead in this daring insurrection were Don Valentin Gomez
Farias, whom your Lordship may recollect as filling the office of Vice President and occasionally administering the Government during the ascendancy of the popular party in the
years 1833, and 1834, and General Urrea, who has within the last three years distinguished himself by a series of attempts of the same description.

"Farias is a political fanatic, whom I believe to have acted from honest motives. Urrea
is a wicked and unprincipled character, who has no other object than his own aggrandise-
ment, and from whose accession to power, had he succeeded, no good whatever could
have been expected.

"On the second morning of the insurrection the Revolutionary leaders thought proper
to set the President at liberty, with the understanding, as is alleged on their side, that he
was to exert his influence to effect an accommodation between the belligerents, which, as
matters then stood, could have only been brought about by some important concessions in
favour of the Revolution: but General Bustamante asserts that he refused to commit himself by any pledge beyond that of endeavouring to put a stop to the effusion of blood.

"The real object of the Insurgents in restoring General Bustamante to liberty I imagine to have been to keep alive, at all events, an influence intermediate between them
and General Santa Ana, who is personally an object of especial hatred to both Gomez
Farias and Urrea, and not less so politically to all adherents to the popular party; for it
was obvious that the continued imprisonment of the President would have afforded to
General Santa Ana an opportunity too favourable to be neglected of assuming per se
the chief civil and military authority; under which circumstances he would have carried on
the war against the Federalists with an energy and determination not perhaps to be expected from him when acting simply in support of the feeble administration of General
Bustamante.

"As it is, I think it by no means certain that General Santa Ana will content himself with
acting a subordinate part on this occasion.

"When the news of what had happened in Mexico reached Vera Cruz, near which place
General Santa Ana resides, it was agreed between him and General Victoria, the Commandant General of the Department, that General Santa Ana should immediately take the
command of the disposable troops in that part of the Country, and proceed to Mexico to
assist in the restoration of order. He accordingly began his march on the 19th, and when
last heard of he had already got as far as Perote, about one third of the whole distance.
He must by this time have received news of the termination of the insurrection in Mexico;
and it remains to be seen whether he will be satisfied to retrace his steps quietly to Vera
Cruz, or whether, pleading the generally disorganized state of the Country, and the too
evident feebleness and inefficiency of the present Administration, he may not think proper
to take upon himself the task of reconstructing the Government upon a different basis, to
the exclusion as well of General Bustamante, as of the parties concerned in the late
Revolutionary movement.

"On the night of the 25th, that previous to the capitulation, General Urrea, and Don
Valentin Gomez Farias, considering their attempt as hopeless, withdrew from the scene of
action. They are accordingly not understood to be included in the capitulation. The other
persons openly engaged in the business are comparatively insignificant: this, and a desire to prevent the further destruction of life and injury to the City are the reasons assigned on the part of the Government for having granted to the Insurgents a free pardon
on condition of laying down their arms; a degree of lenity almost repugnant to justice,
considering the gravity of their offence, and the calamities to which it had given rise.

"We have not heard that movements of any importance in combination with the late
attempt in Mexico have taken place in other parts of the Republick. If any should be attempted it is to be supposed that the failure of the revolt here will lead to their speedy
suppression.

"I must not omit to mention in justice to the parties concerned in the late revolt, that among the measures of reform promised by them, in the event of success, were the repeal of the late addition to the inland duties on Foreign Merchandise, the restitution of what has hitherto been recovered under that head, and the abolition of internal Customs duties throughout the Country. On this account alone the failure of the enterprise, however unhallowed in other respects, is almost to be regretted.

"I have the honour to be with the greatest respect, my Lord, your Lordship's most obedient humble Servant

R. Pakenham"

[13] Gómez Farías, a reformer ahead of his time, later slipped out of Mexico and found refuge in New Orleans. Fanny never mentions him again. He would serve as vice-president of Mexico in 1846, and as acting president for three months in 1847.

[14] The village of La Piedad lay in open country between Tacubaya and Santa Anita. Its church no longer exists.

26. "This Awful Penance"

[1] Calderón's host—whose name, like that of others in this chapter, is derived from the Singer copy—was Gregorio de Mier y Terán, sometimes referred to as the Rothschild of Mexico. He owned two haciendas in the valley of Toluca. From a subsequent reference, it seems likely that Calderón's visit was to the property called San Nicolás Peralta.

[2] The revolution had in reality been over about a month by the date that heads this chapter. Internal evidence suggests that Fanny drew here on a letter written earlier. (In the next paragraph she speaks of the dearth of rain, while three paragraphs later the rainy season is reported to be at its height.)

[3] A brief newspaper article which appeared after his departure characterized the baron—rather a shadowy figure in these pages—as a learned and tactful man; and spoke of the fact that he took with him for ratification at home a treaty of friendship and commerce between Belgium and Mexico. (Diario del Gobierno, September 5, 1840.)

[4] For the last two items Fanny substituted for print "the gentleman's diamond pin, the child's frock."

[5] Marguerite, Countess of Blessington (1789–1849), was a spirited unconventional Irishwoman who in her widowhood took to the pen. One of her best known books, Victims of Society, was published in 1838.

[6] The movements of the four-vessel navy of independent Texas—whose secession in 1836 had never been recognized by Mexico—are best explained in terms of events within Mexico. Yucatán had been conducting since 1839 a federalist uprising and, together with the department of Tabasco, in June 1840 declared its independence from Mexico. On friendly terms with Texas, Yucatán lent support to the Texan naval vessels which at various times from 1840 to 1843 cruised along the Gulf coast and stopped at ports in Yucatán. Calderón, whose government likewise had not recognized the independence of Texas, advised Spanish naval authorities to avoid incidents from any possible encounter with the anomalous Texans. (Despachos Generales, I, 155–56, 160–62.)

[7] Catherine Macleod, youngest child of Fanny's older sister. Kate, as the young girl seems always to have been called, will later appear on the Mexican scene.

[8] Smallpox, brought into Mexico by the Spaniards, had proved an important ally in the conquest of some three hundred years earlier. In the first years of the sixteenth century it is credited with the destruction in Mexico of more than three million aborigines.

Edward Jenner proved the efficacy of vaccination in 1796, and the practice spread quickly thereafter.

[9] This quotation (from Zavala's Ensayo Histórico . . . , I, 56) is part of a discussion of the fact that Hidalgo operated without a plan—at first, even, without a definite goal.

[10] The large house belonging to the Calderóns' friends the Escandóns appears at the extreme left of Plate 39. Fanny and her hosts undoubtedly sat on one of the balconies shown. The noticeable extra width of the street at this point—formerly called the Plazuela de Guardiola—still remains.

[11] According to the Diario del Gobierno of the next day, the Independence Day celebration of 1840 began with a salvo of artillery at dawn, and continued with a Te Deum in the cathedral attended by high officials and a parade from the national palace to the Alameda. It was this parade that Fanny witnessed. Fireworks, somewhat dampened by rain, followed in the evening.

Calderón, as representative of the mother country, was averse to the idea of attending the festivities in general, and of listening to the anti-Spanish Tornel, whom he disliked, in particular. As he explained in a dispatch, he planned to plead illness if invited.

But luckily the feud over precedence, initiated by the Baron de Cyprey the previous May (p. 249), was still smoldering, with the result that no diplomats were in official attendance. They were asked, however, to lend their flags and Calderón, after cautious inquiries of other legations, complied. (*Despachos Generales*, I, 146–47.)

Tornel, a fine orator and a handsome man—and well aware of these assets according to other memoirs of the period—must have made an effective appearance. (For his likeness, see Plate 73.) However, beyond referring to the heroes of the independence as martyrs, he made none of the inimical remarks about Spain that Calderón had anticipated. His main concern was rather with Mexico's difficult present. He prefaced this concern with a mournful review of the rise and fall of individuals and nations, running rapidly through history beginning with Job and including Louis XVI. Independent Mexico, he said, had navigated through a sea of blood and tears for many years without reaching a port. He called on his hearers to swear on the tombs of Hidalgo, Morelos, and Iturbide to guard the heritage of self-government they had won. "There is no hope for us, no future, no happiness, except in the strengthening and triumph of the republic."

Tornel's speech made a strong impression, according to the newspaper *El Cosmopolita* of September 23, which reproduced it. The oration also found its way into more permanent form in a collection entitled *Galería de Oradores Mexicanos en el Siglo XIX*, edited by Emilio del Castillo Negrete (I, 276–87).

The newspaper published by Spaniards in Mexico—*La Hesperia*—dealt with this anniversary of the initiation of Mexico's struggle to achieve independence from Spain through the simple expedient of saying nothing whatsoever about it.

[12] Pieced-together information suggests that the host was Joseph-Charles-Edouard de Lisle, French legation member who had recently inherited the title of Marquis de Siry.

This party marked the beginning of the end of a lively diplomatic fracas to which Fanny makes no allusion at all. While the affair was of no importance—and the reader may skip all that follows with impunity—the account is included for the light it casts on the unforeseeable hazards of Calderón's profession. The story, based on Calderón's dispatch written the next day, September 25 (*Despachos Generales*, I, 148–51), is as follows:

The Comte de Breteuil of the French legation—whom Calderón termed a dissipated, harebrained youth of distinguished family—had directed a letter to a resident Frenchman, to be carried by hand. His servant delivered it by error to the tavern operated by one Francisco Solares, who was Mexican by naturalization though Spanish by birth (from which circumstance Calderón became involved). An employee of Solares opened the letter and, according to his own statement, realized that an error had been made and returned it to the bearer. According to the opposing side, however, he tore the letter across before restoring it, accompanying the action by insulting jibes about France and the French. The truth, Calderón sagely noted, probably lay somewhere in middle ground.

The count, informed of events by his servant, repaired to the tavern and commenced violent action, accompanying blows by forceful allusions to what he considered the cowardliness of both Mexicans and Spaniards. The tavern *mozo*—countering with what ammunition he had at hand—threw a salvo of bottles. The count retreated and sought counsel from his chief, the high-tempered Baron de Cyprey, who ordered him to seek out reinforcements among the resident Frenchmen and return to the attack. The count complied, and the French combatants battered their way into the tavern, whose occupying party meanwhile seems to have augmented its own forces. Insults were hotly exchanged but before any casualties occurred someone notified the local patrol, and the French party withdrew.

Juan de Dios Cañedo, the Mexican Minister of Foreign Affairs, was soon the recipient of a stormy visit from the Baron de Cyprey. The latter demanded arrest and banishment for the taverner and the closing down of his establishment. In the course of a long harangue the baron exclaimed: "I see the hand of the Spanish minister in this!" "Just how?" said Cañedo, who went on to point out Calderón's lack of involvement in the whole affair. The baron, however, stormed on. "This is simply a tavern brawl," maintained Cañedo. "What!" cried the baron, "It's an affair between Frenchmen and Spaniards." "I said a tavern brawl," insisted the Mexican Minister of Foreign Affairs, "the count's high birth should prevent him from carrying on a dispute with a taverner." "Well, the Spanish minister and I are equals!" retorted the baron, "we can fight it out." "You two make of it what you please," concluded the harassed Cañedo.

Whereupon, by recounting the incident to Calderón, Cañedo let the latter know what to expect. Calderón's response was to warn all the resident Spaniards not to permit themselves to be provoked into any incident that might lead to trouble.

In the light of all this, one can imagine the total lack of enthusiasm with which the Calderóns must have set forth for the fête so briefly mentioned by Fanny—as the baron would surely be present.

The unpredictable Baron de Cyprey had, however, cooled off. "To be truthful," Calderón concluded his narration, "I must say that when I met the baron yesterday, at a dinner at the house of a mutual friend, he seemed rather embarrassed and chilly at first. But he soon treated me not only with courtesy but with noticeable cordiality, as if nothing had happened. He promised to come and see me—he owes me a visit—and said that he hoped we would soon meet at his house at a little party he proposes to give."

The affair was widely discussed in the newspapers. Blame was cast about in various directions—upon the count, of course, whose actions caused bitter references to the recent Pastry War; upon Cañedo for allegedly not having been more decisive in this incident involving Frenchmen; and upon Calderón for less specific reasons. Letters from Francisco Solares and the count were published by one paper. Solares, signing himself the editors' secure and attentive servant who kissed their hands, pointed out the utter courtesy and reasonableness displayed in the matter of the initial reception of the count's misdelivered letter. The count, begging the editors to be the recipients of his distinguished consideration, insisted that the newspaper's account of the incident was offensive, indecorous, and a tissue of lies. (*Cosmopolita*, September 23, 26, October 7, and October 14, 1840.)

[13] Iturbide's triumphal entry into the capital on his thirty-eighth birthday, September 27, 1821—rather than his later coronation as emperor, which led to his early downfall—was perhaps for him the high point of his life. He is said to have arranged the route of the troops he headed so that he might be seen from the house of the woman who (although past forty and many times a grandmother) was still Mexico's outstanding beauty: La Güera Rodríguez. As he rode by, he plucked a plume from his hat and sent it to her by one of his aides. (Romero de Terreros, *Bocetos de la Vida Social* . . . , p. 213.)

[14] Fanny here discusses events which preceded Iturbide's entrance into the capital with the Trigarantine Army. The Plan of Iguala and the Treaty of Córdoba were never "confirmed" in the sense of being formally ratified. The thought intended here, evidently, was that the treaty was *based* on the principles and much of the wording of the earlier Plan of Iguala. Even if the treaty had gone into effect, Spain would not have "preserved" Mexico, as the two countries would have been linked solely through the royal house common to both. At the time Fanny was penning these speculations, Brazil—although completely independent—was being ruled by the boy-Emperor Pedro II, brother of young Maria da Gloria, Queen of Portugal.

[15] The Plan of Iguala had been proclaimed by Iturbide in the town of that name (in what is now the state of Guerrero) on February 24, 1821. Furthermore, it was printed on a press Iturbide had sagaciously sent for, and copies of it were distributed. It is believed that the plan's principles had been carefully thought out earlier by a group of creole conservatives who hoped through the success of Iturbide's movement to achieve the independence of Mexico as a constitutional monarchy. The three guarantees—appealing to men of many backgrounds—might be described as national independence; exclusive adherence to the Catholic faith; and equality and union among all classes, including Mexicans and Spaniards. (Its text in English may be found in H. G. Ward's *Mexico in 1827*, I, 525–26.)

Iturbide succeeded in winning over the surviving insurgent chiefs, including Guerrero and later Nicolás Bravo and Guadalupe Victoria. Within six months, with their aid and their troops, he gained control of nearly the whole of Mexico except for the capital. There an acting Spanish viceroy was entrenched with a sizable force. Iturbide was considering an attack upon the city when news came of the arrival in Veracruz of a new representative of the Spanish crown, Juan O'Donojú. Faced with the impossibility of proceeding up from the coast, O'Donojú—a liberal and a realist—made overtures to Iturbide for a peaceful settlement. The two men met at Córdoba in August and then and there quickly drafted and signed a document closely paralleling the Plan of Iguala. Soon afterward O'Donojú prevailed upon his predecessor to quit the capital peacefully, and on September 27, 1821, the anniversary of which date Fanny has just described, Iturbide and his Trigarantine Army entered and were welcomed with frenzied joy. (John Anthony Caruso, *The Liberators of Mexico*, pp. 192–221.)

Later, however, Spain rejected the Treaty of Córdoba signed by O'Donojú, and O'Donojú himself soon died in Mexico. No Spanish prince, therefore, ever was offered the throne of independent Mexico. Instead, Iturbide, who headed an interim regency, was acclaimed as emperor by his troops on May 18, 1822. Fanny, in her paraphrase of the treaty, failed to include the provision—not a part of the earlier Plan of Iguala—that, if Ferdinand VII, his brother, and another stipulated Bourbon prince all declined the Mexican throne, a ruler would be *elected* by Mexico's legislative body. A number of delegates did meet and vote, in a scene of great confusion and noise, for confirmation of what seemed to be an accomplished fact: Iturbide's elevation to the throne.

The unity of purpose which had achieved independence had already begun to disintegrate. Republican and Bourbonist groups both became increasingly disaffected. Iturbide, impatient of dilatory debates and nettled by opposition, resorted to dictatorial measures, including the imprisonment of some of the delegates. Only three months after he had been crowned he dissolved the congress and substituted a smaller legislative body hand-picked by himself. Open revolt against him soon followed. By the following March his reign was over.

[16] Cañedo's decision to resign was not a sudden one. Calderón had reported confidentially to his government some three months earlier the fact that Cañedo, exhausted and heavy-hearted over the trend of public affairs, was planning to quit his post. (Delgado, *España y México en el Siglo XIX*, II, 456.)

[17] The source of this quotation is unknown to the editors.

[18] From John 5:1–15.

[19] These baths still flourish. Located at the base of the Cerro del Peñón, an isolated volcanic hill once an island in Lake Texcoco, they face on a small unpaved plaza that retains something of a village atmosphere. But no longer is the area solitary. The city has reached out to it, and it resounds with the roar of the capital's nearby airport. The building Fanny saw has been modernized and added to, but much of the original construction remains. There is now a doctor in charge, and attendants in sterile garb preside over the private rooms with their deep baths and dressing quarters, furnished with plastic-covered couches—for now, as in 1840, it is considered necessary to rest completely after bathing. The radioactive waters, analyzed by experts, are said to approach in chemical composition those of Vichy and Karlsbad, and are recommended by the management (both for drinking and bathing) to alleviate many ills, including rheumatism, nervous disorders, kidney trouble, and sterility in women. A brochure gives assurance that those in full health—*plena salud*—may also benefit, and that they will emerge with their native vigor intensified.

The chapel, a minute faded jewel within the courtyard of the establishment, enjoys the status of a colonial monument. On the day of our visit in the summer of 1962 it contained this rather surprising notice in Spanish: "We supplicate you NOT to leave money. For the Virgin, flowers and candles—yes."

[20] "And Joshua made them that day hewers of wood and drawers of water for the congregation . . ." Joshua 9:27; also 21 and 23.

[21] From *Hamlet*, Act II, Scene 2.

[22] Waddy Thompson, United States minister to Mexico a little later, attended a similar penitential ceremony and had no doubt of the reality of the self-inflicted penances—as he later saw the blood-soaked cords and recognized, in some of the participants as they came out, various respected persons. "No one in his senses can doubt the sincerity of those who will voluntarily inflict such tortures on themselves." (*Recollections of Mexico*, p. 114.)

[23] Originally Fanny included here the music for four songs. The editors have re-positioned three of them to appear with their words: "*El Palomo*" (p. 183); "*El Aforrado*" (p. 222); and "*Los Enanos*" (p. 224).

Fanny nowhere gave the words for "*El Perico*"—the Poll-Parrot—but they may be found in other sources. The music, with Spanish words only, is given in the magazine *Mexican Folkways*, edited by Frances Toor (Vol. VI, No. 1, pp. 18–19). And the same song, with words in both Spanish and English, appears in *Folk Songs of Many Nations*, compiled and edited by Florence Hudson Botsford (II, 66–67). Like the other light-hearted Mexican songs quoted by Fanny, "*El Perico*" does not translate well. A sample verse runs: "I'd like to be a parrot/So as always to fly in the air/There I'd tell you secrets/And no one would hear them."

In Volume 3 of her Journal, and not a part of *Life in Mexico*, as hitherto issued, Fanny set down, without explanation, some verses in Spanish, which she headed simply "Song." They are difficult to decipher and to translate, but the first verse would appear to say: "My mother whacks me because I love a grenadier, and, to the sound of the whacks, I cry: 'Long live—long live—the cap of fur!' " (A reference, presumably, to the grenadier's headgear.) The chorus consists of three short statements in varying vein, first by Melchior, who says: "Let the little instruments play, happy is the day when God was born"—then by Fernando and Gaspar, continuing the theme of youth versus age.

27. "Like an Old Resident"

[1] It is easy to forget that Calderón's real first name was Angel. In the Catholic calendar October 2 is the day honoring the Holy Guardian Angels.

[2] Joaquín Arrieta was accompanied by his son and his son's friend, one learns from a letter Fanny wrote to her friend Prescott dated October 15, 1840. (Wolcott, *Correspondence of . . . Prescott*, p. 167.) In addition, Arrieta's name is written into the Singer copy, the source for various other identifications provided in this chapter. Three names, left

blank in the Singer copy, seem clear from other notations and from the context. They have been entered in brackets.

[3] This is the school which Fanny, in describing her first visit to it, called Las Vizcaínas.

[4] The museum was moved by Maximilian in 1865 to a structure that the Calderóns came to know well: the large building, adjoining the national palace, which in their day had housed the mint.

The superb Mexican museums of today bear little resemblance to the single crowded installation of the 1840's—although visitors will recognize in the greatly amplified collections some of the objects which Fanny describes. They may also notice, in one of the cases of the Museo Nacional de Historia at Chapultepec, an open copy of her *Life in Mexico*, honored as a vivid account of its time. And in the museum's annex presenting dioramas of Mexican history they will find Fanny portrayed and quoted.

[5] *Tecal*, one learns, is a very white marble—so transparent that it was used sometimes for windows instead of glass.

[6] Miguel Cabrera (1695–1768), one of the best known of Mexican painters and enormously successful during his own lifetime, had Zapotec as well as Spanish inheritance. His output was staggering in quantity, his work frequently mediocre, and—as Fanny will complain—somewhat monotonous. It has been said that almost no church in the capital, and indeed in many parts of Mexico, was without at least one of his paintings. Among his better religious pictures are those in the church of Santa Prisca in Taxco, well known to tourists. His reputation has declined with the passing years, but one picture alone would assure him immortality: a superb portrait, executed in 1750, of the nun who was also a poet, Sor Juana Inés de la Cruz. It is a part of the collection of the Museo Nacional de Historia at Chapultepec.

[7] Gutiérrez Estrada, as the son-in-law of their good friend the elder Countess Cortina, was well known to the Calderóns. He had been a newspaper editor, a cabinet officer, and a diplomat; and he had traveled widely in Europe and the United States. Fanny does not mention his appearance, but, judging from likenesses that remain, he had a splendid, intellectual cast of countenance. (See Plate 78.)

The affair of the pamphlet provoked a thunderous clash of public opinion. There were several steps in its development. Gutiérrez Estrada first wrote a letter to President Bustamante on August 25 which seems not to have caused any special stir; in it, he called attention to what he felt were the failures of the constitutions of both 1824 and 1836, and suggested the need for a constitutional convention. He then wrote a second letter dated September 28, reinforcing the same line of thinking and politely wishing the President peace and prosperity. On October 18 he published his 96-page pamphlet. This incorporated his two earlier letters, and introduced the further idea which was productive of all the excitement—that republicanism in Mexico was a failure and that the country would be better off as a monarchy. The long title of the document might be translated as: *Letter Directed to His Excellency the President of the Republic on the Necessity of Seeking in a Convention the Possible Remedy for the Evils Which Afflict the Republic; and Opinions of the Author Concerning This Same Matter.*

According to the author, the recent "sedition in the capital" served to crystallize his belief that the only means of securing peace for Mexico was to stabilize its government by the establishment of a monarchy. He referred to the recent secession of Texas and to the prevalent disaffection in Yucatán. Repetitions of recent events would, he felt, only result in the complete destruction of Mexico. He cited the freedom enjoyed in Great Britain, France, Holland, and Tuscany, and asked whether a *monarquía democrática* would not be a more effective form of government for independent Mexico, so long accustomed to a rule by kings.

He predicted (p. 58) that unless something was done to remedy the ills and disturbances of government fewer than twenty years would pass before Mexicans would see the flag of the United States waving over the national palace and a Protestant service being conducted in the cathedral. In less than seven years the Mexican capital would in fact be occupied by United States troops. And almost exactly twenty-three years after publication of the pamphlet, the Archduke Maximilian, younger brother of the Emperor Franz Josef of Austria, would receive at his castle on the Adriatic a deputation (by no means as representative of Mexican opinion as the archduke thought) asking him to assume the throne of Mexico. Heading the group and standing a little in front—as the scene is pictured in a representation that hangs in a corridor of Chapultepec Castle—was a tall man with a bold profile: José María Gutiérrez Estrada.

But even the royal Maximilian failed to satisfy the man who worked so long to bring a monarch to Mexico. Gutiérrez Estrada was particularly unhappy over the fact that the Emperor—at once weak, well-meaning, stubborn, and unexpectedly liberal in certain ways—refused to return to the church the properties that had been expropriated and sold to private owners under the earlier Reform government. Gutiérrez Estrada remained in Europe, and died in 1867 a disappointed man, only a few weeks before Maximilian was executed.

8 The "political review" mentioned as the source for this long quotation was the collection in book form of articles by José María Luis Mora: *Obras Sueltas* (I, CCLXXX), on which Fanny has earlier drawn for her characterization of the revolutionary leader Gómez Farías. (These characterizations of public men of the time may be found also in a modern work edited by Arturo Arnáiz y Freg entitled *José María Luis Mora/Ensayos, Ideas y Retratos*.)

9 That Fanny did not read the pamphlet, later if not at exactly this time, one simply cannot believe. She may well have maintained real or feigned ignorance at her husband's suggestion to avoid becoming needlessly involved in a situation which from the start was potentially embarrassing to Calderón, representative of the monarchy which had formerly ruled Mexico, and also known to be a friend of Gutiérrez Estrada.

As a matter of fact, a month before the appearance of the pamphlet, Calderón had informed his government of rumors that some of the clergy were in favor of calling in an Austrian archduke to rule Mexico. And he added that the French minister (the Baron de Cyprey) was alleged to be saying that Calderón was working to bring the Spanish queen's uncle—the discontented Don Carlos who wanted the Spanish throne—to rule over Mexico. (*Despachos Generales*, I, 145–46.) Earlier still—the previous July—Calderón had sent to Spain a "very private" report covering a conversation with Cañedo, then still in office as Mexico's Minister of Foreign Affairs. Cañedo (who was presumably expressing his own ideas, or perhaps was trying to find out Calderón's, or both) spoke gloomily of his country's "many convulsions," and of the likelihood that Mexico would become a monarchy. (Delgado, *España y México en el Siglo XIX*, III, 455–59.)

10 The printer of the pamphlet was the respected Ignacio Cumplido—already mentioned as editor and publisher of the magazine *El Mosaico Mexicano*. He languished for thirty-three days in the city prison (whose heterogeneous inmates Fanny will later see and describe). He let all Mexico know of his indignation. He wrote, printed, and advertised in the December 19 issue of *El Mosaico Mexicano* a pamphlet entitled "*Libertad de Imprenta!* (Liberty of the Press!)" in which he reviewed what had happened, extracted various portions of the testimony given in his case, and in very large type invited the judge who had sentenced him to justify under the law the penalty exacted. A copy of the pamphlet may be found in the Library of Congress copy of Volume IV of *El Mosaico Mexicano*.

11 The President himself, in language with a ring strangely familiar to modern ears, promptly condemned the pamphlet in a special proclamation. "A highly subversive publication," Bustamante warned, was seeking to undermine the Mexican republic. (*Diario del Gobierno*, October 25, 1840.)

In reporting the affair to his own government, Calderón, no republican, made plain his sympathy for the point of view expressed by Gutiérrez Estrada. He was concerned, however, that Santa Anna and other ambitious military leaders might use the proposal as a pretext for seizing the reins of government. (*Despachos Generales*, I, 164–65, 167–68.)

12 Judging by the newspapers, the controversy became even more intense soon after the date Fanny wrote. Later Calderón would become indirectly involved.

La Hesperia, organ of the capital's Spanish residents (see p. 278), at first confined itself almost entirely to reprinting what other newspapers said. In its issue of October 28 there was quoted an article from the paper published by the capital's French residents. This characterized Gutiérrez Estrada as an honorable man, and his ideas as a dream. To make a rabbit stew, it said, one must have a rabbit; and to make a monarchy one must have a monarch—and what royal scion would wish to assume this thorny crown?

The newspaper *El Cosmopolita* of October 31 printed a long, oratorical letter by the Independence Day speaker of a few weeks earlier, General José María Tornel. "Señor José María Gutiérrez Estrada calls me to the arena," he said in preface to eight newspaper pages tabulating the violent ends met by one Roman emperor after another and discussing the general perversity of kings—with quotations from Virgil, Tacitus, Cervantes, Toqueville, and others. The same newspaper on November 4 continued to condemn the pamphlet, and likewise condemned the government for imprisoning Cumplido, its publisher. An article in the November 7 number observed—prophetically anticipating the tragedy of the subsequent French intervention which put Maximilian on the throne of Mexico—that a country is independent only if it governs itself, and that with the coming of a numerous corps of strangers who would accompany a foreign king, Mexico would lose control of its own destiny.

The anti-government paper, *El Mosquito Mexicano*, argued in its November 3 issue—logically enough, as it had earlier censured the government for infringing the liberty of the press—that Gutiérrez Estrada had the undeniable right to say what he pleased.

Much of the public furore, which continued even after Gutiérrez Estrada, the cause of it all, had made his escape from Mexico, developed as a by-product of the main issues.

A verbal battle ensued between General Tornel, who delivered blasts against the memory of Mexico's first Spanish conquerors via articles in *El Cosmopolita*, and those writing for the Spanish newspaper *La Hesperia*. Debate continued even into the new year of 1841. Not all of the exchange was public. One learns from Calderón's dispatches that Tornel on November 23, 1840 had written a bitter personal letter to Calderón, holding him responsible for whatever appeared in *La Hesperia*. Calderón insisted politely (both letters were copied into his dispatch written the next day) that neither he nor any of his staff had anything to do with the newspaper's utterances. (*Despachos Generales*, I, 164–65, 169–71.)

[13] Francisco Javier Echeverría (whose last name Fanny consistently misspelled, not only in her Journal and text, but also in one of her husband's early dispatches to Spain written during a period when she was acting temporarily as his secretary) was in his early forties. Guillermo Prieto describes him as tall, fair, angular, and quiet, with simple courteous manners. He was generous toward charities and maintained the utmost rectitude in his business and political dealings. (*Memorias . . .* , II, 28–29.) His portrait in Manuel Rivera Cambas' *Los Gobernadores de México* depicts a long, attractive, rather melancholy face (see Plate 68).

Señor Echeverría seems not actually to have left his post as Minister of the Treasury for some months. Perhaps he tendered his resignation at this time because he had had his fill of the unpleasant criticism which was being leveled at him by one section of the press. As an example of the provocative style of the newspaper *El Mosquito Mexicano* we quote from an issue of some months earlier (April 17, 1840—Vol. VIII, No. 31): "They say in the arcades and cafés that his excellency Señor Echeverría is going to resign from the cabinet, which news has been received with tears—but of pure joy—because his excellency is killing everyone off with hunger." The article continued with an unspecific accusation that he was using his office to advance his own interests, and made sneering reference to his great wealth. Another blast appeared in *El Mosquito Mexicano* of December 22, 1840: "The moment deeply desired by many has come," it said; "God has so touched the heart of Señor Echeverría as to cause him to leave office." According to another source, however, Echeverría remained in the cabinet until the following March 22. (Riva Palacio, editor, *México a Través de los Siglos*, IV, 460.)

[14] There were three Mexican painters bearing this name, but Fanny is undoubtedly speaking of Nicolás Enríquez. Highly regarded in his own epoch—the last third of the eighteenth century—he is today considered a painter of secondary rank. (Toussaint, *Arte Colonial en México*, p. 355.)

[15] Luca Giordano (1632–1705) was a Neapolitan painter of prodigious fecundity who later worked also in Spain. He painted decorative murals of great size and is said to have early achieved his nickname of "Work-fast Luca" from his picture-dealer father's exhortations to work ever faster. An anecdote survives to the effect that once, when the fiery artist was called to family dinner, he replied: "I'll be there in an instant; I have finished the Christ, and there only remain the twelve apostles." (André Michel, *Histoire de l'Art*, VI, I[e] partie, 118–20.)

[16] It seems probable that Fanny was referring here to Jimeno—Rafael Jimeno y Planes—who was born in 1759 in Valencia in Spain, and who died in 1825, some fifteen years before she wrote. He received his training at the Academy of San Carlos in the Mexican capital, where he won a prize at the age of thirteen. After a period in Spain, he returned again to Mexico where he became director of painting and later director general of San Carlos. Many examples of his work remain in Mexico, among them some vigorous portraits of high quality. The painting within the cupola of the cathedral is an example of his religious work. (Toussaint, *Arte Colonial en México*, pp. 444–48.)

[17] The convent of La Profesa, also called La Casa de los Profesos, formerly had been a Jesuit establishment. It was demolished in 1861 in the course of the period called the Reform, and the street now known as the Avenida del Cinco de Mayo runs through its site. The convent church, built in 1720, still stands as a landmark in the business district, on the Avenida Isabel la Católica at Avenida Madero.

Some, at least, of the paintings that Calderón must have seen in La Profesa exist today. In the choir of the church there are two Cabreras, depicting St. Ignatius Loyola and St. Francis Xavier. The recently formed Museo de Arte Colonial (fronting on the western end of the Alameda) possesses other paintings having to do with the Jesuits and their work, including two by Cabrera.

[18] According to figures of a few years earlier, Santa Teresa la Nueva had twenty-one nuns and no boarders or servants. In contrast, the Encarnación had fifty-six nuns, twenty-one "*niñas*," and seventy-five servants. (José María Luis Mora, *Méjico y Sus Revoluciones*, I, 498.)

From an entry in the Singer copy, we learn that in her visit to the convent, Fanny was accompanied by Señora Adalid, presumably Conchita, wife of José Adalid and therefore sister-in-law of the nun with whom Fanny had formed a ghostly but vital friendship.

[19] Bishop Joaquín Fernández de Madrid was indeed young for his rank: born in 1801, he was still under forty.

[20] "God deliver me from sullen saints!" said the holy, forthright Saint Teresa de Jesús herself. And she is also known occasionally to have danced gaily with a tambourine during the brief periods of recreation allowed under the strict rules she promulgated.

[21] It will be remembered that the nun whom Fanny calls Madre Adalid (as identified previously in the Singer copy) had summoned her to witness the induction of the young girl just mentioned (pp. 260–63).

[22] "La Virgen del Pilar" is a defiant Aragonese song from the time of the Napoleonic invasion of Spain. It deals with the terrible second siege in 1809 of Zaragoza, whose enormous church of Nuestra Señora del Pilar contains a renowned fourteenth-century statue of Our Lady of the Pillar. Though the song is still sung in Zaragoza, efforts to find it in print proved unavailing. The air and one verse are reproduced here by the kindness of Dr. Miguel Querol Gavaldá, of the Instituto Español de Musicología in Madrid, who recalled the song as remembered from his childhood.

"The Virgen del Pilar says/That she doesn't want to be French,/That she wants to be the captain/Of the troops of Aragón."

[23] St. Senanus of Ireland, who lived about 488–560, was first bishop of Scattery Island in County Clare. Thomas Moore's poem, "St. Senanus and the Lady," referring to the bishop's rule that no woman be allowed to set foot on the island, is probably the source here. "And I have sworn this sainted sod/Shall ne'er by woman's foot be trod!"

[24] The name of the capable, gifted Pedro de Gante is commemorated in the north-and-south street cut through the grounds of the once rich and powerful convent of San Francisco. Born in Flanders and reputedly the illegitimate son of the Emperor Charles V, he was founder and director of a very early school affiliated with the convent, where quick-learning Indians were taught, among other subjects, the fine arts and construction techniques. Pedro de Gante is likewise credited with having established many congregations among Indians outside the capital. (Kubler, Mexican Architecture of the Sixteenth Century, I, 119, 153; II, 329–30, 366–67, 463–67.)

Some of the nephews and grandsons of the unfortunate Montezuma were educated at the ancient convent of San Francisco. (Manuel Ramírez Aparicio, Los Conventos Suprimidos en Méjico, p. 211.)

[25] The building occupied by the Monte Pío in Fanny's time—and still today—faced on the cathedral square. It was bought in 1836 from the descendants of Cortés. Fanny refers here, however, to a building earlier used by the Monte Pío: at the corner of what is now the Avenida Juárez and the Calle de San Juan de Letrán. The now no longer existing convent of Santa Brígida was also on San Juan de Letrán, and the secret communication described by Fanny was evidently an emergency link between the two buildings. The convent's church survived until 1933, when it was sacrificed to widen a street.

[26] A reference to Charles V's retirement to a monastery after having abdicated the throne of Spain in favor of his son Philip II.

In the 1840's the convent of San Francisco (Plates 40, 41, and 42) occupied an area that has become two entire city blocks, plus portions of two more. In Plate 39, one is looking east toward the cathedral plaza, along what is today the Avenida Madero. The House of Tiles shows on the left, and the northwest corner of San Francisco's compound is on the right. From this point, the convent façade extended south for what are now two full blocks, and east all the way to the Iturbide palace.

It is difficult to visualize the extent of this and other monastic establishments whose large properties once occupied so much of the capital's present central business district. Most of them were demolished not many years after the Calderóns' stay, as a result of the movement known as the Reform. The chief issues in this struggle—which almost immediately developed into a bloody civil war—were the power and special privileges of the church. Among the results were the nationalization of church properties and the separation of church and state. The movement was initiated during the liberal regime of President Ignacio Comonfort, and was broadened and carried through under his more single-minded and tenacious successor Benito Juárez.

In 1856, on government orders following information that the convent of San Francisco was the center of plotting by the clerical party, San Francisco's walls were breached and an east-west street, now a part of the Avenida 16 de Septiembre, was cut through grounds and buildings. Some years afterward, during a later phase of the Reform movement, the Calle de Gante was similarly cut through in a north and south direction. The convent property was divided into lots and sold off piece by piece. Various of the old buildings continued in altered form with drastically changed occupancy, and as late as the early twentieth century two hotels made use of some of San Francisco's former cells, sturdy old vaulted storerooms, and one of its chapels.

Little of the ancient establishment remains today. In addition to its principal church, entered from the Avenida Madero, there exists one large remnant unknown to many visitors and hidden by later construction: the convent's principal cloister, entered from the Calle de Gante, No. 5. Once an open patio with two-story arcaded walls dating from the seventeenth century, it has been roofed over to serve as a Protestant church.

28. A Second Visit to Santiago

[1] The midnight celebration in the village cemetery of the Day of the Dead, as it survives in a present-day Indian community, is depicted in Plate 141.

[2] Once again evidently the Adalids had imported the celebrated bullfighter Bernardo Gaviño for the entertainment of their guests.

[3] Fanny's text has heretofore defined *atole* as a kind of cake. Whether the error came about because she fastened the term to the wrong dish, or through a long-ago misreading of handwriting, can only be guessed; but *atole*—which is made of corn dough and water, cooked, sieved, sweetened, and sometimes flavored—has the consistency of soup.

[4] For a country bull ring of today—used for bull-baiting rather than bullfighting—see Plate 95.

[5] We have filled in this name as a likely guess. The Calderóns would later see a good deal of the Haros in Puebla.

[6] Fanny dated this and the previous entry the "15th" and "17th," clearly in error in view of their return to Mexico on or before November 12. The dates we have given appear correct in terms of the context.

[7] Fanny had good authority for the figure of five hundred pounds, for her phraseology parallels that of Clavijero's *Historia Antigua de Mégico*—his fourth "dissertation" following his regular text. But this weight given for a mule load is far higher than anything found in other sources of the times. Certainly the figure must have been related to speed, bulk, distance covered, and the kind of terrain covered. Thompson, United States minister a little later, said that mules transporting goods from Veracruz to the capital carried four hundred pounds. (*Recollections of Mexico*, p. 36.) Brantz Mayer, in his second book—*Mexico, Aztec, Spanish and Republican* (II, 347)—defined a *carga* as three hundred pounds. And similarly, H. G. Ward, whose accuracy one somehow relies on, said (*Mexico in 1827*, I, 49) that for a bulky agricultural product, a *carga* was three hundred pounds.

[8] Calderón informed his chief that Gutiérrez Estrada "has hidden himself; some say that he is in the house of the French minister, others that he is in the English minister's, and others that he is in mine—but this is not so." (*Despachos Generales*, I, 167.)

Later Gutiérrez Estrada slipped out of the capital and, with the apparent consent of certain unnamed highly placed persons, left the country on an English man-of-war. (Bustamante, *Gabinete Mexicano*, II, 93.)

[9] Queen Isabel II was ten years old on October 10, 1840. Once again, it was her saint's day—the feast day of St. Elizabeth of Hungary—that was celebrated, rather than her birthday. The reader will recall that in the previous year the Calderóns marked November 19 at festivities in Havana.

[10] From Fanny's own floor plan of their house (p. 145), it is easy to visualize the procession from the drawing room at the front, along the wide gallery, to the dining room at the rear. What is termed here "God Save the Queen" was probably the "Marcha Real" or "Royal March," dating from the eighteenth century.

29. Young Relatives from Home

[1] The noble baroque church of Santo Domingo dominates its historic plaza—two squares north and slightly west of the cathedral—in a neighborhood where there survive many of the buildings and something of the flavor of the Calderóns' time. Among the figures in the richly gilded interior of the church is that of the Virgin of Covadonga, a wide-skirted figure high on the west side of the transept—a replica of the original at Covadonga in northern Spain.

The *Cheval de Bronze* was composed by Daniel-François-Esprit Auber, with libretto by Scribe. A comic opera on a Chinese theme, it was first produced in Paris in 1835.

[2] King Pelayo of Asturias in northwestern Spain fought a great battle against the Moors early in the eighth century. According to tradition, the Virgin of Covadonga intervened to bring victory to the Spaniards—thus beginning the Christian reconquest of Spain.

Many things have changed in Mexico, but the Virgin of Covadonga is still honored at an annual mass (held now on September 8) by Spaniards resident in the capital. When the editors attended in 1962, nearly all the women and girls wore magnificent mantillas of white, black, or écru lace, artfully draped over high-backed combs to fall in ample folds. Some of the children—for many attractive family groups were in attendance—wore Spanish peasant costumes. As in Fanny's day, distinguished personages were present. Among them, his quiet clear voice carrying over what did not exist in 1840, an amplifying system, was the *Arzobispo Primado*, Monsignor Miguel Darío Miranda. Not forgotten in the sermon, delivered by another churchman, was Spain's struggle against the Moors.

Plate 43 shows the Plaza of Santo Domingo as it was before the Reform. Those familiar with the Mexican capital will recognize many surviving buildings. The 1962 celebration in honor of the Virgin of Covadonga is the subject of Plates 44 and 45.

[3] The names of the Calderóns' two companions in trying out Daguerre's new invention (and other names inserted in this and the following chapter) come from the Singer copy. The first was obviously Baron von Gerolt, the expedition-minded diplomat from Prussia who had earlier conquered Popocatepetl.

The second was almost certainly Carl Nebel, an architect-artist born near Hamburg, whose work has been drawn upon as a source for a number of the illustrations in this volume. He had lived in Mexico from 1829 to 1834 and produced a handsome book of colored lithographs, under the title of *Voyage pittoresque et archéologique dans la partie la plus intéressante du Mexique* (first issued in Paris in 1836). In this year of 1840 he was again in Mexico, conducting a lawsuit against Señor García Torres, a Mexican who had recently brought out an apparently unauthorized version of Nebel's work. The controversy illustrates the free and easy attitude of the times toward literary proprietorship. At least one thoughtful writer in the newspaper discussion of the affair urged the need for accord among civilized nations on this important problem. (*Diario del Gobierno*, July 10, August 23, 24, and 25, September 1 and 3, 1840.)

Prescott had not forgotten Calderón's earlier letter (note 22, p. 667) asking to be kept informed on new developments in the art of photography. On April 2 Prescott had reported his meeting on Calderón's behalf with the agent of the Daguerreotype concern, and added that he would order one of the "machines" sent as a gift for Fanny. About two weeks later he wrote Fanny along similar lines, and mentioned the agent as "a person who has come here from France to initiate the Messieurs sauvages in the sublime mysteries of the Daguerreotype . . . a little touch of a humbug, I fancy. . . . He brought with him a number of beautiful specimens, for some of which, executed by the 'great Daguerre' himself, he has the modesty to ask from 500 to 1000 dollars apiece!" On June 5 Fanny wrote to express thanks for the intended gift, "as I think there are few parts of the world where it can be used to more advantage. I hope we shall be able to send you *Chapultepec*, correctly drawn by Nature herself." On October 15 she acknowledged receipt of the device, "which has arrived at last in complete preservation . . . You may depend on receiving its first fruits." (Wolcott, *Correspondence of . . . Prescott*, pp. 116–17, 122, 128.)

With all this by way of prelude, it is sad to have to report that no fruits of the afternoon's efforts at Chapultepec—or of any subsequent photographic endeavors—appear to have survived among Prescott's papers. But at least one of Calderón's daguerreotypes was sent to Prescott (a view of a building which Fanny will later visit). In an accompanying letter, Fanny's brief reference suggests that the achievement was less than satisfactory: "Calderón desires me to say that you will receive along with this . . . the Hospital de Jesús which he daguerreotyped as well as he could . . ." (Wolcott, *Correspondence of . . . Prescott*, p. 284.)

The Calderóns' daguerreotype machine was not the first to arrive in Mexico. According to newspaper advertising, one was raffled off in the middle of March. (*Diario del Gobierno*, March 3, 1840.)

[4] The two visitors were Fanny's niece and nephew, Kate Macleod and her brother Alexander Norman Macleod the younger. Kate was soon to be fifteen and her brother Alex twenty-three. Both were the children of Fanny's older sister Richmond Macleod, who at this time was helping to manage the family school on Staten Island. Kate lived with her mother, but Alex, the only son, seems to have spent the greater part of his time with his father in Jamaica.

According to the maritime news in the *Diario del Gobierno* for November 28, 1840, the young people made the voyage from New York in the American packet ship *Eugenia* in twenty-one days.

[5] "The devil damn thee black, thou cream-fac'd loon!" cried Macbeth to the bearer of bad news in Act V, Scene 3.

The earthquake described must have been run-of-the-mine: two newspapers examined for this and succeeding dates did not bother to mention it. Another recorder of events did note it, but termed it slight. (Malo, *Diario de Sucesos Notables*, I, 189.) Strangely enough, Malo mentioned two months earlier, on September 11 (I, 184) two short but strong earth tremors about which Fanny said nothing.

Another British traveler was struck by the trusting calm displayed by Mexicans during a mild tremor he witnessed from his balcony. There was neither terror nor confusion; merely quiet confident praying as all knelt on the spot while the whole city swayed like a ship at anchor. "When the shock was over, the multitude rose; and each went about his business with a nonchalance which proved how the frequent recurrences of this phenomenon had nerved the public mind." (Latrobe, *Rambler in Mexico*, pp. 136–37.)

[6] The identity of Mr. Bertie, who will shortly disappear from the book, is unknown to the editors. He was, perhaps, a younger son or brother of the Earl of Lindsey or of the Earl of Abingdon, as both of these noblemen bore the surname of Bertie.

[7] Only from the already quoted letter (in note 4, p. 712) which the Protestant Fanny wrote Prescott the previous June do we know the rather offhand method by which she acquired, on the occasion of her visit to the convent of La Encarnación, a patron saint in conformity with Catholic custom.

Francis Xavier, friend and associate of Saint Ignatius de Loyola, aided in founding the Society of Jesus. He was the Jesuits' most notable missionary, and preached in western India, Ceylon, Malaya, the Spice Islands—and even in Japan, where he founded several Christian communities. He was canonized in 1622 and his feast day is celebrated on December 3.

[8] What Fanny saw hanging on the hook was presumably a pelt rather than a carcass, for she would encounter it again a year later. It evidently reminded her of a real or legendary animal which she had seen illustrated in Clavijero's *Historia Antigua de Mégico* (see cut).

One of Clavijero's acknowledged sources was a far older compendium written in Latin by a learned physician whom Philip II had sent to New Spain for the purpose of studying its flora and fauna. A new edition of this rare work was brought out in 1959 by the Universidad Nacional de México, and in it one may see and read about the strange-looking quadruped first catalogued and pictured in the sixteenth century: the *itzcuintepotzotli*, a hunchbacked dog originating in Michoacán; indolent, playful, and fond of its masters. (Francisco Hernández, *Historia Natural de Nueva España*, translated into Spanish by José Rojo Navarro, II, 313–14.)

[9] The Carmelite convent of the Santo Desierto de los Leones was begun in 1606. A few years after Fanny's visit, in 1845, the abandoned church would be converted for a time into a glass factory—considered by some to be a possible cloak for a counterfeiting establishment. (Federico Gómez de Orozco, "El Desierto de los Leones," in *Anales del Museo Nacional*, 4a época, I, 1922, 280–91.)

The Desierto was long a traditional spot for hardy picnickers. An engineer from the United States who made an excursion there with a party of countrymen in the early 1880's noted the accumulated inscriptions of years of visitors, and the soot of innumerable campfires. They explored the many passages and tunnels and, like the Calderóns, came and went by following the rushing stream—a source of drinking water for the capital and a potential source of power for machinery. (Frederick A. Ober, *Travels in Mexico*, pp. 363–68.)

Now easily reached by a good road leading off the highway to Toluca, and also directly from San Angel, the Desierto is today a much-enjoyed national park. In spite of such modern appendages as a parking area, a playground for children, and a restaurant, the walled retreat on its calm pine-forested height keeps an atmosphere of cool green peace. Some of the buildings remain roofless. Some have been partially restored. In several of the patios one comes upon the bloom of unexpected gardens.

[10] This word, which has appeared as *miles* in all previous editions, was altered by hand to read *leagues* in the Carlisle copy of *Life in Mexico*. The correction is clearly necessary in view of other specific references in the text—and in view of what is the true distance. One doubts if many of the ladies attending the picnic accomplished the whole journey, as Fanny did, on horseback. Fourteen leagues amount to some thirty-six miles.

[11] From this and the following paragraph it is clear that something disagreeable went on at the picnic. For clarification we are indebted to Felipe Teixidor's scholarly care in going through the manuscript diary of Carlos María de Bustamante (earlier mentioned by Fanny as a writer on Mexican antiquities), whose lively entry of December 23, 1840, he quotes at length (*La Vida en México*, II, Notas, 155–56).

The day was warm and thirst-producing, said Bustamante (who seems not to have been present at the picnic, a diplomatic affair, but to have heard the story from someone else). The champagne and ale mentioned by Fanny were evidently quaffed only too liberally, and various people noticeably showed their effects. A Frenchman toppled from his horse. The Spanish consul quarreled with the French minister. Some were so far gone as to require help in leaving the scene, among them the daughter of the French minister. She was said to have been removed in a horizontal state, supported on an emergency arrangement of planks borne by four Indians.

None of the newspapers searched by the editors—La Hesperia, El Cosmopolita, not even the stinging Mosquito Mexicano, nor, of course, the Diario del Gobierno—breathed one word about the occasion. Calderón, Pakenham, and the United States minister Ellis said nothing in their dispatches. Perhaps, as diplomats of various nations seem to have been involved, there was a tacit understanding among them to keep the affair quiet. Yet its consequences (especially the fact that Léontine, the daughter of the testy French minister, was inebriated) must have been rolled on a good many tongues.

Visitors to Mexico, critical of some aspects of the local scene, seem to have agreed that upper-class Mexicans in general simply did not get drunk. Waddy Thompson, United States minister a little later, made one anonymous exception, but was otherwise very definite (Recollections of Mexico, p. 150): ". . . As to intemperance amongst respectable people it is almost unknown." A physician with the United States army a few years later confirmed this view (McSherry, El Puchero, p. 159): "The gentry of this country are very temperate, rarely exceeding the bounds of moderation." An Italian observer who had also traveled in the United States said that drunkenness was common among the poorer classes in Mexico, as it was in the northern republic. However, recalling unpleasant scenes witnessed among the higher social strata in the United States, he said: "Such disgusting excess is a stranger among educated people in Mexico." (Barinetti, Voyage to Mexico and Havanna, p. 24.)

Bustamante understandably took a slap at the scandalous behavior of the foreigners, some of whom, evidently, had patronizingly looked down on Mexican manners and customs.

12 This entry has heretofore appeared under date of December 28, clearly an error in view of what follows in the next chapter. We have assumed a misreading of Fanny's handwriting, and have arbitrarily changed it to December 23.

13 Don Anselmo Zurutuza, who made a large fortune, was sometimes called the diligence king of Mexico. He also acquired and operated hotels. (Stuart-Wortley, Travels . . . , II, 55.) As Fanny makes plain when she herself later visits his thriving sugar estate of Atlacomulco, Señor Zurutuza leased the property. The owners were descendants of Cortés living in Europe.

14 The reader may recall Fanny's earlier visit to Tacuba and San Joaquín (pages 186–87). This ride—taken perhaps with Kate and Alex, in Calderón's absence—would, alas, not be a beautiful one today. What was then open country, starting only a few squares from the Calderóns' door, is now completely built up and largely occupied by a nondescript area of poorer dwellings, interspersed with occasional factories and cemeteries. However, many of the landmarks she must have seen still exist. The fine old church with its dismantled convent was presumably that presently serving the parish—originally built by the Franciscans in 1585 and modified in the seventeenth century. It now ranks as a colonial monument.

30. Second Christmas: A Year in Mexico

1 This is the only specific reference to this ornate mid-eighteenth-century church, one of the most delightful and interesting Churrigueresque buildings in Mexico. It directly adjoins the cathedral on the east. Fanny's first impression of it had been negative.

2 The glorious voice belonged to Señorita María de Jesús Cepeda y Cosío, then only seventeen. She is one of the few women included in Francisco Sosa's nineteenth-century compilation, Biografías de Mexicanos Distinguidos (pp. 244–46). Her name in the Singer copy was written in simply as Cosío—her mother's name, which Fanny perhaps took to be her surname.

Following family financial reverses Señorita Cepeda did become a professional—encouraged by such distinguished singers as Cesari and Castellan. (In El Liceo Mexicano—Volume I, 1844, following page 192—the young Mexican girl dedicates a composition to Mme Castellan as her maestra or teacher.) After her debut in 1845 she met with success in Norma, La Sonnambula, and other operas; but her biographical notice contains rather cryptic references to later troubles and disappointments. The singer to whom Fanny compared the Mexican girl was undoubtedly the widely acclaimed Giulia Grisi.

One notices in the brief account of the affair in the Spanish newspaper *La Hesperia* for December 26, 1840 that Fanny is not Doña Francisca, but Doña Fanny. This very concert is described in a modern history of Mexican music. (Campos, *El Folklore Musical de las Ciudades*, pp. 28–29.)

[3] The charming celebration here described is still very much alive in Mexico today. The music the Calderóns heard sung was probably that given by Antonio García Cubas in his account of the *Posadas* in *El Libro de Mis Recuerdos* (pp. 296–98). A modern recorder of Mexican traditions, Frances Toor, has set down an entirely different tune, and somewhat different words, in *A Treasury of Mexican Folkways* (pp. 389–91).

There evidently exist various closely parallel versions of the long exchange of words sung alternately by two groups, one representing Joseph and Mary, outside, and the other the householders, inside. Two verses, as given us by a friend, run:

De larga jornada	After a long day's journey
Rendidos llegamos,	We arrive, exhausted,
Y asilo imploramos	And we implore shelter
Para descansar.	In which to rest.
Quién a nuestras puertas	Who comes to our door
En noche inclemente	On so inclement a night?
Se acerca imprudente	Who imprudently approaches
Para molestar?	To trouble us?

The little drama works up to a climax: "Enter, holy pilgrims . . . This is a joyful night, because we have as a guest the Mother of God."

An old lithograph in the editors' possession depicts such a festivity at about this time (see Plate 48). The scene, labeled "*Las Posadas en la alta sociedad—Posadas* in high society," is contrasted with a companion "Posadas of the lower class"—showing an equally spirited but less well-dressed procession winding past what seem to be numbered tenement doors.

[4] A reference to *Japhet, in Search of a Father* (1836), by Frederick Marryat.

[5] This was the Duchess, who in addition to looking after Fanny's wardrobe, seems also to have acted as housekeeper. In writing later to her friend Prescott, Fanny expresses a good deal of indignation—and helplessness as well—over the unannounced departure of Emilie, who had been with her ever since her marriage, and "who was keeper of everything belonging to me but my conscience . . ." Later in the letter one gets a rather unexpected glimpse of a Fanny downed by the light-fingered, bibulous propensities of some of her servants: "Fortunately, Kate Macleod is with me, or I think for once in my life, I should have sat down in despair—" (Unpublished letter dated January 19, 1841, in the manuscript collection of the Massachusetts Historical Society.)

[6] Not so very speedy, even for the times, as more than four and a half months would elapse before secretary Salvador de Tavira and attaché José Garaycochea would arrive and be presented, on May 19, 1841, to the Mexican government. (*El Cosmopolita*, May 26, 1841.)

[7] The same thought struck the Protestant Poinsett, who wrote about his first visit to Mexico in 1822 not long before he became first United States minister. After accompanying his muleteers to mass in a church crowded with people of all classes, he wrote: "I like the equality on which all people worship the Deity in a catholic church. There are no pews nor seats for the rich. The house of God is open to all, and all without distinction stand or kneel before the altar." (*Notes on Mexico*, p. 186.) See Plate 47 for a similar scene.

[8] This discussion under date of January first—after the New Year's greeting and the specific reference to early mass—Fanny based on a long general disquisition upon the subject of dirt from Volume 3 of her Journal. She concluded it with the observation, made use of elsewhere in this book, that private houses in spite of their immensity were maintained in general in a state of immaculate cleanliness.

[9] One learns later that the newly-rich General Barrera had acquired his grand establishment from the Marqués de Apartado. Like the Calderóns' first house and its neighboring Buenavista Palace, and like the Minería, it was designed by the architect-sculptor Manuel Tolsá. It is located half a block east and a block behind the cathedral, on the southwest corner of the intersection of the Avenida República de Argentina and the Calle de Donceles. The classical gray stone building, three stories high and crowned with a balustrade, is of palatial size. Compared with most older Mexican colonial houses—whose large plain surfaces are relieved by occasional lavish, luscious ornament— General Barrera's house seems today rather forbidding in effect. One cannot help but wonder at the sobriety of Fanny's architectural taste. Her feelings on the subject were presumably deeply rooted in the classic surroundings of her Edinburgh childhood.

[10] The reason for Calderón's return again so soon to *tierra caliente* was apparently to show its beauties to his northern-born wife before orders from Spain might interrupt their plans. He expressed himself frankly in a letter written about this time to their friend Prescott: Political changes in Spain, he surmised, might result in his recall; hence his wish that Fanny also might see something of this land of the embracing sun. (Letter dated January 31, 1841, in the Massachusetts Historical Society, published in part in Wolcott, *Correspondence of . . . Prescott*, p. 199.)

[11] *Nemine contradicente* (no one objecting).
"A barrel of wine, a box of books"—from a terse note in the Mexican shipping news one learns that such agreeable items were among the Calderóns' various importations.

31. To Cuernavaca and the Hacienda of Atlacomulco

[1] From Samuel Butler's *Hudibras* (1663), Part II, Canto II—slightly modified.

[2] The automobile highway between Mexico and Cuernavaca (not the newer high-speed tollway) passes close to Ajusco, through El Guarda, and by Cruz del Marqués (see Plate 103), near the high point of the rise between the two valleys. There are many glimpses of the cobblestone-paved road over which the Calderóns' diligence passed. The town of Huitzilac—shortly to be mentioned—is near Tres Cumbres and was, when the editors last saw it, linked to the outside world by the old pre-independence road.

[3] The pre-Hispanic name meant *near the grove or mountains*, and was modified to its Spanish version of Cuernavaca. (Ferrán de Pol, *Cuernavaca*, p. 6.)

[4] Cortés took Cuernavaca—which was garrisoned by Aztecs, to whom its resident Tlahuicas were tributary—as a part of his campaign to regain Tenochtitlan, from which he had so disastrously retreated the previous summer on the "sad night." A detachment of Spaniards and Tlaxcalan allies made a perilous crossing of the barranca through the branches of trees. Once safely across they repaired a bridge which had been pulled up by the town's defenders, thus enabling their main force to enter the city.

[5] The Franciscan church in whose first chapel Cortés heard mass now ranks as a cathedral. In its massive bulk it is one of the most primitive and hoary in appearance of the fortress-style churches of the early sixteenth century. The "bold arch" may still be seen supporting the choir. The remains of the Franciscan convent stand nearby.
The palace of Cortés is now the seat of government for the state of Morelos. Its arcade looking toward Popocatepetl is probably as Cortés constructed it, but the rest of the building has been extensively rebuilt and frequently restored. (Kubler, *Mexican Architecture of the Sixteenth Century*, I, 199–200.)
Giving credit to his friend, Prescott quoted most of this paragraph in a footnote to Chapter V of Book VII of *The Conquest of Mexico* (II, 281–82)—in order perhaps to give a more personal touch to his brief description of the activities of Cortés after the conquest.

[6] The place where the Calderóns waited for transportation to Atlacomulco was, certainly, the pleasure garden laid out by Manuel de la Borda, son of the rich silver miner José de la Borda who gave Taxco its magnificent parish church. The gardens and the Borda house would become, in the 1860's, a favorite retreat of the Emperor Maximilian and his wife Carlota. The descending terraces of the superb garden may be seen today, still in a state of pleasant disrepair.

[7] On the death of Cortés, his title as Marqués del Valle de Oaxaca went to his son, and subsequently in succession to the two sons of his son. With the death of his last grandson without heirs, the conqueror's male line died out, and the title went through his granddaughter to her daughter. The latter married in 1617 the fourth Duke of Terranova, and *their* daughter, an only child, married Hector Pignatelli, fifth Duke of Monteleone of the Kingdom of the Two Sicilies.
Fanny's reference to Don Lucas Alamán (whom the reader may remember as a director of mining companies and a former minister of foreign affairs) may be confusing here, inasmuch as she earlier used the term *agent* to designate the resident employee in charge of an hacienda. The distinguished Alamán was not an agent in this sense, but was entrusted in general with the administration of the Mexican properties and charities of the conqueror's European descendant, the Duke of Terranova who was also Duke of Monteleone, then living in Naples. The hacienda was leased to Calderón's Spanish friend Anselmo Zurutuza; and on the spot there was the local *administrador*, or agent, who had welcomed the Calderóns' party the previous evening. His name, one reads elsewhere, was Don Lorenzo Robles. (Valadés, *Alamán*, p. 354.)

[8] As Fanny implies, she took these facts from Humboldt, who noted that by 1553 Mexico was exporting sugar to Spain and Peru. His story of the first production of sugar may be found in his *Ensayo Político . . . ,* II, 346–47. The text of the will of Cortés appears in an appendix to Volume IV, one item of which (p. 309) referred to a sugar-works in Coyoacán.

The first sugar mill in Mexico was established at Tlaltenango in 1535, not far from Cuernavaca. (Ferrán de Pol, *Cuernavaca,* p. 10.)

[9] Negro slaves, never very numerous, had played only a minor role in Mexico's economy. Many were freed before the achievement of independence and others simply disappeared during the long revolutionary years of strife and uncertainty. H. G. Ward, writing of early post-independence times, said that as a part of independence day celebrations in the capital there was maintained the custom of liberating a certain number of slaves—and that in the year 1826 it was only with difficulty that Negroes able to benefit from the ceremony could be found. (*Mexico in 1827,* I, 36–37.) However, another British visitor, Captain G. F. Lyon, mentions encountering a few slaves in Veracruz that same year. (*Journal . . . ,* II, 225.)

Later in his book, Ward said (I, 67–68) that some of the sugar planters had earlier followed a policy of freeing annually some of their slaves and encouraging them to intermarry with the local Indian population; and that by the time of his visit the resulting admixture of racial stocks was much in evidence. It was presumably this same population —Indians who had absorbed some small degree of Negro inheritance—who manned the sugar haciendas at the time of the Calderóns' tour.

Leaving aside Texas—independent in effect, but still claimed by Mexico—no slaves remained in Mexican territory at the time Fanny wrote. Morelos had pronounced against slavery in 1813 during the War of Independence, and President Vicente Guerrero abolished it by proclamation in 1829. Legislation passed in 1837 reinforced earlier efforts to end slavery. (Hubert Howe Bancroft, *History of Mexico,* V, 79–80.)

[10] Atlacomulco's ancient buildings—and similarly, in varying degree, those of the other sugar haciendas of the region—were wrecked in Mexico's revolution of the second decade of the twentieth century. In the state of Morelos, the national upheaval was signalized by especial violence and bloodshed amounting to a civil war within a civil war. In the years that have followed, time and neglect have augmented the original damage. However—as Fanny herself has implied in another connection—masonry ages well and, from a purely aesthetic point of view, Atlacomulco when last seen by one of the editors (Plate 102) was strongly appealing even in decay.

[11] Natives of the vigorous state of Durango regard their scorpions with mixed emotions, including a good deal of satisfaction over the quantity and inherently superior potency of their native product. In the capital city of Durango some years ago the editors acquired a pamphlet offering a variety of information, formidable statistics, poetry, and traditions on the subject of the *alacrán*—which, said the author, the Durangueño pretends to hate but really loves.

In the three peak years of 1784–86, according to municipal records, some 600,000 *alacranes* were killed in the city of Durango alone. The author cites an old folk tradition to the effect that there are some people, notably pregnant women, who seem to possess natural immunity to the poison. There are also said to be people—and they are noticed to be of nasty disposition—who, like the unnamed señora cited by Fanny, have the effect of killing off the *alacrán* unfortunate enough to sting them. As to treatment with brandy, still more efficacious was a draft of alcohol especially prepared for emergency use by being infused with *alacranes*.

Times, however, have changed. Serum, well distributed throughout the state, mitigates the dreaded effect of a sting. And when the city of Durango was repaved, insecticides applied during the course of the work greatly reduced the *alacrán* population—so much so that *alacrán* corpses for the local souvenir industry now have to be brought in from outlying areas. (Francisco Atúnez, *Los Alacranes en el Folklore de Durango.*)

[12] Fanny assuredly never encountered a cencoatl. Her information was obviously derived from a too hasty reading of an oddly punctuated passage in José Joaquín de Mora's Spanish translation of Clavijero's *Historia Antigua de Mégico,* which stated (I, 56): "tiene cinco pies, poco mas o menos de largo"—literally, "it has five feet, a little more or less of length." (The rest of her paragraph is likewise derived from Clavijero.)

It is this error which confirms Fanny's use of Mora's version rather than the original Italian or the English translation.

[13] Some of Fanny's material was probably obtained from informants on the spot. Some, as earlier indicated, she took from Clavijero. He denied that salamanquesas were poisonous. He noted the supposedly potent effect of the venom from a tarantula on the

hoof of a horse, but he added that as a resident for some time of an area where they were common, he himself did not believe it.

14 In her published text Fanny confused the town of Cacahuamilpa with the city of Cuautla, sometimes called Cuautla Amilpas—not far from her later route to the east. As this error recurs, and becomes quite misleading, we have corrected it throughout.

32. Cross Country to the Cave of Cacahuamilpa

1 The common names for these trees seem to vary a good deal in spelling, because the Nahuatl word for flower—xochitl—is sometimes altered in compounded names to such spellings as jochitl, sochil, or suchil. The yoloxochitl belongs to the magnolia family, its botanical name being talauma mexicana. Not only does it look like a heart in its shut form, but also an infusion made from its dried blooms is a folk remedy for ailments of the heart. The izguixochitl—or esquisuchil, to give another form—is in one source given the botanical name of bourreria formosa and in another bourreria huanita. The flowering tree that Fanny calls flower of the raven is without doubt cacaloxochitl, whose four-petaled blooms, borne on leafless branches, are a magnificent sight in various parts of Mexico in late winter and early spring. Its botanical name is plumeria rubra. (Diccionario General de Americanismos, by Francisco J. Santamaría; and Mexican Flowering Trees and Plants, by Helen O'Gorman, edited by Elie Wallace Turok.)

2 That Fanny was not exaggerating is clear from the following description by Charles Joseph Latrobe regarding the forbidding barrancas in the Cuernavaca area: "Every Mexican traveller must have remarked the insidious manner in which many of these gulfs commence. In riding along the plains, you perhaps find yourself separated from the companion with whom you are conversing, by a crack or fissure of a few inches in breadth: you proceed carelessly; the rent gapes imperceptibly wider and wider, and increases in depth, till it imperatively demands your attention. Perhaps a very natural dislike to retrace your steps, and ignorance of the real nature and extent of the obstacle, induces you to keep your direction in search of its termination; when, before you are aware, you find a hideous and impassable gulf yawning between you, delving deep for many miles into the face of the landscape, and no alternative left you but to return to its very source. I sketch from experience." (Rambler in Mexico, pp. 246–47.)

3 Miacatlán is one of the haciendas described in a modern work, Antiguas Haciendas de México, by Manuel Romero de Terreros, Marqués de San Francisco (pp. 249–50). It would appear that the noble-looking elderly proprietor was Francisco Pérez de Palacios y Flores de Lozada, whose birth date is given as 1763 and who therefore would have been in his late seventies. He had, however, many years ahead of him, as he died in 1852 at the age of eighty-nine. (There was also a distinguished army officer in the family, Angel Pérez Palacios, who died in 1867 after serving as a general in the United States-Mexican War, and in the later Wars of the Reform.)

When one of the editors visited Miacatlán in 1937, an interesting link with the past was established in the person of an elderly but lively life-long resident on the hacienda— Ceferina Segura. The hacienda owner or patrón of her youth, she said, was Francisco Pérez Palacios y Salazar, whose death some fifty or sixty years earlier was still fresh in her memory. Don Francisco, it would seem likely, may have been the mounted oldest son who greeted the Calderóns and took them to the family's house.

4 The old establishment of Miacatlán, like that of nearly every other sugar hacienda visited by the Calderóns, is largely in ruins. It had passed out of the hands of the Pérez Palacios family long before being wrecked, together with its new machinery, in the revolutionary years of the early twentieth century.

5 Plate 104 shows some of Cocoyotla's fine mass of buildings.

6 H. G. Ward, noting conditions some fifteen years earlier, said that workers on the sugar estates were paid on a piece-work basis, and that an industrious hand was paid six or seven reals a day. (Mexico in 1827, I, 68.) But Brantz Mayer, writing shortly after the Calderóns' time, gave the daily wage as only two and a half to three reals. (Mexico as It Was and as It Is, p. 201.)

7 The identification of Señor Silva, and of Fanny's niece Kate a little earlier, are two lone notations to be found in the Singer copy for this entire sugar-country expedition— with one exception to be noted later.

8 A somewhat later visitor to the sugar haciendas said that a servant entered his bedroom and laid a thick rope around each bed. He was proffered the explanation that scorpions, disliking the hemp's roughness, would not cross it. (Conte, Recuerdos de un Diplomático, I, 307.)

[9] No doubt the wife of Charles Ashburnham, who had been chargé d'affaires of the British legation for a time during Pakenham's absence in 1839. Another writer, Brantz Mayer (*Mexico as It Was and as It Is*, pp. 190–91), explains that Miguel Benito, proprietor of the little ranch near the mouth of the cave, acted as an entrepreneur in securing guides.

33. A Marble Dream

[1] The existence of the cave was not generally known until 1834. At that time, according to tradition, the local Indians kept in hiding there a refugee from the outside world who had earlier befriended them and who was in need of temporary concealment. The ensuing public knowledge caused something of a sensation.

[2] Probably an *amate* or wild fig, whose octopus-like roots go around rocks, or even break them, as they reach for water.
For a picture of the cave's entrance, see Plate 105.

[3] A reference, presumably, to the "woeful city" of Dis, of Dante's *Divine Comedy* (*Inferno*, Canto II, 11.1), with the portal of the cave likened to the city's gate.

[4] There exist various descriptions of the famous cave, but Fanny's perhaps stands without peer. A French visitor adds a small touch: from time to time the members of his party heard a noise like the firing of artillery. They were told it was made by falling rock. (Fossey, *Le Mexique*, p. 307.)
Brantz Mayer, the United States diplomat who toured the sugar country only a few months later, must have approached the cave by a somewhat different route. He described a frightening footpath that narrowed at one point to only a three-inch-wide ledge chipped from the rock, and of passing over it by clinging to overhanging vines. So seldom was the cave visited that an Indian with a hatchet had to clear the way. Members of his party took the precaution of fastening twine to a pillar near the entrance and paying it out as they explored one lofty chamber after another. One of their guides sent up a rocket that soared and lit for an instant, until it struck, the lofty dome-like roof. The detonation echoed and re-echoed in a long thunderous roar, and a sheet of stalactites that was hit clanged like a bell. (*Mexico as It Was and as It Is*, pp. 192–94.)
Those who have visited many caves say that it is the cleanness and brilliancy of the cave of Cacahuamilpa that set it apart from other spectacular caverns.

[5] Fanny's appreciation of Cacahuamilpa and her prediction about it prove to have been well founded: it is now a national park with a steady stream of Mexican and other *turistas*. She could hardly have foreseen what a little more than a century would bring. There are electric lights in place of pine torches; an administration building with gates and tickets instead of the great open mouth and the indignant alcalde; and a parking lot and paved roads from three directions instead of the hair-raising trail.
When first seen by one of the editors in 1937, Cacahuamilpa was open to visitors only on occasional special days. A few electric light bulbs had been installed; but, to stay within the available power, lights had to be turned off behind, and on ahead, as one progressed into the otherwise dark and mysterious depths.

[6] Calderón's letter to the prefect, and the pencilled note he had earlier written to the Indian judge, evidently had no effect upon the future operations of the shrewd Indian officials who ruled over their little world of the town and the cave. From a slightly later account, it is obvious why the local prefect would not have interfered: he himself received a goodly percentage of any fees collected from parties visiting the cave.
When in 1842 a group including Brantz Mayer, United States secretary of legation, and two other diplomats proposed to leave the village for the cave, its Indian guides refused to move without permission from the judge, and took the visitors before him. The barefoot but dignified official then ordered read aloud (by the village schoolmaster, his secretary) the visitors' official documents permitting them to travel unmolested within the republic. After examining them, upside down, he showed himself well able to cope with national and international affairs. The caciques in Mexico's capital and in other lands, he said authoritatively, might issue licenses to travel above ground, but the caves were underground, and to see them they would need his permission, and furthermore would have to pay for it. The fee, first set at ten dollars, was reduced by mutual diplomatic compromise to five: two for him, two for the local prefect, and one for the schoolmaster. Bows were exchanged. The victorious Indian judge commended the strangers for their gentlemanly manners, and instructed their guides to bring them back safely. (Mayer, *Mexico as It Was and as It Is*, pp. 162, 191–92.)

[7] Only a few years before, Don Antonio Silva had augmented the handsome church with a tower (see Plate 104). It was finished in 1837, "the work, material, and its bells"

costing 5,000 pesos. The donor related these facts on a tablet that was still affixed to the church when one of the editors saw Cocoyotla exactly a century later.

[8] The full eclipse was announced on calendars for 7:28 p.m. of Friday, February 5 (feast day of Mexico's beloved Felipe de Jesús).

[9] This was probably Alpuyeca, the only settlement in the area that would seem to fit Fanny's description.

[10] The simple but generously offered hospitality described here hardly suggests a great estate, but Ward mentions the hacienda of El Puente as one of the principal sugar-producing establishments in this part of Mexico. (*Mexico in 1827*, I, 66.) The river crossed and the neighboring village both were named Xochitepec.

[11] Brantz Mayer, United States secretary of legation, describes a visit, as an uninvited but hospitably welcomed guest, to this hacienda, called Temisco. It had been acquired not long before by two brothers, Rafael and Felipe Neri del Barrio. (Fanny will speak warmly about the family of the latter, although she seems never to have realized that he was named for San Felipe Neri, and that the Neri was, therefore, a part of his baptismal name rather than part of his family's surname.) Mayer tells of his astonishment and pleasure in discovering that his host, Rafael del Barrio, who was dressed in rough country clothes, had traveled widely, spoke four languages, and could converse brilliantly on a variety of subjects. There was, he reported, little furniture in the large bare house and his host slept in a hammock, but there were a piano and a fine library. (*Mexico as It Was and as It Is*, pp. 74–76.)

Temisco also appears in the memoirs of a British visitor to the sugar country in the 1850's. It was, the author said, a particularly well managed estate: whereas the owners of some haciendas left everything to their administrators, a son of the family generally lived there. (Edward B. Tylor, *Anahuac*, p. 183.)

The modern traveler on the old road between Cuernavaca and Taxco passes close by Temisco's large buildings that loom up just east of the highway. One of its unusual architectural details is shown in Plate 106.

[12] Fanny entered "7th" here, but from the context it is clear that the next day was intended.

34. Around the Volcanoes

[1] The *oceloxochitl*—a Nahuatl name signifying "ocelot flower"—is shown in the cut. Apparently Fanny should have identified this Indian term with her "tiger's flower," rather than with the "viper's head"—which enjoyed the Indian name of *coatzontecoxochitl* (according to Clavijero, *Historia Antigua* . . . , I, 17–18). The former of these two flowers is also called *cacomite*, and one sees it sold in a dried form in Mexican herb shops as being good for the liver.

[2] The Convento de la Asunción, built by the Dominican friars about 1567, is today a colonial monument noted for its sturdy cloister with barrel-vaulted arcades. There are also remnants of paintings in earth colors.

[3] Don Juan Goríbar (whose wife was Doña María Eca y Músquiz) and his brother Don Faustino were co-owners of Cocoyoc.

[4] The sugarworks of Cocoyoc and its small chapel are in a state of ruin, but its large house with arcades at two levels has undergone recent restoration work and parts have been used as a country pleasure residence. A modern paved road passes under the former hacienda's stoutly built aqueduct.

The cane rubbish that fed this accidental blaze—that is, the dry stalks or *bagazo* left after the juice had been pressed from the ripe cane—would normally have been fed into the furnaces operating Cocoyoc's refinery. From other sources one learns a little more about the usual sequence of the sugar-making process of the time. The cane stalks, from which the leafy parts had been cut for fodder, were pressed between large, slow-moving copper rollers, powered sometimes by horses or mules, but apparently more usually by water. The residue, when dried, provided the bulk of the fuel needed for the boiling process.

From the rollers, the dark grayish-green juice was conveyed by trough to the boiling-house. There it was heated and reduced in a series of great open caldrons. (The boiling froth that was constantly skimmed off was saved for later use in making rum.) Slaked lime and sometimes ashes were added to the mixture as aids in precipitating the non-sugar contents of the juice. When, after boiling, the sugar syrup reached the crystallization stage, it was transferred to large cone-shaped molds, from which the molasses was allowed to drain out at the bottom. These molds were then removed to another building, where the sugar was "clayed," that is, covered with a fine liquid mud, which had the effect of absorbing impurities and whitening the sugar.

Each establishment was thus the focus not only of a large agricultural and livestock operation, but of a sizable industrial operation as well. (*Sketch of . . . Mexico,* anonymous, pp. 219–22; Ward, *Mexico in 1827,* I, 64–69; Tylor, *Anahuac,* pp. 179–81; Gilbert Haven, *Our Next-Door Neighbor: A Winter in Mexico,* pp. 243–44; James B. McNair, *Sugar and Sugar-Making,* pp. 10–16.)

[5] It seems likely that Fanny assembled material on trees new to her from too hasty notes: *cacahuates* are peanuts. Perhaps she meant the *cacahuantli* (whose Latin name is *gliricidia sepium*), beautiful in blossom and useful as a protecting cover for coffee and young cocoa trees. Papaw can mean the papaya.

The tree with the pink tassels, described in the next paragraph, was probably that called *tlacoxiloxochitl* in Nahuatl, *cabello de ángel* in Spanish (angel's hair), and whose botanical name is *calliandra grandiflora.*

[6] This is Fanny's only reference to the hacienda of Calderón, whose name for obvious reasons she remembered. Like several other haciendas in this area, Calderón had its own aqueduct—and a long one—conspicuous from a distance in the level terrain.

[7] Casasano at the time of the Calderóns' visit was also the property of Don Juan Goríbar, their host at Cocoyoc. A prosperous-appearing plant for the production of alcohol serves as the modern successor to the old sugarworks. The hacienda's *casco* or nucleus of buildings is a noble, melancholy ruin—the great two-story main house with its graceful arcades, a roofless shell. (See Plate 107.) Its church, when the editors last saw it, was, however, in good repair—and the tank or reservoir shortly to be mentioned was still there.

[8] The historic city of Cuautla, sometimes called Cuautla Morelos or Cuautla Amilpas—which Fanny earlier confused with Cacahuamilpa—lies only a few miles south of Casasano. In referring to it she wrote: "Politically speaking, Cuautla Amilpas has been the theatre of important events. It was there that the curate Morelos shut himself up with a troop of insurgents, until, the place being besieged by the Spaniards under Calleja, and the party of Morelos driven to extremity for want of food, he secretly abandoned his position, drawing off his forces in the night." The destructive siege mentioned by Fanny lasted seventy-two days, from February 19 to the first of May 1812, and during the silent withdrawal Morelos narrowly escaped capture. The little city would again be caught up in tragedy during the upheavals of the revolution of 1910–20.

[9] Santa Clara's large church (Plate 109) is set off rather than dwarfed by the spectacular rocks behind it, almost small mountains in size (Plate 108). When last seen by one of the editors, however, the atrium was used for the grazing of cattle, and birds nested in the nave of the splendid building.

[10] Fanny reported their departure on February 11, but the context shows that it must have been the following day. It was Joaquín García Icazbalceta—son of the proprietors Eusebio García Monasterio and his wife Ana Icazbalceta—who as a youth of about sixteen saw Fanny fall into a fountain (not at Santa Clara), and who many years later told his granddaughter, who told us, the editors. (See note 2, p. 710.)

Don Joaquín in his turn inherited Santa Clara among other large properties in Morelos, and became a distinguished historian, as well as collector and publisher of important source materials on Mexico's early colonial history.

[11] In approaching Colón, the Calderóns' party crossed the line that now separates the states of Morelos and Puebla. Colón and San Nicolás lie in the area between Atencingo and Matamoros, and were the most southerly points of their journey.

The large cobblestone plaza at San Nicolás, the center for the hacienda's once-dependent village, and the splendid aqueduct marching on arches built for posterity (Plates 110 and 111) suggest what this and other large properties must once have been in their days of isolation and self-sufficiency. (While no effort has been made to determine the true extent of San Nicolás at the time of the Calderóns' visit, the dimensions given—equal to approximately forty-seven miles by thirteen—appear far too generous for an hacienda in this area.)

[12] The "I" in the previous sentence is from the Singer copy. Her printed text credits the pun to an unnamed individual represented only by a blank.

Colón, when the editors last saw it in 1950, was surrounded by brilliant green cane fields in various stages of growth. Like many other sugar haciendas it centered around a roofless, ruined house, but the effect it must have presented in 1841 could easily be imagined. The hacienda's core of buildings was reached through a long, low-walled village street, ankle-deep with dust, and bordered by cottages with steeply-pitched thatch roofs. Cattle and turkeys crowded the side lanes. The hacienda church (apparently added to in the later nineteenth century) was still functioning.

[13] Perhaps the play by Beaumarchais in translation; perhaps the opera by Rossini; or perhaps Paisiello's earlier *Barber of Seville*, said to have been the second opera sung in Mexico—in 1806. (Rubén M. Campos, *El Folklore y la Música Mexicana*, p. 162.)

The role of theatrical troupes in rural Mexico is suggested in an account by a British visitor of 1825 who was a guest at another great sugar hacienda, that of Santa Inés. He tells of driving into the town of Cuautla with his hosts one afternoon to see a play given on a stage (six feet by three) improvised in the town's cockpit. The audience included humbler folk as well as the local gentry. (*Sketch of . . . Mexico*, pp. 216–18.)

Matamoros was some seven miles across-country to the northeast of the hacienda of Colón. Was it perhaps the tireless Fanny—possessed once again (as in Puebla the year before) of "a great desire to see *something*"—who was voted down by less enthusiastic companions?

[14] Literally, a fifteenth-century family of Moors in Granada, whose members feuded with the Zegris—but perhaps here the word is used to mean a Moor in general. Fanny may have read *The Alhambra* by Washington Irving, published in 1832.

[15] The martial effect of the roof-drainage pipes mentioned here may be judged by Plate 112, which depicts not Atlixco but Jonacatepec, near the hacienda of Santa Clara.

An old lithograph of Atlixco is shown as Plate 113. Atlixco's giant tree survived for approximately a century longer before its demise and removal.

[16] Here, as in a few other places, misprints in wording were caught and corrected by hand in the Carlisle copy, presumably by Fanny.

[17] Both Cortés' son by Marina and his much younger son by a marriage later in life were named Martín—and both were believed by the Spanish authorities to be involved in a plot among the Mexican-born sons of the first conquerors. The affair took place after the death of Cortés. One historian, at least, has considered the possibility that under more positive leadership the boldly conceived plan to separate Mexico from Spain at so early a date might have succeeded. (Simpson, *Many Mexicos*, pp. 132–40.)

[18] Careful research on the subject by later Mexican scholars suggests that Marina was born about 1500, not at Painala but close by at Oluta, in the Isthmus of Tehuantepec.

The land grant made to her when she parted from Cortés is thought to have been an island in the Coatzacoalcos River. Supposedly she is buried under an artificial mound at the edge of Jáltipan, where it is a tradition that one day she will return to undo the harm she brought her people. (Miguel Covarrubias, *Mexico South*, pp. 40–41.)

Marina's son Martín Cortés—who was legitimized later by special decree—died in Spain. But *his* son, who bore his famous grandfather's name, returned to Mexico, and his line of descendants lives there today. (Gustavo A. Rodríguez, *Doña Marina*, genealogical chart preceding p. 59.)

[19] It was held in Fanny's time (*Mosaico Mexicano*, I, 205), and long after, that Popocatepetl was Mexico's highest mountain. An atlas of 1885 still gave it first place. While it is now known to be outranked by Orizaba, this fact does not lessen its majestic effect as seen both from the valley of Mexico and from the Puebla side.

[20] This is part of a poem in Spanish, written in 1820, entitled "En el Teocalli de Cholula." The translation was presumably made by Fanny. The poet José María Heredia was born in 1803 in Cuba, was banished for his liberal opinions, and lived for three years in the United States. (While there he wrote, among other poems, one on Niagara Falls.) He settled in Mexico in 1826 and died, in his thirties, in 1839.

For publication Fanny included the Spanish text, and in the Carlisle copy of *Life in Mexico* various typographical errors were carefully rectified, presumably by Fanny herself.

[21] The pyramid of Cholula is an enormous man-made mass whose size is not immediately impressive because, as Fanny says, it resembles a small natural mountain, overgrown with vegetation. Estimates of its size vary in view of the difficulty of measuring the time-worn mound with precision. Even the most conservative figures, however, make it far larger in bulk—although less high—than the Great Pyramid of Cheops. A modern writer in the field of archaeology, Frederick A. Peterson, suggests that it was once much higher than its present measurement of 210 feet. (*Ancient Mexico*, p. 63.) The interior of the pyramid of Cholula has been carefully studied, and its electrically-lit tunnels are now open to visitors.

35. Four Days in Puebla

[1] The identity of Don Antonio, as well as others in this and the following chapter, comes from the Singer copy.

[2] Perhaps it was the performance that was dull. Puebla's Teatro Principal, said to be

the oldest still-functioning theater in the New World, seemed to the editors a delightful building. It stands on its own little square, three blocks north and two blocks east of the principal plaza. Four tiers of arched boxes form an elegant oval around its sloping floor. Seating about seven hundred, it somehow manages to be both intimate and dignified. After a severe fire in 1902 it was out of use until its restoration in 1960, aided by the generosity of a North American resident of Puebla, Mary Street Jenkins.

[3] The Haros' large house still stands, somewhat altered and a story taller, at 219 on the south side of what is now the Avenida General Maximino Avila Camacho, a half-block east of Puebla's principal plaza. A most striking feature remains—the row of rainspouts in the shape of small wheeled cannons that once served to shoot the rainwater from the *azotea* beyond the sidewalk and into the street (see Plate 114).

Not on her first visit, nor here—nor on her third visit still to come—does Fanny mention Puebla's uniquely ornate and festive architecture. Many of its old churches and houses, the Haros' among them, are faced with colored tiles arranged in lively patterns.

[4] The Señora de Haro was Dolores Ovando de Cervantes, a relative of the rich, titled Cervantes family in the capital. Her husband (whose full name is usually recorded as Antonio de Haro y Tamariz) was about thirty. In another book of memoirs he is described as small, dapper, and fragile in appearance. (Prieto, *Memorias* . . . , II, 171–72.) Don Antonio was one of five brothers who left their mark on Puebla. The oldest, Joaquín, had been (and would be again) governor. The youngest, Luis, would found and endow a Puebla hospital. (Hugo Leicht, *Las Calles de Puebla*, pp. 186–87.)

[5] The most remarkable sight in Puebla was and is, perhaps, the Rosary Chapel of the church of Santo Domingo (Plate 115). In the Calderóns' day, however, it may well have been considered gaudy and old-fashioned and therefore not worthy of the attention of distinguished visitors.

[6] The *paseo*, now called the Paseo Bravo, is indeed pleasant, with its fine trees now fully grown, fountains, a drive around it, and various resources for the diversion of children. It is five blocks west of the cathedral.

[7] From internal evidence, it would appear that in what follows Fanny is first presenting the events of Wednesday, and that she later treats the events of Thursday and Friday as if taking place on one day.

[8] Dr. Miguel Ramos Arizpe, at this time sixty-six, had earlier played a rather special role in Mexican history. He was a devout churchman, trained not only in philosophy, theology, and canon law, but in civil law as well. In public life he had shown himself a determined liberal and a shrewd politician. After taking a leading part in framing the federalist constitution of 1824 he became President Victoria's Minister of Justice and Ecclesiastical Affairs (a post he held again in 1832). During his first tenure of office there arrived in Mexico a papal encyclical pointing out the obligation of Mexican churchmen to bring back their pastoral flocks to allegiance to their former king. Following wide discussion, Mexican churchmen instead, under the leadership of Ramos Arizpe, stood with the new republic against the papacy and against Spain. Fanny was evidently familiar with the historian Zavala's description of Ramos Arizpe, contained in his *Ensayo Histórico* . . . , I, 151–52.

Untidy in dress and unprepossessing in appearance, he made an impression of strong force of character on those with whom he dealt. (Manuel Gómez Pedraza, "Don Miguel Ramos Arizpe," in *Museo Mexicano*, II, 105–10; Ward, *Mexico in 1827*, I, 328–30.) Engravings of the period give Ramos Arizpe a rotund face and a determined expression (see Plate 84). An English writer of the 1820's said of him: "I soon became acquainted with a person of singular character and appearance, and who for a time was the most influential person in Mexico, both on account of his great talents and his knowledge of the routine of official business." (Hardy, *Travels in . . . Mexico*, p. 12.)

[9] Francisco Pablo Vásquez had been named bishop of Puebla some ten years earlier and was now well past seventy. As stated in note 7 at the top of page 722, he devoted years of negotiation in Europe to Mexico's effort (which bore fruit in 1837 in a document signed by others) to obtain from the Holy See its recognition of Mexican independence.

[10] In the published text this was printed 1833, but the context shows it in error, and a tablet on the factory itself gives January 7, 1835, as the precise date.

[11] An anonymous article about the vicissitudes of La Constancia Mexicana is contained in the *Calendario de Galván* for 1842 (pp. 61–64). It is of some interest that the "mechanist" who was shipwrecked three times between February 16 and August 18, 1837, bore an Anglo-Saxon name: Calvin Symmes.

[12] In the northwest corner of the Paseo Bravo in Puebla one sees today a statue of the persevering Esteban de Antuñano, "*fundador de la fabril en el país*—founder of the

nation's manufacturing industry." He wears a long frock coat and a large bow tie, and his right hand rests on a symbolic spinning wheel.

In 1962 the editors enjoyed a visit to the factory of La Constancia Mexicana, situated some five miles northwest of Puebla. Behind an attractive shady quadrangle, and hidden by later supplementary construction, lies the solid old plant. Once we had arrived there, it seemed entirely natural to see—and hear—its still pulsing and clattering activity after 127 years of operation.

It was the abundant water power of the Río Atoyac, fed by the snowy slopes of Ixtacihuatl, that drew Antuñano to his country site. Other entrepreneurs followed him, and additional mills were subsequently established on the same stream.

La Constancia's manager reported that, with its present 461 looms, far more power is needed than can be supplied by the mill's historic source. It consequently purchases electricity as needed, though still using the available water supply to power directly the overhead belts, substantially as in Fanny's day.

Antuñano, in laying the foundation for Mexico's industrial revolution, unknowingly was also laying part of the foundation for Mexico's far-reaching political and economic revolution of the twentieth century. Bloody strikes in the cotton-factory areas sparked the smoldering discontent that in 1911 finally ended the long reign of President Porfirio Díaz, and with it the semi-feudal society still reminiscent of that which Fanny saw and described.

[13] A half-block west of Antuñano's statue is the prison, or *palacio penal*. It was damaged in the fighting against the French in 1863, but was finally opened in 1901. (Enrique Juan Palacios, *Puebla, Su Territorio y Sus Habitantes,* I, 275–76.) The orphanage occupied a plain but substantial building, now a public school, two doors north of the church of San Cristóbal.

[14] The building that housed the convent of El Carmen and its adjoining church (now designated a colonial monument) were built in the distinctive Puebla style, and still stand on the plaza of El Carmen at Avenida 17 Oriente and the Calle del 16 de Septiembre. It seems likely that some of the paintings that Calderón admired may be among those now housed in the museum of the convent of Santa Mónica, in which works of art from various former convents are displayed.

[15] Miguel Jerónimo Zendejas was probably the artist mentioned, although his less able son Lorenzo also painted. The older Zendejas, who died in 1815 at a great age, was an extremely fertile painter whose works are hung in a number of Puebla churches. Modern critics have held that some of them show hints of impressionist concepts yet to come. There were three Puebla sculptors surnamed Cora. The most famous was José Zacarías Cora (1752–1816), who worked in the neo-classic style and was creator of Puebla's most important sculptures, including the figure of San Cristóbal in the church of that name. He is also remembered for his statues in the towers of the capital's cathedral. (Toussaint, *Arte Colonial en México,* pp. 354, 359–60.)

[16] Calderón had perhaps met, in Spain, the Mexican diplomat Miguel Santa María who was sent in 1835 to negotiate a treaty of peace and friendship with the mother country. His work came to a successful conclusion with the signing of a treaty at the close of 1836, but he died in Spain, still a comparatively young man, before it was implemented.

[17] Ramos Arizpe and various other prominent Mexicans left Mexico at the end of 1810 to become delegates to the Cortes of Cádiz, a body that gave legislative representation in Spain to colonials. The novel plan was established during the Napoleonic occupation, the provisional government of unoccupied Spain having passed into the hands of a group of liberals. During this period Ramos Arizpe became well known for his outspoken zeal on behalf of his homeland. When Napoleon fell, the restored Ferdinand VII launched a reign of suppression and Ramos Arizpe was sent to prison. After being held in jail for a year and a half in Madrid, he was sent into custodial exile in Valencia, from which he was freed in 1820 by subsequent revolutionary events in Spain. (Manuel Gómez Pedraza, "Don Miguel Ramos Arizpe," in *Museo Mexicano,* II, 105–10; Bancroft, *History of Mexico,* V, 31.)

[18] In view of Fanny's previously expressed architectural preferences, it is not surprising to see her enthusiasm for Puebla's magnificent, rather formal cathedral. It is unconventional in only one significant respect: instead of facing the city's principal plaza, it turns one of its long sides to the square. Its 200-foot towers dominate the Puebla skyline.

[19] Names which suggest themselves, as belonging to Puebla families well known in this period, are Mangino, Marrón, Miranda, or Múgica—but these are merely possibilities drawn from sources of the time.

[20] Bishop Vásquez made his collection of paintings during his long sojourn in Europe.

Perhaps what Fanny calls the bishop's library was the magnificent Biblioteca Palafoxiana, donated by an earlier bishop: it is still today one of the boasts of Puebla.

[21] The Irish William Vincent Wallace was a pianist, violinist, a professor at the Royal Conservatory in London, and the composer, among other works, of the once very popular opera *Maritana*. He made an extremely successful tour in Mexico at this time. Advertisements of the period announce for sale the music of a new waltz—"*La Mexicana, Wals nuevo compuesto por W. V. Wallace.*"

The opera singer Mme Adela Cesari will perform later in the capital.

36. Tales of Robbery and Murder

[1] Antonio Haro y Tamariz was to lead a dramatic life. He fought boldly at Chapultepec Castle in the United States-Mexican War. In 1844, and again in 1853, he served as Minister of the Treasury, and was known as an energetic and honest public official. In 1856, suspected of plotting against the liberal government then in power, he was taken into custody and was on the way to mandatory exile when he escaped and became a leader of a conservative revolutionary group centered in Puebla. After a regular siege, the revolutionaries capitulated, but Haro y Tamariz refused to surrender, eluded those trying to take him, disappeared, and was said to have slipped out of Mexico in disguise on a French ship. (Tylor, *Anahuac*, pp. 111–13; Zamacois, *Historia de Méjico*, XIV, 154–62, 173, 192, 222.) He evidently returned later, for he was among those who welcomed the French forces which preceded Maximilian. Still later—with the consent of his wife and daughter—Haro y Tamariz relinquished family ties to become a lay brother in the Society of Jesus. He died in Rome. (Ortega y Pérez Gallardo, *Historia Genealógica* . . . , I, familia Cervantes; Decorme, *Historia de la Compañia de Jesús* . . . , II, 242 fn.)

[2] The governor of the department of Puebla was General Felipe Codallos.

[3] Fanny seems to have been somewhat confused by the fact that Puebla's grid streets were laid out at an angle to the cardinal points of the compass. The large isolated volcanic cone of Malinche looms almost exactly to the northeast, rather than to the north. The hills of Guadalupe and Loreto were later, on May 5, 1862, the site of Mexico's great victory over the invading French forces, and their fortified crests are now a park.

The sizable mountain of El Pinar (also called El Pinal) lies southeast of Malinche. There is no church on its summit.

[4] In describing this view, Fanny incorrectly had it south instead of west. The events she mentions here all took place during the strife-torn years that began with the close of President Victoria's administration—touched upon briefly in the next chapter.

[5] There had been many compilations and editions under this title. The latest, by G. Thompson and published in London in 1840, was *The Newgate Calendar; containing the lives of the most notorious characters who have violated the laws of their country.* As to the book on the crusades, perhaps Fanny was referring to the *Histoire des Croisades* by Joseph François Michaud, or to *The History of Chivalry and the Crusades* by the Reverend Henry Stebbing (published in Edinburgh in 1829).

[6] That Mexican robbers could be considerate, pious, and interested in music is shown by the anecdotes that abound in memoirs of the period. These seem in part to back up Count Cortina's contention.

A Spanish diplomat in Mexico a few years later says that on one occasion a group of robbers, having stripped a carriage of its baggage, found that their loot included Santa Anna's new wooden leg. They sent it on to the general with expressions of regret over the delay. (Conte, *Recuerdos de un Diplomático*, I, 276.)

Lady Emmeline Stuart-Wortley tells the story of brigands who robbed a party of priests. After having ordered their victims to lie face down in the dust while their baggage was being ransacked, they then courteously but insistently petitioned the padres for absolution from their crimes. (*Travels* . . . , II, 228.)

Charles Joseph Latrobe (in *The Rambler in Mexico*, pp. 142–43) said that García, the noted opera singer, was "set upon by banditti and pillaged, even to his snuff-box, diamond-ring, and pantaloons: after which, the robbers insisted that he should sing for them. He did so—and was hissed most obstreperously by his lawless auditory! It is said that he had borne the pillaging with becoming temper, but the hissing he never forgot nor forgave."

A much later visitor from the United States, Colonel Albert S. Evans, was strongly impressed by stories of the robbers' poise and politeness. "They always apologize for the act, regretting that necessity compels them to do it, and in parting with the traveler, devoutly commend him to the protecting care of Divine Providence. When not too sharply pressed by the Government, the different gangs in any one state usually have a sort of business connection, and, if you desire it, the leader of the first band into whose hands you fall will very courteously write out a pass for you to take along to save you from further molestation. I have one of these passes in my possession." (*Our Sister Republic*, pp. 203–4.) The writer then described the robbery of a friend of his who asked for such a pass, and who suggested also that a small sum be returned to him so that he might eat upon the road. The robber returned the sum asked and pressed also upon the traveler as a gift a small purse which, he said, he had obtained from the stock of a German peddler who had recently passed that way. The traveler proceeded on his route and was soon stopped by another band of robbers who honored the pass and who, moreover, supplied the victim with a horse to take the place of one of his which had gone lame upon the road. "I have a prejudice against being robbed by anybody," concluded Evans, "but if I must be robbed, let it be by a Mexican robber, by all means."

[7] We have assumed here the name of the large and interesting family headed by the Marqués de Apartado, various of whose members the Calderóns came to know well. Two male members appear in the next chapter and also two of its women, and later Fanny will mention five other ladies belonging to the family. The Fagoagas were enormously rich. Humboldt, many years earlier, had spoken of their "*zelo de bien público*—zeal for the public good—and of the fact that their fortune was the largest ever derived from a single mine. (*Ensayo Politico* . . . , I, 244.) The subjects of this anecdote were probably members of the family of José María Fagoaga, who had lived much abroad.

[8] Rafael Beraza, or Veraza as his name was also written—while of no importance to this story—was evidently so remarkable a character that he appears in a number of memoirs of these and much later times. An ex-Spaniard, he was the courier for the English legation, and his tireless speed in making the 260-mile journey between the capital and Veracruz was legendary. In the 1820's he was in the employ of H. G. Ward, who said (*Mexico in 1827*, II, 251–52) that because Beraza had survived yellow fever he went up and down to the coast once or twice a month at all seasons without concern for his health. He seems to have carried private as well as official mail. The Spanish newspaper *La Hesperia* for August 15, 1840, for example, ran a notice to the effect that Rafael Veraza, departing for Veracruz on August 22, would take mail intended for the British packet.

An account of the 1850's indicates that by that time he may have begun to slow down. "Rafael Beraza, the courier of the English Mission at Mexico, used to ride this with despatches regularly once a month in forty hours, and occasionally in thirty-five. He changed horses about every ten or fifteen miles; and now and then, when overcome by sleep, he would let the boy who accompanied him to the next stop ride first, his own horse following, and the rider comfortably dozing as he went along." (Tylor, *Anahuac*, p. 167.)

With the passage of another decade Beraza evidently resorted to a diligence—at least when he wanted to save his energy for a ball. "Not the least remarkable person present was Señor Rafael Beraza, who has filled the post of special courier to the British Embassy for upwards of forty years, to the satisfaction of everybody. Señor Beraza, who is now, I believe, upwards of eighty years of age, is, without doubt, the most active individual in Mexico. He informed me that he had run up from Vera Cruz expressly for the ball, and had arrived in the capital at six o'clock that evening; that, after the ball, he proposed taking the return diligence at four a.m. in order to reach Vera Cruz in time to receive Mr. Scarlett, the newly-appointed British minister . . ." (W. H. Bullock, *Across Mexico in 1864–5*, p. 104.)

[9] The date heading the present chapter (at variance with what Fanny entered herself) is derived from the evidence of this paragraph.

Carlos María de Bustamante in his unpublished diary—carefully sifted, and quoted at pertinent points by Felipe Teixidor—recorded that the wife of the Spanish minister went costumed *a la Escosesa*—in the Scotch manner. So full of "decent people" that dancing was impossible, the ball to Don Carlos was noteworthy for the great luxury of the women, "chiefly of the wife of the so-called General Barrera," and for the extremely costly pearls of the wives of the "infamous money-lenders." (*La Vida en México*, II, *Notas*, 182.)

[10] Lent had actually begun on Ash Wednesday, two days before. The public masked ball had been held on Mardi gras.

37. Distinguished Men of Mexico

[1] H_____ may have been Fanny's brother Henry Inglis, who had remained in Scotland. One doubts, however, that she ever wrote any such letter as here implied. In what fol-

lows, her treatment of the wife of Señor Gómez Pedraza—if related to her subsequent text (p. 542)—suggests that this chapter was written at a much later date, perhaps after her return to the United States.

[2] Posada alone of those here listed will not be the subject of further comment in this chapter. As the reader will remember, he was the jovial Archbishop of Mexico.

[3] Victoria had begun the study of the law when he plunged into the War of Independence.

[4] In fairness to Nicolás Bravo, of whom this is almost the only mention, it should be said that during the War of Independence he had demonstrated impulsive forbearance toward a group of prisoners in his power. Spanish officials had shortly before executed his own father, yet Bravo set his prisoners free. (Ward, *Mexico in 1827*, I, 204.)

Bravo's assignment to conduct to the coast the fallen ex-Emperor and his sizable family and entourage (including relatives, priests, and many servants) was not an enviable one. He was under instructions not to permit any admirers of the magnetic Iturbide—who thought of himself as a retiring monarch—to render him homage, and also to protect him from possible harm from his enemies. Near Jalapa there was an attempt on Iturbide's life, which Bravo and his men frustrated. But on the latter part of the journey, at least, Bravo seems to have become peremptory, and there were times when Iturbide was meanly housed. Fanny's version of the episode almost certainly came from a passage in Zavala's history (*Ensayo Histórico . . .* , I, 251), for which Iturbide's nephew, who accompanied him, was the source.

[5] Gómez Pedraza (pictured in the cut) did serve as president of Mexico for some three months during an interim period in 1833. His attempted return and withdrawal to New Orleans, as described here, had taken place in 1830. Fanny's discussion seems to be derived in part from Zavala's *Ensayo Histórico . . .* (II, 39, 56–58, 140, 336–38). Zavala said that Gómez Pedraza was by nature a man of few words, stoical in manner, but that in public life he was a powerful orator and an able parliamentarian.

He was also portrayed by another contemporary writer, José María Luis Mora. As Fanny quotes Mora elsewhere, she was probably familiar with his frank assessment of Gómez Pedraza as a man of strong character, passionately honest (he left office all but impoverished), but with a hard, rancorous streak. (*Obras Sueltas*, I, LXXVIII–IX.) Later, while the Calderóns were still in Mexico, Gómez Pedraza re-entered public life briefly as Minister of Foreign Affairs, and Calderón's successor spoke of him as friendly and reasonable. (*Despachos Generales*, I, 272–73.)

His wife's father, Juan Francisco de Azcárate, had been a leader in an abortive pre-revolutionary independence movement in August 1808. It was based on the legalistic ground that as Napoleon controlled the Spanish monarchy, authority over Mexico should devolve upon the viceroy, supported by a provisional local government. The ambitious viceroy concurred, but other Spaniards seized him and installed a substitute. Azcárate spent three years in prison but survived until 1831 and thus saw a decade of Mexico's independence. (Teja Zabre, *Guide to the History of Mexico*, pp. 225–26.)

[6] This article on earthquakes, entitled "Terremotos: a la Señorita Doña * * *" may be found in a volume of *El Mosaico Mexicano* for 1840 (IV, 545–53). Faraday's electrical researches a few years earlier no doubt account for two lines of Cortina's poem that is a part of the article: *Eres tú mi máquina eléctrica/Y yo soy tu conductor* (Thou art my electric machine, and I am thy conductor).

Cortina, as one of the Calderóns' first callers, has been described earlier (see p. 92 and also Plate 74). A letter from Fanny to Prescott may serve to add a few touches to Cortina's portrait: "He is a man of good talents, a perfect gentleman and very distinguished in looks and manners, but his head is a sort of *windmill*. He is in a constant whirl, flying here and there, promising, forgetting. Indeed, this last quality is fortunate, for he promises to send you everything in and out of his house that you admire." (Wolcott, *Correspondence of . . . Prescott*, p. 129.)

[7] This play had been first produced in Mexico in 1833. Its youthful heroine, an avid reader of romantic novels, becomes engaged to a devoted, highly eligible young man held in warm esteem by her father. She is plagued by indecision in view of the lack of drama which her future life seems to offer. Her understanding suitor pretends to have been disinherited, and arranges to be dismissed by the father of his affianced. She meets the challenge by running off with him (via a window, although the front door is available), and they are married. Soon wearied of housekeeping in an attic, she accepts, with relief, parental forgiveness—and returns with her amused husband to conventional life.

[8] Manuel Eduardo Gorostiza (referred to as José by Fanny in her published text) has already been encountered as one of her early callers—"decidedly the ugliest man to be seen anywhere" (p. 92). Someone who knew him, although much younger, characterized him as not only a gifted and amusing man, but also an upright one, possessed of in-

herent nobility of character. (Pimentel, *Obras*, V, 40.) Fanny does not happen to mention the fact that he had earlier served as Mexico's minister of foreign affairs. In this year of 1841 his name is mentioned a number of times in newspapers in connection with his effort —later successful—to found an institution for juvenile delinquents. His interest in music and the theater was constant and passionate, and another writer of memoirs recalled the fact that the Gorostiza house was a center for the musical and artistic world of Mexico. (Prieto, *Memorias* . . . , I, 263–64.) In spite of advancing years and poor health, he enlisted at the time of the United States-Mexican War and fought at Churubusco.

9 Fanny is not quite accurate in according only literary fame to Carlos María de Bustamante, whose likeness is shown in Plate 81. At this time he was sixty-seven, but, when younger, he was for many years in the thick of political events. In 1818—during the struggle for independence—he spent eight months imprisoned in the fortress of San Juan de Ulúa, three of them in solitary confinement. In 1823, as an opponent of the authoritarian moves made by Iturbide after he became emperor, Bustamante was imprisoned again. He was a deputy in congress at various times and was a good speaker, but he spoke so often and so long that he sometimes emptied the chamber. According to his modern biographer—who quotes Lucas Alamán—Bustamante was singularly fortunate in his attractive, valiant, and devoted wife, María Manuela García Villaseñor. (Victoriano Salado Alvarez, *La Vida Azarosa y Romántica de Carlos María de Bustamante*, pp. 195–201, 256–57.)

Prescott, in a letter written not long before to Calderón, suggested that Bustamante was interested solely in the Indians' side of the conquest story: "I have long since distrusted him, though Mexican letters are under obligations to his editorial activities." (Wolcott, *Correspondence of . . . Prescott*, p. 136.) Bustamante not only wrote historical works, but also published important source material, and it was his credulity and his extremely free editing that brought criticism from other scholars.

The first of the three books whose titles Fanny lists in English was *Historia del Descubrimiento de la América Septentrional por Cristóbal Colón*, by Manuel de la Vega, edited and published by Bustamante in the Mexican capital in 1826. The second was likewise taken from older material and was entitled *Galería de Antiguos Príncipes Mexicanos*, published in Puebla in 1821. The third—*Tezcoco en los Ultimos Tiempos de Sus Antiguos Reyes, o Sea Relación Tomada de los Manuscritos Inéditos de Boturini; Redactados por el Lic. D. Mariano Veytia*—was published in Mexico in 1826 with notes and additions made by Bustamante "for study by Mexican youth."

Bustamante also wrote histories himself, three of which are cited in these notes. What may prove to be his unique contribution to Mexican history, however, remains at present almost entirely unpublished. It is a diary he kept from December 6, 1822, through the year 1841. Only one manuscript volume out of more than forty is lacking in the long record kept by this opinionated Mexican so deeply concerned with the welfare of his country.

10 The title in Spanish of Bustamante's gift to Fanny was *Mañanas de la Alameda de México*. It was published in two small volumes in 1835, and the quotation Fanny translates comes early in its text (pp. 6–7), following a discussion of the fortunate status of the colonies that had become, respectively, the United States and Mexico. Fanny placed special value on Bustamante's remarks because of his known anti-Spanish point of view.

11 In the original text this word is *lágrimas*—tears—which Fanny, with a feeling for the more reserved English equivalent, altered in translation to "emotion." For greater clarity, the editors have made a few other adjustments in Fanny's translation.

The book referred to is *Historia de la Revolución de Nueva España Antiguamente Anáhuac*, by the Dominican Fray José Servando Teresa de Mier Noriega y Guerra (1765–1827). It was published in London in 1813.

12 A reference, presumably, to José Mariano Beristáin de Souza, author of *Biblioteca Hispano-Americana Setentrional*, published in Mexico, 1816–21.

13 Carlos de Sigüenza y Góngora, born in 1645, was learned in many fields, including astronomy, physics, and Indian antiquities.

The epic poem *El Bernardo*, first published in 1624, was written by Bernardo de Balbuena (born in Spain, but resident some sixteen or seventeen years in Mexico). It is the fanciful story of Bernardo del Carpio, slayer of Roland at the victory over the French at Roncesvalles. According to a modern scholar of the work, John Van Horne, author of *El Bernardo of Bernardo de Balbuena*, the very long and humorless epic is nonetheless enlivened with some colorful passages.

14 The name of Quintana Roo, senator, cabinet officer, outstanding liberal, political writer, and poet, is commemorated in the large territory on the east of the Yucatán peninsula named in his honor. For his likeness, see Plate 82.

His handsome wife, Leona Vicario, reared in affluence and orphaned young, was a colorful figure. She met her future husband as a young lawyer acquainted with her guardian. Although sought in marriage by a rich young man of noble family, her affections were given to Quintana Roo, and like him she became deeply involved in the independence effort, to which she later gave unstintingly of her fortune. Opposed by her relatives in her revolutionary leanings, the spirited girl continued to pursue her own bent. Letters written in cipher, imprisonment under guard in a convent, a dramatic escape to join the insurgents, and marriage to Quintana Roo are only a few episodes of her story. She died in 1842, about the time Fanny was preparing her text for print.

[15] Lucas Alamán (see cut) has appeared in these pages as an organizer of mining ventures (p. 239) and as administrator of the Mexican property of the heirs of Cortés (p. 376). He is described as short in stature, ruddy-complexioned, low-voiced, and extremely deliberate in manner. (Hardy, Travels in . . . Mexico, pp. 10–11.) A Mexican who disagreed politically with Alamán spoke with gratitude of his kindness and admired his learning, but felt that on the subject of government his mind was closed. (Prieto, Memorias . . . , II, 233–35.) Descended through his mother from the Marqueses de San Clemente, he was aristocratic in background and beliefs, and was strongly conservative and pro-clerical. Experience with mob violence in his native Guanajuato during the early phase of the War of Independence seems to have left him with a lasting mistrust of popular rule.

Alamán's range of interests was broad. Trained as a mining engineer in Mexico, he later studied and traveled widely in Europe, and he was at home in several languages. He was active over a long period in mining and industry; he was interested in his country's national museum and its archives; he was concerned with public education and the improvement of livestock; and at a later date he wrote a classic history of Mexico. It was as a powerful political figure, however, that Alamán made his mark at an early age. He was never a popular leader and he never became president; but at different times his strong hand (his ruthless hand, said his opponents) was behind various regimes.

At the time of the Calderóns' stay he was absorbed with personal business difficulties rather than with politics; nevertheless he was thought by some to have had a hand in Gutiérrez Estrada's pamphlet advocating a monarchy for Mexico. Although conservative politically, Alamán favored vigorous economic innovations, and was convinced that Mexico could and would operate its own industries. (Valadés, Alamán, pp. 380, 381–84, 396–98, 408–9.)

Calderón apparently very much liked Alamán. In writing Prescott the previous May, he had called him a "learned and sympathetic friend." (Wolcott, Correspondence of . . . Prescott, p. 125.) In the text as heretofore printed, there appeared a footnote by Fanny saying: "He is now, September, 1842, once more filling the same situation [Minister of Foreign Affairs] under General Santa Anna." She must have been misinformed on this point after her return to the United States, for, according to Mexican government records, José María Bocanegra held the post. Years later, however, in 1853, Alamán did serve as Santa Anna's foreign minister, but died only a few weeks after taking office. (Juan Manuel Torrea, 135 Años de Labor Diplomática al Servicio de México, pp. 11–13, 23.)

Fanny, in writing Prescott a number of years later about Alamán, said: "He was a perfect caballero—his manners very distinguished—of a very gentle and pacific character." (Unpublished letter of October 19, 1859, in the Massachusetts Historical Society.)

[16] It may be remembered that the Calderóns' friend José Morán and his wife the Marquesa de Vivanco were owners of a villa in San Agustín de las Cuevas, as well as the nearby hacienda of San Antonio. The conservative Morán (Plate 79) was commented upon favorably by the outspoken liberal writer José María Luis Mora: General Morán had been a student and a hard worker, punctilious in the performance of his duties, and had risen to his high rank through merit. (Obras Sueltas, I, CCLIII–IV.)

In 1839 Morán was president of the council of state, and in that capacity would normally have served as acting-president of Mexico during several months when Anastasio Bustamante was absent from the capital combatting a federalist uprising. Morán was passed over, however; ostensibly because of his failing health. (Riva Palacio, editor, México a Través de los Siglos, IV, 434.)

[17] Juan Nepomuceno Almonte (see Plate 67), youngest member of the cabinet, was the ambitious Minister of War who had played a leading role as a loyal government man during the revolution of July 1840. Some years later he would serve twice as minister to the United States. He never achieved what he wanted: election to the presidency of Mexico. Abandoning his republican principles, he became a monarchist, and with Gutiérrez Estrada and others he had much to do with bringing the Austrian archduke Maximilian to reign for two strife-torn years as Emperor of Mexico. In 1869, not long after the fall of the empire (under which he held the rank of field marshal), Almonte died in France and was buried in Père Lachaise.

Fanny never specifically discusses Señora Almonte, born Dolores Quesada, whom she must have known as the wife of so prominent an official. The United States minister of about a year later, after observing that with a few shining exceptions the Mexican ladies were not well educated, said: "Mrs. Almonte, the wife of General Almonte, would be regarded as an accomplished lady in any country." (Thompson, Recollections of Mexico, p. 162.)

[18] Juan de Dios Cañedo, it will be recalled, had recently resigned from his post as Minister of Foreign Affairs. He had first achieved prominence in public service before the independence as one of Mexico's elected delegates to the Spanish Cortes, and had continued to hold a prominent place in public life: as a senator, as a diplomat, and twice as foreign minister. His incisive eloquence was memorable. H. G. Ward (Mexico in 1827, II, 712–13) described Cañedo's part in a famous senate debate over the first British-Mexican treaty—particularly in relation to the clause, bitterly opposed by many Mexican senators, which would permit British Protestants the right of burial. Cañedo began by saying that in principle he agreed with his colleagues. Because, however, larger numbers of British heretics might be expected to enter the country as a result of the projected treaty and because many of them would, while in Mexico, leave this life for the doom they so richly deserved, the practical problem of disposing of their unwanted remains had to be faced. To burn them would consume valuable fuel; to eat them he was disinclined; to export them would require legislation to amend the trade regulations. He therefore advised his fellow senators to permit burial. The clause was approved.

Cañedo would be brutally murdered on Holy Thursday 1850. Wide speculation ensued as to whether the crime was politically motivated.

[19] Felipe Neri del Barrio y Larrazábal had earlier served in the chamber of deputies, where he had been known as extremely conservative. With his brother Rafael del Barrio he was owner of the immense sugar hacienda of Temisco (p. 393). His wife was Doña Rafaela de Rengel y Fagoaga who, as inheritor of her father's title, was the Condesa de Alcaraz. Fanny would write a few months later to Prescott that their friend had gone bankrupt, "but his wife . . . has nobly paid the creditors with her jewels." (Wolcott, Correspondence of . . . Prescott, p. 254.)

The man of whom Fanny speaks as the Count de Casa Flores (also spelled Casa Flórez) was Juan María Flores y Terán, later governor of the Federal District. (As earlier explained—in note 11, p. 705—genealogical works show that it was not he but his brother who carried on the family title Fanny used.) One gleans almost nothing about him in other memoirs except that Prieto called him (in Memorias . . . , II, 208) a "typo virreinal"—a viceregal type—with lofty, formal manners. His father had served as viceroy of Buenos Aires and as Spanish ambassador in various European countries, and his grandfather had been viceroy of Mexico. His wife was Doña Manuela de Rengel y Fagoaga.

[20] In the Fagoaga brothers (uncles of the wives of the Señores del Barrio and Flores) one encounters more members of one of the most interesting families in Mexico at this time. Their history has been cited as an example of bountiful luck in the chancy business of mining.

A previous generation of Fagoagas achieved riches from this source, and in 1772 one of them was granted the title of Marqués de Apartado. But in 1780, according to H. G. Ward, their mine at Sombrerete appeared to be depleted, and they had almost abandoned work on it when, at the urging of a secretary, a member of the family decided to risk $16,000 in order to explore a possible new vein. The resulting venture was extremely profitable. Still later, their means were again much diminished. With the utmost difficulty they raised funds once more with which to explore, in 1792, a crucero or crossing from existing works. If the original careful calculations had been faithfully followed, the expensive undertaking would have missed by a single yard the rich vein which was in fact encountered—the source of a bonanza that made the Fagoaga family one of the richest in Mexico—perhaps, said Ward, in the world. (Mexico in 1827, II, 537–39.)

From genealogical sources it appears that Francisco José Fagoaga and his brother, the second Marqués de Apartado, were not (as Fanny has stated) brothers of "the celebrated Don José María Fagoaga" but were, confusingly enough, his first cousins and at the same time his brothers-in-law: that is, Don José María had married their sister. He was celebrated, perhaps, in Fanny's mind because he had been a distinguished scholar as well as a statesman, and a friend of Humboldt, who paid him tribute as an ally of science. He had died in 1837, but the Calderóns enjoyed a warm friendship with his family, consisting of his four intellectual daughters who will appear later in Fanny's story.

[21] Francisco José Fagoaga (Plate 83) had studied and traveled widely in Europe, journeying even to Russia. He had been one of Mexico's earliest statesmen, as one of the colonial delegates sent to the Spanish Cortes. Some years after independence, in the early 1830's, he served as Minister of Foreign Affairs. At the time of the Calderóns' visit he was in his early fifties, and was approaching crises in both health and money matters. A long period spent in Europe had caused serious deterioration in his finances, following

which he undertook banking enterprises with disastrous results. He fell ill, and during this very year of 1841 he went into bankruptcy. To meet his obligations he sold everything, including the collection of paintings which Calderón admired, and likewise the finest private library in the republic. He went through an operation—a pioneer one at the time—for a malady of the liver, and survived for ten more useful years, during which he saw service in the senate.

Unaware of the gravity of these financial troubles, his older brother the Marqués de Apartado, who died in Paris, left his title to Francisco, but much of his immense fortune to Mexican charities—with Francisco as administrator. Francisco Fagoaga carried out his brother's will with the most scrupulous care, and saw to the donation of large sums to the hospital for the insane, the foundling home, and other institutions. He became deeply interested in the Compañía Lancasteriana, an organization devoted to the furtherance of free schools. ("Noticias Biográficas del Ilustre Senador D. Francisco Fagoaga," in *La Ilustración Mexicana*, I, 534–37; Artemio de Valle-Arizpe, *Calle Vieja y Calle Nueva*, pp. 637–59; Torrea, *135 Años de Labor Diplomática al Servicio de México*, p. 27.)

[22] The earlier reference to Padre Lyón appears on pages 163 and 164–65.

Doctor Valentín was, according to an item in *La Hesperia* of December 26, 1840, the *cura* of the Sagrario—the church attached to, but not a part of, the cathedral. (Fanny seems to have obtained Valentín's first name of José from Zavala's *Ensayo Histórico* . . . , I, 158. In all other sources encountered his first name is given as Miguel.)

The Calderóns presumably came to know Valentín well some time during 1841 when he served as president of a newly established cultural institute that Calderón, Cortina, and he—among others—were helping to promote: the Ateneo, modeled on a similar organization in Madrid. (*Ateneo Mexicano*, I, 24.) Current newspapers mention the organization occasionally, and by the following May it was offering lectures and courses open to the general public. (*El Cosmopolita*, May 12, 1841.)

Earlier Doctor Valentín had been a member of the regency that briefly constituted the executive arm of the government just before Iturbide was proclaimed Emperor in May 1822. More recently he had been a conservative member of congress. The preface to an article dedicated to Valentín (in the *Mosaico Mexicano*, V, 481) spoke of him as an eloquent speaker, a wise statesman, and an exemplary churchman.

[23] The previous autumn the Calderóns had visited the hacienda of Francisco Manuel Sánchez de Tagle near San Angel (p. 116), and they will shortly return to it again.

Fanny speaks of Tagle's past role in the independence movement. With many other upper-class Mexicans, he had initially clung to the hope that a Bourbon prince might rule independent Mexico, and for this reason was an opponent of Iturbide in the latter's role as emperor—so much so that for a time he was imprisoned. He later served both as a senator and as governor of Michoacán.

Like Gorostiza, Cortina, and Quintana Roo, Tagle was an example of that not uncommon Spanish-American phenomenon, the man of public affairs known also as a writer. He was a poet of some distinction, and examples of his work have been republished in his native Morelia, as part of a series entitled *Cuadernos de Literatura Mexicana*.

Guillermo Prieto's description of Tagle suggests an attractive warmth of character as a devoted family man and a lover of country living. (*Memorias* . . . , II, 64.) It may be remembered that Conchita Adalid, Fanny's friend, was his only daughter. Surviving likenesses of Tagle (Plate 75) give him a large Roman nose, a piercing gaze, and, even in his later years, a fine head of curling hair. He died in 1847.

38. News from Spain

[1] For publication Fanny deals thus briefly with this major development in their lives. Letters to their friend Prescott and other contemporary sources give us somewhat more background.

When Calderón wrote Prescott at the end of January that he wanted Fanny to see the sugar country because he sensed that political shifts in Spain might result in his dismissal, he did not know that a letter giving news of such developments was already on the ocean—perhaps even on its way up from Veracruz. (A later reference to it in *Despachos Generales*, I, 215, indicates that it was written in Spain on December 1, 1840.) "The constant changes which are going on in Spain," said Calderón to his friend, "make me fear that as I am the friend of Martínez de la Rosa and the others who there belong to the Moderate Party they will dismiss me from this post." (Wolcott, *Correspondence of . . . Prescott*, p. 199 fn.)

Two weeks before the date at the head of this chapter, the newspaper *El Cosmopolita* for March 17, 1841, had picked up rumors of the change: "It is asserted that Señor

Calderón de la Barca, the Spanish minister, has been recalled by his government."
On May 20, seven weeks after the present entry, Fanny will write thus to Prescott: "You probably know that Calderón is recalled as he expected. When we received the intelligence, we took a house in the country, and ordered the sale of all our *effects*—hoping most fervently that Don Pedro Oliver [Calderón's successor] would arrive in time to allow us to spend this summer in the U.S. . . . However, the new Secretary and Attaché have just arrived, and given us the *displeasing* intelligence, that Oliver will arrive in June—thereby *just* making it too late for us to pass through Vera Cruz, where the 'Vómito' is beginning to make great ravages. We now cannot leave this until October or November." On June 18, Calderón will write an even more frank report to Prescott casting light on the uncertainties of their lives at this time: ". . . We find ourselves obliged to live in the country because I am destitute, and we must sell our effects in order to go to Havana . . . the bank of the United States has also wiped out my savings . . ." (Wolcott, *Correspondence of . . . Prescott*, pp. 221, 228–29.)

The Calderóns seem to have acted with decision as soon as they had definite news. Beginning in late March a series of brief advertisements appeared in two of the capital's newspapers. Their wording, literally translated, ran thus, offering for rent: "The large house with all its conveniences, which in the street of San Fernando inhabits the Señor Spanish minister, [who] wishes to disoccupy it, and of the conditions of its rental they will give information at No. 4 of the Bridge of the Holy Spirit: it has no transfer charge." (The cut— typically used for advertisments of larger properties—was probably imported from the United States and undoubtedly bore no slightest resemblance to the Calderóns' house.)

As will appear later, the Calderóns' haste in putting their affairs in order was unrewarded, as the new minister arrived not in June but in August. Calderón continued until that time to serve as Spain's envoy to Mexico.

2 This dwelling house of the former hacienda of Goicoechea still stands and is known as San Angel Inn. No longer in the country, it is now a part of a quiet residential area, at the top of a slight rise in the Avenida Altavista, on the Calle Palmas. A portion of the large building is shown as Plate 116.

3 The village of San Angel, to the southwest and now in what is officially called Villa Alvaro Obregón, has become an integral part of the expanding capital city. There remain, however, tucked away on side streets, a number of handsome old houses and gardens.

The ancient Convento del Carmen, whose church was dedicated in 1617 (Plate 117), is today a museum operated by the Instituto Nacional de Antropología e Historia. The modern visitor may see what Fanny could not: the sparsely furnished but beautiful interior of an old Carmelite convent for men.

4 The name of the Calderóns' friends is derived from the Singer copy—source, together with Fanny's original Journal, of further Adalid identifications in the next chapter.

5 At the Ringling Museum of the Circus in Sarasota, Florida, there are displayed various mementoes of Astley's Amphitheatre in London, including a small model of it as it appeared in 1800. Included also are colored lithographs of Andrew Ducrow, its daring equestrian, in action. Astley's was destroyed by fire in this year of 1841.

6 Fanny has already mentioned, in discussing the pyramid at Cholula and the church built on it (p. 404), beliefs which coupled the apostle St. Thomas with Quetzalcoatl—the fair god who, according to legend, was to return. That such ideas were still alive is evident from the fact that Carlos María de Bustamante, the historian and editor whom the Calderóns knew, as recently as 1829 had speculated in an old work he reissued and annotated on whether St. Thomas had in fact come to Mexico. He indicated that Dr. Miguel Valentín (the elderly churchman described in the previous chapter) had been much interested in this subject, and at one time planned a personal investigation of the inscriptions attributed to St. Thomas. (Fray Bernadino de Sahagún, *Historia General de las Cosas de Nueva España*, edited by Carlos María de Bustamante, I, following p. 277: "Suplemento al libro tercero . . . ," pp. i–xxxi.)

As to the cross presented to Pope Paul V, the tradition surrounding its origin appears, in brief, to be as follows:

Long before the arrival of the Spaniards, a mysterious bearded white man landed at the small Pacific port of Huatulco. He planted a cross there; predicted its future significance; and later departed forever. Toward the end of the sixteenth century English pirates ravaged Huatulco, but the ancient cross withstood all their efforts to destroy it or to drag it away. Its fame spread; and in 1612 Oaxaca's bishop Juan de Cervantes ordered the cross brought into the city: it was lifted out with ease. The revered symbol, much diminished by the removal of splinters by countless visitors, was made into several smaller crosses: one was sent, as Fanny wrote, to the Pope in Rome; one was taken to the cathedral in the capital, and another to Puebla; and one, about two feet in height, was housed in the cathedral of Oaxaca, in the second chapel on the right, where it is today.

Clavijero, the learned eighteenth-century Jesuit writer cited often in these notes, mentioned in his *Historia Antigua de Mégico* (at the beginning of his sixth book) the persistence of beliefs that Christianity had been preached in Mexico long before the conquest. He made it plain that he did not agree.

There do indeed exist ancient sculptured forms of cross-like shape in Mexico, but the cross is an elemental design feature not necessarily connected with Christianity. It is generally recognized today that legends and traditions tend to combine events widely separated in actual time. Thus old traditions of pre-conquest Christian missionaries are not considered historically significant.

[7] A paraphrase, perhaps, from *Hamlet* (Act III, Scene 4): "Look here, upon this picture, and on this,/The counterfeit presentment of two brothers."

[8] The editors have witnessed the use of rockets in Mexico at fiestas, at village weddings, and at the burial of a child. The reader will recall that Fanny heard one set off as a prelude to the ceremony of induction of a nun. Another reminiscence about fireworks may reinforce her anecdote:

H. G. Ward describes in the 1820's the inauguration of a new steam engine for draining a mine in Michoacán. He and a companion stood godfathers to the occasion. The machine was sprinkled with holy water by a local priest, and then blessed, and cakes and wine were distributed to those present; but the ceremony was not complete without a discharge of *cohetes*. (*Mexico in 1827*, II, 689.)

[9] This ball was given on Thursday, March 25th, the day the Calderóns moved to the country. It evoked sharp criticism from the press as profaning the solemnity of an important holy day, the *Encarnación del Divino Verbo*. The newspaper *El Cosmopolita* in its issue of March 27 ran a sarcastic poem on the event—entitled "Dance! Dance!"

[10] Calderón in his dispatch of March 29, 1841 (*Despachos Generales*, I, 186–87) makes plain his relief at having escaped the disagreeable incident.

The usual diplomatic procedure, sensibly evolved to avoid problems of just this kind, apparently would have ranked the flags to the right and left of the Mexican flag in the alphabetical order of the countries represented. According to Calderón, the British flag should have ranked first. The workman who set up the display was, however, a Frenchman who disregarded protocol to give the place of honor, at the right of the Mexican flag, to the banner of France. Pakenham, apprised of the situation before the ball, had asked more than once that it be corrected. But, Calderón surmised, the official in charge—caught between the explosive tendencies of the Baron de Cyprey and the known calmness of the long-resident Pakenham—elected to leave the faulty arrangement alone. Pakenham reacted forcefully. He took out a pen-knife and, as Fanny describes, cut away his country's flag and bore it off.

El Mosquito Mexicano for March 30 (Vol. IX, No. 26) reported that Pakenham had earlier asked General Almonte, Minister of War, to remedy the situation, but that the latter, remarking that he was no *tapicero* (upholsterer), declined. The newspaper laid the greater share of the blame on General Barrera—the rich supplier of army uniforms who has been mentioned earlier—for not comprehending the diplomatic niceties involved.

Pakenham's own account of the matter to his government was unperturbed and certainly reasonable in tone, and he seems not to have troubled his superiors with a blow-by-blow account. "Perhaps if the preference had been given to the Flag of the United States as the Nation which first acknowledged the independence of Mexico, or the Flag of Spain, as the Country from which Mexico is politically descended, such an arrangement might have been justifiable but I could see no earthly reason why on a public occasion, the Flag of France should occupy in this Country, a position denoting preeminence over that of Great Britain." (F. O. 50/144. March 26, 1841. Folio 218. This unpublished Crown-copyright material in the Public Record Office, London, is reproduced by permission of the Controller of H. M. Stationery Office.)

39. Holy Week in Coyoacán

[1] This was a clause in the long, detailed will made by Cortés, who died in Spain in 1547. The convent of nuns, in whose chapel he directed that he should lie, was never built, as funds for its construction were lacking after the conqueror's other bequests were fulfilled. His bones came to rest—after a succession of interments and reinterments in Spain and then in Mexico—in the church of another Mexican foundation he had endowed: the Hospital of Jesús Nazareno in the capital.

[2] The plaza where Fanny and her friends saw the passion play soon to be described is now halved by a street. In spite of this and other changes, however, Coyoacán still re-

tains something of a small-town air; its side streets are peaceful, and a number of its old buildings remain.

3 The members of this group, whose base was a convent in the capital, devoted themselves to caring for the plague-stricken and ill, and to comforting the dying. They wore a black habit, and both on the habit and the cape there was blazoned a large red cross. The organization, whose full name in Mexico was La Congregación de los Padres Regulares de la Buena Muerte, was founded in the sixteenth century by the Neapolitan Saint Camillo de Lèllis. (García Cubas, *Libro de Mis Recuerdos*, pp. 132, 362.)

Their snug country retreat in Coyoacán is easily identified today. Its garden has been subdivided and the house put to commercial use, but time has dealt kindly with the large arcaded establishment, located on the Calle Fernández de Leal, not far from the church of La Concepción.

4 The young Señora de Adalid was the only woman, Mexican or of other nationality, specifically noted by Fanny as handling the reins herself.

It is evident from contemporary accounts that families of means enjoyed keeping various types of equipages and animals in their stables. A Frenchman long resident in Mexico remarked that early in his stay there the strong Mexican-made coaches were almost always drawn by mules. With the importation of European-made carriages, however, horses were also used, and he mentions that some handsome turnouts were pulled by big Kentucky horses. There were, he said, fine-looking large mules in Mexico, but mules lacked elegance: "*Elles gardent toujours quelque chose de la mésalliance.*" (Fossey, *Le Mexique*, p. 221.)

5 Lice or fleas, presumably: it is easy to forget that the germ theory of disease, proposed first in the seventeenth century, would not be generally accepted for several decades to come.

6 From John 18:3. The curate's discourse which follows will be seen to be a close interweaving of what were apparently his own words with material from the gospels— Matthew 26:48, 49, 67; Luke 22:48; and John 18:4–5. Fanny's use of italics is preserved, although it does not correspond exactly with quotations of scriptural wording.

Plate 118 shows a scene such as Fanny was here witnessing.

7 Perhaps this was the Doctor Iturralde who a little earlier had served as rector of the Colegio de San Juan de Letrán. (Prieto, *Memorias* . . . , I, 189, 191.) One notes that a Dr. José María Iturralde—presumably the same man—was listed in the *Diario del Gobierno* of August 31, 1840, as a member of the committee in charge of the Independence Day celebration of that year.

8 Again, a reference to a circus performance evidently recalled from the past. Andrew Ducrow (1793–1842), son of a professional strong man, Peter Ducrow, was an accomplished tightrope dancer and chief equestrian at Astley's Amphitheatre.

9 There are no more open fields where the Calderóns spent Holy Week of 1841. However, Coyoacán's small, charming, eighteenth-century church of La Concepción still survives, its façade ornamented with plaster work in the Moorish style. It faces on its own secluded plaza at the end of the Calle Higuera; and it was across this plaza, presumably, that the procession made its way.

10 Edmund Kean's "Sweet Kitty Clover," if played up to its rapid, jig-like tempo, would have had a peculiarly irreverent effect.

Another traveler to Mexico has commented, however, on the penchant of unsophisticated Mexicans for picking up lively tunes and adapting them to their own use: Edward B. Tylor, visiting an Indian community in the 1850's, maintained that he heard "The King of the Cannibal Islands" played on the harp and violin while a group of local residents danced a quadrille in a reverent and dignified manner—all as part of a religious celebration in the famous convent church of Chalma. (*Anahuac*, p. 212.)

More recently, an ethnologist working in a small town in the state of Michoacán noted the zestful rendition—outdoors, by a local band—of "The Beer Barrel Polka" and "On, Wisconsin!" as part of the celebration of the feast day of the Virgin of Guadalupe. (George M. Foster, assisted by Gabriel Ospina, *Empire's Children: The People of Tzintzuntzan*, p. 221.)

40. On the Subject of Indians

1 The balloonist, who in other records was designated as Luis A. Lauriat, a *profesor de química* (chemistry) from Boston, did make a successful ascent nine days later on Sunday, May 2. His daughter Aurelia, however, was left behind. (*La Unión*, May 5, 1841; Olavarría y Ferrari, *Reseña Histórica del Teatro en México*, II, 4–5.)

A balloon had gone up many years before in 1785 in Veracruz, and the capital witnessed a flight in 1786. The first Mexican to make a balloon ascent was Benito León Acosta, who went up from the city bull ring about a year after the date of this chapter in a balloon gallantly dedicated *al bello sexo mexicano*—to the Mexican fair sex. He came down about a mile away at the Niño Perdido gate and was carried off by an admiring multitude to the palace, where he was congratulated by the President. (Cossío, *Guía Retrospectiva de la Ciudad de México*, pp. 151–53.)

An article on *aerostación* in *El Liceo Mexicano* (I, 174–76) by the sometime Minister of Foreign Affairs Sebastián Camacho not only lauded Acosta as the first son of the Spanish Americas to penetrate the immensity of space, but also concluded with the thought that while efforts at flight had not so far produced useful results, one day they would perhaps have as much effect on the civilized world as the work of the immortal Watt.

[2] As will later appear, this ball, held on the feast day of St. Philip the Apostle, would honor the French monarch Louis-Philippe.

[3] The excursion to San Bartolo must have been a strenuous uphill climb. Today's well-paved Avenida Desierto de los Leones starts near the house the Calderóns were occupying, climbs through various towns, passes close by San Bartolo, and eventually ends on the mountain-top retreat of the Desierto de los Leones—which Fanny has earlier visited, using, however, another route (pp. 360–62).

[4] This is from Byron's series of poems called *Hebrew Melodies:* "She walks in beauty, like the night/Of cloudless climes and starry skies;/And all that's best of dark and bright/Meet in her aspect and her eyes . . ."

[5] As implied by Fanny's numerical listing, colonial-born whites occupied a place lower than those born in Spain, and so on down the scale. Her source was Humboldt's encyclopedic work on New Spain (*Ensayo Político* . . . , I, 154). With Mexican independence, however, Humboldt became obsolete insofar as the legal status of races was concerned. During the colonial period, it was the deliberate policy of Spain not only to maintain the superior position of Spaniards, but also, according to H. G. Ward, to recognize and even promote rivalry among the racially diverse population of Mexico. Early in the War of Independence, Morelos and his supporters had sought to extinguish slavery and the caste system. By the Plan of Iguala—already mentioned by Fanny (p. 331) as a forerunner of inpendence—Iturbide pulled together both factions and races. Article 3 stated that all Mexicans, whether Europeans or Americans by birth, were equal and united. Article 11 specifically emphasized that the distinctions among castes set up by Spanish law were abolished, with equal citizenship granted to all.

In spite of vast social and economic differences—including the fact that minimum-income requirements for voters and office holders were set by the constitution of 1836—no legal distinctions based on race survived in Fanny's day. Some fourteen years earlier, Ward had written: "Castes can no longer be said to exist in Mexico . . . Many of the most distinguished characters of the revolutionary war belonged to the mixed breeds . . . I shall not, I trust, be regarded as a theorist, for supposing that . . . many of the most valuable members of the community will, hereafter, be found amongst those very classes, who were formerly excluded from any share in the direction of the affairs of their country." (*Mexico in 1827*, I, 32, 35–36, 525–26.)

[6] Under Spanish rule the population of New Spain had been divided not merely into castes, but also into clearly defined sub-castes, with special terminology to indicate exact degrees of racial inheritance. And the castes were not only named but also were pictorially represented, in canvases which today are of great anthropological and historical interest. One of the best known of these collections of racial types is a series of sixteen separate canvases, acquired in 1902 by Mexico's Museo Nacional from the Riva Palacio family. The series depicts three races—white, Indian, and Negro—in varying combinations, and each unit in the series shows father, mother, and their resulting child.

The modern writer of a pamphlet describing these historical collections mentions some of the early prohibitions affecting the lower castes—against bearing arms, for example, and walking the streets after nightfall—and the fact that those of mixed blood encountered legal limitations in seeking education or entering professions. (Nicolás León, *Las Castas del México Colonial o Nueva España.*)

In actual practice, racial distinctions in New Spain seem never to have been as rigid as the law implied. Concubinage, and in many instances, legal marriage between Spanish conquerors and Indian girls had taken place at the highest social levels as well as in the ranks. Various prominent families in Mexico and Spain today can trace descent from Montezuma's daughters or others of his family, or from the rulers of neighboring pre-conquest principalities.

Humboldt, who was deeply interested in Mexico's racial composition, noted the fact that in conjunction with the Spanish colonial system of legal distinctions based on race, there also existed comfortable methods for by-passing them. A family with some degree of mixed blood could apply to a high court for a ruling that it was white. If appearances suggested that this was clearly not the case, a decision might still be rendered to the effect that such individuals "may consider themselves white." (*Ensayo Politico* . . . , I, 262.)

7 In this discussion, as Fanny will imply, she draws on Humboldt whose ideas, however, she reinforces with her own observations. The English translation of Humboldt runs thus: ". . . The natives of Mexico patiently suffer the vexations to which they are frequently exposed from the whites. They oppose to them only a cunning, veiled under the most deceitful appearance of apathy and stupidity." (*Political Essay* . . . , I, 169–70.)

8 Prescott, in his *Conquest of Mexico*, said in a footnote (III, 298): "Señor de Calderon, the late Spanish minister at Mexico, informs me, that he has more than once passed by an Indian dwelling, where the Indians in his suite made a reverence, saying it was occupied by a descendant of Montezuma."

That the number of Montezuma's descendants by his lesser consorts may have been sizable is suggested by a footnote in Clavijero which in the English translation (*History of Mexico*, I, 281 fn) reads: "Some historians affirm that Montezuma had a hundred and fifty of his wives pregnant at once; but it is certainly not very credible."

9 Humboldt, an aristocrat by birth, learned in many fields, and widely traveled, concluded his work on colonial Mexico with "this important truth, that the prosperity of the whites is intimately connected with that of the copper coloured race, and that there can be no durable prosperity for the two Americas till this unfortunate race, humiliated but not degraded by long oppression, shall participate in all the advantages resulting from the progress of civilization and the improvement of social order." (*Political Essay* . . . , IV, 282.)

10 The names of the ladies here are guesses. The reader may recall Fanny's earlier praise of Señora Lasquetti's diamonds, which had been concealed in the Spanish legation during the recent revolution. A turban as part of a formal evening costume of the period is illustrated in Plate 60.

11 "Saturday last" was the night of the French minister's ball; consequently Fanny must be in error here. According to a newspaper and to Manuel Mañón's *Historia del Teatro Principal* (p. 82), the benefit for Bernardo Avecilla's family was held somewhat later, on Saturday, May 15. The performance was a translation of the French comedy *Philippe*, by Scribe and others.

12 This name is filled in by guess. Calderón in his dispatches (*Despachos Generales*, I, 214) speaks of Lorenzo Carrera as a Spaniard long resident in Mexico; and another writer, José Ramón Malo, mentions the fact that Carrera owned the hacienda of Coapa—near the road from the capital to San Agustín, and in an area served by canals. (*Diario de Sucesos Notables*, I, 204.) It was Señor Carrera who, at the gambling fête of San Agustín the previous June, impassively won and lost some $16,000.

13 The new attaché's name appears in the newspapers and in Calderón's dispatches. The Comte de Breteuil, mentioned in the next paragraph, is frequently identified elsewhere in the Singer copy. All other identifications in this chapter are directly from the Singer copy.

14 There appears without explanation near the middle of Volume 3 of Fanny's Journal a several-page passage in her handwriting, but consistently set off by quotation marks. Alex Macleod must have been its author because, in a parallel description of this same murder, the wording reads: "I went to the spot where the murder had taken place . . ."

Alex indicated that the murdered man was, like the perpetrator, an Indian. In concluding he added: "If the Government cannot suppress the organized systems of robbery, surely it might punish such wanton atrocities as these. But what can be expected, where there is no trial by Jury, where there is not even an open Court of Justice, and consequently, where every facility is afforded to the bribery and corruption of the Judge." Alex's other remarks were similarly critical of Mexico's separation from Spain and its current governmental situation. They presumably reflected Calderón's views, and perhaps Fanny's also—as she considered them worth copying down and in one or two instances made brief use of parallel wording.

Alex is not heard of in this book again, and was evidently soon to leave Mexico. In the course of writing to her friend Prescott on September 23, Fanny refers to "my nephew Mr. Macleod, who has left this for Jamaica . . ." (Wolcott, *Correspondence of . . . Prescott*, p. 253.) Alex's young sister Kate stayed on and will reappear.

15 Other writers who mention the offspring of Indian-Negro unions do not substantiate Fanny's informants. The observant Humboldt appears to have made no comment on the appearance of *zambos*. And Brantz Mayer said nothing about the looks of a Mexican of this racial mixture whom he encountered. (*Mexico as It Was and as It Is*, p. 178.) Ward, in discussing the workers on the sugar haciendas—Indians many of whom had an admix-

ture of Negro blood—termed the men a "fine athletic race," capable of working with smooth vigor, but wild-looking, noisy, improvident, and much addicted to strong drink. (*Mexico in 1827*, I, 69 and II, 305.) Hans Gadow, writing in 1908, speaks of the Indian-Negroes whom he encountered in a Pacific coastal region as tall and well-built. ". . . Altogether they are often pleasant and good-looking, and bear a surprising resemblance to Melanesians." (*Through Southern Mexico*, p. 428.)

One wonders whether Fanny's allusions could be to pintos, of whom there are various mentions in histories and memoirs of the time. They were victims of *mal de pinta*, a disease which produced mottled or speckled markings on the skin. There existed in the 1850's a military contingent from the south of Mexico whose members, of mixed Indian and Negro inheritance, seem to have been preponderantly pintos. (Wilfrid Hardy Callcott, *Church and State in Mexico*, p. 228 fn.)

[16] It was the twenty-second birthday of the young Queen Victoria, born May 24, 1819.

According to a dispatch Calderón wrote the previous fall, Pakenham had made plain to Mexican officials his indignation over what he considered their dilatoriness in answering his communications. And about two months after Fanny's entry here, Calderón would write his government about the uncomfortable relationship that had developed between Pakenham and Sebastián Camacho, the Minister of Foreign Affairs who had replaced Cañedo. Calderón attributed the increase in tension to the fact that the previous November Great Britain had recognized Texan independence. (*Despachos Generales*, I, 151–52, 224, 338.)

[17] In this and the following four paragraphs—written during the long days at San Angel—the reader may recognize a few phrases or thoughts already made use of elsewhere by Fanny in her published text. She appears to have taken advantage of these three months of almost uninterrupted quiet to write a major portion of Volume 3 of her Journal. In doing so, she obviously worked with a good deal of care, and consequently was able to make later use of whole blocks of what she wrote almost without revision. It was at San Angel, apparently, that she recorded most of her anecdotes, as well as her general discussions on such subjects as servants, Indians, the education of girls, Mexican women, and assorted customs and manners.

At about this time she said in a letter to Prescott: ". . . I always write a volume to Mamma by every packet . . ." (Wolcott, *Correspondence of . . . Prescott*, p. 221.)

[18] "Many begin by dislike and end by fondness," wrote another observer, of pulque. "It is extremely wholesome when drunk discreetly, and of a fair quality, and they who once fall into the general use of it cannot go without it. It is a recorded fact, moreover, that when . . . the Spaniards were persecuted and ordered out of the country, certain of them pleaded to the authorities for leave to remain, on the ground that they could not live without their pulque." (J. J. Aubertin, *A Flight to Mexico*, pp. 177–78.)

41. Dancing, Gambling, and Prayers

[1] San Antonio was, it will be remembered, the hacienda of General Morán and his wife the Marquesa de Vivanco. Luis Cuevas, their son-in-law, already has been mentioned as Minister of the Interior (p. 284). His handsome sister-in-law was presumably the wife of his brother Pepe—José María Cuevas. If so, her name was Asunción Estanillo de Cuevas —"very beautiful and of angelic virtue," and with outstanding accomplishments, according to another chronicler of the time. (Prieto, *Memorias . . .* , II, 289, 438.)

La Güera's granddaughter must have been, according to genealogical sources, either Guadalupe Rincón Gallardo or her sister Rosa. She was presumably new to the capital because she came from the provincial city of Aguascalientes, where her father's family owned a magnificent house (which later became the Palacio de Gobierno of the state).

Identifications provided in this chapter are partly from the Singer copy and partly from the Journal; in some cases from both. The Singer copy is the source for filling in *Guadalupe*, *Escandóns*, and *French* and *English* ministers.

[2] Brantz Mayer, a visitor to San Agustín the year following, said that four sets of costumes were still considered requisite by women for each day at San Agustín: a dress for morning mass at ten; a dress for the cockfight; a dress for the outdoor ball in the late afternoon; and a fourth costume for the ball at the cockpit in the evening. Moreover, no costume was ever supposed to make a second appearance during the three-day fête. (*Mexico as It Was and as It Is*, p. 78.) However, one may note that the most fashionable, according to Fanny, tended to underplay their dresses and jewels.

[3] First performed in Paris in 1814, *Les Anglaises pour rire, ou la table et le logement* was a comedy in one act by Charles Augustin Sewrin and Théophile Marion Dumersan. Frances Trollope said that the first thing British visitors to Paris did was to go to the

Théâtre des Variétés to enjoy hearing themselves satirized. (*Domestic Manners of the Americans,* p. 407.)

[4] This name was left blank in Fanny's Journal.

[5] A reference to a London club housed in an elegant establishment on St. James's Street, where enormous sums were won and lost. Its builder and operator, William Crockford, was in his youth a fishmonger, and is said to have made his start in life by winning, with his partner, one hundred thousand pounds in a single twenty-four-hour gambling session.

Monte, as played by *léperos* on the streets, is shown in Plate 92.

[6] If the bank wins, the banker recovers his share in the *vaca,* and acquires the shares provided by his friends. But if the bank loses, the total loss will, of course, be greater than the banker's share of the winnings.

Fanny is correct in the sense that *vacas* stimulated more gambling, and thus in the long run assured more profit to the banker.

[7] "He dies, and makes no sign." Thus says the king at the death of Cardinal Beaufort in *Henry VI, Part II*—Act III, Scene 3.

[8] An anecdote by the minister from the United States who arrived a few months later indicates that the robber population might have been temporarily swelled by amateurs. "Shortly after I left Mexico, the stage was robbed near Puebla. The robbers all had the dress and bearing of gentlemen. When the operation of rifling the pockets and trunks of the passengers was finished, one of the robbers said to them,—'Gentlemen, we would not have you to suppose that we are robbers by profession; we are gentlemen (somos caballeros), but we have been unfortunate at monte, and that has forced upon us the necessity of thus incommoding you, for which we beg that you will pardon us.'" (Thompson, *Recollections of Mexico,* p. 24.)

[9] The Niño Perdido gate, or *garita,* was the southwesterly entrance to the city, that nearest San Angel. The distance, measured in a straight line, was about six miles.

[10] The director of the mint, said Fanny in a letter to Prescott, "not being paid by the Govt. was too glad to let his house at an enormous ransom." (Wolcott, *Correspondence of . . . Prescott,* p. 248.) His name was Bernardo González Angulo, some years earlier a member of the cabinet. At this time he was under fire for his management of problems relating to copper currency. Presumably González Angulo, like many others, was not being paid because of the financial difficulties being faced by the hard-pressed government.

[11] Not quite a year had elapsed since July 27, 1840, when the federalists had filed out of the national palace in the concluding act of the stalemate revolution of 1840.

The passages quoted in translation over the following several pages comprise substantially all of a story that appeared in the July 1 issue of the *Diario del Gobierno,* a copy of which Fanny pasted into Volume 3 of her Journal. (The events described were those of the day before—June 30—not July 1, as she incorrectly entered in her published text.)

The reader who is interested—as Fanny obviously was—in the utter inappropriateness of the matters described, or in the florid style of oratory characteristic of the period, will wish to read carefully all that follows—in spite of the complication of quotations within quotations, with further quotations within those. However, the going is not easy and nothing important is likely to be lost should a reader skim as far as the paragraph in italics on page 464. At several points, small adjustments have been made in the wording of Fanny's translation in the interest of greater clarity.

[12] The hero of Iguala was Iturbide. The references which follow are to an action in August 1821 at Atzcapotzalco a few weeks before Iturbide entered the capital in triumph; also to an abortive counter-revolution early in 1823 by Spanish troops still remaining in Mexico, put down at Juchi by Bustamante.

[13] William Barnes Rhodes' burlesque tragic opera, first produced in 1790, was a parody of *Orlando Furioso* by Ariosto.

The United States minister who came to know the presidency-aspiring Valencia the year following felt that the general, who had risen from the ranks, possessed both talent and courage, but regretted that he had the education and manners of a parvenu. (Thompson, *Recollections of Mexico,* p. 85.)

42. In Apartments at the Mint

[1] From the roster of the new company Fanny omitted, presumably unintentionally, the name of the contralto Adela Cesari, whom she had heard a few months earlier in Puebla. She will be identified with the group a few paragraphs later.

Fanny in her Journal went on listing other performers until she seems abruptly to have wearied. Her handwriting was hurried, and is difficult to decipher, but none of the names appears to have significance today—except for the director of the orchestra and first violinist, Guglielmo Wallace—the same William Vincent Wallace whom she had heard at a concert in Puebla. The chorus consisted of fourteen men and fourteen women. The orchestra, judging from the names, was a mixture of Italian and local Mexican musicians.

[2] Who the enthusiastic L_____ was (or perhaps it was S_____, for Fanny's handwriting in this instance is hard to decipher) we do not know.

Fanny Tacchinardi-Persiani—around whose talents *Lucia di Lammermoor* had been composed—and Giovanni Battista Rubini were being acclaimed at this period in London and Paris, and must have been much in the musical news that reached Mexico. Only two of this company's singers, Cesari and the prima donna Anaide Castellan (whose real name was Jeanne Anaïs Castellan) are to be found listed in recent non-Mexican works on the history of opera. The fame of the others seems to have gone with the years.

As Fanny points out, Mexico had already heard magnificent voices. The noted tenor-turned-bass, Filippo Galli, had spent several seasons in Mexico. Also remembered were the Spanish-born tenor Manuel García and his gifted daughter Maria Malibran. They and others of García's company spent a period there in the 1820's. The reader may recall that García was said to have been robbed by Mexican highwaymen, forced to sing, and then hissed. (Apparently the whole operatic party was stripped of everything, including its members' earnings in gold, equivalent to some thirty thousand dollars.)

[3] From a later entry, it appears that it was Vaccai's *Giulietta e Romeo* that the Calderóns heard.

[4] The wife of José Iturrigaray, whose period of service as viceroy from 1803 to 1808 included the time of Humboldt's visit.

[5] Fanny quotes freely from Byron's *Parisina*, stanza XIII.

[6] The result of efforts to bring counterfeiters—perhaps less influential ones—to justice was reported in a two-page spread in the *Diario del Gobierno* of January 8, 1840 (Vol. 16, pp. 34–35). It listed the names of persons charged with counterfeiting, the kinds of equipment of which they were found in possession, and the name of the judge involved in each case. From the list one notes that it was not unknown for women to undertake this line of endeavor.

[7] The editors prefer to make no guess as to the identity of General A.—partly because (as the reader may recall) Fanny sometimes deliberately changed initials in the interest of disguising an identity.

[8] For publication Fanny omitted Barrera's name and all subsequent references to him as an individual, substituting "a rich acquaintance of ours, a general, who has been indisposed for some time, and whose illness has now exhibited fatal symptoms."

[9] Probably a reference to James 4:12. "There is one lawgiver who is able to save and to destroy: who art thou that judgest another?"

[10] Speaking, perhaps, of the same lady, a Spanish diplomat of a few years later described Doña Teresa Schneider as an example of the good looks frequently resulting from British-Mexican and German-Mexican marriages. (Conte, *Recuerdos de un Diplomático*, I, 194.)

[11] A likely guess would be that the lady was the wife of the Fernando Mangino who at this time was in Mexico's diplomatic service. He is listed during the 1830's and early 1840's in the *Almanach de Gotha* as secretary of legation and at times chargé d'affaires for Mexico in France.

The Príncipe de la Paz (Prince of the Peace) was Manuel de Godoy, favorite of Charles IV's queen María Luisa, and formerly a powerful but unpopular prime minister. He was still alive and so was his second wife, Doña Josefa Tudó (spelled Tudor by Fanny), Condesa de Castillofiel.

[12] The reference is presumably to Rossini's opera *Semiramide*, first presented in Venice in 1823.

[13] The father of this well-known family was Manuel de la Peña y Peña, who became president of Mexico at an unhappy time a few years later: as head of the supreme court he acted for a time as chief of state during the disorganized period that closed the United States-Mexican War. He has been described as a cautious but powerful personality, slow to make up his mind, but courageous and determined once he had done so. (Prieto, *Memorias* . . . , II, 267–68; Rives, *The United States and Mexico*, II, 584–85.)

[14] Santiago de Compostela is no longer the capital of Galicia, though still Spain's greatest shrine and formerly one of the greatest in Christendom. According to tradition, the body of the apostle St. James (Santiago in Spanish) was miraculously transferred from the Holy Land to Spain in the ninth century.

[15] Santiago, believed to have come in person in aid of fighting Spaniards in the New World, as in Spain, is likely to be represented as Santiago Matamoros—St. James the Moor-Killer—astride a plunging horse and bearing an upraised sword. But he is sometimes shown in the costume of a pilgrim, with scallop shells on his cloak, and the boys wore these decorations associated with his legend.

[16] The ancient fortress-like church of Santiago Tlaltelolco, finished in 1610 and replacing a still older church, is now of course well within the city of Mexico. As earlier explained (p. 702, note 22), the church and other Christian buildings were constructed in the historic area that was the last to fall in the Spaniards' final siege of the Aztec capital. Beside the church, recent archaeological work has uncovered parts of the great pre-Columbian temple often mentioned in the conquerors' accounts.

[17] Except for their final farewell, this is Fanny's last mention of her aging friend La Güera who, one senses, was still at this time vastly enjoying the world and its vanities. During her last years, according to one of her descendants, she turned to a life of piety. She was received before her death into the Third Order of Saint Francis of Assisi—also called the Brothers and Sisters of Penance—an organization whose members, although not cloistered, adhere to the strict rules of the Franciscans' founder. She died in November 1851, just before her seventy-third birthday. Her husband (her third, Juan Manuel Elizalde, a Chilean by birth) later entered the religious establishment—the Convent of La Profesa—across the street from the home he and his spirited wife had shared. (Romero de Terreros, La Vida Social en la Nueva España, p. 216.)

[18] This point of view was expressed in the following statement written a few years later by a surgeon with the invading United States forces. He said: "The Mexican government sits like an incubus on the people . . . and the old people look back with regret to the old régime. They say it is a mockery to speak of the Mexican republic; that they have the burdens of monarchy without its stability. That abuses abounded during the time of the vice-regal sway is admitted, yet in those days it appears there was greater security for life and property. . . . The old nobility retain their titles (by custom); high functionaries affect princely style, and the humbler empleados practice more than courtly servility. . . . The middle classes (that body politic that gives strength and stability to states) are but fragmentary; great landholders and princely merchants represent the aristocracy; the army, the church, shopkeepers, artisans, &c., and adventurers, and place-seekers of all kinds, fill up the space between the ricos hombres and the peons of the soil." (McSherry, El Puchero, p. 182.)

The Calderóns inevitably encountered members of the conservative upper class. Some friends, in discussing the disorders and disillusionments of the early post-independence period, undoubtedly expressed regret for the authoritarian Spanish system which had maintained outward peace and order for three hundred years. Still, one wonders whether the nostalgia for colonial days was as truly general as Fanny, writing here privately, seemed to think. Courteous Mexicans who rejoiced in their country's independence would have hardly said so to the wife of the minister from Spain.

[19] In this quotation we have translated the Spanish of Fanny's Journal.

[20] It seems a likely guess that the Baron de Froissac, mentioned on page 472, and the Baron de Cussac, mentioned here—and about whom the editors know nothing—were one and the same.

[21] For her published text Fanny cut her penetrating facial critique to a mere shell: "She is not at all beautiful, but has a charming face, with a very musical expression." Presumably Castellan sang from Antonio Coppola's opera (1835); or possibly from the much earlier Nina, o sia la Pazza per Amore by Paisiello.

[22] It may be remembered that Mme Castellan's husband had earlier impressed Fanny (p. 468) as "a handsome stick" with no voice.

[23] "Where the virgins are soft as the roses they twine/And all save the spirit of man is divine"—Fanny's favorite, Byron, again: Canto I, stanza 1 of the "Bride of Abydos."

[24] In the Spanish of Fanny's Journal all numerals were written out in full and with clarity. But seven Pater Nosters a day for twelve years (ignoring leap years) would equal 30,660, not 300,670.

[25] Juan Vicente de Güemes Pacheco de Padilla, Conde de Revillagigedo, fifty-second viceroy of New Spain, ruled from 1789 to 1794 with energy and rectitude—combined, as will be seen, with an astonishing degree of nosiness into private affairs. He instituted various reforms in the system of justice, and established and improved schools. He bettered streets and roads, sewers and street lighting, and the water supply of the capital. He made rules restricting the cutting of timber. He carried into execution the project conceived by his predecessors of a botanic garden, opened the School of Mines, and established the national archives.

His ruthless severity toward inefficient subordinates made him many enemies. Charges were made against him to the king in 1795 from which he was eventually completely absolved; not, however, before his death in 1799. He is said to have slept only three or four hours a night, retiring at nine and arising at one in the morning, after which hour he was likely to summon disgruntled officials for consultation. He made it a habit to appear anywhere at any time unannounced so as to learn the state of affairs for himself, and he maintained a box for complaints and information to which only he himself had the key.

According to Fanny's Journal the visit from the mint director actually took place on July 25, the previous Sunday evening.

[26] In the following chapter Fanny presents the anecdotes she heard almost exactly as they appear in her Journal. It seems likely that shortly after her caller left she must have sat down and recorded the stories recounted to her.

43. Calderón's Successor Arrives

[1] Compadre and comadre (meaning literally co-father and co-mother) are terms used among the parents and godparents of a baptized child—and by extension are similarly used among all sponsors of a confirmation or wedding.

[2] According to another account, that by Manuel Payno, in El Museo Mexicano which appeared in 1844 (III, 397–406), it was two weeks later. The murders took place October 24, 1789, very shortly after the Viceroy had assumed office. The perpetrators were executed by the garrote on November 7. To add to the excitement, exactly a week later the aurora borealis appeared in the sky, causing among many a fear of coming doom.

[3] Possibly a heightened version of this same anecdote, or perhaps another example of viceregal peremptoriness, is related by Brantz Mayer in his second book (Mexico, Aztec, Spanish and Republican, I, 263–64). According to the story, the Viceroy was walking about the city one evening at sunset when he came upon a dead-end street leading into a group of squalid tenements. After making inquiries of various officials, he ordered the slum demolished and a street opened through it—to be sufficiently finished for him to be able to drive through it on his way to mass the next morning. Hundreds of workmen labored at top speed all night by torchlight. Early the following morning the viceregal coach bumped through the dusty, rubble-strewn bed of the new street, which was given his name. Whether or not the anecdote is true, the Calle de Revillagigedo, leading south from the Avenida Juárez, still commemorates the energetic and dictatorial viceroy.

[4] For print Fanny not only improved her English, but also narrowed and sharpened her indictment: "Alas! Could His Excellency have lived in these our degenerate days, and beheld certain monks of a certain order drinking pulque and otherwise disporting themselves! nay, seen one, as we but just now did from the window, strolling along the street by lamplight, with an Indita (Indian girl) tucked under his arm!"

[5] Other accounts add more to this store of anecdotes about Revillagigedo. On one occasion he was told by an officer of two impoverished sisters who had neglected that morning to sweep the street in front of their house, on the excuse that their mother had died during the night; and, moreover, that they were distractedly soliciting alms from passers-by for the burial expenses. The Viceroy directed the officer to wait until the alms collected amounted to a dollar and a half, and then to bring the money and the women to him. He appropriated the dollar and a half—the regular fine for failure to sweep the street—but donated to the desolate women the wherewithal for the burial. (Wilson, Mexico: Its Peasants and Its Priests, pp. 263–64.)

Another story of Revillagigedo's all-supervising tendency concerns La Güera Rodríguez. It is told by one of her descendants, Manuel Romero de Terreros, in his Bocetos de la Vida Social en la Nueva España (pp. 211–12).

As very young girls, she and her sister—both endowed with arresting good looks and high spirits—found an excuse to walk every afternoon past the barracks of a regiment whose officers were sons of Mexico's best families. To the shocked amusement of onlookers, the two girls, María Ignacia and María Josefa, were soon on obviously friendly terms with two of the young men on duty there.

Revillagigedo, coming by unexpectedly one day, took in the situation at a glance, and summoned the girls' father for an immediate interview. What, asked the Viceroy, did he do in the afternoons? The Señor Antonio Rodríguez de Velasco replied that he was in the habit of going to the Sagrario to pray. Better, countered the Viceroy, to do his praying at some other hour, and to spend more time watching over his daughters. The Viceroy then decreed that the venturesome girls should be married to the objects of their flirtation. After the long negotiations prerequisite to marriages linking important families—

and some demurring on the part of the young men's parents over the viceregal high-handedness—Revillagigedo's orders were carried out. La Güera's wedding (the beginning of an unhappy marriage) took place in 1794 shortly before she was sixteen. That of her sister followed in about a year and a half.

[6] The new minister, as noted earlier, was Pedro Pascual de Oliver. He was forty-one days between Spain and Havana, but came from Havana to Mexico by steam in four and a half. He landed at Veracruz on August 1 at the height of a bad yellow fever season. After two uneasy days spent in waiting for transportation, he thankfully departed with his family—pausing, however, just as Calderón had, for a prudent call on the powerful Santa Anna at Manga de Clavo. At Jalapa he recuperated for a few days from his long hard journey, in describing which he used exactly the same words—tan largo y penoso viaje—that Calderón had written a year and a half before.

Fanny was apparently in error by some eight days in her memory of the date of Oliver's arrival in the capital. Calderón's last dispatch as Spanish minister was written August 13, and in it he mentioned Oliver's expected arrival the next day. And Oliver in his first dispatch from Mexico reported the date of his arrival as August 14. (Despachos Generales, I, 247, 250, 251–53.)

[7] According to the Guía de Forasteros of 1854 (p. 64), Don Cayetano Rubio lived at No. 12, in the first street of the Indio Triste. The two-block-long street is now a part of the Calle del Carmen and the Calle del Correo Mayor. (González Obregón, The Streets of Mexico, p. 61.) The article Fanny read as the basis for her discussion that follows appeared in the Mosaico Mexicano in 1840 (III, 165–68).

[8] This is Fanny's only mention of a famous Mexican historical source written by Fray Juan de Torquemada: Monarquía Indiana. It was first published in Seville in 1615; but she probably saw the three-volume edition put out in Madrid in 1723.

As to the site of the palace of Axayacatl, confusion on this point has already been dealt with in note 7, pages 710–11.

[9] The figure of the sad Indian that Fanny saw may still be seen at the Museo Nacional de Antropología, which also possesses another figure of the same type, although headless. Because of the extended position of the arms—with both hands making a bottomless cup—and the indentation at the base of each, it is now believed that the large seated figures once held poles for banners.

[10] The name of Ignacio Cubas has been substituted here for that of Cuevas, hitherto printed as a result, perhaps, of a long-ago misreading of handwriting. Don Ignacio Cubas served as director of the archives from 1823 until his death in August 1845. (Mario Mariscal, Reseña Histórica del Archivo General de la Nación, 1550–1946, p. 159.)

[11] Archaeological tunneling under the Pedregal in the twentieth century has revealed that there were indeed people interred beneath its thick lava crust. The lava flow that covered the area spilled out from an eruption of nearby Ajusco about 200 B.C. The ancient graveyard of Copilco has been dated at approximately 900 B.C.

However, it is thought today that the Nahuatl name Mexico means "in the navel of the moon," an interpretation corroborated by the fact that this meaning is also found in references to the city in other indigenous languages. (Letter of April 15, 1964, from John Paddock, chairman, Department of Anthropology, University of the Americas.)

[12] General Mariano Paredes was commandant and governor of the department of Jalisco, of which the city of Guadalajara was the capital. He will figure conspicuously in coming pages. His pronouncement denounced the government and its high taxation, called for a revision of the constitution, and included a demand that the government be put in the hands of an executive with strong powers.

[13] Fanny in her published text reported these events as taking place the previous day, but we here follow her Journal, which agrees with Oliver's dispatch.

[14] This identification is substantiated by a letter Fanny wrote to Prescott from the country about three weeks later: "The new Minister and his lady arrived . . . He is a very polite, bowing sort of personage, and very humble to Calderón, asking his advice in everything, and entre nous without the least experience—au reste an ultra-Liberal. She is of better family than he is, a lady-like little woman, very affected and quite Spanish in her ideas. However we were very amicable. I spent nearly a week before leaving Mexico in driving about with her in the carriage, introducing her to the ladies of the Diplomates and Ministers of the Country, etc., Calderón doing the same to Don Pedro. I also gave her a Tertulia. As yet people insist upon not liking them, but from no personal feeling—merely because they are angry at Calderón's recall." (Wolcott, Correspondence of . . . Prescott, p. 253.)

Oliver had not been in diplomatic life long but had seen service in both Denmark and Belgium. He proved a capable and effective minister. In fact, a recent Spanish ambassador to Mexico asserts that Oliver was better suited to the post of minister to a young republic than Calderón—whom he terms a competent diplomat, but a man nostalgic for the viceregal past, with eyes closed to the new forces shaping Mexico. (*Despachos Generales*, I, Prologue by Pedro Nicolau D'Olwer, pp. XVI, XIX–XX.) Jaime Delgado, in a later study, differs with this appraisal and gives a considerably more sympathetic estimate of the abilities of Fanny's husband. He points out that Oliver's success owed much to the good will resulting from his predecessor Calderón's intelligent groundwork and tact. (*España y México en el Siglo XIX*, II, 217–18.)

[15] Waddy Thompson, the United States minister of a year later, thought that this cemetery—known both as the Panteón de Santa María and also as Santa Paula—was the most beautiful burial ground he had ever seen. It covered some ten acres or more and was surrounded by a fifteen-foot-high stone wall. The rows of coffins Fanny mentions were deposited in orderly ranges of niches within the walls' thickness. Marble tombs were also set among the walks and planting, but the vegetation was luxurious and the effect was that of a large enclosed garden. (*Recollections of Mexico*, pp. 214–15.)

Little remains to mark this peaceful spot—which shows up so plainly on old maps and air views, not far north of the historic small church of Santa María la Redonda—except the chapel which in 1962 the editors saw in a rather forlorn and abandoned state. It faces a small plaza, six blocks north of the Bellas Artes building, at the first Calle de Moctezuma and the Calle Riva Palacio.

[16] What may have drawn Fanny's first attention to the cemetery in general and to this inscription in particular was an article appearing in 1840 in *El Mosaico Mexicano* (III, 350–51), which gave the mother's poem in full. One notes that in the original Spanish it was a sonnet in form.

The Spanish double-naming system, and the prominence of the bereaved family, make it possible to put the infants mourned so long ago into a framework of reality. Their parents were Don Tomás López Pimentel and his wife Mariana de Heras Soto—whose hacienda of Queréndaro the Calderóns will later visit. Others of the couple's children did survive—among them Francisco, who became a distinguished student of Indian languages. Another, Filomena, married the historian Joaquín García Icazbalceta.

44. Manifestoes and the Roaring of Cannon

[1] Bustamante's cross was that presented to him two months earlier at the ceremony celebrating the putting down of the revolution of 1840. The quoted words are paraphrased from the printed congratulatory remarks of General Valencia, head of the army staff (p. 465).

The President, it would appear, was at this time still occupying quarters in the convent of San Agustín, in which he had taken refuge the previous year after the partial destruction of the national palace.

[2] Thus Valencia launched in the capital the second of the two revolutions Fanny witnessed. The text of his pronouncement appeared in *El Cosmopolita* for September 4, 1841 (Vol. 5, No. 71). His concluding words sound far more rousing in their original Spanish: "*El triunfo es seguro, amigos míos, y la causa que proclamamos tan noble, que, vencedores, nos cubrirá de gloria . . .*"

Pedro Cortázar had the year before succeeded the deceased Manuel Cortázar as *comandante* and governor of Guanajuato.

[3] None of the three last-named figures, nor General Juvera, who will appear shortly, is mentioned again by Fanny. Francisco Xavier Pacheco's name appears in contemporary newspapers. General Manuel María Lombardini and General José Mariano Salas each, some years later, headed briefly the government of Mexico. General Julián Juvera, *comandante* of Querétaro, would, like many other prominent officers, figure later in the United States-Mexican War.

[4] Sebastián Camacho was now Minister of Foreign Affairs. The meeting was concerned with a new regulation subjecting to inspection goods imported for the personal use of diplomats, and threatening to confiscate excess amounts. The foreign diplomats registered strong protest against what they felt to be the offensive tone of the regulation.

[5] The manifesto of Paredes on August 8, reported by Fanny on August 18 (p. 489), called for a convention to reform the constitution, the government meanwhile to be headed by a temporary executive with extraordinary powers. Paredes complained of the wreckage of Mexico's commerce and of the government's high taxation; at the same time he also cited the government's failure to protect its citizens in the north against marauding bands of Apaches and Comanches.

[6] Francisco or Francis Morphy, whose name (along with other identifications supplied in this chapter) was written into the Singer copy, appears in the dispatches of both Pakenham and Oliver, the newly arrived Spanish minister. Morphy was a British subject although born in Spain. His part in events shows some of the cross-currents, conflicting interests, and rumors that abounded during these weeks. A rich broker, he was also what would today be called a lobbyist, openly representing and speaking for mercantile interests who wanted a reduction in Mexico's high duties on imported goods. Foreign diplomats, including Calderón, had strenuously objected to the additional internal duties that had been imposed on imported goods by a law of November 1839. Some Mexicans, mostly but not all federalists or liberals, felt that trade was being curtailed and business injured. The members of congress, however, who were paid out of the proceeds of the extra duties, were quite naturally disinclined to repeal the legislation.

Morphy's meeting with Santa Anna followed by his visit to Paredes in distant Guadalajara, in conjunction with pronouncements made by those generals, aroused the government's wrath. As a result, he was about to be deported when, as a British subject, he sought refuge with Pakenham, who harbored him until the revolution was over.

[7] Almonte, as Minister of War, had written to Santa Anna to ask him why he had taken his troops inland, leaving unguarded the coast for whose defense he was responsible. He furthermore ordered Santa Anna not to come to the capital. Santa Anna replied on September 2 with a long letter in which he said, blandly, that he had come (backed up with his troops) only as a pacifier and mediator; that he had heard that catastrophe was imminent; and that he would endeavor to aid in steering the ship of state to safety. The nation was in difficulties and he, Santa Anna, would hold the government responsible if blood were shed. (Bustamante, *Gabinete Mexicano*, II, 144.)

Valentín Canalizo had two months earlier led the parade celebrating the suppression of the revolution of 1840.

[8] In writing Prescott a rapid-fire summary of revolutionary events somewhat later, Fanny said: "The President after eating his usual quantity of eggs, his principal food, addressed his troops, and sallied forth to attack the Citadel, but by the time he reached it, found himself nearly alone. Mexico presented rather a gay appearance. Shots firing— people running—ladies on the balconies—soldiers on the *azoteas*. The Archbishop who lives opposite to us, appeared now and then on his balconies, crossed himself, and vanished." (Wolcott, *Correspondence of . . . Prescott*, p. 248.)

[9] It will be remembered that, in the revolution of the year before, the federalists occupied the national palace—while the government's adherents, headed by Valencia, bombarded the revolutionaries from the Ciudadela, or citadel. In contrast, in this new revolution, Valencia, now opposed to Bustamante, seized the citadel, from which his forces directed their fire at places occupied by the government troops, including the nearby convent of San Agustín where the President had his quarters. Both sides competed in the seizure of large solid buildings, especially churches, as vantage points from which to fire. Even the outlying convent of San Fernando, adjacent to the Calderóns' former house, would soon be involved.

[10] The Salto del Agua, shown in the cut, was the fountain that terminated the southerly aqueduct carrying water from Chapultepec. (It still stands, in the center of the Calle Arcos de Belén at the Calle de San Juan de Letrán.) But presumably what the rebels had seized was the nearby church of La Purísima, often called after the fountain.

[11] A Mexican describing events of this period summed up the motives involved in this and other revolutionary efforts: "You get out so I get in—*Quítate tú para ponerme yo*." (Prieto, *Memorias . . .* , II, 46.)

Oliver, the just-arrived Spanish minister, reported at length to his government on this revolution which broke out in the capital only two days after he presented his credentials. As its underlying causes—aside from the personal ambitions of the leading participants —he cited the sense of the general impotence of Bustamante's government, the low state of the treasury and the government's credit, and the paralysis of commerce. He reported accusations that foreigners (especially the British) were responsible for inciting the revolution, and expressed some worry over the possibility of a revival of the old post-independence hatred of Spaniards—a fear not unfounded, as various rich bankers, some of them Spaniards, were thought to be interested in the fall of Bustamante's regime.

Oliver initially feared a general sack of the capital and asked that a Spanish naval vessel be dispatched from Havana to stand by in case of trouble for Spanish nationals. Writing some few days later, he emphasized the potent influence of Santa Anna over his countrymen, owing to both fear and admiration. (*Despachos Generales*, I, 256–58, 263.)

That the issues were far more complicated than simple black and white is pointed up by the fact, which Fanny will soon note, that various men of known integrity would join the side against the government.

[12] Balderas was almost certainly Lucas Balderas, whom the writer Prieto (in his *Memorias* . . . , II, 124) mentions as a friend and associate of Gómez Pedraza. He was an officer of militia with a reputation for consistently honorable conduct. He fell during the United States-Mexican War—at Molino del Rey. (José María Marroqui, *La Ciudad de México*, I, 488–98.)

Mariano Riva Palacio (whose wife Doña Dolores was the only child of Vicente Guerrero, Mexico's second president, executed in 1831 by the centralist government which had deposed him) was still in his thirties; but he had already acquired a reputation as a moderate of upright character. He would later refuse office under Maximilian, but would accept the Emperor's request to defend him at his trial.

[13] Perhaps Vicente Blanco, a professional pianist mentioned as taking a supporting part in a concert in 1844 with Max Bohrer, a distinguished visiting violoncellist from Munich.

[14] The church of the convent of Nuestra Señora de la Merced is gone. To the Calderóns, however, it must have been clearly visible a few squares south and a little east of where they stood on the roof of the mint. (One of La Merced's cloisters, noted for its sumptuously carved columns, survives at the Avenida República del Uruguay, No. 170.)

For a lithograph of the period which illustrates the usefulness of *azoteas*, see Plate 37.

[15] The *Supremo Poder Conservador* was not an emergency group but an already existing agency established as an integral part of the centralist constitution of 1836 under which Bustamante's regime was operating. Composed of five men of presumably solid position (it was requisite that they be not less than forty years old and possess an income of at least three thousand pesos a year), it was especially charged with the guardianship of the constitution. In effect it was a fourth branch of the government—in addition to the president with his council, the congress, and the judiciary—and had been the cause of much discontent among Mexican liberals, who maintained that it constituted a block to needed reforms. Various of the Calderóns' acquaintances saw service as members.

The emergency grant of powers to President Bustamante permitted him to do away with certain unpopular taxes. Those mentioned by Fanny were presumably the tax on the internal circulation of imports, and a forced annual contribution to the government. (Callcott, *Church and State in Mexico, 1822–1857*, pp. 106–7, 114, and 127.)

[16] Retreat to the Casa de Moneda's strong vaulted lower regions (which Fanny in writing to Prescott termed *bomb-proof*) was a revision, apparently, of a less prudent plan. They had determined, she said, "to go out servants and all on foot to a Convent out of the City, where we have friends amongst the Padres, who though they could not admit women into their Convent, could allow us to pass the night in their Church. I thought this plan very dangerous on account of robbers on the road . . ." (Wolcott, *Correspondence of . . . Prescott*, p. 249.)

[17] Cannon balls had fallen on Oliver's house, on Pakenham's, and on that of the Baron de Cyprey. These diplomats then sent their secretaries to call on General Valencia to protest and to urge him to cease bombarding the city. Valencia (who in writing, at least, referred to himself at this time as chief of the liberating army) told the deputation that he only desired peace, but that—although he was confident that practically all Mexico was on his side—he had found himself obliged to respond to the hostile tactics adopted by his opponents. (*Despachos Generales*, I, 265, 267.)

[18] This letter, dated September 9, would be reproduced later in the *Cosmopolita* of October 16, 1841. As in the revolution of the year before, the regular publication of newspapers was interrupted for some time. But frequent bulletins issued by both sides informed and propagandized the citizenry. The government's *Boletín Oficial* (presumably printed in the national palace) was opposed by the *Boletín de la Ciudadela*, issued by Valencia's insurgents.

[19] Fanny wrote Prescott that "not a corner of a house was to be had for love or money in any of the villages in the environs of Mexico. Dozens of ladies were sitting on the floor of almost every house in Guadelupe . . . crowded together and sleeping on mats." (Wolcott, *Correspondence of . . . Prescott*, p. 249.)

45. Refuge in the Country

[1] For an apt illustration from a Mexican source of about two years later, see Plate 63.

[2] Joel R. Poinsett had met the Fagoaga sisters' father, José María Fagoaga, during his initial visit to Mexico, before he became first United States minister. He found the distinguished Mexican in prison, at the Emperor Iturbide's orders, for having led congressional opposition to the latter's regime. (Poinsett, *Notes on Mexico*, pp. 165–66.) Fa-

goaga's two exiles took place before and after this period of imprisonment. Though born a Spaniard, Fagoaga had made strong remarks about Spain's management of Mexico and was exiled by the viceroy as a man dangerous to peace. (Alamán, *Historia de Méjico*, IV, 237–38.) In contrast, his second exile was ordered during a period of anti-Spanish feeling in the young republic, apparently because he had been born in Spain and had been among those who had wanted independent Mexico to be a Spanish-linked monarchy. (Zavala, *Ensayo Histórico* . . . , I, 81, 141.)

3 Fanny wrote her friend Prescott a few days later from San Xavier. From her long letter, continued over a period of ten days, and from genealogical sources as well, one gets a more revealing glimpse of the personalities of her hostesses. (Prescott, on receiving the letter, may well have been reminded of rich, charitable, frugal Boston women cast in the same mold.)

The ladies were doubly Fagoagas, their father having married his first cousin, a daughter of the first Marqués de Apartado, in 1801. The sisters—presumably in their thirties or perhaps late twenties at the time of the Calderóns' stay with them—were, in order of seniority: Faustina, unmarried; Elena, wife of General Cirilo Gómez Anaya; Lina, married to Joaquín Escandón y Garmendia; and Julia, a spinster like her oldest sister. "Each lady," Fanny wrote to Prescott, "possesses *half a million*, and each has two or three immense haciendas, besides having between them the silver mines of [Bolaños], and large shares in those of La Veta. They are the only learned family in Mexico, having been educated by their father, and having travelled a great deal in Europe. They are especially *dévote*, their whole time being spent amongst padres and convents, and religious and charitable institutions. It is perhaps not fair to say so, when we are living in their house, but I never saw *economy* carried to so incredible an extent in dress and living. This is such an uncommon quality in Mexico, that it is the more remarkable in female *millionaires*. It is a proof of their strength of mind, that having discovered that I am a Protestant, they continue their friendship towards me. They content themselves with giving me to read Tomás A'Kempis, Las Glorias de la Virgen—Verdaderas Eternas, etc." (Wolcott, *Correspondence of . . . Prescott*, p. 250.)

In the absence of any clue to the contrary, it would appear that the Fagoaga ladies must have loyally kept to themselves their astonishing discovery that their friend, the wife of Her Catholic Majesty's minister, was a heretic. One wonders whether the strenuous personally conducted tour of Mexican charitable institutions, upon which Fanny will shortly be launched, might not have resulted from the Fagoagas' wish to demonstrate some of the practical aspects of their faith.

4 The editors first saw San Xavier, home of the Calderóns and of their niece Kate Macleod for four weeks, in the 1950's. It was then the center for a large corporate-owned dairy. The buildings were well kept and the tank mentioned by Fanny survived intact. The hacienda buildings stood on flat rich land only a short distance outside the old town of Tlalnepantla.

The fate of San Xavier exemplifies the rapidity with which developments have been taking place in modern Mexico. The area around Tlalnepantla is now an important industrial zone, and nothing whatsoever remains of San Xavier except its name—now given to the subdivision of modest houses which occupies its site.

5 The ancient church, now a colonial monument, has as conspicuous elements of its façade the glyphs of the two Indian communities that shared in its construction. The word *tianguis* is from the Nahuatl; great markets were one of the Aztecs' most significant social institutions.

6 See Plate 122. Emily Ward, wife of H. G. Ward, who had been chargé d'affaires for Great Britain during Mexico's early republican years, was an intrepid traveling companion to her husband on many of his long journeys in Mexico. His *Mexico in 1827*, cited frequently in these notes, was illustrated with her skillfully executed sketches.

7 Under the law Bustamante, in leaving the capital and personally heading his troops, left his office vacant and a substitute executive was required. Through the unavailability of certain more senior officials, Francisco Javier Echeverría became acting president of Mexico. His position with the Council of State was that of vice-president rather than president as Fanny says. (Zamacois, *Historia de Méjico*, XII, 102–3; Bustamante, *Gabinete Mexicano*, II, 174.)

8 Manuel Escandón's name was written into the Singer copy, and a historian of the time confirms that Escandón and the Spanish financier Lorenzo Carrera threw their support to Santa Anna. (Bustamante, *Gabinete Mexicano*, II, 208.) The pioneer Puebla cotton manufacturer, Esteban Antuñano, would also soon be numbered among those espousing Santa Anna's cause. (*Cosmopolita*, October 23, 1841.)

Except for a quotation which may or may not have been penned after these eventful days, Fanny's Journal has ended. Thus hereafter all identifications in differentiated type derive solely from the Singer copy. (We continue to suggest likely but undocumented names in brackets.)

[9] According to the state records of Puebla, this was not the Calderóns' friend Antonio de Haro y Tamariz but his older brother Joaquín, who had served as governor some years before, in 1828. This second period of service was brief.

[10] From internal evidence, in combination with other accounts of the revolution, it appears that Fanny's dates as originally published were a day late. Accordingly, this and all remaining entries in September have been moved back one day.

[11] General Noriega was presumably Domingo Noriega. General Juan Orbegoso has been mentioned earlier as a contributor to El Mosaico Mexicano.

[12] Poor José seems to have had no recorded last name even in death. The Boletín Oficial—Number 30 of September 24—in informing the public that the perpetrators of the crime had been beheaded, termed him merely José María N., español, porter of a casa máquina. In writing to Prescott on September 23 regarding this incident, Fanny added that they had "recommended him to the new Minister, and he was only waiting till the Olivers had taken a house, when he was to go there as Porter." (Wolcott, Correspondence of . . . Prescott, p. 252.)

[13] We have substituted the name of Quijano for what has previously appeared as Guyame, an error derived presumably from an old misinterpretation of handwriting. General Benito Quijano is recorded as the emissary who went with General Juan Orbegoso to meet with Santa Anna on September 25, 1841, in Ayotla. (Riva Palacio, México a Través de los Siglos, IV, 469.) He had been briefly Minister of War in 1838, and would fight on the liberal side in the coming War of the Reform.

[14] One suspects here another long-ago misreading of handwriting. It seems likely that Fanny wrote "assuring them."

[15] Fanny in writing Prescott a little later said that the insurgent generals had "sent an insolent message to Bustamante, informing him that if he does not surrender in 24 hours, they will attack Mexico, and . . . Bustamante is fortifying the City in all hastel His madness in allowing these troops to unite, when separately, the victory was easyl The result no one can even conjecture." (Wolcott, Correspondence of . . . Prescott, p. 254.)

Oliver, the new Spanish minister, also could not understand Bustamante's permitting his three opponents to unite. He considered the Mexican President a brave soldier, but one who might vacillate in a crisis, and judged that in this instance Bustamante dreaded firing upon his compatriots. (Despachos Generales, I, 263, 268.) It was apparently becoming increasingly evident to Bustamante that influential business men and financiers were supporting Santa Anna. Also at this time General Pánfilo Galindo, comandante and governor of Michoacán, joined the insurgents, together with his troops. (Zamacois, Historia de Méjico, XII, 231–33.)

[16] Santa Anna and Almonte, in opposition to each other at this time, knew each other well. Almonte had been Santa Anna's aide during Mexico's expedition against Texas several years before. Both men had fought at the Alamo; both were captured at the battle of San Jacinto; and subsequently Almonte accompanied his chief to the United States. Not many years later Almonte would again be a Santa Anna adherent.

[17] General Almonte's action was not in approval, but apparently to acquaint the citizens of the capital with "this impudent document," as he will shortly characterize it. (For greater clarity a few adjustments have been made in Fanny's somewhat free, partly abbreviated, and partly expanded translation which follows.)

[18] One account of this sudden, curious counter-pronunciamiento explains that General Almonte, Minister of War, felt that the administration, faced with the practical choice of declaring for federalism or of adopting the uncertainties of the Plan of Tacubaya, should choose the former. (Zamacois, Historia de Méjico, XII, 235.)

President Bustamante's espousal of federalism and the constitution of 1824 was announced at a review of troops in the great square of Mexico, and was accompanied by the ringing of bells and the firing of salutes. A return to the liberal constitution of 1824 had been, it will be remembered, a primary objective of the revolution of the previous year; and in offering this concession to his opponents Bustamante was reversing his prior position, and making a last bid to hold power. Powhatan Ellis, United States minister, apparently thought that Bustamante had at least a chance of saving his regime by this move, as a large number of those opposed to the President were, he thought, not so much Santa Anna supporters as pro-federalists. (William R. Manning, editor, Diplomatic Correspondence of the United States, Inter-American Affairs, 1831–1860, VIII, 477.)

[19] As earlier explained (note 7, p. 782), he had temporarily assumed the presidency. (The constitution of 1836 did not provide for a vice-presidency.) A twentieth-century connection of his family told the editors that Echeverría's brief public career—as Minister of the Treasury and then for less than three weeks as chief of state—cost him a fortune, as he insisted on assuming personally an unpaid obligation incurred by the government. Apparently Echeverría, a patriot and an honorable business man if not an outstanding public servant, became deeply concerned over allegations that he might profit from his post. His personal gift to the government of 672,000 pesos was lost sight of in the difficulties of the times. (Rivera Cambas, *Gobernantes de México*, II, 238–40; Sosa, *Biografías de Mexicanos Distinguidos*, p. 326.)

[20] A proclamation addressed to Bustamante and written the previous day by Santa Anna will illustrate the literary style of the period. His heart, said Santa Anna, throbbed with emotion every time he had to use force against the companions with whom he had fought in the sacred cause of independence. His arms were stretched wide to embrace his old friends. Provided only that they too took to their bosoms the principles now being newly proclaimed by the nation, a veil would be thrown over all differences. (*Cosmopolita*, October 9, 1841.)

[21] The end came on October 6 at the Hacienda of Estanzuela near Guadalupe. Prieto, in his *Memorias* (II, 63) recalled that Bustamante, even as he surrendered his power, retained a sense of executive dignity. A sentinel muttered, as the fallen president passed by, an uncomplimentary remark that referred to him as "the uncle." Bustamante smiled, but said to an officer: "Send my nephew to the guardhouse."

[22] According to another chronicler, the Archbishop went to meet Santa Anna at the door of the cathedral, the elderly churchman bearing in his arms a heavy crucifix of gold. He went on holding it for three-quarters of an hour, waiting until Santa Anna should be pleased to arrive. Not only was the victorious general late; he was also negligently dressed for the occasion. (Carlos María de Bustamante, *Apuntes para la Historia del Gobierno del General D. Antonio López de Santa-Anna*, p. 1.)

[23] The government newspaper—the *Diario del Gobierno*—shifted its tone with practiced ease. Santa Anna, in its issue of October 8, is likened to Caesar closing the temple of Janus (closed in time of peace, open in time of war). He is referred to as invincible, and his opponents have become "the enemy."

Santa Anna had not forgotten the role of quiet home-loving philosopher in which Fanny saw him when she first came to Mexico. He had struck the pose some ten years before in a communication when he was a candidate for the presidency: ". . . Should I obtain a majority of suffrages, I am ready to accept the honor, and to sacrifice, for the benefit of the nation, my repose and the charms of private life. My fixed system is to be called, resembling in this a modest maid, who rather expects to be desired, than to show herself to be desiring." (Mayer, *Mexico, Aztec, Spanish and Republican*, I, 319.) Now once more, on September 9, 1841, he announced that although he had earlier reached a decision never again to leave the bosom of his family, the course of events summoned him to put aside the sweetness of domestic life and to sacrifice himself in defense of justice and liberty. (*Cosmopolita*, October 16, 1841.)

In accordance with the carefully laid plans set forth in the second and seventh articles of "las bases de Tacubaya" (p. 513), Santa Anna was on October 9 made virtual dictator of Mexico by action of a provisional junta made up of representatives, chosen by him, of the various departments. General Tornel headed the junta. The vote was by voice, and was followed by a salvo of artillery. (*Mosquito Mexicano*—No. 82—October 12, 1841.)

[24] Domingo Dufoo was merely an interim appointee substituting until Francisco García should arrive from distant Zacatecas. García, however, declined the appointment and soon died. Dufoo likewise died, and Ignacio Trigueros was then appointed to the post.

As the reader will see, the Calderóns' friend Gómez Pedraza will very soon be in disagreement with Santa Anna, and will give up his position as Foreign Minister—to be replaced by José María Bocanegra. (*Despachos Generales*, I, 272, 290–91.)

[25] In other words, a popular general in the provinces with his own troops to back him was in a stronger position than a cabinet officer in the capital. Paredes would lead a revolt about three years later resulting in Santa Anna's downfall; and, about a year still later, would make himself president for some six months.

[26] Bustamante soon left Mexico for exile, but according to Waddy Thompson, minister from the United States a few months later, his personal reputation for financial integrity remained untarnished. At the time of leaving office, neither he nor Almonte had collected considerable sums due them from the Mexican government. Almonte gave lectures to support himself until subsequently appointed Mexican minister to the United States. (*Recollections of Mexico*, pp. 87, 89.)

46. Back to the Capital

[1] When the editors first saw Santa Mónica, its slumbering atmosphere and sparsely tenanted surroundings seemed remote from the influence of the nearby city. A second visit in 1962 was quickly accomplished by a mere turn off the fine new highway to Querétaro into an embryonic subdivision, called the Jardines de Santa Mónica, where a real estate office and concrete-paved streets awaited the lot buyers who were confidently expected to populate the hacienda's former domain. Slightly removed, in a small island of antiquity, the core of ancient solid buildings still stood, supplemented by unattractive constructions of later date. The massive two-story house was graced by a doorway of splendid proportions and handsome detail. (See Plates 119 and 120 for Santa Mónica's doorway, church, and farmyard.)

[2] Fanny had her own personal interest in Marina, but undoubtedly she was also exploring on behalf of Prescott, who had expressed the hope that a likeness could be found for use in his forthcoming Conquest of Mexico.

However, any connection between Marina and the hacienda of Santa Mónica has been conclusively disposed of by Manuel Romero de Terreros in his Antiguas Haciendas de México (pp. 103–4). Some of Santa Mónica's domain, he says, had once belonged to another sixteenth-century Marina—Marina de la Caballería.

[3] Fanny will soon visit the capital's Cuna (or Cradle), whose formal name was the Casa de Niños Expósitos. At this time the role of foundling institutions in relation to illegitimacy was a subject of much debate in other lands.

[4] According to genealogical records, the four Fagoaga ladies with whom the Calderóns were staying at San Xavier had a first cousin named Doña Matilde Fagoaga y Ovando. She was the wife of Eulogio Villaurrutia, and her father was an uncle of the Calderóns' hostesses.

[5] This is Fanny's only reference to the Masonic lodges whose bitter rivalries dominated Mexican politics during Mexico's early republican years. The Yorkinos or York-Rite Masons (with whom the first United States minister Joel Poinsett had been overtly identified) included various leaders of liberal sympathies. In contrast the Escoseses or Scottish-Rite Masons were more conservative and included those favorable to the establishment of a monarchy in Mexico. As might be expected, most of the Calderóns' friends had been on the side of the Escoseses.

[6] When, some years ago, the editors visited San Mateo, they found on a rise of ground the remains of a low building with an arcaded gallery across the front.

[7] This name, that of the husband of Lina Fagoaga, represents a guess by the editors.

[8] The hacienda called the Lechería—meaning Dairy—belonged, according to Fanny's long letter to Prescott previously quoted, to Doña Lina Fagoaga. The hacienda buildings still stand today, large and bare, within sight of the new super-highway to Querétaro. The house was being lived in when the editors first saw it in 1943 (Plate 121), but in 1962 it appeared to have been closed, presumably because of the encroachment of industry in the area.

[9] During Fanny's own stay in Mexico, an interesting sidelight on this subject is cast by articles in the Diario del Gobierno of February 27 and March 6, 1840. It is evident from the discussions in congress reported there that the Mexican government was paying pensions (or at least had obligated itself to pay pensions currently in default for lack of funds) to three widows of diverse backgrounds. One was the relict of the last Spanish viceroy, Juan O'Donojú, who had signed the unimplemented Treaty of Córdoba. The others were the widows by execution of two quite different deposed chiefs of state, the Emperor Iturbide and the liberal president Vicente Guerrero.

[10] In Santamaría's Diccionario General de Americanismos it is also spelled huisache, derived from the Aztec huixachi, meaning abundantly spined: it is a name given to several kinds of acacias.

[11] This unnamed hotel, according to its advertisements in newspapers of the time, was at the Calle de Vergara No. 10. Writing Prescott two weeks later, Fanny explained thus their refuge in a hotel (their sixth place of residence since first arriving in the capital): "Calderón would accept of no one's house, choosing to be independent for our last few weeks . . ." (Wolcott, Correspondence of . . . Prescott, p. 264.)

[12] Felipe Teixidor gives evidence (La Vida en México, II, Notas, 225) suggesting that the mysterious English couple consisted of the landscape painter Daniel Thomas Egerton, long resident in Mexico, and his more recently arrived mistress Agnes Edwards—known to have stayed at the hotel in the Calle de Vergara during their sojourns in the capital.

They would both be murdered the following April in Tacubaya, where they had a country house. Brantz Mayer, secretary of the United States legation, reported the excitement caused by the brutal affair—still unsolved when he left Mexico. (*Mexico as It Was and as It Is*, pp. 157–58.) The crime was solved eventually through reports of the attempted laundering of the clothes of the perpetrators.

13 *Un Periódico Más* had begun publication on August 12, 1841, less than three weeks before the *pronunciamiento.*

14 This is Fanny's only mention of Juan Alvarez, a mixed-blood liberal leader of renown who would briefly in the 1850's become Mexican chief of state.

15 In a hurried note written two weeks later, Fanny wrote Prescott that brokers were "selling off our things, the most valuable things going for nothing." (Wolcott, *Correspondence of . . . Prescott*, p. 265.)

16 From Hamlet's soliloquy, Act III, Scene 1.

17 When Fanny wrote *Life in Mexico*, in which she frequently gives evidence of thinking of Mexico as the wayward and immature child of Spain, she had not yet seen her husband's country. Years later, writing of political troubles that forced Calderón and herself into exile, a more politically experienced Fanny made a somewhat parallel observation about Spain, distinguishing between fluctuations in national leadership and the national personality: ". . . Yet their noble character has never come out more triumphant than now. Their good qualities are their own—their faults are those of their leaders." (*Attaché in Madrid*, pp. 366–67.)

The poem that follows, dealing with the issue of liberty in Mexico, was presumably written by Fanny, although placed in quotation marks in her published text.

18 The identity of the Baroness von Gerolt is derived from that of her husband the Prussian minister.

19 Fanny had apparently heard, however, of Paredes' great weakness, for a month earlier she had written thus to Prescott: "El Cojo [the Lame One: Santa Anna] is an energetic robber—Valencia a vulgar ambitious upstart. Paredes is the best, but he is *always* drunk." (Wolcott, *Correspondence of . . . Prescott*, pp. 249–50.) Other writers have mentioned Paredes' honesty, his intemperance, and his authoritarian political views. For his likeness, see Plate 71.

20 At a guess, Faustina, unmarried, and oldest of the Fagoaga sisters. A later note will identify her as one of a group of leading women in the capital who were concerned with the welfare of women prisoners in the Acordada.

21 Some time after her last dated entry of August 31, Fanny brought Volume 3 of her Journal to a close with a quotation of French verse. It would seem to have been penned as her comment on Santa Anna's actual or anticipated triumph. We have been able to identify the words as coming from Victor Hugo's *Cromwell*, first published in 1827. Spoken by a Cromwell opponent in bitter admiration after the Protector publicly refused the throne he privately coveted, the words in the English translation run thus:

"They're willing to be crushed and wronged,/But by a Lord Protector, not a king./As a plebeian tyrant he was safe./. . ./His uncrowned brow was deemed the only one/Strong to support the burden of the State;/But on that brow let shine a diadem,/And all things change: to those who loved him most,/'Tis but a King's head, and belongs by right/Unto the executioner."

Was Fanny thinking of Iturbide: of his elevation to the throne some twenty years before, and of his violent end? And was she wondering whether Santa Anna would share a similar fate? If so, she would learn in years to come that he was too shrewd—although he did, during his last brief dictatorship beginning in 1853, go so far as to assume the title of Supreme Highness.

While Santa Anna was of little political importance after his final fall in 1854, he outlived Mexico's second emperor Maximilian who, like Iturbide, met his death before a firing squad. Santa Anna—old, poor, and obscure—died peacefully in his bed in 1876.

(For the record, Fanny's final Journal page closes with these enigmatic words, scrawled at an angle: "a square foot of fine Climate"; nearby, also at an angle, is a small, rough sketch of an unidentifiable head.)

47. The Warmth of Mexican Charity

1 The opera company was evidently making the most of its good fortune in having in its repertoire a work not yet heard in Mexico whose historical background and theme— woven around a Roman leader who fought off the Goths and Ostrogoths, who was plotted against and who suffered, but who died with his reputation as a military leader and

patriot untarnished—could be construed as highly flattering to the new head of state: Santa Anna.

Herbert Weinstock, author of *Donizetti and the World of Opera in Italy, Paris, and Vienna in the First Half of the Nineteenth Century,* has kindly pointed out in a letter to the editors that this Mexican presentation of *Belisario,* which had been enormously successful in Europe following its initial performance in Venice early in 1836, antedated any performance in the United States by some three years.

[2] The hospital of San Juan de Dios still stands and, moreover, still serves as a medical center, although much altered and bearing another name. It adjoins the church of San Juan de Dios, directly north of the center of the Alameda.

Federico E. Mariscal points out that the old Mexican hospitals, marked by noble simplicity and tranquil amplitude in rooms, stairways, and galleries, form a characteristic part of the national architectural heritage. (*La Patria y la Arquitectura Nacional,* pp. 20–30.)

[3] The "chapel" mentioned was the church of Jesús Nazareno. (It is located three blocks south of the Zócalo opposite a small park, on what is now the Avenida de El Salvador, just west of the Avenida Pino Suárez.) In Fanny's day it was directly connected with the Hospital de Jesús Nazareno—the oldest functioning hospital in the New World. This still stands to the south, embedded in modern construction.

If there was left to the church of Jesús Nazareno only the conqueror's *memory,* what had happened to his mortal remains? The Calderóns' good friend Prescott was eager to know, and surviving correspondence shows that they had been seeking an answer on his behalf. By the spring of 1841 Fanny was able to write in her Journal: "I have procured a piece of the *black lace* which trims the sheet in which was wrapped the body of *Cortés.*"

It was common knowledge that in 1823, at a time of strong anti-Spanish feeling in the capital, the conqueror's bones had been hurriedly removed from their well-known resting place—but mystery surrounded their disposition. The Calderóns' Mexican friend Lucas Alamán, as representative of the heirs of Cortés, knew the whole story but was reluctant to divulge it for fear of further trouble—though most helpful in many other ways. Pressed by Calderón, however, he promised to give a full account for transmission to Prescott.

In a letter to Prescott of May 2, 1840, after referring to the emergency removal of 1823, Calderón had written: "Sr. Alamán hid the remains in a chest whose keys I have seen, together with a piece of the lace which adorned the shroud in which was wrapped the skeleton, as it is today, although I did not have the privilege of touching the skull as he promised me."

Much later, after leaving Mexico, Fanny would write to Prescott from Havana on February 16, 1842: "The body of Cortés is in Alamán's own house—concealed. Before leaving Mexico, Alamán promised Calderón to send him a detailed account of all these circumstances . . . Calderón will write now to Alamán, not only reminding him of this, but requesting his permission to disclose to you how the body of Cortés came into his possession . . . for no one in Mexico except Alamán knows where the body is."

The account referred to seems not to have been forthcoming. Ignoring an earlier suggestion by Alamán that "it is . . . best to say that they [the conqueror's remains] were sent to Italy," and presumably lacking permission to use the information provided by the Calderóns, Prescott in the concluding chapter of his *Conquest of Mexico* confined himself to a brief account of the emergency removal of 1823.

Subsequently, early in 1843, Alamán did provide in strict secrecy to Calderón's successor, the Spanish minister Oliver, a memorandum prepared in 1836, consisting of a composite of sworn statements by those who had taken part in certain events of that year. Briefly summarized, this is what it reported:

The midnight removal of the chest of bones in 1823 was followed by its hasty concealment nearby under the floor of the same church. In 1836, taking advantage of a time when repairs were being made in the old building, Alamán sought to retrieve the chest —which was finally located after a three-night search. When it was opened in the adjoining hospital in the presence of trusted witnesses, the remains were verified by virtue of an old document found inside. A portion of the well preserved black lace bordering the rotting winding sheet was removed, to be sent to the Cortés descendants. (It was a fragment of this, no doubt, that Alamán four years later gave to the Calderóns.) Following careful preparations, including repair of the old chest (not a coffin but a narrow, yard-long box) the bones, their wrappings, and their authenticating document were placed first in an inner container—which was locked with a gilded key entrusted to Alamán— and then in the chest. The chest was put in a niche in the wall of the church (the location being well noted) and sealed off so skillfully that no trace of the work remained.

Alamán's confidential letter to Oliver proffering this memorandum of 1836 made no reference to events subsequent to that date, but it did make plain that at the time he wrote (in December 1842) the conqueror's remains were safe in the hidden spot in the hospital's church.

This secret conveyed by Alamán, well guarded for more than a hundred years, finally leaked out in 1946. A small group of searchers located and uncovered the long-concealed niche in the then disused church. The chest was opened the following day in the Hospital de Jesús in the presence of a number of distinguished witnesses who were hastily assembled (among them Lucas Alamán's great-grandson who had inherited the gilded key). Great public interest ensued, and some anti-Cortés sentiment was expressed. The government's Instituto Nacional de Antropología e Historia was charged with the examination, preservation, and suitable disposition of the remains of the Spanish conqueror of Mexico. In due course the small chest with its historic contents—including its old verifying document together with a supplementary new one—was returned to its formerly hidden niche. The spot (within the chancel area of the church, near the east end of its north wall) was marked with a simple tablet.

(See Wolcott, Correspondence of . . . Prescott, pp. 112, 115, 125–27, 135–36, 150, 217, 220, 223, 227, 228, 231, 235, 238, 261–63, 264–65, 277, 284–85; Despachos Generales, II, 191–206; Alberto Carreño, "Hernán Cortés y el Descubrimiento de Sus Restos," in Academia Mexicana de la Historia, VI (Oct.–Dec. 1947), 301–403; Irving A. Leonard, "Cortés' Remains—and a Document," in The Hispanic American Historical Review, XXVIII (Feb. 1948), 53–61; Phyllis Benson, "Bones of Contention," in Modern Mexico, Vol. 19 (March 1947), pp. 7–10; "Mexicans Find the Lost Bones of Cortés," in Life, December 16, 1946, pp. 43–44.)

4 The former sacristy has been separated off from the church and now serves as the office of the director of the hospital, but its splendid coffered ceiling survives.

5 The name of the twice-shot Don Alvaro Muñoz was recorded in the October 3, 1841 entry of José Ramón Malo's Diario de Sucesos Notables, I, 201. The same entry notes the more tragic case of a child who lost both feet during the hostilities.

Alvaro Muñoz was a colonel, and had been a member of the politically conservative Escoseses. (Zavala, Ensayo Histórico . . . , II, 38, 411.)

6 In a later blank left by Fanny, the name Fagoaga was inserted in the Singer copy. The editors have assumed its appropriateness here.

7 Founded in 1766, both the building and the institution of the Cuna, or Casa de Niños Expósitos, survived until 1938.

8 In 1775, Johann Kaspar Lavater, Swiss mystic and philosopher, published the first of four volumes expounding the theory that the character of human beings could be deduced from their countenances.

9 The reader may recall Fanny's query, made to herself in her early and less knowledgeable days, as to what Mexican ladies did with their time (p. 156).

The school being run in the Acordada seems to have developed through a chain of circumstances started by the pamphlet advocating a monarchy for Mexico written by the Calderóns' friend Gutiérrez Estrada. As already noted, a side effect was that its publisher, Ignacio Cumplido, went to jail. The confusion, disorder, and idleness of life in the Acordada made a deep impression on Cumplido, with the result that he wrote a series of articles on prison reform which appeared in 1841 in his Mosaico Mexicano (V, 121–34, 145–53, 169–80, and 313–322). In the fourth of these articles he urged the idea of classes for prisoners. According to a still later article (V, 562–65), the Compañía Lancasteriana, a private organization interested in free schooling, seems to have requested three well-known ladies (all of them Fanny's good friends) to do something about instructing the women prisoners. All accepted the challenge: the elder Countess Cortina apologized for her limited abilities and strength, but promised her aid; Manuela Rengel de Flores (or de Casa Flores as she signed herself) accepted in a brief firm letter; and the Señorita Faustina Fagoaga—who was probably Fanny's guide on her visit to the Acordada—wrote in a letter dated May 26, 1841, that she welcomed the opportunity to help the unfortunate and to pay her debt to society.

10 R. H. Mason in Pictures of Life in Mexico (I, 193) also described a visit to the Acordada and gave figures on its occupants, presumably for about the year 1850. There were, he said, 9,237 persons imprisoned during the year. By far the largest cause of imprisonment was "quarrelling and wounding," accounting for about half. About a fourth were in jail for robbery, and about a tenth for "lesser crimes." Bigamy accounted for 624, and homicide for 222. Picturesque smaller categories—such as "incontinence," "forgery," and "throwing vitriol"—made up the remainder.

11 Although much of this building was destroyed in the cutting through of a street, one sizable segment of it still stands just west of the church of San Hipólito, a block west of the northwest corner of the Alameda. It has become the dwelling-place of many families of modest means who share its ancient patio. This quiet spot is only a few feet from the roar of traffic, but in it parakeets, canaries, and even a few securely tethered hens enjoy the sunshine and open space left from an earlier era.

[12] We have assumed that this was Fray Manuel Pinzón, described in another work as a gentle, persuasive Franciscan, known for his ability to bring comfort to the condemned prisoners under his spiritual care. (García Cubas, *Libro de Mis Recuerdos*, pp. 74, 238.)

[13] Fanny inserted here one of her own rare footnotes, as follows:

"Boston, November, 1842.—*Apropos des bottes*, I copy the following paragraph from a Havana newspaper: 'Mexico, 28th September.—Yesterday, was buried with pomp and solemnity in the cemetery of Saint Paul, the foot which his Excellency, President Santa Anna, lost in the action of the 5th December, 1838. It was deposited in a monument erected for that purpose, Don Ignacio Sierra y Ros[s]o having pronounced a funeral discourse appropriate to the subject.'"

Brantz Mayer, United States diplomat who was in Mexico at this time, described the awning-covered streets and the military procession to the cemetery, the same holy ground Fanny has earlier described (p. 490) under the name of Santa María. (*Mexico as It Was and as It Is*, p. 207.) The inscription, arranged in verse form, that was placed upon the monument ran as follows: "On the 5th of December of 1838/I was lamed but not conquered/Defending in the city of Veracruz/My home and fatherland./I repulsed with glory/The French forces which invaded it./I lost my left foot which I offer to my country/In testimony of the love I bear it./Antonio López de Santa Anna." (Bustamante, *Gabinete Mexicano*, I, 145.)

Not long afterward, following an uprising against Santa Anna, the monument would be destroyed.

[14] "We are getting *Mangas* made," Fanny blithely wrote Prescott, "in order to appear perfectly *à la ranchera*, not to frighten the Indians, for we are to visit very wild tribes. . . . The journey will be very severe from what they say, but Kate and I are ready to support all difficulties." (Wolcott, *Correspondence of . . . Prescott*, p. 264.)

[15] For the following four paragraphs, devoted to a detailed discussion of the temple of Guadalupe and its altars, Fanny drew upon a long article appearing in the 1838 volume of the *Calendario de las Señoritas Megicanas* (pp. 219–40). For clarification we have in several places gone back to the wording of her source. (The word "mark," which appears several times, is a unit of about eight ounces, applicable to either gold or silver.)

[16] Juan de Ortega y Montáñez had been bishop of Michoacán, later served as viceroy, and became archbishop of Mexico in 1701.

[17] This was the convent of Corpus Christi, founded by an early eighteenth-century viceroy in gratitude for his escape from death by a crazed would-be assassin. Its nuns were descendants of the Indian nobility and priestly class, and among the first of them was a descendant of Montezuma. (Rosell, *Iglesias y Conventos Coloniales de México*, pp. 336–39.)

The convent is gone, but its church, with a fine simple classic façade, still stands on the Avenida Juárez at No. 44. (See Plate 50.) No longer a consecrated building, it houses the government-sponsored center for the exhibition and sale of authentic popular arts.

[18] This building, although much modified, still stands as No. 39 on the south side of what is now the Calle de Donceles, in the block east of the Calle de Allende. The institution owed its origin to José Sáyago, a carpenter.

[19] The officer, designated by Fanny for publication as Colonel Y_____ (identified as Yniestra in the Singer copy) was evidently Ignacio Iniestra, who had become a lieutenant colonel and who was involved in the planning and construction of a road between Toluca and Morelia. Iniestra had expounded some of his ideas regarding this new project in the *Diario del Gobierno* of August 7, 1841.

[20] The Comte Ernest de Breteuil has been encountered before. William Robert Ward, a secretary in the British legation, is not to be confused with H. G. Ward, whose *Mexico in 1827* has been frequently cited. The latter had long since left Mexico.

As will shortly appear, Valladolid was the old name for Morelia.

[21] One notes that Fanny was a week late. All Saints Day fell on Monday, November first, the Day of the Dead following immediately on November second. In each case celebration began the previous evening.

Of just what "the illumination" consisted is not clear, but for a modern version of festive lighting, see Plate 20.

[22] In the chapter on Mexico's illustrious men, in which Manuel Gómez Pedraza's stormy political career was outlined (p. 419), Fanny gives some evidence of then knowing his wife—an indication that she later put that material together and interpolated it into her record, presumably after she left Mexico.

Her new-found friend—Juliana Azcárate de Gómez Pedraza—was a gifted amateur painter, according to an anonymous article in an annual of the period (*Museo Mexicano*, IV, 536). She is said to have enjoyed the lasting devotion of her distinguished husband, who exclaimed shortly before he died: "Oh, señora, that one might be eternal, to love you eternally!" (Prieto, *Memorias* . . . , II, 124.)

23 The name of the Señora de Adalid, whose beautiful well-trained contralto impressed Fanny at their first meeting, seems a legitimate guess. Similarly, Count Cortina seems an obvious guess in the next to last paragraph of this chapter.

24 Perhaps it was some other anniversary that the family celebrated, as the feast day of Saint Philip Neri is shown in calendars of the time as May 26. The mother in the family whom Fanny admired was Doña Rafaela de Rengel y Fagoaga, and she was first cousin —by virtue of the fact that their mothers were sisters—of the Calderóns' Fagoaga hostesses at San Xavier. Through her father she had inherited the title of Condesa de Alcaraz. Her two handsome daughters were María Gertrudis and Manuela del Barrio y Rengel. A descendant of the former today carries on not only the title of Conde de Alcaraz but also—in view of the disappearance, some generations ago, of the direct male line of the Fagoaga cousins—their title of Marqués de Apartado.

25 The sword borrowed to show the Calderóns was, it will be remembered, that presented to Valencia by a grateful congress in appreciation for his loyalty to the Bustamante government during the federalist revolution of the prior year. An inscription on the sword ran: "The National Congress, to the valor and loyalty of citizen Gabriel Valencia." (Riva Palacio, *México a Través de los Siglos*, IV, 457.)

48. Toluca, and to the Mines of Angangueo

1 The names provided here seem likely guesses. Matuti and Luis Robles Pezuela— presumably the Señor Robles whose name a few lines later is derived from the Singer copy—were both members of the Ateneo Mexicano, the cultural and scientific organization recently founded by Calderón and some of his friends. According to a letter Fanny had written to Prescott not long before, Robles (a son of Francisco Robles, director of the Minería) had planned to join the expedition. (Wolcott, *Correspondence of . . . Prescott*, p. 264.)

In this and the following three chapters covering the Calderóns' journey to Michoacán, their traveling companions are frequently mentioned: Fanny's niece Kate Macleod, Mr. Ward, the Comte de Breteuil, and Colonel Iniestra. Their names usually, but not always, appear written out in the Singer copy—source also of other filled-in names for these chapters. As their identities in the context are unmistakable, we have consistently restored their names.

2 Unlike the vanished gambling fête of San Agustín, the fair of San Juan de los Lagos in Jalisco still persists, although it now is celebrated on February second. The fair was authorized in viceregal times in honor of a small, revered figure of La Virgen de la Candelaria, and to promote commerce as well as piety. According to Frances Toor, modern folklorist, the great fiesta was formerly enlivened by extensive trading in horses, mules, and burros. (*Treasury of Mexican Folkways*, pp. 184–85.)

3 This battle occurred early in the War of Independence, on October 30, 1810, as Hidalgo and his undisciplined but determined horde approached the capital from Morelia, then called Valladolid. The Spanish government forces decided to give battle at the narrow defile at Las Cruces. They were driven back, with the loss of their artillery, and Hidalgo advanced to within fifteen miles of the capital. There he was seized with indecision, or perhaps with a realization of the scarcity of munitions among his peasant army. He fell back, later to suffer a severe defeat by augmented government forces. (William Davis Robinson, *Memoirs of the Mexican Revolution*, I, 33–37; Ward, *Mexico in 1827*, I, 168–72.)

4 The volcano was the Nevado de Toluca, perpetually snow-covered, and fourth highest among Mexico's peaks.

5 It seems likely that this was the hacienda to which Calderón had paid a visit some two months before (p. 327), and to which Fanny apparently referred in writing Prescott: "But I am inclined to imagine that the landscape is *less* beautiful than in the time of Cortés. They have cut down too much wood—they have an absurd idea that trees are *unhealthy*—and at a great Hacienda . . . where Calderón was lately, he having observed upon the total absence of trees, was informed that they were cut down to prevent the Indians from lying under their shade, and so losing their time instead of working!" (Wolcott, *Correspondence of . . . Prescott*, p. 169.)

6 The Toluca of today, capital of the state of Mexico, bears little resemblance to the solitary small city Fanny saw. Its high altitude—more than a thousand feet above the valley of Mexico—accounted perhaps for the feeling of sunset chill.

[7] To clarify a point of fact: La Gavia belonged not to Don Javier Echeverría (who has been encountered as Minister of the Treasury and acting president of the republic) but to his brother Pedro's wife, Doña Francisca Migoni de Echeverría. However, the hacienda was presumably a center for the entire Echeverría family.

[8] The incursions of *los indios bárbaros* were mentioned frequently in newspaper bulletins and also in books of the period. Horse-stealing expeditions and other depredations by Apaches were frequent in northern Mexico, but the annual September raids of the far-ranging Comanches sometimes wiped out whole villages and were especially dreaded. (Zamacois, *Historia de Méjico*, XII, 216–17; Ruxton, *Adventures in Mexico* . . . , pp. 110–14; *Cosmopolita*, August 7 and 14, 1841.)

[9] From viceregal times, until it was broken up in the 1930's, nothing had been added or subtracted from La Gavia's domain of more than 330,000 acres. At the time the editors first visited La Gavia, only a small area was left, but it was still the home of the much-traveled, trilingual Doña Dolores García Pimentel de Riba, widow of an Echeverría descendant. Thoroughly familiar with *Life in Mexico* and La Gavia's part in it, she welcomed with kindness the two inquiring strangers who had waded the bridgeless stream which separated her from the outside world.

The hacienda buildings, standing on a swell of ground, formed a large open square. The main house—added to since the Calderóns' day—contained, according to Señora de Riba, fifty-six rooms. Its handsome family quarters appeared lovingly tended, but La Gavia's outside was in a state of gentle, aristocratic decline. Señora de Riba's husband Antonio de Riba y Cervantes had been, she explained, a descendant not of the Calderóns' friend Francisco Javier Echeverría, but of his brother Pedro, who also held cabinet rank in the 1840's.

Señora de Riba, descended from the owner of Santa Clara in the sugar country (p. 398), and likewise from the proprietors of Queréndaro in Michoacán (soon to be visited by the Calderóns) was a bountiful mine of information, reminiscence, and suggestions. The editors remember their long rewarding call upon her with special pleasure and gratitude. Some years following this visit she sold the remnants of the once-enormous hacienda to Ramón Albarrán y Pliego—to whom the editors are also grateful for permission to revisit La Gavia in his absence. The greatest change to be seen—even more striking than those in La Gavia's great house and outbuildings (Plates 124 and 125)—was in the surrounding country. Earlier the hacienda buildings stood withdrawn and solitary in a vast rolling grassland. Today much of the same countryside is dotted with small farms and ranchos.

[10] Señora de Riba of La Gavia was unable to identify the hardy little boys by name. They were presumably a mixture among brothers and cousins, and perhaps included one or more Gorospes, sons of Manuel María Gorospe, whose wife was an Echeverría. He will be mentioned on the Calderóns' return to La Gavia a month later.

[11] When Mexicans of means traveled, according to the United States diplomat Mayer, the hazards involved and the dearth of inns called for rather elaborate arrangements. Voyagers usually took bedding, dishes, food, and the servants to prepare it—everything "except a cow and a piano." He also noted that "their long and numerous train should be fully armed and equipped to fight its way if necessary . . ." (*Mexico, Aztec, Spanish and Republican*, II, 344).

Included as an appendix to Ward's *Mexico in 1827* (I, 575) is an account of an expedition that comprised forty-five persons, including servants and cooks, and was "preceded by a musician mounted on a mule, playing a guitar . . ."

[12] In contrast with well-preserved La Gavia, the editors found El Pilar an abandoned and hopeless ruin—reachable only on foot, near the shore of a large modern reservoir. Although its small church was still functioning, the hacienda structures of sun-dried adobe brick—a material for the centuries if kept covered and maintained—had all but melted away. No one in the nearby town of Villa Victoria seemed to have any idea as to the identity of the hospitable Señora M——, long-ago owner of El Pilar.

The provincial lady who, as Iturbide's wife, was briefly the Empress of Mexico was born Ana María Huarte. According to tradition, she was educated in the Convent of Las Rosas in Morelia. She married Agustín de Iturbide in 1805 and became the mother of nine children, the last born not long after her husband was executed. (Only a few years after her death in 1861, a grandson, also named Agustín de Iturbide, would be adopted by the childless Maximilian and Carlota as the heir expected to carry on their dynasty.)

[13] Fanny is here recalling again the historian Clavijero (*Historia Antigua* . . . , II, 308), who cites the French naturalist the Comte de Buffon. The *zorillo*, said a British resident of Mexico of about this period, was a kind of polecat, and the smell exuded from dogs which had killed one was so pungent as to cause a severe pain in the head, "worse than any thing I ever experienced or could have imagined." (Lyon, *Journal* . . . , II, 97.)

[14] From a newspaper article of the time one learns of the interest of various prominent citizens of Michoacán in the construction of the proposed road for wheeled vehicles between Toluca and Morelia. (*Diario del Gobierno*, August 30, 1841.) Three members of a junta or committee concerned with this project will be encountered as hosts to the Calderóns on their journey: Carlos Heimbürger (who will appear in the next paragraph), Tomás López Pimentel of Queréndaro, and Cayetano Gómez of San Bartolo and Morelia.

[15] The editors were pleased but not greatly surprised to encounter in remote Angangueo, as in many other places, admiring readers of *Life in Mexico*. (See Plate 126 for an old view of the town.) Two local mining engineers, Roger W. Loveless and William L. Parker, courteously showed us the old compound—away from and below the town—where the Calderóns' party was welcomed in 1841. It was a large, stoutly walled enclosure with watchtowers in each corner pierced by rifle slits, and within it were the remains of the old refining works. Adjoining were two substantial houses. Our informants pointed out the one in which the Calderóns stayed, with its porch across the front overlooking the sloping land below. By modern standards it was in fact a commodious house, but the fireplaces and the snug scale of the rooms must have produced an effect very different from that of the haciendas and large city houses of the time.

49. Through Morelia and Pátzcuaro to Uruapan

[1] The inventor of homeopathy, Dr. Samuel Hahnemann, was still alive and his theories were esteemed by many. His writings had appeared in the United States in 1836 and created a considerable vogue for the small doses that were one of the most distinctive features of his system. In fact, a homeopathic dose was a weak dilution rather than a concentration such as *mezcal*, potent distilled derivative of the juice of the maguey.

[2] Taximaroa's existence as a community goes back to pre-Columbian times, and fateful encounters between Spaniards and Tarascans took place there during the conquest. Its early settlement by the Spaniards is confirmed by the antiquity of its church and the fine stone cross in its atrium. The town is now called Ciudad Hidalgo.

[3] H. G. Ward had carried "Thompson's small brass camp beds." The length of the legs for a good traveling bed, he explained, should be calculated to raise it just beyond the maximum leap of fleas. Ward's particular brand must have been substantial, as two of them constituted an entire load for a mule. (*Mexico in 1827*, II, 310–11, 317.)

[4] The editors once visited Pueblo Viejo, traveling over a primitive road connecting Huajúmbaro and Zinapécuaro. Their journey was unrewarded except by the sight of a small Indian village—and, farther north, by a distant view of Lake Cuitzeo which (though not mentioned here) lay only a little beyond the Calderóns' route.

[5] Queréndaro's owner was Don Tomás López Pimentel, successively a deputy, a senator, and president of the senate. He is described elsewhere as a shy man in public life, but calm and firm. (Ramírez, *Mexico during the War with the United States*—edited by Walter V. Scholes—p. 26.) He and his wife were the parents of the two infants whose epitaph Fanny quoted on pages 490–91.

When the editors visited Queréndaro, it had passed out of the hands of the Pimentel family and retained only a fraction of its former lands. Its new owners, who were farming the remaining acreage, were proud of their establishment and maintained the large house in good repair.

Queréndaro's layout—like that of the Adalids' Santiago, which the Calderóns had twice visited earlier—demonstrated how a rich hacienda might have been held against marauders. There was a fine deep well in the center of the courtyard, around which extended the heavy-walled house with its appended chapel. Nearby were notably large, staunch barns and outbuildings, and around the whole ran a high thick wall.

[6] "I am monarch of all I survey,/My right there is none to dispute." These are the opening lines of William Cowper's "Verses Supposed to be Written by Alexander Selkirk," the real-life castaway who served as a prototype for Robinson Crusoe.

[7] San Bartolo is no longer a functioning hacienda. Its massive house, outwardly in a fair state of repair, shelters a number of agricultural families—with even the patio divided by a wall. For one of its handsome barns, see Plate 127. The small hacienda church, under which many of the Gómez family lie buried, continues to serve the surrounding countryside.

[8] It was the time of autumnal migration, and the Calderóns were traveling in the flyway between Lake Cuitzeo and Lake Pátzcuaro.

[9] This reference seems to confuse two separate events and different perpetrators:
On the Cerro de las Bateas and another hill, pursuant to the orders of Hidalgo (not

Morelos), eighty Spaniards were put to the sword in November 1810, two months after Hidalgo had touched off the War of Independence by the *Grito de Dolores*. It has been pointed out that such fanatic excesses discouraged many independence-minded creoles from joining Hidalgo's movement at this time. (Ward, *Mexico in 1827*, I, 174–77; Mariano Cuevas, *Historia de la Nación Mexicana*, p. 408.) Pitiless killings of prisoners, hostages, and civilians continued on both sides. Iturbide, then a royalist officer (though later joining the revolutionary effort), General Torcuato Trujillo, the Spanish commander earlier mentioned by Fanny, and another Spanish general, Félix María Calleja, also shot prisoners in large numbers. As many of the Spanish government forces were Mexican-born, the struggle assumed the doubly tragic aspect of a ferocious civil war.

In late December 1813, three years after the bloody Cerro de las Bateas, Morelos was opposed at Valladolid (later called Morelia) by royalist forces, among whose officers was the highly competent Iturbide. Morelos sustained a severe defeat in a confused action during which insurgents fired on their own reinforcements. In a later engagement some distance off, royalist forces were again victorious and Mariano Matamoros, valued aid of Morelos, was taken prisoner. Through an intermediary, Morelos tried to exchange for Matamoros some 200 soldiers whom he had captured from a Spanish regiment. But the viceroy refused, and Matamoros was shot in Valladolid on February 3, 1814. Morelos then retaliated by shooting the 200 prisoners in his power. (Ward, *Mexico in 1827*, I, 206–7; Robinson, *Memoirs of the Mexican Revolution*, I, 66–67.)

[10] Some of Fanny's wording here—as, for example, that Hidalgo operated without a plan, and that Morelos was uneducated—suggests that she used Zavala as her authority. (*Ensayo Histórico* . . . , I, 56.) Morelos, a mestizo, did in fact obtain, as an adult, enough education to qualify for the priesthood at the Colegio de San Nicolás in Valladolid. The Calderóns' friend Lucas Alamán, in the history he would publish some years later, would call Morelos "the most extraordinary man the revolution of New Spain has produced." (*Historia de Méjico*, IV, 314.) Here and in what follows Fanny presents a viewpoint that to some extent, at least, would seem to have reflected her husband's loyalties.

[11] Mexican historians consider that this document—ineffective at the time, because of the military reverses sustained by the revolutionaries—was important, nevertheless, as an early expression of national aspirations and thinking far in advance of the times. (The text of the constitution of Apatzingán may be found in *México a Través de los Siglos*, III, 779–87.) Morelos was constant in his belief in the importance of civil authority, and groups of civilians met first in one place and then in another. There were sorry dissensions among those who took part in these meetings. The congress that produced the document proclaimed at Apatzingán included men of real stature (among those who worked on it, although they were not present at the signing, were Carlos María de Bustamante and Andrés Quintana Roo), but they bickered among themselves, disagreed with Morelos, and in effect hampered the conduct of the liberation effort. Morelos, aware that his own leadership and prestige had waned, considered the safety of these national spokesmen of such importance that he willingly assigned a large body of his troops to the task of protecting them during their trek to a safer spot. Fighting a delaying action against Spanish government troops with a small detachment, and subsequently almost alone, he fell a captive to the royalist forces—as Fanny explains in her next sentence. (Ward, *Mexico in 1827*, I, 181–85, 202–3, 207–10, 212–14; Parkes, *History of Mexico*, pp. 159–63; Teja Zabre, *Guide to the History of Mexico*, pp. 250–52.)

[12] Following the execution of Morelos in December 1815, the fortunes of the revolutionaries sank farther. Except for die-hard groups whose leaders stubbornly held on in the remoter areas, the struggle all but ceased. Finally in 1820 events in Spain led to a change in the political climate of Mexico. In that year the absolutist Ferdinand VII was obliged by the success of revolutionary effort at home to implement once more the Spanish liberal constitution of 1812, drafted during the Napoleonic war by a legislative body in unoccupied Spain. Under the terms of that constitution, Mexicans had sent representatives to the mother country and briefly tasted something of government responsibility— and in 1820 they once again sent representatives to Spain. The re-proclaimed liberal policies of the constitution became perforce the official line in the Spanish colonies. Propertied creoles—many of whom had earlier remained uncommitted, or pro-Spanish, in the face of the disorders and uncertainties brought on by the Mexican insurgents— now saw their conservative system of government, which had survived years of bloody fighting, threatened by the ideology of successful liberal revolutionaries in the mother country. The advantages to such conservatives of an independent Mexico, unencumbered by whatever might emanate from Spain, and in which they themselves might take the initiative, became apparent. It was the formerly pro-Spanish Iturbide who made practical use of the fact that men of widely varying backgrounds, for varying reasons, wanted the same thing: independence. Backed by conservative elements in the capital, including many high officials of the church, Iturbide succeeded in consolidating his own forces and

those of the old insurgent chiefs in the hinterlands or in hiding. For a time the balance of power wavered; then, as Iturbide's movement gained momentum, Spanish power in Mexico crumbled rapidly. While Spanish resistance continued at the fortress off Veracruz, independence for Mexico began in 1821.

[13] Two brothers, Armand and Jules de Polignac, were arrested for their part in a royalist plot against Napoleon when he was first consul of France. Armand (later the Duc de Polignac) is said to have asserted that as the older he should bear the brunt of any blame; whereas Jules (later the recipient of the papal title of Prince de Polignac) urged that he, then a bachelor, should suffer the death penalty in place of his married brother. Both were imprisoned, but both survived to lead eventful lives.

[14] "Full many a flower is born to blush unseen,/And waste its sweetness on the desert air." From Thomas Gray's "Elegy Written in a Country Churchyard."

[15] The lonely baths of Cointzio, when the editors saw them a number of years ago, seemed to be one of those institutions that would never change and never die. A few patrons were picnicking outside (see Plate 134) while others enjoyed in leisurely fashion the benefits of the waters by bathing in the same rather dank building used by Fanny in 1841. The venerable caretaker, whose father had been caretaker before him, said that in the Calderóns' time the baths were the property of the church.

More recently, one hears that Cointzio has added a swimming pool of olímpico size.

[16] From A Midsummer Night's Dream, Act II, Scene 1.

[17] The career of Caltzontzi—whose name is sometimes given as Tangaxoan II—paralleled to some extent that of Montezuma in its somber contribution to the subjugation of his people. He began by refusing, like his father before him, to answer his rival Montezuma's call for help against the mysterious newcomers. Later he received, and permitted to depart unharmed, a small deputation of exploring Spaniards, and promised to recognize the Spaniards' ruler across the seas. Still later, after the arrival of a larger Spanish expedition, Caltzontzi unwillingly accompanied the white men—and the treasure they extracted from him—to Tenochtitlan. There he encountered both affability and threats from Cortés, and was allowed to return home and continue his rule. Subsequently he made other visits to the capital, and embraced Christianity. In 1530, when Cortés was in Spain, Nuño de Guzmán plundered his bloody way through Michoacán. Caltzontzi was defeated after courageous resistance. Unable to produce sufficient treasure to appease the Spanish victors, he was tortured and burned to death. These barbarities were condemned by Mexico's first bishop, Juan de Zumárraga, whose protests were eventually heard in Spain.

Tzintzuntzan was on "the opposite shore" of the lake in that it was on the far side of the peninsula about which Lake Pátzcuaro lies in a great arc. Its name signifies "place of the hummingbirds"—Huitzitzila being the Aztec equivalent. The Calderóns presumably did not visit the town which, now dominantly mestizo, is known for its officially designated archaeological zone—containing five yácatas, or truncated stone pyramids—and an adjacent large and very distinctive churchyard, where there still survive the remains of enormous olive trees planted in the sixteenth century.

[18] This is the chapel of El Humilladero, still standing at the eastern edge of town, on the old road from Morelia. The most ancient Spanish production in Pátzcuaro is the cross, erected in 1552, now inside the chapel. The unpretentious building that was subsequently erected around it shows the forthright result which vigorous Indian craftsmanship could achieve when interpreting Spanish architectural designs of the period. Outside is a later cross, dated 1628. (Monumentos Coloniales, pp. 165–66; Toussaint, Arte Colonial en México, p. 51; Toussaint, Pátzcuaro, p. 119.) The legend that Caltzontzi here met the Spaniards is probably unfounded.

[19] Pátzcuaro actually lies on a sloping plateau considerably above and more than a mile back from the lake shore. (The settlement of Ibarra, near the lake at the railway station, is almost entirely modern.)

Pátzcuaro's founding, like that of scores of other municipalities in Mexico, resulted from confident planning on the part of officialdom in organizing Spain's newly conquered domain. The little settlement, well over 200 mountain miles west of the capital, had by 1547 begun what was planned to be a great five-aisled cathedral, and soon thereafter it was chartered as a city by Charles V. But in the shadow of Morelia, to which the episcopal see was soon moved, Pátzcuaro's growth was slow.

The community's personality is the product primarily of its low, tile-roofed, wide-eaved houses, its several plazas of distinctive quality, and its centuries-old predominantly Indian weekly market. First reached by railroad in 1886, Pátzcuaro became a favorite honeymoon and vacation retreat for Mexicans. When the editors spent their own honeymoon there in 1939, streets were of cobblestone, automobiles sparse, and foreign tourists comparatively few. At night its electric bulbs were pallid and quavering. Señor Miguel Leal, owner of Pátzcuaro's leading general store, served also as town banker. A client's order, written on any scrap of paper to the effect that the bearer should be paid off at Señor Leal's, was as good as hard silver pesos. Today, cobblestones give way to concrete, automobile parking has become a problem, and foreigners are far from curiosities. By night, light bulbs glow brilliantly, and by day calculating machines chatter in the recently enlarged quarters of the Banco de Comercio. Yet Pátzcuaro retains its serenity, and Fanny's description of the older parts of the little city still holds good today. (See Plate 135.)

If the Calderóns' mule drivers had not forgotten the name of Cointzio, Fanny would have arrived in Pátzcuaro in time to have seen, and described for us, its great Friday market, held in accordance with immemorial custom, that briefly fills the quiet main plaza with people and goods, noise and color.

[20] Fanny attributed to the last name of her kindly hosts an initial "H" and entered it as H_____a, thereby giving her editors, more than a hundred years later, the agreeable task of calling upon the baffled but ever-courteous kin of the Huertas, Hinojosas, and other H—— families of the community. Later, armed with the names of Hacha and Pepita based on the Singer copy, the editors resumed their quest. A long-time resident of Pátzcuaro, Don Luis Ortiz Lazcano, at once recalled that the Acha family had received in the past many visitors and at times had used their large establishment as an informal hotel. The house still stands on the south side of the Calle Ibarra, in the first block west of the main plaza; but the Acha family scattered in the twentieth century and no one of the name seems to remain in the Pátzcuaro area.

[21] Pátzcuaro had earlier entertained at least one foreigner—the tireless Humboldt, who in 1803 stayed at a still-existing house called the Casa del Gigante, on the east side of the main plaza. (Antonio Salas León, Pátzcuaro: Cosas de Antaño y de Ogaño, p. 34.)

[22] Don Vasco de Quiroga, born in Spain in 1470 and trained as a lawyer before he entered the church, was a friend of Juan de Zumárraga, first bishop of Mexico—and like him was a Franciscan of liberal views and practical idealism. George Kubler, in his Mexican Architecture of the Sixteenth Century (I, 12–13, 39–40, 224–26), points out that Don Vasco patterned his Indian "hospitals" or communities upon Thomas More's Utopia. Quiroga's broad, imaginative social program brought vigor and stability to his recently war-torn diocese. Modern ethnologists question, however, too literal an interpretation of the legend that he instituted the plan of village specialization in Michoacán, pointing both to old documents and to the fact that the same phenomenon of craft specialization among villages exists in other parts of Mexico. Quiroga and his subordinates wisely built on an existing situation, taught new techniques and modified old ones, and tried to effect an economic balance in the area by encouraging non-competing specialties and market days. The tradition of village specialization persists today: painted trays, guitars, pottery, and copper utensils are only a few examples among nearly a score of major categories. Among Quiroga's legacies was his interest in education, and it has long been a source of local pride that more than an average share of national leaders have come from Michoacán. (Foster, Empire's Children . . . , pp. 10, 130–31, 284; Robert C. West, Cultural Geography of the Modern Tarascan Area, pp. 56–71.)

Quiroga, who had passed sixty when he began his strenuous career in the New World, was still on active duty when he died in 1565 at the age of ninety-five.

[23] The moon was full the following day, Sunday, November 28.

[24] The mountainous descent of 1700 feet from Pátzcuaro down to Uruapan has since 1899 been traversed by railroad. It is a journey of forty-seven miles, and what took the Calderóns most of two days is accomplished in some two hours. Las Palomas and Curu are both served by the line, about seventeen and ten miles respectively before reaching Uruapan.

[25] "Charming the eye with dread,—a matchless cataract / Horribly beautiful ! . . ." From Byron's Childe Harold, Canto IV, Stanzas LXXI and LXXII.

[26] Fanny speaks of Uruapan as an Indian village, but in historical importance and in fact it was far more. Founded by a Franciscan friar about 1540, it became an important trading center between the mountain country and the tropical lowlands that begin a little to the south. (Kubler, Mexican Architecture of the Sixteenth Century, I, 81, II, 493.)

As contrasted with tight, cool, Spanish-style Pátzcuaro, Uruapan—with its thick semitropical vegetation and spread-out Indian cottages—undoubtedly appeared far less urban. Yet its total population was probably larger than Fanny realized. Before being decimated by revolutionary war and disease, it was said to have totaled some 20,000 inhabitants. Uruapan is today a green and attractive small city, but it is no longer Indian. Though still a market center for Tarascans, it lies outside their shrinking cultural area.

[27] Señor Izazaga's wife was presumably Doña Leonarda Izazaga who, one notes, was the only subscriber from Uruapan listed in the new publication El Semanario de las Señoritas Mejicanas.

A brother of the former empress who at this time was identified with Uruapan was Don Manuel Huarte.

[28] José María Izazaga was born at the Hacienda del Rosario in what is now the state of Guerrero, and was educated in Morelia. He had been involved in 1809 in the conspiracy of Valladolid, a pre-revolutionary abortive effort looking toward Mexican independence. The plot was discovered, but the participants' able legal defender extricated them from punishment. Izazaga later fought with Hidalgo and, after independence, was a member of the group that formed the constitution of 1824. (Diego García Loya, *Mosaic of Mexican History*, p. 144; Alamán, *Historia de Méjico*, IV, 289; Rubén García, *Rincones y Paisajes del México Maravilloso*, pp. 125–26.)

[29] In Fanny's published text, this and the date at the start of the next chapter were both entered as the "31st" (of November!). Internal evidence, including later reference to the festival of San Andrés, suggests the revisions provided here and at the next entry.

[30] Again Fanny quotes from Byron's *Childe Harold*, clearly one of her favorite poems: Canto III, Stanza XCIII.

[31] Fanny had evidently read an article on the volcanoes of America in the *Mosaico Mexicano* (III, 80–87).

[32] San Pedro Jorullo, site of the volcano—southeast of Uruapan and a little over thirty miles directly south of Pátzcuaro—had previously been a peaceful sugar cane hacienda. A large area around the central cone was permanently swollen, and roughened by tiny cones six to ten feet high. The two little rivers of Cuitumba and San Pedro (rather than San Andrés, as Fanny had it) reappeared some four miles away as hot springs. In 1780—twenty-one years after the eruption—one could still light a cigar from cracks around the base of the dying volcano, but by the 1820's vegetation was beginning to return along the outer fringes of the area. (Beaufoy, *Mexican Illustrations*, pp. 224–27; Mayer, *Mexico, Aztec, Spanish and Republican*, II, 287–89; Christian Sartorius, *Mexico. Landscapes and Popular Sketches*, pp. 39–40.)

The modern parallel for Jorullo is, of course, Parícutin. In the sight of an astonished farmer, it began modestly enough in a cornfield about fourteen miles northwest of Uruapan on February 20, 1943. During the following eight months it grew awesomely to a height of some 1500 feet, burying one evacuated village, slowly engulfing another with its lava, and intermittently spewing ash as far away as the city of Mexico. Farmers at a safe distance rejoiced in the valuable top-dressing that fell on their fields, while housekeepers in Pátzcuaro, down-wind from Parícutin, philosophically swept up the harsh black particles —useful as scouring powder for their kitchen knives. After serving for almost ten years as a world mecca for geologists, the new volcano subsided and expired.

On the afternoon before Parícutin's birth the editors, some forty miles away, were enjoying the company of a Mexican friend. He complained of a certain malaise, and interposed the prediction that an earthquake would shortly occur. That night the ground shook sharply, the next morning there were new cracks in Pátzcuaro's old Basílica—and, over the rim of mountains to the west, there rose the great column of smoke announcing Michoacán's newest boast.

50. Uruapan and Return to Morelia

[1] In other words, poinsettia—*euphorbia pulcherrima*—named for the first United States minister to independent Mexico, Joel R. Poinsett, who was responsible for introducing the plant to the United States. (According to his own *Notes on Mexico*, page 159, Poinsett also brought back seeds of the spectacular *árbol de las manitas*, but presumably any effort to grow the trees failed.)

[2] This area is undoubtedly that which has so fortunately been preserved as the Parque Nacional Eduardo Ruiz, a riot of rushing water and luxuriant vegetation.

[3] Important ingredients for this distinctive lacquer work included oil from seeds of the *chia* plant (a kind of salvia) and—for hardness and brilliancy—a greasy extract derived from an insect: *coccus axin*, or *aje*. There are preserved magnificent examples of this historic folk art that comprised the decoration not only of the hollowed-out fruit of the calabash tree, but also of boxes, chests, and other articles. The technique survives, although modified by the use of modern pigments and oils. Laborious step-by-step filling in of the incised designs and much hand rubbing is required, and in consequence modern work seldom approaches the old in quality.

[4] The superb falls, south of Uruapan, are today easily accessible by paved road and a safe though steep trail. (See Plate 142.)

[5] A long article discussing this project had appeared in *El Mosquito Mexicano* of June 1, 1841 (Vol. IX, No. 44). Esteban—presumably Etienne in his native France—Guénot was president of the company. According to a later book of memoirs by Mathieu de Fossey, a Frenchman long resident in Mexico, the Chinese mulberry trees prospered, and trained silk workers were brought over from Lyons. M. Guénot was lacking, however, in both natural acumen and business experience, and the venture failed. (*Le Mexique*, pp. 391–92.)

[6] Presumably the hill called La Magdalena, the name also of one of the nine *barrios* or wards demarked and named by Fray Juan de San Miguel, sixteenth-century founder of Uruapan. (Eduardo Ruiz, *Michoacán, Paisajes, Tradiciones, y Leyendas*, pp. 197 fn, 200 fn.)

[7] It would appear that at the time of Fanny's visit Tarascan was spoken by the majority of the residents of Uruapan. Today that language remains a strong force in the mountains to the north and in most of the lake villages of the Pátzcuaro area, but is no longer spoken by the townspeople of Uruapan. (See *Cultural Geography of the Modern Tarascan Area*, by Robert C. West, Maps 9, 10, 11, and 12.)

[8] An old view from approximately this spot is shown as Plate 136. Janitzio, soon to be visited, is the cone-shaped island a little to the left of the center.

[9] Within a few squares of the Acha house there were at least five handsome churches from which to choose, four of them of respectable antiquity. All still exist, although San Agustín has become the city's library. A likely guess is that the Calderóns' hostess took them uphill to what had been started long ago as the cathedral, was in 1841 the *parroquia*, and is now (much renovated after various disasters) the Basílica. In it is enshrined a celebrated image of Nuestra Señora de la Salud (Our Lady of Health), commissioned by Bishop Quiroga himself.

[10] Said by Puck, in Act II, Scene 1 of *A Midsummer Night's Dream*.

[11] Fanny's interest in feather work had evidently been encouraged by reading what Clavijero wrote about it in his *Historia Antigua de Mégico*. Her discussion of the ancient technique and the infinite care it required closely parallels his (I, 374–75), including the fact that a noted practitioner of the art had died some years before in Pátzcuaro. Her thoughts on the unlikelihood that feather work in the old tradition could continue have been borne out in fact. A modern authority on Mexican popular art has pointed out that its decadence dates from the 1840's. (Dr. Atl, *Las Artes Populares en México*, I, 292–93.)

Today's visitor to the Mexican capital can see, in the Museo Nacional de Historia at Chapultepec, an example of the old work: a sixteenth-century feather mosaic representing St. Francis of Assisi.

[12] Fanny and her husband and Kate Macleod, in going to Janitzio with Pátzcuaro's officious prefect (reminiscent of Dickens' Mr. Bumble, head of Oliver Twist's workhouse), must have been among the volcanic island's earliest tourists, although the great Humboldt had visited it in 1803. Only one other mid-nineteenth-century travel account known to the editors so much as mentions what is perhaps today Mexico's best-known indigenous community. Apparently Janitzio remained aloof and even suspicious of strangers until the nineteen-thirties, when the government selected its central cone as the setting for a gigantic monument—larger than the Statue of Liberty—honoring the patriot Morelos. Today an ever-increasing stream of visitors, Mexican and foreign, climbs up the island's stepped stone ways (some perhaps scratching their initials on maguey leaves as they stop to catch breath), mount the spiraling stairs within the statue's hollow mural-covered core, and emerge at the sleeve beneath the upraised fist of the revolutionary hero. Their reward is a full circle view of the beautiful C-shaped lake with its islands, shifting surface textures and colors—the fields and villages along its scalloped shore—the mountains and further mountains beyond. On the way down to their waiting motor launches, they buy miniature replicas of dugout canoes or of the butterfly-shaped nets used by the islanders for fishing in shallow water. Soon they are gone, to be replaced by others.

Pursuing Fanny's trail, one of the editors first visited Janitzio in 1938—and acquired there a vacation house which served as a point of return over many ensuing years. With each visit, new changes were to be seen, taking Janitzio a little farther from the past. Yet the islanders' long tradition of independence—what Fanny so aptly calls "their originality"—to a great extent still survives.

Developments affecting life on Janitzio, as in all Mexico, have been many. There is today a typewriter in the alcalde's modest office. Electricity powers lights, corn-grinding machinery, and resounding radios. In going to market in Pátzcuaro, a combination of motorboat and bus is more often than not a substitute for paddling and trudging, and now trucks instead of oxen bring the still essential dugout canoes—in a roughed-out form—down from the *sierra* to the margin of the lake. But, parallel with such developments, the daily round continues almost undisturbed. Tarascan speech is tenaciously maintained. The enormous nets in which the daily catch is laboriously hauled into long canoes are still knotted by hand from cotton thread spun in the correct, varying thicknesses on the island's many spinning wheels. The women still wear sweeping, lavishly pleated skirts, and their black hair hangs in long braids. In winter, when ducks are plentiful, all but a few of Janitzio's hunters use not guns but triple-pointed spears, deftly cast by means of throwing-sticks of pre-Columbian design.

Janitzio's greatly expanded population presses on the resources of the lake as well as the small island. Many of the men have sought at least temporary employment elsewhere, some few in the United States. Tending further to diminish the isolationism of former days is the fact that a number of families now send their sons to board in Pátzcuaro for schooling beyond the rather limited local offering, and—what was unheard of until recently— a few families send daughters as well.

Plates 137 through 141 show some of the unchanging aspects of Janitzio's lakeside life. The type of dugout canoe shown is without doubt identical in form with that in which the Calderóns' party crossed the lake in 1841.

13 An example of the curiously carved rocks may be seen today on the high promontory directly behind the church and above the town's cemetery.

On the north slope of the island is the bat-cave, inhabited in numbers beyond belief. It is not only the sleeping place for all the bats on the island but also almost certainly for all those of the entire region. They emerge after sunset, in a purposeful, dense, wide black ribbon that streaks for several miles across the darkening sky.

14 Greatly respected on the island today is a descendant of Agustín Campos: José Campos, an able and commanding individual, one of the most forward-looking men of the community. The tablet Fanny saw is still embedded in the base of the bell tower, curiously built a little apart from the church. In time-dimmed characters, with a touch of folk-spelling, it reads: "En el año 1819 se comenso este templo y se concluyó el año de 1822 Agustín_____." But a roughened blank space occupies the former site of Don Agustín's last name—the result, his descendant José Campos said, of jealousy on the part of another branch of the family.

15 Fanny must have reviewed with Prescott the historic process of making tortillas. In a discussion concerning the provisioning of Cortés' troops, he refers briefly to information she gave him in a note near the end of Chapter V of Book VI of his Conquest of Mexico.

In her description above she did not, surely, intend to convey the impression that individual corn kernels are peeled. The dry corn is put into a pot with water and a small quantity of lime, and then cooked gently till soft and swollen, at which point the hulls tend to loosen. One of the happiest innovations for the women of Janitzio—and of all Mexican communities of any size—has been the machine grinding of corn. At the time of our first visit to the island, it boasted a mill powered by an ingeniously converted old and rather temperamental automobile engine. With the coming of twenty-four-hour-a-day power from the mainland, there was installed a new electrically operated mill, owned by José Campos, Don Agustín's descendant. In place of long, monotonous home grinding sessions of two or three hours at their slanted stone metates, Janitzio matrons now go to the mill, exchange the latest news with friends while waiting in line, and, for the payment of a small fee, see the potent machine quickly reduce to dough the wet mass they have brought. But most island housewives still work at their metates to insure final smoothness of the dough before patting it out, and in essence the pre-conquest technique persists.

16 The building which once housed the Convento de las Monjas Domínicas de Santa Catarina was, when the editors last saw it, a tenement on the Calle Portugal, a street whose aspect has been much altered by regrading. A curious low bath-chamber used by the nuns survived the general decay.

17 Don Cayetano's portrait still hangs in Morelia in the home of his great-granddaughters, who, in accordance with the old upper-class Mexican tradition, live in the middle of town within sight of the cathedral. His wife, whom the Calderóns undoubtedly met, was Doña Dolores Alzúa.

18 The early episode of the Poblana dress now having receded far into the past, Fanny apparently uses the term here quite naturally to designate a lady born in Puebla.

19 Morelia's Alameda is a delightful spot now termed the Calzada de los Penitentes or Calzada de Guadalupe (Plate 132), a mall constructed in 1732 as an approach to the Sanctuary of Guadalupe. It is bounded by low stone walls incorporating benches. Beginning at the double bend in Morelia's famous aqueduct (Plate 133), it leads eastward into what in the Calderóns' time was the paseo, now in part a street leading to the south.

20 Just before the beginning of the revolutionary wars, the population of Morelia (Valladolid, as it was then called) was reckoned at 20,000. War and disease brought it to a low of 3,000—as compared with the 15,000 Fanny mentions as the population at the time of her visit. (José R. Benítez, Morelia, p. LVI.)

[21] This was Juan Cayetano Portugal, born in 1783 and therefore well under sixty at this time. Like other churchmen of the period he had been prominent in governmental affairs, but unlike a good many ecclesiastics, he had been a liberal. In addition to having served during Santa Anna's first presidency as Minister of Justice and Ecclesiastical Affairs, he was also a senator and was three times president of the chamber of deputies. A few days after Portugal's death in 1850, news arrived of his elevation to the college of cardinals. (Romero, Noticias . . . del Obispado de Michoacán, I, 20–21.)

[22] Morelia's first cathedral, started soon after the seat of the diocese was moved from Pátzcuaro in 1579, was of wood and adobe. The present building was begun about 1660, the lofty towers reaching completion in 1744. (As in Puebla, Fanny will shortly climb one of them.) The creamy stone exterior, with superb proportions and relatively sober baroque detail, is one of the finest in all Mexico. Facing the city's main boulevard, and flanked on both sides by plazas, the cathedral shows to advantage from every angle, and continues to be the core of its still-beautiful colonial city.

The interior was modified shortly after the Calderóns' visit, in 1844. About 1858 it was despoiled of its fittings, with the result that today it presents little of special interest. (Joseph Armstrong Baird, Jr., The Churches of Mexico, 1530–1810, pp. 99–100.) Among the treasures Fanny admired, a notable one remains and is in service today: the cathedral's silver font, used at the baptism of both Morelos and Iturbide.

Plates 130 and 131 show aspects of the incomparable building.

[23] The dead bishop, kinsman in an older generation to the Calderóns' friend, was the Spanish-born Dr. Pedro Anselmo Sánchez de Tagle. Before coming to Michoacán he had served as bishop of Durango, where he combined generalship with piety in invoking the aid of St. George (the dragon slayer) in a spiritual crusade against that region's famous scorpions. He became bishop of Michoacán in 1757 and died in 1772, and was long remembered for sweetness of character. (Romero, Noticias . . . del Obispado de Michoacán, I, 20; Atúnez, Los Alacranes . . . de Durango, pp. 19–20.)

Portraits of the bishop still hang both in Durango and in Morelia. The family coat of arms is shown also in a modern Mexican genealogical work. Fanny remembered a shorter and slightly different version of the motto, which we have here given in full. (Ortega y Pérez Gallardo, Historia Genealógica . . . , I, "Marquesado de Altamira.")

[24] It seems clear that the Calderóns visited the Colegio Seminario, erected between 1732 and 1770. The handsome building, whose façade is enlivened at each end by small turrets of sprightly design, stands on the main boulevard, across from the cathedral. It now serves as Michoacán's Palacio de Gobierno.

Not in operation at the particular time of the Calderóns' visit was one of the oldest educational institutions in the western hemisphere—the Colegio de San Nicolás de Hidalgo. It originated in a fusion of San Nicolás, founded in 1540 in Pátzcuaro by Bishop Quiroga, and the college of San Miguel in Morelia, and it was the nucleus of today's state Universidad Michoacana. (Benítez, Morelia, p. LXXIII.)

[25] Unrecorded as to origin, twelve pairs of dressed fleas may be seen in the Museo Nacional de Historia Natural in the capital. All are costumed with care—one pair as bride and groom. Judging from warnings in an early twentieth-century guidebook, fleas long continued to find Morelia's benign yet fresh climate an ideal milieu, but they have succumbed to modern insecticides.

51. Friends Revisited; Toluca in Commotion

[1] To foreigners, at least, the term ranchero seems sometimes to have meant cattlemen employed by others, and sometimes independent small farmers or ranchers. Fanny has used the word in both senses. The admiration of other visitors for these stalwart country Mexicans, intermediate in the social scale, reinforces hers. Captain G. F. Lyon, writing of the year 1826, spoke of them as mestizo yeomen of the country: "content in their cabin of mud or stakes,—lively, brave, good-tempered, profoundly ignorant, and careless of every thing beyond their immediate occupations." (Journal . . . , II, 233.) B. N. Norman, writing a little after Fanny, characterized the rancheros as "a mixed race of Mexican and Indian blood. They live on the Ranchos, or large cattle farms, and act as drovers. . . . There is an air of independence, and fearlessness of manner, in the Ranchero, which is quite imposing." (Rambles . . . , pp. 110–11.)

Of the ranchero as a small proprietor, Brantz Mayer said: "He is a person of lofty thoughts and aspirations;—a devoted patriot;—a staunch fighter in all the revolutions . . . a hard rider and capital boon companion over a bottle or in a journey among the mountains. On his small estate he devotes himself to the cultivation of the ground, or leaves this menial occupation to his family whilst he goes off to the wars or to carousals and *fandangos* in the neighboring village *pulquerias."* (*Mexico, Aztec, Spanish and Republican,* II, 28.)

Plate 64 shows rancheros, the nearer of whom displays full-length *manga,* or great calico-lined cloak with a velvet capelet, of the style the Calderóns had purchased for their Michoacán journey.

2 An old French saying, used in a book from which Fanny has already quoted: *A Sentimental Journey through France and Italy,* by Laurence Sterne.

3 The president of the corporation that operates Angangueo's mines today—Licenciado Ricardo J. Zevada—has kindly pointed out that the red color in the river was due not to copper, but to the prevalence of reddish iron oxide in the ores of this district. Ward mentioned such ores, called "*colorados,*" as being near the surface. (*Mexico in 1827,* II, 388–89.)

4 In preparing her material for print, Fanny seems to refer at this point to events not complete until later.

Santa Anna's program to substitute new copper for the miscellany then in circulation—a basically meritorious plan urged by Lucas Alamán—inevitably presented numerous problems in execution. As an indication of the extent of governmental troubles, Bernardo González Angulo, the Calderóns' recent landlord and director of the mint, was suspended from his post for alleged failures in connection with the production of the new copper coinage. (Riva Palacio, *México a Través de los Siglos,* IV, 476–77; Valadés, *Alamán,* pp. 389–91; *Diario del Gobierno,* November 21 and 26, 1841.)

It may be of interest to note that when the new copper money did finally appear, new counterfeit copper was quick to follow. Unfortunately, some of this proved to be better minted and more convincing in appearance than the legitimate article. (Mariano Cuevas, *Historia de la Nación Mexicana,* p. 592.)

5 The use of the reverberatory furnace (in which the flame is reflected from the roof upon the material being treated) must have been fairly new at Angangueo, as Ward did not mention it in his account of these mines. The process made a virtue of the presence of lead and zinc among the various minerals encountered in this area, and obviated the need for expensive imported mercury. In brief, the ores were first roasted to obtain a silver-lead alloy. When this was melted and small amounts of zinc added, the heavier lead tended to sink to the bottom, leaving upon the surface, as the mixture cooled, a scum containing the silver. This was subsequently purified, partly by oxidation in the reverberatory furnace.

At the time of the Calderóns' visit, Angangueo's principal mines were presumably in the hands of The German Company of Eberfeld. Other proprietors followed, and when the editors visited Angangueo some years ago the mines were being operated by the American Smelting and Mining Company. A few years later, following a fire in 1955 involving tragic loss of life, ownership and operation passed to Impulsora Minera de Angangueo, an undertaking formed jointly by the Mexican government, the states of Michoacán and Mexico, and private individuals—including the mines' personnel. We are informed by Mr. W. L. Parker, a long-time resident who welcomed us on our past visit to Angangueo, that many civic improvements have been achieved recently in the once-remote mining town the Calderóns saw in 1841, and that the house where they stayed now serves as the center for an agricultural project to provide fruit trees for planting by local workers.

6 Again, *Childe Harold:* Canto III, Stanza LV. It seems likely that what a few lines earlier is called the "Hymn to the Rhine" was "*Die Wacht am Rhein,*" just written in 1840. It was set to three different melodies before the much later and now familiar one by Carl Wilhelm was written.

7 A reference to the enervating effects of a luxurious winter spent at Capua by Hannibal's hitherto victorious troops.

8 Manuel María Gorospe was in 1841 a member from Puebla in the chamber of deputies.

9 Fanny forgot what she earlier said (p. 563): that letters had been received at San Bartolo reporting the resignation from the cabinet of Señor Gómez Pedraza.

10 Subsequently Santa Anna not only asked for and got funds from the church with which to sustain his government, but also took over a special missionary endowment known as the Pious Fund of the Californias. (Zamacois, *Historia de Méjico,* XII, 259–62; Callcott, *Santa Anna . . . ,* 176–78.)

11 "Their brows with roses and with myrtles bound/(So should desert in arms be crowned)./. . ./None but the brave deserve the fair." From Stanza 1 of "Alexander's Feast," by John Dryden.

Waddy Thompson, minister from the United States—in writing of the period 1842–43—said that Mexico's army had more than 200 generals, most of them without commands. A general who held a command was distinguished from others, according to Thompson, by being termed a *General Efectivo*. (*Recollections of Mexico*, p. 169.)

[12] The name of the Adalids has been entered here, because later notations in the Singer copy make it quite clear that it was with these good friends that the Calderóns spent their last few days in the capital.

The Adalids' handsome house (note 2, p. 687) was on the street then called the Calle de Cadena, and the editors have shown it as the location from which Fanny was writing.

[13] This was General José Morán, who with his titled wife the Marquesa de Vivanco had welcomed the Calderóns on various occasions to their hacienda of San Antonio and their villa at San Agustín de las Cuevas. A newspaper account said that the general had been sadly afflicted with a slow paralysis that dimmed his eyesight and hearing and affected his movements—but not his mental processes. He met his end, said the report, with imperturbable resignation, having made his peace with God. Though his family preferred private services, the government insisted on a brilliant public funeral in his honor. (*Diario del Gobierno*, January 6, 1842.)

[14] Because embalming was then so novel there seems to have been no etiquette governing the situation and the effect of the process on the body of the much-respected general was discussed with perfect frankness. *El Cosmopolita* of December 29, 1841, reported: "His Excellency General Don José Morán died Sunday night; this afternoon he will be interred in the Convent of San Francisco; one is assured that he has been exceedingly well embalmed, and that he is wearing glass eyes and his own natural color." Brantz Mayer, United States secretary of legation—who was disturbed by "the stony gaze of the *glass eyes*"—indicated that the body was left in the convent of San Francisco for a few days, and then taken to the family's hacienda for burial. (*Mexico as It Was and as It Is*, pp. 228–29.)

[15] Jean Nicholas Gannal (1791–1852), the French chemist who developed a method of embalming bodies through the use of solutions of aluminum salts, wrote a book on the subject which had appeared earlier in the year. An article in the *Diario del Gobierno* of March 30, 1841, contained an article on "*Embalsamamiento por el método de Mr. Gannal*," and indicated that the system was already being tried out in the Cuban capital.

[16] The convent of Santa Clara was destroyed by the opening of the Avenida del Cinco de Mayo, but its church exists as a library—the Biblioteca del Congreso de la Unión, on the Calle de Tacuba at the Calle de Allende. In the church of La Enseñanza one may still see grilles such as Fanny described, and also the opening through which the nuns of the convent received the sacrament.

[17] Fanny speaks here of an ill-fated expedition by Texans into New Mexico. Their rather naive plan had been to open up trade, and if possible to induce the residents to throw off Mexican allegiance and unite with the recently established republic of Texas. The story is dramatically told in a book entitled *Narrative of the Texan Santa Fé Expedition*, first published in 1844, by a member of the group: George Wilkins Kendall, a New Orleans newspaper editor who had lightheartedly joined for the sake of his health.

Though enthusiastically manned, the party was poorly equipped for the rugged journey between Austin and Santa Fe. The country through which they had to pass was ranged by hostile Indians. Their guides were vague as to the route and vastly optimistic about the distances involved. Within a few weeks after their start on June 18, 1841, they were both lost and low on food. A few weeks more and they were thirsty and near starvation. Unknown to them, their scouts had been captured and shot. At this point, the party split, sending the hardiest, under Colonel William G. Cooke, on ahead. Both groups fell into Mexican hands. The Mexican governor at Santa Fe decided to send them all to the capital to await justice there. Already weakened by hunger and exposure during their wanderings, they began in October 1841 a forced march of approximately 2,000 miles to the city of Mexico.

They traveled in two contingents. The group of which Colonel Cooke was a part seems to have received reasonably good treatment throughout the long journey. The other, of which Kendall was a member, was put in the custody of Captain Dámaso Salazar, who diverted to his own use the cattle sent along to provide meat for the party, and rationed his prisoners to an ear of corn per day. They stumped along barefoot after their boots wore out, and slept in open corrals. Those who could not keep up were clubbed or shot to death and their ears subsequently cut off to be kept by Salazar as evidence in accounting for his charges. Treated thus by one group of Mexicans they were, during their march, succored by another—kindly townspeople, especially women of small means, who pressed upon their enemy Texans the food that kept most of them alive. Upon reaching El Paso, Salazar turned his prisoners over to General J. M. Elías González who, outraged at the emaciated condition of the men and at Salazar's collection of ears, ordered three days of respite and good food for the prisoners and arrest for Salazar. They were then marched on, still in two groups, reaching Mexico early in 1842.

As Fanny says, the first arrivals were imprisoned in the old convent at Santiago Tlaltelolco, but others would be incarcerated elsewhere. The writer Kendall, together with others suspected of having contracted smallpox, found himself, to his horror, in the lepers' hospital at San Lázaro. Santa Anna made good his threat to have the Santiago group sent out to work on the streets in chains, but the United States minister Waddy Thompson noted that under the indulgent eyes of their guards they contrived to accomplish very little. Thompson said further that the prisoners were well fed—"much better fed than the Mexican soldiers were."

The fate of the prisoners was resolved some months after the Calderóns left Mexico. The newly arrived United States minister Thompson, who wrote his own account of this part of the affair, undertook negotiations for their release—and some, apparently, were freed not long after the Calderóns' departure. Thompson continued his efforts on behalf of the remaining prisoners, and on June 16, 1842—Santa Anna's saint's day—he witnessed at a great review outside the city the ceremony at which Santa Anna set them at liberty. Thompson had been somewhat fearful that the occasion might conclude with a hostile demonstration against the Texans. But, in line with what Fanny sensed, the Mexicans cheered, hands were clasped, coins were flung—and, in one instance, a ragged sarape was offered by a *lépero* to a still more ragged Texan. (Thompson, *Recollections of Mexico*, pp. 92–100; Rives, *The United States and Mexico*, I, 480–84; Riva Palacio, *México a Través de los Siglos*, IV, 476, 486–87; George Wilkins Kendall, *Narrative of the Texan Santa Fé Expedition*.)

[18] Don José María was mentioned earlier by Fanny as the presumed author of articles in *El Mosaico Mexicano* (p. 278).

[19] That Fanny was sincere, and not merely throwing out for publication a few pleasant comments to offset her earlier critical appraisals, is clear from a letter she wrote Prescott from Havana on February 16, 1842. Speaking of Mexican procrastination, as she had experienced it, she refers to "that land of *pulque* and *pronunciamientos*, which after all I left with the greatest regret." (Wolcott, *Correspondence of . . . Prescott*, p. 285.)

52. Revised Impressions

[1] Fanny employs here full names that she earlier (and subsequently, even in the next paragraph) went to the trouble of striking out or abbreviating to conceal identities.

[2] *Todo Lo Vence Amor* (Love Conquers All) was the principal title of this fairly recent burlesque piece—laid in fifteenth-century Zaragoza—by Juan de Grimaldi. In addition to thunder and lightning, its complicated stage effects seem to have included a magical conveyance capable of passing through iron bars (carrying Cupid in aid of the play's lovers), and, as a final climax, the transformation of the Three Graces' sea shell first into a large ship, and then into a fire-spitting marine monster.

[3] The new Spanish minister Oliver was sufficiently struck by Santa Anna's love of sumptuous display and the rumors of his monarchical aspirations as to mention both in a dispatch concerning the Mexican government's New Year's reception and Santa Anna's dinner that followed. The brilliance of the dinner, said Oliver, rivaled anything to be seen in Europe. The reception was the first occasion in which the diplomatic corps officially took part since the quarrel in the cathedral precipitated by the Baron de Cyprey a year and a half before (p. 249). As the reader may recall, the difficulty arose over the question of whether foreign diplomats or members of the Mexican cabinet came next in rank after the president. The dilemma was finally resolved by the acceptance on both sides of an ingenious face-saving geometric arrangement. The diplomats, instead of continuing the line made by Mexican cabinet officials to the right and left of the president, formed two independent groupings drawn up at right angles to that line. Oliver noted that the formula would work for certain structured occasions, but did not provide for those situations "in which it is necessary that one or another pass first, or occupy a place of greater or less distinction." (*Despachos Generales*, I, 311; and II, 8–9.)

[4] In spite of earlier friction, the Calderóns seem to have achieved a genuine friendship with the Baron de Cyprey and his wife. A Spanish diplomat of a little later, in speaking of Mme de Cyprey, noted that she "did the honors of her house very well." (Conte, *Recuerdos de un Diplomático*, I, 292.) After the Calderóns' departure, the baron continued to be something of a thorn in the flesh of the Mexican government. At its urgent request, he was recalled about three years later, after two more spectacular rows. The first, in May 1845, bore a certain resemblance in contour to the tavern affair of 1840 (note 7, p. 740) in that it was initiated by underlings. The locale was a horse bath known

as the Baños de las Delicias—literally, the Baths of Delights. The establishment's employees became involved in a quarrel with a stable employee of the French minister, one or more of whose horses were patronizing the baths. The baron, ignited by the version of events reported to him—which he seems at once to have accepted at full face value—headed an armed expedition to the Baths of Delights in order that he might deal with the matter personally. Needless to say, spectacular violence ensued.

The second episode, in September of the same year, involved a near-duel, precipitated by the baron's having accosted and spat upon his vis-à-vis at the theater. The baron, departing on short notice, went to Paris, and retired permanently from the practice of diplomacy as a career. (Bustamante, El Nuevo Bernal Díaz del Castillo, I, 55–59, 73–74; Despachos Generales, I, 328; Malo, Diario . . . , I, 278, 285–87.)

Maps, earlier provided, cover the Calderóns' return journey to the coast.

[5] The accelerated schedule was inaugurated to speed the handling of foreign mail, according to a letter of complaint in El Cosmopolita for May 22, 1841, written by a diligence passenger who had previously suffered a permanently injured leg.

[6] Fanny's source on the history of San Juan de Ulúa was evidently Humboldt's Ensayo Político (II, 60–61). However, in working from his account—perhaps under pressure in Boston to complete her manuscript—she introduced errors which are corrected here. (She herself evidently later caught one mistake, for in the Singer copy the founding of San Juan de Ulúa was changed by hand from 1682 to 1582.) In the next paragraph she gave the cost of the fortress as four million rather than the forty mentioned by Humboldt—"according to popular tradition."

The name Acolhua—also evidently derived from Humboldt—has been variously interpreted, but is linked with the valley of Mexico. A history of Veracruz published in 1858 says that the island was called San Juan because the Spaniards landed at approximately the feast day of that saint, and that the Indians, when questioned about the evidences of human sacrifice, used the word "Culúa," or "Ulúa." (Lerdo de Tejada, Apuntes Históricos de . . . Vera-Cruz, I, 103.)

[7] Veracruz was taken on the night of May 17–18, 1683. The spectacular amount of the pirates' booty was due to the fact that an immense treasure had been assembled in the city to await official transport to Spain. Most of the inhabitants were packed into a church where they were held for three days without food or water while their houses and strongboxes were ransacked. Some were killed outright; many more died from the experience. Those abandoned on the waterless Isla de los Sacrificios had earlier been forced to carry the spoils to two waiting pirate ships. A few women were carried off.

The pirates were a mixture of French, English, Spanish, and Negro adventurers. Their leaders were men of mystery, whose real identities were obscure. Nicholas Agramont seems also to have been called Van Horn—spelled Banoren or Banoven in Spanish. Lorencillo, according to most accounts, was Lorenzo Jácome, a mulatto—but he is also spoken of as a Fleming, with the name of Laurent de Gaff, or de Graff. (México a Través de los Siglos, II, 638–43; Rivera Cambas, Gobernantes de México, I, 254–57; Parkes, History of Mexico, pp. 126–27.)

[8] The retention of San Juan de Ulúa by the Spaniards after the loss of the mainland not only was a symbol of prestige but also was high in nuisance value. Goods intended for Veracruz were frequently intercepted and a duty collected—for Spain—before they were allowed to land, when they became subject to Mexican customs as well. Or, with the co-operation of Spanish residents living on shore, imported goods could be landed at the castle and smuggled in, thus bypassing Mexican customs and depriving the government of one of its principal sources of revenue. (W. Bullock, Six Months . . . in Mexico, pp. 492–95.) When the Spaniards later undertook to pound the city from the fortress, most of the shipping put in at Alvarado some thirty miles down the coast. (Lerdo de Tejada, Apuntes Históricos de . . . Vera-Cruz, III, 528.)

It was during this very period of hostilities between the Spanish-held fort and the Mexican city that H. G. Ward first came to Mexico, as member of a commission to consider whether Great Britain should recognize Mexican independence. He and his companions paid an initial call on officials in the port and were joyfully received. Some hours later they set out in a small boat to return for the night to their anchored ship. The Mexicans decided to honor the departing visitors with a series of salutes—but forgot "that their guns were shotted and directed against the Castle, which immediately opened its batteries in return." The unhappy British found themselves rowing through a double barrage. (Mexico in 1827, II, 175–76.)

[9] By the "gods" the historian Zavala meant the violent north winds (comparable to those which had kept the Calderóns so long and so tantalizingly off the coast) which made relief to the island fortress hazardous. The quotation is from the author's Ensayo Histórico . . . , I, 336.

[10] José Copinger, last Spanish commandant of San Juan de Ulúa, was said to have been born Joseph Coppinger in South Carolina of Irish parentage, and to have emigrated to Cuba.

The contending forces in the final siege seem to have entertained for one another a good deal of chivalric esteem. Copinger was offered the protection of the Mexican government if he chose to remain in Mexico. He refused, asking for himself only that he be sent to Havana to report to his government and await its judgment. His surrender was contingent on the conditions that the flag of Spain should be respected to the last, and that the emaciated survivors of his garrison should receive hospital care. When the Spaniards left the castle, it was discovered that they had been existing toward the end on rats caught by a talented dog that had been allowed to survive. The Spaniards, after a few days of rest in Veracruz, departed on November 23, 1825. Not until the Mexican ships which carried the Spaniards sailed by the fortress were the Spanish colors hauled down, to the accompaniment of courteous salutes from Mexicans at the fortress and on the mainland. When the ships were out of sight, General Miguel Barragán then raised the Mexican flag with his own hands, and joyful new salvos marked the sovereignty of Mexico over this last vestige of Spanish power.

The old pilot whom the Calderóns had encountered when they approached Veracruz from the sea on December 18, 1839 (p. 53), was evidently a Spanish survivor who had settled in Mexico.

We have substituted in place of Fanny's date of September 15 for the Spaniards' evacuation of the castle—which she seems to have obtained from Zavala's account—that of November 19, derived from a later detailed history of Veracruz. (Zavala, *Ensayo Histórico* . . . , I, 336; Lerdo de Tejada, *Apuntes Históricos de* . . . *Vera-Cruz*, II, 277–83, III, 528; *Sketch of* . . . *Mexico*, pp. 231–35; Bancroft, *History of Mexico*, V, 62–64.)

[11] Fanny's quotation from an unknown French source is confusing. In likening San Juan de Ulúa to the crusaders' Palestinian stronghold of St. Jean d'Acre (captured by the Moslems in 1291 after protracted, hopeless resistance by its Christian defenders), the reference is certainly to the long, stubborn defense of the fort by the last Spanish garrison remaining in Mexico.

[12] Bustamante's aide was José María Calderón. He accompanied his chief into exile, according to an item in the maritime news of about three weeks later. (*Diario del Gobierno*, January 28, 1842.) His father, of the same name, served as governor of Puebla. (Leicht, *Calles de Puebla*, p. 289.)

[13] The Havana-based Spanish warship in which the Calderóns had traveled from Cuba to Mexico happened to be in Veracruz when the fallen Bustamante sought to arrange his departure. So, also, was a visiting French warship. According to the Spanish minister Oliver, he caused the departure of the *Jasón* to be delayed so that Bustamante might be its guest, and furthermore ordered it stocked with extra food befitting so important a passenger (see note 2, p. 674). He gave as reasons for these moves that he was reluctant to let the French outdo Spaniards, and cited Bustamante's friendly conduct toward Spain and Spaniards in Mexico during his two presidencies. Also advanced as a strong reason was the possibility, in view of the uncertainty of the Mexican political scene, that the ousted leader might some day return to power. (*Despachos Generales*, I, 295–96.) Bustamante was on his way to exile in Italy. He would return, however, and would serve his country in the United States-Mexican War.

The uncertainties of wind, weather, and planning are reflected in a notice appearing in the January 6, 1842 issue of the Veracruz newspaper *El Censor* to the effect that the Spanish consul was prepared to receive mail to go aboard the *Jasón*, ready for sail to Havana "at one moment or another."

[14] Prescott's travel gift consisted of two new books: *Incidents of Travel in Central America, Chiapas, and Yucatan*, in two volumes, written by John Lloyd Stephens (New York, Harper & Bros., 1841); and *Biography and Poetical Remains of the Late Margaret Miller Davidson*, by Washington Irving (Philadelphia, Lea and Blanchard, 1841). Margaret Davidson was the younger of two gifted sisters, both precocious writers of poetry —both of whom died very young.

53. To Havana by Way of Tampico

[1] From the witches' incantation in Act IV, Scene 1 of *Macbeth*. The "neat-handed Phillis" of a few lines earlier is from Milton's *L'Allegro*, line 85.

[2] The roots of Tampico and nearby Pueblo Viejo went back to the sixteenth century, but in its sudden recent growth Tampico was a boom town. Independence had brought an end to the tight Spanish controls that had centered Atlantic shipping at Veracruz.

Merchants, especially foreigners, flocked to the river-mouth harbor which, with all its disadvantages, was the best between Veracruz and the Rio Grande. Tampico thus rapidly developed as a major center for the movement of goods to and from Mexico's northern territories. A visitor about two years later observed that the town's situation was delightful, but that its population of some 6000 suffered frightful losses from yellow fever: he reported 2000 deaths there in the year 1843. (Gilliam, *Travels in Mexico*, p. 267.)

[3] Fanny gave his first name as Juan, but it was given as José in a dispatch written by Calderón the previous May (*Despachos Generales*, I, 193).

[4] Late in the nineteenth century the construction of two long jetties at the mouth of the river gave Tampico the safe access Fanny hypothecated. The Pánuco now flows to the Gulf unimpeded by the former shifting shoals of the sandbar. By the turn of the century Tampico had become a flourishing port, serving distant towns of the hinterland by a line of steamboats operating on the Pánuco River, but the town's population still did not much exceed twelve thousand. It was the discovery of oil in 1911 that created the modern Tampico and environs, with a population approaching two hundred thousand. The main city lies about six miles up-river. Where Fanny's pelicans watched over many a drowning crew there is now a lighthouse. A superb beach with rolling surf extends northward.

[5] From "*Les deux pigeons*" in *Fables de La Fontaine* (*Livre neuvième, Fable II*).

[6] The *Tyrian*, according to newspaper accounts, carried $121,773 in *plata acuñada*—coined silver. The passengers, as Fanny earlier indicated, were a young Mexican (identified as José Romero), Calderón and herself, and Kate Macleod—the last two identified merely as Calderón's wife and niece. (*Diario del Gobierno*, February 13, 1842; *Diario de la Habana*, February 2, 1842.)

Altogether the Calderóns were in Mexico from December 18, 1839 to January 19, 1842—or approximately two years and a month.

[7] The young men should have studied an article in the *Mosaico Mexicano* (I, 271) on how to avoid seasickness. Among several suggestions: drink two ounces of brandy in two ounces of sea water; sniff constantly at a lump of mother earth from a supply to be carried in a clay pot or *olla* (a fresh lump to be substituted from the *olla* as necessary).

[8] "Rule Britannia" had first been sung over a century before—in 1740, as the finale to Thomas Augustine Arne's masque *Alfred*. However, both the air and the words by the poet James Thomson have been altered by others.

[9] Don Gerónimo Valdés Noriega y Sierra was a fairly recent appointee, and the Calderóns presumably had never met him.

[10] It is not clear what motives led the Calderóns to decline the invitation of the Captain-General in favor of that of Don Bernardo Hechavarría—in whose house, it may be remembered, Fanny had felt so ill at ease on her first arrival (p. 18). Perhaps Don Bernardo, there in person to offer hospitality, was a familiar and persuasive figure. Possibly Calderón decided against staying at the palace in order to avoid being under obligation to appointees of the new regime in Spain which had recalled him from his post.

Whatever the reason, the Calderóns' choice did not pass unnoticed. About five years later—at a time when Calderón was once again serving as Spanish minister to the United States—the circumstances of his Havana stay were raked up and presented in an extraordinary "very confidential" dispatch prepared by a young United States diplomat, Thomas Caute Reynolds. At the time, the future of Cuba—which had concerned both Jefferson and John Quincy Adams—was the object of much speculation. Beginning in 1845, with the accession of the Democrats to power, southerners in the United States began to urge opening negotiations to purchase Cuba from Spain. This movement grew out of the fear that Cuba might—through aid from England or otherwise—gain independence as a partly Negro republic with slaveholding abolished there, with resulting serious consequences for the institution of slavery in the United States. (Robert Granville Caldwell, *The Lopez Expeditions to Cuba, 1848–1851*, pp. 29–33.)

Young Reynolds, a southerner, was in 1847 acting temporarily as chargé d'affaires at the United States legation in Madrid. Referring mysteriously to secret informants, and with elaborate assurances of their absolute reliability, he presented a lengthy report on supposed international conspiracies affecting Cuba. He included the following regarding Calderón's visit in 1842: ". . . On his return from Mexico, he spent a little time at Havannah, about the period, when . . . fears existed of British designs, and the 'Ethiopico-Cuban Republic' was intended to make its political debût; his associates there are said to have been distinguished for anything but affection towards Spain, and his sojourn in the house of Señor Hechivarria, (a suspected secret partizan of the English Abolitionists), was considered by the Spanish functionaries in the Island, a very grave faux pas: there are not wanting some who even think that had the insurrection broken out and been successful, Señor Calderon de la Barca, so *casually* on the spot, might have been induced, by motives of the purest Creole patriotism, to exchange one adopted country [a reference to Calderón's Argentine birth] for another, and his meagre emoluments as a Spanish diplomatist for the more ample salary and congenial position of a British 'Resident' . . . and Spy-in-Chief in the Ethiopico-Cuban Republic."

Reynolds' dispatch also refers to Fanny: to the fact that she was "a canny Scotchwoman," that she had been, or was, a Protestant (Reynolds was not sure of her then status); that she was alleged to be an abolitionist; and, finally, that she entirely controlled her husband.

When Reynolds' chief, the United States minister Romulus M. Saunders, returned to Madrid after an absence, he took strong exception to his subordinate's action. Saunders made it plain that he considered Reynolds a vain, obnoxious, and not very useful assistant. When challenged as to the reliability of the information presented, Reynolds wrote for the record that he felt it his "imperative duty to *disavow* and *withdraw*" what he had written—and, regarding Calderón specifically, he said, "besides the information *may* be false."

(William R. Manning, editor, *Diplomatic Correspondence of the United States, Inter-American Affairs, 1831–1860*, Volume XI, *Spain*, pp. 424, 425, 436 fn, 466. See also, in the United States Archives, an unpublished letter of December 20, 1847, from Romulus M. Saunders to President Polk, asking for the recall of Thomas Caute Reynolds.)

That Reynolds' statements regarding Calderón's alleged disloyalty were false is abundantly clear from everything known about his prior and subsequent career. Some years later, Calderón was named Spain's Minister of Foreign Affairs, partly, at least, because of his firm record in relation to Cuba. As to Bernardo Hechavarría, the Calderóns' host in Havana both in 1839 and 1842, it seems unlikely that he was a plotter against the mother country in view of his ennoblement by the Queen of Spain in 1851.

[11] This was Doña Loreto Cortina de Gutiérrez Estrada—a sister of Count Cortina. One learns from a letter Fanny will write to Prescott on February 16, 1842, that Doña Loreto had followed her husband (who had fled Mexico as a result of the uproar over his pamphlet on the advisability of a monarchy for Mexico), and that she died in Havana soon after giving birth to a daughter. (Wolcott, *Correspondence of . . . Prescott*, p. 285.) Her remains would be sent back to her own country for magnificent funeral honors, held on April 11 at the church of San Francisco. Principals from the Italian opera company, including Mme Cesari the contralto, sang at the service. (Malo, *Diario* . . . , I, 208; Romero de Terreros, *Cosas Que Fueron*, pp. 189–95.) Gutiérrez Estrada was later married again, and made his life in Europe. As noted earlier, his persisting absorption with the idea of a monarchy merged ultimately into the disastrous plan that brought the Austrian Archduke Maximilian briefly to the throne of a divided Mexico.

54. With Friends in Cuba; Home by Steamer

[1] According to the January 30 issue of the *Diario de la Habana*, Fanny Elssler, together with others in her company, had come from Philadelphia in the 182-ton sailing vessel *Louisa*. Her performances opened on February 12 at the Teatro Principal—presumably the *other* theater referred to by Fanny. Included in her program was *La Sylphide*, still occasionally performed today.

Following the carnival, Lent had begun on February 9, but it seems not to have entirely dampened the gaiety of Havana social life. Fanny wrote to Prescott on February 16: "The Carnival is now over, but I cannot compliment them upon their strictness in Lent." (Wolcott, *Correspondence of . . . Prescott*, p. 287.)

[2] The full name of the Fernandina sugar estate was San José de la Angosta. The other property the Calderóns visited was evidently Valvanera, near the town of Guanajay. It belonged to the Condesa de Villanueva. (Justo Germán Cantero, *Los Ingenios*, unpaged.)

[3] George William Frederick Howard, Viscount Morpeth (later the seventh Earl of Carlisle, and still later Lord Lieutenant of Ireland), had just finished a long tour of the United States, during the course of which he had studied the legal problem that resulted from the inheritance of slaves by British subjects. In Boston he seems to have been liked by—and to have liked in return—several of the Calderóns' friends.

From a letter Prescott wrote on January 3, 1842, which reached Fanny in Havana, and from one that Lord Morpeth later wrote to Prescott, one learns a good deal about both Calderón and Lord Morpeth. Prescott said of Morpeth that he was "a man about forty, who makes capital speeches in Parliament, who tosses off an ode now and then in an annual, and is a most delightful, kind-hearted person in society. I have rarely had the good fortune to meet with a better union of head and heart . . . He reminds me of your husband; and I have ventured as he proposes to go to Cuba to give him a note of intro-

duction to him, as he expressed himself desirous of being acquainted with both of you."
(Wolcott, *Correspondence of . . . Prescott*, p. 278.)

After his Cuban sojourn, Lord Morpeth wrote back to Prescott of his new friends the
Calderóns: "I immediately felt that you were a link between us, and that I had a right to
be intimate with them, which I found it was very well worth while to be on their own
account also. There is great simplicity of character, as well as abundant sense and good
feeling, about him, and I think her most remarkably agreeable and accomplished."
(George Ticknor, *Life of Prescott*, pp. 199–200.)

[4] In expressing herself more frankly to Prescott, Fanny indicated certain reservations
about their Havana sojourn and the warm weight of hospitality pressed upon them. Dinners and balls were again given in their honor as before on their way to Mexico, when
Calderón held high office—"all which, though it may be gratifying, is in reality rather
against Calderón's real interests, only increasing the jealousy already felt in Madrid about
his influence here. For which reason, as well as from motives of economy we have determined to shorten our stay here as much as possible. I think we shall leave . . . in the
packet of April. . . . because the obligation of living on terms of equality with this
golden aristocracy does not suit our present circumstances in the least." Later in the same
letter she says that Calderón has received from Spain only words: thanks from the
Regent for his services, but nothing tangible in the way of a pension due him or travel-
expense money. Calderón, she adds, is very anxious for "some sort of employment, but
the difficulty [is] *what*." (Wolcott, *Correspondence of . . . Prescott*, pp. 286–88—bracketed
word supplied by Wolcott.)

Their financial situation could by no means have been as critical as Calderón gloomily
suggested to Prescott when writing at the time of his recall. Nevertheless, they must
have felt serious concern for ways and means. During the two months Calderón spent in
Cuba he evidently received strong support for the publication of work he had completed
a good many years earlier, in his bachelor days—a translation from German into Spanish
of Johannes von Müller's *Universal History*. When the long four-volume work was published in Boston a year later, some fourteen pages listed *los señores subscriptores* in Cuba
who were its sponsors. To them, in grateful acknowledgment of their aid, Calderón dedicated his work.

[5] In contrast to the sailings of other large vessels, which were advertised in the *Diario
de la Habana* for two or three weeks ahead, that of the *Medway* seems to have been un-
heralded in the press. Only the fact of its departure, under the command of Captain
Smith, was noted in the issue of April 22.

[6] Padre Fúrlong was perhaps the Canónigo Joaquín Fúrlong of Puebla, one of the
eight capable sons of Captain James Fúrlong, formerly of Belfast. Padre Fúrlong was in
charge of the Casa de Ejercicios, a house of retreat for laymen. (Leicht, *Calles de Puebla*,
pp. 165–66.)

[7] Eugène Duflot de Mofras had just completed a long, thorough inspection of the Pacific
Coast, ostensibly to assess future commercial opportunities for French traders in these
beckoning western lands. (The book he wrote is available in English, edited and translated by Marguerite Eyer Wilbur, under the title *Duflot de Mofras' Travels on the Pacific
Coast*.)

A newspaper article in *El Mosquito Mexicano* (June 2, 1840) indicated that Mexicans
were not unaware of possible hidden motives behind the young Frenchman's project.
California, it was predicted, would soon go the way of Texas.

Index

This index to the author's text includes also some references to the background and editorial notes in cases where it appeared that material there might otherwise be overlooked.

Phrases and titles, but not place names, have been listed under their first principal word: thus the newspaper *El Cosmopolita* is to be found under the C's, while the haciendas of El Pilar and La Gavia appear under the E's and L's respectively.

Places in the capital, as the author knew it, have been grouped together under "Mexico, city of."

There is no entry for the author, Fanny Calderón de la Barca. The index taken as a whole is a guide to her opinions, experiences, and encounters.

quits capital for Guadalupe 516; presumably bears Santa Anna no ill-will 522; Calderón calls on 524, 542–43; in Veracruz 614, 616; in Havana 625, 626; 413, 418, 519; Pl. 65

Bustamante, Carlos María de, 418, 420–21, 711 (note 8), 749–50 (note 11), 768–69 (note 11), 793 (note 11), Pl. 81

Bustamante, José María, 278, 602

Byron, George Noel Gordon, Lord (quoted or alluded to), 80, 127, 149, 241, 271, 288, 470, 477, 574, 576

C_____s, General, 379

Cabrera, Miguel, 340, 344, 589

Cacahuamilpa: cave 380, 386–90, Pl. 105; town 385, 390

cacaloxochitl (flower), 381

Cacho, José, 264, 724 (note 10)

cactus. See nopal; órganos

Calderón, hacienda of, 397

Calderón, José María (aide to Bustamante), 613

Calderón de la Barca, Angel: quoted or paraphrased 6, 33, 55, 68, 77, 78, 81, 106, 212, 219, 235, 273, 286, 443–44, 569; interest in photography 12, 357; greeted in Havana 17; hurries Fanny 24; honored by impromptus 24–25, 29–30; on shipboard 42; greeted at Veracruz 53–56; calls on Victoria 58; calls on Santa Anna 64–67; at Jalapa 72; greeted during journey 78–79, 83–84; welcomed to capital 88–89; old friend calls 92; honored by serenade 92, 94–96; received by Bustamante 105–6; theater performance honors him 97, 119–20; bullfight in his honor 97, 126–29; dines with Pakenham 130, 279, 527; interest in paintings 163, 168, 344, 400, 410, 411, 423; at country party 170; visits convent of San Joaquín 186–87; interest in geology and botany 212, 396; dines with archbishop 251; dismisses servant 254–55; belongs to book club 279; friendship with missionary friars 279, 281; friendship with Almonte 307–8; stays at post during revolution 207–9; visits near Toluca 327, 330; his fête day 339; he and Fanny give diplomatic dinner 354, 355; at special masses 356–57, 474; goes to sugar estate 362, 366, 370; incident with Indian official 390–91; has toothache 391; sees Ramos Arizpe 407, 410; calls on Bishop Vásquez 408, 410; is to be replaced 427, 752 (note 10); still continues on duty 428, 446, 452; sends flag to ball for Bustamante 433; country routine 452; visits Mexican archives 489; pays last official visit to President Bustamante 490; sees

Bustamante during revolution 509; visits Bustamante after his fall 524, 542; meets Santa Anna again 528, 542; his political views 734–35 (note 15), 744 (note 11); admired by Prescott and Lord Morpeth 806–7 (note 3); 4, 21, 26, 34, 37, 38, 76, 77, 120, 122, 123, 139, 156, 157, 168, 173, 178, 203, 208, 296, 339, 352, 358, 379, 394, 399, 414, 417, 446, 447, 457, 470, 487, 548, 555, 564, 567, 569, 582, 599, 620, . . . ; Pl. 2

Calderón de la Barca, Pedro, 8

Calendar Stone, 105

Calendario de las Señoritas Megicanas, 288–89, 789 (note 15)

California (Upper and Lower): missions in 279–82; artifacts from 340; historical work on, destroyed 489; French mission to Upper California 626

Calleja del Rey, Félix María, 757 (note 8), 792–93 (note 9)

Caltzontzi, 568

Camacho, Sebastián (Minister of Foreign Affairs in 1841), 497, 770–71 (note 1), 773 (note 16)

camarista (lady of honor), 186

Camilos, Padres, 435–36

Campanero de San Pablo, 35

Campo, Manuel Martínez del. See Martínez del Campo

Campos, Agustín, 585

Campos, Bishop Antonio, 122–24, 189, 720 (note 4)

Canalizo, Valentín, 465, 508, 515, 516–17

canals. See chinampas; Viga canal

Cañas, Manuel de (General de la Marina in Cuba), 22, 37, 40

Cañedo, Juan de Dios (Minister of Foreign Affairs, "Secretary of State"): calls 125, 284; arranges convent visits 188, 205; involved in diplomatic controversy 249, 740–41 (note 12); opposed newspaper tariff 278; described 284; resigns 334; 418, 422, 547, 708 (note 8), 720 (note 5), 744 (note 9); Pl. 66

canoes, 88, 180–83, 343, 446, 550, 584, 586, 618 (note 21), 797–98 (note 12), Pl. 86, 137, 138

canónigo (cannon, chanoine, or prebendary), 263, 407, 565, 588–89

Cape Coast Castle, 15

capellán (chaplain), 163, 205

Cárdenas, Señora de, 28

cargadores (men who carry loads), 197, 328, 504, 547

cariñoso (affectionate), 291

Caritea, Regina di Spagna, 37

Carlisle copy of Life in Mexico, explanation, 723–24 (note 3)

aide, guard 54, 55; Calderón calls on 58;
he calls, is described 58–59; his earlier
history 68, 309, 419, 423, 741 (note 15);
loyal in 1840 revolution 309; courtesy
toward fallen Iturbide 418–19; Pl. 7
Victoria, Queen, 25, 204, 248
Vieyra, Luis Gonzaga, 309, 318
Viga canal, 164, 167, 174–75, 179, 180,
181–83, 343, Pl. 86
Villafuerte, _____, 210
Villanueva, Conde de: his administrador
greets Calderóns 17; calls 24; gives dinner in Calderóns' honor 32–34; shows off
railroad and waterworks 36–37; host with
wife to Calderóns 625; 25, 31
Villanueva, Condesa de: sends flowers 21;
Fanny visits 25–26; described 21, 31, 39;
her son 25, 33, 36, 37; hostess at dinner
33; her costume 36; visits 37; sends gift
of jewelry 40
Virgen de la Concepción, 49
"Virgen del Pilar, La," sung on convent visit,
346
Virgin Mary: Indians' veneration for 194;
plural aspects of, in Indians' view 430–
31. See also the three entries which follow
Virgin of Covadonga, 356–57, Pl. 44, 45
Virgin of Guadalupe: her portrait in congress 117; Calderóns visit her shrine 120–
21, 124, 341, 538, Pl. 89; chapel of the
well 121–22, 341, Pl. 89, 90; her legend
recounted 122–23, 577; her role in War of
Independence 210, 211, 564; her feast
day 359, 592; her portrait in Indian huts
506–7, Pl. 122; history of her shrine 539–
40; 58, 216
Virgin of los Remedios: her legend 210–11;
Calderóns visit her shrine 210–12; brought
into capital 327–28; another church, at
Cholula 404; jewels of 601
Vivanco, Marquesa de (wife of General
Morán): at English ball 247; Calderóns
visit 270, 272; entertains in their honor
275; party at her hacienda 276; gives
posadas at home in capital 365–66; family at Good Friday procession 438; president of foundling hospital 519; Calderóns
visit 526–27; she calls 543; farewells 607;
her death 625. See also Cuevas; Morán
voladores, el juego de los, 86–87
volantes (Cuban carriages), 17–18, 21, 25,
27, 35, 625
volcanoes: near capital (Popocatepetl and
Ixtacihuatl) 87, 116, 146, 149, 152, 216,
335, 361, 396, 413, 428, 608, Pl. 88; Nevado de Toluca 550–51, 554; Jorullo 566,
575–76. See also Ixtacihuatl; Popocatepetl
vómito negro (black vomit). See yellow fever

wages: servants' 257; laborers on sugar haciendas 384; paid in copper 399
Wallace, William Vincent, 411, 468, 774–75
(note 1)
War of Independence, 53, 54, 68, 211, 331–
33, 423–24, 564–65, 589, 611–13, 757
(note 8). See also Hidalgo; Iturbide; Morelos; Victoria
Ward, Henry George: his landlord irked
144; his Mexico in 1827 referred to 240.
Numerous citations in notes
Ward, Mrs. Henry George, 68, 507
Ward, William Robert (secretary of British legation), 300, 416, 541, 549, 550
Washington, George, 450, 525, 600
waterfalls: near hacienda of Santiago 229;
at Santa María Regla 241; of Tzaráracua
579, Pl. 142; near Angangueo 595
wax figures: of nuns 258, 347; of Iturbide
283; Fanny sends as gift 286, 357; Indians' skill in wax and trapo 286; collection to be sent to Spain 286; at Posadas
366; collection in Morelia 590–91
Wellington, Duke of, 466
Wise, Henry Alexander, 272
women: impressions of Havana ladies 32,
39; Veracruz ladies 60; first impressions of
ladies in capital 130; lack of grace 130,
288; lower classes often handsome 130;
Indian women generally ugly, sometimes beautiful 133, 155, 194, 200, 335,
443–44, 457; ladies often untidy in mornings 138–39, 154–55; later impressions of
capital ladies' looks 154–56, 248, 362;
country women often handsome 155–56,
230, 594; warmth of manner 156, 291;
seem to do nothing 156, 168; appear best
when seated 170; skill at embroidery 172,
473–74; education limited 171–73, 286–
88; beautiful hair 200, 320; beauty
among Poblanas 201; do not hunt for husbands or conceal age 230; reasons for becoming nuns 258–59, 267, 406, 410; possess natural gifts 288; praised in Mexican
annual 288–89; morals do not always
match outward decorum 290; not happy
away from Mexico 291; well informed on
politics 329; prone to nervous complaints
330; praise for wives of Mexican leaders
423; good looks at San Agustín fête 455–
56; ladies' concern with charities 519–20,
531–33; their time fully occupied 533

Xaltocan, 180
Xicalango, 401
Ximenes. See Jimeno y Planes